THE URBAN ESTABLISHMENT

The Urban Establishment

UPPER STRATA IN
BOSTON, NEW YORK, CHARLESTON,
CHICAGO, AND LOS ANGELES

Frederic Cople Jaher

UNIVERSITY OF ILLINOIS PRESS   Urbana   Chicago   London

Publication of this work has been supported by a grant from the Oliver M. Dickerson Fund. The Fund was established by Mr. Dickerson (Ph.D., Illinois, 1906) to enable the University of Illinois Press to publish selected works in American history, designated by the executive committee of the Department of History.

LIBRARY OF CONGRESS CATALOGING IN PUBLICATION DATA

Jaher, Frederic Cople.
  The urban establishment.

  Includes index.
  1. Elites (Social sciences)—United States—Case
studies.   2. Upper classes—Massachusetts—Boston—
Case studies.   3. Upper classes—New York (City)—
Case studies.   4. Upper classes—South Carolina—
Charleston—Case studies.   5. Upper classes—Illinois—
Chicago—Case studies.   6. Upper classes—California—
Los Angeles—Case studies.   I. Title.
HN90.E4J33   305.5'2'0973   80–18925
ISBN 0–252–00827–8
    0–252–00932–0 (pbk)

To my Mother for who she is.
To the memory of my Father for who he was.

Contents

Many years ago I talked with Louis Hartz about my plans for a study of the Boston Brahmins. I asked whether he thought that an investigation of several urban élites might not be more significant than an examination of a single upper class. From an intellectual perspective and with an intensity and warmth that his former students know so well, Hartz advised the former course. So encouraged, I embarked on a scholarly odyssey that has taken me to Boston, New York, Charleston, Chicago, and Los Angeles. I chose these places because each represented a different type of city, because collectively they contained a variety of elites, thus enriching the possibility for historical comparisons, and because these cities and their dominant enclaves illuminated important features of the American experience.

In their ability to signify and evoke essential stages and forces in our past, cities are mythic as well as actual communities. To their own inhabitants and to outsiders, Boston, New York, Charleston, Chicago, and Los Angeles embody different styles, accomplishments, and attitudes. No group has equaled the urban upper class in being conscious and proprietary of the symbolic aspect of metropolitan life and in developing, articulating, and projecting a unique and affirmative urban image. Boston and its Brahmins applauded their enclave and city for combining entrepreneurial shrewdness with dedication to intellectual endeavor and civic service. New York and its fashionable and business elites esteemed Gotham and its grandées for their sophistication and economic omnipotence. Charleston's tidewater aristocracy conceived of the place and its people as the citadel of gentility, the theater for the tragic romance of cavalier society, and the refuge from the national devotion to material aggrandizement and mechanical innovation. Chicago's leading citizens regarded themselves and the town as the ultimate realization of the western movement and American industrialism. The aerospace and media moguls of Los Angeles presently esteem their achievements as the jewels and their setting as the crown of post-industrial society. They are the high priests and their metropolis the new Rome of an empire that believes in technology as a god, the grandiose as a moral code, and consumption as paradise. These privileged groups, assisted by local publicists and literati, have been largely successful in gaining acceptance—at home and abroad—for their version of their class and city. Outsiders may have considered Boston and its Brahmins snobbish and stodgy—as much bluestocking as blueblood, New York and its *parvenu* millionaires the center of *arriviste* aggression, Chicago and its tycoons the archetype of blustering Babbitry, Charleston with its languishing gentry a relic of somnolent squiredom, and may now regard the movers and shakers of Los Angeles as the horsemen of an apocalyptic plenty. Even unsympathetic observers, however, have conceded the attributes that these elites attached to themselves and their environs, although they have not always seen the traits as unmitigated virtues.

Impelled by this vision, I set out to examine these elites through the dimensions of outlook, culture, and style. Less lofty but more significant considerations impinged on this strategy when I soon realized that commerce and power played a greater role in these establishments. Whatever their image and repute, their reality would never be recaptured unless I descended to the mundane matters of tax lists, business organizations, family relationships, cultural and charitable institutions, and political activity. I also found that my initial focus between 1790 and 1890, the golden age of the urban patriciates, left their beginnings and endings shrouded in ambiguity. Accordingly, I went back to the colonial era and forward to the present day. What has emerged is as comprehensive an account of these elites as my stamina and intelligence permitted.

I am grateful to my colleagues in the History Department of the University of Illinois, Nunzio Pernicone, David L. Ransel, Thomas A. Krueger, O. Vernon Burton, Joseph L. Love, Richard C. Trexler, Blair B. Kling, and Paul W. Drake, for reading extensive portions of the manuscript. They gave valuable time and judgment, and, in the best sense, encouraged this project. I am indebted for financial assistance to the American Philosophical Society, the Social Science Research Council, the Research Board of the University of Illinois, and the Center for Advanced Study at the University of Illinois, where I was an associate in 1971–72. I thank my research assistants, Jocelyn M. Ghent and Melvin L. Adelman, for their cheerful and indefatigable labor, and

Nancy Edwards and the History Department secretarial staff for typing the manuscript. Finally, I thank Elizabeth Dulany and Nancy Krueger for their editorial assistance.

F.C.J.
April, 1980
Urbana, Illinois

CHAPTER I

Introduction

Appeals to equality and humility echo through the ages, but societies almost invariably discriminate in distributing their assets. From remote beginnings to the present, power, wealth, and status have been unevenly spread among different social strata. The possession of one of these advantages has usually promoted the acquisition of others. History records widespread agreement on the nature and value of the rewards properly bestowed by the community. Focusing on those who amassed a major share of these precious resources in Boston, New York, Charleston, Chicago, and Los Angeles, I analyze the structure and strategy, tactics and thought of the upper levels of society. This perspective is important because the higher ranks have figured prominently in community decision-making. They have played key roles in determining policies that shape the exercise of authority, distribution of resources, levels and modes of conflict and cohesion, and relations with other societies.

The importance of leadership groups has drawn the attention of historians, social scientists, psychologists, philosophers, politicians, *belles lettrists*, journalists, and ordinary citizens. Friends and critics alike have been concerned with the organization of power, wealth, and status, and with the values, habits, and impulses of the upper orders. The most significant and dramatic issue in American elite studies is the current debate between proponents of the view that the United States is ruled by a multifunctional oligarchy, whose members shuttle between command posts of big business corporations, the executive branch of the federal government, the armed services, and the key foundations and universities, and the pluralists, who claim that power is fragmented among pressure groups representing counterbalancing geographical, economic, class, and ethnic interests. This book concentrates on local leadership enclaves. But the prominent citizens of the cities here investigated made or still make an impact on the national as well as the local scene. Through tracing their careers and the involvement of Boston, New York, Charleston, Chicago, and Los Angeles in the national economy and polity, a much needed and largely absent historical dimension will, it is hoped, be added to the controversy over the power structure of contemporary America. This exploration of the past may at least clarify the issue of whether power is today more consolidated or pyramidical than in earlier eras.

Concrete research methods and abstract analytic principles work together, as they do in other scholarly efforts, to shape this venture in elite studies. Common strategies of investigation and organization employed to gather and interpret the data on each enclave and theoretical constructs applied to explain their behavior provide the unifying context for the urban establishments described in the following chapters. Let us turn first to the plan of exploration and presentation and begin with the question of definition.

Those who exercise authority, accumulate wealth, and command respect may be called elites, upper classes, or aristocracies. Conventional usage designates as elite all groups that wield power or possess fortunes or high status. The term also denotes all groups that demonstrate excellence: elite scholars, elite athletes, elite criminals, etc. It is also applied to enclaves within classes. Not every member of the upper class, even in an aristocracy, is equal in power, affluence, or esteem, and those with a disproportionate share of these advantages become an intraclass elite when compared to less endowed members of the stratum. The elasticity of casual usage, however, makes the category too generic, and therefore imprecise. Elites exist at many levels and in many areas of society. But some levels do not have enough wealth, power, and legitimacy, and some areas are too narrow, to gain the celebrity and influence requisite for community leadership. Upper classes and aristocracies, on the other hand, assume generalized hegemony. Military, professional, political, economic, or intellectual elites may exist as separate entities, but enclaves of more comprehensive and consequently more fundamental preeminence in the community must incorporate or control these specialized echelons.

Distinguishing between upper class and aristocracy or patriciate is more difficult but just as essential. Both categories denote a group which holds, or at least has held, the highest and most widely recognized authority in the community. Unlike elites, who are frequently specialized and whose members may find fulfillment through a variety of unrelated affiliations, upper classes and aristocracies are organized to shape all facets of their members' lives and thus make exclusive claims for loyalty. What differentiates these two social orders is not hegemony but mobility. Upper-class status can be achieved by personal effort but patricians are not self-made. This investigation of leadership groups proceeds from their origins, usually as specialized economic elites, to their broadening into upper-class structures through the assumption of political, social, and cultural sovereignty, and finally to their decline as they sought persistence by acquiring aristocratic overtones.

I have used three perspectives in studying these groups: compositional, operational, and intellectual. These approaches are instruments to discover who those groups were, what they did, what they thought, and what was thought of them. Identification required research in tax records to isolate the rich, civil lists to uncover leading government officeholders, business activity to disclose the entrepreneurial elite, memberships in charity, social, and cultural agencies to discover the notables in these sectors of community leadership, and family and genealogical accounts to obtain additional material on these matters and to establish kinship networks. These sources enabled me to construct aggregate economic, political, and social profiles of each enclave at various times in its history and to make interurban as well as intraclass comparisons. I supplemented this "hard" evidence with reputational assessments from within the elite or from outside observers regarding the power and status of various figures in these places.

What these groups did (or failed to do) is the fundamental consideration in this study. It directly addresses the key concerns of elite explorations: Is there a comprehensive ruling class that acts in unity, is sovereignty divided among several elites, or does a kind of issue-mobilized pluralism prevail? Are the privileged productive or parasitical members of society? Where, how, and to what degree do hegemonic groups establish and preserve their dominance? The resolution of these issues lies in functional analysis. Hence I devote the largest share of my efforts to reconstructing the roles and functions of the leadership echelons. In what ways, to what extent, and with what results did they control urban life? This phase of the study focuses on the accomplishments, conflicts, and defeats of the urban upper strata. For this purpose I have consulted contemporary and historical accounts of the professions, business firms, party organizations, political and commercial strife, charitable and cultural institutions, and social clubs, and such primary material as letters, newspapers, and periodicals. When possible I have used decisional analysis to evaluate hegemony. I tried to define and distinguish major issues, to discern the role of the upper ranks in creating or resolving such issues, and to assess the impact of such action on their position in the community.

My final objective has been to reveal the mentalities of these groups: How did they regard themselves? What moved them to attain and lose their standing? Did the personalities, ideas, and priorities in these enclaves remain constant over time or stage of development? Were there variations in outlook and impulse in groups in different cities or in different groups in the same city? Did beliefs and attitudes ever harmonize and thus contribute to intra- and intergroup cohesion and strength, or did they contain contradictions that sowed doubt and dissension and thus undermined the capacity to persevere? Did emotional and intellectual perspectives reflect or challenge the national creed, and did such discrepancy or congruence weaken or advance hegemonic claims? What character traits enhanced the growth or decline of the groups? These inquiries focused on collective and individual personality types and thought processes. In dealing with these questions I consulted books, diaries, and letters written by and about prominent citizens or groups in the cities that I examined.

The findings are presented in five essays, each dealing with one city. These chapters proceed along the same lines. Each is organized through a linear time sequence divided into the crucial stages in the history of the privileged urban group or groups. The chronological periods, in turn, are subdivided according to the major activities of the dominant echelons. These sections focus on entrepreneurial, political, professional, cultural, charitable, and social endeavors. Each essay concentrates on indigenous developments, but includes relevant comparisons with counterparts in other cities. The concluding chapter relates the five case studies to other urban upper strata in the United States, to ruling establishments in Europe, and to the alleged existence of an American oligarchy. The broader ramifications of this investigation illuminate such considerations as the uniqueness of American society, the general implications of the theories of leadership and accounts of hegemonic groups in Boston, New York, Charleston, Chicago, and Los Angeles, and the degree of replication, and consequent validation and larger significance, of the contentions made about the upper strata in these cities.

This study is unified by more than approach (identical methods used to investigate each upper stratum) or organization (the same presentation format for each enclave). A group of concepts, abstractions that interact to form models of elite behavior, interrelate the findings. These paradigms act through a process that social scientists call reification to give more general meaning to the data. As analytic categories they delineate possible behavior patterns of the upper orders and offer explanations for parallel and dissimilar developments that took place in the privileged ranks in these five cities. Stated in simpler terms these theoretical constructs provide the basis for intra- and interurban comparisons among the dominant groups. What follows is an outline of these principles. A more detailed application of the ideas to the historical material is found in the study of the Boston Brahmins. The essays on the enclaves in the other cities assume but do not reiterate the formulas articulated in the introduction and elaborated in the discussion of Boston.

Barring such events as revolutions, coups, civil wars, foreign conquests, economic collapse, or rapid and widespread demographic shifts, the pattern and personnel of community leadership derive from and usually support the traditional social order. Those who exercise authority, however, frequently modify the social system from which they emerged. Since hegemonic groups can lead only by mobilizing the community to cope with the problems of its environment, social change may necessitate creating new institutions, norms, and goals and then coercing or persuading the community to accept these innovations. To retain their position and to preserve the continuity of their society, leaders may also have to modify their own behavior. This process of maintaining and modifying enables dominant groups and individuals to persist by convincing society that they are indispensable for the fulfillment of its ends. Accordingly, influential groups decline because their formulations are rejected, they are no longer thought to reflect the prevailing pattern of social forces, and people lose faith in their ability to organize society for achievement of desired goals. Thus an enclave may deteriorate because it is no longer believed capable of leadership. But it may also descend more abruptly as a result of the cataclysms or radical changes mentioned above.

Put more concretely, the legitimacy of leadership (as opposed to rule by force and terror) combines, in delicate balance, community deference and sufferance. The higher ranks must establish social distance between themselves and the less privileged without cutting themselves off from their followers; they must be exclusive without becoming isolated or irrelevant; and they must have more of what everyone has or wants without making the less endowed feel unjustly deprived. Finally, while higher strata must convince themselves and society that they more perfectly embody commonly held ideals and thus deservedly command a greater share of the community assets, they must also convince themselves and society that they have special qualities that may be universally desired and lauded but inhere uniquely in the upper order. This last justification of hierarchy entails the mystical and charismatic santification of sovereignty.

Such generalizations remain superficial unless they explain the formation of the upper strata, their scope of authority, the duration of their ascendance, and the causes of their decline. Once these explanations are available the behavior of these enclaves, the relations between dominant figures or groups and their followers, and the society's responses to social change can be more precisely analyzed. It is to be hoped that my interpretations of these issues will apply not only to enclaves examined in this book but to other American local or possibly national ruling groups, and to the problem of leadership in general.

A basic theme of this book is the response of the upper orders to their local situation. This situation was both created by their own initiative and determined by forces beyond their control. It shaped their consciousness and activity; it influenced their internal composition and relationships to other groups and to national developments. The changing context (sometimes broadening and sometimes narrowing) in which they operated continually modified their own structure and outlook. Constantly varying internal and external environments dictate that their behavior can be fully explored only by tracing them through their entire existence.

With the partial exception of the Charleston patriciate, the upper strata here examined dwelled in cities. The urban milieu quickens the growth of bureaucracy, division of labor, geographic and social mobility, diffusion of information and education, social and economic change, ethnic variety, community heterogeneity, idiosyncratic lifestyles, segmented relationships, and personal anonymity. These forces encourage turnover at the top, thus inhibiting the development of elites into upper classes and aristocracies. Yet in America and even in Europe the higher ranks have flocked to the city. Courtiers as well as capitalists have found metropolitan life more invigorating and advantageous than the hallowed idylls of rural existence. If town life created or intensified obstacles to stability in the upper orders it also offered unmatched opportunities for the acquisition of wealth, knowledge, and power. The city has always been the center of trade, finance, and other business activities. Educational institutions, cultural efforts, government administration, amusement facilities, and communications networks have been most nurtured and highly developed, and generally located, in or near cities. These facets of urban society have contributed to the cohesion and multidimensional mastery of the upper orders while other aspects have worked in the opposite direction.

The universal qualities of the metropolitan environment do not preclude diverse types of urban communities. Cities differ by age; size; location; stages and rates of growth, decline, or change; demographic characteristics; economic endeavor; government structure; extent of regional and national influence; civic spirit; and cultural tone. If the uniformities of urban existence produce similarities in the upper strata of different cities, these divergences create dissimilarities. Cities also undergo profound transformations over the course of their history. Intraurban changes over time are, in fact, usually greater than interurban contrasts during the same period. Hence the city's upper ranks experience considerable modification at different stages in its development. For these reasons, cities and their hegemonic enclaves must be studied in historical depth. Boston, New York, Charleston, Chicago, and Los Angeles were selected for investigation because they differ from each other in ways that exemplify the variety of urban society, and, therefore, of urban establishments. Conversely, continuities appear in different places and persist over time. These constant elements cause replications in the patterns and structures of leadership in these five cities and consistencies in the behavior and personnel of leadership groups of different eras in the same city.

The rich, the well-born, and the powerful in Boston, New York, Chicago, Charleston, and Los Angeles were not detached individuals or solitary family units. They comprised visible and functional collectivities; therefore it is possible to use social theory to explain their behavior. Concepts from entrepreneurial, family, class, and social group theory, the sociology of knowledge, systems analysis, and social psychology, especially research on achievement and ascriptive personality types, are obviously applicable to this study.

In each city prominent figures congregated through commercial transactions, political alliances, professional societies, business associations, benevolent agencies, cultural organizations, social clubs, church attendance, residence in the same neighborhood, and matriculation at the same schools. These interactions gave rise to ties of friendship and kinship. Institutional and affective types of interrelationships, particularly in those cases where the enclave was relatively long-lived and could effectively exclude or co-opt outsiders, created empathetic feelings in the upper echelons. This consciousness in part derived from the above structural factors, but it also came from shared values, life-styles, experiences, and expectations. Public functions as entrepreneurs, officeholders, lawyers, doctors, philanthropists, and society figures, and less often as intellectuals, contributed to the power, prestige, and sense of group identity in the upper orders. These roles and their rewards showed that the rest of the community accepted the sovereignty of the upper layer. Deference helped fulfill the establishment's expectations, reinforce its self-image, fortify its salience, and enhance its solidarity.

The upper orders constitute reference groups that gave meaning and context to the lives of their members. Since this was the fundamental and universal attribute of these enclaves, the principles of reference group theory compose the essential analytic category of this study. Reference groups define for their members their place in society by providing them with sets of loyalties and emotional bonds, and by clarifying for their adherents the intersection between personal and communal life. The primary reference group is the family, which plays a critical role in determining activities that range from political party affiliation to spouse selection. Most individuals, however, have many roles and some of these lie outside the family. Hence they belong to a variety of reference groups—ethnic, religious, geographical, vocational, political, social, etc.—which anchor them in society and give them self-identity. Elites may form in relatively narrowly bounded reference groups which may not carry over from one area of life to another. Social classes, on the other hand, are more comprehensive. They regulate familial, occupational, economic, political, cognitive, ethical, and esthetic modes of behavior. In a hierarchical social system power, wealth, and status concentrate in upper classes and aristocracies. These groups seek to control the outlook and activities of their members and to influence, if not always to actually formulate or determine, the behavior of the lower levels. Indeed, the essence of a ruling enclave lies in its ability to shape its members and direct others toward the acceptance of its reign. In this country, where hierarchy contends with equality and constituted authority with individual autonomy, privileged ranks have, to a greater or lesser degree, approximated but not consolidated preeminence. Social and economic change and ethnic heterogeneity have also prevented the monopoly of power by creating counter elites that have challenged older establishments.

The groups here studied not only operated under these limitations but were subject to other conditions that influenced their sovereignty. Their dominance peaked when they embodied the spirit and goals and seemed to further the concrete interests, and therefore gained the respect, of the community. In this phase of their existence they were the economic arbiters of their cities. Control over important commercial undertakings, which enabled them to generate wealth, give employment, and oversee the course of metropolitan development, elicited obedience and often admiration from other urban residents. These business elites recognized that political leverage aided entrepreneurship. Their command over municipal government, at least for a time, was not effectively contested because other inhabitants believed in their superiority or were unable to mobilize the resources to defeat them. Ensconced in key commercial and political positions, these enclaves took a proprietary interest in their communities. This impulse involved wealth, power, civic pride, *noblesse oblige*, the need for recognition, and the desire of political-economic elites to strengthen their authority. It propelled such groups into leadership of urban welfare and cultural institutions and programs. Once again the lower classes trusted or could not resist the upper orders. In the course of extending their dominion the elites developed into upper classes.

These multifunctional groups in Boston, Charleston, and Philadelphia, to name an enclave not included in this study, became aristocracies. Given the nature of American democratic capitalism, however, they never wholly escaped their bourgeois-entrepreneurial origins and thus did not become pure patriciates, such as the European nobility, with standing in law and tradition. Nevertheless, these establishments acquired the essential aristocratic attribute of intergenerational bequests of rank and role. This development made ascriptive considerations like birth and kinship overshadow the achievement motive that inspired their family-founding and fortune-hunting ancestors and that remained basic to the American creed. The transition from elite to patriciate thus involved a reordering of priorities from individual to group, from innovation to tradition, and from mobility to inheritance. These upper orders looked upon themselves, and were often similarly regarded by outsiders, as a species of urban gentry, a commercial aristocracy in the northern cities, or more ambiguously a rural-urban squirearchy in Charleston, where low-country planters resided for part of the year in the city-state of tidewater South Carolina.

Kinship was crucial even before the emergence of aristocratic characteristics. From their first appearance as mercantile or agrarian elites, even among the entrepreneurs of post-Revolutionary New York, whose community leadership did not last long enough to assume an aristocratic dimension, commercial needs entailed a reliance upon family connection. Moreover, human impulse, or at least social obligation and defense, has historically encouraged the advancement of relatives. Households in the upper strata of these cities were nuclear in form but extended in substance. Although they generally did not live together, grandparents and grandchildren, uncles, nephews, and cousins, parents and married children constantly interacted. Business firms and medical and legal practices were often partnerships with other relatives, employed kin in responsible positions, and frequently were passed on to collateral or direct descendants. When commercial elites evolved into upper classes, the dynastic principle and family loyalty embraced the entire range of group functions. Tribal and kinship ties influenced public officeholding, preparatory school and college entry, admission to social clubs, militia units, and charity and cultural societies, invitation to dinners, parties, and dances, and ultimately, cemetery interment.

The expansion of hegemony and the emergence of ascriptive norms, patterns, and institutions created an ambience of contradictory forces for those elites that broadened into upper classes and patriciates. By increasing the scope of their sovereignty they fortified each part of it and strengthened their claim to community leadership. Commercial eminence facilitated the assumption of political power, and government influence promoted business enterprise. Money and power, the basic sources of upper-class status, enhanced the opportunity to control such secondary spheres of community life as philanthropy and culture. Civic welfare activities legitimized leadership claims by giving renown to the establishment and providing the means to indoctrinate the urban masses and control dependent groups. Its expanding dominion also consolidated the upper echelon. Group cohesion was enhanced when the establishment fulfilled expectations of leadership roles and distributed rewards of wealth, influence, and fame to its members: Those in the upper rank internalized its values and became more self-confident in their position of authority, thus reinforcing their incentive and capacity for command and the fusion of personal identity with group membership. Internal and external circumstances worked together. Acknowledgment by outsiders of the enclave's superiority integrated the group, and solidarity of purpose and action in turn made it a more effective ruling entity. Urban elites surviving to the aristocratic stage were further united by tradition and intergenerational kinship networks.

If the expansion of the elites into local upper classes and patriciates widened their realm and strengthened their identity, this transition could also weaken their rule and solidarity. These opposing trends, triggered by the same developmental process, constitute the dialectic of upper-class formation and fragmentation. Before assuming authority in altruistic, intellectual, social, and esthetic matters, the elite could concentrate on commercial enterprise and political power. At this stage it focused on the crucial determinants of sovereignty and made the greatest impact on the city. At all levels of society, government and business were considered the vital activities, and success in such endeavors enabled the elite to dominate other aspects of urban life. The additional dimensions of leadership, however, were less important. Moreover, the diversification and extension of its hegemony drew time, energy, and capital away from the main concerns of the community. This deflection of resources occurred at a time when urban conditions stimulated the rise of groups and individuals, such as *parvenu* tycoons or ethnic politicians, seeking to challenge the suzerainty of the older establishments. Emerging elites were undeterred by factors that inhibited the upper orders of more ancient vintage: the former devoted themselves more exclusively to business and government; the latter were bound, or at least constricted, by kinship ties and traditional modes of behavior that hindered an efficient defense of their entrepreneurial and political position.

Forces of a different nature from the dynamics of rise and fall of social class accelerated the disintegration of the old order. *Arrivistes* were encouraged by the American ethos, which preached, if it did not guarantee, equal opportunity in an open society. Older regnant enclaves, on the other hand, seemed by their allegiance to tradition and inheritance to question the commitment to progress, functional specialization, technological growth, rational calculation, individual achievement, meritocratic ideals, and bureaucratic organization that increasingly permeated the national and urban outlook. Impressive rates of economic growth and change and the massive migration of ethnic minorities, which had the greatest impact in places like Boston, New York, Chicago, and Los Angeles, and the Civil War, which gravely wounded the Charleston gentry, also facilitated the emergence of new contenders for leadership.

The older groups were ultimately swept aside. What they attained first they lost first and what they secured last remained longest in their grip. The counter elites, primarily interested in wealth and power, initially displaced the establishment in business and government, while content to adopt a tutorial stance in charity, culture, and fashion. In fact, the newcomers felt that their own elevation in status depended in part upon learning the style of their forerunners. And who could teach them better than the offspring of the old families! Accordingly, the recently endowed sought to join prestigious social clubs, to serve on boards of distinguished benevolent and cultural institutions, to be present at exclusive dinners and dances, and to send their children to proper preparatory schools and colleges. Eventually, however, loss of wealth and influence and changes in national and local values and life-styles resulted in the departure of the older groups from this shadow of their former eminence. The legitimacy of the old hierarchy was demythologized when the symbiosis between community leadership and social distance broke down.

Declining upper classes and aristocracies underwent a process of decomposition which reversed their climb to preeminence. Displacement in one facet of their authority spread to other areas of leadership. Failure to maintain hegemony stimulated internal disintegration as members of the declining enclave were disappointed in their expectations of riches, prestige, and power and discovered that group norms no longer corresponded to reality. This awareness encouraged intramural divisions as segments of the patriciate deserted to join the newly risen or simply left the city. Exogamous marriage, and divorce, for example, became more frequent. Traits and perspectives began to appear which reflected and accelerated the downward course, just as ancestral dispositions and outlooks had reflected and stimulated the push to the top. Family and group founders had been shrewd, self-assertive, and hardworking businessmen and politicians, whose triumphant careers affirmed the national and local commitment to pragmatic activism and upward mobility. Their descendants, who haunted the mansions, clubhouses, and ballrooms of Boston, Chicago, New York, and Charleston were often contemplative, confused, and despairing of themselves, their class, and their nation.

This analysis of rise and fall best explains those enclaves that went the route from elites to aristocracies. The paradigm applies in its most complete form to the Boston Brahmins, although the other upper strata displayed many of its elements and went through various stages of the development from specialized elites to a hereditary urban gentry. But I deal here with different types of cities, hence the histories of their upper ranks do not always converge. Charleston, too, had a patriciate, but its origin was agrarian as well as mercantile, its life-style rural as well as urban, and its demise was more abrupt and due more to a national catastrophe than to local or regional factors. New York, Chicago, and Los Angeles experienced rates of population and economic growth that far surpassed Boston or Charleston. By the mid–nineteenth century New York was the economic capital of the United States, a generation later Chicago became the idol of dynamic, industrial America, and now Los Angeles is the tinseled goddess of the age of consumption and leisure. The older elites in these three cities, unlike those of mellower and slower-growing Boston and Charleston, did not achieve the stability necessary to prolong their economic and political standing or establish themselves as arbiters of high culture and propriety. The proliferation of opportunities for riches, authority, and prestige brought to these places an incessant surge of newcomers who quickly engulfed the older elite, thus creating a rapid circulation at the top that made three generations of upper-class families a rare event and prevented the development of a patriciate.

This book focuses on the nineteenth century, a period when America transformed itself from an outpost of European civilization into the world's premier industrial power. Viewed from the perspective of modernization—the transition from an underdeveloped area into a highly urbanized and industrial society—the groups here studied went through one or more phases of a three-stage process. They originated as functional elites, some expanded their hegemony latitudinally into multifaceted upper classes, and a few longitudinally into aristocracies. Whether these echelons assumed the structure of elites, upper classes, or hereditary enclaves, the forces of economic, demographic, and political growth and change encouraged the emergence of newer functional elites that eclipsed traditional establishments.

From Adam Smith to Talcott Parsons it has become an axiom of modernization theory that economic growth and complexity, political centralization, division of labor, and elite pluralism are mutually dependent. This exploration in elite studies, however, will demonstrate that at different stages of urbanization, a key aspect of the modernization process, elites may evolve into upper classes and then decompose. Thus the relationship between modernization, urban development, and functional differentiation in the upper orders is less simplistic or linear than has previously been suggested. Hegemonic groups in Boston, New York, Charleston, Chicago, and Los Angeles began as specialized elites but aspired to, and frequently attained, a greater scope of community leadership. Ultimately they were deposed by other specialized elites, but their successors have, as in the cases of Chicago and New York robber barons or contemporary Los Angeles tycoons, similarly sought to enlarge their predominance.

CHAPTER II

COLONIAL BOSTON'S PATRICIATE

Massachusetts Bay Colony began as a "Grand Covenant" with God to advance His glory on earth. The New World Canaan commenced as an ordered agricultural village whose civil and spiritual governance devolved upon an oligarchy of magistrates and ministers. Two generations later, Puritan gentlemen still controlled the New England government but could not implement their original vision of the biblical commonwealth. A rapid emergence of mercantile leadership in such port towns as New Haven, Salem, Newburyport, Beverly, and Boston inhibited the realization of a Godly community.[1] Virtually from Boston's initial settlement, a commercial enclave exerted considerable influence over town affairs. This elite assumed authoritative social roles, commanded essential community resources, and developed a collective identity.

Group cohesion came about through joint commercial ventures, residence in the same neighborhood, common organizational membership, intermarriage, and shared outlooks and life-styles. Preeminence depended upon control over vital urban activities and upon arrogation of wealth, high status, and power. The mutually reinforcing phenomena of societal predominance and class integration emerged within a decade of the city's founding. Nearly all thirty-four chief contributors to the building of a school and fort in 1636 were members and officers of the First Church; four-fifths served as assistants, members of the general court, or town selectmen. This group, called "Boston's gentry" by the historian of John Winthrop's Boston, contained eighteen

merchants or sea captains.[2] At an early date prominent traders constituted a multidimensional elite which supported key communal enterprises and occupied important public offices.

Mercantile-inspired urban projects continued in the next century.
Initiatives sometimes sprang from self-interest as in the case of the Long
Wharf project (1707).[3] On other occasions commercial magnates directed their energies and resources to community needs less immediately involved with their purses. In 1718 Thomas and Edward
Hutchinson built a schoolhouse for Boston, and eminent merchants
donated funds to pay schoolmasters and served as overseers of the poor
and school inspectors.[4] In rendering these important services they became the guardians of public welfare, thus substantiating their claim to
community hegemony.

The Revolution caused a large turnover in upper-class personnel and
the advent of industry changed its economic base, but the structure and
mode of leadership remained remarkably constant for over two centuries. This continuity appeared in the persistence of three organizations begun in the seventeenth century. Shortly after the display of mercantile support for the fort and school, tradesmen figured prominently
in the formation of the Ancient and Honorable Artillery Company
(1638); by 1640 almost every merchant in the Bay area belonged. Intended for military purposes, it functioned chiefly as a social club and
until well into the nineteenth century was a gathering place for blueblood Boston.[5] Fifty years later the merchants helped found another
lasting institution, King's Chapel. Anglicanism became the dominant
religion among the upper orders and King's Chapel the favored church
of the governmental and mercantile establishment. Many of Boston's
first families still worshipped there in the nineteenth century.[6] The Artillery Company and King's Chapel integrated the upper class by encouraging good fellowship among peers and sanctifying a common system of beliefs and values. The highly visible rituals of these institutions
also advanced patrician unity and repute by promoting a feeling of
worthiness in their members and making outsiders aware of the honor of
belonging to them.

Harvard College (1636) was a third major source of upper-class cohesion and institutional perpetuity. The college, unlike the Artillery Company or King's Chapel, was created primarily by the Puritan oligarchy. It
quickly became an institution for the colony's eminent clans. Over half
of the seventeenth-century graduates were related to other Harvard
families.[7] Social ties made at school paved the way for later political
advancement. After 1723 classes were ranked by family background and
those in the top half who became general court representatives had an
80 percent chance of becoming leaders in the provincial assembly.
Twenty-two of the thirty-three Massachusetts supreme court judges be-

tween 1692 and 1796 matriculated at Harvard and twenty-six members of the governor's council who served from 1740 to 1755 went to the college and thirty-six sent their sons.[8] Generations of young patricians received a genteel education there. Undergraduate club and dormitory life reinforced endogamous familial, friendly, and business associations and fostered unions with society belles. A degree could be a passport for those not entitled by lineage to membership in the urban aristocracy; promising youths were discerned and developed and the group strengthened by the addition of their talents. Harvard thus became an important stage of socialization, and graduation, a rite of passage and a credential for recruitment in upper-class Boston.

Intermarriage solidified the upper echelon. Marital ties were promoted by business dealings, proximity of living quarters, political coalition, and common membership in voluntary associations. In an age of informal business practices, poor communications, and political nepotism, kinship played a crucial role in attaining riches, place, and power and fulfilled the natural desire to bequeath wealth and status to descendants. By the end of the seventeenth century the great clans of the Puritan ministry and magistracy and the Puritan and newly arrived Anglican merchants were interrelated through blood and marriage. In the eighteenth century these links multiplied and the circle broadened to include the recently risen, and, on occasion, prominent figures from the British provincial government.[9]

Assumption of elite roles and the continuity and cohesion necessary to sustain them ultimately depended upon wealth and power. Without these resources the patriciate could not have attained its position, much less passed it on to later generations. Boston early became the chief colonial port; accordingly its merchants possessed most of the city's large personal accumulations. Of the sixteen fortunes rated at least £100 on the Boston tax list of 1686–87, twelve belonged to merchants, sea captains, shipbuilders, and distillers. These occupations also predominated in the top quarter of this tax roll.[10] The next century's richest Bostonians owned a significantly larger proportion of the city's assessed wealth than did their Puritan predecessors, and affluence increasingly concentrated in the mercantile component. A relatively smaller elite now controlled foreign trade and, as in the seventeenth century, supplemented commercial profits with landholdings and urban real estate.[11] According to the most thorough survey of the distribution of eighteenth-century wealth in Boston, the sixty largest property owners on the 1771 city assessment roll "consisted principally of merchants."[12]

The disproportionate share of wealth held by the mercantile elite was matched by their dominance of high public posts. Nearly two-thirds of the Bostonians who, between 1630 and 1699, became assistants, general court representatives, or selectmen were merchants, or involved in

foreign trade as sea captains, shipwrights, or frequent investors in overseas ventures, the majority being merchants. The maritime stratum also
frequently appeared in a host of strategic local offices as tax assessors,
town auditors, or clerks of the market. Although mercantile officeholders dwindled slightly between 1700 and 1774, over half the Boston
selectmen and representatives were active in commerce, and many
merchants continued to fill important local posts.[13] The small decline in
officeholding was more than compensated for by an enhanced position
in the assembly speakership and the governor's council. Merchants first
controlled the council in 1686 under Governor Joseph Dudley's administration. In the eighteenth century, Bowdoins, Ervings, Hancocks, Bel-
chers, and almost all the overseas magnates received appointments.
Moreover, two of the four native-born provincial governors were merchants, and the great traders or their sons frequently served as speakers
of the assembly; between 1740 and 1760 Bostonians held that post
three-quarters of the time and most of them came from the maritime
group. This segment of elite Boston also was prominent in the provincial
judiciary.[14] Officeholding positioned merchants and their allies to
influence government policy regarding land grants, military supply contracts, sales of town lands, building, market, and shipping regulations,
tax assessments, and trade licenses.

Despite a formidable accumulation of public offices and private fortunes, the mercantile magnates did not inevitably work their will. Their
reverses measure the limits of their own power and cohesion and the
strength of opposing contingents and coalitions. During the early years
the communitarian sentiments of the Puritan oligarchy frequently
checked the pursuit of profit, and agonized Puritan merchants committed themselves both to the Godly commonwealth and the business
ethic.[15] The disappearance of the sovereignty of the saints did not, however, ensure the triumph of the titans of the marketplace. Despite their
backing of the Silver Bank and other deflationary measures in the 1730s
and 1740s, the maritime magnates could not divert the Massachusetts
government from an inflationary money policy.[16] Setbacks might be expected on the colony level, where Boston merchants contended with
aggressive and articulate agrarian interests and traders from the interior.
Even in their own bailiwick, however, they encountered obstacles when
confronted by neighboring farmers, artisans, and small shopkeepers.
Opposition from these quarters prevented the overseas traders from
regularizing the Boston Market and mobilized an antimercantile faction
that often won victories in Boston politics. Several magnates even suffered property destruction because of popular resentment over their
policies and practices.[17]

Mercantile mastery was also curtailed by internal divisions. The great traders united on broad principles of seeking close ties with the British administration, opposing Puritan business restrictions, and attaining a stable and adequate money supply. Sometimes these common impulses resulted in mobilizing the maritime elite to support concrete policies, as in the case of the anti-inflationary initiatives of the 1730s and 1740s. More often these general aims encouraged contention, not coordination. Competition for trade privileges, public offices, land grants, and supply contracts fragmented the maritime elite into cliques vying with each other for commercial and political advantage.[18]

By the eighteenth century one important source of friction within the upper orders had been resolved. Differences over life-style that once divided businessmen and the Puritan oligarchy and Puritan and Anglican merchants gave way to widespread approval of commercial activity, the profit motive, and conspicuous consumption.[19] The multiplication and variety of private schools reveals the triumph of Georgian elegance over Puritan plainness. Seventeenth-century institutions gave instruction in practical subjects like writing or accounting, or prepared their students for college. The sevenfold increase in schools between 1700 and 1774 and the introduction of formerly forbidden subjects, such as dancing, attests to the growing wealth and sophistication of the town and to the urban elite's emulation of European aristocratic culture. Eighteenth-century Boston saw the advent of eleven schools for "Gentlewomen," seventeen for painting, embroidery, and flower-making, nine which gave dancing lessons as part or the whole of their offerings, five dancing or dancing and fencing academies, and nine music schools.[20]

The struggle for independence exposed the fragility behind the imposing upper-class facade. Impressive fortunes, exalted positions in the economic, political, and social hierarchies, and deference from lower orders did not prevent the deposition of some members of the provincial administrative and mercantile establishment: Hutchinsons, Brattles, Olivers, and other aristocrats loyal to British rule suffered exile and confiscation. Revolution, however, did not produce a complete class upheaval. Skill, luck, choice of the winning side, and the advantages of wealth and rank enabled others to survive the conflict relatively intact. More important remnants from colonial times were upper-class institutions that resumed former roles or were recreated. The persistence of the Artillery Company, King's Chapel, and Harvard, and the resurrection of the Merchants Club (1763) as the Boston Chamber of Commerce (1785) limited disruption in the elite.[21] Vocations as well as organizations bridged the gap of war and independence. For a generation after the conflict, great overseas merchants or members of their families dominated the city and for a much longer time retained high social status.

Durability of occupations and institutions in an age of national transformation discloses significant continuity in structure, if not in personnel, in upper-class Boston.

THE BOSTON BRAHMINS

Formation

A segment of the upper strata in Massachusetts Bay emerged from humble beginnings, but the majority had more privileged origins. Most of the leading magistrates and ministers stemmed from the gentry or prosperous yeomanry of England. Maritime magnates of early Boston were usually members of wealthy landowning families or had relatives in London livery companies. Subsequent generations of the colonial upper class owed their position mainly to eminent figures in the clerical, governmental, or commercial elite or to later arrivals with important court or business connections.[22] If inherited advantages facilitated reaching the top, plenty of room existed, at least by the eve of independence, for *arrivistes*. Of the sixty largest property owners on the Boston assessment role of 1771, "between 40 and 45 percent were *nouveaux riches*; indeed one-third were self-made men." Comparable minorities among the richest groups in pre-Revolutionary Philadelphia and New York, again mostly merchants, also achieved success through their own efforts. Relatively easy entry into the first echelon of wealth in northern cities vividly contrasts with constricted upward mobility in the low-country South Carolina and Virginia planter aristocracies.[23] This evidence, limited in time and place, permits no definite conclusions but indicates a more rapid turnover in urban business elites than in the rural gentry.

The vacuum created by the departure of many loyalists made the northern commercial patriciate even more accessible after the Revolution. Jackson Turner Main, studying a sample of merchants drawn from the 1789 Boston city directory, found that half the wealthiest and most distinguished Boston merchants in the 1780s derived from rich or comfortable families, usually in trade, but the rest rose from more modest backgrounds. A similar pattern of increased upward mobility marked the prominent merchants of contemporary New York. The richest Virginians of these years, on the other hand, overwhelmingly stemmed from the colonial gentility.[24] Land, at least in these instances, proved a more stable source of status than did commerce.

Substantial displacement of the Old Guard evoked laments even from members of the establishment who survived the Revolutionary turmoil. In 1777 Elizabeth Gray Otis, daughter of a great Boston merchant, complained: "Those who never knew what it was to live in a gentle way are now the first people here, while others, who were brought up in the most delicate manner, are by these unhappy times reduced to great dis-

tress." James Warren and Stephen Higginson expressed similar sentiments.[25]

Deposition of the pre-Revolutionary upper order was not as extensive
as these observations imply. Main's study of the commercial elite of
the 1780s discloses the varied roots of the enclave that dominated Boston for the next century. A composite profile of this group includes
those few members of the Puritan oligarchy who remained in the top
rank. With their reappearance in the nineteenth-century Boston Brahmin community, Endicotts, Winthrops, and Saltonstalls bridged the gap
between the oldest ruling coterie and its post-Revolutionary successor.
Another source of continuity came from survivals of the provincial
government-mercantile set, Amorys, Quincys, and Otises. But the
struggle for independence created openings for men from humbler local
elites in New England and even more obscure antecedents. Family fortunes were made in trade, piracy, and speculation during the Revolution, and in pioneering postwar commerce with China, India, and the
South Sea Islands. The Higginsons of Salem, the Danas of Cambridge,
and the Jacksons of Newburyport had ranked among the first families of
their hometowns for several generations. Other prominent Bostonians
had respectable and even substantial backgrounds of more recent advent. The Lees of Salem and the Lowells and Tracys of Newburyport
achieved business success a generation or two before independence. But
many self-made men reached the top in the late eighteenth century.
The fathers of William Sturgis, William Gray, and Samuel Eliot, founders of great overseas trading houses, were respectively a sea captain, a
master shoemaker, and an impecunious printer and bookseller. Boston's
richest capitalist, Peter Chardon Brooks, was the son of a poor minister.
The Appleton and Lawrence brothers, incorporated in the enclave in
the next generation, were children of respectable farmers from New
Ipswich and Groton. By the 1820s the Brahmin enclave, composed
eventually of some forty interrelated families, was substantially established.

Leading businessmen often came from small towns, villages, and
farms—a migration from the country to the city, from the periphery to
the center, that frequently appeared in other urban elites. Such movement indicated a willingness to cut roots and break with traditions, a
personality trait suited to entrepreneurship. As the group consolidated,
differences in social and economic origins merged. Newcomers
achieved parity with the Old Guard by moving into the positions and
even into the mansions vacated by the loyalists.[26]

Economic Triumph

Groups acquire influence and high status when the community is
convinced that they have the greatest skill in the roles it considers most

important. In the United States, a dynamic capitalist society, the crucial functions have been economic. Those who create, or are perceived to create, wealth and maximize production have won prestige and power. Dynamic capitalism is based on a continuous creation of opportunity, and this commitment to expansion puts a premium on innovation. The greatest economic growth, the greatest opportunities for success occur when new goods, new resources, new techniques, and new markets are discovered, and when technological and organizational improvements are introduced.

The entrepreneurial origins of the Boston Brahmins reveal how dynamic capitalism rewards men who affirm its values. To those with the resourcefulness to ply new routes, penetrate unexploited markets, provide desired goods, organize vital business enterprises, supply or obtain capital for commercial ventures, and command influence in turbulent political and commercial situations came fame, fortune, and power. British restrictions on trade within the imperial system forced the postwar mercantile elite to discover staples of trade in sealskins from the Oregon country, Hawaiian sandalwood, and Chinese silks and tea; to enter new markets at Canton, St. Petersburg, and Calcutta; and to return to Boston to find eager buyers for their exotic goods. Russell & Co., J. & T. H. Perkins, and later Bryant & Sturgis became the largest foreign traders, and windfalls from their ventures launched many blueblood family fortunes.[27] The success of Boston and other merchants accounted for their predominance among the wealthiest citizens in the northeastern ports. According to the latest and most thorough survey of the antebellum rich in these maritime centers, merchants in 1830 and 1850 (including brokers, auctioneers, and agents) composed respectively 69 and 66 percent of the uppermost 1 percent of affluent Bostonians, and similarly high shares of equivalent enclaves in Philadelphia, Brooklyn and New York.[28]

Overseas commerce integrated the patriciate in other ways than establishing its common economic base. Interdependence was promoted by large risks and spare capital reserves, uncertain communications and commercial intelligence, and the rudimentary state of legal and institutional guarantees in the days before widespread corporate organization. Joint investment minimized the hazards and maximized the financing of long voyages into dangerous territories. In 1784, for example, a group of Boston merchants outfitted the *Columbia* in order to open up the Northwest Coast fur trade.[29] Reliable shipmasters, supercargoes, and clerks could be counted on to carry out instructions, adjust to unanticipated developments, and transmit trustworthy business information, thus overcoming the problems involved in remote and chancy markets. Unable to closely supervise their distant transactions, local merchants needed efficient and faithful employees for accurate data and resourceful action. "I depend . . . more upon your judgment when there," Patrick Tracy Jackson told kinsman Henry Lee, his future factotum in India, "than upon any directions I can now give for the disposal of any of my concerns placed by this authority under your direction—and I wish you to feel hereby authorized to take charge of any property you may find of mine in India."[30]

Shaped by the conditions of overseas commerce, the great firms were networks of personal contacts. Like the royal courts and noble households of a more distant past, they recruited and trained upper-class neophytes. Young clerks, mates, captains, and supercargoes schooled in Russell & Co., Perkins & Co., or by Elias Hasket Derby resembled pages and squires of earlier times. Serving their apprenticeships on deck or at the countinghouse rather than on the battlefield or in the bedchamber, they acquired the wherewithal and experience to start their own shipping businesses or, in later years, to become textile or railroad magnates. Key associates in these organizations increasingly tended to be united by blood and marriage as business enterprise in upper-class Boston assumed its characteristic structure, the family firm. John P. Cushing, William Sturgis, John Murray Forbes, and Robert Bennet Forbes worked for their uncle, Thomas Handasyd Perkins. For several generations the interrelated Lees, Higginsons, Tracys, Jacksons, and Cabots formed partnerships and employed sons, nephews, and cousins. Henry Lee explained to a rejected applicant, "I have several near relations who are in want, and whom I should prefer." Trust and compatibility, as well as family obligations and affection, account for the precedence given to kinfolk. Perkins wrote brother James, on the eve of their partnership, when "strangers . . . connect themselves in business . . . great uneasiness" and "low suspicions" often occur. "On the other hand a connection between brothers is both natural and beneficial; they have fewer distrusts and are more communicative, wh[ich] strengthens their confidence and makes their business but amusement."[31] By the turn of the century, business alliances had led to connubial connections, and foreign trade was in the hands of a group of intertwined families. The family firm, by enlisting or giving business to relatives, encouraged confidence, expanded class and familial resources and commercial opportunities, and mitigated risks and losses. It sheltered failed or weak relatives who might otherwise have fallen from the upper order, thereby contributing to family solidity and class perpetuity in an era of frequent bankruptcy. Robert Gould Shaw recouped the family fortune by being apprenticed to Uncle Samuel Shaw, Perkins protected faltering relatives, and Lee and Henry Lee Higginson reestablished themselves by serving as supercargoes in the firms of kinsmen.[32] A commercial elite stabilized by common interests, coalitions, and intermarriage emerged in the Federalist era.

The quest for wealth and the need for capital and business stability were not satisfied by triumphs in foreign trade or institutions like the family firm. The mercantile elite, like its colonial predecessor, moved into other enterprises to solidify and expand its predominance. For example, life, fire, and marine insurance was an obvious means of generating capital and providing security. Although the first families of Philadelphia supplemented their commercial profits by organizing insurance companies, except for marine insurance, the branch closest to shipping, Boston maritime magnates preferred other endeavors. Marine underwriting, however, made Peter Chardon Brooks Boston's first millionaire and involved other Brahmin traders as well.[33]

Besides overseas commerce, banking was the primary activity of Boston's business elite. Prominent merchants in Philadelphia, New York, Boston, Providence, Salem, and other maritime centers turned to banking as a means of capital accumulation, a field of fruitful investment, and an instrument of economic power. Philadelphia was dubbed "the cradle of American finance" because the Bank of North America (1781), the nation's first chartered bank, and the First Bank of the United States (BUS) (1791) were located there. These financial institutions were founded or directed by members of leading mercantile families.[34] Eminent traders and their allies in Boston and New York followed a similar pattern. Boston merchants of the provincial era had sought a stable supply of money and credit by attempting to charter a bank in the 1740s. This effort failed, but their successors, motivated by the same concerns, founded the first public commercial bank in Boston. The Massachusetts First National Bank of Boston (1784) was organized by Brahmin traders. Since its directors, officers, shareholders, and customers came primarily from this enclave, the Massachusetts senate unsurprisingly discovered in 1792 that loans were "for the most part made to opulent merchants of extensive business and credit. . . ." Serving the most powerful and prosperous group as a source of capital and profits and as a mechanism of exchange, and using conservative policies that stabilized the supply and value of currency and credit, the bank was the largest in New England until 1815. Long after the decline of the mercantile community it exerted considerable influence in Boston. An upper-class enterprise, the bank took on the family structure typical of Brahmin businesses: William Phillips was the second president, his son the sixth, his grandson the eighth, and his daughter-in-law's father the third.[35] Until 1792 the bank monopolized Boston finance, but the appearance of new institutions merely extended the reign of the mercantile magnates. The National Union Bank (1792), the Old Boston Bank (1804), the State National Bank of Boston (1811)—the largest bank in Boston from 1815 to 1827, and the Boston branches of the first (1792) and second Bank of the

United States (1816) were organized, officered, and owned chiefly by Brahmin merchants or their kin.[36]

While gaining control of foreign trade and banking, the commercial elite engaged in another endeavor reminiscent of their colonial predecessors. The great merchants and their allies became landowners, improvers, and speculators. Later they were joined by those who made their fortunes in the cotton industry. Patrician realtors carried over into this field of enterprise the boldness and unprecedented scale of their banking and overseas ventures. The first noteworthy project undertaken by the maritime magnates was the construction in 1785 of what was then the largest toll bridge in America. In 1792 and 1804 blueblood entrepreneurs spanned other Boston outlets with bridges. Around the turn of the century the Mount Vernon Proprietors, a syndicate of elite merchants and their associates, began to develop Beacon Hill, an operation of unprecedented magnitude. Until the 1860s Brahmins conceived, financed, and directed the development of Beacon Hill, Back Bay, and large parts of South Boston and the Waterfront, the city's largest antebellum real estate undertakings.[37]

These initiatives blended private gain with public interest. Bridges, improved wharfage, widened streets, better markets, and building construction facilitated transportation and trade, and upgraded land values, vital interests of the upper class. The economic and esthetic consequences of these efforts, however, benefited the entire community. When in public office, the largest speculators sometimes accomplished highly useful projects. Mayors Josiah Quincy and Harrison Gray Otis cleaned up Boston Common, and Quincy widened Fanueil Hall Market and helped establish the Public Gardens.[38] These activities helped transform the Yankee town into a sophisticated city.

Land speculation contributed to Brahmin wealth and, as another field of cooperative endeavor, united the upper class. Real estate investment particularly promoted group cohesion when it created patrician residential areas. The Proprietors, by developing Beacon Hill as an exclusive neighborhood, exemplified elite enterprise enhancing upper-class integration. Beginning in 1796, Brahmins bought up land and built family mansions on Beacon Hill. To this day parts of the Hill remain an upper-class district, and descendants of the original investors live in some of the old houses. Distinctive ethnic and social enclaves seek their own turf; the Boston gentry were no exception to this dwelling pattern. Residential proximity and retention of ancestral homes became a class emblem both for the elite and for outsiders. *Arrivistes* moved there to legitimize their acquired status and joined oldtimers in fighting to save the historical, genealogical, and esthetic integrity of the neighborhood. Despite the neighborhood's location near the business center, they successfully resisted rezoning even though the introduction of hotels, apartment houses, and commercial structures would raise property values. Cultural and class solidity preempted the profit motive and preserved Beacon Hill as an expression of Brahmin Boston.[39]

Political Power

The assumption of civic authority augmented patrician leadership by co-opting members of the political elite and facilitating and fortifying commercial gains and command over other phases of urban life. Political hegemony was indispensable to entrepreneurial success. Upper-class merchants and bankers obtained many advantages by holding public positions or through friends, relatives, or business associates in government service.

Brahmin influence permeated every layer and branch of government. Boston was the center of New England Federalism, and the party directorate, the Essex Junto, came mostly from interrelated mercantile clans whose eminence dated from the Revolution or the provincial era. Among this group were two U.S. senators (George Cabot and Harrison Gray Otis), six congressmen (Otis, Francis Dana, Jonathan Jackson, Josiah Quincy, John Lowell, and Stephen Higginson), one federal judge (Lowell), one minister to Russia (Dana), one chief justice of the commonwealth (Dana), and two mayors of Boston (Otis and Quincy). Numerous relatives of these statesmen served as Boston mayors and legislators or in the Bay State house, senate, and supreme court. Primarily Federalist, upper-class Boston also contained opposition leaders: Russell Sturgis, John Quincy Adams, William Gray, and the Salem Crowninshields, the most prominent Democratic-Republican family in Massachusetts, had marital and commercial connections with the patriciate.[40]

Officeholding elevated Brahmin status through the highly visible symbols and rituals of the political process. Although public officials and political leaders do not always control decision-making, the Boston political and economic elites merged, and government service advanced class power as well as class or individual honor. Junto members in the national government effectively promoted maritime enterprise. They secured advantageous tariffs, drawbacks on products imported and exported by Massachusetts traders, and tonnage duties which discriminated in favor of Bay State shipping. Alexander Hamilton, a close friend of the junto, played the key role in furthering mercantile interests. His financial strategy also increased the value of public securities, held in large amounts by the merchants; assisted patrician banking institutions; and provided the commercial elite with stable and substantial sources of credit. According to Samuel Eliot Morison, "No section or interest in

the United States was so favored by Washington's and Adams's administrations as maritime Massachusetts."[41]

Overseas trade could best be protected at the national level, but other
Brahmin objectives required the support of the state government. Here,
too, patrician political leaders capably guarded group interests. The initial triumph of the Federalist-mercantile enclave was the state constitution of 1780. Delegations from the port towns of Boston, Salem, Newburyport, and Beverly included prominent merchants and lawyers.
They brought forth a conservative document that protected commerce.[42] In 1786 the patriciate again defeated the agrarian debtor group
from western Massachusetts by helping to suppress Shays's Rebellion.
Governor James Bowdoin, offspring of an aristocratic colonial family of
Boston merchants, acted vigorously to crush the insurgents. He sent out
an expeditionary force financed chiefly by himself and other maritime
titans. Younger members of the gentry contributed by officering an infantry company raised in Boston.[43] Fearing agrarian uprisings, debtor
depredations, and business disasters, the Boston elite enthusiastically
backed the U.S. Constitution. During the bitter struggle over ratification they played a pivotal part in obtaining the necessary votes for acceptance.[44] In these contests the maritime elite bested its most formidable
foe, the agrarian enclave. Federalist-mercantile primacy, once established, became a versatile and influential force in advancing the interests of proper Boston.

In banking, political connections were almost as important as financial assets. Charters had to be secured from the state legislature and
possibly defended against rivals. If subsequent incorporators were relatives or associates of the proprietors of constituted financial organizations, they advanced a common interest by expanding available resources and services. But newcomers might be competitors who could
divert profits, unsettle business conditions, or challenge the established
group. Politics also played a significant role because banks were considered quasi-public institutions and their presidents semi-government
officials. This relationship was underscored by governments keeping
public funds in private financial institutions or using them as fiscal
agents. Such practices expanded a bank's resources, and political leverage was crucial in obtaining these privileges. As a consequence of the
interaction between public bodies and the banks, directors and officers
were frequently chosen for their government influence. America's first
great banker, Philadelphia aristocrat Thomas Willing, president of the
Bank of North America and later of the BUS, was a friend of George
Washington and a partner of Robert Morris, the prominent financier
and Washington's first choice for secretary of the treasury. The chief
executives of the Boston banks were similarly well connected. Bowdoin

was the first president of the Massachusetts Bank, his successor served in the legislature, and Federalist leaders Higginson and Lowell were among the founding directors. Through the influence of its organizers and officers the bank became the fiscal agent of the Commonwealth: it issued notes with the state seal; the government punished counterfeiters of its currency; it held government deposits and made loans to the state. Chief executives of other banks were also politically active: William Gray, head of the State National Bank of Boston and the Boston branch of the first BUS, served twenty years in the state house and senate and refused an appointment as secretary of the Navy. Bank directors and shareholders also often held office, or had familial and commercial ties with government officials.

Brahmin influence in the formulation and ratification of a city charter in 1821 equaled the enclave's role in the conception and adoption of the federal and state constitutions. Representatives of the maritime establishment controlled the committee that wrote this document.[45] The creation of the municipal government and the numerous and important offices filled by patricians indicate their political importance in Boston. This power proved particularly useful in urban real estate operations, which necessitated involvement in local as well as state affairs. Building permits, incorporation charters, location of public improvements, low property assessments, rights-of-way, and purchase of property were secured by power in the Massachusetts and Boston governments. The Beacon Hill venture illustrates the relationship between private interests and political leverage. Mount Vernon Proprietor Otis, who served on the legislative committee that sited the State House near Beacon Hill, had advance notice that land values would rise in that area. Improvements in the Boston Common made under mayors Otis and Quincy further increased the price of real estate in the section. In the 1920s and '30s Beacon Hill inhabitants defeated the zoning board's attempts to commercialize the neighborhood. Other Brahmin enterprises also benefited from political influence. Otis's and Jonathan Mason's participation in the South Boston Bridge project (1805) entailed a legislative package that included the city's annexation of South Boston. Quincy bought a city wharf in 1852 and built warehouses on it.[46] Brahmin administrations also enhanced the interests of rich propertyholders through low tax rates and undervaluations of real and personal holdings.[47] Success in these transactions discloses the ability of Brahmins to manipulate the government through officeholding, organized resistance to competing groups and interests, or other forms of leverage.

Aside from real estate, banking, and trading, the patriciate received government aid for a multitude of lesser enterprises which drew their surplus capital. George Cabot felt that the Beverly cotton factory, in which he had a substantial investment, deserved state assistance. His desire was fulfilled through a land grant, a lottery, a mill franchise, and a monopoly on textile production. Brahmins also received state charters for bridges and turnpikes.[48]

Upper-class entrepreneurs acted much more cohesively than their colonial forerunners. Internal rivalries between Thomas Russell and Cabot over control of transportation routes between Boston and New Hampshire, or competition for public deposits among Brahmin financial institutions, did not disrupt the unified support of upper-class Boston for Federalist political and economic policies.[49] During the heyday of Federalism the patriciate achieved an almost comprehensive degree of political consolidation; even Adams and Gray, the foremost Brahmin Democratic-Republican leaders, did not desert the Federalist party until its precipitous decline during Jefferson's second presidential term.[50]

The Professions

Brahmin ascendancy encompassed the prestigious professions as well as politics and business. Prominent in the legal, medical, religious, and educational elites, the enclave commanded skills that extended its power and wealth, celebrated its position through manipulation of ritual and symbol, affirmed its leadership by shaping community values and initiating civic welfare and cultural projects, and perpetuated itself by recruiting new blood and developing young talent.

Lawyers participated in the formulation and implementation of constitutions, articles of incorporation, and other important pieces of legislation, and in the litigation and adjudication of vital issues. Heavily involved in these matters, the patriciate was well represented at the bench and the bar. John Lowell founded a familial-legal dynasty by counseling the merchants of Boston and Newburyport. Harrison Gray Otis resuscitated his family's failing fortunes through a successful practice in admiralty and maritime litigation.[51] But individual achievement, though noteworthy, could not itself produce long-term Brahmin preeminence in the profession. By dominating the institutions which governed professional standards, education, and entry, the patriciate sought control over the Boston bar. In 1758 Francis Dana, James Otis, John Adams, and others attempted to create vocational order through organizing the first Suffolk County Bar Association. This organization at first had limited success in accomplishing its aims of limiting legal practice to trained and sworn attorneys and of upgrading educational and apprenticeship requirements for admission to the profession. Most of the leading lawyers in Massachusetts belonged to the Suffolk bar, however, and after the Revolution it led the county bar associations in imposing standards that made the law a relatively educated, elitist, and restricted vocation. By 1800 the other associations accepted the Suffolk Bar Association's principles of a fixed term for clerking in a law office under local bar association control as a requirement for admission to practice. Six years later the state supreme court prescribed a uniform code of admission qualifications and examinations. By 1810 over four-fifths of the prominent members of the Suffolk County bar were college graduates, the vast majority from Harvard. The Harvard-Boston legal connection was strengthened when preeminent Suffolk County attorneys, e.g. Daniel Webster and Joseph Story, were instrumental in the appointment of lawyer-politician Josiah Quincy as Harvard's first non-minister president. Quincy reciprocated by helping to rejuvenate the law school at Harvard, and Story became professor of law at the school. The Harvard Law School (1817) was a more permanent upper-class legal institution, but apprenticeship proved the best agency for establishing Brahmin influence. Upper-class lawyers trained younger editions of themselves to take over their practices and succeed to their primacy at the bar. Charles Lowell and John Lowell, Jr., read law with John Lowell, Mason with Quincy, and Robert Treat Paine with his own father.[52] Through this form of tutelage emerged a network of lawyers linked by commerce, politics, and family to the Federalist-mercantile inner sanctum. The elite law office played a class-role similar to the family firm in commerce. Here, too, sensitive problems could be handled by class or family intimates and failed relatives or associates given a second chance. An example of the latter function occurred when Samuel Otis's business losses forced a change of plans in the legal education of his son. Instead of going to the Inns of Court, Harrison Gray Otis studied under John Lowell, who later turned cases over to him.[53] Upper-class legal dynasties that lasted over a century, the Lowells, Danas, and Paines, originated at the same time and matched in repute the leading maritime clans.

Medicine, like law, attracted men from distinguished families who went to college, studied abroad or under eminent domestic practitioners, engaged in research and writing, filled prominent roles in professional schools and organizations, and treated the well-born and the rich. Other physicians, like their counterparts at the bar, with a poorer clientele and less renowned connections and credentials, did not generally achieve civic or professional celebrity. Patricians entered medicine because it was a traditionally important and respected vocation, a branch of science and therefore a field of intellectual endeavor, and a *noblesse oblige* vehicle of social control offering leadership in urban health care and medical aid for the poor. In medicine, as in law, Brahmin control involved an effort to regulate the profession. The Massachusetts Medical Society (1781) was incorporated by patrician John Warren and others to set standards of medical practice and education. Unproductive in its early years, like the first bar association, the society was rejuvenated and professionalized by Warren's son, John Collins Warren, and James

Jackson, son of Jonathan Jackson. Jackson and the two Warrens dominated Boston medicine. The elder Warren helped found Harvard Medical School (1782), the three doctors served as professors on its faculty, the younger Warren and Jackson became presidents of the medical society and helped found Massachusetts General Hospital (1821), where they were respectively chief surgeon and chief physician.[54] The activities of the Warrens and Jackson supplemented by the contributions of other Brahmin physicians, administrators, and fund-raisers gave patricians control over the key institutions that regulated medicine in the Bay State. The Harvard Medical School, Massachusetts General Hospital, and the Massachusetts Medical Society licensed physicians, educated the prominent doctors, decided criteria for professional conduct, conferred the highest medical posts, and assessed the validity of and awarded the honors for medical accomplishments.

Brahmin doctors were active in the laboratory as well as in teaching, administration, and practice. Jackson and John Collins Warren were avid researchers, and with other upper-class colleagues began the *Boston Medical and Surgical Journal*.[55] The achievements of these figures established patrician dominance in Boston medicine, a suzerainty maintained by younger Brahmins who continued to fill leading positions at the key institutions. Subsequent generations of Warrens, Jacksons and Shattucks (another Brahmin clan of physicians) formed medical families in the same dynastic fashion as did their relatives in law, trade, and banking.

As a facet of urban upper-class leadership, medicine played its greatest role in aiding the sickly poor. This mission brought together Brahmin physicians and their relatives among the economic and political elite. The founding of Massachusetts General Hospital exemplified the spirit of patrician civic obligations. Boston lacked facilities for the general treatment of disease, and the indigent were woefully deprived in medical care; therefore, Jackson and John Collins Warren circulated a letter among rich and influential citizens to encourage support for a hospital. "The wealthy inhabitants of the town of Boston have always evinced that they considered themselves as 'treasurers of God's bounty,'" they wrote in 1810; "in Christian countries . . . it must always be considered the first of the duties to visit and heal the sick." The patriciate responded generously to this plea for the stewardship of wealth and assumed management by dominating the board of trustees.[56] Massachusetts General embodied the upper-class functions of medicine by providing posts for Brahmin physicians, by serving as a clinic and a laboratory for their researches and discoveries, by becoming a teaching facility to train neophyte successors (many of them elite Bostonians), and by caring for the underprivileged.

Eminence in law and medicine buttressed Brahmin hegemony. Another important, if less obvious, facet of leadership involved professional activities in religion and education. Upper classes throughout history have sought control over thought and culture to spread their dominion. Churches and schools traditionally cultivated the conceptions, inspired the beliefs, and advocated the arguments that legitimize the authority of the reigning strata. In antebellum Boston, Unitarianism and Harvard became the cultural arm of the Federalist-mercantile establishment, the vehicles for disseminating its ideas and values.

After the Revolution the great merchants embraced Unitarianism. Boston was the center of Liberal Christianity; its leading ministers saved the souls of the maritime magnates at King's Chapel and the Brattle and Federal Street churches; its leading scholars informed the community and deepened their wisdom through the *North American Review* and at the Boston Athenaeum.[57] Staunchly Federalist in politics, faithful defenders and close associates of the economic elite, Unitarian pastors and professors stood guard over the cultural bailiwick of Brahmin Boston.

Harvard went Unitarian in 1805 when Liberal Christian Henry Ware succeeded a moderate Calvinist as Hollis Professor of Divinity; the following year a Unitarian became college president. The educational citadel of the mercantile elite was also a Federalist stronghold because, in the words of its official historian, "Harvard in politics has always reflected the sentiments of the ruling economic class in Boston."[58] Ties between the first families, the college, and the city, forged in the Puritan era, continued after independence. Until late in the nineteenth century many patricians prepared for college at the Boston Public Latin School, for decades the only free high school in the city.[59] After graduating from secondary schools most Brahmins went to Harvard. Since colonial times the college had been attended, supported, directed, and often staffed by the establishment. Like other upper-class institutions it sheltered Brahmins who suffered financial reverses. Related to members of the board of overseers and to generous donors, Stephen Higginson and Jonathan Jackson, when forced to retire from commerce, became treasurers of the college.[60]

During the reign of the mercantile magnates, Harvard's influence over upper-class education increased through the founding of graduate schools in medicine, religion, and law. Links between patrician schooling and professional training were strengthened and the Brahmins enabled to sustain themselves when institutional credentials gradually replaced apprenticeship as a prerequisite for high status in the professions. Notwithstanding new departures in graduate curricula, the college remained the essential educational experience for most students. It imparted the skills and inculcated the values necessary for cultural and vocational attainment. Undergraduate life, where a smattering of the classics combined with good fellowship among peers, created a comprehensive class atmosphere in which morals were taught, manners polished, and connections made. Modeled upon the aristocratic British universities, scholastic demands were light and students clubbed in convivial companionship. Brahmin Andrew P. Peabody, a professor and preacher at the college, recaptured in his reminiscences the leisurely pace of early-nineteenth-century Harvard: "A youth who was regular in his habits, and who made some sort of answer, however wide of the mark, at half of his recitations, commonly obtained his degree, though his college-life might have been interpolated by an annual three-months suspension for negligence."[61]

For those with assured places in society Harvard was a relaxed stage of passage from childhood to the family firm or some other upper-class vocation. For outsiders a Harvard degree might facilitate entry into the urban gentry. Several meteoric careers began in Cambridge. Edward Everett parlayed a brilliant undergraduate record into preeminence as a Brahmin statesman and intellectual. At Harvard he edited the college literary publication and won renown as a poet. In 1813, two years out of college, he became pastor of Boston's elite Brattle Street Church. At this time Mrs. Henry Lee noted in her journal that "Tom [Lee] and the Dr. [James] Jackson were discussing the merits of some of the rising geniuses. This young man seems to be considered as the first on the stage; he is very young to have acquired such a reputation."[62] In 1819 Everett became professor of Greek at Harvard and the next year edited the *North American Review*. He married the daughter of Peter Chardon Brooks and subsequently became a Whig statesman and president of his alma mater. Andrews Norton, another eminent Brahmin Unitarian, duplicated Everett's successful rise. Sons of ministers, they matriculated in the same class at Harvard, returned as professors, wedded daughters of wealthy Brahmin merchants, and achieved reputations as scholars and *belles lettrists*. Higham-born Norton, "the Unitarian Pope," married the daughter of Samuel Eliot (Eliot endowed Everett's chair) and contributed to the *North American Review* and other genteel journals. Reverend Joseph Stevens Buckminster of Brattle Street Church and Harvard President John Thornton Kirkland, associates of Norton and Everett in Brahmin cultural enterprises, rose to eminence in the same manner. Children of poor clergymen, their spectacular scholarship at Harvard admitted them into the establishment.[63]

The advent of these luminaries illustrates the interaction between upper-class intellectual institutions and the city's burgeoning cultural life. The strands of Boston high culture, Harvard, mercantile wealth, and cultivated gentility shaped community values and were woven together in Norton's essay on Kirkland's presidential inauguration. Appropriately, the article appeared in the *Monthly Anthology and Boston*

Review, the organ of the Unitarian-Federalist-mercantile elite. Norton was delighted with "the public interest and regard" long "shewn to our Alma Mater." The "flourishing state of literature . . . and consequently the respectability and happiness of our country itself" depend "upon the taste here cultivated, the sciences taught, the principles here inculcated, and the views opened to those who are to go abroad in society, and be its teachers, guides and governours." The "opulent men of our state, . . . especially . . . the merchants of Boston," have supported the college. "Their liberality has . . . been open to all who had any claim upon it" and especially to Harvard, "whose prosperity should be particularly their care."[64] Educated at Harvard, funded by association with or membership in wealthy maritime families, ensconced in powerful posts in the cultural establishment as professors, ministers, benefactors, and administrators, the leading figures of this era ushered in the renaissance that made Boston the "Athens" of nineteenth-century America.

Culture

The Brahmin impact upon the life of the mind has been exhaustively investigated.[65] An accurate view of upper-class Boston, however, would assign intellectual endeavor a subsidiary priority. The energies of the enclave, at least before the Civil War, were devoted mainly to business and politics—power and wealth constituted the basis of the group's sovereignty and underwrote its cultural efforts. The leaders of Brahmin Boston's first generation were merchants, lawyers, statesmen, and bankers. Only after attaining primacy in these areas did the patriciate establish itself as a cultural elite. Genteel erudition legitimized the interests, justified the arrangements, and proclaimed the values of the ruling order.

Supplementing Harvard and Unitarianism as instruments of cultural leadership, the Brahmins founded societies and journals which helped determine the direction of respectable scholarship and literature. The Massachusetts Historical Society (1791), the Boston Athenaeum (1807), and the *North American Review* (1815), products of the formative period of the patriciate, became permanent monuments of upper-class intellectuality. Their overlapping memberships and sources of support comprised the interlocking cultural complex of Harvard, Liberal Christianity, and elite businessmen. Among the organizers of the historical society, the oldest in the United States, were representatives of distinguished colonial families and institutions such as Harvard librarian John Winthrop and Reverend James Freeman of King's Chapel. Within a few years the membership largely reflected the post-Revolutionary patriciate. Its collections and proceedings provided the basis for the splendid Brahmin historical scholarship of later generations.[66] Dedicated to the past and composed of those committed to the established order, the society preserved the traditions and enshrined the accomplishments of the upper class.

The Athenaeum and the *North American Review* grew out of Boston's first genteel literary association, the Anthology Club (1804). In typically Bostonian fashion it was formed by six clergymen, three merchants, and three lawyers, and all except one of the founders were Unitarian. Club members and contributors to its magazine, the *Monthly Anthology and Boston Review*, included noted Unitarian pastors, future presidents of Harvard, famous physicians, the future founder of the *North American Review*, and other prominent Brahmins and their associates.[67] The *Anthology* was Boston's counterpart to Philadelphia's Federalist publication, the *Port Folio*. The two cities, dominated by similar patriciates, often produced similar cultural effusions. Another example of this parallelism was the Academy of Arts and Sciences (1780), a Brahmin organization modeled on Philadelphia's American Philosophical Society. In addition to its literary activities, the club established a reading room which developed into the Athenaeum. The founders and trustees of the latter mirrored, either in person or in the groups from which they were drawn, the membership of the former. Organized for literary purposes and commercial information, the Athenaeum served both the economic and cultural needs of the patriciate. Like many other Brahmin institutions it was inspired by an English example, in this case the Liverpool Athenaeum. The Athenaeum's acquisition of the libraries of the American Academies of Arts and Sciences, the Boston Medical Society, and King's Chapel exemplifies the interaction among Brahmin intellectual organizations.[68] The declaration of the incorporators, in garbled syntax but with clear intent, called upon the upper rank to impose moral order. This plea for intellectual refinement, the humanization of wealth, and the assumption of community responsibility expresses the essence of upper-class cultural stewardship: "Let men of leisure and opulence, patronize the arts and sciences among us; let us all love them, as intellectual men; let us encourage them, as good citizens. In proportion as we increase our wealth, our obligations increase against the pernicious effects of luxury, by stimulating to a taste for intellectual enjoyment; the more we ought to perceive and urge the importance of maintaining by manners, manners by opinion, and opinion by works in which genius and taste unite to embellish the truth."[69]

Shortly after the *Anthology* folded, its publishers and contributors started a new journal to spread Brahmin values. The *North American Review* was funded by a Boston merchant and founded, edited, and authored by the intellectual contingent from Harvard, the Unitarian pulpit, and Brahmin cultural patrons and *belles lettrists*, including Kirkland, Richard Henry Dana (son of Francis Dana), Quincy, and Edward T. Channing.[70]

Genteel thought perpetuated itself through familial as well as institutional continuity. Henry Ware and Henry Ware, Jr., taught at Harvard's Divinity School, and Channings served as Unitarian preachers and Harvard professors for over a century. The dynastic dimension of high thought in Boston, reflective of similar structures in elite commercial and professional activities, reached an apex in the Eliot-Norton-Ticknor connection. George Ticknor, arbiter of mid-nineteenth-century Boston culture, married a sister of Mrs. Andrews Norton. Ticknor, historian and Harvard professor, was a cousin of the city's leading book publisher. His nephew Charles Eliot Norton, son of Andrews Norton, was the late-nineteenth-century champion of Brahmin gentility and won fame as a fine arts professor at Harvard and a humanistic scholar. Another nephew, Charles W. Eliot, son of Harvard treasurer Samuel Atkins Eliot, directed the college's transition to a great university.

Culture as an instrument of community leadership involved civic promotion in addition to individual, family, and group advancement, moral inspiration, and intellectual refinement. The upper class derived from Boston's national reputation much of its sense of status and accomplishment as a ruling enclave. Intellectual attainment thus became a weapon in interurban competition. In 1815 William Tudor, a founder of the Anthology Club and the Athenaeum, and initiator and first editor of the *North American Review*, tried to organize a "Fine Arts" museum to "give us the start of New York & Philadelphia." According to Tudor, people say "that Boston does & must decline, that New York, Baltimore, & Philadelphia must run away with our population & capital." "They are straining every nerve in rivalship," but the museum "may" put Boston "beyond them, and will produce permanent advantages. If we can make ourselves the capital of arts & sciences, and we have already so many powerful institutions that we may do it, our town will increase in that sort of society that is principally to be desired."[71] Tudor's argument encompassed the chief patrician cultural objectives. This project failed but a subsequent generation of Brahmins prompted by the same impulses succeeded in establishing a museum.

Upper-class cultural and social activities were inseparable. Proper Bostonians combined leisure with mental and moral improvement at Anthology Club dinners or at meetings of a literary society formed by historian William Hickling Prescott in 1818. Shared interests and beliefs and participation in the same institutions created a characteristic lifestyle that, in turn, helped unify the interrelated upper-class clans. Thomas Russell, Thomas Handasyd Perkins, and Harrison Gray Otis were the idols of the genteel set. High society considered the stage and the waltz dangerous frivolities, but cardplaying and dancing at the Sans Souci Club, supper parties and cotillions in Bullfinch mansions, the camaraderie of the Artillery Company and the resplendent dress of rich merchants relieved the Puritan solemnity that still clung to the city.[72]

The Brahmin Outlook

Thus far Brahmin ascendancy has been considered a structural-functional development. But attitudes and ideas, as well as accomplishments and institutions, create a collective identity and stimulate that mutual allegiance necessary for the emergence of a ruling order. Hence the mood, spirit, and outlook of proper Boston must be explored. Such an investigation may uncover a unified, comprehensive set of views, traits, and feelings—a shared consciousness that influences the enclave's behavior in a manner similar to that of the superego over the individual. Common perspectives and attachments enhance cohesion by providing patricians with accepted peer-group values and goals. And the dissemination of this consciousness throughout the community may encourage deference to elite leadership.

The search for a Brahmin ethos properly begins by locating the central concerns of the enclave. For several generations, elite Boston was essentially an entrepreneurial entity. Boston's first families generally owed their position to maritime success. Stephen Higginson, George Cabot, Samuel Eliot, Jonathan Jackson, William Gray, Thomas Handasyd Perkins, William Phillips, and Peter Chardon Brooks were merchant princes before they or their offspring became statesmen, patrons of culture, or intellectual ornaments. Francis Dana, Harrison Gray Otis, John Lowell, and Josiah Quincy, themselves not traders, came from or married into mercantile clans, gave the maritime magnates political and legal service, and became their intimates in such business ventures as real estate speculation. Even the heirs of the founding generation preferred commerce to culture and often discouraged kin from pursuing full-time literary or scholarly careers.

The primacy of business was widely acknowledged and its virtues celebrated by merchants and their political associates. An elegant statement of this conviction was made by Quincy in the U.S. House of Representatives: "The employments of industry, connected with navigation and commercial enterprise, are precious to the people of that quarter of the country [the eastern states] by ancient prejudice, not less than by recent profit. The occupation is rendered ideal and venerable by all the cherished associations of our infancy and all the sage and prudential maxims of our ancestors."[73]

Attachment to the commercial life encouraged characteristics requisite for economic success. Virtue in Brahmin Boston meant diligence, energy, order, thrift, prudence, personal restraint, and self-improvement. These traits, often linked to the pursuit of profit, compose a personality typically idealized by expansive entrepreneurial elites in the capitalist system. Rationalized into a moral code by European and American businessmen and theologians, it has been called the "Protestant ethic," the "bourgeois ethic," the "work ethic," the "gospel of success," and the "spirit of capitalism." This creed, a legacy of New England's Puritan past and Calvinist origins, now became the norm of Massachusetts' newest oligarchy. William Hickling Prescott, Samuel Eliot, William Gray, Jonathan Jackson, and John Lowell, Jr., repeatedly impressed the importance of these qualities upon their children.[74] The congruity between these private virtues and the vital attributes of commercial institutions is strikingly demonstrated in John Lowell's argument for a national bank as indispensable "to punctuality which is the life and soul of credit."[75]

The indefatigably inculcated capitalist ethic even motivated those not inclined toward commerce. Quincy resolved "to be more circumspect,—to hoard my moments with a more thrifty spirit—to listen less to the suggestions of indolence, and so quicken that spirit of intellectual improvement to which I devote my life." Historian Prescott similarly chided himself for lacking industry.[76]

The formula of Jonathan Jackson and Peter Chardon Brooks for commercial success was "attend to your business." Thomas Handasyd Perkins felt that much of his happiness derived from commercial employment, and Patrick Tracy Jackson did not allow his family to deter his single-minded passion for his textile factory. Indeed, the Jacksons and Lees did not develop literary and artistic interests until the third generation.[77] The favorable reception of economic enterprise encouraged the Brahmins to focus their energies upon commerce. Susceptibility to the success formula of hard work and exclusive concentration on business was important in group as well as personal achievement. Undiverted by other interests and activities, at least in the early years, the Brahmins were able to attain the wealth and mercantile mastery that established their preeminence.

While stressing qualities necessary for profit-making, the Brahmins did not ignore the ennobling facets of that pursuit. Memorialists of the merchants piously described the altruism of their subjects. Anna Eliot Ticknor's glorification of her father, Samuel Eliot, typifies the mercantile hagiography of the age: "With nothing to rely upon in youth and manhood but personal industry, self-denial, and determined adherence to truth and honesty through all temptations he gained not only friends, wealth and an honored position in the community, but opportunity to serve that community, and to leave a record of noble liberality."[78] Business enterprise in patrician Boston apparently combined material and moral enrichment.

Testaments from the hearth, the pulpit, or the historical society seem less convincing, however, when weighed against evidence from the countinghouse. Perkins noted the distrust that occurred among partners who were not kinsmen. Henry Lee charged a colleague with caring "but little what may be tho't of his honor or his morality provided he can save his money, pretty much like most of us merchants." Such candor reflected the conduct of the Jacksons and the Lees. They duped buyers, bribed officials, sold spoiled goods, traded with the enemy in wartime, and spread false rumors that enabled them to sell high or buy low. According to their biographer these were prevalent conventions of trade.[79] The Brahmins presented themselves as models of prudence, painstakingly accumulating their assets through productive and careful dealing. Upon closer scrutiny these depictions become as imaginative as some of the operations in which they engaged. Trade in new markets and goods meant high risks and attracted resourceful and resilient rather than restrained types. The maritime elite also speculated in government securities and in transportation, manufacturing, and land ventures. Harrison Gray Otis chastised those who made "every species of property . . . objects of speculation," but took flyers in remote wilderness tracts and, like other patricians, used political influence to realize his schemes.[80]

Scruples, however, were not entirely absent in proper Boston enterprise. Friendships, family relationships, and class interests created a spirit of cooperation and responsibility that tempered the entrepreneurial urge. Moral impulses, as well as regional specialization, may account for reluctance to enter the slave trade. Overseas merchants, however, did not reject opium dealing. Perkins & Co. embarked on this venture with misgivings, but resolved its doubts in the usual outcome of struggles between conscience and cashbook: "We should have got a vessel before this as an opium ship was it not for the stigma that attaches to those who deal in the article, it is considered a very disreputable business . . . we are not therefore inclined to meddle with it without the benefit is great, but if to be got at three dollars we can afford to make *the Mandarin view* it in a more favourable light."[81]

The leading Boston entrepreneurs were imaginative, hard-working businessmen who found gratification in fulfilling their commercial aspirations. They left towns and farms to court success in the city. By uprooting themselves they broke the mold of custom and seized opportunities afforded by changing conditions. As befitted an enterprising group, new men and ideas and fresh fortunes were received with enthusiasm. Anna Ticknor proudly traced the rise of her father from penury to wealth. Jonathan Jackson gave his child money and rank, but perceived them as disadvantages because "self-earned property, especially if hard earned—is generally the best spending property with everybody. It naturally induces habits of reflection and economy."[82]

Aristocracies snub the *parvenu*, appreciate the leisured dilletante, but scorn the specialist whose status depends upon vocational achievement, worship the past, revel in conspicuous display, and usually disdain trade. Eventually the Brahmins shared some of these sentiments, but the formative generation derived its way of life from its entrepreneurial orientation. Emphasis upon self-development and restraint and vocational preoccupation and achievement constituted a bourgeois creed appropriate to a rising class. Commercial skills and advantages were easily fashioned from these traits. Order and neatness made for good bookkeeping, frugality led to capital formation through reinvestment of wealth, prudence prevented ruinous speculation, ambition enlarged entrepreneurial interests and personal fortunes, and devotion to business cut risks and maximized opportunities. Capitalist values and triumphs established Brahmin hegemony because in America deference has been accorded those who dominate the marketplace, amass wealth, and thus affirm the national belief in self-improvement through material accumulation.

Brahmin political activity defended its commercial interests. In the 1780s and '90s the maritime elite supported a strong national government and a powerful executive branch that would repress local uprisings, stabilize business conditions, and assist foreign trade. After 1800, with a hostile party controlling the presidency and Congress and implementing policies that stifled overseas commerce, the patriciate became states' righters. Boston Federalism, however, was more than a mercantile instrument. Party leaders and officeholders were not hirelings of the merchants; indeed no real distinction existed between political and commercial elites. Traders and bankers held public posts, and those who devoted most of their time and energy to politics, for example Quincy and Harrison Gray Otis, participated in business ventures. Interchangeable roles and common concerns made the capitalistic spirit as morally meaningful in politics as in commerce. Merchant-statesman Stephen Higginson, usually a saturnine observer of national affairs, was temporarily heartened because "habits of industry and frugality are taking the place of those of luxury and dissipation." These "new circumstances" have "increase[d] the force and respectability of Government. . . ."[83]

The Brahmins applied the entrepreneurial vision to politics by using their government positions and influence to advance their interests. The political attitudes of these Bostonians similarly expressed the capitalist ethos. Federalists shared with businessmen of later periods distaste for popular rule, distrust of the lower state and national houses as nests of unrestrained democracy, support for the judiciary as a bastion against the threat of the impoverished multitude, suspicion of abstract philosophies of reform, belief that men were driven primarily by material self-interest, and the conviction that the main purposes of government lay in protecting property and promoting business.[84] In patrician Boston the Protestant ethic fused these principles of government with the formulas for upright character and commercial success. Political propriety was conceived in the same terms as correct business or personal conduct. Stephen Higginson, John Lowell, Harrison Gray Otis, and George Cabot thus condemned popular rule for breeding "licentiousness," "indolence, dissipation," "passion," and social disorder.[85]

Federalist leaders sometimes went beyond the general norm of the Protestant-capitalist creed to advocate in matters of state a commercial presence in the form of businessmen or quasi-public financial organizations, or conversely, to assert that politicians should keep out of commercial affairs. Although these prescriptions were inconsistent, they stemmed from a common source, the entrepreneurial bias of the Bostonians. Higginson felt that the Annapolis Convention would fail because too many delegates "are esteemed . . . great Aristocrats" and "few of them have been in the commercial line, nor is it probably they know or care much about commercial subjects." Lowell defended the first BUS because "in the administration of government . . . such an establishment" would be "prudential" and "convenient."[86] When representatives of the maritime interest experienced the shift from Hamiltonian to Jeffersonian policies they opposed government interference in economic activities. "The best guarantees of the interest society has in the wealth of the members who compose it," declared Quincy in a speech demanding the suspension of the embargo on shipping, "are the industry, intelligence, and enterprise of the individual proprietors, strengthened as they always are by knowledge of business and quickened by that which gives the keenest edge to human ingenuity,—self interest."[87] Brahmin fears of unfettered democracy and endorsements of commercial acumen were expressed in words that would have evoked applause in the Union League Club or any other Gilded Age gathering of robber barons.

Although political thought was mainly entrepreneurial in orientation, aristocratic impulses also influenced the patriciate's attitude toward the state. The latter perspective derived from the sizeable segment of inherited wealth and social status in the maritime elite, from the importance of family connections in the enclave, and from the growing self-image of proper Boston as an urban gentry whose position involved more than commercial predominance. Figures like Harrison Gray Otis, Perkins, and Cabot were models of gentility as well as merchants or officeholders. Cabot, for example, lived on his Brookline estate in the fashion of an English squire.[88] The emerging upper-class consciousness was also strengthened by marital and political alliances and personal friendships with other patriciates. Otis's wife was related to the Philadelphia Willings and Binghams, and Quincy's brother-in-law wedded the daughter of Phillip Schuyler.[89] Intimacy gave rise to mutual affinity among eastern seaboard patriciates. Quincy discovered in Virginia Federalists John Marshall and Bushrod Washington "the true New England look, character and spirit." William Wirt, visiting the North, returned the compliment. He found "the people of Boston . . . Virginian in all the essentials of character."[90] These developments encouraged the Brahmins not only to set themselves off from the masses in a manner typical of business elites by asserting that property and commerce engendered civic virtue and wisdom and therefore were entitled to places of power and privilege, but to claim ascendancy as an ascriptive right in a hierarchical social order.

Aristocratic consciousness occasionally expressed itself through Burkean categories such as Quincy's conception of the organic nature of society. The nation, he said, "grows out of the affections [of its citizens]; and has not and cannot be made to have any thing universal in its nature." These ties, nourished over generations by attachments to home and family, made "the first public love of my heart . . . the Commonwealth of Massachusetts. There is my fireside; there are the tombs of my ancestors."[91] Pure emanations of classical conservatism, however, were still rare at this time. More often fixed status and established order were not autonomous values but elements of the social stability necessary to protect wealth and expand commerce. Stephen Higginson approved of "distinctions . . . as to rank and property" and feared that excessive power and ambition, "unrestrained freedom, . . . luxury and dissipation," and a wish to "divide property with their betters" induced the masses to refuse "to submit to their proper stations and modes of living." But the disgruntled merchant made these remarks in the context of supporting a national constitution which he hoped would stimulate trade and prevent another Shays's Rebellion.[92] His objections to democracy were based as much on the Protestant ethic as on aristocratic prescriptions. This criticism of popular rule would be echoed by future generations of businessmen who felt threatened by agrarian movements.

Given the contexts in which they arose and the emphasis upon commerce, belief in the divergence between liberty and democracy, preferences for the concrete over the abstract or restraint over reform, and the identification of property with virtue were not essentially defenses of an *ancien regime* but injunctions against measures that New England Federalists feared might destroy profits, disrupt business arrangements, and hinder capital accumulation. Even Quincy, the most eloquent proponent of constituted authority, tradition, community, and family, argued in Lockean liberal terms: "When all the property of a multitude is at hazard, the simplest and surest way of securing the greatest portion is not to limit individual exertion, but to stimulate it, . . . to leave the wit of every proprietor free to work out the salvation of his property, according to the opportunities he may discern."[93]

The correspondence of commercial and political types and the widespread agreement over principles of polity and economy did not fully extend to culture. While the same values interpenetrated these major areas of Brahmin preeminence, the cultural elite diverged somewhat from the other elites. Nevertheless, Unitarian thinkers, offering intellectual and religious sanction for the Protestant ethic, glorified the accomplishments and defended the primacy of the mercantile magnates and Federalist statesmen. They also shared the patriciate's elitist leanings. Joseph Stevens Buckminster denounced the impulsive and emotional atmosphere which he thought pervaded culture and prevented self-development in the same manner as did Stephen Higginson, Cabot, Lowell, and Quincy. Unitarian essayists' and poets' condemnation of professional writers echoed Quincy's attack on professional politicians. Both types of careerists, criticized for craving money and fame and for abject dependence upon their constituents, corrupted standards of wisdom and morality.[94]

Despite these concordant views, dissimilar conceptions of elitism opened a gap between the intelligentsia and other upper-class elements. Even when intellectuals belong to the ruling order and justify its prerogatives, tensions often exist between them and the commercial and political elites. Seeds of conflict take root in the division of functions between these leadership groups. Arbiters of culture manipulate myths, symbols, values, and ideas; businessmen and statesmen deal primarily with power, products, money, and people. The former flourish in an atmosphere of abstraction and esthetics, the latter pile up tangible resources of authority and wealth. The one is drawn to the contemplative, the other to the active life. When Andrews Norton complained "that in this land, where the spirit of democracy is everywhere diffused, we are exposed, as it were to a poisonous atmosphere," he repeated a grievance of merchants and Federalists. But proper Bostonians in trade and government considered popular sovereignty a threat primarily to property, commerce, and power, while Norton feared that this condition "blasts everything beautiful in nature and corrodes everything elegant in art. . . ."[95] Destruction of the material or the beautiful were not mutually exclusive concerns. Brahmin statesmen and traders were not unaware of art or beauty nor did Brahmin writers and ministers ignore the virtues of Federalism or commerce. The difference lay in tone and priority rather than in total outlook.

Through their appreciation of truth and beauty intellectuals discern in themselves a unique sensibility; through their aloofness from the countinghouse and the assembly they discover in their vocation a superior morality. These sentiments convince cultural elites that they are destined to be moral and philosophical preceptors of society. Harvard professors and Liberal Christian ministers acted in this fashion by designating themselves guardians of propriety, sources of refinement, and inspirers of rectitude in upper-class Boston.[96] Conscious of their higher-mindedness and special claims to leadership, the Brahmin intelligentsia separated themselves from the rest of the patriciate. Other psychological and structural factors reinforced this distinction. The same individuals reached the top in trade and politics because triumph in both fields required identical characteristics, and mastery over the one was deemed indispensable to the other. But transference of such dominance to intellectual endeavor was more difficult. Skill in creating and disseminating ideas, knowledge, and styles involved talents and interests that prohibited a facile interchange of leadership roles. Businessmen and statesmen achieved prominence in culture as institutional managers and benefactors, functions that resembled their primary vocations, rather than as scholars or writers. In the formative generation, upper-class Boston usually co-opted its cultural component. But the shining lights of Harvard and Unitarianism, initially largely imported products, married into the maritime elite. Intermarriage, leisure derived from the consolidation of economic and political primacy, intellectual traditions associated with proper Boston, and the conviction that hegemony included ascendancy in cultural affairs encouraged descendants of the mercantile-political oligarchy to become professors, poets, and pastors. When this happened the cultural elite finally became an indigenous outgrowth of Brahmin Boston.

Self-image and different personality traits separated the cultural from the political and commercial segments of the patriciate. But common interests and values and institutional and familial affiliations brought them together. If the intelligentsia claimed a special variety of leadership, it also assumed the role of spokesman for the establishment. Brahmin intellectuals did not think of themselves as an alienated enclave, but as a force for multiplying the functions, cultivating the sentiments, and improving the quality of patrician leadership. Their self-proclaimed mission was to transform a mercantile elite into an urban upper class.

THE GOLDEN YEARS, 1820–60

The Crisis

Scarcely had the Brahmins emerged as an upper class when they faced extinction. With Federalism eclipsed by Democratic-Republican victories and Commonwealth and overseas commerce severely damaged by Jefferson's Embargo and the War of 1812, the patriciate trembled for its existence. From the Virginia Dynasty's triumph in 1800 through the Democratic-Republican defeat of Harrison Gray Otis in the Massachusetts gubernatorial election of 1823, proper Boston struggled for survival. The maritime elite outlasted these misfortunes only through the extraordinary energy and resourcefulness of its sons and the recruitment of new blood. The achievement of the younger generation transformed the group into an urban aristocracy and prolonged Brahmin predominance for many decades.

The stormy beginning of the nineteenth century evoked dismay and panic among the great overseas traders. Stephen and Henry Lee Higginson and Henry and Joseph Lee failed in 1811.[97] Other merchants escaped bankruptcy but suffered heavy losses due to the embargo and war. Anxiety over vanishing profits turned conservative businessmen like Perkins and Henry Lee into outraged, if temporary, disunionists and converted these self-confident entrepreneurs into harbingers of doom.[98]

The pessimists prematurely predicted the demise of maritime Massachusetts. Boston shipping recovered after 1819, and during the next forty years the waterfront teemed with trading vessels. In 1861, not 1815, war dealt Brahmin overseas commerce a death blow. By this time, however, the bulk of the upper class had withdrawn from shipping. During the first decade of resurgence, however, New York clearly outstripped Philadelphia and Boston as the country's chief port. Commercial supremacy resulted from natural geographical superiority in port and hinterland supplemented by technological innovation and aggressive entrepreneurship. In 1784, three years before Boston, New York merchants financed the original American trading venture to the Far East. A decade later Gotham developed the earliest and fullest use of the auction system for marketing imports. In 1817 New York established the Black Ball Packet Line, the first regularly scheduled freight and passenger service to England. Twenty-five years later Boston finally succeeded in operating a viable packet service to Britain. Delay in adopting ocean-going steamships and refusal to risk investments in alternatives to the Erie Canal were other examples of Boston timidity in the contention for commercial preeminence.[99]

The longevity of Boston's family-structured trading houses, many antedating the Revolution, curtailed maritime innovation. A significant shift of younger and more resourceful traders into textile manufacturing during the commercial crisis reinforced conservative tendencies in the mercantile remnant. Patrick Tracy Jackson, flattened by trading reverses in 1811, Nathan Appleton, and Amos and Abbott Lawrence led this departure. New York's shipping community, more prominently identified with the Tories, underwent a greater turnover of personnel as a result of national independence. Fresh talent coming from more diverse geographical origins stimulated New Yorkers to embrace adventurous policies that more cautious Boston firms adopted much later.[100] Boston merchant Thomas Wren Ward, American agent for the Baring Brothers in the 1830s and '40s, perceived this difference between the maritime elites of the two cities. Ward evaluated the soundness of American firms for the British banking house. His highest rating, "entirely safe," went to Boston merchants and houses, such as William Appleton, Nathan Appleton, and Bryant & Sturgis, in business for over a generation. Bloodlines and business associations weighed heavily in his assessments. The more recent New York firms and entrepreneurs were "quite safe," but not "ranking with those whom I suppose are to continue always beyond question."[101]

The consanguine nature of Brahmin houses created advantages and difficulties. Aggressive and imaginative enterprises of the formative generation became placid family firms as founders hired or bequeathed their business to relatives. Management increasingly depended upon kinship rather than vocational merit. Ascription may encourage trust and stability, but inventive and speculative skills are difficult to pass on. Inheritance enhances imitation of conventional practices and may blunt the desire for material achievement, thus making men less competitive. It constricts the social mobility necessary for an adequate supply of new talent and capital while ensuring posts for those who might ordinarily be eliminated by the exigencies of the marketplace. The dangers of hiring relatives did not escape Brahmin merchants. Robert Bennet Forbes declared that "Captain Cabot, a brother to one of our owners, had never been regularly through lower grades, and although a perfect gentleman, he was not, and never could be, called a sailor." Henry Lee, angry over the misadventures of another Cabot, wrote Francis Cabot: "You will I imagine be strongly solicited to employ some relation of ours . . . but I beg to be excused from having any of my concerns entrusted to them. . . . I have made sacrifices eno. in that way, & have no mind to be ruin'd a second time for the pleasure of serving my cousins."[102] Despite their protests, Brahmin merchants, bowing to family and class conventions, continued to employ relatives.

The perils of family-structured operations appeared in more subtle ways than disappointment over bungling underlings or associates. The maladroit were frequently the maladjusted. Younger Perkinses and Lees, for example, sometimes went into business at the bidding of their elders rather than through any aptitude or wish of their own. Disinterest or incompetence led to financial disaster and early retirement.[103]

Faltering entrepreneurship was compounded as the commercial enclave developed into an upper class. Assumption of multifunctional hegemony weakened devotion to business. Brahmins were expected to serve on governing boards of cultural and charitable institutions while keeping their accounts. Family founders did not assume these roles until they achieved economic success—for them the years of vigorous entrepeneurship remained relatively undisturbed. But their descendants, shouldering class obligations by dint of birth, often scattered their energies during the most productive periods of their lives. Henry Lee, Jr., last of his line in overseas commerce, became an amateur actor, an architect, and an accomplished genealogist. He was respected as an old school gentleman loyal to family, friends, and Boston traditions, but these blueblood virtues attenuated the entrepreneurial spirit. After failing in trade in 1852 he was rescued by obtaining a partnership in Lee, Higginson, & Co., a banking house run by his relatives.[104]

Thomas Handasyd Perkins acknowledged in 1820 that the cotton manufacturers "are more active and more ardent than is the merchant class."[105] His comparison accurately reflected the adverse commercial and geographical conditions that, united with class and familial burdens and psychological disabilities, caused the merchants to lose ground to New Yorkers and to the rising industrial component of Brahmin Boston.

Political disasters accompanied economic debacle. The foreign policy of John Adams distressed the maritime elite, and their discontent deepened into despair during the presidencies of Jefferson and James Madison. Old Guard merchants and statesmen reacted to their loss of national influence by denouncing Democratic-Republican programs and popular rule. The patriciate blamed its displacement upon the insurgence of unrestrained democracy, which it thought could destroy the nation. Fearing for their property, disgruntled over vanishing profits, disgusted with government policies, and outraged at losing national influence, Perkins, Quincy, Lowell, Cabot, Otis, and other Brahmins organized an abortive attempt to secede from the union. The failure of the Hartford Convention (1813) was a milestone in the collapse of Massachusetts Federalism. In 1823 the party was further weakened by defeat in the Commonwealth gubernatorial election. Its candidate, identified as a Harvard-Unitarian aristocrat, lost even Essex County. The death knell sounded a year later when John Quincy Adams, Democratic-Republican presidential nominee, took Boston.[106] The disappearance of Federalism, however, did not end Brahmin political power. A younger generation of upper-class Federalists showed the same resourcefulness as their entrepreneurial counterparts, the one switching to a new line of business, the other to the dominant political party.

Although the newer group saved the Boston Brahmins from oblivion, the Old Guard deemed rejection of Federalism and the sea for Democratic-Republicanism and the factory a repudiation of cherished ways, which made them feel diminished within their own community as well as redundant outside of it. A social dimension was added to the discord by the advent of self-made men in the new breed of entrepreneurs and statesmen.

Aware of their own declining vitality and power, the merchant princes initially responded to the challenge of the textile titans with the bitterness of a beleaguered elite. Perkins warned of "renewed attempts to sacrifice the Commercial Interest to that of the Manufacturers, and unless there is a united effort to defeat the projects of the Manufacturers, they will be successful, and we shall have to lament our supineness when it is too late." Social distance in addition to economic grievance intensified Perkins's hostility to the cotton manufacturers. Regarding the Lawrence brothers as upstarts, he snubbed one of them on Merchant's Row.[107] The Lees were equally uncompromising opponents of the lords of the loom. In 1830 Henry Lee ran for congress against Nathan Appleton. The election was a classic confrontation between the mill and the mast, between the archaic and progressive wings of upper-class Boston. The issue was the protective tariff and the outcome victory for the factory owner. Lee's son, when forced out of trade, chose banking to avoid the indignity and boredom of becoming a mill executive.[108]

A similar split developed between older Federalists and their juniors, who wished to continue their careers and preserve their power by joining or courting the Democratic-Republicans. Senior solons of the Essex Junto despaired over the triumph of the Jeffersonians and raged against defectors from their own ranks. Stephen Higginson felt that Harrison Gray Otis "would sell any or all parties or persons in succession till he reaches the top." Federalist knight-errant Higginson viewed John Quincy Adams in a similar light. Those accused of opportunism thought little better of their elders. "Many of them," wrote Adams to Quincy, "are too much devoted to personal and selfish views to make any sacrifice to party purposes."[109] The cleavage divided upper-class Boston into defenders of the faith, who saw betrayal in flexibility, and pragmatists, who considered recalcitrance a vice of Cronus-rampaging Boston Federalism. Denunciations did not deter desertion. "We are now all Republicans," observed Lee when President James Monroe visited Massachusetts in 1817, "even the Essex Junto."[110]

Trimming sail to survive the gale of democracy meant more than switching party affiliation. Adjustments in attitudes, or at least in rhetoric, appeared among the younger politicians. In 1801 Harrison Gray Otis retired from Congress to "remain a silent spectator of the follies and confusion, of the strife and licentiousness incident to all popular governments and to ours in a most eminent degree." But he returned and subsequently became a U.S. senator and Boston mayor. During his later career Otis discovered, or at least stated, the virtues of popular rule. Addressing the city council in 1830, he rejoiced that "many" in the municipal government's "first ranks rose from humble beginnings and hold out encouragement to others to follow their steps." This felicitous condition of "equality" derived from the enfranchisement of the "great majority," who "constantly" elected "the middling class as respects wealth, the merchants and the working men . . . to all offices in state and city. . . ."[111] An even more remarkable tribute to popular sovereignty came from another former Federalist. Quincy gracefully attributed his defeat for reelection as mayor "to the sound principles of a republican constitution, by which the will of a majority [was] distinctly expressed concerning the continuance in office of public servants."[112] As David Hackett Fischer has observed, old school Federalist leaders became increasingly aloof and bitter while younger members of the party, with their careers before them, adapted to partisan tactics and new political forces.[113]

Fortunately the rift between diehards and progressives stopped short of irrevocable conflict. Older men died off or began to invest in industrial enterprises. Harrison Gray Otis, Robert Gould Shaw, Henry Lee, and Perkins had extensive holdings in railroads and cotton mills. By 1834 seven-eighths of the Boston merchants were identified with the New England textile industry as stockholders, selling agents, or directors.[114] The shift in business interests was facilitated by the fact that the Brahmins originated and dominated large-scale cotton manufacturing in Massachusetts. As mill profits mounted, upper-class Bostonians became more optimistic. "There has been a curious *revival* in the spirit of men and a reaction in the affairs and business of this city which is quite remarkable," declared Otis in 1823. "Two years ago our sun had sunk never to rise again, as many said and more feared." Now "I have never known an impression so deep and general in favor of the prospects as well as actual prosperity of the business people." Grateful for the textile-based economic rejuvenation in which he participated, Otis voted for Nathan Appleton in the congressional election of 1830. Perkins, formerly disdainful of cotton-cloth *parvenus*, was moved by similar sentiments to call Appleton "my friend" and extoll his value "in the councils of the nation."[115] The Lawrences and Appletons were rewarded for their part in recovery by gaining admittance to the patriciate. Intermarriage between the Appletons and Lowells and Lawrences, Bigelows and Prescotts symbolized the amalgamation of Old Guard mercantile families with *arriviste* textile titans.

Political pessimism proved as inaccurate a view of the future as were forebodings over the fate of Brahmin business. Control over Boston was maintained throughout the nadir of patrician politics. The establishment dominated the committee that wrote the city charter, and the municipal executives of the 1820s and 1830s almost invariably came from distinguished families. The first three mayors, John Phillips, Quincy, and Otis, and two of the next four, Theodore Lyman, Jr., and Samuel Atkins Eliot, were Brahmins. Between 1846 and 1851 proper Bostonians Josiah Quincy, Jr., and John Prescott Bigelow served in the office. Numerous patricians were aldermen, common councillors, and overseers of the poor. Noteworthy triumphs occurred at the state as well as the local level, despite the decline of Federalism. Many Brahmins were present in the delegations that Boston and Salem sent to the Massachusetts constitutional convention of 1820–21 and they protected upper-class interests.[116] The state senate remained apportioned according to property, thus ensuring an over-representation of Boston in that body; the judiciary retained its power; and Unitarianism preserved its privileges when attempts to disestablish religion were defeated. Gloomy predictions over the destiny of national affairs also never materialized. As the Jeffersonian spirit waned, Brahmins found Republican policies more congenial. Higher tariffs, internal improvements, and the rechartering of the National Bank enhanced the appeal of the party, especially for the growing industrial enclave in the upper class.

Brahmin Enterprise

By establishing itself in cotton manufacturing during the mercantile crisis of the early 1800s, the upper class mastered the first challenge to its community leadership and ensured predominance for the next two generations. The second generation matched its predecessor in ambition and ability. The entrepreneurial outlook in the form of the Protestant ethic, the primacy of business, willingness to innovate, and absorption of fresh talent passed intact from the maritime elite. Once again the patriciate met the demands of dynamic capitalism, and renewed initiative in creating wealth, opportunity, and economic growth perpetuated preeminence. In structure as well as in spirit and reward the emerging entrepreneurs replicated the experience of their mercantile forebears. The family firm made the transition from shipping to manufacturing. Capital accumulated in textiles financed expansion into other undertakings in a manner reminiscent of trading profits underwriting real estate and banking ventures. Elsewhere industrialization brought disruption, but among the Brahmins it scarcely disturbed institutional and familial continuity. Transformation of the upper-class economic foundation accompanied by considerable enlargement in the scope of its business dealings effected only one relatively minor change in the composition of the patriciate: novel techniques expanded operations, and an increased need for capital opened the ranks of proper Boston to a few newcomers with entrepreneurial and technical skills and financial resources. But the presence of self-made magnates did not entail a circulation of elites. Commercial collaboration, joint participation in political, cultural, and charitable causes, and, finally, intermarriage rapidly assimilated the *arrivistes*.

Brahmin involvement in cotton manufacturing started with the Cabot mills in 1787. This operation soon closed, and the shift to textiles actually began at Waltham, Massachusetts, in 1814, when Patrick Tracy Jackson and his brother-in-law, Francis Cabot Lowell, founded the Boston Manufacturing Company. The Waltham mill, containing a host of mechanical and organizational innovations, was the original modern factory and important industrial corporation in America. Within ten years of its establishment the stockholders more than doubled the return on their investment. Encouraged by this windfall, Boston capitalists built other factories along the Merrimac River and in Maine and New Hampshire. Leaping demand for cotton cloth combined with technological advances that lowered production costs kept mill dividends at an astronomical average of 11.4 percent until 1836 and at nearly 10 percent for the next decade.[117] By 1833, Lowell, Massachusetts, was the largest manufacturing center in the country, and the Brahmins dominated the first great industry in America. Proper Bostonians founded the initial line of manufacturing in which the corporate organization was the characteristic form and now owned the nation's largest corporations. The interrelated Lowells, Jacksons, Lawrences, Appletons, Amorys, Dwights, Lymans, and Coolidges, often called the Boston Associates, figured most prominently in cotton manufacturing. They became the new economic core of blueblood Boston, but virtually every distinguished family furnished shareholders and officers. The industry, owned and managed by interconnected families, was a community enterprise which kinship succession kept in upper-class hands for the rest of the century.[118]

The new backbone of the Brahmin economy benefited from escaping the pitfalls that plagued other businesses. Unlike the early British textile industry, whose hostile labor force multiplied entrepreneurial risks, the Boston proprietors, until the 1840s, employed New England farm girls, whose cultural background and temporary and part-time commitment to their jobs precluded militant resistance to managerial-imposed wage levels or technological innovations. The demand for cheap clothing for slaves also eliminated the problems of acquiring a large and permanent consumer market.

Textiles involved the patriciate in other technological and industrial developments such as factory machinery and railroads. In the 1830s and '40s the Associates built the first long lines in New England to transport mill products to Boston. The Western Railroad (1838), a Brahmin effort to capture western trade from New York, became the longest line in New England, the nation's first transectional road. Aside from the upper-class-controlled Boston & Lowell, Western, and Eastern lines,

Brahmins exerted considerable influence over the Boston & Worcester and the Old Colony railroads.[119] By the mid-1840s Boston was the main source of railroad capital in the country and blueblood entrepreneurs began to extend their operations to the West. John Murray Forbes, nephew and Canton agent of Perkins, was the outstanding organizer of early western ventures. Believing that "a certain amount of boldness is true prudence," Forbes in 1846 embarked on a career capped by the Burlington system, a railroad network stretching from Illinois and Michigan into Iowa, Missouri, Nebraska, and Colorado. At first, upper-class merchants, along with British bankers, were the most active participants in Forbes's scheme. Later the great patrician banking houses—Lee, Higginson, & Co., the Old Colony Trust Co., and Kidder, Peabody & Co.—became the chief suppliers of funds.[120]

Brahmin proprietorship followed the traditional upper-class pattern of kinship and group ties and overlapping business functions. Patrick Tracy Jackson was the prime mover of the Boston & Lowell, and another patrician cotton manufacturer its first president. Blueblood mill executive Francis B. Crowninshield presided over its years of greatest growth and later headed the Old Colony line. Shareholders and other officers of these railroads and of the Eastern, Western, and Boston & Providence lines had similar social origins. The family firm reached its apex in the Burlington system, where Forbes's son-in-law Charles Elliot Perkins succeeded him as president, executives were chosen by social background, and board meetings resembled a family reunion.[121]

Unlike the spectacular financial achievement in cotton manufacturing, railroad enterprise earned spotty profits. Investors in the Boston & Lowell and Forbes's ventures were rewarded with handsome dividends; the former generally averaged 8 percent from 1838 to 1873, while the latter equaled that return in the 1850s.[122] But these successes had to compensate for white elephants like the Western and the Old Colony. Shaky financing and encroachment of New York roads into New England precipitated a collapse in Boston railroad enterprise in the 1850s. Brahmin operators duplicated neither the profits nor the inventiveness of the cotton manufacturers. Technological improvements inflated the fortunes of mill owners, but this spirit of innovation did not carry over as extensively into railroading.[123] Brahmin entrepreneurship, however, made a contribution in this field second only to its role in textiles. Achievements in railroads and cotton manufacturing made proper Boston the strongest industrial force in antebellum America.

The Boston money market, next to New York the largest in the nation, underwrote the industrial achievements of the Brahmins and was dominated by the upper class.[124] Although the Massachusetts First National Bank of Boston declined because of conservative banking and investment strategy, it lost ground to other patrician financial organizations, reflecting in its diminished position the shift of Brahmin interests from trade to industry. The new giant was the Massachusetts Hospital Life Insurance Company (1818), by the 1830s the largest single institutional source of capital in New England.[125] Most of the new bank's funds flowed into blueblood ventures in textiles, urban real estate, and, to a lesser extent, railroads. Massachusetts Hospital Life inherited the patrician structure as well as the predominance of the Massachusetts Bank. In its first century of existence one-third of the officers and directors came from sixteen of Boston's first families, and in typical upper-class fashion three of its presidents were sons of earlier chief executives.[126] In addition to controlling these institutions, bluebloods were officers and major stockholders in five of the seven largest Boston banks.[127] Command over the major sources of capital in Massachusetts permitted the upper class to exercise financial dominion over the state. In 1818 the Associates organized the Suffolk System, an association of Boston banks which forced rural institutions to redeem their own notes in specie, thus curbing inflation by restraining the circulation of these banknotes.[128]

Compared with the volatile money markets of New York and Philadelphia the Hub banks were models of stability. After 1792 the Massachusetts Bank maintained a high specie reserve which sacrificed expansion and profits for security.[129] Massachusetts Hospital Life also proceeded cautiously. As the repository of Brahmin fortunes in the form of trusts, it assumed the role of preserving upper-class wealth for future generations. Hence the institution restricted its activities to safe investments mostly in textiles and carefully chosen Boston real estate mortgages, and was reluctant to seek business outside its class and locale. This strategy eventually curtailed its growth but won praise from aristocratic depositors and shareholders. John Lowell "consider[ed] it the best institution on earth. . . . It is *eminently* the Savings bank of the wealthy."[130] Conservative management coupled with fewer speculative opportunities in a region already more built up than the middle Atlantic area enabled Boston's financial institutions to escape the extreme fluctuations that marked banking and insurance stocks in Philadelphia and New York in the 1830s and '40s. But safety had its price. If the Bostonians avoided the pitfalls of other regions, they also lost the windfalls that accrued to imaginative investment. Capital resources in New York grew more fitfully, but more quickly than in stodgy State Street.[131]

The same figures and families recur as initiators, funders, directors, and officers of Brahmin enterprises. The Lowell clan, the Lawrence brothers, Nathan Appleton, Brooks, Patrick Tracy Jackson, Josiah Quincy, Jr., and Thomas Handasyd Perkins repeatedly appeared in these roles in railroad, insurance, real estate, banking, and manufacturing ventures. The Lymans, Harrison Gray Otis, and others were almost as active. Collectively their achievement concentrated wealth and economic power in the upper class. In their prime the Boston Associates controlled 20 percent of the national cotton spindleage, 30 percent of Massachusetts railroad mileage, 39 percent of Bay State insurance capital, and 40 percent of the city's banking resources.[132]

Political Activity

Economic resurgence was linked with political power. Business required government nurture, and upper-class enterprises at first relied on the residue of Brahmin influence that survived Democratic-Republican victories. As new beginnings matured into powerful corporations they interacted with political activity to enable the establishment to recover its primacy in the Commonwealth and increase its national influence. Similar to the development of mills, railroads, and Massachusetts Hospital Life, new men and new party organizations blended with the Old Guard to reassert upper-class political supremacy. Massachusetts Whiggery, dominated by textile magnates and their allies, became the instrument of leadership.

Rich businessmen dominated the city government of Boston. Between 1825 and 1850, three-fifths of the mayors and over one-third of the common council were merchants, though the proportion of maritime aldermen and councillors declined appreciably after the 1830s. Lawyers, with one-third of the mayors in these years, ranked next to merchants in occupations of chief executives. Attorneys also proliferated in the common council until the 1830s, when they, too, declined in this body, as patrician representation, measured by birth, wealth, and vocational status, began to diminish in municipal office.[133]

Manufacturers, railroad barons, and the new generation of bankers acquired political power in the same fashion and for the same purpose as did their mercantile forerunners. Between 1830 and 1860, when the second great era of blueblood officeholding came to a close, textile magnates Nathan Appleton; his cousin William Appleton; Abbott Lawrence; Samuel Atkins Eliot, son of Samuel Eliot; and banker-railroad promoter Samuel Hooper, scion of a prominent shipping family, served in Congress. Samuel Atkins Eliot, Lawrence's brother-in-law John Prescott Bigelow, and Quincy's son, a railroad promoter, were mayors of Boston. Many patricians also sat in the state legislature and the city council.[134] Once again the upper order assumed leadership in business and politics. Capitalists not only filled government posts, they also financed the Whig party in Massachusetts and had marital and commercial ties with its stellar statesmen, Daniel Webster, Edward Everett, and Robert C. Winthrop. All three were representatives and senators, Winthrop served as speaker of the house, Everett became governor of Massachusetts, and

Webster and Everett were secretaries of state. Webster's daughter married an Appleton, Everett wedded a Brooks, and Winthrop belonged by birth and marriage to the most distinguished clans in Massachusetts. Financial assistance and business affiliations solidified family connections. Nathan Appleton and Lawrence sold textile corporation stock to Webster and contributed to a fund to keep him in office. The great orator was counsel for the Boston & Lowell Railroad and the Boston Manufacturing Company and Everett held stock in the Western Railroad.[135]

The Whig party first appeared in Massachusetts in 1832. Between 1834 and 1848, except for two years, it controlled the governorship, and, excluding one year, both state houses. Every U.S. senator and twenty-seven of the thirty-one Commonwealth congressmen were Whigs, and between 1836 and 1848 the party won Bay State presidential contests. During these years the overwhelming majority of rich Bostonians (86.5 percent of those worth at least $100,000 and 96.3 percent of the city's millionaires) were Whigs.[136] The party dominated Massachusetts, and the Brahmins controlled the party. John Quincy Adams called Lawrence "perhaps the most leading man of Whig politics in Boston," Charles Francis Adams felt that "Abbot Lawrence and Nathan Appleton" constituted "the ruling influence," and David Donald considers Appleton, Lawrence, Webster, Winthrop, and Rufus Choate "the real leaders of Massachusetts Whiggery."[137]

Whig chieftains labored to advance Brahmin business interests. National officeholders fought for a high tariff to protect cotton manufacturing against European competition. Webster, appearing before the Railroad Committee of the Massachusetts legislature in 1845, successfully argued the Boston & Lowell's case against a rival's attempt to break its monopoly over the route between the city and the textile town. The Western, another line dominated by textile capitalists, received even greater favors from the general court. State loans covered three-quarters of construction costs—no other road got as much public aid. Stockholder Everett played a crucial role in procuring public assistance. He was governor when the Western was built, and a commercial, political, and social intimate of Josiah Quincy, Jr., and Elias Hasket Derby, its main promoters.[138]

Whig supremacy in Massachusetts ended when the party split into "Cotton" and "Conscience" factions over the annexation of Texas. Resistance to the extension of slavery created a rift within proper Boston and eventually destroyed the party. Cotton Whigs, led by the textile magnates and Webster, Winthrop, and Everett, sought to maintain friendly relations with the southern planters, suppliers of cotton to the New England mills. A minority of the upper class, opposing the spread of slavery, backed the Conscience faction, and a few Brahmins went even further and joined the abolitionists. The Conscience Whigs became Free Soilers in 1848 and Republicans in the 1850s. Charles Francis Adams, son of John Quincy Adams and son-in-law of Brooks, was one of the leaders of this movement and several bluebloods were among its supporters. Others of distinguished lineage, Edmund Quincy, Wendell Phillips, James Russell Lowell, and Thomas Wentworth Higginson, even more antagonistic to slavery, became abolitionists. The opposition, uniting with the Democrats in 1850, broke the string of Whig victories by preventing Winthrop from succeeding Webster in the senate.[139] Significantly, Brahmin Free Soilers and abolitionists stemmed mostly from colonial or mercantile origins rather than from textile families. Although they came from an older segment of the patriciate, the antislavery leaders were younger than most of the Cotton Whig chieftains. They heralded, as had the defectors from Federalism, the emergence of another generation and a change in party affiliation for the establishment. Similar to the previous dispute between aging conservatives and new leaders, the struggle did not last long enough to threaten group cohesion. The Civil War healed the division and made Republicans of the vast majority of proper Boston. Ironically, intraclass partisan conflict weakened Brahmin political power—Free Soil Democrats like Henry Wilson sometimes rose from humbler strata—while demonstrating, in furnishing principals for both sides, the abundance of patrician leadership talent.

The upper class relished its political and economic ascendancy in Massachusetts, but Boston was the citadel of Brahminism. Pride, place, proprietorship, and tradition, combined with power and prosperity, inspired a high order of civic responsibility and an impressive record of civic accomplishment accompanied, as usual, by indefatigable pursuit of self-interest and class interests. For thirty years after the formation of the city government in 1822 the Brahmins ruled municipal affairs. Political leaders used their influence to promote personal concerns and the schemes of their associates. By the 1820s and '30s Appletons, Lawrences, younger Lowells and Jacksons, and Massachusetts Hospital Life joined older entrepreneurs in urban real estate operations. The development of Back Bay, beginning in the 1860s, was the greatest project of the new generation.[140] Private interests spurred enlightened public policy. Wharves, markets, apartment and office buildings, railroad terminals, land development, and elite neighborhoods appreciated in value through improvements in metropolitan health and order. Brahmin mayors Theodore Lyman, Samuel A. Eliot, Bigelow, Josiah Quincy, and Josiah Quincy, Jr., established a state reform school; paved and repaired thoroughfares in the business section; built public schools, a new jail, a waterworks, a municipal office building, a public market, and an almshouse; modernized the system of relief for the poor and sanitation and public health procedures and organizations; initiated professional police and fire departments; and expanded the park system. Many of these advances began in the administration of Josiah Quincy (1824–30), the greatest of the patrician executives.[141] According to Mayor Bigelow, New York, with three times the population, only doubled the annual government expenditures of Boston. Maintaining a low tax rate while improving the quality of urban life attests to the efficiency and honesty of the blueblood administrations. During the first ten years of city government the tax rate was lower than in the previous decade and did not begin to climb dramatically until the 1850s. The combination of increasing public services while minimizing waste and corruption has led Constance McLaughlin Green to label Boston as America's earliest and best provider of urban welfare.[142]

Philanthropy and Culture

Brahmin civic consciousness extended beyond officeholding and enlightened government policy. Through philanthropic and cultural endeavors the enclave enlarged its sphere of ascendancy; when patrician political power waned these undertakings became the oustanding aspect of its metropolitan leadership. Voluntary associations functioned expressively and instrumentally to perpetuate patrician hegemony. Cultural institutions usually emphasized the former role by articulating and inculcating Brahmin values to foster elite cohesion and legitimize elite leadership. Charitable agencies tended to emphasize the latter role by using proper Boston money and influence to create rewards and punishments that would encourage the underprivileged to accept the virtues of the established order.

With the noteworthy exception of Massachusetts General Hospital, the upper class, before 1830, patronized mainly Harvard and kindred religious and intellectual institutions. Other aspects of city life were deemed the province of the family or the government. The Brahmin concept of social responsibility broadened in the 1820s when the establishment discovered the existence of large numbers of poor and began to doubt the adequacy of traditional benevolence. Destitution, argued contemporary observers, led to delinquency, and enflamed by Jacksonian democracy, the immigrant influx, local riots, and rising rates of drunkenness, pauperism, and arrests for assault and battery, could kindle a social conflagration that might consume the propertied. Fears of class conflict mixed with the higher morality of human sympathy and *noblesse oblige* stimulated public and private efforts to reform the poor and improve the quality of relief. Mayor Quincy, who had chaired the

1821 general court committee on Pauper Laws, which gave the first widespread publicity to the problem of poverty, reorganized the administration of government assistance to the needy. While Quincy changed official practices, Joseph Tuckerman, a prominent Unitarian preacher, started a ministry to the dependent. Tuckerman initiated large-scale welfare and became Boston's foremost dispenser of charity.[143] Motivated by self-interest and altruism, the Harvard-Unitarian-business establishment dominated organized philanthropy. Thomas Handasyd Perkins, aided by other bluebloods, founded the Perkins School for the Blind (1833), Lyman was the chief benefactor of the State Reform School at Westboro and other reformatories, and Amos Lawrence established the Children's Infirmary at Boston. Patricians headed and funded most of Boston's other important charities: Children's Hospital of Boston (1869), the Young Men's Benevolent Association, the Board of Overseers of the Poor in Boston, the Prison Discipline Society, and the Massachusetts Charitable Congregational Society. Robert C. Winthrop and Samuel Atkins Eliot, presidents of several of these agencies, headed the Boston Provident Association, founded in 1851 to coordinate the city's numerous charity organizations.[144] Brahmins were as forthcoming with money as with time and advice. David Sears gave great sums for relief for the poor, Amos Lawrence spent over $700,000 for public causes in his lifetime, and Abbott Lawrence left $150,000 for similar purposes.[145]

Individually and as a group the Brahmins were the greatest donors in Boston. Between 1800 and 1830, according to Quincy, contributions for charitable, moral, religious, and cultural activities totalled $1,801,273. Upper-class institutions received the lion's share of Bostonian largesse. Massachusetts General ($354,000) was the most heavily endowed, followed by Harvard ($222,696). The treasuries of these and other patrician favorites account for over half the expenditure during the three decades. In the next fifteen years, according to another estimator, probably Samuel Atkins Eliot, Bostonians spent $2,938,020 on religion, education, charity, and miscellaneous items. Included in this sum were contributions made before 1830 to a few organizations omitted from Quincy's list. Organizations controlled by the upper class, such as the Lowell Institute ($245,000), the American Board for Foreign Missions ($278,167 given since 1810), Massachusetts General Hospital ($286,513), the Bunker Hill Monument ($100,000), the Perkins School ($82,500), and Harvard ($83,755), account for over half ($1,579,456) the total donation of 1830–45.[146]

Boston generosity seems dwarfed by the beneficence of Gilded Age robber barons, but the assessed wealth of Boston, even in 1845, did not come close to the colossal fortunes of individuals and families of the late nineteenth century. In 1835 Peter Chardon Brooks, the wealthiest Bostonian, was assessed for $768,000, and he was the only millionaire on the 1845 tax assessment list. Property assessments in Boston totaled $59,586,000 in 1830 and $135,948,700 in 1845; in New York the Astor estate in the third generation was worth $200 million, and William Henry Vanderbilt, son of Commodore Cornelius, left the same amount.[147] Although Boston altruism was not, relative to size of fortune, overshadowed by richer New Yorkers of a later era, it fell short of the stewardship-of-wealth ideal widely accepted in the upper class. Total benefactions between 1800 and 1830 came to one-thirtieth of the city's assessed wealth in 1830, and the sum of contributions for 1830–45 does not reach one-fortieth of the 1845 assessment. Admittedly these lists of benefactions are incomplete, and alms-giving on a personal basis went unrecorded; on the other hand, assessors notoriously undervalued property. More important, though generosity substantially exceeded the levels indicated by these calculations, private and business claims always had priority on patrician wealth, and the growing problems of penury withstood the best efforts of proper Boston.

Genteel Boston emphasized inculcating correct moral and intellectual principles in addition to improving living conditions. Well-ordered asylums, penitentiaries, hospitals, and poorhouses contributed to both aims, but the patriciate formed other institutions that specialized in elevating the mind and spirit. Religious, educational, and cultural initiatives sprang from the same combination of social obligation, group hegemony, and fear of class confrontation that engendered care for the indigent, the ill, and the delinquent. Upper-class activity in these areas had two main orientations. Elite institutions directed at proper Boston sought to strengthen in-group cohesion and to train the patriciate in proper modes of leadership. The Athenaeum, Harvard, the historical society, the *North American Review*, and exclusive churches belonged to this category. Institutions organized by the elite to instill in the masses the virtue of established social arrangements were directed primarily to the out-group for the purposes of maintaining patrician predominance. Bible societies, public and Sunday schools, libraries, and other mass education devices served to protect ascendancy in the larger community. Distinctions between internal and external orientation, or between fulfillment of moral or material needs, did not lead to specialization. The same figures superintended or supported altruistic affairs regardless of functional differences, and many societies encompassed several of these roles. David Sears, an influential officer and trustee in many upper-class organizations, spent his mercantile inheritance on "religious, civil, literary, and charitable institutions in Massachusetts and elsewhere." By setting up trust funds for Amherst,

Harvard, the overseers of the poor, and several churches, he "humbly endeavored to benefit the community, promote religion, advance literature and science, encourage the studious, and make the poor comfortable and happy. . . ."[148]

A survey of the posts held by key administrators of upper-class voluntary associations reveals the interlocked leadership of proper Bostonians in politics, business, charity, and culture. Winthrop presided over the Massachusetts Bible Society and the historical society, chaired the board of commissioners charged with building the Boston Public Library, and headed other institutions previously mentioned. Quincy was a trustee of Massachusetts General, treasurer of the historical society, and president of Harvard and the Athenaeum. The founder of the Perkins School for the Blind headed the Athenaeum and the Massachusetts General boards. Samuel Atkins Eliot, textile titans Amos and Abbott Lawrence, and numerous other Brahmins had a similar array of institutional involvements.[149] Organizational interdependence accompanied overlapping leadership. The funds of Harvard, Massachusetts General Hospital, and the Athenaeum were deposited in Massachusetts Hospital Life.[150]

Most of the patrician associations oriented toward internal integration and preparation for leadership originated in the formative age of Brahmin Boston. The advent of mill magnates, the defense of manufacturing rather than maritime interests, and the Unitarian crisis of the late 1840s and '50s did not disturb the basic continuity of personnel and perspective at the historical society, Harvard, the Athenaeum, and the North American Review. Children inherited the places and financial obligations of their fathers, and identification with upper-class organizations and figures sanctified the arrival of the newly risen. The defeat suffered by would-be reformers of Harvard in the 1820s and '30s exemplifies the enduring conservatism. Imbued with notions acquired from their studies in Europe, Edward Everett, George Ticknor, and other insurgents returned with plans to transform the school into a European university. But the Old Guard remained in command, Harvard continued as an upper-class boarding school, and the frustrated young Turks had left by 1835 (a mellowed Everett later returned).[151]

Harvard under the leadership of Quincy, Everett, Samuel Atkins Eliot, and Stephen Higginson remained a bastion of traditionalism. But Unitarianism, another pillar of proper Boston, trembled under the weight of the antislavery controversy. Upper-class sectarian unity was further undermined by an increasing drift toward Episcopalianism.[152] The forces which weakened Unitarianism gave birth to the only major new Brahmin cultural effusion of the period. The Atlantic Monthly (1857) originated in a way similar to the appearance of the North American Review. It, too, was founded by a segment of the upper-class intelligentsia, and James Russell Lowell, the first editor, was also a Harvard professor. The older journal was the organ of the conservative establishment; the *Atlantic*, the voice of younger and more radical patricians like Lowell and Charles Eliot Norton, was more sympathetic to Transcendentalism and abolitionism, then in disfavor with the Old Guard. From the first issue it became the primary vehicle for the publications of Lowell, Norton, Oliver Wendell Holmes, Thomas Wentworth Higginson, and other New England literary giants who made Boston the center of American culture. Due to their fame the *Atlantic* eventually supplanted the *North American* as the chief literary spokesman of patrician Boston and the arbiter of genteel thought.[153]

Aside from the *Atlantic*, new cultural ventures were more significant as precursors of post–Civil War achievements than for their own impact or magnitude. During the 1820s the upper class began an involvement with the fine arts and music. Allegiance to the past and beautification of Boston provided the impetus for this interest. In 1823 prominent Bostonians formed the Bunker Hill Monument Association. The Revolutionary War memorial was completed in 1843. In 1826 the Athenaeum opened the first and for a long time the city's only art gallery. Paintings were collected and exhibited annually, but insufficient interest, funds, and space kept the gallery small.[154] Equally unimpressive were upper-class accomplishments in music. The Boston Academy of Music was founded in 1833 for the same reason as the gallery, to refine the sentiments of the citizenry. Headed by Samuel Atkins Eliot, it introduced Bostonians to symphonic concerts and provided for musical training in the public schools.[155] The monument, gallery, and academy, the outstanding musical and artistic undertakings, were dwarfed by patrician achievements in other cultural fields. These small beginnings, however, led to the Boston Symphony Orchestra and the Museum of Fine Arts, the greatest accomplishments of postwar Brahminism.

The urban gentry was more concerned with cultivating the virtue than the taste of other Bostonians. Public schools, relief for the poor, and prison reform aimed to improve both moral and material conditions. Apart from these efforts, the Brahmins participated in several religious and educational societies designed to uplift the downtrodden. This crusade embodied the second major purpose of blueblood altruism by reaching out to convince the masses that the established order constituted the best social system and to instill in them the values of the upper rank. Amos A. Lawrence spelled out these intentions in explaining that he taught Sunday school at St. Paul's to "prevent the jealousy which springs up in the minds of the poor, or at least diminish it," and "make them endeavor to resemble the rich in their good manners and refinement." His uncle Abbott Lawrence expressed similar sentiments in acknowledging appointment as vice-president of the American Bible

Society. "American democracy and government depends on Christian and biblical moral principles," pontificated the pious mill owner, "therefore it is necessary for the bible to be disseminated throughout America."[156]

Among attempts to inform and inspire, the Lowell Institute won the greatest accolade from contemporary Brahmins. John Lowell, Jr., son of the co-founder of the Boston Manufacturing Company and grandson of Jonathan Jackson, left $250,000 to found the institute, which, next to Stephen Girard's bequest in Philadelphia, was the largest such endowment then made in this country. Lowell, a typical member of the gentility, served in the city council and state legislature and before he planned the legacy had been an incorporator of the Boston Society for the Diffusion of Knowledge (1830) and an Athenaeum president. His scheme reflected the Boston Society experience in its provisions for a series of lectures and for free instruction of mechanics and artisans, ideas borrowed from the lyceum movement and other current popular education agencies. The founder's instructions to the trustees conformed to the prevalent concepts and practices of *noblesse oblige*. Lectures on religion should emphasize the teachings of Christ, avoid "controversy," and demonstrate "the moral doctrines of the gospel." As usual, spiritual sublimation and social harmony formed the essential guidelines. Proper Bostonians, however, were also practical. Lowell hoped to enhance "the prosperity of my native land, New England," which "depended, first on the moral qualities and second on the intelligence and information of its inhabitants." Accordingly, the benefactor recommended talks on applied arts and sciences for their "public utility," and the teaching of drawing and other subjects to upgrade the skills of mechanics and artisans. The governance of the institute reveals the interlocking nature of Brahmin charities and Lowell's familial and aristocratic leanings. The trusteeship had to be held by lineal descendants of the clan, and the Athenaeum board was enjoined to supervise accounts and replace the director if he proved derelict in duty. Still in Lowell hands, the institute continues to perform an educational function in Boston.[157]

Aristocrats shared the burdens of social and cultural responsibility with new men. The memberships and benefactions of ex-farm boys Nathan Appleton and Abbott Lawrence, neither of whom attended college, epitomize the leverage that elite associations provided for the climb of the self-made into the establishment. Appleton belonged to the historical society and the American Academy of Arts and Sciences, became treasurer of the Athenaeum, and received a Harvard M.A. and LL.D. His sons graduated from Harvard, one became a long-term member of the historical society and another a trustee of the Athenaeum, the Museum of Fine Arts, and the public library. The M.A. was a "testimonial of the high respect for your character, personal and literary," wrote President Quincy, "which, in common with your fellow citizens, is entertained by the President and Fellows and Overseers of Harvard University."[158] Appleton's friend and business colleague, Lawrence, trod a similar path to the top. He, too, became a member of the Academy of Arts and Sciences, and was rewarded for being the most generous Harvard donor of his day with election to the board of overseers and an honorary doctorate.[159]

Connection between Brahmin institutions and freshly minted textile tycoons rested firmly on common interest. John Gorham Palfrey, Whig politician, Unitarian scholar, and ex-dean of the Harvard Divinity School, asked Amos Lawrence for a loan to buy the *North American Review*. The prospective owner "believe[d]" that they "agree[d]" on the "importance" of "what principles the work in question should maintain, and I venture to flatter myself that you will give me some credit for attachment to sound principles in morals, politics, and literature." The magazine should "go into hands" that "will prevent it from becoming the instrument of any hurtful influence." Josiah Quincy, Jr., felicitously described the merger between the guardians of the mind with the millionaires from the mill: "Wealth was quite as attractive in those days as it is at present, and it was deemed a happy circumstance that the intellect of the community in one of the adjoining houses should be backed by its purse in the other."[160]

Charitable and cultural activities were conducted along overlapping lines characteristic of patrician enterprises. Eminent businessmen and statesmen took leading roles in ameliorative, esthetic, and educative efforts and control of these organizations rested in the hands of a group bonded by interest, class, and family, and dedicated to preserving the established order. Consequently, accomplishments in these areas, as in commerce and politics, solidified, broadened, and perpetuated the ruling enclave. Calculations of self-interest and social control weighed heavily in these undertakings, but nobler motives were not absent. Civic pride, the stewardship of wealth, concern for the less fortunate, regard for intellectual endeavor, awareness of the obligations of hegemony, and even guilt over the accumulation of vast wealth made *noblesse oblige* more than an instrument of class defense. Celebration of disinterested largesse may be discounted if proclaimed only in the addresses and memorials of distinguished Bostonians. But benevolent sentiments communicated privately made credible the public testament. "We [the Lawrence brothers] have been blessed more than most men," confided Amos Lawrence to his diary, "and have the power, by our use of these blessings, of benefitting our fellow men." Amos A. Lawrence, in his journal, resolved "not [to] forget my duty in using it [wealth], not for my own aggrandizement, but for the advancement of Christ's kingdom upon earth." Massachusetts General Hospital board president William

Appleton emphasized in his commonplace book "my duty to distribute my income, which is large, giving religious objects the first thought, & uniting with others in promoting the Arts and Sciences. I wish to show to myself & the World that a man may be zealous in business, successful in his undertakings without the desire of increasing an ample fortune; able to strive to make money to distribute the same for the good of his fellow beings beyond his own blood."[161] Magnanimity toward, and manipulation of, the distressed co-existed in the same conscience. Good samaritan Amos Lawrence was less than whole-souled when he suggested that the best way to curb the threat that Irish immigrants presented to proper Boston was "to educate the children, and circulate the Bible and good books among them which shall encourage them to do the best they can for themselves." Amos A. Lawrence inherited his father's generosity but gave similarly self-protective reasons for teaching Sunday school. Winthrop succinctly expressed the combined motives of moral obligation and social control in explaining, "the care of the poor, apart from its higher relations to Christian duty is hardly less a matter of police in this great city of ours, than the civil or military organizations which more directly and obviously pertain to the preservation of property or the public peace."[162] Prudence and idealism formed an indistinguishable impulse that brought forth Brahmin philanthropy.

The Professions

Professional achievement constituted another element in the panoply of predominance. It provided proper Boston with a reservoir of expertise that legitimized its assumption of leadership in a variety of urban endeavors. The founding generation established ascendancy in the crucial vocations; its sequel extended this mastery.

Third-generation Warrens and second-generation Jacksons and Bigelows succeeded their forebears in posts at the Harvard Medical School and Massachusetts General Hospital. Bluebloods Oliver Wendell Holmes, Samuel Parkman, and Henry Ingersoll Bowditch embarked on distinguished medical careers and the upper class retained control over the Massachusetts Medical Society. As was usual in patrician undertakings, the same individuals assumed multiple hegemonic roles. Leading physicians and surgeons at Massachusetts General taught at Harvard and became officers of the medical society.[163] Nearly monopolizing these positions, proper Bostonians controlled public health care and influenced standards of medical education and practice.

Lawyers were closer than physicians to the centers of power and wealth because of their greater intimacy with commercial and banking activity, more frequent assumption of public office, and a larger share of the community's foremost fortunes. Among the 459 Massachusetts congressmen between 1789 and 1840 were 292 lawyers, eighty merchants, sixteen ministers, and only fourteen M.D.s. Next to merchants, attorneys appeared more frequently among Boston's richest residents. After 1830 Lemuel Shaw made $15,000 yearly in legal fees and Daniel Webster earned the same amount between 1819 and 1844. Attorneys composed 11 and 10 percent respectively of the wealthiest citizens in 1830 and 1850 while physicians accounted for 3 percent in both years. A similar situation prevailed in other cities. Lawyers and doctors tied for third place in the occupational distribution of the uppermost economic enclave in Philadelphia in 1845–46, but the pattern in New York resembled that of Boston, and the advocates led the healers in the vocations of the most affluent Brooklynites in 1841.[164]

Brahmin supremacy in law was less complete than in medicine. The chief figures of the bar, Daniel Webster, Rufus Choate, Joseph Story, Jeremiah Mason, and Lemuel Shaw did not stem from distinguished Boston families. But Mason's and Webster's daughters married bluebloods, and most of the leading lawyers affiliated politically and culturally with the ruling coterie through Whiggery and membership in the historical society and the American Academy of Arts and Sciences.[165] Upper-class influence manifested itself in typical ways. Certain families, like the Lowells, passed on the vocation, and inbreeding was encouraged by the prevalent forms of legal education. Continuing an earlier custom, aspiring advocates still read law in the offices of leading barristers. These arrangements frequently resulted in partnerships or cases for younger men. Upper-class apprentices were most likely to be selected by the foremost attorneys. Charles Francis Adams and Robert C. Winthrop, for example, studied in Webster's firm. In the 1830s Harvard Law School began to replace private tuition as the main type of training. Richard Henry Dana, Jr., who recouped his family fortunes by counseling textile firms and rising to the top of his profession, graduated from the law school in this decade. Dana's use of social status to build a practice by associating himself with prominent lawyers and businessmen like Choate and the Lawrences, and John Lowell's business in family estates and trusts indicate the advantages possessed by the well-born.[166] Harvard degrees, tutelage in eminent firms, and ties with the wealthy and powerful maximized opportunities for genteel lawyers.

Patrician preponderance in the humanistic callings equaled the enclave's supremacy in the medical profession. As in law and medicine, upper-class institutions and entrée into circles of fortune and influence facilitated success. Harvard professorships, Unitarian and Episcopalian pulpits, the resources of the historical society and the Athenaeum, and the columns of the *North American Review* and the *Atlantic Monthly* were made available to members of the class and clans that controlled and financed these institutions. Inherited or wifely wealth gave Brahmin intellectuals the leisure and education to develop their talents, devote themselves to nonremunerative occupations, and perfect their crafts undiverted by material needs. William Hickling Prescott, disavowing any intention of becoming a "literary hack," articulated the patrician commitment to scholarly and literary careers: ". . . no motives but those of an honest fame and of usefulness will ever be of much weight in stimulating my labors. . . . Fortunately I am not driven to write for *bread*; and I will never write for *money*.[167] Lowells, Jacksons, Warrens, Bigelows, Peabodys, Channings, Holmses, and Nortons lectured at Harvard and preached in the elite churches.[168] Historians Francis Parkman and Prescott and *belles lettrists* James Russell Lowell, Oliver Wendell Holmes, and Henry Wadsworth Longfellow emerged as the brightest stars in Boston's midcentury intellectual renaissance. Excluding Longfellow, who married Nathan Appleton's daughter, they descended from renowned mercantile families, and, except for Parkman and Prescott, were Harvard professors. George Ticknor, historian, Harvard LL.D. and former professor there, fellow of the American Academy of Arts and Sciences, vice-president of the Athenaeum and Massachusetts Hospital Life boards, trustee of the public library and Massachusetts General Hospital, member of the Massachusetts Historical Society, and son-in-law of Samuel Eliot, was the arbiter of genteel culture. He decided whose credentials passed muster in the rarefied society of the Brahmin intelligentsia.[169] From vantage points in literary, educational, religious, and scholarly associations the upper class perpetuated its influence in shaping the moral and intellectual life of the city. The first generation initiated this ascendancy; its successors brought it to fruition.

Proper Boston had little sympathy for the lighthearted and the laggard, but Beacon Hill found relief from toil and responsibility in diversions that characterized high society in other places. Like their New York counterparts, Brahmins entertained themselves at parties, dances, dinners, and clubs. But the less costly Bostonian affairs resembled more closely the activities of southern planters in mixing the convivial with the cultural. Social leaders from the earlier period, Harrison Gray Otis and Thomas Handasyd Perkins, who died respectively in 1838 and 1854, continued to lend majesty to social events, and the younger set, Mrs. Harrison Gray Otis III, Ticknor, Holmes, and Thomas Gold Appleton, supplied wit and wisdom for many a sparkling evening. Early retirement from business, inherited wealth, and increased emphasis upon culture stimulated social activity. Salons appeared, intellectual gatherings multiplied, and Appleton emerged as a man-about-town whose vocation was conversational and culinary triumphs. Older haunts, the Ancient and Honorable Artillery Company and the Wednesday Evening Club (1777), still attracted bluebloods, and serious discussion was combined with good fellowship at the recently founded Thursday Evening (1846), Somerset (1851), and Saturday (1855) clubs.[170]

Brahminism reached its zenith between 1820 and the Civil War. Never again would patrician initiatives be as successful, challengers so ineffective, and sovereignty as complete. Bluebloods who lived past the era looked back upon it as the golden age. In the 1830s "Boston was a synonym for certain individuals and families who ruled it with undisputed sway," recalled Josiah Quincy, Jr., "and, according to the standards then recognized, governed it pretty well."[171] Many Brahmins remembered Boston as a small, homogeneous Yankee town where hierarchy, neighborliness, and order prevailed. The city then, wrote James Russell Lowell, was "more important than at any later period." "Master and servant" came from the same stock, giving the community a "solidarity, an almost personal consciousness rare anywhere, rare especially in America," and engendering a "becoming respect" for "decent authority." Sovereignty inhered in "an aristocracy such as is healthful in a well-ordered community, founded on public service, and heredity so long as the virtue which was its patent was not escheated." The intellectually invigorating forces of commerce and Harvard accompanied the advantages of hierarchy.[172] Pride in the town's cultural eminence moved Holmes to write that "Boston is . . . the thinking centre of the continent, and therefore of the planet . . . I would not take all the glory of all the greatest cities in the world for my birthright in the soil of little Boston."[173]

New York, the antithesis of everything the Brahmins cherished, provided a recurrent basis for unfavorable comparison with Boston. Ticknor, Prescott, Henry Lee, and Richard Henry Dana, Jr., condemned New York for lacking Boston society's "severity towards disorganizers and social democracy." Without "our standard of morals," it was a "showy," aggressive place "rule[d] by demogogues." These views prompted Dana to oppose his daughter's marriage into a rich "New York shoddy family."[174] Blueblood criticism reflected the distaste of the genteel for the brash and boorish. Derision, however, sprang from anxiety rather than assurance. Brahmins were aware that New York's ruling coterie was richer, more powerful, and more cosmopolitan. Southerners better suited Bostonian tastes. Dana lauded the "true gentility" of the Virginia aristocracy. Josiah Quincy, Jr., was equally impressed by a visiting Charleston planter, with "all that charm of a high-bred Southerner which wrought such peculiar fascination upon those inheriting Puritan blood."[175] Midcentury Brahmins, mostly members of distinguished families, preferred Dixie aristocrats to Gotham *arrivistes*.

Wealth

Brahmin supremacy is affirmed by examining Boston tax assessment lists. These compilations are not infallible because holdings were undervalued to avoid taxes, standards of appraisal varied from ward to ward and assessor to assessor, and dishonest assessments cannot be ruled out. Real property was grossly underrated, and underestimation of personal property was even more scandalous due to omission of intangible holdings such as corporate securities.[176] The lists of 1835 and 1860 are here used to construct a profile of the richest Bostonians in the paramount period of Brahmin wealth and power. Tracing the generational origin, officeholding, birthplace, and familial ties to proper Boston of those assessed for at least $100,000 ($50,000 in 1835 because the listing was for one-half the value of the property) measures levels of cohesion, continuity, vintage of wealth, patrician representation, political participation, and kinship among the richest Bostonians.

The wealthiest group possessed a large share of the personal (noncorporate) accumulations in Boston. According to Edward Pessen, the top 1 percent of the propertied in 1833 (those worth at least $75,000) owned one-third of the noncorporate holdings in the city; their 1848 counterparts (those assessed for at least $90,000) owned 37 percent of the noncorporate wealth. The top 1 percent increased its share of property ownership, a trend that began before the Revolution. Salem, several other Massachusetts towns, New York, Philadelphia, and Brooklyn had a similar proportion of maldistributed wealth and, like Boston, the inegalitarian trend grew throughout the antebellum era.[177] By virtue of the commanding position of the economic elite as proprietors, stockholders, and officers in banks, railroads, textile mills, mercantile firms, real estate operations, and insurance companies, this elite also controlled a large segment of Boston's corporate wealth.

Pessen, the most prominent historian of urban elites in the age of Jackson, claims that over nine-tenths of the richest Bostonians, Philadelphians, and New Yorkers inherited fortunes and high social rank.[178] If he is correct, a radical rigidification occurred in the uppermost economic strata of these northeastern cities in the 1800s, for Jackson Turner Main showed extensive penetration of the self-made into wealthy elites of the 1770s and 1780s. Ambiguous and inconsistent definition of inherited wealth and status and factual misinterpretation, however, undermine Pessen's assertion that upward mobility—even from middle-class origins—was virtually curtailed. Pessen argues in *Riches, Class and Power before the Civil War* that "the great majority of wealthy persons appears to have descended of parents and families that combined affluence with high social status."[179] This formulation makes wealth and high status interdependent sources of inherited positions in the upper economic and social order. But Pessen's table on "The Wealth and Status of Parents and Families of the Richest Persons in Antebellum Northeastern Cities" contains the categories "Rich and/or Eminent," "Middling," and "Poor or Humble."[180] This formulation implies that either property or high status may be a source of bequeathed ascendancy. Conceivably, offspring of distinguished lineage may have made their own fortunes because their fathers suffered financial reverses. Pessen's failure to consistently separate social from economic rank obscures this possibility. Robert Gould Shaw, whose father and grandfather were rich Boston merchants bankrupted by the Revolution, went to sea and by the 1830s amassed one of the largest fortunes in Boston.[181] Pessen disregards evidence for Shaw's youthful indigence presented by a "Boston publicist." But Shaw's early financial problems were noted in a biographical sketch by a relative written for the *New England Historical and Genealogical Society Register,* a journal Pessen considers "Excellent" if not infallible.[182] According to Pessen's first formulation, Shaw is self-made because he did not combine affluence with good family, but he also fits Pessen's second formulation of inherited riches and/or eminence because he had distinguished mercantile roots. The family may have maintained high status despite financial disaster, but Shaw's resurrection of the clan's fortune involved considerable upward economic movement compared with the two previous generations. In the long run, social and economic rank go together, but for one or two generations one source of status may remain stable while the other fluctuates.

The rating of Peter Chardon Brooks's family raises a second question about Pessen's evaluations. He is ranked "in the middle" despite direct descendancy from John Cotton and grandfather Peter Chardon, a noted Boston merchant. Assigning Brooks to the middle level suggests that Pessen's ranking standards may be ambiguous. Pessen's criteria for derived as opposed to achieved position are "affluence," "high social status," and parents who were successful "lawyers or doctors."[183] These qualities never receive a more precise definition nor are they correlated with each other. Hence it is impossible to determine whether Brooks is assigned middle-class origin because distinguished ancestry was too remote to compensate for a relatively unsuccessful father, or because his father, a minister, had, according to Pessen, a middle-range vocation.

Yet another drawback in Pessen's formulations arises from his failure to distinguish between descending from prosperous local gentry and inheriting membership in the metropolitan commercial or political establishment. Insufficient discrimination of different types of elites results in this assertion: "A family whose adult heads for four or five generations were among the economic elite of their city or community cannot be said to have experienced upward social movement because their always inordinate wealth kept increasing."[184] This conclusion ignores huge variations in wealth and power among different communities, and, therefore, the dissimilar repute and strength of their elites. To move from the upper order in a New England town to the highest circles in Boston involved a quantum jump in fortune and prestige. Overlooking the communal context of prominence underestimates the vertical mobility entailed in advancing from eminence in lesser to greater enclaves.

A final objection to Pessen's conclusions concerns the proportion of those with unknown socioeconomic backgrounds. His contention that over nine-tenths of the richest Bostonians, Philadelphians, and New Yorkers with identified forebears came from families with established rank and fortune loses significance if the ancestry of large proportions of the uppermost economic strata could not be traced. For those at the apex of the top 1 percent of opulent city dwellers—New Yorkers worth at least $100,000 in 1828 and $250,000 in 1845, Bostonians worth at least $100,000 in 1833 and $200,000 in 1848, and Philadelphians listed in *Memoirs and Auto-Biographies of Some of the Wealthiest Citizens of Philadelphia* (that city's tax records did not disclose total assessed wealth)—Pessen discovered the origins of 90 percent of the New Yorkers, 85 percent of the Bostonians, and 75 percent of the Philadelphians. Except for the latter, the unknowns would not have made much difference in the generational composition of wealth. However, he ascertained the ancestry for between two-thirds and three-fifths of the remainder of the top 1 percent of the wealthy in these cities.[185] If a substantial segment of the unknowns (the more obscure possibly had more humble beginnings) came from the lower strata, Pessen's findings regarding the virtual absence of newly acquired fortunes among the richest urbanites would have to be altered.

Vintage of fortune for the Bostonians examined in this study was determined on the basis of data gathered from reliable genealogical, historical, and biographical material.[186] These sources were cross-checked to reaffirm findings. The rich who, according to these references, came from moderate or poor circumstances and made their own fortunes are designated self-made. City dwellers assessed for at least $100,000 in 1835

Table 1

VINTAGE OF FORTUNE FOR BOSTONIANS ASSESSED
FOR AT LEAST $100,000 IN 1835

Wealth Generation	Number	Percentage of Known Vintage
First	13	27.7
Second	8	17.0
At least second	9	19.1
Three or more	17	36.2
Known vintage	47	100
Total	79	—

and 1860 are grouped in four categories: first generation (self-made), second generation, at-least-second generation, and three or more generations of wealth. At-least-second-generation affluence means that the origin of the family fortune could not be traced beyond the second generation. Relatively recent opulence constitutes the first two categories.

Although only 58 percent of the total number of rich Bostonians could be definitely traced, even if none of the unknowns was self-made, 16.5 percent of the 1835 group would have founded their own fortunes (see Table 1). But the unknown component was almost certainly not exclusively born affluent. If more doubtful biographical documentation is used, another ten Bostonians appear in the first-generation category.[187] This addition makes the knowns 75 percent of the total number and the first-generation segment 40 percent of the knowns. The latter proportion approaches Main's previously mentioned conclusions for the richest Bostonians of 1771 and 1789. He found that 50 percent of the 1789 enclave were self-made, an increase of between 5 and 10 percent over those who achieved their own high financial position in the 1771 group of wealthy residents. The increment of self-made in 1789 may be due to Revolutionary disruption. It is highly possible, therefore, that barring the interference of the war, the representation of the newly rich remained stable for a span of two generations. The 40-percent share of self-made affluents in 1835 gains credence as a measure of first-generation wealth because only one of the eleven designated self-made according to less reliable evidence was disconfirmed by more accurate data, and the thirteen documented as first generation in more valid sources were similarly evaluated in the other biographical sketches.

A substantial share of the rich of 1835 possessed relatively new wealth, first- and second-generation holdings, but at least 36 percent and possibly over 50 percent, if the at-least-second-generation category is included, came from families that had substantial property for a long time. The large aristocratic element validates Pessen's assertion that Boston in the age of Jackson was not an egalitarian society. But the frequency of relatively recently made money indicates plenty of opportunity to rise from the lower strata.

By 1860, the end of proper Boston's greatest era, the number of city dwellers worth at least $100,000 had more than quadrupled (see Table 2). Except for a 10-percent increase in second-generation wealth, however, the frequency distributions remained about the same as in the earlier year. The second-generation movement was caused by the appearance of children of self-made men who had been on the 1830s and '40s assessment lists. Brooks, for example, had six offspring on the 1860 compilation. Since the overall pattern did not change outside of this vintage, the other categories fell slightly and evenly below their 1835 proportions.

Table 2

VINTAGE OF FORTUNE FOR BOSTONIANS ASSESSED
FOR AT LEAST $100,000 IN 1860

Wealth Generation	Number	Percentage of Known Vintage
First	44	24.0
Second	49	26.8
At least second	29	15.9
Three or more	61	33.3
Known vintage	183	100
Total	342	—

If questionable biographical data is used, another sixty-seven could be added to the first generation, raising the portion of known vintages from 54 to 73 percent of the total number of rich residents. The first-generation share of the traced total would then comprise one-third, a segment slightly smaller than in 1835. Unfortunately, the more accurate references do not support the less reliable sources as they did for the earlier year. Only thirty of the 111 self-made appeared in both types of data, and several switches in category had to be made as a result of more accurate information. Even if all the unknowns in Table 2 had inherited wealth, however, close to 13 percent of the 342 rich Bostonians in 1860 would have created their own fortunes. This finding invites no claims of egalitarianism, but indicates some room at the top for Horatio Alger types. When relatively new accumulations are compared with more ancient holdings, openness of opportunity increases. The former compose one-half of the known group, the latter, a minimum of one-third.

Geographical origin is another dimension of mobility (see Tables 3 and 4). Did the rich of 1835 and 1860 come from distant places or did they hail from Boston or nearby locales? The vast majority of those with ascertained birthplaces came from Boston and Massachusetts. Except for one on the 1860 list, the American-born originated in New England. Little change occurred between 1835 and 1860, a condition that duplicated the stability of vintage of fortune over the same period. The particularly high proportion of native Bostonians indicates that urban origin, or at least birth in that city, offered an advantage in acquiring or inheriting money. Boston was the only metropolis in New England, and those born elsewhere came mostly from small towns or rural areas. Simply by virtue of place of residence, the indigenous city dwellers had an edge in participating in large commercial operations, and in tapping capital resources available in the city. They were also more likely to have descended from wealthier families. Opulent Bostonians were a provincial economic elite, a factor that gave the class geographical and cultural

Table 3
_____

GEOGRAPHICAL ORIGINS OF BOSTONIANS ASSESSED
FOR AT LEAST $100,000 IN 1835

Birthplace	Number	Percentage of Known Birthplace
Boston	27	50
Massachusetts	19	35.2
Born elsewhere in the United States	8	14.8
Known birthplaces	54	100
Total	79	—

Table 4
_____

GEOGRAPHICAL ORIGINS OF BOSTONIANS ASSESSED
FOR AT LEAST $100,000 IN 1860

Birthplace	Number	Percentage of Known Birthplaces
Boston	96	47.1
Massachusetts	75	36.8
Born elsewhere in the United States	27	13.2
Born abroad	6	2.9
Known birthplaces	204	100
Total	342	—

cohesion at the expense of cosmopolitan diversity and a limited territorial scope from which to draw talent.

An extensive kinship network discloses another aspect of continuity in the upper economic stratum. This integrative force is measured by the prevalence of marital and blood ties on each list and the persistence of individuals and their relatives from one list to another.[188] Of the seventy-nine wealthiest Bostonians of 1835, fifty-six (70.9 percent) were interrelated; 153 of the 342 in 1860 (44.7 percent) were similarly connected. The rate of persistence was also high: sixty-six of the Bostonians of 1835 (84.8 percent) reappeared themselves or had descendants among the wealthy of 1860; conversely, 132 (38.6 percent) in 1860 had similar ties to those on the earlier list. Family clusters and individual and family persistence predominated among the affluent of 1835 and were still prominent twenty-five years later. The appreciable fall-off in 1860 in these indicators of cohesion is explained mostly by the enormous expansion in the number of rich residents and peripherally by the slightly more diverse geographical origins of these on the later list.

The wealthiest Bostonians considerably overlap with the Brahmin

families. Those born into, married into, or whose direct descendants up
to two generations united with patrician clans have been associated with
this enclave. These standards are used because it is impossible to determine exactly when individuals or families moved into the upper order.
Entry was usually a gradual process of multiplying business and family
ties, inheritances, memberships in patrician organizations, etc. The
linkage with the future generations also connects these lists with the
millionaires of 1892, the last aggregation in this collective analysis of
upper-class Boston. Since the gap between the earliest and latest lists
covers almost sixty years and since members of families admitted to the
patriciate at any time in the nineteenth century are counted as
Brahmins, a three-generation span from family founder to patrician descendant is employed in defining blueblood membership. In 1835, fifty-
two of the seventy-nine (65.8 percent) wealthiest Bostonians belonged
to, or their offspring would enter, the enclave; twenty-five years later,
130 out of 342 (38.0 percent) of the rich had a similar identity. As in the
case of the other family interrelationship and persistence categories, the
Brahmin component dropped from a majority to a substantial segment
of the affluent. The diminution of aristocratic representation was
caused by a sharp drop in textile profits after 1847 and by patrician re-
production and recruitment lagging behind economic expansion and
the proliferation of personal fortunes.[189]

Statistical evaluation of even higher plateaus of wealth is feasible for
only the seventy-four residents assessed at a minimum of $250,000 in
1860. The equivalent 1835 group contained only nine Bostonians.
Newly made affluence is more marked at this level than among the
group worth at least $100,000: first-generation fortunes are 10 percent
higher and old wealth almost 7 percent lower. Virtually no change oc-
curs in distribution of birthplaces, but interrelatedness, persistence from
1835, and upper-class affiliation were respectively 16, 25, and 13 percent
higher than for the entirety of rich Bostonians. The nineteen Bostonians rated at least $500,000 in the 1860 assessments constitute an in-
sufficient number for meaningful quantitative analysis but, relative to
the group at the $250,000-or-more level, they have a 10-percent larger
share of the self-made wealth, a 19-percent higher proportion of interrelatedness, a 16-percent greater rate of persistence, and a 28-percent
heavier representation of Brahmins. The parallel increases of first-
generation wealth and patrician membership at each higher step of
wealth indicates the willingness of the Brahmins to absorb the recently
arrived. Accretions in persistence and family interrelationships show that
the larger the fortune, the greater the likelihood of its holder to have
kinship ties to other wealthy citizens of his time and to appear or have
relatives on the 1835 list. At higher levels of opulence the wealthy were

progressively more integrated by the cohesive elements of family, continuity, and membership in the upper class.

Considerable fusion between the economic and political elites complemented the other forces of cohesion. Party leaders and high public officials, Harrison Gray Otis, Josiah Quincy, Charles Francis Adams, Samuel A. Eliot, Nathan and William Appleton, Amos and Abbott Lawrence, and Robert C. Winthrop ranked among the wealthiest Bostonians. Twenty-four out of seventy-nine (30.4 percent) rich residents of 1835 were common councillors, aldermen, judges, mayors, state legislators, congressmen, senators, and cabinet members. Eighty-one of the 342 affluent city dwellers of 1860 (23.7 percent) occupied similar posts. Apart from the moderate decrease in the proportion of rich who filled public office, one major change occurred between earlier and later times. In 1835 seventeen officeholders (21.5 percent) were Brahmins; twenty-five years later, twenty-seven (7.9 percent) belonged to the enclave. The blueblood component of rich officials fell sharply in 1860, a drop which reflected the waning political influence of proper Boston.[190] The Whig collapse and the growing strength of the Irish in city government accounts for this decline.

Investigation of the vintage of fortune, persistence, geographical origin, family ties, Brahmin component, and political participation of the rich Bostonians reveals an economic elite with extensive intergenerational continuity, clan clustering, common birthplaces, and integration with the social and cultural patriciate. These findings register the presence of a multifaceted upper class that controlled a significant share of public offices and was extensively bonded by birth, marriage, and continuity. In 1835 its predominance and cohesion were impregnable; by 1860 some slippage had occurred in its position. Proper Boston still held sway on the eve of the Civil War, but its grasp was weakening; the task of the next generation lay in reversing this decline.

Outlook

Brahmin thought changed little from the earlier generation. Henry Adams best expressed the inbred universality of this consciousness: "The painful truth is that all of my New England generation, counting the half century, 1820–1870, were in actual fact only one mind and nature; the individual was a facet of Boston. We knew each other to the last nervous centre. . . . Harvard College and Unitarianism kept us all shallow." Other bluebloods gained satisfaction and security from predictability and cohesion. For the embittered aristocrat Adams, genteel Boston's sameness meant narrowness and boredom, and induced in him a "nervous self-consciousness—irritable dislike of America, and antipathy for Boston." What produced such terror and revulsion? The "Type *bourgeois-bostoninen!"*[191] Most patricians of the period conformed to the category, but would have disputed Adams's assessment. For them the bourgeois ethos was an ideal, not an indictment. Punctuality, perseverance, profit, and prudence still set the parameters of propriety. Business as a vocation, stability as a social condition, hierarchy as a principle, culture as an emblem, and self- and civic improvement as an aspiration endured as the prime values of the patriciate. Bluebloods launched and lauded technological invention, industrialization, and new techniques in charity and commercial organization, thus maintaining their position as community leaders and their fame as the foremost entrepreneurs in New England. But the spirit of innovation did not permeate personal behavior, social arrangements, or, except for a tiny minority, intellectual endeavor. This outlook was typical of subsequent business elites, who were also progressive in commercial dealings and conservative on other issues.

All segments of proper Boston—scions of old families, new business titans, and members of the intelligentsia—supported commercial achievement, technological change, and the Protestant ethic.* Patrick Tracy Jackson and Francis Cabot Lowell, who organized the first large-scale mechanized factory in America, received widespread praise from their peers. Thomas Handasyd Perkins, Nathan Appleton, and Amos Lawrence hoped to bequeath their firms to their sons. Textile magnates, aristocrats, political leaders, and cultural celebrities acclaimed the virtues of business, and, following their predecessors, noted businessmen devoted the bulk of their time and energy to their calling. The surest indication of the esteem held for entrepreneurship was the extent of intermarriage between the offspring of capitalists and intellectuals and aristocrats. The daughters of *parvenu* millionaries Nathan Appleton, Abbot Lawrence, and Brooks married respectively Longfellow, Prescott's son, and Charles Francis Adams.[192]

The few patricians who dissented from the entrepreneurial life felt guilty about their misgivings and uncomfortable in their surroundings. Appleton's dilettante son felt himself viewed in Boston as "the pitiful, idle creature who does nothing." Thomas Gold Appleton was tormented by the conviction that he had failed his father and earned the displeasure of his community.[193] The primacy of commerce and the professions associated with it forced Brahmins who later became upper-class culture heroes to escape reprobation by initially seeking careers in more ac-

---

*This discussion summarizes more elaborate evidence and argument presented in my "The Boston Brahmins in the Age of Industrial Capitalism," in Frederic Cople Jaher, ed., *The Age of Industrialism in America: Essays in Social Structure and Cultural Values* (New York: The Free Press, 1968), 194–96.

cepted vocations. Charles Eliot Norton, Holmes, James Russell Lowell, and Parkman repressed literary inclinations for fear that professional success might be compromised or because of parental opposition. Norton, a noted literary and art critic, set out to be a merchant; Prescott turned to history when failing eyesight made a law career impossible; and Lowell tried both business and law.[194] Norton regarded early publication of Lowell's poetry as "scarcely a judicious venture for a young man . . . to whom the repute of being devoted to his profession was important."[195]

Power in Boston society resided in the entrepreneurial elite. Thomas Handasyd Perkins was a model for the Hub gentlemen of his day and Charles Francis Adams, Jr., thought that no Bostonian in the 1840s "stood higher in public estimation than Abbott Lawrence and Nathan Appleton." According to Amos A. Lawrence, "the Merchants were the princes" and founders "of the most powerful families."[196] Late-nineteenth-century Brahmin banker Thomas Jefferson Coolidge remembered the city of his youth as a place where "everybody was at work trying to make money and money was becoming the only real avenue to power and success both socially and in the regard of your fellow man."[197]

Despite the nobility attributed to commerce, its main purpose, as Coolidge recalled, was to enlarge the purse. Brahmin capitalists may have used their assets to aid the underprivileged or court the muses. Business dealing, as asserted, indubitably broadened the mind, and perhaps, as sometimes claimed, even purified the soul.[198] Many enterprises were run by gentlemen whose inherited wealth, family position, and cultural background presumably created a *noblesse oblige* attitude that bridled materialistic cravings and curbed the crudities of scrambling for profits. These estimable traits existed, but they manifested themselves elsewhere than in the headquarters of business establishments. Railroad magnates, mill agents, and cotton manufacturers watered stock, cut wages, increased hours, and blacklisted union organizers just as if they had not gone to Harvard, read the *North American Review*, attended a Brattle Street Church service, or sat on the board of Massachusetts General Hospital.[199] "He still grasps at money tho' he has more than a million," said Amos A. Lawrence of uncle Abbott, "and is the richest man of his age here. . . ."[200]

The acquisitive impulse drove Brahmins to shadowy practices that contradicted their famed probity, but confirmed the prevalence of the entrepreneurial spirit in proper Boston. If moral inconsistency bothered these moguls I have yet to uncover any evidence of it. Perhaps the pangs of guilt manifested themselves indirectly in efforts to reserve a portion of their gains for social redemption. Violation of the Protestant ethic and the entrepreneurial vision, however, was a source of considerable conscious concern. Thomas Handasyd Perkins and Nathan Appleton anxiously regarded the resistance of their sons to frequent injunctions to abjure indolence and to join their fathers in the countinghouse.[201] At the end of the era, attenuation of traits and interests indispensable for successful capitalists threatened family and class continuity. Yet the primary structure of patrician enterprise, the family firm, encouraged these developments. How could the drive for money and commercial conquest, and the virtues of self-reliance and improvement, be absorbed by those who inherited their wealth and position in the firm? This dilemma had emerged once before, but the sons of the maritime elite proved worthy successors to their resourceful fathers. In the 1840s the problem reappeared. At first the family- and class-dominated textile industry was brilliantly successful, but by 1845 the founders died off, grew old and conservative, or became diverted by other endeavors. Younger associates lacked the skill and verve of their elders and were also burdened with civic responsibilities or distracted by cultural aspirations. "We must wait a little before we take up new things," cautioned aging Abbott Lawrence in 1851 when his nephew wanted to make linen cloth, "we must be careful how we move, for we cannot afford to try experiments that may prove expensive." The recipient of this warning had a less dedicated view of the business calling than did his father and uncle at the same age. For the younger Lawrence it was "not a plodding, narrow-minded one pent up in a city, with my mind always in my counting-room." He "would be at the same time a literary man in some measure and a farmer."[202] Amos and Abbott Lawrence, beginning with nothing, initially concentrated exclusively on money-making; their children, born to wealth and social rank and educated to upper-class obligations, could not be as single-minded. Amos Lawrence, for example, told Amos A., "you must be the *literary* and perhaps philanthropic head of the family, perhaps of our name." Blood was running thin in the Appleton clan also. "Neither of Mr. [William] Appleton's son or grandsons who bear his name," noted Amos A. Lawrence, "promise to inherit his energy of perseverance."[203] Faltering leadership undermined textile operations. Machines and techniques grew obsolete as innovation stagnated, kinship-placed executives made mistakes in management, productivity declined, profits dropped, and capital value of assets diminished.[204] When overseas trade collapsed in 1812, a vigorous breed of proper Bostonians recouped losses by admitting fresh talent and entering new fields. A similar challenge awaited the third generation of upper-class Boston.

Bourgeois values were not endogamous prescriptions. Indeed, charitable efforts aimed to export this moral code. Josiah Quincy advocated the replacement of outdoor relief with a House of Industry to promote economy and efficiency in welfare dispensation and teach the poor the virtues of work, self-reliance, and restraint. Robert C. Winthrop, another proponent of centralizing aid to the indigent, expressed similar motives in praising the Boston Provident Association (1851) and agitating for a "Central Charity Bureau."[205] Allegiance to the Protestant ethic served several purposes: as an internal credo it fitted the younger generation for roles of civic and commercial responsibility; as an expression of widely shared sentiments it enabled the upper class to act as a spokesman for the entire community, thus legitimatizing Brahmin leadership; and it was a device for social control. The distressed attracted the sympathies and engaged the sense of obligation of the upper stratum, but were also considered dangerous. Poverty was attributed to lack of participation in the healthy activities of society, a condition that in the case of those deemed recalcitrant, i.e. resistant to amelioration, was blamed on their dissent from wholesome beliefs and respectable habits.

Bourgeois values provided a better rationale for personal and business behavior than for political beliefs. Brahmins were always more susceptible to aristocratic viewpoints in politics. Although electoral defeat forced the enclave to publicly eschew Federalist elitism, proper Boston made an uneasy accommodation to egalitarianism. Defense of inherited privilege did not harmonize with the doctrines of individual opportunity and majority rule.

The upper class, however, was not an *ancien regime* effluvium deposited on the banks of the Charles River. The group lived by the Protestant ethic and the dictates of entrepreneurship, and several of its key figures derived from humble beginnings. As an American social order, it was susceptible to the national deification of the struggle for success. Bourbon tendencies were also checked by the fact that ascendancy involved the expression of widely held values and such tangible matters as maintaining government influence. Advocating birth as a determinant of rank and authority carried the risk of alienating followers and losing elections. These clashing situational and ideological forces made the Brahmin political outlook a conglomeration of inconsistencies and ambivalences.

Andrews Norton exemplified these contradictory perspectives. Repelled by democracy's "poisonous [cultural] atmosphere," Norton nonetheless felt that American laborers, compared to their European counterparts, had the praiseworthy advantages of equal rights, equal protection of law, participation in government, and a better chance to become wealthy. Here no "enormous accumulations of capital" or "hereditary descent" prevented "those of smaller means" from becoming "rich" through "industry, providence and skill." Nathan Appleton and Abbot Lawrence were even firmer champions of American democracy. Appleton conceded that "certain luxurious enjoyments" and "hereditary wealth and honors" give "the favored few" in Europe privileges "unattainable under our system." But these advantages counted little against "the wide diffusion of the means of rational enjoyment—and the all but universal possession of the means of comfortable existence" which prevail in America. Lawrence declared, "our country with all our *bickerings* presents to the world the results of Self Government such as the world has never before mentioned—My pride of Country increases with age. . . ."[206] Expressed in private letters, these convictions were not merely ritualistic affirmations of the national creed or strategems calculated to attract public support in the age of Jackson.

Testaments in praise of equality and democracy must be balanced against commendations of elitism. Even the Alger types were not immune from this belief. Amos Lawrence declared that Jackson's election "goes farther to destroy my confidence in the ability of our people for self government than any other fact." He looked to "the leading people" of the community "to discourage vice and encourage virtue," and preserve "our happy forms of government." When first-generation Brahmins disputed the principle of democracy, as did Lawrence, they still accepted "the value of individual effort and example." Thus they were, like robber barons of a subsequent era, elitist without being aristocratic. Middle-class ideals prompted them to guard their children against the evils of inherited privilege. Amos Lawrence urged Amos A. to "make yourself a better man than your father." Since "men are naturally indolent," they must be taught to "look out for themselves." Sons could surpass their fathers only if "urged by necessity." Accordingly, Amos Lawrence asserted, "My desire is to furnish my sons, facility for getting a living for themselves, but not the means of living in idleness."[207] The Protestant ethic and the entrepreneurial impulse inhibited aristocratic tendencies. Labor not leisure, personal achievement not family inheritance, dedication not dilettantism were the lessons taught the children of family founders.

Amos A. Lawrence perpetuated parental values. Far from regretting that he could not make his offspring independently wealthy, he declared, "I am glad that my children should have the stimulus to exertion which I myself had. Labor has been to me one of the greatest enjoyments of my life, and one of my greatest blessings, and I hope it may be theirs." He also took a dim view of genealogical attempts to connect "the names of the . . . nobility with our democratic ones," for "you may run into a queen's drawg room for one generation, you may be in the kitchen in the next."[208] Lawrence retained paternal prescriptions; Thomas Gold Appleton, with much inner turmoil, rejected them.[209] His rejection, however, may have been subtly encouraged by Nathan Appleton, that paragon of Protestant virtue and defender of self-help and equality. Appleton advised his son "to acquire . . . the education of a gentleman, a tolerable knowledge of Greek and Latin . . . necessary in travelling the road to honour." The elder Appleton also traced ancestors and acquired a family coat-of-arms.[210] Second-generation loyalty to the code of their fathers depended upon paternal commitment to this code. Strongly and consistently held convictions were successfully passed on; when family founders tempered middle-class mores with aristocratic aspirations, their children were likely to be, as was Appleton, confused about their place in society, troubled over their self-image, and doubtful about their father's vocation.

Thomas Gold Appleton illustrates the tendency of bluebloods with bequeathed wealth and high status to adopt genteel values and hence to display greater misgivings about popular government and self-made men. Scions of older families, particularly those removed from commerce, held these predilictions in even more pronounced fashion. Worshipers of gentility were still rare in proper Boston and they did not wholly embrace the life-style of the European gentry, but they herald a trend that became important after the Civil War. "Where in America is to be found that spirit of sport and bluff hearty enjoyment, that is seen in England country gentlemen," complained third-generation patrician Francis Parkman. With business "swallow[ing] much more that is noble, only the army and navy retain some notion of honor and pleasure." Parkman found the masses distasteful, but even he conceded, "There is no permanent aristocracy—the meanest man may raise himself by talent and the highest born sink into insignificance from the want of it."[211] Richard Henry Dana, Jr., had similar views. His father, son of a prominent Federalist, a romantic poet, and a founder of the *North American Review*, hated democracy and favored a monarchy with "established orders," an "established church," and a House of Lords.[212] Richard the younger, filled with a "proper pride of ancestry" and never forgetting that his forebears were "gentlemen & men of honor, & ladies & women of education and refinement," also detested the masses and admired the British nobility and government.[213] Notwithstanding these sentiments Dana worked hard as a lawyer and curried favor with textile magnates.

Despite differences over hierarchy or equality, virtually all Brahmins admired order and moderation. Those who believed that America was a land overflowing with opportunity and abundance, and those who glorified the past and revered established rank found common ground in asserting that social arrangements and institutions needed little change. Communitarian utopias, labor reforms, and abolitionism found few adherents in proper Boston.[214] Descendants of families even more distinguished than the Danas and Parkmans expressed allegiance to both upward mobility and derived social position, and fashioned these beliefs into a defense of traditional institutions and ideas. Josiah Quincy, commemorating the bicentennial of Boston, drew from both sources of conservatism in sanctifying the prevailing order. The "natural and generous affections of man . . . connect[ing] him with ancestry . . . enlarge the sphere of his interests; multiply his motives to virtue; and give intensity to his sense of duty to generations to come, by the perception of obligation to those which are past." In Quincy's mind Burkean concepts cohabited with Lockean liberalism and the Protestant ethic. The history of New England was a continuous and compatible development in which the Revolution and the Declaration of Independence were "the natural and inevitable consequences" of the Puritan quest for civil liberty and religious freedom. The "true glories of the institutions of our fathers" are that "the honors and rewards of society are open equally to the fair competition of all; that the distinctions of wealth, or of power, are not fixed in families; that whatever of this nature exists to-day, may be changed to-morrow, or, in a coming generation, be absolutely reversed." Freedom and equality are "the natural fruits of that patience in toil, that frugality of disposition, that temperance of habit, that general diffusion of knowledge, and that sense of religious responsibility, inculcated by the precepts, and exhibited in the example of every generation of our ancestors." Robert C. Winthrop, appropriately in a biography of ancestor Governor John Winthrop, echoed these ideas. He praised Quincy's evaluation of the Puritans as a self-restrained and pragmatic people who fostered the republican character of New England. Both Winthrop and Quincy had "family pride" and opposed "premature and intemperate [reform] efforts" based on "some broad, unqualified principle of abstract right, without regard to circumstances or consequences."[215] Like many Brahmins, they had an anchor in the past and an eye toward the future. Descended from prominent colonial clans, they were active in charity reorganization and other civic projects and close to Boston businessmen. Winthrop was a political spokesman for the textile industry and Quincy, at his mayoralty inaugural, advocated a "settled policy of mercantile cities to allure and detain capitalists."[216] For them the past, present, and future unified in a timeless outlook which blended their loyalties to history and posterity into a relevant and rooted vision of the social order.

Patrician intellectuals tended to be more aristocratic than other elements of proper Boston. Unlike businessmen or politicians, they were not bound by profit margins or ballot boxes. Success for the upper-class intelligentsia, therefore, did not depend upon absorbing the techniques or expressing the values of middle-class America. Their constituency was each other and like-minded and well-born counterparts placed elsewhere in this or foreign lands. Personal background as well as vocational orientation put distance between the cultural elite and the masses. Prominent Whigs and cotton manufacturers of humble origin prevented Brahmin business and political circles from losing touch with egalitarian notions. The cultural celebrities of Boston, however—Parkman, Dana, Jr., Holmes, James Russell Lowell, Charles Eliot Norton, and Prescott—came from established wealth and family. Of the few exceptions to this condition, Ticknor, son of a rich merchant, and Longfellow wedded rank and fortune. Background and money enabled the intellectual elite to acquire skill and information, avoid hackwork, make good connections, and display polished manners. The life of the mind in Boston required mastery of Greek and Latin, a college education (usually Harvard), European travel, entrée into genteel cultural circles here and abroad, and the wherewithal to adopt a leisurely life-style and live off encomiums rather than royalties. Aloof from the marketplace and the political party, scholars and litterateurs adopted an Olympian posture, a genteel perspective, and an attitude of moral and social superiority.

The right flank of the Brahmin intelligentsia was manned by the romantic reactionaries Richard Henry Dana, Jr., Parkman, and Thomas Gold Appleton. Unremitting in their contempt for the masses, commerce, technology, and democracy, they glorified the past, particularly in the forms of family pride, European culture, and the English gentry. At war with their time, place, and selves they lived a nightmare of fear, doubt, exhaustion, depression, shattered nerves, and psychosomatic ailments.[217]

The most numerous and influential group of blueblood intellectuals combined aristocratic sympathies with an appreciation of American traits and accomplishments. Ticknor, "an old Federalist," painstakingly chose his associates, enjoyed the company of titled Europeans, and disapproved of the revolutions of the 1830s and '40s. Nevertheless, the arbiter of Boston culture preferred American republicanism, prosperity, and progress to foreign social systems.[218] His friend Prescott similarly mixed allegiances to the old and the new. Like Parkman and Dana, Prescott revered the British nobility and shared Ticknor's feelings about contemporary insurgencies. The great scholar evinced other patrician propensities. To "my utter consternation" the "Herald's office" disclaimed his "family crest" and left him "seriously afraid we have not the least blood royal in us." Ancestral worship and praise of aristocracy, however, did not exclude faith in American democracy and approval of textile magnates. The historian manifested the same dual consciousness when thinking about his craft. Repelled by the thought of writing for material gain, he wooed Clio like an ambitious merchant pursued profit: "I must be avaricious of time, even as regards domestic pleasures, not idling an afternoon, if I can help it, & never a morning—This was my enthusiasm once, & must be again. What is worth this? Success in my enterprise & present happiness."[219]

Holmes, as on other issues, with ironic elegance formulated the moderately conservative position. "The Autocrat of the Breakfast-Table," "in most relations of life . . . prefer[red] a man of family" to "the self-made man." Love of literature, pleasant conversation, and polite behavior were better bred than taught. Good manners were more important than a good mind; tact, restraint, and harmony revealed the true gentleman. Treasured artifacts and habits required lineage and wealth. Hence Holmes found "rich people" usually "the most agreeable of companions. The influence of a fine house, graceful furniture, good libraries, well-ordered tables, trim servants, and above all, a position so secure that one becomes unconscious of it, gives a harmony and refinement to the character and manners. . . ." Taste and culture needed careful, long-term nurture. Ancestral customs and homes fostered their development, "mechanical" progress and industrial growth blighted them. Aristocratic leanings and affection for the past, however, did not make the Brahmin *belle lettrist* a hidebound Tory. Proclaiming aristocratic values, Holmes was bourgeois at the core. Desire for repute in medicine delayed his literary output and, like Prescott, he believed in vocational dedication and unceasing labor. If the high-born had their place so did the masses: "I go politically for equality,—I said,—and socially for the quality." The defender of old houses and old ways, in another mood endorsed New England "ultraisms and heresies" as "the natural index, of her intellectual activity." He also expected that contemporary controversy might become subsequent orthodoxy. Urbane tolerance never went beyond ideas. Holmes opposed antislave or temperance legislation as impulsive disruptions of the social order.[220]

Left-wing Brahmin intellectuals, the *Atlantic Monthly* crowd, were mostly a generation younger than the factotums of the cultural establishment. Differences in age, political and intellectual opinions, and personal friction opened a gap between the two groups. Abolitionist sympathizers were unwelcome at Ticknor's home and poets who used Yankee dialect or sought mass appeal drew fire from upholders of classical tradition. James Russell Lowell, a founder and first editor of the *Atlantic*, an abolitionist, a poet who wrote in regional colloquialisms, and, at first, an unqualified democrat, was the most radical upper-class literary figure. He supported Chartism and Garrison, criticized the Cotton Whigs, and praised egalitarian political and social movements. Populism also influenced his literary aspirations. "I am the first poet who has endeavored to express the American Idea," he declared with a Whitmanesque flourish that later horrified Old Guard intellectuals, "and I shall be popular by and by." By the 1850s Lowell began to pull back from some of these advanced positions. He dropped out of the antislavery movement, finding that "the longer I live the more am I convinced that the world must be healed by degrees." Growing more conservative, the former firebrand expressed typically patrician sentiments: nostalgia for the tightly knit, preindustrial community of the past, love of old homes, and emphasis on the virtues of an established order. Lowell, like Holmes, discovered "that the indefinable something which we call *character* is cumulative,—that the influence of the same climate, scenery, and association for several generations is necessary to its gathering head."[221]

Charles Eliot Norton and Lowell, literary associates and close friends, argued against slavery. Although Norton was Ticknor's nephew, the young critic became a Free Soil Republican, admired John Brown, and tried to improve housing conditions in Boston slums. Appreciation of advanced ideas and new forms of expression manifested itself in other areas. Whitman's poetry was "vigorous and vivid." Despite the attack on evolution by Louis Agassiz, proper Boston's favorite scientist, Norton "admire[d] the patience of Mr. Darwin's research, the wide reach of his knowledge," and his ability "to overthrow many old and cumbrous superstitions." Norton's liberalism, however, did not, like Lowell's, stem from faith in the masses. National destiny was a "trust committed to the hands of the intelligent and the prosperous classes." Reform properly came from above, motivated by a patrician sense of duty and a practical desire to halt crime and avoid an uprising of the poor.[222]

Political and intellectual conflicts did not preclude agreement on the uses and values of culture. A vision of moral uplift prompted Lowell to proclaim that the "poet redeems us." In a materialistic society that overvalues science and utility, "imagination" restores the mysterious, the spiritual, the humanistic, and the romantic. Moral refinement through cultural didacticism, the basic tenet of the genteel tradition, found another champion in Norton. He maintained that Whitman's writings deserved respect, but they also contained "passages of intolerable coarseness." To Norton, cultural accomplishments depended upon virtue. The Renaissance, a degenerate era for Norton, lacked the purity and innocence of medieval times; consequently, its literature and art never equaled the earlier age.[223]

The institutional guardians of Boston culture echoed these views. Conservative caretakers of intellectuality shaped Harvard, the bastion of their hopes, according to their beliefs and appealed to its alumni to provide the impetus for their mission. President Quincy's history of Harvard summoned "the wisdom of antiquity" to restrain "an age, almost lawless from its love of liberty" and innovation by inculcating the "great truth" that "the intellectual" must be harmonized with the "moral and religious." Winthrop and Harrison Gray Otis, in addresses to the undergraduates and the alumni, delivered the same message. In a speech significantly entitled "The Obligations and Responsibilities of Educated Men" Winthrop enjoined the alumni never to undermine "public morality," "public faith," and "public order" and to reject "wild and extravagant theories, . . . insubordination to divine or human authority, . . . a rebellion of the intellect against . . . faith, . . . a morbid sentimentalism, or a disorganizing socialism, or a disloyal sectionalism, or an irreverent and impious rationalism," that endanger "our age and country."[224]

The intelligentsia split on several contemporary social issues, but even the radicals held traditional views about culture and society, and constituted too small a minority to disturb the suzerainty of the conservative potentates of mid-century Brahmin thought. Consequently, patrician culture, in the main, continued to rationalize and broadcast values and arrangements that cohered and comforted the upper class.

During the antebellum era the Brahmins developed from a maritime elite into a ruling class. This evolution depended upon the assumption of economic, political, social, and cultural roles necessary for community leadership. Setting goals in many areas and organizing the community for their achievement enabled the enclave to dominate Boston. Multiplication of leadership functions and uniform beliefs facilitated fulfillment of patrician expectations and protected patrician privileges. Unity and power operated reciprocally to exclude unwanted aspirants, defeat challengers, strengthen the loyalties of insiders, and command deference from outsiders.

An important source of proper Boston's supremacy was its harmony with national values. Upper-class initiatives brought success in a nation whose polity is supposed to complement its economy by insuring an open and expansive society where obsolete groups are discarded. Leadership choices based on efficient adjustment to new conditions rather than on inherited status are thus assured. Whether this ideal mirrors reality is beside the point. Democracy and dynamic capitalism are presumed to be mutually dependent upon equal opportunity, competitive choice, innovation, and economic expansion. Yankee merchants and manufacturers were rewarded with prestige, power, and riches partly because their enterprise increased national wealth, created opportunities for those lower on the social scale and thus affirmed the American creed.

Egalitarian and entrepreneurial urges in blueblood Boston were counterbalanced by aristocratic leanings. Gradually the latter gained the upper hand, weakening the leadership claims and abilities of the patriciate. Although these propensities existed throughout the pre–Civil

War period, they began to endanger its hegemony in the mid-1840s. Engaging in the varied activities incumbent upon an upper order fostered Brahmin mastery and cohesion but dissipated the enclave's energy, thus preventing the specialization and concentration of strength indispensable to sustain sovereignty. Increased commitment to tradition and inherited social status, inevitable as a stratum seeks intergenerational perpetuity, breeds class values inimical to the pursuit of wealth and power. Consequently, rising postwar elites in Boston and other cities, more exclusively involved in political or commercial activity, successfully challenged the establishment. Genteel Boston was caught in an inescapable dialectic of stabilization and disintegration: a diversified upper-class community was essential to determine the life-style of members and to direct the different facets of metropolitan society. Diversity, however, led to decline by diverting attention from centers of power and wealth.

TWILIGHT: 1870–1970

Although the Civil War temporarily rescued the cotton industry from the doldrums of the 1850s, the conflict hurt the upper class. Boston aristocrats, like southern planters, rushed to battle, impelled by inherited obligations of communal leadership. Disproportionate losses occurred among the age group and physical and personality type vitally needed to prolong Brahmin ascendancy. Young and vigorous bluebloods were most likely to enter combat and to serve in the ranks of junior officers, which suffered the highest casualties. Hoopers, Shaws, Winthrops, and Lowells were cut down in their prime. The death of Charles Russell Lowell, nephew of James Russell Lowell and a young railroad executive who had intended to open a bronze foundry, deprived the patriciate of probably its most promising figure.[225]

Genteel Boston, its ranks depleted by war, turned to face the disruption of traditional patterns of behavior and status and the threat of emerging elites within and outside the city. The *parvenu* challenge might be overcome through timely adaptation to contemporary conditions, but upper-class vitality could also be sapped by renouncing the claims of the past. This dilemma invests the twilight of the patriciate with a poignance lacking in its previous development.

Business Activity*

Structural and attitudinal obstacles, counterbalanced in the antebellum period, now irreversibly compromised Brahmin enterprise. Blood

*This section summarizes an analysis of late nineteenth- and twentieth-century Brahmin business activity that appeared in my "Boston Brahmins in the Age of Industrial Capitalism," 227–42.

and class ties, epitomized by the family firm, had survived transitions from commerce to industry and organizational changes from proprietorship and partnership to the corporation. As long as the gentry continued to produce or co-opt entrepreneurial talent and control the local business system, the weaknesses of ascriptive business conduct were far outweighed by its perpetuation of class leadership. Although Lee, Higginson, & Co., Calumet & Hecla copper enterprises, and Godfrey Lowell Cabot's carbon-black firm were kinship organizations, the family firm became increasingly archaic in the post–Civil War corporate world. Capital became available chiefly through institutional rather than consanguine contracts, and improvements in transportation and communication systems minimized the necessity of relying on relatives for trustworthy commercial information or for faithful service in distant lands. American capitalism contained strong structural biases toward a competitive, open, and rational market where affective and ascriptive considerations eventually placed the patriciate at a disadvantage when challenged by businessmen uninhibited by tradition, kin, or reference group.

Family trusts raised similar problems of employing capital for business expansion. Many blueblood fortunes were tied up by this device, designed to protect continuity of status over the generations by prohibiting heirs from touching the principal of their legacy. Management was entrusted to upper-class lawyers and bankers to preserve bequests from depredations by impulsive or spendthrift descendants. Conservative trustees invested inheritances in proven enterprises rather than in more profitable but riskier ventures. The inhibitions of William H. Forbes, son of John Murray Forbes and administrator of many genteel accumulations, and Massachusetts Hospital Life Insurance Company, the repository of the bulk of Brahmin family fortunes, kept a substantial amount of these resources in the low-yield securities of older and well-known companies. Caution did not always lead to security. When cotton manufacturing and New England railroads encountered difficultires, "safe" holdings turned into pecuniary disasters.[226]

The family firm and trust did not stifle upper-class endeavor when new men and new types of business were assimilated by proper Boston. Losses in one type of undertaking were retrieved by expansion into other fields. The history of Brahmin banking illustrates this compensatory process. The Massachusetts First National Bank of Boston failed to transcend the eclipse of foreign trade because the directors, accustomed to mercantile dealings, were reluctant to commit the deposits of old families to what they considered risky and undignified industrial enterprises and ignored new techniques in banking. Conservative leadership created an investment vacuum into which moved more energetic and modern financiers. By 1860, the Massachusetts Bank was last among the national banks of Boston in bills of circulation, deposits, bills held on other banks, and total resources. Not until 1900, under midwestern leadership, did the bank reverse its long decline.[227] Its descent, however, did not reflect general economic deterioration in the patriciate. The Massachusetts Hospital Life Insurance Company, the main repository for textile fortunes and the primary source of capital for cotton manufacturers, became the paramount financial institution in New England. Eventually, however, Massachusetts Hospital Life shared the fate of the older institution. Decreasing productivity and profits in textiles undermined its financial base. Brahmin directors, refusing to seek new funds, adopt new methods, add investors, or broaden investment policies, intransigently guarded Brahmin trusts from speculative risks and preserved the exclusiveness of the firm's clientele. In the 1840s Massachusetts Hospital Life began to fall behind the growth of other Boston financial organizations. Between 1900 and 1937 its resources increased only 41 percent while other Boston banks, insurance companies, and trust funds multiplied their capital several times over.[228]

The backsliding of Massachusetts Hospital Life reflected the long-term decline and eventual collapse of the New England textile industry, the upper-class economic base. After the Civil War, cotton manufacturing ceased to be the largest American industry; profits diminished due to increasing costs of production. Many Brahmin companies closed their mills, although a few saved themselves by moving south to take advantage of cheap labor costs and easier access to raw materials. Between 1860 and 1910, dividends averaged an unspectacular 7 percent. In the 1920s, with the industry struggling under depressed conditions, they averaged less than 4 percent.[229]

Thus far, the post–Civil War era seems repetitive of antebellum Brahmin business oscillations. A similar cycle had occurred in maritime and manufacturing enterprise. In the upward phase patricians and their associates pioneer in a branch of business and form kinship- and class-structured organizations to protect their initiatives, promising young men of talent and capital are absorbed into the establishment, and Brahmin firms dominate the field. In the downward phase the industry or trade declines, but the enclave maintains its ascendancy by achieving mastery over newer and more profitable businesses. The decline of the cotton industry completed the second cycle of Brahmin commercial activity. Unfortunately, the gentry—despite several brilliant individual successes—lacked two elements to rise a third time: it no longer admitted self-made men or developed and dominated emerging enterprises. In the first half of the century assimilation of successful participants in new commercial ventures countervailed the regressive tendencies of family trusts and firms by revivifying the upper-class entrepreneurial spirit, affording a fresh supply of talent, and furnishing new sources of capital necessary for commercial expansion. As the decades passed, however, genteel Bostonians became increasingly fussy over matters of birth, education, and style, an attitude which raised barriers for those who had not undergone a multigenerational transformation from businessman to gentleman. Aristocratic constriction resulted in bluebloods no longer preempting positions of wealth. Between 1870 and 1915 over 60 percent of the local millionaires were not included in the listings of old Boston families published by the *Boston Transcript* (the favorite newspaper of the elite).[230] Business ability ceased to be an important prerequisite for access when the commercial elite broadened into an upper class controlling many dimensions of city life. Exclusion enhanced group cohesion, but also encouraged the formation of elites who challenged Brahmin leadership.

When proper Bostonians ventured into new business endeavors they found that, unlike their predecessors, they labored under severe handicaps. Some obstacles resulted from sectional disadvantages, such as high labor costs and poor natural resources. But other adversities— conservative business practices, low profits in textiles, and sluggish growth of capital—were influenced by upper-class habits and perspectives. These geographical and cultural forces combined to terminate the cycle of Brahmin economic performance in the transition phase between downturn and upswing. Brahmin entrepreneurs had enough vitality to explore alternatives to the faltering cotton industry, but not enough capital to exploit imaginative beginnings. In the 1860s, '70s, and '80s aristocrats established themselves in Calumet & Hecla and in the precursors of General Electric and American Telephone and Telegraph. But inadequate financing from patrician institutions and individuals and unwillingness to expand operations enabled better funded and more energetic New York capitalists to drive bluebloods from early positions of leadership.[231]

Even in railroads, where they were better established, proper Bostonians were dispossessed by New Yorkers and other *parvenu* capitalists. Although John Murray Forbes founded the greatest antebellum western railroad empire, he never equaled the scope of James J. Hill or Edward H. Harriman. The Burlington System remained a large regional line while others put together transcontinental organizations. Growing old and lethargic, Forbes refused to expand, and in 1901 Hill absorbed the Chicago, Burlington & Quincy into the Great Northern system. Other Brahmin figures and operations suffered the same fate. In 1890 Jay Gould supplanted Charles Francis Adams, Jr., at the helm of the Union Pacific. Lee, Higginson, & Co., Kidder, Peabody & Co., and the Old Colony Trust Co. had been leading patrician investors in New England and in such western railroads as the Union Pacific and the

Atchison Topeka and Santa Fe. During the 1880s and 1890s New York syndicates assumed major roles in the western lines and even wrested control of New England railroads from Boston capitalists. In railroads, as in the utilities, insufficient material and spiritual resources to meet the demands of expansion chiefly accounted for departure of upper-class moguls.[232]

Although defeats inflicted by upstart tycoons eroded the national power of proper Boston, such reverses did not necessarily destroy local hegemony. Corporate bankruptcies, which would have aborted Brahmin investment and thus collapsed its economic position, were not involved in these contests for control of promising enterprises. But withdrawal curtailed opportunity to accumulate capital indispensable in national commercial competition. Regional leadership, however, was threatened by the rise in Boston of men and companies beyond the influence of the old elite. An example of this new departure was the United Fruit Company, organized and financed by New Englanders of obscure origin. Trade in exotic products with distant lands had been responsible for the formation of the upper class. Yet when United Fruit applied this technique to the import of bananas from South America, the descendants of the old Far East merchants ignored the company. Like the tycoons of United Fruit, Eben Jordan, founder of the largest local department store, and Harvey Parker, owner of the city's largest hotel, arrived too late for genteel acceptance. Immovable genealogical barriers also kept out Elias M. Loew and Howard Johnson, who respectively made millions in movie theatres and restaurants, and several New England railroad magnates.[233]

Brahmin entrepreneurship was not an unrelieved disaster of missed opportunity, diminished stature, or failure to develop brilliant initiatives. Starting in 1882 Godfrey Lowell Cabot built up a carbon-black business that made him reputedly the richest Bostonian. The corporation organized its own engineering firm and research and development plant, indicating that patrician family firms occasionally could move with the times and succeed under modern business conditions. James Jackson Storrow adopted new techniques in selling securities, rejuvenated Lee, Higginson, & Co., reorganized General Motors, and helped found the Nash Motor Co. Charles Francis Adams III served on fifty-six boards of directors, including the Raytheon Manufacturing Company.[234] These triumphs reveal a residue of success amidst proper Boston's entrepreneurial decline, but could not reverse the deterioration exemplified in the 1880s when the New York Stock Exchange passed the Boston Exchange as the nation's largest dealer in industrial securities.[235]

Despite the decline of the Massachusetts Bank and Massachusetts Hospital Life, Brahmins retained greater stature in investment banking than in industry. Bluebloods who opposed J. P. Morgan and his associates for control of G.E. or A.T.&T. were displaced, but proved useful in assisting New York bankers in marketing and underwriting securities. Such cooperation sustained patrician preeminence in Boston and prominence in national investment circles long after industrial hegemony vanished. Upper-class Boston finance also benefited from windfalls like Calumet & Hecla profits, connections with London banking houses, growth of blueblood investment firms, and the reservoir of capital created through accumulations, connections, and institutions built up over decades. Eventually Boston capital, however, was no longer a virtual Brahmin monopoly because several of the city's largest banks were owned and directed by outsiders.[236]

Encroachments by new financiers or new institutions did not initially seriously disturb the position of upper-class bankers. The Massachusetts Bank and Massachusetts Hospital Life lost ground to newer Brahmin houses rather than to other groups. Lee, Higginson, & Co.; Kidder, Peabody & Co.; and the Old Colony Trust Co. (1890) dominated local banking during the period between the Civil War and 1929. A major share of the resources consisted of old family funds deposited for investment. Kidder, Peabody & Co. and Lee, Higginson, & Co. coordinated the great mergers of 1898–1912, which consolidated investment banking in the city, and controlled the institutions that emerged.[237] The success of these firms indicated that proper Bostonians could modernize in high finance.

The three leading investment firms eagerly embraced turn-of-the-century industrial capitalism. They were heavily committed to new and sometimes speculative securities. Between the 1890s and 1913 Lee, Higginson, & Co. and Kidder, Peabody & Co. transferred the bulk of their holdings from conservative low-yield railroad bonds to riskier but more profitable industrials. Old Colony Trust also concentrated chiefly in industrials. Older upper-class institutions limited themselves to backing Brahmin ventures, but these houses invested on an international scale. Provincial operations, mostly supplying money for friends or relatives, strengthened the commercial code of the upper class. Conservatism, honesty, responsibility, and security guided the capital disbursements of the Massachusetts Bank and Massachusetts Hospital Life. Newer blueblood institutions, on the other hand, operating in a national market, involved themselves with companies and capitalists whose rectitude and stability they could neither vouch for nor control. Moreover, customers of Lee, Higginson, & Co., Kidder, Peabody & Co. and Old Colony Trust now came primarily from outside the Boston upper class. Thus ties of blood and friendship no longer reinforced abstract principles of honor and responsibility. The demands of the national market and the impersonality of the new clientele weakened the resistance of traditional group mores to contemporary financial practices.[238] As these three firms changed their strategy and constituency, they adopted new policies, aggressive salesmanship to attract a national clientele of small investors, opening branch offices in Europe and other American cities, and speculation in dangerous but rewarding ventures.[239]

Despite the prodigious capital accumulation and sales of these aggressive Brahmin houses, Boston never regained salience as a source of railroad and industrial capital. Henry Lee Higginson and Thomas Jefferson Coolidge, respectively heads of Lee, Higginson, & Co. and Old Colony Trust, conceded that "New York . . . is the center of all finance." Their assessment reflected the fact that Boston bankers now depended upon underwriting a portion of the corporate issues initiated in the larger city.[240]

Neither impressive profits and sales volume nor association with New York capital saved Lee, Higginson, & Co. and Kidder, Peabody & Co. from disaster in 1929. The former went down in the wreckage of Ivar Kreuger's financial empire, the latter failed because of its involvement with the bankrupt Winchester Repeating Arms Co.[241] Their collapse did not completely obliterate the Brahmin presence on State Street. In 1937 Massachusetts Hospital Life was reorganized by directors descended from original stockholders and officers. Modernized investment policies and administrative procedures increased profits and assets. The State Street Trust Co. and the Boston Safe Deposit and Trust Co., New England's largest independent trust organizations, are also directed by proper Bostonian caretakers of old family fortunes.[242]

These Brahmin strongholds survive despite the declining patrician role in Boston banking. Most bank presidents now come from other parts of the country.[243] The disappearance of aristocratic figures was accompanied by a contraction of the city's prominence in national and regional financial activities. In 1959, the Federal Reserve Bank of Boston reported that the post–World War II growth rate of New England commercial bank deposits was below the national average. Boston's share of New England deposits had decreased 28 percent since 1941, and its share of interbank deposits fell 8 percent since 1945.[244]

The twilight of Brahmin entrepreneurship coincided with the economic decline of Boston and New England. Patrician initiatives enabled Boston to become the headquarters for textile factories, railroad lines, mining corporations, and machine shops while retaining importance in foreign and domestic commerce, and in finance. When the upper class was eclipsed as an entrepreneurial elite, expansion and diversification of the metropolitan and regional economy appreciably slowed. During World War II the president of the Federal Reserve Bank in Boston felt that New England's industrial sluggishness was partly due to Boston's inability to generate new types of manufacturing. This situation he blamed on the large amount of capital locked up in trust funds, an investment device which the banker thought kept local money in conservative, low-return government bonds and old industries. To rejuvenate the economy he persuaded several Boston capitalists to fund new electronics firms, founded by engineers, scientists, and professors, springing up in the metropolitan area.[245] As in the past and in contemporary Los Angeles, local capital resources and organizational and technological talent united to adapt to new conditions and thus promote the metropolitan economy. But the Brahmins did not dominate this resurgence.

The economic profile of the richest Bostonians at the end of the nineteenth century discloses that the patriciate declined in economic strength without losing their personal fortunes. This exploration of the monied elite is drawn from a compilation of America's millionaires that appeared in *The [New York]Tribune Monthly* of June, 1892.[246] After the Civil War, tax assessment lists were no longer published, and the 1892 list avoids some drawbacks of using such evaluations. Over 1,500 businessmen, bankers, lawyers, commercial agencies, and trustees supplied names and sources of fortune of the nation's millionaires. The respondents, because of their vocations, were frequently able to give more reliable information than could tax assessors. This poll, however, should be treated with reservations applicable to impressionistic reports.

Although the proportion of residents whose affluent backgrounds could be traced through reliable sources, 148 out of 216 (68 percent), is higher than for the rich of 1835 and 1860, the pattern of generational origin remained remarkably consistent (see Table 5). Self-made men appear in almost identical percentages in 1835 and 1892 and the Alger types in the later year exceed their counterparts in 1860 by only 5.7 percent. Virtually the same distribution differences occur in the category of oldest wealth in 1835, 1860, and 1892. More change, however, takes

Table 5

VINTAGE OF FORTUNE FOR BOSTON MILLIONAIRES OF 1892

Wealth Generation	Number	Percentage of Known Vintage
First	44	29.7
Second	36	24.3
At least second	11	7.4
Three or more	57	38.5
Known vintage	148	100
Total	216	—

place in the middle vintages. The frequency of second-generation wealth in 1892 was similar to that of 1860 but 7.3 percent larger than that of 1835. At-least-second-generation riches show the greatest diversity between the last and the earlier compilations. The groups of 1835 and 1860 exceed the 1892 segment respectively by almost 12 and over 8 percent. Relatively new wealth (first and second generation) was substantially larger in 1892 than in 1835 and nearly the same in 1860 and 1892. Relatively old accumulations (at-least-second generation or more), about 10 percent greater in 1835 than in 1892, were approximately the same in 1860 and 1892. Brand new and very old wealth show little proportionate change over a period of fifty-seven years, and the gaps in the middle-aged vintages may be due to the availability of more information on the latest group. More abundant data on backgrounds of the millionaires reduced the ambiguity in generational assignments, hence the smaller shares of the unknowns and the at-least-second-generation cohort. If reliable evidence had permitted similar precision on the earlier lists, the gaps between second-generation wealth in 1835 and 1892, and between three or more generations of affluence in 1860 and 1892 might have been closed. This happens by lowering the at-least-second-generation share of the wealthy in 1835 and 1860 to the 1892 level and equally dividing the leftover percentages between second generation and three or more generations of wealth on earlier lists. Such an adjustment also widens the difference between ancient accumulations in 1835 and 1892 and second-generation fortunes in 1860 and 1892, but these discrepancies are relatively small. The sequential similitude of vintage distribution of wealth in nineteenth-century Boston, however, is limited to reliance on trustworthy biographical sources. If less reliable material is used, the generational distribution of wealth changes significantly from 1835 to 1892. At this point, therefore, a tentative and somewhat unsatisfying conclusion must be advanced: according to the most trustworthy information available, the generational origins of the largest Boston fortunes changes relatively little between the Jacksonian era and the Gilded Age.

Another strand of continuity is revealed by comparing the birthplaces of the millionaires with those of the earlier rich (see Table 6). Most wealthy city dwellers with traced birthplaces still came from Boston and Massachusetts, but the proportion of native Bostonians had dropped and a corresponding increase occurred in those born elsewhere. Rich Bostonians, however, continued to stem almost exclusively from New England. Aside from the foreign-born, five millionaires originated outside the region. Of these nine exceptions, four were brought up in the city and at least two had native Bostonian parents. Despite the immigrant influx and the growth of a national economy, the economic elite remained a provincial enclave.

Table 6

GEOGRAPHICAL ORIGINS OF BOSTON MILLIONAIRES OF 1892

Birthplace	Number	Percentage of Known Birthplaces
Boston	56	40.0
Massachusetts	53	37.9
Born elsewhere in the United States	27	19.3
Born abroad	4	2.8
Known birthplaces	140	100
Total	216	—

Other measures of cohesion in nineteenth-century Boston wealth registered more important modifications. Eighty-four of the 216 millionaires (38.9 percent) were related by blood or marriage to at least one other figure on the list. Although this segment manifests a high degree of kinship among the affluent, it represents a precipitous drop from 1835 and a moderate decline from 1860.

Persistence, another integrative force, follows a more mixed trend. Fifty-five of the seventy-nine wealthiest residents of 1835 (69.6 percent) had descendants among the millionaires; 155 out of 342 (45.3 percent) of their 1860 counterparts appeared themselves or had relatives on the latest list. The long-lived fortunes of the 1835 group combined with the large majority of Brahmins among them indicates that upper-class mercantile and industrial wealth was well protected. This conclusion is strengthened by the sharp drop in family persistence, despite the shorter time span, from 1860 to 1892. Proper Bostonians composed a much smaller component of the opulent in 1860 than in 1835. Avoidance of bankruptcy, occasional windfalls like Calumet & Hecla, diversified enterprises, group cohesion, and family trusts enabled the patriciate to preserve its money for several generations. Tracing continuity backward from 1892 reverses the proportions but confirms the persistence of Brahmin wealth. Seventy of the millionaires (32.4 percent) had marital or blood ties with those on the 1835 list, and 113 (52.2 percent) had similar antecedents among the rich of 1860 or themselves appeared on that compilation. The considerably smaller portion of millionaires related to the rich of 1835 (as opposed to those of 1835 who were connected with the millionaires) indicates that the aristocracy was better at preserving their affluence than maintaining their proportion of the far larger total of wealthy Bostonians of two generations later. Blueblood inability to retain its majority share of Boston fortunes is underscored by comparing the millionaires with their 1860 forerunners. A much larger percentage of the former were related to the latter, with its smaller Brahmin segment, than to the rich of 1835.

The divergence between perpetuation and expansion is further exemplified in the component of Brahmins on the 1892 list. Seventy-two out of the 216 millionaires (one-third) had family ties to the patriciate. The size of this segment about equals the share of Brahmins among the rich of 1860, but falls far short of the patrician proportion among the wealthiest Bostonians of 1835. The category of upper-class identity shows that the crucial shrinkage of blueblood representation occurred between 1835 and 1860 and remained the same between the latter date and 1892.

Politics

In the springtime of its existence proper Boston concomitantly acquired political and economic power. These achievements synchronized even though most Brahmin businessmen succeeded in commerce before assuming public office, and elite entrepreneurs, especially the self-made, usually put the countinghouse ahead of the legislative chamber: "I have made up my mind that you will have to go into public life within three years," wrote Amos to Abbott Lawrence, "but you must *not* go, untill you have learnt *one of my boys* the trade. . . ."[247] Notwithstanding individual priorities, for the class as a whole, political and economic hegemony went hand in hand. Merchants and manufacturers counted on descendants of well-established families to defend their interests until they were ready to join these statesmen in government posts. When autumn came upon the patriciate, waning commercial position accompanied loss of political influence. The dual dimensions of leadership emerged concurrently and disappeared concurrently.

The first signs of political decline appeared soon after the Civil War. Brahmin paladins Charles Sumner and John Lothrop Motley were humiliated in the Grant administration. Richard Henry Dana, Jr., was overwhelmingly defeated in the congressional election of 1868 by Benjamin F. Butler, personification of machine politics and champion of the immigrant masses. Dana and his peers endured another reverse when Congress refused to confirm his appointment as minister to Great Britain. These initial indignities were merely a prelude to events in 1880s and 1890s. Massachusetts mugwumpery, embodiment of political Brahminism, proved inadequate in defending genteel Boston against the onslaught of the urban machine. Candidates appealing to newly arrived ethnic groups began to challenge offspring of old New England families. By the 1880s the first son of Erin had been elected mayor as Irish Democrats wrested power from native Yankees. Upper-class Bostonians resisted threats to the establishment with movements for civil service reform and immigration restriction.[248]

Brahmin support for civil service reform, a principle of government opposed by most British aristocrats, illustrates a fundamental difference between Bostonian and British upper classes. Founders of the first families of Boston succeeded primarily through their own accomplishments. British peers and gentry were committed to an older set of values based on the prerogative of rule by birthright. Descendants of famous Boston entrepreneurs were still moved by notions of merit and efficiency which they deemed best served by civil service reform. Their counterparts in Britain were middle- and upper-middle-class reformers who hoped to improve British government by introducing expertise and honesty. By implementing the English system of a permanent college-educated staff of gentlemanly civil servants, the Bostonians sought to accomplish the same ends through similar means. Mugwumpery also functioned to defend Brahmin primacy. This aspect of the crusade served hereditary inclinations in the enclave by attempting to preserve patrician power (this group had the greatest access to the best colleges) against an allegedly corrupt coalition of the masses, the machine, and the *arriviste* magnates.

Prompted by these considerations, bluebloods crusaded to protect the government from the assaults of the *parvenu* and the proletariat. Richard Henry Dana III, an Anglophile and a reformer, justified his mugwumpery by asserting, "I find myself a member of a family with traditions of service and sacrifice which I must perforce follow."[249]

Politically prominent patricians continued to appear despite economic and political defeats suffered by the upper class. From the 1880s to the 1900s Henry Cabot Lodge dominated Massachusetts Republicanism, aided by his Brahmin son-in-law Augustus P. Gardner. Gentility was represented in the Bay State Democratic party by Josiah Quincy III, mayor of Boston (1895–1899) and, as assistant secretary of state, Grover Cleveland's patronage dispenser, by John Quincy Adams III, a party gubernatorial nominee who rejected the post of secretary of the navy in Cleveland's cabinet, and by Robert Treat Paine. The presence of political leaders in party councils, however, did not conceal the fact that proper Bostonians ceased to act as a cohesive group after the flurry of mugwumpery. By the late nineteenth century, Brahmin representation in local, state, and federal governments had plummeted from its antebellum peak.[250] Ethnic heterogeneity fragmented elites in Boston, and an enclave at war with the immigrants could no longer dominate city politics.[251] During the 1890s, despite individual careers, upper-class influence in the Republican and Democratic parties did not match its former salience in Federalist, Whig, and mugwump circles. The patrician position worsened with the passing decades. After 1900 Lodge, the most important aristocratic politician, had to share leadership of the commonwealth G.O.P. with newcomer Winthrop Murray Crane. Gardner died in 1918 and Lodge lost his power in 1922.[252] Eclipse of their class made the next generation of proper Boston statesmen adopt egalitarian personas. Henry Cabot Lodge, Jr., and Leverett Saltonstall, the most prominent genteel officeholders of the 1930–60 period, tried to convey an image at odds with their background and, at least as public figures, identified with the electorate rather than the patriciate.[253]

The lesser proportion of officeholders among the 1892 millionaires compared to the affluent enclave of 1860 reflects the political decline of the economic elite. Thirty-three of the 216 millionaires (15.3 percent) held government positions of the same type as in 1860, a drop of 8.4 percent from the earlier group. The Brahmin rich of 1892, however, more than held their own. Thirteen bluebloods by birth or marriage filled public posts, 39.1 percent of the total proportion of millionaire officials.[254]

Mugwumpery was the last hurrah of the enclave as a formidable political entity. In the 1870s and 1880s Charles W. Eliot, Thomas Wentworth Higginson, Richard Henry Dana III, Henry and Brooks Adams, and others organized a reform club and used the *North American Review* to attack the vulgarity and venality of the political bosses and *parvenu* businessmen who shaped Republican policy and humbled blueblood statesmen. Mugwumps labeled renegade those aristocrats involved in party politics. Genteel civil service reformers looked upon Lodge's regular Republicanism as a betrayal of status for success, propriety for power. Aristocrat William C. Endicott told him that many proper Bostonians "consider that you and any other man who enters politics belong to the criminal class."[255] Lodge argued that pragmatic accomplishment through realistic accommodation justified breaking with the community of his origins by rejecting mugwump purity. When Josiah Quincy III, son and grandson of two patrician mayors, cooperated with Irish ward bosses and organized labor and distributed patronage for Cleveland, he, too, was ostracized for sacrificing gentility to careerism.[256] In politics, as in education and business, those who embraced contemporary values opposed those who recoiled to the refuge of class pride. The Old Guard parried with self-proclaimed rectitude and elitist standards of government recruitment the forward thrust of what it regarded as the unregenerate, the ungrammatical, and the unwashed. Descendants of capitalists who had not hesitated to use politics to maximize wealth and influence, the upper-class reformers could not summon the skill and will to defend themselves against newcomers. Better to yield the field than to adopt the policies of encroachers; better to be victims of class virtue than victors by crass compromise.

The Professions

Proper Boston had mixed success in upholding its prominence in the professions; nonetheless its record here was better than in its unceasing decline in governmental and business dominance. The new industrial and political elites posed a less formidable challenge in intellectual, altruistic, medical, and legal endeavors. Like the original Brahmins, they too consolidated economic and political power before venturing into secondary areas of leadership.

Preeminence was best preserved in medicine. Massachusetts General Hospital and Harvard Medical School expanded their services and continued pioneering research and clinical teaching and practice, thus remaining the finest institutions of their kind in New England. Until well into the twentieth century they remained in the hands of upper-class physicians, trustees, and officers. Family ties at the hospital were so widespread that charges of nepotistic staff appointments were made in the 1920s.[257] Upper-class laymen and doctors echoed their predecessors in expressing a patrician view of the place of medicine in Boston. In 1906 Charles W. Eliot, dedicating new buildings at the medical school, best captured this *noblesse oblige* attitude and pride in kinship continuity. Harvard's president lauded the "influence" exerted over the Boston "medical profession . . . for more than a hundred years by a series of much respected medical personages and strong medical families; and . . . the habit of contributing to public objects from private means, clearly manifested by the first settlers on Massachusetts Bay, and maintained and amplified by the best part of the community in every generation since."[258]

Eliot's paean to class, family, and history missed the fact that J. P. Morgan and John D. Rockefeller made the largest contributions to the buildings. Money for Massachusetts General also increasingly came from nonpatricians. Insufficient financial resources that undermined blueblood entrepreneurship also weakened the enclave's control over medicine. Proper Boston's renowned medical families and other Brahmin physicians continued to staff and direct the hospital for many years, but power gradually passed into other hands. After 1941, no Brahmins presided over the hospital corporation and since the 1930s relatively few served in other offices or on its board.[259]

A similar situation developed in the Massachusetts Medical Society. Between 1859 and 1906 four proper Bostonians headed the organization. Interrelatedness among medical school professors, Massachusetts General doctors, and officers in the society, the basis of Brahmin dominance, continued throughout the nineteenth century. Thereafter, the diminishing upper-class presence in the other institutions evinced itself in the society.[260]

In law, a vocation closer to political and business achievement, aristocrats did not as effectively maintain class prominence. Several bluebloods, such as Richard Henry Dana, Jr., and Oliver Wendell Holmes, Jr., acquired repute at the bench and the bar. Brahmins helped found the new Suffolk County Bar Association in 1875, and John Lowell was president in 1895.[261] These noteworthy figures, however, did not represent a flourishing upper-class element in the profession. The Lowells, Boston's outstanding legal dynasty, began to desert their practices for other activities. A. Lawrence Lowell, for example, became a Harvard professor and president. The further Holmes rose in the judiciary the more remote he became from Boston and his class origins and values. Dana died in 1882 and his son left law at a young age in order to concentrate on charity and civic reform. Harvard Law School did not play a role similar to that of the medical school in fostering Brahmin professional influence. Modernized in Eliot's administration, its deans and faculty rarely came from proper Boston and it never functioned as a patrician vocational bastion.[262]

Even in callings less directly involved with commerce and government the patriciate lost ground. The immigrant influx beginning in the 1840s introduced a large Catholic component into the city. Immigrant groups and sects had their own charities and theological and moral codes. Cultural distance between the newcomers and the aristocracy widened and differences hardened when blueblood contempt and hostility evoked fear and resentment from the recently arrived masses.[263] The city's changing ethnic composition deposed the Brahmins from moral and cultural as well as political leadership.

The major change in upper-class religion was the shift from Unitarianism to Episcopalianism, which reached significant proportions in the 1840s.[264] The Unitarian division over slavery undoubtedly stimulated a movement toward an impeccably conservative sect, but other factors probably weighed more heavily. Until midcentury the liberal, secular rationalism of the Unitarian creed had considerable appeal for the entrepreneurially innovative, the intellectually inclined, and the social reform elements in the elite. Conversion to Episcopalianism occurred at a time when the Brahmins became less progressive in commercial and social matters. Episcopalianism became the high-status religion in nineteenth-century America. Southern planters generally worshipped in its churches and the Philadelphia and New York gentry, often originally of Dutch Reformed, Huguenot, and Quaker persuasion, adopted the faith.[265] American upper classes, triumphant in this world, barricaded themselves behind defenses that bristled with elaborate rules and rituals of respectability. Accordingly, these enclaves rejected evangelical belief, which emphasized spiritualism, simplicity, salvation, enthusiasm, or other-worldliness. Conservative theologically, hierarchical in structure, ceremonial in worship, traditionally aristocratic, and committed to order and decorum, the Episcopal Church better suited patrician interests, tastes, and values. The sect also touched the responsive chord of Brahmin Anglophilism. "Hence he was drawn [in 1838] to the expression of Christian faith as found in the Episcopal Church, the daughter of the Church of England," Massachusetts Episcopal Bishop William Lawrence commented on Richard Henry Dana, Jr.'s, conversion. "He liked background in his family history, he liked it in his church."[266] The triumph of the religion in proper Boston was ensured by the emergence of Brahmins Lawrence, Phillips Brooks, another bishop of Massachusetts, and Endicott Peabody, an Episcopalian divine who became founder and headmaster of Groton School. Lawrence was a brilliant fund-raiser and administrator, Brooks an inspirational preacher beloved by Harvard undergraduates; Peabody, the most influential schoolmaster of his day, instilled the creed into generations of young aristocrats. A firm institutional foundation at St. Paul's School (1855) and Groton (1884) and a coterie of superb leaders made Episcopalianism the most vital religious force in post–Civil War genteel Boston.

As indicated by the founding of St. Paul's and Groton and the influence of Peabody, the Brahmins achieved their greatest professional stature in the field of education. It was the one vocation where upper-class dominion advanced in late-nineteenth-century America. Ironically the two most important and celebrated accomplishments of aristocratic educators, the establishment of private boarding schools and the transformation of Harvard into a great university, weakened the patriciate. The former development took proper Bostonians away from their city at a crucial period of their lives; the latter compromised class ideals and eventually resulted in irretrievable loss of influence.

Antebellum bluebloods were usually educated at the Boston Public Latin School and Harvard. By the late nineteenth century many patricians, disenchanted with the influx of poor immigrants and supplanted in city government by the Irish, migrated to the suburbs.[267] A growing segment of the elite found urban life distasteful and dangerous. Boston and other cities, they declared, fostered corruption, uprooted established elites, and destroyed stable community structure. The foreign-born and the newly rich now controlled the metropolis and were responsible, these critics claimed, for its unhealthy environment.[268] Deploring urban conditions and fleeing to the suburbs, the Brahmins no longer considered Boston Latin a desirable place to educate their young. They turned, instead, to the boarding school to insulate their children from city vices and the pressing immigrant masses. In this respect the proper Bostonians were joined by other eastern seaboard patriciates and by *parvenu* elites from Chicago and other interior cities and subsequently from San Francisco and Los Angeles on the West Coast. In order to educate the offspring of old families and to transform *nouveau riche* youths into gentlemen many new institutions appeared, several older ones were reorganized as boarding schools, and others, begun earlier,

experienced their greatest growth. The years from 1883 to 1896 constituted the most fecund era for noted boarding schools, and the next most
prolific period occurred between 1901 and 1906. At this time Phillips
Andover and Phillips Exeter academies changed from local institutions
catering to middle-class students to prestigious boarding schools. Exeter
enrollment doubled between 1880 and 1905, and St. Paul's largest expansion happened between 1880 and 1900.[269] Most of the high-status
institutions were located in New England, typically in small towns with
high concentrations of native American stock. Those educators who
presented an alternative to the city school met the immediate needs of
the patriciate and received its plaudits, but they also facilitated the surrender of urban leadership, thus accelerating the ultimate disintegration
of the upper class. Although the boarding schools socialized the successors of the older patriciates, they did not prevent newcomers from eventually displacing the aristocrats in positions of commercial and civic importance. The gentility retreated on all fronts. Withdrawal from political
and economic hegemony proceeded simultaneously with educational
and physical abandonment of Boston.

St. Paul's, modeled on elite English public schools, was the first permanent Brahmin-organized boarding school. A cousin of trustee
Charles W. Eliot was its founder, and Richard Henry Dana, Jr., and
other proper Bostonians also sat on the board. At first most of the student body came from Massachusetts, many of them from Boston's leading families. In the 1880s the institution enrolled mainly the sons of rich
industrialists from Philadelphia and New York and was replaced by Groton as the chief school of proper Boston youngsters. Groton, too, was
started by Brahmins and imitated the British public school. Endicott
Peabody and his Gardner and Lawrence relatives began the institution,
and its first board of trustees contained Bishops Brooks and Lawrence
and several present or future Harvard overseers or members of the Harvard Corporation. Unlike St. Paul's, Peabody catered to a clientele of
old families with relatively modest fortunes.[270]

Students at St. Paul's and Groton received a traditional upper-class
inculcation in classical subjects, Episcopal worship, and gentlemanly
behavior. British gentry traditions ruled all activities. "Cricket is the
game at St. Paul's," said its first headmaster, justifying his refusal to
allow baseball; "we trust that she will never resign this her birthright,
inherited from the past." Peabody felt it of prime importance "to have
good manners and be decent and live up to standards. . . . Being a gentleman is a responsibility, that's what it is."[271]

Boarding-school training, by reinforcing aristocratic values, promoted
cohesion among the inheritors of wealth and high status. The genteel
conservatism taught in these institutions did not, however, prepare their
graduates for leadership in an America where the common touch was

necessary for political success and where commercial triumphs did not depend upon Christian morality or a knowledge of Greek and Latin. Peabody even urged Grotonians to avoid Wall Street and seek careers in the professions or in government, especially the State Department.[272] Prep-school boys were ill fitted to adapt to changing conditions or to aggressively exploit business or political opportunities. The historian of St. Paul's admitted that many graduates, when in college, seemed more interested in making the right clubs than in attending their studies. A few years earlier, in 1929, John Jay Chapman, connected by birth and marriage to the upper crust of Boston and New York, more bluntly voiced the same sentiment: "I know the people behind St. Paul's and Groton and St. Mark's," another Episcopalian boarding school where a Lowell had been the second rector and Bishop Lawrence presided over the board of trustees. "They are the stupidest, the nicest and about the most protected and safely rich people in the land. . . . uninformed, timid and comfortable people." These impressions were confirmed by more systematic evaluations. In 1935 *Fortune* surveyed the public and business careers of graduates of Groton, St. Paul's, and other elite private academies. Former schoolboys rarely appeared among the nation's top industrial and government figures, and, despite Peabody's exhortations about leadership and public service, less than 1 percent of the Groton alumni adopted this calling. Almost twenty years later a Harvard psychologist, comparing the course majors of private and public schoolboys at the university, found that the former concentrated on traditional fields of genteel culture like the classics while the latter tended to enroll in pre-professional and technical curricula which prepared them for vocational success.[273] The cultured gentleman, dabbling in humanistic and traditional subjects, thinking of college as a social matter rather than a career necessity, and better suited to the life of leisure than to the pursuit of success, seemed to characterize the twentieth-century products of America's elite form of education.

Until recently the top boarding schools were patronized by the rich and well-born. Beginning in the 1960s, however, the overwhelming representation from the privileged ranks was lessened, though not eclipsed, by a significant increase in scholarship pupils and blacks. The rector of St. Paul's, where a quarter of the students received financial assistance, now took pride in having "every segment of American society at the school."[274]

These institutions trained their pupils for an ascriptive, upper-class leadership rapidly vanishing in America, but many of the boys went on to a college that was adjusting to the modern era. In 1868 Charles W. Eliot became president of Harvard. A progressive Brahmin with little patience for aristocratic esthetes and traditionalists, he applied commercial and technological values and techniques to academic issues and developments. Rationality, efficiency, and practicality transformed Harvard from a provincial, traditional, upper-class college into a great cosmopolitan university. The iconoclast president improved graduate study, extended the elective system, encouraged science at the expense of the old classical curriculum, and introduced a course in civil engineering. These modifications were supported by like-minded bluebloods committed to contemporary times rather than the fading glories of their class. Railroad magnates John Murray Forbes and Charles Francis Adams, Jr., and Calumet & Hecla tycoon Alexander Agassiz embraced Eliot's heresy. Ranged against them were the traditional aristocrats such as Eliot's cousin Charles Eliot Norton and Bourbons Francis Parkman and Richard Henry Dana, Jr. A battle for control of Harvard raged in proper Boston and Eliot became anathema to conservative patricians.[275]

The intensity of the conflict reflected the depth of the issue. The modernists were challenging classical Humanism, a fundamental principle of upper-class culture in Boston and other places. Brahmin thinkers, writers, and patrons of culture developed their capacity to appreciate classical civilization at Boston Latin, Harvard, or on grand tours of Europe. Before the Civil War, proper Bostonians joined southern planters and upper-class New Yorkers and Philadelphians in lauding Hellenism. They showed their love of Greece by visiting that country, sponsoring classical education in local institutions of higher learning, or by aiding Greek revolutionaries in 1830.[276] The virtues that they found in classical Humanism reinforced elitism by celebrating reason, restraint, harmony, balance, tradition, abstract idealism, and the acquisition of tastes and skills, such as a mastery of ancient languages and literature, that required the leisure and education associated with inherited wealth and status. Some of these values, particularly reason and restraint, actually affirmed entrepreneurial impulses; but those which glorified the past and made abstractions, such as forms and ideals, the essential expressions of beauty, morality, and cognition, clashed with modern allegiances to progress, practicality, flexibility, and concreteness and thus undermined the hegemony of the group.

This time, unlike the reform attempts of fifty years earlier, the modernists carried the day. A. Lawrence Lowell, scion of an equally distinguished family, succeeded Eliot in 1909 and continued the progressive trend. A key aspect of the reform program was to encourage the attendance of poor but promising students. Eliot refused to raise tuition and took pride in the scholarship fund because he wanted "the College open equally to men with much money, little money, or no money, provided they all have brains." Lowell worked in a similar fashion to democratize Harvard by introducing the house system, designed to end the invidious distinction between students who lived on the luxurious "Gold Coast" and those quartered in plebian Harvard Yard. Undergraduates placed together in disregard of social or economic preferences, predicted the president, would prevent formation of "cliques based upon similarity of origin and upon wealth" and "make Harvard a more democratic college."[277]

Harvard became a great university at the expense of Brahmin influence. Intellectual orthodoxy, family background, class continuity, and community orientation gradually gave way to expansion, innovation, and expertise in determining admission, appointments, and administrative and curricula policies. The need for money and the quest for excellence increased the number of students, professors, deans, donors, and fellows of non-Brahmin and even recent immigrant stock.[278] In 1929, 55 percent of the undergraduates still came from Massachusetts, in the 1960s only 20 percent. Since the 1950s private-school boys found entry increasingly difficult and in the 1960s as many alumni sons were rejected as were accepted, many from Brahmin families that had gone to Harvard for generations.[279] A similar shift away from provincialism and ascription took place in the governance of the university. In 1900, nineteen of the twenty-five members of the board of overseers came from Boston, in 1925, seventeen of the thirty lived outside the city and the universal Anglo-Saxon composition of the body had been breached.[280] As the Old Guard moved away from Boston and its power and status declined, social and territorial outsiders expanded their representation and influence. After World War II Harvard and the other Ivy League institutions underwent the same alteration as did the prominent preparatory schools. Wealth and distinguished forebears still facilitated, but no longer guaranteed, admission, and these qualities played a significantly smaller role in college life.

Proper Boston's educational leaders undermined the upper class in diametrically different ways. The founders of the boarding schools made their students increasingly incapable of urban leadership by educating them according to values and principles outmoded in contemporary America. They sacrificed relevance and adaptability for tradition and cohesion, and power for style. The Harvard reformers did just the contrary. They created an important national institution, but their achievement necessitated the gradual displacement of genteel beliefs and influence. The vitality, imagination, and ability of Eliot and Peabody, exerted in opposite directions, worked against the survival of their class. Their efforts were not those of wilfull men; they merely reflected the dilemma of a social class in crisis. Adjustment to modern times meant denial of the past and family; in short, disintegration. Clinging to clan and tradition, the Brahmins also lost their *raison d'être*, predominance in Boston.

Waning patrician influence in politics and commerce, the luxury and responsibility of inherited wealth and position, the aristocratic consciousness that prompted multifunctional hegemony, and the assumption of broad-ranging social obligations profoundly influenced the interaction of class and vocation. Many potential Brahmin magnates and statesmen practiced their entrepreneurial and political skills in fields peripheral to the maintenance of class leadership. Early in life Endicott Peabody left Lee, Higginson, & Co., Charles W. Eliot rejected an invitation to become superintendent of the Merrimac Company's Lowell Mills, and A. Lawrence Lowell closed his law practice.[281] What if the monumental accomplishments of fund-raisers, organizers, administrators, and innovators like these men and Bishop Lawrence, all sons of businessmen, had been directed toward protecting Brahmin wealth and power instead of toward religious and educational endeavors? They would not have reversed the deterioration of the patriciate, but they might have improved and prolonged its defense. Perhaps Lowell glimpsed this possibility in remarking, "I'm getting rather worried about the Lowell family, George [Cabot]. There's nobody in it making money any more."[282]

Philanthropy

Developments in upper-class charity closely resembled the situation in the professions. Eminent antebellum altruists like Robert C. Winthrop continued in influential roles and were joined by younger Brahmins like Charles Russell Codman, who succeeded Winthrop as president of the Boston Provident Association, Robert Treat Paine, president of the Associated Charities, and Richard C. Cabot, a pioneer in medical social work. Patrician philanthropy followed the precepts of Josiah Quincy and Winthrop. Younger bluebloods still ministered to the masses out of an aristocratic sense of social obligation and a desire to maintain community control and applied traditional methods of dealing with the indigent and downfallen.[283] Genteel social workers also assumed other conventional class leadership positions, thus continuing the close relationship between altruism, religion, and culture in proper Boston. Codman was warden of Trinity Episcopal Church, president of the Harvard board of overseers, and belonged to the historical society. Paine, likewise a Trinity warden and a friend of its rector, Phillips Brooks, headed the Episcopal Theological Seminary board and served briefly in the Massachusetts house of representatives. Retiring early from law after making a fortune in railroads and mining, he was another example of Brahmin enterprise diverted from primary to secondary fields of endeavor.

Continuity of belief and personnel, however, existed in a radically changed context that, as in other dimensions of urban life, weakened

Brahmin dominance. Until the 1830s Boston had comparatively few social problems. It was still a closely knit community where poverty, prostitution, alcoholism, and crime were relatively infrequent and where
municipal and private agencies seemed adequate for those overburdened with life's strains and deprivations.[284] But the town soon became
a metropolis. Between 1830 and 1850 the population grew from 80,463 to
180,430 and climbed to 247,496 in 1860 and 362,839 in 1880. Poor immigrants, chiefly Irish Catholics, accounted for a major share of this explosive increase. By 1910, 670,585 people lived in Boston and recently arrived and impoverished eastern European Jews and Italians contributed
significantly to the post-1880 rise in number of inhabitants.[285] The city
became overcrowded, slums appeared, crime multiplied, pauper lists
lengthened, and cultural and moral harmony vanished. These problems
were beyond the material and spiritual capacities of the old social welfare organizations. The Provident Association found its resources over-
matched by the widespread poverty caused by the Panic of 1873. Money
was not the only difficulty. Anglo-Saxon benefactors did not welcome or
understand the immigrants, and the newcomers, recoiling from the re-
buffs given them by old Bostonians, resisted patrician efforts and formed
their own benevolent institutions. No longer did Brahmin charity, always offered with Brahmin values, increase upper-class influence or enhance community harmony. The Protestant churches, formerly the
most vigorous philanthropic force in the city, lost much of their moral
credibility among the unfortunate and their influence in social welfare
dwindled.[286]

Upper-class charity was also undermined by the professional trend in
social work. Quincy and Winthrop had earlier argued that a large purse
and a good heart were not enough. Efficient aid was necessary to help
the worthy and discourage dependence. After the Civil War these
figures and the institutions they founded were attacked for the same
reasons that they had once criticized their own forerunners. The Provident Association president was wary of the Associated Charities of Boston (1879). Winthrop felt that the older agency had been founded to
coordinate almsgiving in Boston and eliminate waste; it was not necessary to form another dedicated to the same purpose. The Associated
Charities president disagreed. Paine thought that the association was
loosely administrated and impulsive and permissive in its dispensations.
Like Charles W. Eliot and Endicott Peabody, he encouraged a trend
that hastened the decline of his class. As social work, like other vocations, became a profession, Lord and Lady Bountiful gave way to the
expert. Careerists trained in social work schools to apply the latest progressive and scientific methods of relief replaced upper-class boards of
directors in making the important welfare decisions. The eclipse of patrician philanthropy caused Brahmin social worker Joseph Lee to la-

ment in the 1920s the "passing of control of the destiny of social work from the few choice spirits who created and lovingly fostered it to the great and merciless democracy."[287] His regrets were repeated by other nostalgic Brahmins who agonized over their decline in cultural organizations which their class had once dominated.

Culture and Style

A topography for upper-class decline reveals how the process of ascendance is reversed. A rising class expands its functions, thus broadening its scope of leadership and solidifying itself. Decline entails a shrinking of roles which narrows the dominion of the class. The establishment no longer authoritatively articulates community values and cannot direct society toward their fulfillment. Functions are lost either through inadequate performance or because social change creates a demand for other activities. It would enhance the elegance of this construct if roles were acquired and forfeited in the same order—if, let us say, the upper class amassed wealth, then grasped political power to protect its gains, and finally established its right to social status as reward and recognition for commercial and political sovereignty. The model would be genuinely symmetrical if the declining upper class lost economic functions, suffered political defeats, and ultimately surrendered its claims to social precedence. In fact, the expansion and contraction of patrician hegemony in politics and commerce conform to no such analytic esthetic. Commercial success and political power were not lost or gained in any preordained order, but seem, both in their growth and diminution, to have been mutually dependent.

Cultural and social prestige is one aspect of the expansion and contraction of leadership functions that seems to follow a definite schedule of emergence and decline. High status and honors are rewards for economic and political accomplishments that remain even after these triumphs disappear. A double cultural lag exists in the relation between achievement and prestige: time elapses between the act and its recognition, and to insure prestige, society's memory of the achievement must outlast the performance. Through aristocratic attributes and traditionalism, the upper class is able to maintain this gap between esteem and achievement. Driven out of primary power positions, it defends what is left by retreating behind bastions of taste and culture. No longer able to dominate the corporation or the government, it still rules the museum, the academy, the dinner table, and the club. In the twentieth century the Somerset, Harvard, and St. Botolph clubs still flourished as Brahmin sanctuaries. When the Boston Public Latin School was no longer considered a fit institution for educating their young, Brahmins created New England private schools to seclude proper Bostonians from the urban multitudes. As Harvard became more

heterogeneous and cosmopolitan, the upper class for awhile successfully segregated itself within the exclusive club system and the palatial
dormitories of the "Gold Coast."

Commitment to culture, taste, and life-style to compensate for ebbing
political and economic strength is manifested in the vitality of several
late–nineteenth-century genteel organizations. Except for the Somerset
Club and Harvard's fraternities, proper Boston's antebellum clubs had
been intellectual meeting places where businessmen, professionals, and
men of leisure discussed politics, literature, science, and theology over
sumptuous repasts. After the Civil War several important changes occurred in the club movement. Between the organization of the Somerset and Myopia (1875), only one new aristocratic club, the Union
(1863), appeared. The latter was founded by more radical and younger
Brahmins resentful of the Somerset's tepid support for the war. Several
subsequent clubs, notably the St. Botolph (1879) and the Tavern (1884),
embodied the intellectual orientations of the older conclaves. The
newer institutions, however, emphasized music and the fine arts as well
as the traditional upper-class intellectual interests, a development which
reflected late–nineteenth-century patrician involvement in museums
and symphony orchestras. Moreover, St. Botolph and the Tavern were
partly modeled upon New York's Century Association, an indication
that even in cultural matters New York was beginning to encroach on
Boston's leadership. The other elite clubs begun in these years—Myopia,
Dedham Country and Polo (1887), Essex County (1893), and the Tennis
& Racquet (1902)—were convivial associations primarily dedicated to
golf, fox hunting, polo, tennis, and squash. Myopia, Dedham, and Essex
were country clubs, a national trend in social organization initiated by
the Brahmins. The emergence of country clubs derived, in Boston and
other cities, from the upper-class exodus to the suburbs. Interlocking
and inherited membership in the select clubs, the vast majority of Harvard alumni who belonged, and the substantial presence of members
from that college's prestigious "final clubs," Porcellian, A.D. 1770, Fly,
Spee, Hasty Pudding, and Delphic, created an institutional network
which integrated the patriciate and buttressed a high social status already buckling under the impact of defeat in other aspects of community leadership.[228]

Declining Brahmin vigor elsewhere did not prevent the proliferation
of exclusive clubs or the emergence of the Boston Museum of Fine Arts
(1870) and the Boston Symphony Orchestra (1881). At a time when establishment achievements in commerce and politics were increasingly
due to individual attractiveness or enterprise, the museum, and to a
lesser degree the symphony were class undertakings. These monuments
culminated the enclave's interest in art and music that emerged in the
1820s. Along with the private-school movement and the reform of Har-

vard, they were products of the final surge of patrician intellectual and cultural vitality. These triumphs, however, did not reverse the dwindling influence of upper-class culture. Although leading *belles lettrists* of the genteel tradition still received accolades, in the 1890s new art, music, and literary forms and figures began to displace the Brahmins and their institutions. New York and Chicago became literary, artistic, and publishing centers. Boston, even before World War I, losing its place as the arbiter of high culture, could no longer credibly claim the title Athens of America.

The museum, a typical blueblood institution, was ushered into the world largely through the midwifery of the Athenaeum and Charles C. Perkins, grandson of the great merchant. Perkins's aspirations for the temple of art reflected the mixture of idealism and pragmatism that motivated earlier upper-class efforts on behalf of the genteel tradition. The "highest" function of the masterpieces housed in the museum was "to elevate men by purifying the taste and acting upon the moral nature; their most practical" function was "the elevation of a standard of taste . . . in all branches of industry," and "in all objects made for daily use."[289] Closely related to the Athenaeum and Harvard, the museum immediately became part of the cultural establishment and underwent the same development that marked the history of other patrician organizations. Aristocrats originally dominated everything as staff members, officers, trustees, and donors. After 1900, however, a struggle ensued, as happened at Massachusetts General Hospital and in elite charity societies, because the professional staff challenged kinship and class leadership. Eventually the curators and directors wrested policy control from the patrician board and non-Brahmins began to appear among the trustees and benefactors. Aristocrats still serve as officers and trustees but their influence has diminished. Since World War II, genteel formalism has given way to Madison Avenue promotion campaigns and catchy exhibitions featuring sport in America and modern art, and the sexually explicit scenes on ancient Greek vases have been uncovered.[290]

Although most Brahmin cultural endeavors were cooperative ventures, the symphony was largely the work of Henry Lee Higginson. In the 1840s and 1850s class and paternal demands deterred Higginson from a musical career, but after achieving success in Lee, Higginson, & Co., he returned to his first love. A typical example of an aristocrat dedicated to public causes, Higginson was one of Harvard's most generous benefactors and a member of the corporation for over a quarter-century. In responding to a request for a contribution to the university Higginson voiced the conventional patrician view of culture. "Democracy" reigns and "the gentlemen of this country" can "save ourselves and our families and our money from mobs" if they "lead the new men, who are trying to become gentlemen," through "gifts and . . . efforts to promote education."[291] Motivated by this vision, Higginson almost single-handedly ran and funded the symphony. When assistance was needed he looked to other proper Bostonians for money and advice. The upper class responded by serving as trustees and a Cabot succeeded Higginson as president. The symphony, like the museum, gradually included non-Brahmins among its supporters and directors but aristocrats still play an important role.[292]

The cultural ideals and institutions of the urban gentry aimed to elevate community taste as well as morality, and genteel Bostonians made no distinction between propriety and probity. Shaping standards of esthetics and etiquette gratifies the upper class by enabling it to retain a semblance of former hegemony. The chief purpose of taste, however, provides small comfort for the passing patriciate. Taste attempts to prevent decline by regulating the means to success. By prescribing the manner in which power should be exercised and money acquired and spent, the Old Guard hopes to exclude aspirants and preserve its status. In matters of taste most Brahmins after the Civil War chose the old over the new: the gentleman in business over the aggressive competitor, a classical education to the elective system, the patriarchal kinship group rather than the conjugal unit, ancestral homes to modern apartments, Henry Adams's "Virgin" to the "Dynamo."

This method of avoiding displacement is doomed. The avenues of wealth, power, and prestige in this country are diversified and allow for a degree of open competition, therefore a given enclave cannot impose orthodox standards of ultimate success. No patent of nobility indisputably crowns the career of an American merchant or government official, no entry into aristocratic drawing rooms assures an American Disraeli that he has finally arrived. Preoccupation with defining or defending uniform and traditional patterns of polite behavior encourages an emphasis on style over power or wealth, thus diverting attention and energy from the most crucial factors in preserving hierarchical position. Elaboration of propriety leads to ritualism, to a compulsive repetition of prescribed fashions which rigidly precludes innovation or adaptation. The only relief provided by arbitrating decorum lies in permitting a withdrawal from competition for leadership without admitting defeat. By labeling challengers boorish, the Old Guard can disqualify them as illegitimate. But respectability inadequately compensates loss of power. The unobtrusive Brahmin life-style, often the mark of assured leadership, became a road to anonymity when people were no longer awed or interested by the customs and symbols of the enclave. Restriction became meaningless when few wanted to enter or model themselves upon the patriciate. Proper Bostonians most painfully aware of these matters, the noted Brahmin arbiters of taste Henry Adams, Charles Eliot Norton, and John Torrey Morse, thus became the most bitter observers of the group's eclipse.

The contrasting careers of Thomas Gold Appleton and George Cabot Lodge reveal the shift in Brahmin orientation from wealth and power to style and nuance. Appleton was born in 1812. After graduating from Harvard College and law school, traveling, writing, and painting occupied his time. He had the accomplishments of a dilettante and was noted for his dress, table, and conversation. This role, however, was not a source of gratification in a community which emphasized commercial achievement. A self-acknowledged "painter or poet," he felt "the scorn of my equals." Other patricians considered him "the pitiful, idle creature who does nothing" and he felt "humbled and despicable before men who can build towns" and "turn whole villages into factories."[293]

Lodge also graduated from Harvard, spent much time in travel, and became a gentleman esthete and poet. But he came of age in the 1890s, when culture and leisure were valued considerably higher by prominent Bostonians than in the 1830s and 1840s. Henry Cabot Lodge did not pressure his son to enter a profession, as had capitalist Nathan Appleton, and the younger Lodge did not feel alienated from himself and estranged from his kind.[294]

Defining good taste is a vestige of hegemony preserved at the sufferance of new rulers. The Brahmin life-style was a guide to the *parvenu*, a symbol of his aspirations. Brahmin economic or political organizations, on the other hand, would bar challengers from success. Thus those who defeated mugwumps and took business from family firms wanted to join exclusive clubs, contribute to the correct charities, and send their sons to the right schools. But eventually the ramparts of etiquette and esthetics were breached. Contemporary publishing houses, theater guilds, and universities have destroyed the upper-class cultural monopoly, even in Boston. In preempting this field they substitute bureaucratic standards of specialization and mass-market appeal for personal prestige and class patronage.[295] Prestigious academies and colleges are increasingly open to achieving middle-class children. Modern business, as well, encroaches upon the upper-class style of life. Role, location, and friendship in the bureaucratic corporation are governed at least partly by considerations of organizational efficiency or common work experiences rather than similar origin or family relationship. The final blow to the Brahmin mode of existence is society's withdrawal of upper-class control over matters of taste and culture. Prestige that once sustained position ultimately is forfeited by obsolescence.

Members of new elites now infiltrate the boards of Old Guard institutions, although the Athenaeum, the museum, and the symphony remain comparative strongholds of Brahmin cultural eminence. Several

Jews and Catholics, however, have appeared on the symphony and museum boards in the last forty years. Former patrician preserves, such as the historical society and the Harvard overseers, now having professional as well as class commitment, or outgrowing their local constituencies, draw a significant proportion of members from outside Boston.[296] The Somerset, among the most exclusive clubs in the city, after World War I liberalized its membership requirements in order to meet mounting expenses. Similar financial problems changed admission standards in many selective clubs in Boston, other cities, and even in London.[297] Some organizations, such as the Artillery Company, permeated with smaller tradesmen and middle-class professionals by the end of the nineteenth century, are no longer aristocratic. Other pillars of upper-class respectability, such as the *Boston Transcript*, have disappeared. Brahmin reaction to the departure, diminution, or diversion of these class ornaments ranged from bitterness and nostalgia to the occasional welcome for adjustments to modern times. Morse, an unreconstructed aristocrat, at a meeting of the historical society in 1927, poignantly described the modifications in that venerable organization: ". . . fifty years ago there was more social solidarity. . . . When we came together, there was a . . . familiar saluting of friends. The effect was really quite like that of a club. Of course with the great expansion in the Society . . . the splitting of groups has been inevitable. But it was rather pleasant then to feel intimate with each other's idiosyncracies. . . ."[298]

The anguish evoked by the transformation of these cultural and social agencies reveals their importance to the survival of the group and the self-esteem of its members. Control over social rank is crucial to high status. Followers as well as leaders demand distance between those who command and those who obey. Easy access to social prominence makes it difficult for upper classes to maintain cohesion because in-group relations and values can be destroyed by overwhelming influx. Followers also tend to lose respect for groups unable to protect their own prerogatives. Rigid barriers, on the other hand, prevent revitalization from below and may result in excessive aloofness. If leaders are too remote from the rest of society, they may become irrelevant or rejected. When Boston entrepreneurs broadened into an upper class, recruitment was more effectively controlled because group standards for entry now encompassed all phases of life. As the Brahmins developed aristocratic features, access became restricted. After the second wave of innovation between 1812 and 1820 few new families entered the inner circle.[299] Aspirants were barred by ascribed status, inherited wealth, and emphasis upon slowly acquired taste and style. An exclusive way of life was established through criteria of kinship, neighborhood, age and type of family fortune, education, and membership in prestigious voluntary associations. Socialization began early in childhood through dancing classes and preparatory schools. The process was completed by a gentlemen's education at Harvard.[300] In changing a genteel college into a professionally oriented university, Eliot not only modified an educational system, he also threatened a way of life. After graduation, membership in family firms, exclusive social clubs, and service in selective cultural, educational, and philanthropic organizations maintained barriers and reinforced values and behavior patterns acquired in youth. In the United States a class can set standards for aspirants but it cannot stop social mobility. The Brahmins, therefore, in rigidly regulating access, cut themselves off from American reality and ran the risk of being bypassed by rising elites who found other routes to hegemony. An example of this situation occurred when Louis Brandeis joined the Dedham Polo Club. "It was a club of gentlemen, and Brandeis was soon conspicuously left to 'flock by himself,'" said Morse; ". . . he ceased to frequent the club—his absence was not regretted."[301] Brandeis was considered an outsider by many proper Bostonians, but neither this snub nor their opposition to his Supreme Court appointment prevented him from acquiring power, position, and prestige locally and nationally.

The Brandeis incident illustrates a Brahmin tendency beginning in the 1880s to regroup behind nativist and ancestral barriers in the hope of preserving status and relieving the frustration of failure to meet the challenge of new elites. This desperate device merely made things worse. Joining or forming organizations such as the Immigration Restriction League further isolated the enclave from the basic sources of power and deference in Boston and America.[302]

A unique life-style fortifies high social position by visibly differentiating the dominant class from all outgroups and unites the establishment by enunciating acceptable behavior. According to Abigail Adams Homans, daughter of a Crowninshield and an Adams, proper Boston has "a regular society, a regime under which you live and do the things you ought to do."[303] Upper-class fashions emphasize versatility, leisure, and scarcity. The many-sided gentleman possessing difficult, slowly acquired, and relatively rare skills is easily distinguished from the majority without the wealth, time, and origin to acquire proper modes of dress, speech, manners, and education.

Exclusion was not the only purpose served by versatility and leisure. Given the varied activities of the class, diversified talents and freedom from vocational specialization were necessary to fulfill the functions of community leadership. A typical Boston gentleman might be expected to display competence in business, wisdom in educational matters, prudence in philanthropic policies, judgment in esthetic considerations, and style at social affairs.

Equal to the danger of excessive exclusiveness is the difficulty of maintaining distance. Widespread wealth, mass production, the absence of sumptuary laws or other legal barriers, and universal education make it possible for outsiders to imitate symbols of the insiders' way of life. Another obstacle to the use of style as a means toward legitimizing status and role is its possible irrelevance in indicating hegemony. In America, precedence is at least as much determined by acquired wealth and occupational success, and eminence won this way may threaten the establishment.

If a rising elite integrates itself by engaging the loyalty of its members, decline means disintegration. Control over members varies with control over society. Loss of hegemony diminishes cohesion because individuals cannot assume the roles for which they are conditioned, and group rewards and punishments are ineffective. Inner needs conflict with group values, means no longer lead to ends, and reality contradicts expectation. As group- and self-image diverge, individuals then transfer to other groups or become isolated, confused, and frustrated. In either case vital establishment roles and functions go neglected. In-group disorientation influenced the behavior of many Brahmins. Henry Cabot Lodge, Jr., Leverett Saltonstall, and Endicott Peabody III (a recent governor of Massachusetts) satisfied their power urges by joining organizations outside their class.[304] Henry and Brooks Adams and Charles Eliot Norton found themselves denied the way of life that they had expected and unable to adjust to the existence forced upon them. One example of the refusal to assume roles vital to preservation is the advent of exogamous marriage.[305] Marrying outside their group, many Brahmins undermine the hereditary-familial ties basic to the enclave.

If American society has facilitated the emergence of elites, it also makes them more easily supplanted. Deposition of establishments results not in discontinuity but in reaffirmation of republican values and institutions. New and old ruling groups originally came from similar origins and rose through the same process. Consequently, conflict over hegemony does not cause social upheaval.

Modern industrialism also curtails the life span of the upper class. Bureaucratic development, mass production, the spread of cities, the settlement of the West, and ethnic pluralism accelerated social change and inhibited exclusive life-styles. These developments eroded Brahmin rule by dividing power among many elites. Family firms were not only replaced by new entrepreneurs but also by the modern corporation in which management is usually separated from ownership, executive roles are segmented and specialized, and performance often overshadows heredity. With economic functions increasingly differentiated from kinship networks, business bureaucracies undermined the standing of the Old Guard. Urbanization also disrupted continuity of leadership. The

Boston of 1800 in which the Brahmins rose was a small town compared to the metropolis of 1900. Forty families were able to supply the manpower necessary to dominate a town of 23,000 but not a municipality of 500,000.[306] The city grew heterogeneous as well as huge. An aggregation of mobile masses from dissimilar cultures made it difficult to maintain the intimacy and cohesion requisite for class leadership. Metropolitan life encouraged growth of bureaucracies because specialization and general procedures were needed to administer large and varied groups of people. Division between social and vocational relationships further segmented associations and encouraged the specialization that stimulates bureaucracy and differentiation. Heterogeneous and specialized groups challenged Brahmin dominance by representing other segments of the population. The presence of many elites from diverse groups also enhanced social change by creating alternatives to the traditions of the old upper class. The growing strength of the national economy and the federal government, particularly as proper Bostonians played a declining role in these theaters, further weakened the patriciate. Wealth, power, and status increasingly involved affiliation with national institutions, and citizens of Boston came to depend on governmental agencies rather than local *noblesse oblige* to cope with community problems.

Outlook

Personality interacts with environment, and the passage from ascendance to descendance affected upper-class consciousness as well as upper-class behavior. Proper antebellum Boston consisted mostly of realistic activists who achieved success by combining energy with rational calculation. Lawrences, Prescotts, Jacksons, Perkinses, and Appletons, gratified by their accomplishments, regarded their lives as well spent, fortunate, and happy. "In my own family *every thing* has been *sunshine*," wrote Amos Lawrence in a representative statement; "I have not had a wish *ungratified*."[307] Viewing America's destiny from the perspective of class and personal triumph, despite the growing conflict over slavery, Abbot Lawrence was "among the hopeful one's and look[ed] forward to a brilliant future for our union." Josiah Quincy also believed that "almost everything at the present time seems to me to be better and I do not limit this feeling and opinion to physical improvements and accommodations, but extend it to morals and religion."[308] The sincerity of these testaments of personal satisfaction and confidence in the country is confirmed by their expression between 1843 and 1863, an era of national crisis. Moreover, they appeared in family letters and private memoranda, where public role and repute did not have to be protected.

During the Gilded Age despondency increased. Two related factors, alienation from modern America and awareness of class decline, bred defeatist attitudes of apathy and futility and fears of conspiracy and destruction. Disaffection resulted from the development of proper Boston into an aristocracy and its attendant clash with American culture and social structure. In traditional societies less tension exists between acquisition and perpetuation of high status and power. Values and institutions in relatively static communities tend to harmonize with the wish of rulers to pass on their prerogatives. Human desires for continuity, however, are balanced by human desires for improvement and variety. In communities that welcome social change, attaining and retaining hegemony may involve contradictory behavior patterns because leadership is conferred upon creators of new opportunities who often disrupt transmission of skills and status. The conflict between achieving and preserving leadership plagued the Brahmins. An awareness of the disintegration of established hierarchical patterns began to darken the upper-class outlook. The Boston gentry could neither wholeheartedly embrace the past nor fully accept the new order. Added to the frustrating suspension between history and the present was guilt over not fulfilling ancestral standards or examples. Anachronistic failures, embittered aristocrats withdrew from reality through fantasy, fatalism, and nostalgia, or displayed an aggressive hostility in bigotry toward newcomers, suspicions of conspiracy, or dreams of national disaster.

Despair was the extreme reaction to the eclipse of proper Boston. While some patricians condemned democracy and corporate capitalism for endangering their position and the future of America, others, swept up in the surge of national power and prosperity, praised the advent of unprecedented wealth and power. After all, Brahmins were American citizens as well as Boston aristocrats and many participated substantively and spiritually in the triumphs of the Gilded Age. Even distinction between pessimists and optimists, however, is too broad to grasp the varied response: the most enthusiastic did not approve the system in all its particulars. Several severe critics, on the other hand, saw a residue of promise that might be realized if modern productive and political forces were purified.

A long-lived moral staple of proper Boston, the bourgeois ethic emphasizing systematic labor and entrepreneurial achievement, lost influence as the upper class acquired aristocratic traits and the countinghouse assumed less importance in its life.* Although some continued in commerce, the antebellum situation was now reversed; patricians in other callings achieved national fame and received more community prestige than did blueblood businessmen. Even those still in commerce no longer pursued vocational ends with the avidity of their

---

*This discussion summarizes earlier findings in my "The Boston Brahmins in the Age of Industrial Capitalism," 198–227.

ancestors. In addition to tending business affairs genteel businessmen served on governing boards of upper-class welfare, educational, and cultural organizations. The assumption of civic and social obligations was not in itself a symptom of declining power. Ascendancy depended on retaining variegated leadership, and earlier patricians had diversified hegemonic roles without losing entrepreneurial acumen or dominance. Previous upper-class businessmen, no matter how active in other fields, had nevertheless affirmed their calling; successors sometimes deprecated their own roles, doubted their own abilities, and questioned their own life goals.[309] These ambivalent capitalists echoed the negativism of other Brahmins. No longer did patrician writers invariably celebrate proper Boston business accomplishments. Reflecting the transformation of the group from an entrepreneurial elite into a hereditary upper class, contempt focused on the *nouveaux riches:* they corrupted American life, vulgarized culture, endangered national existence, and displaced established elites.[310] Formerly the patriciate co-opted self-made tycoons, but even some bluebloods who remained in business during the aristocratic phase of proper Boston reprobated freshly minted magnates.[311]

Distaste for businessmen pinpointed general revulsion toward industrial capitalism. Francis Parkman, Richard Henry Dana, Jr., Charles Eliot Norton, James Russell Lowell, Oliver Wendell Holmes, Jr., and the Adamses (Henry, Brooks, and Charles Francis, Jr.) attacked modern times for breeding corruption through materialism, ugliness through technology, and delivering power to the ungrateful and incompetent masses. Steam engines, factories, railroads, and mill towns destroyed beauty, violated the past, leveled inherited rank, and eroded community and order.[312] These critics were spokesmen for both an intellectual and a community elite. As an established enclave they feared to confront new wealth, new relationships, and innovations in technological techniques or social structure. As intellectuals they expressed dismay over emphasis on things instead of ideas, over glorification of undifferentiated quantitative growth rather than qualitative selectivity, and over the mania for money that destroyed literary and artistic imperatives. They were horrified at the triumph of the concrete over the abstract, of action over contemplation, of power over culture.

The negativism of these intellectuals can be traced to the types of existences chosen by or forced upon them. They either forsook or never embarked on mundane careers. Norton and Lowell left law and trade for literature and academia. Holmes was a teaching rather than a practicing physician, and later in life largely gave up medicine for writing. Charles Francis Adams, Jr., after leaving the Union Pacific, devoted himself to familial and antiquarian concerns. For Parkman and Brooks and Henry Adams, isolation from worldly activities resulted in an anguished awareness of denied achievement and suppressed promise.[313]

Class membership, vocational role, and self-image formed the consciousness of these patricians and determined their response to contemporary times. Earlier Brahmins, except in moments of agrarian insurgency and Jeffersonian or Jacksonian triumph, accepted democracy and did not consistently conceive cataclysms in which cities and immigrants became agents of doom. The bitterness of their descendants, however, went beyond condemnations of technology, business organization, and commercial values to encompass immigration, labor unions, class conflict, foreign relations, socialism, political corruption, democracy, and the city. These phenomena were seen as interrelated facets of the potentially fatal malaise of modern times. According to the aristocratic commentators, the catastrophic combination of these evils would eliminate the noble attributes of the Boston gentry, thus causing its downfall and ultimately destroying the nation.[314]

Feeling bypassed in the contemporary era, many patricians became self-asserted relics of the past, hungering for the lost community of their youth—dreaming of antebellum Boston, Quincy, or Cambridge, where ancestral homes lined quiet streets, where everyone belonged and neighborliness prevailed. Henry and Brooks Adams's quest for community led them even further back into history. Brooks's exit from modern times was vicarious immersion in the settlement of his illustrious Puritan ancestors. Henry sought shelter from the bewildering world by fleeing to the twelfth and thirteenth centuries, when, at least in his mind, all social forces united in one faith and everyone moved in the same direction.[315] Inseparable from the longing for lost community was regret over the severing of family ties. Sentimental attachment to ancestral homes revealed the poignancy with which Brahmins regarded the passing of old families.[316]

Brahmin critics confronted industrial capitalism with fundamental opposition to its values and structure. The modern hero was the achieving individual. Free from ties to the past, the community, or the clan, he could move anywhere and adjust to almost anything. Stripped of long-standing attachments or traditions, the emancipated man could more easily meet the needs of a rationalized, bureaucratically structured, dynamic social system. Against the modern demands for efficiency, mobility, adaptability, innovation, objectivity, achievement, and coordination, the genteel objectors raised the claims of loyalty, sentiment, inheritance, tradition, community, and authority. But these defenders of the past, fighting with weapons from another age, were doomed to defeat in a society committed to the present and the future.

Although disgruntled bluebloods agreed in their diagnosis of the forces threatening the country, prognoses differed. Most upper-class observers expected the nation to recover from the diseases attacking the body politic, but they disagreed in locating the sources of America's fundamental vitality. Some patricians, Parkman among them, felt that the persistence of old American homogeneity, moral fiber, and customs could contain the ravages of industrialism. Others, while aware of the danger of the new forces, derived hope from discovering promise in recent developments rather than from the resilience of the past. Lowell's early zest for reform, democracy, and the brightness of the future waned after the Civil War, but current social changes such as increased and widespread distribution of wealth, rehabilitation of European immigrants, and even democracy, if rightly understood, still inspired in him hope for a revivified America.[317]

Norton and Barrett Wendell were more pessimistic than Lowell or Parkman. Unchecked mass rule and unregenerate finance capitalism made them tremble at the prospect of tomorrow.[318] A minority of gloomier patricians were even more certain of imminent disaster. John Torrey Morse, William Sturgis Bigelow, and Henry and Brooks Adams, sharers of a cataclysmic vision, vented deep feelings of self-revulsion and futility. Other Brahmins regretted the advent of new forces that challenged their class, but they did not identify their souls with the threatened demise of their social order. The more optimistic Brahmin critics had professional commitments, and, with the exception of Parkman, institutional affiliations. Richard Henry Dana, Jr., was an ornament of the Massachusetts bar; James Russell Lowell an editor, Harvard professor, ambassador to Spain and England, and world-famous poet and essayist; Oliver Wendell Holmes a noted physician and professor at the Harvard Medical School and a renowned author. Even saturnine commentators Norton and Wendell were Harvard professors. The cataclysmists, on the other hand, withdrew from professional activities for the larger part of their mature lives. Morse stopped practicing law at age forty and became a biographer of minor Brahmin figures and a Boston clubman. Bigelow, while still in his thirties, gave up medicine to study Japanese art and Buddhism. Henry Adams, although an editor, historian, and member of the Harvard history department for nine years, disliked editing and teaching and refused reappointment to the faculty.[319] Brooks Adams, after a short law career, joined his brother as an observer of (but never an active participant in) American life. Unable to draw support and satisfaction from institutional attachments and vocational accomplishments, the Cassandras were left to confront life alone. No alternatives were available to divert or mitigate the intertwining consciousness of class prospects with personal frustrations. Consequently, the morose aristocrats were haunted with feelings of irrelevance, incapacity, and loneliness.[320] Morse, Bigelow, and the Adamses expected revolution or foreign war to bring American civilization to a catastrophic end. A vengeful vision of all-consuming chaos ushered from the agony of irrelevance, anguish, and failure that fermented in their feeble, frustrated, and confused inner selves. The triumph of democracy and big business, the forces in whose victory these pessimists read class defeat, ensured the destruction of America.[321]

The Brahmin critique of industrial capitalism is an aspect of the consciousness that invariably appears in hereditary American establishments. An upper class must present an intellectual, moral, and emotional image to itself and others, and this image is conveyed through its style and reputation. Those at the top must appear to solve problems; they must epitomize society's basic values while inspiring deference among outsiders. Class ideology is the most systematized means of conveying class image. This outlook is effective when it differentiates the elite from lower strata and gains acceptance both within the ruling group and throughout society. America, compared to other nations, is not as sharply structured by class stratification nor as permeated by class consciousness. Similarly, the national creed of majority rule, aggressive accumulation of wealth, competitive achievement, rationally calculated standards of economic efficiency, and equal opportunity is rarely articulated as a systematized set of beliefs. The concrete situation, the practical policy, rather than logic or dogma, have, with the exception of the antebellum South, ruled American political thinkers. Ideology thus becomes a defense against the American creed. Such opposition to the country's reigning values is the product of a self-consciousness that stems from alienation from national norms. Those who have diverged from the prevailing way of life feel the greatest need to justify their disaffection. Ironically then, the most sophisticated ideologies in this nation have been the biggest failures. The more elaborate the rationale the less likely its acceptance because it reflects the growing isolation of its proponents.[322]

This happened in the antebellum South, especially in Virginia and South Carolina, the oldest and most traditional aristocratic strongholds of the section. As the planter gentry moved out of the mainstream of American development it constructed an elaborate defense of its position, which entailed a fundamental attack on Lockean liberalism. It is not a coincidence that America's leading political theorist has been John C. Calhoun, that the region's most popular novelist was Sir Walter Scott, and that the most devastating Tory critic of liberal capitalism was George Fitzhugh, scion of one of Virginia's first families.[323] When the Boston establishment became similarly estranged the expression of its disaffection closely resembled the attack of the southerners. Proper Bostonians also emphasized the virtues of aristocracy, the need for continuity over the quest for change, the timeliness of the past rather than the passing of time. They looked to history, not toward utopia; or at least they saw the good society as an organic growth beginning long ago rather than imposed by abstract rational theories. Status in the community, therefore, inhered in historical institutions such as membership in old schools, old clubs, old firms, and old families. These ties to the past defy rational analysis and are impervious to social climbers. Emotional and deeply rooted, they cannot be evaluated through objective calculation or attained by individual effort.

Adherence to an aristocratic ideology isolated the Brahmins by depriving them of the ability to voice and implement society's goals. The ideology also contradicted their entrepreneurial origins. To the extent that the Bostonians were shaped by their beginnings and influenced by American culture, they could not wholly believe in this philosophy. Conversely, the assumption of aristocratic traits entailed some acceptance of patrician principles.

The self-destructive consequences of adhering to a self-conscious ideology in a pragmatic, matter-of-fact society and to aristocratic tenets in a nation formally committed to democracy explains why the most systematic and firmest defenders of the patrician outlook, Norton, Wendell, Morse, Bigelow, and especially Brooks and Henry Adams (who developed the most consistent and complete conservative dogma), represented the despairing sector of proper Boston. They composed the segment that felt most isolated and oppressed in modern America. Other Brahmin critics, James Russell Lowell and Holmes, for example, vacillated between Burkean impulses and American beliefs in democracy and progress because of dual allegiance to their class and to contemporary society. More optimistic patricians, who felt at home in modern times, turned away from aristocratic conservatism to embrace liberal capitalism.

Many Brahmin businessmen, despite reservations about their calling or their associates, celebrated trusts, tycoons, and technology.[324] Several patricians not engaged in entrepreneurship—Bishop Lawrence; Thomas Wentworth Higginson, the well-known reformer and writer; Justice Holmes; and Harvard presidents Eliot and Lowell—also praised the energy and accomplishments of tycoons and their enterprises.[325] Unsurprisingly, those who affirmed the new order often triumphed under it. Forbes and Charles Elliott Perkins were successful railroad magnates, Henry Lee Higginson a rich banker, Eliot and Lowell progressive academic administrators, and Holmes a Supreme Court judge and a leading legal reformer. These figures evinced the sincerity of their beliefs by applying the latest scientific and business methods in their vocations.[326]

Brahmins who accepted industrial capitalism tended to be less pessimistic about newcomers, class relations, and democracy. Xenophobia, a mania among those feeling displaced, was not as marked among patricians comfortable in contemporary surroundings. Prospects of violent conflict between labor and capital alarmed many aristocrats, but not

Thomas Wentworth Higginson, Eliot, and A. Lawrence Lowell.[327] Brahmins at peace with their age praised egalitarian, industrial society and had little sympathy for the esthetic, intellectual, and class snobbery, or the posture of patrician anguish and disengagement adopted by despondent bluebloods.[328]

Justice Holmes, author Higginson, Presidents Eliot and Lowell, and Senator Lodge, transcending genteel Boston, did not revolve exclusively in its orbit. Nor did magnates Higginson and Forbes, who, while not specifically praising democracy or demeaning Brahmin esthetes, obviously accepted modern conditions. These men, concerned with career and national reputation, adopted contemporary values. In the case of Lodge and Eliot, this meant straining class ties by violating the sacred canons of mugwumpery or classical education. Deriving psychic strength from triumphs in careers which rose above the community of their origins, these figures rooted themselves in the age of industrial capitalism. The imperatives of their world engendered a tough-minded pragmatism, an outlook which resembled the attitudes of proper Bostonians of an earlier day. Vocational success demanded energetic, practical, and disciplined types whose drive for achievement would not be blunted by self-doubt, nonconformity, uncompromising idealism, conservative ideology, or pessimism. Higginson rejected refuge in the past because pride in his accomplishments as a reformer made the present attractive and the future hopeful. Lodge valued concrete gains above aloof righteousness. Ambition, the work ethic, lust for life, and practicality shaped the younger Holmes's attitude toward the world and himself. His positive outlook extended from personal matters to national destiny. Eliot and Lowell shared the jurist's emphasis on vocational involvement, personal achievement, adjustment to changing times, the happy life, and America's bright future.[329]

Patrician optimists accepted the dominant values of their era, attained success, and believed in America. Their despairing peers remained aloof from practical affairs, disappointed in, or indifferent to, career achievement, trapped in self-doubt, paralyzed by excessive introspection, imprisoned in the past, and haunted by visions of impending doom. The interplay between vocational involvement and success and consciousness may be seen in the changing career and outlook of Charles Francis Adams, Jr. When Adams headed the Massachusetts Railroad Commission and the Union Pacific his views were typical of Gilded Age moguls. He avidly pursued power and wealth and praised corporate concentration for leading to a rational, stable, efficient, and socially useful form of capitalism. Buoyant in the incoming wave of industrialism, the transportation tycoon deprecated Brahmin institutions, like the historical society, that he considered irrationally steeped in tradition or preoccupied with family and genealogy.[330] After Adams was deposed by Gould and glimpsed bankruptcy in the Panic of 1893, he turned on former associates and ideas. Like his brothers, he now felt irrelevant and feeble and thought that those who had pushed him aside might destroy America. Existence among proper Bostonians became a refuge from personal defeat and the chaos already engulfing the country. The displaced executive became a historian of ancient Brahmins, a biographer of his father and Richard Henry Dana, Jr., and a historical society president. The once confident entrepreneur, eager to get a toehold in the contemporary world, now venerated clan, class, and the past, and spent his later life wallowing in self-pity.[331]

Adams's experience was a microcosm of the history of his group. For him and for them the path of retreat led from America to Boston, from the present to the past, from business and politics to family and history, from self-confidence to alienation, from dominance to doubt. The transformation of the Brahmins from an entrepreneurial elite into an upper class brought triumph and tragedy. Expansion of leadership meant mastery in Boston, but it bred aristocratic behavior that eroded wealth and power. A reciprocal relationship existed between perspective and practice. Brahmin defeats strengthened resistance to the competitive demands of contemporary life. For the most loyal and compulsive patricians, class values rationalized class failures. But this compensation was dearly bought through an exchange of identity for ideology.

NOTES

1. Bernard Bailyn, *The New England Merchants in the Seventeenth Century* (Cambridge: Harvard University Press, 1955), 38; Sidney Perley, *The History of Salem, Massachusetts, 1626–1719*, 3 vols. (Salem: privately printed, 1924); James Duncan Phillips, *Salem in the Seventeenth Century* (Boston: Houghton Mifflin, 1933); Bernard Farber, *Guardians of Virtue: Salem Families in 1800* (New York: Basic Books, 1972), 111–55, 195–96; Darrett B. Rutman, *Winthrop's Boston: Portrait of a Puritan Town, 1630–49* (Chapel Hill: University of North Carolina Press, 1965).

2. For the list see Rutman, *Winthrop's Boston*, 72–73; for identification of occupation and political position, see Justin Winsor, *The Memorial History of Boston*, 4 vols. (Boston: Ticknor, 1880), I, 560–63 and *passim*; William H. Whitmore, *The Massachusetts Civil List for the Colonial and Provincial Periods* (Albany: J. Munsell, 1870); Robert Francis Seybolt, *The Town Officials of Colonial Boston, 1634–1775* (Cambridge: Harvard University Press, 1939); Nathaniel B. Shurtleff, *A Topographical and Historical Description of Boston* (Boston: A. Williams, 1871), 183–250, 592–687; Bailyn, *New England Merchants*, *passim*.

3. *Professional and Industrial History of Massachusetts*, 3 vols. (Boston: Boston History Company, 1894), II, 39.

4. Seybolt, *The Public Schools of Boston, 1653–1775* (Cambridge: Harvard University Press, 1935), 8, 33, 57–58, 62; James Henretta, "Economic Develop-

ment and Social Structure in Colonial Boston," *William and Mary Quarterly*, XXII (1965), 90.

5. Bailyn, *New England Merchants*, 38; Oliver Ayer Roberts, *The History of the Ancient and Honorable Artillery Company*, 3 vols. (Boston: Alfred Mudge and Sons, 1897), *passim*; for prominent officeholders who were members of the company 1634–1821, see II, 465–68.

6. Henry Wilder Foote, *Annals of King's Chapel*, 2 vols. (Boston: Little, Brown, 1896), I, 89–94.

7. Norman H. Dawes, "Social Classes in Seventeenth Century New England" (Ph.D. dissertation, Harvard University, 1941), 417.

8. Robert Zemsky, *Merchants, Farmers, and River Gods: An Essay on Eighteenth-Century Politics* (Boston: Gambit, 1971), 35–38; Gerard W. Gawalt, *The Promise of Power: The Emergence of the Legal Profession in Massachusetts, 1760–1840* (Westport, Conn.: Greenwood Press, 1979), 39.

9. Bailyn, *New England Merchants*, 105–12, 137–40; Dawes, "Social Classes," 177–93, 209–11, 403–15; Winsor, *Memorial*, I, 574–88, II, 538–63; John A. Schutz, *William Shirley, King's Governor of Massachusetts* (Chapel Hill: University of North Carolina Press, 1961), 174, 179; James H. Stark, *The Loyalists of Massachusetts and the Other Side of the American Revolution* (Salem: Salem Press, 1910), 145–470; Lorenzo Sabine, *The American Loyalists or Biographical Sketches of Loyalists of the American Revolution*, 2 vols. (Port Washington, N.Y.: Kennicott Press, 1966); Nathaniel I. Bowditch, "Gleaner Articles," *Fifth Report of the Record Commissioners, 1880* (Boston: Rockwell and Churchill, 1884); Shurtleff, *Topographical*, 183–250, 592–687.

10. The tax list of the wealthiest Bostonians is reprinted in Winsor, *Memorial*, II, 7–8; Henretta has analyzed the roll in "Economic Development," 78, 80. For a contemporary compilation of some large seventeenth-century personal fortunes see Edward Randolph's report in John Gorham Palfrey, *History of New England*, 5 vols. (originally published 1858–69; New York: AMS Press, 1966), III, 318n, 398. On the same topic see also William B. Weeden, *Economic and Social History of New England, 1620–1789*, 2 vols. (Boston: Houghton Mifflin, 1890), I, 292.

11. Henretta, "Economic Development," *passim*; Jackson Turner Main, *The Social Structure of Revolutionary America* (Princeton: Princeton University Press, 1965), 36, 41, 89, 193; Alice Hanson Jones, "Wealth Estimates of the New England Colonies about 1770," *Journal of Economic History*, XXII (1972), 121–23, 126.

12. Main, *Social Structure*, 193.

13. Winsor, *Memorial*, I, 560–63; II, 533–37; Whitmore, *Massachusetts Civil List*; Seybolt, *Town Officials*.

14. Bailyn, *New England Merchants*, 174–77; Zemsky, *Merchants*, 31–34, 178–79, 218–19, 226–27, 287–314; Francis G. Walett, "The Massachusetts Council," *William and Mary Quarterly*, VI (1949), 605–27; Ellen E. Brennan, *Plural Officeholding in Massachusetts* (Chapel Hill: University of North Carolina Press, 1945), 176–80; Schutz, *William Shirley*, 278–83. Occupational backgrounds of the officials may be found in the above and in Winsor, *Memorial*, I and II; G. B. Warden, *Boston, 1689–1778* (Boston: Little, Brown, 1970); Arthur M. Schlesinger, *The Colonial Merchants and the American Revolution*,

1773–76 (New York: Facsimile Library, 1939); Robert A. East, *Business Enterprise in the Revolutionary Era* (New York: Columbia University Press, 1938); Henretta, "Economic Development," 90. The merchant elites of other port towns showed a similar course of development in amassing great wealth, capturing high office, and intermarrying. Cf. Perley, *History of Salem*; Phillips: *Salem in the Seventeenth Century*; *Salem in the Eighteenth Century* (Boston: Houghton Mifflin, 1937); Benjamin W. Larabee, *The Merchants of Newburyport, 1764–1815* (Cambridge: Harvard University Press, 1962).

15. For a discussion of these points see Bailyn, *New England Merchants*, 40–49; Robert Keane, *The Apologia of Robert Keane*, ed. Bailyn (New York: Harper Torchbooks, 1964).

16. Andrew McFarland Davis, "Boston 'Banks'—1681–1740—Those Who Were Interested in Them," *New England Historical and Genealogical Register*, LVII (1903), 274–81; Davis, "Currency and Banking in the Province of the Massachusetts-Bay and Inflationary Money Policy," *Publications of the American Economic Association*, 3d ser., II (1901), 125–66; Zemsky, *Merchants*, 98–156; 179–80, 265–83, 313–23.

17. Warden, *Boston*, 55ff., 66, 116–21, 140.

18. Bailyn, *New England Merchants*, 47–49, 88–97, 105–12, 137–40, 170–74, 182–89; see also Michael Hall, *Edward Randolph and the American Colonies, 1676–1703* (Chapel Hill: University of North Carolina Press, 1960); Rutman, *Winthrop's Boston*; Zemsky, *Merchants*; Warden, *Boston*; Schutz, *William Shirley*. Those interested in studying the merchants in primary sources should consult N. B. Shurtleff, *Records of the Governor and Company of the Massachusetts Bay Colony in New England*, 5 vols. (Boston: William White, 1853–54); *Diary of Samuel Sewall, Collections of the Massachusetts Historical Society*, V, 5th and 7th ser. (1878, 1882); *Belcher Papers, ibid.*, I, 6th and 7th ser. (1893); Charles Henry Lincoln, ed., *Correspondence of William Shirley* (New York: Macmillan, 1912).

19. Bailyn, *New England Merchants*, 195–97; Thomas J. Wertenbaker, *The Golden Age of Colonial Culture* (New York: New York University Press, 1949), 18–20, 30; Winsor, *Memorial*, II, 451–58.

20. Robert Francis Seybolt, *The Private Schools of Colonial Boston* (Cambridge: Harvard University Press, 1933), 3–11, 16, 82–92.

21. Stark, *Loyalists*, 133–74; Sabine, *American Loyalists*; Winsor, *Memorial*, II, 563; East, *Business Enterprise*, 219–27; Charles M. Andrews, "The Boston Merchants and the Non Importation Movement," *Publications of the Colonial Society of Massachusetts, Transactions*, XIX (1917), 160–65.

22. Bailyn, *New England Merchants*, 31–38, 87, 101–2, 110–11, 192–97; Rutman, *Winthrop's Boston*, 72–75, 182–91, 199–200, 254–55; Shurtleff, *Topographical*, 183–250, 592–687; Winsor, *Memorial*, I, 574–88, II, 538–63; Sabine *American Loyalists, passim*; Stark, *Loyalists*, 145–270; Bowditch, "Gleaner," *passim*.

23. Main, *Social Structure*, 193 for Boston, 183–96 for the other places.

24. *Ibid.*, 191–92 for Boston, 183–85, 189–91 for the other places.

25. Elizabeth Gray Otis to Harrison Gray Otis, July 10, 1777; Samuel Eliot Morison, *Harrison Gray Otis, 1765–1848: The Urbane Federalist* (Boston: Houghton Mifflin, 1969), 33; Joseph Warren and Stephen Higginson quoted in

East, *Business Enterpise*, 227, 214. For similar views regarding the turnover in Salem's elite see Robert E. Peabody, *Merchant Venturers of Old Salem* (Boston: Houghton Mifflin, 1912), 47.

26. For information on the colonial mercantile establishment and its disruption by the Revolution see East, *Business Enterprise*; W. T. Baxter, *The House of Hancock: Business in Boston, 1724–1775* (Cambridge: Harvard University Press, 1945). Studies on the great Boston overseas traders are Samuel Eliot Morison, *Maritime History of Massachusetts, 1783–1860* (Boston: Little, Brown, 1921), 44–49, 76, 129, 165–170 on the formation of the group; Foster Rhea Dulles, *The Old China Trade* (Boston: Houghton Mifflin, 1930); Peabody, *Merchant Venturers*. The most convenient collection of short family biographies of the Boston Brahmins is Mary Caroline Crawford, *Famous Families of Massachusetts*, 2 vols. (Boston: Houghton Mifflin, 1930). For information on the origins of prominent Bostonians see also Thomas G. Cary, *Memoir of Thomas Handasyd Perkins* (Boston: Little, Brown, 1865), 5–9; Charles G. Loring, *Memoir of William Sturgis* (Boston: John Wilson and Son, 1864), 1–15; Robert Bennet Forbes, *Personal Reminiscences* (Boston: Little, Brown, 1878), 26–50; Edward Gray, *William Gray of Salem, Merchant* (Boston: Houghton Mifflin, 1915), 3–13; Kenneth Wiggins Porter, *The Jacksons and the Lees*, 2 vols., I (Cambridge: Harvard University Press, 1937), 6–34; H. W. L. Dana, *The Dana Saga: Three Centuries of the Family in Cambridge* (Cambridge: Cambridge Historical Society, 1941), 1–19; Henry Cabot Lodge, *The Life and Letters of George Cabot* (Boston: Little, Brown, 1877), 1–27; Josiah Quincy, *Memoir of the Life of Josiah Quincy, Jr.* (Boston: John Wilson and Son, 1874), 1–6; Morison, *Life and Letters of Harrison Gray Otis*, 2 vols., I (Boston: Houghton Mifflin, 1913), 12–21; Thomas Wentworth Higginson, *Life and Times of Stephen Higginson* (Boston: Houghton Mifflin, 1907), 10–43; James Jackson Putnam, *A Memoir of Dr. James Jackson* (Boston: Houghton Mifflin, 1905), 4–44; Robert C. Winthrop, Jr., *Memoir of the Hon. David Sears* (Cambridge: John Wilson and Son, 1886), 1–6; L. Vernon Briggs, *Historical Genealogy of the Cabot Family*, 2 vols. (Boston: Charles Goodspeed, 1927); Ferris Greenslet, *The Lowells and Their Seven Worlds* (Boston: Houghton Mifflin, 1946), 3–84, 423–24. There is much genealogical information on Boston Brahmins in the volumes of *The New England Historical and Genealogical Register*.

27. The best general works on the maritime elite are Morison, *Maritime*; East, *Business*, 49–80, 180–263; *Professional and Industrial*, I, 69–155; Peabody, *Merchant*; Dulles, *Old*. For studies of individual merchants and firms see Porter, *Jacksons and Lees*; Carl Seaburg and Stanley Paterson, *Merchant Prince of Boston: Colonel T. H. Perkins, 1767–1854* (Cambridge: Harvard University Press, 1971); Gray, *William Gray*; Loring, *Memoir of William Sturgis*; Cary, *Memoir of Thomas Handasyd Perkins*; John T. Morse, Jr., *Memoir of Col. Henry Lee* (Boston: Little, Brown, 1905). For published accounts by the merchants themselves see Forbes: *Personal*; *Remarks on China and the China Trade* (Boston: Samuel N. Dickinson, 1844); Henry and Mary Lee, *Letters and Journals*, ed. Frances Rollins Morse (Boston: privately printed, 1926). For primary sources see the Perkins Papers, the Samuel Cabot Papers, and the Patrick Tracy Jackson Letterbooks in the Massachusetts Historical Society (hereafter cited as MHS) and the Harvard Business School (hereafter cited as HBS).

28. Edward Pessen, *Riches, Class and Power Before the Civil War* (Lexington, Mass.: D. C. Heath, 1973), 47–52.

29. Morison, *Maritime*, 46, and for other joint ventures see 44, 52; East, *Business*, 256.

30. Patrick Tracy Jackson to Henry Lee, Aug. 20, 1811, PTJ Letterbooks, MHS. For other examples of similar correspondence between merchants and their agents and captains see PTJ Letterbooks and Perkins Papers, MHS, HBS.

31. H. Lee quoted in Porter, *Jacksons and Lees*, I, 92; Thomas Handasyd Perkins to James Perkins, July 14, 1792, Extracts from the Letter Books of T. H. Perkins, 40–41, Perkins Papers, MHS. For a discussion of Brahmin merchant intermarriage and the family firm, see Peter Dobson Hall, "Family Structure and Economic Organization: Massachusetts Merchants, 1700–1850," in *Family and Kin in Urban Communities, 1700–1930*, ed. Tamara K. Hareven (New York: New Viewpoints, 1977), 38–57.

32. Francis George Shaw, "Robert Gould Shaw," *New England Historical and Genealogical Register*, II (1881), 39–41; T. H. Perkins to Robert Bennet Forbes, May 31, 1809, Perkins Letterbooks, MHS; Forbes *Reminiscences*, 26–27; Porter, *Jacksons and Lees*, I, 120. For the similar situation in Salem see Farber, *Guardians*, 75–89, 195–97.

33. Nathaniel Burt, *The Perennial Philadelphians: The Anatomy of an American Aristocracy* (Boston: Little, Brown, 1963), 141–52; E. Digby Baltzell, *Philadelphia Gentlemen: The Making of a National Upper Class* (Glencoe: Free Press, 1958), 87. For Boston marine insurance see N. S. B. Gras, *The Massachusetts First National Bank of Boston, 1784–1934* (Cambridge: Harvard University Press, 1937), 19, 21; Lodge, *Life and Letters of George Cabot*, 568.

34. Burt, *Perennial*, 44–48, 153–58; Baltzell, *Philadelphia*, 89; Fritz Redlich, *The Molding of American Banking, Part 1, 1781–1840* (New York: Hafner Publishing, 1947), 20, 35–38; *Part 2, 1840–1910* (1951), 8–11.

35. Gras, *Massachusetts First National*, 15–20, 34, 75–77, 213, 221, 305–6, 311, 538–40. For the Massachusetts senate quote, 79.

36. *Ibid.*, 710–18; *The National Union Bank of Boston* (Boston: n.p., 1904); Amos W. Stetson, *An Historical Sketch of the State Bank* (Boston: privately printed, 1893); Edwin A. Stone, *A Century of Boston Banking* (Boston: Rockwell and Churchill, 1894), 9–10.

37. Shurtleff, *Topographical*, 385, 417–22; Bowditch, "Gleaner," 77, 84, 100–101, 202–3; Walter Muir Whitehill, *Boston: A Topographical History* (Cambridge: Harvard University Press, 1959), 48–49, 60–67, 76–78, 84–86, 95–98, 146–48; Harold and James Kirker, *Bullfinch's Boston, 1787–1817* (New York: Oxford University Press, 1964), 142–64, 185–205; Walter Firey, *Land Use in Central Boston* (Cambridge: Harvard University Press, 1947), 41–53, 65–70; Aileen Chamberlain, *Beacon Hill* (Boston: Houghton Mifflin, 1925), *passim*.

38. Shurtleff, *Topographical*, 330, 338–39, 357; Whitehill, *Topographical History*, 95–98.

39. Firey, *Land*, 45–55, 87–135.

40. Albert Bushnell, ed., *Commonwealth History of Massachusetts*, 6 vols. (New York: States History Co., 1927–30), III, 581–82, 621–22; *A Catalogue of the Members of the City Councils of Boston, Roxbury & Charleston, 1822–1908. A Catalogue of the Selectmen of Boston, 1634–1822. Also of Various Other*

Towns and Municipal Officers (Boston: City of Boston Printing Department, 1909); Winsor, *Memorial*, III, 194n, 213, 297; Josiah Quincy, *A Memorial History of the Town and City of Boston from September 17, 1630 to September 17, 1830* (Boston: Little, Brown, 1852), 432–42; Charles Warren, *Jacobin and Junto* (Cambridge: Harvard University Press, 1931), 164; Morison, *Maritime*, 167; Josiah Quincy, *Quincy*; Lodge, *Life and Letters of George Cabot*; T. W. Higginson, *Life and Times of Stephen Higginson*; Morison, *Life & Letters of Harrison Gray Otis*; Dana, *Dana Saga*, 21–30; Greenslet, *Lowells*, 48–83; William Bruce Wheeler, "Urban Politics in Nature's Republic: The Development of Political Parties in the Seaport Cities" (Ph.D. dissertation, University of Virginia, 1957), 338–39; Paul Goodman, *The Democratic-Republicans of Massachusetts: Politics in a Young Republic* (Cambridge: Harvard University Press, 1964), 73–75, 108–15; Gray, *William Gray*, 10–11, 38–44. For the political domination in Salem of that city's mercantile-Federalist elite see Farber, *Guardians*, 111–55, 195–96.

41. Morison, *Maritime*, 165. For a discussion of these policies see 164–68. For the role of Brahmin Federalists in representing Massachusetts maritime interests see Lodge, *Life and Letters of George Cabot*, 36–144; T. W. Higginson, *Life and Times of Stephen Higginson*, 69–74; "Letters of Stephen Higginson," *Annual Report of the American Historical Association*, I (1896), 716–840; Edmund Quincy, *Life of Josiah Quincy* (Boston: Ticknor and Fields, 1868), 40–101; Morison, *Life & Letters of Harrison Gray Otis*; Josiah Quincy, *Speeches Delivered in the Congress of the United States, 1805–1813* (Boston: Little, Brown, 1874); John Lowell: *The New England Patriot: A Candid Comparison of the Principles and Conduct of the Washington and Jeffersonian Administrations* (Boston: Russell and Cutler, 1810); *Enquiry into the Question of the Chesapeake and the Necessity and Expediency of War* (Boston: Greenough and Stebbins, 1807), 1–43; *Interesting Political Discussion: The Diplomatic Policy of Mr. Madison Unveiled* (Boston: Russell and Cutler, 1812), 1–53.

42. *Journal of the Convention for Framing a Constitution of Government for the State of Massachusetts Bay, 1779–80* (Boston: Dutton and Wentworth, 1832); East, *Business*, 202; Morison, *Maritime*, 28.

43. Winsor, *Memorial*, III, 193–94; East, *Business*, 264; Morison, *Maritime*, 36–37.

44. Winsor, *Memorial*, III, 195–96; Morison, *Maritime*, 39–40; Anson Ely Morse, *The Federalist Party in Massachusetts to the Year 1800* (Princeton: Princeton University Press, 1909), 40–53. For an example of the Boston elite support of the federal constitution see S. Higginson to John Adams, Aug. 8, 1788, to Nathan Dane, May 22, 1788, "Letters of Stephen Higginson," 719–26, 761.

45. J. Quincy, *Memorial*, 30–31.

46. Bowditch, "Gleaner," 94, 202–3; Shurtleff, *Topographical*, 330, 338–39, 357, 419–22; Whitehill, *Topographical History*, 48–49, 76–78; Firey, *Land*, 128–33; Morison, *Harrison Gray Otis*, 74–79, 219–26.

47. Chester Phillips Huse, *Financial History of Boston* (Cambridge: Harvard University Press, 1916), 37–39.

48. George Cabot to Benjamin Goodhue, Mar. 16, 1790, in Lodge, *Life and Letters of George Cabot*, 34–35; Oscar and Mary F. Handlin, *Commonwealth: A*

Study of the Role of Government in the American Economy: Massachusetts 1774–1861 (Cambridge: Harvard University Press, 1969), 69–70, 102–5, 111.

49. Handlin and Handlin, *Commonwealth*, 99–100, 102–3.

50. Gray, *William Gray*, 38–39; Josiah Quincy, *Memoir of the Life of John Quincy Adams* (Boston: Phillips & Sampson, 1858), 34–37; Goodman, *Democratic-Republicans*, 192–94.

51. Greenslet, *Lowells*, 49, 54–55; Morison, *Harrison Gray Otis*, 51–55, 61–65, 218–19.

52. William T. Davis, *Bench and Bar of the Commonwealth of Massachusetts*, 2 vols. (Boston: Boston History Co., 1895), I, 109–12, 114–15; Morison, *Three Centuries of Harvard* (Cambridge: Harvard University Press, 1946), 238–39; Arthur E. Sutherland, *The Law at Harvard* (Cambridge: Harvard University Press, 1967), 59, 78; Gawalt, *Promise*, 13–30, 41, 46–47, 60–61, 81–118, 131, 139–40, 145, 150, 156.

53. Morison, *Life and Letters of Harrison Gray Otis*, I, 27–29.

54. Walter L. Burrage, *A History of the Massachusetts Medical Society* (Norwich: Plimpton Press, 1923), 16, 70–72, 462–63; Henry R. Viets, *A Brief History of Medicine in Massachusetts* (Boston: Houghton Mifflin, 1930), 104–8, 127–35; Nathaniel Ingersoll Bowditch, *A History of Massachusetts General Hospital* (Cambridge: John Wilson and Son, 1872), 3–55; James Jackson Putnam, *Memoir of Dr. James Jackson*, 266–67, 288–89; *Harvard Medical School 1782–1906* (Cambridge: Harvard University Press, 1906), 1–20.

55. Viets, *Brief*, 108, 139–43; Putnam, *Memoir of Dr. James Jackson*, 220–21.

56. Quoted in Bowditch, *History of Massachusetts General*, 3n; for the other details see 3, 16, 23, 30–31, 45, 52.

57. Foote, *Annals of King's Chapel*, II, *passim*; Winsor, *Memorial*, III, 467–82; Daniel Walker Howe, *The Unitarian Conscience: Harvard Moral Philosophy, 1805–1861* (Cambridge: Harvard University Press, 1970), 6–12, 176.

58. Morison, *Three Centuries*, 185, 187–91, 197; Howe, *Unitarian*, 4–5; James McLachlan, *American Boarding Schools: A Historical Study* (New York: Charles Scribner's Sons, 1970), 19–48.

59. Winsor, *Memorial*, IV, 240–42; Putnam, *Memoir of Dr. James Jackson*, 186–87; Morison, *Life and Letters of Harrison Gray Otis*, I, 6; T. W. Higginson, *Cheerful Yesterdays* (Boston: Houghton Mifflin, 1899), 5; Henry Adams, *The Education of Henry Adams* (Boston: Houghton Mifflin, 1961), 41.

60. *Endowment Funds of Harvard University* (Cambridge: Harvard University Press, 1948); Samuel A. Eliot, *A Sketch of the History of Harvard College and of its Present State* (Boston: Little, Brown, 1848); Josiah Quincy, *The History of Harvard University*, 2 vols. (Boston: Crosby, Nichols, Lee, 1860); Morison, *Three Centuries*; Higginson, *Cheerful*, 5; Porter, *Jacksons and Lees*, I, 120–21, 128.

61. Morison, *Three Centuries*, 181–83, 202–3; Andrew P. Peabody, *Harvard Reminiscences* (Boston: Ticknor, 1888), 202.

62. Mary Lee, "Journal," Aug. 27, 1813, in Henry and Mary Lee, *Letters and Journals*, 200.

63. William R. Cutter *et al.*, eds., *Encyclopedia of Massachusetts Biography*, 12 vols. (New York, Boston, Chicago: American Historical Society, 1916), 266–68; William Newell, *Notice of the Life and Character of Mr. Andrews Norton*

(Cambridge: Metcalf, 1853); Eliza Buckminster Lee, *Memoir of Rev. Joseph Buckminster D. D. and of His Son, Rev. Joseph Stevens Buckminster* (Boston: Ticknor, Fields and Lee, 1849); John Gorham Palfrey, *A Discourse on the Life of John Thornton Kirkland, D.D., LL.D., Late President of Harvard College* (Cambridge: J. Owen, 1840).

64. Andrews Norton, reprinted in *The Federalist Literary Mind: Selections from the "Monthly Anthology and Boston Review,"* 1803–1811, ed. Lewis Simpson (Baton Rouge: Louisiana State University Press, 1962), 126–27.

65. The best analyses of Brahmin culture are Howe, *Unitarianism*; Martin Green, *The Problem of Boston: Some Readings in Cultural History* (New York: W. W. Norton, 1966); McLachlan, *American Boarding Schools*, 19–48.

66. Stewart Mitchell, *Handbook of the Massachusetts Historical Society* (Boston: Massachusetts Historical Society, 1949); Stephen T. Riley, *The Massachusetts Historical Society, 1791–1959* (Boston: Massachusetts Historical Society, 1959).

67. Simpson, ed., *Federalist Mind*, 11–19; Howe, *Unitarianism*, 176.

68. Josiah Quincy, *The History of the Boston Athenaeum* (Cambridge: Metcalf, 1851); *The Influence and History of the Boston Athenaeum* (Boston: Boston Athenaeum, 1907).

69. Quoted in Quincy, *Athenaeum*, 9–10.

70. Howe, *Unitarianism*, 176; Winsor, *Memorial*, III, 637.

71. William Tudor to H. G. Otis, Sept. 2, 1815, in Morison, *Harrison Gray Otis*, 235.

72. Simpson, ed., *Federalist Mind*, 19; George Ticknor, *The Life of William Hickling Prescott* (Philadelphia: J. B. Lippincott, 1863), 73n–74n; Morison: *Maritime*, 124–33; *Harrison Gray Otis*, 42–49, 59–61; Cary, *Memoir of T. H. Perkins*, 264–65; Winsor, *Memorial*, IV, 14–24; Cleveland Amory, *The Proper Bostonians* (New York: E. P. Dutton, 1947), 49–50.

73. Quincy, "Speech on Maritime Protection," Jan. 15, 1812, in Quincy, *Speeches*, 306; cf. Cabot to Timothy Pickering, Feb. 21, 1800, in Lodge, *Life and Letters of George Cabot*, 219.

74. Gray, *William Gray*, 77–81; Samuel Eliot to Sarah H. Eliot, Sept. 3, 1800, in Anna Eliot Ticknor, *Samuel Eliot (1739–1820)* (Boston: n.p., 1869), 155; John Lowell, Jr., to John Amory Lowell quoted in Greenslet, *Lowells*, 211; William Hickling Prescott, *The Papers of William Hickling Prescott*, ed. C. Harvey Gardner (Urbana: University of Illinois Press, 1964), 17–18, 22; Jonathan Jackson to Henry Jackson, Jan. 10, 1789, Feb. 11, 1793, Mar. 19, 1793, Nov. 20, 1793, in Putnam, *Memoir of Dr. James Jackson*, 55–58.

75. John Lowell, *The New England Patriot*, 67.

76. J. Quincy quoted in E. Quincy, *Life of Josiah Quincy*, 71; Ticknor, *Life of William Hickling Prescott*, 186–87, 189, 193–94, 202–6, 341.

77. Peter Chardon Brooks quoted in Cary, *Memoir of T. H. Perkins*, 245; M. Lee, "Journal," Aug. 17, 1813, in Henry and Mary Lee, *Letters and Journals*, 197–98; Porter, *Jacksons and Lees*, 1, 197–98; T. H. Perkins to John P. Cushing, Sept. 18, 1826, Perkins Papers, MHS.

78. Ticknor, *Samuel Eliot*, 195.

79. H. Lee quoted in Porter, *Jacksons and Lees*, I, 104n. For the general business conduct of the Jacksons and Lees see I, 104–10.

80. H. G. Otis to Robert Goodloe Harper, Apr. 19, 1807, in Morison, *Life and Letters of Harrison Gray Otis*, I, 283; cf. I, 42, 230–32.

81. Perkins & Co. to ?, Aug. 7, 1819, Extracts from Perkins & Co. Letters, HBS.

82. Ticknor, *Samuel Eliot*, *passim*; J. Jackson to H. Jackson, Nov. 20, 1793, in Putnam, *Memoir of Dr. James Jackson*, 57–58.

83. S. Higginson to Henry Knox, Apr. 7, 1790, in T. W. Higginson, *Life and Times of Stephen Higginson*, 153–54.

84. For later business attitudes see Francis X. Sutton *et al.*, *The American Business Creed* (New York: Schocken Books, 1962), 184–207.

85. S. Higginson to J. Adams, July ?, 1786, in T. W. Higginson, *Life and Times of Stephen Higginson*, 84; H. G. Otis to Sally Foster Otis, Feb. 15, 1801, in Morison, *Life and Letters of Harrison Gray Otis*, I, 208; G. Cabot to Christopher Gore, Apr. 10, 1801, to T. Pickering, Feb. 14, 1804, to Rufus King, Mar. 17, 1804, in Lodge, *Life and Letters of George Cabot*, 318–19, 341, 344; Lowell, *New England*, 104.

86. S. Higginson, to J. Adams, July ?, 1786, in T. W. Higginson, *Life and Times of Stephen Higginson*, 84; Lowell, *New England*, 67.

87. J. Quincy, "Speech on the Suspension of the Embargo," Apr. ?, 1808; "Speech Against Holding An Extra Session of Congress," Jan. 19, 1809, *Speeches*, 41, and cf. 139; cf. Lowell, *New England*, 104.

88. Lodge, *Life and Letters of George Cabot*, 69.

89. Morison, *Life and Letters of Harrison Gray Otis*, I, 125; E. Quincy, *Memoir of Josiah Quincy*, 78–79.

90. J. Quincy quoted in E. Quincy, *Memoir of Josiah Quincy*, 105–6; William Wirt quoted in Morison, *Life and Letters of Harrison Gray Otis*, I, 218–19.

91. J. Quincy, "Speech Against Admitting Louisiana As A State," Jan. 14, 1811, "Speech On the Invasion of Canada," Jan. 5, 1813, *Speeches*, 224, 396.

92. S. Higginson to N. Dane, Mar. 3, 1787, in T. W. Higginson, *Life and Times of Stephen Higginson*, 109–10.

93. J. Quincy, "Speech On The Suspension Of The Embargo," *Speeches*, 41.

94. Howe, *Unitarian*, 142–48, 174–95; Joseph T. Buckminster, "The Dangers and Duties of Men of Letters," *Monthy Anthology and Boston Review*, VII (1809); Simpson, ed., *Federalist*, 97–100, *passim*; J. Quincy, "Speech on the Influence of Place and Patronage," Jan. 30, 1811, *Speeches*, 231–34; J. Quincy quoted in E. Quincy, *Memoir of Josiah Quincy*, 260–61.

95. Andrews Norton, in *Monthly Anthology and Boston Review*, IV (1807); Simpson, ed., *Federalist*, 57.

96. Seymour Martin Lipset and Richard B. Dobson, "The Intellectual as Critic and Rebel: With Special Reference to the United States and the Soviet Union," *Daedalus* (Summer, 1972), 137–98; Howe, *Unitarianism*, 139–48; McLachlan, *American Boarding Schools*, 194–98; Simpson, ed., *Federalist*, *passim*.

97. Porter, *Jacksons and Lees*, I, 121, II, 969–70.

98. H. Lee to P. T. Jackson, Jan. 30, 1813, in *ibid.*, II, 1076; T. H. Perkins to W. F. Paine, ?, 1815 or '16, Perkins Papers, MHS.

99. Robert G. Albion, *The Rise of New York Port*, *1815–1860* (New York: Charles Scribner's Sons, 1939), 1, 13–14, 389; David T. Gilchrist, ed., *The*

Growth of the Seaport Cities, 1790–1825 (Charlottesville: University of Virginia Press, 1967), 7; Morison, *Maritime*, 233–34; Julius Rubin, "Canal or Railroad? Imitation and Innovation in the Response to the Erie Canal in Philadelphia, Baltimore and Boston," *Transactions of the American Philosophical Society*, LI (1961), 8–21, 25–62, 80–96.

100. Morison, *Maritime*, 21–25, 28, 129; Albion, *Rise*, 21, 235–50; East, *Business*, 184–89, 213–14, 221–38; Hannah Josephson, *The Golden Threads* (New York: Duell, Sloan, and Pearce, 1949), 31–32, 100, 103, 111–13; Caroline Ware, *The Early New England Cotton Manufacture* (Boston: Houghton Mifflin, 1931), 91–92, 734; Malcolm Keir, *Industries of American Manufacturing* (New York: Ronald Press, 1928), 295–97; Victor S. Clark, *History of Manufacturing in the United States* (New York: Peter Smith, 1949), I, 450; Frederic Cople Jaher, "The Boston Brahmins in the Age of Industrial Capitalism," *America in the Age of Industrialism: Essays in Social Structure and Cultural Values*, ed. Jaher (New York: Free Press, 1968), 191–95; John Amory Lowell, "Memoir of Patrick Tracy Jackson," *Hunt's Merchant Magazine* (New York: Hunt's Merchant Magazine, 1848), 4–6.

101. T. W. Ward quoted in Ralph W. Hidy, "Credit Rating Before Dun and Bradstreet," *Bulletin of the Business History Society*, XIII (Dec., 1939), 86–87; Ward quoted in Roy A. Foulke, *The Sinews of Commerce* (New York: Dun & Bradstreet, 1941), 359.

102. Forbes, *Personal*, 80; H. Lee to Francis Cabot, Mar. 3, 1816, in Porter, *Jacksons and Lees*, II, 996.

103. T. H. Perkins to J. P. Cushing, July 12, 1821, to ?, May 7, 1822, Perkins Papers, MHS; M. Lee to H. Lee, Jr., May 20, 1843, Frank Lee to H. Lee, Jr., Sept. 29, 1843, in Porter, *Jacksons and Lees*, II, 1531. For H. Lee, his brothers, and his son see I, 39–40, 120–23; II, 1500–1504, 1532. For similar problems in Salem's mercantile family firms see Farber, *Guardians*, 89–96.

104. William Minot quoted in Morse, *Memoir of Col. Henry Lee*, 395; Porter, *Jacksons and Lees*, II, 1532.

105. T. H. Perkins to James L. Lloyd, May 26, 1820, Perkins Papers, MHS.

106. Morison, *Life and Letters of Harrison Gray Otis*, II, 94, 243, 248; Warren, *Jacobin*, 164–219.

107. T. H. Perkins to LeRoy, Bayard & Co., May 27, 1820, cf. to J. L. Lloyd, May 26, 1820, to Cary & Co., May 10, 1820, Sept. 2, 1820, Perkins Papers, MHS; Amory, *Proper*, 54–55.

108. H. Lee quoted in Porter, *Jacksons and Lees*, I, 44.

109. S. Higginson to T. Pickering, Jan. 2, 1800, Feb. 15, 1804, "Letters of Stephen Higginson," 798, 833, 839; John Quincy Adams to Josiah Quincy, Jr., Dec. 4, 1804, in E. Quincy, *Memoir of Josiah Quincy*, 63–64.

110. H. Lee to P. Remsen and Co., July 8, 1817, in Porter, *Jacksons and Lees*, II, 1257. See also Shaw Livermore, Jr., *The Twilight of Federalism: The Disintegration of the Federalist Party, 1815–1830* (Princeton: Princeton University Press, 1962), 49–54, 59; Morison, *Harrison Gray Otis*, 84–86. For an excellent discussion of the generational split in Federalism see David Hackett Fischer, *The Revolution of American Conservatism* (New York: Harper & Row, 1965).

111. H. G. Otis to S. F. Otis, Feb. 15, 1801, in Morison, *Life and Letters of Harrison Gray Otis*, I, 208; H. G. Otis, *An Address to the Members of the City*

Council on the Removal of the Municipal Government to the Old State House (Boston: John H. Eastburn, 1830), 14–15.

112. J. Quincy, "Farewell Address of Josiah Quincy as Mayor of Boston, 1829," *Old South Leaflets*, VIII (Boston: Old South Meeting House, n.d.), 101.

113. Fischer, *Revolution*, 227–412.

114. T. H. Perkins to Samuel Cabot and Thomas G. Cary, Jan. ?, 1835, Perkins Papers, MHS; Robert K. Lamb, "Entrepreneur and Community," *Men In Business*, ed. William Miller (Cambridge: Harvard University Press, 1952), 110–11; Morison, *Life and Letters of Harrison Gray Otis*, I, 448–50, 454; F. G. Shaw, "Robert Gould Shaw," 54; Porter, *Jacksons and Lees*, I, 123; Keir, *Industries*, 299.

115. H. G. Otis to George Harrison, Mar. 21, 1823, in Morison, *Life and Letters of Harrison Gray Otis*, I, 449; T. H. Perkins to Elizabeth Perkins, May 1, 1852, Perkins Papers, MHS. Nathan's cousin William was brought "into society" by Otis. See William Appleton, *Selections from the Diaries of William Appleton. 1786–1852*, ed. Susan Loring (Boston: privately printed, 1922), Oct. 28, 1848, 132–33.

116. *Catalogue of the Members of the City Councils, passim; Journal of Debates and Proceedings in the Convention of Delegates Chosen to Revise the Constitution of Massachusetts, 1820–1821* (Boston: Daily Advertiser, 1821), 5, 133–36, 175–77, 180, 183, 200–207, 215–16, 250–51.

117. Ware, *Early*, 110–13, 141.

118. For the story of the New England cotton industry see *ibid*.; Lowell, *Memoir of P. T. Jackson*; Josephson, *Golden*; George Sweet Gibb, *The Saco-Lowell Shops: Textile Machinery Building in New England* (Cambridge: Harvard University Press, 1950); Ovra L. Stone, *History of Massachusetts Industries*, I (Boston: S. J. Clarke Publishing, 1930); Keir, *Industries*, 295–300; J. Herbert Burgy, *The New England Cotton Textile Industry* (Baltimore: Waverly Press, 1932); Melvin T. Copeland, *The Cotton Manufacturing Industry of the United States* (Cambridge: Harvard University Press, 1912); H. E. Michl, *The Textile Industries: An Economic Analysis* (Washington, D.C.: Textile Foundation, 1938); W. Paul Strassman, *Risk and Technological Innovation* (Ithaca: Cornell University Press, 1959), 76–115; Nathan Appleton, *Introduction of the Power Loom and the Origin of Lowell* (Boston: B. H. Penhallow, 1858); Paul F. McGouldrick, *New England Textiles in the Nineteenth Century: Profits and Investment* (Cambridge: Harvard University Press, 1968); Robert F. Dalzell, Jr., "The Rise of the Waltham-Lowell System and Some Thoughts on the Political Economy of Modernization in Ante-bellum Massachusetts," *Perspectives in American History*, IX (1975), 229–70. Dalzell advances the interesting argument that the Brahmins embarked on the textile industry for security rather than to maximize profits or from entrepreneurial motivation. This may have been true of their staying in the industry after profits declined in the 1850s, but it is unlikely that financial security was the exclusive reason for leaving trade for the factory in the crucial, early years of textile manufacturing. In this period profits were high, technological advances dazzling, and trade stagnant. Dalzell also mistakenly assumes that the decline in innovation in textile manufacturing after 1830 shows the conservative, security-oriented outlook of the Brahmins. Proper Bostonians, including many of the key textile magnates, in this decade began to

organize the New England railroad system and in the 1840s western railroads, projects which involved risk and inventiveness.

119. For the history of Brahmin enterprise in New England railroads see Edward Chase Kirkland, *Men, Cities and Transportation: A Study in New England History 1820–1900*, 2 vols. (Cambridge: Harvard University Press, 1948); Alvin F. Harlow, *Steelways of New England* (New York: Creative Age Press, 1948); Thelma M. Kistler, *The Rise of Railroads in the Connecticut River Valley* (Northhampton: Smith College Press, 1938); George Pierce Baker, *The Formation of the New England Railroad Systems* (Cambridge: Harvard University Press, 1937); Arthur M. Johnson and Barry Supple, *Boston Capitalists and Western Railroads* (Cambridge: Harvard University Press, 1967), 38–91; Francis B. C. Bradlee, *The Boston and Lowell Railroad, the Nashua and Lowell Railroad and the Salem and Lowell Railroad* (Salem: Essex Institute, 1918); Bradlee, *The Eastern Railroad* (Salem: Essex Institute, 1917); George Bliss, *Historical Memoir of the Western Railroad* (Springfield: Samuel Bowles, 1863); Charles B. Fisher, *The Story of the Old Colony Railroad* (n.p.:n.p., 1919).

120. John Murray Forbes quoted in Thomas C. Cochran, *Railroad Leaders, 1845–1890* (Cambridge: Harvard University Press, 1953), 217. For J. M. Forbes's business career see his *Reminiscences*, 3 vols. (Boston: George H. Ellis, 1902); Forbes Letters, HBS. For upper-class western railroad operations see Johnson and Supple, *Boston Capitalists*; Harlow, *Steelways*, 414–34; Cochran, *Railroad Leaders*; Henry Greenleaf Pearson, *An American Railroad Builder, John Murray Forbes* (Boston: Houghton Mifflin, 1911); Ralph Budd, *The Burlington Railroad's Boston Background* (New York: American Newcomen Society, 1959); Richard C. Overton: *Burlington West* (Cambridge: Harvard University Press, 1941), 26–44; *The First Ninety Years: A Historical Sketch of the Burlington Railroad, 1850–1940* (Chicago: n.p., 1940); *Milepost* (Chicago: n.p., 1949); W. W. Baldwin, *The Making of the Burlington* (n.p.: n.p., 1920); Ernest W. Calkins, "Genesis of a Railroad," *Illinois State Historical Society Proceedings* (1935), 39–72; Forbes, *Letters and Recollections of John Murray Forbes*, 2 vols., ed. Sarah B. Forbes (Boston: George H. Ellis, 1905).

121. See notes 119 and 120.

122. Bradlee, *Boston and Lowell*, 62; Johnson and Supple, *Boston Capitalists*, 120.

123. Kirkland, *Men*, I, 252–55, 299–302, 309, 323–30.

124. H. Parker Willis and Julius I. Bogen, *Investment Banking* (New York: Harper & Bros., 1936), 165.

125. Gras, *Massachusetts First National*, 15–16, 54–132, 710–18.

126. Gerald T. White, *A History of the Massachusetts Hospital Life Insurance Co.* (Cambridge: Harvard University Press, 1955), 5, 12, 12n–13n, 31–32, 34, 81–82, 89–90.

127. *A List of Stockholders in the National Banks of Boston, May 1, 1866* (Boston: Alfred Mudge & Son, 1866), 43–54, 242–51, 264–99, 401–50, 484–98; Gras, *Massachusetts First National*, 19, 55, 70, 127, 142; *The National Union Bank of Boston* (Boston: n.p., 1904), 12.

128. Gras, *Massachusetts First National*, 100–102; D. R. Whitney, *The Suffolk Bank* (Cambridge: Riverside Press, 1878), 8–15.

129. Gras, *Massachusetts First National*, 104.

130. White, *History of Massachusetts Life*, 30–31, 41, 44–45; James G. Smith, *The Development of Trust Companies in the United States* (New York: Henry Holt, 1927), 239–45, Lowell quoted on 245.

131. Walter B. Smith and Arthur Cole, *Fluctuations in American Business, 1790–1860* (Cambridge: Harvard University Press, 1936), 46–51, 113–14.

132. Copeland, *Cotton*, 6.

133. Pessen, *Riches*, 284–87; *Catalogue, passim*.

134. Bushnell, *Commonwealth*, IV, 621–23; *Catalogue, passim*.

135. Thomas H. O'Connor, *Lords of the Loom* (New York: Charles Scribner's Sons, 1968), 35, 66; Kirkland, *Men*, I, 129–33; Baker, *Formation*, 101n; Gibb, *Saco-Lowell*, 61–62.

136. Kinley J. Brauer, *Cotton versus Conscience: Massachusetts Whig Politics and Southwestern Expansion, 1843–48* (Lexington: University of Kentucky Press, 1966), 19; Robert Rich, "'A Wilderness of Whigs.' The Wealthy Men of Boston," *Journal of Social History*, IV (Spring, 1971), 263–67.

137. John Quincy Adams, *Memoirs of John Quincy Adams*, 12 vols., ed. Charles Francis Adams (Philadelphia: J. B. Lippincott, 1874), Nov. 16, 1838, X, 43; C. F. Adams quoted in Brauer, *Cotton*, 133; David Donald, *Charles Sumner and the Coming of the Civil War* (New York: Alfred A. Knopf, 1960), 137; cf. O'Connor, *Lords*, 66.

138. Baker, *Formation*, 101n; Kistler, *Rise*, 152–55; Kirkland, *Men*, I, 127–33.

139. For the struggle between Cotton Whigs and their opponents see Brauer, *Cotton*; O'Connor, *Lords*; Donald, *Charles Sumner*; Arthur B. Darling, *Political Changes in Massachusetts, 1824–1848* (New Haven: Yale University Press, 1925), 150ff; Frank Otto Gattell, *John Gorham Palfrey and the New England Conscience* (Cambridge: Harvard University Press, 1963).

140. Firey, *Land*, 65–70; Whitehill, *Boston*, 84–86; Alexander S. Porter, "Changes of Values in Real Estate in Boston in the Past One Hundred Years," *Collections of the Bostonian Society*, I (1888), 60–62.

141. Huse, *Financial*, 19–106; Winsor, *Memorial*, III, 225–37, 243–44, 251–56; Quincy, *Municipal*, 58–279; Robert A. McCaughey, *Josiah Quincy, 1772–1864: The Last Federalist* (Cambridge: Harvard University Press, 1974), 98–120, 201.

142. Winsor, *Memorial*, III, 255–56; Huse, *Financial*, 58, 86; Constance McLaughlin Green, *American Cities in the Growth of the Nation* (New York: Colophon Books, 1965), 31, 33.

143. J. Quincy chaired a committee investigating poverty and administration of relief in Massachusetts in 1821; the report of the committee is in *Massachusetts General Court, Committee on Pauper Laws, Report of the Committee, 1821* (n.p.). Similar investigations occurred a few years later in New York State and Philadelphia. See David Rothman, *The Discovery of the Asylum: Social Order and Disorder in the New Republic* (Boston: Little, Brown, 1971), 156–57; John Cummings, *Poor-Laws of Massachusetts and New York* (New York: Macmillan, 1895). For general discussions of upper-class philanthropy see Rothman, *Asylum*, 155–79; Howe, *Unitarian*, 236–69. For the rise in immigration, crime, and poverty in Boston between 1820 and 1860 and the growing anxiety about these problems see Stanley K. Schultz, *The Culture Factory: Boston Public Schools, 1789–1860* (New York: Oxford University Press, 1973), 209–51.

144. Winsor, *Memorial*, III, 241n, 271–72; Amos Lawrence, *Extracts from the Diary and Correspondence of Amos Lawrence*, ed. William R. Lawrence (Boston: Gould and Lincoln, 1855), 221–33; Bowditch, *Massachusetts General*, 412–31; Prescott, *Papers*, 72; Freeman Hunt, *Lives of American Merchants*, 2 vols. (New York: Hunt's Merchants' Magazine, 1858), I, 159; William Lawrence, *Life of Amos Lawrence* (Boston: Houghton Mifflin, 1899), 53; Robert C. Winthrop, Jr., *Memoir of Robert C. Winthrop* (Boston: Little, Brown, 1897), 169; Henry James, *Charles W. Eliot*, 2 vols. (Boston: Houghton Mifflin, 1930), I, 28.

145. David Sears, *Record of Deeds and Gifts of David Sears of Boston* (Cambridge: John Wilson and Son, 1886); *Will of Abbott Lawrence* (Boston: John Wilson and Son, 1857), 21–26; Lawrence, *Extracts*, 312.

146. "The Public and Private Charities of Boston," *North American Review*, LXI (July, 1845), 141–47.

147. *List[s] of Persons, Copartnerships and Corporations, Who Were Taxed Twenty Five Dollars and Upwards, in the City of Boston, in the Year[s], 1835, 1845* (Boston: John H. Eastburn, 1836, 1846); Lemuel Shattuck, *Report to the Committee of the City Council Appointed to Obtain the Census of Boston for the Year 1845* (Boston: John H. Eastburn, 1846), 59; Harvey O'Connor, *The Astors* (New York: Alfred A. Knopf, 1941), 186; Wayne Andrews, *The Vanderbilt Legend* (New York: Harcourt, Brace, 1941), 231.

148. Sears, *Record*, 261. For a biographical sketch see Robert C. Winthrop, *Memoir of the Hon. David Sears*.

149. Winthrop, *Memoir of Robert C. Winthrop*, 169, 318; *Influence*, 115; Mitchell, *Handbook*, 97; James, *Charles W. Eliot*, I, 28; Hunt, *Lives*, II, 288–89; Lawrence, *Life of Amos Lawrence*, 56, 58; *Will of Abbott Lawrence*, 11–12, 25; Walter Muir Whitehill, *The Boston Public Library: A Centennial History* (Cambridge: Harvard University Press, 1956), 264–65.

150. White, *History of Massachusetts Life*, 39.

151. David Tyack, *George Ticknor and the Boston Brahmins* (Cambridge: Harvard University Press, 1967), 85–128; McLachlan, *American Boarding Schools*, 76–78, 95–96.

152. Howe, *Unitarianism*, 270–300.

153. Winsor, *Memorial*, III, 679–81; Kermit Vanderbilt, *Charles Eliot Norton: Apostle of Culture in a Democracy* (Cambridge: Harvard University Press, 1959), 59–81; Green, *Problem*, 77–78; Martin Duberman, *James Russell Lowell* (Boston: Houghton Mifflin, 1966), 162–87; Horace Elisha Scudder, *James Russell Lowell*, 2 vols. (Boston: Houghton Mifflin, 1901), I, 419–20.

154. Winsor, *Memorial*, III, 566; Meeting of the Directors of the Bunker Hill Monument Committee, Apr. 1, 1845, Appleton Letters, MHS; Quincy, *History of the Boston Athenaeum, passim*.

155. Winsor, *Memorial*, IV, 423–28.

156. Lawrence quoted in Lawrence, *Life of Amos Lawrence*, 56; Abbott Lawrence to J. C. Brigham, May 5, 1849, Lawrence Papers, MHS.

157. For the terms of Lowell's legacy see Winsor, *Memorial*, IV, 264–65. For other accounts of Lowell and the Institute see Greenslet, *Lowells*, 197–211; Edward Everett, *Memoir of John Lowell, Jun.* (Boston: Little, Brown, 1840); Edward Weeks, *The Lowells and Their Institute* (Boston: Little, Brown, 1966).

158. John H. Sheppard, "A Sketch of Hon. Nathan Appleton," *New England Historical and Genealogical Register*, XVI (1862), 10; Susan Hale, *Life and Letters of Thomas Gold Appleton* (New York: D. Appleton, 1885), 11; J. Quincy to Nathan Appleton, Sept. 13, 1844, Appleton Papers, MHS.

159. Hamilton Andrews Hill, *Memoir of Abbott Lawrence* (Boston: Little, Brown, 1894), 124.

160. Palfrey quoted in Gattell, *John Gorham Palfrey*, 79; Josiah Quincy, Jr., *Figures of the Past* (Boston: Little, Brown, 1926), 118.

161. Lawrence, "Diary," Dec. 17, 1846, *Extracts*, 234–35; A. A. Lawrence quoted in Lawrence, *Life of Amos Lawrence*, 49; Appleton, "Diary," Dec. 31, 1843, *Selections*, 107–8.

162. Lawrence, "Diary," July 23, 1849, *Extracts*, 270; Robert C. Winthrop, "Memorial to the Boston City Council," Oct. 8, 1857, *Addresses and Speeches on Various Occasions*, 4 vols. (Boston: Little, Brown, 1852–86), II, 366.

163. *Harvard Medical School*, 31–32, 37; Bowditch, *Massachusetts General Hospital*, 421; Viets, *Brief History*, 139–41, 143–47, 149; Burrage, *History of Massachusetts Medical Society*, 462–63.

164. Pessen, *Riches*, 47–51.

165. Cutter, *Encyclopedia*, I, 76, 79, 193; Winsor, *Memorial*, IV, 598–606.

166. Sutherland, *Law*, 77–78; Samuel Shapiro, *Richard Henry Dana, Jr., 1815–1882* (East Lansing: Michigan State University Press, 1961), 16–20, 48; Greenslet, *Lowells*, 317.

167. William Hickling Prescott, *The Literary Memoranda of William Hickling Prescott*, 2 vols., ed. C. Harvey Gardiner (Norman: University of Oklahoma Press, 1961), Sept. 24, 1838, 10.

168. Winsor, *Memorial*, III, 415–20; Josiah Quincy, *History of Harvard University*, I, 555–56; Howe, *Unitarian*, 310–12.

169. Tyack, *George Ticknor*, 142ff.; Green, *Problem*, 77–101.

170. Brahmin social life is depicted in Morison, *Life and Letters of Harrison Gray Otis*; Richard Henry Dana, Jr., *The Journal of Richard Henry Dana, Jr.*, 3 vols., ed. Robert F. Lucid (Cambridge: Harvard University Press, 1968); Tyack, *George Ticknor*, 142ff.; M. A. DeWolfe Howe, *Memories of a Hostess: A Chronicle of Eminent Friendships Drawn Chiefly from the Diaries of Mrs. James T. Field* (Boston: Atlantic Monthly Press, 1923); Prescott, *Papers*; Annie Fields, *Authors and Friends* (Boston: Houghton Mifflin, 1897); Roberts, *History of the Ancient and Honorable Artillery Company*, III–IV; Edward Waldo Emerson, *The Early Years of the Saturday Club, 1855–1870* (Boston: Houghton Mifflin, 1918); Alexander W. Williams, *A Social History of the Greater Boston Clubs* (n.p.: Barre Publishing, 1970), 4, 8–11. For a fictionalized account of proper Boston see Mrs. H. G. Otis, *The Barclays of Boston* (Boston: Ticknor, Reed, and Field, 1854).

171. Josiah Quincy, Jr., *Figures*, 253.

172. James Russell Lowell, "A Great Public Character," *The Complete Writings of James Russell Lowell*, 14 vols. (Boston: Houghton Mifflin, 1904), II, 22–24. For similar assessments see Quincy, *Figures*, 54, 145, 153; Edmund Quincy, *Memoir of Josiah Quincy*, 396; Morse, *Memoir of Col. Henry Lee*, 186–87; Henry Cabot Lodge, *Boston* (London: Longmans, Green, 1892), 196–99;

William Minot, *William Minot, 2d* (Boston: David Clapp & Son, n.d.), 7–8, 12; Winsor, *Memorial*, IV, 1–24.

173. Oliver Wendell Holmes quoted in John T. Morse, *The Life and Letters of Oliver Wendell Holmes*, 2 vols. (Cambridge: Riverside Press, 1896), I, 215–16.

174. George Ticknor to George S. Hillard, July 17, 1848, in George S. Hillard, *Life, Letters, and Journals*, 2 vols. (Boston: James R. Osgood, 1876), II, 235; H. Lee to H. Lee, Jr., Jan. 3, 1853, in H. and M. Lee, *Letters and Journals*, 342; Prescott, Apr. 29, 1842, *Papers*, 190–92; Shapiro, *Richard Henry Dana, Jr.*, 153.

175. Richard Henry Dana quoted in Charles Francis Adams, *Richard Henry Dana*, 2 vols. (Boston: Houghton Mifflin, 1891), I, 108–09; Quincy, *Figures*, 97–98.

176. Pessen, *Riches*, 18–22.

177. Pessen, "The Egalitarian Myth and the American Social Reality: Wealth, Mobility and Equality in the 'Era of the Common Man,' " *American Historical Review*, LXXVI (1971), 1020–26; Pessen, *Riches*, 33–40; Robert Doherty, *New England Society* (Northampton: University of Massachusetts Press, 1977), 46.

178. Pessen, "Egalitarian," 1012–13; *Riches*, 85.

179. Pessen, "Egalitarian," 1013; *Riches*, 84–85.

180. Pessen, "Egalitarian," 1012; *Riches*, 85.

181. Shaw, "Robert Gould Shaw," 38–62.

182. Pessen, *Riches*, 88, 237; Hunt, *Lives*, I, 134–37; *New England Historical and Genealogical Register*, VIII (1854), 298.

183. Pessen, "Egalitarian," 1012; *Riches*, 85.

184. Pessen, "Egalitarian," 1013.

185. Pessen, *Riches*, 85–86.

186. The tax assessment lists used for these compilations are *List . . . 1835*; *List of Persons, CoPartnerships and Corporations Who Were Taxed on Ten Thousand Dollars and Upwards, in the City of Boston, in the Year 1860* (Boston: George C. Rand & Avery, 1861).

The biographical sources for the profile of wealth in these years are *New England Historical and Genealogical Register*; Crawford, *Famous Families*; Winsor, *Memorial*; Albert P. Langtry, *Metropolitan Boston. A Modern History* (New York: Lewis Historical Publishing, 1929), IV–V; James Spear Loring, *The Hundred Boston Orators Appointed by the Municipal Authorities and Other Public Bodies from 1770 to 1852; Comprising Historical Gleanings Illustrating the Principles and Progress of Our Republican Institutions* (Boston: John P. Jewett, 1852); Hunt, *Lives of Merchants*; *Biographical Sketches of Representative Citizens of the Commonwealth of Massachusetts* (Boston: Graves & Steinbarger, 1901); Charles Edwin Hurd, *Representative Citizens of the Commonwealth of Massachusetts* (Boston: New England Publishing, 1902); *Biographical Encyclopedia of Massachusetts of the Nineteenth Century* (New York: Metropolitan Publishing and Engraving, 1879); *Men of Massachusetts* (Boston: Boston Press Club, 1903); Daniel L. Marsh and William H. Clark, *The Story of Massachusetts*, 4 vols. (New York: American Historical Society, 1938), IV; Samuel Atkins Eliot, *Biographical History of Massachusetts*, 10 vols. (Boston: Massachusetts Biographical Society, 1911–18); Samuel Adams Drake, *Old Landmarks and Historic Personages of Boston*, 5 vols. (Boston: Little, Brown, 1895); John C. Rand, ed., *One of a Thousand: A Series of Biographical Sketches of 1,000 Representative*

Men Resident in the Commonwealth of Massachusetts. A.D. 1888–1889 (Boston: First National Publishing, 1890); William R. Cutter, ed., *Memorial Encyclopedia of the State of Massachusetts*, 3 vols. (Boston, New York, Chicago: American Historical Society, 1917); Cutter *et al.*, eds., *Encyclopedia of Biography, Massachusetts*; Thomas L. Wilson, *The Aristocracy of Boston; Who They Are, and What They Were: Being a History of the Business and Business Men of Boston for the Last Forty Years* (Boston: published by the author, 1848); *"Our First Men." A Calendar of Wealth, Fashion and Gentility; Containing a List of Those Persons Taxed in the City of Boston, Credibly Reported to Be Worth 100,000 Dollars, with Biographical Notices of the Principal Persons* (Boston: n.p., 1846); Joshua L. Chamberlain, *Universities and Their Sons* (Boston: R. Herndon, 1898); *Boston Past and Present: Being an Outline of the History of the City as Exhibited in the Lives of Its Prominent Citizens* (Boston and New York: John F. Trow, 1874); Cutter, ed., *Genealogical and Personal Memoirs Relating to the Families of Boston and Eastern Massachusetts*, 4 vols. (New York: Lewis Historical Publishing, 1908); Dumas Malone and Robert L. Schuyler, eds., *Dictionary of American Biography*, 22 vols. (New York: Charles Scribner's Sons, 1928–58). In addition to these collective biographical sources, I consulted memoirs, autobiographies and biographies of eminent Bostonians, obituaries in the New York *Times*, and histories of various phases of upper-class Boston life.

187. I have followed Pessen's evaluations in *Riches*, 337–39, 341–42, 344–45, 347.

188. The persistence-of-wealth category from one list to another was, so far as I know, originated by Pessen.

189. Ware, *Early*, 113.

190. A similar decline in upper-class officeholding occurred in Salem, Ware, Northampton, and several other Massachusetts towns. Doherty, *New England*, 82–88.

191. Henry Adams to Henry James, Nov. 18, 1903, Henry Adams, *Selected Letters of Henry Adams*, ed. Newton Arvin (New York: Farrar, 1951), 239–40.

192. N. Appleton, *Introduction*, 8–51; Appleton, "Memoir of Hon. Abbott Lawrence," *Massachusetts Historical Society Proceedings*, III (1856), 69–70; J. A. Lowell, "Memoir of P. T. Jackson," *passim*; R. C. Winthrop: "The Influence of Commerce," *Addresses*, I, 39–70; "The Death of Abbott Lawrence," II, 206–10; *Memoir of Hon. Nathan Appleton* (Boston: John Wilson and Son, 1861); Prescott, *Memoir of Abbott Lawrence*; A. Lawrence, *Extracts*, *passim*; Lawrence, *Life of Amos Lawrence*, *passim*; Edward Everett, "Peter Chardon Brooks," in Hunt, ed., *Lives*, I, 139–80; Jaher, "Businessman and Gentleman: Nathan and Thomas Gold Appleton—an Exploration in Inter-generational History," *Explorations in Entrepreneurial History*, 4 (Fall, 1966), 17–39; W. H. Prescott to Francis Lieber, Dec. 31, 1840, *Papers*, 171. For unpublished evidence of these attitudes see N. Appleton to E. S. Gannett, Jan. 24, 1828, Appleton Papers, MHS; numerous letters of N. Appleton, especially to his son, Thomas Gold Appleton, in the Appleton Papers; Amos Lawrence to Amos A. Lawrence, July 26, 1835, Dec. 4, 1836, Dec. 5, 1836, Amos Lawrence to Abbott Lawrence, Sept. ?, 1832, letters to William Lawrence from William Hickling Prescott, May 15, 1855, A. P. Peabody, Aug. 11, 1855, Jacob Bigelow, Oct. 4, 1855, Robert C. Winthrop, May 19, 1855, John C. Warren, May 22, 1855, Charles Lowell, Sept. 2, 1855, all in

Lawrence Family Papers, MHS; Abbott Lawrence Letters, Houghton Library; T. H. Perkins to E. Perkins, May 1, 1852, to J. P. Cushing, July 12, 1821, Sept. 18, 1826, Perkins Papers. See also Howe, *Unitarian*, 139–48, 226–32.

193. T. G. Appleton to N. Appleton, June 12, 1844, and cf. Same to Same, Dec. 26, 1844, Appleton Papers. For a fuller treatment of the Appleton father-and-son relationship and the place of culture in antebellum genteel Boston see Jaher, "Businessman and Gentleman," 17–39.

194. O. W. Holmes to J. T. Holmes, June 12, 1833, in Morse, *Life and Letters of Oliver Wendell Holmes*, I, 101; H. D. Sedgwick, *Francis Parkman* (Boston: Houghton Mifflin, 1904), 135–36; Edward Everett Hale, *James Russell Lowell and His Friends* (Boston: Houghton Mifflin, 1901); James Russell Lowell to Loring Elmwood, Oct. ?, 1838, in J. R. Lowell, *Letters of James Russell Lowell*, 2 vols., ed. Charles Eliot Norton (New York: Harper & Row, 1894), I, 32–33; Bliss Perry, ed., *Life and Letters of Henry Lee Higginson*, (Boston: Atlantic Monthly Press, 1921), 37, 43, 45, 64–65, 107–10, 121; Ticknor, *Life of William Hickling Prescott*, 55.

195. J. R. Lowell, *Letters*, I, 53; cf. Hale, *Lowell and Friends*, 81–82.

196. Cary, *Memoir of Col. T. H. Perkins*, 49–50; Charles Francis Adams, Jr., *Charles Francis Adams* (Boston: Houghton Mifflin, 1900), 74; Amos A. Lawrence to Amos Lawrence, June 8, 1840, Lawrence Papers, MHS. cf. G. Hillard quoted in Dana, *Journal*, II, 664.

197. Thomas Jefferson Coolidge, *An Autobiography* (Boston: Houghton Mifflin, 1900), 32.

198. N. Appleton to Edward S. Gannett, Jan. 24, 1828, Appleton Papers; N. Appleton, "Memoir of Hon. Abbott Lawrence," 69–70.

199. Bradlee, *Eastern*, 82, 93–94; Kirkland, *Men*, I, 177–78, 447–51, II, 316–22; Kistler, *Massachusetts Railroads*, 220–37; George F. Kenngott, *The Record of a City: A Social Survey of Lowell Massachusetts* (New York: Macmillan, 1912), 115–37; J. C. Ayer, *Some of the Usages and Abuses in the Management of Our Manufacturing Corporations* (Lowell: C. M. Langely, 1863); Josephson, *Golden Threads*, 78–81, 140–41, 212–23, 254, 299; Ware, *Early*, 238–41, 255–56, 269–75; Gibb, *Saco-Lowell*, 216–18; Donald B. Cole, *Immigrant City: Lawrence, Massachusetts, 1845–1921* (Chapel Hill: University of North Carolina Press, 1963), 27–33.

200. Amos A. Lawrence quoted in Josephson, *Golden Threads*, 173.

201. T. H. Perkins to ?, May 7, 1822, to J. P. Cushing, July 12, 1821, Perkins Papers; letters of N. Appleton to T. G. Appleton, Appleton Papers; Jaher, "Businessman and Gentleman," *passim*.

202. Abbott Lawrence quoted in Josephson, *Threads*, 159n; A. A. Lawrence quoted in Lawrence, *Life of Amos Lawrence*, 23.

203. Amos Lawrence to A. A. Lawrence, Nov. 11, 1832, Amos Lawrence Papers, MHS; A. A. Lawrence to Bishop Potter, Jan. 5, 1864, A. A. Lawrence Letterbooks, MHS.

204. Gibb, *Saco-Lowell*, 86, 192–99, 218–20; Ware, *Early*, 113; Strassman, *Risk*, 99–115; Ayer, *Some of the Usages*, 5.

205. J. Quincy, *Municipal*, 35–36, 50, 91–92, 142–44; Winthrop, "Memorial," *Addresses*, I, 361–63.

206. Andrews Norton to N. Appleton, Nov. 11, 1844, N. Appleton to T. G.

Appleton, July 31, 1841, cf. N. Appleton, "Journal of England, Holland and France, 1802," Appleton Papers; Abbott to Amos Lawrence, July 4, 1847, Amos Lawrence Papers, MHS.

207. Amos Lawrence to A. A. Lawrence, Mar. 4, 1833, Nov. 11, 1832, Jan. 6, 1833, Amos Lawrence Papers.

208. A. A. Lawrence quoted in Lawrence, *Life of Amos Lawrence*, 224; A. A. Lawrence to Henry Bond, Apr. 30, 1855, A. A. Lawrence Letterbooks, MHS.

209. For a more complete analysis see Jaher, "Businessman and Gentleman," *passim*.

210. N. Appleton: to T. G. Appleton, Mar. 1, 1826, to S. Appleton, Jan. 3, 1818, Appleton Papers.

211. Francis Parkman, "Old Northwest Journal, 1844–45," *The Journals of Francis Parkman*, 2 vols., ed. Mason Wade (New York: Harper & Row, 1947), I, 289–90; "Oregon Trail Journal, 1846," II, 408.

212. Dana, *Dana Saga*, 34–36; Shapiro, *Richard Henry Dana, Jr.*, 12.

213. Dana quoted in Shapiro, *Richard Henry Dana, Jr.*, 16; Adams, *Richard Henry Dana*, II, 35–36.

214. Edmund Quincy, Thomas Wentworth Higginson, Charles Francis Adams, and James Russell Lowell were a handful of more radical antislavery proponents. But they were a tiny and rejected segment of proper Boston and, except for Wendell Phillips, the reform urges of these bluebloods were short-lived.

215. J. Quincy, *Municipal*, 318, 348, 354, 356; R. C. Winthrop, *Life and Letters of John Winthrop, 1588–1649*, 2 vols. (Boston: Little, Brown, 1869), I, 9; II, 2–3, 188. For Quincy's identical attitude toward social change see Quincy, *History of Harvard*, II, 665–66, 688–89.

216. J. Quincy, *Municipal*, 411.

217. Dana, *Journal*, I: xxxii, Sept. 3, 1843, 213–14, May 16, 19, 1853, 549; II: Nov. 5, 1854, 664, July 20, 1859, 838. F. Parkman to Mary Dwight Parkman, Apr. 15, 1853, in F. Parkman, *Letters of Francis Parkman*, ed. Wilbur R. Jacobs (Norman: University of Oklahoma Press, 1960), I, 103–4, cf. xliv-vii; T. G. Appleton to N. Appleton, July 12, 1844, Sept. 13, 1844, Dec. 26, 1844, Appleton Papers; Jaher, "Businessman and Gentleman," 21–28.

218. The letters of G. Ticknor are in Hillard, *Life Letters and Journals*, II: Ticknor to R. H. Dana, Feb. 22, 1837, 75, to Earl Fitzwilliam, Oct. 17, 1838, 187–88, to Prince John, Duke of Saxony, May 17, 1839, May 14, 1848, July 30, 1848, 190, 213–33, to George T. Curtis, Apr. 22, 1848, 236.

219. W. H. Prescott to Don Pascual de Gayangos, May 30, 1848, Nov. 13, 1848, in Clara Louisa Penney, *Prescott Letters* (New York: Hispanic Society of America, 1927), 77, 82; Prescott, Nov. 19, 1850, *Literary Memoranda*, II, 198; Prescott quoted in Rollo Ogden, *William Hickling Prescott* (Boston: Houghton Mifflin, 1904), 4; Prescott, "Bancroft's United States," *Works*, XX (Philadelphia: J. B. Lippincott, 1904), 299–303; Prescott to William Lawrence, May 15, 1835, Lawrence Family Papers, MHS; Prescott, May 13, 1850, *Literary Memoranda*, I, 143.

220. O. W. Holmes: *The Autocrat of the Breakfast-Table* (Boston: Houghton Mifflin, 1895), 20–23, 57, 62; *The Professor at the Breakfast-Table* (Boston: Houghton Mifflin, 1892), 133, 135, 245–62; Holmes to J. T. Holmes, June 12,

1833, in Morse, *Life and Letters of Oliver Wendell Holmes*, I, 101; Holmes, "Oration before the New England Society of New York at Their Semi-Centennial Anniversary, December 22, 1852" (New York: n.p., n.d.), 34–37.

221. For Lowell's ideas see Lowell to G. B. Loring, Nov. 15, 1838, to Sydney H. Gay, Nov. 3, 1850, in Lowell, *Letters*, I, 34–35, 188; Lowell to C. F. Briggs, Dec. ?, 1848, to Gay, May 21, 1849, cf. Mar. 17, 1850, in Norton, ed., *Complete Writings*, XIV, 201, 212, 214; Lowell: "Cambridge Thirty Years Ago," (1854) and "A Moosehead Journal" (1853), *Complete*, I, 20–21, 76–77.

222. C. E. Norton: "Dwellings and Schools for the Poor," *North American Review*, LXXXV (Apr., 1852), 464–89; "Model Lodging-Houses in Boston," *Atlantic Monthly*, V (June, 1860), 673–80; Norton to Arthur Hugh Clough, Oct. 25, 1857, Mar. 5, 1858, Dec. 6, 1859, to Mrs. Edward Twisleton, Dec. 13, 1859, to Mrs. Elizabeth C. Gaskell, Feb. 7, 1860, to J. R. Lowell, Sept. 23, 1855, to Mrs. Gaskell, Dec. 26, 1859, in C. E. Norton, *Letters of Charles Eliot Norton*, 2 vols., ed. Sara Norton and M. A. DeWolfe Howe (Boston: Houghton Mifflin, 1913), I, 186–90, 196–201, 204–6, 135, 202. For Norton's early social outlook see Norton, *Considerations on Some Social Theories* (Boston: Little, Brown, 1853), quote is on p. 61.

223. J. R. Lowell, *The Function of the Poet and Other Essays* (Boston: Houghton Mifflin, 1920), 11, 17–19, 21–22, 27–29; Norton to Lowell, Sept. 23, 1855, *Letters*, I, 135; Norton, *Notes of Travel and Study in Italy* (Boston: Ticknor and Fields, 1860), 293–94, 299, 303–6, 315–17.

224. Quincy, *History of Harvard*, II, 443, 455–56; R. C. Winthrop, "The Obligations and Responsibilities of Educated Men in the Use of the Tongue and of the Pen" (1852), *Addresses*, II, 48; cf. H. G. Otis, "Address at Harvard's Second Centennial" (1836), in Quincy, *History of Harvard*, II, 662–70.

225. For biographies of Brahmins killed in the Civil War see T. W. Higginson, ed., *Harvard Memorial Biographies*, 2 vols. (Cambridge: Sever and Francis, 1866). The best account of C. R. Lowell is Edward W. Emerson, *Life and Letters of Charles Russell Lowell* (Boston: Houghton Mifflin, 1907).

226. Abbott Lawrence, *Will*, 45; N. Appleton, "Will of Nathan Appleton," May 23, 1855, Appleton Papers; Amos Lawrence, "Wills of Amos Lawrence," Lawrence Papers. For discussion of trust funds inhibiting enterpreneurship see Henry Lee Higginson to F. S. Grand d'Hauteville, Aug. 6, 1915, Higginson Letterbooks, HBS; William H. Forbes quoted in Arthur S. Pier, *Forbes: Telephone Pioneer* (New York: Dodd, Mead, 1953), 99; "City of Boston," *Fortune Magazine*, VII (Feb., 1933), 26–37, 98, 100, 102, 104, 106; Donald Holbrook, *The Boston Trustee* (Boston: Marshall Jones, 1937).

227. Gras, *Massachusetts First National*, 34–55, 74–80, 87–90, 126–27, 132–52, 305–7, 335, 338, 380–81, 538–44, 706–43.

228. White, *Massachusetts Hospital Life*, 5–13, 16–21, 54–70, 72–73, 77, 116–21, 129, 134–38, 150.

229. For cotton-manufacture dividends see Copeland, *Cotton Manufacturing*, 264–65, 395–97; Clark, *Industries*, III, 340–41. For general accounts of the decline of the textile industry see Clark, *Industries*, II, 105, 394, 404–12, III, 171–74, 183, 339–43; Kenngott, *Record*, 160–61; Burgy, *New England Cotton*, 175, 178–206; Thomas R. Navin and Marian V. Sears, "The Rise of a Market for Industrial Securities 1887–1902," *Business History Review*, XXIX (June, 1955),

110; Morton Pepper, "The Development of Cotton Manufacturing in New England and in the South 1900–1923," Edwin F. Gay and Allyn A. Young, eds., *The New England Economic Situation* (Chicago: A. W. Shaw Co., 1927), 101–76.

230. Norton Mezvinsky, "The Social Aristocracy of Boston and New York 1870–1915" (unpublished ms.), 6.

231. N. R. Danielian, *A.T.&T.: The Story of Industrial Conquest* (New York: Vanguard Press, 1939), 40–65; Horace Coon, *American Tel & Tel* (New York: Longmans, Green, 1939), 31–94; John Winthrop Hammond, *Men and Volts: The Story of General Electric* (Philadelphia: J. B. Lippincott, 1941), 147, 193, 195, 223–24; William B. Gates, Jr., *Michigan Copper and Boston Dollars* (Cambridge: Harvard University Press, 1951), 12–45, 81, 121–22, 143–48, 161–79; Alexander Agassiz, *Letters and Recollections of Alexander Agassiz*; G. R. Agassiz, (Boston: Houghton Mifflin, 1913), 56–85; Barrett Wendell, "History of Lee, Higginson & Co. (unpublished typescript, 1919, MHS) 5–6; H. L. Higginson to Francis Lee Higginson, Sept. 29, 1910, to Quincy A. Shaw, Mar. 27, 1911, to C. A. Coffin, July 11, 1913, H. L. Higginson Letterbooks, HBS.

232. Cochran, *Railroad Leaders*, 138–39; C. E. Perkins to Forbes, July 17, 1878, Forbes to Perkins, May 8, 1879, *ibid.*, 336, 431; Forbes, *Reminiscences*, II, 3–4; Forbes to William C. Endicott, Oct. 3, 1833, in Budd, *Burlington*, 12; Edward Chase Kirkland, *Patrician at Bay: Charles Francis Adams, Jr., 1831–1915* (Cambridge: Harvard University Press, 1965), 92–128; Nelson Trottman, *History of the Union Pacific* (New York: Ronald Press, 1923), 200–240; Kirkland, *Men*, II, 60–62; L. L. Waters, *Steel Trails to Santa Fe* (Lawrence: University of Kansas Press, 1950), 195–207; Gurnsey Cam, Jr., "The Influence of New England Capital in America's Railroad Development," in *New England Economic Situation*, ed. Gay and Young, 39–68; Wendell, "Lee, Higginson," 7–8; Edward W. Weeks, *Men, Money and Responsibility: A History of the Lee, Higginson Corporation* (Boston: privately printed, 1962), 12; Kirkland, *Patrician*, 90–91; Johnson and Supple, *Boston Capitalists*, 287–88; 303, 307–9, 319–28; H. L. Higginson Papers, *passim*; H. L. Higginson, Letterbooks, *passim*, HBS; "Lee, Higginson Accounts and Investments," Thomas Jefferson Coolidge Papers, Letterbooks I–IV; "Trust Account Ledger," Old Colony Trust Company, 1901–8, HBS.

233. Frederick Upham Adams, *Conquest of the Tropics* (New York: Doubleday, 1914), 39–95; Charles Morrow Wilson, *Empire in Green and Gold* (New York: Holt, Rinehart & Winston, 1947), 69, 71, 107–9, 206–7; H. L. Higginson to F. L. Higginson, Jr., Sept. 29, 1910, H. L. Higginson Letterbooks; Amory, *Proper Bostonians*, 54, 343–44; Kirkland, *Men*, II, 435.

234. *The Flame*, X (Oct., 1957), 27–33. *The Flame* is the company magazine of Godfrey L. Cabot, Inc. This seventy-fifth anniversary issue was devoted to the history of the company. Amory, *Proper Bostonians*, 346, 348; Alfred D. Chandler, Jr., *Strategy and Structure* (Cambridge: M.I.T. Press, 1962), 120; Lawrence H. Seltzer, *A Financial History of the American Auto Industry* (Boston: Houghton Mifflin, 1938), 164, 252–55; Henry Greenleaf Pearson, *Son of New England: James Jackson Storrow 1864–1926* (Boston: Thomas Todd, 1932), 123–24.

235. Navin and Sears, "Market for Industrial Securities," 115.

236. Thomas P. Beal, *The Second National Bank of Boston* (New York: Amer-

ican Newcomen Society, 1958), 1–2, 7–8, 19; Stone, *Century*, 16–17; *List of Stockholders*, 378–88, 390–400; *The Book of the Shawmut Bank* (Boston: National Shawmut Bank of Boston, 1923); Frederick H. Curtiss, *Fifty Years of Boston Finance 1840–1890* (Boston: n.p., 1930), 7; Gras, *Massachusetts First National*, 161, 166–67.

237. Redlich, *Molding*, II, part 2, 189–90, 379, 394; Curtiss, *Fifty*, 2, 7; Gras, *Massachusetts First National*, 180–84; Navin and Sears, "Market for Industrial Securities," 124–26; *Old Colony Trust Company* (Boston: n.p., 1915).

238. Navin and Sears, "Market for Industrial Securities," 122, 124–26; Redlich, *Molding*, II, part 2, 288; Pearson, *Son*, 190–92; H. L. Higginson Papers, *passim*; Arthur S. Dewing, *Corporate Promotions and Reorganizations* (Cambridge: Harvard University Press, 1914), 171, 183; Paul Goodman, "Success and Failure in Investment Banking," Social Sources of Business Enterprise: Studies in the Longevity of Boston Financial Institutions (unpublished ms.), *passim*; Record of Dividends, Kidder, Peabody & Co., HBS; T. J. Coolidge Papers, "Trust Account Ledger," Old Colony Trust Company, HBS.

239. H. L. Higginson to James J. Higginson, Mar. 27, 1885, to Robert H. Fuller, Dec. 23, 1908, to Frederic W. Allen, Apr. 20, 1915, Higginson Letterbooks; Higginson to B. Wendell, Nov. 14, 1919, MHS; Pearson, *Son*, 90, 100–103, 172–73, 193–95, 238–39; Wendell, "Lee, Higginson," 5, 10–13, 15; Weeks, *Fifty*, 7, 19–20; Redlich, *Molding*, II, part 2, 190, 288, 387–88; *Old Colony*, *passim*; Kidder, Peabody executive quoted in Goodman, "Success and Failure," 24.

240. T. J. Coolidge to C. E. Perkins, Jan. 2, 1899, T. J. Coolidge Papers, HBS; H. L. Higginson to C. A. Coffin, July 11, 1913, to Howard Elliott, Oct. 6, 1913, H. L. Higginson Letterbooks; Redlich, *Molding*, II, part 2, 388; Pearson, *Son*, 196; Weeks, *Men, Money and Responsibility*, 17.

241. Robert Shaplen, *Kreuger, Genuis and Swindler* (New York: Alfred A. Knopf, 1960), 6–7, 77–78, 94, 181, 207, 209, 222, 226–27, 231, 234, 242–43, 250; Dewing, *Corporate Promotions*, 305–22; Harold F. Williamson, *Winchester: The Gun That Won the West* (Washington: Combat Forces Press, 1952), 260–62, 271, 320, 360–63.

242. White, *Massachusetts Hospital Life*, 153–65; Allan Forbes, *Forty Years in Boston Banking* (New York: American Newcomen Society, 1948), 9, 17; *The Log of the State Street Trust Co.* (Boston: privately printed, 1926); William W. Wolbach, *The Boston Safe Deposit and Trust Co.* (New York: American Newcomen Society, 1962), 8–11, 20, 23, 25–26.

243. Richard P. Chapman, *125 Years on State Street* (New York: American Newcomen Society, 1956), 5.

244. The Federal Reserve Bank of Boston, *Commercial Banking in New England 1784–1958* (Boston: n.p., 1959), 38, 41, 43, 45.

245. Jane Jacobs, *The Economy of Cities* (New York: Random House, 1969), 203–7.

246. "American Millionaires," *Tribune Monthly*, 4 (June, 1892), 18–22. Unfortunately the 1892 compilation makes no distinctions between millionaires and multimillionaires; therefore, no comparison can be made between higher levels of wealth in 1892, 1835, and 1860.

247. Amos Lawrence to Abbott Lawrence, Sept. ?, 1832, Amos Lawrence Papers.

248. For studies of the Brahmin response to these late-nineteenth-century developments see my *Doubters and Dissenters: Cataclysmic Thought in America, 1885–1918* (New York: Free Press, 1964), 141–87; John Higham, *Strangers in the Land* (New Brunswick: Rutgers University Press, 1955), 22, 32, 75, 96, 102–9, 134–35, 152; Barbara Miller Solomon, *Ancestors and Immigrants* (Cambridge: Harvard University Press, 1956), *passim*; Ari Hoogenboom, *Outlawing the Spoils: A History of the Civil Service Reform Movement, 1865–1883* (Urbana: University of Illinois Press, 1961), 11, 15–19, 29–46, 73, 115, 149, 200; *Citizens Association of Boston, First Annual Report of the Executive Committee*, 1889 (Boston: Alfred Mudge & Son, 1889), 43–47; Frank Mann Stewart: *The National · Civil Service Reform League* (Austin: University of Texas Press, 1929), 25–27, 72, 85–86, 187–88, 243–44, 270, 272; *A Half Century of Municipal Reform—the History of the Municipal League* (Berkeley and Los Angeles: University of California Press, 1950), 19, 52, 76, 132, 187, 206, 208; Raymond L. Bridgeman, *The Independents of Massachusetts in 1884* (Boston: Cupples, Upham, 1885), *passim*; Geoffrey Blodgett, *The Gentle Reformers: Massachusetts Democrats in the Cleveland Era* (Cambridge: Harvard University Press, 1966).

249. R. H. Dana III, quoted in H. W. L. Dana, *Dana Saga*, 58. For some Brahmin views of the reasons for corruption and the solutions to the problem see C. E. Norton, "Some Aspects of Civilization," *Forum Magazine*, XX (Feb. 18, 1896), 641–52; Moorfield Storey: *Politics as a Duty and as a Career* (New York: G. P. Putnam's Sons, 1889); "The American Legislature," annual address before the American Bar Association, Aug. 22, 1894, *Transactions of the American Bar Association* (1895), 16–17; H. Adams, "Civil Service Reform," *North American Review*, CXIV (Oct., 1869), 443–75; Brooks Adams: "The Platform of the New Party," *ibid.*, CXIX (July, 1874), 47, 60–61; "Review of James Fitzjames Stephens's *Liberty, Equality, Fraternity*," *ibid.*, CXVIII (Apr., 1874), 445–47.

250. Hart, *Commonwealth*, III, 623–26, 688; *Catalogue of Members, passim*.

251. For Brahmin participation in the nativist movement see Solomon, *Ancestors*, 47–54, 84, 88–91, 97ff.; Higham, *Strangers*, 92–93, 96, 99–100, 102, 141–44, 199.

252. Richard M. Abrams, *Conservatism in a Progressive Era: Massachusetts Politics, 1900–1912* (Cambridge: Harvard University Press, 1964), 35–38, 174–75, 261–62; Joseph Huthmacher, *Massachusetts People and Politics, 1919–1933* (Cambridge: Harvard University Press, 1959), 50–58.

253. Amory, *Proper Bostonians*, 72–73; Leverett Saltonstall's collection of speeches, *Six Crucial Years* (n.p.: n.p., 1945), especially "A Toast to the Commonwealth," Mar. 16, 1940, 106–13.

254. "American Millionaires," 18–22; Hart, *Commonwealth*, III, 623–26, 688; *Catalogue of Members, passim*.

255. W. C. Endicott to Henry Cabot Lodge, Jan. 21, 1899, cf. Lodge, "Journal," May 30, 1884, Jan. 19, 1887, Dec. 20, 1890, Francis I. Amory to Lodge, June 26, 1880, H. Lee to Lodge, Mar. 26, 1895, Lodge note to himself, Apr. 11, 1924, Ellen Parkman Vaughan to H. C. Lodge, Jr., Aug. 10, 1932, Lodge Papers, MHS.

256. Lodge, "Journal," Jan. 19, 1887, Dec. 20, 1890, Lodge to Brooks Adams, Feb. 5, 1918, Lodge Papers; Blodgett, *Gentle Reformers*, 141, 243–49. This book contains an excellent discussion of Brahmin attitudes toward political power,

and I have drawn on it for my analysis.

257. Bowditch, *History of Massachusetts General*, 695–729; Grace Whiting Myers, *History of Massachusetts General Hospital*, *1872–1900* (Boston: Griffith-Stillings Press, 1929), 162, 164–65, 180, 185–208; Frederic A. Washburn, *The Massachusetts General Hospital: Its Development*, *1900–1935* (Boston: Houghton Mifflin, 1939), 3–5, 72–73, 111, 126, 162–64, 347, 427–34, 549–60, 568–72, 578–85; *Harvard Medical School*, 31–32, 57, 76, 90, 137, 195–96; Viets, *Brief History of Medicine*, 145–46, 174, 176–78, 183–84.

258. Charles W. Eliot, *Dedication of the New Buildings of the Harvard Medical School* (Boston: Harvard Medical School, 1906). For similar sentiments expressed by H. Lee, Jr., and O. W. Holmes see *Addresses and Exercises at the One Hundredth Anniversary of the Harvard Medical School* (Cambridge: John Wilson and Son, 1884), 45, 54.

259. *Harvard Medical School*, 180–81; Myers, *History of Massachusetts General*, 26, 55, 80, 112, 117, 125, 132, 142, 151; Nathaniel W. Faxon, *The Massachusetts General Hospital*, *1935–1955* (Cambridge: Harvard University Press, 1959), 404–7.

260. Burrage, *History of Massachusetts Medical Society*, 462–66.

261. Davis, *Bench and Bar*, 114–15.

262. Greenslet, *Lowells*, 329–31, 334–39, 348; Jaher, "Proper Bostonians," 214–16, 218; Bliss Perry, *Richard Henry Dana*, *1851–1931* (Boston: Houghton Mifflin, 1933), 110–12, 122–23; Sutherland, *Law*, 165, 185, 214–15, 221, 231, 234, 288, 300.

263. The best account of the immigrant experience in Boston is Oscar Handlin, *Boston's Immigrants: A Study in Acculturation*, *1790–1880* (New York: Atheneum, 1968). See also Schultz, *Culture*, 209–51.

264. McLachlan, *American Boarding Schools*, 140–41.

265. For upper-class New Yorkers active in the Episcopal Church see William Berrian, *An Historical Sketch of Trinity Church*, *New-York* (New York: Stanford and Swords, 1847); *Memorial of St. Mark's Church in the Bowery* (New York: Thomas Whittaker, 1899); Morgan Dix, *A History of the Parish of Trinity Church*, 4 vols. (New York: G. P. Putnam, 1898–1906). For the Philadelphians see Burt, *Perennial Philadelphians*, 74–75.

266. William Lawrence quoted in R. H. Dana, Jr., *An Autobiographical Sketch (1815–1842)* (Hamden, Conn.: Shoe String Press, 1953), 14.

267. Sam Bass Warner, Jr., *Streetcar Suburbs: The Process of Growth in Boston 1870–1900* (New York: Atheneum, 1969), 2, 53, 62–63.

268. C. E. Norton, "The Lack of Old Homes in America," *Scribner's Magazine*, V (May, 1889), 636–40; J. Quincy, *Figures*, 165, 272; E. Quincy, *Memoir of Josiah Quincy*, 396; Minot, *William Minot*, 12; Lodge: *Boston*, 196–99; *Early Memories* (New York: Charles Scribner's Sons, 1913), 16, 207–10; F. Parkman: "The Failure of Universal Suffrage," *North American Review*, CCLXIII (July–Aug., 1878), 1–20; "The Woman Question," *ibid.*, CCLXV (Oct., 1879), 319–20.

269. E. Digby Baltzell, *The Protestant Establishment: Aristocracy & Caste in America* (New York: Random House, 1964), 123–35; McLachlan, *American Boarding Schools*, 92–93, 219–41.

270. Arthur Stanwood Pier, *St. Paul's School*, *1855–1934* (New York: Charles

Scribner's Sons, 1934); McLachlan, *American Boarding Schools*, 158–298; Frank D. Ashburn, *Peabody of Groton* (New York: Coward McCann, 1944).

271. Henry Coit quoted in Pier, *St. Paul's*, 84; E. Peabody quoted in Ashburn, *Peabody*, 222.

272. McLachlan, *American Boarding Schools*, 290.

273. Pier, *St. Paul's*, 351; J. J. Chapman quoted in McLachlan, *American Boarding Schools*, 271; "Twelve Top American Private Schools Don't Have Tradition of Eton and Harrow in Producing Public Servants," *Fortune Magazine*, XIV (Jan., 1936), 48–52, 104–19; Charles McArthur, "Personalities of Public and Private School Boys," *Harvard Educational Review*, 24 (Fall, 1954), 256–62.

274. Rector of St. Paul's quoted in Baltzell, *Protestant*, 324–25, 344.

275. C. W. Eliot: "Why the American Republic May Endure," *Forum Magazine*, XVIII (Oct., 1894), 58; *The Merit System and the New Democratic Party* (New York: National Civil Service Reform League, 1913), 6, 10; Eliot to ?, Nov. 7, 1910, in James, *Charles William Eliot*, II, 207; Eliot to H. L. Higginson, Mar. 31, 1896, Charles William Eliot Letters, Houghton Library, Harvard University; James, *Charles William Eliot*, I, 244–94; Morison: *Three Centuries*, 334–89; *The Development of Harvard University* (Cambridge: Harvard University Press, 1950), 36, 42–44, 259–77, 454–62, 557–58; Hugh Hawkins, *Between Harvard and America: The Educational Leadership of Charles W. Eliot* (New York: Oxford University Press, 1972), 45–68, 92–106. For another discussion of Eliot's beliefs see Jaher, "Proper Bostonians," 215–16. J. M. Forbes to J. D. Washburn, Sept. 11, 1879, *Letters (Supplementary)*, III, 150–51; Forbes, *Reminiscences*, I, 90–91; C. F. Adams to C. E. Norton, Nov. 30, 1883, Charles Francis Adams Letters, Houghton Library; Alexander Agassiz to H. C. Lodge, Apr. 18, 1885, Lodge Papers. For some samples of the opposition see F. Parkman to William Watson Goodwin, Dec. 25, 1891, in Parkman, *Parkman Letters*, II, 251; C. E. Norton to Samuel G. Ward, Sept. 19, 1900, in Norton, *Letters*, II, 300; Vanderbilt, *Charles Eliot Norton*, 181, 200.

276. Stephen A. Larrabee, *Hellas Observed: The American Experience of Greece, 1775–1865* (New York: New York University Press, 1957), 12, 28, 135, 198–99.

277. C. W. Eliot to C. F. Adams, June 9, 1904, in James, *Charles William Eliot*, II, 150–51; cf. Eliot, "Inaugural Address," in Morison, *Development*, 68–69; Morison, *Three Centuries*, 417–18, 467–69, 477–79; Henry A. Yeomans, *Abbott Lawrence Lowell* (Cambridge: Harvard University Press, 1948), 166–70, 183, Lowell quoted on 166.

278. *Endowment Funds of Harvard University, passim*. For the advent of Overseers and Fellows who did not belong to proper Boston see *Harvard University Catalogue[s]*, particularly after World War II.

279. Joan Cook, "Old Boston Families Are Adapting to Changes at Harvard," New York *Times*, Mar. 4, 1967, 90.

280. Baltzell, *Protestant*, 338.

281. Ashburn, *Peabody*, 55–56; James, *Charles William Eliot*, I, 243.

282. A. L. Lowell quoted in Amory, *Proper Bostonians*, 44.

283. Richard C. Cabot, *Social Work* (Boston: Houghton Mifflin, 1919), *passim*; Nathan Irving Huggins, *Protestants Against Poverty: Boston's Charities, 1870–1900* (Westport: Greenwood Publishing, 1971), *passim*.

284. Handlin, *Boston's Immigrants*, 18–19.

285. Massachusetts Bureau of Statistics of Labor, *Census of the Common-wealth of Massachusetts 1905* (Boston: Wright & Potter, 1909), I, 815–17.

286. Handlin, *Boston's Immigrants*, 52–53, 118–22, 160–63, 183–85, 215; Huggins, *Protestants*, 144, 193–94.

287. Huggins, *Protestants*, 63–65. For the professionalization of social work in general see Roy Lubove, *The Professional Altruist* (Cambridge: Harvard University Press, 1965), *passim*, Joseph Lee quoted on 50.

288. For the best account of Brahmin social clubs see Williams, *Social History*, *passim*.

289. Charles C. Perkins quoted in Walter Muir Whitehill, *Museum of Fine Arts, Boston: A Centennial History*, 2 vols. (Cambridge: Harvard University Press, 1970), 9.

290. The best account of the museum is found in *ibid*. For another study of its formation see Neil Harris, "The Gilded Age Revisited: Boston and the Museum Movement," *American Quarterly*, XIV (Winter, 1962), 545–46. For lists of officers, trustees, and contributors see Whitehill, *Museum*, II, *passim*; *Museum of Fine Arts Annual Report[s]*.

291. H. L. Higginson to ?, Mar. 8, 1890, in Perry, *Life and Letters of Henry Lee Higginson*, II, 329.

292. For H. L. Higginson's life and thoughts see *ibid*. The best history of the orchestra is M. A. DeWolfe Howe, *The Boston Symphony Orchestra* (Boston: Houghton Mifflin, 1931). For lists of trustees and donors see *Boston Symphony Orchestra Programs*, published in each symphony season. I am also grateful to Lanning Humphrey, Associate Director of Public Relations and Archivist of the Boston Symphony Orchestra, who permitted me to see the orchestra's press releases, which contained much information about the symphony and its trustees.

293. T. G. Appleton to N. Appleton, July 12, 1844, cf. Same to Same, Dec. 26, 1844, Appleton Papers. For a more extended analysis see Jaher, "Businessman and Gentleman," 17–40.

294. H. Adams, *Life of George Cabot Lodge* (Boston: Houghton Mifflin, 1911), 34, 38, 69, 144–49. On H. C. Lodge's attitude toward his son's literary endeavors see H. C. Lodge quoted in John A. Garraty, *Henry Cabot Lodge: A Biography* (New York: Alfred A. Knopf, 1953), 192.

295. For a general discussion of the inability of schools and clubs to maintain the status of the old upper class see Baltzell, *Protestant*, 339–79. For the situation at Harvard see Cook, "Old Boston Families," 90.

296. The best way to trace the change in personnel is to check memberships and lists of officers periodically published by these institutions. See *The Boston Athenaeum Reports*, *Harvard University Catalogues*, *Museum of Fine Arts Annual Reports*, *Boston Symphony Orchestra Programs*, *Proceedings of the Massachusetts Historical Society*.

297. Laurence Curtis to H. C. Lodge, Feb. 9, 1920, Lodge Papers. For the financial difficulties of other Boston clubs see Williams, *Social History*, 75, 126. For the decline of London clubs see New York *Times*, May 12, 1968, 74, Aug. 21, 1969, 10.

298. John Torrey Morse quoted in Riley, *Massachusetts Historical Society*, 20–21.

299. Henry Wadsworth Longfellow, Edward Everett, and Louis Agassiz were the last significant additions to the class. These men entered in the 1840s and '50s and their acceptance into the group indicated the growing Brahmin preoccupation with intellectual endeavor. For the closing of the class see Amory, *Proper Bostonians*, 53–54.

300. *Ibid.*, *passim*; Firey, *Land Use*, 103–6, 115, 120–21, 335; Morison, *Three Centuries*, 358, 417–22.

301. Morse to Lodge, Feb. 3, 1916, Lodge Papers.

302. For an analysis of the Brahmin role in founding the Immigration Restriction League see Higham, *Strangers*, 102–3. For the contribution of the Brahmins to the Watch and Ward Society and the motivation for their participation see Paul S. Boyer, "Boston Book Censorship in the Twenties," *American Quarterly*, XV (Spring, 1963), 3–25. For a general account of the Boston establishment and immigrants see Solomon, *Ancestors*. Among specific Brahmin attacks on the newcomers are Norton, "Some Aspects," 641–52; H. C. Lodge, "The Census and Immigration," *Century Magazine*, LXVII (Jan., 1904), 466–73. For the anti-Semitic remarks of H. Adams see Worthington Chauncey Ford, ed., *The Letters of Henry Adams, 1858–1918*, 2 vols. (Boston: Houghton Mifflin, 1920), I, 388, II, 33, 95. For the anti-Semitism of B. Adams see B. Adams to H. Adams, Mar. 25, 1896, July 26, 1896, Oct. 15, 1896, Brooks Adams Letters, Houghton Library. A. L. Lowell, M. Storey, and C. F. Adams, Jr., opposed Brandeis's appointment—see Amory, *Proper Bostonians*, 324. For other Brahmin opposition to Brandeis see Morse to Lodge, Feb. 13, 1916, Barrett Wendell to Lodge, June 30, 1916, Lodge Papers. For other unfavorable references to Jews see Lodge to William S. Bigelow, Feb. 22, 1913, Edward E. Hale to Lodge, Feb. 16, 1901, Lodge Papers. For a general study of tendencies among American elites to embrace nativism see Wallace Evan Davies, *Patriotism on Parade: The Story of Veterans and Hereditary Organizations in America, 1783–1900* (Cambridge: Harvard University Press, 1955).

303. Abigail Adams Homans, New York *Times*, Mar. 11, 1965, 26. For a further description of these facets of Boston society see Amory, *Proper Bostonians*, 115–17.

304. It can be claimed that the political success of these figures and the persistent prominence of their families indicates the sustained strength rather than the eclipse of the class. Further support for this argument is the example of the Kennedy family. The Kennedys, it has been suggested, assimilated elements of the Brahmin style. This criticism, however, represents a different emphasis rather than a contradiction of the thesis. Until the Brahmins totally disappear there will be residual advantages in their social position. It is to be expected that families and individuals will preserve prerogatives of leadership. The more significant perspective in analyzing Brahmin political behavior, however, is that if being well-born provides an initial advantage, career success depends upon achievements in spheres and organizations which are not controlled by prominent Bostonians. The Massachusetts Whigs of 1840, and even the Massachusetts Republicans of the post–Civil War period, were much more amena-

ble to patrician influence than present-day Bay State political parties. The Whigs had been controlled by Boston textile magnates and their associates, and the Republicans were financed by men like H. L. Higginson and J. M. Forbes, ornamented by J. R. Lowell and R. H. Dana, Jr., and, for a time, bossed by H. C. Lodge. Nor does the behavior of the Kennedy clan evince the sustained power of the Brahmins. The Kennedys are part of a new breed, children or grandchildren of business magnates who have inherited wealth and acquired a *nobless oblige* attitude of public service. William Scranton, Averell Harriman, and Nelson Rockefeller are other prominent members of this group. They share with public-spirited scions from older families not a desire to pattern themselves on the Boston establishment (most of them are not Bostonians) but rather a common attitude, the analysis of which is a central theme of this book. This type of statesman signifies the tendency for descendants of successful businessmen to seek individual gratification or to broaden class and family hegemony through politics, academic life, or the arts.

305. The author personally knows of several cases in the last two generations of the Minot and Channing families where marriages to people of non-Bostonian middle-class origins took place. In at least two cases Jews married into the family. For more examples of exogamous marriage see Amory, *Proper Bostonians*, 344.

306. The actual figures are: 1800, 24,937; 1900, 560,892. United States Census Office: *Second Census, 1800* (Washington, D.C.: Apollo Press, 1802), 14; *Twelfth Census of the United States, Taken in the Year 1900*, Population, Pt. I (Washington, D.C.: U.S. Government Printing Office, 1901) lxix.

307. Amos Lawrence to Mark Hopkins, Apr. 6, 1847, cf. to Mrs. Caroline Lee Hertz, Oct. 14, 1852, Amos Lawrence Papers; Lawrence, *Extracts*, 234–35, 268, 318. For similar expressions of satisfaction see N. Appleton to T. G. Appleton, Dec. 31, 1831, Appleton Papers; Prescott, *Literary Memoranda*, May 4, 1845, 150; T. H. Perkins to J. P. Cushing, Sept. 18, 1826, Perkins Papers; James Jackson to Anna C. Lowell, Oct. 2, 1843, in Putnam, *Memoir of Dr. James Jackson*, 359; Amos A. Lawrence to Mrs. A. A. Lawrence, July 31, 1863, Lawrence Letterbooks.

308. Abbott to Amos Lawrence, Dec. 14, 1851, Lawrence Papers; J. Quincy, "Diary," Mar. 24, 1853, in E. Quincy, *Life of Josiah Quincy*, 504.

309. H. L. Higginson to Sir Hugh Levick, July ?, 1918, to Mrs. George R. Agassiz, July ?, 1918, in Perry, *Life and Letters of Henry Lee Higginson*, 507, 520–21, Higginson quoted on 275; Higginson to T. W. Higginson, Jan. 14, 1879, T. W. Higginson Letters, Houghton Library.

310. F. Parkman to the Boston *Daily Advertiser*, Sept. 4, 1861, June 30, 1863; Parkman, *Letters of Francis Parkman*, I, 143, 160; Parkman: "Review of H. H. Bancroft, *The Native Races of the Pacific States*," *North American Review*, CXX (Jan., 1875), 34; "Failure," 16–17; J. R. Lowell, *The Works of James Russell Lowell* (Boston: Houghton Mifflin, 1890), VI, 6, 26–27; Lowell, *Complete*, I, 327; B. Adams to H. Adams, Apr. 22, 1896, B. Adams Letters; B. Adams, *The Law of Civilization and Decay*, 2nd ed. (New York: Alfred A. Knopf, 1943), 303–5; H. Adams to Mrs. Elizabeth Cameron, June 10, 1888, Sept. 15, 1893, to Charles Milnes Gaskell, Nov. 26, 1893, Jan. 23, 1894, in Ford, ed., *Letters of Henry Adams*, II, 33–35; Charles Francis Adams, Jr., *An Autobiography, 1835–1915*

(Boston: Houghton Mifflin, 1916), 190; William Minot to H. C. Lodge, Mar. 18, 1880, Lodge Papers; Lodge, *Early*, 209; R. H. Dana, Jr., quoted in Shapiro, *Richard Henry Dana, Jr.*, 184.

311. J. M. Forbes to John N. A. Griswold, May 12, 1880, in Cochran, *Railroad Leaders*, 338; Francis Lee Higginson to H. L. Higginson, June 20, 1888, H. L. Higginson to Barrett Wendell, Nov. 14, 1919, H. L. Higginson Papers, MHS.

312. C. E. Norton: *Tercentenary Festival of Emmanuel College* (Cambridge: C. J. Clay and Son, 1884), 29; *Address Read at the Opening of the Slater Memorial Museum* (Norwich, Conn. n.p., 1888), 22; Norton to Sir Mountstuart E. Grant-Duff, Nov. 8, 1895, to L. Stephen, Jan. 8, 1896, to E. L. Godkin, July ?, 1900, to S. G. Ward, Sept. 19, 1900, Apr. 14, 1901, in Norton, *Letters*, II, 235–37, 293–94, 300, 304–5; F. Parkman: "The Tale of the Ripe Scholar," *The Nation*, XCV (Dec. 23, 1869), 559; "Bancroft," 130; *Journals*, 43, 60; Parkman to H. R. Casgrain, Sept. 30, 1890, in Wade, *Francis Parkman, Heroic Historian* (New York: Viking Press, 1942), 438; J. R. Lowell, *Works*, VI, 27; Lowell to William Dean Howells, Nov. 2, 1865, William Dean Howells Letters, Houghton Library; Lowell, *Writings*, I, 20–21, 327; R. H. Dana, Jr., quoted in Shapiro, *R. H. Dana, Jr.*, 23; H. Adams, *Education*, 343–44; 346; B. Adams, "Introductory Note," in H. Adams, *The Degradation of the Democratic Dogma* (New York: Macmillan, 1919), v–viii.

313. F. Parkman to M. D. Parkman, Apr. 15, 1853, in Parkman, *Letters*, I, 103–4; H. Adams to Gaskell, Sept. 25, 1868, Nov. 25, 1877, in Ford, ed., *Adams Letters*, I, 145, 302, II, *passim*; Jaher, *Doubters and Dissenters*, 158–88.

314. C. E. Norton: "Some Aspects," 650, 666; *Memorials of Two Friends* (New York: n.p., 1902), 101–2; Norton to J. B. Harrison, July 23, 1882, to L. Stephen, June 25, 1898, in Norton, *Letters*, II, 135, 270–71; F. Parkman: "Failure," 6, 20; "Woman," 312, 318–20; Parkman to H. R. Casgrain, May 9, 1875, in Parkman, *Letters*, II, 82; J. R. Lowell, *Works*, VI, 10–11, 205; C. F. Adams, Jr., "The Protection of the Ballot in National Elections," *Journal of Social Science*, I (June, 1869), 107, 110–11; H. C. Lodge, "Census," 737; B. Wendell, *Privileged Classes* (New York: Charles Scribner's Sons, 1908), 114, 122; Moorfield Storey, *The Democratic Party and Philippine Independence* (Boston: George H. Ellis, 1913), 7; J. T. Morse to H. C. Lodge, Apr. 21, 1920, W. S. Bigelow to Lodge, Feb. 20, 1913, May 21, 1913, Lodge Papers; H. Adams to Gaskell, Nov. 26, 1893, Jan. 23, 1894, to B. Adams, Sept. ?, 1895, June 11, 1897, to Mrs. Cameron, Jan. 25, 1903, Feb. 7, 1904, Aug. 20, 1905, to B. Adams, Nov. 1, 1910, to Mrs. Cameron, June 22, 1911, in Ford, ed., *Adams Letters*, II, 34–35, 82–83, 120–21, 393, 424, 460, 551, 570; B. Adams: "The New Industrial Revolution," *Atlantic Monthly*, LXXVII (Feb., 1901), 164; "War as the Ultimate Form of Economic Competition," *Scribner's Magazine*, XXXI (Mar., 1902), 352; *America's Economic Supremacy* (New York: Macmillan, 1900); B. Adams to H. Adams, Mar. 7, 1896, July 5, 1901, Jan. 9, 1906, May 21, 1905, Jan. 1, 1908, B. Adams Letters; Higham, *Strangers*, 102–3; Solomon, *Ancestors*, *passim*.

315. C. E. Norton to S. G. Ward, Apr. 26, 1896, in Norton, *Letters*, II, 244; Norton: "Reminiscences of Old Cambridge," *Cambridge Historical Society Proceedings*, I (1905), 13; "The Lack of Old Homes," 636–40. J. R. Lowell, *Writings*, I, 20–21; Lowell to Miss Jane Norton, Sept. 9, 1856, in Lowell, *Letters*, I, 270–71;

John Holmes to Waldo Higginson, Mar. ?, 1891, in J. Holmes, *Letters of John Holmes to James Russell Lowell and Others*, ed. William Roscoe Thayer (Boston: Houghton Mifflin, 1916), 249–50; C. F. Adams, Jr., *Autobiography*, 7–8; C. F. Adams to C. E. Norton, Jan. 26, 1906, Charles Francis Adams, Jr., Letters, Houghton Library; H. Lee quoted in Perry, *Henry Lee Higginson*, 83; H. Adams: *Education*, 260, 384–85, 434–35, 459; *Mont St. Michel and Chartres* (Boston: Houghton Mifflin, 1905), 45, 276; H. Adams to John Hay, Nov. 7, 1900, to Alan Stanburrough Cook, Aug. 6, 1910, in Ford, ed., *Adams Letters*, II, 301, 546–47; H. Adams to Hay, Sept. 7, 1895, to B. Adams, May 6, 1899, in Harold Dean Cater, ed., *Henry Adams and His Friends* (Boston: Houghton Mifflin, 1947), 347, 463; H. Adams, "Prayer to the Virgin of Chartres," *Henry Adams: Letters to a Niece*, ed. Mabel LeFarge (Boston: Houghton Mifflin, 1920), 131; B. Adams: *The Emancipation of Massachusetts* (Boston: Houghton Mifflin, 1887), *passim*; "Can War Be Done Away With?" *Publications: American Sociological Society*, X (Dec., 1915), 106, 115; B. Adams quoted in M. DeWolfe Howe, *Who Lived Here* (Boston: Little, Brown, 1952), 12.

316. Lowell, *Writings*, I, 76–77; Norton: "Lack," 636–40; "Reminiscences," 11–23; O. W. Holmes, *A Moral Antipathy* (Boston: Houghton Mifflin, 1913), 31; C. W. Eliot to Mrs. William James, Feb. 6, 1900, in James, *Charles W. Eliot*, II, 100.

317. Parkman, "Failure," 13; Lowell, *Works*, VI, 25, 36, 96.

318. C. E. Norton to L. Stephen, June 24, 1898, to E. Lee-Childs, June 26, 1898, to Ward, Oct. 10, 1898, to Godkin, July 7, 1900, to W. L. Mackenzie King, Jan. 26, 1903, in Norton, *Letters*, II, 270–73, 276, 293–94, 333; Norton: "Some Aspects," 654; "Memorials," 101–2; "The Public Life and Services of William Eustis Russell," *Harvard Graduates Magazine*, V (Dec., 1896), 191; Wendell, *Privileged*, 112, 114.

319. Harold Clark Durell, "John Torrey Morse," *New England Historical and Genealogical Register*, XCI (Oct., 1937), 307–12; Frederick C. Shattuck, "William Sturgis Bigelow," *Proceedings: Massachusetts Historical Society*, LX (Nov., 1926), 15–19; H. Adams, *Education*, 103, 301–8, 327, 382.

320. J. T. Morse to H. C. Lodge, Mar. 20, 1892, May 14, 1918, W. S. Bigelow to Lodge, Apr. 3, 1912, F. C. Shattuck to Lodge, Apr. 28, 1921, Lodge Papers; H. Adams to Gaskell, Jan. 4, 1897, to Mrs. Cameron, Feb. 7, 1904, Feb. 8, 1904, to Mrs. Chanler, Aug. 11, 1905, to Mrs. Cameron, Jan. 13, 1910, to C. F. Adams, Jr., Nov. 10, 1911, in Ford, ed., *Adams Letters*, II, 120, 423–24, 529, 547, 576; B. Adams to H. Adams, Sept. 21, 1893, June 24, 1895, Oct. 13, 1895, Aug. 17, 1896, July 5, 1901, Dec. 21, 1899, Oct. 6, 1904, Mar. 20, 1915, B. Adams to M. DeWolfe Howe, June 22, 1921, B. Adams Letters.

321. J. T. Morse to Lodge, Mar. 20, 1892, Nov. 14, 1892, May 14, 1898, Jan. 3, 1912, May 14, 1920, W. S. Bigelow to Lodge, Apr. 3, 1912, May 30, 1912, May 21, 1913, Feb. 20, 1913, June 3, 1918, Lodge Papers; H. Adams, *Degradation*, *passim*; H. Adams to E. H. Davis, Feb. 3, 1911, Jan. 12, 1912, *Yale Review*, XI (1921), 220; H. Adams to B. Adams, Sept. ?, 1895, to Mrs. Cameron, Aug. 4, 1896, to B. Adams, June 11, 1897, June 11, 1898, to Mrs. Cameron, June 25, 1903, Feb. 7, 1904, Aug. 20, 1905, to Mrs. Chanler, Apr. 11, 1909, to B. Adams, Sept. 20, 1910, Nov. 11, 1910, to Mrs. Cameron, June 22, 1911, in Ford, ed., *Adams Letters*, II, 82–83, 114–15, 129–30, 184n, 393, 424, 460, 517,

549, 551, 570; H. Adams to Gaskell, Dec. 17, 1908, in Cater, *Adams and Friends*, 514; Adams, *Education*, 343–44, 384–85, 388, 396; B. Adams: *Civilization and Decay: The Theory of Social Revolutions* (New York: Macmillan, 1913), *passim; Emancipation*, 1919 ed., 152–67; "Collective Thinking in America," *Yale Review*, VIII (Apr., 1919), 623–40; "The Heritage of Henry Adams," Introductory Note, in H. Adams, *Degradation;* "Can War," 103–24; B. Adams to H. Adams, Mar. 7, 1896, Apr. 22, 1896, July 12, 1896, July 2, 1905, Jan. 9, 1906, Apr. 15, 1908, Feb. 10, 1910, Mar. 2, 1910, B. Adams Letters.

322. For a discussion of this point see Louis Hartz, *The Liberal Tradition in America: An Interpretation of American Political Thought Since the Revolution* (New York: Harcourt, Brace, 1955).

323. Rollin Gustav Osterweis, *Romanticism and Nationalism in the Old South* (New Haven: Yale University Press, 1949); William R. Taylor, *Cavalier and Yankee: The Old South and American National Character* (New York: Doubleday, 1961); Hartz, *Liberal*, 145–200.

324. J. M. Forbes, paper possibly written in 1895, *Letters (Supplementary)*, III, 296–97; Charles Eliot Perkins to H. L. Higginson, Mar. 8, 1900, H. L. Higginson to C. W. Eliot, Dec. 15, 1914, in Perry, *Henry Lee Higginson*, 433–34, 442–43; Higginson to Lodge, Oct. 19, 1907, Feb. 19, 1908, Lodge Papers.

325. W. Lawrence, *Life of Amos Lawrence, passim;* T. W. Higginson, *Part of a Man's Life* (Boston: Houghton Mifflin, 1905), 103–4, 110; C. W. Eliot, "Why," 58; Yeomans, *Abbott Lawrence Lowell*, 233–35; Oliver Wendell Holmes, Jr., to Sir Frederick Pollack, Aug. 10, 1908, Sept. 1, 1910, Dec. 31, 1911, in M. DeWolfe Howe, Jr., ed., *Holmes-Pollack Letters*, 2 vols. (Cambridge: Harvard University Press, 1941), I, 141, 167, 187; Holmes to Dr. John C. H. Wu, June 21, 1908, *Justice Holmes to Dr. Wu* (New York: Central Book, n.d.), 48.

326. C. W. Eliot to H. L. Higginson, Mar. 31, 1896, Charles William Eliot Letters, Houghton Library; Eliot to ?, Nov. 7, 1910, in James, *Charles William Eliot*, II, 206; Eliot, *Merit System*, 6, 10; Morison, *Three Centuries*, 417–18, 477–79; Yeomans, *Abbott Lawrence Lowell*, 166, 169–70, 174, 183; O. W. Holmes, *Collected Legal Papers* (New York: Harcourt, Brace & World, 1920), 167–202, 210–43, 310–16; Holmes, *The Common Law* (Cambridge: Harvard University Press, 1963), *passim.*

327. On the defense of the Chinese see J. M. Forbes to G. F. Hoar, Apr. 2, 1882, *Letters (Supplementary)*, III, 174. For praise of the Irish see T. W. Higginson, *Cheerful*, 345–46; C. W. Eliot, *America's Contributions to Civilization* (New York: Century, 1897), 130–31; Eliot to ?, Nov. 21, 1892, in James, *Charles William Eliot*, II, 52–54. For views on capital and labor see T. W. Higginson, *Atlantic Essays* (Boston: James R. Osgood, 1871), 25; C. W. Eliot, *The Fortunate or Happy Conditions for a Life of Labor* (n.p.: Electrical Manufacturers Club, 1913), 23–24; A. L. Lowell, *Facts and Visions* (Cambridge: Harvard University Press, 1944), 154–55.

328. T. W. Higginson: *Atlantic*, 65; *Part*, 300–302. C. W. Eliot to L.B.R. Briggs, Mar. 13, 1901, to C. F. Adams, June 9, 1904, to James Bryce, Nov. 13, 1916, Mar. 6, 1918, in James, *Charles William Eliot*, II, 134–35, 150–51, 271, 279; Eliot, "Inaugural Address," 68–69; B. Wendell, "Conflict of Idolatries," *Harvard Graduates Magazine*, XXVII (Sept., 1918), 4, 15–16; Yeomans, *Abbott Lawrence Lowell*, 166, 169–70, 174, 183; Morison, *Three Centuries*, 417–18,

477–79; Lodge to Morse, Apr. 7, 1921, to B. Adams, Feb. 5, 1918, Lodge Papers; O. W. Holmes, Jr., to Pollack, Jan. 28, 1914, *Holmes-Pollack*, I, 211.

329. T. W. Higginson, *Cheerful*, 362–63; Lodge, "Journal," Jan. 19 ,1887, Dec. 20, 1890, Lodge to B. Adams, Feb. 5, 1918, to Mrs. Chanler, Sept. 9, 1921, Lodge Papers; Holmes to Pollack, Jan. 17, 1887, Mar. 22, 1891, Aug. 9, 1897, July 31, 1902, Dec. 28, 1902, Dec. 31, 1911, Mar. 24, 1915, Dec. 11, 1928, Apr. 5, 1932, *Holmes-Pollack*, I, 30, 37, 75–77, 102, 187, 235, II, 234, 307, and *passim*; M. DeWolfe Howe, ed., *Holmes-Laski Letters* (Cambridge: Harvard University Press, 1953), 2 vols., *passim*; Holmes, *Speeches by Oliver Wendell Holmes* (Boston: Little, Brown, 1934), 27, 103; C. W. Eliot: *The Ninetieth Birthday of Charles William Eliot* (Cambridge: Harvard University Press, 1925), 29–30; "Some Reasons," 145; Eliot to William James, Jan. 20, 1895, to James Fords Rhodes, Mar. 25, 1914, to C. F. Adams, Apr. 26, 1914, to Bryce, Jan. 6, 1920, Sept. 20, 1921, in James, *Charles William Eliot*, II, 86–87, 237–39, 281, 296; A. L. Lowell, *Facts*, 10, 37, 41, 120–30, 154–55; Lowell quoted in Yeomans, *Abbott Lawrence Lowell*, 398.

330. C. F. Adams quoted in Kirkland, *Patrician*, 79–80; Adams: *Chapters of Erie* (Ithaca: Great Seal Books, 1946), 95–98, 135–39; "The Railroad System," *North American Review*, CIV (Apr., 1867), 492–93, 502; *Railroads: Their Origin and Purpose* (New York: G. P. Putnam's Sons, 1888), 78ff.; C. F. Adams to T. W. Higgins, May 9, 1882, in C. F. Adams, Jr., Letters, Houghton Library; Adams, "Boston," *North American Review*, CIV (Apr., 1867), 1–25, 557–91.

331. C. F. Adams, Jr., *Autobiography*, 190–95, 198, 202, 210–11; Adams quoted in Kirkland, *Patrician*, 127, 178–79, 185, 219; *ibid.*, 178–84.

CHAPTER III

Sweeping statements about class behavior obscure the variety of responses that different environments elicit from enclaves of the same social stratum. The life-styles of court and country nobility in England and France, for example, often diverged more than that of urban merchant and royal courtier. A comparison of New York's successive and competing leadership groups—with each other and with the Brahmins—indicates significant variations in upper strata from different urban contexts. These enclaves differ in origins, velocity of status and personnel changes, beliefs, and behavior.

Long-lived hegemonous groups neutralize the challenge of new men either by co-option or by effective exclusion. Persistence creates a stable, homogeneous leadership structure. Genteel Boston and Philadelphia were powerful upper classes through most of the nineteenth century. The greater magnitude and speed of social and economic change in New York, however, encouraged a circulation and fragmentation of elites. Descendants from prominent colonial and federal families composed the "Knickerbocker set," the dominant echelon of the second quarter of the nineteenth century was the great overseas merchants, and post–Civil War banking and railroad clans constituted yet another exalted circle. These New Yorkers lacked the institutional and familial solidarity and continuity of patriciates in the other cities. Fading enclaves disintegrated as renegade members deserted to stronger and wealthier *arrivistes*. Conversely, power, unity, and perpetuity enable elites to expand their sovereignty and bequeath it to descendants. The demise of the colonial-federal families, substantially complete by 1810, terminated aristocratic control over a broad range of urban activities. Subsequent elites controlled or contended for control of trade, politics, culture, or fashion, and some overlap existed among these groups, but none developed into an aristocracy by prolonging its multifaceted leadership for several generations.

COLONIAL BACKGROUND

The "better sort" in New York, one of the more aristocratic colonies in North America, constituted an intimately connected group of manorial grandees, overseas merchants, and leading lawyers. The majority of the eminent clans (Morrises, Philipses, Schuylers, Van Rensselaers, Van Cortlandts, Beekmans, Livingstons, and Delanceys) established themselves by 1700. They controlled land patents, high military and civil offices, and mercantile regulations and operations, and achieved wealth, social standing, and influence with the royal administration. Each facet of their leadership reinforced the others, and the whole was fortified by intermarriage. Dynastic upheaval in England, rebellious outsiders, reforming royal governors, even rifts within the elite failed to dissipate their sovereignty.

The early patriciate resembled the southern gentry rather than the Puritan merchants, magistrates, and ministers who ruled seventeenth-century Massachusetts Bay Colony. Huge land grants in the Hudson Valley enabled estate proprietors to live in baronial splendor that rivaled the planters of Virginia and South Carolina and rarely existed in relatively egalitarian New England. Primogeniture and entail sometimes kept large concentrations of real property in eighteenth-century New York and the South from being divided or alienated, thus preserving inherited economic and social position. In New England, except for Rhode Island, partible descent was the custom, making it more difficult to bequeath family estates intact and to maintain a landed gentry.[1] New York politics, dominated by city merchants and great landlords, was also more elitist than the Massachusetts government. The governor's council was typically the aristocratic stronghold in the colonies. New York councillors, like those in Virginia and South Carolina, came from older and richer families than did their Massachusetts counterparts. "The New England Governments are all formed on Republican Principles," asserted Lieutenant Governor Cadwallader Colden. "The Government of New York on the contrary is established as nearly as may be after the model of the English Constitution."[2]

The Landed Gentry

The Pells, Morrises, Lawrences, Van Rensselaers, and other family-founding proprietors of the great estates in Long Island and the Hudson

Valley, like the initial Tidewater dynasts, usually came from prosperous burgher or yeoman antecedents. A minority, however, had more humble roots: Frederick Philipse began as a carpenter; Philip Pietersen Schuyler's father was a baker; Robert Livingston, son of a minister, started as a bookkeeper; Oloff Stevense Van Cortlandt came to New Amsterdam as a soldier in the Dutch West India Company. As indicated by family background, the landed gentry, sharing another characteristic of the southern planters, involved itself in commerce. Livingston, Van Cortlandt, Kiliaen Van Rensselaer, Philipse (the most prominent merchant of his time), Schuyler, and John Lawrence (the Long Island grandee) bought their land with profits made in trade. Livingston, Nicholas Bayard, and William Beekman started as merchants, and Lewis Morris had been a trader-planter in the West Indies. Their descendants, even after several generations in the squirearchy, continued in commerce and intermarried with the maritime elite of New York City. Country estates contained flour mills and breweries, and their proprietors lent money, trafficked in furs, and owned ships. The gentry themselves or through offspring in commerce traded the products from their rural properties. Virtually every great landed clan also ranked among the foremost mercantile families of the province. They lived more in New York City (the Philipses, Van Cortlandts, Beekmans, and Bayards) and Albany (the Schuylers) than on their estates. The first two generations of Van Cortlandts and Philipses were absentee landlords whose urban operations overshadowed agricultural interests; the Beekmans and Bayards were primarily commercial clans; the Livingstons distributed their talents equally in trade, law, and land; and Schuylers and Van Rensselaers belonged to the New York City maritime elite. Extensive urban real estate holdings forged another tie between the landlords and the cities.[3]

Political power promoted the enterprises of the landed and mercantile magnates. Officeholding and influence with British officials enabled them to obtain patents, franchises, and military supply contracts, and to receive the government protection that increased fortune and power. The aristocratic nature of the political system was manifested by widespread nepotism, placing successive generations of consanguine upper-class families in high public posts. Of 137 top executive, legislative, and judicial officers between 1750 and 1776, 110 (80 percent) were from the great landowning families.[4] Patrician predominance did not exclude intramural rivalries over offices, influence, and economic advantages, and between Dutch and English economic and political leaders. But factionalism, except for the Leisler Rebellion, did not lead to fundamental rifts until the Revolution. Shifting alliances, common agreement over class sovereignty and political legitimacy, kinship, and the absence, until the end of the provincial period, of well-organized opposition to the great merchants and landlords, prevented such clashes from threatening the ruling order.[5]

English administrators (and those who identified with them), although dependent on the indigenous elite, often felt frustrated by its power. Colden complained that "the leading Men of the Country" had engrossed most of the land in New York for "trifling Quit Rents" because they controlled the assembly and "forced the Governor and Council to yield" in order to get "financial support" from the landlords. Despite Colden's attacks and manorial and mercantile influence, the assembly was less elite than other branches of the government. A recent student of provincial politics estimates that a substantial minority of the legislators were prosperous yeomen and country shopkeepers. Royal officials, Colden, in another mood, and Governor George Clinton worried about the democratic learning and lower-class composition of this body.[6]

The judiciary and the council were less uncertain aristocratic bastions. "The persons of most Independence [wealth] here are the Descendants of the first Settlers of the country . . . related to all the best families in the Province," declared Governor Henry Moore in 1767; "from such connections, and from their own Landed Interests, it must frequently happen in causes of consequence where Land is the subject of contention, that they or some of their relations will be eventually interested and Justice delayed by the Judges being unqualified to sit." Colden agreed: the "Judges & Principal Practitioners at the Bar, are either [land] Owners' Heirs or strongly connected in family Interest with the Proprietors," and uphold the landlords against "the Executive powers of Government."[7] The bench and the bar were also intimately connected with the great merchants and defended maritime as well as landed interests. Livingstons, Morrises, Van Cortlandts, DePeysters, DeLanceys, Smiths, Lawrences, and Philipses sat on the supreme court. Along with other prominent merchants and lawyers, they received appointments to the vice-admiralty and lesser tribunals and as attorney generals. Kinship frequently determined the course of justice as lawyers, judges, defendants, and plaintiffs often came from interrelated upper-class clans.[8]

From its inception representatives of eminent families held the majority of places on the council. Governor Moore nominated Robert R. Livingston because: "He is a branch of the most considerable family in this Province; his father [has a] great landed Estate, which will come to him, undivided, as he is an only son. He is married to the richest Heiress in this Country" and "must very shortly be the greatest Landholder without any exception, in this province;" which "cannot fail of giving him great weight here, and puts it very much in his power to support the

Government."[9] Moore also noted that Livingston had sat in the assembly and on the supreme court. In short, he had the aristocratic credentials necessary for a councillor.

The Hudson Valley and Long Island merchant-barons and their relatives also played important political roles in New York City and in Albany, thus serving their urban commercial interests. In New York City, between 1653 and 1700, Oloff S. Van Cortlandt, John Lawrence, Philip Schuyler's father-in-law, and Nicholas Bayard became burgomasters and mayors, and others, e.g., Frederick Philipse, occupied lesser posts. Among the eighteenth-century mayors were sons of Van Cortlandt and Bayard, manorial grandee Caleb Heathcote, and prominent merchants William Beekman, Abraham and Johannes DePeyster, David Provoost, John Cruger, and John Cruger, Jr. Many maritime leaders were business associates and kin of the landlords, and the urban branch of the Livingstons furnished aldermen and assemblymen.[10]

The Lawyers

For Colden the upper strata consisted of "First the Proprietors of the large Tracts of Land," "Second The Gentlemen of the Law," "The Merchants make the third class."[11] Leading seventeenth-century lawyers, however, rarely came from or established distinguished families, and New York City magistrates and judges of the vice-admiralty and supreme courts initially were laymen. In later years the vocation advanced in prestige and power and attracted the upper class. College-educated lawyers became increasingly frequent; between 1758 and 1781 one-fourth of the graduates of King's College went into the profession. After the 1690s virtually all vice-admiralty justices were lawyers and so were most supreme court judges after the 1730s. The recorder (corporation counsel) of New York City was invariably a lawyer, and several holders of that office served simultaneously on the governor's council. Offspring of the Smith, Livingston, Watts, Jay, Morris, and Delancey families embarked on legal careers, served in high judicial and political posts, and counseled the landed and maritime elites.[12] Apart from enhancing the power and purses of their class and tending their own political and commercial interests, patrician attorneys sought to upgrade their profession. William Livingston and William Smith, Jr., believed that classical learning was necessary for lawyers and in the 1760s led the fight to raise education requirements and licensing standards. Along with other patrician barristers, they founded the New York Moot, a society devoted to discussing the law and elevating professional standards. Its deliberations influenced court decisions. Attempts at improvement aimed to weed out the incompetent, and, through licensing (thus controlling admission to the bar), to make the law a gentleman's career.

Longer terms of apprenticeship and a baccalaureate prerequisite would exclude the poor and base-born. But the genteel reformers were unable to make their wishes legal regulations, and the supreme court set shorter training periods and lower levels of education.

Elite practitioners in colonial New York and Boston had similar aspirations. Suffolk County attorneys also sought to elevate educational and admission requirements for the profession. New York's bar, however, largely due to Puritan hostility toward lawyers, achieved considerably higher status than did its New England counterpart. The New York Bar Association (1748) began ten years before its Suffolk County equivalent and served as a model for the latter. Between 1761 and 1780 the share of Harvard graduates entering the legal profession constituted one-half that of King's College alumni who became lawyers. And only six of the thirty-three Massachusetts supreme court judges between 1692 and 1776 were trained lawyers, far fewer than among the New York supreme court justices during the same period.[13]

The Merchants

Colden's distinctions among upper-class New Yorkers meant little because mutual interests and kinship intertwined these groups. Agrarian aristocrats participated in commerce; conversely, leading urban businessmen frequently acquired vast up-country estates and speculated extensively in interior and city holdings, sometimes jointly with manorial lords.[14] The upper strata also cooperated in politics. Ruling-class factionalism never took the form of city-country conflicts; the elite divided into cliques that included lawyers, merchants, and landowners. Upper-class solidity emerged from even more intimate connections. New York's foremost commercial clans—the DeLanceys, Rays, Whites, Provoosts, DePeysters, Van Dams, Jays, Wattses, and Verplancks—intermarried with Hudson Valley barons as well as with each other, and eminent lawyers came from both enclaves.

The rural and urban elites stemmed from the same middle-class antecedents. Under Dutch rule, merchants, Dutch West India Company officials, and large landholders constituted the urban upper order. The leading men—the Van Rensselaers, Stuyvesants, DePeysters, Kips, and Rutgerses—had usually been ministers, officials, merchants, and scholars in Holland. Few of the gentry emigrated, but several members of the inner circle rose from humble origins. Govert Loockermans had been a cook's mate and Hendrick Kip a tailor. Regardless of former status, kinship soon united the prominent families. Later additions to the upper class also came from primarily the middle class, some from comfortable yeoman and burgher stock, others self-made. Among the former were Augustus Jay, John and Henry Cruger, Jonathan Fish, Thomas Buchanan, Theophylact Bache, and the Delafields and Clarksons. The Barclays and DeLanceys, who derived respectively from high military and civil officials in England and wealthy minor French nobles, were among the few with more distinguished ancestry. Like their counterparts in Boston, the founders of the American branches of these families sometimes had relatives in British and Dutch overseas trading houses. James Jauncey, Henry White, Elias Desbrosses, and Abraham Isaac Verplanck, who made their own fortunes, indicated that the city's commercial growth provided opportunities for new men. During the eighteenth century, the mercantile enclave was the most accessible sector of the upper class. Jackson Turner Main, studying the backgrounds of early members (1768–69) of the New York Chamber of Commerce, an organization of merchants with great wealth and high status, concluded that 45 percent belonged to the colonial aristocracy, 15 percent to good families, and one-third to two-fifths were self-made, a distribution similar to that of contemporary business elites in Boston and Philadelphia.[15]

Initially the upper class was mostly Dutch, but New York City quickly became a center of varied nationalities and this ethnic diversity permeated the upper stratum. French Huguenots (Delanceys, Jays, and Pintards), English and Scots (Fishes, Waltons, Smiths, Barclays, Delafields, and Clarksons), and Germans (Beekmans) gave the patriciate a heterogeneity lacking in Anglo-Saxon Boston.[16]

Great merchants and landholders accumulated the largest fortunes in New York City. Among the highest taxpayers in 1655 were traders Govert Loockermans, Johannes DePeyster, several Kips, William Beekman, and Jeremias Van Rensselaer. The tax lists of 1674 and 1676 were topped by Frederick Philipse, Oloff S. Van Cortlandt, John Lawrence, DePeyster, Jacob Leisler, and other members of the maritime-landed elite. The wealthiest citizens on the assessment roll of 1730 included the DePeyster, Roosevelt, Beekman, Philipse, Bayard, Delancey, Clarkson, Schuyler, Van Cortlandt, and Jay families—a majority of merchants interspersed with a few landed gentlemen. The tax lists of 1664 and 1676 show a significant penetration of English merchants into the upper ranks of wealth over the twelve-year span, a consequence of the British conquest of New Netherland. These rolls also indicate the elitist structure (compared to New England) of the colony. The richest 5 percent of the 1676 taxables in New York City and in Boston in 1687 owned 39 and 27 percent of the assessed wealth in their respective cities in these years.[17]

New York merchants (for the same reasons as their Boston equivalents) pursued wealth by forming partnerships with friends and relatives or through family firms. Relatives staffed branch offices in other North

American cities and at strategic points along foreign shipping routes, forged ties between European and American trading houses, and provided access to goods from the interior. Young kinsmen acquired experience as clerks, ship captains, and agents, and then benefited from the influence of their elders when they launched their own enterprises or took over established firms.[18]

Overseas traders, like those in Boston and the rural gentry, diversified their operations. They speculated in urban lots and wilderness tracts, lent money, and were the major holders of municipal bonds. Government influence enlarged these interests, and the commercial elite shaped public policy through officeholding, business association, and family ties. From the beginning the merchants dominated municipal government. The ten mayors between 1665 and 1673 and five of the eight between 1731 and 1746 were merchants; great traders proliferated on municipal councils from Stuyvesant's Nine Men to the board of aldermen and represented the city in the assembly. Prominent merchants and their allies sat on the mayor's court and the court of admiralty and filled many other strategic government positions. The maritime elite also controlled key provincial offices. Bayards, Van Dams, Kips, DeLanceys, DePeysters, Crugers, Beekmans, Henry White, William Wallace, William Walton, John Watts, and other merchants were secretaries and treasurers of the colony, high court judges, councillors, and lieutenant and acting governors. Throughout the provincial era, landlords and New York City merchants dominated the council. British governors allied with the magnates to gain profits while in office and to get supplies for their troops. Political leverage on the local and colonial level secured permission to build public markets, pave streets, acquire water rights, construct roads and bridges, obtain land grants and trading privileges, provision the armed forces, and enabled merchants to defy maritime restrictions.[19]

British officials complained about the power of the merchants as they did about the influence of the landowners. Governors George Clinton and Henry Moore argued that "the Assembly is directed by Merchants" who thus "weaken the Administration, by which these Laws [of trade] are to be put in execution," by "mak[ing] the [customs] Officers sensible, that the only way for them to prosper, or to be rewarded, is by neglecting their duty, and that they must suffer by a performance of it." Despite these feelings, the merchants, as did the landed gentry, received appointments because of wealth and social status. "He is in every way qualified for the post," wrote Governor James Montgomerie, justifying his choice of Stephen DeLancey for the council; "his father is an eminent merchant, a member of the Assembly, one of the richest men of the province, and he his eldest son." DeLancey also had other credentials: a Van Cortlandt mother, a Heathcote wife, large estates in Manhattan, and vast holdings in Westchester and Ulster counties.[20]

Institutions and Life-Style

The urban elite displayed, through wealth, distinctive life-style, civic leadership, institutional cohesion, intermarriage, and convivial activity, the attributes typical of a metropolitan ruling class. The fortunes of Oliver DeLancey (£100,000), William Bayard (£75,000), James Beekman (£25,000), John Watts (£20,000), and others enabled them to cluster in fashionable neighborhoods, reside in imposing mansions, entertain lavishly, own carriages, and dress resplendently. Unlike rich Bostonians, affluent New Yorkers hunted, raced and bred horses, and attended the theater. Less somber than the New Englanders, they were not scandalized by gambling or dancing. Waltons and Livingstons served as managers of the Dancing Assembly in the 1750s and '60s.[21] Men of substance enlivened their leisure in relaxed surroundings at taverns and the weekly meetings of the Social Club. The fashionable and sophisticated existence of New York's merchants led Governor Francis Lovelace, in 1688, to assert that "these people have the breeding of courts. . . ." But patricians of a more serious turn of mind, annoyed at "noisy fops," organized the Society for the Promotion of Useful Knowledge where they improved their "valuable moments in useful knowledge."[22]

In addition to widely if not universally shared social customs and habits, the aristocracy strengthened its leadership and cohesion by founding a series of voluntary associations that increased patrician influence over urban life and reinforced upper-class values. Although these organizations varied in function, their overlapping membership came primarily from distinguished mercantile clans supplemented by socially and professionally prominent lawyers of the same families. The New York Chamber of Commerce (1768) exemplifies the point. It was formed by the maritime elite to protect business enterprise by encouraging integrity in commercial contracts and a stable currency system. The pre-Revolutionary presidents were great merchants and assumed other leadership roles: John Cruger, Jr., served as mayor and speaker of the assembly; Wallace, White, and Walton were councillors; Elias DesBroses was an alderman and a warden and vestryman of Trinity Church; Theophylact Bache was also a Trinity vestryman and president of the St. George Society and Society of New York Hospital; Isaac Low attended the continental congress. Most of its leaders and many members, ornaments of the colonial establishment, became Tories.[23]

Commercial support and solidarity were not the only types of cohesion offered by upper-class associations. Trinity (1698) was the mother church of the Episcopal Diocese of New York. After the English conquest, notable Dutch Reformed and French Huguenot families—Provoosts, DeLanceys, DePeysters, and others—converted to Anglicanism, thus enhancing sectarian unity in the establishment. Along with the Morrises, Heathcotes, and other prominent New Yorkers, they became vestrymen and important donors. Henry Barclay, the second rector, married a DeLancey and sired a family of famous merchants, and David Provoost served as an associate minister shortly before the Revolution. Rectors and ministers of Trinity sanctified the rites of passage for the aristocracy by officiating at baptisms, marriages, and funerals, and burying the foremost parishioners in the churchyard. Inherited status was reinforced through intergenerational ownership of family pews. Institutional guardian of upper-class religion, Trinity opposed the Leisler faction and joined the chamber of commerce in backing the British during the war for independence.[24]

Trinity's tie with King's College (1754) was characteristic of the interaction among upper-class institutions. The church gave the land on which the college was built, seven of the original trustees were Trinity vestrymen, commencement exercises were held there, and Samuel Johnson, first King's College president, was an assistant minister at Trinity. King's College, now Columbia University, was also linked to other upper-class organizations. Before the Revolution four of the original eight trustees of the New York Society Library and sixteen merchants, including Henry and John Cruger, White, and Walton, served on its board of governors. Patricians studied at King's and the elite gave crucial financial support. The school soon became an educational emblem of the urban gentry and won Colden's praise for "prevent[ing] the growth of Republican Principles which already too much prevail in the Colonies." Colden correctly labeled King's an establishment stronghold, but its founding precipitated a conflict typical of upper-class factionalism. William Livingston, William Smith, and John Morin Scott became embroiled with the James DeLancey group over the terms of the charter. This struggle disclosed the limits of religious and political harmony within the upper order. The Whig triumverate opposed the pro–royal government DeLancey party, and, as Presbyterians, they feared that the college might become an Anglican sanctuary. A compromise settlement provided for a minority on the board to represent the Dutch Reformed and Presbyterian faiths.[25]

Livingston and Smith, still wary of Episcopalian influence, founded the Society Library (1754) as a Presbyterian cultural counterweight to the college. The library was quickly infiltrated by Anglican merchants: fifty-seven of the first eighty-three subscribers were traders, and Crugers, Wattses, Waltons, Barclays, and DeLanceys preponderated among the trustees.[26]

Upper-class organizations looked outward to the needs of the community as well as serving the special interests or concerns of their own group. During the seventeenth century, leading men assisted the indigent by becoming overseers of the poor, or, as aldermen, by supplementing public funds with private contributions. By the early 1700s the administration of municipal relief centered in the common council and the wardens and vestry of Trinity Parish. Wealthy parishioners sometimes left bequests for the poor and the church also conducted a charity school for orphans and destitute children.[27] More specialized forms of charity emerged later in the colonial era. In 1756 merchants Philip Livingston, Andrew and Henry Barclay, James Murray, and John Watts, lawyers William Livingston and John Morin Scott, and other patricians incorporated St. Andrew's Society. Boston, Philadelphia, Charleston, and Savannah already had such societies and the founders used the Philadelphia organization as their model. The New York version assisted and secured employment for needy Scotsmen. The Marine Society (1769) cared for sailors' widows and orphans and aided poor seamen. Its initiators and officers came from the same group and were sometimes the same people who formed and headed the chamber of commerce and St. Andrew's.[28] In 1771 patrician benefactors, many of them active in the other welfare associations, prompted by a suggestion originally made in Trinity Church, incorporated the Society of New York Hospital. The hospital began as a "charitable institution" for "the poor diseased who are so indigent as to be helpless without the public aid. . . ." Eighty of the ninety-two founders of the society were merchants; its first president, John Watts, and virtually all the pre-Revolutionary board of governors, came from the maritime elite.[29]

While the New Yorkers were less socially inhibited than the Bostonians, the latter city had a superior intellectual atmosphere. The Dutch settlers, unlike the Puritans, were not a bookish people, and even after the English conquest, Boston and Philadelphia continued to surpass New York as an educational and cultural center. "Tho' the province of New York abounds certainly more in riches than any other of the northern colonies," wrote Colden in 1748, "yet there has been less care to propagate knowledge or learning. The only principle of life propagated among the young people is to get money, and men are esteemed according to what they are worth. . . ."[30] Intellectual deficiencies and a passion for money-making did not prevent New York's urban elite from manifesting a civic responsibility comparable to that of the genteel Bostonians. Assuming identical communal obligations, both enclaves founded corresponding institutions, King's Chapel and Trinity Church, Harvard and King's colleges, Massachusetts General and the Society of New York hospitals.

Boston and New York upper classes exhibited other common features. Primarily maritime elites, their businesses were structured along similar lines: each achieved integration through close commercial and kinship ties; they wielded substantial political power and dominated the same branches of government; finally, both were open to new men. The patriciates resembled each other far more than they diverged, but New York's upper class was more varied ethnically, more frivolous, and less intellectual than its Boston peers. More important, the mercantile elite merged with the landed gentry, making the colony a city-state with a more powerful and cohesive aristocracy than emerged from the interior village and port-town elites in Massachusetts Bay.

Nevertheless, the sovereignty of the landed-mercantile upper order was limited by internal cleavages, opposition from outsiders, and issues and areas where the establishment did not intervene. The king's representatives and their provincial adherents increasingly desired an orderly state of affairs, which meant peace with the Indians, restricted penetration into the wilderness, resistance to large land grants, and obedience to trade regulations. These policies set the aristocratic segment that identified with officialdom against those politicians, landowners, and entrepreneurs who maximized their wealth and influence by measures that interfered with the strategies and undermined the power of the British and their allies. On the other hand, alliance with royal rule provided an alternative route to economic benefits and political power. Consequently, the political situation remained fluid. The leading factions repeatedly switched sides, at one time constituting the court party; at another, confronting it. These squabbles were dominated by aristocratic chieftains, but during Leisler's Rebellion and increasingly after the 1720s, they afforded opportunities for the lower ranks to participate in politics and obtain the advantages of government influence. Opponents of the royal administration increasingly appealed to egalitarian sentiments and sought to enlist the support of the middle classes. Dissension in the higher echelons thus led to concrete, if often temporary, gains such as curtailment of commercial monopolies, tax relief for interior merchants at the expense of those from New York, and the defeat of landowners by yeomen in assembly elections. The other important breach in aristocratic rule was the capacity of lower strata to retain some autonomy in personal and local concerns. Middle-class officials filled most of the public posts in the counties, towns, and villages outside of New York City and ran the daily affairs of their communities. The great landlords, their grandeur and influence notwithstanding, complained about recurrent difficulties in collecting rents and evicting squatters.[31]

If the upper class did not reign supreme nor exist as a harmonious entity, it dominated the provincial polity and economy. Different factions were always headed by distinguished families, and advances made by the lower ranks with which they associated were usually impermanent and by-products of the struggle for their own interests. Despite the efforts of English administrators and the resistance of smaller farmers, the landed-maritime elite continued to amass vast acreage, to escape imposts and admiralty laws, and to trade with the enemy. Tenants often avoided rent-collectors, and squatters plagued the landlords, but agrarian uprisings were crushed by the militia and the rebellious arrested and sentenced by establishment-controlled magistrates. As the Revolution approached, however, challenges to the aristocracy became more formidable. An increase of popular appeals and participation, agrarian violence, and electoral defeats of landed gentlemen began in the 1750s, climaxed in insurrection, and culminated in independence. These conflicts disturbed but did not annihilate the upper class. Revolution deposed a considerable segment of the old order, but many survived with purse, power, and position intact.

Numerous patricians opposed independence and went into permanent exile. A large part of upper-class New York left with the British troops, but this departure did not entail an abrupt or complete turnover at the top. Some Tory sympathizers—Theophylact Bache, Frederick DePeyster, and Thomas Buchanan—staying at home or returning after the war, saved the bulk of their property and regained their commercial and social position. Those whose estates were confiscated and who never came back did not necessarily represent a total loss for the aristocracy. Most of the forfeited holdings wound up in the hands of upper-class merchants, landowners, and politicians, frequently acquired by relatives who chose the right side in the conflict. James DeLancey's New York City real estate was bought up by Livingstons, Lawrences, Lewises, Fishes, Roosevelts, and Beekmans; a substantial share of Frederick Philipse's land was obtained by the Van Cortlandts and John Lawrence; Henry White, Jr., purchased a large part of his father's holdings; John Watts's sons bought up his estate; and William Bayard's property was acquired by Nicholas Bayard and Gilbert Van Corlandt. The property of Roger Morris, Henry Wallace, and other aristocrats had the same ultimate disposition. Moreover, much of the upper order backed the Revolution. Many of the above purchasers of Tory estates, along with the Schuylers, Van Rensselaers, Jays, and most of the Morrises, became patriotic leaders and engaged in political and commercial activities that preserved their standing.[32]

Continuity in personnel was matched by institutional continuity. The chamber of commerce, King's College, Trinity Church, the New York Society Library, the Society of New York Hospital, and the St. Andrew's and Marine societies retained their functions, and descendants of the foremost colonial clans continued to direct their activities.

If the persistence of aristocrats and their societies prevented a radical disruption of the upper order, the Revolution had an impact on the ruling class by creating opportunities for new men and by unleashing new political and economic forces. Established arrangements and conditions were unsettled by egalitarian appeals, increased political participation of the middle classes, formation of new government institutions, departure of loyalists and the dispersal of part of their estates into small freeholds, inflation, and the reorientation of trade routes. Changing circumstances undermined traditions of deference and hierarchy and elevated outsiders into the upper class. Thomas Eddy arrived penniless in New York City in 1777 and amassed a fortune handling the monies of those in British prisons; Comfort Sands, previously an unimportant trader, became rich and respected through wartime commercial activity; the conflict also made the fortune and fame of William Duer; Alexander Hamilton's army connections laid the basis for a brilliant career as a lawyer, financier, and statesman. Political as well as business enterprise elevated unknowns to power and prominence. Alexander MacDougall, John Lamb, and Isaac Sears became leaders of the popular party. These achievements were sometimes as temporary as they were spectacular. Sears and Lamb soon slipped back into obscurity, but Eddy, Hamilton, Sands, and Duer made more permanent gains and their descendants appeared in the highest rank of nineteenth-century fashion and affluence.

The entry of the low-born accompanied by the exit of many aristocrats suggests that the Revolution caused a significant, if limited, turnover in the upper class. This conclusion is substantiated by Main's analysis of a sample from those designated "merchants" in the 1786 New York City directory: one-quarter were sons of wealthy landowners or merchants and, at most, another one-tenth derived from well-to-do families. Approximately two-thirds, a substantially higher proportion than in the prewar maritime elite, were self-made. Moreover, Main estimated that one-quarter of the sample had apparently emigrated to the city.[33] Although "merchant" usually meant wealthy wholesalers and the directory differentiated between them and shopkeepers and retailers, Main realized that it probably included some with little property. Accordingly, he made a more precise evaluation of the backgrounds of rich merchants by identifying the wealthy business men on the 1791 tax list for the city's elite East Ward. Coming up with a list comparable to the 1768–69 chamber of commerce membership, he concluded that half had risen from humble beginnings, a rate of mobility significantly higher than in the prewar group.[34] Similar shares of new and old wealth prevailed among pre-Revolutionary Boston and New York merchants, and identical accretions of self-made men appeared in the post-Revolutionary maritime elites, indicating that the impact of the Revolution upon social mobility was the same for mercantile enclaves in both cities.

Changes in upper class composition failed to appreciably alter its habits. Overseas trade remained central to the city's commercial life.

The great merchants still predominated in the urban upper rank, and partnerships and family firms reappeared as the characteristic business organizations. Patrician social life and civic endeavor followed colonial precedents, and the high rate of intermarriage did not vanish after the birth of the republic. As a result of the personal and structural continuities that outlasted the Revolution, newcomers quickly settled into established upper-class ways. Duer and Hamilton wedded daughters of distinguished colonial families and Eddy became active in patrician altruistic organizations. Although the struggle for independence precipitated disintegrative forces, the process of decline was cumulative rather than abrupt. Manors eventually disappeared and colonial families gradually withdrew from commerce and government, but for at least another generation the Old Guard remained potent in business and politics and, for an even longer time, in society.

1780–1860

The Landed Gentry

Although the patriotic gentry kept their holdings, land speculation, soil exhaustion, rent wars, falling agricultural prices, the growing influence of small farmers in the legislature, and the dispersion of confiscated estates gradually resulted in the break-up of large tracts of land into small freeholds. Patents and manors first disappeared in the lower Hudson Valley. Further upstate the squirearchy held on for a longer period, but the Schuyler's Saratoga estate was sold in the 1840s, and by 1850 most of Livingston Manor had been alienated and the last patroon was liquidating his possessions in Rensselaerwyck, the final vestige of the manorial grants.[35]

Even before their estates disappeared, the gentry withdrew from trade. The Beekmans, unable to adjust to new commercial conditions, forsook the sea for urban real estate; the Schuylers, Van Rensselaers, and Van Cortlandts retired to their estates or focused on up-country interests.[36] While patricians still participated in canals, railroads, and Albany banks, except for the Livingston and Lawrence families and one or two Schuyler descendants, they no longer figured significantly in the commercial life of New York City. Philip Livingston became the first president of the New York branch of the Bank of the United States. Robert R. Livingston used his political influence to get a charter for the Manhattan Water Co., an anti-Federalist banking venture, to obtain exclusive steamboat navigation privileges on the Hudson River, and served as an Erie Canal commissioner. The family departed from business during the early national period, but the Lawrences remained eminent capitalists throughout the antebellum era. Members of the clan were bank directors and wealthy merchants: for nineteen years Issac

Lawrence presided over the New York branch of the Second BUS; Cornelius Van Wyck Lawrence, a mayor of the city, headed the Bank of the City of New York and became a trustee of several insurance companies, and collector of the Port of New York.[37] The Lawrences aside, the elites of Albany, New York City, Long Island, and the Hudson Valley ceased to comprise a city-state patriciate; the ruling class now centered in the merchants, industrialists, and bankers of Gotham.

As the landed gentry's economic base withered away, its political influence gradually waned. At first, few hints of eventual eclipse were evident. Between 1789 and 1800 Philip Pietersen Schuyler, Gouverneur Morris, John Lawrence, and John Armstrong (a Livingston brother-in-law) served in the U.S. Senate. Until the War of 1812 Van Rensselaers, Van Cortlandts, and Livingstons regularly appeared in New York's congressional delegation, in the state legislature, at state and federal constitutional conventions, in high judicial positions, on the council of revision, and as canal commissioners. For a generation after independence, kinship politics loomed large in government affairs. This colonial tradition reached its post-Revolutionary apex in the officeholding of the Livingstons and their in-laws. Brockholst Livingston was a state and federal supreme court justice; Robert R. Livingston, chancellor of the state of New York, secretary for foreign affairs, and minister to France; Edward Livingston, a congressman, mayor of New York, minister to France, and secretary of state; and Maturin Livingston, recorder of New York City. In-laws Armstrong, John Jay, James Duane, and Governor Morgan Lewis held an equally imposing array of public posts.[38]

Despite its formidable government positions, the landed aristocracy never fully reasserted its provincial predominance, and, by 1820, although several scions of distinguished families later had notable careers, the enclave had given way to professional politicians of lesser origins and greater constituencies. Signs of weakness appeared even before the demise of the Federalists and at a time when the grandees proliferated in the government. During the 1780s the majority of state assemblymen and senators came from moderate propertied groups; in the colonial legislature the upper class usually preponderated. Moreover, this shift occurred because of an influx of upstate representatives, many from formerly baronial bailiwicks.[39] The patrician position worsened with the triumph of the Democratic-Republicans because most landed-gentry families were Federalists. Even those who belonged to the victorious party did not preserve their power. The Livingstons were ousted by the Clintonians in 1808. The deposition of the Clinton faction in 1820 by the Albany Regency ended the long reign of family dynasties in New York politics.[40]

A confluence of institutional, psychological, and economic factors brought about the political demise of the estate proprietors. A major source of disintegration was the erosion of upper-class assets and influence through shrinking land ownership, withdrawal from commerce, tenant uprisings, squatter encroachment, falling agricultural prices, and comparatively slow population and economic growth in the areas controlled by large landowners. Institutional changes, lower suffrage requirements, increased power of the small farmers in the legislature, elimination of the council of revision, an elite stronghold that acted as a check on the assembly, and displacement of dynastic elites by political machines seeking mass support, also contributed to the decline. Division of large estates into small holdings multiplied the number of yeoman freeholders who, no longer tenants of patentees and manor owners, deferred less to the landlords. Continued immigration of New Englanders, coming from a region of small farmers, further enhanced yeoman independence.[41]

Attenuation of aristocratic rule diminished the ability of large landowners to protect their interests. Notwithstanding the protests of the Beekmans, Morrises, and Livingstons, the assembly confiscated Tory estates, permitted small farmers to purchase forfeited acreage with depreciated state securities, and raised land taxes.[42] The constitutional convention of 1821, where the patriciate was weaker in numbers and influence than in the conventions of 1777 and 1788, enlarged the electorate and increased the power of the lower house.[43] Outraged by their deteriorating situation, landed gentlemen resisted the new forces, but dwindling resources sapped their strength and they could not reverse the inevitable.[44]

Upper-Class Economic Activity in New York City

For a generation after the Revolution, the maritime elites of Boston and New York resembled each other. Each consisted primarily of merchants and bankers with close business and family connections, performed identical civic and political roles, and exhibited similar mobility patterns. Although similarities outweighed differences, the groups were not identical. The superior cultural accomplishment of the Brahmins and the Unitarian creed of the upper-class Bostonians in contrast to the Episcopal beliefs of their New York peers had relatively little effect on the economic behavior of these patriciates. But the comparatively cosmopolitan ethnic and geographic origins of the New Yorkers and the relationship of heterogeneous backgrounds to entrepreneurial vigor and acumen helped determine the fate of these two elites and the outcome of the struggle for commercial preeminence between the ports.

On the eve of independence, New York handled less shipping tonnage than Philadelphia, Boston, and Charleston. Revolution wrought greater havoc there than in the other ports, where British occupation had been briefer and less destructive. The city, however, made a quicker commercial recovery than did Boston because postwar British trade regulations more severely handicapped New England shipping. By 1797 it surpassed Philadelphia and Boston in exports and imports, but New York's lead was not consolidated until the decade of 1815–25. Before then threats of war or actual belligerence and the strategy of Britain and France influenced the flow of goods to and from the Eastern Seaboard. After 1815 the nation settled into a century of peace with Europe, and permanent channels of shipping were established. Stability enhanced New York's advantages in climate, geography, and mercantile resourcefulness.[45]

Physical advantages over Philadelphia and Boston, a relatively ice- and fog-free harbor, fewer storms, better location for coastal and foreign trade, and a richer, more extensive, and more accessible hinterland, were supplemented by technological inventiveness and aggressive entrepreneurship. New York pioneered in finding new markets for American shipping after British restrictions inhibited traditional trading patterns, in improving business methods, and in developing a tributary back-country. The initial commercial expeditions to the Far East (1784 and 1787) embarked from the Hudson River port. The *Empress of China*, which inaugurated the China trade, was partly financed by Philadelphia capitalists and commanded by a Massachusetts mariner, but subsequent initiatives came exclusively from New York. Beginning in 1794 Gotham developed the earliest and fullest use of the auction system for marketing imports. Selling goods by auction, eliminating middlemen between foreign exporters and domestic wholesalers, facilitated the disposal of cargoes and made New York a more attractive entrepot than those of her competitors, who processed merchandise in conventional ways. In 1817 the auction system was completed and perfected by state legislation. Two other events occurring in that year brought uncontested commercial leadership to the city: authorization to build the Erie Canal and formation of the Black Ball Packet Line. Sailing packets were even more important than auctions in directing European goods to New York. The first regularly scheduled freight and passenger service between the United States and Great Britain, the Black Ball Packet Line anticipated viable equivalents in Philadelphia by four years and in Boston by almost twenty-five years.[46] The Erie Canal, completed in 1825 after New York had widened its lead, preserved the city's mastery by diverting western trade from Baltimore and Philadelphia. The canal, begun when the longest American waterway, the Middlesex Canal in Massachusetts, extended for only twenty-eight miles and was in financial trouble, was another triumph of New York enterprise. Once again the other ports responded inefficiently and belatedly. During the 1830s and 1840s Philadelphia, Baltimore, and Boston, using costly combinations of railroads and canals, tried to reach the West, but Philadelphians refused to risk their own capital and relied on insufficient and unwise state funding and planning, and Boston merchants also proved reluctant to invest in routes to the interior.[47]

Failure to innovate in foreign commerce can be construed as demonstrating the wisdom of Boston and Philadelphia businessmen if they concentrated on undertakings where the geographical advantages of New York were irrelevant. New York originated maritime improvements, but Boston Brahmins proved equally inventive when they founded America's modern textile industry. Similarly, many prominent Philadelphia families began because of vigorous entrepreneurship in chemical companies, coal mining, and iron manufacturing between 1800 and 1830.[48] Redirection of talent and energy in other cities, therefore, might explain New York's leadership in packet lines, but it cannot account for the belated adoption of the auction system. More important, New Yorkers achieved dominance in trade during the thirty years (1785–1815) when the issue was fully contested.

New York completely overshadowed its commercial competitors. Although Boston ranked second in foreign commerce during the 1830s and 1840s, she could not protect herself from the encroachments of her overbearing neighbor. Now the richest and most populous urban center and reigning over the best-developed back-country, New York attracted goods bought by Boston merchants and carried in Boston-owned vessels. Beginning in the 1820s Boston tea ships in the Far Eastern trade started to dock in Manhattan and in the 1850s the bulk of Boston's wholesale cotton trade was also marketed there. A contemporary expert estimated that [between 1839 and 1842] "one-third of New York's commerce was carried on Massachusetts' account, or in Massachusetts vessles." According to Samuel Eliot Morison, 23 percent of New York's overseas imports in these years were owned by New Yorkers, while 83 percent of Boston's imports had been bought abroad by local merchants. The New England port relied more exclusively on local resources and its mercantile capital was diverted from its own growth to the expansion of New York commerce. In 1860 two-thirds of the nation's imports and one-third of its exports passed through New York. Textile imports alone exceeded the combined total imports of Boston, Philadelphia, and Baltimore.[49] Primacy in trade led to economic and demographic preeminence. New York passed Philadelphia (1800–10) to become America's largest city in population, and its urban, metropolitan, and hinterland population increased faster than that of Boston or Philadelphia in the antebellum period. Commerce was then the primary factor in capital accumulation, and the nation's shipping and trade center became the chief money market. By every measure of economic growth, rising population, expansion of capital resources, and assessed property values, New York forged ahead of her rivals. This triumph disheartened residents in other cities. The Philadelphia author of an 1859 essay lamenting that city's eclipse in growth of trade, capital, and population, sadly conceded New York's superior energy and initiative in canal and railroad building and in entrepreneurial zeal and inventiveness.[50]

Business supremacy had ancillary economic effects just as important though less easily quantified. Predominance was a magnet that drew the talented, skillful, and ambitious; slower growth rates in other cities afforded fewer opportunities. Philadelphia and Boston and their tributary regions suffered a net loss of human resources to New York, a situation which enabled the latter to widen its lead over other mercantile communities. "All the other cities of the United States are centres of local business," declared a writer in *De Bow's Review* in 1848; "New York, however, is the centre of national capital and trade."[51] He exaggerated New York's hegemony, but the city had become the economic capital of the United States.

TRADE

In an era of unspecialized commercial roles, most financiers, insurance agents, and realtors were former merchants or still continued in that occupation. Until at least the 1840s, trade was the fundamental business activity in New York, and the great merchants were the most revered and the richest entrepreneurs. "This city is the creation of Commerce," said ex-trader Charles King, president of Columbia College and member of a distinguished New York commercial and political clan, and "the merchants of Amsterdam . . . have made it what it is." Attorney George Templeton Strong, another member of the social and economic elite, managed Mrs. William H. Aspinwall's property "because William H. Aspinwall is a rich man and a merchant prince and one of our first citizens, and because I desire that men should say, 'Yes, I know Aspinwall's wife had property in her own right, a man named Strong is her trustee.'"[52] With the praise of eminent lawyers and educators ringing in their ears, it is not surprising that businessmen also proclaimed the primacy of their calling. According to Knickerbocker chamber of commerce president James DePeyster Ogden, "Commerce is ever found to either precede or accompany the march of rational freedom and of equal rights." Auctioneer and mayor Philip Hone declared that Boston and New York "have risen, and prospered, and grown great, upon the foundations which were laid by commerce. Their charitable, scientific, and literary institutions have been, in most instances, funded and endowed by the munificence of merchants." In its own right, even more than through patronage, "commercial enterprise" informs the intellect and "refine[s] the social condition of man." In a place and age that admired commerce above all other vocations, the kings of the countinghouse were considered the finest New Yorkers. John Pintard, merchant, insurance company executive, and institutional trustee, remembered Archibald Gracie as "the most respected merchant in this city . . . esteemed & beloved above every other citizen of his time." Among the living he ranked merchants William Bayard and Matthew Clarkson as the most "highly respected" men in the metropolis. [53]

The repute and resources of the mercantile community were reflected in its domination of the wealthiest stratum of antebellum New Yorkers. According to the most complete and recent study of pre–Civil War affluence in northeastern shipping centers, merchants, auctioneers, brokers, and agents composed 78 percent and 70 percent respectively of the top 1 percent of affluent New Yorkers of 1828 and 1854. [54]

The maritime elite which achieved so much and was rewarded so handsomely consisted of aristocrats from noted colonial stock and newcomers chiefly from the Middle Atlantic and New England states and Europe. The provincial patriciate was represented by LeRoy, Bayard, & Co. (1790), for a time the largest shipping house in the city, and by H. & G. Barclay (1814), by the sugar refineries and hardware and glass emporia of the Roosevelts, by John and Isaac Lawrence and their relatives scattered in thirty New York firms, and by overseas traders William Walton, Jr., Daniel Ludlow, Henry Remsen, David Clarkson, Nicholas Cruger, Francis Lewis, Jr., and Peter Schermerhorn. Clarksons, Bayards, Lawrences, and Barclays were multigenerational aristocrats; Roosevelts and Remsens had ranked just below them in the provincial hierarchy; Walton, Schermerhorn, and Lewis had fathers or uncles who reached the pinnacle shortly before the Revolution. This enclave persisted because personal property did not suffer as much confiscation as real property; hence Tory traders survived the Revolution in better shape than loyalist landowners. When the chamber of commerce reconstituted itself in 1784 most of the British supporters and fence-sitters again became members, and ex-Tory John Alsop, prewar vice-president, was elected president. Patriots, of course, were better situated to retain their wealth and commercial position. Whig merchants Comfort Sands, Francis Lewis, and others expanded their fortunes by supplying the Continental Army. [55] Reactivation of old connections also preserved continuity between pre- and post-war commercial elites. Former Tory James Beekman wrote Effingham Lawrence that he had returned to New York and "once more entered in Trade," with sons William and Abraham. Discovering that Lawrence was "established in the Commission way [in London], and as you have been well acquainted with our Family and Circumstance there, we think it needless to observe anything further with respect to Recommendation, but request you will be pleased, if agreeable to ship us per first vessel the Sundries" ordered and "allow us the usual Credit." Lawrence shipped the goods.[56]

Connections facilitated but could not guarantee prosperity. Failure to adjust to new trading conditions soon caused the Beekmans' collapse. By the 1820s most of the old elite had left trade. Involvement in William Duer's ruin sent Pintard to debtor's prison; the trading crisis of the 1800s bankrupted Sands and incurred heavy losses for Daniel Ludlow, who inherited his father's firm in 1769; and the War of 1812 caused the dissolution of S. & L. Clarkson. LeRoy, Bayard, & Co., the last remaining patrician firm except for H. & G. Barclay, lost out to packet lines, which took business away from older houses, and went bankrupt in 1826. Mercantile demise did not impoverish the Hoffmans, Clarksons, Verplancks, and Beekmans, who retained much of their wealth and lived off real estate investments or went into the professions. Departure from trade, however, diminished Old Guard influence in New York's economic life.[57]

The exodus of established firms and merchants, accompanied by vast commercial expansion, created opportunities for new men. They came from the British Isles, from New York State (mostly Long Island and Westchester), and chiefly from New England. The influx began around the time of the Revolution when Eddy moved from Philadelphia, Cornelius Ray, Walter Bowne, the Lawrences and Hickses from Long Island, and John Delafield and Gracie respectively from England and Scotland. Between 1790 and 1820, when New York forged ahead of the other ports, the incoming wave crested. Jonathan Goodhue, Arthur Tappan, Thomas Tileston, and the Lows (who migrated a few years later in 1829) came from Massachusetts; the Griswolds, William E. Dodge, Pelitiah Perit, the Howlands, and Anson G. Phelps from Connecticut; James Boorman and Robert Lenox from Scotland; and John Jacob Astor from Germany. These figures dominated commerce. Boorman & Johnson and later Phelps & Dodge were the largest iron importers, the Tappans ran the largest retail dry-goods store in the 1830s, G. G. & S. Howland (later Howland & Aspinwall) became the greatest firm in South American trade, A. A. Low & Brothers was the leading New York house in the Far Eastern market of the 1840s, N. L. & G. Griswold owned more ships than any other firm in the 1830s, and John Jacob Astor, the richest antebellum American, made his first fortune in the Far East and fur trades.

The primacy of former New Englanders was registered by the fact that from 1845 to 1875 every chamber of commerce president, except for an eight-month period, hailed from that region.[58] Benjamin Robert Winthrop, a native New York descendant of that distinguished Massachusetts family, admitted that "New England has indeed been outstripped in the race with New York for commercial enterprise and prosperity," but asserted that "a strong infusion of . . . the New England element" was largely responsible for New York's "rise in power and greatness with a rapidity that has no parallel in the history of the world." The displaced Knickerbockers resented the intrusion, but commercial and marital ties prevented this hostility from creating a permanent rift in upper-class ranks.[59]

The newcomers came from all levels of society. Phelps, an orphan, and Tileston, a printer's apprentice, started at the bottom, as did John and Philip Hone and Astor. On the other hand, Goodhue was the son of a U.S. senator, Samuel Hicks derived from a prominent and prosperous landowning family, and the Griswolds claimed a distinguished colonial lineage. Most came from the middle- or upper-middle range and several were children of merchants who had been bankrupted by the War of 1812. Moses Taylor's father was an Astor agent and the parents of Dodge, Robert Bowne Minturn, and Arthur and Lewis Tappan were failed merchants.

The advent of outsiders, many of whom worked their way to the top, gave New York its reputation for vigorous entrepreneurship and vividly contrasted with Boston's older and more conservative maritime elite. Coming from different regions and backgrounds and therefore less bound by tradition than were more homogeneous enclaves, they had the flexibility to try new techniques and the spirit to take profitable, if dangerous, risks. The comparative stability and respectability of the Bostonians led Thomas Wren Ward, as described in chapter 2, to give them higher credit ratings than the upstart New Yorkers.[60]

Newcomers brought with them more than imagination and resourcefulness. Some emigrated with skills honed in firms in other places, with connections and patrons acquired elsewhere, and with capital accumulated from previous endeavors. The Lows clerked for Russell & Co., retained ties to that house where their uncle was a partner, and had conducted a thriving shipping business in Salem. Goodhue was schooled in a Salem countinghouse, and William Gray was one of his patrons; Delafield had connections with British merchants; and Gracie was trained in a Scottish firm. Joseph Howland and Arthur Tappan similarly received their training and were prosperous traders before moving to New York.

Although the family firms in Boston were older, the institution also prevailed in New York. Grinnells, Barclays, Bayards, Griswolds, Lows, Tappans, Howlands, Hones, and Schiefflins formed partnerships with their brothers; Phelps associated with his Dodge son-in-law; and Gracie took his daughter's husband, Charles King, into the business. Families associated in business frequently intermarried, for example, the Howlands and Aspinwalls and the Grinnells and Minturns. When they came

of age, offspring of the founders frequently joined the firm. Schiefflin &
Co., LeRoy, Bayard, & Co., A. A. Low & Brothers, Phelps & Dodge,
Howland & Aspinwall, and other firms became intergenerational businesses. A widespread kinship network soon emerged from the unions
of Grinnells and Howlands, Goodhues and Clarksons, Delafields and
Kings, Lorrilards and Griswolds, Howlands and Hones, and other matrimonial alliances between the major maritime families.

The magnates interacted in other ways typical of port cities and of
their colonial predecessors. Merchant princes shipped goods in each
other's vessels, served apprenticeships in each other's firms, and assisted
each other's children. No New York firm equaled the position of Elias
Hasket Derby or J. & T. H. Perkins as a mercantile academy. Many
great traders were schooled at other ports, but John Delafield, Jr., James
DePeyster Ogden, and Gardiner G. Howland worked for LeRoy,
Bayard, & Co.; and Taylor clerked for G. G. & S. Howland. While
employed as clerks or supercargoes, many launched small ventures or
rose to partnerships. Nicholas Gouverneur Ogden, initially a supercargo
for John Jacob Astor & Son, became their agent in the China trade, and
Joseph C. Delano began as a captain and wound up a partner in Grinnell, Minturn & Co. Leading traders also aided their juniors by opening
credit lines or introducing them to other merchants. Gracie and
Matthew Clarkson helped Goodhue in this fashion.

The aggressive New Yorkers rapidly advanced the town's commerce,
but their daring sometimes resulted in disasters avoided by more cautious Bostonians. If willingness to take chances helped make New York
the primary port and commercial emporium of the country, it also resulted in a shorter life span for her firms compared to such dynasties as
the Cabots, Lees, and Gardners, who were established foreign traders
before the Revolution and continued in that calling respectively until
1838, 1852, and after the Civil War. Russell & Co., incorporated in 1818,
did not dissolve until the 1890s, and the Dabneys, who began in 1807,
lasted until 1892. Compare the longevity of these Bostonians with
Samuel Ogden, ruined in 1808 because he unwisely financed a revolution in Latin America, and Gracie, who went under in the War of 1812.
Foreign visitors and New Yorkers repeatedly commented on the
speculative impulses and uncertain existence in the city's commercial
community. A chain of bankruptcies triggered by the Panic of 1837
prompted George Templeton Strong to lament the inconstancy of New
York business. During another crisis, in 1857, he noted: "All confidence
is lost, for the present, in the solvency of our merchant-princes—and
with good reason. It is probable that every one of them has been operating and gambling in stocks and railroad bonds." In the same decade
Nathaniel Griswold estimated: "The average [number of merchants]

who have succeeded [in the last fifty years] have been about seven in the hundred; All the rest [went] bankrupt."[61]

Failure was frequent, but not always permanent. Arthur Tappan, and Talbot, Olyphant & Co., a great Far Eastern house, fell in 1837, and Phelps & Dodge suspended payments but all resumed operations. Although impetuous enterprise could bring ruin, it also contained a spirit of resilience. "Throw down our merchants ever so flat," wrote Philip Hone in 1845, "they roll over once, and spring to their feet again."[62] Family and business connections and diversified interests, as in Boston, often rescued temporary failures. John Delafield, Jr., after losses incurred in the War of 1812, turned to banking, as did James Gore King and Archibald Gracie, Jr., upon the dissolution of their firm. Charles King, involved in the ruin of Archibald Gracie, became a partner in Talbot, Olyphant & Co. and later found a sinecure as president of Columbia College. Others were less fortunate. Hone never fully recovered from his son's bankruptcy and his own losses in the 1830s. Jeremiah Thompson, foremost cotton trader in the world and an organizer of the Black Ball Packet Line, permanently folded in 1827. Thomas H. Smith, a notorious plunger who carried on most of New York's Canton trade in the 1820s, suffered the same fate in 1826.

Speculative impulses were less restrained than in Boston partly because fewer New York fortunes were tied up in family trusts.[63] Greater freedom of investment permitted wealth to expand more rapidly; risky projects, however, did not always bring huge returns. Many New York mercantile fortunes had long vanished when prudent Bostonians still lived handsomely off ancestral accumulations. New Yorkers also lived more extravagantly than Bostonians, consuming assets that might have protected them from business losses or provided an inheritance for their heirs.[64] Character defects and faltering entrepreneurship in later generations also decimated the maritime elite. The younger Bayards did not possess their father's acumen; the last LeRoys and Alexander Hamilton, Jr., dissipated themselves in drink, debauchery, and unwise investment.[65] The mercantile community was further reduced by changes in class and economic outlook which encouraged withdrawals from trade. Some merchants, e.g., Jonathan Sturges, retired early in life; others, like John Jacob and William B. Astor, shifted to real estate; and offspring of both groups sought leisured existences or occupation in the professions. Banking became more profitable than trade, and many merchants shifted their interests accordingly. James A. Roosevelt transformed the family glass business into a financial house; Adrian Iselin left the dry-goods trade to found Adrian Iselin & Co., an investment banking firm; and Howland & Aspinwall added a commercial banking operation. These developments had already begun to erode the dominion of foreign trade over the business community when the Civil War sent American shipping into a long-term decline. Howland & Aspinwall and Grinnell, Minturn & Co. lost their eminence as a result of the conflict, Goodhue & Co. folded in 1861, and N. L. & G. Griswold terminated in the next decade.[66]

Symptomatic of the maritime elite's decline was the deterioration of the chamber of commerce, its long-time spokesman. "In later years the Chamber has been less attractive to the commercial body," wrote its historian Charles King in 1857; "the meetings have been negligently attended, and hastily dispatched, and as a consequence the influence of the Chamber has declined." Six years later Pelitiah Perit, former partner of Goodhue, nostalgically recalled that the great merchants of fifty years ago "held a prominence which at the present time is not accorded to those of the same position. There was some remnant of aristocracy at that time, which has since become obliterated."[67]

INSTRUMENTS OF CAPITAL ACCUMULATION

Trade, especially overseas ventures, was conducted largely on credit, much of it advanced by European businessmen and bankers. American merchants, faced with high risks and lacking capital, formed financial institutions to provide a steady and plentiful flow of credit that would discourage bankruptcy, expand undertakings, and widen profit margins. Commercial needs did not exhaust the potential benefits of banking. Merchants speculated in government securities, and banks, by purchasing the public debt, would increase the value of such holdings. The maritime elite provided most of the major shareholders in financial institutions, thus banking profits would add to their wealth. These expectations were not disappointed. Banks discounted merchants' bills and notes and established a firm credit base which attracted foreign funds and underwrote business activities. High dividends, cautious lending policies, ample cash reserves, and infrequent failures (before the Panic of 1837) made banking, compared to the pitfalls of trade, a profitable and stable force in the urban commercial community.[68]

The Bank of New York (1784), like the first banks in Providence, Boston, and Philadelphia, was founded, directed, and owned by upper-class merchants. Its incorporators included Comfort Sands (a president of the chamber of commerce), and Nicholas Low, and its first seven chief executives came from the commercial elite, for example Herman LeRoy, founder of LeRoy, Bayard, & Co. and Matthew Clarkson of S. & L. Clarkson.[69] Hamilton, a pivotal figure as a founding director, writer of the bank charter and legal counsel, and secretary of the treasury, was intimate with the mercantile elite. While in the West Indies he served an apprenticeship with Knickerbocker overseas houses, partners in these firms became his patrons, sons of merchants were his close friends at King's College and later studied under him while he handled their fathers' legal affairs. The rising politician and lawyer eagerly promoted the interests of the foremost traders. He opposed the formation of a land bank, which the urban merchants fought as an unwise alternative to the Bank of New York, an institution based on specie and merchandise and designed to keep control of credit in their hands. He introduced the Bank of New York's first cashier to the Bank of North America, where he could learn the techniques of finance. The welfare of New York's commercial community and its bank continued to receive high priority when Hamilton entered Washington's cabinet. The Federalist statesman consulted merchants from New York, Boston, and other cities in drafting his Report on Public Credit; deposited government monies and foreign loans in the Bank of New York; relieved a credit crisis in the city by using public funds to shore up the bank's stock and to increase its abilities to buy securities and extend credits to hard-pressed merchants; aided the bank in resisting the chartering of competing corporations; and opposed the raising of import duties. New York bankers and merchants reciprocated these indulgences. The bank made loans to the national government, assisted Hamilton's factory venture, and passed his wife's banknotes; LeRoy, Bayard, & Co. lent him money, and local businessmen took up a collection to pay off his posthumous debts.[70]

The bank's policies reflected the interests of its proprietors. Its main business consisted of issuing short-term loans for merchants, such advances often being made on the basis of merchandise as collateral. Restrictive credit grants, mostly to shareholders and other members of the maritime inner circle, prompt recall of due loans, and high reserves provided the merchants with a reliable reservoir of funds and stockholders with yearly dividends averaging over 8 percent between 1791 and 1884.[71]

New York's second bank, a branch of the Bank of the United States, opened in 1792 over the objections of the Bank of New York, which feared a withdrawal of federal funds, the dominance of Philadelphia banking (the parent BUS was located in that city), and the loss of its monopoly. A period of initial uneasiness soon gave way to rapport between the institutions because Hamilton kept some government funds in the older bank and still did business with it, Philadelphia's overlordship did not materialize, leading merchants controlled both banks (eight directors of the BUS branch held similar positions in the Bank of New York), and their policies harmonized. Mutual interests and ties moved the Bank of New York to petition Congress for renewal of the BUS charter in 1811.[72]

Establishment of the BUS branches brought an end to urban bank monopolies. Six banks existed in the United States before the branches appeared, by 1800 there were twenty-nine, and by 1816, 246. Within seven years nominal banking capital doubled in the eastern seaports.[73] Banks multiplied in response to the demand of a growing economy for more credit, to an intercity rivalry that promoted instruments encouraging commerce and enlarging capital resources, and to outcries from Republican businessmen and politicians that the older banks, all Federalist, discriminated against their interests. The last reason prompted the formation of the Manhattan Company (1799) by Republican merchants and politicians. Despite Republican origins the Manhattan had close connections with the Federalist mercantile-financial elite: Hamilton drew up its charter and argued for incorporation; among its initial directors were directors or relatives of board members of the BUS, its New York branch, and the Bank of New York; and stockholders of the older banks also appeared or had kin among Manhattan shareholders. These interconnections, however, did not stop Federalist businessmen from opposing its charter, and the institution became an issue in the election of 1801. Within a few years the Federalist directors departed and the Manhattan became politically partisan and began to extend credit to Republican artisans and shopkeepers. The Manhattan introduced new features into local finance; it was the subject of an interparty squabble; its loan and discount policies were liberal compared to older banks; credit was extended for longer terms, on less security, and to those who did not belong to the upper class.[74]

The Merchants' Bank (1803) was founded by the Federalist-mercantile elite to counteract the influence of the Manhattan and because older banks were reluctant to fund new enterprises. Hamilton again wrote the incorporation charter and patrician traders and financiers controlled the institution. The original president was later a director of the Second BUS branch bank in New York, his successor was a brother and partner of a founding director of the Bank of New York, the third chief executive had been on the board of the Bank of New York and married the daughter of its third president. The Merchants' aggressive credit policy, however, was largely the work of a new man, Lynde Catlin, its first cashier and later president.[75]

Burgeoning commerce and aggressive entrepreneurship created an incessant demand for capital. Accordingly, the business elite, seeking to retain control over New York's economy, continued to organize new financial institutions. In 1812 the directors and stockholders of the New York branch of the BUS, defunct by congressional fiat, reconstituted it as the Bank of America. During the same year the Phoenix Bank petitioned for a charter because of "the difficulty of inducing persons to invest in untried enterprises." Both institutions were run by prominent overseas traders or their relatives. Oliver Wolcott, the Bank of America's first president, had been the original head of the Merchants' Bank. He was succeeded by William Bayard of LeRoy, Bayard, & Co., former director of the New York branch of the first BUS and the Bank of New York.[76] Five years after the formation of the Phoenix Bank and the Bank of America, the New York branch of the Second BUS was chartered. Its organizers, stockholders, and officers were drawn from the same group that dominated older financial institutions. Isaac Lawrence, who headed the bank for all but the first few months of its existence, was previously a director of the Bank of New York.[77]

The ownership and management of the Chemical Bank (1825) continued the traditional mixture of old patricians and prominent post-Revolutionary merchants. Unusual for incorporated upper-class financial institutions in New York City, it had a kinship-structured leadership. The second, third, and fourth presidents were related to each other, and one of the vice-presidents was succeeded by his son. In this case, ascriptive administration proved successful. The large surplus of the Chemical Bank made it the only New York bank to maintain specie payments in the Panic of 1857; in 1860 it had the highest ratio among local banks of net profits to capital.[78]

Private (unincorporated) banks offered another important source of credit for the mercantile elite. These firms often developed from upper-class mercantile, insurance, and note-brokerage houses and became the chief conduits of foreign funds for long-term loans. By the 1850s they financed most of the city's foreign trade and dealt extensively in corporate securities such as railroads.[79] Prime, Ward & King (1824), the largest private bank in New York, was prototypical of these financial institutions. Note-broker Nathaniel Prime, Samuel Ward (originally his clerk), and James Gore King (a well-connected commission merchant), were the founding partners. They were succeeded by their children and other relatives, the firm assuming the family structure characteristic of this type of enterprise. Other participants in the business were interrelated offspring from prominent maritime-financial-political clans. The principals of the firm were also officers and directors in chartered banks. Notwithstanding patrician leadership, it proved more venturesome than the older banks, operating in the commercial paper market generally avoided by conservative financiers who preferred to make loans based on specie or merchandise. Ties with Baring Brothers enabled the house to exert considerable financial leverage and occasioned its greatest feat when King obtained a gold loan from Baring which permitted New York's banks to resume specie payments in 1838. The Panic of 1837, however, weakened the firm; ten years later it dissolved and the Kings formed their own banking business.[80]

Brown Brothers & Co. had similar origins and structure. In 1825 James Brown established a New York branch of his father's Baltimore dry-goods business and eight years later turned it into an investment firm. The Browns married Howlands and Delanos, and the latter entered the house. The importance of kinship in private banks, at first unprotected by incorporation, is illustrated by Brown's explanation of his invitation to a relative to join the branch office: "We are going to lose our confidential man," whose "place will be filled by James Brown, my cousin . . . who was brought up in our office at Baltimore. . . . We need someone here . . . in whom we can respose entire confidence; as we brought James M. up from the stump we know all about him and his habits which are unexceptional. . . . I am gratified at being able to bring in Stewart's brother."[81] As banking supplanted trade as the fundamental source of profits and power, other upper-class family firms, as noted above, were transformed from mercantile to financial establishments.

Old Guard merchants labored to meet New York's commercial needs by proliferating financial institutions and liberalizing the extension of credit, but even in the heyday of patrician banking, outsiders encroached on upper-class dominance. The City Bank of New York (1812) and others did not have the usual complement of distinguished traders among their founders and officers.[82] Other alterations in New York banking further diminished aristocratic influence. Inter- and intraurban cooperation among banks in the major shipping centers enhanced the cohesion and power of the Federalist-maritime enclave, but newer banks were sometimes incorporated by rival groups and, as in the case of the Merchants' Bank and the Manhattan Company, financial warfare ensued.[83] Departures from cautious and traditional investment and credit strategies were another indication of decline in the Old Guard. "A great number of new banks were also established by men who possessed neither capital or experience," complained Wolcott, criticizing the rise of new figures and new policies, "the credit of which rested solely on the breath of public opinion."[84] As the Knickerbocker traders passed from the scene so did the gentleman merchant-banker. No longer were leading financiers or bank directors almost invariably from noted families and firms. Business grew more complex, and functional specialization differentiated merchants from financiers. After 1825 the chief officers of the Merchants' Bank and the Bank of New York had usually started as clerks and tellers and worked their way up to presidencies from positions as cashiers. In the 1790s, "the president and directors of a bank were other sort of people from those of the present day," declared Hone in 1847; "proud and aristocratical, they were the only nobility we had (now we have none); powerful in the controlling opinions of the city, . . . and woe to them who bowed not down to the . . . dispensers of bank favours." A few years later a bank president described his colleagues in these words: "One had acquired wealth by selling dry goods, and therefore he was fit to be a bank president; another had been equally successful in making shoes; another had been a ship chandler, and fortunate in the schooner coasting-trade, another had been a stage-driver; not a few were men of the narrowest minds, wholly lacking in mercantile education, and without the ability to conduct the simplest commercial correspondence."[85]

Multiplication of financial institutions, overextended and speculative credit policies, and inadequate reserves led to a host of banking disasters. Before 1809 no failures had occurred in the United States; between 1811 and 1825 several New York banks collapsed. In 1838 the legislature passed a general incorporation law for banks; within three years the number of banks doubled in the state, and of the first eighty that appeared, twenty failed.[86] The Panic of 1837 impartially wrecked newcomers and older financiers. Strong's uncle, head of the Dry Dock Bank, John Delafield, Jr., and Samuel Ward went under.[87] Conservative patricians Alexander Hamilton, Jr., David B. Ogden, William Alexander Duer, and the chamber of commerce blamed incontinent incorporation for destroying confidence and causing inflation and failure and called for national and state banks to restore stability.[88]

Alarmed by disaster and displacement, the Old Guard made a last attempt to stem the tide and reassert their power. Their vehicle was the Bank of Commerce (1839), organized for mercantile transactions and loans. "I really think that this institution will be important in keeping the other banks in order," Thomas Wren Ward wrote Baring Brothers, urging them to subscribe to its stock. "It will be a conservative money bank in which . . . the best men in the city of New York, have a large stake." The Bank of Commerce, at its founding the largest in the country next to the former BUS in Philadelphia, was among the few great New York banks in which the patriciate retained leadership after the Civil War.[89] Other measures to curb financial promiscuity, however, revealed the weakness of the traditional elite. The New York Safety Fund System (1829) and the New York City Clearing House Association (1835) were run mainly by newcomers.[90]

Ranking the incorporated banks discussed above according to amount of capital held by New York City banks in 1824, 1834, and 1853 offers a profile of antebellum upper-class financial institutions (see Table 1).[91]

Although the Bank of New York, conservative in administration, slipped from its 1780s preeminence, other upper-class organizations, the Bank of America and the Bank of Commerce, retained their high standing. The Merchants' Bank also underwent a relative decline, but except for 1834, when the Manhattan Company edged out the Bank of America, institutions founded and controlled by the Old Guard held first place. The Manhattan, however, run by new men with comparatively liberal and aggressive financial policies, was the most consistently highly placed throughout the period. By 1853 the order of precedence

Table 1

EIGHT NEW YORK BANKS RANKED ACCORDING TO CAPITAL HELD BY
THE CITY'S BANKS IN 1824, 1834, AND 1853

	1824		1834		1853	
Bank of New York	7[a]	($1,000,000)	5[a]	($1,000,000)	7[a]	($1,500,000)
Manhattan Company	2[a]	(2,000,000)	1	(2,050,000)	2	(2,050,000)
Merchants' Bank	5	(1,490,000)	4	(1,490,000)	10	(1,490,000)
Bank of America	2[a]	(2,000,000)	2	(2,001,200)	3[a]	(2,000,000)
Phoenix Bank	9[a]	(500,000)	11[a]	(500,000)	13	(1,200,000)
New York Branch of Second BUS	1	(2,500,000)	-		-	
Chemical Bank	-		17[a]	(400,000)	44[a]	(300,000)
Bank of Commerce	-		-		1	(5,000,000)

[a]Tied for this position with other banks.

became less important as a measure of upper-class economic power because the leadership of the other banks was passing out of patrician hands.

Commercial crises affected all the port cities, but New York's money market was particularly volatile. Upper-class conservatives dominated Boston banking throughout the nineteenth century, but their counterparts in financial New York were largely displaced before the Civil War. Relatively rapid turnover of leadership stimulated, as it did in trade, more adventurous activities and institutional instability. In 1815 New York banks kept a lower capital-to-debt ratio (cash reserves against notes and deposits) than did institutions in Philadelphia and Boston, and from 1834 to 1845 Boston banking securities avoided the spasmodic fluctuations of New York bank stock.[92] A record of unsavory dealings, less frequently found in Boston, contributed to the hazards of New York finance. In 1819 and 1820 Pintard noted embezzlements in the Phoenix, Merchants', and Mechanics' banks. A Livingston and a DePeyster in-law were involved in these peculations.[93] On the other hand, aggressive entrepreneurship paid off in high profits and innovative techniques, and in making New York the nation's financial center. Its bankers formed the original commercial paper and call-money markets, and its banks usually averaged higher yearly dividends than did those in Boston.[94]

Capital formation is more accurate than foreign trade as a measure of New York's economic predominance. Pursuing alternatives to shipping became by 1815 an intelligent response to New York's mercantile primacy. Urban economies ideally orient themselves around endeavors that maximize regional advantages, but all forms of business need capital, and the city that won financial supremacy would dominate the economy of the eastern seaboard. The comparative financial standing of New York, Boston, and Philadelphia, the chief contenders in this contest, can best be traced through the instruments of capital accumulation—banks, insurance companies, and stock exchanges.

Philadelphia has been correctly dubbed "the cradle of American finance." The Bank of North America (1781), the nation's earliest state-chartered bank, and the First BUS (1791) were located there. The founders of the original state-chartered banks in Boston and New York sought officers and advice from the older institution. Philadelphia soon lost its early lead in banking sophistication and resources. Excluding the BUS, New York and Boston banks by 1812 had more capital than those in Philadelphia. In the 1820s New York became the money market of the nation: New England and New Jersey banks kept larger balances in New York financial institutions than in those of Philadelphia or Boston, and entrepreneurs from other states came to Gotham banks to float loans for internal improvements.[95] In 1831 capital in New York banks totaled $18,130,000; Boston banks were next with $13.9 million, followed by Philadelphia banks with $10,792,000. Thomas Wren Ward recognized New York's supremacy; he told Baring Brothers in 1839 that "the Bank of America, the Manhattan and the Bank of Commerce by uniting can keep the other banks in the city right and I think act strongly on Philadelphia and Boston for the same object."[96]

Next to trade and banks, stock exchanges and insurance and trust companies constituted the major sources of capital in the port cities, and they too were initially controlled by the maritime elite. Merchants, accustomed to acting as private commission agents, played a similar public role in marketing government securities, made investments for foreign customers, and committed substantial sums of their own to purchases of the state and federal debt. Due to the extensive involvement of Herman LeRoy, William Bayard, John Delafield, Nicholas Low, John Pintard, William Duer, Gouverneur Morris, and others, speculation in government issues centered in New York.[97] Security dealers rapidly branched out from public securities to handling the private issues of banks, canal and insurance companies, and, later, railroads. Their activities became institutionalized through brokerage houses and the New York Stock Exchange (1792). August H. Lawrence, Pintard, and

Benjamin Winthrop helped found the exchange. Between 1831 and 1851 John Ward, Edward Prime, and David Clarkson consecutively headed the exchange. Banks, insurance companies, and eminent merchants and bankers comprised the membership, revealing in their interlocked functions the coinciding facets of the upper-class commercial community. Descended from distinguished colonial families or from figures who emerged in the Revolution or early national era, patrician securities dealers in the 1850s shared the displacement of the older maritime-banking elite.[98]

Speculation equaled overseas trade as a graveyard for upper-class fortunes. In the 1790s Walter Livingston, Pintard, and William Duer were ruined by misadventure in public debt manipulation; in 1819 the Livingston partner in a brokerage firm tried to recoup his losses by stealing money from the Merchants' Bank; and abortive investments resulted in waves of bankruptcies during the Panics of 1837 and 1857. Stocks in New York companies tended to fluctuate more widely than Boston issues, increasing the possibilities of speculative failure in the former city and making brokerage firms a potent factor in unsettling Gotham's money market.[99] Businessmen and their associates, outraged by the disastrous consequences of impulsive investment, condemned speculation in securities. Hone, financially embarrassed by his son's bankruptcy and his own losses on the market, witnessing the widespread failures of the 1830s and '40s, labeled "stock-jobbing a most profligate and ruinous system of gambling; infinitely worse than any of which the laws take cognizance." The ruin of his father-in-law evoked identical sentiments in Strong. He concluded after a bitter indictment against stock speculation that "geniality and high principle do not abound" on "Wall Street."[100] Feverish activity on Wall Street, however, as in trade and banking, was also prompted by unrivaled economic growth. In 1816 the New York stock market overtook Philadelphia's exchange as the busiest in the country. By the 1830s Wall Street had achieved national predominance. Its market quotations, reproduced in Philadelphia, Boston, Baltimore, and other places, set the standard national values, and its brokers were America's largest traders in state and federal, bank, canal, and insurance company shares, and primary promoters of new issues.[101]

The exchange in the 1820s, still a small operation, had fewer than fifty members, and trading rarely exceeded 100 shares daily.[102] At this time insurance companies more significantly influenced capital formation. In this field, too, merchants excelled. Supremacy over other sources of capital, desire for yet another profitable venture, and dire need for protection against losses in fire and at sea moved Eddy, Delafield, and Bowne to become leading insurance underwriters and other magnates and bankers to organize and run insurance companies. The firms instituted and controlled by the commercial elite were the Mutual Assurance Company (1787), the first corporation in New York formed to provide compensation for shipping and buildings destroyed by fire; the United Insurance Company (1796) and the Insurance Company of New York (1796), the city's initial marine insurance firms; the United States Insurance Company (1797); and the Eagle Fire Insurance Company (1806). Hamilton drew up the incorporation deed for the Mutual Assurance Company and served as general council at the United Insurance Company. Lenox was president of the Mutual Assurance Company, Nicholas Low was president of the United Insurance Company and the Insurance Company of New York. Gracie was chief backer of the latter and also headed it. Delafield founded and headed United States Insurance, and Moses Rogers presided over the Eagle Fire Insurance Company.[103]

Insurance underwriting was a perilous undertaking. The city's unstable business conditions made New York insurance stock a less secure investment than stock in the calmer Boston firms.[104] Other dangers were created by the commercial crisis of 1808–19 and frequent property losses due to sinkings, captures, and urban conflagrations. One catastrophe, the New York fire of 1835, wiped out most of the fire insurance firms. Insurance companies were also weakened by defalcations; several of these transgressions were committed by members of aristocratic families.[105]

Prosperity in the late 1820s added to the number of insurance organizations; by 1824 New York had at least thirty-four firms providing protection against shipping and fire disasters.[106] In 1842 the maritime-banking elite, apparently undeterred by fraud or fire, organized the Atlantic Mutual Insurance Company, the largest marine and general insurance firm in North America during the 1850s; the Mutual Life Insurance Company, the first purely life insurance firm in New York; and three years later, the New York Life Insurance Company, which sold general insurance and executed trusts. The Atlantic Mutual Insurance Company was controlled in dynastic fashion by the Joneses, a distinguished colonial family. Alfred Pell, of similar ancestry, helped found the Mutual Life Insurance Company, and James DePeyster Ogden, offspring of another notable provincial clan, headed the New York Life Insurance Company. A number of eminent and well-born businessmen sat on the early boards of these institutions.[107]

The checkered past of insurance underwriting and the recent advent of life insurance induced the incorporating directors of the Mutual Life Insurance Company to solicit endorsements from prominent citizens to attract customers and to draw up a charter which, forbidding investment in railroad, manufacturing, and canal stock, restricted the company's holdings to mortgages and unencumbered real estate in New York state and government bonds. As a further safeguard the company pledged not to issue its first policy until $500,000 in applications had been obtained. Such caution was amply rewarded—by 1865 only $827 was irretrievably lost out of $20 million invested. Despite upper-class leadership and conservative investment strategy, it broke new ground by popularizing mutual policies, pioneering in selling policies through personal solicitation, and developing actuarial tables that became standard in the field. For decades the Mutual Life Insurance Company was the largest insurance firm in America; between 1842 and 1913 it paid out one-quarter of the total amount of life insurance premiums in the country.[108] The New York Life Insurance Company also adopted aggressive marketing techniques. It employed salesmen, many of them in the newly settled West, and set up agencies in many parts of the country. By 1854 New York Life had sold 3,430 policies valued at $10 million and accumulated $900,000 in capital.[109]

Notwithstanding this dazzling display of upper-class entrepreneurship, by the 1850s the grasp of the Old Guard noticeably weakened. The proportion of aristocratic bankers and merchants among trustees and executives drastically declined in New York Life, Mutual Life, and Knickerbocker Fire Insurance. Even the most progressive patrician organization, Mutual Life, placed limits on its aggressiveness. Mutual's president dismissed Henry B. Hyde, who wanted to underwrite risky insurees, and Hyde founded the highly competitive Equitable Life Assurance Company (1859). Other companies inaugurated by the old elite, such as Gracie's first Atlantic Mutual Insurance Company, had long since dissolved. Many firms destined to become postwar giants, e.g., Equitable Life and the Manhattan Life Insurance Company (1850), were not dominated by the Old Guard, although a few patrician merchants and bankers acted as original trustees.[110]

The same features made New York paramount in insurance, finance, and commerce. Unlike Philadelphia firms, e.g., the Insurance Company of North America (1792) and Penn Mutual (1784), whose boards even today contain a heavy representation from old families, their New York counterparts have not been so dominated since the 1850s. Sharper business methods lured clients and capital from Boston firms. The higher rates of Massachusetts Hospital Life Insurance Company, in its early years monopolizing life insurance in the Commonwealth, diverted many potential customers to New York and Philadelphia underwriters. In the 1780s and '90s Philadelphia pioneered insurance organizations. By 1806 New York firms passed those in Philadelphia in total capital; by 1824 more insurance companies existed there than in Philadelphia and Boston put together, and the total capital of its institutions exceeded that of the other two cities and Baltimore combined.[111]

Trust companies, the latest appearing of the major instruments of capital formation, developed out of insurance firms. The former were originally conceived as an additional security service naturally provided by those already affording protection through life, marine, or fire policies. The complexity of operating in both fields, however, soon led to a separation of functions similar to the differentiation of banking from trade. Trust companies specialized in offering safe deposit for funds, real estate title-searching and conveyance, and investment guidance. Acting as fiduciary agents, usually for wealthy heirs, they soon resembled—and often merged with—banks rather than insurance companies. Besides handling private and corporation wealth, trust organizations assumed an important role in the urban economy by using their funds to provide long-term credit, particularly in the form of buying railroad and canal bonds and mortgages.[112]

Three companies managed by urban gentry, the Farmers' Fire Insurance & Loan Company (1822), the New York Life Insurance and Trust Company (1830), and the United States Trust Company (1853), typified the functions and structure of investment trusts. Early New York institutions replicated the structure of Massachusetts Hospital Life Insurance Company, the first trust company in the United States. Farmers' Fire & Loan, the earliest in the city, followed the Boston example by quickly dropping its insurance business and by its patrician leadership. New York Life and Trust paralleled the development of the new Farmers' Loan & Trust in being organized by Old Guard bankers and merchants and rapidly divesting itself of insurance functions. The officers and trustees of these firms included descendants from virtually every Knickerbocker manorial and mercantile clan and representatives of the subsequent maritime-banking-insurance elite.[113]

Reflecting on New York Life and Trust's initial purposes of underwriting life insurance and handling estates, its incorporators had "in view safety more than profit" and, stressing the "duty they have to perform of protecting the property of others," they declared that "they will in no instance dispose of money intrusted to them, but upon ample security." They also recognized the advantages of an elite directorate: "None will be elected to vacancies [on the board] but men of established reputation for prudence, capacity, and integrity." By 1840 New York Life and Trust held $3.5 million in trust funds and it eventually became the chief repository of old family fortunes.[114] New York Life and Trust accepted only private accumulations, but the United States Trust Company received both personal and corporate deposits. United States Trust also differed from older firms in beginning exclusively as a fiduciary agent. Its leadership, however, was typical of patrician trust organizations: August H. Lawrence, for example, was the first president. In this case, elite leadership proved incapable of stimulating growth, and the company stagnated until 1900.[115]

According to their declared purposes and public opinion, two types of capital-accumulating institutions existed in midcentury New York. Commercial banks and brokerage houses tended to be speculative enterprises; insurance and trust companies, preservative enterprises. The former were often founded to supply venture capital and sometimes explicitly announced this intention in their charters. The latter claimed to provide protection for life and property and emphasized this service in their incorporation papers. Although many insurance companies failed and some suffered employee embezzlement, there are indications of restrictive insuring and investment policies. Conclusive evidence of the comparative investment and administrative strategies of these two types of organizations awaits a thorough examination, if possible, of the major financial and insurance institutions. Whether or not insurance and trust firms were actually safer than banks or brokerage houses, the former more frequently attempted to project a conservative public image. Seeking to convey a sense of responsibility appropriate to their stated roles and the desires of their clientele, they attracted an upperclass management less likely to engage in commercial banking and stock dealing. The latter were dominated first by Knickerbocker merchants and then by traders of New England origin. They were owned and run by businessmen in the prime of their commercial power, quest for profits, and entrepreneurial zeal. These figures were also sometimes involved in the insurance and trust organizations and new men were more prevalent in New York insurance companies than in those from Philadelphia, but descendants of the colonial landed and mercantile gentry were more heavily represented as officers of these institutions than as stockbrokers or bank officers. In the 1840s and '50s, roughly a generation after the Knickerbocker merchants had fallen from their pinnacle in trade and finance, Bownes and Lenoxes could be found with greater frequency in the directorates of insurance and trust firms than on the boards of the other instruments of capital accumulation. Old names were valued in companies seeking business among those who wanted protection from calamity and security for their children, and undoubtedly the Old Guard felt more at home in this kind of endeavor. An aristocratic presence facilitated testimonials to the prudence and respectability of such institutions and lent credence to the conservative declarations of their charters. These efforts met with success. Philip Hone and others who deplored the departure of patrician financiers and the impulsiveness and inexperience in banking and speculative circles did not include insurance and trust organizations in their condemnations.

TRANSPORTATION

Commerce, finance, and insurance did not exhaust the energy and ingenuity of upper-class businessmen. Indeed, their quest for capital, trade, and profits involved them in transportation schemes designed to enlarge the market for New York imports and exports. In these ventures the urban elite cooperated with the upstate gentry, seeking to improve transit for its agricultural products and to enhance the value of its land-holdings. This incentive produced the outstanding entrepreneurial achievement of the post-Revolutionary squirearchy: the Erie Canal. The canal culminated this rural-urban alliance, but earlier efforts paved the way for that spectacular accomplishment. In the 1790s Philip Schuyler, as a canal president and director and state senator, became the most active waterways promoter, securing charters and state aid for short canals that were forerunners of the Erie. Eddy, Sands, Gilbert Aspinwall, Philip Hone, John Duer, John Lawrence, and Rufus King participated in these and other canal ventures, and James Livingston pushed them in the assembly.[116]

In 1810 the legislature appointed Gouveneur Morris chairman of a commission, which included Eddy, DeWitt Clinton, and Stephen Van Rensselaer, to explore the route for the Erie Canal. A year later they and Chancellor Livingston served on the commission to build the waterway. Cadwallader D. Colden, grandson of the provincial lieutenant governor and a member of the legislature, along with Eddy and Clinton, helped get government support for the project. William Bayard, president of the chamber of commerce and a prominent merchant and bank direc-tor, raised money, and in 1818 the Bank of America, the Manhattan Company, and the Phoenix Bank took the first flotation of New York canal loans. Colden, celebrating its completion, captured the spirit be-hind the undertaking. He predicted that the Erie and other canals would make "New York . . . a greater emporium than ever called herself the mistress of commerce."[117]

In addition to fostering internal improvements, upper-class figures promoted steamshipping. Chancellor Livingston pioneered in coastal and upstream steam navigation, built the first steamboat (1797) to ap-pear on the Hudson, and acquired a monopoly on the river's steamboat lines. Chiefly through his activities the first American coastal and river shipping using this kind of power originated in New York. Colden, an officer of the first ferry company to use steam propulsion, noted that immediately after application of the steam engine to navigation, Livingston wrote to his "friends" and "through their interference an act was passed by the [state] legislature" in 1803 "by which the rights and exclusive privileges of navigating all waters of this state by vessels pro-pelled by fire or steam, granted to Mr. Livingston" in 1798 "were ex-tended for the term of twenty years. . . ."[118] Nicholas J. Roosevelt, an-other Knickerbocker, ranking next to Livingston as an aristocratic inventor and promoter, also developed steam engines and opened the Mississippi River to steamboat traffic.[119]

Railroads appeared several years earlier in New York than in Massachusetts and gradually replaced canals as conduits to the interior. Manorial descendants and members of the business elite participated in the creation of the new transportation system. Among the officers and promoters of the early lines were Stephen Van Rensselaer, Augustus Jay, Nicholas Fish, Peter G. Stuyvesant, Philip Schuyler, James Gore King, Gardiner G. Howland, Anson G. Phelps, William E. Dodge, and George T. Olyphant, son of the great East India merchant. They were active in the Mohawk & Hudson (1826), the state's original railroad; the New York and Erie (operational in 1843), the first trunk line to enter the city; the Delaware & Hudson (started as a canal company in 1823); the New York & Albany (1833); the Auburn & Syracuse (1834); the New York & New Haven (1844), which linked the city with Boston; the Mohawk Valley (1851); and the Hudson River (1851).[120]

Aristocrats in these projects were often either figureheads or ineffective promoters and administrators. Van Rensselaer, a founder and original president of the Mohawk & Hudson, was merely the titular head of the line; when the railroad finally became profitable in the 1840s, most of the upper-class officers had long since left. Similarly, the 1841 bankruptcy of the New York and Erie drove out most of the patrician element; its later success occurred under the administration of newcomers Phelps and Dodge.[121] But not all the aristocrats were figureheads or failures. Robert Schuyler, Hamilton's nephew and Philip Schuyler's grandson, was the original president of the New York & New Haven. The leading American railroad tycoon of his day, he also headed the Illinois Central, the New York & Harlem, and the Vermont Valley and served as treasurer in four other lines. The Delaware & Hudson proved another exception to the trend of patrician management by generally operating in the black, especially under Olyphant's presidency in the 1850s and '60s.[122]

In the late 1840s New York's Old Guard and maritime-financial elite became interested in western lines. Their efforts produced the Illinois Central (1851), one of the earliest, soundest, and largest Mid-American roads. Illinois Central was a wholly eastern creation: Schuyler was the chief promoter and first president, the great merchant Jonathan Sturges succeeded him, and Sturges's son-in-law, John N. A. Griswold, the son of eminent trader George Griswold, became the third chief executive. Some members of this venture ranged even further afield. William H. Aspinwall and his fellow Illinois Central directors John Alsop and Thomas W. Ludlow (the president) organized the Panama Railroad in 1848.[123]

Railroad capitalists exhibited the promotional zeal, mobilization of political influence, quest for respectability, versatile entrepreneurship, and shady dealing familiar in other New York business operations. Catlin was the original treasurer of the Mohawk & Hudson while president of the Merchants' Bank, and the organizers initially met there. The economic and political power of the founders of the New York and Erie helped obtain a $3 million grant from the legislature in 1836. Its original directors asserted that "the great majority of the present stockholders . . . are merchants or landowners in the city of New York." Their first report predicted that "the proposed work will not add less than one-third to the present population and trade of the city of New York, and augment in an equal degree its landed wealth." Such expectations made it "difficult to fix within any moderate bounds, the value of the proposed road, or the amount of travel and transportation which it is destined to create and accomodate."[124] Railroad ventures were also marred by the duplicity that infected other business undertakings. An inveterate speculator, Schuyler issued false shares of New York & Harlem stock and bankrupted the New York & New Haven by defrauding it of over $2 million.[125]

Knickerbocker bluebloods and New England–born merchants and bankers made a crucial contribution to early railroad enterprise. Their initiatives, particularly the Erie and Hudson Lines, giving the city direct freight routes to the Great Lakes, enabled New York to turn back the renewed challenge from Boston, Philadelphia, and Baltimore for mastery of western trade, and, consequently, to maintain commercial primacy. During the final stage of this triumph, however, the Old Guard, as in other business activities, had been supplanted by a new breed. When most of the roads established by the upper class were annexed by the New York Central System in 1853, making it the chief trunk line to the West, Tileston alone of the old elite was active in the consolidation. The Hudson River line did not merge with the Central until 1869, but by 1855 Grinnell was the last patrician on its directorate. Ex-ferryboat deckhand Cornelius Vanderbilt acquired control of most of these roads. Beginning in 1857 he began to move in on the financially troubled New York & Harlem, where the old upper class had some administrative influence, and during the Civil War won full control over that line and the Hudson River railroad and in 1867 took over the New York Central.[126] Ironically, the only major line in which the Old Guard retained an appreciable post–Civil War influence, the Illinois Central, was the most geographically remote of its antebellum domestic railroad endeavors.

MANUFACTURING

By 1830 New York City and State had become the leading manufacturing city and state in the Union.[127] Upper-class businessmen, preferring other enterprises, contributed little to these accomplishments.

Philadelphia and Boston patricians, falling behind New Yorkers in commerce and capital accumulation, more readily shifted to industry.[128] The New York establishment, on the other hand, did not collectively or consistently commit itself to any line of manufacturing. A Roosevelt or a Livingston might construct steamboats, but such interests were neither the primary endeavors of their families nor were they passed on to future generations. An occasional mercantile firm, W. H. Schieffelin & Co. (1794) in drugs and Phelps & Dodge (1834) in copper and iron mining, achieved industrial eminence. But Schieffelin & Co. remained primarily a wholesale distributor and Phelps & Dodge did not concentrate on mining until the 1880s.[129] The Society for Establishing Useful Manufactures (SUM) (1791), a textile corporation, was the lone enterprise in which the urban gentry participated as a group. Hamilton originated the scheme, and his fellow directors and shareholders included Pintard and several Livingstons. Notwithstanding this mobilization of political and economic power and the aid of a grateful Bank of New York, the enterprise collapsed in 1796. The SUM emerged, as did parallel efforts by other urban elites—the Cabots' Beverly Manufactory (1787) in textiles and the Philadelphia Society for the Encouragement of Manufactures (1787)—from a mixture of speculative profit-seeking and a wish to make the new nation powerful and self-sufficient.[130] Initially sharing the zeal of eminent Bostonians and Philadelphians, patrician New Yorkers thereafter neglected industry. Failure to undertake industrial enterprise ultimately eroded the position of the mercantile elite. Moses Taylor, a rare exception and New York's last great general entrepreneur, embarked on mining ventures in the 1840s. Railroads, utilities, and coal and iron ore increasingly preoccupied him and sustained his prominence in the business community until he died in 1891.[131] Many aristocratic clans in Philadelphia and Boston likewise persisted in local leadership because they made a successful transition from trade to manufacturing. The San Francisco maritime elite of 1850–80, on the other hand, which imitated much of its New York predecessor's social and economic behavior, also did not industrialize and suffered the same fate as had its eastern preceptor.[132]

REAL ESTATE

Real estate endeavors coincided more closely with traditional urban upper-class economic functions. Many descendants of the maritime-banking enclave and the colonial gentry lived off the proceeds of Manhattan lots long after their families had left active business. Except for the Brevoorts and Stuyvesants, the richest city landowners, the Beekmans, Rhinelanders, Schermerhorns, Astors, and Goelets had begun as merchants or urban processors of agricultural products. Metropolitan acreage was also the favorite investment of blueblood institutions such as Columbia College, Sailors' Snug Harbor, and Trinity Church. Like the merchants and bankers of other cities, the New Yorkers also sought windfalls in underdeveloped tracts in New England, upstate, and the West. These ventures were generally less successful than real property holding in the city.[133] Contradictory impulses, speculative gain, and secure, high-status investment inspired the acquisition of land. The desire for quick profit led to repeated buying and selling in the hope of wringing a fortune from volatile land values. Preservation of inherited wealth, an honored aspiration of history's aristocracies, especially in the forms of rural estates and urban family mansions, arose from a presumption of permanent proprietorship untainted by the cash nexus, dubious dealing, and high risk associated with trade, manufacturing, and capital accumulation.

Despite interurban rivalry, considerable interaction occurred among New York, Boston, and Philadelphia elites. Pintard was involved with Boston merchants in trading projects in the 1780s and '90s, and the first American voyage to Canton was launched by capitalists and seamen from the three cities. Many transplanted New Englanders who became important New York merchants had been schooled in Boston firms and retained these early connections. Businessmen in New York, Boston, and Philadelphia also formed land-speculating companies and became stockholders and directors of the Bank of North America and the Bank of the United States. The Massachusetts First National Bank kept deposits with the Bank of New York and the Bank of North America; the last two financial institutions established a mutual credit to accommodate their common customers; banks of different cities collected payments on and for each other and accepted each others' notes and checks, exchanged information, and occasionally circulated personnel. Upper-class New Yorkers and Bostonians also organized the Michigan Central and Illinois Central railroads in the 1840s and '50s.[134] Commercial cooperation and common interests harmonized policies regarding the funding of the public debt, stabilizing currency values, generating capital, and government encouragement of overseas shipping.

WEALTH

The survival of many aristocrats and the emergence of Knickerbocker merchants were important features of the urban economy in the post-Revolutionary era. Thereafter outsiders, many of them New Englanders, gradually displaced patricians in overseas trade, but the Old Guard retained substantial influence in banking, insurance, transportation, and real estate enterprise. In the 1850s the Knickerbockers and their mercantile successors markedly declined in all phases of business endeavor except real estate. Analysis of the social structure of New York's wealthiest strata tends to support these contentions, although the appearance of *parvenu* entrepreneurs was somewhat hidden by the fact that old fortunes persisted after heirs no longer went into business. Measuring these data against similar information about Boston's richest citizens provides a comparative dimension for elite studies.

The index of antebellum affluence in New York is based on the tax assessment lists of 1828 and 1856–57.[135] While these are compilations of personal rather than corporate wealth, they include the officers and proprietors of the city's great commercial and financial houses. Investigating New York's richest residents takes on greater significance because, as in Boston, the wealthiest 1 percent of the population owned a disproportionate and increasing share of the city's personal property. In 1828 this group (those assessed for at least $35,000) held 23 percent of the total noncorporate wealth, and in 1840 the group (those assessed for at least $55,000) held 40 percent of this wealth.[136] For reasons already discussed, Pessen appears to have underestimated the share of self-made wealth in New York as well as in Boston. He claims that only the two Astors and possibly the three Lorrilards on the 1828 list of those rated as worth at least $100,000 derived from humble or moderate circumstances and that 95 percent inherited wealth or high status.[137] A much larger share of the rich, however, fashioned their own fortunes. The father of merchant-banker Samuel Whittmore, for example, is described in the *New England Historical and Genealogical Register* as "never a financial success himself."[138] Pessen's evaluation of the vintage of fortune in midcentury is more in accord with the findings here presented: "About seventy-five percent of the New York City families constituting the plutocracy of the so-called industrial era of the mid-1850s were families that comprised the elite of the merchant-capitalist era of a generation earlier," (see Tables 2 and 3).[139]

Table 2

VINTAGE OF FORTUNE FOR NEW YORKERS
ASSESSED FOR AT LEAST $100,000 IN 1828

Wealth Generation	Number	Percentage of Known Vintage
First[a]	15	39.5
Second	4	10.5
At least second[b]	2	5.3
Three or more	17	44.7
Known vintage	38	100
Total	59	—

[a]Those coming from moderate or poor circumstances.
[b]Wealth at least second generation and possibly older.

Table 3

VINTAGE OF FORTUNE FOR NEW YORKERS
ASSESSED FOR AT LEAST $100,000 IN 1856–57

Wealth Generation	Number	Percentage of Known Vintage
First	56	28.9
Second	45	23.2
At least second	19	9.8
Three or more	74	38.1
Known vintage	194	100
Total	440	—

These findings are based on relatively reliable historical, biographical, and genealogical sources.[140] If questionable material from Moses Yale Beach, *The Wealth and Biography of the Wealthy Citizens of the City of New York*, and Walter Barrett (Joseph Scoville), *The Old Merchants of New York*, had been used, the percentage of self-made rich residents and of those with traced vintages would have soared, but this information often proved erroneous. The proportion of those with known vintages was 64.4 percent in 1828 and 44.1 percent in 1857. Hence the conclusions drawn from these tables are based on substantial but incomplete evidence. It is possible that the lacunae in the data create a bias toward old wealth inherited from distinguished families, for this type of affluence is more frequently recorded.

Comparing the rich of 1828 and 1856–57 reveals a diminution in both polar categories, with ancient accumulations dropping less sharply than newly made money in the twenty-eight-year span. Very recent and very old wealth comprise the lion's share in 1828 because aristocrats—Van Rensselaers, Stuyvesants, Livingstons, and Pells—preserved their provincial prosperity, and many merchants—John Jacob and Henry Astor, and John and Philip Hone—recently made it to the top. Relatively new (first- and second-generation) fortunes comprise half the 1828 total and relatively mellowed accumulations (at least second and up) the remainder, indicating that the enclave included both continuity and fluidity. A generation later the middle vintages of wealth (second and at least second) had appreciably increased. The old families did not disappear, but the number of New Yorkers worth at least $100,000 had multiplied sevenfold, shrinking the aristocratic share of opulent residents. The 1856–57 list also comes at the end of the mercantile era when family-founding Astors, Hones, Lenoxes, and Lorrilards had descendants on the compilation and when transplanted New Englanders, like the Phelpses, had also acquired middle-aged fortunes.

Looking back on Main's findings for the economic elites of 1768–69 and 1791 discloses that shortly before the Revolution and in 1828 roughly the same proportion prevailed of self-made and inherited riches. This congruence apparently breaks down for the other contrasting dates, 1768–69 and 1856–57, and 1791 and 1828 and 1856–57. The subsequent divergence between the eighteenth-century and the later groups is accounted for by the increase in first-generation affluence immediately after the Revolution as against the decrease in this vintage in the nineteenth-century compilations. The growing discrepancy may be due to discontinuity caused by the Revolution or to the possibility that new money may be underestimated in the later assessments because of the paucity of information regarding sources of wealth.

Contrasting the assessment of lists for Boston in 1835 and for New York in 1828 shows the former with 11.8 percent fewer self-made figures and 8.5 percent fewer ancient fortunes. New York's edge in mellowed wealth arises from the fact that its colonial aristocracy survived in better shape. On the Boston list Thomas L. Winthrop alone came from a family that matched the descendants of New York's gentry in historical importance. On the other hand, Boston had 6.5 percent more second-generation affluence and 13.8 percent more at-least-second-generation affluence. Boston's lead in these categories occurred mostly because its merchants and their children in manufacturing had established themselves a generation before the New Yorkers. Indeed, the profile of 1835 opulence in Boston more closely resembles that of New York in 1856–57, when Gotham's mercantile community had also matured over a generation. Both cities' vintage profiles correspond even more closely in the 1860 Boston list and the 1856–57 New York list. The differences in the categories are: New York, 4.9 percent more first-generation wealth, 4.8 percent more third-or-more-generation wealth, 3.6 less second-generation wealth, and 6.1 percent less at-least-second-generation wealth. The coinciding trend reflects the movement of Gotham fortunes into the second generation while some Boston merchants, like William Gray, grandson of the family founder, now possessed property at least three generations old.

Percentages of known birthplaces, 76.3 in 1828 and 50.9 in 1856–57, reasonably high for the earlier compilation but incomplete for the later, condition the comparison between these dates (see Tables 4 and 5). The geographical origins of the wealthiest citizens indicate that New York's attainment of national economic leadership drew men from far-flung birthplaces. The proportion of native New Yorkers dropped substantially in the generational interval; correspondingly, the share of those coming from elsewhere in the United States increased by the same amount. Moreover, in 1828 half of those born in other states came from Connecticut and New Jersey, areas contiguous to New York, and the

Table 4

GEOGRAPHICAL ORIGINS OF NEW YORKERS
ASSESSED FOR AT LEAST $100,000 IN 1828

Birthplace	Number	Percentage of Known Birthplaces
New York City	22	48.9
New York State	6	13.3
Born elsewhere in United States	8	17.8
Born abroad	9	20.0
Known birthplaces	45	100
Total	59	—

Table 5

GEOGRAPHICAL ORIGINS OF NEW YORKERS
ASSESSED FOR AT LEAST $100,000 IN 1856–57

Birthplace	Number	Percentage of Known Birthplaces
New York City	84	37.5
New York State	27	12.1
Born elsewhere in United States	65	29.0
Born abroad	48	21.4
Known birthplaces	224	100
Total	440	—

rest from New England. Thirty years later, a slightly larger share of those born in other states came from contiguous areas, but others hailed from more distant places like Virginia, Maryland, Louisiana, and Kentucky. As reflected in the origins of many great merchants, the metropolis attracted outside talent mainly from New England, especially from Connecticut and next from Massachusetts. Four of the rich on the earlier list and eleven on the later list moved in from Massachusetts.

On the first lists of the two cities New Yorkers had more varied geographical origins than did Bostonians. Native Bostonians had only a marginal edge over native New Yorkers, but those from Boston or Massachusetts had a twenty-three-point lead over those born in New York City or State, and no foreign-born were among the Hub's wealthiest citizens. On the assessments of the next generation the comparative cosmopolitanism of New York became even more marked. Native Bostonians were ahead of native New Yorkers by 9.6 percent and natives of Boston and Massachusetts were 34.3 percent more frequent in proportion to natives of New York City or State. Moreover, New Yorkers born elsewhere in the United States sometimes came from distant regions, a characteristic not typical of those who moved to Boston. New York also had an 18.5 percent margin over Boston in foreign-born rich residents. Foreign-born Bostonians overwhelmingly came from the British Isles, but New Yorkers came from a variety of European countries.

Apart from generational and geographic measures of cohesion, kinship ties among individuals on the same list and appearance of family members and individuals on both compilations provide additional assessments of integration in the upper economic strata. Thirty-one of the 1828 New Yorkers (52.5 percent) were related by blood or marriage to others on the list; 163 of the 1856–57 group (37.0 percent) were similarly connected. The rate of persistence was higher than the degree of interrelatedness for the 1828 enclave: forty-four (74.6 percent) reappeared or had relatives on the later list. In 1856–57, however, the reverse occurred: 134 (30.0 percent) had appeared or had kin on the 1828 assessment. The enormous expansion in the numbers of rich residents, a consequence of New York's spectacular economic growth, brought wealth to many newcomers, and they intermarried more with each other than with the older families of 1828. Conversely, the higher degree of persistence of the 1828 wealthy meant that changes in the profile of the economic elite were due to expansion not to the disappearance of inherited fortunes. Interrelationship and persistence considerably diminished over the thirty-year span because of the significantly higher proportion of rich born outside the city in 1856–57 and the tremendous increase in the number of wealthy citizens between the earlier and later lists.

Family relationships among affluent Bostonians in 1835 and 1860 followed the same declining trend, but remained more prevalent than in New York. Bostonians had an 18.4 percent edge in interrelatedness in the first list and a 7.7-point lead in the last. This higher proportion is explained by the slower growth and more insular geographical origins of the Hub's moneyed circle. A countervailing factor, however, operated to narrow the gap. By 1856–57 Gotham had made up more than half the lead in interrelatedness held by Boston in the earlier assessments. This gain reflects the post-1846 sharp decline in textile profits, which inhibited the growth of Brahmin fortunes. Bostonians were also ahead of New Yorkers in rates of persistence by 10.2 percent in the earlier compilation and by 8.6 percent in the later compilation. The causes for the variance in family relationships apply to the differences in continuity.

Membership in the upper class is the last cohesive indicator. For New York we designate as patrician the enclave of colonial families and great Knickerbocker and New England–born merchants whose formation was completed by the 1820s. As in the case of the Brahmins and for the same reasons, membership includes those or their direct descendants up to two generations with marital or blood ties to this group. The aristocratic component of New York wealth in 1828 was thirty-three (55.9 percent); in 1856–57, 144 (32.8 percent). Boston, too, suffered a decline in upper-class membership from earlier to later lists, but it was ahead of New York by 9.9 percent on the first compilation and 5.2 percent on the last. The intra- and interurban differences in this category result from the same factors influencing the degrees of persistence and interrelatedness.

Does the profile of the economic elite change at even higher rungs of wealth? The eighty-four rated at $250,000 and above in 1856–57 constitute the only group sizeable enough to permit useful statistical measurement. This enclave showed no important changes (variations of no more than 4 percent) in vintage of fortune and in upper-class representation from the totality beginning at $100,000. An 8.1 percent larger segment of the eighty-four had belonged or had relatives in the 1828 list than had those assessed for a minimum of $100,000. Two linked categories showed greater differences between these levels of wealth. The richer group had a 14.2 percent greater proportion of interrelatedness and a 12.5 percent larger share of natives of the city. The thirteen New Yorkers assessed for at least $250,000 in 1828 and the eighteen worth at least $500,000 in 1856–57 show an even larger percentage born in New York and much higher levels of old family membership, persistence, and interrelatedness compared to lower steps of wealth on their respective assessment lists. No significant change occurred in the distribution of old and new fortunes except for a 13.6 percent rise in first-generation affluence between the $500,000-and-above level over the $250,000-and-above stratum in 1856–57. This difference may be due to the much greater proportion of those with known vintages at the top rung. At the highest level of wealth, 88.9 percent of the generational sources could be traced; at the $250,000-or-more level, 51.2 percent. The discrepancy in tracing lends credence to the argument that as the unavailability of data on generational background of wealth increases, the possibility of underestimating self-made accumulations grows larger. Those assessed for at least $500,000, all things being equal, were more likely to draw the attention of biographers and genealogists than those at lower levels of wealth. This contention is supported by the finding that three or more generations of riches in the top rank of 1856–57 was 6.2 percent less than in the at least $250,000 category and 4.8 percent lower than for the entirety beginning at $100,000. Unfortunately, so few belonged to the richest cohort that a slight change in numbers creates an enormous shift in percentages. Aside from the newly risen at the top level of opulence in 1856–57, the indicators point toward greater cohesion, continuity, and upper-class membership at each higher step on the pyramid of affluence, a trend similar to that of Boston. At each higher stage progressively larger proportions of wealthy Bostonians than New

Yorkers, however, were interrelated, belonged to the patriciate, and persisted from one list to the other.

Examination of the tax assessment lists of the two cities shows that wealthy residents of Boston were more integrated and more aristocratic than their New York counterparts. These findings reflect institutional differences between the urban business structures. Boston firms tended to be older and more frequently family-structured and market conditions generally more stable. Hence the higher rates of patrician, persistent, and family wealth in that city. Another factor contributing to the weaker forces of integration in New York was the more rapid multiplication of fortunes in that city. Boston still had an edge in kinship and generational cohesion and continuity of fortune, in the 1850s; however, its margin narrowed. The initial gaps were wider because the old New York merchants declined before 1825, thus opening up opportunities for new men. Brahmins later encountered losses in the textile industry, thus bringing the indicators closer together. The universal decline in these categories in both cities, including that of ancient wealth, resulted from the rapid expansion of antebellum fortunes and the corresponding departure of Old Guard merchants. Growing diversification of the birthplaces of New York's affluent inhabitants also undermined cohesion in that elite.

Politics

Elites in New York and Boston involved themselves in politics for the same reasons and in the same manner. Their proprietary attitude toward government derived partly from commercial interests. John Alsop, John Brevoort, John Jay, August and Frederick Van Cortlandt, and the Society of New York Hospital, for example, held more than one-third of New York City's Corporate Debt Due on Bond in 1784.[141] Aside from business concerns, the rich and well-born sought to influence the government to assist the philanthropic and cultural activities that fortified upper-class civic hegemony. Bostonians and New Yorkers pursued these goals through serving in government and by establishing commercial and personal ties with public officials.

Nowhere was government leverage more crucial and business and politics more intimately associated than in banking. Incorporation, deposits of public funds, suppression of competitors, and a stable and ample supply of credit depended upon favorable municipal, state, and national action. Conversely, government at all levels employed financial institutions to help implement public policy. Hamilton, as previously described, performed vital services for the Bank of New York, which reciprocated by assisting the federal administration's fiscal activities. The Federalist monopoly in New York banking was broken when the Manhattan Water Company, initially a waterworks, was formed because

Republican leaders, such as Aaron Burr and Chancellor Livingston, and Federalist merchants, such as John Murray, president of the chamber of commerce and director of the Bank of New York, and Gulian Verplanck, president of that bank, convinced the common council to reverse its original preference for a publicly owned utility. The state legislature subsequently granted the corporation a banking charter, and Fedceralist businessmen and politicians, alarmed when the bank aided the Democratic-Republicans, successfully went to the same body to incorporate the Merchants' Bank. In both cases bribery facilitated the bank charters, and both institutions assisted their respective parties.[142]

In other enterprises cooperation between businessmen and public servants resulted in profits and privileges for those with entrée into government circles. The importance of politically influential promoters of transportation ventures was mentioned above. Federalist congressmen from New York got tariffs reduced on goods imported at the Hudson River port and defeated attempts to discriminate against British shipping in which city merchants were involved. Banker-merchant-politician Richard Varick and overseas trader Benjamin Romaine received water rights from the municipality while trustees of the corporate property of New York; John Jacob Astor amassed the largest single share of these shore lots; and merchants Isaac Roosevelt, John Alsop, and Walter Livingston were granted similar privileges by the municipality. Varick also bought city property while mayor. Future mayors Marinus Willett and Cadwallader Colden obtained ferry franchises from the city, and Willett's line ran to his Long Island wharf. William B. Astor successfully petitioned the common council to request the state legislature to change the health law so that furs could be brought to New York during the summer, James Gore King, New York and Erie Railroad president and senior partner in Prime, Ward & King, influenced the legislature to give a state credit of $3 million to construct the line.[143] Personal attachments with key public figures worked to businessmen's advantage. John Jay invited merchant Nicholas Cruger and LeRoy Bayard & Co. to exploit a proposition suggested to Jay by a Dutchman. Taking time from ambassadorial duties in 1794, Jay wrote Cruger, "I esteem and like" LeRoy Bayard, & Co., and "their acquaintance with the commerce of Holland and their connections in that country would afford facilities to all parties." Another case of politico-commercial symbiosis existed in the relationship of minister to France Gouverneur Morris with the firm of James and William Constable. Morris, involved in shipping ventures and land speculation with this house, informed William Constable, "I shall keep a good look out and give you the best [business] intelligence I can." Statesmen also exploited their positions to secure commercial advantages for their children. Rufus King, former Federalist U.S. senator and recently resigned minister to England, used his friendship with Sir

Francis Baring to place his son Charles, who desired a mercantile career, with Baring Brothers.[144] Tax and assessment policies that favored corporations and wealthy property holders were among the benefits obtained by those with influence in the right quarters. Real and personal property was consistently underassessed, and not until 1823 were bank stocks, bonds, and mortgages made taxable. In that year only $91,462 was collected from corporations and in 1827 and 1828, an even lesser amount. Municipal property revenues were ludicrously small. In 1805 the city collected $127,095 from this source; in 1825, $387,449, and in 1835 the levy had not yet reached $1 million.[145]

The upper order manipulated government policy by entering public office or by associating with politicians. Out of these interactions emerged, as in Boston, the Federalist-mercantile elite. Prominent New Yorkers correctly envisioned the treasury headship as a pivotal post in this alliance. "Our Minister of the Finances," asserted Gouverneur Morris, should be "habituated to business on the most extensive scale, . . . a regularly bred merchant . . . who has been long and deeply engaged in that profession."[146] In this case, at least, the hopes of the New York aristocrat were realized. Hamilton, his assistant William Duer, and Oliver Wolcott, the next secretary of the treasury, belonged to or were allied with the city's business elite.

Merchant-bankers were particularly active in public life because of the relationship between government and finance. The early presidents of the Bank of New York almost invariably had political backgrounds. Matthew Clarkson had served in both state houses. Heads of other banks had similar credentials. Wolcott was president of the Bank of America and Merchants' Bank. Another Merchants' president, Richard Varick, had been attorney general of New York, recorder and mayor of the city, and speaker of the assembly. Bank directors and stockholders also frequently held office; one-fourth of the 283 federal, state, and municipal officeholders from New York City between 1778 and 1815 were bank directors.[147]

Merchants, including those who were not bankers, were also active in politics: 117 of the New York officeholders between 1778 and 1815 were or would become foreign traders; of the 114 common councillors from 1783 to 1801, nearly one-third (thirty-six) were merchants. Another twenty-three were lawyers, many of whom belonged by interest and family to the maritime enclave. Since its formation in 1686 the upper occupational groups (merchants, lawyers, and large landowners) had been overrepresented, relative to their numbers in the city population, on this body. From 1734 to 1775 they held as many seats as did artisan, farmer, and shopkeeper aldermen and assistant aldermen. From 1789 to 1800 an egalitarian trend occurred, which returned common councillors with more prestigious occupations to approximately the same minority share that they constituted from 1686 to 1733. A similar pattern existed in these three eras regarding the occupations and political offices of councillors' fathers and in the degree of rotation in that office. During the middle period, councillors were more likely to be sons of merchants, lawyers, large landowners, and government officials and to remain in office for a longer term than in the early colonial or national periods.[148]

Between 1783 and 1801 New York City representatives presided over the assembly in eight of seventeen sessions despite the city's 9 percent share of lower house seats. Speakers Varick, Gulian Verplanck, John Watts, Jr., and Samuel Osgood were members of the Federalist-mercantile group, and Watts and Verplanck had distinguished colonial forebears. Long Island and New York City legislative delegations, especially in the state senate, for a generation after the Revolution contained numerous members of blueblood clans and of the business elite. Also active at the state level were Governors John Jay and Morgan Lewis, sons of prominent New York merchants, while James Kent, Robert R. Livingston, Samuel Jones, and other upper-class judges presided over courtrooms from the municipal chambers to the state supreme court.[149] The well-born and the rich were also prominent in national bodies. Between 1789 and 1800 city residents Rufus King, Aaron Burr, and Gouverneur Morris were U.S. senators. King, who speculated extensively in government securities and was a director of the Bank of New York and the National Bank, married John Alsop's daughter and sired James Gore King. Merchant Nicholas Low handled his business affairs and finances. Burr helped found the Manhattan Company, and Morris speculated in the national debt and was associated with New York merchants in several overseas trading voyages. Senator John Lawrence, from Queens County, came from a family of famous merchants, bankers, and landowners, and Senator Philip Schuyler, from Albany, Hamilton's father-in-law, was heavily involved with urban capitalists through canal ventures. The congressional delegations included men of the same type.[150] New York's mayors between 1784 and 1815—James Duane, a Livingston son-in-law; Varick; Edward Livingston, who assisted in the Manhattan Company charter effort; and merchant Marinus Willett, descendant of the original (1665) mayor—were upper class by birth or marriage. Wealthy merchants, eminent lawyers, and offspring of aristocratic families also became recorders, city treasurers, city commissioners, and aldermen.[151]

The majority of the important merchants, bankers, and lawyers, whether of colonial gentry stock or of more recent arrival, were Federalists. The party drew its strength from the same sources as it did in Massachusetts and for the same reasons. New York merchants and landlords also feared that an agrarian-dominated assembly might expropriate the rich and desired a strong national government to encourage shipping, protect property, fund the national debt, stabilize currency, and generate capital. New York, even more than Boston, especially in the affluent, commercial wards, was a Federalist stronghold and its patriciate supported ratification of the national constitution. Schuyler, Morris, Jay, Hamilton, and King, Federalist chieftains in New York, belonged by birth or marriage and business interest to the Knickerbocker gentry or the maritime elite. Compared to their Democratic-Republican counterparts, Federalist officeholders in New York City between 1789 and 1815 had: (1) higher property assessments, (2) higher proportions of merchants and sons of merchants; of bank and insurance company directors; of members of upper-class organizations like the chamber of commerce, the Society of the Cincinnati, the New York Society Library, and the St. George's and St. Andrew's societies, of Episcopalians, of college graduates and trustees, of relatives also holding office, and (3) greater likelihood of being reelected to the same public posts or chosen for other public posts. Conversely, Democratic-Republican officeholders had larger shares of mechanics and sons of mechanics, and came, as in the case of Massachusetts, from newer families; only one member of that party was on Mrs. John Jay's "dinner and supper list" of 1787–88, a Who's Who of society in that era.[152]

The commercial elite supplemented personal and business friendships and control of the Federalist party by using voluntary associations to influence government action. The chamber of commerce, the chief pressure group, memorialized appropriate public bodies to form a national bank, build the Erie Canal, improve the harbor and waterfront, and aid New York railroads. Among its presidents were Federalist merchants and bankers Alsop; Cornelius Ray, president of the New York branch of the second BUS; William Bayard, president of the Bank of America and partner in LeRoy, Bayard & McEvers; Robert Lenox; Alsop's grandson James Gore King; Rufus Prime, another partner in Prime, Ward & King; and Peletiah Perit. Prime, Lenox, Bayard, and King served as state legislators or aldermen, and between 1778 and 1815 forty-two (19.6 percent) of New York City's officeholders belonged to the chamber.[153]

Even in the heyday of Federalism, merchants, bankers, and landed gentlemen did not always have their own way or speak with one voice on every issue. Federalist merchants split over chartering the Manhattan Company; in 1789 the common council denied the petition of several upper-class property owners for improvements in their houses and lots; anti-Federalists under George Clinton controlled the governorship and assembly between 1777 and 1795; Manhattan paid higher per capita taxes than other counties; and the legislature broadened the franchise over the objections of the Federalists.[154]

Unlike Boston, a Federalist bastion until the 1820s, the Republicans captured New York in 1804 and generally held it thereafter, a result of the Republican-controlled legislature lowering suffrage requirements in the metropolis. Although the Republicans usually came from families of lower wealth and rank than the Federalists, neither their backgrounds, the structure of their party, nor their principles or actions created class-cleavage politics. Federalist insurance and banking concerns were chartered by Republican-controlled legislatures and administrations, and state aid for internal improvements, which strengthened commercial interests, also passed Republican governments. The party's structure in the city helps explain Republican accommodation to the maritime-banking elite. Candidates from both parties came mainly from the wealthy business wards, and until 1792 the richest ward elected a Clintonian alderman. Sixty percent of the bank director officeholders were Federalist, but 40 percent were Clintonians and later Republicans; 32.4 percent of the Federalist officeholders were Episcopalians, as were 22 percent of their opponents; 20.4 percent of the Federalist officeholders were merchants' sons, as were 12 percent of the opposition; one-fourth of the Federalist officeholders had college degrees, as did 15 percent of the other party; 64.3 percent of the Federalist officeholders had at least one relative in a government position, as did 61.4 percent of the other side; 18.3 percent of the chamber of commerce officeholders were Federalists, but 11.6 percent were Clintonians and Republicans.[155] Moreover, the Livingstons, Lewises, and the relatively newly risen Clintons gave the Republicans a dynastic family leadership not unlike that of the Federalists.

After Jefferson's victory, the Federalist party in New York, as in Massachusetts, Pennsylvania, and the South, began to lose younger adherents. Schuyler, Jay, and Morris remained loyal but Verplanck, Colden, Peter A. Jay (son of John Jay), and Hamilton's children, preferring successful careers to consistent consciences, became Republicans and adopted the technique of popular appeal. In the 1820s one-fourth of the Clintonian leadership were ex-Federalists.[156] The defectors' complaints about the steadfast nestors resembled the charges that younger Boston Federalists made against their seniors. Verplanck saw in John Jay a deficiency in "a *knowledge of men* and a disregard of the causes of popular impression . . . with too unbending and inflexible dispositions on various occasions." Like the Old Guard Bostonians, ancient New York party chieftains responded by accusing the waverers of opportunism. Rufus King, even after the Federalist defeat of 1816, "would not suffer the self-humiliation & reproaches of the changlings, I could name, for the highest offices & applauses, that could be given them."[157] Words of derision for the inconstant notwithstanding, King later switched parties. The transition was perhaps easier in New York, where the Federalists had more experience with Republican rule and realized that it did not mean destruction of wealth and position and where the Federalist leadership was less alienated from the national administration than in Massachusetts.[158]

Changing parties involved more than rhetorical allegiance to democracy. Although the Clintonians were labeled the conservative and even pro-Federalist wing of Republicanism, they supported the elimination of the councils of revision and appointment, which served as conservative checks on the assembly, advocated the replacement of legislative caucuses with state conventions for gubernatorial nominations, favored county elections for local posts, were more sympathetic than the Martin Van Buren faction to debtor tenants and firmer than the Bucktails in taxing absentee landlords and in investigating manorial land titles and the Holland Land Company. The latter was a land-speculating organization which involved several Federalist merchants.[159]

Emergence of a mass electorate and the professional party manager, accompanied by loss of deference accorded traditional elites and the economic decline of the Knickerbockers, forced Federalists to adopt new parties and perspectives. Joining the winning side prolonged individual careers, but patrician sovereignty did not survive transplantation. Foreign traders, gentlemen bankers, and aristocrats never dominated the Republicans, Democrats, and Whigs as they had the Federalists. The new leaders, Thurlow Weed, William L. Marcy, Van Buren, Silas Wright, and Fernando Wood, were men of obscure origins who had more rapport with the populace and with the growing ethnic minorities in New York City. They were not businessmen who intermittently entered politics to protect their interests or bluebloods who procured public posts through family influence. Specialization and professionalization of politics, akin to that of business, increasingly separated businessmen and gentlemen from officeholders and party chieftains. The dynastic politics of provincial times and the post-Revolutionary generation gave way to machine politics which meant interparty competition, preoccupation with winning offices and elections, the discipline of patronage, and the emergence of careerists who made politics a life-long and full-time vocation. These conditions discouraged merchants, bankers, and patricians unwilling to commit the time or energy, or make the compromises necessary for political success. In Massachusetts, where old families remained more powerful commercially and politically and where antebellum machines developed later and never achieved the power of the Albany Regency or Tammany Hall, old-style upper-class politics survived in better shape.

A shift away from wealthy and upper-class officeholding accompanied the decline of Federalism. Between 1778 and 1800 one-third of the public servants from New York City were merchants when they entered office. The mercantile share of officeholding decreased by one-half between 1800 and 1815. Government officials who were mechanics or farmers did not increase; a rise of lawyers made up the difference.[160] But lawyers were generally less wealthy than merchants and more likely to be professional politicians. During the second quarter of the nineteenth century nearly three-fourths of the mayors were merchants, followed by lawyers, who accounted for one-fifth of the chief executives. New York also resembled Boston in that these two professions ranked first and second among the city councillors of 1825–37, merchants constituting over a fourth of that body. As in Boston, however, the democratizing tendency between 1838 and 1850 registered itself in the displacement of merchants as the most frequent calling, a decline of lawyers, and the expansion of artisans, laborers, mechanics, and farmers on the board of aldermen.[161] A sample of city-dwelling officeholders from 1835 to 1860 (federal officials in executive, diplomatic, and senate posts and congressmen between 1839 and 1849, the state legislators of 1840, and aldermen between 1842 and 1845, totaling 140 officeholders) consisted of 36 percent (fifty) lawyers and only 11 percent (fifteen) merchants and 2 percent (three) bankers. Of those holding municipal positions, only four of forty-five aldermen were merchants while fourteen were retailers. Four of the ten mayors, however, were overseas traders.[162] These occupational changes reflected important modifications in the shares of wealthy, upper-class officeholders. Sixteen of the fifty-nine New Yorkers (27.1 percent) and fifty-five of the 440 New Yorkers (12.5 percent) assessed for at least $100,000 respectively in 1828 and 1856–57 were or would become assistant aldermen, aldermen, judges, mayors, state legislators, governors, congressmen, senators, cabinet officers, ambassadors, or would fill other high positions in city, state, and federal administrations.[163] Eleven (18.6 percent) on the first list and twenty-four (5.5 percent) on the last were by birth or marriage from distinguished families, or their descendants up to two generations would enter distinguished families. A decline in wealthy officeholders and an even greater decrease of government officials belonging to the opulent upper class had occurred during the years. Relating the 1828 findings to the equivalent data on the Bostonians worth at least $100,000 in 1835 shows the latter having a 3.3 percent edge in officeholding and a 2.9 percent margin in upper-class public servants. Given the small percentage variances and the size of the groups measured, these differences are negligible. An interurban comparison of the later lists shows that rich Boston public servants of 1860 had an 11.2 percent edge and upper-class Boston public servants a 2.4 percent edge over their New York counterparts of 1856–

57. A contraction of affluent officeholders and an even sharper shrinkage in wealthy upper-class government servants occurred between the earlier and later assessments in both municipalities. As the Civil War approached, however, a considerably larger proportion of rich Bostonians and a slightly larger percentage of wealthy Brahmins held public posts than did their economic and social peers in New York. Affluence and officeholding did not diverge as much in Boston, and the patriciate was marginally more involved in government because greater proportions of rich Bostonians were born in or near their city, the genteel element among the wealthiest Bostonians was larger, and, despite the growing specialization of functions, that city's leading families maintained a more vigorous role in both business and civic affairs.

Professionalization and democratization of the political process undermined Old Guard influence. After 1820 the Knickerbocker element disappeared as party chieftains and officeholders, just as it vanished in various phases of business.[164] The fading of the old dynasties and their allies did not entail an abrupt or complete abandonment of public life. An occasional aristocrat turned up in the municipal government or the legislature, and several generations of Joneses were active in city and state government, especially on the supreme court, until the 1870s. Whig Hamilton Fish was governor in 1848 and Democrat John Alsop King in 1856; Rufus King returned to the U.S. Senate as a Democrat in 1820, and Fish was elected to that body in 1851. Verplanck, Colden, and Cornelius Van Wyck Lawrence served as congressmen at various times in the 1820s and '30s, as did James J. Roosevelt, J. Phillips Phoenix, and Fish in the 1840s. But these figures constituted a tiny minority of New York City officeholders and held little power in their party organizations. The New England–born merchants as a rule stayed out of politics, although Moses Grinnell became a Whig congressman. New York's mayoralty was the post most consistently held by merchants and upper-class types. After 1820, however, they appeared less frequently in that office. Colden (1818–21), Philip Hone (1826–27) (last of the Federalist mayors), Walter Bowne (1823), Lawrence (1834–37), and Robert H. Morris (1841–44), the final Knickerbockers, served in that capacity during the antebellum period.

Upper-class service, however, did not inevitably entail aristocratic style or the promotion of patrician power. Morris was a Tammany Democrat and Fish got started in the seventh ward under an ex-teacher and a cloth merchant whom he admired for manipulating "city alms" and "city patronage." Fish later came under the tutelage of Whig state boss Weed, a former blacksmith's helper. As governor he disliked making family appointments and refused pleas of brother-in-law Richard Morris for a state post.[165] For every aristocrat willing to adjust to the system many more warned against the new developments or shunned public office. William A. Duer, president of Columbia College, and Verplanck, former state legislator and congressman, and James A. Hamilton, son of Alexander Hamilton, condemned "party discipline," "partizan attachments" and "patronage" for Tammany Hall triumphs and the emergence of "an unmitigated and uncontrolled Democracy" which jeopardized the republic.[166] Strong expressed even more intense revulsion for contemporary politics. He rejected an aldermanic nomination in 1857 because election "would shorten my life. Whatever good name I have would be lost, for one can't touch the city government without being defiled, and my business income would disappear, for the office would demand every minute of my time." Strong also felt that he lacked the "capacity to do any real service against the sons of Belial, and should injure myself by taking the place without accomplishing any good whatever."[167] The eminent lawyer's disavowal of candidacy encompasses the patrician arguments against political involvement and anticipates the Gilded Age conviction that municipal service was an activity which gentlemen properly disdained. Even before the Civil War, genteel New Yorkers began to display the classical signs of a patriciate conscious of its own decay and alienated from its city.

When the Republicans divided during the Age of Jackson, former Federalists and the economic and social elite in Boston and New York overwhelmingly embraced Whiggery.[168] The new party, favoring internal improvements and a stable banking system, best represented their interests and values. Before Jackson removed the national government deposits from the BUS, wrote Federalist-turned-Whig Hone, "The merchants were doing a good and profitable business." Now "public confidence is shaken, personal property has no fixed value, and *sauve qui peut* is the maxim of the day." A few years later Strong noted "the increasing tendency of the Whig Party to absorb all the wealth and respectability, and to the Democratic (so-called) to take in all the loaferism of the nation. . . ."[169] New Yorkers who favored Whiggery, for the same reasons as their Boston allies, generally embraced the Cotton wing of the party and were compromisers in 1860. After Secession, Bostonians and New Yorkers of wealth, business eminence, and high status usually became Republicans.[170]

Principles as well as interest guided upper-class political thought, organization, and action. Elitist views of aristocratic and wealthy New Yorkers paralleled the outlook of their Boston peers. Well known to contemporaries and historians were the objections of Morris, Jay, King, Schuyler, Hamilton, and others to unchecked majorities and radical reforms as threats to order, property, liberty, and progress.[171] The next generation of bluebloods echoed this antipathy. Although the gentry at the state constitutional convention of 1821 were less numerous than at the charter meeting of 1777, a sprinkling of aristocrats, mostly descendants of 1777 delegates, made it the last body in which the Old Guard was prominently represented. These figures generally opposed attempts to lower suffrage requirements, shorten terms of office, weaken the judiciary, and strengthen the assembly at the expense of other branches and houses of government. Chancellor James Kent, Jeremiah Van Rensselaer, and Peter A. Jay withheld their signatures from the constitution because it exemplified the nationwide "passion for universal suffrage" and might unleash the propertyless majority against the privileged minority.[172] Other New Yorkers of Knickerbocker extraction and mercantile vocation shared the elitist persuasion. "To elevate, then, the character of the mechanic and the working man is the duty of your representative in the Assembly," said James William Beekman in 1848, in a Burkean announcement of candidacy. Pintard, Strong, and even self-made Philip Hone denounced popular rule because they feared that the mass electorate in New York fostered demagoguery, gave power to Irish voters, corrupted politics, unsettled business, threatened property, and encouraged mob violence. Duer, in a more oblique attack, told Columbia students in 1848 that college studies "will furnish you with greater power to wield or control that mighty engine" ["public opinion"].[173]

Upper-class Federalists and their patrician successors believed in the classical conservative doctrines of human imperfection, the sanctity of private property, a preference for concrete experience over abstract theory, and a distrust for radical social reconstruction. But their perspective, like that of the Brahmins, was elitist in the plutocratic rather than the aristocratic sense. Even the most antidemocratic, Morris and Hamilton, or the best born, Morris and Jay, were not American versions of Burke or de Maistre. Entrepreneurs themselves, sons of merchants, or closely associated with businessmen and bankers, they belonged to the most advanced commercial echelon in America and were unlikely to glorify inherited landed proprietorship. Property for them consisted of personal and national assets that could swell or shrink depending upon diligence, innovation, prudence, and the nurture of the state. Economic growth involved tangible resources of trade and manufacture and liquid assets of credit and capital. Finally, national economic growth was measured through the calculus of personal profits and appreciated values of bank stock and the public debt. Pioneers equally in politics and economics, they viewed government as an institution to coordinate and encourage capitalistic endeavor. Stability and order were, for them, rational conditions of economic growth, not the bastions of a hallowed past.

Committed to an achieving rather than an ascriptive establishment and rejecting European-type aristocracies, Federalist leaders felt that America's social order consisted of property and numbers, and they sought to incorporate both elements in an overlapping and countervailing system of government. Many bluebloods naturally approved of patrician statesmen and dynastic politics, but powerful officials from humble backgrounds have also placed relatives in public posts and aristocrats have accepted promising newcomers into their families. Schuyler told Hamilton he was "happy at the Connection you have made with my family" and asked his son-in-law Hamilton to "consider me as one who wishes in every way to promote your happiness."[174] Federalist patricians conceived of the upper order as a stratum of enterprising and wealthy businessmen, landowners, lawyers, and politicians, not as an estate with four quarterings of nobility. Proud of its ancestry, this enclave nevertheless absorbed newly risen successes.

Another premise of classical conservatism rejected by many New York Federalists, e.g. Morris, and in which respect they differed from their Boston cohorts, was a religious establishment. Most of the aristocratic delegates at the 1821 constitutional convention voted against a state-supported church or against making Christianity the only legally sanctioned religion.[175]

A brief examination of the ideas of Hamilton, the most intransigent opponent of democracy, and Morris, the most aristocratically inclined, shows that even in extreme cases Federalist leaders were not inflexible defenders of a mythic ancient regime. Although they argued that at least one branch of the government should serve for life and saw some virtue in hereditary rule,[176] neither statesman advocated an oligarchy nor conceived of the upper strata as a transplanted European nobility. "But who are the aristocracy?" asked Hamilton at the New York ratifying convention of 1787: "Indeed every man distinguished [by wealth and ability] . . . is an aristocrat." In the speech recommending a British type of government, Hamilton opposed "the granting of titles of nobility." Hamilton occasionally advocated monarchy and believed that "the wealthy" had better "character" and were "probably more favorable to the prosperity of the state" than were "the indigent," but he rejected aristocratic rule and at times even expressed republican sentiments. "Asserting my own political creed," he wrote in a private letter of 1792, "I am *affectionately* attached to the Republican theory. I desire *above all things* to see the *equality* of all political rights exclusive of all *hereditary* distinction firmly established by a practical demonstration of its being consistent with the order and happiness of society."[177]

Morris, too, equated "Aristocracy" with "the Rich." He felt that "our government" must "depend on the influence which property shall acquire; for it is not to be expected that men who have nothing to lose will feel so well disposed to support existing establishments as those who have a great interest at stake."[178] But the propertied class he envisaged was not the historical gentry. This scion of manorial New York thought that the French nobility had "oppressed and insulted" the people and he praised the Revolution for abolishing "feudal tyranny." Moreover, European systems of government could not be reproduced here. Ideally, "the principal authority is vested in a permanent senate," but politics should be shaped by "experience" and the "materials for an aristocracy do not exist in America. . . ." There is little "of family, wealth, prejudice, or habit to raise a permanent mound of distinctions," or create "regular gradation of ranks among our citizens. . . ." Our upper class was based on wealth and in this nation "the industrious poor soon become rich, the idle and debauched soon perish." Ambivalent about a hereditary upper order, Morris supported the moderate faction in the French Revolution and found "good things" both in Burke's *Reflections on the Revolution in France* and in Paine's rejoinder, *The Rights of Man*.[179]

Moderates Jay and King, who also distrusted the masses and radical reform, were less alarmed over the progress of national affairs and more willing to adapt to democracy. Morris, Hamilton, and Schuyler despaired over Jefferson's election, but Jay repeatedly counseled against panicky predictions about imminent expropriation of property and "overturn" of order. "At present, democracy prevails too much," he wrote in 1807, but "the time may come when it prevails too little." Jay also did not denigrate the intelligence or virtue of the people as bitterly as did Hamilton and Morris.[180] King was even more receptive to new developments: Jefferson's victory left him "calm" and "convince[d]" that "Evils in respect to the Great Measures of the Government are not likely to happen." His party's "failure" in the state elections of 1816 "should discourage the Federalists from maintaining a fruitless struggle. It has probably become the real interest & policy of the Country, that the Democracy should pursue its own natural Course. Federalists of our age must be content with the past." A year later he pronounced "our political system . . . better fitted to our character and conditions, and more certain to promote the growth of the strength and wealth of the nation than any other system."[181]

Upper-class Federalist ideology stemmed from bourgeois values and allegiance to the business creed as well as from a realistic assessment of political possibilities. Correct government was practical and stable, protecting property and bolstering commerce and banking. Morris asserted that "commerce . . . tends greatly to that established order of things which can alone exist with justice, public and private." Jay advocated a government of "stability" and "strength," which would appeal to "the better kind of people, by which I mean the people who are orderly and industrious; who are content with their situations and not uneasy in their circumstances." Hamilton, like Jay, felt that the "better kind of people" supported the Constitution. This group was "the commercial interests," who wanted "a government capable of regulating protection and extending the commerce" and of curbing "domestic violence and the depradation which the democratic spirit is apt to make on property." During Washington's presidency, when these ends were being served, particularly through the efforts of the secretary of the treasury, King told Morris that "we are . . . the happiest people in the world. Our government is established, it performs as much as its friends promised, and its administration has evidently advanced the prosperity of its citizens." The senator noted that "Our Commerce & navigation continue to increase. . . . The sound state of public credit, and the Establishment of Banks, have already given aids to commerce, and will soon afford assistance to manufacturing & agriculture."[182]

The Federalist leaders were imbued with the bourgeois spirit. A teen-aged Hamilton declared, "My Ambition is [so] prevalent that I condemn the grov'ling and condition of a Clerk or the like, to which my Fortune condemns me and would willingly risk my life tho' not my Character to exalt my Station . . . I mean to prepare the way for futurity . . . we have seen such Schemes successful when the Projector is Constant. . . ." Ten years later, now a successful army officer, he wanted a "well-bred" wife with a large "fortune." Later, having arrived, he urged son Philip "to exert yourself [in study], that you may make us every day more and more proud of you."[183] Better-born Federalists also voiced the Protestant ethic. Rufus King, child of a prosperous Maine farmer and merchant, warned son Edward not to drink, gamble, or borrow money. "Regularity, order, . . . early rising, with industry and the prudent regulations of passions," he advised the youth, "not only conduce to health and wealth, but are the infallible agents, by which great results are produced." John Jay, whose grandfather had been a wealthy New York merchant, whose father retired early from the countinghouse to a country estate, and whose grandparents included a Bayard, a Van Cortlandt, and a Philipse, instructed his son's tutor to inculcate "habits of punctuality and industry [which] are so important through life that they cannot be too early and carefully formed." He dispensed the same wisdom to his children, pressing upon them the necessity of "prudence" and "virtuous exertions" motivated by "duty" and the rewards of "Providence." The gayer and more sophisticated Gouverneur Morris expressed identical notions: "Genius and science are pleasing and ornamental, but morals and industry are useful and essential . . . idleness is the root of all evil . . . young people should be kept at work in some business, which may enable them afterwards to earn a living for themselves and their families." In America, where the professions "are overstocked, . . . Commerce and the useful arts present a wider and more fertile field."

Nor was Morris the only patrician to express these sentiments. Republican Edward Livingston praised his child for "diligence" and recommended that the boy avoid drinking and late hours in order to "rise early and study hard."[184]

Federalist suspicions of the masses and notions of the purpose of government inspired subsequent generations of the upper rank. Blueblood constitutional delegates of 1821 and Pintard, Hone, and Strong differed little from their predecessors. Jeffersonian and later Jacksonian triumphs evoked similar anxieties about social unrest, economic instability, attacks on property, and popular rule. Nonetheless, later aristocrats, at least publicly, were not as antidemocratic. In the 1830s, '40s, and '50s, Verplanck, James A. Hamilton, William A. Duer, James Depeyster Ogden, and Charles King saw dangers in party machines and partisan conflict, but they overcame these doubts with faith in America's "Free institutions," "steady," "industrious," "enterprising and energetic," and "educated" populace, absence of European class distinctions or inherited rank and privilege, widespread distribution of wealth, preference of "wise innovation" over "time-honored usage," and rule by "the will of the people." An "equality in political rights" and economic opportunities enabled the "humblest individual" with "talent" and determination to rise above those born with advantages of wealth or high social status. These virtures, claimed as uniquely American, would bring unprecedented "happiness," "wealth," "power," and integrity to the young republic.[185]

Other members of the establishment looked more balefully upon national and local prospects. Hone and Strong viewed their personal plights and the deteriorating position of the patriciate as a symptom of decay and disaster. Pessimism, too, derived from Federalist-patrician sources. But a discussion of genteel accomplishments in the professions, charity, and culture properly precedes an analysis of upper-class dismay.

The Professions, Education, and Religion

Boston's blueblood professionals provided the Brahmins with economic and political services and amplified elite influence over the metropolitan community. Lawyers, doctors, ministers, and professors promoted group hegemony and cohesion by multiplying patrician leadership opportunities, sharpening its skills in important and respected vocations, legitimizing its mastery, and acting on behalf of the established order as agents of social control. Upper-class New York professionals functioned in a similar but less successful manner. The patrician bar, at least up to the 1820s, was probably superior in quality and more powerful than its Boston counterpart; Knickerbockers, however, did not match Brahmin achievements in medicine, education, and theology.

As in Boston, law ranked just behind commerce in influence and remuneration. Except for merchants, attorneys, constituting 7 percent of the richest New Yorkers in 1828 and 9 percent in 1845, appeared most often among the wealthiest city dwellers. Physicians, with 1 and 3 percent respectively in these years, tied for seventh in 1828 and for fourth in 1845.[186] Law was dominated by the upper class more completely than were any other professions. The origins of the aristocratic legal community antedate the Revolution. William Smith, Jr., Samuel Jones, Richard Morris, and William Livingston were the senior members of the bar in the 1770s and Duane, John Jay, Peter B. Livingston, Jr., and Gouverneur Morris began to win repute at this time. Increasing numbers of college graduates and gentlemen in the calling, high judicial posts filled by lawyers, greater prestige and fees, formation of professional societies, and attempts to raise the level of practice indicated an upgrading of vocational status and quality that took place throughout the eighteenth century, especially after 1750. Upper-class attorneys were trained in the offices of, and their business came mostly from, their social and economic peers. William Livingston clerked for James Alexander and William Smith and later handled the mercantile and manorial interests of his blueblood relatives, friends, and commercial associates. Gouverneur Morris studied under Smith and Duane and counseled his Livingston in-laws, members of the provincial gentry, and high British officials. Well-connected attorneys also advised upper-class organizations. Duane conducted legal matters for Trinity Church, and Thomas Jones acted in a similar capacity for King's College. Eminent members of the bar engaged in business ventures with the aristocracy and frequently held high public posts. Livingston served in the assembly, Smith sat on the governor's council and became chief justice of the colonial supreme court, and cousins Samuel and Thomas Jones were recorders of New York City.[187]

Independence did not disrupt traditional patterns in genteel legal circles. John Jay, Edward Livingston, Brockholst Livingston, Robert R. Livingston, James Kent, Gouverneur Morris, Samuel Jones, Jr., Duane, Alexander Hamilton, Morgan Lewis, and Josiah Ogden Hoffman ranked among the leading New York lawyers between 1785 and 1815. They belonged to distinguished families, participated in the ventures and handled the personal and institutional affairs of the maritime and banking elite, and began as clerks for and later trained aristocratic luminaries of the bar. An increase in the proportion of college-educated lawyers and the establishment of licensing requirements by New York's supreme court in 1797 improved professional standards. Hamilton's career illustrates many of these developments. James LeRoy and Pierre Van Cortlandt clerked for him, his clients included the first three banks formed in the city, the largest mercantile firms and magnates, James LeRoy & Sons, James Barclay, Nicholas Low, Cornelius Ray, and the baronial families.[188] Leaders of the bar, especially Hamilton, Morris, Burr, and the Livingstons, continued to be important political figures. Many patrician lawyers served in the municipal government as mayors and common councillors and between 1784 and 1800 virtually monopolized the post of recorder.

After the War of 1812 the old elite lost its grip on political and commercial affairs and its legal component similarly declined. Upper-class professional inbreeding continued through clerkships and partnerships in blueblood firms and practices with a patrician clientele. Successive generations of Beekmans, Joneses, Delafields, Hamiltons, and Jays became lawyers. Hamilton Fish studied under Peter A. Jay and went into partnership with J. Rusten Van Rensselaer and later with William Beach Lawrence. Jay's partner was James I. Roosevelt and Gulian Verplanck read law with Hoffman and Edward Livingston.[189] "The principal lawyers of the city," wrote James A. Hamilton, "who were the friends or contemporaries of my father, gave me their business."[190] Blueblood practitioners increasingly devoted themselves to administering patrician estates rather than the affairs of major banks and businesses. James Hamilton, Peter Jay, Hamilton Fish, and David S. Jones concentrated chiefly upon real estate and chancery litigation and family trusts for their clientele of relatives and associates. They also counseled upper-class organizations; for example, Fish handled the affairs of St. Mark's Church and land titles for the Erie Railroad. Some upper-class lawyers withdrew not only from more vital professional and commercial activities, but from active practice and even from the law itself. Kent, the Joneses, and Livingstons turned from litigation to politics, the bench, or scholarship; Verplanck and several Beekmans retired early or never practiced. A few Delafields, who combined a legal practice with gentleman farming and preferred intellectual pursuits to the law, continued halfheartedly in the calling.[191] The various forms of withdrawal show, as they did in Boston, the tendency of the Old Guard to vacate primary areas of wealth and power, diversify their interests, and scatter their energies. Different routes of disassociation led to the same point: inevitable displacement by single-minded, resourceful newcomers.

These trends were both reflected and countervailed in Wells and Strong (later Strong, Bidwell, and Strong), New York's largest antebellum law firm. Wells and Strong was founded in 1818 by Strong's father, George Washington Strong, scion of a well-known though not aristocratic Long Island colonial family, and John Wells, an upstate Federalist. Three generations of Strongs became partners and its clerks included several patrician novices. The firm concentrated mostly on probate, trust, and real estate matters, especially on the affairs of aristocratic clients. It also counseled patrician business and charitable organizations such as the Mutual Life Insurance Company and the Orphan Asylum

Society. The Strongs perfectly fitted their role as upper-class advocates. They were prominent in high society and trustees in patrician cultural, educational, and altruistic societies. Father and son, cautious conservatives in economic, social, and legal matters, abhorred speculation and indebtedness and emphasized precedent over legal innovations. Had the firm restricted its practice, clientele, and membership to the Old Guard, it would have suffered the same fate as other patrician practitioners. Fresh blood, however, was brought into partnership and self-made successes like John Jacob Astor enlisted its services. Under new management in the 1870s, it shifted litigation activities and was retained by several premier financial and industrial corporations.[192]

Upper-class New York was less prominent in the medical profession. Philadelphia, joined by Boston in the early nineteenth century, was the center of American antebellum medicine. Despite the earlier advent of medical facilities and organizations in New York, educational facilities were better and the community of physicians more harmonious and its morale higher in Boston. New York Hospital (created in 1771 by the Society of New York Hospital) admitted its first patients thirty years before Massachusetts General Hospital. The medical department of King's College (1768) appeared fourteen years earlier than Harvard Medical School, and a local New York City medical society existed in the 1760s. The Revolution, which devastated New York more severely than Boston, and internal rivalries, which plagued the pre–Civil War New York medical establishment, dissipated this lead. Conflicting factions formed competing associations and schools. Not until the College of Physicians and Surgeons (1806) affiliated with Columbia in 1811 did a permanent medical school emerge.[193]

Elite New York and Boston physicians had parallel career patterns. Members of the New York County Medical Society (1806) founded the College of Physicians and Surgeons and staffed New York Hospital. Doctors' organizations agitated for stricter license and fee laws to regulate admission into the profession and set standards of practice. Similarity in structure, however, did not mean replication of personnel. Compared to Boston, few upper-class medical families emerged, although bluebloods financed and directed hospitals and clinics. Leading early nineteenth-century doctors David Hosack, Samuel Mitchell, and John W. Francis hobnobbed with high society but did not come from patrician clans. The upper order possibly avoided the calling because of incessant disputes among contending medical faculties and societies. More likely, its relatively poor showing was due to a stronger propensity toward materialism and practicality than existed in Brahmin Boston. Knickerbockers preferred law, a vocation more attuned to these values. When occasional genteel physician-dynasties appeared, such as the Beekmans and Delafields, they did not match the achievements of the

Warrens, Jacksons, and Cabots in Boston. Moreover, many doctors in the two most famous New York medical families never practiced.[194]

Upper-class ministers and educators also lagged behind their Brahmin equivalents in wealth and in vocational attainment. Professors and pastors jointly accounted for 1 percent of the richest Bostonians in 1850, but these vocations were absent from lists of wealthiest antebellum New Yorkers.[195] Public education in Boston developed earlier and was better supported than in New York. Boston, in 1832, with less than two-thirds of New York's population spent nearly twice as much on schools.[196] Brahmins often went to Boston Latin; genteel New Yorkers enrolled exclusively in posh private institutions to meet the right people and absorb class mores. Pintard wanted his grandsons placed in cousin Samuel Bayard's school because it "is composed of children of our most respectable families, which is a great advantage as it keeps them from vulgar associations."[197] Columbia Grammar School (1763), connected with Columbia College, was the foremost patrician academy.

Upper classes in New York and Boston were primarily interested in higher education, chiefly in Columbia and Harvard. A high degree of continuity prevailed between King's College and Columbia. Descendants of the colonial aristocracy were heavily represented on its board of governors and among its presidents, officers, and students. William A. Duer, Charles King, and Benjamin Moore and his son served as presidents, Livingstons, Lawrences, and Ogdens as treasurers. Ties with Trinity Church also persisted. Many trustees and officers were Trinity wardens and vestrymen. Moore served as rector of Trinity and bishop of the diocese of New York, and Samuel Provoost, another rector and Episcopal bishop of the diocese, sat on the Columbia board. Graduation exercises until the 1830s were frequently held at Trinity. Columbia reciprocated this ritualistic interaction between upper-class institutions in 1787 by closing classes at Provoost's ordination and requiring the student body to attend the ceremony, and in 1846, when the trustees marched in the processional to dedicate the new Trinity Church.[198]

Columbia, like Harvard, was a Federalist stronghold, hence many party leaders and public officials were alumni or trustees who aided the college. In 1784 the legislature and the council of revision created the Board of Regents of the University of the State of New York. This body was formed chiefly to rejuvenate Columbia, which had been destroyed during the British occupation, and was dominated by graduates and trustees of the college. Over the objections of upstate Republicans, the board granted the school a considerable amount of state financial assistance. When the board was no longer controlled by friends of Columbia, former Professor (now Chancellor) James Kent rescued the school by voting as a member of the council of revision to veto an attempt to transfer power of appointing trustees from the college to the regents.[199]

Columbia and Harvard were ornaments of the New York and Boston establishments, but the Knickerbockers participated less than the Brahmins in scholarship and teaching. Few upper-class New Yorkers became Columbia professors and the school had no equivalent to the Norton or Channing dynasties at Cambridge. Nor was it, like Harvard, a breeding and recruiting agency for talented undergraduates who could enrich the elite. Intellectual endeavor meant less to the Gotham patriciate and the Columbia professoriate did not replicate the Harvard faculty's pivotal role in the creation of an upper-class intelligentsia.

Each college's endowment came largely from the local upper order, but the New York institution did not receive as much material support and resourceful direction from its city's patriciate; consequently it was inferior in quality and repute. Probably with Harvard in mind, President Duer said that Columbia "cannot boast of the rich endowments which some similar institutions, in other states received from private citizens,—whose examples well merit the imitation of your own merchant princes."[200] Except for medical education, Harvard's specialized and graduate schools appeared earlier: Columbia began its School of Mines in 1864, but the Lawrence School of Science opened in 1847; Columbia Law School started in 1858, thirty-nine years after the Harvard Law School. These belated initiatives indicated upper-class New York's comparative reluctance to transform its college from a provincial patrician school into a modern university willing to incorporate progressive intellectual developments. The denial of a professorship to noted chemist J. Wolcott Gibbs in 1854 was another example of conservative parochialism hindering institutional excellence. Gibbs was supported by several patricians, but other aristocratic trustees carried a majority against the appointment of a Unitarian. The college remained faithful to the Episcopalian insularity of the upper class and Gibbs went to Harvard.[201]

Columbia's weaknesses bothered several patrician trustees. Alumnus Strong, serving on a trustees' committee of 1858, complained about the students' lax study habits and the mediocrity of the undergraduates and the faculty. He wanted the college to hire the most famous professors, including Gibbs, improve its faculties and curricula, start an engineering school, introduce controversial scientific and political ideas in courses, and tighten undergraduate standards. These recommendations reflected the view that Columbia could "gain conspicuous position and power" in the metropolis only "by appealing to the dominant wants and impulses of the time, and should, therefore, place itself in close contact with the centres of population and activity." The committee did not go as far as Strong desired. But, in arguing that rich, upper-class students should no longer receive special treatment by being indulged in gentlemanly indolence and that an upgrading of academic standards and the imposition of stricter discipline was necessary, it pressed for relevance and careerism instead of the traditional class education.[202] Hamilton Fish, another alumnus-trustee, shared this outlook. He brought in Francis Lieber to fill a chair in political science, advocated expansion of the college and the opening of a school of mines, improvement of the law school, and the creation of a faculty of political science, and supported Gibbs. Ten years after Strong's statements, however, Fish still deplored the shoddy scholarship and teaching of the faculty, an inadequate physical plant, poor undergraduate study habits, low academic standards, and a sparse student body.[203]

Columbia and Harvard experienced the same dispute between inbred, upper-class traditionalists and those committed to professional excellence and modernized education. For the conservatives, Greek and Latin studies epitomized genteel culture; for the reformers, the classical curriculum blocked rational recruitment of faculty and students and the introduction of updated and practical subject matter. Alumnus-trustee Gulian Verplanck straddled the issue by asserting that the classics and the newer disciplines, tradition and inventiveness, were both desirable and harmonious. Philip Hone, who had not gone to college, sought "to enforce the claims of classical learning" against "a host of utilitarians" whose "innovation[s] threaten to destroy the foundations of learning. . . ." Scrambling to a place among the gentility, he declared, "[I] would give one-half I possess in the world to enjoy the advantages of a classical education. Oh that my sons knew how to appreciate their opportunities of acquiring knowledge, and would profit by their father's experience!" Aristocrat Ogden Hoffman, another old graduate on the board of trustees, also disdained the "bigoted utilitarian argument." Classical studies refined the intellect, "elevat[ed] the moral feelings," and checked excessive and impulsive innovations by preserving the past and guiding the vox populi.[204] President Duer expressed similarly elitist feelings by telling his undergraduates "to fit yourselves for public life" and use their education to lead the masses toward a higher morality. In praising the graduates, particularly multigenerational alumni on the board, he reaffirmed the tradition of a provincial institution controlled by the local patriciate. Among the Columbia trustees were "a second Jay, an Ogden and a Jones," whose "intercourse and sympathies of business drew closer between them the ties of personal friendship . . . they were Christian gentlemen and scholars. . . ." Arguments in support of insular elitism replicated Old Guard Brahmin assertions about the place and meaning of Harvard. President Moore, however, in opposing the recommendations of the trustee committee, which advocated higher academic standards, voiced a practical plea absent in more intellectually confident proper Boston: with "lax views, so prevalent, respecting the value of thorough scholarship conducive to success in the ordinary pursuits of life, it may be doubted whether public opinion in this city would sustain so strict a course . . . there must be some allowance unless we are ready to reduce our classes to the comparatively small number who are in earnest in the pursuit of a good education."[205]

Strong, among the foremost critics of established educational patterns and ideas, nevertheless declared that Columbia, "to be of real value must found its teaching on a 'positive Christian basis'" that was "not a legitimate subject of Academic discussion."[206] A Trinity vestryman, his unwillingness to subject religion to the same inquiry that he demanded for education indicated that upper-class New York closed ranks on matters of fundamental belief. The patriciate anticipated the Brahmins by several generations in adopting Episcopalianism. Until the 1830s Trinity was still the reigning upper-class church, incorporating through its colonial past and aristocratic tone the hierarchy, tradition, and ornate ritualism that attracted southern planters and eastern seaboard elites to the Episcopal faith. Wardens and vestrymen invariably came from the best families and Trinity's marriage and burial ceremonies, pewholders, and benefactors extensively involved the same stratum. The first five bishops of the diocese (1786–1854) had been rectors or assistant ministers of the parish and until 1830 the bishopric and the rectorship were combined in the same person. The first two bishops, Provoost and Moore, whose consecutive service lasted over thirty years, belonged to noted Knickerbocker clans and were on Mrs. Jay's list. Trinity's aristocratic leaning long outlasted the Federalist patriciate. "One thing which we need is young men of good education, of good families and breeding, & of high education to give themselves to the Sacred Ministry," wrote Bishop Horatio Potter, in 1855, urging protegé Morgan Dix to become an assistant minister.[207]

Trinity was the wealthiest, as well as the most prestigious, church in New York. In 1856 Strong estimated its urban landholdings, exclusive of accrued rents, at over $1.6 million.[208] Its resources, connections, and congregation enabled Trinity, at least until the 1830s, to maintain predominance. In 1813 and 1832 the parish defeated an attempt to put a street through the churchyard. The city's Episcopalians elected the vestry until 1814, when the state legislature, at the church's behest, limited this right to the congregation. Trinity also beat back repeated efforts of heirs of the original owners of the King's College land grant to regain the family property. In the 1840s and '50s, when Trinity's supremacy had waned, the parish retained sufficient strength to again prevent the common council from constructing a thoroughfare through the burial grounds, to stop the legislature from repealing the act of 1814, and to keep Columbia's property in the college's hands. Trinity's wealth, power, and precedence made it the mother church of the diocese and a prime supporter of important charitable and cultural organizations. It gave land and money, and helped found several upper-class houses of worship, St. Mark's in the Bowery (1799), Grace Church (1805), St. Michael's (1807), and St. George's (1811), as the city grew in population and area. Trinity assisted in the formation of the General Theological Seminary (1819), Sunday schools for indigent children, the Episcopal Charity School, missions to the city poor and the heathen abroad, the Free School Society, and the New York Society Library. William Berrian, the eighth rector, estimated that Trinity up to 1846 had given away $2 million in loans, gifts, and land grants.[209]

After 1830 Trinity's eminence dimmed. Old families that controlled and funded the parish were eclipsed in power and opulence by recently arrived businessmen and politicians. For the first time in fifty years its rectors were not bishops of New York, and conflicts arose between the now separate powers in the parish. Newer shrines diverted upper-class membership as old and new elites moved uptown and squabbles occurred in the 1840s between Trinity and these churches over parish governance. Trinity was charged with niggardly donations to the diocese, and in the 1850s a public dispute arose over the uses of Trinity's affluence and the size of its charitable contributions. "The condition and character of our congregations have materially changed," declared Rector Berrian in 1855, dwelling upon modifications in the church, the congregation, and the neighborhood. "The Gospel may still be preached to the poor . . . to the strangers who visit our city . . . to the young men engaged in mercantile or medical pursuits . . . to the casual attendants led thither by curiosity or convenience. . . . With these several classes our churches may once more be filled to overflowing."[210] Berrian's comments reflect a sense of dislocation in the upper-class community and an awareness that it had been replaced by more functional, depersonalized, and alienated groups. He recognized, as did others connected institutionally or personally with the Knickerbocker enclave, that unities based on class, family, and tradition had been destroyed by the segmental, modern metropolis. The rector called upon the parish to adjust to these new conditions, but Trinity's values and officers could not respond, thus losing much of what remained of the church's moral leadership.

As Trinity declined, St. Michael's, St. Mark's, and Grace challenged its reign over sectarian and altruistic activities. St. Mark's, dominated by the Stuyvesants and other ancient families, catered to the Old Guard. St. Michael's had a larger complement of New England and New York merchants of later vintage. Both churches underwent the experience of Trinity, the rich and well-born moved away, and the congregation changed.[211] Grace, founded by relics of the colonial gentry and by the Knickerbocker foreign traders, was soon taken over by the post-1820 mercantile-banking elite. By the 1840s it was the wealthiest parish in the city. Hone and Strong, members of a vanishing social order, deplored the rector's penchant for "pomps and vanities" and the *nouveau riche* congregation, whom they considered vulgar showoffs. The New York *Herald* reported these traits more favorably in covering the consecration of the new church building: "The Church was filled with one of the most beautiful congregations we ever saw gathered together. Youth, elegance, and jewelry were combined." High pew rents and successive moves uptown into the new exclusive neighborhoods kept Grace fashionable. Its standing with the *arrivistes* was reinforced during the 1840s, when Isaac Brown, the first of a series of *déclassé* arbiters of high society, became sexton. He labeled Grace "the most fashionable and exclusive of our metropolitan 'courts of Heaven.'"[212] The former upstate carpenter occupied an unprecedented position among the older eastern seaboard elites and played a role, in refining upstart wealth and guiding freshly minted society, unique to New York. Unlike patriciates in such places as Charleston, Boston, and Philadelphia, the upper order in New York fragmented into the Old Guard and the emerging "smart set." Brown became the master of ceremony for the latter, and it was not coincidental that Grace was the base of his operations.

Brown's official post and unofficial function illustrates an important dimension of upper-class religion in New York. Patrician faiths in Boston and New York shared certain elements. Sectarian rites, symbols, and doctrines fortified elites in both cities. For the Brahmins, however, religion had another purpose. Unitarianism contributed to proper Boston's preeminence as a cultural enclave. Upper-class New Yorkers, however, followed Episcopal traditions at a time when their Bostonian peers embraced the intellectual vitality of Liberal Christianity. Genteel Boston had no Grace Church, but elite New York had no Unitarian pastor-professor-philosophers.

Culture

Trinity was a grander edition of King's Chapel and Columbia a lesser version of Harvard. Other elite cultural institutions exhibited equally close resemblances in type of membership, structure, and aim, although those in Boston were usually older, better financed, better known, and superior in quality. New York also had its historical society (1804) and Athenaeum (1825), founded respectively thirteen and eighteen years after their Boston equivalents. The New York Historical Society paralleled its New England counterpart in purpose and personnel. James Kent, in an 1828 presidential address, sought "to elevate the pride of ancestry."[213] Homage to the past undoubtedly was well received by an organization whose antebellum presidents included Peter G. Stuyvesant, Gouverneur Morris, and Peter A. Jay, and of which Benjamin Moore of Trinity and Columbia was the original vice-president and Pintard, the longtime recording secretary. Apparently the wealthy and influential founders and members were reluctant patrons of historical studies; the institution was near bankruptcy in 1826 when President Frederic DePeyster saved its library by getting $5,000 from the state legislature. A few years later banker John Delafield helped put the organization on firmer financial footing by assuming a portion of the debt. Its strained circumstances reflected patrician New York's relatively weak support of cultural activities. In 1791 Pintard noted that New York lagged behind Boston in historical research. President Kent reiterated this complaint thirty-seven years later.[214] This situation may have been due to the decline of the Knickerbocker element in affluent commercial circles. Successors of this enclave, often coming from New England, did not as strongly identify with New York's past; hence their efforts and contributions went elsewhere. Boston's business community, more insular in origin and still dominated by the Brahmins, was more highly motivated to support the Massachusetts Historical Society.

The founders of the New York Athenaeum had similar feelings about the inadequacy of New York's intellectual accomplishments. "New York is now probably the only city, of equal size and prosperity in the civilized world," said the incorporators in 1824, "in which an association for the purpose of encouraging and promoting the popular sciences and liberal arts is not to be found."[215] Athenaeum organizers and officers came largely from the group that managed the historical society. Jay, Delafield, and Kent occupied important posts in both institutions and Columbia presidents Moore and King were among the founders of the library and reading room. But a stronger presence of more recent wealth, for example, Secretary William Gracie, appeared in the Athenaeum. Rich businessmen may have been attracted because "its object" was "the cultivation of Science" in addition to "Literature and the Arts." Aware of the commercial elite in its ranks, the Athenaeum Associates declared: "It is to the merchants of the City of New York that their townsmen and the Union look for such support and patronage of science and literature." The associates expected a successful response to this appeal because of civic pride, the moral obligations of wealth and urban leadership, and the desire to bequeath a legacy of cultural accomplishment which would enshrine mercantile donors in the nation's history long after their fortunes had disappeared. The Athenaeum plea resembled those made on behalf of Boston's cultural institutions to that city's plutocracy, but the Brahmin response was more generous, and, as the associates asserted, those who gave more freely were better remembered.[216]

Knickerbockers and subsequent elites also participated in numerous other intellectual organizations. The New York Society Library, among the oldest and most socially prominent institutions in the city, continued to draw its shareholders and trustees from aristocratic families, but also admitted to its ranks Hones, Grinnells, Howlands, and even dry-goods king Alexander T. Stewart. Despite the infusion of new wealth, the library's historian noted in 1856 "how unfavorably we compare with Boston and Philadelphia" in contributions from "moneyed men."[217] Other cultural associations formed by the urban gentry and the newer elite include the Lyceum of Natural History in the City of New York (1818), the Literary and Philosophical Society of New York (1818), and the American Academy of Fine Arts (1802).[218] Astor Library (1849), created by a $400,000 bequest by the family founder, was funded and directed largely by men of first- or second-generation affluence and high status and by famous New York authors.[219]

Despite these activities *belles lettres* had less significance in patrician New York than in proper Boston. New York did not have a cultural establishment of interrelated publishers, writers, and merchant Maecenases like the Brahmin intelligentsia. Leading New York publishers George Palmer Putnam and James Harper did not emulate Boston bookman James T. Fields as a society figure. The Hudson River port had fewer, poorer, and shorter-lived highbrow journals, and they lacked the genteel backing, management, and authorship of the Brahmin magazines. Boston supported the only permanent American literary publication, the *North American Review*, years before the *Knickerbocker Magazine* (1833), *American Monthly Magazine* (1833), and *Harper's Magazine* (1847) demonstrated that New York journals could last beyond a brief period. These monthlies catered to a middlebrow audience that did not have the intellectual pretensions or credentials of the readerships of the *Review* or the *Atlantic Monthly*. Several well-known authors of the "Knickerbocker School" were not even native New Yorkers, but Washington Irving, son of a merchant, and James Fenimore Cooper, a minor upstate squire married to a DeLancey, had tangential connections with the urban oligarchy. The most noted patrician authors were Verplanck and his nephew by marriage, Charles Fenno Hoffman. Poet, editor, and writer of songs and travel sketches, Hoffman was the original editor of the *Knickerbocker*. Verplanck, the outstanding New York aristocratic intellectual of his time, served in both state houses, in Congress, as a governor of New York Hospital, as first vice-president of the historical society, as trustee of Columbia, the Society Library, and the Public School Society, as vice-president of the American Academy of Fine Arts, as vestryman and warden of Trinity Church, as professor at the General Theological Seminary, as vice-chancellor of the Board of Regents of the University of the State of New York, and as president of the Century Association. He wrote legal and theological treatises, satirical sketches, topical magazine pieces, and an edition of Shakespeare. With the typical defensiveness of a New York intellectual, Evert A.

Duyckinck, a "Knickerbocker" editor and critic, felt that if Verplanck had lived in Boston he would have equaled James Russell Lowell in literary honors.[220] Charles Astor Bristed, grandson of John Jacob Astor and satirist of the smart set, and Henry Brevoort, Jr., whose father made millions in Manhattan real estate, completed the corporal's guard (compared to the Brahmin authors) of upper-class New York literati.

Patricians in the New York intelligentsia were less moralistic, didactic, and intense than proper Bostonians. Sketches, satire, and fiction, rather than theological tomes or multivolume histories, engaged the efforts of most Gotham bluebloods. New York writers, not integrated into a comprehensive upper class, were also more contentious. Intellectual factionalism reflected the fragmentation of the commercial and professional communities. Disharmony brought reproofs from Brahmins, who considered it a reason for the superiority of New England culture. Many New Yorkers shared this view, but, as in business, diversity promoted creativity and originality. The New Yorkers embraced indigenous themes and techniques; they were more cosmopolitan and Rabelaisian and less committed to a genteel tradition that, too often, uncritically imitated British culture. The ferment of the metropolis attracted eccentric outsiders like Edgar Allan Poe and Herman Melville, whose works were frequently cited as examples of the lack of restraint that ruined New York literature. Proper Bostonians took pride in their city being called the Athens of America, but history has been kinder to Irving, Poe, and Melville than to Longfellow, Holmes, and Lowell.[221]

Relative to the Brahmins, New York elites were deficient in intellectual achievement. Upper classes in both places made equally small contributions to the development of music in their respective cities.[222] In art, however, New York outshone Boston. The same forces conducive to vigor and originality in the city's literature also stimulated painting. Elites typically participate in this cultural endeavor when their members act as collectors and patrons and when they promote organizations to exhibit and teach art and elevate taste. Before the Civil War the Atlantic ports were the national art centers. Wealth and the cosmopolitan life concentrated in these places, and their upper orders organized the institutions and provided the patronage and audiences which attracted artists, as Athens, Rome, Florence, and Venice had done in earlier eras. Civic leadership and pride, moral uplift, esthetic interest, a desire to symbolize wealth and attain status through owning beautiful objects, and the encouragement of artistic creation and display of taste according to patrician canons motivated elite involvement. Aristocratic sponsorship became a weapon against materialistic vulgarity, a means of separating the Old Guard from the *nouveau riche*, and a compensation for displacement in other aspects of leadership. *Parvenus* turned to this activity to gain social acceptance by demonstrating that they too had refined tastes and esthetic concerns.

Until the War of 1812 Philadelphia was the leading art center in the country, for a generation thereafter Charleston, Boston, and New York vied for preeminence, and on the eve of the Civil War New York forged ahead. Boston's noted collectors, Thomas Handasyd Perkins, Harrison Gray Otis, David Sears, Nathan Appleton, and Peter Chardon Brooks, preferred European Old Masters and neoclassical conventions. Several wealthy New York collectors—Verplanck, John Murray, Jr., and James Lenox, who inherited wealth and social standing—shared the traditional taste of the Bostonians. Others, mostly self-made members of the social and business elite, like Johnathan Sturges and especially Philip Hone, bought American art and supported native-born painters.[223] Many collectors cultivated artistic activity, and their more modern and indigenous interests were reflected in the greater vitality of organizations and achievements in New York than in Boston. The American Academy of Fine Arts, founded primarily by Chancellor Robert R. and Mayor Edward Livingston, was the nation's first important art academy. Its purpose, according to Chancellor Livingston, was to train painters, "polish" our civilization, and perpetuate "whatever may be useful, virtuous and laudable to society." Academy president John Trumbull referred to the Livingstons and other founders of manorial stock as "Gentlemen of Taste and Fortune." Formed by aristocrats, the academy became the bastion of European-dominated, classical styles.[224] In 1826 the National Academy of Design was organized in opposition to the American Academy's stodginess and because artists objected to control of the institution by businessmen-trustees. National Academy patrons included many Knickerbockers, but Hones, Gracies, Griswolds, and Astors represented the new oligarchy. When it temporarily folded in 1839, a successor institution, the American Art Union (1839), was founded. The union also was dedicated to encouraging national art, and the majority of its incorporators and committee of management—Samuel Ward, Moses H. Grinnell, Hone, and Sturges—were recently risen plutocrats. Modernistically stressing American subjects and techniques, the union also committed itself to traditional aims of upgrading popular moral and esthetic values by eschewing "sensual" pictures and emphasizing simplicity, naturalness, truth, and purity.[225] These organizations and patrons made midcentury New York, richer than Boston and with a culture freer of institutional and patrician control and more attuned to new subjects and styles, the artistic center of America. The city attracted the most painters, had the largest exhibitions and art market, and the most influential artists and artistic organizations.[226]

Throughout history, elites have used art, literature, religion, and education to indoctrinate society with the ideas and values of the dominant order. Respectable intellectuals are instructors of moral and intellectual leadership for those who should command and inspirers of acceptance in those who should obey. "It is upon the diffusion of sound and wholesome knowledge among the people," said Duer, exhorting Columbia undergraduates to support New York's cultural and charitable associations, "not merely of their political rights and duties, but of their religion and moral obligations—that, under Heaven, the duration of the government and prosperity of the nation depend. . . ." This "inculcation . . . is enforced by the dictates of a conservative forecast, and genuine philanthropy." Verplanck, Charles King, Philip Hone, and George Templeton Strong echoed these sentiments.[227] Culture was not only a device used to discipline the masses; it also purified the privileged, thus fitting them to rule. Pintard emphasized this function in describing the purpose of the Academy of Arts and Sciences. "Gross dissipation always prevails where refinement is not cultivated," declared the academy's secretary; "The vices of polished society" increase "as wealth & its consequent indulgences more & more abounds," hence "we must aim at giving proper direction to young minds, find out new resources for occupation & *killing* time, among which Theatres, Operas, Academies of Arts, Museums, &c. are to be classed as the means to attract & prevent the growth of vice & immorality." Pintard, officer in a host of altruistic and cultural societies, expressed the sense of stewardship that impelled upper-class Bostonians and New Yorkers to devote themselves to these activities: "We all owe a debt to Society as well as to God for the blessings we enjoy, and I wish to discharge my share." Utilitarian arguments were sometimes conceived more narrowly than in terms of community well-being or spiritual improvement. The founders of the Lyceum of Natural History hoped that the "method" and "habit" of scientific "investigation . . . may be advantageously applied in other and perhaps more important [i.e. business] affairs." Verplanck felt that "good taste is always the parent of utility"; it enhanced efficiency and comfort in addition to propriety.[228]

Influential Bostonians and New Yorkers had identical impulses and ideas regarding the merit of intellectual and cultural endeavor and founded similar organizations. Nevertheless, important differences existed between the patriciates. Brahmins were more generous donors and more directly involved as creators, professionals, and managers. Consequently, the intellectual elite in Boston achieved closer integration with the commercial and social hierarchy. The New York intelligentsia overlapped to a lesser degree with other elites, therefore the city's cultural life tended to be less formal and traditional. The livelier and more venturesome New Yorkers sometimes thought that culture could be fun and that the theater, as well as the pulpit, the library, and the classroom, might foster mental and moral enlightenment. "Mankind cannot always be praying nor working," asserted Pintard, suggesting the opera and the stage as worthwhile leisure pursuits. The "theatre," Hone agreed, "should come in for a better share of support. . . ."[229]

Attendance at dramatic or musical performances, however, was not entirely impelled by desire for entertainment or uplift. "Great crowd: all the aristocracy and 'gig respectability' and wealth and beauty and fashion of the city there on the spot," observed Strong of a philharmonic concert. "For myself being superior to such vanities I selected the little side gallery." His description reveals the anger of an aristocrat being displaced by upstart swells who made culture a vehicle of self-advertisement. Opera-going became a similar rite for the recently arrived; many first- or second-generation holders of wealth and social prestige had boxes at the Italian Opera House.[230] Their presence foreshadowed the ritual of Mrs. Astor's circle at the Metropolitan Opera House of fifty years later. Such display of riches and status horrified more modest and confident elites in Boston and Philadelphia, who resented frivolous exploitation of cultural activity. "This opera of ours is a refined amusement, creditable to the taste of its proprietors and patrons," wrote Hone in 1848. "A beau parterre in which the flowers of New York society" brighten "under the sunshine of admiration"; and "our young men" learn "the habits and forms of elegant social intercourse," and "acquire a taste" of "refined and elegant nature. . . ."[231] Hone balanced the moral-didactic concept of culture, commonly held by eastern seaboard urban patriciates, with an attitude unique to New York. Brahmins would have subscribed to the aim of embellished taste, though they might have preferred another source, but turning a cultural event into an occasion for attracting attention through physical beauty or conspicuous consumption offended their sense of propriety. Blue-blood Boston, however, did not contain an enclave desperately seeking social acceptance through public notoriety.

Mood, as well as style and accomplishment, differentiated elite New Yorkers and Bostonians. Gotham patricians, measuring their historical societies, magazines, libraries, and colleges against Boston and Philadelphia, felt inferior and defensive. These anxieties were intensified by similar evaluations made by foreign visitors and intellectual snubs administered by genteel Bostonians and Philadelphians. According to Pintard, the "Athens of America is Phil. This city is only the Pyraeum of Athens. . . . I know full well the contempt with which we are regarded by our rival sisters B[oston] and P[hiladelphia]." He expressed an attitude widespread in New York commercial and professional circles, but concluded on a note of optimism not always shared by upper-class New Yorkers. Pintard expected the city's wealth to enable it to "excell all others in the U.S. as well in Arts & Sciences as in commerce," and attributed the condescension of other metropolises partly to "jealousy of our vast superiority in commerce. . . ."[232]

Brahmins tended to be enthusiastic participators in the life of the mind. James W. Beekman, trustee of Columbia and the Society Library and executive committeeman of the historical society, expressed the relative aloofness of the Knickerbockers. He preferred "the man of taste," who enjoys the creations of genius, to the genius himself, who suffers the tensions of ambition and is flawed by Byronic passions.[233] Beekman inherited a fortune that enabled him to remain remote from the hustling, highly charged atmosphere of his city. Intellectual disengagement reflected a class retreat from commercial and political activity. A vacuum in patrician-dominated culture was opened by the withdrawal of the old families. New elites in commerce and politics did not fill this void. Their members frequently came from other regions and countries and tended to pursue profits and power single-mindedly and to be less certain of their place in the intellectual and social hierarchies. Thus the New York intelligentsia did not, as in Boston, coordinate with the urban patriciate. Fragmentation of elites in business and politics inhibited the emergence of a unified establishment culture and prevented the continuity and cohesion necessary for the existence of a metropolitan aristocracy. Shorter-lived and narrower-ranged New York elites never achieved the comprehensive dominance over city life attained by upper orders in Boston, Philadelphia, and Charleston.

Philanthropy

Upper-class philanthropic and cultural efforts overlapped in personnel and aim. John Pintard devoted as much time to being vice-president of the American Bible Society, secretary of the Sailors' Snug Harbor, president of the Bank for Savings, and a founder of the Society for the Prevention of Pauperism as he did to his offices in cultural societies. Philip Hone divided his civic responsibilities among the board of trustees of Columbia, the Trinity vestry, the vice-presidencies of the historical society, the Institute for Instruction of the Deaf and Dumb, the American Seamen's Fund Society, and Bloomingdale Asylum, and as a governor of New York Hospital. Peter A. Jay, a trustee of the General Theological Seminary, Columbia, and the Society Library, a president of the historical society, and a Trinity vestryman, also headed the boards of New York Hospital and the Public School Society. Eminent philanthropists in New York involved themselves simultaneously, like their Boston counterparts, in several projects, and their multiple interactions created a community of like-minded altruists. Thus did Pintard "possess the full confidence of my new associates [at the Bible Society] many of whom however are companions in other Institutions & all personally know me."[234] Hone, Jay, Pintard, and others were active in charitable and cultural societies because both types of organizations offered opportunities for social control and exercising and displaying class leadership and rationales for holding wealth and wielding power.

New York's commercial and social elites, along with proper Bostonians, feared that urban vice, tumult, and poverty threatened the established order and they supported a panoply of institutions to combat these forces. They founded agencies to alleviate the physical needs and improve the outlook of the unfortunate. New York Hospital, New York Eye and Ear Infirmary (1820), New York State Women's Hospital (1855), and St. Luke's Hospital (1858) ministered to the diseased poor. A number of institutions, for example the American Bible Society (1816), several savings banks for workingmen and relief organizations for the poor, and the New York Temperance Society (1829), attacked the problems of crime and destitution by giving money, imparting skills to the indigent, securing employment for the jobless, reforming the penal and legal system, uplifting morality, and encouraging thrift. Groups particularly subject to debility or deprivation, or who had special claims on the sentiments and obligations of the affluent, received special treatment. In this category belonged the Colored Orphan Asylum (1836), Leake and Watts Orphan House (1843), the New York Institution for the Instruction of Deaf and Dumb (1816), New York Institution for the Blind (1831), and the Association for the Relief of Respectable Aged Indigent Females (1837). Institutions providing for sailors, Episcopalians, and Presbyterians, the Marine Society, the Seamen's Bank for Savings in the City of New York (1844), Dry Dock Savings Institution (1848), St. Andrew's Society, and St. George's Society (1770) served groups with vocational or sectarian affinities to the commercial elite.

Philanthropic scions of the provincial gentry were joined by businessmen of Quaker and New England stock, or native New Yorkers whose prestige and fortunes postdated the colonial era. The new elite, with greater wealth, power, and civic involvement, gradually displaced the aristocrats. Knickerbocker salience in such cultural institutions as Trinity, Columbia, and the historical society outlasted its reign over charity. Culture, which entailed style, education, and leisure, proved a stronger Old Guard bastion than charity, which depended on wealth and seemed more relevant to pressing metropolitan needs. New York Hospital remained a patrician preserve, but *arriviste* merchants and bankers assumed control of ancient institutions like the St. Andrew's and Marine societies. They also took the initiative in subsequent and more important undertakings. Thomas Eddy and John Murray founded the Public School Society of the City of New York (1805), which from 1814 to 1842 virtually monopolized free public schooling in the city, and Eddy was the prime mover in the Bank for Savings in the City of New

York (1819), the largest local savings bank.[235] Brahmins, better preserving their ascendancy than did Knickerbockers, ranked among the leading Boston philanthropists. Pintard alone of the New York bluebloods matched their stature.

A rising tide of poor immigrants and depressed trading conditions increased pauperism and created a public welfare crisis during the second decade of the nineteenth century. The municipal government resisted increased expenditures for poor relief and voluntary associations assumed an ever larger role in aiding the indigent. Many of the agencies cited above were founded after 1816–17, when the city relief budget, despite the local government's restraint, soared to an unprecedented height.[236] Their multiplication drew praise from Pintard, who believed that such "institutions" were "bless[ed]" by "a gracious Provid[ence]" and who "favored private initiative as a way of easing the financial burden upon the municipality and its taxpayers." The generosity of "a few public spirited men," he declared at the formation of the Society for the Prevention of Pauperism in New York City (1818), will "relieve the city from a poor tax of $80,000." The first board of trustees of the Bank for Savings similarly claimed that "the habits" which the Bank "induces hold out the best pledge for a reduction in the public burdens, as they are connected with indigence and want. . . . They teach a man to depend on his own exertions, encourage industry, frugality, cleanliness, and self-respect and effectually prevent those who are so fortunate as to be influenced by them, from applying either to public provision, or private bounty for support." The trustees of the Public School Society, too, felt that in promoting mass education they would equalize economic burdens in the community and decrease taxes by curbing poverty and thus broadening the revenue base.[237] The argument that altruism lessened relief costs especially appealed to leading philanthropists, who, as affluent New Yorkers, paid the highest taxes.

Government participation in upper-class welfare agencies exemplifies the interlocked political, economic, and social components of the establishment. New York Hospital received legislative grants of money and the mayor and common councillors were ex-officio members of its board. The Society for the Prevention of Pauperism provided that five of its managers be appointed by the common council and eleven members of the society between 1817 and 1823 were councillors before 1825. In 1802 the city fathers gave a plot of land and $600 to the Humane Society (1787), the city's earliest private charity association. A year later the state legislature authorized a lottery for a home at the Society for the Relief of Poor Widows with Small Children. The Orphan Asylum Society was also granted a lottery revenue and after 1811 a yearly stipend of $500 by the municipality. In 1813 the legislature decreed that the city's share of the state school fund be paid to the Free School Society and a few groups maintaining charity schools.[238]

The private charities were dominated mainly by merchants. Of the 109 Humane Society trustees between 1787 and 1831, ninety-six had identified occupations and fifty-eight were merchants. Businessmen made up 56 percent of the trustees and seven-ninths of the officers of the Public School Society and a similarly large proportion, between 1818 and 1823, of the officers and managers of the Society For Prevention of Pauperism.[239] Despite the intensive participation of merchants and bankers, Pintard, Strong, Charles King, and William Jay denigrated the parsimony of institutions like Trinity Church, of businessmen like John Hone, Stephen Whitney, and William B. Astor, and the benevolence of the commercial elite as a whole, particularly compared to their counterparts in Boston and Philadelphia.[240]

Their comments mirrored the complaints of culturally concerned New Yorkers over mercantile neglect in that dimension of urban leadership. How valid is this criticism? Pintard, Strong, and King made statements unsupported by details about the donations and activities or about comparative expenditures between prestigious and wealthy New Yorkers and Bostonians. John Jacob Astor's bequest of $507,000 to public causes (2½ percent of an estate worth over $20 million) substantiates this view, but Anson G. Phelps, who accumulated far less in his lifetime, left $600,000 for benevolent purposes.[241] Some evidence, however, consistently points to the inferior performance of New York elites. Intramural accusations regarding indifference to cultural and charitable obligations were not raised in upper-class Boston, which repeatedly expressed pride in the generosity of its benefactions. Although the charges of the critics were not always backed by hard data, they were prominent philanthropists and members of the upper class. As institutional trustees, business partners, and relatives of the elite, and in the case of Strong, a lawyer with rich and well-born clients, they were knowledgeable about charitable expenditure. Argument from analogy further suggests the inadequacy of the New Yorkers. Despite the greater wealth of the metropolis, its cultural institutions did not usually match their Boston equivalents. Participants in New York's cultural organizations were frequently the same people or came from the same enclaves initiating welfare projects. In activities both charitable and intellectual, such as education, Bostonians spent more than New Yorkers. During the 1820s, at a time when both urban governments were dominated by patrician merchants, the New York administration spent less than half of what Boston did on public elementary education, i.e., schooling for the poor.[242]

The evidence suggests considerable interurban variance in altruism, but the relative generosity of different elites cannot be precisely determined until the percentage of their contributions is calculated in proportion to their wealth. Firmer evaluations of upper-class benevolence would emerge from investigating the resources and disbursements of similar patrician organizations in Boston and New York, the humane societies, the institutions for the handicapped, associations to assist seamen, savings banks for the poor, etc. A typology of charitable causes is also needed before any feasible comparisons can be made: How were energies and contributions distributed? Did different urban elites tend to concentrate their efforts in their own cities or did a larger share of their aid go to other localities or to national or international charities? Possibly Brahmins were more involved than were upper-class New Yorkers in local social welfare, but the latter might have been more forthcoming in national and international activities. In the 1820s, for example, New Yorkers donated more to the Greek independence movement than did Bostonians.[243] Perhaps the comparative vitality of proper Bostonians encouraged closer identification with local affairs and gave them a greater capacity for action than occurred in the waning Knickerbocker enclave. New elites in New York, frequently born outside the city or even the region, may have had weaker ties to the metropolis; conversely, their cosmopolitan origins may have directed their humanitarianism beyond their adopted home. Comparative analyses of urban philanthropy illuminate the role and image of urban elites. Historical research in this subject, however, has not advanced enough to permit much more than interesting speculation.

Regardless of differences in commitment or generosity, upper-class Boston and New York philanthropists alike failed to remedy metropolitan problems. In 1848 almost seven times as many New Yorkers received public outdoor relief as had in 1812–13. Accordingly, poor rates soared and, as in Boston, new types of institutions appeared in the 1840s and '50s to cope with the deteriorating conditions and increasing numbers of the indigent. The New York Association for Improving the Conditions of the Poor (1844) resembled the Boston Provident Association in establishing a comprehensive relief system with visitors in every district of the city. The AICP, along with the Prison Association of New York (1844), and several charities founded in the 1850s—the Five Points House of Industry, the Children's Aid Society, and the New York Juvenile Asylum—conducted their affairs through salaried professionals. Not only was *noblesse oblige* replaced by career social workers, but prestigious organizations no longer had intimate ties with municipal and state governments. By the 1840s upper-class public officials decreased in number. Leaders in the welfare agencies, now much less likely to have served in public posts, began to criticize political officeholders for failing to improve living conditions.[244]

Prominent New Yorkers and Bostonians formed similar charitable institutions, faced similar problems, and were prompted by similar aims. Social control, community leadership, and the stewardship of wealth motivated these elites. Good Samaritans sought to overcome poverty and vice, symptoms of a disorder in which they read a threat to urban life and their own prerogatives and property, by inculcating traits of thrift, industry, self-dependence, and self-restraint. These qualities they thought vital in their own successes, taught their children, and hoped to instill in the lower classes. Accordingly, when New Yorkers and Bostonians searched for the most efficient and economical means to restore social harmony and protect themselves they came up with similar solutions.

An important difference between the Bostonians and New Yorkers was that the latter anxiously contemplated the destiny of their city and their own survival. Such forebodings appeared earlier in Manhattan because its greater economic volatility and more ethnically mixed populace endangered established elites at a time when the Brahmins felt relatively secure. Pintard regretted the reforms of the 1821 constitution that granted "universal suffrage, to a mass of people esp[eciall]y in this city, which has no stake in society. It is easier to raise a mob than to quell it, and we shall hereafter be governed by rank democracy." In the 1830s and 1840s Philip Hone blamed the influx of the foreign-born for making New York like "the large cities of Europe; overburdened with population, and where the two extremes of costly luxury . . . and improvident waste are presented in daily and hourly contrast with squalid misery and hopelessness." The "ignorant" and "obstinate" Irish, "without a feeling of patriotism or affection in common with American citizens, *decide the elections in the city of New York.*" Strong, a trustee of the Seamen's Bank for Savings and a member of the finance committee of St. Luke's Hospital, had similar views. "Wretched, filthy, bestial-looking Italians and Irish," he wrote in 1838, the "dregs of human nature" were being naturalized at City Hall. Twenty years later he was almost certain that "democracy and universal suffrage will not work in crowded cities."[245]

Immigration, rising pauperism, rapid economic growth, turnover in social and commercial elites, party strife, and Jacksonian democracy signified to the Old Guard its own demise and the disintegration of the urban community. Charles King and Clinton Roosevelt feared that "individualism" had unleashed an irresponsible selfishness that compromised "the public weal." Patricians found evidence of vanishing solidarity (by which they also meant the old hierarchy) in other phases of city life. Pintard deplored the modern tendency of New Yorkers to constantly change their domiciles. Verplanck expressed a similar sentiment in anticipating by over a generation the Brahmin regret at the disappearance of the old houses. George Templeton Strong and Philip Hone condemned party factionalism for endangering America and Strong also criticized the "irreverance, presumption, indecency," in that "epidemic of religious fever" called "revival[ism]."[246]

For the apprehensive, charity, by promoting restraint and gratitude among the masses, defended against social disorder and loss of elite leadership and property. Strong wished the Astors and Whitneys to use philanthropy to reassert hierarchical control and urged "the wealthier classes to seek out and aid the poor" as a "great good to be set off against manifold signs of social degeneracy and disease."[247] In 1828 the executive committee of the Public School Society asserted: "If we would preserve our free institutions" the masses must be educated; therefore "our schools are the very foundation upon which rest the peace, good order and prosperity of society." Twelve years later this body petitioned the common council for funds so that Irish Catholic immigrants will "abandon any unfavorable prejudices . . . and become familiar with our language, and reconciled to our institutions and habits. . . ." The "best interest for all will be alike promoted by having their children mingle with ours in the public seminaries of learning." In 1854, Charles King also advocated free public schools to "educate a restless, questioning generation of citizens; which takes nothing for granted, nothing for settled; and which especially claims and exercises the right to make and unmake its laws and government at its own pleasure."[248]

Nobler impulses than self-preservation also stimulated upper-class philanthropy. Piety inspired the Jay family, Arthur and Lewis Tappan, Pintard, Eddy, and William E. Dodge. They felt obligations of Christian as well as class stewardship and saw themselves as instruments of divine will. Altruists usually mixed the secular responsibilities of wealth and rank with godly injunctions. Eminent attorney Robert Troup, president of the Society for the Relief of the Destitute (1827), said in 1827, "the rich can not live without the necessaries provided for them by the labour of the poor; and consequently, that the former in assisting the latter, do but pay a debt which is justly their due." The "Society" was "confident" that "God, who has amply given to man, takes delight in seeing him give to his necessitous fellow creatures. . . ." Personal pleasure derived from helping the unfortunate also inclined the charitable toward good works. The trustees of the Savings Bank for the Poor gladly advised "many of the depositors . . . to promote careful habits and moral feeling. The gratification which they have received, in numerous instances, has amply repaid the attending committee for this gratuitous labor."[249]

Similarly motivated New York and Boston benefactors agreed on the best strategy to aid the dependent. They would separate the worthy from the worthless and promote orderly behavior in the most economical, efficient, and rational manner. Pintard, in a representative statement, explained that "the intent of this Society [For the Prevention of Pauperism] is not to afford alms but labour, so that there shall be no pretext for idleness, to give [th]e means of occupation to the industrious, to educate their children & to expel the drones from Society," and to "meliorate the condition of the labouring community and amend their morals." Its directors named "Ignorance," "Idleness," "Intemperance in drinking," "Want of Economy," and "Imprudent and Hasty Marriages" as the causes of poverty. This familiar conservative litany blamed pauperism on personal weakness rather than systemic deficiencies. The society proposed to divide the city into districts, place its members in charge of inspections and records, and have these workers assist the indigent to become independent.[250] These methods, then considered the cheapest and most progressive and efficient tactics to curb pauperism, have remained, to this day, guiding principles for welfare agencies.

Society

High society in New York, as in Boston and Philadelphia, overlapped with elites in other areas of urban life. Businessmen, statesmen, and professionals, wastrels with inherited incomes, genteel intellectuals, and civic-minded patricians congregated at summer spas, parties, dinners, dances, clubs, concerts, the opera, and except for the relatively solemn Brahmins, at theatrical performances and horse races. Coinciding patterns of behavior in New York and Boston were due to similar interests and structures rather than to intimate contact. A branch of the Winthrop family moved down from New England in the eighteenth century and became active in New York legal and banking circles. Rufus King had many ties with the Massachusetts Federalist-maritime elite, George Templeton Strong and Philip Hone sometimes visited Boston and had Brahmin friends, Strong's sister wedded a Derby, and the Tileston and Hemenway families intermarried.[251] Despite some social connections and business and political alliances, each enclave focused primarily on its own baliwick.

Similarities between Boston and New York elites coexisted with significant differences. Increasingly after 1820 greater diversity, more rapid circulation, and newer and larger fortunes appeared in the upper ranks of New York. These developments militated against cohesion and confidence in the upper strata of that city.

Foreign visitors and members of other urban elites thought that high society in New York was ruled by *parvenu* capitalists who lacked polish and culture. The *nouveau riche*, the critics charged, compensated for their recent emergence, shaky status, and temporary reign by a vulgar show of wealth and by admitting upstarts while practicing gross and comical forms of social snobbery. Commercial volatility and orientation, claimed these commentators, created a rapid turnover in high social circles and precluded refinement. These observers regarded patriciates in Charleston, Philadelphia, and Boston as more permanent, traditional, exclusive, and cultivated.[252]

Immediately after independence, New York high society displayed the qualities that set it off from other port city patriciates. Noah Webster in 1789 found New York the most social and hospitable "town in the United States. The principal families associating in their public amusements with the middle class of well-bred citizens render their rank subservient to the happiness of society, and prevent that . . . affectation of superiority in certain families in Philadelphia [which] has produced in that city . . . the reputation of being inhospitable."[253] New York aristocrats saw the democracy and expansiveness of their social affairs in a less favorable light. Margaret Beekman Livingston in 1792 contemplated "fortunes tumbling in ye Laps of very many people in so rapid a manner as never before has been the case. . . . Dissipation takes place proportionably—is it not a Query whether riches acquired by frugality and industry which are nurseries for Public Virtues as well as domestic Happiness—or wealth acquired by speculators and Brokers . . . which in all probability will expand in Balls, Entertainments, Sumtious Buildings and superb furniture in which Gambling is carried on in large sums lost and won."[254] Early condemnation of display, dissipation, and newly risen intruders reverberated down through the decades. In 1819 and in the 1820s and '30s Pintard lambasted "the fashionable who wish to nullify out *antient* ways. . . ." Society events were a "serviel imitation of foreign manners" [which embodied] "a spirit of luxury & refinement [that] has in the course of my days been gaining ground, propelled by the rapid accumulation of wealth. . . ."[255] Hone, Strong, and Bristed reiterated this refrain in the 1830s, '40s, and '50s. The Hone and Strong diaries chronicled the round of dances, parties, Saratoga summers, and other features of upper-crust social life, and Bristed wrote a novel on this theme. Identifying with the Knickerbocker residue, they denounced "extremes of costly luxury in living," introduced by "a fluctuating mushroom aristocracy" of "speculating, bank-swindling, money worshipping" *arrivistes*. "Society" was "comfortless, joyless, insipid," snobbish, superficial, and dissipated. Dedicated to the pursuit and display of wealth and lacking style or pedigree, it also shocked the modest and discreet Boston bluebloods.[256] Pintard and Hone suffered pangs of inferiority because of financial reverses and felt that in wealth and stature they did not match midcentury moguls. These perspectives, however, did not necessarily distort their impression of New York society. Foreign tourists and Bristed, unaffected by loss of fortune and status or undisturbed by the challenge of new elites, made the same evaluations. Moreover, the data on vintage of antebellum New York fortunes supplemented by institutional evidence affirms the contentions that the upper class was less cohesive, predominant, persistent, and public-spirited than the Boston elite.

This lack of achievement and solidarity accounts for the self-criticism expressed in upper-class New York at a time when patricians in Boston, Philadelphia, and Charleston had high opinions of themselves. Pintard, Hone, Strong, Duer, and Charles King disparaged their enclave, as well as new elites, for deficiencies in character, intellect, cultural accomplishment, and commitment to social welfare. Strong was especially censorious. He chastised the Century Association, Grace Church, the Society Library, Columbia, Peter G. Stuyvesant's tightness, John Jay, Jr.'s, mindless and effeminate reform sentiments, Peter Schermerhorn's passionate attachment to rents and investments, Robert B. Minturn's pomposity, Ogden Hoffman's self-indulgence, William B. Astor's and John C. Hamilton's parties, and the degeneracy of Jacob and Robert LeRoy.[257] Negative class appraisals appeared over a generation before similar self-judgments in genteel Boston. Their earlier presence in New York was due to the fact that the Knickerbockers and their mercantile and banking successors of the 1820s were already being deposed by tycoons, party bosses, and social swells while the Brahmins still dominated Boston.

Attacks on the rootlessness and disorganization of New York society brought forth repeated attempts to create distinctions and institutions which would provide form and order. Ancestral and convivial associations appeared, and deference was given to bluebloods and social leaders and arbiters. The Society of the Cincinnati in New York (1795) functioned, as did the parent organization and chapters in other cities, to rally those who valued their Revolutionary antecedents. The St. Nicholas Society of the City of New York (1835) also sought to preserve old customs and clans. Both organizations chose their early members from the Knickerbocker ranks, reflecting the influence of family pride in patrician circles.[258] Although Columbia presidents Duer and Charles King professed faith in the masses and in equality of opportunity, they also perceived advantages in distinguished lineage. Duer was gratified by kinship succession among the college trustees, and King told his grandson to "remember you have a great name in trust. Be careful not to tarnish it." Pintard felt "pride & elevation when I contemplate such near relations [Bayards and Boudinots] so highly respectable in society and so eminently distinguished in their day & generation, and I devoutly pray that no conduct of mine or my successors may reproach our name and family." He also admired "the Independent fortunes, high education, refined minds & polished manners of the Nobility & gentry of Eng^d. . . ."[259]

Exclusive clubs, though containing many patricians and elite businessmen among their founders, less successfully served as Knickerbocker bastions than did ancestral societies. The Union Club (1836) was a purely social organization. The Century Association (1847) sought to promote culture as well as conviviality. It became a meeting place for artists, authors, and intellectually inclined aristocrats, merchants, and professionals.[260] These clubs, because they admitted newcomers as well as bluebloods, were upbraided by society censors Hone and Strong for unselectivity, stupidity, and frivolity—defects often attributed to New York's *beau monde*.[261]

Dinners, parties, dances, and exclusive neighborhoods like Washington Square complemented formal associations in organizing high society. Midcentury hostesses Mrs. James D. Roosevelt, Mrs. Hamilton Fish, Mrs. Henry Brevoort, and Mrs. William Schermerhorn continued a tradition of feminine leadership established during Washington's first administration by Sarah Van Brugh Livingston Jay. Invitations to their homes signified social acceptance. Males had more time, interest, and energy for society in Boston and Philadelphia, where they did not confront the intensely competitive and chancy conditions that prevailed in New York's commercial community. These cities, too, had aristocratic hostesses, but civic and business leaders dominated genteel circles.[262] Although secondary to the society queens, Gotham men helped sustain the fashionable world. Strong in 1860 was "elected" by a "synod of men about town" to a "committee of twenty, which is hereafter to take charge of polite society, regulate its institutions, keep it pure, and decide who shall be admitted hereafter to 'Bachelors' Balls and other annual entertainments. The committee is perpetual and fills its own vacancies. It is to pass on the social grade of everybody, by ballot—one blackball excluding." Among his "colleagues" were "Charles King, Hamilton Fish, Anson Livingston, John Astor . . . ."[263]

As the Civil War approached, New York society still resembled other eastern seaboard centers. Social leaders stemmed from the aristocracy, and society had not yet attained the frenetic dazzle, stupendous extravagance, and rarity of blueblood credentials of the Gilded Age smart set. But intimations of the future already significantly differentiated New York social circles from polite society in other places.[264] Vain attempts to retain Old Guard influence by maintaining exclusiveness through the Bachelors' Balls reveals the uncertain status and extensive permeability in the *haute monde*. Unsettled conditions made Isaac Brown the first of New York's social arbiters. Since the well-heeled were often not the well-born, Brown, and his successors Ward McAllister and

Harry Lehr, sorted out pretense from precedence and balanced wealth and birth to legitimate the fragile exclusiveness of the fashionable elite. These figures advised hostesses on every procedure from placing musicians to patronizing the proper florist. Brown's excellent memory for lineage, social credentials, and biographical details proved invaluable in his chief function, advising on invitations. A consummate snob, he separated society into "old family, good stock" or "a new man" who "had better mind his p's and q's, or I will trip him up." When employed by the recently arrived, the Grace Church sexton cautioned guests from old families that "this [affair] is mixed, very mixed." But there were limits even to Brown's suzerainty. "I cannot undertake to control society beyond fiftieth street," he warned at the close of his reign.[265] Upper Fifth Avenue, beyond Brown's domain, became the fashionable neighborhood after the Civil War.

Other differences notwithstanding, antebellum upper classes in New York and Boston were fundamentally business enclaves. Capitalists were civic leaders, commercial interests motivated elite political activity, and charities were largely conducted by magnates and funded with profits won in the marketplace. Entrepreneurs were certain of the superiority of their profession and the personal values and attributes that best promoted success and virtue, and their notions were generally accepted throughout the upper order. Federalist statesmen, aristocrats Charles King and James DePeyster Ogden, Knickerbocker civic leader Pintard, newly risen Philip Hone, and lawyer-trustee George Templeton Strong endorsed thrift, industry, prudence, personal restraint, and self-dependence and acknowledged the priority of commerce.[266] Businessmen naturally praised the Protestant ethic and the primacy of the counting house. When Bayards, Roosevelts, Schuylers, Kings, Hamiltons, and Gallatins approved of their sons entering financial and shipping firms, it is little wonder that Delafields, LeRoys, Aspinwalls, Dodges, Pintards, and Hones hoped that their offspring would do the same. Theodore Winthrop, of the New York branch of that family, resembled his literary-inclined Brahmin contemporaries in resolving to forego writing poetry for a "practical" life in the 1840s as a clerk in the Pacific Steamship Company. He declared that the owner of this enterprise "commands more and more my admiration." The traits that aristocrat Winthrop respected in William H. Aspinwall were "self-command! attention! energy!"[267]

Bourgeois belief in self-development and vocational achievement, as previously noted in the attitudes of Verplanck, James A. Hamilton, William A. Duer, James Depeyster Ogden, and Charles King, led them to intermittent acceptance of political equality and majority rule. Jonathan Goodhue, a representative figure of the maritime successors of the Knickerbocker elite, agreed with the optimistic viewpoint of the older patriciate regarding spiritual, social, and material progress. He expressed the conventional allegiance of successful businessmen to the Protestant ethic and open opportunity. This creed was voiced in a highly personal document, an 1848 testament to his family, where he disparaged "the extraneous circumstances of official position, family connections, or great wealth."[268] Emphasis upon personal effort and responsibility, however, did not always result in egalitarian sentiments. Ascriptive norms and aspirations sometimes coexisted with achievement values, thus creating a worship of aristocratic breeding. Knickerbockers like King, Pintard, and Duer unsurprisingly revealed this ambivalence, but second-generation Strong and Bristed, grandson of the *bete noire* of the patriciate, scorned the "recently elevated," and *parvenu* Hone praised "highly respected gentlemen of the old school" as New York's "only nobility" and lauded James Roosevelt, Arthur Barclay, Charles King, William A. Duer, and Ogden Hoffman for being the "elite of the city."[269]

1865 TO THE PRESENT

Throughout history aristocracies have assumed military roles. American patriciates followed this tradition in serving, since colonial times, as officers of elite militia units. Apart from class convention and attraction to ritual, armed service has strengthened the sense of authority with which upper orders identify and has satisfied their need to display *noblesse oblige*. Antebellum riots in northern cities reinforced among the privileged an awareness of the advantages of militia service, and during wartime it seemed proper that the upper classes, with their feeling of community proprietorship, should hasten to the fray. Unlike the European nobility, decimated by recurrent battles, American elites escaped carnage until the Civil War. Southern aristocrats suffered grievous depletion in the fighting, and the Brahmins lost a number of promising young men. Philadelphia, where Copperhead sentiment inhibited genteel enlistment, and New York, where newer and more commercially oriented elites lacked the romantic impulses of Charleston planters or the social responsibility of proper Bostonians, escaped relatively unscathed. Several leading industrial and banking families in Philadelphia established themselves or spectacularly improved their fortunes during the war. New York's moguls and future robber barons were among the greatest beneficiaries of belligerence. Daniel Drew, J. P. Morgan, Jim Fisk, John D. Rockefeller, August Belmont, Cornelius Vanderbilt, Jay Gould, and Andrew Carnegie profited from the war through government contracts, financial manipulations or increased volume of sales, or, while still in junior positions in banking, railroads, and industry, they honed the skills that eventually brought them fame, power, and affluence.[270] Genteel New Yorkers, like Strong and Hamilton Fish, uncomfortably aware of freshly minted Civil War fortunes, deplored the emergence of the newly risen.[271] But the Knickerbocker-maritime enclave had been declining for over a decade before 1860; hence the Civil War was not, as in Charleston or Boston, a primary force in undermining or dispossessing a sovereign enclave.

Upper-Class Economic Activity and Wealth

Postwar tycoons replicated many of the characteristics of earlier New York economic elites. Fisk, Rockefeller, Drew, Gould, Vanderbilt, railroader Edward H. Harriman, transit magnate Thomas Fortune Ryan, and financiers George F. Baker and Levi P. Morton sprang from middling or humble origins. Morgan, son of a banker, and utilities' titan William C. Whitney had affluent backgrounds. The city continued to attract many of its leading capitalists from other areas. Fisk, Morgan, Morton, and Whitney were native New Englanders; Rockefeller, Drew, Gould, and Baker hailed from upstate New York; Ryan from Virginia; Carnegie from Scotland; and many great Jewish bankers and retail merchants, such as August Belmont, the Schiffs, Lehmans, and Warburgs, emigrated from Germany. Most Jewish capitalists rose from poverty, but several came from rich European families.[272] Regardless of birthplace or vintage of wealth, the new elite represented a substantial break with the Old Guard. Discontinuity at the top had occurred earlier, when New England–born merchants preempted the place of the Knickerbockers. Eventually the enclaves merged to form the midcentury patriciate, which now lacked the vitality to incorporate newcomers. Arrivistes entered society as members of Mrs. Astor's Four Hundred, a crowd that evoked contempt in traditional social circles. When rejected by the smart set, as in the case of the Harrimans and the Goulds, they remained outside fashionable society.

Proper Bostonians made a successful transition from trade to manufacturing and after the Civil War continued to dominate New England investment banking and played a significant role in several important industries. Their New York counterparts, edged out of economic leadership in the 1840s and '50s, had little influence in the apex of New York's imperium over American capitalism. The insurance companies, banks, brokerage houses, and railroads they founded either vanished or were absorbed into corporations dominated by the robber barons, or, if they survived under old management, were dwarfed by newer firms. The changing composition of the business elite was reflected in the chamber of commerce, where Old Guard merchants gave way to newer wholesale and retail dealers. At the time of World War I only a tiny residue remained of the maritime elite. Extensive turnover in commercial corporations meant that New York firms rarely lasted beyond three generations. Nine local companies in 1927 held membership in the Assembly of Centenary Firms of the United States of America, and only one, Schiefflin & Co., operated under patrician management. Schiefflin & Co. and William Iselin & Co. (1808), a textile sales house, were the sole organizations still under upper-class control among the century-old New York businesses in 1942.[273]

Insurance firms started before the Civil War—Knickerbocker Fire Insurance, Mutual Life Insurance. Continental Insurance Company, Manhattan Life Insurance, and Equitable Life Assurance—at best had an occasional blueblood as window-dressing on their boards, and subsequent firms, such as Metropolitan Life (1868), the largest in the country, were run by newcomers. The robber barons proliferated on insurance company boards and the affairs of the three largest, New York Life, Equitable, and Mutual, were dominated by J. P. Morgan.[274] Although aristocrats more frequently served as directors (but almost never as officers) of older banks, the situation was basically the same in both institutions of capital accumulation. Roosevelt & Sons, Brown Brothers & Co., and Adrian Iselin & Co. were still under family control in the twentieth century, but their stature in the financial world paled next to those dominated by new capitalists. The most important investment banking and trust houses in the late nineteenth and early twentieth centuries were the Manufacturer's Trust Co., the Chase National Bank (1877), the National City Bank of New York, Kuhn Loeb & Co., the First National Bank, Farmers' Loan & Trust, Guaranty Trust Co. (1864), and J. P. Morgan & Co. National City was controlled by the Rockefellers, and directors of the other institutions included leading Gilded Age capitalists. The heads of the great banks, George F. Baker of First National, James Stillman of National City, and Morgan, came from New England and upstate New York, and Jacob Schiff, of Kuhn Loeb & Co., was born in Germany.[275] There is little point in reviewing the well-known robber baron rule in railroads, utilities, oil, steel, and other industries, but the supremacy of the tycoons over remnants of the Old Guard is illustrated by Harriman's ouster of Stuyvesant Fish in 1906 as president of the Illinois Central Railroad. Fish, one of the few Knickerbocker executives in an industrial enterprise, headed the line in which the old upper class retained its greatest influence. He was discharged by Harriman, the real power in the organization, because Mrs. Fish, who succeeded Mrs. Astor as the Queen of society, refused to admit the Harrimans into the fashionable set.[276]

Institutional evidence for the decline of the Old Guard, relative to its pre–Civil War rank and to the position of Brahmin contemporaries in Boston, is reaffirmed by an analysis of the 1892 *Tribune Monthly* list of millionaires (see Table 6).[277] Measured against the 1828 and 1856–57 list of New Yorkers assessed for at least $100,000, the self-made among the

Table 6

VINTAGE OF FORTUNE FOR NEW YORK MILLIONAIRES OF 1892

Wealth Generation	Number	Percentage of Known Vintage
First	255	31.4
Second	189	23.3
At least second	92	11.3
Three or more	276	34.0
Known vintage	812	100
Total	1,368	—

1892 rich decreased by 8.1 percent from the earliest and increased by 2.5 percent from the midcentury enclave. The 1892 group, with fortunes that went back at least three generations, was respectively 10.7 percent and 4.1 percent smaller than in 1828 and 1856–57. The share of second-generation wealth in 1892 was 12.8 percent larger than in 1828 and the same as in 1856–57. The segment of at-least-second-generation affluence in 1892 was over double that of 1828 and nearly identical to that of 1856–57. Between 1828 and 1892 the vintage distribution of wealth moved substantially from brand new and ancient accumulations to the middle categories. Between 1856–57 and 1892 only slight variations appeared. The generational pattern for late-nineteenth-century fortunes was set before the Civil War. Livingstons, Schermerhorns, Rhinelanders, Stuyvesants appeared on every nineteenth-century list and some, like the Astors, shifted from first to third generation between 1828 and 1892. But old wealth in 1892, as in 1856–57, was engulfed by a massive tide of newcomers. Hence the share of ancient accumulations remained what it had been on the eve of the Civil War. A significant segment of the *nouveaux riches* of 1892 consisted of Jewish bankers and merchants. As a result of the *arriviste* influx, 55 percent of the millionaires possessed relatively young fortunes (no more than two generations old) and the rest inherited property of older vintage. This profile of wealth, however, is not conclusive because only 59.4 percent of the total number of millionaires could be reliably traced. The proportion of those with known backgrounds is relatively close to the rich of 1828 but significantly greater than the 1856–57 group.

New York millionaires tended slightly toward more recent vintage of fortune than did Boston millionaires. A 1.7-percent-larger share of the former was first-generation while 1.0- and 4.5-percent-greater proportions of the latter had respectively inherited second and three or more generations of wealth. The New Yorkers, however, had a 3.9 percent edge in wealth of at least two generations' standing so that the proportions of relatively old and relatively new wealth in the two groups of millionaires were almost identical. However, 8.6 percent more of the 1892 Bostonian vintage backgrounds could be identified. Since the Alger types usually came from more obscure families, newly made riches might be underestimated on the New York list, thus perhaps widening the gap between the two cities in that category.

More significant differences emerge through an examination of the geographical origins of the monied elites of 1892 (see Table 7). About half (51.2 percent) of the birthplaces of the New Yorkers were identified, a proportion similar to that of the 1856–57 affluent residents, but a 25 percent smaller share than the rich of 1828. Incomplete information, therefore, permits only tentative conclusions about the geographical distribution of the millionaires and about variations with earlier compilations and the Bostonians. Comparing the three lists of affluent New Yorkers, the share of 1892 rich residents born in the city was 7.2 percent less than in 1828 and 4.2 percent more than in 1856–57. Approximately the same percentage in the three compilations came from New York State; 9.6 percent more of the *Tribune* enclave hailed from other parts of the country than did the wealthy of 1828, conversely 1.6 percent more of the 1856–57 group were born elsewhere in the United States than were the millionaires; the wealthy of 1828 and 1856–57 exceeded the proportion of the 1892 rich born abroad respectively by 1.7 and 3.1 percent. Despite a slightly smaller share of foreign-born, the millionaires were less insular than their predecessors of 1828; a smaller percentage of the millionaires were natives of the city and a larger share originated in other regions of the nation than New York City or State. As in the case of vintage frequency, differences between the rich of 1856–57 and 1892 were slight.

Gotham millionaires indigenous to New York City had a marginal (1.7 percent) edge over Hub millionaires native to Boston. But the rich Bostonians of 1892 born in Massachusetts exceeded by one-fourth the percentage of their New York peers born in the Empire State; an 8.1 per-

Table 7

GEOGRAPHICAL ORIGINS OF THE NEW YORK MILLIONAIRES

Birthplace	Number	Percentage of Known Birthplaces
New York City	292	41.7
New York State	88	12.6
Born elsewhere in the United States	192	27.4
Born abroad	128	18.3
Known birthplaces	700	100
Total	1,368	—

cent greater segment of the affluent New Yorkers came from elsewhere in the United States, and a 15.5 percent larger share were born abroad. Although the wealthy New Yorkers of 1892 barely edged their Boston equivalents in being natives of their respective cities, the former were more cosmopolitan. The relative geographical diversity of the New Yorkers is further revealed in their comparatively far-flung birthplaces. Twenty millionaires hailed from the South and thirty-three from the West. Only twenty-eight came from the Middle Atlantic region, an area comparable to that of New England for Boston, which was the source for most Boston millionaires not born in Boston or Massachusetts. New York continued to draw talent away from other regions because it was the national economic center. Leaving aside the thirty-four Connecticut-born millionaires as coming from a state that bordered New York and Massachusetts, seventy-seven of Gotham's millionaires originated in New England, including forty-two from the Commonwealth. On the other hand, New York lost little talent to Boston. Only three of the Hub millionaires came from the Middle Atlantic states, and one of the two from New York City had Boston parents and was raised there.

Frequency distributions of vintage of fortune and geographical origin measure the degree of cohesion that existed among the New York millionaires. Further evidence of integration is the extent of family ties within the enclave and between it and the wealthy of 1828 and 1856–57. Five hundred and eighty-six (42.8 percent) of the millionaires were related to each other by blood or marriage, a decrease of 9.7 percent from the affluent of 1828 and an increase of 5.8 percent from those in 1856–57. Degree of persistence is determined by the share of the millionaires who appeared themselves or had ancestors on the antebellum compilations and by the proportions of those on the earlier lists similarly related to the moneyed elite of 1892. One hundred and eighty-two (13.3 percent) of the millionaires had antecedents among the 1828 group and 400 (29.2 percent) among the 1856–57 group. A much stronger rate of persistence occurred in the other direction: thirty-six (61.0 percent) of the affluent of 1828, and 190 (43.2 percent) of the rich of 1856–57 had descendants or themselves appeared on the 1892 compilation. In this category, as in the others, the significant change was registered on the midcentury list. The same proportion of the 1892 elite was related to the wealthy of 1856–57 as were the midcentury rich to their predecessors of 1828. Economic growth swelled the ranks of opulent New Yorkers and even though many millionaires had ties with the older economic elites, they composed less than a third of the *Tribune* enclave.

New York millionaires had a slightly higher (3.9 percent) degree of kinship than their Boston equivalents but a lower rate of persistence. The proportions of affluent Bostonians of 1892 with antecedents among the wealthy Bostonians of 1835 was 19.1 percent (nearly two and a half times) larger than the share of opulent New Yorkers of 1892 related to the rich of 1828. Boston millionaires with kinship ties to Bostonians assessed for at least $100,000 in 1860 had a 23.0 percent greater representation than Gotham millionaires similarly related to the wealthy New Yorkers of 1856–57. Reversing the direction of continuity still leaves the Bostonians with an advantage: 8.6 percent more of the descendants of the rich of 1835 appeared on the 1892 Boston compilation than occurred over the 1828–92 span in New York; 2.1 percent more of the rich in 1860 reappeared themselves or through their descendants on the *Tribune* list for Boston than did New Yorkers of 1856–57 connected in like fashion with their local economic upper order of 1892. New York's millionaire interrelatedness, a measure of horizontal integration in time, surpassed that of their Boston counterparts because many *arriviste* Gotham millionaires had siblings, wives, and children who were also amply propertied. The rate of persistence, a measure of vertical integration through time, was higher among Boston millionaries because the Brahmins better preserved their economic ascendancy than did the Knickerbockers and the antebellum maritime magnates in New York.

The last category of cohesion, the presence of patricians—members of Knickerbocker and prestigious antebellum mercantile families among the millionaires of 1892—directly focuses upon the vitality of aristocratic New York. Two hundred and seventy-eight (20.3 percent) of those on the *Tribune* list were born or married into, or their children and grandchildren (as of 1892) belonged to, the old upper class. This proportion was 35.6 percent less than the aristocratic segment of the 1828 rich residents and 12.5 percent smaller than the blueblood representation among the wealthy of 1856–57. The shrinkage of the patrician component considerably exceeded the contraction that took place over the same period of time in the category of three or more generations of wealth because many of those with an inherited fortune, like Chauncey DePew, stemmed from upstate elites, or, as in the case of the six Vanderbilts, belonged to sectors of wealth outside the Old Guard.

The superior commercial vitality of the Brahmins is shown in their heavier representation on the 1892 list. One-fifth of the New York millionaires belonged to the old upper class compared to one-third of the Bostonians. The Brahmin presence in the upper rank of wealth fell appreciably less between the eve of the Civil War and 1892 than did patrician New York's, despite the fact that the provincial aristocracy of New York perpetuated itself more extensively than did the Massachusetts Bay Colony establishment. On the 1892 list were four Livingstons, three Stuyvesants, a Van Rensselaer, two Beekmans, four DePeysters, two Morrises, and a host of other descendants from prominent colonial clans. Many offspring of old families appeared on all three lists of wealthy New Yorkers. With the exception of the Winthrops and an Endicott in 1892 (and a larger number of Winthrops appeared among the New York millionaires), the pre-Revolution elite of Massachusetts is absent from the corresponding groups of rich Bostonians.

The greater persistence of the nineteenth-century Brahmins is partly the result of a slower and smaller numerical growth of personal fortunes in post–Civil War Boston, a fact that also explains the larger share of third-generation or more fortunes and continuity with antebellum rich residents. The mercantile community's superior adaptation to industrialism is another reason for the comparative longevity of Brahmin wealth. Millionaire Bostonians included a host of offspring from Brahmin mercantile families. New York's equivalent group had rougher sailing. Grinnell, Goodhue, Jacob LeRoy, and Tileston appeared on the list of 1857–58, but their direct descendants were not on the 1892 compilation. Others, like George Griswold and several Howlands, married into families that continued among New York's wealthiest, but left no rich male heirs to perpetuate their name. The failure of the pre–Civil War maritime elite to reproduce themselves as extensively as did the Knickerbockers on the 1892 list accounts for the higher degree of persistence from 1828 to 1892 than from 1856–57 to 1892, despite the shorter time of the latter interval.

Type of wealth influenced the proportion of patrician fortunes that survived into the 1890s and demonstrates the commercial impotence of New York's Old Guard. Type, as distinguished from source, of wealth designates the chief economic activity which sustained patrician fortunes in 1892. A Brahmin, Knickerbocker, or New York maritime fortune might have begun in one kind of endeavor, but subsequent accretions may have been due to success in other fields. The previous discussion of the old upper-class segments in the two cities sought to ascertain the maximum patrician influence upon nineteenth-century affluence in New York and Boston. This phase of the analysis concentrates on the economic backbone of the patriciate in 1892. Omitted, therefore, from Tables 8 and 9 are those made patrician by marriage, by progeny, or by maternal descent. In each of these cases, it seems more plausible to attribute wealth to the nonpatrician source.

An investigation of the primary type of wealth among the blueblood millionaires can be valid only if restricted to the patrilineal core, to patricians who inherited their wealth from patrician fathers, and to offspring of patrician parents who added to their own fortunes or married other patrilineal bluebloods who expanded ancient accumulations. Old types of wealth in the following tables designate riches gained through preindustrial occupations, overseas trade, mercantile banking,

Table 8

PRIMARY TYPE OF WEALTH
FOR NEW YORK PATRICIAN MILLIONAIRES OF 1892

Type of Wealth	Number	Percentage
Patrician millionaires	128	100
Old	100	78.1
Mixed	16	12.5
New	12	9.4

Table 9

PRIMARY TYPE OF WEALTH FOR BRAHMIN MILLIONAIRES OF 1892

Type of Wealth	Number	Percentage
Brahmin millionaires	47	100
Old	24	51.0
Mixed	6	12.8
New	17	36.2

and, chiefly, urban real estate. These activities are labeled old whether the descendants of their originators still pursued them or lived off ancestral efforts in such lines. New types of wealth constitute accumulations that derive from industrial capitalism: wealth inherited or made in mining, railroads, or manufacturing, or in investment banking that financed such enterprises. Mixed forms of wealth denote those who owed their economic position to old and new business endeavors, or denote cases where it was impossible to tell which form accounted for the major part of the fortune. Tables 8 and 9 show that a considerably larger segment of the fortunes of blueblood Bostonians derived from modern enterprises than did the wealth of aristocratic New Yorkers.

The patrilineal core, more economically viable in Boston, also comprised a larger share of the patriciate of that city. Of the 278 bluebloods by birth, marriage, or progeny among New York's millionaires of 1892, 128 (42.0 percent) can be designated intrinsic aristocrats. The Boston portion is forty-seven out of seventy-two (65.3 percent). Brahmins were appreciably more endogamous (23.3 percent) than their New York counterparts. A greater proportion of the New York Old Guard married outside their enclave, probably because they controlled a lesser share of urban wealth and economic power than the Brahmins and were more often tempted toward alliance with the new rich in order to avoid financial decline. By the end of the century genteel Bostonians and New Yorkers constituted aristocracies whose unity depended upon intragroup conjugal ties. According to the proportion of intrinsic members of the old upper class among the Boston and New York millionaires and the comparative share of urban wealth and economic power controlled by these patricians, the New York gentry was in a more advanced stage of disintegration.

Politics

Economic and political power were intertwined facets of upper-class leadership. Consequently, the greater vigor of Brahmin entrepreneurs enabled proper Boston to escape as severe a political decline as occurred in the New York patriciate. Nevertheless, from the Gilded Age to the present, members of old New York families appeared in public office. Theodore and Franklin D. Roosevelt served as New York governors and U.S. presidents, John T. Hoffman was mayor of the city right after the Civil War and then became governor of the state, Seth Low headed the urban government in the early 1900s, and Newbold Morris served in several municipal posts in the mid-twentieth century. Other descendants of the Knickerbocker-maritime elite sat on the city council or in the state legislature. Bluebloods in New York, as well as in Boston, were particularly attracted to diplomacy. Hamilton Fish was Grant's secretary of state, and John Jay in the 1860s and Peter A. Jay and Montgomery Schuyler in the 1920s headed various foreign missions. Nevertheless, the share of offices held by the Old Guard substantially declined. Between 1789 and 1835, 79 percent of the officers of the chamber of commerce held political posts, in 1870 one-third had. Only a third of the latter served in policy-making posts—elected judicial, legislative, or executive offices—or as high party officials. The rest were lower party functionaries, appointed administrators, members of agencies, boards, or commissions; or served in posts of honor rather than substance. Society leaders appeared even more infrequently than business leaders in public life and in policy-making roles. About one-fourth of the 1870 officers of the exclusive Knickerbocker and Union Clubs were in government service, and less than one-fifth of the Union officers occupied policy-making positions. Between 1890 and 1910 the proportion of chamber of commerce officers holding government posts increased to two-fifths, and one-third of the officers of three major business associations—the chamber, the Clearing House, and the Merchants' Association—were in public life. But these organizations had long ceased to be, or never were, patrician-dominated. The share of Union and Metropolitan club officers filling government jobs during these decades was one-fifth. In this period the share of chamber officers in policy-making positions fell to one-fifth and that of Union and Metropolitan officers was one-tenth. About the same proportion of the three business association officers held public posts in 1930–36 as had their predecessors in 1890–1910. A slightly larger representation of the elite club officers entered government service in 1930–36 than in 1890–1910, but none came from the Knickerbocker and less than one-third from the Union, the most aristocratic of the clubs. Metropolitan officers, an organization based on wealth and less exclusive than the other clubs, contributed most of the social leaders in public life. Only 10 percent of the business leaders and an even smaller proportion of social leaders held policy-making positions in 1930–36.[278]

Industrial tycoons and their descendants were generally more powerful than the bluebloods. A few held high office—William C. Whitney, Cleveland's secretary of the Navy; Levi P. Morton, congressman, New York governor, minister to France, and Benjamin Harrison's vice-president; and, more recently, Nelson Rockefeller and W. Averell Harriman—but the main function of this group was party financing. August Belmont was the major contributor to the New York Democrats and national chairman of the party in the 1860s. Cleveland Dodge (from one of the rare antebellum families that remained among the business elite after the Civil War), James W. Gerard, Thomas Fortune Ryan, Ralph Pulitzer, Herbert H. Lehman, and Bernard M. Baruch also gave large sums to the Democrats, while Chauncey DePew, several generations of Rockefellers, Payne Whitney, Edward H. Harriman, Henry H. Rogers, and J. P. Morgan helped underwrite the Republicans. Remnants of the pre–Civil War establishment, with their comparatively slender resources, were not large donors to political organizations. The few robber-baron statesmen constituted an exception to the virtual disappearance of the richest late-nineteenth-century New Yorkers from political office. Only fifty-four of the 1,368 (4.0 percent) millionaires of 1892 held the same types of public posts as did the wealthy of 1856–57.[279] Eleven percent more of the Boston millionaires held the same types of government offices.

Older elites declined in New York politics, similarly but more precipitately than bluebloods in Boston, through loss of commercial eminence and displacement by urban machines who voiced the values, served the needs, and captured the votes of the immigrant masses. Major patrician political figures in New York, as in Boston, placed party regularity above Old Guard values. Hoffman was a Tammany Democrat and Hamilton Fish supported Grant in 1872 and voted for Blaine in 1884 despite upper-crust mugwumpery. Both Roosevelts, starting out in plebian clubhouses, overcame family and class resistance to pursue their careers. Theodore Roosevelt was warned by "men of cultivated taste and easy life," that "politics were 'low'; that the organizations were not controlled by 'gentlemen'. . . ." Throughout his career Roosevelt suffered the slights of aristocrats who considered themselves morally superior to partisan organizations and struggles. Like Henry Cabot Lodge, to whom

he frequently complained, Roosevelt deprecated blueblood civic reformers. Their censorious purity, he believed, stemmed from snobbery,
ignorance, indolence, and impotence. He and Lodge agreed that practical and even machine politics was the route to personal power and accomplishment and the best way to improve national conditions and retain patrician influence. They preferred compromise, hard work, adaptability, and democracy to aloofness, exclusiveness, over-sensitivity, and
futile idealism.[280] FDR also endured peer disapproval. His mother told
Cornelius Vanderbilt that "when he was running for the State Senate
. . . I was the only sympathizer he possessed among his own people."
They thought it "shameful and ridiculous for" a young patrician "to
associate himself with dirty politicians" and "hoped for his own sake that
he would be defeated." As president he was called "a traitor to his class"
and Endicott Peabody, FDR's old headmaster, defended him against
outraged Groton alumni.[281]

Stuyvesant Fish embodied the Knickerbocker type abhorred by
Theodore Roosevelt. In 1888 Fish wrote that "young men of means and
leisure should take public office, but am unable, and very decidedly unwilling to do so myself." But public "abuse" caused William Waldorf
Astor and other upper-class friends and acquaintances to be "driven
out" of running for office and made it impossible "for a man to go into
politics, and retain his self-respect and the confidence of his neighbors."
Fish, Strong, and Astor avoided politics or suffered early defeat for public office, and, consequently, turned against majority rule and government service.[282] Other aristocrats hoped to rectify these matters by remaining active without surrendering to party orthodoxy. This group
emerged in the battle against William Marcy Tweed, the infamous but
possibly mislabeled Tammany boss of the 1860s. Many tycoons were
allied with Tweed, thus giving the blueblood crusaders a chance to strike
out against the *parvenu* in business as well as in politics. In 1871 the
reformers formed a Committee of Seventy, which included several
upper-class civic organizations, and a host of bankers moved less by
moral or class indignation than by fear of rising taxes and impaired
municipal credit. The following year the good government forces, the
Union League Club, the Citizens' Association, and the Young Men's
Municipal Reform Association elected William F. Havemeyer, a respectable businessman who inherited a sugar-refining fortune, as a reform mayor.[283]

The reform movement of the late nineteenth and early twentieth centuries contained Jays, Delafields, Grinnells, Lows, and Roosevelts, who
acted from the same grievances and adopted the same strategies as did
the Brahmin crusaders. They would resist the onslaught of new elites,
ethnic minority–dominated city machines, and industrial magnates by

counterattacking with civil service laws, secret ballots, and the election of honest and economy-minded officials. Since their values and prescriptions were superficial and irrelevant, and sometimes deleterious, to the needs of the urban masses and powerful business interests, their victories were rare and their achievements impermanent. Good government advocates in New York and Boston formed similar organizations. Their haunts in Gotham were the Union League, the Century and University clubs, the New York Civil Service and Citizens' associations, the Citizens' Union, and the Reform and City clubs. The Bostonians and New Yorkers worked together in the National Civil Service and National Municipal clubs and the mugwump movements of 1872 and 1884. Upper-class reformers in both cities were active in social, cultural, charitable, and professional organizations. In New York they were officers of the city bar association, the chamber of commerce, and exclusive social clubs. Between 1890 and 1910, for example, 16 percent of the officers of the Union Club were members of the Reform Club and 42 percent belonged to the City Club. Subsequently, patrician participation dwindled: in 1930–36 none of the officers of the Union, Knickerbocker, or Metropolitan clubs were members of these civic organizations.[284] Turn-of-the-century crusaders were also prominent in the Charity Organization Society and the Association for Improving the Condition of the Poor, the leading welfare agencies in the city, and served as Columbia University trustees. Columbia presidents Seth Low and Nicholas Murray Butler were also leading reformers.[285]

Except for Low and a few others, the Old Guard played a minor role in local or national good government organizations. Few upper-class types appeared among the founders of the New York Civil Service Reform Association (1877) or the Good Government Club, and those in the Social Reform Club (1895) were largely inactive showpieces. The City Reform Club (1882), where bluebloods were more important, was barely alive in 1887. Only seven of the thirty members of the executive committee of the New York Civil Service Reform Association from 1877 to 1883, whose birthplaces Ari Hoogenboom was able to trace, were natives of the city, while sixteen came from New England. Gerald W. McFarland collected 410 names of New York Independents in 1884; only 100 were in the Social Register and a scant 16 belonged to the Union Club.[286] The patriciate made a poor contrast to the Danas, Adamses, Codmans, Eliots, and other Brahmins who helped organize the opposition to Grant and Blaine, dominated the Citizen's Association of Boston (1887), and were more influential in the Massachusetts Civil Service Reform League than were their New York peers in the New York Civil Service Reform Association. No New York aristocrat headed the National Civil Service Reform League (1881), although several were high officers, but Richard Henry Dana III and Charles William Eliot served as presidents. Brahmin members of the Massachusetts Civil Service League were instrumental in founding the national body; upper-class New Yorkers took no part in its formation. Boston bluebloods in the Massachusetts legislature drew up and led the successful fight for the passage of civil service bills; New York aristocrats did not provide similar leadership in Albany.[287] The superiority of the Boston reformers prompted Knickerbocker Montgomery Schuyler to remark to the National Civil Service Reform League in 1920 that "in New York we are apt to think . . . that our institutions are in peril and things are not what they used to be. . . ." He was "ashamed" that the city was not like Boston, where a police strike had just been defeated and the mayor had snubbed the president of the Irish Republic.[288]

The Knickerbocker-maritime establishment exerted a relatively weak influence in reform movements because its declining power, wealth, status, and confidence depleted patrician resources in the fight for good government. Unlike the Brahmins, the New York gentry also shared power with multimillionaire industrial capitalists and their allies in law and banking. Rockefeller, Morgan, Henry Villard, and other robber barons were officers, members, and contributors in the major national and local good government associations.[289] Psychic and material deficiencies hastened withdrawal from urban leadership, a resignation of upper-class functions which further weakened the Old Guard and diminished its identification with the city. Increasingly the old order centered its concerns in, and derived its comforts from, participation in ancestral societies and social clubs.

Blueblood Bostonians also participated more extensively in foreign affairs. The state department solicited the advice of patricians like Brooks Adams and Charles William Eliot. Instead of consulting New York aristocrats, Washington turned to publishers, tycoons, and corporate lawyers in that city.[290] Brahmins were vigorous, too, in opposing foreign policy. Eliot, Thomas Wentworth Higginson, Charles Eliot Norton, and Charles Francis Adams, Jr., were active in the antiimperialist movement. Patrician New Yorkers stayed out of the controversy over territory acquired in the Spanish-American War.[291]

Professions and Culture

Deterioration in the core functions of urban leadership affected accessory roles. A survey of old family influence in professional and cultural activities in the late nineteenth and early twentieth centuries, as in business and government, discloses an acceleration of the decay already evident in the 1850s and much worse than contemporary Brahmin debilitation.

Blueblood New Yorkers still entered the legal profession, but concentrated on real estate and trust administration for a largely genteel clientele. Consequently, they were increasingly remote from the corporate law practices of leading attorneys and found themselves at the periphery of the profession. Aristocrats participated in the reorganization of the New York City Bar Association in 1870, but the officers of the reconstituted body were not drawn from the patriciate.[292] The foremost Gilded Age lawyers, Joseph Choate, Chauncey DePew, and John L. Cadwalader, hailed respectively from Massachusetts, upstate New York, and Pennsylvania. Strong, Bidwell, and Strong retained its preeminence, but operated under different direction and now served the industrial elite. Cadwalader, a Philadelphia aristocrat, became a partner in the 1870s and transformed it into a modern practice specializing in banking and corporate litigation. Cadwalader and Taft's attorney general George W. Wickersham, who later joined the firm, brought in the business of several modern financial and industrial giants. In 1914, when ex-President Taft entered the firm, it was renamed Cadwalader, Wickersham & Taft.[293]

Well-born New York lawyers had once proliferated at the top of the legal profession. Physicians of distinguished lineage were much rarer. St. Luke's Hospital had several Delafields on its staff; in 1858 one became president of the College of Physicians and Surgeons and his son later taught there. Doctors of elite ancestry, however, ranked neither in number nor in repute with those of Philadelphia and Boston. New York had no equivalent of nationally known old family figures like S. Weir Mitchell, Cadwalader Morris, or the Wood and Wister medical dynasties of Philadelphia, or the Homans, Cabots, Warrens, Codmans, and Minots (one of them a Nobel laureate) in Boston.[294] The inferiority of New York's patrician physicians was reflected in the superiority of internationally famed Massachusetts General Hospital over its social counterpart, New York Hospital. The latter was ultimately surpassed by Mt. Sinai Hospital, a favorite charity of wealthy New York Jewry.

As patrons, rather than practitioners, aristocrats made a better showing: Robert B. Minturn and Murray Hoffman (president of its board) were active in founding St. Luke's. James H. Roosevelt left $1 million to begin Roosevelt Hospital (1863) and in 1918 a Roosevelt still headed its board. Several great merchants and Alexander Van Rensselaer served on the original board of managers of the Presbyterian Hospital in the City of New York (1868). James Lenox, first board president, gave the institution $500,000 in land and bequests and younger Lenoxes and Dodges continued the family tradition of acting as officers of the hospital. The outburst of patrician altruism that within one decade led to the formation of three hospitals for the sickly poor did not prevent newcomers from permeating this Old Guard preserve. In 1866 J. P. Morgan was a manager of St. Luke's and subsequently the Vanderbilts donated huge sums to the College of Physicians and Surgeons; *parvenu* lawyers and capitalists and their children also made generous contributions to New York Hospital and were elected to its board of governors. Rising costs, however, now prohibit hospitals from relying primarily on private beneficence. Philanthropy met only 4 percent of the 1971 budget of New York Hospital.[295]

Although old New Yorkers were more active in education than in medicine, here too their accomplishments faded, they were successfully challenged by younger elites, and their achievements did not measure up to those of the Brahmins. Knickerbocker, maritime, and later elites, like proper Bostonians, sent their sons to private schools where Episcopalianism, classics, and cricket constituted a code of gentlemanly deportment which instilled patrician behavior patterns. The New Englanders preferred Groton, which emphasized careers in public and professional life. After 1875 St. Paul's became the favored place for offspring of the Vanderbilts and other tycoons.[296] Members of descendants of the New York maritime establishment also acted as administrators and donors, but did not match the accomplishments of the Brahmins who founded Groton, St. Paul's, and Milton Academy and supplied headmasters at Groton and St. Mark's. Nevertheless, the New Yorkers had some substantial attainments: the bequest of one overseas trader made possible the formation of Lawrenceville School. Henry Augustus Coit of St. Paul's, after Endicott Peabody the most influential headmaster, was the grandson of a merchant who wedded a Howland. An occasional notable New York also was a trustee of Groton and St. Paul's.[297]

Placing children in private schools did not preclude patrician concern over public education. Suspicion of the common people continued to nag the Old Guard, and mass schooling still seemed the best antidote for the dangers of republican rule. Upper-crust civil service reformers in New York, as well as in Boston, locked in combat with immigrant-supported machines, often looked upon the foreign-born and their children as particularly in need of indoctrination in "common schools" and felt that parochial education was a Roman plot to undermine public education and other institutions and principles that sustained the nation.[298]

Primary and secondary schooling, whether private or public, was not the major focus of the upper class. Columbia University continued to engage its chief, but inadequate, efforts. After the war, Fish and Strong reiterated their earlier dissatisfaction. In 1868 Strong denounced "wealthy and distinguished alumni" for neglecting the college. Since "the Revolution," Columbia has been "low in public favor, compared with Harvard, Princeton, and Yale, and has almost wholly turned away from its Treasury the great current of private munificence—donations and bequests—that has sustained and enriched those institutions. . . . Columbia College has been, at least till within the last ten years, a 'one horse concern'. . . ."²⁹⁹ Strong's critique came when Harvard, under the imminent leadership of Eliot, was about to mature into a great national university. Partly as a reflection of the academic inferiority of Columbia (Harvard's introduction of the elective system antedated and was more complete than Columbia's), the Old Guard and the industrial titans began to withhold their presence as well as their purses. Old families like the Roosevelts and Fishes, who had sent generations of their children to Columbia and served as trustees, now enrolled their sons at Harvard. The newer elite of Morgans, Vanderbilts, and Astors usually studied at Harvard or Yale. Money followed matriculation. A few aristocrats continued to support Columbia generously, but their fortunes were insignificant compared to the *arriviste* multimillionaires. Even when the latter gave to Columbia, their largest contributions went elsewhere. Peter Cooper preferred Cooper Union, Vanderbilts gave mostly to Vanderbilt University and Yale, Rockefellers to the University of Chicago, and Morgan and Baker to Harvard.³⁰⁰ Boston bluebloods, on the other hand, concentrated their resources and sent their sons to Harvard and Groton. New York multimillionaires frequently were not natives of the city, and their political concerns, industrial empires, and educational benefactions were not primarily local. These involvements show them to be a national upper order with commitments whose geographical scope far surpassed the relative insularity of the Brahmins.

Old family alumni still looked to Columbia to defend traditional values. In 1876 John Jay warned the Alumni Association against "infidelity and atheism." He exhorted "our Alma Mater" to defend "that Protestant faith" upon which "King's College was originally established, and upon" which "must depend the purity of national morals and perhaps the continuance of national life." Columbia's limited adoption of the elective system and the founding of the School of Mines were necessary adaptations to contemporary needs, but should not "undervalue the dignity which quiet permanence confers upon institutions of learning, nor the effect of such classic associations upon the mind and character of the student, and even upon the casual visitor."³⁰¹

Attempts to keep Columbia a patrician bastion were doomed by changes in the administration, student body, and sources of financial assistance. The old order continued to give, but the greatest donors, except for Seth Low and the Schermerhorns, were Cornelius Vanderbilt, Morgan, the Dodges, Rockefeller, and several Jewish bankers.³⁰² An influx of newcomers also modified the undergraduate body. "While doubtless the old New York stock will always be represented, Columbia is not likely ever again to be a fashionable college, *per se*," reported the college dean in 1914.[303] He was reflecting on the intrusion of immigrant and *nouveau riche* sons in Columbia classrooms. After World War II the upper class constituted a miniscule minority of the students. A list of the alma maters of members of the New York Social Register in 1963 shows Yale first with 2,234 graduates, Harvard second with 1,746, and Columbia fifth with 311. The distribution of the college enrollments of the sons of the 1963 social registrants indicated that Columbia was becoming progressively less attractive to the social elite: Harvard, where 171 of the younger generation studied, ranked first, and Columbia, with nine, stood fourteenth. An identical situation prevailed among high society women. In 1963 Barnard, with only six daughters of social registrants, tied for fifteenth on the list of colleges. The decline of Barnard and Columbia was also part of a general diminution of Ivy Leaguers in the inner social circle. Before 1950 two-thirds of the children of the socially prominent had attended Harvard, Yale, or Princeton; in 1963, only 45 percent.[304]

The disappearance of patrician benefactors and undergraduates was accompanied by changes in the administration and by Columbia's transformation into an outstanding university. Patricians rarely became faculty members and Low was the sole upper-class president of the college. After the 1880s a new breed, represented by Morgan and Cornelius Vanderbilt, were elected trustees. In the 1920s members of elite Jewish clans began to serve and old New Yorkers steadily departed until in 1957 none were on the board.[305] Their withdrawal was more precipitous and more complete than that of the Brahmins at Harvard. Twentieth-century Columbia bore little resemblance to the upper-class antebellum school. At the 1927 celebration of his twenty-fifth anniversary as president, Butler announced that he was "building the university into the industrial and economic life of our time" and recommended that its graduates take jobs in large corporations. "It is temperament and capacity to grow and to move that count," he claimed. "We are making two traditions. One is part of the great tradition of human aspiration and achievement . . . the other is the great tradition of our own University, and the part which it can and must play in the centuries that lie before this American democracy." Like one of Sinclair Lewis's Rotarian boosters, he wanted Columbia to "swing into the marching step of the great tradition. . . ."[306]

Upper-class religious activity offered no exception to the retreat of the Old Guard from leadership. Disarray in its ranks had begun before the Civil War and spread in subsequent decades as exclusive churches continued to lose worshippers and benefactors. Grace Church, more attuned to the faith of the fashionable, became the dominant shrine of the New York Episcopal diocese. Up to 1924 seven rectors had served there;

four became bishops and two headed the diocese; none belonged to the city's aristocracy. Schenectady-born rector Henry Codman Potter became bishop of New York in 1887; several of his relatives were on Ward McAllister's Four Hundred list. The favored clergyman of the smart set, he sanctified its births, weddings, and funerals.[307] While Grace attracted fashionable New York, Trinity continued to decline. Sixteen years after Berrian drew attention to the impoverishment and atomization of its congregation and neighborhood, his successor, Morgan Dix, denounced churches, like Grace, for moving uptown to retain their wealthy and well-born communicants. "Now that the pride and the show, the class-notions and caste-privileges, of the fashionable world have ebbed away from" the old downtown churches "and none are left here but the . . . neglected and forgotten of gay society," these old shrines should "become sanctuaries for men of all classes and conditions." Dix took pride in Trinity's charitable activities, which swelled attendance at his services and assuaged the loss of wealthy and socially prominent parishioners.[308] Despite dedication to the "lost sheep" who now filled its pews, Trinity, with gross assets of $14,000,000 in 1908, was the richest church in the United States. In that year it also faced another controversy over its tenement-house holdings. Other relics also persisted. Many aristocrats remained active as wardens and vestrymen, and traditional ties between Trinity and blueblood institutions such as Columbia and New York Hospital were kept up by parish officials who served on the boards of various patrician institutions. Nonetheless, aristocratic influence was waning: the proportion of old stock decreased in the administration of the church and was no longer represented among the rectors and assistant ministers. Rector William Thomas Manning (1908–21) came from a poor family of Texas and Nebraska farmers and in 1919 ended the aristocratic practice of pew rents.[309]

The rise of the new elite in upper-class Episcopalianism was dramatically displayed in that grandiose undertaking, the Cathedral of St. John the Divine. Among the cathedral trustees were several bluebloods, but trustees Cornelius Vanderbilt, August Belmont, and John Jacob Astor gave much more money and Morgan was the financial and spiritual force behind the project.[310] The waning power of the aristocracy was a microcosm of the diminished role of this sect in the religious life of the city. Immigration from Ireland, Italy, and eastern Europe reduced Protestantism to the point where it had less influence over civic morality and politics than did the Catholic archbishop.

Brahmin ministers and educators played a crucial role in the intellectual life of Boston. Genteel New Yorkers, infrequently drawn to these callings, were deprived of an important institutional base for the formation of a patrician intelligentsia. Reluctance to enter professions dealing with ideas manifested the relative low priority of intellectuality within the antebellum establishment. This situation changed little after the Civil War. European visitors and native New Yorkers continued to comment on the impoverished state of culture (especially in contrast to Boston) in both fashionable and polite society. Edith Wharton "was a failure in Boston because they thought I was too fashionable to be intelligent, and a failure in New York because they were afraid I was too intelligent to be fashionable." Knickerbocker Wharton "grew up in an environment where the [creative] arts are simply non-existent" and "authorship was still regarded as something between a black art and a form of manual labor."[311] If the serious-minded were stifled in New York, they sometimes blossomed in the culturally stimulating Brahmin atmosphere. Isabella Stewart Gardner, daughter of a New York dry-goods merchant, became Boston's leading art patroness. Julia Ward Howe, child of banker Samuel Ward and cousin of Ward McAllister, was another Gotham heiress who bloomed there. If not for marrying Boston reformer Samuel Gridley Howe, she said, "I should probably have remained a frequenter of fashionable society, a musical amateur, and a *dillettante* in literature."[312]

Although Old Guard Manhattan ranked behind Brahmin Boston in intellectual accomplishments, it produced historian Theodore Roosevelt and novelist Wharton. Even if one elite indisputably overshadows another in creative talent, such comparisons are misleading indicators of upper-class cultural contributions. The historical function of urban gentries has not been to breed great minds but to support them. Patronage is the real test of cultural attainment in the patriciate, and old New Yorkers, also inferior to proper Bostonians in this respect, performed better as benefactors than as practitioners of the arts and sciences. Until well into the twentieth century, bluebloods served as Columbia trustees and several gave generous gifts. Patrician influence in the New York Society Library and the historical society remained even more pervasive. Before World War II aristocrats predominated among the library officers and trustees and up to the 1930s among its donors; in the 1960s with Frederic R. King as chairman of the board, they still held high positions. The historical society was controlled by the same group, although newcomers, for example, Goulds, Vanderbilts, and Morgans, have, since the 1880s, gradually infiltrated its membership. The society president in 1947 was Fenwick Beekman, Columbia graduate, New York Hospital physician, and Society Library trustee.[313] Bluebloods even had the intellectual vitality to organize, in 1878, the Thursday Evening Club, similar to proper Boston's Saturday and Wednesday Evening clubs. Here Columbia professors mixed with scholarly patricians and a few plutocrats with elevated tastes.[314]

Millionaires without mellowed social credentials, barred from Knickerbocker-maritime circles, gravitated to the Four Hundred. The

crowd of Mrs. Astor and Mrs. Fish was intellectually barren. Knickerbockers May King Van Rensselaer and Theodore Roosevelt acidly attacked the vacuity of this group.[315] A few habitués of the Four Hundred
shared the evaluation and sometimes even the sentiments of aristocratic
critics.[316] Ward McAllister himself recognized that "any number of cultivated and highly respectable, even distinguished men [were] outside of
fashionable society." Only at unselective "large ball[s]" do "we go outside of the exclusive set and invite professional men, doctors, lawyers,
editors, artists, and the like." The inner circle, according to the list
McAllister gave the New York Times in 1892, contained one artist, one
author, one editor, two architects, and a publisher out of 273 names that
he dubbed "The Four Hundred."[317] The paucity of intellectuals and
artistic interests in the fashionable enclave accounts for its rare participation in cultural activities. At the height of its brilliance, during the
1882–83 Manhattan social season, 849 of its events, excluding weddings,
made the society pages of the New York Tribune. Among these news-
worthy affairs appeared three art exhibits and thirty-six lectures. Culture
claimed 12 percent of the publicized activities. In 1900 such gatherings
had increased by only 1 percent.[318]

Despite the tendency to denigrate highbrow interests of robber barons and other freshly minted millionaires and the mindlessness of the
Astor group, plutocrats contributed more than did aristocrats to the
formation of New York's famous cultural institutions. While old families
centered their concerns around the historical society and the New York
Society Library, newcomers created institutions which eclipsed the ancient organizations in cultural achievement. Here again an important
difference existed between genteel New Yorkers and their counterparts
in Boston and Philadelphia; the latter started the great museums and
orchestras in their cities.[319]

The Metropolitan Museum of Art (1870) was the work of the industrial elite. In fact, shortly after the Civil War a disdainful historical society rejected a proposed merger with the museum because its board of
trustees lacked distinguished pedigrees. Without aristocratic endorse-
ment and with déclassé millionaires like John Jacob Astor and August
Belmont at first dubious about its survival, the museum struggled along
in the early years. In the 1870s the trustees repeatedly exhorted wealthy
New Yorkers to donate money and made the usual unfavorable comparison between the niggardliness of rich residents and elite support of
museums in Philadelphia and Boston. Until 1905, when Morgan headed
its board, art scholars rated the Metropolitan inferior to the Boston
Museum of Fine Arts. Through his management and munificence, collections were upgraded and acquisitions increased, making the Metropolitan, by the 1920s, the largest and richest museum in the Western

Hemisphere. A few aristocrats sat on the board, but they were over-shadowed in numbers, influence, and beneficence by trustees Morgan, Henry Clay Frick, Baker, the Lehmans, Lewisohns, and other Gilded Age capitalists and their children.[320] The new breed of art collector magnates and millionaires was also responsible for the Museum of the City of New York (1923), and the Frick Collection (1920), the Museum of Modern Art (1929), the Whitney Museum of Modern Art (1930) and the Solomon R. Guggenheim Museum (1937) established respectively by Henry Clay Frick, the Rockefellers, Whitneys, and Guggenheims.[321]

The Old Guard also played a peripheral role in music. The confronta-tion over control of opera in New York discloses its impotence when challenged by the robber barons. The Metropolitan Opera Company was organized in 1880 after the patrician-dominated Academy of Music snubbed William H. Vanderbilt's $30,000 offer for a box seat. Vander-bilt, Jay Gould, and other *parvenus* financed a new opera company. This contest between age and ambition ended in defeat for the older order: the Academy Opera failed to survive the challenge of the Met-ropolitan Opera because, in the words of the academy's manager, "I cannot fight Wall Street." From the 1900s to the 1920s Jewish banker Otto Kahn was the main contributor and stockholder in the Metropoli-tan Opera Company. He was responsible for bringing in Arturo Tosca-nini and making other improvements in the quality of the perfor-mances.[322] The New York Philharmonic Society was the other major civic musical organization. Although Strong and E. H. Schermerhorn headed its board in the 1870s, tycoons and Jewish millionaires and their families, for example, Henry Harkness Flagler, Oswald G. Villard, and Mrs. Charles S. Guggenheimer, subsequently became the chief patrons and managers of the society.[323]

The new moneyed elite also became the force behind the New York Public Library (1895), yet another of the city's late nineteenth-century cultural monuments. It emerged from the union of the Astor, Lenox, and Tilden libraries. Astor and Lenox trustees came from old families, as did the original board of the public library. An Old Guard dominion in the 1890s, the New York Public Library had fewer books than the Boston Public, Harvard, and University of Chicago libraries. In the twentieth century, however, when Morgans, Schiffs, Whitneys, and Bakers took control, it became, next to the Library of Congress, the largest in the United States.[324]

Patricians still preponderated in traditional associations whose re-stricted membership and appeal made them minor factors in urban cul-tural life. When the old upper class failed to join emerging organizations which sought to reach a broader audience in the community (as in the case of the refusal of the historical society to unite with the Metropolitan Museum), the bluebloods retained command of an organization less important as an intellectual force than the one they rejected. When the patriciate contested the rivalry of a new cultural association under upstart management (as in the case of the Academy of Music versus the Metropolitan Opera), they found themselves bested by *arrivistes*. When they initially controlled a new institution attempting to appeal to a larger audience (as in the case of the public library), its growth lagged until the new breed took over and used superior resources and skills to elevate the enterprise to national preeminence. When the old establishment gradually gave way to a new order (as in the case of Columbia), its decline coincided with the enlargement and revivification of the institution. In the twentieth century the orchestra, opera, university, and library, along with salience in book- and magazine-publishing, the theater and radio, made New York the cultural capital of the western hemisphere. But the relics of the antebellum elite, deficient in material resources, management skills, and intellectual commitment, contributed little to this supremacy. A similar eclipse awaited the captains of industry and finance and their families. Supporters of the Metropolitan Opera, the Philharmonic, and the Metropolitan Museum now claim that new personnel and new fortunes patronize and direct these institutions. IBM, Ford Motor Company, and other modern corporations give generously to New York's noted cultural institutions, and their executives increasingly appear among their trustees.[325] The supremacy of New York and its elites is also threatened by the emergence of the Southern California way of life as the ideal American existence. Movies and television, located in Hollywood, along with the growth of major museums, universities, and libraries, and modern industries such as the aerospace complex, have provided the West Coast, especially Los Angeles, with the confidence, wealth, and style to rival New York for national cultural leadership.

Charity

Loss of political, professional, and commercial leadership did not at first prevent the urban gentry from maintaining a conspicuous role in culture and philanthropy. Rising elites were more concerned with gathering wealth and power than disseminating ideas or disbursing unconsolidated fortunes. When the newcomers felt secure in their wealth, they would come to dominate the city's major charities. Until that time the Old Guard faced less competition than in contests over control of business or government. The postwar vitality of the Knickerbocker-maritime establishment was demonstrated in its founding of hospitals for the poor and the New York Societies for the Prevention of Cruelty to Animals and to Children, organized respectively in 1866 and 1875. In the 1890s this enclave held a major share of the offices of both societies and retained significant if decreasing influence in the administration of the older savings banks for the poor and the Marine Society.[326]

Several aristocrats were noted altruists. Columbia graduate Elbridge T. Gerry was a founder and officer of the Societies for Prevention of Cruelty to Animals and to Children, chaired a municipal commission of inquiry into public care of the insane and the New York State Commission on Capital Punishment, and served as a governor of New York Hospital. Tenement-house reformer Theodore Roosevelt, Sr. was active in both charitable and cultural associations as a member of the executive committees of the Museum of Natural History and the Metropolitan Museum of Art, vice-president of the State Charities Aid Association, a commissioner of the State Board of Charities, and a member of the Children's Aid Society. For a time bluebloods also figured prominently in modern charity movements. Louisa Lee Schuyler was the main force in the formation of the State Charities Aid Association in 1872, Seth Low and James Gallatin participated in tenement-house reform and Low served on the State Board of Charities, and Alfred and James R. Roosevelt helped found New York's foremost late-nineteenth-century welfare organization, the Charity Organization Society of the City of New York (1882). Particularly during the first quarter-century of its existence, many COS officers came from the old upper class.[327]

Erosion of power and wealth ultimately weakened Old Guard philanthropic leadership. Other factors in its decline were an increasing patrician alienation from the city, especially from the foreign-born element, who received much of the public and private aid, and beginning in the 1850s, the rise of widespread disenchantment with humanitarian reforms. Finally, the professionalization of social work replaced old upper-class figures with vocationally trained and oriented settlement-house and social workers.[328] New agencies like the COS put professionals in charge of policy and administration and rationalized relief. As a result of these developments, organizations once dominated by the patriciate began to disappear, as did the Public School Society in 1853. Their functions were assumed by public bodies like the board of education or newer private associations where aristocrats had less influence. Ancient charities still extant became primarily social clubs, as happened in the St. George's and St. Andrew's societies, or aristocratic members and officers were gradually replaced by newcomers as in the Marine Society, the savings banks for the poor, and also, incidentally, at St. George's and St. Andrew's. Some organizations formed later in the pre–Civil War period also shifted purposes. After 1900 the Bank for Savings in the City of New York concentrated on finance rather than uplift.[329]

Blueblood attainments equaled neither antebellum nor Brahmin achievements. Upper-class Bostonian altruism was also entering its twilight era—for the same reasons that undermined old New York philanthropy. But Robert C. Winthrop, Charles Russell Codman, Richard C. Cabot, and Robert Treat Paine were more influential and lasted longer than their New York counterparts. After 1890 New York settlement-house workers assumed initiatives in tenement-house reform. Early COS trustees included, and its generous patrons were almost exclusively, newly risen industrialists and bankers. Even when benevolent associations were founded for similar reasons as in the antebellum era, the old upper class often took a minor role. In 1894 the COS formed the Provident Loan Society to alleviate, for the deserving indigent, hardships incurred by the 1893 depression. Members of the old and new elites belonged to the lending agency, but most trustees came from the latter enclave.[330]

Fashionable society was even more remote from philanthropy than were the Knickerbockers. Neither Louisa Lee Schuyler, the leading lady of the charity movement in the 1870s, nor her successor, Brahmin Josephine Shaw Lowell, who moved to New York in that decade to become the chief founder of the COS and was the first woman on the board of state commissioners of charities and a key promoter in modernizing relief dispensation, belonged to the smart set. Conversely, the Four Hundred rarely participated in social welfare activities. Only thirty of the 849 (4 percent) events reported in the New York *Tribune* society page during the 1882–83 social season involved charitable purposes. In 1900, despite the intervention of a severe depression, the percentage merely doubled.[331] If the bequests of the richest in the group are any reflection of the disposition of smaller fortunes, the smart set displayed no more sense of public welfare individually than as a unit. Mrs. Astor's husband left $145,000 (0.33 percent) of his millions to public purposes. William H. Vanderbilt allowed philanthropy 0.75 percent of an estate of $200 million. Some of the *nouveaux riche* outside the charmed circle left equally small sums for social welfare. Morgan allocated less than $1 million out of a $68 million fortune to legacies for cultural and philanthropic projects.[332] The wills of these noted multimillionaires, however, do not necessarily reflect a lifetime of niggardliness. Vanderbilt and Morgan had given millions for various causes before they died.

Investment bankers and captains of industry outside both polite and fashionable society had become the primary supporters of benevolent enterprises. Bishop Potter called Jacob Schiff New York's foremost late nineteenth-century philanthropist, and banker James Loeb was another important charity donor. Of the seven leaders in charitable and cultural matters, named by the New York *Times* in 1912, Isaac N. Seligman, Schiff, and Felix Warburg belonged to Jewish banking and mercantile families excluded by the Four Hundred and patrician society, and Morgan was a lone wolf. R. Fulton Cutting and Robert W. DeForest were the only premier philanthropists with Knickerbocker connections and none belonged to the McAllister enclave. Among the twelve placed just below these luminaries, three came from the antebellum elite, the remainder were eminent Gilded Age capitalists (including two Jewish bankers) and, once again, none belonged to the Four Hundred. The *Times* article also listed the members of the executive boards of the Metropolitan Museum of Art, the American Museum of Natural History, the COS, the New York Zoological Society, the National Child Committee, the Russell Sage Foundation, the Society to Protect Children from Cruelty, the AICP, and New York Hospital. Except for the last two—both founded before the Civil War—the directors of these organizations were largely or wholly from the new breed of millionaires.[333]

Leading philanthropists, especially Gilded Age tycoons, did not limit their gifts to local institutions. In 1896–97, for example, Schiff and Morris K. Jesup were among the foremost contributors to Armenian relief, and New York donations doubled those from Boston. In 1907 the wife of Russell Sage, with a bequest from him of about $20 million, established a foundation bearing his name, and Thomas Fortune Ryan gave the Catholic Church over $20 million in gifts and legacies. During World War I, Schiff, Nathan Straus, and the Guggenheim brothers contributed large sums to Jewish War Relief.[334]

The trustees of New York's largest philanthropic and cultural institutions overlapped in the same manner as had their antebellum predecessors, but the personnel now came from a different enclave. Their roles, however, were more circumscribed than those of their forerunners because dispensation of charity was more controlled by professional managers. Moreover, municipal political machines, the Catholic Church, and religious and ethnic associations played an unprecedentedly key role in aiding the underprivileged. Upper-class charity was dealt another grievous blow during the 1930s when the magnitude of needs and financial reverses prevented the moneyed elite from effectively coping with adversity. In 1931 fund-raisers for the Red Cross, the Community Chest, and unemployment assistance organizations in Philadelphia and New York complained about inadequate gifts from rich residents. This had always been true. Private efforts never met the problems of the dependent, and the two greatest post–Civil War relief organizations in New York, the AICP and the COS, for the duration of their existence up to 1931 received respectively only 264 legacies, funds, and gifts, and 173 gifts to capital funds.[335]

Society

The decline of the old upper class intensified self-doubt and pessimism regarding the destiny of the city and country, aristocratic anxieties that predated the Civil War. Edith Wharton, George Templeton Strong, John Jay, Edward King, William Ingraham Kip, Stuyvesant Fish, Jr., William C. DeWitt, May King Van Rensselaer, Robert B. Roosevelt, and Frederic J. and John Watts DePeyster argued (nostalgically but inaccurately) that the antebellum establishment had created an orderly, organic community with high standards of rectitude, firm roots in the past, and no place for "parvenuism."[336] Relics of the passing order now discovered that old values and ways had not persisted. "The mighty city of today knows little or nothing of our traditions," rued F. J. DePeyster. "Strangers in our own city. . . . Life here has become so exhausting and so expensive that but few of those whose birth or education fit them to adorn any gathering have either strength or wealth enough to go at the headlong pace of that gilded band of immigrants and natives, 'The Four Hundred.'"[337] Edith Wharton and Theodore Roosevelt contended that weaknesses in the aristocracy had caused its eclipse. Roosevelt was caustic and Wharton sympathetic, but both acknowledged that failure of will, inflexible conservatism, and rejection of the responsibilities of political and economic leadership accounted for this decline. Most of the Old Guard, unable to look inward and confront its shortcomings, attributed its demise to demagogues who hoodwinked the bovine masses and to robber barons who seized commercial supremacy from a class too noble to adopt their malevolence. Beleagured patricians saw in democracy, immigration, racial degeneracy, and industrialism the essence of the modern era and the enemies of the fallen elite.[338]

Overwhelmed by defeat and self-pity, the eclipsed establishment sought unity and comfort in the founding of ancestral and patriotic societies, where lineage and style outweighed wealth and power: the national and local Society of the Cincinnati, the St. Nicholas Society, the St. Nicholas Club of the City of New York (1875), the Holland Society (1885), the Colonial Order of the Acorn (1894) and its New York chapter, the New York Society of the Order of the Founders and Patriots of America (1896), the Order of Colonial Lords of Manors in America (1911), and the national organizations founded in the 1890s, the Colonial Dames of America, the Sons and Daughters of the American Revolution, and the Order of Colonial Dames. In these societies the Old Guard could vent bitterness over being shunted aside by upstarts and, through their genealogical and historical research and publication, keep alive old traditions and vicariously experience the glory of their forebears. Almost invariably the members and officers of these societies came from the fading aristocracy.[339] Their purposes and impulses are best illustrated in the statements of their adherents, constitutions, and by-laws. Hamilton Fish, Frederic J. DePeyster, and William C. DeWitt respectively praised the Cincinnati, St. Nicholas, and Holland societies for "purity in the actual lineal descent" of their members, "as a rallying ground for Knickerbockers," and for offering refuge "when a race is being outnumbered and overrun in its own land." The constitutions of the St. Nicholas Club, the Holland Society, and the New York chapter of the Acorn committed these organizations to preserve the history of their forebears and promote solidarity among the descendants. De-Peyster hoped that the example of "our Dutch ancestors" would inspire St. Nicholas Society aristocrats to halt the "deluge of poverty, ignorance, disease, and crime threatening to engulf our good city." The local branch of the Acorn similarly dedicated itself to the "principles transmitted by our forefathers." Only the wisdom of "the past" could stem the "tide of foreign immigration," which threatened "our national characteristics" and "endanger[ed] the stability of our cherished institutions."[340]

Upper-class social clubs with purposes other than ancestral worship provided meeting places for aristocrats and more recent elites. At the Century Association, Union, University (1865), Union League (1863), Knickerbocker (1871), Coaching (1875), Tuxedo (1886), Metropolitan, (1891), and Brook (1903) clubs, patricians mingled with Morgans, Astors, Vanderbilts, Belmonts, and, as the decades passed, even with Rockefellers. Special club interests, which emphasized wealth (Tuxedo and Coaching), culture (Century), college attendance (University), and economic or political influence (Metropolitan and Union League), led to admissions on bases other than lineage. The Old Guard continued to belong, but their numbers gradually dwindled.[341]

Although these organizations were limited to the educated, the cultured, the rich, the powerful, and the well-born, they represented a regression from aristocratic exclusiveness, from an age when the rites of high society were conducted in old family houses. Clubhouses were not as intimate as domiciles nor invitations as restricted as in the old days. Just as a man might do business with people whom he would not invite to his club, so he might elect someone to the club whom he would not entertain at home. Thus McAllister and Harry Lehr, anathema to the Old Guard, rubbed shoulders with them in the Union and Metropolitan. After World War I the clubs were undermined by high service costs, the Depression, the suburban movement of the socially and financially prominent accompanied by the advent of the country club, the accent on family togetherness, and an increasing preoccupation with golf and tennis—sports for which the city clubs had no facilities. As a result, the Metropolitan in 1934 had a huge deficit and has survived by admitting Conrad Hilton, Dale Carnegie, and Stavros Niarachos. The influx of freshly minted millionaires prevented bankruptcy, but one member said in 1958: "The Club will never be what it was in the old days. Today's members don't seem to have the time or the inclination to devote themselves to club life." The Knickerbocker, undergoing similar financial problems, was rescued when Nelson Rockefeller bought the clubhouse and allowed the members to meet there rent-free for forty years. Current members of the Union League and Union complain about indiscriminate admissions policies.[342] The decline of the latter, New York's oldest and most exclusive club, exemplifies the disintegration of urban club life. The Union had been founded chiefly by Old Guard merchants and lawyers. Clubmen usually belonged to several social organizations, and Union members helped form the Union League, Metropolitan, Brook, and other exclusive clubs, and the Knickerbocker was created by younger men tired of waiting for openings in the Union. In 1920 the Union had over 1,500 members, in 1932 it had 1,300 and the waiting list disappeared. Twentieth-century nominees lacking impeccable social credentials, Vanderbilts, Harrimans, Belmonts, Rockefellers, and even an occasional Jew, have passed through the sacred portals. *Arriviste* admissions did not change the club's conservative outlook, give it a more youthful orientation, drive out the patricians, or stop the decline in membership. In 1969 there were barely 1,000 members, mostly social registrants. One-fifth were listed in *Poor's Register of [business] Executives*, the largest single occupation being stockbrokers. Sons inherited the places of their fathers, and many members descended from the original founders. Continued exclusiveness resulted in a membership lacking national fame or power; only a tiny minority were in the 1969 edition of *Who's Who*. But the president said in that year: "We want no salesman here, nobody who pushes himself. We are a small club and that type of personality would not be acceptable to our members."[343]

Social, cultural, and charitable institutions facilitated interaction among the elites in upper-class New York, but each group remained distinct. The "Faubourg St. Germain set," presided over by Mrs. Hamilton Fish, Mrs. Theodore Roosevelt, Sr., and Mrs. Lewis Rutherfurd, was similar to patrician enclaves in Philadelphia, Boston, and Charleston. Its modest, unpublicized, and self-contained world encompassed the Academy of Music and quiet evenings in lower-Manhattan brownstones. Inherited status, allegiance to the past, relatively small fortunes, an anonymous life-style, and contempt and envy for the Four Hundred defined Faubourg values and attitudes.[344] For the aristocrats fashionable society was no longer polite society. Typically for New York, though the two groups differed in customs, leaders, origins, vintage and source of wealth, and neighborhood, they shared certain experiences, personnel, and values. Fishes and Astors went to Harvard in the 1880s, Philip Schuyler and George F. Baker served together as trustees of the public library, and several descendants of old families associated with new wealth. But it is simplistic to designate these cases as examples of merging elites. Fellowship at school, at board meetings, and even at social clubs does not necessarily unify family-structured social groups, though it may enhance the opportunity for integration. Transferring membership from one group to another does not inevitably signify assimilation. Mrs. Astor, born Caroline Schermerhorn, by lineage and upbringing easily qualified for the Faubourg set, but this fact did not endear her enclave to Knickerbocker critics Mrs. Van Rensselaer, Kip, Mrs. Wharton, Theodore Roosevelt, or Frederic J. DePeyster. Renegades do not increase interaction between the deserted group and the body they join or form. The surest evidence of closeness between two enclaves is the presence of dual allegiance, common values, and mutual influence. The most powerful of the Four Hundred—Mrs. Astor, Mrs. Vanderbilt, Mrs. Fish, McAllister, and Lehr—did not, either by choice or stock, belong to old New York. Moreover, their behavior differed substantially from that of bluebloods in New York or elsewhere. The Four Hundred, as McAllister put it, balanced "the nobs" (birth) and "the swells" (wealth). He praised Mrs. Astor for valuing "ancestry; . . . bringing it in, in all social matters," without failing "to understand . . . the importance and power of the new element; recognizing it, and fairly and generously awarding it a prominent place."[345]

I have elsewhere discussed the Four Hundred and will here summarize those qualities which differentiated it from social elites in other Atlantic port cities and made it a model for newer sets in such places as Chicago.[346] Mrs. Astor's circle was relatively open to new wealth, uncertain of tradition and prerogatives, unconcerned with civic leadership, internally divided among cliques, dominated by strong-willed females, dependent upon publicity and costly and conspicuous display to establish and sustain its status, subject to marital disruption which destroyed the family continuity vital to bequeathing upper-class status, and eager to import European titles, artifacts, and styles to substitute for its own lack of rooted credentials and conventions. Patrician Boston and Philadelphia, comparatively closed aristocracies, shunned newspaper notoriety, sought to preserve traditional roles of urban leadership, had simple life-styles and stable family relationships, and were guided by grand old men like Henry Lee Higginson or George Wharton Pepper.

Neither the Four Hundred nor the Old Guard constituted an upper class. They were social elites with little influence over other aspects of civic leadership. The urban gentry withdrew from other functions; the smart set never sought them. Most of the great business and community leaders—Morgan, Harriman, Rockefeller, the Jewish financiers—were not on McAllister's 1892 list. In fact, only twenty-three of his adherents appeared in Who's Who in America (1899–1900).[347]

High society was no longer, as in Boston or Philadelphia, linked to predominance in other areas of municipal life. Moreover, trends started in the last days of the Four Hundred—divorces, marriages with titled Europeans, and lionizing of athletes, actors, and actresses—made it a transitional order between New York's *haute monde* and the Café Society that flourished between the world wars in that city, London, and Paris. The international set was even more remote from conventional patrician circles. Café Society combined Hollywood and Broadway celebrities, European nobles, debutantes, Astor, Whitney, and Vanderbilt playboys from New York, Philadelphia Wideners, party-giver Elsa Maxwell, and gossip columnist "Cholly Knickerbocker" (Maury H. Paul). Instead of being rooted in a single city, this fashionable elite spanned the Atlantic. It forsook the traditional gathering places of previous upper orders for the Stork Club and El Morocco. New wealth and celebrity, personified by William R. Hearst, the Schiffs, Selznicks, and heiresses Doris Duke and Barbara Hutton, replaced the grand dames and drones of the Four Hundred.[348]

Every passing elite sees in its own decline the disappearance of cherished virtues. Regret, bitterness, and sentimentality shape the views of social critics from fading enclaves. Knickerbocker commentators evaluated mid and late nineteenth-century fashionable circles from the perspective of their own displacement. After World War I, when Newport and Fifth Avenue gave way to the international set, vestiges of Mrs. Astor's crowd, once considered vulgar interlopers, similarly complained about vanishing tradition, refinement, and established social rank. Café Society in turn waned after World War II, by which time New York society as a whole was in terminal disarray. Social secretaries now have difficulty in supplying social registrants for parties and dances, and organizers of assemblies and balls cannot get enough eligible escorts for these affairs because college boys find them formal and phony. Discotheques, square dances, travel, quiet visits with friends, political campaigns, and ecological, civil rights, or antiwar movements offer rival attractions for the younger generation.[349]

Ironically, in their twilight era interrelationships expanded among Atlantic seaboard upper classes. The increased interaction centered in New York, the country's social and economic capital. The city's elites had cosmopolitan geographical roots and the children of its tycoons and aristocrats joined the younger generation of genteel Bostonians and Philadelphians at the same eastern boarding schools and Ivy League colleges. Descendants of Philadelphia's first families settled in New York, several belonged to the Four Hundred and married Goulds and Astors. At the extremes of absurdity and achievement one wedded Lehr and another became a distinguished New York lawyer and patron of important cultural institutions. Proper Bostonians also migrated to New York. Endicott Peabody's father joined the House of Morgan, and

Henry Lee Higginson's brother also belonged to the city's banking fraternity. Theodore Roosevelt's first wife was a Shaw, and a Rockefeller married a Sears. Brahmins entered the smart set, and Josephine Shaw Lowell became a leader in social welfare activity. Greater participation of Brahmins in various aspects of New York life, however, did not end, and perhaps exacerbated, the long-standing Knickerbocker resentment for New Englanders. Robert B. Roosevelt told the Holland Society in 1886 that the Yankees had "crowded themselves forward . . . in social life, in public prominence, and above all in politics," and "pushed" the "old residents of New York . . . into the background." Two years later Hamilton Fish wrote his brother Stuyvesant, who also disliked Boston bluebloods, that the Brahmins were "cowardly" and conceited and accused them of stupidity, "bigotry, and coldheartedness and insincerity." His nephew, Stuyvesant Fish, Jr., in 1942 considered "the so-called intelligentsia of Boston . . . narrow-minded, self-satisfied, smug Puritans."[350]

The death of New York society reflected the displacement of the industrial capitalists, the third great upper order in the city. The Rockefellers were an exception to the ruin of many twentieth-century Astors, Vanderbilts, Morgans, Paynes, and Whitneys. Divorces, fast living, exogamous marriages to adventurers, and indifference to business dissipated patrimonies, diminished commercial power, and disintegrated kinship groupings necessary for class survival. A new generation of moguls, in Detroit, Pittsburgh, Delaware, and Texas, or the technocrats and bureaucrats who managed the mammoth corporations, dispossessed the robber barons and their families.

NOTES

1. Richard B. Morris, "Primogeniture and Entailed Estates in America," *Columbia Law Review*, XXVII (Jan., 1927), 24–51. For the landed gentry of colonial New York see Charles Worthen Spencer, "The Land System of Colonial New York," *New York State Historical Association Proceedings*, XVI (1961), 150–64; Ulysses Prentiss Hedrick, *A History of Agriculture in the State of New York* (Albany: New York State Agriculture Society, 1933); Alice P. Kenney, *The Gansevoorts of Albany: Dutch Patrinians in the Upper Hudson Valley* (Syracuse: Syracuse University Press, 1969); Harold D. Eberlein, *The Manors and Historic Homes of the Hudson Valley* (Philadelphia: J. B. Lippincott, 1924); William S. Pelletreau, *Historic Homes and Institutions and Genealogical and Family History of New York*, 4 vols. (New York: Lewis Historical Publishing, 1907); Edward L. Merritt, "Col. Henry Beekman and his Times," n.p., paper read at the Meeting of the Ulster County Historical Society, June 5, 1933; John A. Krout, "Behind the Coat of Arms: A Phase of Prestige in New York," *New York History*, XVI, (1935), 45–52; Milton M. Klein, "The American Whig: William Living-

ston," (Ph.D. dissertation, Columbia University, 1954); George W. Schuyler, *Colonial New York, Philip Schuyler and His Family*, 2 vols. (New York: Charles Scribner's Sons, 1885); Alexander C. Flick, ed., *History of the State of New York*, 10 vols. (New York: Columbia University Press, 1933–39) I, II; S. G. Nissenson, *The Patroon's Domain* (New York: Columbia University Press, 1937); Irving Mark, *Agrarian Conflicts in Colonial New York, 1711–1775* (New York: Columbia University Press, 1940); Maunsell Van Rensselaer, *Annals of the Van Rensselaers* (Albany: Charles Van Benthuysen & Son, 1888); Ruth L. Higgins, *Expansion in New York* (Columbus: Ohio State University Press, 1931); Cuyler Reynolds, *Hudson Mohawk Genealogical and Family Memoirs*, 2 vols. (New York: Lewis Historical Publishing, 1911). The Order of Colonial Lords of Manors in America, Baltimore, published a series of pamphlets on New York manors: John H. Livingston, *The Livingston Manor*, no. 1 (1915); Lucy D. Akerly, *The Morris Manor*, no. 4 (1916); Howland Pell, *The Pell Manor*, no. 5 (1917); Mrs. James Marsland Lawton, *The Van Cortlandt Manor*, no. 6 (1920); Edward H. Hall, *The Manor of Philipsborough*, no. 7 (1920); Mrs. William B. Beekman, *The Beekman Family*, no. 15 (1925); Montgomery Schuyler, *The Schuyler Manor*, no. 16 (1926); Mrs. Anson Phelps Atterbury, *The Bayard Family*, no. 18 (1928); Julius Goebel, Jr., *Some Legal and Political Aspects of the Manors in New York*, no. 19 (1928); Kiliaen and Miss Florence Van Rensselaer, *The Van Rensselaer Manor*, no. 21 (1929); Montgomery Schuyler, *The Patroons and Lords of Manors of the Hudson*, no. 23 (1932). Sung Bok Kim, *Landlord and Tenant in Colonial New York: Manorial Society, 1664–1775* (Chapel Hill: University of North Carolina Press, 1978). For a comparison with Virginia planters: Clifford Dowdey, *The Virginia Dynasties* (Boston: Little, Brown, 1969).

2. Jackson Turner Main, *The Upper House in Revolutionary America, 1763–88* (Madison: University of Wisconsin Press, 1967), 11–13, 43–44, 54–59, 68–81; Cadwallader Colden to the Lords Commissioners for Trade and Plantations, September 26, 1763, *The Colden Letterbooks*, 2 vols., *Collections of the New York Historical Society* X, XI, (1876–77), I, 236–37. (Hereafter referred to as *NYHS Colls.*)

3. Virginia D. Harrington, *The New York Merchants on the Eve of the Revolution* (New York: Columbia University Press, 1935), 11–14; James Grant Wilson, ed., *The Memorial History of The City of New York*, 4 vols. (New York: New York Historical Co., 1892–93), IV, 523–24; Flick, *History of the State*, II, 290–91, 369, 371, 381, 390–91; Irene D. Neu, "The Iron Plantations of Colonial New York," *New York History*, XXXIII (Jan., 1952), 3–25; Klein, "American Whig," 11–13, 25–27, 158–59; David T. Valentine, *History of New York* (New York: G. P. Putnam, 1853), 76, 118–19, 187, 239; Schuyler, *Colonial New York*, I, 276–77; A. J. F. van Laer, ed., *Van Rensselaer Bowier Manuscript* (Albany: University of the State of New York, 1908), 329–30; Philip L. White, ed., *The Beekman Mercantile Papers*, 3 vols. (New York: New York Historical Society, 1956); Donald R. Gerlach, *Philip Schuyler and the American Revolution in New York* (Lincoln: University of Nebraska Press, 1964), 48–56, 92–93; *Ships and Shipping of Old New York* (New York: Bank of Manhattan Co., New York, 1915), 30–31; Catherine Van Rensselaer Bonney, *A Legacy of Historical Gleanings*, 2 vols.

(Albany: Weed, Parsons, 1875), I, 20–21, 40–41; I. N. Phelps Stokes, *The Iconography of Manhattan Island*, 5 vols. (New York: Robert H. Dodd, 1915), I–IV, *passim*; Patricia U. Bonomi, *A Factious People: Politics and Society in Colonial New York* (New York: Columbia University Press, 1971), 60–68. Robert C. Ritchie, *The Duke's Province: A Study of New York Politics and Society, 1664–1691* (Chapel Hill: University of North Carolina Press, 1977), 25–152.

4. Mark, *Agrarian Conflicts*, 94.

5. This analysis of New York politics is based on the following sources: Higgins, *Expansion*; Spencer, "Land System"; Herbert Osgood: *The American Colonies in the Seventeenth Century*, 3 vols. (New York: Macmillan, 1904), II, 132–33, III, 450, 459–60, 466; *American Colonies in the Eighteenth Century*, 2 vols. (Goucester, Mass.: Peter Smith, 1958), I, 237–39, II, 51–71, 83, 109–15, 448–82; Martha J. Lamb, *History of the City of New York*, 2 vols. (New York: A. S. Barnes, 1877), I; Gerlach, *Philip Schuyler*; Flick, *History of the State of New York*, I–V; Schuyler, *Colonial New York*; Charles W. Spencer, "Sectional Aspects of New York Provincial Politics," *Political Science Quarterly*, XXX (Sept., 1915), 397–424; Staughton Lynd, *Anti-Federalism in Dutchess County* (Chicago: Loyola University Press, 1962), 23–27; Jerome R. Reich, *Leisler's Rebellion: A Study of Democracy in New York, 1664–1720* (Chicago: University of Chicago Press, 1953); Stanley Nider Katz, *Newcastle's New York: Anglo-American Politics, 1732–53* (Cambridge: Harvard University Press, 1968); Charles Worthen Spencer, *Phases of Royal Government in New York, 1691–1719* (Columbus: Fred J. Heer, 1905); Ross J. S. Hoffman, *Edmund Burke: New York Agent* (Philadelphia: American Philosophical Society, 1956); Carl Lotus Becker: *The History of Political Parties in the Province of New York, 1760–1776* (Madison: University of Wisconsin Press, 1910); "Nominations in Colonial New York," *American Historical Review*, VI (Jan., 1901), 260–75; Clinton Williamson, *American Suffrage from Property to Democracy* (Princeton: Princeton University Press, 1960), 27–29, 43–46, 50–57; Klein: "American Whig"; "Democracy and Politics in Colonial New York," *New York History*, XL (July, 1959), 221–47; John William Leonard, *History of the City of New York, 1609–1919* (New York: Journal of Commerce and Commercial Bulletin, 1910), 74, 145, 153–54, 169–85; Mark, *Agrarian Conflicts*; Krout, "Behind the Coat of Arms"; Ritchie, *Duke's*, *passim*; Main, *Upper House*, 43–67, 54–59; Bonomi, *Factious People, passim*. Those who wish to follow the politics of New York through primary sources should consult: Cadwallader Colden, *The Letters and Papers of Cadwallader Colden*, 9 vols., *NYHS Colls.*, 1918–27; *The Colden Letterbooks*; E. B. O'Callaghan, ed., *Documents Relating to the Colonial History of the State of New York*, 15 vols. (Albany: Weed, Parsons, 1856–83). For a roll of government officials in colonial New York see Edgar A. Werubi, *Civil List and Constitutional History of the Colony and State of New York* (Albany: Weed, Parsons, 1889), 62, 269–70, 305–14, 443.

6. C. Colden to John Popple, Secretary of State for the Colonies, Dec. 4, 1726, O'Callaghan, *Colonial Documents*, V, 806; cf. Colden to the Lords Commissioners for Trade & Plantations, Sept. 20, 1764, *Colden Letterbooks*, I, 363; Bonomi, *Factious People*, 8–10; Main, *Upper House*, 59; C. Colden to Dr. John

Mitchell, July 6, 1749, *NYHS Colls.*, LXVIII (1935), 33; George Clinton to the Duke of Newcastle, Dec. 12, 1746, O'Callaghan, *Colonial Documents*, VI, 462–63.

7. Henry Moore to the Earl of Shelburne, Feb. 21, 1767, O'Callaghan, *Colonial Documents*, VII, 906; C. Colden to Henry Seymour Conway, Dec. 13, 1765, *Colden Letterbooks*, II, 70, 72–78; cf. Colden to the Earl of Egremont, Sept. 14, 1763, I, 231–32.

8. Alan Chester, ed., *Legal and Judicial History of New York*, 3 vols. (New York: National Americana Society, 1911), I; Charles P. Daly, *Historical Sketch of the Judicial Tribunals of New York, 1623–1846* (New York: John W. Amerman, 1855), 11–12, 14–19, 26, 49; Mark, *Agrarian Conflicts*, 89–91, 94, 130–63; Paul M. Hamlin and Charles E. Baker, *Supreme Court of Judicature of the Province of New York, 1691–1704*, 3 vols. (New York: New York Historical Society, 1959), I, 84–93, III, 3–220; Hamlin, *Legal Education in Colonial New York* (New York: New York University Press, 1939), 206–8; Colden to the Earl of Halifax, Jan. 23, 1765, and Colden to the Lords of Trade, Jan. 27, 1765, O'Callaghan, *Colonial Documents*, VII, 701–3.

9. Henry Moore to the Earl of Hillsborough, Jan. 1, 1769, O'Callaghan, *Colonial Documents*, VII, 148.

10. Lamb, *History of the City of New York*, I, 161, 221–22, 230–31, 260; Wilson, *Memorial History*, II, 49–54; Stokes, *Iconography*, I–IV, *passim*; Leonard, *History of the City of New York*, 92, 112, 137, 160, 174, 231; Valentine, *History of New York*, 193, 195–197.

11. Colden to Conway, Dec. 13, 1765, *Colden Letterbooks*, II, 67.

12. Daly, *Historical Sketch*, 11–12, 14–19, 26, 49, 51; Hamlin, *Legal Education*, 110–12, 115–49, 202–3; Hamlin and Baker, *Supreme Court*, I, 99–108, 3–220; Dorothy Rita Dillon, *The New York Triumverate* (New York: Columbia University Press, 1949), 21, *passim*; George William Edwards, *New York as an Eighteenth Century Municipality* (New York: Columbia University Press, 1917), 216; Mark, *Agrarian Conflicts*, 91; Harrington, *New York Merchant*, 14, 35; Klein, "The Rise of the New York Bar: The Legal Career of William Livingston," *William and Mary Quarterly* XV (July, 1958), 334–58.

13. Hamlin, *Legal Education*, 35–40, 202–3; Klein, "Rise," 335, 355–57; Dillon, *New York Triumverate*, 21–27. For the data on Massachusetts lawyers see Gerard W. Gawalt, *The Promise of Power: The Emergence of the Legal Profession in Massachusetts, 1760–1840* (Newport, Conn.: Greenwood Press, 1979), 8–9, 12, 39, 144.

14. Harrington, *New York Merchants*, 132–42.

15. Main, *Social Structure*, 187–89.

16. For the family and geographical backgrounds of New York merchants see *ibid.*, 187–89; Van Rensselaer, *History of the City of New York*, I, 474–76; Stokes, *Iconography*, I–V; John Austin Stevens, Jr., *Colonial Records of the New York Chamber of Commerce, 1768–1784* (New York: John F. Trow, 1867); Charles W. Baird, *History of the Huguenot Emigration to America*, 3 vols., (Baltimore: Regional Publishing, 1966), II, 148–200; Margherita Arlina Hamm, *Famous Families of New York*, 2 vols. (New York: G. P. Putnam's Sons, 1902); Pelletreau, *Historic Homes*; Chester, ed., *Legal and Judicial*, I, 308–22. Many of the old New York families also have published histories, e.g., *The Clarksons of*

New York, 2 vols. (New York: Bradstreet Press, 1875); Laura Jay Wells, *The Jay Family of La Rochelle and New York* (Baltimore: Order of Colonial Lords of Manors in America, 1938); Stuyvesant Fish, *Ancestors of Hamilton Fish and Julia Ursin Niemcewitz Kean and His Wife* (New York: Evening Post Printing Office, 1929); John Ross Delafield, *The Family History of the Delafields*, 2 vols. (New York: privately printed, 1945).

17. For the largest New York City taxpayers in 1655 see Julia M. Colton, *Annals of Old Manhattan, 1609–1664* (New York: Brentano's, 1901), 179–80; for the 1674 list see "Tax List of New York 1674 (New Orange) during the Dutch Occupation," O'Callaghan, *Colonial Documents*, II, 699; cf. Wilson, *Memorial History*, I, 362; for the 1676 roll see "New York Assessment and Tax List, 1676," *New York Genealogical and Biographical Record*, II (1871), 36–38; for the 1730 list see "New York City Assessment Roll, February, 1730," *ibid.*, XCV (1964), 27–32, 166–74, 197–202. For the advent of English merchants and the comparison with Boston see Ritchie, *Duke's*, 136–39.

18. For the commercial behavior of New York's merchants see Harrington, *New York Merchants*; White, ed., *Beekman Mercantile Papers*, I, II; White, *The Beekmans of New York in Politics and Commerce, 1647–1877* (New York: New York Historical Society, 1956); *Ships and Shipping; Letter Book of John Watts, 1762–75, NYHS Colls.*, LXI (1928); Flick, *History of the State of New York*, II, 336–72. Additional information is scattered through the standard histories of New York City by Valentine, Leonard, Lamb, and Wilson.

19. For the political activities and officeholding of the New York merchants see Werner, *Civil List*, 62, 269–70, 305–14, 443; Harrington, *New York Merchants*, 16–17, 38–46, 292–308; Spencer, *Phases*, 51; Stokes, *Iconography*, I–IV, *passim*; Leonard, *History of New York City*, 72–74, 95, 99, 111–12, 127, 137, 145, 153–55, 159–60, 169, 171, 177, 180, 216, 218, 231; Valentine, *History of New York City*, 76, 114, 116, 118–23, 193–97, 228–29, 231, 240, 242; White, *Beekmans*, *passim*; Lamb, *History of New York City*, I, 90, 161, 221–22, 230–31, 244, 260, 270–72, 397–99, 420, 444, 483–84, 517, 560–64, 568, 577, 673, 678, 723; Edwards, *New York as an Eighteenth Century Municipality*, *passim*; Ernest S. Griffith, *History of American City Government: The Colonial Period* (New York: Oxford University Press, 1938), 133–37, 326–27, 348–49, 389, 401; Flick, *History of the State of New York*, I, 300–301, II, 192–93, 370–71, 387, III, 148–50; Wilson, *Memorial History*, I, 350–51, II, 49, 177–78, 355, 413–14; Mark, *Agrarian Conflicts*, 91–93; Sullivan, *History of New York*, V, 1913–14, 1938–42, 1956; Main, *Upper House*, 54–59; Julius Goebel and T. Raymond Naught, *Law Enforcement in Colonial New York* (New York: Commonwealth Fund, 1944), 239–49; Bonomi, *Factious People*, *passim*; Ritchie, *Duke's*, 43–44, 59–62, 99–101, 112–14, 121–22, 181, 185; Chester, ed., *Legal and Judicial*, I.

20. George Clinton to the Lords of Trade, Oct. 4, 1752, O'Callaghan, *Colonial Documents*, VI, 765; cf. Henry Moore to the same, June 24, 1766, VII, 833; Montgomerie quoted in O'Callaghan, ed., *The Documentary History of the State of New York* (Albany: Charles Van Benthuysen, 1851), IV, 1038–40.

21. Harrington, *New York Merchants*, 18–19, 27–34; Esther Singleton, *Social New York under the Georges, 1714–1776* (New York: D. Appleton, 1902), 19, 22–23, 27, 259, 262–70, 301–2; White, *Beekmans*, 404–7, 475–77, 482; Wilson, *Memorial History*, II, 306, IV, 456–74; Martha J. Lamb, "The Golden Age of

Colonial New York, *Magazine of American History*, XXIV (July, 1890), 1–30; Carl Bridenbaugh, *Cities in Revolt: Urban Life in America, 1743–76* (New York: Alfred A. Knopf, 1955), 141–46, 163–67, 334–72; Howard Mumford Jones, *American and French Culture, 1754–1848* (Chapel Hill: University of North Carolina Press, 1927), 217–90, 308–14, 326–49.

22. Francis Lovelace quoted in Bridenbaugh, *Cities in the Wilderness: The First Century of Urban Life in America, 1625–1742* (New York: Alfred A. Knopf, 1938), 98; Wilson, *Memorial History*, II, 474–75; Klein, "American Whig," 117–18.

23. John King, *The Charter and By Laws with a History of the Chamber of Commerce of the State of New York* (New York: John M. Elliot, 1855), 55; James Bucklin Bishop, *A Chronicle of One Hundred and Fifty Years: The Chamber of Commerce of the State of New York, 1768–1918* (New York: Charles Scribner's Sons, 1918), 17–29; Charles King, *History of the New York Chamber of Commerce* (New York: William Van Norden, 1849), 50–60; Stevens, *Colonial Records*.

24. Charles C. Tiffany, *A History of the Protestant Episcopal Church in the United States of America* (New York: Charles Scribner's Sons, 1903), 166–81; "Old New York and Trinity Church," *NYHS Colls*. (1870), 145–408; William Berrian, *An Historical Sketch of Trinity Church, New York* (New York: Stanford and Swords, 1847), 14–161; Morgan Dix and Charles T. Bridgeman, *A History of the Parish of Trinity Church*, 6 vols. (New York: Columbia University Press, G. P. Putnam's Sons, Morehouse-Barlow, 1898–1962), I, *passim*.

25. Harrington, *New York Merchant*, 33–34; Nathaniel Fish Moore, *An Historical Sketch of Columbia College* (New York: Leavitt, Trow, 1846), 3–52; John B. Pine, *King's College: Now Columbia University, 1754–1897* (New York: G. P. Putnam's Sons, 1896), 3–38; J. Howard Van Ameringe, "History of Columbia University," *Universities and Their Sons*, ed. Joshua L. Chamberlain (Boston: R. Herndon, 1898), 571–731; *Catalogue of Governors, Trustees, and Officers and of the Alumni and Other Graduates of Columbia College, 1754–1882* (New York: Macgowan & Slipper, 1882); *Gifts and Bequests: Land Buildings and Equipment, 1754–1928* (New York: Columbia University Press, 1929); *Columbia University Gifts and Endowments, 1754–1904* (New York: Columbia University Press, 1904–5); C. Colden to Governor William Tryon, Aug. 22, 1774, O'Callaghan, *Colonial Documents*, VII, 486; Klein, "American Whig," 338–437; Dillon, *New York Triumverate*, 31–53.

26. John MacMullen, *A Lecture on the Past, the Present, and the Future of the New York Society Library* (New York: John F. Trow, 1856); *The New York Society Library: Shareholders and Officers* (New York: n.p., 1914); Harrington, *New York Merchant*, 35.

27. David M. Schneider, *The History of Public Welfare in New York State, 1609–1886*, 2 vols. (Chapel Hill: University of North Carolina Press, 1938), I, 66–69, 83; "Old New York and Trinity Church," 300–301; Raymond Mohl, *Poverty in New York, 1783–1825* (New York: Oxford University Press, 1971), 37–51.

28. George Austin Morrison, Jr., *History of St. Andrew's Society of the State of New York* (New York: n.p., 1906), 7–30, 181–245; *St. Andrew's Society of the State of New York: Annual Report, 1952* (New York: n.p., 1952); *The Marine Society* (New York: Henry Bessey, 1913), 5, 26, 31, 53–110.

29. Quote from the charter in "Condensed History of the Society of New York Hospital Compiled from its Records, 1769–1821," typescript, Columbia University Library, 3; *ibid.*, 3–5; *Charter of the Society of the New York Hospital* (New York: G. P. Scott, 1833), 3–6, 66–70; *Charter . . . etc.* (New York: Daniel Fanshaw, 1856), 119–40; *Charter . . . etc.* (New York: D. Van Nostrand, 1872), 83–91, 99–110; *The Society of New York Hospital, Commemorative Exercises, One Hundred and Fiftieth Anniversary* (New York: privately printed, 1921), 16, 41, 91–94.

30. Thomas J. Wertenbaker, *The Golden Age of Colonial Culture* (New York: New York University Press, 1949), 47–48; Bridenbaugh, *Cities in the Wilderness*, 286–89, 401; Colden quoted in Singleton, *Social New York*, 314–15.

31. I have based this assessment on Bonomi, *Factious People, passim.* For other discussions of the issues described here see Kim, *Landlord*, 208–415; Reich, *Leisler's Rebellion*; Klein, "American Whig," 568–72; Gerlach, *Philip Schuyler*, 107, 206; Becker, *History of Political Parties*; Spencer, "Sectional Aspects"; Mark, *Agrarian Conflicts*; Klein, "Democracy and Politics," 221–47.

32. Lorenzo Sabine, *The American Loyalists* (Boston: Little, Brown, 1847); Flick, *Loyalism in New York during the Revolution* (New York: Columbia University Press, 1901); Oscar Theodore Barck, Jr., *New York City during the Revolution* (New York: Columbia University Press, 1931); Wilson, *Memorial History*, III, 8–9; *New York City during the American Revolution: Being a Collection of Original Papers from the Manuscripts in the Possession of the Mercantile Library Association of New York City* (New York: Columbia University Press, 1939); Harrington, *New York Merchants*, 348–51; Robert Abraham East, *Business Enterprise in the American Revolutionary Era* (New York: Columbia University Press, 1938), 103–11, 124, 184–94, 221–25, 237–38; Thomas C. Cochran, *New York in the Confederation* (Philadelphia: University of Pennsylvania Press, 1932), 46, 84; Lamb, *History of New York City*, II, 83, 88–90, 101–5, 252, 296–99, 303–4; Becker, *History of the Political Parties.*

33. Main, *Social Structure*, 189–190.

34. *Ibid.*, 190–91.

35. David Maldwyn Ellis, *Landlords and Farmers in the Hudson-Mohawk Region, 1790–1850* (Ithaca: Cornell University Press, 1946), *passim*; Simon W. Rosendale, "Closing Phases of the Manorial System in Albany," *NYHS Proc.*, VIII (1909), 234–45; Lynd, *Anti-Federalism*, 71–81; Edward P. Cheyney, *The Anti-Rent Agitation in the State of New York, 1839–1846* (Philadelphia: University of Pennsylvania Press, 1887), *passim*; David Murray, "The Antirent Episode in the State of New York," *Annual Report of the American Historical Association*, I (1896), 137–73.

36. For the decline of the Beekmans see White, *Beekmans*, 486–525.

37. George Dangerfield, *Chancellor Robert R. Livingston of New York, 1746–1813* (New York: Harcourt, Brace, 1960), 291–93, 382–85; Wilson, *Memorial History*, III, 187–95; Hamm, *Famous Families*, I, 236–40.

38. Werner, *Civil List*, 314–82, 156–58, 277–91, 476–86; Chester, ed., *Legal and Judicial*, I, 336–444; Jabez D. Hammond, *The History of Political Parties in the State of New York, from the Ratification of the Federal Constitution to December, 1840*, 3 vols. (Syracuse: Hall, Mills, 1852), I, 42, 44, 49, 54, 62–63, 70, 101, 153–54, 180, 371, II, 2–3, 60–64; Ellis H. Roberts, *New York: The Planting*

and Growth of the Empire State, 2 vols. (Boston: Houghton Mifflin, 1890), II, 529–32; *Reports of the Proceedings and Debates of the Convention of 1821, Assembled for the Purpose of Amending the Constitution of the State of New York* (Albany: E. and E. Hosford, 1821), 27–28; Alfred B. Street, *The Council of Revision of the State of New York* (Albany: William Gould, 1859); Charles Z. Lincoln, *The Constitutional History of New York*, 5 vols. (Rochester: Lawyers Co-operative Publishing, 1906), I, 608–9, 704–7; Charles Havens Hunt, *Life of Edward Livingston* (New York: D. Appleton, 1864); Dangerfield, *Chancellor Robert R. Livingston*; Edward P. Alexander, *A Revolutionary Conservative: James Duane of New York* (New York: Columbia University Press, 1938); Edwin Brockholst Livingston, *The Livingstons of Livingston Manor* (New York: Knickerbocker Press, 1910), 198ff.; Dixon Ryan Fox, *The Decline of Aristocracy in the Politics of New York* (New York: Columbia University Press, 1919), 31–46, 122–30, 140–43, 151–54; Ray B. Smith, *History of the State of New York*, 1776–1922, 4 vols. (Syracuse: Syracuse University Press, 1922), I, 68, 72, 88, 122–25, 200, 216, 267, 300–301, 355, 358.

39. Main: *Upper House*, 133–43; "Government by the People: The American Revolution and the Democratization of the Legislatures," *William and Mary Quarterly*, XXIII (July, 1966), 399–400.

40. Lynd, *Anti-Federalism*, 71–81, 85; David Hackett Fischer, *The Revolution of American Conservatism: The Federalist Party in the Era of Jeffersonian Democracy* (New York: Harper & Row, 1965), 60–72, 94–109, 120–21, 126, 211–18; Alfred F. Young, *Democratic Republicans of New York: The Origins 1763–1797* (Chapel Hill: University of North Carolina Press, 1967), 42–46; Fox, *Decline*, 185–91; Shaw Livermore, *The Twilight of Federalism: The Disintegration of the Federalist Party, 1815–1830* (Princeton: Princeton University Press, 1962), 67–79, 110–16; Hammond, *Political Parties*, I, 451; Lincoln, *Constitutional History*, I, 471–72, 608–9; Dangerfield, *Chancellor Robert R. Livingston*, 399ff.; Douglas T. Miller, *Jacksonian Aristocracy: Class and Democracy in New York, 1830–1860* (New York: Oxford University Press, 1967), 11–18.

41. Lynd, *Anti-Federalism*, 71–81; Fischer, *Revolution of American Conservatism*, 211–18; Young, *Democratic Republicans*, 156–57, 203–7, 533–36; Alvin Kass, *Politics in New York State* (Syracuse: Syracuse University Press, 1965), 12–19, 81–90, 136; Robert V. Remini, *Martin Van Buren and the Making of the Democratic Party* (New York: Columbia University Press, 1959), 8–9, 97; Chilton Williamson, *American Suffrage from Property to Democracy, 1760–1860* (Princeton: Princeton University Press, 1960), 196–97.

42. Young, *Democratic Republicans*, 27–28, 63–65; Fox, *Decline*, 264–69; Smith, *History of the State of New York*, I, 267–68, 300–301, II, 15–17, 23; Ellis, *Landlords*, 205–6.

43. *Reports of the Proceedings*, 63–64, 148, 158, 220, 274–75, 296, 551–52.

44. For the comments of upper-class conservatives see *ibid., passim*; Young, *Democratic Republicans*, 60–62, 504–5.

45. Robert G. Albion, *The Rise of New York Port, 1815–1860* (New York: Charles Scribner's Sons, 1939), 5–13; David T. Gilchrist, ed., *The Growth of Seaport Cities, 1790–1825* (Charlottesville: University of Virginia Press. 1967), 58–60.

46. Albion, *Rise*, 7, 38–46, 194–96, 276–80; East, *Business Enterprise*, 254–56;

Sidney Irving Pomerantz, *New York: An American City, 1783–1803* (New York: Columbia University Press, 1938), 152; Gilchrist, ed., *Growth*, 70–71.

47. For the Erie Canal and its impact on New York City shipping see Albion, *Rise*, 83–94; Henry Wayland Hill, *An Historical Review of Waterways and Canal Construction in New York State* (Buffalo: Buffalo Historical Society, 1908), 63ff.; Nobel E. Whitford, *History of the Canal System of the State of New York*, 2 vols. (Albany: Brandow Printing, 1906), I, 31–81, II, 1130–33; Alvin F. Harlow, *Old Towpaths* (New York: D. Appleton, 1926), 44ff. For the response in other cities see Albion, *Rise*, 378–82; Julius Rubin, "Canal or Railroad? Imitation and Innovation in the Response to the Erie Canal in Philadelphia, Baltimore and Boston," *Transactions of the American Philosophical Society*, LI (1961).

48. E. Digby Baltzell, *Philadelphia Gentlemen: The Making of a National Upper Class* (New York: Free Press, 1958), 95–106; Nathaniel Burt, *The Perennial Philadelphians: The Anatomy of an American Aristocracy* (Boston: Little, Brown, 1963), 179–211.

49. Samuel Eliot Morison, *The Maritime History of Massachusetts, 1783–1860* (Boston: Houghton, Mifflin, 1961), 228, 275–76; Arthur M. Johnson and Barry Supple, *Boston Capitalists and Western Railroads* (Cambridge: Harvard University Press, 1967), 15, 36; Albion, *Rise*, 386.

50. Gilchrist, ed., *Growth*, 29–31, 41–44, 73–74. The assessed wealth of New York City more than doubled that of Boston in 1835 and 1840. See *De Bow's Review*, "The City of Boston," IV (Oct., 1847), 261–62; T. P. Kettell, "The Commercial Growth and Greatness of New York," V (Jan., 1848), 37–38; G. W. Baker, *A Review of the Relative Commercial Progress of the Cities of New York & Philadelphia* (Philadelphia: Jackson Printer, 1859), *passim*.

51. For the exodus of Philadelphia merchants to New York see Rubin, "Canal or Railroad?" 19; Kettell, "Commercial Growth," 42.

52. Address of Charles King, *Proceedings of the Chamber of Commerce of the State of New York at the Opening of Their New Rooms, June 10, 1858* (New York: John A. Douglas, 1858), 7, 10–11; George Templeton Strong, *The Diary of George Templeton Strong*, 4 vols., ed. Allan Nevins and Milton Halsey Thomas, (New York: Macmillan, 1952), Jan. 31, 1856, II, 252–53.

53. "An Account of the Celebration by the New York Historical Society of Their Fortieth Anniversary," NYHS *Proc.* (1944), 97; Philip Hone, *An Address Delivered before the Mercantile Library Association, October 3, 1845* (Boston: William D. Ticknor, 1843), 7; John Pintard, *Letters from John Pintard to His Daughter Elizabeth Pintard Davidson*, 4 vols., 1816–33 (New York: New York Historical Society, 1940–41), Apr. 13, 1829, III, 72, Sept. 19, 1826, II, 300.

54. Edward Pessen, *Riches, Class and Power before the Civil War* (Lexington, Mass.: D. C. Heath, 1973), 47–48.

55. East, *Business Enterprise*, 190–91, 221–23; Wilson, *Memorial History*, IV, 535; Pomerantz, *New York*, 79–80; 90; Harold C. Syrett, ed., *The Papers of Alexander Hamilton* (New York: Columbia University Press, 1961), I, 95–96.

56. James Beekman to Effingham Lawrence, Nov. 3, 1784; White, ed., *Beekman Papers*, III, 1115; Lawrence to Beekman, Jan. 4, 1785, 1117.

57. Albion, *Rise*, 236; *Ships and Shipping*, 36–43; *Clarksons*, II, 168; Hamm, *Famous Families*, I, 75, 170–90.

58. The information for this analysis of the New York mercantile community

is provided by the following studies: Albion, *Rise; Ships and Shipping;* F. Gray Griswold: *The House Flags of the Merchants of New York* (New York: privately printed, 1926); *Clipper Ships and Yachts* (New York: E. P. Dutton, 1920), 1–70; East, *Business Enterprise;* George W. Sheldon: "The Old Packet and Clipper Service," *Harper's New Monthly Magazine,* LXVIII (Jan., 1884), 217–37; "The Shipping Merchants of Old New York," *ibid.,* LXXXIV (Feb., 1892), 475–91; William Thompson Bonner, *New York: The World's Metropolis* (New York: R. L. Polk, 1924), 697–883; Flick, *History of New York State,* VIII, 161–90; Myron H. Luke, "The Port of New York, 1800–1810" (Ph.D. dissertation, New York University, 1953); Walter Barrett (Joseph Scoville), *The Old Merchants of New York City,* 5 vols. (New York: Thomas R. Knox, 1885, originally published 1862) is colorful but unreliable. For accounts of individual merchants and firms see Freeman Hunt, *Lives of American Merchants,* 2 vols. (New York: Derby and Jackson, 1858); Mary W. Tileston, *Thomas Tileston, 1793–1864* (privately printed, 1925); D. Stuart Dodge, *Memorials of William E. Dodge* (New York: Anson D. F. Randolph, 1887); Richard Lowitt, *A Merchant Prince of the Nineteenth Century: William E. Dodge* (New York: Columbia University Press, 1954); Howard Thomas, *Marinus Willett* (Prospect, N.Y.: Prospect Books, 1954); *Clarksons;* Delafield, *Delafield: The Family History;* Carlos Martger, *William E. Dodge: The Christian Merchant* (New York: Funk & Wagnalls, 1890); Benjamin R. C. Low, *Seth Low* (New York: G. P. Putnam's Sons, 1925); William T. Cobb, *The Strenuous Life: The "Oyster Bay" Roosevelts in Business and Finance* (New York: William E. Rudge's Sons, 1946); Phyllis Mary Bannan, "Arthur and Lewis Tappan: A Study in New York Religious and Reform Movements," (Ph.D. dissertation, Columbia University, 1950); *One Hundred Years of Business Life, 1794–1894: W. H. Schiefflin & Co.* (New York: privately printed, 1894); *One Hundred and Fifty Years Service to American Health—Schiefflin & Co.* (New York: privately printed, 1944); Hall Roosevelt and Samuel Duff McCoy, *Odyssey of an American Family* (New York: Harper & Bros., 1939); George Wilson, *Portrait Gallery of the Chamber of Commerce of the State of New York* (New York: Chamber of Commerce Press, 1890); Kenneth Wiggins Porter, *John Jacob Astor: Businessman,* 2 vols. (Cambridge: Harvard University Press, 1921), I, 132–407. Much information can be found in these primary sources: Pintard, *Letters,* 4 vols.; Strong, *Diary,* 4 vols.; Philip Hone, *The Diary of Philip Hone,* 2 vols., ed. Bayard Tuckerman (New York: Dodd, Mead, 1889); Philip Hone, *The Diary of Philip Hone,* ed. Allan Nevins (New York: Dodd, Mead, 1936).

59. Benjamin Robert Winthrop, *Old New York* (New York: Edmund Jones, 1862), 4. For Knickerbocker resentment of the New Englanders see Albion, *Rise,* 250–52.

60. Albion, *Rise,* 235; Thomas C. Cochran, "Business Organization and the Development of an Industrial Discipline," *The Growth of an American Economy,* ed. Harold F. Williamson (New York: Prentice-Hall, 1944), 304–5; Ralph W. Hidy, "Credit Rating before Dun & Bradstreet," *Bulletin of the Business History Society,* XIII (Dec., 1939), 81–88.

61. Strong, *Diary,* Feb. 21, 1840, I, 131; Sept. 27, 1857, II, 355. Nathaniel Griswold quoted in Albion, *Rise,* 285–86. For similar comments from foreign visitors see Bayard Still, *Mirror for Gotham* (New York: New York University

Press, 1956), 92, 133, 172.

62. Hone, *Diary*, ed. Tuckerman, Aug. 11, 1845, II, 261.

63. Albion, *Rise*, 253–54.

64. For comments on New York extravagance see: Pintard, *Letters*, Mar. 5, 1819, I, 172; Dec. 12, 1829, III, 100; Hone, *Diary*, ed. Tuckerman, Jan. 22, 1834, I, 88–89; Strong, *Diary*, Dec. 23, 1845, I, 269; Dec. 18, 1856, II, 313; Jan. 22, 1857, II, 319; Charles Astor Bristed, *The Upper Ten Thousand: Sketches of American Society* (New York: Stringer & Townsend, 1852); Still, *Mirror*, 25–27, 60, 92–93, 117, 119, 133–34, 141–42, 148–59, 172–73, 188, 190, 211, 227–30, 277, 283, 287.

65. Strong, *Diary*, Dec. 24, 1857, II, 377–78; Mar. 29, 1860, III, 18; May 2, 1860, III, 25; Pintard, *Letters*, Mar. 15, 1819, I, 172.

66. Griswold, *House Flags*, 34; Albion, *Rise*, 246; Junius Henri Browne, *The Great Metropolis* (Hartford: American Publishing, 1869), 666–67.

67. King, *Charter*, 158; Address of Pelitiah Perit, *Proceedings of the Chamber of Commerce of the State of New York, May 7, 1863* (New York: John W. Amerman, 1863), 7.

68. The best studies of antebellum banking are: Gilchrist, ed., *Growth*, 104–47; Bray Hammond, *Banks and Politics in America from the Revolution to the Civil War* (Princeton: Princeton University Press, 1957); Fritz Redlich, *The Molding of American Banking*, 2 parts (New York: Hafner Publishing, 1947); Syrett, ed., *Hamilton Papers* also contains much information on early banking.

69. Redlich, *Molding*, I, 20; Henry W. Dommett, *A History of the Bank of New York, 1784–1884* (New York: G. P. Putnam's, 1884), 121–25, 136–39.

70. Syrett, ed., *Hamilton Papers*, I, 9–30, III, 6–7, 520–24, VI, 431, VII, 90, 133–34, 190, 209, 232, VIII, 304–5, 396–97, 440, 494–95, 504, 513, 518, IX, 68–71, 172, 176, 301, 518–20, X, 562–63, XI, 28, 152–55, 193–95, 225, 264, 494, 505–6, 666–67.

71. Dommett, *History of the Bank*, 29–30, 38, 62; cf. William T. Hardenbrook, *Financial New York* (New York: Franklin Publishing, 1897), 79–119.

72. Hardenbrook, *Financial*, 193; Dommett, *History of the Bank*, 64–65.

73. Hammond, *Banks*, 127, 146; Gilchrist, ed., *Growth*, 118.

74. Beatrice G. Reubens, "Burr, Hamilton and the Manhattan Company," *Political Science Quarterly*, LXXIII (Dec., 1957–Mar., 1958), 100–125, 578–607; Redlich, *Molding*, I, 22, 35; Hammond, *Banking*, 149–64.

75. Philip G. Hubert, Jr., *The Merchants' National Bank of the City of New York, 1803–1903* (New York: Trow Directory Printing & Binding, 1903), 1–80, 102; Hammond, *Banks*, 202–5; Hardenbrook, *Financial*, 192–226; Redlich, *Molding*, I, 35.

76. Quote from the charter in Gilchrist, ed., *Growth*, 123–24; Delafield, *Family*, I, 252; Tileston, *Thomas Tileston*, 16; Porter, *John Jacob Astor*, II, 473–74; Bonner, *New York: The World's Metropolis*, 409; *The Bank of America: A Brief Account of an Historic Financial Institution and Its Site* (New York: Bank of America, 1918), 18–22, 26–29; Redlich, *Molding*, I, 36.

77. Hardenbrook, *Financial*, 176–91.

78. *History of the Chemical Bank, 1823–1913* (New York: privately printed, 1923), 12–13, 28–29, 44–52, 57, 103–65.

79. Hammond, *Banking*, 672–73, 686, 701–4; Margaret G. Myers, *The New York Money Market* (New York: Columbia University Press, 1931), 67–69; Arthur H. Cole, "Evolution of the Foreign Exchange Market of the United States," *Journal of Business and Economic History*, I (May, 1929), 384–421.

80. Redlich, *Molding*, II, 67–69, 72, 77, 333–34, 350; Charles King, *A Memoir of the Life of James Gore King* (New York: George W. Wood, 1854); Hunt, ed., *Lives*, I, 186–204, 295–97; Strong, *Diary*, Feb. 21, 1840, I, 131; *The New York Stock Exchange* (New York: Historical Publishing Co., 1886), 61; Ralph W. Hidy, *The House of Baring in American Trade and Finance* (Cambridge: Harvard University Press, 1949), 109, 351.

81. John Crosby Brown, *A Hundred Years of Merchant Banking* (New York: privately printed, 1909), *passim*; James Brown to Thomas B. Curtis, Aug. 12, 1847, 215–16.

82. *The National City Bank of New York, 1812–1912* (New York: n.p., 1912), 4–5; *History of the Chemical Bank*, 7, 40–42.

83. Gilchrist, ed., *Growth*, 116–18; Redlich, *Molding*, II, 245–304; Hammond, *Banking*, 197–205.

84. Oliver Wolcott quoted in Gilchrist, ed., *Growth*, 119.

85. Hone, *Diary*, ed. Tuckerman, Feb. 8, 1847, II, 297; quote in Henry Wisham Lanier, *A Century of Banking in New York, 1822–1922* (New York: George H. Doran, 1922), 213. For another example of an aloof upper-class banker who was contemptuous of newcomers see James Gallatin, *The Diary of James Gallatin* (New York: Charles Scribner's Sons, 1916), 80.

86. Hammond, *Banks*, 572–600; Myers, *New York Money Market*, 94–99, 427–28; Robert E. Chaddock, "The Safety-Fund Banking System in New York State, 1829–1866," *Publications of the National Monetary Commission*, IV (1911), 247–52.

87. Strong, *Diary*, Apr. 27, 1837, I, 62.

88. Alexander Hamilton, Jr.: *A Letter by Alexander Hamilton on the Subject of Banks and the Currency* (New York: n.p., 1839); *Banks and the Currency* (New York: n.p., 1837); William A. Duer, *A National Bank: Its Necessity and Most Advisable Form* (New York: n.p., 1841); David B. Ogden: *Remarks on the Currency of the United States and the Present State and Future Prospects of the Country* (New York: n.p., 1840); *Additional Remarks on the Currency of the United States* (New York: Wiley and Putnam, 1841); *Memorial of the Chamber of Commerce of the City of New York for a National Bank, May, 1841* (New York: J. P. Wright, 1841).

89. Thomas Wren Ward quoted in Hammond, *Banking*, 598; *Articles of Association of the Bank of Commerce in New York* (New York: George F. Hopkins, 1839); 5; *One Hundred Years of Banking Service, 1839–1939* (New York: privately printed, 1939), 7–17, 44–45; Hardenbrook, *Financial*, 227–51.

90. Chaddock, "Safety-Fund," *passim*; Redlich, *Molding*, I, 78–79, 88–95, II, 48–52; Hardenbrook, *Financial*, 1–62.

91. Table 1 constructed from statistics in *History of the Chemical Bank*, 7, 17–20, 40–42.

92. Gilchrist, ed., *Growth*, 126–27; Walter B. Smith and Arthur H. Cole, *Fluctuations in American Business, 1790–1860* (Cambridge: Harvard Univer-

sity Press, 1935), 46–51, 113–14.

93. Pintard, *Letters*, Mar. 15, 27, 1829; July 11, 1830, I, 172, 174–75, 302–3.

94. Gilchrist, ed., *Growth*, 114–15, 120.

95. N. S. B. Gras, *The Massachusetts First National Bank of Boston* (Cambridge: Harvard University Press, 1937), 4; Alexander Hamilton to Gouverneur Morris, Mar. 21, 1784; William Seton to A. Hamilton, Mar. 27, 1784, *Hamilton Papers*, ed. Syrett, III, 523–24, 526; Gilchrist, ed., *Growth*, 110–111; Myers, *New York Money Market*, 109–10, 200–201; Joseph Edward Hedges, *Commercial Banking and the Stock Market before 1863* (Baltimore: Johns Hopkins University Press, 1938), 68–71.

96. H. Parker Willis and Jules I. Bogen, *Investment Banking* (New York: Harper & Bros., 1929), 165; Ward quoted in Hammond, *Banking*, 598.

97. E. James Ferguson, *The Power of the Purse* (Chapel Hill: University of North Carolina Press, 1961), 71–105; Joseph Stancliffe Davis, *Essays in the Earlier History of American Corporations*, 2 vols. (Cambridge: Harvard University Press, 1917), I, 168–371.

98. Francis L. Eames, *The New York Stock Exchange* (New York: Thomas G. Hall, 1894), 13–25, 72–73; William Armstrong, *Stocks and Stock-Jobbing in Wall Street* (New York: New York Publishing, 1848), 32–40; *History of the New York Stock Exchange* (New York: Financier Co., 1887); *The New York Stock Exchange* (New York: Historical Publishing Co., 1886).

99. Syrett, ed., *Hamilton Papers*, XI, 126, 131–32, 161, 173, 185–190; Pintard, *Letters*, Mar. 15, 27, 1819, I, 173–75; Smith and Cole, *Fluctuations*, 46–51, 113–14.

100. *Hone Diary*, ed. Tuckerman, June 6, 1844, I, 227–28; Strong, *Diary*, May 8, 1851, II, 45–46; cf. May 27, 1851, 48–49; Oct. 4, 1853, 131.

101. Myers, *New York Money Market*, 8, 200–201; Gilchrist, ed., *Growth*, 106; Smith and Cole, *Fluctuations*, 40.

102. Gilchrist, ed., *Growth*, 106.

103. *The Knickerbocker Fire Insurance Company of New York from 31st January, 1787, to 21st October, 1875* (New York: Francis & Loutrel, 1875), 3–50; Pomerantz, *New York*, 192; Sullivan, *History of New York State*, V, 2187–88; Julius Goebel, ed., *The Law Practice of Alexander Hamilton*, 2 vols. (New York: Columbia University Press, 1964, 1969), II, 405–6.

104. Smith and Cole, *Fluctuations*, 46–51, 113–14.

105. Lester Zartman, ed., *Property Insurance: Marine and Fire* (New Haven: Yale University Press, 1921), 80; Pintard, Jan. 2, 3, 1828, *Letters*, III, 12; Nevins, ed., *Hone Diary*, Sept. 2, 1842, 643–44; July 19, 1845, 740–42.

106. Gilchrist, ed., *Growth*, 108–9.

107. Hunt, *Lives*, I, 415–22; Philip N. Schuyler, *The One Hundred Year Book* (New York: A. S. Barnes, 1942), 192, 228–30; Thomas Jones, *History of New York during the Revolutionary War*, 2 vols. (New York: New York Historical Society, 1879), I, lxxi-ii; *The First Ninety-five Years of the Mutual Life Insurance Company of New York* (New York: privately printed, 1938), 8–10, 14, 30–31; Shepard B. Clough, *A Century of American Life Insurance* (New York: Columbia University Press, 1946), 30–33; James W. Hudnut, *Semi-Centennial History of the New York Life Insurance Company, 1845–1895* (New York: New York Life

Insurance Co., 1895), 1, 3, 7, 392–94; Lawrence F. Abbott, *The Story of the New York Life Insurance Company* (New York: New York Life Insurance Co., 1930), 35–36.

108. Clough, *Century*, 32–33, 35, 59–75, 89–91, 98–105; R. Carlyle Buley, *The Equitable Life Assurance Society of the United States, 1859–1964*, 2 vols. (New York: Appleton-Century-Crofts, 1967), I, 40–44; Charles Kelley Knight, *The History of Life Insurance in the United States to 1870* (Philadelphia: University of Pennsylvania Press, 1920), 103; *Ninety-five Years*, 60.

109. Hudnut, *Semi-Centennial History*, 30, 50; Abbott, *Story of New York Life*, 47, 51.

110. Clough, *Century*, 97. For lack of upper-class influence in the founding of other insurance companies in the 1850s see William Loring Andrews, *The Continental Insurance Company of New York, 1853–1905* (New York: privately printed, 1906); *Home Life Insurance Company: A Record of Fifty Years, 1860–1910* (New York: privately printed, 1910); *Milestones Making Three-Quarters of a Century of Achievement, 1853–1928* (New York: privately printed, 1928); *Proudly We Say Hanover Insurance Company: Seventy-five Years of Progress* (New York: Stillson Press, 1927).

111. Burt, *Perennial*, 141–52; Baltzell, *Philadelphia Gentlemen*, 87; Knight, *History of Life Insurance*, 83–84, 105; Roy A. Foulke, *The Sinews of American Commerce* (New York: Dun & Bradstreet, Inc., 1941), 123–28, 165–66; Zartman, ed., *Property Insurance*, 16–23; Gilchrist, ed., *Growth*, 109.

112. James G. Smith, *The Development of Trust Companies in the United States* (Henry Holt, 1927), 251–56, 283–316.

113. Lanier, *A Century of Banking*, 275–316; Edward T. Perine, *The Story of the Trust Companies* (New York: G. P. Putnam's Sons, 1916), 11–18, 109–110; *Rates and Proposals of the New York Life Insurance and Trust Company* (New York: Clayton & Van Norden, 1830), 5–6.

114. *Rates*, 13, 21; Smith, *Development*, 25–28; Perine, *Story*, 31, 109–12.

115. *Promises Fulfilled* (New York: United States Trust Company, 1953), 26–54.

116. Hill, *Historical Review*, 37, 47–48, 60; G. Morris quoted in Ellis H. Roberts, *The Planting and Growth of the Empire State*, 2 vols. (Boston: Houghton Mifflin, 1890), II, 529–30; Harlow, *Old Towpaths*, 30–45; Flick, *History of New York State*, V, 299–308; East, *Business*, 307–8; Davis, *Essays*, II, 158–65; *A Century of Progress: The History of the Delaware and Hudson Co.* (Albany: J. B. Lyon, 1925), 23.

117. Whitford, *History of the Canal System*, I, 31–81, II, 1130–33; Hill, *Historical Review*, 72–73, 81, 85; Redlich, *Molding*, II, 329–31; *The Advantages of the Proposed Canal from Lake Erie to Hudson's River. Fully Illustrated in a Correspondence between the Hon. Gouverneur Morris and Robert Fulton, Esq.* (New York: n.p., 1814); *Opening of the Building of the Chamber of Commerce of the State of New York: A Brief History of the Chamber of Commerce of the State of New York, 1768–1902* (New York: Press of the Chamber of Commerce, 1902), 108–9; Cadwallader D. Colden, *Memorial of the Celebration of the Completion of the New York [Erie] Canals* (New York: W. A. Davis, 1825), 52 and *passim*;

Anne Cary Morris, ed., *The Diary and Letters of Gouverneur Morris*, 2 vols. (London: Kegan, Paul, Trench, 1889), II, 532–42; Hunt, *Lives*, I, 334–35.

118. Albion, *Rise*, 143–64; J. Leander Bishop, A *History of American Manufactures from 1608 to 1860*, 2 vols. (Philadelphia: Edward Young, 1868), II, 79–81, 94–99, 118–19; Cadwallader D. Colden, *The Life of Robert Fulton* (New York: Kirk & Mercein, 1817), 66 and *passim*; Dangerfield, *Chancellor*, 291–93, 382–85; Wilson, *Memorial History*, III, 187–95.

119. Roosevelt and McCoy, *Odyssey*, 178–79.

120. Frank Walker Stevens, *The Beginnings of the New York Central Railroad* (New York: G. P. Putnam's Sons, 1926), 1–25, 250–55; *Century of Progress*, 161, 724–26; *The First Annual Report of the Directors of the New York and Erie Railroad Co.*, *September 23, 1835* (New York: G. P. Scott, 1835), 36; *Second Report of the Directors of the New York and Erie Railroad Company* (New York: Egbert Hedge, 1841), 16; John Livingston, *The Erie Railway: Its History and Management* (New York: John Polhemus, 1875), iii-xxxvi; Lowitt, *Merchant Prince*, 159–61; Albion, *Rise*, 164, 238, 246, 384; Alvin F. Harlow: *The Road of the Century* (New York: Creative Age Press, 1947), 4, 6–9, 42–43, 64; *Steelways of New England* (New York: Creative Age Press, 1946), 180–83.

121. Stevens, *Beginnings*, 21, 95–97, 107–8; *Second Report*, 16; Livingston, *Erie*, iii-xxxvi.

122. Harlow, *Steelways*, 187; *Century of Progress*, 161.

123. William K. Ackerman, *Historical Sketch of the Illinois Central Railroad* (Chicago: Fergus Printing, 1890), 21–24, 39–54, 73, 151–53; Carlton J. Corliss, *Main Line of Mid-America* (New York: Creative Age Press, 1950), 23–41; Howard G. Brownson, "The History of the Illinois Central Railroad to 1870," *University of Illinois Studies in the Social Sciences*, IV (1915), 285–466; Albion, *Rise*, 368.

124. Stevens, *Beginnings*, 8–10; *Second Report*, 3–4; *First Annual Report*, 17–18.

125. Strong, *Diary*, July 6, 1854, II, 178; Harlow: *Road*, 129; *Steelways*, 187–89.

126. Stevens, *Beginnings*, 362–64; Edward Hungerford, *Men and Iron: The History of the New York Central* (New York: Thomas Y. Crowell, 1938), 71–73, 162; Harlow, *Road*, 162–69.

127. Sullivan, *History of New York State*, V, 2258–65.

128. Baltzell, *Philadelphia Gentlemen*, 95–106; Burt, *Perennial*, 179–211.

129. *One Hundred Years*, 9–46; *One Hundred and Fifty Years*, 1–71; Lowitt, *Merchant Prince*, 139–88.

130. Davis, *Essays*, I, 347–522; Syrett, ed., *Hamilton Papers*, IX, 24–25, 144–45, X, 345–46, XI, 280–81, 424–25, 505–6, XII, 27, 217–18; Samuel Rezneck, "The Rise and Early Development of Industrial Consciousness in the United States, 1760–1830," *Journal of Economic and Business History*, IV (Aug., 1932), supplement, 784–811.

131. Daniel Hodas, *The Business Career of Moses Taylor: Merchant, Financial Capitalist, and Industrialist* (New York: New York University Press, 1976), 80–156, 265–66, 283–84.

132. Peter R. Decker, *Fortunes and Failures: White-Collar Mobility in Nineteenth-Century San Francisco* (Cambridge: Harvard University Press, 1978), 240–41.

133. The best accounts of Manhattan real estate are in: Stokes, *Iconography*, I–VI, *passim*; Arthur Pound, *The Golden Earth: The Story of Manhattan's Landed Wealth* (New York: Macmillan, 1935); Porter, *Astor*, II, 914–52. For speculation in wilderness tracts see A. M. Sakolski, *The Great American Land Bubble* (New York: Harper & Bros., 1932); Paul D. Evans, *The Holland Land Co.* (Buffalo: Buffalo Historical Society, 1924).

134. East, *Business Enterprise*, 256, 287; Albion, *Rise*, 195; Gilchrist, ed., *Growth*, 116–17; Hammond, *Banks*, 125, 197; Gates, *Illinois Central*, 44; Harlow, *Road*, 219, 230; Corliss, *Main Line*, 23–24.

135. The 1828 tax-assessment list was compiled from manuscript sources by Edward Pessen and is found in his "The Wealthiest New Yorkers of the Jacksonian Era: A New List," *New York Historical Society Quarterly*, LIV (Apr., 1970), 155. The 1856–57 list was based on records in the tax commissioner's office and was compiled and published by William Boyd as *Boyd's New York City Tax-Book; Being a List of Persons, Corporations & Co-Partnerships, Resident and Non-Resident, Who Were Taxed According to the Assessors Books, 1856 & '57* (New York: William H. Boyd, 1857).

136. Edward Pessen, "The Egalitarian Myth and the American Social Reality: Wealth, Mobility and Equality in the 'Era of the Common Man,'" *American Historical Review*, LXXVI (Oct., 1971), 1022–23; Pessen, *Riches*, 33–34.

137. Pessen, "Egalitarian," 1006, 1012; *Riches*, 85.

138. *New England Historical and Genealogical Register*, CVIII (1954), 29.

139. Pessen, "Egalitarian," 1017.

140. Information on vintage, family relationships, and birthplaces was gathered from the following biographical sources (the verification methods used were identical to those used for the wealthy antebellum Bostonians): Moses Yale Beach, *The Wealth and Biography of the Wealthy Citizens of the City of New York* (New York: New York Sun, 1845); William Armstrong, *The Aristocracy of New York: Who They Are, and What They Were* (New York: New York Publishing, 1848); Barrett, *Old Merchants*; Charles Morris, ed., *Makers of New York: An Historical Work Giving Portraits and Sketches of the Most Eminent Citizens of New York* (Philadelphia: L. R. Hamersly, 1895); Morris, *Men of Affairs in New York* (Philadelphia: L. R. Hamersly, 1906); Lyman H. Weeks, *Prominent Families of New York* (New York: Historical Co., 1897); Hamm, *Famous Families*; William R. Cutter, ed., *Genealogical and Family History of Southern New York and the Hudson River Valley*, 3 vols. (New York: Lewis Historical Publishing, 1913). Other volumes by the same editor and publisher that were here consulted are *Genealogical and Family History of Central New York*, 3 vols. (1915); *Genealogical and Family History of Northern New York*, 3 vols. (1910); *Genealogical and Family History of Western New York*, 3 vols. (1912); *Genealogical and Family History of the State of Connecticut*, 4 vols. (1911); *New England Families: Genealogical and Memorial*, 4 vols. (1915); *Historic Homes and Genealogical Memoirs of Middlesex County, Massachusetts*, 4 vols. (1908); *Genealogical and Personal Memoirs of Families of Boston and Eastern Massachusetts*, 4 vols. (1908); L. R. Hamersly, ed., *Who's Who in New York City and*

State (New York: Who's Who Publications, 1905); Stephen Birmingham, *"Our Crowd": The Great Jewish Families of New York* (New York: Harper & Row, 1967); Robert G. Albion, "Commercial Fortunes in New York," *New York History*, XVI (1935), 150–68; *The Men of New York* (Buffalo: George Matthews, 1898), II; Daniel Van Pelt, *Leslie's History of the Greater New York* (New York: Arkell Publishing, 1898), III; *Biographical Directory of the State of New York, 1900* (New York: Biographical Dictionary Co., 1900); Mitchell C. Harrison, ed., *New York State's Prominent and Progressive Men: An Encyclopedia of Contemporaneous Biography*, 3 vols. (New York: New York Tribune, 1901); Julius Chambers, *The Book of New York: Forty Years' Recollections of the American Metropolis* (New York: Book of New York Co., 1912); Mae F. Herringshaw, *Herringshaw's City Blue Book of Biography: New Yorkers of 1917* (Chicago: Clark J. Herringshaw, 1917); George F. Black, *Scotland's Mark on America* (New York: Scottish Section of America's Makers, 1921); John D. Crimmins, *Irish American Miscellany* (New York: published by the author, 1905); Reynolds, ed., *Hudson-Mohawk*; Reynolds, *Genealogical and Family History of Southern New York*, 3 vols. (New York: Lewis Historical Publishing, 1914); Pelletreau, *Historic Homes and Institutions*; Pelletreau and John H. Brown, *American Families of Historic Lineage, Long Island Edition*, 2 vols. (New York: National Americana Society, 1914); Mary Powell Bunker, *Long Island Genealogies* (Albany: Joel Munsell's Sons, 1895); Thomas H. Evans, ed., *Men of Affairs of the Empire State* (New York: Thomas H. Evans, 1895); James Parton et al., *Sketches of Men of Progress* (New York: New York and Hartford Publishing, 1870–71); Edwin R. Purple, *Contributions to the History of Ancient Families of New Amsterdam and New York* (New York: privately printed, 1881); Charles T. Gritman, "Genealogical Data of Many Families," 3 vols. (typescript); Lanier, *A Century of Banking*; Tunis G. Bergen, *Genealogies of the State of New York*, 3 vols. (New York: Lewis Historical Publishing, 1915); Charles Elliott Fitch, *Encyclopedia of Biography of New York*, 8 vols. (New York, Boston, and Chicago: American Historical Society, 1924); William H. MacBean, *Biographical Register of St. Andrew's Society of the State of New York*, 2 vols. (New York: St. Andrew's Society, 1922); Charles J. Werner, *Genealogies of Long Island Families* (New York: Charles J. Werner, 1919); *St. Nicholas Society of the City of New York: Genealogical Record* (New York: St. Nicholas Society, 1905, 1916, 1923, 1933), I–IV; *Memorial Biographies of the New England Historical and Genealogical Society, 1845–1897*, 9 vols. (Boston: New England Historical and Genealogical Society, 1880–1908); Wilson, *History of New York* (biographical volumes), 2 vols.; "Supplement" by E. Cleave in *The History of New York City from the Discovery to the Present Day by William L. Stone* (New York: E. Cleave, 1868); David McAdam, *History of The Bench and Bar of New York*, 2 vols. (New York: New York History Co., 1897); Stokes, *Iconography*; Samuel Francis, *Medical Biographies of Distinguished Living New York Physicians* (New York: G. P. Putnam, 1867); Wilson, *Portrait Gallery*; *History of St. George's Society of New York from 1770–1913* (New York: St. George's Society of New York, 1913); John D. Crimmins, *St. Patrick's Day: Its Celebration in New York and Other American Places, 1737–1845* (New York: John D. Crimmins, 1902), 328–448; Edward H. Hall, *A Volume Commemorating the Creation of the Second City of the World* (New York: Republic Press, 1898); C. F. Deihm, *Merchants of Our Second*

Century (New York: C. F. Deihm, 1889); Frank W. Norcross, *The History of the New York Swamp* (New York: Chiswick Press, 1901); Joseph L. Chamberlain, *Universities and Their Sons*, 5 vols. (Boston: R. Herndon, 1900); *Encyclopedia of Contemporary Biography of New York*, 6 vols. (New York: Atlantic Publishing and Engraving, 1878–90); John F. Sprague, *New York, the Metropolis: Its Noted Business and Professional Men*, 3 vols. (New York: New York Recorder, 1893); Stephen Fiske, *Off-Hand Portraits of Prominent New Yorkers* (New York: George R. Lockwood & Son, 1884); Henry Hall, ed., *America's Successful Men of Affairs: An Encyclopedia of Contemporaneous Biography* (New York: New York Tribune, 1895), I–II; Dumas Malone and Robert L. Schuyler, eds., *Dictionary of American Biography*, 22 vols. (New York: Charles Scribner's Sons, 1928–58); *Who's Who in America, 1899* (Chicago: A. N. Marquis, 1899); New York *Times* obituaries. In addition, numerous memoirs, biographies, and autobiographies of upper-class New Yorkers, New York city and state histories, and specialized accounts of New York business, cultural, charitable, and social organizations were consulted.

141. Hardenbrook, *Financial*, 342.

142. Pomerantz, *New York*, 188, 283; Young, *Democratic-Republicans*, 222–30; Dangerfield, *Chancellor*, 291–93; Hammond, *History of Political Parties*, I, 313–39; Hammond, *Banks*, 149–64, 579.

143. Young, *Democratic-Republicans*, 156–58; Hunt, *Lives*, I, 191–92; Stokes, *Iconography*, V, 1212, 1218, 1419, 1452, 1552, 1594, 1610–11, 1637.

144. John Jay to Nicholas Cruger, Sept. 11, 1794, Henry P. Johnston, ed., *The Correspondence and Public Papers of John Jay*, 4 vols. (New York: G. P. Putnam's Sons, 1890–93), IV, 57; Gouverneur Morris to William Constable, May 6, 1790, Gouverneur Morris, *A Diary of the French Revolution*, 2 vols. (Boston: Houghton Mifflin, 1939), I, 510; Rufus King to W. Hope, Mar. 9, 1805, Charles R. King, ed., *The Life and Correspondence of Rufus King*, 6 vols. (New York: G. P. Putnam's Sons, 1894–1900), III, 447. King decided not to apprentice his son to Baring Brothers and sent him instead to an Amsterdam firm.

145. D. C. Sowers, *The Financial History of New York State from 1789 to 1812* (New York: Columbia University Press, 1914), 16–21; John Christopher Schwab, "History of the New York Property Tax," *Publications of the American Economic Association*, V (Sept., 1890), 85, 88.

146. Gouverneur Morris quoted in Jared Sparks, *The Life of Gouverneur Morris*, 3 vols. (Boston: Gray & Bower, 1832), I, 228.

147. For biographies of early New York bankers, revealing their political activities, see Hardenbrook, *Financial*, 85ff. Philip Willis, "Social Origins of Political Leadership in New York City from the Revolution to 1815," (Ph.D. dissertation, University of California at Berkeley, 1967), 168, 172.

148. Willis, "Social," 156–57; Pomerantz, *New York*, 46.

149. Bruce M. Wilkenfield, "The New York City Common Council, 1689–1800," *New York History*, III (July, 1921), 249–74; Pomerantz, *New York*, 60; Werner, *Civil List*, 277–80, 314–22; Chester, ed., *Legal*, I, 336ff., II, *passim*, III, *passim*; John Theodore Horton, *James Kent: A Study in Conservatism* (New York: Appleton–Century, 1939).

150. Young, *Democratic-Republicans*, 171; Sparks, *Life of Gouverneur Mor-*

ris, I, 265–66, 281; Morris, ed., *Diary*, I, 543–45; King, ed., *Life and Correspondence of Rufus King*, II, 73.

151. "A List of the Members of the City Government, 1653–1870," *Valentine's Manual of the Corporation of the City of New York* (New York: Edmund Jones, 1870), 609–22; Stokes, *Iconography*, V, 1487, 1503.

152. Linda Grant De Pauw, *The Eleventh Pillar: New York and the Federal Constitution* (Ithaca: Cornell University Press, 1966); E. Wilder Spaulding, *New York in the Critical Period, 1783–1789* (New York: Columbia University Press, 1932), 7–8; King, ed., *Life and Correspondence of Rufus King*, I, 544–45, 583; Young, *Democratic-Republicans*, 47–52, 75–82, 89–90, 109–28, 171, 176–77; Pomerantz, *New York*, 98, 134–37; Fox, *Decline*, 11–31, 151–52, 183–84; Willis, "Social Origins," 4, 11–12, 16–17, 71–93, 97–98, 159–62, 164–69, 172, 211–12, 222–24, 236–37, 244, 249, 258, 266, 287–89, 308–13. For the Massachusetts Democratic-Republicans see Paul Goodman, *The Democratic-Republicans of Massachusetts: Politics in a Young Republic* (Cambridge: Harvard University Press, 1964), 73–75. Mrs. Jay's "Dinner and Supper" list of 1787–88 is reprinted in Dixon Wecter, *The Saga of American Society: A Record of Social Aspiration, 1607–1937* (New York: Charles Scribner's Sons, 1937), 196–204; William Bruce Wheeler, "Urban Politics in Nature's Republic: The Development of Political Parties in the Seaport Cities in the Federalist Era" (Ph.D. dissertation, University of Virginia, 1967), 222–26.

153. *Memorial of the Chamber of Commerce of the City of New York for a National Bank, May 4, 1841* (New York: J. P. Wright, 1841); *Opening of the Building of the Chamber of Commerce of the State of New York: A Brief History of the Chamber of the State of New York* (New York: Press of the Chamber of Commerce, 1902), 108–13; King, *Charter*, 62, 90, 102, 110–11, 114, 120, 127; John Austin Stevens, Jr., "A Historical Sketch of the Chamber of Commerce," *Centennial Celebration of the Chamber of Commerce of the State of New York, April 6, 1868* (New York: John W. Amerman, 1868), 16–21; Bishop, *Chronicle*, 47–48, 52–56, 59–60; Willis, "Social Origins," 236–37, 244.

154. Pomerantz, *New York*, 61–62, 66; Stokes, *Iconography*, V, 1256.

155. Willis, "Social Origins," 65, 144, 168, 172, 204–5, 236–37, 288–89.

156. Fischer, *Revolution*, 33–49, 60–62, 94–97, 117–20; Hammond, *History of Political Parties*, I, 451; Livermore, *Twilight*, 69–79, 110–16, 299–311; Fox, *Decline*, 198–99; Kass, *Politics*, 76, 81–87, 172–78.

157. Gulian C. Verplanck quoted in Fischer, *Revolution*, 35; Rufus King to Christopher Gore, May 15, 1816, King, ed., *Life and Correspondence of Rufus King*, V, 535.

158. Fox, *Decline*, 177–83.

159. Kass, *Politics*, 81–87, 98–109.

160. Willis, "Social Origins," 159–62.

161. Pessen, *Riches*, 284–87.

162. Gabriel Almond, "Plutocracy and Politics in New York City" (Ph.D. dissertation, University of Chicago, 1938), 40–46.

163. See notes 135 and 140 for references to the lists and biographical backgrounds, and Werner, *Civil List* and "A List of the Members of the City Government," for political posts.

164. Fox, *Decline*, 415–16; Smith, *History of New York*, II, 15–17; Michael Wallace, "Changing Conceptions of the Party in the United States: New York, 1815–1828," *AHR*, LXXIV (Dec., 1968), 453–79; Fischer, *Revolution*, 29–32. The fall-off can be seen by surveying "A List of the Members of the City Government," and Werner, *Civil List*; cf. Pessen, *Riches*, 286.

165. Allen Nevins, *Hamilton Fish: The Inner History of the Grant Administration* (New York: Dodd, Mead, 1936), 24–25, 30–31, 33–34.

166. William Alexander Duer, *Address to the Peithologian and Philolexian Society, July 24, 1848* (New York: n.p., 1848), 10; Gulian C. Verplanck, *The Advantages and the Dangers of the American Scholar: A Discourse* (New York: Wiley and Long, 1836), 57–59; James A. Hamilton, *Reminiscences of James A. Hamilton* (New York: Charles Scribner, 1869), 430–36.

167. Strong, *Diary*, Nov. 12, 1857, II, 371–72.

168. Frank Otto Gattell, "Money and Party in Jacksonian America: A Quantitative Look at New York City's Men of Quality," *Political Science Quarterly*, LXXXII (June, 1967), 235–42; Fox, *Decline*, 415–16, 431–37, 440–49; Tuckerman, ed., *Hone Diary*, II, 35, 44, 47, 49.

169. Tuckerman, ed., *Hone Diary*, Dec. 31, 1833, 86; Strong, *Diary*, Nov. 5, 1838, I, 94.

170. Philip S. Foner, *Business and Slavery: The New York Merchants and the Irrepressible Conflict* (Chapel Hill: University of North Carolina Press, 1941).

171. Expression of these sentiments may be found scattered in the following works: Johnston, ed., *Correspondence*; Morris, *Diary of the French Revolution*; Sparks, *Life of Gouverneur Morris*; Morris, ed., *Diary and Letters*; King, ed., *Life and Correspondence*; *Reports of the Proceedings and Debates of the Constitution of 1821*; Syrett, *Hamilton Papers*, IV, 192, 207–8, 254, 258–59, 262, 265, V, 43, 425; Dangerfield, *Chancellor*, 97–98, 210–11; Harold Wesley Thatcher, "The Social Philosophy of William Livingston" (Ph.D. dissertation, University of Chicago, 1935), 246–47; Brockholst Livingston, *Democracy: An Epic Poem* (New York: n.p., 1794); Max Farrand, ed., *The Records of the Federal Convention of 1787*, 4 vols. (New Haven: Yale University Press, 1966), I, 288–92, 359, 424, 511–12, 541, 583, II, 6–7, 30–31, 54, 113, 403–4.

172. *Reports of the Proceedings*, 115–16, 148, 158, 274–75, 283, 287, 360, 368–69, 413, 443, 445, 554; Peter A. Jay to John Jay, Jan. 5, 1821, Johnston, ed., *Correspondence*, IV, 455.

173. James W. Beekman quoted in White, *Beekmans*, 574; Pintard, *Letters*, Jan. 15, 1822, II, 121; Tuckerman, ed., *Hone Diary*, Dec. 17, 1835, March 4, 1837, I, 184, 264; Nov. 4, 1840, II, 50; Nevins, ed., *Hone Diary*, Dec. 7, 1838, Apr. 12, 1839, Apr. 12, 1843, 367, 388, 648; Strong, *Diary*, Nov. 5, 1838, Nov. 6, 1838, Apr. 27, 1844, I, 94, 236; June 7, 1852, June 5, 1858, Dec. 6, 1858, II, 96, 404, 425; Duer, *Address*, 13–14.

174. Philip Schuyler to A. Hamilton, Jan. 25, 1781, Syrett, ed., *Hamilton Papers*, II, 543–44; cf. same to same, Feb. 25, 1781, II, 575.

175. Morris, *Diary of the French Revolution*, Feb. 28, 1790, I, 430. *Reports of the Proceedings*, 576–77.

176. Syrett, *Hamilton Papers*, IV, 192–265; G. Morris to Aaron Ogden, Dec. 28, 1804, Sparks, *Life of Gouverneur Morris*, III, 218.

177. Syrett, ed., *Hamilton Papers*, V, 41, 43, IV, 266; A. Hamilton to Marquis

de Lafayette, Oct. 6, 1789, IV, 425; Hamilton to Edward Carrington, May 26, 1792, XI, 443.

178. G. Morris quoted in Farrand, ed., *Records*, I, 512, 545; Morris, *Diary*, 1802, II, 428; cf. Morris to Robert B. Livingston, Oct. 10, 1802, Sparks, *Life of Gouverneur Morris*, III, 172.

179. G. Morris to George Washington, Nov. 22, 1790, Sparks, *Life of Gouverneur Morris*, II, 118; to Thomas Jefferson, June 10, 1792, II, 178–180; to Aaron Ogden, Dec. 28, 1804, III, 218; to John Parish, June 20, 1802, III, 169; Morris, *Diary*, Apr. 8, 1791, I, 156; 1811, II, 524–25.

180. John Jay to William P. Beers, Apr. 18, 1807, William Jay, *The Life of John Jay*, 2 vols. (New York: J. & J. Harper, 1833), II, 310; to James Anderson, Mar. 18, 1795, II, 253; to William Vaughan, May 26, 1796; to William Wilberforce, Oct. 25, 1810, Johnston, ed., *Correspondence*, IV, 216, 336. For Jay's calm reception of Democratic-Republicanism: Jay to Jedidiah Morse, Apr. 24, 1800; to R. Peters, Mar. 4, 1814, July 24, 1809, IV, 266, 318, 387–88. An example of Jay's moderation was his coolness toward the Order of the Cincinnati: Jay to G. Morris, Feb. 10, 1784, III, 111–12.

181. Rufus King to Robert Troup, Feb. 3, 1801, King, ed., *Life and Correspondence*, III, 381–82; to Christopher Gore, May 15, 1816, V, 535; to Jonathan Mason, July 4, 1817, VI, 75.

182. G. Morris to Walter Rutherfurd, Dec. 3, 1789, Livingston Rutherfurd, *Family Records and Events* (New York: De Vinne Press, 1894), 137; Jay to G. Washington, June 27, 1786, Johnston, ed., *Correspondence*, III, 204–5; Syrett, ed., *Hamilton Papers*, IV, 275–76; R. King to G. Morris, Sept. 1, 1792, King, ed., *Life and Correspondence*, I, 424.

183. A. Hamilton to Edward Stevens, Nov. 11, 1769, Syrett, ed., *Hamilton Papers*, I, 4; to John Laurens, Apr. ?, 1779, II, 36; to Philip Hamilton, Dec. 5, 1791, IX, 560.

184. R. King to Edward King, Jan. 1, 1816. King, ed., *Life and Correspondence*, V, 497; cf. same to same, Dec. 16, 1815, V, 494; J. Jay to Henry Davies, Feb. 10, 1803, Johnston, ed., *Correspondence*, IV, 297; Jay quoted in Jay, *John Jay*, II, 428–31; G. Morris to Mrs. Sarah Burns, Mar. 19, 1806, Sparks, *Life of Gouverneur Morris*, III, 234; Edward Livingston quoted in Hunt, *Life of Edward Livingston*, 190, 192, 221, 223.

185. Gulian C. Verplanck: *An Address Delivered at the Opening of the Tenth Exhibition of the American Academy of Fine Arts* (New York: G. & C. Carroll, 1825), 5, 34; *Advantages*, 17–18, 60; James Hamilton to ?, Feb. 27, 1848, Hamilton, *Reminiscences*, 361; Duer, *Address*, 19; James De Peyster Ogden, *Lecture on National Character* (New York: J. P. Wright, 1843), 26–27, 30–31; Charles King, *Progress of the City of New York during the Last Fifty Years* (New York: D. Appleton, 1852), 47–53, 63, 79–80.

186. Pessen, *Riches*, 47–48.

187. Hamlin, *Legal Education*, 35–37, 111–12, 116–19, 125–26, 134–49, 202–3; Daly, *Historical Sketch*, 51; Klein: "Rise," 335, 338–47, 355–57; "American Whig," 73–74, 89–90, 158–59, 164–70, 568–72; Alexander, *A Revolutionary Conservative*, 24–27, 35–36, 52–67; Sparks, *Life of Gouverneur Morris*, I, 5; Jones, *History of New York*, I, lx, 97; Dillon, *New York Triumverate*, 21–27, 169–70, 175–76.

188. Harry J. Carman, "The Professions in New York in 1800," *Columbia*

University Quarterly, 23 (1931), 161–66; Horton, *James Kent*, *passim*; Pomerantz, *New York*, 46, 53–54; Daly, *Historical Sketch*, 49; Hamlin, *Legal Education*, 117, 125–26; Syrett, ed., *Hamilton Papers*, III, 6–7, 604, 622; IV, 154; Goebel, ed., *Law*, II, *passim*.

189. Daly: *Historical Sketch*, 65; *Gulian C. Verplanck: His Ancestry, Life and Character* (New York: D. Appleton, 1870), 17ff.; Lucien B. Proctor, *Bench and Bar of New York* (New York: Diossy, 1870), *passim*; Horton, *James Kent*, *passim*; White, *Beekmans*, xxix-xi; Delafield, *Family History*, I, 261; Pelletreau, *Historic Homes*, I, 261, III, 191; Jones, *History of New York*, I, lxxi; Wells, *Jay Family*, 41–42; Nevins, *Hamilton Fish*, 13–15; Hamilton, *Reminiscences*, 45–46; John Jay, *Memorials of Peter A. Jay* (New York: G. J. Thieme, 1929), 74, 81, 99, 104, 124, 151; William Cullen Bryant, *A Discourse on the Life, Character and Writings of Gulian C. Verplanck* (New York: New York Historical Society, 1870), 14–15.

190. Hamilton, *Reminiscences*, 45.

191. See note 189 for references.

192. Henry W. Taft, *A Century and a Half at the New York Bar, Being the Annals of a Law Firm and Sketches of Its Members* (New York: privately printed, 1938), 3, 11, 17–18, 24, 26–34, 43, 47–48, 57, 64–65, 69–72, 99, 109, 123–124, 159–60, 165–66, 168–70, 174ff.

193. Richard Harrison Shryock, *Medicine and Society in America, 1660–1860* (New York: New York University Press, 1960), 1–82, 141–42; James J. Walsh, *History of Medicine in New York*, 5 vols. (New York: National Americana Society, 1919), I, 150–52, 363–77, 413–15, 420; Daniel H. Calhoun, *Professional Lives in America: Structure and Aspiration, 1750–1850* (Cambridge: Harvard University Press, 1965), 20–58, 195; F. H. Bosworth, *The Doctor in Old New York* (New York: G. P. Putnam, 1898), 277–317; Wilson, *Memorial History*, IV, 392–412; Benson J. Lossing, *History of New York City* (New York: Perine Engraving and Publishing, 1884), 138; Sullivan, *History of New York*, V, 2056–61; Carman, "Professions," 169–75; John Wakefield Francis, *An Historical Sketch of the Origin, Progress, and Present State of the College of Physicians and Surgeons of the State of New York* (New York: C. S. Van Winkle, 1813); John C. Dalton, *History of the College of Physicians and Surgeons* (New York: Columbia University Press, 1888), 1–102.

194. J. W. Francis, *Old New York* (New York: W. J. Middleton, 1846), 84–89; Walsh, *History of Medicine*, V, *passim*; Delafield, *Family History*, I, 275; White, *Beekmans*, xxix-xi; Beekman, *Beekman*, 19, 25; Wells, *Jay Family*, 47–51; Sullivan, *History of New York*, V, 2027–2126; S. Francis: *Distinguished Living New York Surgeons* (New York: John Bradburn, 1866); *Medical Biographies*.

195. Pessen, *Riches*, 50.

196. William O. Bourne, *History of the Public School Society of the City of New York* (New York: G. P. Putnam's, 1873), 153.

197. Pintard, *Letters*, Sept. 3, 1822, II, 132.

198. Dix, *History*, II, 124, IV, 279.

199. Sidney Sherwood, *The University of the State of New York: History of Higher Education in the State of New York* (Washington, D.C.: U.S. Bureau of Higher Education, 1900), 49–58, 142–44; Horton, *James Kent*, 236–37.

200. Compare: *Endowment Funds of Harvard University* (Cambridge: Harvard University Press, 1948) with *Columbia University Gifts and Bequests*; Duer, *Address*, 19–20.

201. Strong, *Diary*, II, 141ff.; Nevins, *Hamilton Fish*, 98.

202. *Report of a Committee of the Trustees of Columbia College* (New York: John W. Amerman, 1858), 11, 17–24, 26.

203. Nevins, *Hamilton Fish*, 97–98.

204. Verplanck, *Dangers*, 16–26; Tuckerman, ed., *Hone Diary*, May 2, 1832, I, 52–53; Ogden Hoffmann, *An Address before the Association of the Alumni of Columbia College*, May 2, 1832 (New York: G. & C. Carvill, 1832), 11–12, 16–24, 27.

205. Duer, *Address*, 11, 13–14, 25; *Report*, 15–16.

206. *Report*, 26.

207. Horatio Potter to Morgan Dix, Aug. 8, 1855, Dix, *History*, V, 26.

208. Strong, *Diary*, Jan. 22, 1856, II, 325.

209. Dix, *History*, IV, 264–74, 294–99, 388–92, 430–46, 449–50; Berrian, *Historical Sketch*, 386.

210. William Berrian quoted in Dix, *History*, IV, 415. For the antebellum history of Trinity Church see Dix, *History*, II–IV, V, 7–10, 72–92, 99, 113–15, 162, 164, 293–94; Berrian, *Historical Sketch*, 162ff.; James Grant Wilson, ed., *The Centennial History of the Protestant Episcopal Church in the Diocese of New York, 1785–1885* (New York: D. Appleton, 1886), 45–83, 126–41, 150, 370–416; W. H. DeLancey, *The Title, Parish Rights and Property of Trinity Church, New York, August 19, 1857* (Utica: Curtiss & White, 1857); William Jay, *A Letter to the Rev. William Berrian on the Resources, Present Position, and Duties of Trinity Church* (New York: Anson D. F. Randolph, 1856); James G. Wilson, *Samuel Provoost* (New York: privately printed, 1887); John B. Peters, *Annals of St. Michael's* (New York: G. P. Putnam's Sons, 1907), 28–29, 88, 98–99.

211. *Memorial of St. Mark's Church in the Bowery* (New York: Thomas Whittaker, 1899); James H. Rylance, *The Centennial of St. Mark's Church* (New York: Thomas Whittaker, 1895); Peters, *Annals*. For a survey of other New York churches and their upper-class rectors and officers, see Wilson, *Centennial*, 204–350.

212. William Rhinelander Stewart, *Grace Church and Old New York* (New York: E. P. Dutton, 1924); Nevins, ed., *Hone Diary*, Feb. 5, 1846, 754; Strong, *Diary*, Sept. 10, 1867, IV, 149; New York *Herald*, Mar. 8, 1846, quoted in Stewart, *Grace*, 161; Isaac Brown quoted in Lloyd Morris, *Incredible New York* (New York: Random House, 1951), 21.

213. James Kent, *An Anniversary Discourse, Delivered before the New York Historical Society, December 26, 1828* (New York: G. & C. Carvill, 1829), 6, 32.

214. R. W. G. Vail, *Knickerbocker Birthday, a Sesqui-Centennial History of the New York Historical Society* (New York: New York Historical Society, 1954), 17–20, 30–32, 60–61, 67–68; Robert H. Kelby, *The New York Historical Society, 1804–1904* (New York: n.p., 1905), 1–3, 36, 56–57, 83–91; John Pintard to Jeremy Belknap, Apr. 6, 1791, *Collections of the Massachusetts Historical Society*, 6th Ser., IV (1891), 490; Kent, *Anniversary Discourse*, 5.

215. *An Address of the Committee of the New York Athenaeum to the Public*

(New York: J. W. Palmer, 1824), 3; cf. *Report of the Committee Appointed to Amend the Constitution of the New York Athenaeum. Address of the Associates to the Public of New York* (New York: J. W. Palmer, 1825), 3.

216. *Constitution and By-laws of the New York Athenaeum* (New York: J. W. Palmer, 1825), 3; *Report*, 3–5; *Address*, 4–5.

217. MacMullen, *Lecture*, 25. For the membership see *Shareholders and Officers and Trustees of the New York Society Library* (New York: New York Society Library, 1914).

218. *Charter, Constitution, and By-laws of the Lyceum of Natural History in the City of New York* (New York: Daniel Fanshaw, 1835); *The Charter, Laws and Regulations of the Literary and Philosophical Society of New York* (New York: C. S. Van Winkle, 1818); *The Charter and By-laws of the American Academy of the Fine Arts* (New York: David Longworth, 1817); Mary Bartlett Cowdrey, *The American Academy of Fine Arts and the American Art Union* (New York: New York Historical Society, 1953), 3–48.

219. Harry Miller Ludenberg, *History of the New York Public Library* (New York: New York Public Library, 1932), 6–92; Wilson, *Memorial History*, IV, 78–82; Porter, *John Jacob Astor*, II, 1271.

220. Daly, *Gulian C. Verplanck*; Bryant, *Discourse*; Evert A. Duyckinck quoted in Perry Miller, *The Raven and the Whale: The War of Words and Wits in the Era of Poe and Melville* (New York: Harcourt, Brace, 1956), 84.

221. The best account of literary New York between the 1820s and the Civil War is Miller, *Raven*. See also Wilson, *Memorial History*, IV, 54–77.

222. There were, for example, few antebellum upper-class New Yorkers active in forming the Philharmonic Society of New York. James Gibbons Huneker, *The Philharmonic Society on New York and Its Seventy-fifth Anniversary: A Retrospect* (New York: n.p., 1917), 3; Henry Edward Krehbiel, *The Philharmonic Society of New York: A Memorial* (New York: Novello, Ewer, 1892), 33–35; John Erskine, *The Philharmonic Symphony Society of New York* (New York: Macmillan, 1940), 1–60; Wilson, *Memorial History*, IV, 169–80.

223. Lillian B. Miller, *Patrons and Patriotism: The Encouragement of the Fine Arts in the United States, 1790–1860* (Chicago: University of Chicago Press, 1966), 105–27, 144–59, 224–25; Neil Harris, *The Artist in American Society* (New York: George Braziller, 1966), 4–5, 10, 101–9, 262–82; Tuckerman, ed., *Hone Diary*, May 15, 1832, I, 535; Nevins, ed., *Hone Diary*, Nov. 27, 1839, 433.

224. Robert R. Livingston quoted in Winifred E. Howe, *A History of the Metropolitan Museum of Art*, 2 vols. (New York: n.p., 1913), I, 234; John Trumbull quoted in Cowdrey, *American Academy*, 3–4. For other data on the academy see Miller, *Patrons*, 91–96; *Charter, passim*.

225. Cowdrey, *American Academy*, 48–61, 100–168; Miller, *Patrons*, 160–72; Howe, *History*, 29–30, 45–57; Harris, *Artist*, 90–102; Eliot Clark, *History of the National Academy of Design, 1825–1923* (New York: Columbia University Press, 1954), 58–65, 243–44, 276–78.

226. Harris, *Artist*, 108–9, 262–82.

227. Duer, *Address*, 20–21; Verplanck, *Advantages*, 49–50; C. King, *Address*, 28, 33, 40–46; Strong, *Diary*, June 17, 1844, I, 238; Tuckermann ed., *Hone Diary*, Nov. 15, 1841, II, 98; King, *Proceedings of the Chamber of Commerce*, 13.

228. Pintard, *Letters*, Aug. 13, 1816, I, 25–26; *Charter . . . of the Lyceum*, 7; Verplanck, *Address*, 20–21.

229. Pintard, *Letters*, Aug. 13, 1816, I, 25–26; Tuckerman, ed., *Hone Diary*, Nov. 5, 1841, II, 98.

230. Strong, *Diary*, Nov. 18, 1843, I, 215; Jan. 26, 1847, I, 288; Tuckerman, ed., *Hone Diary*, Sept. 16, 1833, I, 73.

231. Nevins, ed., *Hone Diary*, Jan. 21, 1848, 832.

232. Pintard, *Letters*, Apr. 13, 1831, III, 240. For comments on New York's cultural inferiority by other city-dwellers see Albion, *Rise*, 251–52; Miller, *Raven*, 31–33. For unfavorable comparisons between New York and Boston and Philadelphia see Burt, *Perennial*, 26, 371, 388; Miller, *Raven*, 288–90. For critical observations from foreign observers see Still, *Mirror*, 143.

233. White, *Beekmans*, 561.

234. Pintard, *Letters*, Jan. 2, 1817, I, 45.

235. The best general studies of antebellum New York charity are: Mohl, *Poverty*; Schneider, *History of Public Welfare*, I; Henry J. Cammann and Hugh N. Camp, *The Charities of New York, Brooklyn and Staten Island* (New York: Hurd and Houghton, 1868); J. F. Richmond, *New York and Its Institutions, 1609–1872* (New York: E. B. Treat, 1872). For New York Hospital see *Charter . . . 1833, 1856, 1872*; "Condensed History"; *Commemorative Exercises*. For other organizations see *Marine Society*; Morrison, *History of St. Andrew's*; *St. Andrew's . . . Annual Report, 1852*; Charles W. Bowring and Francis H. Tabor, *A History of St. George's Society of New York from 1770 to 1913* (New York: St. George's Society of New York, 1913); *A Sketch of the Origin, Progress, and Work of the St. George's Society of New York* (New York: Henry Dawson, 1887); Henry Otis Dwight, *The Centennial History of the American Bible Society*, 2 vols. (New York: Macmillan, 1916); John A. Krout, "The Genesis and Development of the Early Temperance Movement in New York State," *Quarterly Journal of the New York State Historical Association*, IV (Apr., 1923), 79–98; *Constitution of the Society for the Relief of the Destitute* (New York: Rutger's Press, 1827); *By-laws of the Trustees of the Public School Society of New York* (New York: M. Day, 1833); Bourne, *History of the Public School Society*; Thomas Boese, *Public Education in the City of New York: Its Condition and Statistics* (New York: Harper & Bros., 1869), 25–84, 99–126; S. S. Randall, *History of the Common School System of the State of New York from Its Origin in 1795 to the Present Time* (New York: Iveson, Blakeman, Taylor, 1871), 14–15, 29–31, 43–49, 71–77, 119–38, 312–14; A. Emerson Palmer, *The New York Public School* (New York: Macmillan, 1905), 16–131; William W. Cutler, "Status, Values and the Education of the Poor: The Trustees of the New York Public School Society, 1805–1853," *American Quarterly*, XXIV (Spring, 1972), 69–85; M. H. Heale, "From City Fathers to Social Critics: Humanitarianism and Government in New York, 1790–1860," *Journal of American History*, LXIII (June, 1976), 21–41; John G. Leake, *The Last Will and Testament of John G. Leake: Act of Incorporation of the Leake and Watts Orphan House in the City of New York* (New York: J. B. Jansen, 1837); *A Sketch of the Origin and Progress of the Humane Society of the City of New York together with the Act of Incorporation and By-laws, etc.* (New York: Van Winkle and Wiley, 1814); Emerson Keyes, *History of Savings Banks in the United*

States, 2 vols. (New York: Bradford Rhodes, 1878), I, *passim*; Joseph Husband, *One Hundred Years of the Greenwich Savings Bank* (New York: n.p., 1933); Charles E. Knowles, *History of the Bank for Savings in the City of New York, 1819-1929* (New York: n.p., 1929); James H. Collins, *Ninety Years of the Greenwich Savings Bank* (New York: Bartlett Over Press, 1923); Andrew Mills, *That's My Bank! The Story of Dry Dock Savings Institution, 1848-1948* (New York: n.p., 1948); *One Hundred and Fifteen Years of Service, 1829-1944* (New York: Seamen's Bank for Savings in the City of New York, 1944).

236. Mohl, *Poverty*, 86–88, 90, 115–18.

237. Pintard, *Letters*, Mar. 9, 1821, II, 11, cf. May 16, 1821, II, 41, Oct. 20, 1818, I, 151–52; "First Report of the Bank for Savings in the City of New York," reprinted in Knowles, *History*, 176–77; Bourne, *History*, 117–18.

238. M. J. Heale, "City Fathers," 24–25; *Sketch*, 7.

239. Heale, "City Fathers," 23; Mohl, *Poverty*, 131; Cutler, "Status," 74.

240. Jay, *Letter*, 3–20; Pintard, *Letters*, Nov. 28, 1818, I, 155–56, Nov. 7, 1820, I, 343, Apr. 14, 1834, IV, 38–39; Strong, *Diary*, May 5, 1852, II, 92, Nov. 15, 1854, II, 200, Jan. 21, 1855, II, 209, Feb. 17, 1860, III, 9; *Proclamation of the Chamber of Commerce on the Death of Pelatiah Perit* (New York: John W. Amerman, 1864), 14.

241. Porter, *John Jacob Astor*, II, 1096; Merle Curti, *American Philanthropy Abroad* (New Brunswick, N.J.: Rutgers University Press, 1963), 145.

242. Mohl, *Poverty*, 180; "Public and Private Charities in Boston," *North American Review*, LXI (July, 1845), 137.

243. Curti, *American Philanthropy*, 22–32, 38–39.

244. Heale, "City Fathers," 29–36.

245. Pintard, *Letters*, Jan. 15, 1822, II, 121. Tuckerman, ed., *Hone Diary*, Jan. 29, 1847, II, 293–94, Dec. 17, 1835, I, 184, cf. Sept. 20, 1832, I, 64, June 2, 1836, I, 210; Strong, *Diary*, Dec. 6, 1838, I, 94, June 5, 1858, II, 404.

246. King, *History*, 11; Clinton Roosevelt, *The Mode of Protecting Domestic Industry Consistently with the Desires Both of the South and the North by Operating on the Currency* (New York: McElrath & Banks, 1833), 9; Pintard, *Letters*, Apr. 28, 1832, IV, 44; Gulian C. Verplanck (Francis Herbert), *The Talisman for 1830* (New York: Elam Bliss, 1829), 339–47; Strong, *Diary*, Mar. 24, 1858, II, 391.

247. Strong, *Diary*, Nov. 15, 1854, II, 200, cf. Jan. 21, 1855, II, 209.

248. The Executive Committee of the Public School Society quoted in Bourne, *History*, 110–13, 185.

249. *Fiftieth Anniversary of the Founding of the New York Historical Society November 20, 1854* (New York: John F. Trow, 1854), 70–73, 368; John Jay, *Memorials*; Tuckerman, *William Jay*; W. Jay, *Life of John Jay*; J. McVickar, *A Christian Memorial of Two Sisters* (New York: Stanford & Delisser, 1858); Bayard Tuckerman, *William Jay and the Constitutional Movement for the Abolition of Slavery* (New York: Dodd, Mead, 1894). Martyn, *William E. Dodge*; Dodge, *Memorials*; Bannan, "Arthur and Lewis Tappan"; Pintard, *Letters*, Apr. 5, 1820, I, 280–81; R. Troup quoted in *Constitution*, 5; "First Report," 174.

250. Pintard, *Letters*, Oct. 20, 1818, I, 151–52. For other examples of these sentiments see Bourne, *History*, 3–4, 11, 14–24, 37, 85–89, 103–4, 110–13, 117–18; Knowles, *History*, 43, 173–77; *Constitution*, 5, 17; Schneider, *History*, I,

318–19, the directors are quoted on 212–14.

251. King, ed., *Life and Correspondence*, 6 vols., *passim*; Tuckerman, ed., *Hone Diary*, I, 3, 4, 7, 107, 131, 136, 156, 159, II, 40, 195, 265, 352; Nevins, ed., *Hone Diary*, 358–59, 749; Strong, *Diary*, I, xxi, II, 126–27, 293.

252. Thomas E. V. Smith, *The City of New York in the Year of Washington's Inauguration 1789* (New York: Anson D. F. Randolph, 1889), 95–99; Jones, *American and French Culture*, 278; Still, *Mirror*, 25–27, 60, 72–73, 117–19, 133, 141–43, 158–59; Francis J. Grund, *Aristocracy in America* (New York: Harper Torchbooks, 1959), 26–27, 36, 44–46, 81, 91–92, 139–213. For a similar view by a Philadelphia aristocrat see Burt, *Perennial*, 26. For the comments by Boston Brahmins see previous chapter.

253. Noah Webster quoted in Smith, *City*, 119.

254. Margaret Beekman Livingston to T. A. Vanderkemp, Feb. 1, 1792, Julia Delafield, *Biographies of Francis Lewis and Morgan Lewis*, 2 vols. (New York: Anson D. F. Randolph, 1877), II, 42–43.

255. Pintard, *Letters*, Jan. 25, 1819, I, 165, Mar. 9, 1821, II, 10, Dec. 12, 1829, III, 133, Jan. 1, 1833, IV, 117.

256. Tuckerman, ed., *Hone Diary*, Jan. 29, 1847, II, 293–94; Strong, *Diary*, May 27, 1844, I, 236, Dec. 24, 1845, I, 270, cf. Feb. 16, 1852, II, 117, Dec. 18, 1856, II, 313, Oct. 22, 1860, III, 52; Bristed, *The Upper Ten Thousand*, *passim*.

257. Strong, *Diary*, I, Aug. 18, 1847, 298, II, Mar. 31, 1840, 11, Dec. 27, 1850, 31, June 27, 1852, 98, Jan. 14, 1854, 149, May 1, 4, 8, 1856, 268–70, Dec. 18, 1856, 313, Dec. 24, 1857, 377–78, III, Feb. 17, 1860, 9, Mar. 6, 1863, 303–4.

258. John Schuyler, *Institution of the Society of the Cincinnati in New York* (New York: Douglas Taylor, 1886); *The Institution of the Society of the Cincinnati* (New York: John M. Elliot, 1851); *The St. Nicholas Society of the City of New York* (New York: Walter N. Dennis, 1945); Florence E. Youngs, ed., *Portraits of the Presidents of the Society* (New York: n.p., 1914); *St. Nicholas Society Genealogical Record*, III (New York: St. Nicholas Society, 1923).

259. C. King quoted in Gertrude King Schuyler, "A Gentleman of the Old School: Some Reminiscences of Charles King," *Scribner's Magazine*, LV (May, 1914), 616; Pintard, *Letters*, Oct. 18, 1817, I, 85, Mar. 21, 1828, III, 19, cf. Dec. 18, 1816, I, 41.

260. Reginald Townsend, *Mother of Clubs: Being the History of the First One Hundred Years of the Union Club of the City of New York, 1836–1936* (New York: William Edwin Rudge, 1936); *Officers, Members, Constitution and Rules of the Union Club of the City of New York 1914, 1947* (New York: n.p., 1914, 1947); John H. Gourlie, *The Origin and History of "The Century"* (New York: William C. Bryant, 1856); *The Fiftieth Anniversary of the Founding of the Century* (New York: Century Association, 1897); *The Century, 1847–1946* (New York: Century Association, 1947); *The Century Association Year-Book* (New York: Century Association, 1962); Harris, *Artist*, 279.

261. Nevins, ed., *Hone Diary*, May 13, 1842, 601; Strong, *Diary*, Jan. 8, 1849, I, 342.

262. E. F. Ellet, *The Queens of American Society* (New York: Charles Scribner, 1868), 44, 452–53; Burt, *Perennial*, 60–61, 535; Baltzell, *Philadelphia Gentlemen*, 336.

263. Strong, *Diary*, Apr. 13, 1860, III, 20.

264. The best accounts of New York society 1820–60 are Pintard, *Letters*, the diaries of Hone and Strong, and Bristed, *Upper*. Additional information may be found in Edith Wharton, *A Backward Glance* (New York: D. Appleton Century, 1934), 5–7, 21–23, 55–60, 65–70, 79, 92, 95, 120, 143; Abram C. Drayton, *The Last Days of Knickerbocker Life in New York* (New York: George W. Harlem, 1890); Ellet, *Queens*, 290–92, 452–53; William Ingraham Kip, "New York Society in the Olden Times," in Stone, *History*, 93–108; May King Van Rensselaer and Frederic Van DeWater, *The Social Ladder* (New York: Henry Holt, 1924), *passim*; Miller, *Jacksonian Aristocracy*. See also Frederic Cople Jaher, "Style and Status: High Society in Late-Nineteenth-Century New York," *The Rich, the Well-Born, and the Powerful: Elites and Upper Classes in History*, ed. Jaher (Urbana: University of Illinois Press, 1973), 260–63.

265. Isaac Brown quoted in Ward McAllister, *Society as I Have Found It* (New York: Cassell Publishing, 1890), 124. Accounts of Brown are in Ellet, *Queens*, 453; Morris, *Incredible*, 21; Wecter, *Saga*, 209–10; Cleveland Amory, *Who Killed Society* (New York: Harper & Bros., 1960), 115–17; M. E. W. Sherwood, *An Epistle to Posterity* (New York: Harper & Bros., 1897), 179.

266. See above for references and examples of the ideas of the Federalist statesmen King and Ogden. For Pintard's notions see Pintard, *Letters*, June 18, 1819, I, 199, Sept. 14, 1820, I, 326, Dec. 12, 1828, III, 50, Oct. 13, 1829, III, 100, Mar. 22, 1831, III, 232. For Hone see Tuckerman, ed., *Hone Diary*, Nov. 10, 1834, I, 119, Feb. 25, 1846, II, 271. For Strong's attitudes see Strong, *Diary*, May 27, 1844, I, 236, Dec. 24, 1845, I, 270, May 8, 1851, II, 45–46.

267. For Pintard's preference for a mercantile occupation for his grandson see Pintard, *Letters*, June 18, 1819, I, 199, Apr. 16, 1828, III, 28, May 18, 1830, III, 146–47, July 15, 1833, IV, 163. For Hone's similar feeling about his son's vocation see Nevins, ed., *Hone Diary*, Mar. 8, 1836, 201. Theodore Winthrop, *The Life and Poems of Theodore Winthrop* (New York: Henry Holt, 1884), 22, 72–73.

268. Jonathan Goodhue to his wife and children, Feb. 7, 1848, reprinted in Hunt, *Lives*, I, 363–64.

269. Bristed, *Upper, passim*; Tuckerman, ed., *Hone Diary*, May 27, 1835, I, 143–44, Feb. 8, 1847, II, 297; Strong, *Diary*, Oct. 13, 1860, III, 49.

270. Burt, *Perennial*, 21–22, 121, 177, 189–90, 274–76, 281; Stewart H. Holbrook, *The Age of the Moguls: The Story of the Robber Barons and the Great Tycoons* (Garden City, N.Y.: Doubleday, 1954), 18–128; Matthew Josephson, *The Robber Barons: The Great American Capitalists, 1861–1901* (New York: Harcourt, Brace, 1934), 12–20, 32, 37–49, 59–74.

For a more extended discussion of the role of the Robber Barons and their families as a New York elite, see Frederic C. Jaher, "The Gilded Elite: American Multimillionaires 1865 to the Present," in *Wealth and the Wealthy in the Modern World*, W. D. Rubenstein, ed. (New York: St. Martin's Press, 1980), 189–276.

271. Hamilton Fish quoted in Nevins, *Hamilton Fish*, 87; Strong, *Diary*, Mar. 21, 1865, III, 567.

272. For biographical and institutional details of the triumph of post-Civil War New York capitalists see especially Josephson, *Robber Barons*; Holbrook, *Age*; Sprague, *New York, the Metropolis*; Charles A. Conant, *The Progress of the*

Empire State (New York: Progress of the Empire State Co., 1913); Birmingham, "*Our Crowd*"; cf. n. 140 for other sources.

273. Bishop, *Chronicle*, 271–92; Stokes, *Iconography*, II, 27; Schuyler, *One Hundred Year Book*.

274. Buley, *Equitable*, 1360–64; Lovejoy, Jr., *Old Reliable, passim*; *New York Life Insurance Company Goodfellowship News, Century Edition* (Apr. 12, 1945), *passim*; Hudnut, *Semi-Centennial*, 366; Andrews, *Continental, passim*; Abbott, *Story*, 247–48; *Knickerbocker*, 50; Clough, *Century*, 177–96; Alexander, *Brief History*, 39; *First Ninety-five Years*, 30–46; Wendell Buck, *The Old Reliable* (New York: Manhattan Insurance, 1950), *passim*; *The Metropolitan Life Insurance Co.* (New York: privately printed, 1908), *passim*; Josephson, *Robber Barons*, 409.

275. Hardenbrook, *Financial New York*, 119, 226, 251; *One Hundred Years*, 23–33; Lanier, *Century*, 313; Perine, *Trust Companies*, 109–10, 195–200, 278–87; *1877–1922: The Chase National Bank of the City of New York* (New York: privately printed, 1922); *The Five Decades of Bankers Trust Co.* (New York: n.p., 1953); Redlich, *Banking*, II, 181, 187, 360–65, 381–88; Sprague, *New York*, especially vol. III; Josephson, *Robber Barons*, 290–315, 375–455.

276. Stuyvesant Fish, *1600–1914* (New York: J. J. Little & Ives, 1942), 237–38.

277. "American Millionaires," *Tribune Monthly*, 4 (June, 1892), 57–85. For biographical sources see nn.140 and 272.

278. Almond, "Plutocracy," 77–91.

279. "American," 57–85; Werner, *Civil List*, 277–80, 314–22; Chester, ed., *Legal*, I, 336ff., II, *passim*; Louise Overacker, *Money in Elections* (New York: Macmillan, 1932), 138ff.; James K. Pollock, Jr., *Party Campaign Funds* (New York: Alfred A. Knopf, 1926), 127–28; Irving Katz, *August Belmont: A Political Biography* (New York: Columbia University Press, 1968), *passim*.

280. Theodore Roosevelt, *An Autobiography* (New York: Macmillan, 1913), 63. For Roosevelt's thoughts on politics and reformers see 59, 63, 94–96, 149–50, 163–64; Roosevelt: *American Ideals* (New York: G. P. Putnam's Sons, 1901), 35–46, 83, 102–3; *The Strenuous Life* (New York: Century, 1902), 1–3, 72, 81–82, 280–82; *The Letters of Theodore Roosevelt*, 6 vols., ed. Elting Morison (Cambridge: Harvard University Press, 1951–54), I, 76, 80, 87–88, 90, 112, 115, 128, 131, 138, 193, 197–98, 245, 254, II, 269–97, 490–92, 535, 703, 889, 1228–29, III, 86, 107, 114–15, IV, 914, 1037, 1041, 1083, VI, 1048.

281. Mrs. James Roosevelt quoted in Cornelius Vanderbilt, *Farewell to Fifth Avenue* (New York: Simon and Schuster, 1935), 244. Endicott Peabody to Franklin Delano Roosevelt, Dec. 24, 1935, Nov. 12, 1936; E. Peabody to Ellery Sedgwick, Nov. 7, 1932, Endicott Peabody Papers, Houghton Library, Harvard University.

282. Stuyvesant Fish to T. T. Wright, Feb. 8, 1888 in Fish, *1600–1914*, 203–4. For the attitude of the Astors see Harvey O'Connor, *The Astors* (New York: Alfred A. Knopf, 1941), 140–58.

283. Robert B. Roosevelt, *Is Democracy Dishonesty?* (New York: Journeymen Printers' Co-Operative Association, 1871); Dennis Tilden Lynch, *"Boss" Tweed* (New York: Boni and Liveright, 1927); Seymour Mandlebaum *Boss Tweed's New York* (New York: John Wiley & Sons, 1965); Alexander B. Callow, Jr., *The Tweed Ring* (New York: Oxford University Press, 1966).

284. Almond, "Plutocracy," 98–99.

285. For the history of the civil service and Mugwump movements in New York see Marlene Stein Wortman, "The Mugwump in New York, 1865–1884: A Study of the Culture and Institutions of Reform" (Ph.D. dissertation, University of Chicago, 1966); Gerald W. McFarland, "The New York Mugwumps of 1884: A Profile," *Political Science Quarterly*, LXXVIII (Mar., 1963), 40–58; Richard Skolnick, "The Crystallization of Reform in New York City, 1890–1917" (Ph.D. dissertation, Yale University, 1964); Ari Hoogenboom, *Outlawing the Spoils: A History of the Civil Service Reform Movement, 1865–1888* (Urbana: University of Illinois Press, 1961); Frank Mann Stewart: *The National Civil Service Reform League* (Austin: University of Texas Press, 1929); *A Half Century of Municipal Reform: The History of the National Municipal League* (Berkeley and Los Angeles: University of California Press, 1950); Lorin Peterson, *The Day of the Mugwump* (New York: Random House, 1961); Paul P. Van Riper, *History of the United States Civil Service* (Evanston: Row, Peterson, 1956); Wallace S. Sayre and Herbert Kaufman, *Governing New York City: Politics in the Metropolis* (New York: Russell Sage Foundation, 1960), 694–98; Low, *Seth Low*, 47–56. For contemporary accounts see Richard Welling, *As the Twig Is Bent* (New York: G. P. Putnam's Sons, 1942); E. L. Godkin, *The Triumph of Reform* (New York: Souvenir Publishing, 1895); *Report* [s] *of the Executive Committee of the New York Civil Service Reform Association, 1892, 1915* (New York: New York Civil Service Reform Association, 1892, 1915); *Proclamations at the Twentieth Anniversary of the Union League Club, February 6, 1883* (New York: Union League Club, 1883); *John Jay: The President's Address at the Last Meeting in the Old Club House* (New York: Union League Club, 1867); *The National Republican Party: Its Principles, Pledges and Opportunities* (New York: G. P. Putnam's Sons, 1885).

286. Hoogenboom, *Outlawing*, 190–92; McFarland, "New York Mugwumps," 49.

287. For comparisons between upper-class New Yorkers and Bostonians which reflect the greater vigor of the Brahmins see Stewart, *National*, 23–27, 270–73. Contrast the accounts of Boston reformers in the following references with those of New York in n. 285. *Citizen's Association of Boston, First, Second, Third, Fourth Annual Report*[s] *of the Executive Committee, 1889–91* (Boston: Alfred Mudge & Son, 1889–91); Raymond L. Bridgeman, *The Independents of Massachusetts in 1884* (Boston: Cupples, Upham, 1885); Philip Putnam Chase, "Some Cambridge Reformers of the '80s," *Cambridge Historical Society*, XX (Apr., 1927), 24–52; Geoffrey Blodgett, *The Gentle Reformers: Massachusetts Democrats in the Cleveland Era* (Cambridge: Harvard University Press, 1966).

288. "Address of the Hon. Montgomery Schuyler," *Proceedings at the Annual Meeting of the National Civil Service Reform League*, XLIX (1920), 17, 21–22.

289. Stewart, *Half*, 179, 187; Wortman, "Mugwumps," 335–37; Skolnick, "Crystallization," 132–37, 302; *Report . . . 1915*, 60.

290. Ernest R. May, *American Imperialism: A Speculative Essay* (New York: Atheneum, 1968), 45–56, 59–72.

291. "National Convention of the Anti-Imperialists," *Public Opinion*, XXIX (Aug. 15, 1900), 277–78; "Bryan's New Allies," New York *Times*, Nov. 30, 1899, p. 6; "Eastern Conference of Anti-Imperialists," New York *Tribune*, Feb. 24,

1900, p. 2; Robert L. Beisner, *Twelve against Empire: The Anti-Imperialists, 1898–1900* (New York: McGraw-Hill, 1968), *passim*; Thomas A. Bailey, "The Election of 1900: A Mandate on Imperialism," *Mississippi Valley Historical Review*, XXIV (June, 1937), 43–52; Fred H. Harrington, "The Anti-Imperialist Movement in the United States," *MVHR*, XXII (Sept., 1935), 211–30.

292. Chester, ed., *Legal*, III, 59–61.

293. Taft, *Century*, 174ff.

294. For Philadelphia's upper-class physicians see Burt, *Perennial*, 107–13. Compare the small number of New York patrician doctors on the staff of New York Hospital with the numerous Brahmins at Massachusetts General Hospital. For New York Hospital see *Commemorative*, 95–96. For MGH see previous chapter.

295. Wilson, *Memorial History*, IV, 438–444; David Bryson Delevan, *Early Days of the Presbyterian Hospital in the City of New York* (New York: privately printed, 1926); Walsh, *History*, III, 760–66, 770–71; Cammann and Camp, *Charities*, 3; Dalton, *History*, 153; *Condensed*, 39–40; *Commemorative*, 94; New York *Times*, May 17, 1971, p. 31.

296. James McLachlan, *American Boarding Schools: A Historical Study* (New York: Charles Scribner's Sons, 1970), 183–84, 236–37; Arthur Stanwood Pier, *St. Paul's School, 1855–1934* (New York: Charles Scribner's Sons, 1934), 167, 219.

297. McLachlan, *American*, 161, 251; Pier, *St. Paul's*, 353; Roland J. Medford, *History of Lawrenceville School, 1810–1935* (Princeton: Princeton University Press, 1935), 50–51.

298. For prominent New York civil service reformers who expressed these views see James William Beekman, *The Founders of New York* (New York: St. Nicholas Society, 1870), 30, 35; John Jay: *National*, 6–7; *Address of the President, June 23, 1866, Union League Club of New York* (n.p., n.d.), 54.

299. Strong, *Diary*, Feb. 3, 1868, IV, 185–86. For Fish's criticism see Nevins, *Hamilton Fish*, 97–98.

300. Holbrook, *Age*, 338–49; Merle Curti and Roderick Nash, *Philanthropy in the Shaping of American Higher Education* (New Brunswick: Rutgers University Press, 1965), 76–77, 142–49, 192; Wayne Andrews, *The Vanderbilt Legend* (New York: Harcourt, Brace, 1941), 326, 391; Columbia University: *Gifts and Endowments; Gifts and Bequests*.

301. Jay, *Centennial*, 22, 40, 43–46.

302. Columbia University: *Gifts and Endowments; Gifts and Bequests*.

303. Frederick Paul Keppel quoted in Gene R. Hawes, "The Colleges of America's Upper Class: Alma Maters of Men Listed in the New York Social Register 1963," *Saturday Review of Literature*, 69 (Nov. 16, 1963), 69.

304. *Ibid.*, 69–71.

305. *Columbia University Catalogue[s], 1899–1940* (New York: Columbia University Press, 1899–1940); *The Role of the Trustees of Columbia University* (New York: Columbia University Press, 1957).

306. *A Dinner Tendered to Nicholas Murray Butler to Mark the Twenty-fifth Anniversary of His Inauguration as President of Columbia University* (New York: Columbia University Press, 1927), 21–22, 26–27.

307. Stewart, *Grace Church*, 415; Elizabeth Drexel Lehr, *King Lehr and the Gilded Age* (Philadelphia: J. B. Lippincott, 1935), 77–78. Mrs. Lehr was the wife

of Harry Lehr, who succeeded Ward McAllister as the majordomo of the Four Hundred.

308. Morgan Dix, *Twenty-fifth Anniversary of the Consecration* [*of the Church Building*] (New York: American Church Press, 1871), 4–7, 9–10.

309. For the twentieth-century history of Trinity Church see Bridgeman, *Trinity*, VI, *passim*.

310. *Cathedral Church of St. John the Divine* (New York: St. Bartholomew's Press, 1926), 6, 60–61, 66–101.

311. Edith Wharton, *A Backward Glance*, 68–69, 119, 121, cf. 61, 79, 195. For a similar evaluation by a foreign observer see E. Catherine Bates, *A Year in the Great Republic*, 2 vols. (London: Wardle Downey, 1887), I, 251–52.

312. Julia Ward Howe, *Reminiscences, 1819–1899* (Boston: Houghton Mifflin, 1899), 80.

313. New York Society Library, *Shareholders and Officers; New York Society Library Annual Report*[s], *1930, 1940, 1949–50, 1966* (New York: New York Society Library, 1930, 1940, 1949–50, 1966); Vail, *Knickerbocker*, 203; Kelby, *New York Historical*, 54–119.

314. Georgina Schuyler, *The Beginnings of the Thursday Evening Club* (New York: privately printed, 1920).

315. Van Rennselaer and Van De Water, *Social*, 108–10, 134–35; Roosevelt, *Letters*, III, 114–15, 535, IV, 1299, V, 223, 352, VI, 882, 1002.

316. Frederick Townsend Martin, *The Passing of the Idle Rich* (Garden City, N.Y.: Doubleday, Page, 1911), *passim*. Mrs. Winthrop Chanler quoted in Cleveland Amory, *Who Killed*, 120.

317. Ward McAllister interview, New York Daily *Tribune*, Mar. 25, 1888, p. 11; McAllister interview, New York *Times*, Feb. 16, 1892, p. 5.

318. Almond, "Plutocracy," 156, 158, 272. For a fuller account of New York fashionable society see Jaher, "Style and Status," 258–84.

319. For the influential role of upper-class Philadelphians in the Philadelphia Orchestra, the Pennsylvania Academy of Fine Arts, the University of Pennsylvania Museum, and the Philadelphia Museum of Art see Burt, *Perennial*, 343–56, 469–70; Baltzell, *Philadelphia*, 393–94.

320. The best history of the Metropolitan Museum of Art is Calvin Tomkins, *Merchants and Masterpieces: The Story of the Metropolitan Museum of Art* (New York: E. P. Dutton, 1970). Other sources are: Howe, *History; A Metropolitan Art Museum in the City of New York* (New York: Trow & Smith, 1869); *Address of the Officers of the Metropolitan Museum of Art, to the People of New York* (New York: Francis & Loutrel, 1871); *The Metropolitan Museum of Art: The Fiftieth Anniversary Celebration MDCCCLXIX–MCMXX* (New York: n.p., 1920); *The Metropolitan Museum of Art: Seventy-fifth Anniversary Celebration* (New York: n.p., 1945). For the rejected merger of the historical society and the museum see Van Rensselaer and Van De Water, *Social Ladder*, 128–29.

321. *Museum of the City of New York: Annual Report*[s] *1927, 1957–58* (New York: n.p., 1928, 1958); James Thrall Soby, *The Museum of Modern Art* (New York: n.p., 1958); Dwight MacDonald, "Action of 53rd St.," *New Yorker* (Dec. 12, 19, 1953), 49–82, 53–72.

322. Wecter, *Saga*, 332; Andrews, *Vanderbilt*, 262–64; Edward Robb Ellis, *The Epic of New York City* (New York: Coward McCann, 1966), 377–80; Bir-

mingham, *"Our Crowd,"* 305.

323. Huneker, *Philharmonic*, 3, 45; Krehbiel, *Philharmonic*, 164–73; Erskine, *Philharmonic*, 1–60.

324. Ludenberg, *History*, 6, 10, 62, 104, 305–6, 537–39; *After One Hundred Years* (New York: New York Public Library, 1948), *passim*.

325. New York *Times*, Mar. 8, 1965, pp. 1, 32.

326. Wilson, *Memorial History*, IV, 450–54; *Marine*, 53–110; Husband, *One Hundred Years*, 35–38; Collins, *Ninety Years*, 185–87; Mills, *That's My Bank*, 102–6; *One Hundred and Seventy-five Years*, 41–44; Knowles, *History*, 179ff.

327. Weeks, *Prominent*, 230; *Theodore Roosevelt, Sr., a Tribute: The Proceedings of a Meeting of the Union League Club, New York City, February 14, 1878* (New York: privately printed, 1878), 7–31; Robert W. De Forest and Lawrence Vieller, eds., *The Tenement House Problem*, 2 vols. (New York: Macmillan, 1903), I, 98–100, 333, 363–64; Schneider, *History*, II, 20–21, 31, 144; Lillian Brandt, *The Charity Organization Society of the City of New York* (New York: B. H. Tyrrel, 1907), 15–16, 167–220.

328. On the disenchantment with reform see David J. Rothman, *The Discovery of the Asylum: Social Order and Disorder in the New Republic* (Boston: Little, Brown, 1971), 237–95. On the professionalization of social work see "Charter and Constitution of the C.O.S.," reprinted in Brandt, *Charity*, 303–18; *Papers Issued by the Charity Organization Society of the City of New York during Its First Five Years, 1882–86* (New York: John J. O'Brien, 1887); William Rhinelander Stewart, *The Philanthropic Work of Josephine Shaw Lowell* (New York: Macmillan, 1911); Josephine Shaw Lowell, *Public Relief and Private Charity* (New York: G. P. Putnam's Sons, 1884). For an analysis of the new ideas in philanthropy see Marvin E. Gettleman, "Charity and Social Classes in the United States, 1874–1900," *American Journal of Economics and Sociology*, XXII (Apr., July, 1963), 313–29, 417–26.

329. Morrison, Jr., *History of St. Andrew's*, 249–91; *St. Andrew's Society of the State of New York: Annual Report, 1952* (New York: n.p., 1952), 6, 47–78; *Marine*, 53–110; Bouring and Tabor, *History of St. George's*, 211–91; *St. George's Society of New York: Annual Report[s] and Constitution, 1925, 1961* (New York: n.p., 1925, 1961), 35–50, 51–67; Husband, *One Hundred Years*, 35–38; Collins, *Ninety Years*, 185–87; Mills, *That's My Bank*, 102–6; *One Hundred and Seventy-five Years*, 41–44; Knowles, *History*, 149–50, 179ff.

330. James Ford, *Slums and Housing*, 2 vols. (Cambridge: Harvard University Press, 1931), I, 123–24; *The Provident Loan Society of New York, 1894–1944: Fifty Years of Lending* (Philadelphia: William F. Fell, 1944), 9, 45–48; Brandt, *Charity*, 167–220, 266.

331. Almond, "Plutocracy," 156, 158, 272.

332. O'Connor, *Astors*, 231–32; Andrews, *Vanderbilt*, 236; Holbrook, *Age*, 337.

333. "'Interlocking Directors' in Charities and Good Works," New York *Times*, Dec. 29, 1912, Magazine Section, Part 5, p. 8; cf. Dec. 30, 1912, p. 6; Curti, *American*, 65–78, 122–35, 148–49, 172, 176, 186, 212, 243; Josephson, *Robber Barons*, 317–24; Holbrook, *Age*, 347–49; Birmingham, *"Our Crowd,"* 322–26.

334. For some Jewish charities see Birmingham, *"Our Crowd,"* 188, 288,

324–26, 358; Moses Rischin, *The Promised City: New York's Jews, 1870–1914* (New York: Harper Torchbooks, 1970), 103–11, 198, 206–9, 241.

335. Abraham Epstein, "Do the Rich Give to Charity?" *American Mercury* (May, 1931), 25–27.

336. Kip, "New York Society," 101; cf. Van Rensselaer and Van De Water, *Social Ladder*, 21–22; Wharton, *Backward*, 5; John Jay, *The Battle of Harlem Plains* (New York: New York Historical Society, 1876), 38.

337. Frederick J. DePeyster, "Speech at the St. Nicholas Society Dinner," *New American Gazette*, VII (Nov. 30, 1891–Jan. 7, 1892), 2.

338. For Edith Wharton's views see *Backward*, 6–7, 22–23, 55–56, 92. For some other examples of aristocratic thoughts on modern times, the eclipse of the patrician enclave, and the dangers of the present and future see John Watts DePeyster, *An Address Delivered before the Historical Society of New Brunswick, Canada, July 4, 1883* (New York: Charles H. Ludwig, 1883), 2; Robert B. Roosevelt and William C. DeWitt, "Speeches at the Holland Society Dinner," *New American Gazette*, III (Jan. 31, 1886), 10–11; F. J. DePeyster, "Speech at the Pass Festival," *ibid.*, VII (Apr. 18, 1892–May 19, 1892), 4; R. B. Roosevelt, *Early New York: Address Delivered before the New York Society of the Order of the Founders and Patriots of America, January 15, 1904* (New York: n.p., 1904), 7, 15; J. W. DePeyster, "Reminiscences 1876," in Frank Allaben, *John Watts DePeyster*, 2 vols. (New York: Frank Allaben Genealogical, 1908), I, 113–14, 150; Strong, *Diary*, IV, Dec. 19, 1868, 236, May 20, 1869, 245–46, Sept. 30, 1869, 256, Nov. 11, 1869, 259–60, Mar. 25, 1872, 416, July 22, 1873, 488–89; Van Rensselaer and Van De Water, *Social Ladder*, 6, 21–22, 31–32, 35–37, 157–62.

339. For the history of these organizations, lists of members and officers, and constitutions and by-laws see *St. Nicholas Club of the City of New York: Constitution and By-laws* (New York: n.p., 1926); *Yearbook of the Holland Society, 1930–37* (New York: n.p., 1937); *St. Nicholas Society; St. Nicholas Society Genealogical Record*, III; Youngs, ed., *Portraits*; Schuyler, *Institution*; William Sturgis Thomas, *Members of the Society of the Cincinnati 1929* (New York: Tobias A. Wright, 1929); *The Colonial Order of the Acorn: Yearbook 1894* (New York: Dempsey & Carroll, 1894); *New York Chapter of the Colonial Order of the Acorn Yearbook 1931* (New York: n.p., 1931); *The Order of Colonial Lords of Manors in America: Address of Mrs. Albert Levin Richard* (Baltimore: n.p., 1912), 29–32; *Publications of the Order of Colonial Lords of the Manors in America: Year Book[s], 1936, 1947, No[s]. 26A, 30A*; Wallace Evans Davies, *Patriotism on Parade: The Story of Veterans' and Hereditary Organizations in America, 1783–1900* (Cambridge: Harvard University Press, 1955), 57, 80–81, 92.

340. Hamilton Fish to John Schuyler, Feb. 22, 1892, *New American Gazette*, VII, 1–2; DePeyster, "Speech," 2–3; DeWitt, "Speech," 11; *St. Nicholas Club*, 7; *Order . . . Yearbook 1936*, 13; *Holland Society . . . 1930–37*, 6; *Colonial . . . Acorn Yearbook*, 4; *New York Chapter . . . Acorn*, 9, 13–15.

341. For New York clubs, clubmen, and club life see Townsend, *Mother; Officers . . . Union*; Gourlie, *Origin; Fiftieth; Century Association; Union League Club of New York, Charter, Articles of Association and By-laws, May, 1868* (New York: n.p., 1868); *Proceedings at the Dinner of the Early Members of the Union League Club of the City of New York, May 20, 1880* (New York: Kones

& Toby, 1880); Henry Bellows, *Historical Sketch of the Union League Club of New York, 1863–1879* (New York: G. P. Putnam's, 1879); *The Union League Club of New York* (New York: Jacques, 1932); William Irwin, Earl Chapin May, and Joseph Hotchkiss, *A History of the Union League Club of New York City* (New York: Dodd, Mead, 1952); James W. Alexander, *A History of the University Club of New York, 1865–1916* (New York: Charles Scribner's Sons, 1915); *The Charter, Constitution, Officers and Roll of Members of the University Club in the City of New York, 1865–66, 1900, 1929, 1961* (New York: published by the club, 1866, 1900, 1929, 1961); Reginald Rives, *The Coaching Club* (New York: Derrydale Press, 1935); *Officers, Constitution, By-laws and List of Members, Metropolitan Club, 1936, 1952* (New York: n.p., 1936, 1952); *The Brook, 1903–30* (New York: privately printed, 1930); *The Elite Catalogue of Clubs for 1890–91: The Annual Club Book for New York and Vicinity* (New York: New York Club, 1890); *Clubmen of New York* (New York: Republic Press, 1898).

342. Amory, *Who Killed*, 210; Lucy Kavaler, *The Private World of High Society* (New York: David McKay, 1960), 40.

343. Townsend, *Mother*, *passim*; "The Union: Mother of Clubs," *Fortune Magazine* VI (Dec., 1932), 45–47, 100–103; Robert M. Thomas, Jr., "Union Club Still There—Someplace between Skull and Bones and Dow Jones," New York *Times*, Dec. 11, 1969, p. 90.

344. Wecter, *Saga*, 331–32; W. Jay Mills, "New York Society before Its Great Transformation," *The Delineator*, LXIV (Nov., 1904), 747–52.

345. McAllister quoted in Amory, *The Last Resorts* (New York: Harper & Bros., 1952), 189; cf. McAllister, *Society*, 161, 224, 246.

346. Jaher, "Style and Status," 258–84.

347. John W. Leonard, ed., *Who's Who in America* (Chicago: A. N. Marquis, 1899). This edition includes people who died between 1895 and 1899. Possibly a few of the Four Hundred died between 1892 and 1895 who might have been included, but this would not substantially affect the proportion on McAllister's list who made *Who's Who*.

348. "The Yankee Doodle Salon," *Fortune Magazine*, XVI (Dec., 1937), 123–29, 180, 183–84, 186; Geoffrey T. Hellman, *Mrs. DePeyster's Parties and Other Lively Studies from the "New Yorker,"* (New York: Macmillan, 1963), 165–66; Kavaler, *High Society*, 73–93, 227–35; Amory, *Who Killed*, 131–88, 522ff.; Lanfranco Rasponi, *The International Nomads* (New York: G. P. Putnam, 1966), *passim*.

349. Amory, *Who Killed*, 11, 109–14, 522ff.; Juliana Cutting, "Society Today and Yesterday," *The Saturday Evening Post*, CCV (Apr. 1, 1933), 10–11, 59, 61–62, (May 6, 1933), 16–17, 64, 66, (June 24, 1933), 14–15, 69–70, 72, 74; Fish, *1600–1914*, 290; Kavaler, *High Society*, 61; New York *Times*, Dec. 17, 1967, p. 80.

350. Robert B. Roosevelt, "Speech," 10; Hamilton Fish to Stuyvesant Fish, July 24, 1888, Fish, *1600–1914*, 24–25; *ibid.*, 1.

CHAPTER IV

Northern urban elites differed from the upper order in Charleston. The northerners flourished in an entrepreneurial atmosphere and languished when zest for the marketplace was inhibited by aristocratic impulses. Newcomers, undeterred by family and historical loyalties, eventually dispossessed old patriciates. The leading economic and political enclaves in the Northeast became the model for elites in the young western cities. Although the higher strata in the North felt ambivalent about republican rule, their commercial activities helped realize the American Dream within and beyond their municipal borders. Displacement increased the declining elites' opposition toward democracy, economic growth, and social change, but intensified intransigence hastened their defeat by rigidifying responses to new forces and distancing them from the concerns of most Americans.

Industrialism and immigration altered city life in the North in ways that undermined the traditional establishments. Charleston, however, a region dominated by the planter class, was relatively untouched, until after the Civil War, by demographic and technological developments that threatened patricians elsewhere. Northern upper classes existed in an increasingly urbanized milieu. By 1860 over one-third of the Northeast population lived in towns or cities of at least 2,500 residents, and the metropolises of Boston, Philadelphia, and New York were within a few hundred miles of each other. Even in the more recently settled Midwest—Indiana, Illinois, Michigan, and Wisconsin—14 percent of the inhabitants in 1860 dwelled in places of at least 2,500 people. In that year the slave states had no large cities except for New Orleans and

Baltimore. On the eve of the Civil War a scant 7 percent of the lower South population resided in towns or cities, and outside of New Orleans only Charleston, Mobile, and Savannah, in the Confederacy, had 15,000 or more inhabitants. The three latter, whose combined population totaled 92,000, were urban islands dominated by rural areas.[1]

The tidewater South was agrarian in interest and "cavalier" in outlook. Rooted in the land, the family, and the past, and dedicated to hierarchy and paternalism, after 1830 the rural gentry became increasingly disaffected from the national commitment to mobility, progress, and equality. Throughout the future Confederacy, especially among the planters, spread the conviction of being a beleagured minority whose economic and political power was declining compared to other parts of the nation and whose way of life was increasingly under attack by other Americans. The gulf widened, tensions became unbearable, and relief was sought through armed rebellion. As a consequence the section endured two additional experiences which differentiated it from the rest of the nation—insurrection and defeat. Although Charleston was a trade and financial center, its upper class shared the destiny of the squirearchy because the city serviced the plantations and served as the residence of many planters.

Throughout its history, approximately ninety families comprised upper-class Charleston. Seventy percent of these clans stemmed from the colonial patriciate of South Carolina; the others emerged in the nineteenth century. Aristocratic families married chiefly among themselves, a practice still frequently followed. *Parvenu* capitalists and statesmen or their children, however, did make matches with the well-born. Newcomers were not numerous and usually accepted traditional values; hence they were easily absorbed into the establishment. Charleston was the market of the low-country parishes, and the power and wealth of its leaders derived mostly from land and trade. The dominant enclave consisted of plantation owners and urban businessmen (who often divided their resources between agriculture and urban capitalism and their residences between their estates and their town houses) and was a rural-urban gentry.

For two crucial reasons the unique character and experiences of the South had a more powerful impact on Charleston than did the regional locations of the other cities in this study. The South differed more from the rest of the country than did any other section. The Palmetto port reflected this divergence and developed in another way that embedded it more deeply in its surroundings and further separated it from the experience of Boston, New York, Chicago, and Los Angeles. When the United States won independence, New York and Boston were emergent national cities. Chicago and Los Angeles began as regional centers, but they, too, eventually dominated important sectors of the nation's economic and cultural life. Charleston, however, regressed as the decades passed. The most populous and leading commercial town in the colonial South, before the Revolution Charleston rivaled northern ports in population and in trade and shared their entrepreneurial outlook. After independence Charleston was overshadowed by her northern competitors and the town drifted away from the bustling commercial spirit typical of maritime centers to become a locus of the plantation life-style, a middleman in tidewater traffic, and a second home for great landowners.

Tidewater attitudes were most clearly articulated when Carolina aristocrats contrasted themselves with northerners. Statements by Joseph Alston in 1800, Frederick A. Porcher in 1857, and Robert Barnwell Rhett in 1865—members of leading low-country Charleston families established in early colonial times—convey a class image contradictory to the bourgeois ideals of upper orders in New York and Boston. South Carolina had the most "polished . . . society" in the United States, wrote Alston to his bride, a daughter of Aaron Burr; its "gentlemen," with "large fortunes . . . and little disposed by the climate to the drudgery of business or professions," have "leisure" to be "well informed, agreeable companions, and completely well bred." Compared to "the more commercial citizens of the northern states," slave owners were proud, generous, honorable, impulsive, and sensitive, but "inferior" in "steadiness and perseverance."[2] Porcher reiterated Alston's view of the agrarian gentry. Written on the eve of the Civil War, however, his portrayal contained ominous overtones. "The planter class" had "a catholicity of taste as well as of feeling, and an elevated view of all subjects, particularly public affairs, which commands respect, because it is felt that the views are neither the suggestions of private interests nor the convenient opinions of a paid advocate." These qualities conditioned the "southern gentleman," unlike northern employers, not to "regard the laborer merely" as "money value" but as "our friend, our dependence, our hope." Nevertheless, northern "activity" and "progress" "contrast[ed]" with southern "sluggishness" and "conservatism." Porcher believed that "our destiny" forbade "competition" with the North and prevented the acquisition of "great wealth." He asked those driven by an insatiable quest to excel and accumulate: "Is the heart of man never to expand the warm influence of home, and all its associations of family, of kindred, and of friendly affections? Is man to become a mere money-making, cotton-spinning, iron-founding machine?" This "unceasing struggle after more" was characteristic of an urban environment foreign to southern civilization and "beyond the direct influence of the slave-holding power. . . . Boston, or New York, or Cincinnati . . . is destined to be the centre of opinion, and to give the law to the rest of the country." Consequently, for Porcher "our place in the

Union is . . . provincial" and "our peculiarities will have to be defended, excused, ridiculed, pardoned. We can take no pride in our national character because we . . . do not contribute to its formation." He concluded: "We can never be other than dependants and inferiors so long as we continue to live with them on a footing of political alliance. Let us hold them as we hold the rest of mankind, enemies in war, friends in peace. . . ."[3] Defeat during the Civil War did not still the voice of aristocratic dissent. "There is an incongruity between the two peoples from their very natures," declaimed Rhett shortly after the war. He offered a conventional catalogue of the antinominous traits of the sections. The northerner is "cautious and reticent," lacks "honor, . . . cultivates privacy and individuality, . . . is skeptical, prying, officious, harsh, dogmatic, aggressive, and fond of novelties misnamed progress." He "looks upon government as an instrument of aggrandizement, to make money or to rule others." The southerner is "frank and open, gregarious, . . . free in the use of money, . . . values" honor "beyond life, . . . distrusts change and reverences the past," and regards government "as an instrument of protection, for securing justice and leaving to all under its authority the privilege of seeking their own happiness in their own way." Rhett wondered if "people of such different characteristics and antagonistic views can live voluntarily under the same Free Government."[4]

THE COLONIAL ERA

In colonial times the gap between the regions was considerably narrower. Tidewater society in provincial South Carolina and Virginia was bourgeois in origin and entrepreneurial in spirit. Carters, Byrds, and Lees speculated in lands and copper mines, built textile and grain mills on their plantations, owned ships, lent money at interest, and engaged in overseas and coastal trade.[5] Carolina planters undertook similar projects and Charleston became the leading southern port.

According to the "Fundamental Constitutions of Carolina" (1669, 1670), the original proprietors planned to concentrate landholding and political power in the hands of a local "hereditary Nobility." Wilderness conditions, abundance of land and scarcity of settlers, and the inadequate funds of the early arrivals, however, precluded the development of "landgraves" and "caciques" who were to own the "Seignories," "Baronies," and "Manors" and to dominate the provincial "Grand Council."[6] Although a noble order failed to survive, by the 1690s gentry appeared in the coastal parishes. A large proportion of its land and power remained in the hands of direct descendants until the Civil War, a continuity that surpassed the longevity of elites in New York City and Boston. Low-country planters, however, were not an exclusively rural enclave. They spent half the year in town, escaping the heat and malaria of the rice fields, belonged to Charleston's cultural, convivial, and charity societies and churches, and often represented the city in the commons house of assembly. The squires speculated in urban real estate, participated in business ventures with merchants, married into ranking maritime families, and sometimes sent their sons into trade. Conversely, the most prosperous burghers acted as factors, suppliers, and shippers for the planters, and usually owned plantations as supplementary sources of income, symbols of high status, places of retirement, or desirable pursuits for their children.

The upper order consisted of planters and merchants of chiefly English (either from the home country or the West Indies) and Huguenot extraction, whose antecedents, like the colonial patriciates of Virginia, New York, and Massachusetts, were mostly middle class. They came largely from families of minor gentry, comfortable yeomen, merchants, and sea captains. Among the founders of clans destined to remain conspicuous in the city and state until 1861 were Stephen Bull, an offspring of the lesser British gentry, and Edward Middleton, a London and Barbadian merchant. Bull and Middleton received huge land grants and held high positions in the proprietary government. Ralph Izard, whose father was a British landholder, was soon similarly well placed. Thomas Pinckney, designated a "gentleman" upon arrival, had enough money to buy a plantation. The upper stratum also contained many who rose from humble beginnings. The fathers of Charleston's wealthiest pre-Revolutionary merchants, Henry Laurens and Gabriel Manigault, began respectively as a saddler and a cooper; the first Read made the family fortune in a ropewalk establishment in that city; William Rhett was formerly a British sailor; and the Elliotts started out as indentured servants. These and other prominent figures whose descendants remained influential in the nineteenth century were among the early settlers. Bull, Middleton, John Van Der Horst, Thomas Drayton, and Daniel Heyward arrived in the 1670s; Izard, Pinckney, and the first Allstons, Hugers, Smiths, Horrys, Rhetts, Balls, Elliotts, Prioleaus, Manigaults, Gaillards, Peronneaus, Brewtons, and Ravenels in the 1680s and '90s; the Mottes, Harlestons, Barnwells, and Moultries between 1700 and 1710; and in the next two decades the Laurenses, Porchers, Pringles, Lowndeses, Rutledges, and De Saussures.[7] The vast majority soon acquired plantations. Fifty of the 440 Carolinians who, in 1860, owned at least 100 slaves on one plantation in the state came from these and other prominent forebears, and many of their estates were inherited from the original proprietors.[8]

Founders of distinguished families also bought Charleston real estate, and several built wharfs on their property. Some of these urban holdings exhibited a dynastic continuity equal to that of rural possessions. A plot of land bought by Rawlins Lowndes in 1762 was not sold until 1851, and city lots obtained by Isaac Mazyck in 1717 still belonged to his twentieth-century kin. Several stately Charleston mansions built at the height of colonial prosperity in the two decades before the Revolution sometimes housed direct descendants many times removed from the original owners. The Izard and Pinckney homes, the latter constructed before 1740, were the living quarters of those families until the Civil War; the Pringle house remained in the family until 1886; and twentieth-century Mottes, Hugers, and Brewtons inhabited their ancestral domiciles.[9]

Land and slaves were the primary assets of the agrarian elite. Since their value depended heavily upon shipment of rice and indigo and upon the slave trade, these activities constituted the gentry's chief contribution to the market economy. The patriciate was also active in the Indian trade in leather and skins, land speculations in Carolina, Florida, and Georgia, selling firewood to Charleston, operating retail stores disbursing supplies to smaller farmers, occasionally chartering ships to send their products directly to England and more frequently building schooners to take goods to Charleston, buying provisions for the plantation, exporting naval stores, owning ferry franchises, and laying out roads. Several planters were innovative entrepreneurs: a direct ancestor of the Heywards inaugurated Carolina rice planting in 1685, Eliza Lucas Pinckney reintroduced indigo culture in the early 1740s, and thirty years later Daniel Heyward began to manufacture cotton on his estate.[10]

Commercial, political, and marital ties with the maritime elites of Charleston and Georgetown further drew the planters into mercantile capitalism. Scions of great landholding families appeared among Charleston's eminent eighteenth-century businessmen. Thomas Middleton, Benjamin Smith, Andrew Rutledge, Samuel Prioleau II and III, and Jacob Motte were offspring of low-country planters, and Henry Laurens clerked in the countinghouse of Landgrave Thomas Smith's grandson. Thomas Pinckney and Isaac Mazyck were planter-merchants, and Pinckney's son William helped form the first fire insurance company in North America.[11] A planter background helped attract business. Laurens, the greatest Charleston trader of his day, advised a London connection to deal with Brewton and Smith because "of the Elder Mr. Smith . . . whose extensive acquaintance and ability in dispatch of business as well as influence with the Planters are at least equal to those of any other Man in the Province."[12] Another tie between the mercantile and agricultural elites was forged by planters' sons who became lawyers for overseas traders. John Rutledge reversed paternal depletion of the family estate, becoming Carolina's leading attorney in the 1760s and handling the legal affairs of Miles Brewton and Laurens.

Charles Pinckney ranked just behind him in the pre-Revolutionary Charleston bar.[13]

A capitalistic spirit and the Protestant ethic encouraged the business activities of the squirearchy and the Charleston merchants. "I make no doubt this will prove a very valuable Commodity in time," wrote Eliza Lucas, later the wife of Pinckney, of her experiments in indigo culture. Her journal and letters reiterated the homilies uttered by northern merchants. "Use all your diligence to improve yourself," she advised herself and her kin. Avoid "Sloth or Idleness" and be neither "luxurious or extravagant."[14] Planter Elias Ball, Jr., told his son, then living in Charleston, not "to lay out your money so foolishly," not "to let your head turn too much on Dress," and "to mind your business and study more than you do."[15] The parents of second-generation planter-merchant Peter Manigault gave him similar advice, and he repeatedly reassured them about his frugality, diligence, and serious-mindedness. In the 1770s Manigault urged these virtues upon his nephew, so that "you will make your Entry into the Great World, with greater Advantage." John Rutledge made identical recommendations to his brother, a law student in London.[16] The most comprehensive allegiance to the bourgeois creed was expressed by Laurens. In 1755 the great trader reported that his relative and partner, George Austin, "must make a Voyage to England next Year to place him [Austin's son] some where more to his advantage than to pore over Latin and Greek Authors of little utility to a young Man intended for the Mercantile Business."[17] Laurens affirmed utility, self-improvement, impulse control, and material achievement. Some Laurenses "retained the French pride of family and were content to die poor," he wrote in 1774. "My father was of different sentiments; he learned a trade, and by his great industry acquired an estate with good character and re-established the name of his family." The merchant-statesman praised his parent for being "careless of his ancestry." In his own life and in admonishments to his children Laurens emphasized "Vigilance," "Industry," "Temperance," and "Self-Denial." Accordingly, he condemned dancing, horse-racing, gambling, and duelling, and catechized his children with the burgher faith of self-betterment and vocational success.[18]

Sharing the traits and values and engaging in the activities that brought success in Georgetown and Charleston, the planters acquired many of the assets of South Carolina. On the eve of the Revolution the wealthiest 10 percent of the landholders owned over half of the slaves and the acreage in the colony and nearly 60 percent of its personal property. This group possessed a larger percentage of provincial wealth than did tidewater Virginians, held the largest concentrations of land and slaves, and were the richest agricultural aristocracy in America.[19]

Commercial interests and bourgeois beliefs, however, coexisted with conservative impulses and a leisured outlook. Inherited holdings, wealth, and status together with genteel values inhibited innovation, foreshadowed the traditionalism of the nineteenth-century rural gentry, and diverted energy and resources to luxury and amusement. Low-country planters even lagged behind their counterparts in Virginia and Maryland in adopting scientific agricultural methods.[20] Alexander Garden, the colony's foremost scientist, noted in 1755 the "very few Mechanical Machines here in this Province to facilitate labor." The "planters" do not "Encourage . . . any Discovery in Machines, though there are no Men who stand more in need of this Assistance." The physician, botanist, rector of St. Philip's, and Anglican commissary for the Carolinas attributed unwillingness to mechanize to the planters' "Desire to remain in a well trodden Path, that they have been accustomed to." Alexander Hewatt argued that manufacturing would never develop so long as cheap land was readily available. The former minister of the Presbyterian Church of Charleston noted that artisans and merchants used their profits to buy land and settle on plantations. He went even further than Garden in criticizing the squirearchy. "Carolinians," declared Hewatt in 1779, were "slovenly husbandmen" and "managed" their "estates" in a "negligent manner. . . . Those planters who had arrived at easy or affluent circumstances employed overseers; or having little to do . . . indulge[d] themselves in rural amusements, such as racing, mustering, hunting, fishing, or social entertainments."[21] Merchants desiring to expand trade through marketing new products occasionally became impatient with patrician planters whose reluctance to experiment interfered with commerce and cut profits. Laurens remarked in 1748 that a good market price for rice checked indigo culture because of "our Planters in Common chusing to go on in the old Rhoad while it will answer, rather than Venture in any new enterprize. . . ." He said that planters of little wealth or status were indigo pioneers and their success overcame the reluctance of rich and well-born estate owners to enter the field.[22]

Overseas traders in Charleston and Georgetown composed the other wing of the upper order. The introduction of rice culture in the 1680s furnished South Carolina with a staple that launched the mercantile communities of her two êntrepots. Maritime and agricultural elites were interdependent: merchants shipped the planters' crops, advanced them credit, conducted their legal and financial affairs, imported their slaves, and supplied them with the goods and services necessary for a gentry life-style. Charleston merchants also controlled the commerce of Georgia, the Carolinas, and Florida, dominating the Indian trade, exporting furs, naval stores, and lumber from these regions, and establishing retail stores for settlers in the interior. During the eighteenth century Charleston became the leading southern city in population, wealth, and trade, and conducted maritime operations on a scale equal to northern ports. In 1730 more vessels were loaded at Charleston for European destinations than at New York and Philadelphia in 1732. Shortly before the Revolution, South Carolina ranked behind Massachusetts Bay and Pennsylvania but ahead of New York in shipping tonnage entering and leaving the colony.[23] As in other urban ports, merchants engaged in insurance underwriting, moneylending, and primitive banking, enterprises related to maritime activities.

Typically for that age, Charleston's business structure depended heavily upon personal contacts. Friends and relatives participated in joint ventures, formed more permanent alliances, and employed their own kin or relatives of business associates. This ascriptive network also extended to connections with British firms. In common with northern commerce, personal ties were necessary to obtain reliable market information, loyal service, and adequate sources of capital. Benjamin Smith, Laurens, Isaac Mazyck, the leading trader in early Charleston, and other merchant princes entered partnerships with in-laws, sons, brothers, and fathers; Gabriel Manigault, one of the richest men in America, bequeathed his firm to his child.[24] The importance of kinship prompted Laurens to advise a British firm to deal with Thomas Loughton Smith and Roger Smith, respectively the sons of merchant brothers Benjamin and Thomas Smith, because "The connexions capital and application to business of these younger gentlemen together with the aid of their fathers and other able friends will give them an ascendant [position] over some houses and enable them to do much for the interest of their constituents in the African [slave trading] branch as any House in the place, both in obtaining good prices and making faithful remittances."[25]

Two possible deterrents to upper-class harmony never substantially emerged in colonial South Carolina. Common interests, vocational interchange, and intermarriage prevented conflicts between planters and merchants. A second potential source of division, ethnic diversity, also failed to develop. As in New York, the upper rank of the business community contained a large number of non–Anglo–Saxons; in Charleston's case, Huguenots. Most of the family founders of this enclave emigrated in the 1680s and '90s, shortly after the revocation of the Edict of Nantes (1685). In 1699 the Huguenots comprised one-tenth of the provincial population, in 1722 one-fifth of Charleston residents. At first the Huguenot merchants suffered trade restrictions and at least one of them contemplated leaving the colony. After 1700, however, extensive intermarriage with English planters and merchants and conversion to Episcopalianism indicated Huguenot assimilation.[26]

Charleston resembled northern ports in distribution of wealth as well as in business methods and structure. The richest 10 percent of Charleston's inhabitants around the time of the Revolution owned approximately five-eighths of the city's wealth, a distribution of wealth identical to that of contemporary Boston and Philadelphia. Affluent Charlestonians, however, were generally more opulent. Barely one-fifth of the Bostonians left personal estates exceeding £1,000 (provincial currency), but nearly 30 percent of the Charlestonians did. The largest estate probated in 1775 in Boston was about half the value of the largest in Charleston. Five estates probated in the northern town in that year were valued above £1000 sterling compared to thirty-six in the southern port. The higher level of wealth in Charleston was due to the presence of many planters: one-fourth of the value of estates probated in excess of £1000 (provincial currency) consisted of slaves and twenty-three of the decedents worth over £1000 sterling were planters, another four were widows who may have been married to planters, and four were farmers. Occupational frequencies disclosed another similarity with Boston. About one-fourth of those employed in each city followed commercial vocations. Four of the Bostonians leaving estates of more than £1000 sterling, however, were merchants, while only one Charlestonian at this rank of affluence was so designated. Another significant difference between the moneyed elites indicates the relative persistence of the southerners. Several of the richest Charlestonians who died shortly before 1775, including Peter Manigault, bequeathed property and power to nineteenth-century descendants. None of the richest Bostonians who died around that time transmitted their assets to heirs that far in the future.[27]

Commercial elites in Charleston and the North had similar values and accomplishments. Charleston merchants, too, were resourceful entrepreneurs. They pioneered in the rice and indigo trade, developed the back-country, and organized the first fire insurance company in America. Among the incorporators and officers of the Friendly Society for the Mutual Insuring of Houses against Fire (1735) were Gabriel Manigault and other maritime luminaries.[28] Acquisitiveness was another trait shared by colonial businessmen of all regions. An Anglican rector in Charleston wrote in 1702 that "people here are more mindful of getting money and their worldly affairs than they are of Books and Learning." Peter Manigault in 1767 noted that "Money was the first object that possessed" kinsman Benjamin Huger's "Mind" in wedding an heiress, and that this "natural" motive accounted "for the many Bargains & Sales in the matrimonial Way, which we frequently see attended with some Share of Happiness."[29]

The pursuit of material gain and social recognition created a restlessness characteristic of commercial elites. Hewatt, who castigated planter indolence, felt that "in point of industry the town was like a beehive, and there were none that reaped not advantages more or less from the flourishing state of trade and commerce." The "merchants" were "a respectable body of men, industrious and indefatigable in business. . . ." Just before the Revolution a letter in the South Carolina *Gazette* described the "lives" of upper-class Charlestonians as "one continued Race: in which everyone is endeavoring to distance all behind him; and to overtake or pass by, all before him. . . . Every Tradesman is a Merchant, every Merchant is a Gentleman, and every Gentleman one of the Noblesse." This observer contrasted the striving urbanites with the rural "Gentry, who can aim no higher, plunge themselves into Debt and Dependence to preserve their Rank."[30]

Common practices and beliefs did not make Charleston merchants mirror-images of their northern counterparts. Toward the end of the colonial period many overseas traders at an early age forsook the countinghouse for rice and indigo fields. This migration heralded the mass departure of the upper class from urban commerce, which made the nineteenth century patriciate a homogeneous and conservative social order. Beginning in the 1740s Gabriel Manigault, Miles Brewton, Benjamin and Thomas Smith, and others retired to their low-country estates and after 1764 Laurens "resigned the bulk of his commission business."[31] Early retirement, which deprived the business enclave of talent, energy, and resources, was approved in the urban community. The *Gazette* obituary of "Benjamin d'Harriette, formerly an eminent Merchant," mentioned that he "had retired from Business some years— Knowing when he had enough." In 1770 Peter Manigault also realized he had had enough: "As my Fortune is in such a Train that I think I may in a Year or two, if I live, devote the Rest of my Time to my own Ease & Quiet."[32] The compulsive quest for profit and repute which drove northern businessmen to intensify and prolong their efforts was being undercut by the lure of the leisured gentry, an aspiration which soon became the uncontested ideal for the patriciate.

The interdependence of enterprise, wealth, and power led to similar political behavior among the upper orders of South Carolina, Virginia, New York, and Massachusetts. The economic interests of the commercial and agrarian elites necessitated political leverage, and the provincial government was generally controlled by low-country planters and Charleston merchants. Beginning in the 1670s the first of a long series of Bulls, Izards, Middletons, and Ravenels entered the council and the commons house of assembly. For forty-five of the years between 1689 and 1776 members of the planter-mercantile oligarchy acted as chief executives of South Carolina, and of the forty-nine councillors between 1720 and 1763, eighteen were large planters and sixteen overseas traders. Family connections played a crucial role in obtaining public office.

Three generations of Bulls served on the council, and three of William Bull's daughters married into the Drayton and Middleton clans; the latter two families supplied seven more councillors. These three clans were in turn connected with the Izards, Blakes, Fenwicks, and Pinckneys, and the entire dynastic complex provided one-fourth of South Carolina's colonial councillors and nineteen of the forty-nine who served between 1720 and 1763. Leading Charleston merchants also served on this body.[33] It was more aristocratic than the Massachusetts Bay Council and similar in class structure to those of Virginia and New York. South Carolina governors looked for the same traits in their candidates as did the royal executives in New York. Governor William H. Lyttleton called one of his nominees "an English Gentleman of an exceeding fair Character who has been settled for many years in this Province, and is esteemed one of the richest Merchants in it," a description which echoed Governor Moore's nomination of Robert R. Livingston to the council in New York.[34]

The same figures and their relatives and peers dominated the assembly. After the 1730s, however, most aristocratic planters eschewed the assembly and Charleston merchants comprised the majority of its leaders. The departure of the planters gave this body an increasingly nonaristocratic composition as the Revolution neared. Although half the representatives of 1765 came from old families, 40 percent were self-made. Nearly half were merchants, lawyers, and physicians, though most of these were also large landowners and two-thirds of the assemblymen were wealthy. While the Virginia House of Burgesses was more aristocratic and rural in membership, South Carolina's assembly had a larger presence of wealth, family, and country gentry than did its cognates in New York and especially in Massachusetts.[35]

Great planters and merchants also filled other high offices that enabled them to promote their economic interests. Councillor and merchant Benjamin de la Conseillere was colonial treasurer in 1721, Gabriel Manigault and John Motte occupied that post from 1735 to 1770, when Henry Peronneau, Jr., Motte's son-in-law, succeeded him. John Barnwell served as deputy secretary and comptroller of South Carolina, William Rhett as colonel of the provincial militia, vice-admiral of the colonial navy, receiver general, surveyor general and comptroller of customs; William Bull as lieutenant governor and commissioner of Indian affairs; Ralph Izard headed the Indian commission and his son became the provincial attorney general; Charles Pinckney was chief justice of the supreme court and his son became commissary general; Barnwell and Councillor and merchant James Crockatt went to England as agents of the colony. Planters also held local offices, stepping-stones to provincial posts, such as road, causeway, and parish church commissionerships, and served as parish vestrymen. The latter imposed poor taxes and supervised education, assembly elections, and relief for the indigent.

The aristocratic political system duplicated the situation in Virginia, except that in South Carolina planters shared government influence with urban merchants, and the more fluid entry into the upper class permitted men like Laurens, John and Andrew Rutledge, Christopher Gadsden, and Charles Pinckney, coming from less successful older families or relatively recent immigrants, to acquire considerable power in the 1760s. Notwithstanding the achievements of these newcomers, dynastic politics created an aristocratic atmosphere in civic matters. In 1770 Lieutenant Governor William Bull II noted "a gratuitous execution of many branches of Power under a desire of shewing a public spirit and easing the public expences." Some assemblymen "disdain[ed] taking any pay," and other upper-class officials likewise served without salary.[36]

The mercantile component of the patriciate wielded considerable power. In 1719 merchants filled seven of twelve places on the council and also controlled it in the late 1720s and 1740s. Appointments to that body had to be cleared with the board of trade and the maritime elite had relatives and partners in London who influenced the board's decisions. After the 1730s a majority of the assembly leaders were merchants; overseas traders usually held the colonial treasurership; from 1726 to 1731 and 1749 to 1756 the colonial agent was a merchant; and, since the provincial courts sat in Charleston, the traders exerted an important influence over the judiciary. Like the planters in their parishes and the merchants in northern cities, overseas magnates served in local posts; the urban traders were as fire masters and market, workhouse, and street commissioners.[37]

Agrarian and maritime elites were bonded by economic and family ties. Political activity, by enhancing the ability of these groups to protect their mutual privileges and interests, further unified the enclaves. Harmony prevailed even in the recurrent controversy over currency inflation. Until the prosperity of the 1740s, planters occasionally, due to indebtedness to Charleston and Georgetown merchants, sought relief through modest emissions of local bills of credit. The mercantile community, largely because it included a number of squire-traders, usually split between moderates and hard-money advocates. Most of the prominent low-country agriculturalists and overseas traders, however, were moderates and succeeded in defeating up-country schemes for massive issues of local paper that might endanger the trading and creditor interests of the merchants. One of the rare confrontations between planters and shippers, won by the latter, arose over whether purchasers or importers should pay the duty on African slave cargoes.[38]

Apart from issues affecting the general well-being of the commercial community, businessmen with political connections exploited public office for personal gain. Treasurer Alexander Parris, in debt to Councillor Joseph Wragg, gave the merchant government money for business ventures. Treasurer John Motte also made private loans from public funds and let merchants delay duty payments. Laurens was first elected to the lower house in 1757 and in that year was also appointed commissioner of fortifications for Charleston, a post which governed the purchase of armaments for the city. Christopher Gadsden, Robert Brewton, and other merchant commissioners during the French and Indian War were similarly positioned to improve their own businesses as well as Charleston's defenses.[39]

Despite its influence, the maritime elite did not always defeat other interest groups. In 1727 the assembly limited the jurisdiction of Charleston courts, a move urban businessmen objected to because it curbed the number of debtor trials in the city. In the early 1740s the lower house increased the proportion of provincial taxes imposed on Charleston and decreased the interest rate on loans; both measures were opposed by the city merchants.[40] Infrequent setbacks did not develop into a fundamental threat to the rule of the indigenous elite until the end of the colonial era. In 1756 the board of trade began to fill the council with placemen and upheld governors who suspended independent councillors. As a result several aristocrats refused appointments to that body, thus taking the first step toward patrician opposition to the imperial system. The struggle between native leaders and British governors was intensified in 1762 when Thomas Boone refused to seat duly elected Charleston representative Gadsden. Gadsden and upper-class allies Rawlins Lowndes, John Rutledge, and Charles Pinckney became patriot leaders in the Revolution. Despite these conflicts, the merchants, prosperous and protected under the imperial trading network, initially resisted opposition to the Stamp Act and cooperation with the Yankee-inspired boycott of British goods. But the Townsend Acts, which increased surveillance of colonial shipping and led to the seizure of Laurens's vessels even though he was not a smuggler, turned the moderates into nonimporters and stimulated patrician support for independence.[41]

Like their peers in the North, distinguished South Carolinians entered the professions. Economic and political activities involved the upper class in legal matters and attracted the wealthy and well-born to a calling which functioned to preserve the social order and to experiment within it, and to enlarge the influence and resources of the upper rank. Hence law became an avenue for monetary accumulation, social prestige, and political power and a vocation for gentlemen. The earnings of eminent members of the bar (John Rutledge, the leading lawyer in the province, made £3,000 in 1765 and £9,000 ten years later, and Josiah Quincy, Jr., estimated in 1773 that the top attorneys received £2,000–3,000 sterling yearly) enabled them, as in the case of Rutledge and

Charles Pinckney, to recoup fallen family fortunes.[42] Prominent attorneys were based in Charleston, the commercial and political center of South Carolina. They often came from second-generation planter or commercial clans, as was the case with Rutledge and Pinckney. An illustration of law attracting the scion of a relatively recently risen family was the decision of John Laurens to become a lawyer because, as he declared, "I never have loved merchandise."[43] Thus was another merchant's son lost to trade. The newer and humbler family backgrounds of lawyers, as compared to planters, is indicated by the former's longer service in the assembly before elevation to the council and their more protracted wait between nomination and appointment to the latter.[44] The pre-Revolutionary bar was small in number and, like the upper stratum of the business world, success was facilitated by family and personal connections. Rutledge studied with his uncle Andrew and in turn sponsored his brothers Hugh and Edward, giving them their first cases. Julius Pringle, son of family-founding Charleston merchant Robert Pringle, read law with Rutledge, and the sons and nephew of Pinckney became lawyers. Widespread patrician membership in the profession can be seen from the "List of Attorneys Enrolled at Charleston, South Carolina from 1772 to May, 1779, Inclusive." It included eight Elliotts, four Hugers, three Pringles, three Grimkés, three Manigaults, four Pinckneys, four Prioleaus, six Rutledges, four Lowndeses, and others of distinguished lineage.[45]

The colonial bar in Boston and New York similarly drew the well-born, but the medical profession in South Carolina and Virginia differed from New York and Massachusetts by attracting a number of upper-class types. Some of the founders of the province's powerful clans—John Moultrie, Elisha Poinsett, and John Rutledge—were educated as physicians. Before the Revolution, William Bull, John Moultrie, John Moultrie, Jr., and Robert Peronneau practiced medicine. The greater representation of blueblood southerners was partly due to the health care needs of the plantation. A measure of the social standing of doctors was their activity in such elite associations as the Charleston Library and the St. Cecelia, St. Andrew's, and South Carolina societies, and in the appearance of physicians in the assembly and other public offices.[46]

Patrician membership in medicine and law continued after independence. Several religious, charitable, and cultural organizations also bridged the gap between colony and state. Charleston's Episcopal shrines of St Philip's (1710) and St. Michael's (1751), the city's First Presbyterian Church (1731), and the French Protestant Church (1681–82) were frequented by elite planters and merchants from their formation until at least the Civil War. Like Trinity in New York and King's Chapel in Boston, St. Philip's pewholders and officers were drawn from the upper class and housed the rites of passage in the same manner as did the northern churches. Although patricians did not become ministers, they were wardens and vestrymen of the parish and provincial commissioners for the Anglican Church. Aristocratic planters also became officers in other low-country parishes. St. Philip's rectors supervised Anglican activity in the Carolinas, parish officers monitored the elections of Charleston municipal officials from 1716 to 1775, and the church was the greatest initiator of public welfare projects in the colony. In 1751 St. Michael's Parish in Charleston was created. It, too, attracted patrician worshippers, donors, vestrymen, and wardens and took a prominent role in urban charity. The Society for the Relief of the Widows and Children of Clergymen of the Church of England in the Province of South Carolina was organized there in 1762.[47] The ritual, traditional high status, and control over important public functions attracted the wealthy and well-born to the Church of England. As indicated by lack of theological controversy and by the rarity of clergymen from distinguished families, respectability rather than religious feeling motivated adherence to Anglicanism. Yankee Josiah Quincy, Jr., visiting St. Philip's in 1773, described the urbane attitude of upper-class Carolinians when he noticed: "It was very common in prayer as well as sermon-time to see gentlemen conversing together."[48]

Although the upper rank embraced mainly Episcopalianism, the French Protestant (Huguenot) and the First Presbyterian churches catered to elite congregations before and after the Revolution. Elias Prioleau was the first pastor of the Huguenot shrine and, despite numerous conversions to the more socially prestigious Anglican faith, Mazycks, De Saussures, Porchers, Grimkés, and Ravenels, even after the Civil War, served as elders of the church. The flock of the First Presbyterian Church, from colonial times to secession, consisted mostly of rich Scottish merchants with a scattering of bluebloods such as the Bee family.[49]

Public welfare initiatives came largely from the maritime-agrarian elite, and the major institutional force in organized philanthropy was St. Philip's. In 1712 the legislature made the vestries of South Carolina parishes responsible for the appointment of overseers of the poor in each parish and for taxation and medical aid for the impoverished. St. Philip's, therefore, managed most of the early benevolence in Charleston. In 1736 the vestry built the first hospital in the province, St. Philip's Workhouse and Hospital for the Poor. Thirteen years later, the same body founded the Marine Hospital for sailors. The church also took leadership in educating indigent children. In 1712 the Free School at Charleston (1710) and the school of the Society for the Propagation of the Gospel (1711), both organized by prominent planters and merchants, merged and were put under the direction of St. Philip's. In addition to these efforts, St. Philip's was the largest institutional source of relief for the poor, contributing £1,000 in 1734 and £1,534 in 1738 for this purpose. Similar types of charity were undertaken in other coastal parishes by planter vestrymen.[50] Charleston, along with Philadelphia and New York, lagged behind Boston in relief appropriations. In the early eighteenth century the three northern towns spent much more on the dependent than did Charleston, but by the 1750s its welfare expenditures considerably exceeded those of the New York government.[51]

Apart from religious and public charity, private and secular urban institutions assisted the unfortunate. Like its sister branches in New York and Boston, the St. Andrew's Society of Charleston (1729) helped fallen members and their families. Run chiefly by prosperous Scottish merchants, it soon acquired a membership that included many leading families. The society was the earliest lay charity in the province and the oldest American St. Andrew's association. Throughout the nineteenth century it was headed by blueblood Charlestonians and Scottish merchants. Another long-lived humanitarian organization, the South Carolina Society (1736), was formed to aid widows and other needy members of the society and to educate their children. Originally dominated by Huguenot merchants, it soon included English and Scottish magnates and tidewater aristocrats. This society became the richest and most generous charitable organization in the colony. From the 1750s to the Revolution, Henry Laurens, Jacob Motte, Charles Pinckney, Miles Brewton, Peter Manigault, and other Charleston luminaries served as stewards (chief officers) of the society. Charleston, like Boston, had an Ancient Artillery Society (1757), which also began as a patrician militia company and outlasted the Revolution. This association, too, performed charitable and social functions. Gadsden became the first commander, and its colonial officers included prominent merchants, lawyers, and planters.[52] The southern port, as did New York, also formed a St. George's Society (1733), which, along with the German Friendly (1766) and Fellowship (1762) societies, assisted immigrants, paupers, and the insane while also serving as a social club.

Aside from institutional involvement, planters and merchants made individual benefactions. The most generous were also usually active in Charleston's cultural and charitable associations. Miles Brewton left £2,000 sterling for a college in South Carolina; Benjamin Smith, a vice-president of the Charleston Library Society, willed £500 sterling for a college in the province and £1,000 each to the city poor and the South Carolina and Charleston Library societies; Benjamin d'Harriette bequeathed £7,000 to charity (£3,000 to the South Carolina Society); and Gabriel Manigault made a legacy of £5,000 to the South Carolina Society.[53] Through personal and associational benevolence, planters and merchants exercised a role typical of elites throughout history. Public welfare leadership enabled the establishment to assume a highly visible leadership over important functions and large segments of the community.

Control over culture is another conventional method used to solidify upper-class sovereignty. As in Virginia, Massachusetts, and New York, higher education was viewed as a bulwark for patrician hegemony. Unlike these other colonies, South Carolina had no college, a situation partly due to the fact that many aristocrats went to England for schooling. Among the 114 Americans educated at Middle Temple, Inner Temple, and Lincoln's Inn, London's elite law schools, forty-four were from South Carolina while only five came from New York and three from Massachusetts.[54] Nevertheless, several planters and merchants left large sums for a college, and Laurens regarded its absence as "a great reproach upon our Public Character." Acting Governor William Bull II, requesting the assembly in 1770 to create a free school and a college to be located in Charleston, advanced a typical aristocratic argument for the proposed college: it was necessary for those "who by their opulent fortunes will be placed in the foremost rank of public servants."[55] Civic pride, class necessity, and material resources made the plan feasible, but the Revolution terminated the project.

Charleston also lagged behind New York and Boston in such features of urban culture as scientific, literary, and other intellectual accomplishments, the introduction of printing presses, and newspapers and numbers of books published, but it was the first American city to establish a free, government-supported, lending library (1698), a forerunner of the Charleston Library Society (1748).[56] The latter, like other charitable and cultural projects, owed its development chiefly to the maritime elite. Among the seventeen founders were nine merchants, two planters, two lawyers, and one physician. Gabriel Manigault presided over the society and lodged it rent-free. Many planters, belonging to the library and other voluntary associations in the city, inaugurated organizations in the rural parishes or in Georgetown which imitated urban institutions. Georgetown's Winyah Indigo Society (1740), a social club, intellectual center, library, and free school, was modeled upon Charleston societies.[57]

Membership of political and economic leaders in several voluntary associations discloses an interlocked elite that dominated commerce, government, charity, education, religion, culture, and high society. St. Andrew's president Dr. John Moultrie belonged to the South Carolina and Charleston Library societies. Gabriel Manigault and Henry Laurens were officers of the South Carolina and the Charleston Library societies and wardens or vestrymen at St. Philip's, and served in the assembly. Many of the members of elite organizations also belonged to the St.

Cecilia Society (1762), presently Charleston's premier and oldest social club.

The upper class easily equaled northern elites in artistic interests and accomplishments. In 1732, four months after the first public allusion to a colonial concert, which appeared in Boston, a publicly advertised musical performance took place in Charleston. During the decade before independence and throughout the nineteenth century the St. Cecilia, America's oldest musical society, dominated musical life in the city.[58] The stage was another patrician passion. Charleston's first theatrical season began in 1743 and a theater, the third in the colonies, was built in 1736. Plays, like concerts, were attended by the rich and well-born, and benefit performances for charity were sometimes given.[59] Resident painters came to Charleston around 1725, and in the 1730s the first drawing schools appeared. Prominent Carolinians had their portraits done by Benjamin West, John Singleton Copley, and Thomas Gainsborough, another sign of growing wealth and sophistication.[60] In art, as in music, the theater, religion, and education, the patriciate adhered to British institutions and styles. Charlestonians, wrote Eliza Lucas Pinckney in 1749, "live . . . much in the English taste." Reverend Alexander Hewatt, living in England in 1779, recollected that Carolinians aped British "luxury and extravagance."[61] Architecture, even more than art, attracted the aristocracy, and amateur and professional builders were closer to the gentry than were their northern colleagues to that region's upper classes. William Gerard de Brahm, Dutch constructor of the city's fortifications, wedded William Drayton's sister; Drayton, a well-connected planter and officeholder, dabbled in architecture and may have built the Charleston courthouse; and Peter Horlbeck, a German architect, became a Georgetown planter and founded a distinguished Carolina family.[62]

Charleston's reputation for amusement, elegance, and gentility derived from the extroverted grandeur of rich planters and merchants, an aristocratic atmosphere, and artistic interests. "The inhabitants . . . live in a very gentile manner," wrote Eliza Pinckney in 1742, "the ladies and gentlemen gay in their dress." Twenty years later *London Magazine* reported that "the rich people have handsome equipages; the merchants are opulent and well bred; the people are thriving and extensive in dress and life; so that everything conspires to make this town the politest, as it is one of the richest in America."[63] Charleston, with clubs, horseracing, dancing, conviviality, gambling, and fine wines and food, resembled New York rather than Boston. Visitor Quincy was impressed by Miles Brewton's mansion, which "exceeds [Boston merchants] Mr. Hancock's, Vassal's, Phillips's." The *haut monde* encompassed St. Cecilia balls, planters and merchants conversing about slaves and rice at the Friday-night Club, livelier evenings of feasting and cardplaying at the Monday-night Club, and horse races and dinner parties.[64]

Grace, gastronomy, and courtliness did not capitvate Quincy to the point of indiscriminate praise. The proper Bostonian made criticisms of the upper order that northerners and even some southerners would later repeat with increasing frequency and bitterness. The inhabitants were "divided into opulent and lordly planters," conspicuous in "magnificence and ostentation," and "poor and spiritless peasants and vile slaves." "Cards, dice, the bottle and horses" preoccupy "the gentlemen planters and merchants. . . ." Acknowledging the "hospitality and politeness" of the Carolinians, their guest "questioned what proportion there is of true humanity, Christian charity and love."[65] Quincy underestimated patrician political activity, and his reservations about upperclass altruism reflected New England's ethnocentric moral judgments, which, in the nineteenth century, so antagonized other regions, especially the South. Although arrogant and sometimes inaccurate, he pointed up certain traits, social distance between hierarchical groups, extravagance, and indolence that subsequent observers, including planters, would attribute—in encomium or in condemnation—to the gentry. As long as the entrepreneurial spirit flourished in Charleston and on the plantations, Quincy's description presented a flawed vision of the upper class. Its social origins, commercial pursuits, moral code, and civic activity bore marked resemblance to northern elites. At the close of the colonial era, however, the champions of burgher enterprise began to desert the wharf for the plantation. This transition increasingly differentiated the Charleston establishment from those in the northern ports.

THE ANTEBELLUM ERA

Revolution did not destroy the aristocracy. Patrician religious, cultural, and philanthropic organizations survived the upheaval with their leadership virtually intact. Nor did independence create a significant turnover in the upper class. A few prominent native-born merchants and planters fled to England; however, the exodus consisted mostly of British and Scottish overseas traders. Numerous Tories suffered amercement or confiscation of their estates, but the disabilities of emigration and expropriation were considerably eased in 1783 and 1784 when many, including forty-seven Charlestonians, were removed from the amercement list, confiscation was reduced to a fine, and a number of exiles were permitted to return. By 1786 most of the seized property had been restored and the economic ravages of independence stopped short of impoverishing the gentility.[66]

Economic Functions

COMMERCE

Although the birth of the republic did not trigger a massive circulation of elites, it precipitated or encouraged several economic changes in the ruling enclave. Most important was the decline of the mercantile elite, a result of disrupted imperial trade routes, contempt for commerce, and concentration of prestige, wealth, and power in the squirearchy. Several prewar merchants or offspring of old maritime magnates, however, reappeared or entered business in the 1780s. In 1783 Gadsen sought to recoup his fortune by going into partnership with his sons. A year later Edward Darrell, his brother-in-law Josiah Smith, Jr. (a relative of Benjamin and Thomas L. Smith), Josiah's cousin George Smith, and Daniel De Saussure formed Smith, De Saussure and Darrell, the foremost native post-Revolutionary firm in Charleston. City merchants and cotton and rice factors of 1809 still included many patricians, but the leading traders were largely postwar arrivals, usually of British and Scottish extraction. "The old merchants whose fortunes were easy, unwilling to risk their capital, gently retired from business. A new set who had little to lose by boldly venturing served their country and rapidly advanced their own interests," wrote David Ramsay, a Charleston capitalist-politician and son-in-law of Henry Laurens; "few Carolinians had resources left to enter into competition with British merchants."[67] American firms in Charleston in the late 1780s began to complain about English dominance, and Nathan Appleton, visiting Charleston in 1805, noted that "business here appears to be carried on . . . almost wholly by Jews. . . ." Of the twenty-one leading commercial houses in Charleston between 1795 and 1816, only one was owned and managed by a native of South Carolina.[68]

Connections with England, which facilitated the acquisition of capital and entreé into European markets, gave immigrant merchants an important advantage. But their displacement of indigeneous businessmen also occurred because of the social stigma now attached to trade. Edward Trescot, one of the Revolutionary maritime elite, after independence became a planter and his sons stayed on the land. Merchant Gadsden and Charleston lawyer-planter-statesman Charles Pinckney, grandson of a Charleston merchant, in the 1780s expressed the new priority of values. They considered "trade . . . only the handmaid to her *mistress*, agriculture." The nation "must depend principally upon the farmers and planters," who are "attached to the truest interests of their country." The "merchants were mere *Birds of Passage*" who changed their residence to seek "their fortunes." "Foreign trade" was America's greatest of "enemies" and the "source" of "future national calamities."[69] Ebenezer S. Thomas, editor-owner of the Charleston *City Gazette*, stated that by the 1790s "the aristocracy" felt it "disreputable to attend to business of almost any kind. . . . All the merchants with a very few exceptions were from the Eastern States, or Europe."[70] The eclipse of Carolina-born merchants and the declining status of trade and of the port was reflected in the Charleston Chamber of Commerce. Founded in 1784 and restricted to American-born businessmen, it lay dormant between 1795 and 1828.[71]

Preeminent merchants in the second quarter of the nineteenth century continued to hail primarily from outside the state. In the beginning of this period Georgetown planters' sons no longer became Charleston factors and traders, and the déclassé status of commerce was further confirmed by the fact that only about 1 percent of the 440 great slave owners of 1860 were originally urban businessmen or their children.[72] Robert N. Gourdin, son of a low-country squire and a member of an important midcentury mercantile house, noted that his brother Henry, who entered an export firm in 1819, was the first planter's son "to embark in a business [i.e. overseas commerce], on which the elite of the community looked down." A northern businessman, residing in Charleston, asserted in 1839 that five-sixths of the city's merchants were Yankee or foreign-born.[73]

The displacement of native-born businessmen may have adversely affected local capital accumulation. Adam Tunno died in 1833, leaving $130,000 in loans, cash, and investments. The bulk of these assets were tied up in ventures outside the state.[74] This example, too isolated for conclusive evidence, suggests that transplanted Charleston merchants were less committed than indigeneous entrepreneurs to keeping their capital at home. Perhaps the former, in their lifetime, could not cultivate the intense local allegiance that the latter inherited from previous generations.

Toward the end of the antebellum era, commerce became a more respectable occupation in genteel circles. In 1840 Thomas noticed that in recent years "numerous" Charleston businessmen were "descendants of those who once considered business degrading, but now see, that to secure to themselves the benefits of that commerce . . . they must take their commercial business out of the hands of British and Eastern agents, and attend to it themselves."[75] Among these descendants transacting "commercial business" on the eve of the Civil War were Ravenels and their Huger kin in Ravenel & Co., formed shortly after 1800 and the earliest post-Revolutionary overseas shipping house established by members of the agrarian aristocracy; Samuel Prioleau, a principal in John Fraser & Co.; and a number of scions of equally prestigious families. Despite this influx, the greatest midcentury merchants still generally derived neither from blueblood stock nor from the native-born. George A. Trenholm, head of John Fraser & Co., the city's leading merchant, was a native Charlestonian of undistinguished ancestry. John F. Blacklock, a partner of Robertson & Blacklock, the largest rice house in the city, was the son of a British-born Charleston merchant. Henry W. Conner of Conner & Wilson, a factorage and commission mercantile firm, and wholesale grocer George W. Williams, a self-made emigrant, originated in North Carolina.[76]

Post-Revolutionary changes in personnel did not appreciably modify maritime operations. Relatives and friends continued to form partnerships, as in the cases of Smith, De Saussure and Darrell, Gadsden and his sons, and Robertson & Blacklock. Typical of port cities, Charleston merchants organized a chamber of commerce to promote trade, stabilize currency, and regulate credit. Chamber officers and members were leading merchants, but the nineteenth-century presidents, like Conner and Trenholm, were mostly *parvenus*.[77] The relationship between planters and factors also varied little from colonial times. "My friend Alexander Robertson [a partner in Robertson & Blacklock] stood squarely behind me," reminisced planter J. Motte Alston. "They [Robertson and Blacklock] were both cousins of my mother's and were very devoted friends of mine. . . . When I . . . entered the profession of rice planting . . . Mr. Robertson came to me and said 'your grandfather made me what I am, and I wish to return all his kindness to you.' No man ever had a firmer friend than he. . . . Any amount of money I wanted in reason (from $1,000 to $20,000) I could have and no security asked. I never had a note in the book though I was at one time $45,000 in debt."[78] Social relations within the maritime elite also replicated the provincial experience. Successive generations of ancient Charleston business families, e.g., Colcocks and Gadsdens, went into trade. As a rule the *arriviste* element intermarried, e.g., the Trenholms and the Robertsons, rather than uniting with the aristocratic mercantile and agricultural groups. Alexander Robertson and John F. Blacklock, however, were cousins of the Alstons, and a few other self-made businessmen married daughters of the aristocracy.

Economic problems accompanied the downgrading of business. Compared with other regions and other parts of the South, the state's agricultural productivity and wealth rose sluggishly throughout most of the antebellum era. Soil exhaustion, the westward movement of the cotton kingdom, and the drop in cotton prices between 1819 and 1833 depressed land values and caused a net emigration rate which inhibited population increase. Hinterland stagnation compounded Charleston's disadvantage of having a smaller and more sparsely populated backcountry than did Baltimore, Boston, New York, Philadelphia, or New Orleans. Port activity depended upon shipping products to and from the surrounding rural area, hence the deterioration of South Carolina's agricultural position diminished Charleston as a maritime center. Trade in

Boston, Philadelphia, and New York flourished despite the decline of northeastern farming because of compensatory business expansion with emerging cities and towns in their back-countries. The relatively slow rate of urban development in the South denied Charleston this route to mercantile growth. By 1791 Charleston ranked well below the chief northern ports in total shipping tonnage handled and after 1819 the city experienced a long-term contraction and permanent eclipse in direct commerce with Europe. Between 1800 and 1804 tonnage in foreign trade averaged close to 40,000, a level not reached or surpassed until the 1850s. The antebellum value of imports, except in 1839, never rose above the 1821 total of $3,007,114. Exports reached $11,338,016 in 1825, a figure not surpassed until 1834 and not consistently exceeded until the decade before secession. Between 1856 and 1860, when Charleston peaked as a maritime center, the value of its exports and imports totaled less than one-fifteenth of that of New York and less than one-third of that of Boston, and was lower than that of Philadelphia and Baltimore. During these four years the southern city handled 5 percent of the exports (less than New Orleans and Mobile) and 0.5 percent of the imports of the United States.[79] A progressively larger share of South Carolina's staples were shipped from northern ports, which prevented Charleston from developing into a national commercial center and reflected the Palmetto State's colonial relationship to the North. Northern merchants took the plantation business away from Charleston factors because North Atlantic harbors provided cheaper and faster service for southern exports and imports. Northern sea lanes were closer to British cotton markets and the introduction of steam navigation made distance more important than favorable trade winds; the establishment of packet lines between Boston and New York and England and of coastal packets between these cities and southern ports expedited the shipment of southern goods in northern vessels; and northern merchants had better access to the domestic textile industry. Another adverse development, the decline of the West Indies, deprived Charleston merchants of a hitherto profitable outlet. Charleston's commercial position was also undermined in the South due to migration of cotton culture and to superior transportation systems and proximity to the West which enabled Savannah, Mobile, and New Orleans to draw business away from the low-country port and capture its up-country trade. The ebb of commerce was dramatically registered when real estate values in Charleston's business district began to fall.[80]

Although Charleston gradually lost out to other national ports, her salience as the low-country business center became greater. By the 1850s competitors in Beaufort, Georgetown, and other towns had disappeared and Charleston factors almost exclusively handled the decreasing share of the coastal plantation trade still conducted by local merchants.[81]

Problems in agriculture and trade did not lead to mass bankruptcies among planters and merchants. South Carolina's economy grew more slowly than did those of other states; nonetheless an absolute expansion of productivity and prosperity took place. Relative loss of position in commerce and agriculture hurt urban businessmen more than planters. The latter expanded their holdings as erosion of land and diminishing crop yields forced smaller farmers off the soil and out of the state. Emigration also held back urbanization and a larger demand for edibles which might have encouraged crop diversification and production of foodstuffs.[82] These factors, along with the decline of a vigorous yeomanry, precluded any successful challenge to plantation predominance. Economic constraints affected the commercial elite more adversely. Merchants suffered from the curtailed development of the back-country, which constricted their primary market. Planters had alternative outlets in northern shipping houses, while Charleston firms almost exclusively depended upon hinterland markets and products. Hence the commercial decline of the city limited the power and wealth of businessmen without threatening the mastery of the agrarian elite. Impediments to the development of towns and the emergence of an influential bourgeoisie removed another potential source of resistance to planter sovereignty.

Although the relative economic decline of South Carolina did not impair the local status of her rural gentry, it contributed to a feeling among planters and urban businessmen of being bypassed by other regions and newer states in the South and consigned to permanent inferiority within the Union. These anxieties manifested themselves politically in the nullification crisis of 1828–33, which placed South Carolina in the vanguard of a movement that eventuated in secession. Growing disaffection with the Union also deepened concerns about the economic situation of the region, particularly South Carolina and Charleston. Many became convinced that they were in bondage to the North and actively promoted a series of southern commercial conventions to escape this subordination. The first four (1837–39) focused on proposals for increasing direct trade between the South and Europe, a project deemed vital for achieving sectional autonomy and keeping southern capital at home.[83] During the 1840s and 1850s Robert Barnwell Rhett, a South Carolina assemblyman and attorney general, a U.S. senator and representative, and a delegate at several southern commercial conventions, and Henry Laurens Pinckney, speaker of the state's lower house and a congressman, claimed that Charleston's maritime resurgence depended on southern political autonomy. Rhett and Pinckney were fire-eaters, editors of the well-named Charleston *Mercury*, and descended from distinguished planter and mercantile stock. "So long as the Union lasts," wrote Pinckney in 1858, "Charleston and Savannah will be mere suburbs of New York and Boston. For our cities to be independent in trade, they must be independent politically of the North."[84]

Despite the sentiments expressed in the conferences and in the pleas of South Carolina's foremost capitalists and statesmen, schemes for expanding intercourse between Charleston and Europe ended in failure. The squirearchy refused to invest in projects to establish trade between Charleston and European firms, or in packet services to foreign ports. Planters preferred to send their crops to, and buy their goods in, New York, Boston, and Philadelphia, thereby undercutting efforts to foster Charleston commerce and retain capital within the state. Beginning in 1836 several attempts were made to organize transatlantic packet lines, but foundered when bankers and planters would not supply adequate funds and because of navigation obstructions in the harbor. In 1860 the first regular packet sailed to England, but the Civil War ended this service. Agitation for foreign commerce, a revitalized economy, and regional emancipation did not prevent an increase in the 1830s and 1840s of the North-South coastal trade, northern exports of southern crops, and a decrease of Charleston-owned vessels in foreign shipping. Charlestonians lagged behind their counterparts in northern ports in substituting steam for sail, organizing packet lines, and making harbor improvements. Between 1789 and 1860, next to California, Texas, New Jersey, and New Hampshire, South Carolina ranked last in federal expenditure for internal improvements.[85]

Geographical disadvantages and the distribution of power, wealth, and prestige inhibited commercial progress and eroded the entrepreneurial traits that had distinguished Charleston's colonial merchants. A visitor in 1839 declared that the city's businessmen's "character may not be remarkable for that persevering industry and close attention to minutiae in business which are so remarkable in the New England merchants. . . ."[86] Alarmed by the state's economic deficiencies and motivated by a growing defensiveness toward the North, Carolinians agonized over the situational adversities and spiritual inadequacies. New men—William Gregg, a West Virginia orphan who became South Carolina's leading manufacturer, and U.S. Senator and Governor James Hammond, once a poor up-country schoolteacher—bemoaned the tidewater traditionalism and the waning entrepreneurial impulse that hastened the flight of wealth and population.[87] In the early 1820s, when the city failed to recover from the Panic of 1819 as speedily as the rest of the country, Charlestonians began to worry about their economic destiny. In 1827 the *City Gazette* and the *Courier* criticized the eclipse of the port. A year later a chamber of commerce committee reported, "Charleston has for several years past retrograded with a rapidity unprecedented. Her landed estate has within eight years depreciated in value one-half. Industry and business talent driven by necessity have sought employment elsewhere. Many of her houses are tenantless and the grass grows interrupted in some of her chief business streets." In 1833 railroad president Elias Horry, offspring of the rural gentry, agreed with the chamber assessment of the 1820s and charged that these "evils" were "progressing" throughout the South while "Northern and Eastern States and Cities" increased in "influence and prosperity." Two decades later James Johnson Pettigrew, later a paladin of the coastal chivalry and then a Charleston law apprentice, grumbled that "The Life of half-employment one is compelled to lead here is tiresome beyond description."[88]

The economic decline of the city reduced the aristocracy's disdain for commerce. In 1842 William Elliott, a planter who served in both houses of the state legislature and was president of the Beaufort Agricultural Society, asserted the primacy of agriculture over other business activities. Nine years later, Elliott urged Charlestonians to expand trade with the West by constructing railroads and increasing shipbuilding and manufacturing. He now praised the merchants for their "activity, sagacity, integrity," but conceded "that they lack[ed] the dashing adventurous enterprise which distinguished the merchants of some other cities." Robert Y. Hayne, lawyer, railroad president, Charleston mayor, South Carolina governor, U.S. senator, and an officer of the commercial convention of 1838, went even further in supporting urban capitalism. Offspring of a noted but poor plantation family, he advanced funds to son William in 1839 to enter a partnership with an old Charleston importer "to rear up a young brood of Carolina merchants which I believe to be indispensable to put our Southern America on a right footing."[89] Such affirmations undoubtedly encouraged the reentry of patricians into trade and bolstered the confidence of the upper-class residue that had persisted through the decades of disrepute. James Gadsden's ancestor Christopher Gadsden had been an early spokesman of the superiority of agriculture over trade. The eminent capitalist and president of the Southern Commercial Convention of 1838 told the Charleston Mercantile Society in 1846 that Charleston rivaled northern cities until "the adoption of the American constitution." Since then "her commerce remained stationary" because of "the unequal distribution of the public revenue, and the continued prosperous condition of our agricultural pursuits; which attracted and confined enterprise and capital in that channel alone and made us indifferent and neglectful of commercial interests, which others seized and appropriated." Now, with capital going into trade and transportation, "Carolina has awakened to the truth, that her commercial and manufacturing interests are identified with those of her agriculture, and equally merit attention, ingenuity, enterprise and capital." He looked to the "intelligence, perseverance and energy" of the Charleston merchants to "rescue . . . the inheritance of your fathers . . . by resuscitating and restoring the commercial prosperity of your native city." A year later William J. Grayson, a Charleston lawyer and tidewater planter who represented the city in both state houses and in Congress and served as collector of the port, effusively praised the morality, intelligence, enterprise, and cultural and philanthropic leadership of the merchants. Patrician advocacy made commerce once again a respectable calling. In the 1850s Charleston artist Charles Fraser and mayor and congressman William Porcher Miles, descendants of distinguished families, noted with approval the return of aristocrats to trade and the readmission of businessmen into the city's select social circles.[90]

CAPITAL ACCUMULATION

Charleston traders, like other maritime enclaves along the Eastern Seaboard, sought to augment profits and sources of credit through banking, insurance underwriting, and speculations in the public debt. Participation of leading attorneys and political and agrarian elites in these operations unified the upper class in a manner similar to such interactions in northern cities. South Carolina's original bank appeared in 1791, when the Bank of the United States opened a branch in Charleston. With the incorporation of the Bank of South Carolina in 1792, a decade after the first bank in Philadelphia and eight years after similar institutions began in Boston and New York, a local bank at last appeared.

The BUS branch was controlled by the city's maritime elite, at first chiefly by the firm of Smith, De Saussure and Darrell. Its first president and cashier were partners in that firm, another partner was an original director, and yet another Smith, Charleston's Federalist congressman William Loughton Smith, was a director in the parent institution and exerted considerable influence over its branch. Most of the local directors were either newly risen or blueblood merchants. Edward Rutledge represented the Federalist political elite on the board.[91] In 1819 the Second National Bank organized a branch in Charleston. *Parvenu* commercial magnates along with a generous sprinkling of aristocratic businessmen proliferated among the officers and directors. The Charleston branch became the center of federal banking in the South and after the New York and New Orleans branches (centers respectively of U.S. banking for the Northeast and the West and Southwest) did the most business of the BUS branches.[92] The local BUS set the pattern for antebellum Charleston banks: the Bank of South Carolina, the Union Bank of South Carolina (1810), the Planters & Mechanics Bank of

South Carolina (1810), the Bank of the State of South Carolina (1812), the Bank of Charleston (1834), the Southwestern Railroad Bank (1838), the Farmers & Exchange Bank of Charleston (1852), and the People's Bank of Charleston (1852) were founded and managed by merchants, included key political figures as officers and directors, and catered chiefly to the city's commercial interest. In one respect alone, the *parvenu* enclave of the maritime elite generally overshadowing the patrician component, did institutions organized in the 1850s diverge from this prototype.[93]

The Bank of Charleston, formed to replace the defunct Second BUS branch, developed into the largest financial institution in antebellum South Carolina and was the only Charleston bank that survived the Civil War. Henry Gourdin, assisted by Conner and other prominent merchant bankers and statesman Robert Y. Hayne, was mainly responsible for its organization. Merchants Ker Boyce and Conner headed the bank between 1838 and 1850. Its major function, conventional for the city's commercial banks, was to aid the wholesale shippers.[94]

Since the other South Carolina banks, all located in Charleston, served primarily the port's commercial interests, the Bank of the State of South Carolina "had its origin," its president told the state senate in 1843, "in the distresses . . . especially [of] the Agricultural interest. . . ." The act of incorporation instructed the bank to assist agriculture through making long-term loans backed by real estate and establishing branches in the interior.[95] Fearing new competition and a diversion of capital, Charleston merchants and legislators opposed the institution. Stephen Elliott, who introduced the charter bill in the state senate and became the bank's original president, found that "the mercantile interest was rather hostile." In return he opposed the influential role that urban businessmen played in banking.[96] Beaufort planter Elliott's background and bias against commerce shaped his administration. He established branches in Georgetown and the interior and favored long-term loans with land as collateral over more profitable short-term commercial and mercantile transactions. In 1831 Charles J. Colcock, a prominent lawyer and justice of the South Carolina court of appeals and scion of a distinguished Charleston mercantile clan with ties to the squirearchy, succeeded Elliott and continued this policy until he retired in 1839.[97]

Without stinting on agricultural assistance, the bank, especially its main office in Charleston, gave considerable support to the city's commercial interests. "In the city and towns," noted a president in the 1840s, "our chief customers are merchants." Businessmen on its board used their positions to obtain credit for themselves or their friends; loans to directors who were factors usually covered their advances to planters.

These accommodations, often made to risky recipients on insufficient collateral, sometimes resulted in uncollected debts and evoked complaints by legislative investigating committees and apologies by bank officers. Aside from personal loans to entrepreneurs, the bank made credit available to the Charleston commercial community after the fire of 1838, thus saving many businessmen from bankruptcy. Under Colcock and President William Elmore, who had extensive manufacturing and railroad interests and was concerned over the economic stagnation of Charleston, it endorsed the bonds of the Louisville, Cincinnati, and Charleston Railroad Company and advanced considerable sums to that enterprise and to the South Carolina Railroad Company. Charleston capitalists supported these projects in the hope of increasing the city's foreign and interior trade.[98]

In many respects—leadership of merchants, prominent politicians acting as officers and directors, and the mixture of newly risen and blueblood businessmen—banking in Charleston resembled financial activity in Boston and New York. Former high government officials frequently occupied important posts in financial institutions. The Bank of the State of South Carolina presidents usually had been officeholders in the state or national governments. Daniel Ravenel, chief executive and cashier of the Planters & Mechanics Bank, was a former assemblyman, and Christopher G. Memminger, its solicitor from 1830 to 1850, was a Charleston alderman and head of the Ways and Means Committee of the South Carolina House of Representatives. James Hamilton, Charleston mayor, U.S. congressman, and South Carolina governor, was the first president of the Bank of Charleston. The Bank of the State particularly needed political influence because it was the fiduciary agent of the South Carolina government, its president and directors were appointed by the legislature, and that body closely supervised its activities. The Special Joint Committee of the legislature on the Bank of the State at Charleston declared in 1847: "None but a man of considerable strength in the Legislature can be elected its President and all its Directors rest on the same foundation for their appointment, and the keeping of their places." As a result of their influence with the state government, the bank and its officers carried considerable weight in South Carolina politics. Hayne, solicitor and director of the Charleston branch of the second BUS, was well aware of the power of the Bank of the State. In 1819 he told National Bank president Langdon Cheves, "nothing is to be feared from the Legislature of this state [regarding the BUS] unless unfavorable representations should be made by the President & Directors of our State Bank, in Charleston. That Bank as you know is the favorite child of the State & the confidence reposed in Mr. Elliott is so great, that any statement coming from him will be deemed conclusive. I certainly deem it of the last importance to preserve a good understanding with that Bank."[99] The Bank of the State constituted a formidable but not sovereign force in South Carolina's financial affairs. The limits of its authority were revealed in President Colcock's unsuccessful resistance to the founding of the Bank of Charleston. This opposition did not create a deep rift in the banking community. The older institution became the largest shareholder in the new one, and Conner and Elmore, later chief executives respectively of the Bank of Charleston and the Bank of the State, were friends and fought antibank forces in the state legislature.[100]

Another similarity between banking in South Carolina, New York, and Massachusetts was the financial ascendancy of each state's urban center. Charleston virtually monopolized banking in South Carolina. Until 1824 all banks in the state were located in that city. In 1860 half of the eighteen banks in South Carolina operated in Charleston, but $11,033,275 of the $14,962,962 banking capital in the state was held in Charleston banks.[101]

Significant differences also appeared between Charleston and northern banks. Long after the latter began to appoint professional financiers as chief officers, merchants and former public officials still headed the former. A planter's son who clerked in Robertson & Blacklock in the 1840s referred to George A. Trenholm, head of John Fraser & Co. and a Bank of Charleston director, as "the absolute master of local banking and the cotton trade."[102] The continued predominance of merchants and ex-politicians reflected the slower progress of capitalism in Charleston than in the North. Economic life in the southern city had not yet developed the specialization achieved elsewhere.

At a time when Boston banks heavily involved themselves in manufacturing ventures, Charleston's mercantile-controlled institutions still concentrated on commerce. Trenholm in 1837 wrote planter R. F. W. Allston, describing the precedence of the merchants before even the landed gentry, that Charleston banks refuse "country" notes unless endorsed by a "city . . . Merchant who must pay it up." Investment "in real Estate is generally deemed impolitic and unsafe for a Banking Institution, no matter what class of the Community may be the borrower."[103] Concentration of liquid capital in Charleston and control of financial institutions by the maritime elite meant that merchants had ample credit. Reluctance on the part of banks to fund packet lines and other schemes for direct foreign trade did not therefore arise from a desire to thwart overseas traders.[104]

Financial institutions shied away from these projects because of their conservative outlook. Unlike New York bankers, Charleston financiers adopted cautious policies. "The old banks in Charleston did not accustom themselves to handling, to any extent, foreign exchange," observed George W. Williams, a prewar wholesale merchant and Charleston's leading postwar financier; "they were very conservative in their business." This comment indicates the decline of the city's European trade and the insularity of its bankers. The Bank of the State and those in Charleston resembled Boston institutions in keeping a high ratio of capital reserves against circulating notes. In addition, the legislature made it difficult to incorporate new banks and, unlike other states, severely limited their indebtedness. These constraints constricted the supply of credit, but won approval from the commercial elite who controlled the extant banks, feared competition from new ones, and wanted sound money to maintain their own credit ratings and forestall agrarian debtors. Safe banking conditions prevented the failure of any Charleston institution prior to the Civil War, a striking contrast to the volatile money market of New York. On the other hand, antebellum Charleston had far fewer banks and much less banking capital than did other cities. The Bank of South Carolina was organized with a much smaller capital stock than the banks of New York and Massachusetts eight years earlier. As the decades passed, Charleston financial institutions in numbers and capital resources fell further behind those in Baltimore, Boston, New York, and Philadelphia. By 1851 banks in the southern city numbered less than one-fourth of those in Boston, one-ninth of the combined total in New York City and Brooklyn, and less than one-half of those in Philadelphia. The total capital of the Charleston institutions amounted to less than one-half of Boston's, under one-sixth of New York's and Brooklyn's combined total, and also ranked behind Philadelphia and New Orleans.[105]

Conservatism in Charleston financial circles was encouraged by bank officers from Old Guard backgrounds. New York banking after the 1830s drifted out of the hands of the Knickerbocker elite. Charleston merchants, however, dominated the city's banks until the Civil War, and the upper class was well represented in influential posts. Elias Horry presided over the Bank of South Carolina and Samuel Wragg was its cashier in the 1820s; Daniel Ravenel was cashier of the Planters and Mechanics Bank in the 1820s and president in the 1830s; Elliott headed the Bank of the State; and Henry Ravenel presided over the Union Bank in 1845–59. In the 1840s and '50s many tellers, clerks, and bookkeepers were also aristocrats.[106]

Charleston and northern merchants engaged in insurance underwriting to protect property, compensate shipping losses, and generate capital. In 1795 and 1797 the first post-Revolutionary insurance companies were chartered in South Carolina. Like their predecessor, the Friendly Society for the Mutual Insuring of Houses against Fire, they located in Charleston and sold fire insurance. In 1800 South Carolina, with two insurance corporations, ranked behind Massachusetts (five), Pennsylvania (four), and New York (three). Charleston merchants were influential in this field of business, dominating the boards of the South Carolina and Union Insurance companies. In the 1830s a Middleton headed South Carolina Insurance and several aristocrats served as directors. But neither the urban nor rural gentry matched the New York and Boston patrician presence in insurance enterprise. By the 1840s none of the Charleston firms contained blueblood directors or officers.[107]

The maritime elite and its political allies shared with similar groups in the North an affinity for speculation in the public debt. Charleston businessmen, along with New York merchant Nicholas Low and the house of LeRoy & Bayard, subscribed heavily to the state debt, and among the large investors were Smith, DeSaussure and Darrell and the Charleston branch of the first BUS. Laurens was the most extensively committed; others included Rawlins Lowndes (a planter and president [governor] of South Carolina in 1778), Josiah Smith, Jr., Federalist senator Ralph Izard (father-in-law of subscribers Gabriel Manigault and William Loughton Smith), and Charles Cotesworth Pinckney, then a Federalist assemblyman and party chieftain whose niece married Lowndes's son. Smith, De Saussure and Darrell also acted as the agent for London speculators.[108] The project was undertaken by the interrelated low-country, commercial, banking, and political elites. Upper-class speculations in the 1780s and 1790s set a precedent, reinforced by its role in antebellum banking, for continued involvement in securities and commodity dealing. Several Charleston brokers of 1860 came from distinguished families.[109]

TRANSPORTATION

The achievements of the tidewater elites in canal, turnpike, and railroad enterprise reveals a streak of innovative, technological entrepreneurship rarely associated with upper-class southerners. Unlike manufacturing and trade, planters and merchants jointly participated in the construction of transportation facilities, especially in the pre-railroad era. Since colonial times the landed gentry had been parish turnpike and ferry commissioners. After independence, the desire to move rice and cotton to Charleston and other ports and to increase land values kept estate owners active in transportation ventures. City merchants, dependent upon the back-country for cargoes and profits, shared these interests. Consequently, canals and turnpikes attracted capital from agrarian and commercial sources and, as was the case with the Hudson Valley grandees and the New York merchants, fostered cooperation between the squirearchy and the maritime magnates.

The Santee Canal (1786) was the first noteworthy waterway in South Carolina, one of the earliest in the South, and, before 1800, the largest in the country. It was designed to open inland navigation between the Santee and Cooper rivers, thereby facilitating connections between

Charleston and its hinterland and enhancing the city's domestic and foreign commerce. Planters sought benefits by employment of their slaves as canal labor, inflated land values along the passage route, and the promise of cutting costs of food shipped from interior farms. The appearance of merchants and planters on the board of the Santee Canal Company signified the rural-urban appeal of the project: Governor William Moultrie served as president and John Rutledge as vice-president. Ralph Izard, a prime initiator of the enterprise, along with William Loughton Smith, who became president in 1809, invested heavily in the company. Throughout its existence, prominent planters, capitalists, and statesmen involved themselves in the Santee management. Unanticipated costs, the spread of cotton growth into the Piedmont and the overland movement of that crop, lack of speed, frequency of accidents, and a shallow water level prevented extensive use of, or substantial profits from, the canal. In the 1840s it was preempted by a railroad connection between Charleston and the interior and was closed in 1858.[110]

The second largest waterway in eighteenth-century South Carolina, the Catawba Canal (1787), was inaugurated for the same purposes and by the same men that founded the Santee Canal Company, but proved a financial albatross and was abandoned. This group of planters, politicians, bankers, merchants, debt speculators, and canal builders in 1787 built yet another waterway. Their initiatives anticipated canal construction in New York, Massachusetts, and Pennsylvania—in the 1790s South Carolina surpassed these states in the number and magnitude of such undertakings.[111] A generation later, planters were still active in canal enterprise. Between 1823 and 1825 several squires constructed a waterway along the Santee to take goods from Georgetown to Charleston.[112]

The Charleston Bridge Co. (1808) built the greatest toll bridge in the state. Rural and urban gentry served on its original board and as officers in the 1830s and 1840s. Turnpike and canal construction dominated internal improvements before the advent of railroads, and Joel R. Poinsett, son of a wealthy Charleston planter-physician, zealously promoted these projects when he served on the South Carolina board of public works during the 1820s.[113]

In the 1830s transportation entrepreneurs shifted to railroads. New York and Massachusetts capitalists expected railroads to expand their vigorous manufacturing and commercial enterprises. For Carolinians, railroads were a more desperate and defensive device to rejuvenate a stagnant economy. The South Carolina Railroad (1830) was the initial instrument to reverse the diversion of up-country and foreign commerce from Charleston. Urban capitalists like William Aiken (the first president) and Ker Boyce were the original promoters and directors. Stephen

Elliott sold the company's stock in Charleston, the project was primarily funded by the city's business community and government, and the Bank of the State purchased large amounts of SCRR securities. Until the Civil War the chief executives and directors came mostly from the old and new wings of Charleston's banking-maritime elite. Elias Horry succeeded Aiken and John Ravenel (head of Ravenel & Co.), Mitchell King, James Gadsden, Henry W. Conner, and Hayne subsequently headed the road. The SCRR used the first locomotive in America built for actual railroad service and the first steam locomotive in the nation. It was also the first steam railroad to carry passengers, mail, and freight, and the first to have banked curves and a branch line. It had the first long-distance steam engine line, and when completed in 1833, became the longest line in the world. Despite these achievements, the railroad failed to recover commerce for Charleston, its earnings disappointed expectations, costs were higher than planned, and dividends were intermittent. An interesting if minor reason for the lines's failure was the refusal of the Charleston citizenry and government to let the road enter the city, therefore stopping it several miles short of the waterfront.[114]

In 1835 the SCRR promoters sought to improve Charleston's commercial position by building a railroad to Cincinnati. The Louisville, Cincinnati, and Charleston Railroad (LCCRR) again managed and financed chiefly by the urban mercantile and banking community and its political allies, folded in 1843, largely due to inadequate funding and an internecine squabble over the best route to the West. The Committee of Fifteen appointed to report on the feasibility of the line gave the usual geopolitical justification for such ventures: the northern attack on "slavery" threatened the "existence" of the South and could destroy "the Union"; an "intercourse with the Western States" might "avert this dire calamity." The committee further asserted that the construction of railroads in northern and other cities should "admonish the citizens of South Carolina, of the impossibility of their remaining stationary, while all around them are pressing forward." Robert Y. Hayne, who chaired the committee and became president of the line, also exhorted Charleston to retain "front rank among the cities of the South." He was alarmed over "wasteful cultivation of her [South Carolina's] soil and the state of almost 'colonial vassalage' to which her trade has been reduced." Irreparable loss of "prosperity, honor and renown" could be "counteract[ed] by the opening of fresh avenues to trade and new and more profitable employment of labor and capital." Access to the West would enlarge the Charleston market sufficiently to create a demand for direct shipment of goods to and from Europe, hence according to Hayne the "railroad, with the aid of the South Western Railroad Bank [the institution organized to finance the road], will achieve for us [Charleston] this important and peaceful victory [over the North]."[115]

The railroad became the panacea for the economic problems of Charleston, Carolina, and the South. In the 1840s and '50s southern commercial conventions emphasized internal improvements, especially railroads to the West, as the solution for the section's faltering growth; James Gadsden in the 1840s and William Elliott in the 1850s suggested the same formula for halting the decline of Charleston.[116] Out of this atmosphere came the Blue Ridge Railroad Co. (1852), the last attempt to establish a Charleston connection with the West. Its two presidents, Henry Gourdin and Edward Frost (former member of the state legislature and the state Supreme Court), were upper-class Charlestonians. With the aid of Christopher Memminger the project received considerable support from the municipal and state governments. This venture, too, failed to divert western traffic and collapsed in 1859.[117] The Northeastern Railroad Co. (1852), yet another abortive attempt to improve Charleston commerce, this time in the opposite direction, involved the business elite. The Northeastern was promoted and headed by the principals of Ravenel & Co. Nathaniel Russell Middleton, a planter who moved to Charleston and a former assemblyman and city treasurer in the 1850s, was treasurer of the road.[118]

Antebellum railroad development in South Carolina was unimpressive both in scope and in the realization of its purposes. State aid was less generous than in Virginia and North Carolina. Assistance from this source was curtailed by planter objections over possible increases in public debts and taxes and because plantations, located at the river bottoms, did not need alternatives to water transport. The Charleston government, on the other hand, more directly concerned with revivifying urban commerce, invested heavily in the Blue Ridge Railroad Co., the SCRR, and other projects. Although railroads drew more support from the city's business community than did harbor improvements or steamship companies, they were insufficiently funded and inefficiently managed. The LCCRR collapsed from deficiencies in capital and leadership and the SCRR suffered from the same problems. In 1849 James Gregg, active in SCRR affairs and a relative of the state's leading manufacturer, touched on these grievances in explaining his dissatisfaction with the new president. James Gadsden's appointment was opposed by "all the [Charleston] banks, the City Council, Insurance companies & societies, all the merchants, the large stockholders. . . . Gadsden regards the present as the greatest triumph ever gained in Charleston over the money power, the Bank of Charleston, Ker Boyce, William Gregg [another director] & the Graniteville Company." Since Gadsden came from the patriciate and his foes were *arriviste* entrepreneurs, Gregg may have been responding to a rift between old and new business elites. More important than personal or group differences, however, was the observation that "the money power of our City has certainly not the connection with this interprise which usually exist[s] in other Cities."[119] This conclusion derived from the assertion that Gadsden, Wade Hampton, Boyce, and James Adger, the wealthiest capitalists involved in the enterprise, had not increased their stock subscriptions. As a result of these drawbacks, between 1850 and 1860 South Carolina ranked ninth in adding railroad mileage among the states that later left the Union and slipped from third to fourth place in railroad mileage in the Confederate states. While railroads helped bring up-country and south-western products to Charleston, contributing to a 71 percent rise in the value of the city's exports and imports from 1850 to 1860, the lines did not capture western trade or dramatically improve overseas commerce. Nor did the railroads, as in the North, expand South Carolina's indus-trial base or diversify her economy. In fact, by making cotton shipments more accessible for Charleston, the lines extended the plantation sys-tem, thus inhibiting self-sufficiency, the retention of capital, and the development of manufacturing and international trade. "Of all the grand projects which cost millions of dollars," wrote William J. Grayson of the railroads, "one or two only served any practical end."[120]

MANUFACTURING

Charleston fell behind other maritime centers in every important sec-tor of commercial capitalism. The city's economic eclipse, well under way before the advent of large-scale manufacturing in America, was made irrevocable by the peripheral participation of South Carolina in the industrial revolution. Boston merchants perpetuated Brahmin as-cendancy by turning from the wharf to the mill; Charleston traders, faced with an even graver crisis, failed to make this transition. Unable to fashion opportunity out of adversity, the mercantile elite locked itself into a subordinate position vis-à-vis the agrarian aristocracy.

Before 1812, an age of comparative entrepreneurial vigor, rural and urban patriciates cooperated in several industrial undertakings. Begin-ning in 1776, with the spinning and weaving of cotton and woolen cloth on Daniel Heyward's estate, and ending in 1808, with the formation of the South Carolina Homespun Co. in Charleston, several cotton and rice mills were established in the low-country. Homespun, the first state-chartered manufacturing firm and the most important of these ventures, was planned by upper-class capitalists frequently at the fore-front of other major business enterprises. Seeking an alternative route to profits because Jefferson's embargo stifled shipping, they helped or-ganize the project. David Ramsay, an original director of the Charleston branch of the first BUS, became president, and several leading mer-chants were original directors. Six years later the Brahmins, similarly embarrassed by trade restrictions, organized the Boston Manufacturing Co. But the Charleston factory was not as well funded and after heavy losses suspended operations in 1815. Failure to get a state loan and the refusal of the municipality to make available a cheap and accessible source of waterpower, harbingers of planter and urban resistance to factories, complicated the company's affairs.[121]

A relatively positive attitude toward manufacturing prevailed in the early 1800s and was articulated in William Loughton Smith's speech at the laying of the cornerstone of the Homespun factory and in Ramsay's communication to the *Courier*. "The shuttle and the loom," declared Smith, "operating on the products of your fields, will in this century emancipate you from commercial thralldom" and provide an antidote to the stagnation in foreign trade. Ramsay expected that "many factories will soon be established over this state and indeed all the states."[122]

Subsequent developments belied these expectations. A disappointed Ramsay complained in 1815 about "stagnation of all business. Our people have not the versatility necessary to substitute manufactures or new works of industry for foreign commerce. Too many fold their hands & do nothing but complain of old times." After the war, urban businessmen returned to trade; most of the mills, small in scale, insufficiently capitalized, and producing for a local market, went bankrupt in the Panic of 1817. While industry flourished in the North, Carolinians closed their factories. In 1816, when a group of New Englanders founded the first permanent South Carolina cotton factory at Spartanburg, textile production began to spread to the Piedmont—its eventual home. The greatest expansion in cotton manufacturing occured between 1828 and 1838; sixteen mills were founded in this decade, most of them in the up-country. But the largest companies, containing the bulk of the capital, labor force, and spindleage in the industry, remained in the mid- and low-country. Thereafter, except for William Gregg's Graniteville Manufacturing Co. (1846), the industry declined; Graniteville excepted, fewer spindles operated in 1860 than twenty years earlier.[123]

The Charleston Cotton Manufacturing Co. (1847) was the first textile establishment to appear in the city since 1815. Unlike Homespun, this corporation was not organized by the upper class although it was later owned by Ravenel & Co. The company existed only five years, sharing the fate of three other contemporary short-lived cotton mills in Charleston. Few cotton factories were sited in the city, but the business community provided most of the capital for the textile industry. Charleston lawyer George McDuffie (a Georgia-born orphan who became a congressman, U.S. senator, and South Carolina governor), Mitchell King, and Ker Boyce were large shareholders in the Vaucluse Manufacturing Co. (1833) and the Graniteville Manufacturing Co. The latter, modeled on New England factories and the largest and most modern mill in the South, had a preponderance of *parvenu* Charleston merchant-bankers among its directors and chief financial supporters. Capitalists interested in the textile industry unsurprisingly also committed their time and resources to railroads. Rural and urban aristocrats, however, rarely participated in manufacturing, and the newly risen businessmen did not invest huge sums or assume managerial responsibilities.[124]

South Carolina cotton manufacturing faltered for the same reasons as did railroads. In both fields of antebellum industrialization, Palmetto entrepreneurs proved unable to provide adequate funding or direction. Insufficient liquidity was compounded by absentee ownership, technological conservatism, a sparse skilled labor force, constricted markets due to low population density and little urban growth, competition from domestic production on plantations and from more modern, cheaper, and more efficient northern processes, and an anti-industrial outlook. Even railroads, which in New England had a symbiotic relationship with Massachusetts manufacturing, worked against industrial development because the lines radiated out of Charleston instead of being centered in the Piedmont. These factors accounted for the low profits and frequent failures that plagued textile mills. Other industries encountered the same problems. Shipbuilding was more expensive in South Carolina than in New England or Philadelphia. Iron manufacturing, like textiles, suffered from paltry financing, low profits, and bankruptcy, and also declined after 1840.[125] These adverse developments contributed to South Carolina's fall, between 1850 and 1860, from fourth to fifth place in manufacturing in the southern states. Between 1850 and 1860 the state's industrial establishments decreased by 16 percent while factories in the United States rose by 14 percent. In that same decade capital employed in South Carolina manufacturing expanded by 14 percent; the national increase was 89 percent. South Carolina, seventh among the southern states (Maryland plus the Confederacy) in capital invested in industry in 1840 and 1850, slipped to tenth in 1860. From 1850 to 1860 the value of manufactured products in the state rose 22 percent, 64 percent below the national average. During this decade it was the only southern state whose increase in per capita manufacturing output fell below the U.S. average.[126] As a result, an integrated economy which might have curbed agricultural dominance and freed the state from its dependence upon the North failed to emerge.

The most recent and systematic examination of planter involvement in southern industry shows that only 18 percent of the South Carolina manufacturers owned more than fifty slaves. While 46 percent of the manufacturing capital in the state was owned by planters (proprietors of at least 100 acres of land who grew export staples), this group had a four-to-one ratio of capital investment in agriculture over industry. The leading industrialists of 1850–60 (owners of the top twenty firms or the top 1 percent, whichever was larger, as measured by value of output) in

South Carolina alone, of the six southern states where such data was available, invested more in agriculture than industry. The state's largest manufacturers were primarily planters, and rice milling was the only industry that significantly involved the landed gentry. They had steam powered mills on their estates, processing their own and their neighbors' crops, and some squires shipped the finished product directly to rice factors in Charleston. The largest mill in South Carolina, the West Point Mills Co. located in Charleston, was financed by local merchants, members of the city's first families, agrarian aristocrats, and Carolina statesmen.[127]

Despite the rarity of textile factories within its environs, Charleston was the industrial center of South Carolina. But the city ranked far behind other municipalities in manufacturing. In 1840, 3.5 percent of its residents worked in trade or industry, compared to New York's 13.8 percent, Baltimore's 8.3 percent, and Boston's 5.7 percent. According to a Charleston census of 1848, 6.5 percent of the population found employment in manufacturing, but in 1861 this figure fell to 2.1 percent. In 1860, Charleston ranked twenty-second among American cities in population and eighty-fifth in manufacturing (as determined from a composite measurement of capital invested, number of employees, and value of product), and was surpassed by New York and Philadelphia (respectively first and second in both categories), Boston (fifth in population and fourth in manufacturing), and Mobile, Richmond, and New Orleans. After the War of 1812, the tidewater gentry, blueblood Charlestonians, and entrepreneurs of newer vintage, with the exception of rice mills and railroads, did not intensively engage in manufacturing.[128]

The city's poor showing stemmed partly from the hostility and indifference that many Carolinians felt for industrialism. William Gregg, James Hammond, Elias Horry, William Elliot, William B. Heriot (secretary-treasurer of the chamber of commerce), and James Gadsden argued that prosperity and independence involved the development of manufactures. But the upper class had at best a secondary interest in such ventures. Land and slaves preoccupied the planters and, except for railroads, Charleston tycoons concentrated primarily on trade and banking. A Charlestonian in 1828 expressed "astonishment, that such an apathy should pervade our community against the encouragement of mechanics."[129] The tariff conflicts and nullification crisis of the late 1820s and early 1830s turned apathy into opposition. Many unionist leaders participated in textile enterprises, and the nullifiers regarded them as subversive protectionists. Political candidates became vulnerable to accusations of cotton mill investments, a hitherto noncontroversial issue in electoral battles. In the 1840s, during the search for solutions to the state's economic decline, the virulence vanished, but obstacles to industrialization did not disappear. Pre–Civil War South

Carolina had no general statute of incorporation, which created difficulties in chartering manufacturing as well as financial and transportation companies. Anti-industrial attitudes in Charleston took the form of passing an ordinance in 1836, substantially reaffirmed in 1845, prohibiting the erection of steam mills or the use of steam engines within the municipal boundaries except for a restricted area and then only with the consent of the urban government.[130] Inadequate investment, mediocre management, miniscule profits, financial disasters, slow growth, legal restraints, and a hostile culture discouraged the proponents of industry. William Gregg felt that it "will be the work of an age" to "upturn all our slothful & anti economical habits & make us as it were by magic a great Manufacturing people." His friend and associate, James Hammond, had the same opinion of southerners and warned that without "the manufacturing and commercial spirit . . . they are gone."[131]

South Carolina shared with most of the South a deteriorating economic position in the Union and a tangential involvement in urbanization and industrialization. Northern metropolises grew in population, wealth, and influence because they added industry to their commercial base, or provided the capital and served as the headquarters for great manufacturing corporations. Charleston and other southern cities lost ground because they were increasingly restricted to servicing shrinking agrarian hinterlands. The declining proportion of national wealth composed by agricultural products and such raw materials as lumber limited their financial and shipping activities and hindered their population growth. Urbanization, capital accumulation, and economic autonomy were further stifled when southern towns did not match northern and western cities in exchanging products brought to town for goods originating in the metropolitan area, its back-country, or the region. The urban South suffered high rates of emigration, a flight of capital to the North and West, and an increased reliance on relatively nonproductive functions, such as the resort trade and part-time residence of planters.[132]

These developments undermined urbanization in the South. The section's one-fifth share of cities in 1790 with more than 10,000 inhabitants was not surpassed until the 23.1 percent figure of 1820, the high point until after World War II. The South's rate of urbanization (by population in cities) lagged about fifty years behind the national average. In 1840–50 the South reached the national level of 1790, in 1900 it equaled that of 1850, and in 1940, that of 1890.[133]

Economic stagnation and opposition to the entry of working-class whites hindered population growth in Charleston and South Carolina. The low-country port had a much higher ratio of native- to foreign-born than did Boston, New York, and Chicago; Wilmington, North Carolina, and Richmond, Virginia, alone of towns with more than 10,000 people in 1850, had lower proportions of foreigners. Charleston also had a lower share of native Americans from other states relative to those born in the city or state than did Boston, New York, Chicago, and the other large cities in 1850. A similar situation prevailed in the state. According to the 1850 census, 92.3 percent of the white population was American-born, compared to 69.0 percent in Massachusetts and 68.6 percent in New York. Only 4.6 percent of the American-born South Carolinians emigrated from other states while 9.8 percent of the population in New York and 14.2 percent in Massachusetts were born elsewhere in the United States. In 1850 barely 3 percent of the Carolinians were foreign-born compared to 21.5 percent in New York and 16.6 percent in Massachusetts.[134]

Before independence Charleston had yet to experience the demographic symptom of urban malaise. Between 1720 and 1740 it had the highest rate of population expansion among the five most populous colonial towns and between 1730 and 1740 moved from fifth to fourth place. In 1775 the port had 12,000 inhabitants and in 1790 was still the fourth largest American city. In 1860 Charleston, with 40,522 residents, ranked among the four southern cities with more than 15,000, but stood twenty-second in the nation while New York, Philadelphia, and Boston persisted in the top five places. It also lost ground to Piedmont towns and never again equaled before the Civil War its 1790 share of the state's residents. South Carolina suffered the same sluggish growth. Between 1800 and 1870 its portion of the nation's population shrank from 6 to 2.8 percent. During this era the state trailed the national average in population increase, density of population per square mile, and proportion of city dwellers. Conversely, it exceeded America's average in balance of out-migration over in-migration.[135]

Emigration of native sons meant loss of talent as enterprising Carolinians rose to leadership elsewhere. Of the twelve graduates of Charleston's College of South Carolina who became antebellum governors, five served in other states; of twenty-one who became judges, ten sat on the bench in other states.[136] Loss of people and their skills was linked to the failure to expand trade, transportation, and manufacturing, and perceived as an independent element in the decline of Charleston and South Carolina. It is "truly afflicting, for one so much under the influence of *local* attachment," wrote Hugh Swinton Legaré in 1835, "to think of the old families of the State leaving their homes in it forever." Legaré, a Charleston lawyer who represented the city in the assembly and in congress, served as attorney general of South Carolina and the United States, and stemmed from both the rural and urban gentry, feared that the flight of the well-born showed "how terribly *uncertain* our whole existence in the South is."[137] An enfeebled economy could not offer the opportunities or rewards that drew or kept people. The thinly populated interior and the absence of concentrated settlements in turn limited the size of the market and labor force for trade and manufacturing, circumscribed the pool of available talent, and prevented revitalization of the upper orders by infusions of new blood and the emergence of a powerful urban elite.

PLANTERS

In 1860 ninety-seven of the 440 slave owners with 100 or more slaves on a single plantation in South Carolina resided in Charleston at least part-time. Conversely, only a few leading urban capitalists, e.g. Elias Horry, Alexander Robertson, and George A. Trenholm, belonged to this group.[138] The backgrounds and behavior of the 440 planters reflect ancient antecedents, territorial insularity, and lack of commercial and industrial involvement. Forty-nine of the ninety-seven with Charleston homes belonged to distinguished pre-Revolutionary clans. These included six Allstons or Alstons, three Izards, six Heywards, three Middletons, two Lowndeses, and three Pringles. Another eighteen married into these families, making a total of sixty-seven (69.1 percent) related to the aristocracy.[139] A much larger proportion of aristocrats persisted in the agrarian than in the commercial enclave of the city elite. Similarly, estate proprietors who were also Charleston-based were more likely to have such forebears than were their affluent contemporaries in New York and Boston. As shown in the comparison between the late-eighteenth-century Virginia gentry and the mercantile elites of New York and Boston, the tidewater squirearchy had more extensive aristocratic origins than did the urban upper orders. Large slave owners of distinguished ancestry among those not living in Charleston, however, were much rarer due to the more frequent presence in this group of up-country *parvenus*.

Only forty-one (9 percent) of the 440 were born outside of South Carolina, thirteen hailed from elsewhere in the South, eleven originated in the North (six from rich South Carolinians vacationing there), and seventeen were foreign-born. The planters who also lived in Charleston were even more inbred: three came from abroad, four from the North, five may have been and the rest definitely were native South Carolinians.[140] The birthplaces of this group were less diverse than those of leading Charleston or New York capitalists, and were comparable in homogeneity to rich Bostonians.

All other things being equal, such as age of settlement, landed elites tend toward a greater degree of inherited wealth and status and insularity than do commercial elites. Real estate is finite and immoveable while personal property is more easily transferred and, in the form of capital and production, is limitless in growth potential. Hence it is easier to exclude newcomers from a landed gentry than from a mercantile, indus- trial, or banking enclave. The preservation or expansion of personal property often depends upon a series of contacts and contracts which must be continually renewed and therefore can be canceled or inter- rupted within one lifetime or over a generation. The planters' rights to their estates were less easily breached since they did not involve renew- able types of interactions and were inherently continuous. Real prop- erty thus lent itself more readily to the kinship, traditionalism, and ro- mantic allegiance to blood, community, and class that characterize ascriptive social systems.

The marginal nonagricultural involvement of the large planters, even those who resided in Charleston, shielded the landed gentry from com- mercial or industrial permeation. Of the 440 great slave owners, ten were directors of the Bank of the State, and six of these ten had Charles- ton residences. An additional fifteen were heavily involved in enterprises other than agriculture, including six railroad presidents, one cotton mill owner, and Charles T. Lowndes, president of the Bank of Charleston. Only three of the fifteen, including Lowndes and Thomas F. Drayton, president of the Charleston and Savannah Railroad, also lived in town.[141] Planter investments reflected the primacy of their landed activities. Slaves made up most of the value of Edward Trescot's estate, much diminished from the fortune he accumulated in commerce, at his death in 1818. Arthur Heyward left $135,000 in personal property, all but $7,000 in slaves.[142] A mere corporal's guard of the squirearchy participated extensively in commerce and industry, and residence in Charleston, the state's leading business center, obviously did not draw the planters into urban capitalism.

Despite the general absence of planter leadership in nonagricultural enterprise, the landed elite, including those with less than 100 slaves in one place, sat on the boards of every important bank and railroad in South Carolina. Several estate owners sought to invent or improve in- dustrial machinery, and some low-country barons began to agitate for commercial and industrial progress.[143] Others, however, even in the 1850s when trade and other types of business became increasingly re- spectable in patrician quarters, continued to oppose such undertakings. Edward J. Pringle believed that investments in anything but land and slaves endangered the plantation system. "Slavery is right because the ruling class declare it to be right," claimed Frederick A. Porcher, an antagonist of railroad building, internal improvements, and commercial expansion. "Let the planter class feel itself inferior to . . . the merchant class," he warned, "and it will no longer have to defend an institution condemned by them."[144] This resistance stemmed from traditional preferences and priorities and from fears that economic change might encourage elites that would challenge the hegemony of the rural establishment. By the 1850s the gentry ambivalently contemplated commercial and industrial growth. Predictions that South Carolina and her social system could survive only through the advent of railroads, factories, and a vigorous mercantile enclave were confronted with forebodings that such developments would weaken the tidewater patriciate. Anxiety over possible displacement had a real basis: during the 1850s the coastal districts had the smallest slave-growth rates in the state, and Charleston lost one-half of her black population while white working-class inhabitants significantly increased.[145] Many planters feared that the loss of slaves eroded the economic and social base of the plantation system and that the emergence of a free artisan class might unleash egalitarian forces dangerous to the oligarchic social structure. Resistance to commerce also rose out of tensions between Charleston factors and their estate owner customers. If planter J. Motte Alston found merchant Alexander Robertson supportive, planter William Elliot felt exploited by George A. Trenholm's firm.[146] Although planters did not usually assume a prominent part in the trade, banking, railroad, and manufacturing ventures of Charleston and South Carolina, they played an influential role in the urban economy as providers of agricultural exports, as part-time city-dwellers, and as an enclave that influenced business and population growth. The impact of the rural elite in these areas was mainly negative: as agriculturalists their exhaustion of the soil and unwillingness to adopt innovations hindered crop yields, thus limiting the amount of goods shipped out of Charleston; as investors they put their money into land or slaves rather than into mills or railroads; as politicians they did not push for federal or state expenditure on internal improvements; as businessmen and consumers they discouraged immigration of white workers; as part-time members of the urban upper class they were more interested in developing Charleston as a recreational and cultural than an economic center; as agrarian traditionalists they looked with indifference or suspicion upon local entrepreneurs in commerce and industry.[147]

Politics

Charleston entrepreneurs and tidewater planters wielded considerable political power as officeholders and party factotums, or through kinship, social, and business associations with those in public life. A recent study of the South Carolina political elite of the 1830s showed that twenty-six of the seventy-five leaders made their homes in Charleston.[148] Influence in municipal, state, and national government fortified upper-class status by nurturing vital interests and by developing the skills, exercising the functions, and acquiring the prestige of leadership. High public posts in Charleston, as in Boston and New York, were often held by capitalists and lawyers who belonged to the urban elite. Unlike the situation in northern towns, however, planters also were elected to office. Mayors (intendants until 1836) between the 1780s and 1830s usually came from the squirearchy and the business elite. As in the northern cities, patrician chief executives fell off after this decade, and William Porcher Miles was the lone aristocratic mayor (1855–57) between 1841 and the Civil War. Aldermen (wardens before 1836) also included a heavy representation from the old families, and the Old Guard decline that occurred in the 1830s was less abrupt than that in the mayoralty.[149]

This decline of the patriciate occurred in a context familiar to the experience of other American cities. Even though Charleston had, relative to northern towns, a more aristocratic style and a homogeneous and native-born population, by the 1850s populist machines, factions, and ethnicity played an increasingly important political role. William D. Porter, Michael P. O'Connor, and Andrew G. McGrath received the support of the Irish community when they ran for public office, and most tickets included a representative of the German contingent.[150]

Aristocrats in Charleston politics did not, any more than in colonial times, raise the tone of elections or the quality of government. Governor Charles Pinckney called the 1800 presidential campaign in Charleston "corrupt." Grayson described the city campaigns of the 1820s as contests in which "one party was abused as aristocrats, the other as a rabble or mob. But . . . they differed on no important principles or purposes; they both bought votes at equal prices, and sought personal objects by similar means." Liquor flowed and fists flew on election days. "The only matter in dispute was whether one or the other should control the power and emoluments of the city government." Frederick A. Porcher, another low-country planter and Charleston resident, declared that the 1830 intendant contest between Henry Laurens Pinckney and James Reid Pringle, won by the latter, involved corrupt voting practices on both sides. According to James L. Petigru, the next election, in which Pinckney defeated Henry A. De Saussure, "was conducted very scandalously in many respects."[151] Charlestonians pursued the spoils of victory no less avidly than they did electoral office. William J. Grayson recalled that, in his various government posts, acquaintances and office seekers unremittingly entreated favors for themselves or their friends.[152]

Miles rose above this degrading routine with an enlightened administration reminiscent of Josiah Quincy's notable Boston reign of the 1820s. He replaced the night watch with a professional police force, established a house of correction for juveniles, improved sanitation and health facilities by building a pest house to halt contagion and filling in and draining marshland, and funded the city debt through a bond issue. For once an aristocrat validated the elitist rhetoric of South Carolina orators.[153]

Patricians initially dominated state as well as municipal bodies. Between 1779 and 1814 South Carolina governors invariably were tidewater estate proprietors with residences in Charleston. Eighteen of the first twenty-one chief executives dwelled in the city and not until 1816 did an up-country planter assume this office. After 1822 other parts of the state were better represented, but planters and capitalists from the coastal districts preponderated until 1860. The early governors were usually aristocrats, e.g., John and Edward Rutledge, Thomas and Charles Pinckney, John Drayton, Henry Middleton, and Joseph Alston. Beginning in the 1820s men of humbler origins and even the self-made, such as Robert Y. Hayne, Thomas Bennett, and James Hamilton (also mayors of Charleston), William Aiken, and George McDuffie held the office. This group, however, owned plantations.[154]

Low-country urban and rural elites were somewhat less prominent in the lieutenant governorship, but controlled the state senate. Although the Revolution increased the up-country and middle-class segments of the upper house, compared to the colonial council, planters from the coastal parishes maintained their dominance. The South Carolina, Maryland, and Virginia state senates were the most aristocratic pre–Civil War government bodies in the United States. Charlestonians David Ramsay, James Reid Pringle, and Henry Deas presided over the South Carolina state senate, and other bluebloods also sat for the city. Urban entrepreneurs were represented by James Hamilton and Ker Boyce. Here, too, the patrician presence waned after the 1830s; Elliot Huger (1838–42) was the last blueblood in the Charleston delegation, but aristocratic senators proliferated in the other low-country districts until the Civil War.[155]

Jackson Turner Main, contrasting the South Carolina assemblymen of 1765 and 1785, noted a substantial drop in median number of slaves and acreage, in levels of wealth, in rural and urban aristocrats, and in low-country representatives. Nonetheless, the well-born from Charleston and other parts of the coast continued to hold many seats. Between 1782 and 1805 patrician Charlestonians and tidewater planters Hugh Rutledge, John F. Grimké, John J. Pringle, Jacob Read, Robert W. Barnwell, Theodore Gaillard, and William Cotesworth Pinckney served as speakers. Throughout the antebellum era Charleston was represented by members of distinguished Old Guard clans. In the 1830s and 1840s aristocrats still represented Charleston, but their numbers declined from previous decades, and recently risen capitalists Ker Boyce and William Aiken joined the delegation.[156]

The political power of the great planters is also indicated by the extensive officeholding of the 440 large slave owners of 1860: 122 (27.7 percent) had served in the state legislature and seven of them became governor. Three other pre–Civil War chief executives had 100 or more slaves, but the holdings of two lay partly outside of South Carolina and another died in 1855. Fifty-two, while not serving in the state government, were local magistrates, intendants, wardens, or sheriffs, and another four were delegates to the southern rights convention of 1852 or the secession convention of 1860. Thus 178 of the 440 (40.5 percent) occupied federal (all of the congressmen and U.S. senators had served in the legislature), state, or local offices, or were convention delegates. Of the ninety-seven residing in Charleston only twenty-two (12.9 percent) were state senators or representatives, but another twenty-one were local officials (usually in their plantation parishes rather than in town) who had not been members of the state government. Five more sat in the conventions without holding other public offices. Few of these slave owners held local or federal positions in the city. This group consisted of one mayor, four aldermen, one collector of the port of Charleston, one master of chancery for Charleston County, and one trustee of free schools in Charleston.[157]

Among the state houses of the lower South in 1850 and 1860 (South Carolina, Georgia, Florida, Alabama, Mississippi, Louisiana, and Texas), Palmetto State legislators in 1850 had the highest median real and personal property and the largest proportion of planters and of those owning twenty or more slaves. In 1860 South Carolina topped the other states in these catagories, except for median real property holding: 53.5 percent of the South Carolina legislators in 1850 and 55.4 percent in 1860 were planters.[158] Planter predominance was fostered by constitutional arrangements which gave more legislative seats to the low-country than to inland areas and by South Carolina after 1808, fearing internal turmoil that might weaken it in struggles with the national government, not following other South Atlantic states in holding constitutional conventions which democratized their political structures. South Carolina surpassed even Virginia as the most oligarchic southern state. The Carolinians clung longest to property qualifications for office, coastal domination, elite local governments, choice of governors and presidential electors by the legislature rather than the people, legislative representation determined by amount of taxes paid as well as population, and a system of representation which let the coastal districts control the state senate.[159] "The government of South Carolina is that of an aristocracy," wrote James Hammond in 1850. "When a Colony, many families arose in the Low Country who became very rich and were highly educated. They were the real noblemen and ruled the Colony and State —the latter entirely until about thirty years ago, and to a very great extent to the present moment."[160]

The salience of the well-born, however, did not exclude the emergence of *parvenu* leaders who lived in Charleston. David Ramsay, son of an Irish immigrant, hailed from Pennsylvania; George McDuffie derived from Georgia yeomen stock; Christopher Memminger, born in Germany, began life in this country in a Charleston orphanage; state attorney general, Speaker of the U.S. House of Representatives, and U.S. Supreme Court Justice Langdon Cheves, originally from the up-country, worked as a day laborer; James L. Petigru, Charleston alderman and recorder, attorney general of the state, and U.S. district attorney for South Carolina, stemmed from a family of farmers and ministers too poor to send him to college; Civil War governor Andrew G. McGrath was the son of an Irish immigrant; and, from the German community, Jacob F. Mintzing and John Schnierle served as mayors in the 1840s. Despite their obscure origins, many of the *arrivistes* acquired plantations or married into the old upper class. McDuffie and Petigru wedded daughters of low-country planters; Cheves, McDuffie, and Ramsay (husband of a Laurens), acquired plantations; and Memminger's daughter married a Middleton.[161]

The analysis of the top seventy-five political figures in the 1830s confirms the waning but still formidable influence of planters, low-country residents, and old families. Next to law, plantation ownership was the most frequent occupation. Twenty were primarily planters and another nine managed their estates as a secondary vocation. Conversely, merchants, industrialists, and financiers rarely appeared among the foremost statesmen. Low-country inhabitants and the Palmetto patriciate were well represented in the elite: thirty-one lived in coastal districts, sixteen belonged by birth to the tidewater aristocracy, and five more came from distinguished up-country clans.[162]

Leverage in the state government was important to Charleston entrepreneurs. In the absence of a general statute of incorporation, special laws were necessary to secure charters for banks, railroads, and manufacturing companies. The major financial and transportation organizations, as previously observed, had powerful politicians among their officers. A similar situation prevailed in industrial undertakings. "He wants a 'retired Statesman' to . . . 'lead' in his project," wrote James Hammond in 1848 of Abbott H. Brisbane's attempt to start "a Machine Factory in Charleston." Brisbane asked Hammond, Cheves, and McDuffie to assume this task. Boyce and Hammond enabled Gregg to get a charter for the Graniteville Manufacturing Co., two ex-governors were among the twenty original stockholders of the West Point Mills, and the Nesbitt Iron Co. shareholders included a governor, a congressman, an ex-congressman, a judge, and three state legislators.[163] The legislature also provided benefits to businessmen whose political connections gave them access to the state treasury. George A.

Trenholm, Charles T. Lowndes, and Henry Gourdin, Charleston merchants, public officeholders, and heavy investors in the Blue Ridge Railroad, successfully used their influence in 1860 to obtain state subsidies for the line.[164]

Financial favors for cooperative officials forged another tie between businessmen and politicians. In the 1830s, Robert Barnwell Rhett, chairman of the assembly ways and means committee and attorney general of South Carolina, was a close associate of President William Elmore of the Bank of the State and had a brother on its board of directors. When Rhett encountered money problems in 1837, he borrowed extensively from the bank and in 1841 owed it $70,000. Politician Benjamin F. Perry reminisced that the bank "became in a measure, a political machine, and the politicians were very freely accomodated with loans by the board of directors." The Bank of Charleston adopted the same policy. In 1842, on payment of 10 percent of the liability, the bank freed its solicitor, Petigru, from his obligation as an endorser of notes of bankrupt James Hamilton, Jr. Aid to politicians sometimes carried to the grave. Charleston blueblood and *parvenu* capitalists subscribed to pay off the posthumous debts of John C. Calhoun; an identical fund had been created for Alexander Hamilton by wealthy New York merchants, bankers, and Federalists.[165]

Urban and rural elites were also active on the national scene. During the Confederation and Federalist eras the families who had ruled the colony continued in control, and the state and city backed a strong national government that would fund public debts; encourage manufacturing, banking, and commerce; support internal improvements and a protective tariff; and resist yeomanry radicalism. In 1785 the Charleston Chamber of Commerce joined the New York chamber and Boston merchants in agitating for congressional control over trade regulations. Both state houses approved the measure and also advocated giving Congress tax powers. In the Confederation congress, South Carolina's predominantly patrician delegation usually voted with the nationalistically inclined big states like Massachusetts and Pennsylvania, and against the small states. The upper class shared the concerns of northern elites in opposing mechanics and up-country farmers, fearing expropriation of wealth, and deploring excessive democracy and a weak central government unable to aid business effectively.[166] Just as the coast fought the Piedmont in the legislature, so the Charleston merchants triumphed over mechanics in the city when in 1784 Richard Huston, backed by the maritime and planter residents, won the intendant race.[167]

The South Carolina members of the 1787 constitutional convention in Philadelphia were leading lawyers and planters from the city and low-country. A year later Charleston and the tidewater parishes sent upper-class delegates to the state ratifying convention. From Charleston came the usual mixture of blueblood merchants, planters, and lawyers. The coast voted overwhelmingly for ratification, carrying the state against up-country opposition. Rural and urban elites, like their northern equivalents, approved the constitution for reasons of political stability and economic growth.[168] Upper-class Federalists dominated the city, state, and were influential in the federal government until 1800. In the 1790s John Rutledge served as chief justice of the U.S. Supreme Court, Thomas and Charles C. Pinckney respectively as ministers to Britain and France, and William Loughton Smith left Congress for the Portugese mission. The federal district court judges and the U.S. district attorney of South Carolina belonged to distinguished low-country clans. Federalist leaders in Charleston also controlled customshouse appointments. A Charleston merchant and brother-in-law of Smith became naval officer. The collector of the port, another city merchant, was related by marriage to U.S. senator Jacob Read. Upon obtaining the collectorship in 1795, James Simons wrote Read, a BUS director and member of the Charleston commercial elite, that "I shall entertain an affectionate and grateful sense of your affectionate attention and conduct towards me; and I shall endeavor, by a friendly and polite deportment to give satisfaction to the Mercantile Gentlemen."[169] Federalists Read and Ralph Izard were U.S. senators during this period, and Smith, Thomas Pinckney, and John Rutledge, Jr., represented Charleston in the House. Other low-country districts also sent patrician Federalists to Congress. Izard, Smith, Ramsay, Gabriel Manigault, John and Edward Rutledge, and Charles and Charles Cotesworth Pinckney, the leading Federalists, were mostly Charleston-based attorneys and planters bound to the maritime-banking elite by their law practices, kinships, and business involvements. Advocating assumption of state and national debts, a powerful central government, and Hamilton's financial plans, they became the political arm of the urban commercial community. The "respectable part of the mercantile interest" supports you, Smith assured the secretary of the treasury in 1793.[170]

Shortly thereafter South Carolina Federalism began to disintegrate. Charles Pinckney became a Republican in 1792 and, a few years later, Edward and John Rutledge, Jr., deserted to the Jeffersonians. In the late 1790s the Rutledges returned to the fold and the party enjoyed a brief resurgence. Electoral reverses, however, generated the same rifts as occurred elsewhere. Youthful careerists, dissatisfied with defeat, criticized the uncompromising attitudes and impractical techniques of their elders.[171] As younger men left, the party fell back on the Old Guard. Federalist leader Henry William De Saussure told John Rutledge, Jr., in 1800, "All the elderly men, of high Character, . . . will come out efficiently at the election [for the state legislature] & many of them will be candidates." Party nestors preferred purity to victory. "Many of our new-comers," wrote Christopher Gadsden in explanation of the Republican triumph in 1800, "brought on a strange reversement in our State. Our old-standers and independent men of long well-tried patriotism, sound understanding, and good property, have now in general very little influence in our public matters." He regarded "our planet [as] a mere bedlam," and felt "happy" that his "passage over this life's Atlantic is almost gained."[172]

While the Republicans captured the state government and national elections in 1800, Charleston and the low-country remained true to the ancient faith, showing the same persistence that characterized Boston and New York. "The Weight of Talent, Wealth and personal and family influence Brought against us," and "the influence of Banks and federal officers and English merchants," Charles Pinckney wrote Jefferson, cost the Republicans a victory in the city. Pinckney reported that his role in Jefferson's triumph "insured to me the hatred and persecution of the federal party for ever and the loss of even the acquaintance or personal civility of many of my relatives." Smith endured the same ostracism when he turned Republican in 1807.[173] But the demise of Federalism did not cause permanent conflicts in the upper class. In the early 1800s Governor John Drayton, Assembly Speaker Theodore Gaillard, Justice of the State Supreme Court John J. Pringle, and several Alstons were Republicans.[174] Moreover, the rich and well-born, still potent in the national government, continued to champion the interests of the squires and merchants. John Gaillard was U.S. senator from 1803 to 1826, and during the same period John Rutledge, Jr., Charles T. Lowndes, Langdon Cheves, Henry Middleton, Charles Pinckney, Joel R. Poinsett, and William Drayton represented Charleston in the House. Until the 1830s figures of equal eminence monopolized the judgeships of the U.S. district court in Charleston, the Charleston postmastership, the collectorship of customs at the port, and frequently served as U.S. attorneys for South Carolina. Up to 1824 upper-class and *parvenu* politicians supported high tariffs, a national bank, the U.S. Supreme Court, the doctrine of congressional implied powers, and federally funded internal improvements, and opposed the Hartford Convention. These policies reflected the interests of the agrarian and business elites.[175]

From the 1830s to the Civil War, even though the low-country aristocrats diminished in state power, they remained prominent federal officeholders. From 1823 to 1852, Robert Y. Hayne, William C. Preston, Daniel Elliot Huger, Robert W. Barnwell, Robert Barnwell Rhett, and William F. De Saussure were U.S. senators. Between 1826 and 1861 William Drayton, Henry Laurens Pinckney, Hugh Swinton Legaré, Isaac E. Holmes, and William Porcher Miles were among the city's congressmen. Only one representative, William Aiken, came from the newly risen capitalists. Patrician Charlestonians also retained the city postmastership until 1867 and the customs collectorship until 1865.[176]

As South Carolina proceeded from opposition to the tariff, to nullification, and, finally, to secession, Charleston, once the citadel of South Carolina Federalism, remained the unionist stronghold. Resistance to nullification came especially from the East Bay overseas traders, involved in the national rather than the local economy, who feared disruption of profits and whose railroad investments made desirable federally financed internal improvements, and from members of old and conservative planter and city families. Opposing them were artisans, retailers, planter residents of Charleston, and capitalists who feared an attack on slavery and the decline of the region and the state within the Union, and sought to make Carolina and the South economically independent of the North. In 1830 the Charleston unionists elected James Reid Pringle over Henry Laurens Pinckney in the contest for mayor and sent Joel R. Poinsett to the assembly. Two years later the states righters won the city election when Pinckney beat Henry A. De Saussure. For both campaigns the margin of victory was slender, reflecting the close division of the urban patriciate into both camps. Aristocrats in the Charleston delegation at the convention of 1832–33, called to vote on nullification, joined the tidewater patriciate in support of the antinationalist position. The controversy, however, failed to create a fundamental confrontation between the clashing upper-class factions. Unionists, primarily older men whose political influence had waned, gradually died off or retired, and South Carolina became more uniformly disenchanted with the Union in the late 1850s.[177]

Agitation over the Wilmot Proviso and enforcement of the Fugitive Slave Law again brought South Carolina fire-eaters into conflict with the federal government, and again Charleston was the loyalist bastion. Although separatist candidates in the state election of 1851 swept most of the low-country, they met overwhelming defeat in the city. Charleston merchants, along with aging statesmen Langdon Cheves, William J. Grayson, James L. Petigru, Joel R. Poinsett, Christopher Memminger, Alfred Huger, and James Simons, led the cooperationists. The state convention of 1852, by a two-thirds vote, tabled a motion to withdraw South Carolina from the United States. But an assertion of the right of South Carolina to leave the Union decisively passed with the unanimous concurrence of the upper-class delegates from the city and the tidewater area.[178]

By 1860 the extremist and moderate alternatives were immediate and unilateral secession or action in concert with other southern states. In 1858 states righter Miles replaced National Democrat Aiken as Charleston's congressman, and Memminger, moderate until that year, became a secessionist. Miles and planter William Grimball identified Charleston and especially "its mercantile interest" as "the most union loving and conservative portion of the State. . . ." Two years later most of the low-country elite resisted the radical secessionists. Its vehicle was the "1860 Association," organized and dominated by upper-class Charleston planters, professionals, and merchants who lived in Ward No. 1, the most exclusive section of the city, and supported by a majority of the coastal planters. Although they suffered one defeat in the city, the moderates ultimately prevailed in the struggle to keep Charleston a cooperationist bulwark. This time, however, they failed to halt secession.[179]

On the eve of rebellion the patriciate remained influential. William Gilmore Simms suggested that the secession party "put on its ticket a Rutledge, a Heyward, a Gadsden if one can be found of right lineage and decent ability."[180] At the South Carolina secession convention, Charleston's twenty-two delegates consisted of six planters, two planter-lawyers, one banker, three merchants, and one insurance company president. Fifteen had marital or blood ties with the agrarian aristocracy. One hundred of the 170 delegates were planters and leading merchants, and capitalists like the Gourdins, William Gregg, and Henry W. Conner also attended. Real property holdings per member averaged $35,349 (median $18,875), and personal property, $68,704 (median $50,000). The average slaveholding per delegate was 58.8 (median 37.0).[181]

Before the Civil War, South Carolina had the most oligarchic government in the nation, and Charleston and other coastal parishes repeatedly opposed measures to liberalize the political system.[182] The state government reflected a more open and intense commitment to hierarchy than prevailed in the North and provided a legitimacy for elite rule that, after the death of Federalism, was muted outside the South. Upper-class Federalist leaders in South Carolina shared the distrust for popular sovereignty that emanated from their allies in other sections. Charles and Charles Cotesworth Pinckney, Edward, John, and John Rutledge, Jr., Henry W. De Saussure, Francis Kinloch, William L. Smith, Christopher Gadsden, and David Ramsay condemned "levelling Principles," politicians with a mass following, and powerful lower houses; sought to curb the potential influence of voters with little or no property; and deprecated enlightenment theories regarding the natural virtue of mankind.[183]

Edward Rutledge conveyed to his son, about to depart for France in 1796 as private secretary to Minister Charles C. Pinckney, the proprietary, family, and class interests in government service that made aristocrats distrust social change and mass political participation: "The family my Son from which you have descended; the style of your education; the long and steady attachment of your uncle Pinckney towards you; the early acquaintance which you have formed with public men; the habits to which they themselves are accustomed of considering your nearest connections, as the property of their Country, form such a combination of circumstances as forbid the idea of private life." Fearing domestic disorder because of "constant migrations from every part of Europe," the elder Rutledge felt it "incumbent on the descendants of those, to whom America is indebted for her Independence to vindicate the rights of their Country and maintain them with as sacred a piety, as they would the reputation of their ancestors."[184]

Unlike post-Federalist patrician statesmen in the North, who either believed or at least publicly expressed democratic principles, the Carolinians persisted in the traditional creed. Their thought increasingly diverged from that of elites elsewhere in the country by the addition of a defensiveness which fixed the source of southern political and economic troubles in northern urban capitalism and a hostile federal system. A typical example of blueblood distaste for modern politics occurred in an 1818 exchange between Grayson and Daniel Elliot Huger, a Charleston lawyer-planter, member of both state houses, and a U.S. senator. Huger deplored democracy for making public officials servile demagogues and "thought it would be impossible for a man of any self respect to enter the arena of political strife." The choice was "rule or be ruled by the base," answered Grayson. In "a democracy or in any government" no "educated and influential property holder" can "rightfully or safely stand . . . apart" from "the conflict of parties."[185]

From the 1820s to the 1850s, in private letters, essays, speeches, and legislative bodies, Frederick A. Porcher, Edward J. Pringle, Henry W. Ravenel, Stephen Elliott, Daniel E. Huger, Robert Y. Hayne, William Gilmore Simms, Hugh Swinton Legaré, James Hammond, William J. Grayson, and George McDuffie negated majority rule as corrupt, impulsive, violent, and radical. They advocated an orderly and hierarchic social structure, grounded in slavery and ruled by a well-born, well-educated elite that abhorred change. These upper-class statesmen and their allies claimed that their values reflected southern attitudes and customs and that adherence to the cavalier creed would preserve the integrity and institutions of the South and enable the section to escape northern degeneracy and encroachment.[186]

The Professions

Law and medicine attracted the largest numbers of patrician professionals. Except for the prominence of the squirearchy, medical and legal vocations in Charleston differed little in structure and function from those in Boston and New York. The bar, from the colonial period to the Civil War, drew many aristocrats and also offered opportunities for talented seekers of fame, fortune, and power. Business interests needed skilled advocates, and successful political careers awaited those able to master the intricacies and ramifications of legislation. Antebellum Charlestonians Charles Fraser and newspaper editor Jacob N. Cardozo noted that "the law has always been considered a road to preferment in Carolina, and best calculated by its liberal studies to prepare a young man for public as well as professional life."[187] The mixture of *parvenu* and patrician and the expertise and aggressiveness of leading lawyers, however, caused some uneasiness about the calling. Knowledgeable attorneys on occasion intimidated aristocratic legislators. Planter William Elliott, an assemblyman from 1818 to 1832, felt unqualified "in the arena of debates with the regular gladiators, 'the lawyers.'" Nearing the end of his service in the lower house, he declared, "The lawyers . . . are literally *everything* here and *we* nothing." Petigru, Charleston's foremost attorney, asked, in 1835, "Can there be any bar in the Democracy?" American lawyers "disguise the truth by ambiguity and call the attorneys barristers . . . . as long as the employments are not kept distinct the profession must continue a trade, and there is no order of men from whom fit judges are to be selected and on whom the Bench can rely for assistance in the decision of cases or for support against popular clamor."[188]

Notwithstanding Petigru's fear of plebian pettifoggers, upper-class lawyers (by birth or achievement) rose to high places in the profession, politics, and the judiciary. Between the 1780s and secession aristocrats repeatedly sat on the state supreme court and lesser tribunals and served as state attorney generals and recorders (chief judicial officers of the city court) in Charleston.[189]

The luminaries of the Charleston bar in the 1790s were Edward and Hugh Rutledge; Thomas, Charles and Charles Cotesworth Pinckney; William Loughton Smith; John Julius Pringle; William and John Read; John F. Grimké; and Isaac Bee Holmes. Most were Federalist leaders or related to the party chieftains, close to urban entrepreneurs, and members of interrelated, aristocratic clans. Charles Pinckney and Hugh Rutledge, for example, were brothers of statesmen Thomas Pinckney and John Rutledge and married daughters of Henry Middleton. The elite derived its income largely from real estate, commercial, and admiralty law. Leading lawyers were retained by Charleston and British merchants seeking to collect or avoid maritime debts, administered upper-class estates, and often directly participated in urban business schemes. Smith, Grimké, Hugh Rutledge, and Charles Pinckney engaged in canal enterprises and sat on bank boards. The importance of commercial practice as a source of income is indicated by the impoverishment of John Rutledge. When Charleston's preeminent lawyer of the 1770s and 1780s returned to practice in the 1790s, he could no longer get mercantile clients.[190] Prominent attorneys resembled prudent merchants. Charles Pinckney had a reputation for keeping close accounts and being strict with debtors. "William Smith is so fond of business," reported Joseph Manigault, "that he pities the idle fellows he sees about Charleston." Smith alienated upper-class friends and relatives because he took his debtors to court. "I knew him [to be] attentive to his disbursements," said George Izard, "and fond of economy in his own person."[191]

After 1800 the Old Guard gradually gave way to a younger generation. The new elite consisted of bluebloods Henry, William, and Daniel De Saussure, William Drayton, Daniel Elliott Huger, Legaré, Samuel Prioleau, John Gadsden, and more humbly born Mitchell King, Langdon Cheves, Robert Y. Hayne, and Timothy Ford. The leaders, like their predecessors, held high government positions, counseled mercantile, financial, and transportation firms, and served as officers of banks and railroads.[192] Attorneys proliferated among the top seventy-five political leaders in South Carolina during the 1830s: twenty-one devoted themselves primarily to legal careers; another twenty conducted practices as a secondary calling, including eleven of the eighteen professional politicians in this group. Henry W. De Saussure, one of the leaders, son of a rich Beaufort merchant, became president of the state senate, Charleston intendant, chancellor of the court of equity, and president of the court of appeals. The influential jurist claimed that few of Charleston's outstanding lawyers devoted themselves exclusively to law.[193] Their business and political interests reflect the pragmatism of leading attorneys. Edward Rutledge warned his son that law would provide the basis for his income and political advancement and advised him "to practice it as extensively as possible; . . . it must be entered upon as a business. . . ." Thomas S. Grimké, another key power-wielder of the 1830s, told younger brother Henry, his law pupil and subsequent partner, that law "is necessarily a practical science and whoever expects to derive practical benefits from it must pursue it as a practical study. . . ." Thomas assured Henry, "you would certainly derive a great advantage in the management of the [family] property from possessing our Father's [John F. Grimké] knowledge of law." This attitude caused difficulties for Legaré, a renowned classicist and a member of the political elite. He had trouble obtaining cases because, "according to the vulgar argument, so finished a scholar was sure to be a mere *theorist*."[194]

For upper-class professionals, family, personal, class, and business connections continued to be essential in legal training and building a profitable practice. Henry W. De Saussure studied with Charles Cotesworth Pinckney, and Daniel Elliott Huger, William Lowndes, and Benjamin Elliott, Jr., with Henry W. De Saussure. Samuel Prioleau, son of a merchant, started as a clerk in an overseas trading house and later became a law clerk for William Drayton. When Prioleau established his own firm he handled the affairs of Adam Tunno and other notable maritime figures. Newcomers also ascended through patronage from aristocrats. Daniel Elliott Huger and Thomas Heyward sponsored Petigru, and assemblymen Huger and James Reid Pringle obtained for Petigru the Beaufort district solicitorship, thus expanding his law practice. Petigru came to Charleston in 1820 and formed a partnership with James Hamilton, Jr. The latter secured a large share of Drayton's business after Drayton became the recorder, and Petigru was similarly aided, in 1822, when Hamilton became intendant. Petigru later took in Henry C. King, son of his friend Mitchell King, and upon assuming the U.S. district attorneyship for South Carolina, appointed his own child as assistant. The elder King, a Scotsman, received cases through friendships with leading Charleston lawyers. Timothy Ford, originally from New Jersey, who became a city councilman, state legislator, and president of the Charleston Library Society, was a partner and brother-in-law of Henry W. De Saussure and later wedded the daughter of Prioleau. Robert Y. Hayne studied under Cheves, took over his clients when Cheves went to Congress, and married the daughter of Charles Pinckney.[195]

Like the Rutledges and Pinckneys of former times, legal dynasties developed in several families. Benjamin Elliott and Benjamin Elliott, Jr., John F. Grimké and his sons, and the firm of De Saussure & Son (1834) disclose typical upper-class kinship continuity. Ties were formed laterally, as well as vertically, through the intermarriages of Prioleaus and Hamiltons, Draytons and Gadsdens, and other examples given above. Despite self-made successes, the formidable patrician presence at the head of the bar and frequent alliances between the families of leading lawyers sometimes discouraged new men from pursuing a legal career. Lacking "family, friends or fortune," poet William Gilmore Simms left the profession because he "would never be anywhere more jealously resisted, than in a proud, wealthy community such as that in which I was born." William Henry Trescot, grandson of Charleston merchant-planter Edward Trescot, expressed a more positive view of this "old boy" network. He read law in the office of his maternal uncle, became a leading commercial attorney and associate in the Blue Ridge Railroad, and acquired a plantation by marrying into the Bull family. According to him, the business and professional life of Charleston in the 1850s was "leavened by the spirit of family connection and local prejudice." The "leading interest of its social and industrial life was represented at the bar by young men of character and ability, in whose fortunes the community were personally concerned; and the city was scarcely large enough for that sort of professional success which is entirely independent of personal connection."[196]

Medicine, as in the provincial era, was a favored calling for elites in South Carolina and elsewhere. Planter R. F. W. Allston's mother wanted him to study "physic" to "save yourself the expense of doctors' bills on your plantation and in your Family." Several planters became doctors, but, as with law, the most famous practitioners resided in Charleston. The versatile David Ramsay, also a leading Charleston physician, claimed that "the Study of medicine becomes daily more fashionable, and the first people in the State now educate their sons for physicians."[197] His contention was borne out by the emergence of medical dynasties in the Ramsay, Huger, and Moultrie families and by the frequent appearance of doctors in numerous other aristocratic clans. Here, too, family fortune and status facilitated professional success. The 1792 "fee-bill" of the Medical Society of South Carolina noted that no Charleston M.D. became financially independent through his practice alone.[198]

As in other cities, Charleston's medical elite regulated the profession by forming a society that controlled licensing and by dominating urban health care and the local medical school. The founders of the Medical Society of South Carolina (1789) included Ramsay and were state legislators and congressmen, presidents of the St. Andrew's and Charleston Library societies, and managers of the St. Cecilia Society. The society set medical fees and in 1817 became an examining board to license Charleston physicians. It encouraged medical education by agitating for the organization of the Medical College of South Carolina (1821), which was located in Charleston and was the original medical school in the South. The society also dominated charity and municipal health care, founding and running the Charleston Dispensary for the Poor, the Humane Society, and the Society for Treating Alcoholics, supplying physicians for the Poor House Hospital, operating Roper Hospital, and furnishing trustees for Shirras Dispensary. In addition, it promoted medical and other scientific research and established a botanical garden and society. As in Boston and New York, blueblood doctors dominated the society, the medical college, and the health services. Nearly twenty aristocrats headed the society between 1789 and 1861. President Ramsay was physician at the Charleston Dispensary for the Poor, Vice-president William Harleston Huger at the Charleston Orphan House, and upper-class doctors served on the staff at the Marine Hospital and as trustees of Roper Hospital. President Thomas G. Prioleau was dean of the medical school and Presidents James Moultrie, Peter C. Gaillard, Henry R. Frost, and other bluebloods were pre–Civil War faculty members.[199]

The extensive professional commitment of the upper strata is indicated by the fact that eighty-nine of the 440 large slave owners of 1860 pursued or were trained for careers in law, medicine, or the ministry. Similar to their political and commercial engagements, the ninety-seven who also lived in Charleston were even more active: twenty-four studied or practiced these professions. Forty-eight of the 440 slaveholders were doctors, thirty-eight were lawyers, and only three were ministers.[200]

Culture

Law and medicine served concrete upper-class interests. The teaching, ministerial, literary, and artistic professions attracted fewer blue-bloods and focused on less tangible but vital patrician concerns involving style, thought, and values. Antebellum Carolinians articulated typically southern cultural perspectives. Stephen Elliott, in an 1859 address to the College of South Carolina undergraduates, expressed a widely held regional viewpoint when he asserted that slavery made the South a land of "high culture. . . . A Planter can pursue his inclination for study or travel, for reading or art," and that from "a society of men of wealth and of leisure—ought to arise that patronage which shall give us men of learning of every kind." Some Charlestonians and visitors to the city contended that southern and Carolinian culture was flourishing or superior to northern intellectual endeavor. Ramsay noted in 1808 that "free inquiry and the enlivening energy of representative government" engendered impressive intellectual growth in the state. An English tourist in 1842 perceived "more general acquaintance with the popular writers of Europe among the society of Charleston than in that of Boston, with less of pretension."[201]

Claims about the refinement of the planter class and the slave society notwithstanding, most native commentators disparaged the state and the city's cultural accomplishments. Such deprecation paralleled widespread feelings of economic decline and political displacement and resembled the doubts of upper-class New York intellectuals regarding their metropolis rather than the self-confidence of the Brahmin intelligentsia about Boston. In the 1780s, in the *South Carolina Gazette and General Advertiser*, a Charleston newspaper, newcomer Timothy Ford, and Ramsay, who at least publicly became more optimistic, accused the townspeople (including planters and other patricians) of being frivolous, dissipated, and uninterested in the arts and sciences. Subsequent generations reiterated these charges. In the 1820s Charles Cotesworth Pinckney complained about the apathetic attitude toward fine arts among upper-class Charlestonians, and Stephen Elliott, seeking funds to establish an academy of fine arts in the city, criticized the lack of support "from our wealthy and fashionable citizens."[202] During the next decade the *Courier* deplored the indifference which, it editorialized, had killed off the Academy of Arts, the Academy of Art and Design, and the *Southern Literary Journal* and crippled the Literary and Philosophical Society and the Charleston Library. In the 1840s and '50s, James Hammond claimed that outside of oratory and politics southerners were not drawn to intellectual activity.[203] Hammond's friend, William Gilmore Simms, a newspaper and magazine editor and the South's leading author, argued that southern writers, lauded elsewhere, "perish" for want of material and psychic support at home. Poetry, painting, and architecture suffered a similar fate compounded by "monstrous abortions of taste" and by businessmen considering them not "useful" occupations. Simms felt that South Carolina, which failed to nurture Washington Allston, contributed to the cultural delinquency that plagued states below the Mason-Dixon line. Intellectual shortcomings were inseparable from other forms of regional inferiority, a condition that Simms attributed to its leaders. Plantation owners let "Northern States . . . supply" southern "wants" and cultural ideas. According to Simms, the north "ruled us, through the languour which we owed to our wealth and the deficient self-esteem naturally due to the infrequency of our struggle in the common marts of nations." His anger reflected the conviction that his "birthplace" [Charleston] refused "to acknowledge [his] claims" and made him feel like "a stranger."[204] Feelings of rejection were not paranoid fantasies. Planter J. Motte Alston remembered southerners as "ever a book-reading but not a book-writing people" who "rather looked down upon" their most famous poet. Moreover, Paul Hamilton Hayne, nephew of Robert Y. Hayne and Simm's successor as Carolina's foremost poet, harbored the same anxieties about the status of culture and his own reputation in the region and in his home state and city. Boston, the Athens of America, seemed infinitely more attractive to Hayne.[205] The testimony of Simms and Hayne may be tainted by their personal and professional disappointments. However, James Warley Miles, a blueblood Charlestonian in the coveted post of assistant minister at St. Michael's Church, "confess[ed]," as "a Southerner," to "mortification" over "a miserable deficiency in any well organized efforts . . . to further the cause of learning." In Charleston, anyone "devoted to the pursuits of scholarship and learning, would find no" decent "library . . . and no learned society or association to . . . aid him."[206]

Eminent Carolinians in science, art, and letters and the major intellectual, religious, and educational institutions of the state centered largely in Charleston. These schools, churches, and societies were dominated by elites, who, as in other places, enlarged their prestige and influence by controlling these organizations. Hence, any gaps that they discerned, or that otherwise existed, in the cultural framework must be attributed to weaknesses of resources or resolve in the upper class.

From colonial times until secession the upper orders in Charleston and the tidewater parishes provided most of the support and direction for low-country Episcopalianism. Aristocrats served as vestrymen or wardens at, donated money to, worshipped and were baptized, married, and buried at, St. Philip's, St. Michael's, St. Paul's (1810), St. Peter's (1833), Grace (1846), Church of the Holy Communion (1851), and Christ Church (1854). The squirearchy also involved itself in the religious affairs of the parishes where their plantations were located. In addition, the upper class was heavily represented in sectarian charities and at diocesan conventions. The patrician minority of other faiths worshipped at Charleston's French Protestant and First Presbyterian churches.[207] Extensive upper-class participation in religion is indicated by the facts that 282 out of the 440 (64.1 percent) of the great slave owners of 1860 and sixty-three of the ninety-seven (64.9 percent) who also resided in Charleston were church officers or benefactors of religious causes. Twenty of these city dwellers were officers in urban congregations, especially in those mentioned above.[208]

Rural and urban elites, through their avocational interests, dominated religious, charitable, and cultural activities while their primary leadership and professional commitments lay in agriculture, commerce, politics, medicine, and law. Relatively few patricians entered the ministry, but several became pastors of important Charleston churches and influential officers of the South Carolina diocese. Christopher E. Gadsden, grandson of the merchant, was rector at St. Philip's (1814–52) and Anglican bishop of South Carolina (1840–52). Other aristocratic rectors were Thomas Frost (1801–4), James DeWar Simons (1809–14), and John Barnwell Campbell (1852–58). Upper-class ministers also occupied pulpits in other influential and fashionable parishes. As Frederick A. Porcher put it: "Eminent success [for Episcopal divines] might lead to the possession of a Charleston pulpit. . . ."[209]

St. Philip's and St. Michael's continued to reign over South Carolina Episcopalianism. Five of the first six South Carolina bishops came from these shrines, and several rectors of other Charleston churches previously served there as assistant ministers. The two churches also played an important role in metropolitan life. The city's largest buildings, they housed public meetings and the deliberations of civic and patriotic societies. Their associated charity organizations assumed a significant share of poor relief and their influential vestry obtained city council appropriations for building repairs and municipal ordinances which enabled them to avoid urban discomforts. In 1807, for example, the Charleston intendant, a St. Michael's vestryman, secured a council ruling preventing horses and carriages from galloping past churches during services.[210]

Upper-class attitudes toward faith, as in most other things, were conservative in matters of organization, morals, and theology. Charles Cotesworth Pinckney, warden and vestryman at St. Philip's, a founder of the Charleston Bible Society, and vice-president of the American Bible Society, "dread[ed] innovation in the service of our Church." In

1803 the St. Philip's and St. Michael's vestries called a state Episcopal convention in order to revitalize the faith in South Carolina. Old Federalists and low-country patricians sucessfully led the movement to uphold the authority of the Episcopal heirarchy over the laity and the clergy of individual churches.[211] Patrician rector Paul Trapier was discharged by the St. Michael's vestry in 1846 because he wanted to admit to communion only those who had been confirmed. He attributed his departure to challenging "long established usages" in "a congregation made up in large part of old families, priding themselves upon ancestry and attached to the church rather because their fathers had been than from enlightened acquaintance with its principles" or from strong moral or religious convictions. Porcher attributed the success of South Carolina Episcopalianism to upper-class religious traditions. "The calmness and seriousness of the ritual commends it to every person of taste" and is preferable "to the wild enthusiasm" of revivalism. Stephen Elliott, an aristocrat who became Episcopal bishop of Georgia, in an 1862 sermon voiced the reactionary extreme, even by tidewater standards, when he blamed the moral degeneracy of America on "cast[ing] to the winds all conservatism." Opposing "monarchy and an established Church, we declared war against all authority. . . ." Opposition to "the one struck at the whole constitution of civilized society as it ever existed"; opposition to "the other denied the fall and corruption of man."[212]

Religion for the aristocracy was a moral censor that not only disciplined the passions of the masses but furnished the upper order with a model of propriety. This patrician ideal constituted an important, if secondary and somewhat contradictory archetype to the legendary southern cavalier. Both myths stemmed from Renaissance and Puritan England, and the paradigm of the Christian gentleman is exemplified long before the Revolution in the parental advice given by Ann Broughton, and Eliza Lucas and Charles Pinckney. Broughton in 1719 urged son Nathaniel to renew "vows and promises . . . made for you in your baptism," and "neglect no known duty, nor commission of any evel"; as "your chefest cair," prepare for "eternity" and "depend on the all-mighty for life and all things, and it is impieous to live without acknowledging that dependence by praying to him." A less personal and more familial and civic aspect of this genre appeared in the instructions Charles Pinckney willed in 1752 so that his son might become a worthy "head of his family," serve "his country," and "honour . . . his stock and kindred." Pinckney direct[ed] that Charles Cotesworth "be virtuously, religiously and liberally brought up. . . ." Eliza Lucas, wife of the senior Pinckney, emphasized the private and pietistic strain in Christianity. Mrs. Pinckney resolved "to keep a steady eye to His commands, and to govern myself in every circumstance of life by the rules of the Gospel of

Christ, whose disciple I profess myself, and as such will live and dye."
Urging her brother and son to live accordingly, she recommended "piety, . . . humility and charity."[213] During the nienteenth century Christian precepts continued to be invoked as a guide for patrician behavior.
John F. Grimké, assembly speaker, Charleston intendant, state supreme
court justice, St. Philip's pewholder, and delegate to South Carolina
Episcopal conventions, told his son in 1818 that "humility, which constitutes the greatest ornament of a Christian character," could not be obtained without practising "the principles of the religion we profess." The
"faultless model of the gentleman," wrote William J. Grayson in 1853, is
"furnished by the exalted characters of devout and holy men."[214]

Differences in the cavalier and Christian conceptions of gentility
created a conflict within the upper class over dueling. In 1804 several
prominent aristocrats appealed to Carolina clergymen to end this practice because it was "in direct hostility to the principles of Christianity."
Charles Cotesworth Pinckney, in 1826, helped form the Charleston Society to oppose such combats. Robert Barnwell Rhett, former president
of the Charleston Bible Society, rejected challenges because "I am a
professor of the religion of Christ."[215] Beginning in 1812 several anti-
dueling laws were enacted, but cavalier pride prevailed over Christian
pacifism and they were ignored. Christian sentiments occasionally led to
a broader condemnation of violence. Thomas S. Grimké, eminent
Charleston lawyer, philanthropist, reformer, and St. Paul's warden, opposed war as well as dueling. He wanted to establish "the Christian per-
fection of humility, forebearance, love and forgiveness. . . ."[216]

Education, like religion, occasionally engaged bluebloods vocationally, but more often as students, financiers, trustees, or officials. Similar
to religious and other cultural or charitable endeavors, patricians participated in a *nobless oblige* spirit that usually precluded professional
employment. Like elites elsewhere, the low-country aristocracy promoted schooling as a means of socializing the upper and lower classes,
the former to command, the latter to obey. Instrumentalism, however,
too narrowly defines the role that education played in upper-class life.
Along with religion it inculcated skills and values necessary to preserve
community leadership and achieve group unity. Academies and colleges brought well-born youths together to share common experiences
and reaffirm social and familial contacts. Control over public school systems reinforced elite leadership by enabling it to perform an important
communal service and to instill in the masses an acceptance of the prevailing social order.

Elementary schools in Charleston and the tidewater parishes existed
chiefly for the poor and were controlled by aristocratic organizations. In
1826 the South Carolina Society founded separate academies in Charleston for boys and girls; the St. Andrew's Society and the Charleston Or-

phan House also provided schooling for parentless and pauper children. The patrician Winyaw Indigo Society of Georgetown (1740), the John's Island Society (1779) of St. John's, Colleton County, and the rich squires of St. James, Goose Creek Parish, ran primary schools in the plantation parishes.[217]

Aristocrats, particularly Christopher Gadsden, Stephen Elliott, and Governors Arnoldus Van Der Horst, Charles Pinckney, and Henry Middleton, began agitating in the 1790s for a state system to educate paupers. In 1811, during Middleton's administration, Elliott guided a bill through the legislature establishing a state school system. Later studies and legislation for improvement of the system came from the same group, e.g., Stephen Elliott, Jr., and Edward Frost in the 1830s, and R. F. W. Allston in the 1840s. Charleston spent more per pupil and totally for schools than any other district and after the reforms of 1856–57 had the only system in South Carolina comparable to the North. The commissioners of free schools for the city of Charleston, appointed by the state legislature, ran the system. This post attracted leading entrepreneurs and statesmen and many patricians. Capitalist and planter educators sometimes confused altruism with self-interest. In 1849 school funds raised by tax assessment were invested in the South Carolina Railroad, a line in which School Commissioners Robert Y. Hayne and Elias Horry had been presidents.[218]

The motives of the commissioners received concise expression in their 1846 report to the legislature. Without schools the board expected "beggary, wretchedness, sloth," mob "violence," "political seduction" by "our unprincipled leaders," and "deficience [of] the authority of the law." Education promoted personal success as well as community order. Unlearned, "poor youth[s] could neither make skillful farmers, nor enterprising and successful merchants nor ingenious and intelligent mechanics, but would be fit only for the drudgery of bodily labor, or be confined to the narrow limits of manual dexterity."[219]

In 1856–57 the Charleston school board, headed by Christopher Memminger, who was assisted by commissioners drawn mostly from the urban patriciate, transformed the city schools from a pauper into a universal educational system. Using New York as a model, the curriculum was broadened, the tax rate raised, new schools built, additional teachers hired, a step system leading to high school implemented, a girls' high school and a normal school organized, and the number of pupils sharply increased. Memminger's 1858 report on the public schools articulated the bourgeois impulses that often inspired innovations made by upper-class Charlestonians. After asserting the importance of mass learning in a nation under popular rule, he argued that Charleston could become "a centre of industry and commercial enterprise" only if "superior intelligence and education" guides "those who are practically to conduct the business of life. A well educated mechanic, or storekeeper, or merchant" can "advance his business." The "united success of many such men . . . advanc[es] that community to the position of a great mart of trade and industry."[220]

Except for Charleston in the 1850s, public primary and secondary education was not successful. The state did not develop the potential talents of its citizenry to the degree that occurred elsewhere in America, thus inhibiting the economic and cultural growth of South Carolina. In 1857 Massachusetts spent $1,006,795 on public schools while South Carolina disbursed $200,000 and was the only antebellum southern state without a permanent public school fund. Few reforms were made in the system, and between 1812 and 1860 governors and independent and legislative investigating committees labeled it a failure due to state-wide apathy, lack of a centrally organized administration, ill-paid and bad teachers, insufficient financing, poor quality of education, and a pauper rather than universal orientation. An 1847 legislative investigating committee was appalled that other southern states "outstrip us in this benevolent and great work of diffusing knowledge among the people."[221]

Societies dominated by rural aristocracies tend to support mass education less than do burgher elites. The latter place more emphasis upon the acquisition of the classroom skills—reading, writing, and mathematics—that later prove advantageous in business. Cities, the historical centers of the professions and the life of the mind, also show greater concern for education as a preparation for intellectual and vocational endeavor. Since the bourgeois vision of individual achievement and upward mobility flourished more strongly in the urban North than in Old South plantations and since schooling was considered a fundamental prerequisite for wordly success, public education advanced further in Massachusetts and New York than in South Carolina. The landed gentry, however, displayed more interest in higher learning. By the nineteenth century, colleges had long established themselves as important agencies for socializing the patriciate by instilling genteel manners, associations, and culture. The planter-ruled Palmetto State devoted a larger share of its educational appropriations for this purpose than did the less aristocratic North and West. Massachusetts in 1857 spent one-tenth of its education budget for colleges ($107,901) while South Carolina, with only one-fifth of the Massachusetts expenditure on public schools, allocated more than half of its education appropriation ($104,790) to higher learning. South Carolina had the highest ratio among the states in 1860 of college students to white population and the South had a greater proportion of college students per white capita than any other part of the country. With a population one-fourth of that of Massachusetts, South Carolina had five more colleges and outnumbered every New England state in colleges, college students, and teachers. The total income of her colleges equaled that of Massachusetts and surpassed every other New England state.[222]

The significance of higher education to the squirearchy is indicated by the fact that 222 of the 440 great slave owners of 1860 and 220 of their fathers attended institutions of higher learning. The parents were more likely to be educated in Europe or in the North and their children in the South. Great slaveholders who lived in Charleston were even more likely (fifty-four out of ninety-seven or 55.9 percent) to go to college and matriculate in the North. The largest enrollments were in the College of South Carolina (ninety-five) and the College of Charleston (twenty-five), the most elite schools in South Carolina.[223]

The College of Charleston (1785) was the first such institution chartered in South Carolina. It got off to a shaky start due to sparse patronage and attendance by upper-class Charlestonians and was criticized for this performance by founding trustee David Ramsay and other local patricians. Between 1794 and 1805 and 1811 and 1825 no degrees were given and it functioned as a secondary school. The College of Charleston became a college in 1825, and by 1830 enrollment reached its nineteenth-century peak. Finances improved because of sizeable donations from Thomas S. Grimké and Elias Horry, and the advent, in 1826, of a yearly municipal appropriation. Another crisis occurred in the 1830s when the nullification controversy hurt funding and attendance. Unionist William Drayton was president of the board in the early 1830s and Grimké was another unionist trustee. The college closed in 1835 and reopened the next year under city funding. Poor management compounded inadequate revenue and political unpopularity in creating problems. Aristocrat Thomas Bee, Jr., principal (president) from 1798 to 1805, was a cloistered scholar and an ineffective administrator. In 1823 the board rejected the request of the medical society to establish a medical school at the institution, partly for lack of financial support and students but also out of fear that it would hinder the development of a liberal arts college. Consequently, the medical school became an independent institution. Attempts to enlarge the curriculum, liquidate the secondary school, and take advantage of the reverses suffered by the College of South Carolina in the 1820s and '30s were also rejected by the board. In 1850 a writer in De Bow's Review charged that "the advantages of the college" were not "diffus[ed] . . . widely."[224] In leadership, intellectual quality, and endowment the College of Charleston did not equal antebellum Harvard or Columbia.

The college was an integral part of the interlocked upper-class business, political, intellectual, social, and religious structure, and its deficiencies reflected weaknesses in the cultural atmosphere of Charleston. Virtually all the original trustees were members of the Charleston

Library Society, and the president and vice-president of the society sat on the college's board. Faculty members belonged to the society and headed the Elliott Society of Natural History, the Charleston Museum, and the South Carolina Historical Society. The first and fourth principals were also respectively rectors of St. Philip's and St. Michael's and later became bishops of the Episcopal Diocese of South Carolina. Nathaniel Russell Middleton, principal from 1857 to 1880, had been city treasurer and a railroad magnate and helped form the Carolina Art Association. Many professors (as at Harvard but not Columbia) and most of the trustees came from the urban elite and the low-country gentry. Between 1789 and 1862 Thomas Bee, Jr., Hugh Rutledge, John J. Pringle, Thomas Lowndes, William Drayton, Elias Horry, Thomas S. Grimké, Henry Deas, and Mitchell King in that order headed the board.

Close ties between the municipality and the college also resulted from the mayor's position as an ex-officio trustee, and Robert Y. Hayne, a regular trustee when mayor, began the annual government allocation for the institution. The civic pride invested in the school was voiced by one Charlestonian during a fund-raising drive in 1847: "Let us emulate the noble Bostonians," he declaimed in a plea echoed by New Yorkers seeking similar inspiration for cultural efforts, "in our manifestations of love and liberality to our native city . . . and render her . . . in learning, arts and refinement, the Athens of the South." This spirit materialized in donations and in the community prominence of many alumni. Thomas S. Grimké, Horry, and Ker Boyce were generous benefactors of the college and among its graduates were Charleston and tidewater bluebloods and eminent figures like Daniel Elliott Huger, Langdon Cheves, Paul H. Hayne, and Nathaniel Middleton.[225]

Upper-class control of the college was unblushingly depicted by Frederick A. Porcher, professor of history and belles lettres from 1848 to 1888. He "had reasonable hopes of being the professor" because "everything in this country depends upon favor and influence. . . . My brother-in-law" was an "Alderman of the City" with "a seat among the trustees," and "the Mayor" was "favourable to my appointment. Among the Board of Trustees I had other friends, and a number of well wishing [friends] outside." He might have added that the principal and four-fifths of the faculty were related to him when he acquired his post.[226] Porcher's account of his successful candidacy revealed an aristocratic unconcern about the dubious merit of ascriptive privilege.

The College of South Carolina, subsequently the University of South Carolina, was chartered as a state institution in 1801 and located at Columbia. The initiative for this institution, like that of the College of Charleston, came from aristocrats, chiefly Thomas Rhett Smith and Henry W. De Saussure in the assembly, Charles Cotesworth Pinckney in the senate, and Governor Drayton. De Saussure and other patricians connected with the College of South Carolina felt that the up-country would eventually rule the state and hoped that the school would educate the new rulers and help heal the rift between the interior and the coast.[227] The trustees frequently came from the distinguished clans that proliferated on the College of Charleston board, and Hugh Rutledge, Daniel Elliott Huger, Henry W. De Saussure, James L. Petigru, Langdon Cheves, Robert Y. Hayne, Henry Middleton, and James Hamilton, Jr., served at both institutions. But nullifiers, up-country planters, and powerful state political figures were more numerous, and unionists rarer, among state college trustees. Cultural leaders Grayson and Legaré also served on the board. The aristocracy was somewhat more involved in the administration and faculty at the Charleston school, but Stephen Elliott, Jr., son of the president of the Bank of the State, Robert W. Gibbes, and Robert Barnwell, president from 1835 to 1841, were professors at the College of South Carolina. Alumni in government posts included eleven of the twenty-one South Carolina governors between 1824 and 1865; at least one U.S. senator from South Carolina between 1830 and 1860; and, with one exception, the assembly speakers between 1824 and 1860. In 1858, fifty of the 112 members of the lower house and nineteen of the forty-three in the upper house were former undergraduates. The student body, especially after 1820, when South Carolina grew more insular and increasingly sent its sons to local schools, frequently stemmed from urban and rural elite stock, but the college also served, as did Harvard, as a passport to success for talented youngsters from obscure origins such as George McDuffie, James L. Petigru, and Christopher Memminger. Before the Civil War the low-country, particularly Charleston, had the highest percentage of its students in proportion to its share of the state population, and the great majority of undergraduates came from the coast and the Piedmont, the major slaveholding sections of South Carolina.[228]

Like the College of Charleston, the school at Columbia stressed the classics, and attempts in the 1840s and '50s to introduce electives were defeated by the traditionalists. A pillar of conservatism, the College of South Carolina drew up-country criticism for being a tidewater citadel. If the debating societies accurately reflected student opinion, it was indeed a bastion of planter values. During the 1830s these organizations defended slavery and nullification, in the next decade they called for secession, and they opposed unlimited white suffrage and popular election of governors and presidential electors. Although the college supported social orthodoxy and powerful political movements; educated the upper class; trained future state leaders; and the governor, lieutenant-governor, assembly speaker, and state senate president were ex-officio members of its board, it was not amply funded. In the late 1820s the legislature appropriated about $10,500 yearly to the college compared to the $16,000 and $15,000 that the Universities of Alabama and Virginia respectively received from their states.[229]

Southern patricians shared with the European gentry and nobility an inclination for military training, a legacy of the age of chivalry notably absent in northern and western urban commercial elites. Except for West Point, the major military academies—Annapolis, the Virginia Military Institute, the Arsenal, and the Citadel—were located in the South, the last two in Charleston. Southerners were also disproportionately represented, relative to their share of the national population, at West Point, in the officer corps, especially in the higher ranks, and in the infantry. In accord with the European aristocratic tradition, southerners constituted a majority of the cavalry officers.[230] Carolina bluebloods reflected the sectional military commitment. Senator Ralph Izard sent his son to a German military school and secured a commission for him in the U.S. Army. William Loughton Smith urged the secretary of war in 1798 to encourage "respectable men to give good military educations to their children, which can be most effectively done by rapid promotions of those who have been well educated." Some Charlestonians preferred the Navy, and John Rutledge, Jr., used his influence to obtain an appointment as midshipman for his brother. Planter William Lowndes, Charleston resident and congressman from the Beaufort District, in 1815 wanted his "sons to be, one a good general, the other a good admiral."[231] Frederick A. Porcher noted that in the 1820s prominent Carolinians frequently sent their children to military schools, especially to Partridge Military Academy in New Hampshire. In 1826 the fifty South Carolinians there comprised one-sixth of the cadets; among the twenty-six Charlestonians were several from renowned families. In 1842, as distaste for the North led Carolinians to attend southern schools, the Arsenal and the South Carolina Military Academy (the Citadel) were founded. The former was patterned after the Virginia Military Insitute and the latter upon West Point.[232] Apart from service and education, Charlestonians manifested their interest in military affairs by sustaining in the 1850s, with 40,000 residents, twenty-two militia companies. The romantic impulse of the cavalier vision was not the only source for militarism. Eminent Charleston lawyer Richard Yeadon in 1854 declared that "slavery and its exposure of us to hostile machinations render it doubly incumbent on . . . Southern states, to cherish a military spirit and to diffuse military science among our people."[233]

The landed gentry's interest in education is shown by the fact that 172 of the 440 (39.1 percent) of the large slave owners of 1860 acted as patrons, officers, and trustees of colleges or academies and medical schools, commissioners of free schools in their parishes, and members of societies that maintained local primary schools. Seventeen were trustees of the College of South Carolina and over 100 were commissioners of free schools. Thirty-five of the ninety-seven (36.1 percent) also living in Charleston were similarly involved, six were trustees of the College of South Carolina and four of the College of Charleston.[234] The rural gentleman's conception of his role in this and other public posts was expressed by Professor Porcher in 1849. The ex-planter argued for public schools and pauper education and against centralizing the public school system or paying school commissioners and other officials: "We confess that we still have faith in the benevolence, the integrity and the public spirit of the Carolina Gentleman, and we are proud to see them assume parish and district offices to which no compensation is attached." The school commissioners "now act under that high sense of moral obligation which so eminently characterizes our country gentlemen. A paid controller or a salaried board would convert this obligation into one of law purely."[235] Thus did the Tory ideal of local sovereignty resting upon *noblesse oblige* leadership prescribe the planter role and public responsibility.

Most upper-class Carolinians, New Yorkers, and Bostonians, and virtually all American colleges, were committed to a curriculum of Greek and Latin. A minority of the patrician intelligentsia, however, dissented from the genteel tradition, and arguments on both sides of the issue were identical in both regions of the country. Thomas S. Grimké was the foremost proponent of educational reform. In 1827 he asserted that indoctrination in ancient subjects encouraged immorality and imitation and undermined republicanism and Christianity. Grimké advocated modern science, history, literature, and "the agricultural and mechanical arts" as conducive to the happiness and improvement of the people. Hugh Swinton Legaré answered Grimké with a conventional defense. He envisioned "a cultivated and a literary nation," a goal which required "the study of the classics . . . to make accomplished, elegant and learned men—to chasten and to discipline genius, to refine the taste, to quicken the perceptions of decorum and propriety, to purify and exalt the moral sentiments. . . ." Self-made McDuffie and Simms reiterated Grimké's agruments and aristocrat and College of Charleston professor James Warley Miles shared Legaré's perspective, but social origins did not necessarily determine the lineup in this debate. Grimké had distinguished lineage, and Grayson, a scion of coastal planters, also contended that schools of "mechanical arts" were "as beneficial to the people as those that give lessons in Latin and Greek. . . ." On the other hand, newly risen Petigru advised his nephew to acquire "the marks of a polite education."[236] Opponents sometimes arrived at the same conclusion: Simms felt that lack of a classical training had excluded him from the social and cultural elite and Petigru claimed that such credentials facilitated admission to high status. Except for Simms, the principals in this controversy were trustees of the College of Charleston and the College of South Carolina.

Religion and education were the main upper-class cultural concerns, but other activities, more specialized and less obviously involved with maintaining social order, also drew patrician attention. Characteristic of aristocracies throughout history, low-country bluebloods dabbled in science, *belles lettres*, and the arts, more as partons than as practitioners. Intellectual life centered in Charleston, where, like Boston, the upper stratum dominated the intelligentsia. The southerners, however, neither rivaled the Brahmins nor had a vigorous intellectual community, as did New York, outside elite circles.

The existence of a metropolitan center in a territory ruled by a landed gentry helped make Carolina preeminent in southern science. Charleston housed the Charleston Museum, the Medical College of South Carolina, the College of Charleston, the Medical and Agricultural societies of South Carolina, and the Elliott Society of Natural History. Urban capitalists, e.g., Christopher Memminger and George A. Trenholm, and socially prominent and politically powerful figures— James Hammond, Henry Laurens Pinckney, Joel R. Poinsett, Thomas S. Grimké, John Drayton, and Stephen Elliott—promoted science on the national and local levels and engaged in amateur research.[237] Money, organization, and encouragement attracted the professionals (teachers and researchers) necessary for a scientific community. Planters were interested in natural history, chemistry, and medicine, particularly as these disciplines touched on estate problems. Many of them, living in Charleston, came in contact with scientists and financed and more directly participated in scientific efforts. Finally, the leisure available to urban and rural aristocrats sometimes led them to research and experimentation.

Appropriate to the concerns of upper-class Carolinians, the Agricultural Society of South Carolina (1785), the second oldest in the nation, was the first scientific organization founded by the elite. Its aristocratic officers and members included the foremost planter-statesmen. The institution's accomplishments in improving agriculture and husbandry through scientific methods, however, were at best intermittent. Porcher, a member of the society, called it in the 1830s "only a social club."[238] More significant in the annals of Carolina science were the Charleston Museum (1777) and the Elliott Society of Natural History (1853). The former, the oldest in the country, in the 1850s under the curatorship of Francis S. Holmes became the outstanding natural history musuem in the South. It began under the auspices of the patrician Charleston Library Society, and Holmes, a Charleston blueblood, was professor of natural history and geology at the College of Charleston, where the museum was located for twenty years.[239] The Elliott Society had close connections with the museum and the college, meeting at the school, storing its books in the college library, and making contributions to the museum. Lewis R. Gibbes, the first president, taught at the college and Holmès was the original secretary. Other antebellum officers also came from leading Charleston clans. Before the Civil War the society regularly published its investigations and deliberations.[240]

In addition to institutional involvement, several patricians were botanists, geologists, biologists, chemists, physiologists, and medical researchers. This group—Stephen Elliott, Henry W. and St. Julien Ravenel, Frederick P. Porcher, Lewis R. and Robert W. Gibbes, Middleton Michel and Francis S. Holmes—comprised Carolina's leading scientists. All but Elliott were born in the second decade of the nineteenth century in or near Charleston, did their best work in the 1850s in that city, and received considerable encouragement from membership in or recognition by local scientific bodies and through studies or faculty posts at local colleges and professional schools. Their achievements gave national recognition to the scientific community. In 1850 the meeting of the American Association for the Advancement of Science was held for the first time in Charleston, several local scientists were original members, and in 1861 Robert W. Gibbes became a vice-president.[241]

Upper-class attitudes toward science encompassed traditional aristocratic dilettantism along with the bourgeois utilitarianism that permeated American elites. In 1807 Governor John Drayton, an amateur botanist, expressed the avocational ideal. The study of plants was "connected with the purist principles of morality and religion," a "delightful recreation" that "unbend[s] the mind from more serious pursuits." This notion of a genteel hobby was far removed from the professional commitment of the institutional and college-based patrician researchers of the 1850s and from Thomas F. Grimké's feelings that scientific studies would advance American morals, freedom, power, and wealth.[242]

Although control over arts and letters reposed in the same class and in the same city, Carolinians did not match scientific with humanistic accomplishments. A survey of efforts in literature, history, art, and music properly begins with the Charleston Library Society, the best library in the South and the oldest and most influential cultural organization in antebellum South Carolina. It possessed the largest book collection in the city, sponsored the Charleston Museum, inspired low-country library societies, and participated in the administration of the College of Charleston. High social and cultural status enabled it to attract such luminaries as presidents Charles Cotesworth Pinckney, Henry W. De Saussure, Stephen Elliott, Joel R. Poinsett, Frederick A. Porcher, and David Ramsay. Despite its importance and influential membership, the society for a century and a half received only one cash bequest.[243] The Literary and Philosophical Society of South Carolina (1813), which housed the Charleston Museum for twenty years, was another Charleston blueblood institution. Among its founders and presidents were Ramsay, Stephen Elliott, John Drayton, and Joel R. Poinsett. The society languished in the 1830s and probably disappeared in the 1840s.[244] The South Carolina Historical Society (1855), organized in Charleston, was antedated by at least one generation by historical societies in Massachusetts, New York, and Pennsylvania. Similar institutions had been established in Virginia, North Carolina, and Georgia in the 1830s and in Maryland in 1844. Like the other historical associations, and for the same reasons, it was inaugurated and controlled by the patriciate, and Petigru became the original president.[245]

Apart from institutional involvement, the urban upper class participated in literary life as authors and magazine editors and patrons. Unlike northeastern metropolitan elites, several aristocrats were newspaper editors. During the 1830s and 1840s Henry Laurens Pinckney and Robert Barnwell Rhett brought out the Charleston *Mercury*, a nullification organ, and in 1858 Rhett's son became publisher. Periodicals like the *Southern Review* (1828–32), founded by Hugh Swinton Legaré and Stephen Elliott, the *Southern Quarterly Review* (1842–56), and *Russell's Magazine* (1857–60) helped make Charleston the literary center of the South. William Gilmore Simms published several short-lived monthlies and Paul Hamilton Hayne co-edited *Russell's Magazine*. The fragility of the city's intellectual life, however, is revealed in the ephemeral nature of these journals at a time when Boston and New York had permanent publications. Charleston intellectuals, patricians, businessmen, and politicians occasionally tried to rescue these magazines from bankruptcy, but their aid, relative to personal fortunes or to the requirements for survival, was inadequate.[246]

Many planters, Charleston intellectuals, and statesmen, spurred by creative impulses, opportunities afforded by leisure, the desire to reaffirm and disseminate values, and the necessity of defending the southern way of life against northern attacks, became writers, and much of their work appeared in the above-mentioned magazines. Upper-class male authors concentrated on history, travel sketches, and political, social, and cultural essays, and except for poets James Mathewes Legaré and Paul Hamilton Hayne, eschewed fiction. That genre attracted blueblood women, e.g., Susan Petigru King, the society novelist of the 1850s and '60s, and poets Catherine Gendron Poyas and Louisa S. McCord, Cheves's daughter. The Revolutionary generation—John and William Henry Drayton, William Moultrie, David Ramsay, and Henry Middleton—wrote about provincial and early national South Carolina. John Drayton, James J. Pettigrew, Joel R. Poinsett, and William Elliott

authored travel and local-color sketches. William J. Grayson and Hugh
Swinton Legaré, members of the Charleston literary set which included
Simms, Paul Hamilton Hayne, and Pettigrew, concentrated on social
and cultural subjects.[247] Outside of careerists Hayne and Simms, authorship was mostly a genteel or instrumental activity. Measured by the
great slave owners of 1860, writing was not a widespread avocation
among the rural elite. Thirty-five of the 440 planters had published at
least once and twelve were among the ninety-seven with Charleston residences.[248] The higher percentage in the latter group attests to the
incentives provided by living in the state's publishing, literary, and intellectual center. Standards of literary taste, as in so many other matters, were puritanical and British. Sir Walter Scott ranked as the South's
favorite novelist because he abjured "purient sensuality" and "vulgarity," cherished "female purity" and linked Victorian sentimental morality with feudal chivalry, thus expressing values lauded by the squirearchy.[249]

Charleston's reputation for culture, refinement, and gaiety derived
largely from musical, artistic, and theatrical activities. Wealthy planters,
leaving their estates to escape heat and malaria, and yearlong upper-
class residents had the wealth, leisure, and desire to cultivate these features of city life. During the early nineteenth century, concert performances continued to be directed, as in colonial times, by the exclusive
St. Cecilia Society.[250] Aristocrats, however, took a more intense and
professional interest in art and architecture, but mostly limited themselves to consumer and institutional roles. The rich and well-born patronized renowned American painters and collected pictures, but
Charleston could not until the 1880s for any length of time sustain a
public art gallery. The South Carolina Academy of Fine Arts (1816),
whose initiators included Joel R. Poinsett and Stephen Elliott, failed
because the upper class refused to contribute funds. Simms's attempt to
establish an academy of arts and design in 1838 did not last out its first
year, and Washington Allston, Carolina's greatest artist, fled to the more
congenial atmospheres of Boston and Italy. The final prewar attempt to
organize an institution for the exhibition and advancement of art, the
Carolina Art Association (1858), included among its founders Principal
Nathaniel R. Middleton of the College of Charleston, Governor Robert
F. W. Allston, the first president, several other aristocrats, and William
Aiken. In 1861 inadequate revenue and a Charleston fire ended its existence until the 1880s.[251] Charleston as an art center lagged far behind
wealthier and more cosmopolitan New York, Boston, and Philadelphia.

Deficient as patrons and organizers, upper-class Carolinians easily
equaled the northern elites as artists and architects. Charleston's most
popular artists—Charles Fraser, John Irving, Jr., Washington Allston
and his pupil George W. Flagg, Henry B. Bonnetheau, and Thomas

Sully—belonged by birth or marriage to leading tidewater families. The most prominent patrician architect in post-Revolutionary Charleston was Gabriel Manigault, a lawyer and rice planter, College of Charleston trustee, and a member of the South Carolina Society. He built several private homes in the city, the orphan house chapel, and possibly the Bank of the United States building. Thomas Bennett, father of the governor, was another planter-builder and designed the orphan house. Fraser, son of Mary Grimké, and Edward Brickell White, who had an Allston mother, were other gentlemen architects who owned plantations and belonged to exclusive cultural and social associations. Their northern counterparts, Charles Bullfinch and James Renwick, Jr., were considerably rarer. Bostonian Bullfinch, New England's leading architect in the Federalist era, had an elite mercantile background and a Harvard degree. His contemporary, Manigault, derived from similar antecedents. They agreed that architectural knowledge was one of the accomplishments of a gentleman and designed homes for their local upper classes. Bullfinch also built the Massachusetts State House and Harvard's University Hall. New Yorker Renwick, too, came from and married into distinguished mercantile families. He graduated from Columbia and designed Grace Church, where his relatives worshiped, St. Patrick's Cathedral, and the Smithsonian Institution. The gentlemen architects expressed the traditional outlook of the class and clientele by imitating European styles. Manigault had been educated in London and Switzerland and Bullfinch made the Grand Tour of Britain and the Continent that was then the capstone of a patrician education. Manigault's model was the eighteenth-century English Adams brothers, who used classical ornamentation in the mansions they created for the gentry. Bullfinch adopted the Georgian style, and Renwick, in the 1840s and '50s, imported the European Romantic revival, as expressed in the Gothic and Romanesque modes.[252]

Southerners patronized the same famous painters, sought to form the same type of art institutions, and had the same Victorian taste as did northern elites. Frederick A. Porcher, in 1852, expressed the prevalent esthetic-moral standard: "To the civilization formed under the influence of Christianity, nakedness is revolting and humiliating." Nude Greek statues compromised "that modesty which lies at the source of all beauty."[253]

Typical of such strata throughout America, aristocrats eminent in politics and the professions were also active in cultural institutions. Stephen Elliott, coastal planter and Charleston resident, embodies the ideal of the multiply-engaged patrician. He was an assemblyman and state senator, and in the latter office the prime mover of the Free School Bill of 1811 and the incorporation of the Bank of the State in 1812. While president of the bank, Elliott helped found the medical society and the medical college and served as professor of botany there. The planter-statesman-financier wrote a *Sketch of the Botany of South Carolina and Georgia*, co-edited the *Southern Quarterly Review*, founded and became president of the Literary and Philosophical Society, helped promote the Academy of Fine Arts, and headed the Charleston Library board and catalogued its books.[254] Elliott was unsurpassed, but Charles Cotesworth Pinckney, Ramsay, Porcher, Henry W. De Saussure, and Robert W. Gibbes were also distinguished by political, professional, and intellectual endeavors. A more general index of upper-class cultural involvement is provided by a survey of large slaveholders of 1860 belonging to scientific societies, art associations, and the historical society. Since most of these bodies met in Charleston, the ninety-seven who also resided there had a much higher percentage of memberships. Twenty-three of the 440 slave owners were in the historical society (twelve lived in Charleston), nineteen in scientific organizations (eight had homes in the city), six in art associations (all dwelling in Charleston), and five of the latter in the Carolina Art Association.[255]

While Old Guard planters, politicians, and professionals undertook cultural leadership, the urban business community did not participate as vigorously as did northern capitalists. Counterparts to the Appletons and Lawrences of Boston or to the Hones and Pintards of New York did not emerge in the southern port, even on the scale that their slenderer resources permitted. Aristocratic distaste for commerce and the accompanying hiatus of bluebloods from trade may have discouraged rich moguls from entering a preserve of the patriciate. Their reluctance deprived organizations of funds, energy, and talent. Intellectual life in Charleston thus suffered a disadvantage not as severely felt in Boston, New York, or Philadelphia.

Charity

Upper-class Charlestonians and northerners, out of humanitarianism, civic leadership, and a desire to maintain social order, sponsored agencies to meet the spiritual, educational, and physical needs of the poor.[256] These charities naturally involved leaders in the professions, business, politics, and culture. Hence philanthropy was another dimension of community hegemony that strengthened the elite.

Institutions existing from colonial times, the South Carolina and St. Andrew's societies, under Old Guard management and membership, continued to support the same causes, chiefly education for indigent children.[257] The older associations also participated in the founding of new public welfare organizations. St. Andrew's contributed £50 to the erection of the Charleston Orphan House (1790), established by the city to care for and educate impoverished parentless youngsters. The orphan house, the first municipally supported orphanage and the third oldest in the nation, was chiefly the work of merchant John Robertson. Its commissioners, elected by the city council, included the foremost businessmen, politicians, lawyers, physicians, and society figures. Control over its private donations and public stipends resided in a board of trustees composed of the mayor, city treasurer, and chairman of the commissioners. The latter, during the antebellum period, was usually an aristocratic civic leader, e.g. John Huger, Rawlins Lowndes, and Henry A. and Henry W. De Saussure.[258]

The Shirras Dispensary (1811) and Roper Hospital (1845), which ministered to the sickly poor, also owed their existence to the generosity of *arriviste* Charleston merchants. Both, however, were directed and staffed by elite physicians and medical society officers. Alexander Shirras, a Scottish overseas trader, was an officer of St. Andrew's Society, and William Roper was chairman of the orphan house commissioners and a commissioner of the poorhouse. The last great pre–Civil War welfare agency for the indigent similarly originated in a legacy from a self-made Charleston capitalist. An ex-cabinetmaker's apprentice, English-born William Enston in 1860 left $400,000 for a hospital and home for the aged and sick.[259]

Apart from these philanthropies, wealthy and well-born Charlestonians and planters assisted dependent sailors and clergymen and formed sectarian institutions that brought relief and Christianity to the urban poor. Notable among these charities were the Charleston Bible Society (1810), the Protestant Episcopal Society for the Advancement of Christianity (1810), the Ladies Benevolent Society (1813), the Charleston Female Domestic Society (1821), the Charleston Port Society for Promoting the Gospel Among Seamen (1823), and the Harriott Pinckney Home for Seamen (1853). In addition to administering these organizations, upper-class altruists served as commissioners of the poorhouse and workhouse.[260]

Many patricians were leaders in benevolence as well as in the professions, politics, and culture. Thomas S. Grimké, for example, was renowned for giving to charity more than half his yearly income.[261] Urban businessmen of humble birth participated much more extensively in welfare than in intellectual organizations. Their relative salience in charity partly stemmed from the fact that some forms of assistance, e.g., to sailors, were considered a special obligation of shipowning merchants. Moreover, philanthropy was supposed to help make the dream of success come true for others as it had for some of the self-made magnates. Businessmen benefactors also saw relief services as more protective of property and order than were the Charleston Library or the historical society. As in Boston and New York, charity in the 1820s was becoming a systematic enterprise based on bourgeois values. Public welfare in Charleston took on the prevailing outlook that innovative methods and pragmatic rationality would enhance social control and upward mobility. Urban capitalists, therefore, felt more at home in undertakings prompted by these ideas than in institutions of high culture which dedicated themselves to an aristocratic worship of the classics, courtly ideals, and the past. Roper expressed the modern view of charity in 1822 when he introduced a resolution ratified by his fellow poorhouse commissioners that "permanent provisions for persons in the uninterrupted possession of health has served but to the increase of pauperism; it is thence incumbent on the commissioners of the poor, when dispensing public charity to discriminate between . . . those whose dependence arises from sickness, decrepitude and unavoidable calamity, and . . . all whose indigence is induced" by "an aversion to habits of industry and economy." Henry W. De Saussure voiced the broader principles behind progressive philanthropy in commemorating the sixty-sixth anniversary of the orphan house: "Physical wants supplied, food, raiment, shelter and education provided, systematic habits of order and regularity established, and discipline enforced," declared the chairman of the orphan house commissioners, "are the social obligations of a Christian community—they lay the foundations of a moral character, and form the elements of future usefulness in life. The habit training of the boys in the Institution, disciplines them for that course of useful, honorable employment in the various walks of life befitting their condition; and many respectable mechanics, merchants, engineers, and efficient members of society, are to be found among our beneficiaries. Their duties as practical men of business and good citizens in the middle classes of society, are generally fulfilled with honorable industry and commendable propriety and fidelity. In mercantile pursuits they have been often successful."[262]

"Charity is carried rather to excess in Charleston," wrote David Ramsay, active in the Charleston Dispensary for the Poor and the Charleston Bible Society. Compared to contemporary Boston, however, little was spent on welfare or culture. The South Carolina Society, the city's largest nineteenth-century benevolent agency, dispensed $7,360 in 1826 and $8,305 in 1848, expenditures over twice that of any other charitable or intellectual organization in the city. Several Boston institutions exceeded these disbursements and that city appropriated considerably more on a per capita basis for public schools and poor relief than did Charleston.[263]

Society

Various genres of southern gentlemen—the Christian, the scholar, and the cavalier—emphasized different virtues: piety and charity, or intellectuality, or virility in battle, dueling, and hunting. Virtually all patricians, however, defended the slave basis, traditional outlook, patriarchal form, and hierarchical perspective that constituted the essence of southern gentility. Social interactions in Charleston and the surrounding plantations strengthened the upper class by reinforcing its values and traits, impressing the lower ranks, and forming a distinctive pattern of life that resisted encroachment. Relations within high society were conducted through hallowed institutions like the St. Cecilia Society and the South Carolina Jockey Club (1792) and the hunting, riding, and racing organizations in the plantation districts, through events like the Jockey Club and St. Cecilia balls, race week, and mock tidewater tournaments, and, less formally, through the Cossack and Conversation clubs, gatherings over sumptuous repasts at regal mansions, and summer migrations to Charleston and exclusive resorts in South Carolina, Newport, Rhode Island, and Saratoga Springs, New York. Reflecting the long-standing bias against trade, newly risen capitalists, frequently northern emigrants, were barred from *haut monde* ornaments like the St. Cecilia. Consequently, they started their own associations, most notably the New England Society (1819).[264]

Foreign and northern visitors and settlers in South Carolina called Charleston and the adjacent parishes the most genteel place in America. These observers felt that generations of inherited rank made the low-country aristocracy courtly, commanding, courageous, and congenial.[265] Charlestonians sometimes reciprocated these plaudits. Before New York became a symbol of brash and decadent capitalism, disdained as enemy headquarters, tidewater and Knickerbocker elites sometimes mingled. During the Federalist era, common political and economic interests were nurtured by warmer relationships. Carolina bluebloods were welcomed at John Jay's home, then the center of Gotham society. Ralph and Henry Izard married respectively a DeLancey and a Colden, Lewis Morris an Elliott heiress, and John Read the daughter of a Knickerbocker merchant.[266] During the 1850s, however, William Porcher Miles and William J. Grayson considered New York a Babylon of pretentious, upstart millionaires. Philadelphia and especially Boston were more respected. Grayson felt that Philadelphia shared, though to a smaller degree, the coldness and superficiality of New York, but Petigru sent his daughter to school in that city where "she sees better society than she would do at home." Boston received the most widespread and unqualified praise. Washington Allston made a permanent home in the vicinity and Paul Hamilton Hayne longed to move there. Grayson "found Boston the most agreable [sic]" northern city because "the manners of Charleston and Boston were thought to approximate more nearly than those of any other places in the country." Hugh Swinton Legaré was impressed by "the liberality which Harvard experienced from the opulent merchants of Boston" and asked whether "any society" was "more entirely devoted to liberal pursuits than" Boston.[267]

The indigenous elite naturally echoed the encomiums that outsiders gave it. Joseph and J. Motte Alston, Frederick A. Porcher, John Drayton, Hugh Swinton Legaré, David Ramsay, Robert Barnwell Rhett, Grayson, Elizabeth Ann Poyas, William Porcher Miles, and William Elliott praised the intellect, refinement, benevolence, and chivalry of the squirearchy. Charleston residents E. S. Thomas and Charles Fraser attested to the exclusiveness of the urban fashionable set during the 1790s. Grayson and Fraser even judged that high society had since improved due to a decline in "licentiousness," drunkenness, and lewd "conversation."[268]

A minority of northern and European critics, including lawyer Timothy Ford, who settled in Charleston, derogated the upper class for harsh treatment of slaves, indolence, alcoholism, extravagance, and indebtedness.[269] Surprisingly, with the exception of the handling of the Blacks, many aristocrats, e.g., John Drayton, Ramsay, Porcher, Miles, Grayson, and R. F. W. Allston, shared these reservations.[270] Patricians dwelled more obliquely on other weaknesses. Porcher regretted that custom dictated his becoming a planter despite inability and lack of interest. William Lowndes, Ramsay, and Porcher pointed out that women often ran the estate and rescued the family from debt. Blueblood urbanites occasionally discouraged their children from being full-time agriculturalists. John F. and Thomas S. Grimké opposed Henry Grimké's wish to become an up-country farmer because it dulled the spirit, dimmed the intellect, and lowered social status. Adele Petigru's family warned her against marrying R. F. W. Allston, who lived in the country all year and would isolate her from the fashionable set in Charleston.[271]

Many Virginia and Carolina patricians were aware of their drawbacks and absorbed the national glorification of bourgeois values.[272] John F. Grimké recommended "a more industrious habit of employment" to his son, and Martha Laurens Ramsay enjoined her child to practice "industry and self-denial," piety and frugality. "The gentleman," wrote Grayson, is "distinguished from the cavalier or noble as not resting on law, custom or privilege." An "offspring of popular institutions," he "is independent of all aristocratic distinctions." The "finest specimens" of gentility "may be found in the humblest condition of life." The scholar-planter-statesman also rejected as a European "estimate" the historical attribute of leisure as a mark of gentility. "Property" in America "passes too easily from hand to hand, to furnish the successive generations of idlers necessary to make the grand distinctive qualifications of the gentleman easy, graceful, and natural. We are all *parvenus*, pretenders, or snobs." Charles Fraser, noting the improvement of contemporary Charleston society, commented that in the 1790s, "the merchant had not that position to which his contribution to the prosperity of the community entitled him and which is now so readily and justly recognized. . . . *Then* fortune and cultivation could alone place men at the head of society—men, place themselves there *now*."[273] Criticism of the gentry and commitment to middle-class ideals came largely from estate owners who were primarily city dwellers and mainly involved in urban activities. Their ambivalence about agrarian life reflected the ambience in a town that was the capital of a coastal plantation society. As townsmen they shared the outlook of metropolitan elites, as squires they defended the rural aristocracy. Ramsay, for instance, acknowledged that "a sense of honor is general; but, like charity, is sometimes carried too far" and "degenerated into a vice."[274]

Businessmen received social recognition when many aristocrats accepted commerce as a legitimate upper-class calling and convinced themselves that self-preservation depended upon the commercial recovery of Charleston and the economic autonomy of the South. Several observers, however, declared that the admission of fresh blood into the upper class diminished the influence of the Old Guard. E. S. Thomas asserted that the "distinguished men of the present day are self-made. . . ."[275] Their intrusion dismayed defenders of the old order. "I ask of heaven only that the little circle I am intimate with in Charleston should be kept together while I live," said Hugh Swinton Legaré in 1833; "We are . . . the *last* of the race of South Carolina; I see nothing before us but decay and downfall. . . ." Twenty years later William Porcher Miles also anguished over the decline of the squirearchy and Charleston society. In "the olden time planters constituted the almost sole society," but "good sense and necessity have long since given many gentlemen to trade, and merchants who reside constantly in town, now constitute one of the largest, most influential and cultivated portions of our community." Although Miles concurred with Fraser on the desirability of the rejuvenated commercial community, he came to the opposite conclusion about Charleston society. Extravagance and termination of primogeniture caused "many" families "of consequence" to sink "into poverty and obscurity. . . . Sons of decayed gentlemen had to . . . work hard and constantly" and "social intercourse died out." Charleston's "polished society" deteriorated "because we have become gradually *Americanized*. The earnest pursuit of money . . . for the mere vulgar ambition of being known as a 'rich man'" replaced the pursuit of "culture which alone can make wealth enjoyable. . . ." The "Puritan spirit . . . of New England, has spread . . . to the region once granted by Charles II, to his courtly favorites."[276]

If insiders Miles and Fraser thought fashionable Charleston less exclusive and its patriciate less influential, outsiders William Gilmore Simms and James Hammond objected to its imperviousness. Simms perceived Charleston to be divided into "old and new communities" that "perpetually confront each other. . . . The modern is daily growing more and more insolent and obtrusive; but the ancient is formidable in sheer stubbornness." Notwithstanding his dissatisfaction with the conservatism and aloofness of the aristocracy, qualities which most bluebloods and visitors found attractive, Simms joined upper-class observers in announcing its decline and predicting its demise. "Note the falling off in our [coastal parishes] in social tone," he wrote William Elliott in 1849. The "causes of degeneracy" were "the evils of Revolution—the abolition of the Rights of Primogeniture—" and "intermarriage" between the "aristocracy" and "the commoner." The suicidal practice of "crossing the breed" contradicted the way "British nobility has been made the most splendid race of men in the world."[227]

In society, as in business and politics, Carolinians increasingly expected ultimate disintegration. Convinced of the ebbing power and wealth of their master class, they saw its blight endangering the social order. Every aspect of their world was threatened, and despair generated an aggressive defensiveness that led to secession and war.

1860 TO THE PRESENT

The Civil War

Northern aristocracies faded away, but Old South patriciates encountered an abrupt disaster in the Civil War. Military tradition, the cavalier myth, determination to defend southern civilization, and elitist attitudes emphasizing special obligations to protect the social order, lead in battle, and face danger prompted bluebloods to volunteer for armed service. Since the younger generation bore the brunt of combat and proliferated in ranks most susceptible to casualties, a large portion of the gentry that might have provided leadership and sustained the class in subsequent decades disappeared in the prime of life. Aside from a high mortality rate, extensive property destruction as a result of the conflict being fought mostly in the South traumatized the upper class and prevented a postwar patrician restoration.

These factors applied with particular intensity to South Carolina. Twenty-three percent of its male citizens of military age were killed, the highest rate of any seceding state and more than double the Confederate average. According to one estimate South Carolina lost 40,000 out of an 1860 population of 146,000 white males.[278] Carnage in the upper order was equally widespread. Nearly half of the exclusive Washington Light Infantry of Charleston (1807) died in action; one-third of these casualties were commissioned or noncommissioned officers. Memoirs and family histories show, with a poignancy only hinted at by statistics, that none of the aristocratic clans escaped attrition.[279]

Property was also consumed in the struggle. Charleston, Columbia, and the tidewater plantations were devastated, trade strangled in the Union blockade, factories and railroads were destroyed, and liquid capital vanished. Between 1860 and 1867, land values decreased by 60 percent; emancipation cost slave owners an estimated $200 million; production of rice in 1870 dwindled to less than half that of 1860; banking resources in Charleston fell from $41 million in 1860 to $400,000 in 1867. According to one analysis, total property value in South Carolina shrank from $400 billion in 1860 to $50 million in 1868.[280] Many of the large planters, now bankrupt, left the land and, along with their wives and children, sought employment in Charleston or outside the state and region as teachers, storekeepers, manual laborers, seamstresses, and boardinghouse keepers. Urban dwellers also flew from adversity, and the exodus of the city and country gentry weakened its ability to regain ascendancy.[281]

Despair over personal and property losses and fear of a black insurrection overwhelmed the aristocracy. As early as 1863 R. F. W. Allston saw signs that the landed gentry was "inferior to the Northern fiends" and was "giving way" to the "devastation" of their plantations. Immediately before and after surrender, Susan R. Jervey, planter William Henry Ravenel and his Charleston relatives, and Harriott Middleton panicked at the prospect of a black "insurrection" and felt that the low-country and the "old order" were in a state of "confusion, disorder, discontent, violence, anarchy," and "total ruin." Even after the initial shock of defeat wore off and the most dire prophesies did not materialize, pessimism continued unabated among some aristocrats. In 1869 Paul Hamilton Hayne declared, "My section is *dead* beyond any hope of resurrection."[282]

Economic Functions

Defeat and destruction dispossessed many planters, and the late-nineteenth-century outflow of Rhetts, Gadsdens, Haynes, Prioleaus, Barnwells, Mazycks, Manigaults, and Rutledges to the North or to other parts of the South steadily eroded the patriciate in Charleston and the plantation parishes. A larger number of aristocrats, however, retained ownership of family estates until at least the 1880s and a few well into the twentieth century. But falling real estate values and the subsidence of rice growing gradually reduced their holdings. Even at the turn of the century, low-country plantations were worth only one-fifth to two-thirds of prewar value. Rice growing, an important tidewater crop, diminished in productivity and profit due to competition from the Southwest, where it was grown more efficiently and cheaply because of the earlier and greater application of machinery, superior irrigation methods, and an absence of hurricanes and floods. The disappearance of Charleston rice factors created marketing difficulties for the planters, and storms and inundations between 1888 and 1913 wiped out most of the remaining squirearchy. By 1900 only a rare old proprietor still survived, and Theodore D. Ravenel, who ceased operations in 1927, was the last large commercial rice planter in South Carolina. After World War I many of the plantations were bought up by a new ruling enclave, becoming the country seats of northern capitalists.[283]

The Charleston economy reflected the disintegration of its hinterland. Real and personal property assessments in 1870 totaled $32,137,477 and declined in every subsequent decade, falling to $17,246,142 in 1900. The 1920 assessment of $26,461,840 was below that of 1870. Shrinking values resulted from deterioration in the urban economy. Charleston real estate prices in 1904 plunged to their lowest point since 1880.[284] Moreover, the city continued to fall behind other Atlantic ports as a shipping center: in 1860 it ranked third in exports and fifth in imports among the six principal Atlantic ports; in 1883 it placed sixth in these categories and handled 2.5 percent and .05 percent respectively of the nation's exports and imports, one-half the share of the former and one-tenth of the latter that went through the harbor in 1860.[285] Banking declined not only relatively but absolutely. In 1898, capital in South Carolina banks barely equaled one-third the amount of 1860. Depletion in financial resources was accompanied by an unprecedented number of failures. Between 1865 and 1888 several banks—the State, the Union, the Planters and Mechanics, the Southwestern Railroad, and the People's—folded.[286] Except for the last named, these had been controlled by the antebellum mercantile-political elite. Charleston also slipped as a regional transportation center as southern railroads bypassed it to carry cotton to Norfolk, Virginia, and the rice crop diminished. Higher freight and terminal charges and services inferior to other cities also undermined the transportation network. In 1860 South Carolina ranked fourth among the southern states in railroad mileage, in 1880 seventh, in 1890 ninth, and between 1880 and 1890 ninth in mileage increase. The South Carolina Railroad, the state's largest railroad, failed to recover after the war. Increasingly a local line, its earnings and stock value decreased while its corporation debt mounted. In 1878 it went bankrupt and three years later passed into the hands of New Yorkers. During the late nineteenth century several other roads, built by antebellum Charleston capital, were also acquired by northerners. Inadequate financing and poor harbor facilities further weakened business enterprise. A revealing sidelight of this situation was the *News and Courier* discontinuing in 1889 its annual "Trade Review" because of the stagnating economy.[287]

Economic adversity inhibited population growth, thus continuing antebellum trends of an excess of out- over in-migration, a lower than national average rate of population expansion until 1940, and South

Carolina's place at the bottom of states in proportion of urban residents. Between 1870 and 1920 the Piedmont, primary locus of the postwar textile industry, expanded faster than did the low-country, and Charleston grew less rapidly in population than did up-country cities. The twenty-second largest American city in 1860, it was sixty-eighth in 1900 and 129th in 1940.[288]

Sluggish commercial and demographic development evoked pessimism and pleas reminiscent of prewar days. The chamber of commerce advocated in 1880 the building of a railroad to the West to regain trade captured by northern cities. Merchant William L. Trenholm, son and partner of George A. Trenholm, the great Charleston capitalist and Confederate secretary of the treasury, told the chamber in 1884 that Charleston had failed to fulfill her colonial economic promise because of hostility or indifference to commerce, conservative business practices, and inadequate maritime and railroad facilities.[289] In 1899, during a depression in Charleston and a time when other cities were seeking to emulate the success of the Chicago World's Fair of 1893, an Inter-State and West Indian Exposition was organized to advertise local trading advantages. Several aristocratic notables in the political and business affairs of the city were on the executive committee. But inclement weather, refusal of many South Carolina firms—particularly cotton factories—to contribute funds, delay in building the exposition, and failure to get a federal appropriation resulted in a huge financial loss and a low turnout. Executive committeeman R. Goodwin Rhett, when mayor, reported that the enterprise did not bring in much new business.[290] Accordingly, chamber vice-president and utilities executive Philip H. Gadsden and other businessmen continued to dwell on the flagging economy. Ex-mayor Rhett, many years later, described the period between 1865 and 1904 as an age when "a feeling soon became prevalent that opportunity for successful business in Charleston was shrinking and that one must move westward to find a promising opening." The "flower of the youth of Charleston" departed and "drained the city of much of its vitality." Haynes, Barnwells, Rhetts, Hugers, and other aristocrats were among those who left.[291]

Despite this exodus, between the Civil War and World War I, Elliotts, Pringles, Rhetts, Gadsdens, Ravenels, and Gaillards stayed on as merchants, factors, realtors, insurance agents, and executives of banking, utility, railroad, and phosphate-manufacturing concerns. The largest mercantile houses, however, did not have Old Guard owners. Stanland & Downing, the preeminent southern brokerage firm for general merchandise, was a branch of a New York company, and A. Norden & Co., the foremost southern cotton export firm, was founded by a German who came to Charleston after the war. Smyth & Adger, the greatest cotton factors and commission merchants in Charleston, similarly contained no upper-class partners, although the founder of the conjoined families, James Adger, had come to Charleston in the 1790s and the postwar principals of the firm possessed third-generation wealth. Antebellum upper-class survivors figured more prominently in banking, though they exerted less influence than before secession. Bluebloods served as bank officers and directors of the Southwestern Railroad, the Charleston, the Union, the People's, and the Planters and Mechanics banks. Presidents of the Bank of Charleston, still South Carolina's largest financial institution, between the Civil War and the world wars included Charles T. Lowndes and Ernest H. Pringle; during the same period Mayor Rhett and his son headed the People's Bank. George W. Williams, the state's leading banker, general entrepreneur, and richest man, however, was a self-made Georgia-born millionaire. Except for phosphate fertilizer production, the patriciate tended to remain aloof from industry, as before the war.[292] But manufacturing, especially textiles, now played a much larger role in South Carolina's economy, and the absence of the Old Guard constituted a graver threat to aristocratic ascendancy in the 1880s and '90s than in earlier decades.

Phosphate fertilizer manufacturing represented the major initiative launched by postwar urban bluebloods, and its windfalls restored several damaged fortunes. Here too, the old order did not control the largest firms. In 1867 St. Julien Ravenel and Francis S. Holmes discovered phosphate deposits in the vicinity of Charleston. Local capitalists were initially reluctant to invest in an untried venture. Accordingly, Holmes and others organized the Charleston Mining and Manufacturing Co. (1867) with funds from Philadelphia. At the same time Ravenel founded the Wando Fertilizer Co. The Atlantic Fertilizer Co. (1870), the largest firm in the field in Charleston, employed Ravenel as a chemist and had a few patricians on its board. Several other fertilizer corporations, e.g., the Stono Phosphate Co., were headed by members of the Old Guard, and upper-class mercantile houses, e.g., W. C. Bee & Co., acted as selling agents for the factories. The greatest companies, Charleston Mining and Manufacturing, Pacific Guano, and Atlantic Phosphate, were neither run by patricians (although they organized the first firm) nor used aristocratic agents. By the early 1890s the industry declined due to competition from Florida, Tennessee, and Algiers, and exhaustion of local phosphate deposits.[293]

As a consequence of the infrequent presence of bluebloods in the largest business enterprises, none of the seven Charlestonians listed in the *Tribune Monthly*'s 1892 compilation of American millionaires had distinguished low-country lineage. In 1860, three of the twenty-four residents with property assessed for at least $100,000 had such pedigrees, and the bulk of the holdings of many other rich patrician city dwellers were in land and slaves owned elsewhere.[294]

Shortly after 1900 Charleston's economy began to surge forward. In 1903 a navy yard was located in the city, in the next few years harbor and railroad facilities appreciably improved, and between 1904 and 1911 urban property values increased 50 percent.[295] Yet in 1914 Mayor John Grace, a reform Democrat, reported that in New York, Boston, and Philadelphia "is wealth and culture and growth, and here is poverty, ignorance and decay." Grace attributed the town's backwardness to a "narrow-minded" and "irreconcilable aristocracy and oligarchy," which discouraged new blood and innovation. The attitude abhorred by Grace prompted a 1920s upper-class businessman to state, "It is to my interest to see the town grow. But I feel that if it grows commercially, it is bound to change in other ways and become more modern and more like other cities. I hate to think of that." In 1939 author DuBose Heyward, a descendant of the antebellum gentry, also acknowledged "a stubborn clinging to the modes of life and thought that have been tried and proved." Heyward felt that Charlestonians were "not particularly concerned" about accumulating a "large fortune."[296]

Since 1940 Charleston has experienced an economic renaissance. Between 1940 and 1944 the metropolitan area population rose almost two-thirds and the city acquired its first great industry, a hydroelectric power project that enabled it to house heavy industry. During World War II Charleston obtained a federal port terminal and between 1940 and 1948 the value of manufacturing and retail trade tripled and bank clearings almost tripled. *Sales Management Magazine* rated Charleston among the top ten American cities in business expansion during the first six months of 1948 and *Business Week* listed it as one of the most progressive cities in America. After the war the House Armed Services Committee, headed by a Charleston congressman, located many military installations in the vicinity and the Charleston Naval Shipyard and Naval Base became the major industry. Charleston held its position as the premier South Atlantic port, and agriculture now contributed a miniscule portion of the region's income.[297]

During this resurgence the presence of the Old Guard in business enterprise substantially waned. In the 1940s none of the bank presidents were old Charlestonians, although several securities brokerage houses and insurance firms were headed by aristocrats. A. F. Pringle & Co. (1918), the largest chemical fertilizer plant in Charleston County, was an exception to the general absence of bluebloods from manufacturing. The postwar rarity of upper-class officers in business, professional, and trade associations, compared to the posts held between the Civil War and World War I by Rhetts, Laurenses, Jerveys, Gadsdens, Frosts, and Heriots in the chamber of commerce and the Commercial Club, further indicated patrician displacement.[298] The disappearance of this class-conscious conservative enclave helped reshape the image of the city.

Herbert Ravenel Sass, a local antiquarian and blueblood, claimed "that this city from its earliest days has been the home of a dynamic people" and rejected "the legend of a beautiful but languid and indolent lotus-eater." The president of the College of Charleston board and the Carolina Art Association repudiated the "pernicious Charleston legend" that "one tight and exclusive social group" dominates the town. "Charleston is genuinely friendly and hospitable to newcomers." A few may "concern themselves with magnolias and moonlight and ancestors," but most are "tough and realistic businessmen and workers. . . ."[299]

Politics

Death in battle weakened the coastal patriciate, and the advent of the Piedmont-centered textile industry stimulated population and economic growth in that area. These developments accelerated the late antebellum shift of power from the tidewater to the interior. At the state convention of 1865 the latter defeated the former and increased up-country legislative seats at the expense of Charleston and distributed senate seats according to population rather than taxes. During Reconstruction, the old elite, of course, underwent an eclipse. When the conservative Democrats, led by Wade Hampton, triumphed in 1876, low-country artistocrats remained in a subordinate position. Less than one-fourth of the Redeemer chieftains came from this section, and descendants of ancient families held virtually none of the higher state or federal offices. With a few exceptions, most notably Duncan Clinch Heyward (governor, 1903–7), Burnett Rhett Maybank (governor, 1939–41, U.S. senator, 1941–54), Burnett Rhett Maybank, Jr. (lieutenant governor, 1959–63), and attorney generals Charles Richardson Miles (1882–86) and Joseph W. Barnwell (1894–96), their exclusion has continued.[300]

The Old Guard was more potent in local politics. Until the 1960s at least one state legislator from Charleston had aristocratic ancestry. Just as before secession the upper class was proportionately more significant in the upper than in the lower house. In municipal government bluebloods made their best showing. Peter C. Gaillard (1865–68), R. Goodwin Rhett (1903–11), Thomas P. Stoney (1923–27), Burnett Rhett Maybank (1931), and J. Palmer Gaillard (1973) were mayors; bluebloods have occasionally served as recorders and police chiefs and more regularly as commissioners on the boards of health, school, parks, airports, city planning and zoning, port utilities, sewage, cultural institutions, and public charities, and as aldermen.[301]

Business eminence accompanied stellar political careers oftener than in antebellum times. Heyward was the leading rice planter in South Carolina and president of a warehouse company in Columbia; Rhett was president of the South Carolina Loan and Trust Co. and the People's National Bank and a director in twenty-five Charleston corporations;

P. C. Gaillard was a prominent cotton broker, and Burnett Maybank, a textile merchant. The other upper-class officeholders usually had similar if less imposing credentials.

Even before the Civil War the aristocratic influence in municipal politics began to wane and several new men became mayors. Afterward aristocrats constituted a small, if steady, minority on the city council and on the public boards. Moreover, in state and local government the traditional elite lost its power as a class, though an occasional individual like Maybank achieved outstanding success. In this respect genteel Charleston recapitulated the destinies of Knickerbocker New York and Brahmin Boston.

After the war the "best people" of Charleston resumed the moderate politics for which they had been previously castigated by southern fire-eaters. At the convention of 1865 several blueblood city delegates advised the repeal of the secession ordinance. Henry Deas Lesesne requested the convention to pledge that slavery would never be reestablished and Edward Frost wished to give the Blacks civil rights and in a short time full political privileges. Although the aristocracy did not play a major part in his victory, it supported Wade Hampton against both the Reconstruction administration and the "Straight Outs" who wanted to harshly repress the freedmen, and later against the Tillmanites.

Frost, former Blue Ridge Railroad president and member of both state houses and the state judiciary, and Lesesne, also a former member of the South Carolina senate and house and postwar solicitor of the Bank of Charleston, accommodated new political forces.[302] A steadfast defense of the past, however, characterized the upper-class majority. Those primarily interested in culture tended to be staunch guardians of "the lost cause." J. J. Pringle Smith told the historical society in 1879 that the Palmetto State had never been morally or constitutionally wrong in contesting the federal government. Society president Frederick A. Porcher argued that carpetbaggers misled the Blacks, well treated by their antebellum masters, and that Reconstruction illustrated that "without property qualification the legislature became corrupt with members selling votes and using their seats to make money." Daniel Elliott Huger Smith, a historical society vice-president and a local chronicler, agreed that slaves were tenderly cared for and deplored emancipation as unnecessarily cruel.[303] Poet Paul Hamilton Hayne, an exile in Georgia, and novelist Gabriel Manigault were the most comprehensive and intransigent denunciators of the modern age; in the defeat of the South they discerned the doom of the nation. A "Mobocracy," Hayne called the United States in 1878. "Centralism," "diverse Nationalities," "miscegenation," radicalism, corruption, "emancipation," and "a general overthrow of class distinctions" would result in "some Monarchical form of rule, destined in time, to degenerate into absolutism." Manigault, in *The United States Unmasked* (1879), argued that the defeat of the Confederacy had removed the South's "wholesome, elevating, and conservative influence" and unleashed in the nation immigrant-produced racial inferiority, class confrontation, and demagogic rule of the propertyless. To these evils he added the degeneration of the family, urbanization, industrialism, loss of exports due to the destruction of the plantation system, and "lawlessness and violence." The only consolation for this embittered aristocrat was that "in bringing an avalanche on the South, [its] enemies have covered themselves with the same mass of ruin."[304]

The Professions

After the war, genteel Charlestonians maintained professional salience more effectively than other types of leadership. They continued to excel at the bar despite the political and economic decline of their order. Aristocratic attorneys, like their antebellum forerunners, studied under and drew their clients and partners from among their peers, counseled upper-class business, cultural, charitable, and religious institutions, and were the most politically active members of the Old Guard. Two-term assemblyman Benjamin Huger Rutledge, one of the city's most successful late-nineteenth-century lawyers, and his relative Henry Edward Young studied under Petigru. Charles Richardson Miles, who clerked for Isaac W. Hayne, became an assemblyman and state attorney general in addition to being a master in chancery, solicitor of St. Philip's Church, and president of the College of Charleston board. James Barnwell Heyward, an outstanding twentieth-century Charleston real estate attorney, clerked for Joseph W. Barnwell. The latter, a member of both state houses, South Carolina attorney general, and chairman of the Charleston County Democratic Committee, was administrator of many old fortunes and the holdings of Charleston Episcopal churches. He was famed for never losing the principal of a fund entrusted to him. Rutledge and Young, Miles and Lesesne formed partnerships, and generations of De Saussures started as apprentices and became partners in De Saussure & Son, which, even in the late nineteenth century, handled much of the state's legal business. Another family firm bridging the Civil War—McCrady, Sons & Bacot—had one of the largest real estate practices in late-nineteenth-century Charleston. A noteworthy twentieth-century Charleston partnership consisted of M. Rutledge Rivers, his son, and their relative Arthur Rutledge Young. They all held public office and were kin of other distinguished lawyers, and during World War I Young was president of the Charleston county and state bar associations. The firm conducted legal matters for the South Carolina Power Co., Southern Bell Telegraph, and several other utilities and banks. It epitomized the willingness of some patricians to break with tradition by involving themselves with the newest and wealthiest economic forces in South Carolina. Earlier examples of this entrepreneurial vigor were William Elliott, Jr., who represented Columbia textile corporations and managed utility companies in that city; Henry E. Ravenel, Jr., a lawyer for and director in several cotton mills; Assembly Speaker James Simons, whose clients included wealthy financial institutions of Charleston's German community; and Assemblyman Philip H. Gadsden, president of Charleston Consolidated Railway, the Charleston Gas and Electric Company, and other utilities.[305]

Medicine was more remote than law from the centers of power and wealth, hence the patrician presence in this calling played a smaller role in preserving aristocratic ascendancy. But the distinction achieved by upper-class doctors buttressed the local establishment by maintaining its historical prominence in the profession, its influential civic functions of supervising public health institutions and administering medical care to the poor through direction of municipal and private charities and hospitals, and its tradition of scientific activity. The professional structure, as in law, remained intact after the war. Patrician physicians usually received their training at the South Carolina Medical College and, as in law, from relatives or associates of equal social rank. Like their antebellum predecessors, they taught at the medical college, served as physicians and trustees or commissioners of the same charity hospitals and orphanages, the city and state boards of health, and in high posts in medical societies. The careers of the foremost upper-class physicians exemplify the prominence of the bluebloods, the interlocking facets of their professional hegemony, and the importance of kinship connections. Among those who received part of their training from their social peers or relatives were Thomas Grange Simons, Jr., William Harleston Huger, and Francis Le Jau Parker. Medical as well as legal dynasties were established after the war or prolonged from the antebellum era. Drs. Jacob Ford Prioleau, Francis P. Porcher, and Middleton Michel had physician fathers, and Robert A. Kinloch's son practiced medicine. Kinloch and Porcher achieved national recognition for their research by being named vice-presidents of the American Medical Association. Porcher and his son, Parker, Prioleau, and Peter G. De Saussure headed the South Carolina Medical Association. Simons, Kinloch, Parker, and Michel headed the South Carolina Medical Society. Huger, Simons, De Saussure, and Prioleau served on the state or city boards of health. Many of the doctors were faculty members of the medical college and Prioleau served as dean. These professors, association presidents, and health commissioners were on at least one of the medical staffs or administrative boards of the leading Charleston hospitals and charities.[306]

Medical school was but one form of education in which the Old

Guard participated. After the Civil War many patricians, now in straitened circumstances and deprived of their plantation livelihoods, opened academies and became teachers and administrators in Charleston's school system, and later generations of bluebloods followed the same careers. Between the Civil War and World War II, several aristocrats were on the Charleston High School faculty, and in the 1870s and 1880s E. Montague Grimké and William Simons and from 1911 to the 1930s Andrew B. Rhett were superintendents of schools. Aristocrats also often served on the board of public school commissioners and as clerks of that body. Remnants of the old elite also formed and ran private schools. The principal academies in Charleston in 1883 included Miss S. D. Pinckney's, Miss De Saussure's, and Miss F. A. Porcher's schools for boys and girls, and at the turn of the century Charles J. Colcock, Jr., was headmaster of Porter Academy.[307]

A typical genteel academy was Mrs. Hopson Pinckney's Boarding and Day School for Young Ladies, of which Mrs. Pinckney was principal and owner. "This institution offers to Parents and Guardians the advantages of a Finishing School of Young Ladies," read an advertisement in 1875, "combined with the comforts of a refined home. . . . Attention is given to the cultivation of the mind, the affections and the manners," and "all the usual branches of useful and ornamental education." Listed references included many bluebloods. Testimonials coming from *arriviste* businessmen and the mayor praised Mrs. Pinckney's "polished home circle" and ability to make "ladies of our daughters," and cited her as an "authority for gentle civilities and rules of conduct."[308] As in the North, private academies reinforced upper-class mores and indoctrinated children of the *nouveaux riches* with patrician propriety.

The regular appearance of aristocrats on the high school faculty, administration, and board of trustees proved no bar to the adoption of more practical and progressive policies than prevailed in the academies. In 1901 an extensive scholarship and a commercial course of study was introduced. Nine years later James Simons, president of the board, arguing the case for industrial education (adopted in 1912), asserted that the trustees were "the servants of the people." The latter determined "what kinds of schools they want" and "whether intelligent labor should be dignified." It "is impossible to make every boy an able and well educated man, but I believe in giving every boy a chance to become such."[309] As in commerce and politics, aristocrats identifying themselves with broader, municipal endeavors tended to be more modern-minded than those, like the blueblood proprietors of academies, who served the distinctive interests of the old elite.

The major educational concern of the aristocracy continued to be higher learning, and the College of Charleston still enlisted the primary efforts of this group. The war-devastated college closed in 1865-66, recovery then ensued until 1880, when a sharp decline in funds and students (only ten undergraduates matriculated in 1883) and the withdrawal of municipal support from 1885 to 1891 again impoverished the institution. After 1892 another resurgence occurred. Many administrators, trustees, professors, and students still came from the patriciate, and Nathaniel Russell Middleton was president from 1857 to 1893, but, as in the case of the high school, the curriculum was modernized. Between the Civil War and World War II a number of upper-class lawyers and businessmen headed the board. Although the establishment retained a formidable presence at the college, its influence gradually lessened. After 1900 there were few blueblood faculty members, and upper-class trustees and students were less prevalent than in the old days. The college persisted, however, in providing a huge share of the Charleston professional community: in 1912, 35 percent of the bar, 28 percent of the physicians, and almost all the teaching staff of the high school were alumni.[310]

The University of South Carolina was even less of an upper-class preserve. Although several patricians remained prominent in the administration and the faculty from 1865 to the 1880s, e.g., Presidents Robert W. Barnwell (1865–73) and William Porcher Miles (1880–81), populist attacks and loss of appropriations under Governors Benjamin Tillman and Cole Blease precipitated a decline that lasted until the 1920s. Few of the higher state officials from the 1880s to the 1930s, contrary to antebellum times, went to the university.[311]

Episcopalianism constituted another Old Guard commitment. From the Civil War to the present many aristocrats have been ordained in this faith and some became rectors of exclusive Charleston churches. Bluebloods served as wardens, vestrymen, solicitors, and other officers in these congregations and had an appreciable, if subsiding, presence in the twentieth century. The bishops of the South Carolina diocese from 1907 to 1943 had distinguished tidewater lineage. The diocese treasurer and its chancellors (chief legal officers) from 1915 to 1950 had similar antecedents.[312]

The postwar privations of exclusive churches offer further evidence of upper-class decline. St. Philip's, St. Paul's, St. Michael's, and Grace were severely damaged and depleted during the conflict, and a committee appointed in 1868 to survey the physical and financial condition of South Carolina's Episcopal establishment reported widespread devastation and disarray. The committee noted that impoverishment of the diocese and financial problems in Charleston prevented St. Philip's from being "Habitable" until a wealthy contributor repaired the ravages of war and that St. Michael's needed "public subscriptions, and voluntary concerts" to pay "customhouse dues upon their bells." During Reconstruction cordial relations between St. Michael's and the city government broke down. In 1886 its vestry exaggerated a kernel of truth in announcing, in a manner reminiscent of New York's Trinity rectors William Berrian and Morgan Dix, that "the Congregation is a small one and has no wealthy members now. It belongs largely to the past, in its membership as in its building."[313]

Despite its novel assumption of humility, St. Michael's still sought an elite role in the community. "In what may rightly be termed a special sense," declared its rector in 1915, whose ancestors had been vestrymen, "St. Michael's is regarded by visitors, as well as by our own citizens, as the Church of this City. . . ." The Episcopal establishment, reflecting local sentiment, backed segregated shrines and a separate organization for Blacks.[314] But when changes came, even St. Michael's ultimately adapted. In the 1920s younger men replaced older officials, and the traditional practice of pew rent gradually disappeared. The old order, however, manifested its conservatism by delaying until 1942, long after it had vanished in patrician churches in other cities, the final end of this elitist custom.[315]

Charity

Medical and religious activities involved the upper class in public and private forms of altruism. The previously mentioned orphanages and hospitals were publicly and privately funded and administered. The municipality, as shown by allocations in the city budget of 1880, was primarily concerned with groups whose dependency resulted from physical as well as financial circumstances. Of the $57,000 appropriated for public welfare, the orphan house and the City Hospital of Charleston, which treated sick paupers, each received $20,000; the Alms House $8,000; the seven physicians to the poor $5,000; and the Ashley River Asylum, a home for the penurious aged, $4,000. After the war aristocrats never sat as commissioners of the Alms House or the Ashley River Asylum, rarely at the City Hospital, and often, but in a minority, on the orphan house board. The patriciate, however, was more active on the staffs of these institutions. Upper-class physicians frequently served at the Alms House, the hospital, and the asylum, and the orphanage doctor was invariably a blueblood until well into the twentieth century. The secretary and treasurer, usually a combined office, of the orphan house board were generally patricians.[316] The orphan house remained a favorite upper-class charity. In 1902 a blueblood found among its "Commissioners . . . grandsires and great grandsires, grandsons and sons, holding the position of their fathers in an honorable way."[317] Such statements contained a degree of accuracy, but the segment of well-born commissioners had shrunk from pre-secession days and donations were at no time in the institution's history either large or primarily due to the patronage of the old elite. An indication of the significance of organized benevolence in urban leadership was an 1865 *Courier* report that "no institution . . . deservedly enjoys a greater hold on the affections of our people than does the Orphan House of Charleston."[318] Naturally the upper class sought to identify with so cherished an enterprise.

Shirras Dispensary, closely connected with the St. Andrew's Society and the Medical Society of South Carolina, Roper Hospital, which the medical society helped administer, and the William Enston Home were other charitable associations in which the Old Guard prominently participated as managers and staff members. But even at Roper Hospital, where patricians were as active as in the orphanage, the major contributors were *parvenus*. Aristocrat William T. Wragg, long-term secretary-treasurer of the William Roper Fund, expressed the middle-class rationale for institutionalized relief in claiming that the "patients are not from the vicious or pauper classes, who are provided for at the public expense, but are from among the industrious working poor."[319]

Next to medical care for the needy, religious charities commanded upper-class loyalties. To the present day, descendants of distinguished families have labored in historic Episcopalian societies and in such newer efforts as the Church Home Orphanage (1906), the Ladies' Home (1909), and the Young People's Service League (1924). These endeavors, unlike the medical organizations, were exclusively private in funding and administration. Sectarian aid to the unfortunate was also directly dispensed through patrician churches, which, as in other cities, increased their welfare agencies after the Civil War. Several ancient philanthropies, neither religious nor medical in origin, continued under genteel domination. During the twentieth century the Ladies Benevolent Society, the oldest women's organization in the United States, catered to the ill and aged poor, and the Harriott Pinckney Home for Seamen was directed from 1853 to 1913 by Pinckneys. Aristocrats still frequently became officers of the Charleston Port Society, but their influence was not as extensive as in the Pinckney Home or the Benevolent Society and the major benefactors were not Old Guard Charlestonians. Supplementing its role in older institutions or types of altruism, the traditional elite, by forming the Home for Mothers, Widows and Daughters of Confederate Soldiers (1867), demonstrated a reserve of vitality that enabled it to deal with new problems. Many pre–Civil War upper-class associations persisted and a few new ones emerged, but several of the old welfare organizations, the St. Andrew's and St. George's societies, became primarily elite social clubs, and the South Carolina Society lost its educational functions to the public school system and folded in 1880.[320]

Some aristocrats, such as Thomas Pinckney—physician, rice planter, and trustee in several elite religious charities—were prominent altruists. Modern philanthropy, especially the YMCA, also attracted elements of the Old Guard, particularly lawyers and politicians involved in progressive sectors of urban life. Many of the greatest figures and all the largest donors in Charleston charities, however, were recent attainers of affluence and status. Self-made banker George W. Williams chaired the orphan house board from 1894 to 1903. Andrew Buist Murray, late-nineteenth-century Charleston's preeminent benefactor and a wealthy capitalist educated at the orphan house, also became chairman and was a member of the Charleston Bible and St. Andrew's societies. He gave $1,013,000 to public causes, including $200,000 to the orphanage and $100,000 to the College of Charleston.[321] Although aristocrats still head several welfare organizations, newcomers now predominate. The only patricians prominent in such institutions in 1950 were the presidents of the Charleston County Tuberculosis Association and the East Cooper River Community Chest Council, and an officer of the Episcopal Church Home.[322]

While its financial condition prohibited the large monetary contributions of other urban patriciates, the Old Guard gave generously of time and professional talent. The Brahmins, a wealthier group with equal civic pride, played a larger role in Boston benevolence. Genteel New Yorkers, on the other hand, withdrew more completely after 1900 from humanitarian causes than did upper-class Charlestonians or Bostonians.

Culture

Civic, class, and career commitments and vocational expertise propelled patrician capitalists, professionals, and officials into philanthropy and culture. Upper-class involvement also was motivated by a desire to maintain community leadership and to create an ethical and ideological rationale for such ascendancy. Aristocrats, especially those with the skill and energy to excel in other fields, applied these traits to benevolent projects. Individuals often simultaneously managed several charitable and intellectual organizations. Although the chief benefactors of the needy were usually newly risen businessmen, patrician professionals and politicians, particularly educators and attorneys, took the lead in cultural activities. Joseph W. Barnwell headed the historical and library societies and the Art Association. Edward McCrady, Jr., represented Charleston in the lower state house and served on the St. Philip's vestry, as a medical college and library society trustee, and as vice-president of the historical society. Wilmot G. De Saussure of De Saussure & Son, an assemblyman and harbor commissioner, was president of the library and St. Andrew's societies.[323]

Civil War did not disturb Old Guard suzerainty over such ancient institutions as the library and historical societies and the museum, which were as much social as cultural organizations. In the 1860s and '70s patricians were curators of the museum, and until World War I many bluebloods served on its staff and as trustees, administrators, and patrons. The museum was finally housed in its own building in 1907 and incorporated eight years later. Thomas Pinckney, whose great-uncle chaired the founders' committee in 1773, became the first president of the board of trustees. Beginning in the 1920s the old family presence gradually dwindled, but even earlier the main financial support came from *arrivistes*. The museum building was a gift of a merchant and adopted citizen of Charleston, and Andrew Buist Murray, that noted underwriter of public causes, gave $100,000. After the Civil War the museum added cultural and historical memorabilia of South Carolina to its natural history and geological collections, thus becoming a guardian, along with the historical society, of the local past.[324] The latter also continued under elite leadership. Among its post–Civil War presidents were Porcher in the 1880s, Charles Cotesworth Pinckney in the 1890s, Joseph W. Barnwell during the first quarter of the twentieth century, and Samuel Gaillard Stoney in the 1950s. President Barnwell's 1919 remark that Charlestonians were "securely intrenched in our own views" captured the spirit of the society. Stoney, a local historian and genealogist living on the family planatation who fought to preserve Charleston landmarks and also headed the museum board, received an obituary in the *News and Courier* in 1968 that indicated the stature of genteel cultural figures in that town. A "Charleston institution," he was "a widely recognized symbol and source of community pride."[325]

The aristocracy demonstrated a reserve of vitality by rejuvenating old cultural institutions and founding new ones. An example of the former was the 1880s recovery, from its Civil War–Reconstruction hiatus, of the Art Association. Under the leadership of Nathaniel Russell Middleton, then president of the College of Charleston, it held an exhibition in 1880. Under Gabriel E. Manigault's presidency in the 1880s and '90s the organization underwent a renaissance, procuring a yearly stipend from the legislature, giving art fairs and shows, and buying paintings. The multiple leadership functions of aristocrats Middleton, Manigault (a museum curator), and Joseph W. Barnwell (a recording secretary of the association) disclose an interlocking blueblood directorate that dominated the older cultural institutions of Charleston. During the Great Depression the association once again declined; this time, however, it was rescued by a newer elite and the generosity of the Charleston County government. With new management came a different outlook. Modern art was now exhibited, and the association controlled WPA art and theater projects in the vicinity. Unlike its role in some other cultural organizations, the upper class was as open with its purse as with its time and energy. In 1903 James S. Gibbes, a Charleston merchant descended from a colonial South Carolina governor, left the association $119,322, and recently several aristocrats have given large bequests. The Gibbes legacy, jointly administered by the mayor and the association, became the James S. Gibbes Memorial Art Gallery (1904). The *noblesse oblige* impulse behind this gift was expressed by the donor in 1883. He desired "to assist in fostering in our young and growing generation a taste for the Fine Arts in this the home of my forefathers and the loved city of my heart."[326]

The launching of the South Carolina Poetry Society (1920), a model for similar organizations in other southern states, indicated that the patriciate could still advance urban culture by undertaking new ventures. This spirit permeated the proclamation issued by the originators, which combined customary regional defensiveness with a zest for the intellectual life and a willingness to accept change. The founders believed that "culture in the South is not merely an *ante bellum* tradition, but an instant, vital force," and were utterly "weary of the reiterated pronouncements from commercial publishing centers in the North and West that America is vocal only in that territory." Several patricians belonged to its writers' groups and helped revivify the organization in 1940 after it became a Depression casualty. The society also deteriorated, in the fashion of other Charleston associations, as one member put it, by becoming "one-tenth poetry and nine-tenths society."[327]

Supplementing their functions in private institutions, bluebloods contributed to urban culture by appearing with regularity on such municipal bodies as the Charleston Art Commission and the Historical Commission of Charleston, and, in the case of the Manigaults, by owning, since 1894, the *Evening Post* and, since 1926, the *News and Courier.* Apart from institutional involvement the upper class participated more creatively in intellectual endeavors, primarily as *belles lettrists*. Charleston's most famous literary figure was DuBose Heyward. Born into an impoverished aristocratic clan, he was a founder and president of the poetry society, on the board of the art association, resident dramatist and prime mover behind the restoration of the Dock St. Theater, and the first Charlestonian elected to the National Institute of Arts and Letters.[328]

Despite varied and extensive aristocratic engagement, old complaints reemerged charging the South, South Carolina, and Charleston with denigrating arts and letters. Simms and Paul Hamilton Hayne continued to deplore the neglect of creative talents in the region. Michael P. O'Connor, Charleston lawyer and congressman in the 1870s and '80s, agreed that South Carolina ignored art and literature. The financial troubles of the art association, the College of Charleston, and the historical society reinforced these attitudes. In 1884 society president Porcher solicited the municipal government for a yearly appropriation to replace the state stipend halted in 1861. He argued that "poverty has greatly diminished the membership, and, without aid, the society is unable to publish."[329]

Since the Civil War, aristocratic culture has functioned primarily to transmit ancestral values and traditions. Paladins of the past—Paul Hamilton Hayne, Alice R. Huger and Daniel Elliott Huger Smith, Samuel Gaillard Stoney, Anna Wells Rutledge, J. Motte Alston, and Harriott Horry Rutledge Ravenel—kept old memories alive through organizational activity, poems, novels, essays, memoirs, histories, biographies, and genealogies. In common with Virginians and other southerners, they mythified the plantation South into a harmonious and hierarchical society of pure, self-sacrificing women; elegant, noble, and brilliant cavaliers; and grateful, docile slaves. Their conservatism had a "lost cause" poignancy that intensified the self-pity and sentimentality with which they contemplated the past, rued the present, and feared the future. Reaffirmation of old ways necessarily entailed condemnation of modern times. Democracy, industrialization, and black liberation were departures from the Golden Age—vile forces unleashed by unscrupulous politicians, robber barons, and radical reformers who, untouched by the ennobling experiences of the low-country gentry, were bent on wiping out the vestiges of decency and high culture.[330] Thus persisted the prewar conflict, still seen by bluebloods as a confrontation between old and new, continuity and change, elitism and equality, the sublime and the sinister, the South and the North. Little had changed in this ongoing tidewater defense, for the outcome of civil war had confirmed in the patrician remnant the antebellum consciousness of an enfeebled, beleaguered enclave doomed by an onslaught of the dynamo and the demagogue.

Society

High society in Charleston resembled the Old Guard bastions of Philadelphia and Boston. Unlike New York's Four Hundred, aristocratic families and agencies dominated the inner circle, and its foremost figures achieved considerable repute in culture, the professions, and politics. Since antebellum times, the St. Cecilia Society has been the reigning social organization; its main activity, the St. Cecilia dances, climaxes the social season; its leadership comes from the oldest low-country clans and its outlook reflects their values. "Membership in this society," said ex-Mayor Rhett in 1940, "early became the criterion of social standing in the city." Joseph W. Barnwell and Stoney served as post–Civil War presidents. In common with the Philadelphia Assembly and New York's Bachelor balls, its dances were run by men, for Charleston society, like that of Boston and Philadelphia, differed from the Astor set in being male-dominated. Actresses and divorcées are barred from the balls along with spouses and children of members who marry outside their enclave, and, as with genteel affairs in Boston and Philadelphia, publicity is shunned. St. Cecilia membership is almost exclusively inherited and based on lineage, although barriers were recently lowered to admit a few affluent *arrivistes*. According to DuBose Heyward, the society "preserved the aristocratic traditions" by adhering "to a code of manners and morals of an earlier day." Its semiannual balls, "the social events of the year, . . . are examples of social decorum and formal elegance. . . . It is not uncommon to see upon the dance floor at the same time representatives of three generations of the same family."[331]

The Jockey and Cotillion (1867) clubs and the Charleston Ancient Artillery Society were other gathering places for the well-born. The old elite also fortified itself by revivifying the St. George and Artillery societies and founding the Huguenot Society of South Carolina. These efforts indicate the increased patrician attraction to organizations which emphasized kinship ties and loyalty to the past. The St. George's Society was formed in 1733 to assist unfortunate Englishmen and their progeny in South Carolina. Moribund between 1890 and 1897, it was reorganized largely under patrician leadership. During the first half of the century the Artillery Society had few aristocratic officers or members, but after 1865 bluebloods became more numerous in membership and prominent in its direction.[332] The Huguenot Society (1885) typified the nationwide resurgence of ancestral and patriotic associations. Its constitution dedicated the society to "commemorate" the history, "perpetuate the memory, . . . promote the principles and virtues of the Huguenots," and to "discover, collect and preserve" data "relating to genealogy or history of" that ethnic group. Admission was open to direct descendants of pre-1787 Huguenot or other French Protestant immigrants, pastors of French Huguenot congregations in South Carolina, and students of Huguenot history. The bulk of the membership has come from distinguished low-country French Huguenot stock, and its presidents include Wilmot G. De Saussure, Horry Frost Ravenel, Thomas W. Bacot (also head of St. George's), Alfred Huger, and Stoney. The 1889 presidential address of Daniel Ravenel expressed the traditional and familial orientation of the organization: "pride of birth and ancestry" should provide "an incentive to higher life." Those with distinguished "breeding" should derive "satisfaction" from their origins, have a strong sense of self and group identity, and ought to be worthy of their "lineage."[333]

Aristocrats headed a variety of ancestral associations and social clubs, including the Society of Colonial Wars, the Order of the Cincinnati in South Carolina, and the Charleston Club. As late as 1950 descendants of the antebellum gentry headed the Artillery Society, the Huguenot Society, the English Speaking Union, the Ivy Garden Club, the Who's

My Neighbor Society, and were high officers in the Carolina Plantation Society.[334]

Intermarriage and perpetuation of ancient customs constituted other strategies for maintaining group cohesion. Although dueling ended in the 1870s, annual knightly tournaments were still held in the 1930s at the Charleston Azalea Festival. Offspring of old families continued to unite and Charleston, unlike New York, did not provide wives for titled Europeans.[335]

Genteel Charlestonians, along with the Brahmins and Knickerbockers—and for the same reasons—surrendered social leadership long after they retreated from more important areas of urban life. In common with these other patriciates they now reign over matters of little significance outside polite society. Withdrawal into a world of reminiscences and genealogies ill-fitted the aristocracy for more weighty contests of leadership and inadequately compensated for irrelevancy to the community that lay beyond the old clans. A transplanted northern businessman could not gain entry into the St. Cecilia Society, but his well-born stenographer belonged.[336] None knew of their decline better than upper-class cultural and social luminaries. From the Reconstruction era to our own times they have bemoaned the burial of the past under the onrushing present. Paul Hamilton Hayne, Gabriel Manigault, and J. Motte Alston shrunk from "beholding St. Paul's [Parish] once more," bewailed the "decay and poverty" that befell their class, and grieved over the war deaths that "prematurely cut off" the "most valued scions" of the "well-known families" and destroyed "the noble aspirations in the South." Manigault thought that those left on the battlefield were "happier than the part that survived," and Alston "often felt that death and not life was the boon to be craved."[337] Despite Charleston's reputation for preserving the most aristocratic society in the country, Stoney said in 1960 that "here you've got Society *a la carte* and you've got Society *a la mode*. And both of them are a long way from the blue plate special." In 1941 South Carolina's poet laureate, Archibald Rutledge, made a pathetic if slightly sardonic admission of impotence by deferring to the tycoons who had recently purchased tidewater baronies. His family plantation bordered on "a colony of multimillionaires" who "have been most gracious to me and often come informally to visit this rustic native. . . . The work that the wealthy men from the North have done in restoring the desolate and abandoned plantations in the coastal region of the South is about as fine as anything that has come to my view."[338]

Charleston's multivariate and persistent upper-class community leadership resembles Brahmin Boston rather than the specialized, contentious, and short-lived elites in New York. The upper ranks in Boston and Charleston, however, differed in that the former preserved its eminence by adapting to industrialization and democracy while the latter maintained its position because its defense of tradition fulfilled an important need in a section where blood ties and old ways still gave meaning to life. The genteel New Englanders, more talented in and committed to business and having escaped the holocaust of war, outlasted the Charlestonians as a significant urban economic force. But the enclaves evinced marked similarities and eventually met the same fate. Both held onto vestiges of political leadership long after the Knickerbockers disappeared from the scene, and in the twentieth century they sought cohesion, status, and gratification in kinship ties, polite society, high culture, and patrician philanthropy. If the Brahmins had an edge in intellectual, commercial, and financial vitality and in charity activities, the Charlestonians have better perpetuated their role in setting the tone for the fashions and rituals of the *beau monde* in their city.

NOTES

1. U.S. Bureau of the Census, "Urban Population in the U.S. from the First Census (1790) to the Fifteenth Census (1930)," reproduced from typescript, 1939. For an analysis of the antebellum South lagging behind all other parts of the country in urbanization and industrialization see Gavin Wright, *The Political Economy of the Cotton South: Households, Markets, and Wealth in the Nineteenth Century* (New York: W. W. Norton, 1978), 109–25. Wright attributes the South's relatively slow growth in these areas to the profitability of large-scale agriculture. The plantation system, whose economic advantages depended heavily upon slavery, provided an alternative form of investment and economic activity otherwise absent in the United States. Wright also argues that the interests of the rural gentry did not necessarily lie in promoting local commerce, industry, immigration to the city, or other features of urban capitalism.

2. Joseph Alston to Theodosia Burr, c. 1800, in George Rogers, Jr., *The History of Georgetown County, South Carolina* (Columbia: University of South Carolina Press, 1970), 189.

3. Frederick A. Porcher, "Southern and Northern Civilization Contrasted," *Russell's Magazine*, I (May, 1857), 98–104, 106.

4. Robert Barnwell Rhett, "A Farewell to the Subscribers of the Charleston Mercury," in Richard M. Weaver, *The Southern Tradition at Bay* (New Rochelle, N.Y.: Arlington House, 1968), 149. For another example of South Carolinian defensiveness toward the North see William Gilmore Simms, "Summer Travel in the South," *Southern Quarterly Review*, new ser., II (Sept., 1850), 24–65. For other states and more general treatments of the Southern upper-class ideology see Weaver, *Southern*; Thomas Nelson Page: *The Old South* (Chautauqua, N.Y.: Chautauqua Press, 1919); *The Old Dominion: Her Making and Her Manners* (New York: Charles Scribner's Sons, 1918); Rollin G. Osterweis, *Romanticism and Nationalism in the Old South* (New Haven: Yale University Press, 1949); W. J. Cash, *The Mind of the South* (New York: Alfred A.

Knopf, 1941); William Taylor, *Cavalier and Yankee: The Old South and American National Character* (New York: George Braziller, 1961); Louis Hartz, *The Liberal Tradition in America* (New York: Harcourt, Brace, 1955), 143–77; Eugene D. Genovese: *The Political Economy of Slavery: Studies in the Economy and Society of the Slave South* (New York: Vintage Books, 1967); *The World the Slaveholders Made* (New York: Pantheon Books, 1969); Francis Pendleton Gaines, *The Southern Plantation* (New York: Columbia University Press, 1925); C. Vann Woodward, *The Burden of Southern History* (New York: Vintage Books, 1960), 17–22.

5. Louis Morton, *Robert Carter of Nomini Hall* (Princeton: Princeton University Press, 1941); Bernard Bailyn, "Politics and Social Structure in Virginia," *Essays in Colonial History*, ed. James Morton Smith (Chapel Hill: University of North Carolina Press, 1959), 90–115; Thomas J. Wertenbaker, *The Shaping of Colonial Virginia* (New York: Russell and Russell, 1958); Louis B. Wright: *The First Gentlemen of Virginia* (San Marino, Calif.: Huntington Library, 1940); *The Cultural Life of the American Colonies, 1607–1703* (New York: Harper & Bros., 1957), 5–13; Clifford Dowdey, *The Virginia Dynasties* (Boston: Little, Brown, 1969).

6. Mattie E. E. Parker, ed., *North Carolina Charters and Constitutions, 1578–1698* (Raleigh: Carolina Tercentenary Commission, 1963), 128–240; M. Eugene Sirmans, *Colonial South Carolina: A Political History, 1663–1763* (Chapel Hill: University of North Carolina Press, 1966), 9–37. For the origins and circumstances of the earliest settlers see Alexander S. Salley, "Narratives of Early Carolina, 1650–1708," *Narratives of Early American History*, ed. J. Franklin Jameson (New York: Charles Scribner's Sons, 1911), 184; Peter H. Wood, *Black Majority: Negroes in Colonial South Carolina* (New York: Alfred A. Knopf, 1974), 17, 23, 28.

7. The best sources for the genealogies and histories of upper-class South Carolina families are *Transactions of the Huguenot Society of South Carolina* and *South Carolina Historical and Genealogical Magazine*. These journals are subsequently cited as *Transactions* and *SCHGM*. More convenient but less complete information is contained in *Cyclopaedia of Eminent and Representative Men of the Carolinas of the Nineteenth Century*, 2 vols. (Madison, Wis.: Brant and Fuller, 1892); Helen Kohn Hennig, *Great South Carolinians* (Chapel Hill: University of North Carolina Press, 1940); J. C. Hemphill, *Men of Mark in South Carolina*, 4 vols. (Washington, D.C.: Men of Mark Publishing Co., 1907–9); Frampton Ellis Smith, *Some Historic Families of South Carolina* (Atlanta: Foote & Davis, 1905); Arthur Henry Hirsch, *The Huguenots of Colonial South Carolina* (Durham: Duke University Press, 1928); Daniel Ravenel, *French and Swiss Protestants* (Baltimore: Genealogical Publishing, 1969); Jonathan P. Thomas, Jr., "The Barbadians in Early South Carolina," *SCHGM*, XXXI (Apr., 1930), 75–92. For other data on distinguished South Carolinians and their families see David Duncan Wallace, *The Life of Henry Laurens* (New York: G. P. Putnam's Sons, 1915), 7; Edward McCrady, *The History of South Carolina under the Proprietary Government, 1670–1719* (New York: Macmillan, 1897), 369.

8. For the early acquisition and long-lived holding of plantations among the

low-country aristocracy see A. S. Sattey, Jr., *Warrants for Lands in South Carolina, 1680–92* (Columbia, S.C.: State Company, 1911); Rogers, *History, passim*; Henry A. M. Smith: "The Baronies of South Carolina," *SCHGM*, XI (Apr., 1910), 86–87, (Jan., 1911), 9, XII (July, 1911), 116–17, XIII (Jan., 1912), 5–11, (July, 1912), 119–25, XV (Apr., 1914), 63–72, (Oct., 1914), 153, 156; "The Upper Ashley; and the Mutations of Families," *ibid.* XX (July, 1919), 151–98; "The Ashley River: Its Seats and Settlements," *ibid.* XX (Jan., 1919), 3–51, (Apr., 1919), 75–122; "Old Charleston and Its Vicinity," *ibid.* XVI (Jan., 1915), 14–15, (Apr., 1915), 57–58, 65–66; "Charleston and Charleston Neck," *ibid.* XIX (Jan., 1918), 3–76; "Goose Creek," *ibid.* XXIX (Apr., 1928), 76–79, (July, 1928) 167–72, (Oct., 1928), 267–72; Albert Morel Lachicotte, *Georgetown Rice Plantations* (Columbia: University of South Carolina Press, 1955); Samuel Gaillard Stoney, *Plantations of the Carolina Low Country* (Charleston: Carolina Art Association, 1938), 47–48, 54–55, 57–59, 61–62, 81–82; Herbert Ravenel Sass, *The Story of the South Carolina Low Country*, 3 vols. (West Columbia, S.C.: J. F. Higer Publishing, 1956), I, *passim*; Harriette Kershaw Leiding, *Historic Houses of South Carolina* (Philadelphia: J. B. Lippincott, 1921), 81–82, 107–8, 114, 124, 134–35, 140, 142–44, 173–75, 202–5, 240–42; Chalmers Gaston Davidson, *The Last Foray: The South Carolina Planters of 1860, a Sociological Study* (Columbia: University of South Carolina Press, 1971), 15–16.

9. Henry A. M. Smith, "Charleston—the Original Plan and the Earliest Settlers," *SCHGM*, IX (Jan., 1908), 1–10, 26; Alice Huger Smith, *The Dwelling Houses of Charleston, South Carolina* (Philadelphia: J. B. Lippincott, 1917), 77–78, 93, 120, 223, 260–62; Leiding: *Historic*, 5; *Charleston: Historic and Romantic* (Philadelphia: J. B. Lippincott, 1917), 101, 107, 118.

10. Anne Simon Deas, *Recollections of the Ball Family of South Carolina and the Comingtee Plantation* (n.p.: privately printed, 1909), 9, 15, 33–35, 40; Lewis C. Gray, *History of Agriculture in the Southern United States to 1860*, 2 vols. (New York: Peter Smith, 1941), I, 110, 135, 192–93; Stoney, *Plantations*, 21–28; Leila Sellers, *Charleston Business on the Eve of the American Revolution* (Chapel Hill: University of North Carolina Press, 1934), 25–48, 85, 87, 152, 162–68; David L. Coon, "Eliza Lucas Pinckney and the Reintroduction of Indigo Culture in South Carolina," *Journal of Southern History*, XLII (Feb., 1976), 61–77; Verner W. Crane, *The Southern Frontier* (Ann Arbor: University of Michigan Press, 1964), 108–9, 119–22; Rogers, *History*, 27, 41–43, 45–46, 50–51; Samuel DuBose, "Address Delivered at the Seventeenth Anniversary of the Black Oak Agricultural Society [1858]," in T. Gaillard Thomas, *A Contribution to the History of the Huguenots of South Carolina* (New York: Knickerbocker Press, 1887), 5; Harriet Horry Ravenel, *Eliza Pinckney* (Spartanburg, S.C.: Reprint Co., 1967), 7–9, 104–6; Eliza Lucas, *Journals and Letters* (Spartanburg, S.C.: Reprint Co., 1967), 5, 9, 13, 15–16; Augustus Kohn, *The Cotton Mills of South Carolina* (Charleston: Daggett Printing, 1907), 7; E. M. Lander, Jr., "The South Carolina Textile Industry before 1845," *Proceedings of the South Carolina Historical Association* (1951), 19; Sirmans, "Politicians and Planters: The Bull Family of South Carolina," *Proceedings* (1962), 34; Broadus Mitchell, *The Rise of Cotton Mills in the South* (Baltimore: Johns Hopkins Studies in Historical and Political Science, ser. XXXIX, 1921), 11–19.

11. Rogers, *History*, 304–5; "The Thomas Pinckney Family of South Carolina," *SCHGM*, XXXIX (Jan., 1938), 15–16; W. Robert Higgins, "Charlestown Merchants and Factors Dealing in the External Negro Trade," *SCHGM*, XLV (Dec., 1964), 206–17; Myrta J. Hutson, "Early Generations of the Motte Family of South Carolina," *Transactions*, no. 56 (1951), 57–61; Gabriel E. Manigualt, William H. Huger, William C. Ravenel, and Robert Wilson, "Historical Sketch of the Prioleau Family in Europe and America," *Transactions*, no. 6 (1899), 28; Smith, *Some Historic*, 10–11; Elizabeth Anne Poyas, *The Olden Time of Carolina* (Charleston: S. G. Courtenay, 1855), 67; Richard Barry, *Mr. Rutledge of South Carolina* (New York: Duell, Sloan, and Pearce, 1942), 31, 70.

12. Henry Laurens to John Knight, June 12, 1764, in *Documents Illustrative of the History of the Slave Trade*, ed. Elizabeth Donnan, 4 vols. (Washington, D.C.: Carnegie Institution, 1935), IV, 391–92.

13. Barry, *Mr. Rutledge*, 56–62, 65–69, 247.

14. Eliza Lucas to George Lucas, June 4, 1741, in Lucas, *Journals*, 13; Eliza Lucas Pinckney quoted in Ravenel, *Eliza Pinckney*, 114, 116; E. L. Pinckney to G. Lucas, ?, ?, 1742, in *The Letterbook of Eliza Lucas Pinckney*, eds. Elise Lucas and Marvin R. Zahniser (Chapel Hill: University of North Carolina Press, 1972), 51–52.

15. Elias Ball, Jr., quoted in Deas, *Recollections*, 75, 78.

16. Peter Manigault to Mrs. Gabriel Manigault, Oct. 10, 1750, in "Peter Manigault's Letters," *SCHGM*, XXXI (July, 1930), 179–80; same to same, Feb. 20, 1750, *ibid.* (Oct., 1930), 271–72, Mar. 12, 1750, 276; P. Manigault to G. Manigault, July 30, 1751, *ibid.* XXXII (Jan., 1931), 46; same to same, Oct. 18, 1752, 56–57, Mar. 15, 1753, 122–23; P. Manigault to Francis Huger, June 5, 1770, in Maurice A. Crouse, "The Letterbook of Peter Manigault," *SCHGM*, LXX (July, 1969), 186. John Rutledge to Edward Rutledge, July 30, 1769, in John Belton O'Neal, *Biographical Sketches of the Bench and Bar of South Carolina*, 2 vols. (Charleston: S. G. Courtenay, 1859), II, 121, 123–24, 126–27.

17. H. Laurens to J. Knight, June 26, 1775, in *The Papers of Henry Laurens*, ed. Philip Hamer (Columbia, S.C.: University of South Carolina Press, 1968), I, 271–72.

18. H. Laurens to ?, Feb. 25, 1774, in Hamer, "Henry Laurens—Neglected Patriot," *Transactions*, no. 70 (1965), 4–5. For Laurens's values and attitudes see H. Laurens to Gidney Clarke, Feb. 21, 1756, in *Laurens Papers*, ed. Hamer, I, 101; H. Laurens to Levi Durand, July 19, 1763, *ibid.* III, 502; "Letters from Henry Laurens to His Son John Laurens, 1773–1776," *SCHGM*, III (Jan., 1902), 86–96, (July, 1902), 139–49, (Oct., 1902), 207–15, IV (Jan., 1903), 26–35, (Apr., 1903), 99–107, (July, 1903), 215–20; H. Laurens to Martha Laurens, Aug. 18, 1771, in David Ramsay, *Memoirs of the Life of Martha Laurens Ramsay* (Boston: Samuel T. Armstrong, 1812), 55; Wallace, *Laurens*, 33, 441n.

19. Jackson Turner Main, *The Social Structure of Revolutionary America* (Princeton: Princeton University Press, 1965), 57–66.

20. Gray, *History*, I, 178.

21. Alexander Garden to the Royal Society, Apr. 22, 1755, in "Correspondence between Alexander Garden and the Royal Society of London," *SCHGM*,

LXIV (Jan., 1963), 16–17; Alexander Hewatt, "An Historical Account of the Rise and Progress of the Colonies of South Carolina and Georgia," originally published in 1799, in *Historical Collections of South Carolina*, 2 vols., ed. B. R. Carroll (New York: Harper & Bros., 1836), I, 377, 512.

22. H. Laurens to William Stone, May 18, 1748, and to Richard Pattison, Oct. 23, 1756, in *Laurens Papers*, ed. Hamer, I, 138–39, II, 343.

23. Sellers, *Charleston Business*, 11; David MacPherson, *Annals of Commerce*, 4 vols. (London: Nichols and Son, 1805), III, 570–71.

24. For intermarriage within and between the maritime and agrarian elites see Alexander S. Salley, ed., *Marriage Notices in the South Carolina Gazette and Its Successors (1732–1812)* (Albany: John Munsell's Sons, 1902). For data on the Charleston commercial community see references in note 7; Sellers, *Charleston Business*; George Rogers, Jr., *Evolution of a Federalist: William Loughton Smith of Charleston (1758–1812)* (Columbia: University of South Carolina Press, 1962); Richard Walsh, ed., *The Writings of Christopher Gadsden* (Columbia: University of South Carolina Press, 1966); Higgins, "Charlestown Merchants"; Donnan, *Documents*, IV; Maurice A. Crouse: "Gabriel Manigault: Charleston Merchant," *SCHGM*, LXVIII (Oct., 1967), 220–31; "Letterbook" *ibid.*, LXX (Apr., 1969), 79–96, (July, 1969), 177–96; Gabriel E. Manigault, "The Manigault Family of South Carolina," *Transactions*, no. 4 (1897), 48–84; Wallace, *Life*; Hamer, ed., *Laurens Papers*; "Correspondence of Henry Laurens," *SCHGM*, XXVIII (Jan., 1927), 144–63, (Oct., 1927), 207–25, XXIX (Jan., 1928), 26–40, (July, 1928), 193–211, XXX (Jan., 1929), 6–26, (July, 1929), 134–67, XXXI (Oct., 1929), 134–67, 199–214, XXXI (Jan., 1930), 26–45, (July, 1930), 209–27; "Journal of Robert Pringle, 1746–47," *ibid.*, XXVI (Jan., 1925), 21–30, (Apr., 1925), 93–112; "Izard-Laurens Correspondence," *ibid.*, XXII (Jan., 1921), 1–41. For Georgetown merchants see Rogers, *History*, *passim*.

25. H. Laurens to Ross and Mill, Sept. 2, 1768, in *Documents*, ed. Donnan, IV, 425.

26. Hirsch, *Huguenots*, 60n, 90–102, 186–87, 262; cf. Robert Wilson, "The Huguenot Influence in Colonial South Carolina," *Transactions*, no. 4 (1897), 26–38.

27. Main, *Social Structure*, 59–60; Alice Hanson Jones, *American Colonial Wealth: Documents and Methods*, 3 vols. (New York: Arno Press, 1977), II, 887–1022, III, 1473–1619, 1855–56, 1933–37, 2096–2125, 2153–56, 2165–67.

28. Hirsch, *Huguenots*, 243–44.

29. Edward Marston quoted in Sirmans, *Colonial*, 59; P. Manigault to R. Izard, Aug. 26, 1767, in Crouse, "Letterbook," 87.

30. Hewatt, "Historical," 506, 510; Carl Bridenbaugh, *Myths and Realities* (Baton Rouge: Louisiana State University Press, 1952), 115–16.

31. Rogers, *Evolution*, 29, 76; Manigault, "Manigault," 58–60; Wallace, *Laurens*, 69–70; Amery R. Childs, *Planters and Businessmen: The Guignard Family of South Carolina, 1795–1830* (Columbia: University of South Carolina Press, 1957), 3–5; Sass, *Low Country*, I, 188–89; Rogers, *History*, 64, 98–99; Mary Pringle Fenhagen, "Descendants of Judge Robert Pringle," *SCHGM*, LXII (July, 1961), 153; George C. Rogers, "The Conscience of a Huguenot,"

Translations, no. 67 (1962), 3; Sellers, *Charleston Business*, 58–59; Crouse, "Gabriel Manigault," 228; Edward McCrady, *History of South Carolina in the Revolution, 1775–1780* (New York: Macmillan, 1902), 183.

32. South Carolina *Gazette* quoted in Hirsch, *Huguenots*, 223; P. Manigault to Daniel Blake, Oct. 19, 1770, in Crouse, "Letterbook," 187.

33. Jack P. Greene, *The Quest for Power: The Lower Houses of Assembly in the Southern Royal Colonies, 1689–1776* (Chapel Hill: University of North Carolina Press, 1963), 34–35; M. Eugene Sirmans, "The South Carolina Royal Council," *William and Mary Quarterly*, XVIII (July, 1961), 375–76, 378, 380; Leonard Woods Labaree, *Conservatism in Early American History* (Ithaca: Cornell University Press, 1959), 11–14.

34. Governor Lyttleton quoted in Sirmans, "South Carolina," 373.

35. Sirmans, *Colonial*, 245–47. For a list of assembly leaders see Greene, *Quest*, 459–60, 475–88; Jackson Turner Main, "Government by the People: The American Revolution and the Democratization of the Legislatures," *William and Mary Quarterly*, XXIII (July, 1966), 394–407.

36. William Bull II quoted in Greene, *Quest*, 34.

37. Sirmans, *Colonial*, 126, 200, 247, 251–52; Ella Lonn, *The Colonial Agents of the Southern Colonies* (Gloucester, Mass.: Peter Smith, 1965), 394–95; Hamer, ed., *Laurens Papers*, I, 244–45.

38. Sirmans, *Colonial*, 109–10, 126, 145–49, 160–61, 200–207, 269–70; Sirmans, "South Carolina," 382–83; Sellers, *Charleston Business*, 71–74; Hirsch, *Huguenots*, 139–44; Richard M. Jellison: "Antecedents of the South Carolina Currency Acts of 1736 and 1746," *William and Mary Quarterly*, XVI (Oct., 1959), 556–57; "Paper Currency in Colonial South Carolina: A Reappraisal," *SCHGM*, LXII (July, 1961), 134–47.

39. Sirmans, *Colonial*, 252–53; Hamer, ed., *Laurens Papers*, II, 539.

40. Sirmans, *Colonial*, 154, 248.

41. *Ibid.*, 311–14; Sirmans, "South Carolina," 389–91; Jack P. Greene, "The Gadsden Election Controversy and the Revolutionary Movement in South Carolina," *Mississippi Valley Historical Review*, XLVI (Dec., 1959), 474–92; Rogers, *Evolution*, 38, 48–50, 74; Sellers, *Charleston Business*, 186–210.

42. Barry, *Mr. Rutledge*, 94; Josiah Quincy, Jr., "Journal 1773," *Massachusetts Historical Society Proceedings*, XL (June, 1916), 446–47.

43. John Laurens to James Laurens, Apr. 17, 1772, *The Army Correspondence of Col. John Laurens* (New York: Bradford Club, 1867), 14.

44. Sirmans, "South Carolina," 380–81.

45. Barry, *Mr. Rutledge*, 12, 14, 65–67, 132–33; "The Letters and Will of Robert Pringle," *SCHGM*, L (July, 1949), 145–46; "The Thomas Pinckney Family of South Carolina," *SCHGM*, XXXIX (Jan., 1938), 15–35; "List of Attorneys Enrolled at Charleston, South Carolina from 1772 to May, 1779, Inclusive," reprinted in O'Neal, *Bench and Bar*, II, 599–604.

46. Joseph Ioor Waring, *A History of Medicine in South Carolina, 1670–1825* (Columbia: South Carolina Medical Association, 1969), 59, 68–69, 82, 212–13, 268–76, 303, 336–37, 343.

47. Edward McCrady: *A Sketch of St. Philip's Church* (Charleston: Walker, Evans & Cogswell, 1901), 15–23, 54–62; "An Historic Church," *Year Book 1896. City of Charleston, So. Ca.* (Charleston: Lucas & Richardson, 1897), 317–74;

Frederick Dalcho, A *Historical Account of the Protestant Episcopal Church in South Carolina from the First Settlement of the Province to the War of the Revolution* (Charleston: E. Thayer, 1920), 27–180, 183, 190–91, 245, 255–57, 292; A. S. Salley, ed., *Register of St. Philip's Parish Charlestown, South Carolina, 1720–58* (Charleston: Walker, Evans & Cogswell, 1904). George S. Holmes, "The Parish Church of St. Michael, in Charles Town in the Province of South Carolina," *Year Book 1886. City of Charleston, So. Ca.* (Charleston: Walker, Evans & Cogswell, 1887), 281–327. George W. Williams, *St. Michael's, Charleston, 1751–1951* (Columbia: University of South Carolina Press, 1951), 12–22, 74–76.

48. Quincy, "Journal," Mar. 7, 1773, 444.

49. "The Huguenot Church," *Year Book 1885* (Charleston: News and Courier Book Presses, 1886), 297–313; Hirsch, *Huguenots*, 60n, 98; A. H. Missildine, "Historical Sketch of the First Presbyterian Church, 1731," *Year Book 1882* (Charleston: News and Courier Book Presses, 1883), 397–98.

50. Joseph Ioor Waring, "The Marine Hospitals of Charleston," *Year Book 1939* (Charleston: Walker, Evans & Cogswell, 1941), 172–73; Waring, *History of Medicine*, 25–26, 57, 110; McCrady, "Historic," 334–36; Edgar L. Pennington, "The Reverend Thomas Morritt and the Free School in Charleston," *SCHGM*, XXXI (Oct., 1930), 34–44; McCrady, *Sketch*, 25; H. P. Archer, "The Public Schools of Charleston," *Year Book 1886*, 173; "List of Contributors to the Negro School in Charleston," reprinted in *Year Book 1884* (News and Courier Book Presses, 1885), 213; Dalcho, *Historical*, 255–56, 292.

51. Carl Bridenbaugh: *Cities in the Wilderness: The First Century of Urban Life in America, 1625–1742* (New York: Alfred A. Knopf, 1960), 232–37; *Cities in Revolt* (New York: Alfred A. Knopf, 1955), 126, 172–74.

52. John Drayton, A *View of South Carolina* (Charleston: W. P. Young, 1802), 215; J. Bachman Chisolm, "St. Andrew's Society of Charleston," *Year Book 1894* (Charleston: Walker, Evans & Cogswell, 1895), 274–94; J. H. Easterby, *History of the St. Andrew's Society of Charleston, South Carolina, 1729–1929* (Charleston: Walker, Evans & Cogswell, 1929); *The St. Andrew's Society of Charleston from 1729 to 1901* (Charleston: Lucas & Richardson, 1901), 3–4, 24–30; *Rules of the Incorporated South Carolinian Society, Originally Established at Charleston the First of September, 1736* (Charleston: Markland & McIver, 1795), iii, vii, 23–35, 42–59; Dr. ? Milligen, "A Short Description of the Province of South Carolina," originally written in 1763, in Carroll, *Historical*, II, 488; *A Sketch of the History and Rules of the Charleston Ancient Artillery* (Charleston: Walker, Evans & Cogswell, 1940), 9–10, 15.

53. Hirsch, *Huguenots*, 218–19, 223, 259–60; "Wills of South Carolina Huguenots," *Transactions, passim*; Edgar W. Knight, ed., A *Documentary History of Education in South Carolina before 1860*, 5 vols. (Chapel Hill: University of North Carolina Press, 1949), I, 53, 351, 353–54; A. S. Salley, Jr., "William Smith and Some of His Descendants," *SCHGM*, III (July, 1903), 25; Susan Legaré Clement Simmons, "Early Manigault Records," *Transactions*, no. 59 (1954), 39.

54. Colyer Meriwether, *History of Higher Education in South Carolina* (Washington, D.C.: U.S. Government Printing Office, 1889), 25–26.

55. Laurens quoted in J. H. Easterby, A *History of the College of Charleston*

(Charleston: Scribner Press, 1935), 14; William Bull II quoted in Easterby, "The South Carolina Education Bill of 1770," *SCHGM*, XLVIII (Apr., 1947), 98. For other upper-class support for a college in Charleston see Easterby: *History of the College*, 10–14; "South Carolina," *passim*.

56. Alexander Hewatt, "An Historical Account of the Rise and Progress of the Colonies of South Carolina and Georgia," originally published in 1779, in *Historical Collections*, ed. Carroll, I, 504, 507. Hewatt was pastor of the Presbyterian Church of Charleston from 1763 to 1775. Cf. Bridenbaugh: *Cities in Revolt*, 181–83, 205, 384, 408–15; *Myths and Realities*, 86, 99–108; Frederick P. Bowes, *The Culture of Early Charleston* (Chapel Hill: University of North Carolina Press, 1942), 75–101.

57. Anne King Gregorie, "The First Decade of the Charleston Library Society," *Proceedings of the South Carolina Historical Association* (1935), 3–10; Hirsch, *Huguenots*, 161; "Original Rules and Members of the Charleston Library Society," *SCHGM*, XXIII (Oct., 1922), 163–70; Edgar Legaré Pennington, "The Beginnings of the Library in Charles Town, South Carolina," *Proceedings of the American Antiquarian Society*, XLIV (Apr., 1934), 159–87; Francis Lander Spain, "Libraries of South Carolina: Their Origins and Early History, 1700–1830," *Library Quarterly*, XVII (Jan. 1947), 28–41.

58. O.G. Sonneck, *Early Concert-Life in America (1731–1800)* (Leipzig: Breitkopf & Hartel, 1907), 10–11, 16, 18; "Rules of the St. Cecilia Society, 1773," *SCHGM*, I (July, 1900), 223–27; Quincy, "Journal," Mar. 3, 1773, 441–42.

59. Lola Willis, *The Charleston Stage in the XVIII Century* (Columbia, S.C.: State Co., 1924), 7, 10, 40–44, 70, 175–82, 215–16, 426; "Extracts from the Journal of Mrs. Ann Manigault, 1754–1781," *SCHGM*, XX (Jan., 1919), 52–63, (Apr., 1919), 128–39, (July, 1919), 204–12, (Oct., 1919), 256–59, XXI (Jan., 1920), 10–23, (Apr., 1920), 59–72, (July, 1920), 112–20; Hewatt, "Historical," I, 507–8; Milligan, "A Short," 478–79.

60. Anna Wells Rutledge, "Artists in the Life of Charleston," *Transactions of the American Philosophical Society*, new ser., XXXIX, part 2 (1949), 111–13, 116–17.

61. E. L. Pinckney to Mrs. ? Boddicott, May 2, 1749, in *Letterbook*, eds. Pinckney and Zahniser, 7; cf. Milligen, "A Short," 490; Bridenbaugh, *Myths and Realities*, *passim*; Hewatt, "Historical," I, 505.

62. Beatrice St. Julien Ravenel, *Architects of Charleston* (Charleston: Carolina Art Association, 1945), 22–24, 44, 69–72.

63. E. L. Pinckney to Thomas Lucas, May 22, 1742, in *Letterbook*, eds. Pinckney and Zahniser, cf. same to Mrs. Bodicott, May 2, 1749, *ibid.*, 39, 7; London *Magazine* quoted in Rutledge, *Artists*, 109; cf. Hewatt, "Historical," 505, 507–8; Milligan, "A Short," 478–79.

64. Quincy, "Journal," 444, 450–51; W. H. Mills, "The Thoroughbred in South Carolina," *Proceedings of the South Carolina Society* (1937), 15–18; Hirsch, *Huguenots*, 183–85; John Beaufain Irving, *The South Carolina Jockey Club*, 4 parts (Charleston: Russell & Jones, 1857), part 1, 33–36. For other social clubs see Bowes, *Culture*, 120–21; Bridenbaugh, *Myths*, 79.

65. Quincy, "Journal," 444.

66. "Josiah Smith's Diary 1780–81," *SCHGM*, XXXIV (Oct., 1933), 194–99; Ella Pettit Levett, "Loyalism in Charleston, 1761–84," *Proceedings of the South*

Carolina Historical Association (1936), 3–17; Robert Barnwell, Jr., "The Migration of Loyalists from South Carolina," *Proceedings* (1937), 34–42; Charles G. Singer, *South Carolina in the Confederation* (Philadelphia: University of Pennsylvania Press, 1941), 123; Rogers, *History*, 107–18.

67. Walsh, ed., *Writings*, 253n; Rogers, *Evolution*, 97–103; Richard Hrbowski, *Directory of the District of Charleston, 1809* (Charleston: John Hoffman, 1809), *passim*; David Ramsay, *History of South Carolina from Its First Settlement in 1670 to the Year 1808*, 2 vols. (Newberry, S.C.: W. J. Duffie, 1858), II, 132, 134.

68. Donnan, *Documents*, IV, 474–77, 504–6, 509, 510, 513–16, 521–24; E. S. Thomas, *Reminiscences of the Last Sixty-five Years*, 2 vols. (Hartford, Conn.: Case, Tiffany and Burnham, 1840), I, 40; Rogers, *History*, 337–38; Rosser Howard Taylor, "The Gentry of Ante-Bellum South Carolina," *North Carolina Historical Review*, XVII (Apr., 1940), 117; Morris and Brailsford to Thomas Jefferson, Oct. 31, 1787, "Letters of Morris & Brailsford," *SCHGM*, LVIII (July, 1957), 135; Nathan Appleton, "Journal, January 8, 1805," Appleton Papers, Massachusetts Historical Society.

69. Robert Nicholas Olsberg, "A Government of Class and Race: William Henry Trescot and the South Carolina Chivalry, 1860–1865" (Ph.D. dissertation, University of South Carolina, 1972), 23, 25.

70. Christopher Gadsden letter in the South Carolina *Gazette*, Aug. 5, 1784, quoted in *Writings*, ed. Walsh, 236–37; Charles Pinckney, "Speech at the South Carolina Ratifying Convention, May 14, 1788," *Debates on the Adoption of the Federal Constitution*, ed. Jonathan Elliott, (New York: Burt Franklin, n.d.), IV, 321–23; Thomas, *Reminiscences*, I, 34; cf. Charles Fraser, *My Reminiscences of Charleston* (Charleston: John Russell, 1854), 57.

71. *Roll of Officers of the Charleston Chamber of Commerce during the First Century of Its Corporate Life, as Far as Ascertainable. Roll of Members on the 103rd Anniversary* (Charleston: Walker, Evans & Cogswell, 1887), 5–6; W. L. Trenholm, *The Centennial Address before the Charleston Chamber of Commerce, February 11, 1884* (Charleston: News and Courier Book Press, 1884), 13–14.

72. Davidson, *Last*, 6–8.

73. Robert N. Gourdin quoted in Taylor, "Gentry," 117; Herbert Wender, *Southern Commercial Conventions* (Baltimore: Johns Hopkins University Studies in History and Political Science, XLVIII, 1930), 44.

74. Olsberg, "Government," 23–24.

75. Thomas, *Reminiscences*, I, 41.

76. Manigault *et al.*, "Historical Sketch," 31–32; "Notices of Conspicuous Members of the Gaillard Family," *Transactions*, no. 5 (1897), 97–98; "Obituary of Robert N. Gourdin," *Transactions*, no. 3 (1894), 30–31; Ravenel, *Ravenel*, 55–59; A. S. Salley, Jr., "Captain John Colcock and Some of His Descendants," *SCHGM*, III (Oct., 1902), 216–41; John G. Van Deusen, *Economic Bases of Disunion in South Carolina* (New York: Columbia University Press, 1928), 205–6; *Directory of the City of Charleston, 1860*, 2 vols. (Savannah: J. M. Cooper, 1860), II, 6–8; A. Toomer Porter, *Led On! Step by Step* (New York: G. P. Putnam's Sons, 1898), 44, 47, 112–13; *Cyclopedia*, I, 362–67, 543–45; Arney R. Childs, ed., *Rice Planter and Sportsman: The Recollections of J. Motte*

Alston, 1821–1909 (Columbia: University of South Carolina Press, 1953), 67; "Henry W. Connor," *De Bow's Review*, X (May, 1851), 578–81; J. H. Easterby, ed., *The South Carolina Rice Plantation* (Columbia: University of South Carolina Press, 1945), 37–42.

77. *Roll*, 5–9; Trenholm, *Centennial*, 13–19.

78. Childs, ed., *Rice Planter*, 67.

79. "South Carolina—Her Agriculture, etc.," *De Bow's Review*, XIX (Nov., 1855), 530–33; Alfred G. Smith, Jr., *Economic Readjustment of an Old Cotton State: South Carolina, 1820–60* (Columbia: University of South Carolina Press, 1958), 4–8, 17, 19–20, 29–32, 43–44, 47–60, 84–85; A. E. Parkins, *The South: Its Economic and Gecgraphical Development* (New York: John Wiley & Sons, 1938), 449–50, 480–81; Van Deusen, *Economic*, 332; "Progress of the South and West," *De Bow's Review*, IX (Sept., 1950), 309; Trenholm, *Centennial*, 4; Blaine A. Brownell and David R. Goldfield, *The City in Southern History: The Growth of Urban Civilization in the South* (Port Washington, N.Y.: Kennikat, 1977), 85–86.

80. Robert Mills, *Statistics of South Carolina* (Charleston: Hurlbut and Love, 1826), 161–63; Samuel Derrick, *History of the South Carolina Railroad* (Columbia, S.C.: State Co., 1930), 1–11; Gray, *History*, II, 696, 900; "The Report of the Superintendent of Public Works of South Carolina for the Year 1825," *Internal Improvements in South Carolina, 1817–28*, ed. David Kohn (Washington, D.C.: privately printed, 1938), 385; MacPherson, *Annals*, IV, 326; *South Carolina Resources and Population, Institutions and Industries* (Charleston: Walker, Evans & Cogswell, 1883), 384; Van Deusen, *Economic*, 182–219; *The Cause of the Decline of Real Estate in the City of Charleston* (Charleston: J. B. Nixon, 1847), 2, 5, 9.

81. Rogers, *History*, 335–38; Russell, *Diary*, 136; "Journal of Arthur Brailsford Wescoat, 1863, 1864," *SCHGM*, LV (1954), 71–102; F. A. Porcher, "Historical and Social Sketch of Craven County," *Southern Quarterly Review*, new ser., IX (Jan.–Apr., 1854), 404.

82. Smith, *Economic*, 34, 42–44, 59–60, 106–7.

83. Wender, *Southern*, 9–48; John G. Van Deusen: "The Ante-Bellum Southern Commercial Conventions," *History Papers, Trinity College Historical Society*, XVI (1926), 9–17; *Economic*, 197–202.

84. For the reflections of Robert B. Rhett and Henry L. Pinckney see Van Deusen, *Economic*, 217–18.

85. Van Deusen, *Economic*, 192–94, 200–13, 335; Robert Royal Russel, *Economic Aspects of Southern Sectionalism, 1840–61* (Urbana: University of Illinois Press, 1922), 113, 118.

86. Charles August Murray quoted in J. Rion McKissick, "Some Observations of Travelling in South Carolina, 1800–1860," *Proceedings of the South Carolina Historical Association* (1932), 47.

87. William Gregg: "Manufactures in South Carolina and the South," *De Bow's Review*, XI (Aug., 1851), 123–40; "Domestic Industry—Manufactures at the South," *ibid.*, VII (Feb., 1850), 134–60; "Southern Patronage to Southern Imports and Southern Industry," *ibid.*, XXIX (July–Dec., 1860), 77–83, 226–32, 494–500, 623–31, 771–78; "Practical Results of Southern Manufacturers," *ibid.*, XVIII (June, 1855), 777–91; "Essays on Domestic Industry, or

An Inquiry into the Expediency of Establishing Cotton Manufacturers in South Carolina," reprinted in D. A. Tompkins, *Cotton Mill, Commercial Features* (Charlotte, N.C.: D. A. Tompkins, 1899), 207–35; James H. Hammond, "Progress of Southern Industry," *De Bow's Review*, VIII (June, 1850), 501–22. For similar sentiments from another upcoming up-country politician see James L. Orr, "Development of Southern Industry," *ibid.*, XIX (July, 1855), 1–22. Another example of official concern over these matters in "Report of the Superintendent of Public Works . . . 1825," 385.

88. The Charleston newspapers and the committee report are quoted in Derrick, *Centennial*, 3; Elias Horry, *An Address Respecting the Charleston and Hamburgh Railroad* (Charleston: A. E. Miller, 1833), 5–6; James Johnston Pettigrew quoted in Olsberg, "Government," 50.

89. William Elliott: *The Planter Vindicated: His Claims Examined—to Be Considered, a Direct Producer and Chief Tax-payer of South-Carolina* (Charleston: Burges & James, 1842), 4; *The Letters of Agricola* (Greenville, S.C.: Southern Patriot, 1852), 3–5, 7; Robert Y. Hayne to James H. Hammond, Jan. 18, 1838, in Russell, *Economic*, 28.

90. James Gadsden, "Commercial Spirit at the South," *De Bow's Review*, II (Sept., 1846), 119, 121–23, 126, 129–32; William J. Grayson, "The Merchant—His Character, Position, Duties," *ibid.*, III (Feb., 1847), 93–94, 96; Fraser, *My Reminiscences*, 52–53, 57; William Porcher Miles, "American Literature and Charleston Society," *Southern Quarterly Review*, VII (Apr., 1853), 406.

91. J. Mauldin Lesesne, *The Bank of the State of South Carolina* (Columbia: University of South Carolina Press, 1970), 6; W. A. Clark, *The History of the Banking Institutions Organized in South Carolina prior to 1860* (Columbia: Historical Commission of South Carolina, 1922), 40; Rogers, *Evolution*, 188–89, 227, 231–32.

92. Clark, *History*, 46; C. H. Catterall, *The Second Bank of the United States* (Chicago: University of Chicago Press, 1903), 396–97.

93. For lists of officers and directors and brief histories of these banks see Clark, *History*, 42, 54–57, 65–67, 71–74, 140–44, 169–73, 187–89, 191–96, 212–13.

94. *Ibid.*, 114–20, 125, 204–7; George W. Williams, *History of Banking in South Carolina from 1712 to 1900* (Charleston: Walker, Evans & Cogswell, 1903), 9–10.

95. "President's Report to the South Carolina Senate, December, 1843," *A Compilation of All the Acts, Resolutions, Reports, and Other Documents in Relation to the Bank of South Carolina* (Columbia: A. S. Johnston and A. G. Summer, 1848), 562; "The Act to Establish a Bank, on Behalf and for the Benefit of the State," *ibid.*, 1, 5.

96. *Compilation*, xvi; Lesesne, *Bank*, 15; "Report of the President and Directors of the Bank of the State, 1814," *Compilation*, 346; "Report . . . 1819," *ibid.*, 385.

97. *Ibid.*, 360–61, 384–85, 392, 397, 401, 411, 426, 708; Clark, *History*, 97–98, 196–97.

98. *Compilation*, 94, 124, 138–39, 146–47, 159, 198, 228, 321, 422, 435, 484, 499, 508, 540–51, 695–96. Elmore quoted on 323.

99. "Report of the Special Joint Committee [of the Legislature] on the Bank

of the State at Charleston, 1847," *ibid.*, 312; R. Hayne to Langdon Cheves, Oct. 9, 1819, in Theodore D. Jervey, *Robert Y. Hayne and His Times* (New York: Macmillan, 1909), 90–91.

100. Williams, *History*, 10; Lesesne, *Bank*, 143–44.

101. Smith, *Economic*, 194.

102. Porter, *Led*, 112–13.

103. George A. Trenholm to Robert F. W. Allston, Apr. 18, 1837, in Easterby, *Rice*, 69.

104. Smith, *Economic*, 195–99, 208–9, 215–17; Van Deusen, *Economic*, 210–11.

105. Williams, *History*, 9; *Compilation*, 602, 689; Smith, *Economic*, 195–98, 215–17; Clark, *History*, 288; "City Banking Capital," *De Bow's Review*, X (May, 1851), 587; Joseph S. Davis, *Essays in the Earlier History of American Corporations*, 2 vols. (Cambridge: Harvard University Press, 1917), II, 80, 103; Bray Hammond, *Banks and Politics in America from the Revolution to the Civil War* (Princeton: Princeton University Press, 1957), 144–45.

106. See note 93.

107. Davis, *Essays*, II, 22–23, 235; Hrabowski, *Directory . . . 1809*, 11; *The Charleston Directory 1835–36* (Charleston: Daniel J. Dowling, 1835), 141, 149; *Directory of the City of Charleston and Neck for 1849* (Charleston: A. J. Burke, 1849), 141–42.

108. Walsh, ed., *Writings*, 252; "Letters of William Loughton Smith to Edward Rutledge," *SCHGM*, LXIX (Jan., 1968), 229–30; Rogers, *Evolution*, 193–98, 205–8, 235–36, 239–40.

109. *Directory . . . 1860*, II, 56.

110. Frederick A. Porcher, *The History of the Santee Canal* (Charleston: South Carolina Historical Society, 1903), *passim*; Porcher, "The Memoirs of Frederick Porcher," *SCHGM*, XLIV (Apr., 1943), 68–70; Henry Savage, Jr., *River of the Carolinas: The Santee* (New York: Rinehart, 1956), 242–51; Ulrich Bonnell Phillips, *A History of Transportation in the Eastern Cotton Belt to 1860* (New York: Columbia University Press, 1908), 15–16, 35–43; Rogers, *Evolution*, 131–33; "Report of the Superintendent of Public Works to the Legislature of South Carolina for the Year 1823," *Internal*, ed. Kohn, 257–67; William Loughton Smith to E. Rutledge, Dec. 4, 1791, Feb. 13, 1792, in "Smith Letters," 231, 241–42; *Directory . . . 1809*, 139; *Directory . . . 1849*, 138.

111. Davis, *Essays*, II, 23, 146–48; Rogers, *Evolution*, 133–34, 361–62.

112. Rogers, *History*, 328–29.

113. Phillips, *History*, 62, 88–89; *Directory . . . 1809*, 140; *Directory . . . 1835–36*, 141; *Directory . . . 1849*, 139; J. Fred Rippy, *Joel R. Poinsett, Versatile American* (Durham, N.C.: Duke University Press, 1935), 79–80.

114. Derrick, *Centennial*, 12–18, 21, 80, 116–21, 208–9, 322; Horry, *Address*, 8, 14–37; *Compilation*, 484, 499; Kohn, ed., *Internal*, 592; Phillips, *History*, 132–62, 202–20; Jervey, *Robert Y. Hayne*, 216–17, 384–86; Smith, *Economic*, 159–60; *Directory . . . 1835–36*, 141; *Directory . . . 1849*, 139; *Directory . . . 1860*, II, 34.

115. *Proceedings of the Citizens of Charleston, Embracing the Report of the Committee and the Address & Resolutions Adopted at a General Meeting in*

Reference to the Proposed Rail-road from Cinncinnati to Charleston (Charleston: A. E. Miller, 1835), 17, 20, *passim;* Derrick, *Centennial,* 131–33, 170–89; Jervey, *Robert Y. Hayne,* 384–85, 400–409, Hayne quoted on 454–58; Smith, *Economic,* 160–69; Van Deusen, *Economic,* 223–42; Phillips, *History,* 168–202.

116. Wender, *Southern,* 49–207; Van Deusen, "Ante-Bellum", 21, 95; Gadsden, "Commercial," 132; Elliott, *Letters,* 4–5.

117. Van Deusen, *Economic,* 348–49; Smith, *Economic,* 174, 182, 188–90; Phillips, *History,* 377–80.

118. Ravenel, *Ravenel,* 69; Phillips, *History,* 354–55; *Directory . . . 1860,* II, 34; Cheves, "Middleton," 245.

119. John F. Stover, *The Railroads of the South, 1865–1900: A Study in Finance and Control* (Chapel Hill: University of North Carolina Press, 1955), 5, 31–34; James Gregg to J. H. Hammond, Feb. 18, 1849, in "The Advent of William Gregg and the Graniteville Co.," ed. Thomas P. Martin, *Journal of Southern History,* XI (Aug., 1945), 411.

120. Smith, *Economic,* 191; Phillips, *History,* 220, 388; William J. Grayson, "The Autobiography of William John Grayson," *SCHGM,* L (Oct., 1949), 214.

121. Kohn, *Cotton,* 7, 11–21; Mitchell, *Rise,* 11–14; Lander: "South Carolina," 19–21; *The Textile Industry in Antebellum South Carolina* (Baton Rouge: Louisiana State University Press, 1969), 3–4, 7–10; Richard W. Griffin, "An Origin of the New South: The South Carolina Homespun Co., 1815–18," *Business History Review,* XXXV (Autumn, 1961), 402–14; R. F. W. Allston, "Rice," *De Bow's Review,* I (Apr., 1846), 343; *Directory . . . 1809,* 138.

122. W. L. Smith and D. Ramsay quoted in Rogers, *Evolution,* 378, 379n.

123. David Ramsay to Jedidiah Morse, Jan. 9, 1815, in Robert L. Brunhouse, "David Ramsay, 1749–1815," *Transactions of the American Philosophical Society,* IV, part 4 (1965), 179; Lander: *Textile,* 10–21, 27–29; "South Carolina," 21, 26, 49–50, 79–80; Victor S. Clark, *History of Manufactures in the United States,* 2 vols. (Washington, D.C.: Carnegie Institute of Washington, 1916, 1928), I, 537–38, 541, 622; Mitchell, *Rise,* 21.

124. Lander, *Textile,* 31–32, 56–58, 63–65; Broadus Mitchell, *William Gregg* (Chapel Hill: University of North Carolina Press, 1928), 39–41, 275n, 276–79, 281n–82n, 308n; Van Deusen, *Economic,* 272, 274; Lander, "South Carolina," 24; Kohn, *Cotton,* 211–17; Lander, "Manufacturing in South Carolina, 1815–1860," *Business History Review,* XXVIII (Mar., 1954), 64–65; Gregg: "Essays," 220–23; "Southern," 494.

125. Clark, *History,* I, 591; Lander, "The Iron Industry in Ante-Bellum South Carolina," *Journal of Southern History,* XX (Aug., 1954), 355.

126. Lander, "South Carolina," 26; *South Carolina Resources,* 576; Gray, *History,* II, 1043; Fred Bateman, James Faust, and Thomas Weiss, "The Participation of Planters in Manufacturing in the Antebellum South," *Agricultural History,* XLVIII (Apr., 1974), 278n.

127. Bateman, Faust, and Weiss, "Participation," 285–86, 288, 292, 295–96; Easterby, *South Carolina,* 25, 32–33, 113, 140; Rogers, *History,* 334–35; Allston, "Rice," 343; Lander: "Manufacturing," 64; "Ante-Bellum Milling in South Carolina," *SCHGM,* LII (July, 1951), 130–31.

128. Lander, "Manufacturing," 61; Leonard P. Stavisky, "Industrialism in

Ante-Bellum Charleston," *Journal of Negro History*, XXXVI (July, 1951), 318, 320n–21n; J. L. Dawson and H. W. De Saussure, *Census of the City of Charleston, South Carolina for the Year 1848* (Charleston: J. B. Nixon, 1849), 31–35. For lack of upper-class participation in Charleston factories see Van Deusen, *Economic*, 294–95; *De Bow's Review*, X (May, 1851), 562.

129. For the sentiments of Gregg and Hammond see note 87; Gadsden, "Commercial," 121–22; Elliott, *Letters*, 5–6; "Proceedings . . . in Reference . . .," 10; W. B. Heriot, "Commerce, Naval, and Military Resources of Charleston," *De Bow's Review*, III (June, 1947), 516–28. Letter to the Charleston *Gazette*, Mar. 4, 1828, in Ulrich B. Phillips, *Plantation and Frontier*, 2 vols. (Cleveland: Arthur H. Clark, 1910), II, 354.

130. Chauncey Samuel Boucher, "The Ante-Bellum Attitude of South Carolina towards Manufacturing and Agriculture," *Washington University Studies*, vol. III, part II, no. 2 (Apr., 1916), 243–44; Lander, "South Carolina," 31–32; Stavisky, "Industrialism," 315n; Gregg, "Domestic," 140.

131. William Gregg to J. H. Hammond, Dec. 1, 1848, in Martin "Advent," 407–8; J. H. Hammond to William Gilmore Simms, Mar. 26, 1850, in Boucher, "Ante-Bellum," 256.

132. Rupert B. Vance and Nicholas J. Demerath, eds., *The Urban South* (Freeport, N.Y.: Books for Libraries, 1971), *passim*.

Since Charleston was the capital of the low-country plantation parishes and the part-time residence of many planters, slavery as a means of profit and capital accumulation had a great impact on the local economy. A debate rages over whether slavery was an economic asset or liability in the South, and the ultimate resolution may be the judgment that no generalization holds for the section as a whole. The findings of Alfred H. Conrad and John R. Meyer in their important defense of southern slavery as a viable financial institution indicate that it may have been less profitable and productive in South Carolina than elsewhere in the region. Reported yields per prime cotton field hand in nine areas of the South between 1849 and 1859 showed coastal South Carolina ranking fourth from the bottom. Upland South Carolina stood last, and the coast was only barely ahead of the next two lowest places. In annual hiring rates for slaves in the southern states in 1860 South Carolina had the cheapest rates for males and the third cheapest for females (Alfred H. Conrad and John R. Meyer, *The Economics of Slavery* (Chicago: Aldine Publishing, 1964), 58, 73). South Carolina's low hiring rates may have been related to a comparatively slow growth in demand for slaves in Charleston. A recent estimate of the average annual rate of growth in the demand for slaves by decade in ten southern and border cities, three urban aggregates (Old South cities, New South cities, and border cities), and the United States placed Charleston next to last among the cities in 1820–30, tied for third from last in 1830–40, fifth in 1840–50, and last in 1850–60. Except for 1840–50, when Charleston's growth rate in demand for slaves exceeded that of the New South cities, it ranked behind the urban aggregates and the United States (Robert William Fogel and Stanley L. Engerman, *Time on the Cross: Evidence and Methods*, 2 vols. (Boston: Little, Brown, 1974), II, 154). This data is too fragmentary for any conclusive evaluation about the positive or negative consequences of slavery in capital investment or accumulation in Charleston and the low-country. It does suggest, however, that in some important aspects of returns on capital invested in slaves, this part of the South lagged considerably behind other parts of the section and was lower than the regional mean and median. This evidence also suggests—by extension—that in some significant respects the economy of the town and the state was expanding at a slower rate than for the region as a whole.

133. Vance and Demerath, eds., *Urban*, 28, 32–33.

134. For examples of hostility to white immigrants in Charleston see Christopher G. Memminger to J. H. Hammond, Apr. 28, 1849, in Boucher, "Ante-Bellum," 255–56; Stavisky, "Industrialism," 307, 307n. "Nativity of the Leading Cities of the United States," *De Bow's Review*, XIX (Sept., 1855), 262–63; "Nativities of White Population of the United States," *ibid.*, XVIII (Oct., 1854), 431.

135. Bridenbaugh: *Cities in the Wilderness*, 303n; *Cities in Revolt*, 216; Parkins, *The South*, 449–50; Stavisky, "Industrialism," 318n; Julian J. Petty, *The Growth and Distribution of Population in South Carolina* (Columbia: Industrial Development Committee of the State Council of Defense, 1943), 61–66, 74, 115, 141–44; *South Carolina Resources*, 384–90; Tommy Rogers, "The Great Population Exodus from South Carolina 1850–60," *SCHGM*, LXVIII (Jan., 1967), 14–21.

136. Rogers, "Great," 15.

137. Elliott, *Agricola*, 3; Orr, "Development," 405; Derrick, *Centennial*, 3; Gregg: "Essays," 213; "Manufactures," 133; "Practical," 791; "Domestic," 137, 140; Heriot, "Commerce," 528; Hugh Swinton Legaré to Alfred Huger, Nov. 21, 1835, in *Writings of Hugh Swinton Legaré*, 2 vols., ed. Mary S. Legaré (Charleston: Burges J. James, 1846), I, 221.

138. *Charleston Directory . . . 1809, passim* for residents listed as planters; Frederick A. Ford, *Census of the City of Charleston, South Carolina, for the Year 1861* (Charleston: Evans & Cogswell, 1861), 21–230, for planter residents of 1861; Rogers, *History*, 318–21; Davidson, *Last*, 170–267.

139. Compiled from data in Davidson, *Last*, 170–267.

140. Compiled from data in *ibid.*, 5–16.

141. Compiled from data in *ibid.*, 170–267.

142. Olsberg, "Government," 24, 33.

143. *Ibid.*, 178.

144. Pringle, *Inquiry, passim*; Porcher, "Prospects," 453.

145. *A Century of Population Growth: From the First Census of the United States to the Twelfth, 1790–1900* (Washington, D.C.: U.S. Government Printing Office, 1909), 133–36, 139–40, 206; Petty, *Growth*, 76–79; Smith, *Economic*, 191–92; *Compendium of the Seventh Census of the United States: 1850* (Washington, D.C.: Public Printer, 1853), ix, 334–40; *Compendium of the Eighth Census of the United States: 1860* (Washington, D.C.: U.S. Government Printing Office, 1866), iii–lxvi, 348.

146. Porcher, "Prospects," 453–54; Olsberg, "Government," 43–44, 83.

147. For a more elaborate discussion of this type of impact on South Carolina and elsewhere in the South see Genovese, *Political, passim*.

148. Diane Cook Norton, "Social Composition of the South Carolina Politi-

cal Elite of the 1830s," unpublished manuscript (1972), 29–32.

149. *Year Book 1881* (Charleston: News and Courier Book Presses, 1882), 367–77.

150. Olsberg, "Government," 81–84.

151. Charles Pinckney to T. Jefferson, Oct. 12, 1800, in "South Carolina in the Presidential Election of 1800, Letters of Charles Pinckney," *American Historical Review*, IV (Oct., 1890), 114; William J. Grayson, *James Louis Petigru: A Biographical Sketch* (New York: Harper & Bros., 1866), 93–94; Porcher, "Memoirs," *SCHGM*, XLVI (Jan., 1945), 37–38.

152. Grayson, "Autobiography," *SCHGM*, LI (Apr., 1950), 106.

153. Clarence M. Smith, Jr., "William Porcher Miles, Progressive Mayor of Charleston," *Proceedings of the South Carolina Historical Association* (1942), 31–33.

154. *Year Book 1884*, 335–37; Emily B. Reynolds and John R. Faunt, eds., *Biographical Dictionary of the Senate of South Carolina, 1776–1964* (Columbia: South Carolina Archives Department, 1964), 8–9.

155. Main, *Upper House*, 114–24, 131–32; Reynolds and Faunt, eds., *Biographical*, 170–340.

156. Main, "Government," 403–4; Ramsay, *History*, II, 82; *Directory . . . 1835–36*, 133; *Directory . . . 1849*, 151; Reynolds and Faunt, eds., *Biographical*, 170–340.

157. Compiled from data in Davidson, *Last*, 170–267.

158. Ralph A. Wooster, *The People in Power* (Knoxville: University of Tennessee Press, 1969), 39–41.

159. D. Huger Bacot, "Constitutional Progress and the Struggle for Democracy in South Carolina during the Revolution," *South Atlantic Quarterly*, XXIV (Jan., 1925), 61–72; William A. Schapen, "Sectionalism and Representation in South Carolina," *Annual Report of the American Historical Association*, I (1900), 367, 377, 408, 417–19, 424, 435–36; Fletcher M. Green: *Constitutional Development in the South Atlantic States, 1776–1860* (Chapel Hill: University of North Carolina Press, 1930), 109–20, 167–296; "Democracy in the Old South," *Journal of Southern History*, XII (Feb., 1946), 3–23; Chauncey S. Boucher, "Sectionalism, Representation and the Electoral Question in Antebellum South Carolina," *Washington University Studies*, IV, part II (Oct., 1916), *passim*; Charles S. Sydnor, *The Development of Southern Sectionalism* (Baton Rouge: Louisiana State University Press, 1948), 275–89. The antidemocratic devices continued despite the facts that an 1810 amendment to the state constitution reinforced a long-term trend liberalizing voting requirements, that after 1824 universal white manhood suffrage prevailed in legislative and congressional elections, and that between 1824 and 1860 voter participation peaks in South Carolina elections compared favorably with half of the other states in the Union (see James M. Banner, Jr., "The Problem of South Carolina," *The Hofstadter Aegis: A Memorial*, eds. Stanley Elkins and Eric McKitrick, (New York: Alfred A. Knopf, 1974), 81–83). The persistence of high qualifications for holding office and other oligarchic restraints, despite extensive voter participation, can be explained by the widespread deference accorded to elites in South Carolina.

160. Hammond, *Diary*, Dec. 7, 1850, quoted in James Petigru Carson, *Life*,

Letters and Speeches of James Louis Petigru (Washington, D.C.: W. H. Low-dermilk, 1930), v.

161. Henry D. Capers, *The Life and Times of C. G. Memminger* (Richmond, Va.: Everett Waddey, 1893), 12; Edwin L. Green, *George McDuffie* (Columbia, S.C.: State Co., 1936), 7–8; Brunhouse, "David Ramsay," 12–14, 25–26; Carson, *Life*, 1–28, 58–59, 80, 182; *Cyclopedia*, I, 61–63, 130–31, 243–45; Elizabeth Merritt, *James Henry Hammond, 1807–1864* (Baltimore: Johns Hopkins University Press, 1923), 9–10; Jervey, *Robert Y. Hayne*, 15, 40–41, 50–51, 107, 534; Reynolds and Faunt, eds., *Biographical*, 292; B. F. Perry, *Reminiscences of Public Men* (Philadelphia: John D. Avil, 1883), 241–42.

162. Norton, "Social," 25–32.

163. J. H. Hammond to W. G. Simms, Dec. 1, 1848; cf. William Gregg to Hammond, Dec. 1, 1848, in "Adventure," ed. Martin, 406–8; Genovese, *Political*, 199; Lander, "Manufacturing," 64.

164. Olsberg, "Government," 82–83.

165. Laura A. White, *Robert Barnwell Rhett: Father of Secession* (New York: Century, 1931), 33–34; Perry, *Reminiscences*, 99; Carson, *Life*, 217–20; Charles M. Wiltse, *John C. Calhoun, Sectionalist, 1840–1850* (Indianapolis: Bobbs-Merrill, 1951), 430–33, 446.

166. Singer, *South Carolina*, 9, 30–37, 69–87, 94–101, 165–66. For examples of these sentiments see C. Gadsden, "Letter to the *Gazette*, of South Carolina," July 11, 1784, in *Writings*, ed. Walsh, 216; Gadsden to George Washington, May 13, 1787, and to John Adams, July 24, 1787, *ibid.*, 242, 244; D. Ramsay to T. Jefferson, Apr. 7, 1787, and to Benjamin Rush, Nov. 10, 1787, in Brunhouse, "David Ramsay," 115–16. John Rutledge, Charles Cotesworth Pinckney, and Charles Pinckney, South Carolina delegates to the Federal constitutional convention, advocated property qualifications for officeholding and elections, opposition to direct election of the president, and a strong national government to foster business, protect property, and preserve law and order. For their views see Max Farrand, ed., *The Records of the Federal Constitutional Convention of 1787*, 4 vols. (New Haven, Conn.: Yale University Press, 1966), I, 69, 130–32, 137, 147, 196, 211, 410, II, 30, 81, 205, 248–49, 340, 360, 511, 534, 536–67, III, 106–23, 355.

167. Richard Walsh, *Charleston's Sons of Liberty: A Study of the Artisans* (New York: Columbia University Press, 1959), 114–27.

168. *Journal of the Convention of South Carolina Which Ratified the Constitution of the United States, May 23, 1788* (Atlanta: Foote & Davis, 1928), 39–49; Elliot, ed., *Debates*, IV, 318–41; George C. Rogers, Jr., "South Carolina Ratifies the Federal Constitution," *Proceedings of the South Carolina Historical Association* (1961), 41–63.

169. James Simons to Jacob Read, July 10, 1795, quoted in Rogers, *Evolution*, 185.

170. For lists of federal government officials, see *Year Book 1883* (Charleston: News and Courier Book Presses, 1884), 6, 14, 457–58; *Year Book 1884*, 338–49; W. L. Smith to Alexander Hamilton, Apr. 24, 1793, in *The Papers of Alexander Hamilton*, ed. Harold C. Syrett (New York: Columbia University Press, 1969), XIV, 338. For other examples of support for Hamilton and the national gov-

ernment see W. L. Smith to E. Rutledge, July 5, 1789, Aug. 9, 1789, Feb. 13, 1790, Feb. 26, 1790, Nov. 10, 1791, Apr. 28, 1793, in Smith, "Letters," *SCHGM*, L (Apr., 1968), 6, 20, 104, 229–30, 241–42; Ralph Izard to E. Rutledge, Dec. 29, 1789; W. L. Smith to G. Manigault, Aug. 3, 1790, in "South Carolina Federalist Correspondence," *American Historical Review*, XIV (July, 1909), 778–79. For the history of the South Carolina Federalists see Ulrich B. Phillips, "The South Carolina Federalists," *ibid.*, 529–43; Barry, *Mr. Rutledge*, 303ff.; Elizabeth Cometti, "John Rutledge, Jr., Federalist," *Journal of Southern History*, XIII (May, 1947), 186–219; Marvin R. Zahniser, *Charles Cotesworth Pinckney* (Chapel Hill: University of North Carolina Press, 1967), 86ff.; George C. Rogers, Jr.: *Charleston in the Age of the Pinckneys* (Norman: University of Oklahoma Press, 1969), 116–23; *Evolution*, 97ff.; Lisle A. Rose, *Prologue to Democracy: The Federalists in the South, 1789–1800* (Lexington: University of Kentucky Press, 1968); John H. Wolfe, *Jeffersonian Democracy in South Carolina* (Chapel Hill: University of North Carolina Press, 1940); Charles Cotesworth Pinckney, *The Life of General Thomas Pinckney* (Boston: Houghton Mifflin, 1895), 92ff.; Gabriel E. Manigault, "Ralph Izard, The South Carolina Statesman," *Magazine of American History*, XXIII (Jan., 1890), 60–73.

171. David Hackett Fischer, *The Revolution of American Conservatism* (New York: Harper & Row, 1965), 40–41, 401–5.

172. Henry W. De Saussure to John Rutledge, Jr., Aug. 14, 1800, quoted in Rose, *Prologue*, 248; C. Gadsden to J. Adams, Mar. 11, 1801, in *The Works of John Adams*, ed. Charles Francis Adams (Boston: Little, Brown, 1854), IX, 579–80.

173. C. Pinckney to T. Jefferson, Oct. 12, 1800, and Dec. ?, 1800, in "South Carolina," 122, Rogers, *Evolution*, 385.

174. Wolfe, *Jeffersonian*, 171, 182.

175. *Year Book 1883*, 6, 14, 457–58; *Year Book 1884*, 338–49; David F. Houston, *A Critical Study of Nullification in South Carolina* (Cambridge: Harvard University Press, 1896), 6–9, 28–30; Green, *George McDuffie*, 76–83; Wiltse, *John C. Calhoun, Nationalist, 1782–1828* (Indianapolis: Bobbs-Merrill, 1944), 98–108, 120–22, 131–36, 288–89; William W. Freehling, *Prelude to Civil War: The Nullification Controversy in South Carolina, 1816–1836* (New York: Harper Torchbooks, 1968), 89–113.

176. *Year Book 1883*, 6, 14, 457–58; *Year Book 1884*, 338–49.

177. Freehling, *Prelude*, 177–80, 196–97, 201–2, 224, 229, 254–59, 304, 365–69; Schapen, "Sectionalism," 441–42, 445; Sydnor, *Development*, 207–21; *Journals of the Convention of the People of South Carolina: Assembled at Columbia on the 19th of November, 1832, and again, on the 11th of March, 1833* (Columbia: A. S. Johnson, 1833), 19–24; White, *Robert Barnwell Rhett*, 14–16; Houston, *Critical*, 32–142; Rippy, *Joel R. Poinsett*, 130–64; Charles J. Stille, "The Life and Services of Joel R. Poinsett," *Pennsylvania Magazine of History and Biography*, XII (1888), 257–58, 275–77, 294–300; Jervey, *Robert Y. Hayne*, 278–317; Green, *George McDuffie*, 99–119; Carson, *Life*, 78–171; Legaré, *Writings*, I, 207, 215, 221; Thomas Smith Grimké, *To the People of the State of South Carolina* (Charleston: n.p., 1832); William Elliott, *Address to the People of St. Helena Parish* (Charleston: William Estill, 1832); Wiltse, *John C. Calhoun, Nullifier, 1829–1838* (Indianapolis: Bobbs-Merrill, 1949); Banner, "Problem," 60–93.

178. Philip May Hamer, *The Secessionist Movement in South Carolina, 1847–1852* (Allentown, Pa.: H. Ray Haas, 1918), 54–55, 74–75, 85–92, 123–24; White, *Robert Barnwell Rhett*, 108–9, 135, 173; Steven A. Channing, *Crisis of Fear: Secession in South Carolina* (New York: Simon and Schuster, 1970), 168–74, 184–87; Wiltse, *Calhoun, Sectionalist*, 398–99, 409; Laura White, "The National Democrats in South Carolina, 1852 to 1860," *South Atlantic Quarterly*, XXVIII (Oct., 1929), 37–89; *Journals of the Convention of the People of South Carolina Held in 1832, 1833, and 1852* (Columbia, S.C.: R. W. Gibbs, 1860), 137–39, 143, 147–53; Banner, "Problem," 60–93.

179. Miles and Grimball quoted in Channing, *Crisis*, 258–260. For the role of Charleston see Harold D. Schulz, *Nationalism and Sectionalism in South Carolina, 1852–1860* (Durham, N.C.: Duke University Press, 1950), 104, 126, 129, 151–52, 200–201, 223; Charles Edward Cauthen, *South Carolina Goes to War, 1860–1865* (Chapel Hill: University of North Carolina Press, 1950), 34–43; Channing, *Crisis*, 173, 178–79, 182–90, 258, 260–62; Olsberg, "Government," 252–304.

180. W. G. Simms to William Porcher Miles, Nov. 12, 1862, in Clement Eaton, *The Civilization of the Old South* (Lexington: University of Kentucky Press, 1968), 240.

181. *Journals of the Conventions of the People of South Carolina Held in 1860, 1861, and 1862, Together with the Ordinances, Reports and Resolutions, etc.* (Columbia, S.C.: R. W. Gibbs, 1862), 5–7, 847–52; Ralph Wooster, "Membership of the South Carolina Secession Convention," *SCHGM*, LV (Oct., 1952), 169, 187–88, 191–94; John Amasa May and Joan Reynolds Faunt, *South Carolina Secedes* (Columbia: University of South Carolina Press, 1960), 94, 96, 100, 136, 151, 155, 157–60, 175–76, 180, 184–86, 194, 199–201, 204–5, 209–11, 213, 221.

182. Bacot, "Constitutional Progress," 67–68; Wolfe, *Jeffersonian*, 46, 49–51; Boucher, "Sectionalism," 17, 45–48; Green, *Constitutional*, 117–29.

183. Charles and Charles Cotesworth Pinckney and John Rutledge wanted the state legislatures rather than the people to elect members of the House of Representatives, Rutledge and C. C. Pinckney wanted the House apportioned by taxes rather than by population, Rutledge and Charles Pinckney wanted the president elected by national legislature rather than by popular vote and the Senate rather than the House to originate money bills, and Pinckney and Rutledge desired high property qualifications for the presidency, Congress, and judiciary. For their views see Farrand, ed., *Records*, I, 69, 130–32, 137, 147, 196, 350, 360, 534, 536–37, II, 30, 81, 224, 248–49; C. Pinckney to Rufus King, Jan. 26, 1789, and to James Madison, Mar. 28, 1789, III, 355; E. Rutledge to John Jay, June 26, 1776, in *Letters of Members of the Continental Congress*, 8 vols. ed. Edmund C. Burnett, (Washington, D.C.: Carnegie Institution of Washington, 1921–36), I, 518. For other examples of antidemocratic beliefs see William L. Smith, "Oration at Charleston, July 4, 1796," in *Pro-Slavery Thought in the Old South*, ed. William S. Jenkins (Chapel Hill: University of North Carolina Press, 1935), 61; C. Gadsden to Samuel Adams, July 4, 1779, and "Letter to the *Gazette*," July 11, 1784, in *Writings*, ed. Walsh, 163–64, 216; J. Rutledge, Jr., to E. Rutledge, July 4, 1797, quoted in Rogers, *Evolution*, 202–3; D. Ramsay to Benjamin Rush, Aug. 6, 1786, in Brunhouse, *David Ramsay*, 105; H. W. De

Saussure to Richard Bland Lee, Feb. 14, 1795, quoted in Rose, *Prologue*, 57; Francis Kinloch quoted in Rogers, *History*, 177.

184. E. Rutledge to Henry Rutledge, Aug. 2, 1796, *SCHGM*, XLIV (Apr., 1963), 69.

185. Grayson, "Autobiography," 222; Frederick A. Porcher: "Eulogy of Calhoun, 1850," *De Bow's Review*, X (Feb., 1851), 237; cf. "The Free School System in South-Carolina," *Southern Quarterly Review*, XVI (Oct., 1849), 39, 46.

186. Edward J. Pringle: "The People," *Southern Quarterly Review*, IX (Jan., 1854), 33, 37–41, 43–44, 46, 48–57; *Slavery in the Southern States* (Cambridge, Mass.: John Bartlett, 1852), 19, 30–31; McDuffie quoted in Green, *George McDuffie*, 146–47. For more examples of South Carolina conservative elitism see J. H. Hammond: "Speech in the United States Senate, March 4, 1858," *Congressional Globe*, 35th Congress, 1st Session, Appendix, 71; Speech in the House of Representatives, Feb. 1, 1836, *Debates in Congress*, 25th Congress, 1st Session, 2460; *Selections from the Letters and Speeches of the Honorable James H. Hammond* (New York: John F. Trow, 1866), 226, 281, 305; *Two Letters on Slavery in the United States* (Columbia, S.C.: Allen, McCarter, 1845), 10, 35–36; Legaré, *Writings*, I, 43, 57, 271–72, 352; Grayson, "Autobiography," *SCHGM*, LXIX (Apr., 1948), 102, L (July, 1949), 143, (Oct., 1949), 209, LI (Jan., 1950), 31–32; Mary Simms Oliphant, Alfred T. Odell, and T. C. D. Saves, eds., *The Letters of William Gilmore Simms*, 5 vols. (Columbia: University of South Carolina Press, 1952), II, 493, III, 173, 175, IV, 42, 229, 302; Henry W. Ravenel, "Address before the Black Oak Agricultural Society, 1852," quoted in Easton, *Civilization*, 204–5; James Hamilton, Jr., H. L. Pinckney, George McDuffie, and Daniel Elliott Huger quoted in Freehling, *Prelude*, 89, 132, 144–47, 152, 241–42, 256, 258; Stephen Elliott, "Sermon Delivered at Christ Church, Savannah, February 28, 1862," in Jenkins, *Pro-Slavery*, 239–40.

187. Fraser, *My Reminiscences*, 69–70; J. N. Cardozo, *Reminiscences of Charleston* (Charleston: Joseph Walker, 1866), 37–39.

188. William Elliott quoted in Lewis Pinckney Jones, "William Elliott, South Carolina Nonconformist," *Journal of Southern History*, XVII (Sept., 1951), 364; James L. Petigru to H. S. Legaré, May 31, 1835, in Carson, *Life*, 174.

189. O'Neall, *Biographical*, II, 597–99.

190. *Ibid.*, I, 307; Mrs. St. Julien (Harriett Horry Rutledge) Ravenel, *Charleston: The Place and the People* (New York: Macmillan, 1912), 301; Robert Molloy, *Charleston: A Gracious Heritage* (New York: D. A. Appleton Century, 1947), 86; Fraser, *My Reminiscences*, 71; Rogers, *Evolution*, 112–18, 121–23, 250–52, 357–59; Barry, *Mr. Rutledge*, 311, 358–59, 362n; Zahniser, *Charles Cotesworth Pinckney*, 116–17.

191. *Ibid.*, 277; Joseph Manigault and George Izard quoted in Rogers, *Evolution*, 359.

192. Fraser, *My Reminiscences*, 76; Ravenel, *Charleston*, 401; Cardozo, *Reminiscences*, 37–39; O'Neall, *Biographical*, I, 180–84, 305–64, II, 243–52.

193. Norton, "Social," 26–28; O'Neall, *Biographical*, I, 217–31; Perry, *Reminiscences*, 62.

194. E. Rutledge to H. Rutledge, Aug. 2, 1796, *SCHGM*, XLIV (Apr., 1963), 71; Thomas S. Grimké to Henry Grimké, Feb. ?, 1818, in Adrienne Koch, "A Family Crisis: Letters from John Faucher Grimké and Thomas Smith Grimké,"

SCHGM, LXIX (July, 1968), 191; Paul Hamilton Hayne, *Lives of Robert Young Hayne and Hugh Swinton Legaré* (Charleston: Evans & Cogswell, 1878), 131–32.

195. O'Neall, *Biographical*, I, 180, 324–25, 357–58; II, 3–37, 250–52, 378–89, 402–7, 488–90, 542–43; Fraser, *My Reminiscences*, 78; Carson, *Life*, 40, 52, 62, 226, 281; Capens, *Life*, 15–19, 28; Timothy Ford, "Diary of Timothy Ford," *SCHGM*, XIII (July, 1912), 133.

196. W. G. Simms to James Lawson, Dec. 29, 1839, in *Letters*, eds. Oliphant *et. al.*, I, 164–65; William Henry Trescot, *Memorial of the Life of J. Johnston Pettigrew* (Charleston: John Russell, 1870), 24.

197. Charlotte Ann Allston to R. F. W. Allston, in *Rice*, ed. Easterby, 13; Rogers, *History*, 311; Ramsay, *History*, II, 61.

198. *Directory . . . 1809, passim*; *1860*, II, 32; Waring, "Medical Huguenots in South Carolina," *Transactions*, no. 72 (1967), 8–10; Waring, *History*, 144, 343–44, 347–49.

199. Ramsay, *History*, II, 59, 63; Brunhouse, "David Ramsay," 28, 154n; Edward F. McGrady, "An Historical Address Delivered before the Graduating Class of the Medical College of the State of South Carolina," *Year Book 1896* (Charleston: Walker, Evans & Cogswell, 1897), 392–95, 404, 412–13, 416–19, 432; "Shirras Dispensary," *ibid.*, 141–45; Waring, *History*, 118–29, 160, 167–70, 212–13, 245, 275–76, 278–79, 310–11, 318–20, 347; *Directory . . . 1860*, II, 32; Waring, "Marine," 175–76, 179; "William Harleston Huger, 1826–1906," *SCHGM*, VII (Jan., 1907), 54–56.

200. Compiled from data in Davidson, *Last*, 170–267.

201. Stephen Elliott, *Annual Address before the Clariosophic and Euphradian Societies of the South Carolina College, 1859* (Charleston: Walker, Evans, 1860), 14–15; Ramsay, *History*, II, 212–13; James Silk Buckingham, *Random Shots and Southern Breezes*, 2 vols. (New York: n.p., 1842), II, 138.

202. South Carolina *Gazette and General Advertiser*, Feb. 5–7, 1784, quoted in Rutledge, "Artists," 130–31; Ford, "Diary," Oct. 10, 12, 1785, 191–92, 203; D. Ramsay to B. Rush, May 1, 1787, in Brunhouse, *David Ramsay*, 112; C. C. Pinckney quoted in Zahniser, *Charles Cotesworth Pinckney*, 276; Stephen Elliott to Joel R. Poinsett, Jan. 9, 1822, in Rippy, *Joel R. Poinsett*, 198.

203. Charleston *Courier*, Aug. 27, 1839, quoted in Jervey, *Robert Y. Hayne*, 503–4; Hammond, "The North and the South," *Southern Quarterly Review*, XV (July, 1849), 292.

204. W. G. Simms to Philip C. Pendleton, Feb. 1, 1841, in *Letters*, eds. Oliphant *et. al.*, I, 220–21, 224; cf. same to George Frederick Holmes, July 15, 1853, III, 245; Simms, "Summer Travel," 31; Simms to Thomas Caute Reynolds, July 15, 1844, in *Letters*, eds. Oliphant *et. al.*, V, 383; cf. same to W. P. Miles, May 27, 1855, V, 242.

205. Childs, ed., *Rice*, 111; Paul Hamilton Hayne to James Russell Lowell, Dec. 28, 1860, in Kate Harbes Becker, *Paul Hamilton Hayne: Life and Letters* (Belmont, N.C.: Outline Co., 1951), 27; P. H. Hayne to Horatio Woodman, Aug. 19, 1860, in Jay B. Hubbell, *The South in American Literature, 1607–1900* (Durham, N.C.: Duke University Press, 1954), 746.

206. James Warley Miles, "Journal of the American Oriental Society," *Southern Quarterly Review*, VII (Apr., 1853), 273.

207. Albert Sidney Thomas, *A Historical Account of the Protestant Episcopal*

Church in South Carolina, 1820–1857 (Columbia, S.C.: R. L. Bryan, 1957), 167–467, 657–789; Dalcho, *Historical*, 465–563; Williams, *St. Michael's*, 18–19, 22, 57; Holmes, "Parish," 314–20, 343–47; McCrady, *Sketch*, 54–62; McCrady, "Historic," 346–72; "Huguenot," 303–13; Missildine, "Historical Sketch," 397–403; William Way, *The History of Grace Church, Charleston, South Carolina: The First Hundred Years* (Durham, N.C.: Seeman Printery, 1948), 3, 9, 26, 130–32, 184–98.

208. Compiled from data in Davison, *Last*, 170–267.

209. For a list of South Carolina clergymen see Thomas, *Historical*, 637–41; Porcher, "Memoirs," 137.

210. Williams, *St. Michael's*, 78–80.

211. C. C. Pinckney quoted in Zahniser, *Charles Cotesworth Pinckney*, 271; Rogers, *Evolution*, 388–89.

212. Paul Trapier quoted in Williams, *St. Michael's*, 60; Porcher, "Memoirs," 137–41; Elliott, "Sermon," 239–40.

213. Mrs. Thomas Broughton to Nathaniel Broughton, Dec. 5, 1716, in "Broughton Letters," *SCHGM*, XV (Oct., 1914), 175–76; C. Pinckney quoted in Zahniser, *Charles Cotesworth Pinckney*, 3; E. L. Pinckney, "Resolutions," in Ravenel, *Eliza Pinckney*, 116; E. L. Pinckney: to C. C. Pinckney, Feb. ?, 1761, 209–10; to G. Lucas, ?, 1743, 64–66; to Lucas, ?, 1742, in *Letterbook*, eds. Pinckney and Zahniser, 51–52.

214. John F. Grimké to H. Grimké, Mar. 7, 1818, in Koch "Family," 181; W. J. Grayson, "The Character of the Gentleman," *Southern Quarterly Review*, VII (Jan., 1853), 61. For another upper-class view of the importance of religion in shaping character see Poyas, *Olden*, 202.

215. Lorenzo Sabine, *Notes on Duels and Duelling* (Boston: Crosby, Nichols, 1855), 322–23, 325–29; Jack Kenny Williams, "The Code of Honor in Ante-Bellum South Carolina," *SCHGM*, LIV (July, 1952), 123, 126–27; D. Ramsay to B. Rush, Sept. 27, 1804, in Brunhouse, *David Ramsay*, 156–57.

216. T. S. Grimké, *Address on the Truth, Dignity, Power and Beauty of the Principles of Peace, and on the UnChristian Character and Influence of War and the Warrior* (Hartford: George F. Olmstead, 1832), 25–26; cf. Grimké, *People*, 15.

217. Ramsay, *History*, II, 201–2; Knight, ed., *Documentary*, I, 66–86, 335–36, 351; Knight, *Public Education in the South* (Boston: Ginn, 1922), 33–34; Meriwether, *History*, 109–16, 236–47; John Furman Thomason, *The Foundations of the Public Schools of South Carolina* (Columbia: State Co., 1925), 93–97.

218. Thomason, *Foundations*, 116–18, 127–28, 140–41, 145, 150, 157–58, 175; Archer, "Public," 199–200; Knight, *Public*, 215–75; Nita K. Pyburn, "The Public School System of Charleston before 1860," *SCHGM*, LXI (Apr., 1960), 86–91; J. Perrin Anderson, "Public Education in Ante-Bellum South Carolina," *Proceedings of the South Carolina Historical Association* (1933), 4–7.

219. "Commissioners of Free Schools of St. Philip's and St. Michael's Parish, 1846 Report to the Legislature," *Documentary*, ed. Knight, V. 121.

220. *Year Book 1880* (Charleston: News and Courier Book Presses, 1881), 116–17; Pyburn, "Public," 93–98; Capens, *Life*, 110–14; Knight, *Public*, 228;

Archer, "Public," 184–87; Thomason, *Foundations*, 161; C. G. Memminger, "Report on Public Schools (1858)," *Documentary*, ed. Knight, V, 197–98.

221. James Stirling, "Letters from the Slave States," *Documentary*, ed. Knight, IV, 205; Knight, *Public*, 215–27, legislative committee of 1847 quoted on 222–23.

222. Stirling, "Letters," 205; *De Bow's Review*, 3d ser., XXII (1857), 517; Anderson, "Public," 3–4; David Duncan Wallace, *The History of South Carolina*, 4 vols. (New York: American History Society, 1934), III, 47–48.

223. Compiled from data in Davidson, *Last*, 18, 21–39, 170–267.

224. Richard Beale Davis, "The Ball Papers: A Pattern of Life in the Low Country, 1800–1825," *SCHGM*, LXV (Jan., 1964), 8; D. Ramsay to J. Morse, Feb. 26, 1813, in Brunhouse, "David Ramsay," 172; Easterby, *History*, 63; Porcher, "Memoirs," 46–47; "Progress," 308.

225. Quoted in Easterby, *History*, 105. This account of the history of the College of Charleston is drawn from Porcher, "Memoirs," 107–8, 150–62; Easterby, *History*, 18–152, 258–333; Meriwether, *History*, 57–68, 246–47; Henry E. Shepard, "College of Charleston," *Year Book 1893* (Charleston: Walker, Evans & Cogswell, 1894), 238–46.

226. Porcher, "Memoirs," 105, 107–8, 152.

227. H. W. De Saussure and R. Izard quoted in Ravenel, *Charleston*, 587–88; Grayson, "Autobiography," 88.

228. Daniel Walker Hollis, *The University of South Carolina*, 2 vols. (Columbia: University of South Carolina Press, 1951), I, 257–58, 262–63.

229. E. Merleton Coulter, *College Life in the Old South* (Athens: University of Georgia Press, 1951), 174. This account of the College of South Carolina is based on M. La Borde, *History of South Carolina College* (Charleston: Walker, Evans & Cogswell, 1874), 22–549; Hollis, *University*, I, *passim*, II, 9–10, 13–15; Meriwether, *History*, 165, 199–211.

230. Marcus Cunliffe, *Soldiers & Civilians: The Martial Spirit in America*, *1775–1865* (New York: Free Press, 1973), 337–42, 360–69; Russell F. Weigley, *History of the United States Army* (New York: Macmillan, 1967), 199. Even today the South preponderates among American military leaders: see Morris Janowitz, *The Profesional Soldier: A Social and Political Portrait* (New York: Free Press, 1960), 88–89.

231. W. L. Smith to James McHenry, Aug. 4, 1798, in Rogers, *Evolution*, 344–45; *ibid.*, 345–46; William Lowndes to Mrs. Elizabeth Pinckney Lowndes, Jan. 8, 1815, in Mrs. St. Julien Ravenel, *The Life and Times of William Lowndes* (Boston: Houghton Mifflin, 1901), 146–47.

232. Porcher, "Memoirs," 146–48; "South Carolinians at Partridge Military Academy, 1826," *SCHGM*, LXI (Jan. 1960), 11–12; "The S.C. Military Academy (the Citadel)," *Year Book 1892* (Charleston: Walker, Evans & Cogswell, 1893), 207–8, 215; Meriwether, *History*, 72–75.

233. Osterweis, *Romanticism*, 127, Richard Yeadon quoted on 125.

234. Compiled from data in Davidson, *Last*, 170–267.

235. F. A. Porcher, "Free School Systems," 39, 46.

236. T. S. Grimké, *An Address on the Character and Objects of Science*

(Charleston: A. E. Miller, 1827), 20–23; Adrienne Koch, "Two Charlestonians in Pursuit of Truth: The Grimké Brothers," *SCHGM*, LXIX (July, 1968), 164–67; C. B. Galbreath, "Thomas Smith Grimké," *Ohio Archaelogical and Historical Quarterly*, XXXIII (1924), 309–10; Legaré, *Writings*, II, 551; McDuffie, "Annual Message to the Legislature, 1835," quoted in Green, *George McDuffie*, 150–51; W. G. Simms to J. Lawson, Dec. 29, 1839, in *Letters*, eds. Oliphant *et. al.*, I, 159; J. W. Miles quoted in Thomas Cary Johnson, Jr., *Scientific Interests in the Old South* (New York: D. Appleton-Century, 1936), 91–92; Grayson, "Autobiography," 92–94; Petigru to Phillip Porcher, June 16, 1851, in Carson, *Life*, 289.

237. Johnson, *Scientific*, 67–68, 84, 87, 101–3, 190; Stille, "Life," 301; Rippy, *Joel R. Poinsett*, 203–13; Grimké, *Address*, *passim*; John Drayton, *The Carolinian Florist, 1807* (Columbia: University of South Carolina Press, 1943), 1–2.

238. Chalmers S. Murray, *This Our Land* (Charleston: Carolina Art Association, 1949), 18–128; Porcher, "Memoirs," 48.

239. William G. Mazyck, "The Charleston Museum, Its Genesis and Development," *Year Book 1907* (Charleston: Walker, Evans and Cogswell, 1908), 13–38; Johnson, *Scientific*, 54.

240. Johnson, *Scientific*, 149; Mazyck, "Charleston," 28–30; Horatio Hughes, "The Elliott Society," *Proceedings of the South Carolina Historical Association* (1938), 25–31; Davidson, *Last*, 111–13.

241. Johnson, *Scientific*, 80–81, 84–88, 124, 128, 132–38, 143–44, 146–47.

242. Drayton, *Carolinian*, 1–2; Grimké, *Address*, 73.

243. Spain, "Libraries," 35–36; Hubbell, *South*, 95–96; "Items from the South Carolina and Georgia Almanac, 1793," *SCHGM*, XXXIII (Jan., 1931), 74; *Directory, 1809*, 137; *1835–36*, 143; *1860*, II, 35; Wallace, *History*, II, 56–57.

244. Johnson, *Scientific*, 128, 137; *Directory, 1835–36*, 144; Mazyck, "Charleston," 15, 37–38.

245. *Collections of the South Carolina Historical Society*, I–II (1857–58); *Directory, 1860*, II, 36; Walter Muir Whitehill, *Independent Historical Societies* (Boston: Boston Atheneum, 1962), 34–47; Arthur S. Link and Rembert W. Patrick, *Writing Southern History* (Baton Rouge: Louisiana State University Press, 1968), 53.

246. White, *Robert Barnwell Rhett*, 35, 56–60, 145; Hubbell, *South*, 468; George A. Wauchope, *The Writers of South Carolina* (Columbia, S.C.: State Co., 1910), 13–15; *Letters*, eds. Oliphant *et. al.*, III, 209n.

247. Edd Winfield Parks, *Segments of Southern Thought* (Athens: University of Georgia Press, 1938), 93–94, 149–50; Wauchope, *Writers*, 64–65, 74–75, 78, 149, 151, 155, 159, 223, 249, 319, 322.

248. Compiled from data in Davidson, *Last*, 170–267.

249. William Elliott, "Review of Anne of Geierstein," *Southern Review*, IV (Nov., 1829), 498–522. For another example of praise of English culture and an acknowledgment of its influence on South Carolina's gentility see William Porcher Miles, "American," 384–86, 404.

250. Sonneck, *Early*, 18, 27, 29.

251. Rutledge, *Artists*, 124–25, 130–31, 138–40; George C. Rogers, Jr., *Charleston in the Age of the Pinckneys* (Norman: University of Oklahoma Press,

1969), 159–60; Rippy, *Joel R. Poinsett*, 197–200; Davidson, *Last*, 140–44; G. E. Manigault, "History of the Carolina Art Association," *Year Book 1894*, 243–44, 247–53; Harold A. Mouzon, "The Carolina Art Association," *SCHGM*, LIX (July, 1958), 125–28.

252. Davidson, *Last*, 136–39; Ravenel, *Architects*, 53–59, 79–80, 84, 87, 97, 100–102, 157–58, 181. Wayne Andrews, *Architecture, Ambition and Americans: A Social History of American Architecture* (New York: Free Press, 1964), 82, 96–99, 129–30.

253. F. A. Porcher, "Modern Art," *Southern Quarterly Review*, V (Apr., 1852), 100, 105; cf. William Lowndes to Elizabeth Pinckney Lowndes, Apr. 29, 1812, in Ravenel, *Life*, 108.

254. John Hampton Hock, "Stephen Elliott," *Annals of Medical History*, VII (Mar., 1955), 164–68.

255. Compiled from data in Davidson, *Last*, 170–267.

256. See, for example, the charities of the largest slaveholders of 1860 in *ibid.*, 170–267.

257. Easterby, *History*, 63–70, 90–91, 95, 98, 107–09; Chisolm, "St. Andrew's," 287–92; *St. Andrew's*, 25–50; *Rules*, 41; Thomason, *Foundations*, 93–97; *Directory*, 1835–36, 153; Mills, *Statistics*, 428–29.

258. Ravenel, *Life*, 45–48; J. S. Buist, "Address Delivered on the 112th Anniversary of the Charleston Orphan House," *Year Book 1902* (Charleston: Walker, Evans & Cogswell, 1903), 175–81; Newton B. Jones, "The Charleston Orphan House, 1860–1876," *SCHGM*, LII (Oct., 1961), 203–5; Benjamin Joseph Klebaner, "Public Poor Relief in Charleston 1800–1860," *SCHGM*, LV (Oct., 1954), 210–20; *Charleston Orphan House: Centennial Celebration* (Charleston: Walker, Evans & Cogswell, 1891), 27–63; *Year Book 1880*, 61–66.

259. "Shirras Dispensary," 139–42; *Year Book 1880*, 44–50, 71–72; "Roper Hospital," *Year Book 1905* (Charleston: Calder-Conklin, 1906), 3–28; "William Enston Home," *Year Book 1882*, 111–17.

260. For accounts of various upper-class eleemosynary institutions and their officers, members, and donors see *Directory*, 1809, 139; 1835–36, 134–35, 155–58; 1849, 135–36, 147; Thomas, *Historical*, 657–71, 696; "Items," 76, 78; C. E. Chichester, "Historical Sketch of the Charleston Port Society," *Year Book 1884*, 313–34; Margaret Simons Middleton, "A Sketch of the Ladies Benevolent Society," *Year Book 1941* (Charleston: Walker, Evans & Cogswell, 1942), 215–56.

261. Koch, "Two," 159.

262. William Roper quoted in Klebaner, "Public," 214; H. W. De Saussure quoted in *Charleston Orphan House*, 72.

263. Ramsay, *History*, II, 214–15. The basis for the comparison on educational, cultural, and charitable institutions is taken from Mills, *Statistics*, 207, 428–32; Dawson and De Saussure, *Census*, 40–41. For Boston see "The Public and Private Charities of Boston," *North American Review*, LXI (July, 1845), 141–47; Lemuel Shattuck, *Report to the Committee of the City Council Appointed to Obtain the Census of Boston for the Year 1845* (Boston: John H. Eastburne, 1846), 102–5.

264. For accounts of upper-class life in Charleston and on the plantations see Cardozo, *Reminiscences*, 73–74; Fraser, *My Reminiscences*, 50–51, 59, 61–66,

100–110; Ravenel, *Charleston*, 384–85, 394–99, 426–32, Porcher, "Memoirs" (Jan., 1944), 36–38, (Apr., 1945), 78–92, (Oct., 1946), 214–27; Grayson, "Autobiography," 26–27; Katherine M. Jones, ed., *The Plantation South* (Indianapolis: Bobbs-Merrill, 1957), 153–56, 166–67; Alston, *Rice*, 19, 133; Elizabeth W. Allston Pringle, *Chronicles of Chicora Wood* (Boston: Christopher Publishing House, 1940), 145–46; Poyas, *Olden*, 143; Davis, "Ball," 1–15; Irving, *South Carolina*, 14ff.; F. A. Porcher, "Historical and Social Sketch of Craven County," 396, 404, 407, 411–12, 414; Lawrence Fay Brewster, *Summer Migrations and Resorts of South Carolina Low-Country Planters* (Durham, N.C.: Duke University Press, 1947); J. H. Easterby, "The St. Thomas Hunting Club," *SCHGM*, XLVI (July, 1945), 123–31; Richard B. Harwell, "The Hot and Hot Fish Club of All Saints Parish," *SCHGM*, XLVIII (Jan., 1947), 40–47; William Oliver Stevens, *Pistols at Ten Paces: The Code of Honor in America* (Boston: Houghton Mifflin, 1940), 31–33, 91–92, 103, 131–34; John Lyde Wilson, *The Code of Honor or Rules for the Government of Principals and Seconds in Duelling,* (Charleston: James Phynney, 1858); Sabine, *Notes,* 322–29; Mills, "Thoroughbred," 19; William Way, *History of the New England Society of Charleston, South Carolina for One Hundred Years, 1819–1919* (Charleston: New England Society, 1920).

265. For samples of these opinions see Clement Eaton, ed., *The Leaven of Democracy* (New York: George Braziller, 1963), 199–201, 208–10; Jones, ed., *Plantation,* 81, 86, 121, 153–56, 166–67, 174; Isaac Weld, Jr., *Travels through the States of North America and the Provinces of Upper and Lower Canada during the Years 1795, 1796, 1797,* 2 vols. (London: John Stockdale, 1807), I, 267; Abiel Abbot, "The Abiel Abbot Journals, a Yankee in Charleston Society, 1812–1827," *SCHGM,* LXVIII (Oct., 1967), 246; Adam Hodgson, *Letters from North America during a Tour in the United States and Canada,* 2 vols. (London: Hurst, 1824), I, 48–49; N. Appleton, Jan. 2, 8, 18, Feb. 4, 1805, "Journal 1804–05"; Charles Eliot Norton to A. H. Clough, Apr. 5, 1855, in *Letters of Charles Eliot Norton,* 2 vols., eds. Sarah Norton and M. A. DeWolfe Howe (Boston: Houghton Mifflin, 1913), I, 122–23; McKissick, "Some," 48.

266. Rogers, *Evolution,* 116, 142.

267. Miles, "American," 383; Grayson, "Autobiography," 218–19; J. L. Petigru to Jane Petigru North, May 13, 1839, in Carson, *Life,* 194; Legaré, *Writings,* II, 279.

268. Drayton, *View,* 220; Miles, "American," 400–404; Ramsay, *History,* II, 214–15, 229–30; J. Alston to A. Burr, c. 1800, in Rogers, *History,* 189; Rhett, "Farewell," 149; Elliott, *Annual,* 14–15; Porcher: "Southern," 98–104, 106; "Memoirs" (Jan., 1944), 32, 37; Grayson: "Autobiography," 102; "Character," 74; Alston, *Rice,* 110; H. S. Legaré to A. Huger, Dec. 15, 1834, in Legaré, *Writings,* I, 218; Elizabeth Ann Poyas, *Our Forefathers, Their Homes and Their Churches* (Charleston: Walker, Evans, 1860), 161.

269. Ford, "Diary," 143, 191–92; Abbot, "Abiel," 122–23; "Ebenezer Kellogg's Visit to Charleston, 1817," *SCHGM,* XLIX (Jan., 1948), 6, 9.

270. Miles, "American," 404–5; Porcher, "Memoirs" (Apr., 1945), 80, 87–88, (Jan., 1947), 24; Ramsay, *History,* II, 217–23, 229–30; Grayson, "Autobiography," 27; Drayton, *View,* 221; R. F. W. Allston to John C. Calhoun, July 28, 1847, in "Correspondence Addressed to John C. Calhoun," *Annual Report of*

the American Historical Association (1929) eds. Chauncey S. Boucher and Robert P. Brooks, 388.

271. Porcher, "Memoirs" (Jan., 1945), 39, (Jan., 1947), 24; Lowndes quoted in Ravenel, *William Lowndes*, 61; Porcher, "Memoirs," 95; Ramsay, *History*, II, 229–30; J. F. Grimké to H. Grimké, Mar. 6, 1818, and T. S. Grimké to H. Grimké, Feb. ?, 1818, in Koch, "Family," 182–88; Pringle, *Chronicles*, 57–58.

272. The best discussion of this and other themes respecting the genteel South is Taylor, *Cavalier, passim*.

273. J. F. Grimké to H. Grimké, Mar. 6, 1818, in Koch, "Family," 184; Martha Laurens Ramsay to David Ramsay, Jr., June 13, 1810, July 18, 1810, Aug. 26, 1810, Nov. 21, 1810, Mar. 5, 1811, in Ramsay, *Memoirs*, 254–56, 261–63, 269–71; Grayson, "Character," 55, 66–69; Fraser, *My Reminiscences*, 57–58.

274. Ramsay, *History*, II, 215.

275. Thomas, *Reminiscences*, I, 34.

276. H. S. Legaré to I. W. Holmes, Apr. 8, 1833, and to A. Huger, Dec. 15, 1832, in Legaré, *Writings*, I, 215, 218; Miles, "American," 404–6.

277. W. G. Simms to J. H. Hammond, Aug. 18, 1852, and to W. Elliott, Mar. 7, 1849, in *Letters*, eds. Oliphant *et. al.*, III, 195–96, II, 493; Simms, "Charleston, The Palmetto City," *Harper's New Monthly Magazine*, XV (June, 1857), 6.

278. Robert H. Woody, "Some Aspects of the Economic Condition of South Carolina after the Civil War," *North Carolina Historical Review*, VII (July, 1930), 353; John Porter Hollis, *The Early Period of Reconstruction in South Carolina* (Baltimore: Johns Hopkins University Press, 1905), 25.

279. *Year Book 1883*, 543–46; *An Historical Sketch of the Washington Light Infantry of Charleston*, S.C. (New York: D. A. Appleton, 1875), 6–7; Ravenel, *Ravenel Records*, 64; Pringle, *Chronicles*, 147, 163, 174, 183, 190, 219; Mary Boykin Chesnut, *A Diary from Dixie* (Boston: Houghton Mifflin, 1949), *passim*; "Middleton Correspondence, 1861–1865," *SCHGM*, LXIII (Jan., 1962), 33–41, (Apr., 1962), 61–82, (July, 1962), 164–74, (Oct., 1962), 204–10, LXIV (Jan., 1963), 28–38, (Apr., 1963), 95–113, (July, 1963), 158–77, (Oct., 1963), 212–29, LXV (Jan., 1964), 33–44, (Apr., 1964), 98–109.

280. Hollis, *Early*, 10–15, 25–26; Francis B. Simkins, "The Problems of South Carolina Agriculture," *North Carolina Historical Review*, VII (Jan., 1930), 47, 59–61, 66; Lesesne, *Bank*, 169; Derrick, *Centennial*, 225; Rogers, *History*, 404–10, 419–25, 434–36, 453; Simkins and Woody, *South Carolina during Reconstruction* (Chapel Hill: University of North Carolina Press, 1932), 3–12, 284, 286–87, 315–16; Woody, "Some," 352–54, 362–64; Ravenel, *Ravenel Records*, 115–16; Sidney Andrews, *The South since the Civil War* (Boston: Ticknor and Fields, 1866), 1–11, 28–37.

281. Samuel Gourdin Gaillard, "Recollections of Samuel Gourdin Gaillard," *SCHGM*, LVII (July, 1956), 129–30; Nanny Bostick De Saussure, *Old Plantation Days* (New York: Duffield, 1909), 87; Ravenel, *Ravenel Records*, 116; Alston, *Rice*, 125; Arney R. Childs, ed., *The Private Journal of Henry William Ravenel* (Columbia: University of South Carolina Press, 1947), xviii–xx, 209, 237–38, 243, 257, 261, 301, 303, 370, 394, 397; Easterby, ed., *South Carolina*, 18–19, 214; Murray, *This Our Land*, 144–46, 151; Susan R. Jervey and Charlotte St. Julien Ravenel, *Two Diaries from Middle St. John's Berkeley, South Carolina, February-May, 1865* (St. John's, S.C.: St. John's Hunting Club, 1921), *passim*;

Pringle, *Chronicles*, 289, 320; Chesnut, *Diary*, 395, 425, 431, 467, 483, 498, 503–5, 520; Harriott to Susan Middleton, June 17, Aug. 19, 1865, in "Middleton," 108–9, cf. 98–109; Anne F. Scott, *The Southern Lady from Pedestal to Politics, 1830–1930* (Chicago: University of Chicago Press, 1970), 92–93; P. H. Hayne to Elizabeth Bartow Stoddard, Mar. 6, 1869, and to Horace E. Scudder, Dec. 11, 1869, in Becker, *Paul Hamilton Hayne*, 31–33, 35–36; Hayne to Bayard Taylor, Mar. 2, 1869, in *The Correspondence of Bayard Taylor and Paul Hamilton Hayne*, ed. Charles Duffy (Baton Rouge: Louisiana State University Press, 1945), 16–17; Hayne to John Esten Cooke, July 24, 1866, to Richard Henry Stoddard, Mar. 16, 1869, and to H. E. Scudder, Dec. 11, 1868, in *A Collection of Hayne Letters*, ed. Dan Morely McKeithan (Austin: Unversity of Texas Press, 1944), 46–47, 89, 107–8; Simkins and Woody, *South Carolina*, 18–20; Andrews, *South*, 223; Belton O'Neall Townsend, "South Carolina Society," *Atlantic Monthly*, XXXIX (1877), 674–75; Wallace, *History*, III, 222.

282. Easterby, ed., *South Carolina*, 197–98; Jervey and Ravenel, "Diaries," Feb. 27, 1865, 7; Childs, ed., *Private*, Mar. 7, 1865, 209, cf. Mar. 12, 1865, 222; Harriott to Susan Middleton, Aug. 19, 1865, "Middleton," 108–9; P. H. Hayne to B. Taylor, Apr. 22, 1869, in *Correspondence*, ed. Duffy 29.

283. Rogers, *History*, 454–55; Archibald Rutledge, *Home by the River* (Indianapolis: Bobbs-Merrill, 1941), 14; Robert Goodwyn Rhett, *Charleston: An Epic of Carolina* (Richmond: Garrett and Massie, 1940), 322, 339–41; Wallace, *History*, IV, 846, 848; White, *Robert Barnwell Rhett*, 241–42; Ravenel, *Ravenel*, 105–6, 112, 115–16, 118–19; Leiding, *Historic*, 182–84; Stoney, *Plantations*, 47–48, 54–55, 57–59, 61–62, 73, 77–79, 81–82; Lachicotte, *Georgetown*, 22–26, 33, 46–49, 64–65, 78–82, 85–87, 102–8, 119–24, 135–37, 139–44, 155–58, 181–83, 186, 193–94; David Doar, "Rice and Rice Planting in the South Carolina Low Country," *Contributions from the Charleston Museum*, VIII (1936), 7–42; Theodore D. Ravenel, "The Last Days of Rice Planting," *ibid.*, 43–53; Heyward, *Seed*, 27–28, 42–43, 50, 85, 159, 211–12, 242; Smith, "Ashley," 23, 40, 45, 91–94, 190–91, 194–96; Smith, "Charleston," 13, 37–38, 70–71; Childs, ed., *Private*, 405; Archibald Rutledge, *Santee Paradise* (Indianapolis: Bobbs-Merrill, 1956), 112; Patience Pennington (Elizabeth Waties Allston), *A Woman Rice Planter* (Cambridge: Harvard University Press, 1961), xxx–xxxi; Pringle, *Chronicles*, 14; Murray, *This Our Land*, 170–74.

284. *Year Book 1887* (Charleston: Lucas Richardson, 1888), 6; *1890* (Charleston: Walker, Evans & Cogswell, 1891), 24–25; *1900* (Walker, Evans & Cogswell, 1901), 13; *1910* (Charleston: Daggett Printing, 1911), xiii, 40; *1920* (Walker, Evans & Cogswell, 1921), 61.

285. Trenholm, *Centennial*, 50.

286. John Jay Knox, *A History of Banking in the United States* (New York: Bradford Rhodes, 1900), 569; J. V. Nielsen, Jr., "Post-Confederate Finance in South Carolina," *SCHGM*, LVI (Apr., 1955), 85–91.

287. Rhett, *Charleston*, 315–26; Stover, *Railroads*, 5; Derrick, *Centennial*, 244–57; Rhett, "Mayor Rhett's Annual Report," *Year Book 1910*, xvi; August Kohn, "The Charleston of To-day," *Year Book 1909* (Charleston: Walker, Evans & Cogswell, 1910), 3.

288. George R. Sherrill and Robert H. Stoudemire, *Municipal Government in South Carolina* (Columbia: University of South Carolina Press, 1950), 2, 5;

Vance and Demerath, eds., *Urban*, 28, 32–34; Petty, *Growth*, 65–66, 85–86, 110, 115–16, 141–58.

289. *Year Book 1880*, 83–85; Trenholm, *Centennial*, 6, 9, 23–25, 33–36, 41–42.

290. J. C. Hemphill, "A Short Story of the South Carolina Inter-State and West Indian Exposition," *Year Book 1902* 103–71; Rhett, "Mayor," xvi–xvii.

291. "Immigration to the South, Report of Philip S. Gadsden to Mayor Robert G. Rhett," *Year Book 1907*, 1–12; Rhett, *Charleston*, 322.

292. For information on post–Civil War business firms and figures see *An Historical and Descriptive Review of the City of Charleston*, 2 vols. (New York: Empire Publishing, 1882), I, 41–44, 48–51, 57–60, 62–64, 66–67, 70–73, 98–99, 102–3, 105, 114–16, 127–28, 140; *Charleston Directory, 1866, Compiled by Burke & Boinest* (New York: Brown, 1866), 63, 85; *The Charleston City Directory, 1886, Compiled by Ross A. Smith* (Charleston: Lucas & Richardson, 1886), 4, 20–21, 464, 729; *Charleston Chamber of Commerce Year-Book, 1912–13* (Charleston: Charleston Chamber of Commerce, 1913), 68–70, 73–74, 79; Arthur Mazyck, *Guide to Charleston* (Walker, Evans & Cogswell, 1875), *passim*; *Cyclopedia*, I, 362–72, 449–78, 543–45, 612–14; Hemphill, *Men*, I, 87–89, 158–61, 351–55, 436–40, II, 436–37, III, 180–83, 404–7; Clark, *History*, 254–57, 260; Thomas Petigru Lesesne, *History of Charleston County, South Carolina* (Charleston: A. H. Cawston, 1931), 131–34; E. Merlton Coulter, *George W. Williams: The Life of a Southern Merchant and Banker, 1820–1903* (Athens: University of Georgia Press, 1976), 140ff.

293. *The Trade and Commerce of the City of Charleston, South Carolina from April 1, 1865 to September 1, 1872* (Charleston: News Job Presses, 1873), 50–51; *Historical*, I, 26, 70–75; Mazyck, *Guide*, 173–83; Philip E. Chazal, *The Century in Phosphates and Fertilizers: A Sketch of the South Carolina Phosphate Industry* (Charleston: News and Courier Book Presses, 1894), 38–48.

294. "American Millionaires," *Tribune Monthly*, 4 (June, 1892), 53; *List of Taxpayers of the City of Charleston for 1860* (Charleston: Evans & Cogswell, 1861).

295. Rhett, "Mayor," xvii–xxiii.

296. John Grace, "Mayor Grace's Annual Review," *Year Book 1914* (Charleston: Walker, Evans & Cogswell, 1915), xxv–xxviii, xxx–xxxi, xxiv; anonymous quote in Maude Parker, "Charleston," *Saturday Evening Post*, CCI (Sept. 23, 1927), 124; DuBose Heyward, "Charleston: Where Mellow Past and Present Meet," *National Geographic*, LXXV (Mar., 1939), 277, 281.

297. *Charleston Grows* (Charleston: Walker, Evans & Cogswell, 1949), 4, 40, 43–44, 47, 128.

298. *Ibid.*, 61–129. For the earlier period see *Roll*, 5–9; *Chamber of Commerce Annual Report*, 1916, 1, 1917, 1. For the post–World War II era see *Charleston Grows*, 155–63.

299. Herbert Ravenel Sass, "The Charleston Story," *Charleston Grows*, 1–3; Harold A. Monzon, "Cultural Charleston," *ibid.*, 282–83.

300. Andrews, *South*, 71–72; William Watts Ball, *The State That Forgot* (Indianapolis: Bobbs-Merrill, 1932), 183–84; Alfred B. Williams, *Hampton and His Red Shirts: South Carolina's Deliverance in 1876* (Charleston: Walker, Evans & Cogswell, 1935), 38, 59; Simkins and Woody, *South Carolina*, 485–547; William

J. Cooper, Jr., *The Conservative Regime: South Carolina, 1877–1890* (Baltimore: Johns Hopkins University Press, 1968), 208–12; Reynolds and Faunt, eds., *Biographical*, 8–12; *Year Book 1883*, 6, 14, 457–58; *1884*, 338–49.

301. For state officials see Reynolds and Faunt, eds., *Biographical*, 170–340; *Historical*, I, 17–20; *Cyclopedia*, I, 132–37, 144–46, 148–50, 163–66, 661–63; Hemphill, *Men*, I, 120–32, II, 9–10, 158–61; Wallace, *History*, IV, 304–5; Sass, *Story*, II, 2–6, 456, 458–59. For city officials between 1865 and 1880 see *Year Book 1881*, 368–77; for subsequent lists of city officials see *ibid.*, *1880–1951*.

302. Andrews, *South*, 57–58, 72–74, 88–89; Childs, ed., *Private*, 385; J. J. Pringle Smith, *Address Delivered before the South Carolina Historical Society on Their Twenty-second Anniversary, May 5, 1877* (Charleston: Lucas & Richardson, 1879), *passim*; Daniel Elliott Huger Smith, *A Charlestonian's Recollections, 1846–1913* (Charleston: Carolina Art Association, 1950), 152–62; Gaillard, "Recollections," 129; F. A. Porcher, "The Last Chapter of Reconstruction in South Carolina," *Southern Historical Society Papers*, XII (1884), 173–81, 193–205, 241–53, 309–21, 554–58, XIII (1885), 47–87; Becker, *Paul Hamilton Hayne*, 84, 86; P. H. Hayne to Edward C. Stedman, Apr. 17, 1882, in *Collection*, ed. McKeithan, 285–86; Williams, *Hampton*, 33, 82–83; Cooper, Jr., *Conservative*, 202–10; C. Vann Woodward, *Origins of the New South, 1877–1913* (Baton Rouge: Louisiana State University Press, 1971), 19; Francis B. Simkins, *The Tillman Movement in South Carolina* (Durham, N.C.: Duke University Press, 1926), 92–94, 207, 224; *Year Book 1883*, 567–68.

303. Smith, *Address*, *passim*; Porcher, "Last," 77, 79; Smith, *Charlestonian's*, 132–34.

304. P. H. Hayne to Daniel J. Wilkinson, Aug. 1, 1878, in "The Southern Dilemma: Two Unpublished Letters of Paul Hamilton Hayne," ed. Richard B. Davis, *Journal of Southern History*, XVII (Feb., 1951), 67–68; Hayne to Susan Hayne, Feb. 4, 1886, in "Seven Unpublished Letters of Paul Hamilton Hayne," ed. William Stanley Hoole, *Georgia Historical Quarterly*, XXII (Sept., 1938), 284; Hayne to Julia C. R. Dorr, Aug. 30, 1884, in "A Southern Genteelist: Letters by Paul Hamilton Hayne to Julia C. R. Dorr," *SCHGM*, LIII (Jan., 1952), 19–20, 24; cf. Hayne to S. Hayne, Aug. 28, 1884, in Hoole, ed., "Seven," 275; Hayne to W. G. Simms, Apr. 25, 1869, to J. E. Cooke, Mar. 16, 1877, and to Moses Coit Tyler, Nov. 20, 1876, in *Collection*, ed. McKeithan, 92, 107–8, 362; Hayne, *Lives*, 5–8; Gabriel Manigault, *The United States Unmasked* (London: Edward Stanford, 1879), 72, 96, 106–7, 116–18, 120, 122–24, 130–31, 136–38, 142, 147, 149.

305. Walter Ablen, *Governor Chamberlain's Administration in South Carolina* (New York: G. P. Putnam's Sons, 1888), 216; *Cyclopedia*, I, 144–46, 148–51, 163–66, 661–63; *Historical*, I, 50–51, 81–82, 101–2, 128–29; Hemphill, *Men*, I, 50–51, 186–88, II, 8–10, 157–61, 320–21, III, 354; Wallace, *History*, IV, 186–88; *Transactions*, no. 3. (1895), 26–28; Sass, *History*, II, 449, 455–56, 458–59, 473–74; Lesesne, *History*, 237–43, 290.

306. Hemphill, *Men*, II, 258–61, 299–301, III, 234–36, 344–45, IV, 287–88, 388–40; *Cyclopedia*, I, 325–28, 330–33, 359–62, 657–59; Sass, *Story*, III, 541–42, 688; Lesesne, *History*, 321–22; *Historical*, I, 170–75; Mazyck, *Guide*, 58; "Shirras," 139–45; "Roper," 3–28, *Year Book 1880–1951*.

307. *South Carolina*, 467; *Charleston Directory, 1866*, 58; Lesesne, *History*,

201; Hemphill, *Men*, I, 72–75; Eugene C. Clark, "A History of the First Hundred Years of the High School of Charleston," *Year Book 1943* (Charleston: Walker, Evans & Cogswell, 1946), 194–247; Archer, "Public," 199–204; *Year Book 1880–1951*.

308. Mayzck, *Guide*, advertisement, n.p.

309. James S. Simons, "The High School of Charleston," *Year Book 1910*, 6–7, 15–16; Clark, "History," 196, 200, 223–24, 226.

310. Easterby, *History*, 153–57, 194, 258–332; Meriwether, *History*, 63–68; Rhett, *Charleston*, 345–46; Shepard, "College," 240–46; *Year Book 1912*, 312. The Citadel was another municipally supported institution in which the upper class frequently served on the board of visitors, but, unlike the College of Charleston, rarely on the faculty or enrolled as students. "South Carolina," 214, 235; Meriwether, *History*, 72–75.

311. Meriwether, *History*, 199–210; Hollis, *University*, II, 80–296.

312. Thomas, *Historical*, 212–65, 654, 712–15; McCrady, *Sketch*, 4; Williams, *St. Michael's*, 110–21, 316–32; Way, *History*, 184–98.

313. "Committee Report," reprinted in Thomas, *Historical*, 75; Williams, *St. Michael's*, 108, 112.

314. Rector John Kershaw quoted in Williams, *St. Michael's*, 88; Thomas, *Historical*, 88–99.

315. Williams, *St. Michael's*, 124.

316. *Year Book 1880*, 40, 192–97. For lists of commissioners of these institutions see *ibid.*, *1880–1951*; *Centennial*, 38, 55–63.

317. J. S. Buist, "Address," 177; cf. Rev. Charles S. Vedder quoted in *Centennial*, 22.

318. "Legacies and Donations to the Orphan House Funds," *Year Book 1881*, 32–34. The Charleston *Daily Courier*, Dec. 27, 1865, quoted in Jones, "Charleston," 214.

319. "Shirras," 140–46; "Roper," 3–28; *Year Book 1880*, 44–50, William T. Wragg quoted on 58. For lists of trustees and physicians at these institutions, *Year Book[s] 1880–1951*.

320. Thomas, *Historical*, 225–30, 254–65, 695–96; Way, *Grace*, 144–49; Middleton, "Sketch," 236, 238, 240–56; Chichester, "Historical," 317, 319–22; "The Confederate Home," *Year Book 1884*, 361–70; Knight, *Public*, 33–34; Rhett, *Charleston*, 79; Easterby, *History*, 117–18.

321. Hemphill, *Men*, II, 157, 436–37; Lesesne, *History*, 131–33; Reynolds and Faunt, eds., *Biographical*, 300; Rhett, *Charleston*, 344; *Year Book 1929* (Charleston: Walker, Evans & Cogswell, 1930), 348–49; Coulter, *George W. Williams*, 234–36.

322. *Charleston*, 191–240.

323. Hemphill, *Men*, IV, 396–97; Lesesne, *History*, 201; Reynolds and Faunt, eds., *Biographical*, 176–77; *Cyclopedia*, I, 163–66; "General Wilmot G. De Saussure," reprinted from the Charleston *News and Courier*, Feb. 2, 1886, *Year Book 1886*, 210–15.

324. Mayzck, "Charleston Museum," 20–30, 36–37, 43–44; *Bulletin of the Charleston Museum*, IX (Jan., 1913), 15, XI (Nov., 1915), 53–55, XII (Dec., 1916), 3, XIV (Jan., 1918), 2, XVII (Fourth Quarter, 1922), 26, 47–48; *Year Book 1916* (Charleston: Jonathan F. Furlong, 1917), 404; *Year Book 1925* (Charleston:

Southern Printing & Publishing, 1926), 251–253; *Year Book 1927* (Charleston: Jonathan F. Furlong, 1928), 232–33, 239.

325. *Collections*, V (1888), XIV (1897); *SCHGM*, IX (1908–9), XVI (1915–16), XXV (1924–25), XXXV (1934–35), LV (1953–54), LXIII (1962); Joseph W. Barnwell quoted in Way, *History*, vi; Charleston *News and Courier*, July 31, 1968, reprinted in *SCHGM*, LXIX (Oct., 1968), 269.

326. Manigault, "History," 266–73; Mouzon, "Carolina," 127–38; "The James S. Gibbes Memorial Art Gallery," *Year Book 1904* (Charleston: Lucas-Richardson, 1905), 81–85; James S. Gibbes to William A. Courtenay, Mar. 13, 1883, *Year Book 1883*, 171–72.

327. Quote from Frank Durham, "South Carolina's Poetry Society," *South Atlantic Quarterly*, LII (1953), 277–80, 282–83; Durham, *DuBose Heyward: The Man Who Wrote Porgy* (Columbia: University of South Carolina Press, 1954), 24–27.

328. *Year Book[s] 1920–1951; Charleston Grows*, 110–12; Wauchope, *Writers*, 61–63, 71, 74–77, 85, 322; Durham, *DuBose Heyward*, 136–39.

329. W. G. Simms to Charles E. A. Gayarre, Mar. 13, 1868, in *Letters*, eds. Oliphant *et. al.*, V, 115; P. H. Hayne to B. Taylor, June 16, 1875, to M. C. Tyler, Dec. 3, 1878, and to John G. James, Apr. 3, 1878, in Becker, *Paul Hamilton Hayne*, 66, 96, 112–13; Hayne to B. Taylor, Apr. 26, 1875, and July 14, 1877, in *Correspondence*, ed. Duffy, 68, 90; Hayne to M. P. O'Connor, June 11, 1875, and O'Connor to Hayne, June 8, Aug. 21, 1875, in Mary Doline O'Connor, *The Life and Letters of M. P. O'Connor* (New York: Dempsey & Carroll, 1893), 102–3; F. A. Porcher to the Mayor and Aldermen of Charleston, Nov. 11, 1884, *Year Book 1884*, 166.

330. Glorifications of the Charleston and plantation past may be found in the following works: Smith and Smith, *Dwelling*; Bayard Wootten and Samuel Gaillard Stoney, *Charleston: Azaleas and Old Bricks* (Boston: Houghton Mifflin, 1937); Mrs. St. Julien Ravenel, *Charleston*; Rhett, *Charleston*; Samuel Gaillard Stoney, *This Is Charleston* (Charleston: Carolina Art Association, 1944); Anna Wells Rutledge, *Artists*; Stoney, *Planatations*; Smyth *et al.*, *Carolina*; Sass, *Story*; Heyward, *Seed*; DuBose Heyward, *Charleston*; Elizabeth Ann Poyas, *Days of Yore; or Shadows of the Past* (Charleston: William G. Mazyck, 1870); Mazyck, *Guide*; De Saussure, *Old*; A. R. H. Smith and H. R. Sass, *A Carolina Rice Plantation of the 1850s* (New York: William Morrow, 1936); Rutledge, *Home*; Pringle, *Chronicles*; J. Motte Alston, *Rice Planter*; Ravenel, *Ravenel*; H. R. Sass, "Mixed Schools and Mixed Blood," *Atlantic*, CXCVIII (Nov., 1956), 45–49; Manigault, *The United States*; Porcher, "Last"; Childs, ed., *Private*; P. H. Hayne's letters in references cited above.

331. Rhett, *Charleston*, 79–80; Heyward, *Charleston*, 286; Parker, "Charleston," 22, 121, 124; Smith, *Charlestonian's*, 143; Ravenel, *Charleston*, 426–28; Lucy Kavaler, *The Private World of High Society* (New York: David McKay, 1960), 133–34, 183–84; Cleveland Amory, *Who Killed Society* (New York: Harper & Bros., 1960), 90.

332. *Sketch*, 50ff.; *Charleston Grows*, 258; *The St. George's Society of Charleston, South Carolina* (Charleston: Walker, Evans & Cogswell, 1898), 18–21.

333. *Transactions*, no. 1 (1889), 13–17. For lists of officers and members see *ibid.*, no. 1 (1889), 7–8, 20–24, no. 8 (1901), 16–24, no. 50 (1945), 63–84, no. 60

(1956), 30–53, no. 70 (1965), 62–69; Daniel Ravenel, "President Ravenel's Address, 1889," *ibid.*, no. 1 (1889) 53–54; cf. Robert Wilson, "The President's Address," *ibid.*, no. 16 (1909), 11–12.

334. *Charleston Grows*, 256, 258, 264, 266–68.

335. Stevens, *Pistols*, 254–55; Heyward, *Charleston*, plate IV, facing p. 292. See biographical and genealogical sources listed in previous footnotes; A. E. Hartzell, *Titled Americans* (n.p., 1915), 357.

336. Parker, "Charleston," 22.

337. P. H. Hayne to C. E. A. Gayerre, Jan. 27, 1885, in David Kelly Jackson, *American Studies in Honor of William Kenneth Boyd* (Durham: Duke University Press, 1940), 227–28; Hayne to Wilkinson, Aug. 1, 1878, in "Southern," ed. Davis, 69; Manigault, *United States*, 147; Alston, *Rice*, 147.

338. Stoney quoted in Amory, *Who*, 53; Rutledge, *Home*, 164–65.

CHAPTER V

Recent origin, an interior location, and early identification with heavy industry distinguishes Chicago from Boston, New York, or Charleston. The seaboard ports exuded elegance, cosmopolitanism, cultural achievement, and pride in their historical roles and had aristocratic elements in their social structures. The midwestern metropolis epitomized the raw and powerful adolescence of industrial America. Even New York, the nation's *parvenu* capital, had roots in the past and an ascriptive group that influenced its upper class. Did Chicago's elite, often labeled vigorous but vulgar and devoid of old families and traditions, behave differently from these other enclaves?

THE ANTEBELLUM ERA

The first settlement (1803) was a military and Indian trading outpost, and the village stagnated until the defeat of the Black Hawk tribe in 1832. In 1829 Chicago's population totaled thirty; five years later, 1,300; in 1850, 29,963; and in 1860, 109,263. This demographic explosion reflected spectacular economic growth. Real and personal property valuation in Chicago amounted to $1,441,314 in 1843 and $37,053,512 in 1860. The aggregate worth of the 211 square miles of land in what would be the 1933 corporate limits increased from $168,000 in 1833 to $60 million in 1861. Exports in 1836 were worth $1,000 and imports $325,203; in 1845 they respectively reached $1,543,518 and $2,043,445. In 1848 the railroad had not yet appeared in Chicago; four years later a line connected it with the East, and in 1856 it was the hub of ten trunk lines with

2,033 miles of track. By the 1850s Chicago had become the largest primary grain, wheat, and lumber market in the country and was the railroad center of the West, and early in the Civil War it surpassed Cincinnati as the nation's premier meat-packing town.[1] Chicago emerged as the colossus of the West because its hinterland contained the world's most productive agricultural area and because it was the terminus of the world's greatest internal waterway. The city soon dominated East-West traffic and the processing and shipment of farm products.

Prosperity was punctured by the Panics of 1837–42 and 1857–61. Real estate values collapsed, businesses failed, banks disappeared, and capital fled the city. Between 1836 and 1842 land prices fell more than three-quarters and only one of the ten Chicago banks in 1854 survived to 1860.[2] Such reverses had a severe impact on the newly formed upper class. William B. Ogden, the city's business and civic leader, complained in 1841 that "property which sold for hundreds, even thousands, is not now worth even ten dollars." The "ancient dynasty" (the wealthy elite of 1836) was "deeply embarassed" by the crash and "men of families of more recent date seem a good deal in the ascendant."[3]

Ogden's "ancient dynasty" typically consisted of transplanted north-easterners, versatile entrepreneurs who assumed community leadership. A few derived from the largest taxpayers of the 1820s, but most of the older group, employed by John Jacob Astor's American Fur Co., were shunted aside by the arrivals of the next decade. The Kinzies were the preeminent old family. Astor agent John Kinzie came to Chicago in 1804. By the 1830s the Kinzies were in their second generation of wealth and influence. John's son James became a school trustee, the first sheriff of Cook County, an insurance agent and president of the Chicago Board of Underwriters, a real estate speculator, and Chicago's first auctioneer. He sold the land given to the Illinois and Michigan Canal Co. to finance construction. John H. Kinzie, like his brother and father, worked for the fur company, became private secretary to the territorial governor, first president of the Village of Chicago, registrar of public lands, canal collector of tolls, receiver of public moneys, a large landowner, a founder of the Illinois Savings Institution, and an influential member of the exclusive St. James Episcopal Church. The newcomers were epitomized by Ogden, son of a bankrupt New York merchant. Arriving in 1835 to tend his brother-in-law's real estate investments, he became the town's foremost real estate operator and railroad promoter, a key figure in the building of the canal, a banker and newspaper publisher, a lumber company organizer, a financier of Cyrus H. McCormick, the original mayor, a sponsor of the city's earliest higher educational establishments, vice-president of the Chicago Historical Society, director of the board of trade, and a society leader. His salience stemmed largely from being an agent for eastern capitalists who provided the wherewithal for Chicago's early development. New Hampshire–born Gurdon S. Hubbard was cut from the same pattern. The child of a failed lawyer, Hubbard entered Illinois in 1818 and settled permanently in Chicago in 1834. He began as a fur company clerk and later became an independent fur trader. As an assemblyman he introduced the bill for the incorporation of the canal and was instrumental in making Chicago its terminus. Hubbard was Chicago's initial banker and insurance underwriter, the first meat packer who shipped to the East, founder of Chicago's earliest real estate firm, an incorporator of the city's original waterworks, partner in a steamship line between Buffalo and Chicago, a forwarding and commission merchant, and an organizer and director of the Illinois Savings Institution. He was an alderman, president of the Chicago Board of Underwriters, an organizer of the Chicago Board of Trade, a member of the historical society, and a founder of St. James Church. Another prominent Chicagoan, lawyer Jonathan Y. Scammon was born in Maine, where his father served in the state legislature. College-educated, he arrived in 1835 and became a court clerk and judge, school and bank commissioner, and primary shaper of the city school system. Scammon was also a railroad, bank, and insurance company president, a realtor, a leader in the city's cultural institutions, and framed the Illinois banking law of 1852. These figures, Francis C. Sherman, Levi D. Boone, Silas B. Cobb, Isaac N. Arnold, John D. Caton, Mark Skinner, John Wentworth, and others constituted an overlapping group of ninety-three predominant capitalists, lawyers, politicians, and officers of cultural and charitable organizations. Criteria for elite designation are influence in important community issues, control of the largest business establishments, service in high public office, leadership in civic welfare associations, and the testimony of such prominent contemporaries as Wentworth, John V. Farwell, Scammon, Hubbard, Arnold, Ogden, Mrs. William Blair, Mrs. Martha Freeman Esmond, William Bross (an early journalist and government official), and William Corcoran, who, in 1868, became librarian of the Chicago Historical Society.

A collective portrait of the antebellum ruling enclave, based on biographical data, discloses that the vast majority moved to the city in the 1830s and '40s; only eleven lived there before 1832. A majority of the elite originated in New England and New York and were self-made.[4] Vintage of fortune could be definitely discovered in slightly over half the cases (see Table 1). Although a majority made their own money, the numerous unknowns, many of whose parents were merchants, professionals, and locally prominent officeholders, indicate that the findings in this category may not be representative of the entire enclave.

Table 1

VINTAGE OF FORTUNE OF CHICAGO'S ANTEBELLUM
BUSINESS, POLITICAL, AND SOCIAL LEADERS

Wealth Generation	Number	Percentage
First	36	69.2
Second	9	17.3
At least second	6	11.5
Three or more	1	1.9
Total known	52	100

Geographical origins were more comprehensively determined (see Table 2). Thirty-three of the notables were born in New York and only three in Chicago or Illinois, eight west of Pennsylvania, and five outside the United States. Their birthplaces do not correspond to the nativity distribution of the urban populace. In 1850 slightly more than half the residents were foreign-born. While transplanted New Yorkers were the largest single source for the elite, only 13 percent of the inhabitants came from that state, and Chicagoans from the middle Atlantic region constituted 15.6 percent of the city's population. Yankees, the second largest segment of the upper class, composed only 6.3 percent of the residents.[5] The upper class, a new elite in a new community, differed from contemporary patriciates in Boston, New York, Charleston, and Philadelphia in that much smaller segments originated in the area or inherited their affluence.

Economic Activities

The multifunctional elite dominated the economy. Its members formed the first banks and insurance, manufacturing, and utility companies, and pioneered in retail and wholesale trade, transportation ventures, and real estate operations. Connections with eastern capitalists were crucial in establishing their primacy. While businessmen in older cities began to specialize, these entrepreneurs engaged in diverse ventures. In versatility and access to sources of credit in more settled and

Table 2

BIRTHPLACES OF CHICAGO'S ANTEBELLUM
BUSINESS, POLITICAL, AND SOCIAL LEADERS

Birthplace	Number	Percentage
New England	34	41.0
Middle Atlantic states	35	42.2
Elsewhere	14	16.9
Total known	83	100

wealthier places, the Chicagoans recapitulated the experiences of prominent Bostonians and New Yorkers of the early national era.

REAL ESTATE

When the village was platted in 1830, the heaviest taxpayers of the previous decade or their relatives purchased the lion's share of Chicago's first land sale. The successful arrivals of the 1830s and '40s also began as real estate speculators. Ogden, the town's foremost real estate dealer, Hubbard, Wentworth, Walter L. Newberry, and others founded their fortunes on profitable land transactions. Property values soared after 1833 as a result of peace with the Indians, an influx of newcomers, a building boom, and the 1834 chartering of the canal. Aggregate real estate value within the environs of Chicago of 1933 rose from $168,000 in 1833 to $10 million in 1836. If windfalls resulted from inflated investments, disasters sometimes plagued speculators. The Panic of 1837 devastated the new city and turned the victors of 1836 into the victims of 1837. Land values declined precipitately to a nadir of $1.4 million in 1842. Demographic and economic expansion increased them to $125 million in 1856, but another depression ensued and they diminished to $60 million in 1861.[6]

TRANSPORTATION

Prosperity depended upon channeling East-West trade through Chicago. Land speculators and merchants, therefore, were the main promoters of canals, roads, bridges, and railroads. An early example of the interrelationship between government influence, real estate values, and transportation projects occurred in 1839, when ex-mayor Ogden convinced the city to build a bridge across the Illinois River in order to sustain property values in the business district. The bridge was financed through tax revenues and private subscriptions organized by Ogden.[7] The Illinois and Michigan Canal linked the Lake Michigan port with the Mississippi River, captured the upper Mississippi Valley commerce, and made Chicago the key transfer point of interregional commerce. The realization of the most important enterprise of the 1830s discloses the strategic position of the elite. Assemblyman Hubbard introduced the canal bill in the legislature, lobbied for its acceptance, and served on the first board of canal commissioners. In 1843 Assemblyman Arnold helped get a state loan for its completion. Ogden acted as the agent for the contractors and arranged eastern backing for canal bonds. Auctioneer Kinzie sold the land given to the company to aid construction and his brother served as an original canal commissioner and collector of tolls. When land prices escalated after construction started, these and other members of the upper class made fortunes in acreage they bought alongside the canal site.[8]

Upon completion in 1848 the waterway was the chief route for East-West trade, but its preeminence was short; in 1846 construction commenced on the first railroad out of Chicago. The Galena & Chicago Union was promoted by the elite. Scammon and Ogden handled the stock subscriptions in Chicago, Ogden became the first president, and Scammon, Newberry, and William H. Brown subsequently headed the enterprise. Local lines were usually controlled by the elite. Ogden headed the Chicago, St. Paul, & Fond du Lac and the Illinois & Wisconsin. State Senator Perry H. Smith helped obtain a land grant for the former line and became its vice-president; grain merchant Charles Walker helped form the Galena & Chicago Union and later became acting president of the Chicago, Iowa & Nebraska; and Norman B. Judd, state senator and law partner of Scammon, was legal advisor for many roads in the Chicago vicinity. The city council, prompted by Scammon and Ogden, readily granted the venturers rights-of-way for termini points of the roads' choice. Most of the large railroads in the region, however, were dominated by New Yorkers, although the Chicago & North Western (1859) proved an exception until absorbed by Wall Street in 1868. Under Ogden and Smith it took over several smaller lines mentioned above.[9] While notable Chicagoans did not run the larger systems they rendered important services. In 1854, for example, Scammon and Ogden secured a right-of-way into Chicago for the Michigan Central. Land speculation provided an impetus for railroad as well as canal construction. The chief promoters were realtors seeking opportunities to enhance their investments. Galena & Chicago Union director Wentworth, a vigorous proponent of railroads, as a congressman in 1852 assisted the Illinois Central charter through the state legislature and helped procure a federal land grant for the road. Wentworth owned 120 acres of Chicago real estate and thousands of acres along the canal, and the building of the Illinois Central enhanced his holdings. Political involvement with railroads sometimes created rifts within the elite. Rivalry between the Michigan Central and Illinois Central led Wentworth to run unsuccessfully for mayor against Walter S. Gurnee in 1852 because the latter vetoed a right-of-way bill for Illinois Central entry into Chicago.[10]

TRADE AND MANUFACTURING

Most of the prominent railroad and canal promoters were also merchants and manufacturers hoping to make Chicago the key exchange point for western agricultural products and finished goods from the East. Chicago began as a trading post, and the 1820s elite consisted mostly of Indian and fur traders. Their successors among the leading pre–Civil War merchants, unlike the magnates of Boston, Charleston, and New York, were retailers as well as wholesalers. Upper-class Chicagoans ran the earliest general and drug stores, taverns, and hotels. In the 1830s and '40s alderman, mayor, and assemblyman Francis C. Sherman was proprietor of the grandest hotel. Department store owners in northeastern cities, who emerged long after the establishment was formed, lacked prestige in polite society. In Chicago, such tycoons inherited the high status of the early general storekeepers. John V. Farwell in 1844, Potter Palmer in 1852, Marshall Field in 1856, and Levi Z. Leiter in 1857 came to Chicago to launch their careers. Palmer in his own emporium and Farwell, as partner in Cooley & Wadsworth, the leading retailers of the 1840s and '50s, established themselves before the Civil War. Through the efforts of her upper-class merchants, geographical site, and transportation network, Chicago went from a single store in 1831 to second place behind New York in 1864 as a dry-goods mart. Hubbard, George W. Dole, Newberry, and John H. Kinzie were the prominent early lumber merchants. The last three and Arnold were the foremost antebellum commission merchants in interregional trade. Charles Walker was the greatest grain dealer in the country, a railroad organizer, and president of the Board of Trade of the City of Chicago (1848). William and Chauncey Blair, founders of one of Chicago's most distinguished families, began the wholesale hardware business in Chicago in the 1840s. By the Civil War the city was the wholesale center for the West.[11]

In the undifferentiated economic world of early Chicago, lumber and grain traders owned saw and flour mills, early meat packers were commission agents who handled many commodities and dressed beef and pork as a sideline, and many dry-goods traders also engaged in manufacturing. Dole, Chicago's first general storekeeper as well as its first meat packer, exemplified the diversified entrepreneurs who dominated business and politics. This capitalist, also an insurance agent, a land speculator, a bank director, an original trustee of the town, and a city treasurer, formed with Newberry's brother, Newberry & Dole (1839), a large grain-shipping house. This firm sent the initial grain shipment to the East, was the first to place boats on the canal, and was among the first to build steamers for use on the Great Lakes. Other outstanding general entrepreneurs were Hubbard, a hotel owner, meat packer, commission merchant, and realtor; Gurnee, a leading leather and hardware merchant and a manufacturer of building stones; and Mayor Charles M. Gray, the premier industrialist of the 1840s, a building and bridge contractor, street commissioner, fire department officer, and steamer and railroad freight agent.

Manufacturing became significant after Chicago emerged as a distributing center. Before 1840 little industry existed because the city and hinterland were sparsely populated, the inhabitants lived simply, and factories required more capital than did commercial establishments.

Meat packing, the original industry, grew out of cattle slaughtering to provision the fort. Although it became the city's leading manufacturing line, not until 1845–50 did Chicago begin to rival Cincinnati and St. Louis in supplying the nation with meat. As late as 1850 the largest packinghouse was a branch of a New York firm. Meat packing, like other major antebellum primary industries in Chicago, grain and lumber processing, developed through access to nearby raw materials and initially served local needs. By the 1840s merchants and processors in these industries were shipping their goods east and in the next decade Chicago became nationally known in these fields. Iron- and steelmaking began on a large scale when the Galena & Chicago Union contracted with Hiram H. Scoville in 1848 to build freight and passenger cars, but not until after the Civil War did the city achieve prominence in heavy industry. By 1860 Chicago stood first in the nation in agricultural implement production, second in meat packing, and third in railroad car production. Apart from these industries, Chicago and Illinois ranked relatively low among cities and states in volume and value of manufacturing.[12] Nevertheless, the momentum for future greatness was under way. Cyrus H. McCormick established his agricultural machinery works in 1848, George Pullman's Pullman Palace Car Co. was organized in 1859, and Richard Crane started Crane Brothers Manufacturing Co. in 1855.

The upper class also controlled utilities enterprise. George W. Dole headed the original waterworks, the Chicago Hydraulic Co. (1836). Its directors came from the elite, as did the organizers of the Chicago City Hydraulic Co. (1851), which absorbed the earlier corporation. The Chicago Gas Light and Coke Co. (1849), which received the first municipal franchise to furnish gas, was also organized by business-political leaders. Hugh T. Dickey, a lawyer, Cook County judge, Chicago alderman, and director of several insurance companies, became president, and Judd was the corporation lawyer. A similar enclave in 1855 organized the People's Gas Light and Coke Co. In 1848 the telegraph came to Chicago, and John D. Caton, president of the Illinois & Mississippi Telegraph Co., became known as "the Telegraph King of the West." A former New York harnessmaker's apprentice, he was Judd's law partner, chief justice of the Illinois supreme court, and a land speculator. Ogden and other prominent city officials and businessmen in the 1850s helped form the first street railway and omnibus lines.[13]

INSTRUMENTS OF CAPITAL ACCUMULATION

Chicago replicated the early stages of banking and insurance underwriting in older commercial centers. The low level and local orientation of business transactions in the 1830s generated no need for an elaborate banking system, and frontier conditions inhibited capital accumulation. During an era when banking and insurance in eastern cities were becoming specialized functions and long after they had been institutionalized, Chicago underwriters and financiers extended credit and security on an individual basis as part of their varied commercial involvements. Lyman J. Gage, Chicago's foremost late-nineteenth-century financier, noted that "the first bankers in a community are usually . . . successful merchants, lawyers and men of versatility and ready adaptation."[14] Those with eastern connections naturally took the lead in banking and insurance since capitalists in that region constituted the main source of funds for early Chicago enterprise. Similar circumstances once prevailed in Boston, Charleston, Philadelphia, and New York, where merchants with access to British credit accommodated their colleagues in trade. The career of Hubbard, the city's original banker, illustrates the conditions of early Chicago finance. Engaged in many different endeavors, he kept an account in Buffalo, New York, allowed other businessmen to draw on this source, and kept their sums on deposit. In the absence of incorporated private banks, moneylenders of this type furnished credit to local entrepreneurs.[15]

The first financial institution, the Chicago branch of the Bank of the State of Illinois (1835), provided eastern exchange at a low discount, thus facilitating interregional trade. The bank ran into trouble in 1839 because of imprudent speculation in the pork market and disappeared in 1843. As the urban economy matured, additional institutions appeared. The Chicago Marine and Fire Insurance Co. (1837) was the original private insurance corporation in the city. Chicago Marine did a banking business as a sideline, which it transferred to the Marine Bank (1852). The initial chartered bank in the city, in the 1850s it had the largest amount of capital and note circulation in Chicago. Other institutions of this era included Newberry & Church (1844) (the second largest financial firm of the 1850s), the Merchants' and Mechanics' Bank (1852), the Illinois Savings Institution (1856) (the first mutual savings bank in the West), and the Merchants' Savings Loan & Trust Co. (1857) (the oldest trust company in the West and for a time the largest bank in the city). Members of the urban elite organized these institutions. Newberry was a partner in Newberry & Church, John H. Kinzie headed Illinois Savings and the Chicago branch of the State Bank, Scammon was president of Marine Insurance and the Marine Bank and attorney for the Chicago branch of the State Bank, and Judd and Arnold introduced the bill to charter Merchants' Savings in the state legislature. Connecticut-born William H. Brown, original cashier of the Chicago branch of the State Bank, moved to Chicago in 1835 and became president of the school board, an assemblyman, real estate operator, promoter and president of the Chicago Locomotive Co., president of the Galena & Chicago Union, president of the historical society, an organizer and leader in the fashionable Second Presbyterian Church, and a trustee in several philanthropies. Merchants' and Mechanics' president, ex-mayor Boone, and former assemblyman John H. Dunham, original head of Merchants' Savings, had similarly imposing business and civic credentials. Hubbard, Ogden, Dole, and Wentworth were also directors and officers of one or more of the early banks. Upper-class control of banking led the Chicago *Democrat* to note that "a large number of our wealthiest businessmen have taken stock" in Merchants' Savings. "The President and Vice-President are well known as among our most wealthy and conservative businessmen, who will take all possible care of the character and credit of the institution."[16] Similar announcements in New York and Boston newspapers greeted the openings of elite-managed banks in those cities.

Internecine conflicts, impulsive investments, and the Free Banking Law of 1852, largely the work of Scammon, which encouraged inflation, unbacked notes, and wildcat banking, made the life of most financial institutions hazardous and short. Even before the Panic of 1857 most of the Chicago banks had folded. Of ten banks incorporated in 1854, only three lasted until 1856, and the Marine Bank, the lone survivor after the Panic, collapsed in 1860.[17] According to Wentworth, "Chicago's early struggles" were "embarassed by banks without capital," run by "bankers" in "high positions in social circles and in churches." Protected by "charters," they "robbed our State, our Country, our City, our school fund, our historical society, our charitable institutions, our widows, our orphans, and all our laboring-classes."[18] Upper-class officers and stockholders, however, because of diversified interests, did not lose their fortunes when banks failed. Unincorporated firms still funded local enterprises when chartered institutions closed down.

Chicago's foremost entrepreneurs, particularly those involved in banking, initiated insurance underwriting. Hubbard, the original banker, also wrote the first insurance policy. Realtor, mayor, corporation director, and civic benefactor Benjamin W. Raymond, Scammon, John H. Kinzie, and Dole also doubled as bankers and insurance agents. Hubbard was the first president of the Chicago Board of Underwriters (1849) and Kinzie and Dole held that post in the 1850s. Other early agents were Julius Wadsworth and Thomas Dyer (president of the board of trade), partners in Wadsworth, Dyer and Chapin, the largest local packinghouse of the 1840s and '50s. Until the appearance of Chicago Marine & Fire Insurance, underwriters acted mostly for eastern firms. Thomas Church, realtor and dry-goods merchant, alderman, member of the board of health, and Whig candidate for mayor, was a founder and president of the company. Thirteen years later Scammon became chief executive and major shareholder and the board continued to be dominated by eminent businessmen and politicians. During the 1850s upper-class figures regularly appeared on the boards of the Chicago Mutual Insurance Co. and the Great Western Insurance Co., and Church headed the Chicago Firemen's Insurance Co.[19]

Politics

As in other cities, political power and commercial success went hand in hand. Through holding public posts or through intimate connections with officials, upper-class entrepreneurs obtained the charters, franchises, rights-of-way, land grants, internal improvements, and funds that enhanced their business ventures and fortunes. The foremost lawyers and businessmen predominated in municipal and county government, represented Chicago in Congress and in the state legislature, and were local Whig and Democratic chieftains.[20] Besides holding office the elite performed crucial services for the town. Ogden, the city's fiscal agent in 1836, negotiated a loan with eastern capitalists that saved municipal credit. In that year the city charter was drawn up by a delegation including Caton, John H. Kinzie, and Newberry, who later served on the committee that petitioned the assembly for its approval.[21]

A collective profile of the mayors from 1837 to 1868 discloses the high social and economic standing of these officials. Chicago party leaders, congressmen, state legislators, aldermen, municipal and county commissioners, and other key public servants also came from the elite. Only two of the nineteen mayors in this period, a blacksmith and a bartender, were not prominent businessmen. The vast majority, such as Ogden, meat-packing partners Chapin and Dyer, Wentworth, Gurnee, and Boone, were versatile capitalists whose political careers were subordinate to commercial concerns. Eight were chiefly in real estate, an equal number in merchandising and trade, six were active in railroad development, and three in banking and building contracting. All but three hailed from New York and New England, all were native Americans and all but one arrived in Chicago before 1837. Fourteen held public office before their election and seventeen served in other government posts after their term. Few came from distinguished families, only three were college-educated, and two more were lawyers. Humble in origin, once in Chicago they performed the varied functions of an upper class by supplementing political and business with cultural and philanthropic leadership.[22]

Professions

Law and medicine were the most prestigious professions in Chicago, Boston, Philadelphia, New York, and Charleston. By the time of the lake port's settlement, the older cities, due to their original role as outposts of English civilization or Christianity, and their wealth and comparatively long history, had developed a rich cultural life which also drew their patriciates to the ministry, education, and arts and letters. Callow Chicago lacked the conditions and traditions that attracted other upper classes to these callings.

Next to businessmen, lawyers comprised the largest segment of the upper order. Legal skills facilitated political and commercial activities, thus elevating members of the bar to positions of urban leadership. Attorneys often participated in government and business as entrepreneurs and officials in addition to being called upon for specialized expertise. They were state, county, and municipal administrators and legislators, judges, and city attorneys, officers in business corporations, and land speculators. The drawing up of the state loan bill for the canal by Justin S. Butterfield and James H. Collins, Chicago's leading firm, illustrates the significance of prominent lawyers in critical community matters.[23]

Unlike eastern legal establishments, the bar did not gain cohesion through widespread descent from interrelated families or by its luminaries being trained at the same colleges or in the practices of relatives or class associates. As in the business elite, integration resulted from partnerships or broader alliances based on common interests. Top-ranked lawyers practiced together, cooperated with each other in political bodies, sat on the same corporate boards, and served as trustees of the same civic associations. Scammon, for example, practiced with Buckner S. Morris and Judd, and Caton with Collins, Ebenezer Peck, Grant Goodrich, and Judd.[24]

Physicians were more remote than lawyers from the pinnacle of wealth and power but several belonged to the elite. Some doctors, e.g., banker and mayor Levi D. Boone, won renown primarily from non-professional activities. Boone, however, served on the city board of health and was first president of the Cook County Medical Society (1850). John T. Temple, another entrepreneur-physician, was the first contractor to handle the U.S. mail going out of Chicago, operated a stagecoach line, and was a constructor of buildings and of a section of the canal. But he devoted most of his time to medicine and served on the board of health and as a founder and trustee of Rush Medical College (1837). Daniel Brainerd, like Temple and Boone, an arrival of the early 1830s, was the most eminent antebellum doctor. Son of a prosperous New York farmer, he graduated from Philadelphia's Jefferson Medical College, published research papers, was on the board of health, was a founder and professor of Rush Medical College, and was an organizer of the medical society and of Chicago's first general hospital (1847).[25]

By the 1850s Chicago's medical elite, like its counterparts in older cities, held key posts in hospitals, medical schools, and societies and served on the board of health. This group drew on economic, political, and social resources acquired through activities in other fields and contacts with other members of the urban upper order. Conversely, businessmen, lawyers, and politicans joined leading physicians on the boards of Chicago's medical schools and hospitals. Newberry, Skinner, Caton, John H. Kinzie, Judd, Brown, Hubbard, Dole, Goodrich, and Ogden were trustees and officers of Rush Medical College, Hahnemann Medical College (1860), Illinois General Hospital of the Lake (1849), St. James Hospital (1854), City Hospital (1856), Illinois Charitable Eye and Ear Infirmary (1858), and Mercy Hospital (1859). As in other cities, physicians and other leading citizens derived professional and civic distinction and community influence from managing indigent and public health care.[26]

Charity

Medical aid to the poor stemmed from a spirit of *noblesse oblige* typical of many ruling echelons in history. Upper-class philanthropy received further impetus from the reform movements that swept America in the 1830s and '40s. Chicago's early elite was unexceptional in the motives and means of its benevolence. In common with other European and domestic patriciates, the upper class sought to solidify its position, maintain social order, express civic pride, and gratify its conscience. Capitalists, lawyers, politicians, and their wives managed and supported such institutions as the YMCA (1841), the Chicago Orphan Asylum (1849), the Chicago Home for the Friendless (1858), and the Chicago Nursery and Half-Orphan Asylum (1859). Among the incorporators of the Chicago Relief and Aid Society (1857), the most notable humanitarian organization, were Arnold, Judd, Dole, Philo Carpenter, Brown, John H. Kinzie, Skinner, and Dunham. This agency did not restrict itself to special categories of dependence and kept abreast of modern methods by sending out visitors to check on the recipients of its largesse. The elite also participated in contemporary reform movements. Raymond, Carpenter, and Brown were active in the Young Men's Temperance Movement (1835), the Washington Temperance Society (1840), and the Chicago Temperance Savings Association. Charles V. Dyer, another prominent physician-capitalist and the original vice-president of the Illinois Charitable Eye and Ear Infirmary, Wentworth, and Carpenter were prominent abolitionists. Brown and Ogden were officers of the Chicago branch of the American Colonization Society (1839).[27]

Despite this array of welfare agencies, older forms of altruism still existed. Mary Drummond, daughter of Judge Thomas Drummond, in her memoir of the 1850s, claimed that "there was 'no organized charity,' as we know it nowadays, but there was much of that now despised 'basket charity' when friendships were formed between rich and poor."[28] She forgot about institutionalized philanthropy, but her remembrances of "lord and lady bountiful" show that the personal touch had not yet vanished from upper-class charity.

Culture

The interlocking group that dominated business, politics, the professions, and charity assumed another conventional urban leadership role in spiritual and intellectual matters. Within a generation of Chicago's founding, historical, scientific, and musical societies and several libraries were established. The elite, reminiscent of its eastern counterparts, however, focused mainly on education and religion, which were widely associated with philanthropy and commonly considered the primary instruments of moral uplift and social control.

Settled chiefly by New Yorkers and New Englanders, Chicago in 1840 had a higher literacy rate than western cities with fewer migrants from these regions, an achievement which reflected an intense interest in schooling.[29] Upper-class participation in public education began in 1826 with the election of leading citizens as original school trustees. Scammon drafted the public school law of 1837, which established the city school system. Eminent Chicagoans regularly served as school inspectors and as school agents for Cook County, and Scammon and Brown were antebellum presidents of the school board. The upper class contributed money to the school system, and Ogden and Scammon were respectively president and vice-president of the North Western Educational Society (1847), which promoted public schooling.[30]

Distinguished Chicagoans participated in an equally vigorous fashion in establishing institutions of higher learning. Scammon, Newberry, Brown, Ogden, Boone, Arnold, and their associates were benefactors and trustees of Chicago's first college, University of St. Mary of the Lake (1844), Female Seminary (1843), Northwestern University (1850), and the first University of Chicago (1856).[31]

Extensive interaction occurred in educational, religious, and charitable endeavors. They aimed to disseminate identical principles of community and private behavior, and religion was thought to encourage Christian culture and benevolence. "Most of our young people who sought to be philanthropic," observed Mary Drummond of the 1850s, "worked through their churches, and religious observances seemed to enter more closely into our home lives than is the case today."[32] An important event in sectarian benevolence happened when St. James, the oldest and most prestigious Episcopal church, established the hospital of the same name. Christian nurture, however, went beyond the efforts of exclusive congregations. Leading citizens imitated their equivalents elsewhere by organizing the Chicago Bible Society (1835) and forming Sunday schools, city missions, and sectarian institutions of higher learning.[33] Upper-class laborers for the Lord were often moved by personal piety. Methodist merchant Farwell, YMCA president and initiator and superintendent of the Illinois Street Mission (1856), undertook "religious duties" to gain "redeeming grace" and become "an exemplary follower of my Lord and Master."[34]

Between 1833 and 1835 the major Protestant sects organized their initial congregations and elite Chicagoans invariably played key roles. Dole, Brown, Carpenter, and Philip F. W. Peck were founders and elders of the First Presbyterian Church (1833). Temple helped establish the First Baptist Church (1833), Carpenter was active in the First Methodist Society (1832) and deacon of the First Congregational Church (1851). John H. Kinzie donated the land for St. James Episcopal Church (1834), and with Hubbard and Giles Spring, the town's original attorney, comprised the initial vestry. In the 1840s the upper class continued to establish such fashionable churches as the Second Presbyterian (1842) and Grace Methodist Episcopal (1847).[35] These shrines functioned even more to integrate the newly privileged than to aid the unfortunate. In the 1870s Wentworth regretted that "Christian[s]" no longer took "strangers in the city, to church with them . . . to lead them to a high social position with their religious instruction." He "honor[ed]" those "weekly church sociables, where young men are brought forward into respectable social intercourse, as well as moral developments."[36] Upper-class Chicago, adopting the conventional usage of patrician religion, differed from cities where Episcopalianism was the high-status sect only in the variety of denominations which attracted its elite.

The advent of the Chicago Lyceum (1834), modeled on the Boston Lyceum, the Chicago Historical and Antiquarian Society (1836), the Chicago Athenaeum (1836), the Mechanics' Institute (1847), the Chicago Historical Society (1856), the Chicago Academy of Sciences (1857), and the Young Men's Association (1858) indicated that Chicago early shared in what Gunther Barth calls the atmosphere of "metropolism," i.e., values and institutions common to many American cities. The intertwined business-political-philanthropic elite again provided the early officers and members of these associations. As in other towns the historical society became a stronghold of upper-class intellectual life. Scammon, in an 1868 presidential address, expressed the typical upper-class view of cultural leadership. Since Chicago and Illinois "made us what we are," we must "endow . . . the Chicago Historical Society, the University of Chicago, the Academy of Sciences, the Chicago Astronomical Society, or any other of our public institutions. . . . Every man who has made his fortune, or found his home, his prosperity, or his happiness in this land, owes it to Chicago, owes it to the State of Illinois, owes it to his duty and his God, to see that those institutions, which it is our duty now to found are placed upon a solid basis."[37]

Patriciates in older cities usually supported arts and letters as collectors and institutional trustees and benefactors, but sometimes, especially in Boston and Charleston, also as painters, architects, and authors. The Chicago upper class, in its formative years, had not the leisure, interests, traditions, or resources to match these accomplishments; nonetheless it laid the foundations for future development. The first literary magazine appeared in 1845. Unlike Boston, pre–Civil War intellectual periodicals were short-lived and without patrician patronage. Newspapers in the 1830s and '40s, on the other hand, were owned and edited by Caton, Wentworth, Scammon, Newberry, Dole, Goodrich, Brown, Ogden, Judd, and Arnold. Journals in the hands of well-connected proprietors made profits from government patronage and promoted their publishers' views and interests.[38]

Upper-class Chicagoans displayed another aspect of metropolism in art and music. Ogden, Skinner, Newberry, realtor Samuel H. Kerfoot, and lawyer Ezra B. McCagg imitated patricians in other places by collecting paintings. In 1859 the first public art exhibit was organized, largely from these private collections. Before the Civil War, however, art schools and galleries had not yet appeared.[39] Music associations began earlier. The Old Settlers' Harmonic Society (1834) gave concerts, and the Chicago Musical Union (1857) performed operas. Both organizations were patronized by the upper class: Benjamin Raymond was an early president of the Harmonic Society and Levi D. Boone headed the Musical Union.[40]

Eminent Chicagoans, mostly New Englanders or upstate New Yorkers of New England stock, shared the solemnity of Boston bluebloods rather than the gaiety of patrician New Yorkers and Charlestonians. During the early 1790s bluenose Brahmins opposed the revival of theatrical performances in Boston and forty years later this same issue divided elite Chicagoans. In both cases, however, proponents of the stage triumphed.[41]

The 1850s represented a milestone in upper-class maturity. In this decade emerged the historical society, the academy of sciences, the first public art show, the musical union, Northwestern University, the old University of Chicago, Hahnemann Medical College, the Chicago Theological Seminary, several hospitals and shelters for the dependent, and the Relief and Aid Society. The political and economic elite, in the third decade of its existence, extended its suzerainty to civic welfare and culture.

Society

Multidimensional hegemony enables the elite to perform the functions of an urban upper class. Business partnerships, political alliances, and participation in voluntary associations also solidified the ruling enclave by promoting interpersonal contact and mutual values and interests. While Chicago's upper rank could not yet turn to inherited status, power, or wealth as a source of cohesion, it did achieve unity in other ways typical of older patriciates. Spatial proximity supplemented interlocked undertakings and institutions as an integrating force. Virtually all the town leaders were extensive land speculators and in the 1830s bought large lots on the near North Side, thus creating the original exclusive neighborhood.[42] The numerous and diverse activities jointly participated in by members of the upper class fostered in a natural sequel economic and political cooperation, friendship, and intermarriage. Matrimony united Ogdens with Scammons and McCaggs, Smiths with Laflins, and other distinguished families made similar matches.

"During the winter of 1833–34," reminisced Caton, "a large immigration rushed in from all parts of the country," who "sought to cultivate acquaintance and . . . lay the foundation for what might be called society." An Englishman living in Chicago between 1833 and 1851 claimed that in 1835–36 "society seemed to take upon itself a more decided form, rising from the chaos in which it had before been." He attributed its incipience to the arrival of eastern land speculators and women and the rise in wealth.[43]

At first society, relative to older establishments, was simple and unstratified. Knickerbocker author Charles Fenno Hoffman, a visitor in the winter of 1833–34, Caton, Wentworth, and Joseph T. Ryerson, an iron manufacturer and institutional trustee who arrived in 1842, agreed that in the 1830s and '40s "society" was "simple," lacked "conventional restrictions," "people were all poor," and no one was "fashionable and exclusive." According to these observers, residents of different faiths, birthplaces, educational levels, and sophistication mingled together, and public balls included "a medley of all ranks, ages, professions, trades and occupations."[44]

Levels of expenditure were necessarily low when even in the boom of the 1830s men worth $10,000 were considered rich. Depressed conditions after 1836 further discouraged display. In 1839 fashionable women went to the First Presbyterian Church in a dung cart. Ryerson doubted "whether a lady's dress for a party cost more than from five to ten dollars. . . ." William Blair's wife said that during the Panic of 1837–42 everyone was poor, there were only two carriages in the city, and people wore old clothes, and that even in the prosperous 1850s party-givers made their own refreshments. "Naturally, in a smaller city, and with less wealth there was more simple living," recalled Mary Drummond of the 1850s. "At many of our parties ice-cream and cake . . . were considered 'an elegant sufficiency.'"[45]

Despite these claims of poverty and egalitarianism, even in the 1830s an inner circle of the powerful and affluent frequently met at Ogden's home. The "Managers" who organized the winter ball of 1834 came from this group.[46] "It is a remarkable thing to meet such an assemblage of educated and refined and wealthy persons as may be found there," wrote Harriett Martineau, visiting Chicago in 1834. Four years later the sister-in-law of Cyrus McCormick predicted that "we will soon have as many acquaintances as we want, and of the best in the city." Wentworth also discerned early social distinctions in noting, "most of the families of wealth, education and high social position, about the time of our incorporation, were settled on the North Side." The "fashionable people . . . would invite our young men to their parties," but "when we had a party on the South Side, instead of coming themselves, the ladies would send their domestics."[47] By the 1850s habituées of the fashionable set were able to identify its foremost figures. Drummond named the Arnolds, McCaggs, and Scammons as society leaders and Blair listed the wives of several civic and economic notables as the chief hostesses. The hierarchy of this decade emerged from the stratification which surfaced in the 1830s and solidified shortly thereafter. According to Caton, "gatherings at private houses, where dancing, plays, and charades constituted their amusements," and "public balls . . . familiarized them [convivial Chicagoans of the 1830s] with each other." Ryerson remembered a higher degree of cohesion in the 1840s, the "small circle of business and professional men, and others of note were generally well acquainted with or known to one another, and whenever there was a social gathering there would be a good deal of mixing in."[48]

Religious traditions and beliefs, a family-centered life, and an absence of opulence contributed to the straightlaced tone of the 1840s and '50s. Ryerson recalled that "balls ended at eleven or twelve, parties at ten or eleven." Drummond felt that "everything in that era centered in the home. . . . Even fathers were a part of family life. There were no dinner-parties for young people. . . . 'Square-dances' were popular. . . ."[49]

Notwithstanding its recent advent and relative restraint and equality, society patterned itself upon older urban establishments, an aspiration which inevitably imposed an eastern patrician style on upper-class Chicago. Cotillions and balls started in 1833, and in 1834 dancing teachers made their appearance. During the 1840s the New England, Excelsior, and St. Andrew's societies were formed and their officers and members, as usual, included community leaders. In that decade, too, appeared dancing assemblies. The premier events of the social seasons of the 1850s were the Bachelor's Assembly Balls, run by an elite corps of managers. The privileged sent their daughters to the Chicago Academy, the select private academy of the 1850s and '60s. Exclusive affairs, organizations, values, and fashions were borrowed from the East: two Boston women directed the Chicago Academy; the Bachelor's Balls took their name and style from New York; the first three-story brick private house, built by Ryerson's sister in 1850, the most splendid home in the city, imitated Philadelphia residences; the regional, Old Settlers', and St. Andrew's societies imitated similar associations in Atlantic Coast ports; and dressmakers visited recent emigrés or visitors from the East to copy the latest fashions.

The tendency of upper orders to look backward prompted in Chicago the founding of the Old Settlers' Society (1855). Eligibility was restricted to pre-1837 arrivals, and Scammon, John H. Kinzie, and Hubbard were among the first officers. Yet another relic of the East appeared a few years later when a group of distinguished citizens organized a literary club which read plays and Dickens. "Chicago isn't composed of rough and ready pioneers," wrote Martha Freeman Esmond, daughter of a Chicago lawyer, to a New York friend in 1858. "There never were so many delightful and cultivated people to the square yard as there are here. They are all from the East or South, you know, and have brought the traditions and ideals of those older communities with them."[50]

Thought

Local tycoons, like other entrepreneurial elites, identified wealth, diligence, and devotion to commerce with good character. Preoccupied with personal achievement and material gain and lacking aristocratic roots, intellectual interests, or a contemplative outlook, Chicago capitalists expressed the unreflective instrumentalism ingrained in American life. Industry, venturesomeness, and success were reigning values among businessmen. By these criteria Scammon praised Ogden for "His practical mind and enterprising spirit."[51]

New cities attracted plungers and promoters; hence audacity, until temporarily suppressed by the Panic of 1837, characterized local magnates. The parade of boosters began with John Kinzie in the 1820s, predicting that Chicago would prosper, and became important because of its location and fertile soil. "When you are dealing with Chicago property," advised Ogden prior to the fall in land values, "go in for all you can get and then go on with your business and forget all about it." This impulsive optimism moved Wentworth to remark that early "society lived upon . . . faith in the future of Chicago. Nearly everyone had laid out a town and men exchanged lots with each other, very much as boys swap jack-knives."[52]

Making money was the chief aim of these volatile manipulators, and those with the largest fortunes received the most respect. William Blair's "wealth estimated at nearly 100,000 dollars" impressed Mrs. Esmond; "in character and public esteem none stands higher." But Farwell perceived a disagreeable side to the acquisitive spirit: "Men are all greedy for gain, . . . yet they are never satisfied. Such is the testimony of all who have been eminently successful in courting dame nature."[53]

Scammon offered a more flattering explanation than greed for staying in business after accumulating a fortune and many commercial conquests: "No one can be happy, except in the degree in which he is occupied in some useful employment." Diligence was well regarded. "To be busy is my delight," wrote Farwell. "There is nothing like it to keep one in good spirits at all times and under all circumstances." Perseverance, especially when combined with piety, won the approval of the elite. "He [Farwell] is a hard worker, and a leader in Sunday school and church matters," mentioned Esmond; "everyone likes and admires these men." What the upper class lauded in individuals it attributed to the city. The "busy activity of the people," said Arnold in 1877, was "then, as now, a trait so characteristic [of Chicago]."[54]

Ambition, prudence, and other forms of impulse control were deemed invaluable in the pursuit of success. "Economy . . . of time" and "everything else should be coupled with a preserving and noble ambition," advised Farwell. All "desires must be limited by means that we possess of gratifying them or else penury will blast the most flourishing prosperity. . . . The sluggard and the spendthrift can never be useful . . . in a world where action is the watchword and economy the sentinel of all honest wealth."[55]

This version of the good life worked best in a society dedicated to equal opportunity and achievement through individual merit. Therefore, early Chicagoans subscribed to the egalitarian as well as the entrepreneurial tenets of the American creed. "Father, like most men, made fun of Colonial societies," declared William Hibbard's daughter. When asked about his lineage, the hardware magnate replied that "all he knew was that his father was an honest man, and that he had tried to be one also." Ogden merged the work ethic with the Alger ideal in reassuring an impoverished mother, "If your sons are healthy and willing to work, they will find enough to do, and if they cannot begin at the top let them begin at the bottom, and very likely they will be all the better for it." Suggesting himself as an example, he noted "I was . . . an orphan, . . . graduated at a log-school-house, and, at fourteen, fancied I could do anything. . ., and ever since, madame, I have been trying to prove it, and with some success." Personal virtues became community qualities. Ryerson, Blair, and Drummond attested to the humble origins of the elite and the former believed that "every man in those days stood on his own merits."[56]

1865–1918

Economic Activities

By 1890, after fifty years of more rapid population growth than any city in the world, Chicago was the second largest American metropolis.

The era of spectacular expansion ended after 1900, when Detroit and Los Angeles grew much quicker and Chicagoans were not multiplying much more rapidly than New Yorkers, Clevelanders, or San Franciscans.[57] Economic progress kept pace with the increase in residents. Between 1873 and 1892 the aggregate value of land in the 1933 corporate limits rose twelvefold, and between 1892 and 1915 another 50 percent. Commercial growth particularly escalated property values in the central business district. The Loop comprised 12.5 percent of the total urban land value in 1873, 23.3 percent in 1892, and 40 percent in 1910.[58] Between 1870 and 1902 Illinois had more railroad mileage than any other state, and Chicago was the hub of this network.[59] A strategic geographic location and a superb transportation system made the metropolis by the 1870s the merchandising emporium of the West. By 1875, for example, the city was the nation's leading clothing-distributing center. In that year the value of its wholesale trade reached $250 million, by 1890 this exchange had nearly doubled, by 1910 it was more than five times that of 1890, and it then increased almost one-third in the next eight years.[60] Chicago attained industrial prominence after it became a commercial and agricultural center. Illinois stood seventeenth among the states in iron and steel production in 1870, but climbed to fourth a decade later. In 1880 Chicago ranked next to Pittsburgh in iron and steel manufacturing. Although the latter retained first place, Chicago's share of the industry grew faster between 1869 and 1929. Indeed, except for 1889–99 amd 1914–19, the lake city outpaced the other five leading centers in value added in iron and steel production. Chicago's share of the state's manufacturing increased steadily from less than one-half in value of production in 1870 to almost three-quarters in 1890. In that year Chicago was second to New York in value of industrial production. By 1914 the city's proportion of Illinois manufacturing fell off slightly to two-thirds, but it held second place nationally. In 1890 the city ranked first in agricultural implements, meat packing, railroad car building, tinware, foundries and machine shops, piano and organ works, and furniture making, and second in leather tanning, railroad shop and construction work, clothing, and cooperage. In these industries Chicago either held its status or advanced from a relatively low position in the 1860s. Between 1860 and 1890 the value of manufactures in the city rose from $13,555,671 to $664,568,000 and in 1910 reached $1,867,329,000.[61] Chicago matured somewhat later as a financial center, but in the 1870s it surpassed St. Louis to become the major financial fulcrum of the Midwest. Between 1880 and 1900 it forged ahead of Philadelphia and Boston in bank clearings and deposits and by 1900 placed behind only New York as a money market. Between 1865 and 1913 banking capital in the city increased more than sixfold, a faster growth than in New York.[62] Growth and change in the urban economy were accompanied by local tycoons adopting the functional specialization of their eastern counterparts. While the moguls of this era still had diversified interests, unlike their forerunners, they tended to concentrate on one line of endeavor.

In 1879 wealthy Chicago realtor Samuel H. Kerfoot said that real estate "has proven during the past thirty years, as compared with all other subjects of investment or places of deposit, the best and ultimately the safest." The "colossal fortunes in the country" were invested in urban acreage, and "in all the large cities the heavy estates own the property."[63] The post–Civil War elite emulated its predecessors in this type of speculation. In 1894, for example, Pullman owned more than $2 million and Levi Z. Leiter, Field, and Palmer in excess of $4 million worth of acreage in the business district. A list of owners of Loop lots in that year included many other leading Chicagoans.[64] As in Boston and New York, the foremost proprietors usually made fortunes in other fields and then bought land, often to improve the sites and surroundings of their business establishments. The magnitude and diversity of their wealth enabled such investors to withstand depression-blighted values. Palmer epitomized the operations of great realtors. The city's outstanding dry-goods tycoon, in 1864 he sold his department store to Field and Leiter and devoted himself to real estate and the Palmer House hotel. In 1868 he induced his successors to move to his State Street property and transformed that run-down block of boardinghouses and saloons into the center of the retail and wholesale dry-goods trade. He further enhanced the value of his investment by street improvements and by building the Palmer House. In 1905 he left a fortune of $8 million, consisting of $2.9 million in urban real estate and $3.5 million in the hotel. Other magnates also made huge profits. Philip D. Armour, at his death in 1901, had $5 million worth of real estate, and Cyrus H. McCormick, in 1884, left $2.5 million worth of city land. While only 5 percent of the former estate was tied up in real property, one-quarter of the latter was so invested. Leiter and Field committed even larger amounts to land. Nine million dollars of Leiter's $14 million legacy was thus invested. Field's real property holdings at his death constituted $38 million ($31 million in the Loop) of a fortune estimated at between $150 and 200 million.[65]

The richest investors rode out the Panic of 1873, which more than halved Chicago land values, and profited enormously in the boom years from 1878 to 1892, when Loop values soared 500 percent. During the Panic of 1893 prices did not decline as precipitously as in the previous depression and decreased only slightly in the business district. Between 1892 and 1910 Loop values rose four-fifths. Real estate profits also increased because this form of property was grossly underassessed for tax purposes. Undervaluation enhanced its attractiveness as an investment and attested to the political influence of large holders. In 1894, when business district values reached $319,999,999, assessments totaled $23,490,310 and the lots and buildings owned by the elite were rarely rated above 12 percent of actual worth and generally much lower. A sample of thirty choice residential properties scattered throughout the city were assessed in 1893 at an average of 7.78 percent of actual value. Cook County real estate assessments in 1873 totaled $18,351,314, 9.91 percent more than in 1893, when Indiana assessments exceeded those of Illinois by one-third.[66]

Extensive proprietors capitalized on their influence as bank officers and stockholders. Financial institutions were heavily engaged in selling local real estate mortgage bonds and giving credit to realtors. Such operations sometimes embarrassed bankers and their organizations. Samuel J. Walker, a prominent realtor and bank president reputedly worth $15 million in 1873, lost his property by 1877. Scammon's Marine Bank suffered its second and final liquidation in 1874 because he borrowed money to cover disastrous land speculations. Three years later four more banks failed due to the imprudent investments of their officers.[67]

Reverses and pitfalls, however, did not deter plungers from remaining optimistic about Chicago's capacity to overcome holocausts that periodically leveled property values. "I will invest in R. E. in Chicago," wrote Charles B. Farwell, brother and partner of John V. Farwell, in 1863. "It is to be the largest & most wealthy city outside of New York in the United States." Palmer recalled, "I had not been in Chicago a year before I was convinced that no human obstacles could check its growth." He "had connections" in "New York and New England," and "invited them to look over the field with a view to their letting me have their capital for investment purposes." By 1861 he "brought into Chicago . . . over ten millions of eastern capital, a proportion of which receiving myself I invested in real estate and buildings, they form a foundation of support for my merchandizing interests." Accordingly, he "bought State Street, not only to improve it, but made it a foundation for his dry-goods business." Cyrus H. McCormick and his brother William were motivated by similar confidence in the city's destiny. During the early years, profits from C. H. McCormick & Bros. went back into the business or into urban lots. William, who made these purchases, predicted in 1863 that "*Chicago must* be a success if any city in this country will be. The best men and capital are here and coming here."[68]

COMMERCE

By the 1850s and '60s Chicago dominated the grain, meat, and lumber trades and became the midwestern dry-goods emporium. Interior merchants who formerly bought in the East now placed their orders in the lake city because Chicago drummers flooded rural areas, good transportation facilitated the distributing network, the city was the heart of a bourgeoning agricultural hinterland, the development of Chicago banking gave businessmen easier access to credit, and after 1870 Chicago began importing directly from Europe. Before the Civil War no mercantile house in Chicago had sales exceeding $600,000; in 1868 seventy-eight firms had a turnover of over a million a year.[69] At this time Field established himself as the premier merchant in Chicago. In 1867 Field, Leiter & Co. transacted $9,071,597 worth of business, the largest sales volume of any commercial or industrial firm in the city. John V. Farwell & Co. was second with $7,109,714. Next to department-store owners, commission merchants in the grain trade conducted the most extensive commerce. Munn, Norton & Co. ranked first in 1867 with sales of $3,929,670, and B. P. Hutchinson & Co. and Rumsey Brothers & Co., each with sales of over $3 million, placed among the top five concerns. J. W. Doane & Co. was then the leading wholesale grocery, doing a business of over $2.5 million, and the foremost hardware dealers, with sales of over $1 million, were Hibbard, Spencer & Co., Hale, Ayer & Co., and William Blair & Co.[70] The heads of these houses belonged to the upper class and exercised leadership in a variety of civic affairs.

Grain dealing, with an estimated $4 billion in capital in 1875, was the largest enterprise in Chicago and made the city notorious for commercial volatility and corruption.[71] The agricultural commodities trade was dominated by a few firms. They owned warehouses where grain was stored and established oligopolistic control by holding stock in each other's companies and obtaining railroad rebates and favorable transportation rates denied to smaller competitors. Grain elevator proprietors, because of their storage facilities and wholesale outlets, gambled on futures, seeking to corner commodity markets and thus manipulate prices. Conflicts between speculators, large and small operators, and merchants and warehousemen, fraud, brilliance, luck, or imprudence resulted in sensational losses and gains. Leading nineteenth-century speculators, Benjamin P. Hutchinson, Nathaniel K. Fairbank, Norman Ream, and Philip D. Armour, won and dropped millions in the "pit," as the Chicago Board of Trade Grain Exchange was called. Most of these plungers recovered their fortunes, but several firms went under. Munn & Scott failed in 1871, heavily involving George Munger, for years the foremost elevator owner and a president of the board. A similar fate befell John W. Rumsey & Co. in 1881, and Charles Henrotin, a prominent capitalist and society figure, was closed out in 1887 by a successful Hutchinson bear raid on a wheat corner organized by Henrotin and others. Joseph Leiter, son of the dry-goods magnate, lost between $2 million and $3 million to Armour in an abortive attempt to corner the wheat market in 1897–99. Collusion and corruption abounded, but the board, empowered by the state to regulate the market, was run by the most notorious speculators; hence laws were violated, attempts to implement stronger controls defeated, and malingerers escaped unpunished.[72] "Speculation stimulates enterprise; it creates and maintains proper values; it gives impulse and ambition to all forms of industry—commercial, literary, and artistic; it arouses individual capacities; it is aggressive, intelligent, and belongs to the strongest of the race," said the board secretary in 1891, voicing the spirit of the exchange. Speculation "founded Chicago, and developed the great West, which is the basis of the Nation's prosperity and the impelling commercial power of the continent."[73]

The grain trade attracted meat packers like John Cudahay and Armour and reaper manufacturer Cyrus H. McCormick. Conversely, speculator Hutchinson's Chicago Provision Co. was between 1868 and 1878 the largest Chicago meat-packing establishment. These diversified endeavors ran counter to the trend toward specialization among the entrepreneurial elite. But pork and beef processors also sold their products, sought "corners," and gambled in meat-market futures, and these operations involved some of them in grain speculations. Many grain traders, on the other hand, had originally carried on cattle slaughtering and packing as a sideline. Speculative fever was intensified by the cooperation of Chicago banks. They financed the major plungers, most of whom were directors of financial institutions. The power of the commission merchants over the banks enabled the board in 1864 to force local banks to deflate currency by refusing to base grain transactions on depreciated state bank notes and by insisting upon conducting business only in federal legal tender treasury paper. The banks then accepted at par value only the national bank issues and were forced to redeem state bank emissions on the same terms.[74]

If the grain trade made Chicago a synonym for commercial chaos, department stores upheld a reputation for honesty. John V. Farwell, Palmer, Field, Leiter, and Harlow Higinbotham won their fortunes and, unlike their eastern equivalents, upper-class status in retailing. Cooley & Wadsworth, the largest antebellum dry-goods enterprise, acted in the manner of Perkins & Co. as a merchandising schoolhouse. Farwell came to Chicago from an Illinois homestead in 1844 and began as a clerk in the firm; he later married Francis B. Cooley's daughter and inherited the business. Leiter and Field, upon arriving in the city, became employees, and Higinbotham, subsequently a Field partner, also started in the house. In 1865 the firm became John V. Farwell & Co. Farwell's associates were his brother and brother-in-law; his sons later inherited the store. The senior partner won fame as a sound family man, hard worker, and generous benefactor of public and Christian welfare causes.[75]

Farwell arrived in town with $3.50, but Palmer, his great rival, son of a prosperous dairy farmer, came in 1852 with $3,000 from his father and $2,000 salvaged from unsuccessful general store ventures in upstate New York. More imaginative than Farwell and his partners, Palmer introduced methods later expanded by Field. Innovations included money-back guarantees and giving credit accounts to female customers. Palmer charged the lowest prices in town, a feat accomplished by doing his own buying in New York and Europe, thus eliminating middlemen. Through these devices and courteous service, elegant and clean furnishings, ordering the latest fashions, and advertising more than any other store in town, he attracted a vast clientele, especially among the rapidly growing number of rich residents. Daring and ingenuity paid off in 1861, when Palmer purchased a huge quantity of goods at a time when Cooley & Farwell were reluctant to buy because of the impending crisis. A wartime spending spree made Palmer a fortune and the town's leading dry-goods dealer. Palmer combined intrepid inventiveness with prosaic but essential traits of hard work, prompt payment of bills, and shrewd credit evaluations. The Bank of Commercial Ratings, a predecessor of Dun & Bradstreet, early judged him as "Making money, economic business not too much extended, attends closely to business, does not pay large interest, good moral character, credits prudently given, not sued, pays promptly. Credit good."[76]

Following medical advice Palmer, age thirty-eight, sold out to Field and Leiter. Field left his father's Massachusetts farm for a Pittsfield general store clerkship. According to Farwell, then a junior partner in the house where the twenty-two-year-old Field first worked after settling in Chicago in 1856, "He had the merchant's instinct. He lived for it, and it only." When Field opened his own store Farwell called him "a supreme goods manager and salesman; he had the confidence of the buying public; his standing with eastern houses and home banks was clean. He was known as an indefatigable worker, one who would not neglect his business affairs for any personal pleasures." Another admirer, William McCormick, wrote in 1864 that Chicago capitalists "speak in strong terms of Mr. F. as a close, calculating & safe business man who devotes himself to his business." Palmer, Farwell, and Field had reputations for industry, sobriety, and reliability, and faith in the future of the city. Field moved there "feeling that I had finally reached the gateway to the West. The opportunities to make money and advance in Chicago struck me as extraordinary."[77]

In 1862 Field became a partner in Cooley, Farwell & Co.; three years later he and Leiter associated with Palmer. They bought him out in 1867 and Leiter left the firm in 1881. With Leiter handling credit and finance and Field administration and merchandising, the store flourished. The new management continued proven policies of low prices, approval purchases, refunds, courteous service, close credit terms, and prompt repayment, and initiated the use of electric lights and the bargain basement. By the mid-1880s the enterprise was earning the highest net profits in American dry-goods merchandising and in 1905 was the largest single national importer of foreign goods.[78] Unlike John V. Farwell & Co., which remained second to the Field store in business volume but lagged ever further behind, Marshall Field & Co. was run like a modern corporation rather than a family firm. Higinbotham felt that "the department store . . . stands for centralization, for relentless commercial utility as opposed to craft sentiment, for economy of opportunity and conservation of energy, for comprehensiveness and completeness, for quickness, accuracy and system." These "twentieth century traits . . . find picturesque expression in the great metropolitan department store." Selection of partners and executives through merit rather than kinship exemplified modernism. Except for Field's brother Joseph and his nephew Stanley, no major figure in the firm was related to the founder. A "storekeeper" who "selects his assistants because they are relatives is not at liberty to make the selections on the broader lines of their real qualifications," asserted Higinbotham.[79] Field paid high salaries to executives but lower-than-average wages to salesmen and clerks. Employee loyalty was secured through relatively good working conditions, high retirement and sick-leave benefits, and the prestige derived from working in the store. Between 1865 and Field's death in 1906 yearly sales increased from $8 million to $72,634,000 and annual net profits from $240,000 to $4,797,700. Profits also swelled because the lots on which his wholesale and retail establishments stood were assessed at a fraction of their real value. Although Field was a noted business and civic leader, he still placed more than four-fifths of his orders in New York and only 6 percent in Chicago, yet another sign that even the mightiest magnates depended upon Manhattan.[80]

Mass market retailing propelled several entrepreneurs and their descendants into the upper class while undermining the hierarchical social structure. Rich and well-born consumers were customarily served by dressmakers, haberdashers, and interior decorators who came to their homes and offered personal attention and goods designed to individual taste. Department stores sold standardized items in an impersonal manner. These establishments weakened the patrician monopoly of fashion. Bourgeois buyers could now imitate elite styles of dress and furniture, thus diminishing the distance between social strata. Mass marketing also encouraged more rapid changes in fashions, which eroded the traditionalism that supported patrician status. Unaware of these leveling tendencies, upper-class shoppers like Mrs. Potter Palmer, dazzled by the new store, patronized Marshall Field's, and subsequent elites frequented Bloomingdale's and Sak's Fifth Avenue in New York, I. Magnin in Los Angeles and San Francisco, Gump's in San Francisco, and Nieman-Marcus in Dallas.

Besides the grain and dry-goods trades, upper-class businessmen conducted a variety of enterprises. Such undertakings included wholesale grocers Franklin MacVeagh, William M. Hoyt, John W. Doane, Franklin D. Gray, and Otho and Albert A. Sprague; wholesale drug proprietor Melville Fuller; wholesale hardware dealers Blair, Hibbard, Adolphus C. Bartlett, and Seneca D. Kimbark; iron jobbers Joseph T. and Edward T. Ryerson; wholesale milliners Edson and Elbridge Keith; high society jeweler Charles D. Peacock; lumber merchants Turlington W. Harvey, Jesse Spalding, Edward E. Ayer, Martin Ryerson; and leather dealer John Clark.

TRANSPORTATION AND UTILITIES

Chicago was the focal point of regional and national railroad systems, and its salience as a distribution and manufacturing center depended upon its transportation facilities. Nevertheless, the business elite, contrary to its predominance in industry and commerce and its counterparts in New York, Boston, and Philadelphia, did not play an autonomous role in railroad enterprise. The midwestern network was built without any important contribution of Chicago capital, and before 1900 none of the great western lines with central offices in Chicago used that city's stock exchange. Even after World War I, when Chicago investment banking became more prominent, flotations still originated mostly in Wall Street. The Illinois Central, the Chicago, Burlington & Quincy, the Michigan Central, and the Chicago, Rock Island & Pacific, as well as a host of smaller, local roads were controlled by eastern, usually New York, capitalists.[81] The Chicago & Northwestern, one of the largest midwestern systems, was the greatest venture in which city residents exerted significant influence. Self-made magnates Henry and Albert Keep and Marvin Hughitt served as presidents through most of the years between the Civil War and World War I, and bankers, merchants, and industrialists were directors. Easterners, however, dominated the board and the executive committee, and financial control reposed in Manhattan even if operations were directed from Chicago.[82] Chicago tycoons were generally on the periphery of railroad operations: Field held over $4 million in railroad securities and sat on the board of several large roads, Pullman assisted Henry Villard's manipulations in the 1870s and '80s, Armour owned $25 million in railroad stocks and was a large shareholder and a director in the Chicago, Milwaukee and St. Paul line, and McCormick was a stockowner and director in the Union Pacific. But the major resources and efforts of these tycoons lay in other enterprises. An exception to this rule was Henry H. Porter, son of a Massachusetts lawyer, who came to Chicago in the 1850s, as had the Keeps and Hughitt. Before turning to the organization of steel companies in the 1880s, Porter was a railroad promoter and a director in several Chicago lines and the Union Pacific and headed the Chicago, St. Paul, Minneapolis & Omaha.[83]

Businessmen, municipal politicians, and the railroads developed mutual interests. Leading grain merchants, meat packers, and industrialists like Armour and McCormick received rebates and special shipping rates, often from lines in which they were large investors. Field and Armour owned stock and were active in local and such interregional lines as the Baltimore & Ohio because of their interest in sending goods to the East.[84] Cooperation between entrepreneurs, railroad executives, and politicians resulted in ludicrous underassessment of railroad capital stock in Cook County and throughout the state. Between 1873 and 1898 total railroad property valuation in Illinois actually decreased by 65 percent.[85] Influence also obtained other benefits. In 1869 the municipal government let the Illinois Central, the Chicago, Burlington & Quincy, and the Michigan Central pay $800,000 for land worth $2.6 million. Railroads, however, did not always override the public interest. The governor vetoed the land deal and in 1887 the city and state thwarted an Illinois Central attempt to annex the Chicago lakefront.[86]

Urban transit, requiring less capital than railroads, was initially locally financed and controlled. By the 1880s the city's commercial banks and the private firm of N. W. Harris & Co. marketed traction company bonds, and bankers like Chauncey Keep (son of railroad president Henry) and Charles G. Dawes were trustees and reorganizers of street railway corporations. Bartlett, Field, Armour, Albert Sprague, Leiter, Cyrus H. McCormick, banker Charles L. Hutchinson (son of the great grain speculator), and especially meat packer Samuel Allerton also acted as directors, investors, and promoters. Field's influence caused trolley lines to stop at and run special cars to his establishment. By the late 1880s, however, the dominant capitalists, Charles T. Yerkes and Samuel Insull, were held in contempt by the upper stratum because of their recent arrival, the unsavory connection between traction franchises and municipal fraud, notorious stock-watering, and inefficient and unsafe service. When Yerkes came from Philadelphia and, backed by that city's financiers, emerged as the czar of street railways, a combination of reformers and Field, Leiter, and Allerton fought him, even though the three entrepreneurs owned stock in his companies. Insull, on the other hand, though never accepted in exclusive society, became a civic leader and was financed by Chicago capital.[87] In common with other corporations, and for the same reasons, traction assets were notoriously undervalued for revenue purposes. In 1894 one line was taxed on 1.23 percent of its capital stock, another on 8.67 percent, and a third was assessed for $30,000 in property value.[88]

The upper class participated more vigorously in other utilities. Distribution of gas and heat was generally controlled by members of the elite, except for the decade of 1887–97, when Yerkes, again with Philadelphia money, organized the Chicago Gas Trust. An early example of upper-class political influence occurred in 1865, when Hugh T. Dickey still headed the Chicago Gas Light and Coke Co., and Albert M. Billings, the Peoples' Gas Light and Coke Co. The city council in that year lifted ceilings on power rates and these corporations collusively set higher prices. Former Vermont harnessmaker's apprentice Billings and his son successively headed from 1862 to 1910 the Peoples' Gas Light and Coke Co., which after 1897 monopolized the field. Another illustration of government manipulation occurred when Assemblyman J. Russell Jones, a railway president and telegraph company director, helped Cummings change Peoples' corporate charter in order to enlarge business. During the 1880s the Gas Trust undertook an electric power operation which involved Field and several other economic leaders. Electric power distribution came under the control of Insull in 1892; for the next generation he dominated utilities enterprise and in 1919 took over Peoples' Gas. Eminent citizens also participated in other utility organizations. Robert T. Lincoln, corporation lawyer and son of the President, Porter, and John Crerar, a capitalist and social figure, financed the Chicago Telegraph Co. (1881). In 1892 Insull became president of the Chicago Edison Co., a firm in which many first- and second-generation upper-class Chicagoans were involved.[89] Influential participants in the gas, electric, and telegraph companies ensured, like other utility corporations, the significant underassessment of capital stock.[90]

INDUSTRY

By value of production in 1892, meat packing, iron and steel, textiles, brass and copper, lumber processing and wood manufacturing, and wood and iron works (wagons, agricultural implements, hydraulic elevators, etc.) were in that order the leading industries in Chicago.[91] Except for clothing manufacture, a light industry with many small firms, the upper class dominated these enterprises. From the early years of settlement through World War I meat packing was the paramount industry. Long-term primacy, however, did not entail continuity of firms. Of twenty-four establishments operating in 1857, five still existed in 1871 and only one remained among the chief firms. Upper-class Chicagoans ran the three major packinghouses of the early 1870s.

Hutchinson's Chicago Provision Co., the top firm, was bought in 1872 by Albert E. Kent of A. E. Kent & Co., the third largest. Culbertson, Blair & Co. held second place; two of the three partners were also grain speculators and related to hardware mogul William Blair. By the 1880s self-made millionaires Nelson Morris, Armour, and Gustavus F. Swift, born respectively in Germany, New York, and Massachusetts, dominated the industry. Morris arrived in 1857, Swift and Armour not until 1875. The other large packers were also humbly born: Allerton came from upstate New York in 1859 and the Cudahy brothers, originally from Ireland, moved to Chicago in the 1870s. Family firms prevailed. Sons of the Cudahays, Morris, Swift, Allerton, and Armour inherited their fathers' businesses and a Morris daughter married Gustavus F. Swift, Jr. Armour, who put his brothers in charge of branches of the company in other cities, assured his nephew that "I will always be loyal to anybody with the Armour name. . . ."[92] Like other upper-class-directed enterprises, creative entrepreneurship abounded, in this case seizing on technological improvements like the refrigerator car to expand operations. Swift inaugurated extensive shipments to the East, sending out frozen beef in the 1870s, and originated the transatlantic dressed beef trade. Armour became involved a little later but improved on Swift's techniques by establishing branch houses or selling agencies to distribute his products. Swift had used older marketing methods, relying on his New England family and business connections, forming partnerships with local butchers, or using commission merchants. Armour & Co. also led the way in developing such by-products as soap, glue, and fertilizer. The code of conduct in this business was no better than in grain dealing. A U.S. Senate investigating committee discovered a beef trust which regulated prices and production standards. Big firms received rebates from railroads in which they owned stock, paid off city officials in order to obtain a low-cost water supply, and fought meat-inspection laws, and meat packers speculated in pork and beef corners. The industry was mainly locally financed, chiefly by the Continental Bank and its successor institution the Central Trust Co., meat packers being extensive stockholders in both organizations.[93] Astronomical profits enabled packer families to enter the upper order. Swift & Co. was capitalized at $300,000 in 1885, $15 million in 1896, and $25 million at Swift's death in 1903. Armour & Co. profits were $199,000 in 1873, $2 million in 1893, and $21 million in 1918. Its net worth totaled $258,000 in 1873 and $12 million in 1893. Value of product for the entire industry increased 900 percent between 1870 and 1890.[94]

Located in the breadbasket of the nation, Chicago became the center for agricultural implements production. Rapid expansion of farming made this industry, like meat packing, a windfall undertaking. Between 1860 and 1890 capital invested in Chicago farm machinery enterprises increased from $682,000 to $26,468,443 and value of production from $529,000 to $11,883,976.[95] The foremost manufacturers were William Deering & Co. Harvesting Machine Works (1870) and the McCormick Harvesting Machine Co. (1848). Cyrus H. McCormick, offspring of a middling Virginia farmer, achieved preeminence through the superiority of his machines, prompt servicing of defective reapers, extension of credit for purchases, and the pioneering use of advertising techniques and traveling salesmen. Company sales concentrated in the plains and prairie states, the regions of most spectacular agricultural expansion. Within ten years of coming to Chicago, McCormick was a millionaire, and by 1895 was selling more than one-third of all the grain- and grass-harvesting machines in the world. The Deering and McCormick concerns were family firms with children following fathers at the helm. "Cyrus is a great comfort to me," wrote McCormick of his son and namesake. "He has excellent judgment to business matters and I find myself leaning on him more and more."[96]

McCormick, Jr., succeeded his father in 1883 and eventually headed the International Harvester Co. (1902), a consolidation of Deering, McCormick, and three other companies. But the farm machinery industry encountered trouble. The McCormick Co. had to borrow heavily and paid no dividends between 1899 and 1901, and between 1897 and 1901 domestic sales of harvesting implements stagnated. Although the new concern was financed and organized by J. P. Morgan, the McCormicks held the largest share of stock, had the most directors, and thus, unlike other Chicago-based companies created by eastern capitalists, retained control over operations.[97] The younger McCormick in a 1916 essay repudiated the "ruthless and wasteful practices" of "older days." He was the public-spirited executive, a contradiction of his father and an increasingly fashionable type in modern managerial capitalism: the Harvester Company was now governed by a "code of business laws and morals" prohibiting "unfairness toward a competitor or a customer." According to McCormick, International Harvester refused to oversell farmers, improved employee welfare and relations with management, sought only "a reasonable profit," and above all aspired to community "service."[98]

Chicago's proximity to Michigan ore deposits and Pennsylvania and Illinois coal, together with the need for metal in such industries as railroad cars and agricultural machinery, gave rise to iron and steel production. Between 1857 and 1890 capital investment in that industry rose from $1,763,000 to $55,621,515 and value of production from $3,887,084 to $68,991,294.[99] The first large ironworks, the North Chicago Rolling Mill (1857), where the original American steel rail was rolled, was founded by a Detroit resident backed by Boston money. In 1871 Orin W. Potter, who married the niece of the founder, became president of the company and later board chairman of the successor firm, the Illinois Steel Co. (1889). His son was also an executive in these corporations. Other members of the upper class also took part in iron and steel manufacturing. Porter was president of the Union Steel Co. (1863) and board chairman of the Federal Steel Co., a forerunner of the U.S. Steel Corp., and a member of the group that bought Illinois Steel, another maker of railroad cars. Arthur B. Meeker helped organize the Chicago Iron Co. (1867) and subsequently headed the Joliet Iron and Steel Co. (1871). The Ryersons operated Joseph T. Ryerson & Son, Inc. (1842), the largest independent iron and steel company until it merged with Inland Steel in 1935. The Scovilles owned the Scoville Iron Works (1848), makers of machinery, steam engines, and railroad cars. These were the biggest steel and iron firms in the metropolitan area until the formation of U.S. Steel (1901). Eastern capitalists and executives controlled the mammoth trust, but Chicago magnates had some influence over its policies. President Charles M. Schwab claimed that Field, a director and large shareholder, prevented the corporation's removal to Pittsburgh.[100] Similar to other upper-class-owned businesses, the manufacturing enterprises benefited from low assessments. In 1903, for example, Illinois Steel paid no taxes.[101]

Two of Chicago's famed families got their start in industries associated with iron and steel production. George Pullman, an upstate New Yorker of modest background, began the construction of sleeping cars soon after coming to Chicago. Like other stellar entrepreneurs, Pullman succeeded because his product was more reliable than that of competitors, he innovated technical improvements, e.g., the use of dining cars, and entered an industry on the verge of explosive growth. Between 1889 and 1911 the assessed value of the Pullman Palace Car Co. multiplied from $1,091,360 to $10,297,865, and its real worth is indicated by the fact that its total assessment in 1893 was 4.92 percent of actual assets. The corporation differed from many other elite businesses in not being a family firm. Its directors and major shareholders included local tycoons, as well as Morgan and several Vanderbilts. At his death director Field owned the most stock, worth $7.5 million, and Pullman cars used Field & Co. sheets, carpets, and pillows. The great merchant was instrumental in making Robert T. Lincoln head of the firm after Pullman died.[102]

R. T. Crane & Co. was founded by New Jersey–born Richard Teller Crane, another poor boy who made millions in Chicago. Staked by uncle Martin Ryerson, Crane opened a brass and bell foundry. With the help of ex-mayor and hotel owner Sherman, he received a contract to heat the Cook County courthouse. Crane had the "good fortune to become acquainted with a number of prominent businessmen," and "consulted them when in doubt concerning business matters." In the 1860s, in partnership with brother Charles, he expanded into iron pipe and machinery making. Between 1890 and 1910 Crane & Co. experienced explosive growth because the advent of electricity increased the demand for steam engines. The firm adopted or discovered new production methods and opened branches in other cities. An important sideline was the manufacturing of elevators, and Crane's connections enabled him to put in lifts in Hibbard Spencer & Co., Field & Co., John V. Farwell & Co., and other major Chicago enterprises. Beginning when Chicago had a small population and a limited market, Crane diversified his products to increase sales. As the city grew, however, he followed the trend toward specialization, eventually concentrating on pipes and fittings. For decades Crane & Co. ranked among the top five concerns in the nation in the making of plumbing fixtures, heating equipment, and engine valves and fittings. In 1912 Crane left a fortune of at least $20 million. He was succeeded by R. T. Crane, Jr., under whom business continued to expand, especially during World War I.[103]

Elite Chicagoans participated in a variety of other industries. The great lumber merchants, Harvey, Thomas W. Avery, Spalding, Ayer, August A. Carpenter, etc., were usually the leading lumber manufacturers, operating saw and planing mills. Nathaniel K. Fairbank owned N. K. Fairbank & Co. (1864), soap and lard makers, Erskine M. Phelps and uncle and nephew Charles N. Henderson and Charles M. Henderson were in shoe manufacturing, and Henry W. King had a large clothing factory. Many of the city's leading entrepreneurs organized the Elgin National Watch Co. (1864). Raymond became the first president and was succeeded by Avery.[104] Most of the renowned capitalists specialized in one type of manufacturing, but several diversified their efforts. Harvey owned the Harvey Steel Car Works which in 1892 built the first steel railroad cars, and Avery headed the Chicago Brass Co.

CAPITAL ACCUMULATION

Chicago emerged as a major money market after it became a transportation, commercial, and industrial center. The Chicago Clearing House Association was formed in 1865, twelve years after its New York predecessor. Other basic institutions also developed relatively late. N. W. Harris & Co., the first investment bond house, appeared in 1882. Chicago was made a central reserve city in 1887, i.e., a place where other banks deposited part of their reserve funds as prescribed by the National Bank Act of 1863, and in the same year the Chicago Stock Exchange was permanently organized. Boston and Philadelphia had a long period of financial autonomy before succumbing to New York. Chicago banks from the beginning depended on the latter's banking and securities institutions and kept large balances with New York financial institutions. Finance in the midwestern metropolis was dominated by the local elite, but this group acted as intermediaries for eastern capitalists. As previously mentioned, the midwestern railroad system was capitalized largely from the East, and before 1900 none of the great lines with central offices in Chicago used the local stock exchange. Although the metropolitan area was the leading locus of industrial trusts and many of the titanic combinations had their headquarters in the city, Chicago bankers and brokers were on the periphery of the great corporate mergers. The town's financiers engaged mostly in extending credit to small and local enterprises and not until 1918 did its investment houses bring out a major securities issue. An early partner in N. W. Harris & Co. recalled that their market was "in the East, and only by very slow degrees in Chicago. It was an event then to sell a bond in the West."[105]

Although tributary to New York, by the 1870s Chicago dominated the West. During this decade country banks in the region transferred their balances from New York to Chicago. As the section matured economically, Chicago became America's second largest money market. The city "attained this high place of financial importance in a few short years," reported Central Trust Co. of Illinois President Charles G. Dawes in 1907. The "volume of business transacted by its banks is second only to that of New York City."[106]

Chicago's major financial organizations were in upper-class hands until World War I. The First National Bank of Chicago (1863) was the biggest in the city from 1876 to 1910, and in 1901 the second largest in the United States. Along with the Corn Exchange and Commercial National Banks, it was the chief source of credit for the grain trade. Chicago's leading commercial lender concentrated on short-term credit and kept a low cash reserve, thus making capital available for businessmen. First National also led Chicago banks into international finance, developing an extensive foreign exchange department. The presidents between 1863 and 1916 were distinguished civic as well as financial figures. Lyman J. Gage and James B. Forgan chaired the Chicago Clearing House Committee and the former became president of the American Bankers' Association and McKinley's secretary of the treasury. In 1898, with Dawes serving as comptroller of currency, Chicago bankers controlled the two most important federal financial posts. First National's first two presidents assumed office after mercantile success; thereafter career bankers took over. Close cooperation with the entrepreneurial elite prevailed from the beginning. President Forgan in 1918 declared that "the best directors banks can have, and those they now do have, are the men connected with the leading commercial and manufacturing industries, whose close touch with business affairs makes them the best judges of credits in their various communities. . . . The best loans in the banks are those to its directors, who are engaged in the legitimate, successful, and profitable enterprises of the communities in which they live." The First National board, with its numerous eminent capitalists, embodied this dictum.[107]

Repeated mergers concentrated banking in even fewer hands in Chicago than in New York. The Continental and Commercial Bank (1910), the largest institution to emerge from these couplings, for a time ranked first in the nation in banking resources. On its board sat the heads of several large railroads, Armour & Co., and Pullman Palace Car, and other great merchants and meat packers. Elite Chicagoans, either self-made or inheriting their wealth and status, proliferated as officers and major stockholders in the foremost financial institutions. Bank presidents between the Civil War and World War I included William F. Coolbaugh of the Union National, until 1876 Chicago's greatest bank; Chauncey B. Blair of the Merchants' National, which later became the Corn Exchange; Chauncey J. Blair, Julian S. Rumsey, Ernest A. Hamill, and Charles L. Hutchinson, of the Corn Exchange, most of whose clients belonged to the Board of Trade; Solomon A. Smith and John W. Doane of the Merchants' Loan & Trust; Byron L. Smith of the Northern Trust Co.; John J. Mitchell of the Illinois Trust and Savings, Insull's main source of funds; and Samuel M. Nickerson of the First National. Field had about $5 million invested in banks and was influential in Merchants' Loan & Trust, and McCormick and Pullman were also heavily involved, the former as a founder and the latter as a director. The Morrises were large stockholders in First National and active in shaping its policy. Philip D. Armour owned $10 million in bank stock, especially in the Continental and Commercial banks, and was a director in the former.[108]

Many bank executives came to Chicago as fledglings and rose from the ranks, but bureaucratic promotions did not entirely exclude kinship ties. Byron, son of Solomon A. Smith, served under him as vice-president of Merchants' Loan & Trust, and Byron's son, in turn, was vice-president of Northern Trust when he was president. Josiah L. and Isaac G. Lombard respectively headed Fifth National and its descendant, the National Bank of America. Chauncey J. Blair followed his parent Chauncey B. Blair as president of Merchants' National. Forgan's brother headed Union National when it merged with First National and then became vice-president of the latter. When George M. Reynolds became board chairman of Continental and Commercial his brother succeeded him as president. Family and class connections were especially visible in the branch of banking that managed family fortunes. "Perhaps the greatest problem confronting the man of means is how best he can dispose of his wealth so that his heirs shall enjoy it without the danger of dishonest agents dissipating the fund," Gage told the American Bankers' Association in 1903. "This problem . . . the trust company, in its legal capacity as administrator, executor, guardian, or trustee is established to solve." The one-time Merchants' Loan & Trust cashier felt that expertise, collective wisdom, perpetuity, and surplus capital to cover losses and errors of judgment made this type of institution an ideal protector of inherited wealth.[109] Merchants' managed the estates of Field and other eminent Chicagoans, and its presidents, cashiers, and directors were frequently members of distinguished Chicago families. The Illinois Trust & Savings Co. (1873), along with Merchants', the largest institution of its kind in Chicago, had a similar directorate.[110] The national banks also acted as guardians of upper-class affluence. Forgan handled several multimillionaire estates.

Money is a symbol of success and a source of anxiety, and those entrusted with it cultivate an aura of prudence about themselves, their institutions, and their calling. "What right have I to give away the property of which I am custodian," exclaimed Solomon A. Smith, refusing to use Merchants' funds for city relief after the 1871 fire. "Why I tell you, he is the closest fellow financially, I ever did know," remarked Wentworth of Byron L. Smith. Gage and Forgan felt that they and their colleagues were "conservative, always supporting the side of order and precedent," abhorred "innovations," "never speculated in stocks" to make a quick "profit," and were "punctilious and severe." The banker's "guiding stars are sobriety, rectitude, integrity," and "diligence and perseverance." Dawes celebrated "the strong, reliable, independent, and conservative banking system of Chicago. . . ."[111] Such praise belied a reality of risk and recklessness, fraud and failure. During the Panic of 1873 twenty-one Chicago banks collapsed. Several of the largest suspended operations, including Union National, whose president committed suicide. Illinois contributed the outstanding national bank failures in the Panic of 1893. The National Bank of Illinois, second largest in Chicago, went under because of a vice-president's speculations, and he, too, killed himself. In 1905 and again in 1912–14 catastrophe hit the financial community. These disasters resulted from inadequate reserves, unwise investments, lax state banking laws and institutional examinations, promiscuous chartering of state and private organizations, cheating executives, and defaulting directors.[112]

The frequency of prominent businessmen as bank stockholders and directors ensured cooperation between commerce, industry, and finance. During an 1893 run on Illinois Trust and Savings, depositors received their money at Armour's office and the Field store, thus building confidence in its resources. Bankers reciprocated by aiding businessmen. In 1905 former comptroller Dawes intervened with Theodore Roosevelt on behalf of J. Ogden Armour, a director in Dawes's Central Trust Co., to prevent prosecution of meat packers under the Sherman Anti-trust Act. Financiers and other magnates also worked together on civic projects. Gage, Doane, Hutchinson, and Nickerson raised money for the Chicago World's Fair, sold its bonds, and went to Washington to get congressional support. Gage headed the fair's financial committee and board of directors.[113] Occasionally, however, friction developed between financial and other entrepreneurial interests. One conflict, already noted, in 1864 between the board of trade and the bankers, resulted in defeat for the latter. In 1893, however, Field, Philip D. Armour, and other magnates complained that bank loans were too small. This time the bankers prevailed, despite the opposition of Gage, and refused to expand credit. Bankers also acquired prestige and power by assisting the municipal government. During the Panic of 1873 First and Third National and Merchants' Loan & Trust advanced money to help pay the municipal debt. Political influence meant low property assessment. The capital stock of Cook County banks in 1893 had an aggregate value of $56,394,350; these assets were assessed for $357,353. Cook County bankers' credits in 1890 were valued for tax purposes at $30,308, a considerable drop from the 1875 assessment of $349,573.[114]

Brokerage and insurance firms supplemented banks as instruments of capital accumulation, New York speculators gravitated toward the stock exchange, and Chicago's greatest plungers manipulated grain and meat futures on the board of trade. Not until the 1880s did the city's financial establishment embark on any substantial scale in securities investments. Before World War I commercial banks and brokerage houses played a minor role in capital formation and credit extension, specializing in local and regional ventures such as farm mortgages and timber, municipal, and traction bonds. After 1900 investment companies and banks participated in underwriting national issues, but initiated no important corporate flotations until the Armour & Co. $60 million debenture issue in 1918.[115]

Elite Chicagoans wielded considerable influence in the brokerage business. McCormicks and Armours were shareholders in N. W. Harris & Co., and Nickerson and Gage gave advice and financial support. Edward L. Brewster & Co. (1872) also catered to an elite clientele, handling the investment portfolios of tycoons and acting as the chief local negotiator of Chicago Edison Co. securities. Like N. W. Harris, it was a family affair with the founder's son inheriting headship of the house.[116] The upper class also dominated the Chicago Stock Exchange: Charles Henrotin, William B. Walker, Granger Farwell, and Edward L. and Walter S. Brewster served as presidents and equally eminent figures as treasurers and on the board of governors.[117] Extensive overlap existed between officers of the exchange and the board of trade. Orson Smith, Chauncey J. Blair, and Byron L. Smith were officers of both organizations.

Life insurance enterprise also attracted affluent moguls. Companies founded in the 1860s were usually capitalized at between $100,000 and

$300,000 and invariably had leading bankers and businessmen as executives and directors. By the 1880s, however, the upper class no longer dominated insurance underwriting.[118]

Several interesting patterns characterize the business elite between the Civil War and World War I. Leading capitalists were generally self-made successes who moved to Chicago from the East during the 1850s.[119] Except for the bankers they were almost exclusively entrepreneur-proprietors who founded their own establishments, rather than organization men promoted through the corporate hierarchy. The foremost magnates mixed daring and innovation with careful attention to mundane details. Swift said that Philip D. Armour "was a born speculator" with "the power to speculate safely" and "keep a great number of irons in the fire all the time. . . . Armour's attention to the details of his vast business was marvelous . . . and to that can be attributed much of his success."[120] This combination and the foresight to enter fields about to expand phenomenally resulted in spectacular entrepreneurship. No single type of institutional structure predominated in these triumphs. Family firms, as might be expected because of the earlier advent of mercantile enterprise, were more prevalent in commerce, corporate bureaucracies in industry and banking. By 1906 the giants—McCormick, Pullman, Armour, Field, etc.—had died, their places taken, depending upon the form of their organizations, by children, by unrelated underlings, and occasionally, as in the Pullman Palace Car Co., by outsiders. Until World War I no qualitative difference in managerial skill seemed to distinguish these dissimilar types of succession. The business elite consisted of the wealthiest residents and also possessed the greatest civic influence and social prestige. Hence, business achievement anchored upper-class hegemony. Finally, compared to aging patriciates in older cities, Chicago's upper order adapted to economic change. Magnates engaged in endeavors typical of their eastern equivalents, such as banking and railroads, but they were also involved in department stores, plumbing fixtures, and other enterprises eschewed by more traditional upper classes. Such flexibility and resourcefulness may be attributed to the lesser weight of inherited rank and ascriptive values in the western elite. "You [New Yorkers] defer too much to what you call society," explained Dawes in rejecting the presidency of New York's Knickerbocker Trust Co. "They called it the 'society bank.' Now that the bank is smashed where are the second generation men? I don't see them here helping to put it together." The great banker did not like "men of inherited power and inherited business position" as "business associates."[121] Dawes underestimated the role of inheritance in Chicago banking circles. New York tycoons, unlike those in other older cities, also displayed the same verve as did Chicagoans, but their sovereignty over social and cultural matters was challenged by an aristocracy absent in the newer metropolis. Perhaps this situation, rather than entrepreneurial differences, prompted this unflattering view of New York banking. Regardless of its validity, Dawes's comment accurately depicts the self-image of Chicago capitalists, who contrasted themselves to the East as a new breed of western frontiersmen. Consequently, they expressed a dynamic egalitarianism that, according to the popular myth, represented the essence of America's virtue and power.

WEALTH

The titans of the business community amassed the gigantic fortunes in the city. Palmer, Farwell, and wagonmaker Peter Schuttler, according to the assessor of internal revenue for the First District of Illinois, were the only Chicagoans earning over $100,000 in 1863. Spectacular annual earnings mounted into multimillions over the lifespans of the leading magnates. In addition to the mammoth legacies of Field, Crane, Palmer, Armour, McCormick, and Leiter, Morris left $18 million, Swift, $12 million, Pullman, $7 million, Cobb and Martin A. Ryerson, $6 million each, and Albert Keep, $5 million.[122]

The moneyed elite of the 1860s, similar to its predecessor, tended to be recent migrants. Federal income tax records listed 216 residents who made at least $10,000 in 1863. Of the 115 whose date of arrival could be ascertained, twenty-six moved to the city in the 1830s, twenty-nine in the 1840s, fifty-two in the 1850s, and eight in the early 1860s.[123] Brown, Ogden, Newberry, Scammon, and Church appeared on this list, but the majority came after 1850. A similar situation prevailed at higher incomes. Among the fifty-six earning a minimum of $25,000, of those with discovered dates of entry, five had lived in the city since the 1830s, seven since the 1840s, seventeen since the 1850s, and one thereafter. Among the twelve making $50,000 or over, of those with known dates of arrival, one came in the 1830s, two in the 1840s, and four in the 1850s.

Recent residence was accompanied by recent fortune. Like the pre–Civil War elite, the high income earners of 1863 were overwhelmingly architects of their own affluence (See Table 3). Indeed, the proportion of self-made men in the later exceeded those in the earlier group by one-fifth. Except for the oldest category of derived wealth, frequencies of inherited riches were smaller in the subsequent list. While those with at least three generations of money were twice as frequent in 1863 as before the war, the numbers were negligible in both groups. Although the urban economic and social structure was aging, upward mobility, contrary to conventional wisdom, actually expanded. This phenomenon was due to the explosive growth of Chicago from the 1850s to 1865. Similar generational distributions obtained at higher earnings: twenty-six of the twenty-nine (89.4 percent) and all nine with known vintage of

Table 3

VINTAGE OF FORTUNE FOR CHICAGOANS
EARNING AT LEAST $10,000 IN 1863

Wealth Generation	Number	Percent
First	76	89.4
Second	1	1.2
At least second	5	5.9
Three or more	3	3.5
Total known	85	100

wealth among those making respectively at least $25,000 and $50,000 had humble beginnings. The high-income earners of 1863 diverged in generational frequency distributions from Bostonians of 1860 and New Yorkers of 1856–57 assessed for at least $100,000 and Charlestonians who owned at least one hundred slaves on one South Carolina plantation in 1860. About a quarter of the rich residents of the northern coastal cities were self-made, and one-third of the Bostonians and 45 percent of the New Yorkers had inherited wealth at least three generations old. Chicagoans making $25,000 and $50,000 shared with Bostonians assessed at $250,000 and New Yorkers at $250,000 and $500,000 the trends of showing no change or an increase in first-generation wealth compared to the entire group of affluent citizens in their respective places. Dissimilarity between the Chicagoans and the southerners was even more marked: 69 percent of the Charlestonians belonged to the old South Carolina families.

In geographical, as in generational, origin the high-income earners of 1863 resembled the earlier elite (See Table 4). New York State, birthplace of forty-six of those making at least $10,000, was still the largest source of wealthy Chicagoans and had nearly the same percentage as in the pre-war upper-class. New England remained second; however, its representation decreased slightly from the previous list. Eight with known birthplaces came from west of Pennsylvania, twelve were born abroad, and none in Illinois. Those with higher incomes had similar origins. The nativity of thirty-five of the fifty-six Chicagoans making a

Table 4

BIRTHPLACES OF CHICAGOANS EARNING AT LEAST $10,000 IN 1863

Birthplace	Number	Percentage
New England	45	36.6
Middle Atlantic states	54	43.9
Elsewhere	24	19.5
Total known	123	100

minimum of $25,000 was established: thirteen of the sixteen from the Middle Atlantic states originated in New York and ten in New England. Birthplaces for eight of the twelve Chicagoans earning $50,000 or more were found: one was a Yankee and four of the five from the Middle Atlantic states came from New York. The nativity of the rich did not correspond with that of the city population. In 1860 half the residents were foreign-born, 12.7 percent hailed from the Middle Atlantic region, and 6 percent from New England.[124] Because of the relatively recent settlement of Chicago, its wealthy inhabitants differed greatly in geographical origins from the more insular economic elites in Boston, New York, and Charleston. Half the New Yorkers and five-sixths of the Bostonians worth at least $100,000 respectively in 1856–57 and 1860, and over nine-tenths of the great slaveholders living in Charleston, hailed from their home city or state.

Incomplete portions of known generational and geographical origins condition the findings regarding the high income earners of 1863. Vintage of wealth for those making at least $10,000 included only 39.4 percent of the total group. Virtually the same generational frequency distribution, however, occurred at the $25,000-and-over level where 51.8 percent of the backgrounds were discovered. At the $50,000 minimum, the self-made comprised an even higher percentage of the total, and vintage of fortune was determined for three-fourths of the group. A similar situation prevails in geographical origins. Those with ascertained birthplaces constituted 56.9 percent of the entire enclave and 62.5 percent and two-thirds respectively at upwards of $25,000 and $50,000. Another reservation about the high-income earners concerns the equation of income with wealth and high status. Large-income earners in 1863 might have encountered mishaps that prevented their subsequent inclusion among the richest residents. Chicago, however, was a new community and its opulent citizens had little opportunity to accumulate fortunes over many years or benefit from ancestral acquisitions. Consequently, income more accurately defines wealth in Chicago than in older cities. Moreover, the 1863 group included Scammon, Ogden, Brown, McCormick, Palmer, Nickerson, Newberry, Farwell, and other notable citizens. Finally, the pre–Civil War establishment had similar vintage and birthplace trends that caused it to differ markedly and in the same way from contemporary elites in Boston, New York, and Charleston.

Another indication of the congruence of wealth and income was the rate of persistence between the 1863 enclave and the 1892 *Tribune* list of Chicago millionaires. Sixty-seven of the 216 (31.0 percent) Chicagoans in the earlier enclave appeared or were related to those on the later list.[125] Twenty-three of the fifty-six (41.1 percent) making at least $25,000 and nine of the twelve earning $50,000 or more were similarly related to the millionaires. Akin to inherited wealth, the Chicagoans fell considerably below the level of the Boston and New York affluents in this dimension of continuity of fortune. Of Bostonians worth at least $100,000 in 1860 and New Yorkers similarly rated in 1856–57, 14 and 12 percent more respectively were so connected to the 1892 millionaires of their cities.

Cohesion among affluent residents may be measured horizontally as well as vertically. Forty-nine (22.7 percent) of the Chicagoans who earned at least $10,000 in 1863 were related by blood or marriage to at least one other member of this group. Nineteen (33.9 percent) who made $25,000 or more were so related and nine at the pinnacle of $50,000 and above had kinship ties with others on the list. Here, too, Chicagoans lagged considerably behind their contemporaries in Boston and New York. Bostonians assessed for at least $100,000 in 1860 and New Yorkers with an identical property valuation in 1856–57 had respectively 100 and 14 percent larger shares of this type of interconnection. The three elites, as in the case of persistence, showed increased interrelatedness at higher stages of wealth. Commercial integration, as defined by business partnerships or offices in the same companies, exclusive of common corporate directorships, exceeded the frequency of kinship ties. One hundred and seventeen (54.1 percent) of the Chicagoans who made at least $10,000, thirty-four (60.7 percent) who made at least $25,000, and eight who earned a minimum of $50,000 were in business with one or more members on the list.

Relative to the wealthiest Bostonians and the great Charleston slaveowners of 1860 and the richest New Yorkers of 1856–57, the high-income Chicagoans tended by huge margins to be self-made, to have smaller percentages of old fortunes, to be born outside the state or the city where they made their money, to have lower rates of persistence, and to be less interrelated. This evidence supports the widely held notion that newer settlements have higher rates of upward mobility than do older communities.[126]

Did Chicago's wealthiest echelon come to resemble those of older places as the town developed into a mature metropolis? The answer lies in a collective analysis of the 1892 millionaires and a comparison between them and the antebellum elite, the high-income earners of 1863, and the Boston and New York millionaires of 1892 (See Table 5).[127]

While the percentage of self-made millionaires had dropped nearly one-fifth from that of the high-income earners of 1863, it remained about the same as among the antebellum elite. Second-generation wealth was much higher in 1892 than 1863, but again close to the pre–Civil War group. Relatively mellowed fortunes, the last two categories, composed approximately the same share in 1863 and 1892. At-least-two-generation-old fortunes, however, were proportionately larger in

Table 5

VINTAGE OF FORTUNE OF CHICAGO MILLIONAIRES OF 1892

Wealth Generation	Number	Percentage
First	125	70.6
Second	36	20.4
At least two	5	2.8
Three or more	11	6.2
Total known	177	100

the former and in the three-or-more category in the latter list, but this difference may result from later accumulations being easier to trace. Among the antebellum notables, money at least three generations old comprised less than one-third the share of the latest compilation. But this discrepancy, too, may be a factor of more available data on the millionaires' backgrounds: the share of those with at least two generations of wealth was four times smaller in 1892 than in the antebellum group. In any case, the numbers in the last two categories are too few for meaningful comparisons. Although the city was more than a generation older than in the 1850s, upward mobility had not appreciably diminished, and the proportions of new and old wealth among its millionaires contrasted significantly with that of equivalent contemporaries in Boston and New York. A caveat of incompleteness may also be entered here. The vintage of wealth of 177 of the 278 millionaires (63.7 percent) was identified, roughly the same proportion as in the eastern cities. The segment of first-generation millionaires exceeded their Boston and New York counterparts by about 40 percent. Conversely, the share of three or more generations of wealth among the westerners was 32 and 28 percent respectively smaller than that of Boston and New York millionaires.

Because the birthplaces of 227 of the 278 millionaires (81.7 percent) were discovered, there is no issue of insufficient evidence. As on the earlier lists, few came from Chicago or Illinois (See Table 6). Fourteen

Table 6

BIRTHPLACE OF CHICAGO MILLIONAIRES OF 1892

Birthplace	Number	Percentage
New England	67	29.6
Middle Atlantic states	69	30.4
Chicago	14	6.1
Elsewhere in the United States	38	16.7
Abroad	39	17.2
Total known	227	100

were native city dwellers and four more were born in Illinois. Fifty-eight hailed from New York, still the single largest source of wealthy residents, and the Middle Atlantic and New England regions continued by far to be the greatest suppliers of rich Chicagoans. The Northeast representation, however, had shrunk from four-fifths on the first two lists to three-fifths on the latest list. Conversely, those born in Ohio, Wisconsin, Indiana, Michigan, and Illinois had substantially increased, numbering 43 (15 percent) of the total with known birthplaces. This rise was due to the expanded population and economy of the Old West. As in the earlier compilations, the origins of the millionaires did not correspond to the population of the entire city: in 1890, one-third of the residents were foreign-born, 39.7 percent came from Illinois, 46.1 percent from the Old West, and only 1.8 percent from New England and 5.9 percent from the Middle Atlantic region.[128] In geographical as in generational origin, millionaire Chicagoans differed from their peers in Boston and New York. Over three-quarters of the Yankees and more than half of the New Yorkers originated in the state or city of their 1892 domicile.

Leaving aside the fourteen indigenous Chicagoans, the year of entry for 155 of the 264 millionaires was identified. Sixteen came in the 1830s, twenty-nine in the 1840s, sixty in the 1850s, thirty in the 1860s, seventeen in the 1870s, and three in the 1880s. The 1850s was still the predominent decade of entry for the richest residents. Unlike the 1863 compilation, however, the major share (two-thirds) of the wealthiest inhabitants of 1892 had lived in Chicago for at least a generation. This change is due to the aging of the city and to the fact that it takes longer to become a millionaire than to make a large yearly income. The relative longevity of the millionaires indicates the emergence, as measured by temporal continuity, of a more cohesive elite by 1892.

The same share of millionaires, eighty-eight of 278 (31.7 percent) were or had relatives on the 1863 list as the 1863ers or their kin on the 1892 collectivity. Hence this level of integration did not change despite the maturation of the society and economy. A one-fifth smaller portion of Chicago millionaires had family ties with their rich predecessors than did Boston millionaires to their forerunners of 1860, but edged New Yorkers with such bonds to the wealthy of 1856–57 by 1.5 percent.

Although no modification occurred in the representation of blood or marital ties between the 1863 and 1892 economic elites and vice versa, interrelatedness among the millionaires exceeded that of the high-income earners by 14.4 percent. One hundred and one (37.1 percent) were united by blood or marriage. In this type of cohesion alone did the opulent Chicagoans approximate the level of continuity of both eastern millionaire enclaves, coming to within 2 and 4 percent respectively of the Bostonians and New Yorkers. Kinship was more extensive among Chicago millionaires than among the 1863 cohort, but fewer of the 1892 rich conducted joint business enterprises. Excluding directorships in the same corporations, eighty-four (30.2 percent) were in business with at least one other millionaire, a drop of almost one-quarter from the 1863 enclave. The growing institutionalization and specialization of business and the advent of the family firm limited the formation of the numerous and sometimes short-lived partnerships characteristic of earlier times.

Chicago millionaires still differed in generational and geographical origins from those in Boston and New York, but in several respects the wealthy enclaves of the three cities drew closer together than in the past. A slightly larger portion of the richest Chicagoans of 1892 were born in the West, in Illinois, and in Chicago than were their predecessors. The millionaires matched their New York equivalents in appearing or having relatives on earlier lists of wealthy residents. And affluent Chicagoans, Bostonians, and New Yorkers of 1892 recorded virtually the same degree of interrelatedness.

THOUGHT

Field, Higinbotham, Armour, Swift, Hutchinson, Crane, Gage, and Insull held conventional bourgeois notions about personal virtue, the requisites for and desirability of commercial success, and the unique role and merit of the businessman. According to their pronouncements and the testimony of relatives and associates, these tycoons were preoccupied with their enterprises, combined mastery of detail with entrepreneurial vision, adopted progressive productive, organizational, and marketing methods, and avoided extravagance, particularly in the early years, to plough profits back into the business. They possessed indomitable will, unshakable self-confidence, shrewd judgment, a passion for hard work, and incredible self-discipline. The magnates pursued wealth, but largely as a symbol of power and accomplishment. They felt optimistic about Chicago and their contribution to its growth and welfare, and saw their enterprise as harmonizing self-interest with obligations toward family, employees, the community, and the nation.[129]

Hints of anxiety cast a shadow over these claims of rectitude and gratification. At times, Cyrus McCormick acknowledged in 1845, "I would almost sink under the weight of responsibility hanging upon me." Pit speculator Hutchinson went insane. Philip D. Armour disclosed another possible source of strain in saying that it "bother[ed] Father" that "I always seemed to be gaining more of this world's goods than he and was always in advance of him, instead of his being able to help me." Mrs. Reginald De Koven, a daughter of statesman and dry-goods merchant Charles B. Farwell, thought commercial life in Chicago "one of almost killing stress and strain. Wealth gained by the wealthy of the Middle West gives its possessors little of the joy of life and all of its responsibilities, its efforts and its cares."[130]

Dissonance and doubt surfaced more distinctly and frequently in the younger generation, which bore the added burden of fulfilling the demands of famous fathers. I am "spoken of as the son of the 'great reaper man,'" Cyrus McCormick, Jr., wrote his father. "It makes me feel keenly the tremendous responsibility of the position in which you have put me, and to fill it creditably and according to your wishes is my constant aim & care."[131] An Armour executive claimed that Philip D. Armour forced J. Ogden Armour to enter the firm, leave Yale, and forego a career in architecture. Friction over life-styles may have involved more than vocational preferences. "Ogden . . . thought there would be something he would like to do instead of grubbing for money when we already had more than enough," Armour allegedly told John B. Sherman, founder of the Union Stockyards. "He thinks he should retire. I told him to be at the Yards in his working clothes at seven on Monday morning." Direct testimony reveals Armour's doubts about his sons. The meat packer "always felt that I could run Armour and Co." alone because "I always felt within myself resourceful and inherently strong. That is very necessary in anybody managing a large concern." He mentioned this to one son "as I think you need a little back bone in your makeup." Philip D. Armour also perceived "a feeling around among the concern that the young element isn't as resourceful or as strong in its determination as 'the old man' has been. . . ."[132] The Swifts experienced the same generational discontinuity of values and habits. "No doubt there is a great difference between the types of men required to build a great business and to carry it on," suggested Louis F. Swift, comparing himself and his brothers with their father. "He had to work as he did to build Swift & Co." The "habit of work was so strongly fastened on him that he could not shake it off. The rest of us were fortunate. The period of worst struggle, once over, found us young enough to change our working methods to what accorded better with the requirements of the job. I have never since those early days yearned to live all my working hours with the business." Helen Swift Morris, daughter of Gustavus Swift and wife of Nelson Morris's son, pointed out another difference between first- and second-generation businessmen in describing the responses of her husband and father to the packer anti-trust prosecution: "Mr. Edward Morris was a nervous, hypersensitive man. . . . After a court session, Mr. Morris would return, completely worn out, unable to eat, unable to sleep. . . ." Swift was carefree and relaxed during the trial. The "Chicago Tradition," said Frazier Jelke, whose parent made a fortune in oleomargarine, "was hard on the second generation. . . . few sons of outstanding success made names for themselves or kept pace with their sires."[133]

Changing business conditions and dissimilar backgrounds sometimes made the commercial practices of filial successors vary markedly from those of their fathers. Armour and McCormick placed little value on intellectual activity and higher education. McCormick also wanted his son to enter the firm rather than college and only his wife's insistence kept the youth at Princeton. When head of International Harvester, young Cyrus discerned a role for educated executives that the old "reaper king" would have deplored: Business "stand[s] with law, ministry, and medicine in its claims upon the time and attention of any man who wishes his life to be one of service and sacrifice in a noble cause." In the *Daily Princetonian* of 1916, McCormick exhorted the undergraduates to seek a business career, and, unlike his own father, "to be a good 'mixer' and not have an air of aloofness to those around and with him." The son, who, as previously mentioned, wanted to be a modern corporate manager rather than a replica of this robber baron father, felt that "In team work there is strength."[134]

Politics

Upper-class Chicagoans, like other elites, used public office, party posts, and financial assets to obtain government favors for their interests and projects and to sustain their community leadership. Officeholding is the most obvious, though not necessarily the most consequential means of political control. Aside from the statistically insignificant highest income level in 1863, the proportions of wealthy citizens who at some time held such municipal, county, state, and federal offices as mayor, county commissioner, city comptroller, city or county treasurer, alderman, judge, customs collector, minister or ambassador, governor, federal or state legislator, and U.S. cabinet officer, remain remarkably constant over time and at different plateaus of high earnings and wealth (See Table 7). An interurban comparison shows that Chicagoans making at least $10,000 in 1863 had an 8.4-percent-smaller segment of officeholders than did Bostonians worth at least $100,000 in 1860, a one-third smaller share than the great Charleston slaveholders, and a 2.8-percent edge over New Yorkers assessed for $100,000 and above in 1856–57. The percentage of former, current, or future officeholders among the

Table 7

HIGH-INCOME EARNERS OF 1863 AND MILLIONAIRES OF 1892
WHO HELD PUBLIC OFFICES

Income	Total Number	Number in Office	Percentage in Office
$10,000 and above (1863)	216	33	15.3
$25,000 and above (1863)	56	11	19.6
$50,000 and above (1863)	12	4	33.3
Millionaires of 1892	278	46	16.5

Chicago millionaires was slightly more than for the 1863 cohort. Public officials were now a rarity among the richest New Yorkers and a 1.2-percent-smaller enclave among the Boston millionaires than among their Chicago counterparts. Public servants among the Chicago millionaires, as among the income elite of 1863, were overwhelmingly self-made men. Twenty-nine of the thirty-five officeholders (82.9 percent) with known vintage of fortune were first generation, three second generation, one at least second generation, and two had three or more generations of inherited wealth.

The Union League Club of Chicago (1879), a prestigious body formed chiefly by leading capitalists, illustrates the interconnections between entrepreneurial eminence, wealth, high status, and politics. Among its members up to the 1920s were at least one of the city's congressmen, eight U.S. senators, three ambassadors or ministers, four federal circuit and four federal district court justices, and U.S. vice-president Charles G. Dawes.[135]

Wealthy and socially prominent officeholders were usually businessmen whose service was intermittent and supplementary to their commercial activities, but several members of the upper class embraced political careers. Charles B. Farwell, a Union League founder, served almost continuously from the 1840s until the 1890s as a county official, congressman, and U.S. senator. Carter H. Harrison began his career as a county commissioner in 1872, went to Congress in 1874, and was mayor of Chicago from 1879 to 1887 and in 1893. A more typical pattern, however, occurred in the Medill-McCormick-Patterson clan, who accumulated more posts than any other patrician kinship unit. Family founder Joseph Medill, publisher of the Chicago *Tribune*, resigned after a few unhappy months as mayor and later reflected that "Politics and office-seeking are pretty good things to let alone for a man who has intellect and individuality. Generally he will get more happiness out of life, I am sure, tending to his business, respecting God, his conscience, and the grand jury, and doing only what those three powers will let him." Medill's son-in-law, Robert S. McCormick, nephew of Cyrus, became a career diplomat who headed missions to France, Austria, and Russia. Ambassadorships, though prestigious, were remote from issues vital to the power and wealth of eminent Chicagoans. Robert R. McCormick, son of Robert S. McCormick, served briefly (1904–6) as an alderman and president of the sanitary district. After resigning from municipal government he advised against "politics as a profession."[136] Robert R.'s cousin, Joseph Medill Patterson, during the same years was an assemblyman and a municipal commissioner of public works. Patterson and McCormick soon forsook politics for the family newspaper, but the latter's brother, Medill McCormick, left journalism for politics. In 1912 he was elected to the state house, in 1916 to Congress, and in 1919 to the U.S. Senate. After his death in 1925, his wife ran successfully for Congress. Medill was the only officeholder of this clan with a continuous, professional involvement in domestic politics.

Public servants of the Patterson-McCormick stripe revealed a tendency for inheritors of wealth and social position to dabble in, and less often to embrace, government careers. John V. Farwell, Jr., was a Cook County commissioner, William Kent, son of the meat packer, in 1895–97 led the reform forces on the city council, and Palmer's child also was a two-term alderman. Hempstead W. Washburne, whose father Elihu B. had been a top-ranked lawyer, eight-term Congressman, minister to France, secretary of state, and president of the historical society, became city attorney in 1885 and mayor in 1891. Carter H. Harrison and his son created the only patrician political dynasty, the latter serving as mayor from 1897 to 1903 and 1911 to 1915.

Upper-class Chicagoans entered the foreign service, a branch of government particularly attractive to American patriciates. Robert S. McCormick, Lambert Tree, Hobart Chatfield-Taylor (son of a great lumber manufacturer and son-in-law of Charles B. Farwell), Richard Teller Crane's sons and grandson, millionaire railroad lawyer Frederick H. Winston, and traction magnate J. Russell Jones headed foreign missions. Elite Chicagoans were also consulted by the government on foreign policy. But the westerners lacked blueblood opinion leaders in international relations like Bostonians Thomas Jefferson Coolidge, Brooks Adams, or William C. Endicott. Instead, as in New York, the advice of big businessmen was sought by the State Department.[137]

Party posts and contributions provided the upper class with another source of political influence. Seven of the 1892 millionaires were delegates to Republican and Democratic national conventions. Dawes ran the McKinley and Roosevelt campaigns in the West, Philip D. Armour gave money to a private fund to restore McKinley's personal fortune, and Cyrus H. McCormick, the most politically active of the supermagnates, helped fund the state and national Democratic organizations, chaired the State Central Democratic Committee, sat on the Democratic National Committee, and ran for Congress in 1864.[138]

Power and payoffs created additional opportunities for rich capitalists to dominate politicans. "Here in person, or represented, were the two most prominent men of Chicago, neither of whom I had met or even seen so I felt a little fluttery," recalled the U.S. collector of internal revenue at Chicago, after a Leiter and Field secretary visited him. "I'll be elected," asserted Alderman "Bathhouse" John Coughlin; "I have the business interests with me. . . . Because when anyone wants me to do anything I do it courteously. Marshall Field, Mandel Brothers, the First National Bank. They're all with me." John Powers, another notorious aldermanic boodler, said, "You can't get elected to the [city] council unless Mr. Yerkes says so."[139]

Deference accorded to leading businessmen produced government policies advantageous to their primary concerns. The tycoons led the annexation movement of the 1880s which absorbed Hyde Park and other suburbs into the city. Fearing that a suit might someday be brought against Field, the state's attorney for Cook County refused to prosecute violators of an Illinois factory law prohibiting employment of children. Dawes used his influence with the state treasurer to gain backing for a collateral law that favored large Chicago national against state banks, and during the Panic of 1907 he convinced the secretary of the treasury to deposit federal funds in Chicago banks to halt the currency drain on these institutions. Meat packers were on good terms with Chicago police, who gave them protection in labor disputes.[140] After the Haymarket Riot the governor agreed to commute the death sentence of the anarchists if Chicago's foremost citizens appealed for mercy. Gage called a meeting of fifty magnates. Although he and Palmer desired clemency, Field prevailed against them. "Afterward many of the men present came around to me," reminisced Gage, "and said they . . . would have been glad to join me in such an appeal, but that in face of the opposition of powerful men like Marshall Field, they did not like to do so, as it might injure them in business, or socially."[141] The most consistent example of the ability of wealth to manipulate government was the underassessment of real and personal property. In 1895 a mayor's commission valued the property of the central business district at ten times its assessed worth, and in 1894 total property in the city was assessed for nearly $20,000,000 less than in 1869. Several leading merchants and manufacturers, the president of the Chicago Real Estate Board, the mayor, and the city comptroller charged that assessments were criminally low, thus favoring the rich and adding to the tax burden of the poor, and that undervaluation occurred because wealthy property owners contributed to party campaigns and bribed assessors.[142] Yet not until 1898 did property assessments equal the total of 1873. Inadequate assessment created a low revenue base. Chicago, the third largest American city in 1885, ranked ninth among the thirteen most populous in property value for taxes, sixth in total taxation, and last in per-capita taxes. Boston, New York, and Philadelphia topped these categories. In the early 1900s Chicago had lower per-capita property valuations, revenues, money raised by taxes, and expenditures than did Boston, New York, Philadelphia, or St. Louis. The city spent less per capita on police, street cleaning, and public health than did these municipalities.[143]

While using the political system to further its interests, the upper class, for a variety of reasons, found itself at odds with the urban government. Although the proportions of rich and well-born officeholders changed little between 1863 and 1892, the Old Guard was pushed to peripheral places in party leadership and public office. After 1870 premier entrepreneurs and their offspring served mostly in park commissionerships and on the board of education. Seventeen of the twenty-four 1892 millionaires appointed to these offices held no other post. These positions, like foreign service, were marginal to the preservation of group power. Prominent millionaires seeking more important offices usually lost out. Tree and Franklin MacVeagh were defeated U.S. Senate candidates, and Cyrus H. McCormick never received a much-coveted nomination for governor or senator. Professional politicians with support among the ethnic minorities now dominated elections. Washburne was the last upper-class mayor, and the victories of the elder Harrison ushered in the new order. Despite genteel origins, Harrison reflected the rise of ethnic politics and professional politicians. Hence he was even less popular in upper-class Chicago than were Theodore Roosevelt and Henry Cabot Lodge with the Knickerbockers and the Brahmins. Mayor Harrison refused to suppress liquor, gambling, and prostitution, feeling that they were inevitabilities of urban life, defended free speech and association for anarchists, and won labor support by backing the eight-hour day. His stand on these issues and his following among the immigrant masses roused the opposition of the great capitalists and the Union League. In 1881, 1885, and 1893 he respectively bested establishment nominees leather manufacturer John Clark, Crane, and Allerton.[144]

Machine politicians, whose power base lay in the immigrant wards, tolerated gambling, saloons, and brothels, style-of-life issues that offended transplanted northeasterners and other American-born members of the old establishment. These politicians, among whom the Harrisons were an exception, were amenable to bribery and the selling of public utility franchises. New tycoons—banker John R. Walsh, Yerkes, and Insull—through campaign contributions and bribes, collaborated with bosses with an ethnic following, Coughlin, Powers, "Hinky Dink" Michael Kenna, William Lorimer, and "Big Bill" Thompson. This triumphant alliance made the old elite feel displaced by elements that violated its belief in honest, efficient, and economical government.

Self-made financier Gage, second-generation-gentleman Hobart Chatfield-Taylor, and Wayne MacVeagh regretted the departure from local government of "substantial and successful business and professional men." Taylor, Medill, and MacVeagh attributed the spread of urban vice and corruption to immigration and popular sovereignty.[145] These critics typified the flight of the upper class from elective office to the civil service crusade. Disenchanted with municipal administration, the traditional elite participated in organizations dedicated to eradicating evil and ending the supremacy of those who had driven out the old upper order. Taylor agitated for civil service and ballot reform and opposed Yerkes. MacVeagh, original president of the Citizens' Association of Chicago (1874), a trustee and organizer of the Civic Federation of Chicago (1893), vice-president of the National Civil Service Reform League, and a founder of the National Municipal League, in 1885 introduced a civil service reform act in the Illinois legislature, and fought Harrison. Gage, an organizer and first president of the Civic Federation and an initiator of the Municipal Voters' League (1896), in 1895 lobbied in Springfield for a civil service bill. Medill, a member of the Citizens' Association, like Gage belonged to the Union League, which championed civil service and ballot reform. The *Tribune* editor agitated for the merit system and election reform and opposed Yerkes and Harrison.

The Citizens' Association, the Union League, the Chicago Civil Service Reform League (1882), the Civic Federation, and the Municipal Voters' League were the leading reform organizations. The Citizens' Association, the oldest continuous municipal reform society in the country, inaugurated the movement against corrupt government in 1875 with a successful fight to modernize the city charter. Until World War I it was a vehicle of the social and economic elite: its presidents included MacVeagh, Edson Keith, Carpenter, Melville E. Stone, also a vice-president of the Union League, and other millionaire magnates. Union League president Ferdinand W. Peck, Charles L. Hutchinson, Richard Teller Crane, Martin A. Ryerson, Marshall Field, and the sons of Philip D. Armour and John V. Farwell were officers and executive committeemen. Two-thirds of the thirty-four Chicago cultural leaders identified by Helen Horowitz were active in the Association: three as presidents and six as members of the executive committee. Along with the Union League, many of whose members belonged to the Association, it led the clean government forces in the 1870s and 1880s. A conservative body, the Association contributed $30,000 to the militia during the Railroad Strike of 1877, opposed the Eight Hour Day walkout of 1885, and took a hard line against the Haymarket prisoners.[146] The Chicago Civil Service Reform League was made up mainly of Union League and Association members, an alliance solidified by the presidency of Stone. This organization, the earliest exclusively civil service reform group in Chicago, in the 1880s unsuccessfully promoted good government bills in the state legislature.[147]

During the next decade the reformers won their greatest victories. Washburn, helped by the civil service organizations, was elected mayor. In his administration (1891–93) the police department was reorganized, gambling was curbed, utility companies' taxes were increased and their fees were cut, and building codes were improved. A state civil service act passed in 1895 and the city adopted the merit system. In 1898 the crusaders defeated Yerkes's attempt to obtain long-term street railway licenses and drove him from the city, and between 1898 and 1905 purged the aldermen who had been bought by Yerkes and were selling off traction and other utility franchises.[148] The Federation, composed mainly of businessmen interested in tax and charter reform and urban improvements, and its creation, the Municipal Voters' League, spearheaded these triumphs. Society queen Mrs. Potter Palmer was a founder and original vice-president of the Federation. Its presidents included Gage, William T. Baker, grain commission merchant and president of the board of trade, realtor-banker Josiah L. Lombard, also an Association vice-president, and iron manufacturer Franklin H. Head. Membership came largely from the Union League and Commercial clubs and the Association: many had great wealth and upper-class backgrounds and the majority were college-educated, native-born, overwhelmingly from northeastern forebears, and were professionals, businessmen, and financiers. The Federation was an all-purpose civic agency, organized for vice removal, educational improvements, labor problems, and municipal government reform. Although successful in civil service reform and in the fight against Yerkes, it failed on some fundamental issues, e.g., charter revision, and in its chief post-1910 effort, modification of the tax structure.[149] The political arm of the Federation became the Municipal Voters' League, specifically formed to combat corruption in Chicago government and eliminate boodling aldermen. Gage took the lead in organizing the League, most of whose members were businessmen, professionals, and academics who also belonged to the Association. Former Alderman Kent headed the League, aided by crusading millionaire newspapermen Medill, Victor Lawson, and Herman H. Kohlsaat. Apart from agitating for the merit system, it backed young patricians like Robert R. McCormick and Kent for public office and campaigned for the prosecution of saloon owners who violated city ordinances.[150] Its ideology and policy opposed machine bosses and their adherents among the foreign-born.

The reformers, conducting municipal administration according to the business corporation ideal of efficiency and honesty, believed in replacing bossism with educated and upright public servants, and curbing saloons and gambling. These nostrums and hostility or indifference to tax inequities, unions, and aid to the disadvantaged made the crusade unattractive to the urban masses, especially the ethnic minorities. Reform victories were intermittent and accomplishments superficial. The attempt to secure charter revision in 1907 was defeated at the polls, partly because it contained restrictions on liquor selling and saloon hours. During the same year the Union League, previously at the forefront of reform, united with Lorimer and Democratic bosses Coughlin and Kenna to elect a corrupt Republican mayor because they feared municipal ownership of traction lines more than dirty politics. The clean government advocates thus faltered in 1907 and suffered another loss in

1911 when Carter Harrison, Jr., beat their candidate, alderman and University of Chicago political scientist Charles E. Merriam. The reform era terminated in 1915 with Thompson elected mayor and the Federation and the Municipal Voters' League in disarray.[151]

The movement was doomed by the conservatism of its leaders. Many eminent capitalists and reformers held stock in traction and other utilities companies; therefore they opposed public ownership, a remedy for a primary source of political corruption. MacVeagh and Field, for example, fought against city ownership of transit lines. Field, Leiter, Pullman, Swift, Armour, McCormick, and Medill, except for Field's suggestion that Pullman seek arbitration in the Railroad Strike of 1894, consistently attacked unions and broke strikes. Reformers Stone, Head, and Charles L. Hutchinson, long-term treasurer of the Association, and the Association policy, were anti-union.[152] "American businessmen are properly rewarded for great energy, entrepreneurial spirit, and hard work," proclaimed Head in 1888. "They are mostly self-made men and through these virtues have become employers rather than employees and have created wealth for national prosperity and the prosperity of their employees. Criticisms that the fortunes are undeserved or ill gotten or much greater than the masses are criticisms calculated to set class against class, employed against employer, and to arouse the basest passions of our nature." Admiration for capitalists led reformers, as Mac-Veagh put it in 1895, to apply "business methods in city government." Open identification with big business was a form of elitism that limited the crusaders' commitment to social change and their chances of victory. Behind the rhetoric of rectitude lay contempt for the masses. MacVeagh told the Association that "the universal right to vote and right to hold office" has "succeeded in our great cities at least, in binding hand and foot the best part of the community, and placing political power in the hands of the baser elements of the people."[153] Accordingly, the reformers consistently supported the candidacy of Kent, Patterson, and McCormick. Their nominees, however, often inhibited by the same distaste for the masses, were reluctant campaigners and officeholders. For Kent, active in many important reform organizations, the "worst . . . experience" of his aldermanic campaign was "fight[ing]" for "an office I did not want except as an opportunity of rendering service." Echoing eastern elite mugwumps, he declared that "for a sensitive man it is an immense sacrifice to act as a candidate under any conditions. . . . The miserable task of shaking hands with people you despise, the pressure of petty grafters of all sorts, these and many other such trials. . . ."[154]

Few upper-class reformers questioned the distribution of wealth or the purity and prerogatives of the social and business elite. One exception was Louise de Koven Bowen, by birth and marriage linked to

Chicago's leading families, president of Hull House, and a social welfare and civic reform activist who used her leverage as stockholder in Pullman, Sears Roebuck, International Harvester, and U.S. Steel to complain about working conditions at their plants. She criticized low wages and long hours in local department stores and campaigned for a national minimum wage for women, and a national labor law, and against job, educational, and social discrimination against women and Blacks. But she also had "sympathy with the capitalists," thinking that the worker "often acts as badly as" the employer.[155] Joseph Medill Patterson was temporarily a greater champion of the underdog. Haunted by guilt over being an "idle-rich young man," in 1906 he resigned as reform public works commissioner and joined the Socialist party. Patterson now attacked amassers of great fortunes, like Field, and their legatees and advocated the labor theory of value, redistribution of wealth, and nationalization of industry.[156] Within ten years, however, he was vice-president of the family paper and a staunch reactionary.

In Chicago, even more than in Boston and much more than in New York, upper-class women participated in municipal reform. Political activity was but one facet of their civic prominence, a role encompassing charity and culture. Indeed, philanthropy drew them into reform. The Chicago Woman's Club (1876), which evolved from a cultural into a social welfare and reform organization, agitated for good government and full citizenship rights for women. Among its presidents were Ellen M. Henrotin and Helen S. Shedd, wives of famous Chicago businessmen, and its membership included Pullman's daughter, Louise de Koven Bowen, and the spouses of Palmer and Medill McCormick. In 1876 the club petitioned the mayor to appoint women to the board of education, in 1896 it organized the Chicago Political Equality League to promote women's suffrage and officeholding, in 1904 it endorsed a bill to give females the vote, in 1905 it supported civil service reform, and in 1909 it backed the enfranchisement of women in city elections.[157] Genteel ladies and society hostesses, apart from belonging to the Woman's Club, undertook a variety of political activities and functions. Federation vice-president Palmer managed her son's aldermanic race and sought an ambassadorship for her husband. Bowen was the only female member of the state Council of Defense in World War I, an associate Republican national committeewoman, president of the Woman's Roosevelt Republican Club, the Woman's City Club, and the Equal Suffrage Association, and an officer in the National Women's Suffrage Association. Mrs. Emmons Blaine, Cyrus McCormick's daughter, was a member of the board of education, Mrs. Medill McCormick was a congresswoman and a Republican national committeewoman, and Mrs. Kellogg (Janet Ayer) Fairbank, a member of two of the city's leading families, was a suffragette and a member of the executive committee of the Democratic national committee. Several of these figures were indefatigable campaigners against political, vocational, economic, and social sexism.[158] In a series of addresses at or concerning Chicago World's Fair of 1893 Palmer anticipated the arguments of modern-day women's liberationists. She attacked "the theory . . . that the sphere of woman is her home—that it is unfeminine, even monstrous, for her to wish to take a place beside or to compete with men in the lucrative industries. . . ." The president of the board of women managers of the fair, of which Henrotin was vice-president, wanted women to become "not only self-supporting, but able to assist in maintaining their families when necessary." She was "not a believer in the pedestal theory—never having seen an actual example of it—" and "suspect[ed] the motives of anyone advancing it." Women's "powers are the same as that of her brothers," and "like encouragement and fostering care may develop her to an equal point of usefulness."[159]

The Professions

As the Great Lakes settlement matured into a metropolis, the elite continued to derive power, prestige, and remuneration from its ties with the legal profession. Incentives to enter law and its contribution to upper-class ascendancy differed little from earlier days or from older, eastern patriciates. After the Civil War, however, Chicago's top-ranked attorneys were more likely to specialize in a given branch of litigation than had their antebellum predecesors. In the 1830s and '40s, when land speculation seemed the quickest road to wealth, many leaders of the bar devoted a large share of their general practices to real estate, as both lawyers and proprietors. When Chicago emerged as the nation's transportation center, the legal elite shifted its focus to railroad litigation.

Several eminent attorneys launched their careers in the offices of their predecessors. Real estate counselors L. C. P. Freer and George H. Manierre studied respectively with James H. Collins and Scammon. Paul Cornell, another real estate attorney, started out in the firm of Mark Skinner and Thomas Hoyne, corporation lawyer Edward Isham began with Hoyne, and railroad attorney Henry W. Blodgett with Scammon and Judd. Others, however, reflected the modern trend of attending law school. Many distinguished firms, as in the past, were family affairs. Father and son Edwin C. and Walter C. Larned had a large real estate practice. Brothers Daniel K. and Henry Tenney, and the latter's son Horace, represented the greatest Chicago banks and businesses. Railroad solicitors William C. Goudy and Frederick H. Winston and Isham took their sons into their firms. Prominent, but unrelated, lawyers also frequently practiced together. Freer and Cornell, Hoyne and railroad attorney Benjamin P. Ayer, and Isham and Lincoln, another railroad lawyer, formed partnerships. Lucrative fees and related business dealings made millionaires out of many leaders of the bar.[160]

Outstanding attorneys, as in other cities, took the initiative in professional organization and education. Leadership in these activities considerably overlapped, attesting to an extensive degree of integration among the legal elite. Presidents of the Chicago Bar Association (1874) included McCagg, Judd, railroad counselor Wirt Dexter, and other luminaries. Goudy, the first president, and Hoyne, the first vice-president, were among its founders. The Chicago Law Institute (1857), modeled on the New York Law Institute, which furnished practitioners with a fine law library, was headed by several officers of the association and many other renowned attorneys. Hoyne chaired the board of counselors of the law department of the old University of Chicago (1859–88), a body dominated by the famous practitioners who advised the great corporations and dominated the association and the institute.[161]

Professional self-evaluations varied markedly. Isaac N. Arnold "congratulate[d]" the Illinois Bar Association in 1881 "that thus far, the good name of our noble profession has been unstained. Fidelity to every trust, integrity and intelligence in the discharge of every duty, has characterized its members, whether at the Bar, or upon the Bench." Hoyne, an orphan who arrived in the city in 1837, a year after Arnold, and became mayor in 1874, secretary of the Chicago Astronomical Society, a founder of the public library, and married the daughter of noted physician John T. Temple, was more pessimistic. The "railroad corporations have come to assume the same relations [as the great merchants] toward the legal profession," he said in 1882. Through "unscrupulous use of money," they "command the most abject servility from their legal service . . . to engage in their basest service, for whatever purpose, either to establish or subvert as well public as private rights," to establish monopolies, and to "coerce citizens and subordinate society!" Superior court judge Elliott Anthony, Republican national convention delegate and an organizer of the public library, warned that "the practice of law ought not to be reduced to a simple trade or an ordinary collecting agency. . . ."[162]

The influence of distinguished lawyers extended beyond professional boundaries and business circles. They became judges or other officials in local, county, state, and federal governments, and participated as trustees in a variety of cultural and charitable institutions. These upper-class ties were strengthened by more intimate connections. Railroad counselor Tree married the daughter of Field, Goudy wedded Judd's child, Cornell was a brother-in-law of grain merchant Lunt, and George M. Kimbark's and Ayer's daughters entered the McCormick, Fairbank, and De Koven families.[163]

Unlike other elites, Chicagoans rarely took up medicine. The few who did, however, evinced the standard pattern of patrician practioners: They followed ancestral careers, studied and taught at institutions funded and directed by the rich and the well-born, and served on the staffs of prestigious hospitals and medical charities. Temple Stoughton Hoyne, grandson of Dr. Temple and son of lawyer Hoyne, graduated from Hahnemann Medical College and became a professor and treasurer in that institution. Newcomer Henry B. Favill, who moved to Chicago in 1893, also exhibited attributes found in high society doctors in different cities. Favill was on the Rush Medical College faculty and headed the Chicago Medical Society, the City Club of Chicago, and the Municipal Voters' League, served as a director of the United Charities, belonged to the selective Commercial Club, and had a son who was also a doctor. Other socially prominent physicians had careers similar to those of Favill and Hoyne. Frank Billings, for example, nephew of Albert M. Billings of the Peoples' Gas Light and Coke Co., was dean of Rush and a founder of the University of Chicago Medical School, and, along with other members of the family, of the university's hospital, Albert Merritt Billings Memorial (1916). Medicine shared with law a tendency toward interlocking leadership. As in the earlier period and similar to other metropolitan medical establishments, professors at the top medical schools staffed the best hospitals, both types of institutions depending heavily on upper-class support and management, and became officers in the local medical society.[164]

Elite Chicagoans did not replicate upper-class Bostonians, Charlestonians, and New Yorkers by achieving fame as physicians, educators, or ministers. Reluctance to enter these callings may be attributed to the city's lack of intellectual traditions or sectarian commitments compared to those of older urban establishments. The westerners, however, did excel in journalism, an occupation considered undignified by patriciates in New York, Philadelphia, and Boston. Between the Civil War and World War I, millionaire publishers William Bross, Medill, and Alfred Cowles of the *Tribune*, Melville Stone and Victor Lawson of the *Daily News*, Herman H. Kohlsaat of the *Record-Herald*, and William P. Nixon of the *Inter Ocean* and the *Record-Herald*, dominated journalism. They differed from publishers among the antebellum elite in specializing as newspapermen. In this capacity they were creative entrepreneurs: Bross was the original professional commercial journalist in the city; the *Tribune* used the first copper-faced type in Chicago, was the first machine-folded newspaper, and inaugurated in Chicago a household department for women; the *Daily News* was the city's first penny daily; Stone hired Chicago's initial columnist; and Lawson, in 1921, founded the earliest newspaper-owned radio station in the Midwest.[165]

The lords of the press belonged to the most exclusive clubs and sometimes took public office: Medill as mayor, Bross as alderman and lieutenant governor, Nixon as Collector of the Port of Chicago, and Stone on the board of education. Nixon and Kohlsaat were Republican national convention delegates. Except for Bross and Nixon, these figures also played key roles in civic reform. The editor-owners were also officers or directors in such cultural and civic organizations as the Chicago World's Fair, the Athenaeum, the Chicago Academy of Sciences, and the Chicago Festival Opera Association. Several also had extensive outside business interests, e.g., Kohlsaat and Medill in real estate and Stone as a bank president.

Offspring of the great newspaper proprietors married into other upper-class families, Medill and Kohlsaat daughters wedded respectively the nephew of Cyrus McCormick and the son of Palmer, and Joseph Patterson married Higinbotham's daughter. Medill and his McCormick and Patterson descendants established the only dynasty in Chicago journalism, owning newspapers in Cleveland, New York, and Washington.[166]

Charity

Charitable activities, as in earlier days and among elites in other places, attracted rich and well-born Chicagoans. Philanthropic motives and values changed little from the pre–Civil War decades and were similar to those of other contemporary urban patriciates. But major modifications occurred in the structure, if not in the function and meaning, of upper-class benevolence. Humanitarian institutions became larger in scale, centralized in organization, and professional in outlook and management. While the first development did not weaken the role of the upper stratum, whose wealth had also grown, the latter developments eventually curbed its influence by gradually replacing *noblesse oblige* amateurs with full-time careerists. For a time, however, the commitment of the affluent to the dependent was strengthened by the withdrawal of the establishment from government agencies to voluntary associations. Displacement from and distrust for municipal administration impelled urban elites to use private organizations for both political and philanthropic purposes.

Hospitals and benevolent societies founded by the antebellum upper order continued under the same type of patronage. Between the Civil War and World War I Lunt, Gage, Cyrus McCormick, George Armour, Sprague, John V. Farwell, John V. Farwell, Jr., and Charles L. Hutchinson helped run and support the YMCA and the orphan asylum. Henry Field chaired the board of the Home for the Friendless, a body that included wealthy and socially prominent capitalists. Some of the older institutions expanded their roles. The Relief and Aid Society, the largest local nineteenth-century relief agency, became the distributor of public and private assistance to victims of the 1871 fire. Its officers included Marshall Field, Pullman, Leiter, and many other community notables. The society coordinated Chicago charity, sending relief applicants to appropriate upper-class agencies and disbursing aid to these institutions.[167]

After the Civil War a number of organizations appeared resembling older ones in their particularistic approach to social problems and in elite management and financing. Among these institutions were the Old Ladies' Home, St. Luke's Free Hospital, and the Chicago Hospital for Women and Children, all founded in 1865; the Halstead Street Mission (1866), which gave workingmen and their children free industrial training and a kindergarten; the Newsboys' Home (1868); the Foundlings' Home (1871); the Armour Institute (1874), a medical dispensary and kindergarten; the Chicago Floating Hospital (1874), for the care of poor sick women and children; the Free Kindergarten Association (1881); and Presbyterian Hospital (1883). The Lake Geneva Fresh Air Association (1887) provided summer vacations in the country for slum children. The Children's Aid Society (1890) was formed to improve the condition of penurious youngsters, teach them trades, and find respectable homes for them. The St. James Episcopal Church sponsored a day nursery, convalescents' home, home for the aged and home for orphans, organized in 1892, and home for juvenile offenders (1893). St. Luke's Hospital and the St. James associations were founded by upper-class congregations respectively of Grace and St. James churches, and Arthur Ryerson became president of St. Luke's. Hibbard, head of the Foundlings' Home, and Carter H. Harrison were the largest contributors to this institution. Armour Institute was created by the meat-packing clan. Winston, Higinbotham, and Crane were presidents respectively of the Floating Hospital and the Free Kindergarten and Lake Geneva associations. Scammon, Crerar, Gustavus W. Swift, Gage, William Blair, and Cyrus H. McCormick, Jr., were founders and officers of the other organizations. Many of these philanthropists were active in several charities.[168]

Relief and remedial expenditures, either on a long-term basis or after a disaster, indicate the inadequacy of patrician benevolence for alleviating the distressed. Between October, 1871, and April, 1874, the Relief and Aid Society spent $4,415,454 to help victims of the fire and $581,328 for other assistance. In 1894, one of the worst depression years in American history, the society distributed $104,178, and its aid to the indigent averaged $30,000–40,000 annually during the late nineteenth century. The Civic Federation, a welfare as well as a reform organization, in 1899 gave $176,000 in money and clothing supplies to the poor. In 1893–94 the Children's Aid Society dispensed $5,716, and in the more prosperous year of 1891 the Lake Geneva Association and the Newsboys' Home disbursed $4,981 and $4,764 to their respective causes. Between 1876 and 1916 the Chicago Woman's Club, the wealthiest and most exclusive of the socially minded women's groups, contributed $457,401 to various charitable, cultural, and educational efforts.[169]

When the profit motive and civic beautification linked up with philanthropic impulses, the greatest efforts were made and the best results materialized. Inspired by New York's park movement, the elite backed similar projects in Chicago. As in Boston, New York, and Los Angeles, realtors and traction magnates favored these enterprises because they upgraded land values and contributed to the building boom. Other community leaders supported parks because they made the city more attractive and healthy and allegedly provided for the masses recreational outlets to relieve social strains that otherwise might erupt in attacks upon the wealthy. Three park districts were created in 1869, and by 1880 Chicago stood second only to Philadelphia in total park space. After a hiatus between 1880 and 1895, the business elite and prominent reformers, e.g., Kent and the Merchants' Club, became active in park expansion and in the founding of smaller green spaces and playgrounds. Prompted by the vast increase in the urban populace, especially among the poorer, immigrant minorities, this phase of the movement lasted until 1912.[170]

The park and playground movements were closely associated. Park commissioners administered the playgrounds, and Kent, in 1894, donated one of the early sites, a playground lot for Hull House. Brahmin Boston pioneered in this, as in many other civic activities, and Chicago, as usual, imitated the example of eastern cities and their older patriciates. The modern park and playground movement originated in Boston in 1886 and blueblood Joseph Lee was its chief theoretician and long-term (1910–37) president of the Playground and Recreation Association of America. At the height of the movement (1903–13) New York, followed by Chicago, expended the largest government sums for playgrounds. Organized play represented another elite-inspired reform directed toward uplifting and disciplining the urban masses. Specifically it sought to make poor children, frequently of foreign birth or parentage, productive and patriotic future citizens of industrial America.[171]

Newer kinds of institutions emerged even while traditional organizations were flourishing. The Chicago Charity Organization Society (1886) adopted the latest techniques of professionalization and centralization, but it, too, was originally dominated by Old Guard capitalists. Gage was a key force in the 1880s, and between 1886 and 1909 MacVeagh served as president. Of fifty-six directors in this period (89 percent of the total) with identified social and occupational backgrounds, fourteen were merchants, ten bankers, and seven lawyers. The average director belonged to two upper-class clubs and many to the Civic Federation, another example of genteel privatism in politics and charity as an antidote to public corruption.[172] Settlement houses represented another attempt to implement new types of philanthropy. Located in slum neighborhoods, their resident heads were usually more sympathetic to the poor than were the absentee altruists who ran the older organizations. Board members of the settlement houses included Mrs. Emmons Blaine, Louise de Koven, Kent, Lawson, Edward L. Ryerson, and Charles Crane; the Civic Federation, the Woman's Club, and the Woman's City Club assisted in the movement.[173]

Long before genteel females became active in settlement houses they participated extensively in benevolent enterprises. Wives and daughters of the Pullman, Medill, Hibbard, Scammon, Judd, Armour, and other distinguished clans acted as officers or trustees of the Home for the Friendless, the Hospital for Women and Children, the orphan asylum, St. Luke's and Passavant hospitals, the St. James' nursery and convalescents' home, the home for juvenile offenders, and other philanthropies. The Woman's Club sponsored free kindergartens, initiated the Truant Aid Society (1889) and the School Childrens' Aid Society (1894), and raised money for the Illinois Industrial School for Boys and other humanitarian ventures. Several grand dames were philanthropic and political activists. Bowen served as treasurer of Hull House, vice-president of the United Charities, executive committeewoman of Chicago's Council for Social Agencies, vice-president of the Woman's Board of St. Luke's, and president of the women's board of Passavant.[174] Chicago upper-class women far surpassed those in New York in their commitment to social welfare.

Upper-class males also filled multiple leadership posts. Scammon served as an alderman and state senator, and headed the board of education. He helped organize Hahnemann Hospital, the Old Ladies' Home, the Illinois Humane Society, and the Chicago Hospital for Women, presiding over the board of the latter. Massachusetts-born Elbridge G. Keith, a self-made millionaire, arrived in Chicago in 1858 and became president of the National Bank of Chicago and the Chicago Clearing-House. He was also president of the YMCA and the orphan asylum, and treasurer of the Bible Society, the Home for the Friendless, and the Bureau of Charities. Keith was a Republican national convention delegate, a ward boss, a member of the board of education, a director of the World's Columbian Exposition, and headed the Union League, Commercial Club, and Bankers' Club. Railroad president and millionaire railroad supplies manufacturer and wholesaler John Crerar, banker and board of trade president Charles L. Hutchinson, multimillionaire hardware wholesaler Adolphus Clay Bartlett, and self-made clothing manufacturer Henry W. King had equally impressive civic credentials.[175]

Alms-giving varied widely, as much a matter of personal taste as were investments of time and talent. Bartlett left only $62,000 to charity. But this small legacy he claimed was due to a lifetime of donations, including $155,000 to the University of Chicago. Richard T. Crane, on the other hand, designated $2,135,000 (10.8 percent) of his estate for public purposes. Armour biographers estimated that he gave away $15 million while alive and left the Armour Mission and Institute $2.8 million (2.8 percent) of his fortune. Cyrus H. McCormick, like most of the super-rich, turned to benevolence after becoming a millionaire. While alive McCormick dispensed about $550,000, and within five years of his death $475,000 (4.75 percent) of his fortune went for humanitarian causes, mostly to educational and religious institutions and to the YMCA. Marshall Field's altruistic expenditures also postdated his commercial success. He donated approximately $2.5 million between 1890 and 1901 and at his death another $8.2 million (about 5 percent of his estate), mostly to the Field Museum of Natural History. Out of an accumulation of $20 million, Mrs. Palmer allotted $515,000 to civic organizations and $100,000 worth of paintings to the Chicago Art Institute. Cobb left $255,000 (slightly over 4 percent of his fortune) to charity, and Insull, until 1920, averaged only $3,000–4,000 a year for civic causes. Lesser business potentates were sometimes more generous. Charles L. Hutchinson willed at least $455,000 to charitable and cultural institutions. Harris, the broker and YMCA vice-president, gave away more than $555,000 in his lifetime and another $500,000 in bequests. Martin A. Ryerson, son of Martin Ryerson and another Commercial Club president, earmarked two-ninths of his $6 million legacy to the art institute. Charles J. Hull, a poor boy from Connecticut who became a real estate lawyer and operator, posthumously contributed $7 million to public institutions. Crerar left nearly $3.5 million to charity and only $500,000 to relatives. Hobart Williams, scion of a great realtor, assigned his entire $5 million estate to charity, most of it to upper-class Chicago agencies, despite leaving the city long before he died.[176] Donations varied according to individual conscience and capacity, but usually went to patrician-patronized welfare and cultural associations.

Apart from upper-class money and management, high society and philanthropy intersected at charity balls. One historian of Chicago's *beau monde* dates its birth at the Charity Ball of 1868. This affair was run by Medill, Pullman, Arnold, Ogden's brother, and Scammon. These annual events, later conducted by Mrs. Palmer, combined the socially elect with anyone who could afford admission. They became well-publicized displays of lavish consumption and modest altruism; the celebration of 1889 netted $12,000 for benevolent causes. Smaller, less fancy dances—like the affair given in 1871 by Mrs. Harrison for the Half-Orphan Asylum—were organized for specific charities.[177]

Elite benevolence resembled in values and motives, as well as in organization, upper-class philanthropy in other cities. Bowen was "brought up with the idea that some day I would inherit a fortune, . . . that the responsibility of money was great, and that God would hold me accountable for the manner in which I used my talents." Chicago Woman's Club members Henriette G. Frank and Amalie H. Jerome expressed a secular version of the stewardship of wealth, claiming that "women of leisure and culture, animated by a noble desire to solve some of the knotty problems left to us by the past are a potent factor for good, and a force that should not be despised."[178] Several tycoons found that charity eased their anxieties. Cyrus H. McCormick felt that "works of benevolence" counteracted "an increase in cares and responsibility" brought on by "increased means and success in business life. . . ." Others emphasized altruism and amelioration. Philip D. Armour spent millions to educate the "children of the unfortunate and to give needy work." Armour Institute of Technology, his favorite charity, was both "a character training school" and "a manual training school." Richard T. Crane made the fullest statement about the motives and consequences of upper-class philanthropy. He, too, believed it "preeminently the duty of rich men and women to expend their surplus wealth largely in improving the condition under which the poor, the unfortunate, the degraded, and the criminal class live." This obligation was reinforced by "the fact that in many cases the wealth of the rich has been wrung from the poor." Self-defense also motivated largesse. The destitute masses reminded Crane of France prior to the Revolution of 1789 and he warned that irresponsible wealth created anarchists. The remedy for maldistribution of wealth was "the dispersing of the great fortunes" at the deaths of their makers so that "the bulk of them should go to the poor."[179] His millions, however, were not disposed of in this fashion.

Culture

Between the Civil War and World War I, high culture in Chicago, as in earlier times and other places, was deemed a worthy endeavor of the urban gentry. Upper-class activity in Chicago differed from Boston, New York, and Charleston in that the western elite had fewer careerists in education, religion, the arts and letters, and science; its leading cultural figures had a more democratic outlook; a specific event gave great impetus to its intellectual and esthetic endeavors; and it played an important role in mass communications through newspaper ownership. In addition, its major efforts, the public library, museums, opera, and symphony, lagged at least one or two decades behind the founding of comparable institutions, except for the New York Public Library, in New York and Boston. Most of these differences and widespread imitation of eastern culture resulted from the relatively recent advent of Chicago and its establishment. As mentioned above, many self-made tycoons placed little value on higher learning or on artistic or intellectual callings. When Reginald De Koven left John V. Farwell & Co. for music, his wife remembered that her husband's uncle, John De Koven, and her father, Charles B. Farwell, "expressed the opinion that music should be considered as a diversion and should not be seriously followed."[180] Similar disapproval was encountered by Brahmin literati at an early stage of the Boston aristocracy. The Columbian Exposition of 1893, better known as the Chicago World's Fair, was the event that fostered the cultural as well as the business life of the city. It was conceived, funded, and directed by the establishment. Gage, Baker, and Higinbotham were successive presidents of the exposition board of directors. Martin A. Ryerson chaired the committee on exhibitions, Ferdinand W. Peck the financial committee, Mrs. Palmer headed the lady managers, Burnham and Root, the favorite architectural firm of the elite, planned and supervised construction, and virtually every eminent Chicagoan appeared on the board of directors.[181] Notwithstanding various differences, the upper class shared with peer groups in other cities the fundamental features of elite culture. Metropolitan establishments patronized and managed the same types of institutions, and their activities functioned as an insignia of rank, a symbol of community leadership, a means of ideological cohesion, and a vehicle for social order. Multipurposed genteel culture in Chicago and other towns reflected the fact that its foremost proponents invariably were outstanding capitalists, professionals, philanthropists, and society figures.

RELIGION

Religion strengthened the upper class through common membership in select churches and sectarian charities, and by imposing deferential norms upon the lower classes through such agencies as Sunday schools and church-related benevolent organizations. Many antebellum shrines, St. James, the First and Second Presbyterian, Grace, and the First Congregational, retained their patrician status. Leading Chicagoans were trustees and officers of these churches and their clergy had intimate ties with the elite. Robert W. Patterson, son of the minister of the Second Presbyterian, married Medill's daughter, and several ministers of the Episcopal Church of the Ascension were offspring of early city merchants.[182] In these churches were performed the rites of passage—baptism, communion, marriage, and funerals—that solidified the patriciate. St. James and Grace were the most exclusive congregations. "It was a well-known saying" in the 1870s, declared Hibbard's daughter, "that no one was 'in society' unless he or she belonged to St. James. . . ."[183]

The upper class participated in church charities, the YMCA, and the Bible Society. In 1885, for example, Harvey headed the latter association. Despite this involvement, Cyrus H. McCormick alone of the great tycoons made an avocation of Christian service. Presbyterian causes, particularly the relocation of the New Albany Seminary to Chicago, preoccupied him.[184]

EDUCATION

The elite was more involved in educational than in religious matters. Distinguished Chicagoans originated the public school system, and after the Civil War continued to serve with regularity on the board of education. Four of the six millionaires of 1892 in this post established or belonged to leading families. Board service appealed to upper-class imperatives of civic duty and leadership, and to its conviction that public schools upgraded the masses and preserved order. Politicians who displaced the establishment from municipal government regarded this quasi-honorific office, safely removed from powerful and profitable positions, a natural vehicle, like park commissionerships, for the cultural pretensions and superior education of the gentility. Nonetheless, patrician influence, as measured by frequency of board memberships or policy-making initiatives, declined considerably from its antebellum peak. The elite supplemented its official role in mass education by sponsoring kindergartens and manual training. The upper-class Free Kindergarten and Froebel associations took the lead in establishing early schooling, especially for the poor. In 1884 the Chicago Commercial Club, a conclave of tycoons and patricians, financed the Chicago Manual Training School.[185]

The privileged considered management of public schools an elite responsibility, but, like other patriciates, sent their children to private academies. This choice again exemplifies the upper-class impulse to withdraw from public institutions. During the 1870s, Lake Forest Academy, Harvard School, and Ira Allen's Academy were attended by boys from Chicago's first families. A couple of decades later they went to Chicago Latin School. Their sisters attended the Chicago Academy and, after it closed, Dearborn Seminary.[186]

As patrician influence ebbed in public schooling it increased in private institutions of higher learning. In this respect, too, the establishment coincided with older urban elites. Business and civic leaders were trustees of Rush, Woman's, and Hahnemann medical colleges and of the Chicago Homeopathic College. The favorite causes of Philip D. Armour and Cyrus H. McCormick were respectively the Armour Technological Institute and the McCormick Theological Seminary.

Armour founded and gave the institute $5 million. Swifts, Pattersons, Deerings, and Lunts made handsome donations to Northwestern University, and, along with others of equal repute, sat on its board of trustees.[187]

The University of Chicago (1891), like Columbia, Harvard, the College of Charleston, and the University of Pennsylvania, was the favorite local educational institution of its city's establishment. Field, Ogden, Hull, and Martin Ryerson, second president of the board of trustees, each donated over $500,000, and Yerkes, Sidney A. Kent, Cobb, Bartlett, and Charles L. Hutchinson were also generous benefactors. More than half of the original trustees were or had been major corporate, railroad, or banking officials, or possessors of great wealth, and many were linked with such other upper-class organizations as the art institute, the public library, the Union League, Chicago, and Commercial clubs, the Auditorium Association, or the elite Jewish organization, the Standard Club. Hutchinson introduced the prospective university to the business elite and arranged for the appeal to match John D. Rockefeller's initial grant to take place at the Commercial Club. Martin A. Ryerson's appointment as president of the original board was applauded by university planners because he was "universally respected, with plenty of leisure, with great wealth and very close to the wealthiest and most liberal citizens." The service on this body of Hutchinson (the original treasurer), Ryerson, and Ferdinand W. Peck further gratified the friends of the university because "We shall have in the responsible financial positions three of the leading young businessmen of the city . . . & we shall then have a pull on the wealth of Chicago that we can get in no other way. Those three men can raise more money than any other three men in Chicago."[188] The endowment, however, differed from the financial bases of upper-class colleges in older cities. Plebian-born, nonresident Rockefeller's gifts made up better than four-fifths of the total contributions in the first quarter-century of the university's existence.

The paradox of exogamous funding accompanied by endogamous upper-class management may be explained by the tendency of eminent Chicagoans, as well as elites in Philadelphia and New York, to go to or enroll their sons at Yale, Harvard, and Princeton rather than Columbia or the Universities of Chicago and Pennsylvania. Although trustees at the latter institutions were frequently from the local upper order, this situation illustrates the emerging metropolism which standardized patriciates from different cities. Not only did Chicago's upper class attempt to replicate an Ivy League institution to gain status for the enclave and city, the establishment also sent its children to eastern prep schools and colleges where they could learn patrician behavior firsthand. "Social conditions" in education "were always paramount with our good mother," recollected patrician Arthur B. Meeker, Jr. She made her youngest daughter go to a "place in Virginia where the girls rode to hounds every day and nearly everybody was a Biddle." Another, contradictory, reason for the relative stinginess of notable Chicagoans was that many of the richest magnates disparaged higher learning. Armour and McCormick wished their sons to enter the family firm rather than college, Crane denounced universities as a fraudulent waste of money, time, and talent, and Field and Insull thought that undergraduate life frustrated the youthful quest for self-improvement and occupational advancement.[189] Armour, Field, McCormick, Crane, and Insull were self-made successes, but inherited wealth showed more respect for higher education. The most active trustees, Hutchinson, Peck, and Ryerson, were second-generation gentlemen of affluence.

Aside from policymakers on the board, elite Chicago performed social services for the university. President William Rainey Harper asked Mrs. John J. Glessner to start the Monday Morning Reading Class (1894) for newly arrived faculty wives to become acquainted with genteel ladies. Robert Morss Lovett remembered from his undergraduate days "the hospitality of a section of the merchant aristocracy. . . . Families of Spragues, Bartletts, Glessners, McCormicks exercised a kindly patronage."[190]

ARTS, LETTERS, AND SCIENCE

Support for religious and educational enterprises that stirred civic pride, promoted public welfare, and enhanced upper-class cohesion and community control transcended historical eras or city limits. Little difference existed in the manners and motives of those who worshipped at Grace Church in New York or in Chicago, or in the values and aims of opulent donors or trustees at the University of Chicago or at Harvard. Continuity also manifested itself in cultural activities of more limited scope and resources. Chicago's historical society and academy of sciences continued to flourish under the same upper-class patronage and supervision as in former times and resembled their analogues in other places. Between 1861 and 1877, Newberry, Scammon, Arnold, and Washburne headed the society, and Scammon and other local eminents presided over the academy. Upper-class figures often simultaneously acted as officers, trustees, and major contributors in both organizations.[191]

While the historical society kept up its researches and publications and the academy of sciences its experiments, expeditions, museum, and journal, other old upper-class associations foundered. The Mechanics' Institute and the Chicago Lyceum, which offered reading matter and lectures to workers, declined after the Panic of 1857. The Chicago Library Association, formerly the Young Men's Association, was bankrupted by the 1871 fire. Conversely, traditional upper-class institutions continued to emerge. The Chicago Astronomical Society was formed in 1862, chiefly through the efforts and money of Scammon, its first president.[192] The disappearance of the older libraries was more than compensated for by the creation of the Newberry Library (1885) with a $2 million posthumous grant from its namesake, and the Crerar Library (1895), made possible by a $2.5 million legacy from Crerar. The donor and trustees of the Newberry were leading professional, business, and cultural leaders, several of them veterans of earlier library societies. They conceived of the institution as a noncirculating, research library managed by an economic and social elite for the use of a scholarly elite. The originator and trustees of the Crerar Library came from the same social stratum. Crerar's legacy, as stated in his will, was prompted by conventional upper-class cultural and charitable impulses—the Christian and civic stewardship of the rich, especially in the city where they made their fortune, a desire to build character, and a Victorian moral code.[193]

Helen Horowitz aptly dubs most of the patrician-sponsored libraries and historical and scientific societies particularistic undertakings run by the elite for special groups such as scholars and genteel dilettantes. The academy of sciences and the astronomical society had a clientele of professional investigators and amateur dabblers, the Young Men's Association was a subscription library, the lyceum charged rent for books on loan, and the Newberry library and the historical society offered its services to historians, antiquarians, and memorialists. Upper-class clubs devoted to the pursuit of knowledge or the muses constituted another variety of patricularistic association, combining, as did the more formal organizations, intellectuality with sociability. The exclusive Fortnightly Club (1873), Chicago's oldest and most intellectually renowned woman's club, was dedicated to improving the mind through lectures and essays on literature, art, and history. A candidate had to be nominated by two members who vouched for her mental qualities, social status, and potential usefulness in the organization. Mrs. Franklin MacVeagh was a president, and the wives of Palmer, Field, and other great capitalists were members. The Fortnightly, the Chicago Woman's during its early years, the Friday (1887), the Wednesday, and the Junior Fortnightly clubs had identical interests, drew their membership from the same social stratum, and ladies frequently joined several of these associations. Fortnightlies de Koven and Henrotin initiated the Friday Club and the former became its first president. "These organizations," wrote Henrotin, "in the beginning were simple in form and usually literary or purely charitable in character, such subjects as religion, suffrage, and political economy being carefully shunned. Friendly intercourse and self-improvement were the objects sought."[194] Other associations of this type were the Anonymous Club (c.1875), a gathering of North Side upper-class men and women who put on amateur theatrical productions and wrote literary essays, and the Caxton Club (1895), a collection of rich and prestigious bibliophiles. A number of organizations—the Twentieth Century Club (1889), the Little Room (1893), the Contributors' Club, and the Cliff-Dwellers (1909)—mixed socially prominent patrons with artists and writers, thus serving as intermediaries between patricians and the intelligentsia. The Little Room, which included industrialist and civic reformer Franklin H. Head, sculptor Lorado Taft, poet Harriet Monroe, publisher Melville Stone, Jr., and novelist H. C. Chatfield-Taylor—Chicagoans with intellectual interests and inherited social status and riches—typified such organizations.[195]

The formation of traditional upper-class cultural institutions was overshadowed by the advent of new types of elite-run institutions. Horowitz suggests that the appearance of the Chicago Public Library (1872), Chicago Symphony Orchestra (1891), Field Museum of Natural History (1893), and the transformation of the Chicago Art Institute (1879) in the 1880s signified the emergence of upper-class cultural associations that were larger in size and sought to reach the urban community rather than a restricted enclave.[196] This shift in emphasis paralleled new departures in philanthropy represented by the Relief and Aid Society, the Charity Organization Society, and the United Charities.

The movement for a public library began in 1871–72, mainly through the urging of Mayor Medill and his newspaper. Scammon, Ogden, Field, McCormick, and other local luminaries were among the founders, and Hoyne headed the first board of trustees. Incorporators of the earlier libraries came from the same enclave, and many active in the public institution had been involved in the private societies. Hoyne, for example, once presided over the Young Men's Association. Of 100 leaders in public and private library movements, listed by a historian of the public library, most immigrated from the East, especially from New England, two-thirds were professionals, and all but nine of the remainder were businessmen.[197]

Many elite Chicagoans were interested in art as patrons or collectors, and the art institute, therefore, became an upper-class cause. It was part of the museum movement that engaged eastern urban aristocracies whom the westerners often emulated. A number of leading Chicagoans owned large collections of paintings, and many became active in the institute and donated their pictures. Their individual efforts and the founding of the Chicago Academy of Design (1866) and the Society of Decorative Art (1878), both under upper-class sponsorship, paved the way for the institute. The academy trained artists and exhibited paintings. The society, started by grand dames "to bring to our city the knowledge of such arts," later transferred many of its holdings to the institute.[198] In 1879 the academy was replaced by the institute, a typical venture to refine public taste and morality through elite tutorship. These aims would be accomplished through a museum where art would be viewed free of charge by people from all walks of life, and through institute lectures and exhibitions held in such public places as the city schools. Art is not "something apart from daily life," wrote Hutchinson, head of the board of trustees and the chief force in the institute. He expressed the organization's philosophy that art "exists for the common heart and for ordinary culture." In "the humblest walks of life you will find the most conspicuous examples of virtue" and "a true appreciation of Art." This populist argument concluded that "Art for art's sake is a selfish and erroneous doctrine . . . a service of Art for those who live and work and strive in a humdrum world is the true doctrine and one that every Art Museum should cherish." Consequently, the "institute should be measured by the service it renders to the community in which it stands." The "Trustees of our Art Museums . . . are endeavoring to diffuse information about Art and to develop a just appreciation of Art among the masses." Applying this dictum locally, Hutchinson proudly asserted that "the Art Institute is nobly democratic. It exists for the people, and they appreciate its advantages." The institute, which Hutchinson evaluated according to Boston and New York standards of genteel culture, had also brought credit to the metropolis. In 1888 he felt that Chicago was culturally "one of the most barren cities." By 1907 he was no longer "ashamed of Chicago as an art center. Few cities have relatively accomplished as much during the past twenty years. In no other city is the influence of art more directly felt by the masses."[199] A measure of the institute's success in reaching the people was that in the year 1910–11 it had 861,000 visitors compared to 703,000 for New York's Metropolitan Museum of Art, despite Gotham's larger population, and 224,000 for the Boston Museum of Fine Arts, despite the Hub's greater reputation as a cultural center. It also exceeded the Philadelphia Academy visitorship and had been outdrawing these institutions since 1897. On the other hand, its endowment fell far short of the New York and Boston museums. The discrepancy in support between the Chicago and New York museums may have reflected the location of the latter in the nation's wealthiest metropolis, but Chicago, in turn, was richer than Boston.[200]

Museum trustees constituted a who's who of the upper social and economic echelon. After short terms by George Armour and Leiter, Hutchinson headed the board from 1880 to 1924 and Martin A. Ryerson and Gage respectively were its long-term vice-president and treasurer. Hutchinson and Ryerson, the most active figures, were mainly responsible for acquisitions. The upper class contributed money and art as well as time and energy. Its most valuable gifts were, beginning in the 1890s, the acquisition of the art collections of Higinbotham, Ryerson, Henry

Field, Albert A. Munger, Mrs. Palmer, and Samuel M. Nickerson.[201]

The inner workings of elite boards were disclosed by Palmer, whose husband was an institute trustee, requesting that Hutchinson, "so old and valued a friend," make her son a director. Possibly fearing that friendship alone might not "realize my wish," she mentioned that the Palmers took a "great interest in the Institute and would like to give evidence of it."[202] Another son also became a director and was later president of the institute.

In architecture, as in art, the East influenced upper-class standards. Between the 1870s and World War I, America's multimillionaires, particularly New York's robber barons, engaged in an orgy of competitive and conspicuous expenditure. Resplendent mansions and mausoleums and imposing skyscrapers symbolized their triumphs and established their credentials. Thus did they carry on a tradition of the wealthy and the mighty at least as old as ancient Egypt. The foremost architect of the 1870s and '80s was Henry Hobson Richardson, a devotee of the Romanesque fashion. A member of Harvard's elite clubs, he settled near his Brahmin friends in a Boston suburb. Richardson was responsible for several Brahmin mansions, a couple of buildings at Harvard, and Boston's Trinity Church. His most famous followers were Charles Follen McKim, William Mead, and Stanford White. McKim and White were draftsmen for Richardson before going into partnership with Mead. In the 1880s and '90s the principals in the firm built Newport mansions and Manhattan townhouses for New York's premier capitalists and society figures, and planned the Pennsylvania Railroad station and the Columbia University campus in that city. McKim, Mead and White also created the Boston Public Library edifice (1887), an indication that in architecture, as in other facets of culture, the Athens of America was beginning to defer to New York, the Rome of America. New Yorker Richard Morris Hunt competed with McKim, Mead and White for clients among the Vanderbilts, Astors, and other Gilded Age giants. Potential patrons could choose between the French Gothic style of Hunt or the Italian Renaissance imitations of McKim, Mead and White. Along with Richardson and McKim, Morris studied at the École des Beaux Arts, and, like many architects for the affluent, he married into a distinguished maritime family.

Although most wealthy and well-known Chicagoans preferred local talent, noted eastern architects were also sought after by an upper class eager to emulate Atlantic Coast elites. White helped design the summer home of Cyrus H. McCormick, Richardson constructed the Field Wholesale Building and the homes of Wayne MacVeagh and John J. Glessener, and Hunt built Field's residence. According to renowned Chicago architect Louis H. Sullivan, Burnham, the favorite builder for the town's elite, as superintendent of construction at the World's Fair wanted to place all the exposition work with the eastern masters and apologized to them for the presence of western designers. Repudiating his earlier iconoclastic work, Burnham became a champion of classicism and left the planning of the fair to Hunt and McKim, Mead and White.[203]

Chicago architects differed from the easterners in emphasizing function, engineering, and innovation over tradition and ornament and in being more apt to celebrate than conceal the business functions of their commercial skyscrapers. This was the essence of Sullivan's greatness, but it was also true of Burnham and Root (1873), despite Burnham's later embrace of traditionalism and John Wellborn Root's tutelage by James Renwick, Jr. In the 1880s and '90s, proper Bostonians had long become an aristrocracy and New York capitalists were undergoing gentrification. But Chicago's *parvenu* tycoons were relatively unabashed and unpolished titans of the marketplace and wanted their business edifices to proclaim their entrepreneurial achievements. In other respects, however, Chicago architects resembled their eastern counterparts. Burnham and Root created houses, clubs, office and cultural buildings, and monuments for the elite. The fashionable Chicago architects moved easily in exalted circles of culture, commerce, and society. Burnham married the daughter of a stockyard entrepreneur, was close to Theodore Thomas, conductor of the Chicago Symphony, helped raise funds for it, and served on its board. Among Burnham's other friends were Ryerson, Ayer, and Hutchinson; he was also a director in the Continental and Commercial Bank and constructed its building, and belonged to the Union League, Commercial, and Chicago clubs. Dankmar Adler and Sullivan, who built the auditorium (1889) for Ferdinand W. Peck to house the Chicago Opera festival, joined the Union League, and Sullivan was also in the Chicago Club. The auditorium, like many other civic projects, was first aired at the Commercial Club and much of the money was raised there and at the Union League. After 1900 Howard V. D. Shaw was the prime builder of the patriciate's domiciles and public buildings. Shaw belonged to several country clubs, became treasurer of the Second Presbyterian Church and a trustee of the United Charities and of the art institute. He married a child of a millionaire shoe jobber and clubman, and his daughter wedded a partner in a firm that handled wills, trusts, and divorces for Chicago's leading families. Like Burnham, his style derived from Europe. Dramatic innovator Frank Lloyd Wright, however, received no commissions from the establishment. After World War I the center of modern architecture moved farther west to San Francisco and Los Angeles. Many modern architects relocated there from the East. California, with its newer elites and affinity for *au courant* impulses, became to mid-twentieth-century architectural innovators what Chicago has been to the revolutionaries of an earlier day.[204]

Art, commerce, civic pride, and upper-class leadership coalesced in Burnham's Plan of Chicago. The idea originated in the Merchants' Club in 1906 and was taken over, in the next year, by the Commercial Club when the two organizations merged. Civic reformer MacVeagh, Bartlett, and John V. Farwell, Jr., were on the club's Committee for the Plan. The Commercial Club gave $300,000 for the project, with additional support from the business and social establishment and municipal bond issues. The plan aimed to improve transportation facilities and traffic movement in the business district, to beautify the city through developing the park system, and in general to bring order and esthetics to Chicago's economic growth. Burnham told the Merchants' Club that his plan would beautify the city, but "of far more immediate importance" it would stimulate "material prosperity." He discerned "among our well-to-do people" a tendency "to spend much time and money elsewhere . . . because life at home is not so pleasant." The Plan would halt this "constant drain upon the resources of the town. . . ." Despite powerful backing, its proponents accomplished before World War I only the widening of a few downtown avenues.[205]

The Field Museum of Natural History was the scientific counterpart of the art institute. Organized, funded, and administered by the elite to educate the masses, they rose out of the museum movement that swept the country in the last third of the nineteenth century. The Field Museum was engendered by the natural history display at the World's Fair and was initially housed in the fair's fine arts building. Peck, Pullman, Leiter, Armour, and other leading citizens were among the founders. Capitalist Edward E. Ayer headed the first board of trustees, and this body long remained an upper-class preserve. Field gave $1 million after Ayer told him that his fame might vanish "unless you do something outside of a business way to perpetuate it." The campaign for the museum was identical to those that launched the art institute and the University of Chicago. "At the various Chicago clubs I came into familiar association with the leading men of the city at the table and at card games," said Ayer, "so I began on all occasions to urge the importance of our getting material for a museum at the close of the World's Fair. . . . These men endorsed and backed up my remarks. Of course Marshall Field was the richest we had among us in those days . . . and on social occasions when I would meet Mr. Field I began to talk to him (as others did, too) about giving a million dollars to start with."[206] Ayer's pleas were successful. Field contributed $1,430,000 before he died and left the museum $8 million, his family donated another $10 million, and Stanley Field became president of the board in 1908. Pullman, Higinbotham, Harris, several Cranes, and Ayer were also generous contributors. Like the institute, the museum reached the urban community through lecture services for the public schools, lending out exhibits, and sponsoring tours for school children.[207]

Like New York, Boston, and Charleston, music in Chicago did not tap upper-class resources to the same degree as did art, architecture, and science. Nevertheless, the establishment patronized amateur opera performances at the Apollo Club (1875), modeled on its Boston namesake, and semiannual orchestral concerts given by the Chicago Music Festival Association (1881). The symphony and the opera, to a greater extent than the art and natural history museums or the public library, were directed toward the elite. Opera in Chicago, as in New York, was an opportunity to show off high society. President Peck of the Chicago Festival Opera (1884) conceived of the auditorium to house opera in a different way than the "Met" functioned for Mrs. Astor's Four Hundred. He "regard[ed] the Metropolitan Opera House of New York where the whole structure is sacrificed to boxes with infinite scorn and patriotic distaste." The auditorium should represent "the future and not the corrupted past."[208] Despite Peck's wishes, Chicago imitated New York. The auditorium contained expensive season boxes bought, for reasons of civic pride and conspicuous consumption, by the great capitalists, several of whom were festival directors. The maiden season banquet took place at the Union League, whose members included auditorium boxholders, auditorium association directors, and eight of the ten original festival directors. Not until 1910 did the city have its own opera company. Again the influence of New York was in display: original directors included Otto H. Kahn, Harry Payne Whitney, and other New York multimillionaires. Harold F. McCormick, son of the reaper king, who became president of the Chicago Opera Company, and Dawes, vice-president, were the chief fund-raisers. John C. Shedd, Field's successor, Richard T. Crane, and Charles L. Hutchinson were among the Chicago directors. By 1914 the New Yorkers had left, but the company had also gone bankrupt. The following year the Chicago Opera Association appeared, led and supported by the principals of its defunct predecessor. Until 1922 its deficits were made up by the Harold F. McCormicks. At the first performance, Arthur Meeker, surveying the splendor of his enclave, "had never seen the pagentry of the East better staged than right here."[209]

Pianist, music critic, and light opera composer Reginald De Koven, one of the few upper-class figures professionally committed to the arts, argued in the 1880s that westerners are "behind our brethren of the East in our appreciation for, or encouragement of, music as an art or means . . . to refine and elevate the popular taste." The absence of an orchestra in Chicago is a "disgrace to our culture and public spirit." If "our leading men" emulated "Henry Lee Higginson and the Boston Symphony" and took "the initiative . . . the rest would be easy."[210] De Koven's plea was answered in 1889 by the formation of the orchestral association. Primarily through the efforts of C. Norman Fay, president of the Gas Trust and the Chicago Telephone Companies, the association founded the Chicago Symphony Orchestra. Fay in 1910 complimented the founders, contributors, and trustees for doing "for Chicago what Major Higginson has done singly in Boston, and indeed they could not have had a better exemplar either in deed or in manner." Fairbank, the first president and once head of the festival association, Fay, and other prominent capitalists and civic leaders helped underwrite the orchestra. Subsequent officers and trustees came from the same group and frequently were descendants of the founders. The orchestra was an upper-class institution. Conductor Theodore Thomas married Fay's sister, the first concert was a society event, and thirty-two of the original fifty-one guarantors were Union Leaguers. Unlike the museums or the public library, high-priced seats and programs exclusively devoted to old masters prevented the symphony from disseminating culture to the larger community. It resembled the opera in having limited funds, a limited audience, and continual deficits. George E. Adams, ex-president of the association, captured its aristocratic spirit at the dedication in 1904 of Burnham's Orchestra Hall. "Disinterested patrons," he declared, must exist if "art is to find its highest expression."[211]

In this address Adams also expressed a democratic vision shared by Hutchinson and Peck. This persistent, if not always dominant, theme in patrician Chicago's cultural endeavors received firmer emphasis from the newer western elite than from the gentry in Boston or Charleston. Orchestra Hall "is not the easy gift of millionaires," claimed Adams. The "poorest contributor of the smallest sum has the same right as any other to look on this beautiful building with pride and a sense of ownership." In "this country the most effective patron of Art is an association like this, in which rich and poor, learned and unlearned men and women, merchants and bankers, professional men and workingmen, join hands to serve the higher life of the community in which they live." Adams concluded on a note of civic pride and promise present at every inaugural of the city's great cultural monuments and institutions. Chicago had again proved her reputation as "the most public-spirited city in the world" and demonstrated her "noble" future as "a centre of influence, intellectual and artistic as well as industrial, a school of the nation, as Pericles declared that Athens was the school of Greece."[212]

The upper-class commitment to literature, as to music, was weaker than in art. Novelists Hamlin Garland and Henry B. Fuller claimed that Chicago supported artists, sculptors and architects, but not writers, and Garland left the city for this reason. Bluebloods in Boston, New York, or

Charleston won renown as poets, novelists, essayists, or historians, but Chatfield-Taylor was a rare exception to the dearth of authors from distinguished Chicago families. Late-nineteenth-century Chicago became the intellectual capital of mid-America, a consequence of its economic predominance in this region and its tremendous population expansion. The business and social elite, however, played a marginal role in the literary phase of this upsurge. *America* (1888–91), the earliest upper-class magazine, was a short-lived, highbrow *belles lettres* and political journal, founded and edited by Chatfield-Taylor. De Koven was the music critic, and financial backing came from several prominent businessmen. *The Weekly Magazine* (1876–84), another ephemeral literary and political effusion, was funded by Pullman, Charles B. Farwell, and Field. The *Dial* (1880) was the only permanent intellectual organ founded in these years, but neither its staff nor money came from magnates or old families. In the next generation *Poetry Magazine* (1912) was supported by Burnham, Hutchinson, Edward L. Ryerson, Insull, and second-generation Deerings, Palmers, McCormicks, and Pullmans. While printing traditional and genteel verse like conventional upper-class periodicals, the foremost modern poets appeared on its pages. Melville Stone's son published the *Dial* and other literary periodicals. Despite these efforts, Garland in 1894 felt that "rich and powerful" Chicago "could not establish—or has not established—a paying magazine, and its publishing firms were mostly experimental or not very successful. . . ."[213]

Upper-class cultural figures were no more in touch with the finest Chicago writers, such as Theodore Dreiser and Carl Sandburg, than they were with its best architect. Except for the mass-circulation dailies controlled by members of leading families, the establishment also had little impact on the literary taste of the urban community. Moreover, the *Tribune*, which in 1918, under Robert R. McCormick's editorship, achieved the largest metropolitan circulation, acquired readers through the popular appeal of organized sports reportage, comics features, sensational crusades against venereal disease, patent medicines, and large fortunes, and through an aggressive and even violent offensive in the newspaper circulation wars.[214]

Horowitz, using the standard of trusteeships or officerships in at least two major cultural institutions, compiled a list of thirty-four Chicago cultural leaders between the 1880s and World War I. Most of them, e.g. Field and Higinbotham, were capitalists, or, like Charles L. Hutchinson, Martin A. Ryerson, and Harold F. McCormick, sons of tycoons, or, as in the case of Burnham and Harper, closely associated with the business-social inner circle. Among these figures were noted civic reformers and philanthropists. Horowitz discovered that almost all were members of the Chicago Club, two-thirds belonged to the Commercial

Club, and more than one-third presided over that club. They lived on the Near North Side or on Prairie Avenue just south of the business district, and, unlike other big businessmen and their children, did not move to the East Coast or the suburbs. About half originated in New England and, characteristic of the upper class, they did not participate in municipal government. In short, their cultural functions were one dimension of a multifaceted sovereignty traditionally exercised by upper classes. After 1900 the older group died out, replaced by younger leaders more friendly to modern intellectual trends, a shift in orientation apparent in the differences between *America* and *Poetry* and in the art institute making American and contemporary paintings part of its collection.[215]

Before the advent of the museums, the symphony, and the World's Fair, Hutchinson, De Koven, Gage, and Arnold criticized the disparity between the esthetic and intellectual growth of Chicago and its commercial and demographic expansion.[216] After the 1890s renaissance, they were much more satisfied with the accomplishments of their city and class. Hutchinson, as noted above, now praised Chicago's artistic achievements. "Libraries, museums and endowments for the development of the arts and sciences are the transmuted products of coal and iron," remarked Mrs. De Koven in 1902, "and the patrons of art are as earnest and conscientious in the distribution of their wealth as they were in its early accumulation." This optimism received its strongest expression in 1917 from Chatfield-Taylor, who proclaimed that Chicago equaled New York in educational and cultural achievements.[217]

Society

Intermarriage, friendship, residential propinquity, and social clubs and affairs continued to solidify upper-class Chicago after the Civil War. Family ties increased, a natural development in an aging but still powerful establishment. The millionaires of 1892 were significantly more interconnected by blood and matrimony than their affluent predecessors of 1863. Blairs wedded McCormicks, Keeps, Higinbothams, and De Kovens; Farwells united with De Kovens and Chatfield-Taylors; Fields joined with Catons and Trees; McCormicks with Medills, Blairs, and Dexters; and other leading clans similarly intertwined. Exclusive neighborhoods encouraged intermarriage and other interrelationships. From the 1860s to the 1890s the upper order lived mainly on Michigan and Prairie avenues. Of the approximately 6,000 people listed in the 1885 *Elite Directory and Club List of Chicago*, 556 had homes on these streets. At one time forty of the sixty members of the Commercial Club resided within five blocks of each other on Prairie Avenue. After 1885, led by Mrs. Palmer, the elite began to move to Lake Shore Drive. During the summer the privileged enclave had a colony at Lake Forest or mingled with elites from Boston, Philadelphia, Charleston, and Detroit at Newport, Rhode Island, and Bar Harbor, Maine.[218] "Life in the Seventies, Eighties, and Nineties must have been less agitated and in many ways pleasanter than after the turn of the century," asserted socialite Arthur Meeker, Jr. "For one thing, everybody still knew everybody . . . my mother lists the owners of every house from Sixteenth to Twenty-Second Streets on [Prairie Avenue] as old and dear friends."[219]

During the 1860s and '70s high society, according to the leading belles of these decades—Addie Gregory, Mrs. De Koven, Abby Farwell Ferry, Elizabeth Voluntine Rumsey, Louise Bowen, and cotillion leader and Assembly Ball committeeman Chatfield-Taylor—remained simple, virtuous, democratic, and family-centered. Yankee dressmakers fitted debutantes for their coming-out parties, French-style invitations were rare and still considered pretentious, and lemonade, ice cream, and coffee were served at parties, which ended at midnight. Hostesses wrote their own invitations, cleaned house, and helped prepare the food for these festivities, and artists and theater folk rarely entered proper homes.[220]

After the 1870s society figures and native and visiting observers continued to differentiate Chicago from Boston and New York society by attributing to the westerners warmth, openness, and equality. By the 1880s, however, a fashionable set emerged, ruled by Chicago's first grand dame and patterned upon New York's Four Hundred. Events like those in other cities—dancing classes, coming-out parties, formal dinners, Derby Day in Washington Park, the Assembly Ball, and Mrs. Palmer's New Year's Day Ball—featured the social season. Palmer's court consisted of the leading families, with the exception, as in New York, of some tycoons. The charmed circle developed into a near replica of its New York forerunner as high society became more expensive and exclusive and dominated by calculating and determined women. Fancy-dress balls replaced casual dances, catered affairs superceded informal parties and suppers, and costly mansions furnished with European, usually French, artifacts housed the world of wealth and fashion. Society reporters, periodicals, and newspapers publicized the doings of the smart set, and rifts occurred among rival hostesses. The worlds of society and the theater began to intermingle. The elite changed homes, neighborhoods, and spouses more rapidly than in Boston, Philadelphia, or Charleston, and Swift, Palmer, Armour, and Field, until he remarried, regarded the social swirl as a frivolous waste of time and energy better applied to business matters. Rich and well-born Chicagoans also resembled older elites in their aspirations to mate with prominent and titled foreigners. Fifteen Chicago girls had made such matches before 1915, far behind the 193 New Yorkers, but only slightly fewer than the twenty Philadelphians or the seventeen Bostonians, and well ahead of any other western city. Wealthy and status-seeking Chicagoans employed New York architects, imitated the Four Hundred coaching craze, and bought carriages that were copies of Vanderbilt vehicles. When Mrs. Marshall Field gave the famous $75,000 Mikado Ball in 1886, the Japanese village extravaganza was created by Sherry's of New York rather than by Herbert M. Kinsley, Chicago's upper-class caterer. At Newport Mrs. Palmer won acceptance in New York's *beau monde* and in 1898 Mrs. Astor recognized Chicago society by giving a dinner in her honor.[221] But Carter Harrison, Jr., a man-about-town as well as a politician, deplored the appearance of "a small group patterned on New York's Four Hundred [that] arrogates to itself leadership in things social. The newspapers, eager for society items, play it up; frequently the families of their proprietors belong to the charmed circles. It affects an authority that in older lands is based on blood, official position, titles of long standing or recent acquirement."[222]

In two important respects the smart set differed from its New York model. "Chicago has never had a male leader of society like Ward McAllister," remarked Gregory. Kinsley advised hostesses on dress, ballroom etiquette, jewelry, and protocol at receptions, but he did not rival the exogamous arbiters of high society in Gotham.[223] Chatfield-Taylor, who introduced British coachmen to the city, most nearly resembled the New York prototype. In role he replicated McAllister and in personality, Harry Lehr. According to Meeker, whose father ran the Assembly Balls, Chatfield-Taylor tried "to impress a sense of protocol and precedence on one of our most relaxed and least naturally stiff communities." Ferry, an intimate friend, remembered him a "a regular gossip. . . . He noticed everything a woman had on and could tell all the latest news; he was a fascinating talker, too."[224] But Chatfield-Taylor stemmed from distinguished Chicago stock, wrote novels and essays, and edited literary magazines in addition to planning and leading dances and imposing rules of etiquette at tribal rituals. His extrasocial concerns and accomplishments also characterized society queens. Palmer and Henrotin were active in charitable and civic causes, and the former was also an art connoisseur. Artists, actors, intellectuals, and statesmen attended Palmer's affairs. Her contemporaries and successors were cut from the same cloth. Mrs. Herbert (Harriett Hubbard) Ayer, a society leader in the 1870s, scandalized Chicago matrons by inviting theater people to her Sunday French breakfasts. After her husband's bankruptcy she went on the stage and later became a successful cosmetics manufacturer and a journalist. Mrs. Alfred (Minnie Murdock) Mason, daughter-in-law of a former mayor of the city, was an ex-actress and a novelist. Mrs. Kellogg Ayer Fairbank, amidst her social, political, and philanthropic activities, found time to write novels. Mrs. Harold F. (Edith Rockefeller) McCormick endowed a hospital, financed the Chicago Opera, wrote poetry, played the cello, read several languages, and practiced psychiatry.[225]

Unlike the Four Hundred, this circle involved itself in civic and cultural enterprises, a reflection of the broader urban role assumed by upper-class Chicago women.

The bourgeoning field of American women's history has thus far been concerned mainly with the middle and working classes. The absence of systematic studies of upper-class females makes possible only the most tentative conclusions about the wealthy and socially prominent who lived in the cities investigated in this book. An impressionistic survey of biographical data indicates that those from Chicago and Los Angeles were more apt to break with genteel conventions by assuming civic leadership or undertaking vocations. "Respectable" women may have been freer in the more recently settled West because its urban establishments were more egalitarian and less oriented to the past than were Eastern Seaboard elites. Several Brahmin ladies were noted for their intellect and philanthropy, but they expressed these qualities in traditional ways, such as conducting salons or being active in elite charity organizations or in reforms to lighten the burdens of underprivileged women and children. New York society figures were less intellectually inclined or socially responsible, but one member of the Four Hundred proved an exception to this generalization. Mrs. Oliver H. P. Belmont, who as Mrs. William K. Vanderbilt won social acceptance for her first husband's family, later became a women's suffrage activist and evinced a serious interest in architecture. Significantly, these developments appeared in the early 1900s when Belmont was in her fifties, after she had divorced her first and outlived her second spouse, and when the Astor set was fading. Belmont's life in many ways paralleled that of Mrs. Potter Palmer, but the latter was more forceful in civic affairs. A few of Belmont's younger contemporaries, including the second Mrs. W. K. Vanderbilt and the daughter of E. H. Harriman, had a more orthodox sense of *noblesse oblige* which they displayed in social welfare work. Another younger contemporary, Mrs. John D. Rockefeller, Jr., was perhaps the key founder of the Museum of Modern Art. This type of accomplishment, even in 1929, was unique among well-bred eastern women.

By the 1890s Chicago society had a formal, exclusive, and hierarchical structure. Self-made successes Field, Armour, Farwell, Hibbard, and Insull professed indifference about lineage and praised the upwardly mobile. But Farwell spent large sums on genealogical investigation and his daughter traced the family back to British royalty. Hibbard disdained ancestral societies, but his child became a Colonial Dame. Field and Leiter girls married titled Englishmen. Cyrus McCormick searched for aristocratic antecedents, acquired a family coat-of-arms, wanted his daughter to be presented at the Court of St. James, and craved the attention of European nobility.[226] Accompanying the quest for distinguished forebears and contemporary coronets was a growing aloofness in familial and social relationships. "You must realize," said Mrs. Palmer, "that the Palmer family is quite an institution." She granted audiences only upon appointment with her secretary. Edith McCormick was even less accessible, speaking to her private secretary and chief steward alone of her employees and seeing her children by appointment. Meeker, Jr.'s, mother would not let him accept invitations from the newly rich or attend their parties. Assembly Balls and Palmer's New Year's Day celebrations erected formidable admission barriers, and robber barons Yerkes and Insull were denied entry into the inner circle, just like their déclassé counterparts Harriman and Gould in New York. "By the time I was born [in 1902]," wrote Meeker, society "had become a tightly organized, smoothly working organization, to enter which was no longer easy. Money wouldn't do it any more; we can all think of rich vulgarians who battered on the doors in vain."[227]

Despite these developments, the Four Hundred and other eastern patriciates, at least until Palmer's Newport conquest, snubbed the westerners. McAllister, visiting the World's Fair, caused a tempest between the New York and Chicago elites by disparaging Chicago society. The staid Philadelphia *Evening Bulletin*, accustomed to a modest upper order typical of Atlantic seaboard aristocracies, castigated the Chicago press for pandering to the notoriety craved by the *haut monde* of the city. Robert R. McCormick at Groton in the 1890s found that "the Boston and New York boys . . . looked down upon us Middle Westerners." Upper-crust Chicagoans responded ambivalently to the coastal gentility. The patriciate imitated the Four Hundred and sent their offspring to eastern academies and colleges. Newberry's daughter attended the same New York boarding school as did aristocratic Gothamites and Bostonians. In that metropolis and at European spas she hobnobbed with blueblood easterners. But she was bored at her first society dinner and regarded Stuyvesant Fish as "little less than an idiot."[228] Carter Harrison, Jr., also denigrated Gotham's smart set. On the other hand, Mrs. De Koven, circulating in New York society because of her husband's Newport connections, felt that "the Four Hundred really did include what was best in New York in those days. . . ." A few years later, however, New York "Society" was a "flaring plutocracy," now "uninteresting" and approaching a "welcome" state of oblivion. The passing of the Astor crowd combined with "the unwieldy size of the city has broken that [high society] solidarity." But "Boston society" upheld "the rule of the 'closed corporation.' " A "patriarchal institution," based upon "the family," the Brahmins were "the pinnacle of society." De Koven had been accepted in New York, but "realize[d] that a stranger although enthusiastically received, should never dare to hope to be really a Bostonian." McCormick, more cruelly treated by well-born New York and Boston Grotonians, responded with severer judgments of the Atlantic

Coast patriciates.[229] Pleased or outraged by their experiences, some Chicagoans became fellow travelers of eastern elites, but seldom forged closer bonds. Aristocratic Philadelphians, Bostonians, and New Yorkers sometimes intermarried; the westerners made no matrimonial alliances with these families. Even unions with *arriviste* New Yorkers, the Rockefeller and McCormick wedding being a notable exception, rarely occurred before World War I.

Metropolitan club life was the institutional equivalent to the female-dominated fashionable world. "The men of Chicago had first ventured into a social life outside home and church circles through clubs," said Gregory, "and the women soon followed their example." The exclusive club coincided with high society. Yerkes, whose family was snubbed by the smart set, never won full acceptance from his fellow Union Leaguers. Clubs also had a business side. "The knowledge that an employee belongs to a club that is not distinctly beyond his means is not a detriment to his advancement," advised Higinbotham.[230] Elite association memberships, the Chicago (1869), Commercial (1877), Calumet (1878), Union (1878), Union League (1879), and Washington Park (1883), often overlapped and were passed on from father to son. The Chicago Club succeeded the Dearborn Club (1861), the city's first upper-class club. The older organization was incorporated by prominent civic and commercial figures, and a year after its bankruptcy leading citizens formed the Chicago Club. Conviviality mixed with business deals at the "millionaires' table," where Lincoln, Isham, Field, Fairbank, Pullman, and Crerar met daily for lunch. Meeker, Jr., captured the duality of club life in noting that "much of his [father's] business was done at the [Chicago] club; big deals and cocktails seemed to have an affinity for each other."[231] The Calumet appealed to younger upper-class types and to cultural interests, holding a yearly art show. By World War I it was a casualty of suburban flight and wifely resistance. The Union also flourished among the younger set and faded for the same reasons and at the same time. It, too, had a cultural affinity, sponsoring concerts.[232] Gregory, whose father belonged to the Commercial Club, called it "the most characteristic and influential one in Chicago." Selectivity was maintained by setting a limit of sixty members. Former president, club historian, and second-generation wagon manufacturer John J. Glessner stated: "To be eligible for membership a man must have shown conspicuous success in his private business, with a broad and comprehending sympathy with important affairs of city and state, and a generous subordinating of self in the interests of the community. . . ." The Commercial Club, through its varied civic initiatives, met these criteria. Modeled on its Boston namesake, founders and presidents included Leiter, Franklin MacVeagh, Gage, Cyrus H. McCormick, Jr.,

Bartlett, Charles L. Hutchinson, and Martin A. Ryerson.[233] Seventeen of the twenty-three presidents between 1878 and 1903 were on the 1892 list of millionaires. The Union League began, according to a founder, out of a "demand for a gentleman's club in the heart of the city . . . which would conduct a first class restaurant and whose membership would be exclusive." Like older branches in eastern cities, it originated as a patriotic, Republican organization. The most politically active of the gentlemen's clubs, it was, next to the Commercial Club, the most culturally influential. Seven of the twelve Columbian Exposition executive committeeman and all three presidents were Union Leaguers. Most members were prominent capitalists and civic figures and many business transactions were conducted at the club.[234] The Washington Park Club was chartered "to promote good fellowship among its members. . . ."[235] Dedicated primarily to the turf, its racing days were special events in the social season. Sixty-eight percent of the 1892 millionaires (189 out of 278) joined these clubs: the Chicago enrolled 115, Washington Park, 96, Union League, 86, Calumet, 85, Commercial, 50, and Union, 41. Most belonged to more than one of these associations.

Many other clubs of varying importance and duration also appeared. Among them were the Chicago Yacht, the Merchants', the Illinois, the Iroquois, the Luncheon Society, and the Twentieth Century. The latter, patterned after New York's Nineteenth Century Club, was linked to the smart set. Its founder felt that "when a distinguished foreigner and people from other parts of the country come to Chicago, they want to meet the representative society people. They don't care about being bored with a lot of men who have a local reputation as men of genius. . . . They want to meet people whose names are known as men and women of fashion."[236] Hence, the formation of this short-lived club.

Chicago came of age between 1871 and 1893. The town's quick recovery from the great fire was hailed by the first Inter-State Industrial Exposition (1873). Headed by Potter Palmer, it was organized by the usual group of civic and commercial titans and put on yearly exhibitions to celebrate and publicize Chicago's industrial achievements.[237] Twenty years later the city's arrival as a commercial and cultural giant was symbolized by the Columbian Exposition. During these years Chicagoans and visitors lauded the metropolis for its raw power, aggressive energy, and spectacular growth. They made Chicago the archetype of industrial America, but often denigrated its intellectual and social atmosphere. Eminent citizens answered criticism with strident claims of excellence and attacks on detractors that carried an undertone of doubt and inferiority, particularly when the defenders emulated Atlantic Seaboard patriciates.[238]

The establishment spearheaded Chicago's triumphs and proclaimed its confidence in the city and in its own deeds, but affluence, achievements, and honors often obscured disappointments and tragedies that initiated the enclave's eventual disintegration. Leslie Carter, society leader, president of the chamber of commerce, the Chicago Dock Company, and St. Luke's Hospital board, divorced his wife in 1889 for adultery and killed himself in 1906. The strong-willed Chicago capitalists, perhaps because they devoted themselves largely to business and civic affairs, frequently led miserable family lives. The Armours, Fields, and Insulls had unhappy marriages, sons of Field and Gage were drunkards and suicides, Cyrus McCormick's nephew made a misalliance with Joseph Medill's daughter and died of melancholia in a nursing home, Field's daughter got divorced, Yerkes left his first wife, and the Harold McCormicks separated. "A number of Prairie Avenue's most respected matrons" kept "lurid secrets," reported Meeker, Jr. "Men went quietly insane in several of these grim old houses and took their lives for business or personal reasons. More marriages were failures than not. . . . In their old age the millionaires' relicts were liable to take to drink or drugs." Mrs. De Koven, possibly thinking about these unfortunate cases and their destructive effect upon the family, the backbone of upper-class continuity and cohesion, felt that "many a spendthrift son dissipates his father's fortune, with the result that a third generation rarely survives to show the advantages of money turned to the gracious enjoyment of stable fortune with all its evolution of refinement and gentle breeding."[239]

Even before the Roaring Twenties and café society, divorce, drugs, drunkenness, and death began to undermine the upper class in Chicago as well as in New York. The western elite also suffered a massive flight to distant places, a source of erosion spared New York, Boston, and Philadephia patriciates, but endured by the Charleston aristocracy after the Civil War. Pleasant climes and exciting and elegant environments lured eminent Chicagoans. Harriett Ayer went to New York, Gage never returned after serving in McKinley's cabinet, and reformer Kent moved to California. Mrs. Palmer left for Florida and London, the Leiters for Washington so they could arrange better matches for their daughters, and the second Mrs. Field, society leader Mrs. Arthur (Delia Spencer) Caton, the hardware heiress, also moved to the capital. Chatfield-Taylor, shortly before escaping to California, remarked in 1917 that Chicago's "few men of leisure" live elsewhere "and tarry within [Chicago] only long enough to collect rents or cut off coupons." This exodus saddened the old cotillion leader, who ruminated on Chicago in a way that elderly Brahmins reflected on Boston, Cambridge, or Quincy: "Time was when I knew a goodly proportion of the passers-by in the downtown streets—men, like myself of New England blood. . . . Now

. . . I search the scurrying crowds in vain for a familiar face. . . . Bewildered by the hurly-burly of my native city, I—a lonely figure of a pristine day—try then to comprehend the multifarious changes a few short years have wrought in its life and character, try to realize that within my own lifetime more than two million people have been added to its population."[240]

MODERN TIMES

In contemporary America the train has given way to the car and the jet, play has become as respectable as labor, and consumption as virtuous as production. Thus Chicago, with its harsh climate, railroads, heavy industry, and reputation for hard, but remunerative, work, no longer represents the national ideal. Cities in other parts of the country and in Chicago's own region, such as Detroit, the automobile capital, captured the new spirit and outpaced the economic and population growth of the Great Lakes metropolis. Compared to more recent and faster-growing urban centers, Chicago has increasingly become thought of as a shabby and deteriorating residue of pre–World War I America. And the enclave responsible for many of the city's triumphs now moves in the shadow of decay.

The Economy

Even before the Great Depression, Chicago's economy slowed down. Between 1910 and 1928 land values in the Loop rose 62 percent, an unprecedentedly low rate over so many years, and for the first time property values in the business district increased less than in the city as a whole. During the Crash, however, land values in the Loop did not fall as much as the city's average.[241] The dollar value of wholesale trade expanded 50 percent between 1921 and 1929, a stagnating pace relative to the 1875–1910 era, but somewhat better than the 1910–18 period, which included two minor panics. Between 1948 and 1963 it grew by over one-fifth, exceeding during these years Boston wholesale commerce (actually decreasing in dollar volume), but behind New York (enlarged by over one-third), Charleston (nearly doubled), and Los Angeles (augmented by 225 percent). Between 1948 and 1967 the dollar volume of retail trade in Chicago rose less than one-third, compared to Boston's slightly more than one-third, New York's by half, two-and-a-quarter times for Los Angeles, and over two-and-a-half times in Charleston.[242] Dollar value of manufacturing expanded barely $200,000 between 1921 and 1929, the smallest increase since the depression decade of the 1890s, and then fell by more than one-third between 1929 and 1931. The 1925 dollar value of manufactured products declined 15 points from its 1919 apex, while New York's increased 3 points. Using

1914 as a base, Chicago five years later had an 18 percent higher growth rate than New York in value added by manufacturing, but by 1925 the cities were deadlocked. The western town, long accustomed to outrank the national average in this variable, now lagged behind. It was under the nation's mean between 1914 and 1919, and decreased between 1919 and 1925, when the average rose by 2 points. Overall diminution, however, did not affect every industry. While Pittsburgh remained first in iron and steel manufacturing between 1919 and 1929, Chicago grew faster in value added than any of the five largest iron and steel areas in the country. Moreover, its equipment was more modern and production costs cheaper than in Pittsburgh. But iron- and steelmaking comprised only about 10 percent of the total value added in manufacture by Chicago industries in the 1920s. Between 1949 and 1967 value added by manufacturing in Chicago climbed nearly six times, a little ahead of New York's rate and a little behind Boston's, but much less than Charleston's nine times and Los Angeles' sixteen times.[243] Sluggish manufacturing growth reflected the fact that several once important industries either declined, such as railroad car building, or, as in meat packing, moved to other places. Chicago made a better showing in capital accumulation. Between 1913 and 1929 the financial resources of New York grew faster, but Chicago banks recovered more quickly from the Depression than those in any other city except San Francisco. Between 1919 and 1930 Chicago investment banking outpaced the national average increase in size and number of firms and security flotations organized. After World War I local banking and securities houses participated more vigorously in handling large national corporate issues, but still depended upon New York's financial institutions and stock exchange and chiefly funded local and regional enterprises. Although Chicago held its own against other money markets, its growth declined considerably relative to the past. Bank clearings rose by 50 percent between 1921 and 1929, but they climbed by 194 percent between 1898 and 1915 and doubled between 1911 and 1920. Because of the Depression they diminished by one-third between 1928 and 1932. After World War II total dollar value of bank deposits in Cook County no longer increased more than in other cities. Between 1949 and 1970 deposits in Cook County banks expanded about three-and-a-half-fold, a rate slightly behind banks in Los Angeles and Charleston counties and barely ahead of those in New York City.[244]

Demographic stagnation accompanied and inhibited economic growth. The urban population almost doubled between 1898 and 1925, but decreased by 165,000 between 1927 and 1933. Between 1940 and 1960 Chicago residents decreased by 27,451, New York's by 44,568, Boston's by 139,475, and Charleston's by 4,300, while Los Angeles nearly doubled in numbers of inhabitants.[245]

REAL ESTATE

Buying and selling land laid the foundations for many inherited fortunes. In the 1920s and '30s descendants of old families remained active in real estate and related enterprises. Grandsons and great-grandsons of Matthew Laflin, the versatile entrepreneur and land speculator of the 1840s, administered family business interests, including its Chicago properties. The grandchildren of Thomas Hoyne formed a realty firm in the 1890s which managed several large estates, and John B. Drake's offspring retained control over their father's hotels. Land ownership, which sustained many upper-class accumulations, still could lead to disaster through imprudent speculation. J. Ogden Armour lost $17 million and went bankrupt as a result of a rash plunge, between 1913 and 1920, into California acreage.[246] Property continued to be grossly underassessed for tax purposes, the more valuable the house usually the lower the rate of valuation. The Loop, however, had the highest average of assessed against sales value of any area of Chicago, 74.1 percent in 1927, an enormous increase from old ratios and an indication that patrician rentiers were losing political power.[247]

COMMERCE

The great merchants no longer primarily derived from the Old Guard entrepreneurial enclave. Newcomer Julius Rosenwald was the foremost retailer and richest man in Chicago during the era between the world wars. Sears, Roebuck & Co. embodied a different concept in merchandising than did the urban department store. Sears was a low-priced, unfashionable mail-order house catering to rural customers. Notwithstanding the advent of new men and new ideas, several dynasties managed to survive the perils of the pit and the panics of the 1890s and early 1900s. The grandson and great-grandsons of George A. Seaverns, a prominent grain merchant and speculator of the 1850s and '60s, continued the family business. Grandchildren of society jeweler and clubman Elijah Peacock, who began in 1837, perpetuated the firm. Others who inherited status, fortune, and vocation included John A. Carpenter, who worked in a mill, railway, and vessel supply house founded by his grandfather, Albert A. Sprague, son and partner of the organizer of Sprague, Warner & Co. (1862), the largest wholesale grocery in the United States, and Eames MacVeagh, son and successor of wholesale grocer Franklin MacVeagh. This group, however, represented a tiny margin of the largest traders of the 1920s and '30s. The greatest mercantile establishments were modern corporations rather than family firms. Farwell & Co. underwent this transition in 1926 when the Farwells sold out to Carson, Pirie, & Scott. Marshall Field & Co. was never a kinship-structured concern. Field's nephew, who resigned as first vice-president in 1917, was the last Field official, and after World War I the family no longer held the largest block of stock. The presidents were self-made men and immigrants to Chicago who occupied a high place in the business elite. Shedd, Field's immediate successor, played a key role in building the LaSalle St. Bridge, and the next head of the store, James Simpson, chaired the Chicago Plan Commission and served as a director of the Federal Reserve Branch Bank and Commonwealth Edison. In the 1930s Macy's of New York passed the Chicago emporium in having the world's largest sales volume. The average turnover and sales volume of Field & Co. was now lower than most of the great urban department stores. Its growth was slowly contracting even before Field's death. Under new management in 1934, the store lost money but subsequently recovered. In the 1940s and '50s it still numbered among its clientele foreign and national celebrities and the local upper class. Nevertheless, it shared Chicago's economic decline: profits in 1951 fell nearly $6,000,000 from 1944.[248]

INDUSTRY

In the 1920s and '30s descendants of Old Guard industrial clans generally lost control of ancestral enterprises or suffered reverses due to their own mismanagement. Richard T. Crane, Jr., presided over the Crane Co. during its great expansion in World War I, but after his death in 1931 the family ceased to run the corporation, although it retained more than two-thirds of the stock. Joseph T. Ryerson & Son, Inc. (1842) became the largest independent iron- and steelmaker under the reign of the founder's son. In 1936, then directed by a grandson, it was absorbed by the Inland Steel Co. Inroads occurred even in meat packing, the industry where family proprietorship was most prevalent. Cudahys, Swifts, Morrises, Allertons, and Armours inherited their fathers' businesses. Several of these companies encountered heavy losses under the direction of the younger generation. Cudahy Packing (1884) endured the severest crisis in its history in 1937–38, a consequence of unwise expansion in the early 1930s. Armour & Co. experienced the most disastrous case of upper-class maladministration. Failure to cut back inventory after the World War I bonanza together with the recession of 1919–22 turned a 1918 profit of $21 million into a 1921 deficit of $31 million. Catastrophic land investments and losses in other Armour operations cost the family control of the company and ruined J. Ogden Armour. The Chicago bankers who reorganized the enterprise in 1922 also absorbed Morris & Co., thus ending the independent existence of yet another family firm. This debacle also consumed Arthur Meeker's $3 million fortune. Armour never recovered from the catastrophe. "I don't suppose I shall ever be happy," he said. "The thing that would make me happiest just now would be to know that I could get roaring drunk and wander about the Loop for two days with no one paying the slightest attention to me."[249] International Harvester was an exception to the usual course of development. Cyrus McCormick, Jr., chaired the board from 1918 until his death in 1935, and after World War II, Brooks McCormick was a powerful force in the company.[250]

MISCELLANEOUS ENTERPRISES

Continuity between the pre– and post–World War I decades occurred in several other enterprises. In the 1920s Insull still controlled the gas and electric companies and elevated railways in the city and its suburbs; however, he went bankrupt in 1929. George W. Dixon inherited the headship of his father's firm, the Arthur Dixon Transfer Co., one of the largest freight-handling concerns in the world. Second-generation members of the establishment continued to own the city's preeminent publishing houses. Reuben H. Donnelley increased the business of R. R. Donnelley and Sons, a firm organized by his father, by printing the city telephone books. Ogden T. McClurg, a grandnephew of William B. Ogden, inherited the presidency of A. C. McClurg & Co. The newspapers also remained in the hands of patrician entrepreneurs and their families. In the 1920s Victor Lawson still ran the Chicago *Daily News* and pioneered in the radio industry. After 1919, when Joseph Patterson left for New York to start the *Daily News*, Robert R. McCormick assumed sole charge of the *Tribune* and retained command until his death in 1955. Shortly before World War II the *Tribune* had the world's largest circulation. McCormick also headed the Tribune Co., a McCormick-Patterson empire of newspapers, a Chicago radio station, and paper mills that in 1947 was worth between $75 and 100 million. Marshall Field III reversed the course of Patterson by moving from New York to Chicago to publish the Chicago *Sun* (1941), a liberal rival of the *Tribune*. McCormick tried to stop the new paper, but it succeeded far better then Field's abortive journalistic venture in New York, the *PM*. Shortly after the war, Field's holdings included two publishing houses, two newspapers, an encyclopedia, four radio stations, and a vast amount of Chicago real estate.[251]

FINANCE

Descendants of the old elite played an even more marginal role in post–World War I railroads and banking than in other enterprises. They were no longer active in transportation, and in finance they were much less influential in their city than were the second-generation Morgans and Whitneys and the third-generation Rockefellers in the New York money market. Most of the important Chicago banks were headed by recent arrivals to the city.[252] Upper-class figures were more important in the brokerage business. Walter S. Brewster, a partner in the securities firm founded by his father, headed the Chicago Stock Exchange in the early 1920s. Solomon A. Smith, from that distinguished banking clan, was then treasurer of the exchange. Alfred E. Hamill, son of a chief executive of the Corn Exchange and Illinois Merchants' banks, and nephew of the president of the Chicago Board of Trade, was a partner in Hathaway and Co., an investment house with offices in New York and Chicago. Marshall Field III, among his other enterprises, was a founder of Field, Glore & Co. (1921), an investment firm with branches in New York, Chicago, and Paris. Inheriting little of his grandfather's aloofness, Field's notion of a successful securities salesman was that of the 1920s huckster. The securities dealer must be "a natural-born salesman," with "the knack of making friends. . . ." In "the selling game . . . dress neatly. People always like to do business with a young man who looks every inch a success. Always talk to a man about his business, not about yours. Show him how he can make some money, and he is interested." In 1929 Field, Glore created the Chicago Corporation, according to its prospectus a "financial corporation designed to supplement the existing credit facilities of the Middle West." Among the directors were Field and his uncle, and newcomers like the presidents of the Marshall Field, Armour, and Pullman companies. Other charter members included the vice-president of International Harvester, the senior partner of one of Chicago's largest law firms, and Edward F. Swift, vice-president of Swift & Co. Despite the corporation's avowed aim, most of its capital gravitated to New York. The Continental Chicago Corporation, organized in 1929 by Field, Glore and the Continental Illinois Bank and Trust Co., was another example of cooperation between patrician and *parvenu* businessmen. The first board consisted of six directors from the Chicago Corporation, including Swift, Stanley Field, and the president of Armour & Co., and Continental Illinois' board chairman, newcomer Arthur Reynolds, who had moved to Chicago and seven years earlier had helped rescue Armour & Co. Several other investment trusts, the Chicago Investors' Corporation (1929) and the Continental Illinois Co., were started by this same interlocking group. In 1936 Field retired from high finance.[253]

WEALTH AND INFLUENCE

Variations in entrepreneurial success created different destinies for old fortunes. J. Ogden Armour went bankrupt; Joseph Leiter's estate, depleted by foolish speculations going back to 1897, according to his lawyer amounted to $775,000 in 1926; extravagance, bad real estate investments, and the stock market crash forced Edith McCormick, once worth $40 million, to sell securities, mortgage her home, and move into an apartment. Meeker, Jr., reported that the Depression devastated the old upper order. Several distinguished families, however, enlarged their affluence. Richard T. Crane, Jr., was the second richest man in Chicago when he left an estate of $50 million. Cyrus H. McCormick, Jr., was one of the city's wealthiest residents at his death in 1936. His cousins Robert R. McCormick and Joseph Medill Patterson also expanded their families' assets; the former in 1955 left an estate of $20 million. Meeker, Sr., rebounded from the Armour cataclysm to make a second fortune, and yet a third after he lost millions in 1929.[254]

The accomplishments of Field and McCormick descendants led some businessmen to conclude that Chicago, even after World War II, was still run by a plutocracy of magnates, several of them from old families. An owner of a firm that grossed over $100 million yearly asserted that Brooks McCormick, Marshall Field III, and two newcomers to the city controlled the metropolis. But *Tribune* editor Donald Maxwell denied the existence of a ruling cabal of businessmen.[255] The Chicago Plan and other evidence suggests that a hegemonic enclave did not exist and virtually proves that the old elite did not wield great power. Unlike blueprints in other cities, the plan attained a large measure of success by contributing to improved rapid transit, a comprehensive park system, and better movement of freight and passenger traffic. These strides occurred in the 1920s under the leadership of Chicago Plan Commission chairmen who were not patricians, and the *bête noire* of the upper class, Mayor William Hale Thompson, exerted considerable influence over the project. The existence of other elites, competing interests, and the retirement of old families from active business management worked against an omnipotent, homogeneous, or patrician oligarchy. Business leaders divided on crucial urban affairs issues, such as the 1950s disputes over the Chicago Transit Authority subsidy and the Fort Dearborn Project to renew the Loop.[256]

Politics

Old Guard political decline helped reduce its hold over the urban economy. In the 1870s the establishment began to withdraw from government officeholding, in the 1900s urban reform, the last political movement in which it participated as a cohesive unit, began to wane, and after World War I the upper class encountered increasing difficulty in protecting its privileges or initiating commercial and civic projects. A few patricians held public posts, but their numbers dwindled from previous decades and they served mostly in appointive or honorific posts and on the state or national level. Absence from elective, substantive, and municipal positions signified loss of community influence. Typical of upper-class officeholders in the 1930s and '40s were Ambassadors Richard T. Crane III and John Cudahy, Carter Harrison, Jr., chairman of the state public works administration and collector of internal revenue in Chicago, and Edward L. Ryerson, Jr., who headed several Illinois commissions on relief and unemployment. Mayors and city councilmen, however, were drawn almost exclusively from lower- and lower-middle-class and ethnic minority backgrounds. The most politically influential magnates of the 1920s, Insull and Rosenwald, were reviled by the traditional elite for their religious beliefs or moral standards. By the 1930s even they had lost power. Insull, hard pressed by creditors, fled the city. Rosenwald, defeated by Thompson and other foes, announced in 1930 that he no longer "contribute[d] money to [political] campaigns. Experience has taught me that ninety percent of all the money I have given for such purposes is wasted."[257] Civic crusader, University of Chicago political scientist, former alderman, and mayoralty candidate Charles Edward Merriam declared in 1929 that indifference, clashing interests, and aloofness from the citizenry prevented Chicago's leading capitalists from acting as a group or from translating their wealth and economic power into political leverage. Merriam asserted that a fragmented and feudalized system of autonomous bosses dominated the local government. A generation later, Edward Banfield, another political scientist surveying the business and political structure of the city, came to the same conclusion.[258] Thompson's manipulation of the Chicago Plan, rising tax rates on Loop properties, and internecine squabbles among tycoons over important urban projects lent credence to the argument that the upper class, if one existed, was ineffectual.

The Old Guard no longer held office or effectively opposed municipal administrations which did not reflect its interests or values. Few wellborn Chicagoans remained active in civic reform associations, and these organizations were considerably weaker than in their heyday.[259] Flaccid leadership, rifts within the business community, and hostility toward ethnic minorities and organized labor, which undermined the movement twenty years earlier, still plagued these organizations. They were now further debilitated by the departure of upper-class crusaders, who had devoted much energy and money to good government. The Citizens' Association, the Civic Federation of Chicago, the Municipal Voters' League, the Commercial Club, and the Union League repeatedly called for reform, but were unable to defeat Thompson or to dissolve the alliance of traction and utility magnates with city hall.[260] In the 1920s and especially in the New Deal most of the Old Guard, like other elites attempting to salvage wealth and status, opposed liberal policies and abhorred radical programs. Franklin Delano Roosevelt was an epithet in the Union League of Chicago, despite being the nephew of a former club president. The xenophobia and antilabor traditions of upper-class Chicagoans, once trumpeted by Chatfield-Taylor in *America* and Medill in the *Tribune*, were perpetuated by the McCormick-Patterson clan in their newspapers. Marshall Field III, a supporter of labor, Roosevelt, the poor, and the blacks, championed a minority viewpoint in upperclass Chicago.[261]

Since World War II, Lodges, Saltonstalls, and Peabodys in Boston, Morrises, Fishes, and Roosevelts in New York, and Charleston aristo-crats filled important elective and appointive offices at the city, state, and national level. The offspring of families that established themselves in late-nineteenth-century New York—New Deal secretary of the treasury Henry Morgenthau, New York governor and U.S. senator Herbert Lehman, New York governor and ambassador Averell Harriman, and Nelson Rockefeller, another governor of that state and U.S. vice-president—also made a better record in modern public life than did their Chicago equivalents. The latter's poorer showing cannot be attrib-uted solely to machine politics or ethnic minority voters. These condi-tions existed in Boston and New York. The gentry in Charleston and Boston, however, and to a lesser degree in New York, had a stronger tradition of participation in government than did the western elite. And the politically active scions of families who achieved high economic and social standing in the Gilded Age—Harriman, Lehman, and Rocke-feller—belonged to clans still prominent in banking and industry.

Philanthropy

Rich Chicagoans of modern times, regardless of social origin, donated larger sums to public welfare than had their predecessors or forebears. Cyrus H. McCormick, Jr. and Marshall Field III, born to affluence, humane in outlook, and possessing a quality of *nobless oblige* that some-times graces those with inherited wealth and status, were more generous than the ruthless founders of their fortunes. McCormick contributed millions to educational and religious causes such as the YMCA and the Presbyterian Theological Seminary. Field organized the Field Founda-tion (1940) for child welfare and improved race relations. By 1947 his philanthropy amounted to approximately $50 million and he allocated 15 percent of his yearly income for public welfare causes. Robert R. McCormick, more mean-spirited than his rival or his cousin, neverthe-less outspent his ancestors. He committed the bulk of his fortune to the Robert R. McCormick Charitable Trust, whose beneficiaries included Passavant Hospital, the United Charities of Chicago, and Northwestern University. Apart from paying the Chicago Opera deficits, the Harold F. McCormicks founded the John Rockefeller McCormick Institute for In-fectious Diseases. Self-made multimillionaires were just as benevolent. Victor Lawson, who gave one-tenth of his annual income to charity, in 1925 left at least $2,060,000 (nearly 15 percent of his estate) to Christian welfare organizations. After 1920 Insull became an avid donor and fund-raiser in organized charity. Rosenwald, president of the Associated Jewish Charities of Chicago, was an ecumenical philanthropist. The United Charities, the YMCA, the University of Chicago, and the Museum of Science and Industry were among his favorite projects. He gave away an estimated $63 million in his lifetime.[262]

Altruism was not limited to almsgiving. Upper-class leadership in humanitarian agencies lasted much longer than in political organizations. Entrepreneurial and public welfare involvement went hand in hand; both activities indicated personal resourcefulness and a commitment to Chicago. Many of the foremost benefactors headed family firms. Edwin L. Ryerson, Jr., in addition to chairing state unemployment and relief commissions, presided over the Chicago Council of Social Agencies, the Hospital Planning Commission of Metropolitan Chicago, and the Community Fund of Chicago, and served as vice-president of St. Luke's Hospital board. John A. Carpenter, Walter S. Brewster, and George W. Dixon respectively headed the Illinois Children's Home and Aid Society, the United Charities, and the Chicago Home Missionary Society. Alfred E. Hamill was a director at Presbyterian Hospital and the Chicago Home for Incurables and vice-president of the orphan asylum, and Marshall Field III sat on the boards of Hull House, Illinois Children's Aid Society, and St. Luke's and Provident Hospitals.[263]

Hospital service is a prestigious activity for genteel women. Such work merges high status with the traditional female role of nursing the sick. A principal task of contemporary debutantes consists of working 100 hours in Passavant Hospital. Several generations of distinguished families have sat on boards at Passavant, St. Luke's, and other upper-class-sponsored hospitals. A study of three female upper-class and three middle-class Chicago hospital boards shows the former to be more exclusive and more kinship-connected. Seventy-six percent of the patrician boards preferred their trusteeships to all their other organizational affiliations. Forty percent of the upper-class boards, compared to 10 percent of the middle-class boards, were from related families. Recently, however, the need for money has made these elite institutions more inclusive. Twenty-five percent of the patrician boards did not appear in the Social Register. "There was a policy decision to get outsiders," said one upper-class director. "If you ask the public for money, you can't go in for an ingrown or too exclusive group."[264] Admission of outsiders indicated the intrusion into exclusive voluntary associations, as into government and business, of the newly risen. Arriviste participation in philanthropy, however, preceded the emergence of nouveaux riches in these charities. Before World War I Rosenwald had served on municipal commissions concerned with public welfare and as a Hull House trustee.[265]

Culture

In common with the gentry of Boston, Philadelphia, and Charleston, and the robber baron families of New York, and for the same reasons, the Chicago patriciate maintained its status in charity, culture, and society while being eclipsed by new enclaves in politics and business. Leisure, tradition, *noblesse oblige*, and an eastern prep-school and Ivy League education were advantages in ballroom and dinner-table etiquette, high culture, and philanthropy. Such endeavors were insulated from the accumulation of power and wealth, central concerns of upstart elites, and thus became the last bastion of patrician leadership. In this remnant of metropolitan influence, offspring of Chicago's upper class repeated previous patterns of multiple trusteeships, overlapping involvement in charitable and cultural activities, and the convergence of commercial and cultural eminence.

The old establishment, if no longer predominant, remained prominent in several intellectual institutions. Between the world wars, Edwin L. Ryerson, Jr., was president of the Crerar Library Board. Joseph M. Cudahy and William McCormick Blair, in the 1940s and '50s, headed the historical society and their peers were officers and benefactors. The president of the Chicago Academy of Sciences from 1938 to 1956 was the grandson of a founder. Another example of institutional continuity was the Union League's perpetuation of its association with Chicago culture by inaugurating the Union League Civic and Arts Foundation (1949) to encourage historical research and musical and artistic talent in the Midwest.[266]

The upper class also sustained an important role in endeavors, unlike the library, the academy, or the society, whose scope and clientele was community-wide. The Old Guard assisted universities and seminaries located in or near Chicago. Cyrus H. McCormick, Jr., gave $1.5 million to the Presbyterian Theological Seminary and Lawson willed $250,000 to the Chicago Theological Seminary. The newspaper McCormicks and Pattersons presented millions to Northwestern University, where Joseph Medill Patterson and Robert R. McCormick in 1920 founded the Medill School of Journalism. Field, ever a maverick, contributed to Roosevelt University, an unfashionable but modern type of urban college. Patricians continued to act as trustees of schools whose origins, endowments, and past management owed so much to their ancestors among the nineteenth-century establishment. Edwin L. Ryerson, Jr., headed the University of Chicago board in the 1930s, and Marshall Field III and Marshall Field IV served as trustees, as did Harold F. McCormick, also a trustee of the McCormick Theological Seminary. Albert A. Sprague sat on the Rush Medical College board, and George W. Dixon was a Northwestern University trustee. Upper-class allegiance to higher learning stopped short of direct participation as administrators, teachers, or students. "Our boys and girls are sent east to school and college," wrote Meeker, Jr., in an insider's account of the upper order published in 1955;

"nobody thinks of attending the universities of Chicago and Illinois; we feel they are meant for the hordes of young people from our vaguely known hinterland."[267]

Aristocratic Chicago best preserved its cultural ascendancy in the art institute and the Field Museum. During the 1920s and '30s many patricians gave the institute money, artifacts, and paintings. Potter Palmer, Jr., in 1933, Chauncey McCormick in 1946, and William McCormick Blair in 1966 headed its board, and other post–World War I trustees and officers have stemmed from equally distinguished and old families. After curtailment of services and exhibitions during the Depression, the institute recovered its vitality. At the end of World War II visitors equaled in numbers those who came to the Metropolitan Museum of Art, despite New York's larger population, and its membership exceeded that of any other American museum. This showing unfortunately did not extend to creators—artists continued to move to New York.[268]

The Field Museum was another patrician stronghold. In 1943 Stanley Field had been president for thirty-five years and trustees included two other Fields, an Armour, and a Blair. Twenty-three years later the same families controlled the board and it was headed by a Palmer. Younger Fields kept up the family tradition of supplementing service with support. By 1943 Marshall Field III had donated $2,852,000 and Stanley Field $1,592,000 to the museum.[269]

Patronizing the symphony and the opera is a recurrent feature of urban upper-class life. After World War I the great Chicago families contributed many officers and supporters of the Orchestral Association. In the 1920s Charles H. Hamill, and from 1938 to 1952 Edwin L. Ryerson, Jr., headed the association.[270] The opera, however, passed out of patrician hands. In 1922 the Opera Association failed and was reorganized by Insull. The Chicago Civic Opera Company retained the elite officers of its predecessor, but the utilities tycoon, president and chairman of the financial committee, became the prime force. The Harold F. McCormicks, who gave $10 million to finance civic opera, were now overshadowed by Insull's endowment. He cut costs, successfully campaigned for increased funds, and expanded attendance by lowering prices and putting on special performances of popular productions. The Insull-inspired new opera house opened in 1929. This theater had fewer boxes, and they were placed in the rear, antagonizing Gold Coast patrons accustomed to the opera as a forum for displaying wealth and high status. Although many of the officers were patricians, Insull, despite a déclassé social standing, so predominated that the company did not survive his financial collapse.[271]

Post–World War I developments of the academy of sciences, the historical society, the art institute, the Field Museum, and the symphony exhibited substantial continuity with the past. Insull's democratization of Chicago opera, however, highlighted significant modifications in personnel and policy in high culture. The Old Guard, notwithstanding its personal opinion of *parvenu* moguls, now accepted their leadership in several institutions and admitted them to the boards of other organizations. Money and power might not secure entry into high society, but these desperately needed resources overcame exclusiveness in prestigious cultural and charitable institutions. Jews appeared on the boards of the opera and the institute, and a recent chancellor of the University of Chicago is of that faith. Rosenwald, the city's most munificent benefactor, donated over $4 million to the University of Chicago and financed the Museum of Science and Industry, giving it more than $6 million. Emphasizing technology and invention, the present and the future, it represented a new concept in the museum movement. Other *nouveau riche* tycoons, Rosenwald's brother-in-law Max Adler and Shedd, were responsible respectively for the planetarium and aquarium.[272]

Changes also occurred in Old Guard cultural involvement. Adoption of eastern ways, a consequence of attending schools in that region, and the leisure provided by an inherited income, resulted in members of distinguished families becoming practitioners as well as benefactors and administrators in arts and letters. Mrs. Kellogg Ayer Fairbank wrote novels, and her sister, Mrs. Margaret Ayer Banks, produced a Pulitzer Prize–winning work of fiction. Mrs. Reginald De Koven authored two novels, a historical monograph, and an account of her life. Alfred E. Hamill was a poet and published a study of Petrarch's life, Lloyd Alan Laflin wrote plays, Meeker, Jr., combined an autobiography with a sketch of Chicago society, and John A. Carpenter composed music. Robert R. McCormick published three books on public affairs, Joseph Medill Patterson wrote three novels and had three plays shown on Broadway, Eleanor Medill Patterson authored two novels and her daughter, Felicia, also wrote a novel. Their foe, Field, published a work on social problems.[273]

Patricians became active in institutions outside of Chicago, indicating the acceptance in eastern circles of the prairie upper class and the tendency of members of different metropolitan elites to participate jointly in national institutions. Cyrus H. McCormick, Jr., was a Princeton University trustee, and Edwin L. Ryerson, Jr., a fellow of the Yale Corporation, a trustee of the Carnegie Endowment for International Peace, and a member of President Eisenhower's Board of Consultants on Foreign Activities, which supervised the CIA and other overseas intelligence operations. Field was another exemplar of the interaction of urban elites. Living in New York from 1921 to 1941 and marrying into an aristocratic New York mercantile family, he was president of the New York Philharmonic Society and the board of directors of the Metropolitan Opera, a trustee of the Metropolitan Museum of Art, and a director of several banks in that city. Field and Rosenwald philanthropy also went beyond local limits.[274]

Society

Divorce, the Depression, flight, and the encroachment of café society withered high society in Chicago and other places. A modicum of order was preserved in the 1920s when reigning prewar hostesses—Mrs. Fairbank, Mrs. Walter S. Brewster, Mrs. Arthur Ryerson, Edith McCormick, and Mrs. Meeker presided over the *beau monde*—and by membership in the elite clubs. But the traditional kinship and institutional structure could not withstand the forces of disintegration. Palmers, Fields, McCormicks, Blairs, and Pattersons endured a series of broken marriages and began to seek spouses outside the charmed circle. The younger generation grew bored with conventional social affairs, preferring the company of Hollywood stars and café society habitués. Prestigious events no longer barred those with questionable family antecedents or social credentials. Mrs. Ryerson, Chatfield-Taylor, the Meekers, and Joseph Medill and Eleanor Patterson left the city; other patricians, Marshall Field III and Mrs. McCormick, were absent for long periods. The flight from downtown to the North Side, to the suburbs, or to more remote places replicated similar movements by the Brahmins and other urban elites. "Millionaire Row" on Prairie Avenue gradually became a black neighborhood. By the 1950s one-quarter of the social registrites lived out of town. By the 1930s several society leaders were broke, in exile, or dead. Depression-ravaged fortunes ended the Assembly Ball and Twelfth Night Ball and made formal dinners give way to cocktail parties.[275] The decline of the old clans was registered in the low correlation between listings in the 1940 editions of the Chicago *Social Register* and *Who's Who*. Eleven percent of the registrites made *Who's Who*, the lowest proportion of the social elites in eleven large cities. The share of those who belonged to both the achievement elite and the social elite in the other urban centers ranged from 20 percent in New York and Cleveland to 30 percent in Washington. Philadelphia tied for second place with 29 percent and Boston was third with 28 percent.[276] As was the case with other metropolitan gentries, the passing of the old establishment did not go unmourned among its members. From Chatfield-Taylor and the Gold Coasters of the 1920s to William Blair and Meeker, Jr., in the 1950s patricians dwelled on the vulgarization of society, the physical and spiritual disintegration and departure of the upper class, their feeling of alienation and displacement, and the deterioration of their city. When "I'm there [in Chicago]," Meeker, Jr., felt "dépaysé, which implies that where you were at home you aren't so any longer."[277]

NOTES

1. Bessie Louise Pierce, A History of Chicago, 3 vols. (New York: Alfred A. Knopf, 1937–57), I, 44, II, 76, 481–82; Homer Hoyt, One Hundred Years of Land Values in Chicago (Chicago: University of Chicago Press, 1933), 55–56, 58, 483; John Moses and Joseph Kirkland, History of Chicago, Illinois, 2 vols. (Chicago: Munsell, 1895), I, 141; A. T. Andreas, History of Chicago from the Earliest Period to the Present Time, 3 vols. (Chicago: A. T. Andreas, 1884–86), I, 183, 571; J. W. Norris, Norris' Business Directory and Statistics of the City of Chicago for 1846 (Chicago: Fergus Printing, 1883), 15; Howard Copeland Hill, "The Development of Chicago as a Center of the Meat Packing Industry," Mississippi Valley Historical Review, X (1923), 262.

2. Hoyt, One Hundred, 39–41, 74–80, 470, 487; Moses and Kirkland, History, I, 129; Francis M. Huston, Financing an Empire, 4 vols. (Chicago: S. J. Clarke, 1926), I, 153–67; F. Cyril James, The Growth of Chicago Banks, 2 vols. (New York: Harper & Bros., 1938), I, 121–22, 143–60, 191, 231–43, 268–80; Pierce, History, I, 67–71, 124–25, 190–91, II, 119–20.

3. William B. Ogden to James Allen, Jan. 15, 1840, and to H. Moore, Jan. 25, 1841, reprinted in Hoyt, One Hundred, 40, 42.

4. For a list of the largest taxpayers of 1825 see Andreas, History, I, 101; Moses and Kirkland, History, I, 76. For designations by prominent contemporary figures see Isaac N. Arnold: Reminiscences of the Illinois Bar Forty Years Ago (Chicago: Fergus Printing, 1882), 133; William B. Ogden and Early Days in Chicago (Chicago: Fergus Printing, 1882), passim; John V. Farwell, Some Recollections of John V. Farwell (Chicago: R. R. Donnelley & Sons, 1911), 55–56; Herma Clark, ed., Dear Julia: Letters from Martha Freeman Esmond to Her Friend Julia Boyd of New York in the days "When Chicago Was Young" (Chicago: W. D. Bauman, 1933), 13, 17; Carolina Kirkland, ed., Chicago Yesterdays (Chicago: Caughaday, 1919), 68, 84, 130–31; Paul M. Angle, The Chicago Historical Society (New York: Rand McNally, 1956), 37; Gurdon S. Hubbard, The Autobiography of Gurdon Saltonstall Hubbard (Chicago: R. R. Donnelley & Sons, 1911), 27, 34; Mabel McIlwaine, ed., Reminiscences of Early Chicago (Chicago: R. R. Donnelley & Sons, 1920), 142; William Bross, History of Chicago (New York: Jansen, McClurg, 1876), 23–25, 56; Pierce, History, I, 190–91. For biographical data on the antebellum elite see Moses and Kirkland, History; Andreas, History; Huston, Financing, II–IV; Josiah S. Currey, Manufacturing and Wholesale Industries of Chicago, 3 vols. (Chicago: Thomas B. Poole, 1918), II, III; Chicago: Its History and Its Builders: A Century of Marvelous Growth, 5 vols. (Chicago: S. J. Clarke, 1912), IV–V; Charles H. Taylor, ed., History of the Board of Trade of the City of Chicago, 3 vols. (Chicago: Robert O. Law, 1917), III; David Ward Wood, Chicago and Its Distinguished Citizens or the Progress of Forty Years (Chicago: Milton George, 1881); Paul Gilbert and Charles Lee Bryson, Chicago and Its Makers (Chicago: Felix Mendelsohn, 1929); Album of Genealogy and Biography, Cook County, Illinois (Chicago: Calumet Book & Engraving, 1897); A. N. Waterman, Historical Review of Chicago and Cook County, 3 vols. (Chicago and New York: Lewis Publishing, 1908); Portrait and Biographical Record of DuPage and Cook Counties, Illinois (Chicago: Lake City Publishing, 1894); Biographical Sketches of the Leading Men of

Chicago (Chicago: Wilson & St. Clair, 1868); Thomas Wakefield Goodspeed, *The University of Chicago Biographical Sketches*, 2 vols. (Chicago: University of Chicago Press, 1925); *In Memoriam: Founders and Makers of Illinois* (Chicago: S. J. Clarke, n.d.); *The United States Biographical Dictionary and Portrait Gallery of Eminent and Self-Made Men: Illinois Volume* (Chicago and New York: American Biographical Publishing, 1876, 1883); *The Biographical Encyclopedia of Illinois of the Nineteenth Century* (Philadelphia: Galaxy Publishing, 1875); Isaac N. Arnold, *William B. Ogden*; Donald E. Fehrenbacher, *Chicago Giant: A Biography of "Long John" Wentworth* (Madison: American History Research Center, 1957); Henry E. Hamilton, *Incidents and Events in the Life of Gurdon Saltonstall* (Chicago: Rand McNally, 1888); Clint Clay Tilton, "Gurdon Saltonstall Hubbard and Some of His Friends," *Illinois State Historical Society Transactions for the Year 1933*, no. 40, 81–178; W. B. Bushnell, *Biographical Sketches of Some of the Early Settlers of Chicago* (Chicago: Fergus Printing, 1876); Hubbard, *Autobiography*; *Industrial Chicago*, 6 vols. (Chicago: Goodspeed Publishing, 1891–96), vols. III–VI; Mrs. John (Juliette Magie) H. Kinzie, *Wau-Bun: The Early Days in the North-West* (Chicago: R. R. Donnelley & Sons, 1932), xxvi–vii, xlv, xlvii. For a more elaborate study of an overlapping group see Jocelyn Maynard Ghent and Frederic Cople Jaher, "The Chicago Business Elite: 1830–1930. A Collective Biography," *Business History Review*, L (Autumn, 1976), 288–328.

5. Pierce, *History*, I, 174–78, 418.

6. Hoyt, *One Hundred*, 24, 26, 32–47, 52–54, 98–99, 470; Moses and Kirkland, *History*, I, 82, 540–46; *Fergus' Directory of the City of Chicago, 1839* (Chicago: Fergus Printing, 1839), 47–49; Andreas, *History*, I, 124–25, 130–31, 136–37, II, 569; Pierce, *History*, I, 57–59, 124–25, II, 140, 143–46, 148–49; *Industrial*, IV, 17–24.

7. Pierce, *History*, I, 340–41.

8. James W. Putnam, "An Economic History of the Illinois and Michigan Canal," *Journal of Political Economy*, XVII (1909), 272–95, 337–53, 413–33; Putnam, *The Illinois and Michigan Canal* (Chicago: University of Chicago Press, 1918); Elmer A. Riley, *The Development of Chicago and Vicinity as a Manufacturing Center prior to 1880* (Chicago: University of Chicago Press, 1911), 84, 92–93; Pierce, *History*, I, 46–47, 58–61, 119–22, 149, 151n; Currey, *Manufacturing*, I, 135; Hoyt, *One Hundred*, 26–27, 45–53, 60; Moses and Kirkland, *History*, I, 97, 109, 119–20; Bross, *History*, 25; Andreas, *History*, I, 165–72; Tilton, "Gurdon Saltonstall Hubbard," 140, 149–50; Hamilton, *Incidents*, 169–70; Hubbard, *Autobiography*, xviii–xix.

9. W. H. Stennett, *Yesterday and Today: A History of the Chicago and North Western Railway System* (Chicago: n.p., 1910), 8–49, 55–57, 75–76; Moses and Kirkland, *History*, I, 416–84; Pierce, *History*, I, 51–52, 56–57, 75–76, 115–18, II, 146–47; Goodspeed, *University*, I, 46–47, 50–51, 101; *Industrial Chicago*, VI, 276–78.

10. Andreas, *History*, I, 617, II, 136–37, 462–63; John Wentworth, *Congressional Reminiscences* (Chicago: Fergus Printing, 1882), 39–42; Paul W. Gates, "The Disposal of the Public Domain in Illinois, 1848–1856," *Journal of Economic and Business History*, III (1930–31), 232; Fehrenbacher, *Chicago*, 109–10, 113–15; Pierce, *History*, II, 200–201.

11. Taylor, *History*, I, 70, 102, 135, 137, 149, 167, 218; Moses and Kirkland, *History*, I, 86, 89, 93, 287–88, 308–62, 560–66; Hotchkiss, *Industrial*, IV, 286–87; Andreas, *History*, I, 98–99, 106–11, 629–30; Judson F. Lee, "Transportation: A Factor in the Development of Northern Illinois Previous to 1860," *Journal of the Illinois State Historical Society*, X (Apr., 1917), 17–18, 24; John V. Farwell, *Some*, 55.

12. Hill, "Development," 251–54; Hotchkiss, *Industrial*, I–V, *passim*; Rudolf A. Clemen, *The American Livestock and Meat Industry* (New York: Ronald Press, 1923), 84, 92–108; Riley, *Development*, 22–23, 37–40, 54–57, 63–68, 72–73, 97, 101–2; S. S. Schoff, *The Industrial Interests of Chicago* (Chicago: Knight & Leonard, 1873), *passim*; Bross, *History*, 23, 50–52; Taylor, *History*, I, 102–3, 162–64, 173, 245; Moses and Kirkland, *History*, I, 389–92, 429–30; Andreas, *History*, II, 326–38, 680–81; Pierce, *History*, I, 137, 143, 148.

13. Wallace Rice, *75 Years of Gas Service in Chicago* (Chicago: Peoples' Gas Light and Coke, 1925), 3–6, 19–20; Arthur Charles Cole, *The Era of the Civil War, 1848–1870* (Springfield: Illinois Centennial Commission, 1919), 31; R. E. Heilman, "Chicago Traction," *Publications of the American Economic Association*, 3rd ser., IX (1908), 1–2; Harry P. Weber, *An Outline of Chicago Traction* (Chicago: n.p., 1936), 5–6; Moses and Kirkland, *History*, II, 528–29, 538–40; Andreas, *History*, II, 118–21.

14. Lyman J. Gage, "Banks and Banking," in Moses and Kirkland, *History*, I, 516.

15. Huston, *Financing*, I, 138; George William Dowrie, *The Development of Banking in Illinois* (Urbana: University of Illinois Press, 1913), 128.

16. Chicago *Democrat*, June 12, 1857, 2. For the history of early Chicago bankers and banking see William H. Harper and Charles H. Ravell, *Fifty Years of Banking in Chicago: The Merchants' Loan and Trust Co.* (Chicago: n.p., 1907), 31–40; James, *Growth*, I, 194–200, 203–4, 215–30, 255–57; Edward T. Perine, *The Story of the Trust Companies* (New York: G. P. Putnam's Sons, 1916), 104–6, 117; Huston, *Financing*, I, 108–24, 138, 141–42, 147–48; Moses and Kirkland, *History*, I, 517–18; Andreas, *History*, I, 159, 532–38, 547–49, II, 626–27; Pierce, *History*, 152–53, 156–59, II, 119–20.

17. James, *Growth*, I, 231–43, 268; Huston, *Financing*, I, 153–67; Andreas, *History*, I, 159; Pierce, *History*, II, 119–20, 128.

18. John Wentworth, *Address at the Calumet Club, May 18, 1852* (Chicago: Fergus Printing, 1882), 70.

19. Andreas, *History*, I, 549, II, 635–41; Pierce, *History*, I, 159; *Industrial*, IV, 657–77.

20. For lists of officeholders and their biographical backgrounds see Theodore Calvin Pease, *The Frontier State, 1818–1848* (Springfield: Illinois Centennial Commission, 1918), 283; Cole, *Era*, 190, 218–20; Pierce, *History*, I, 368–71, 376, 379–80, 421–23; Fehrenbacher, *Chicago*, 39, 52–55, 60, 68, 83, 121–22; Arnold, *Reminiscences*, 133; Fergus, *Directory . . . 1839*, 39; Fergus, *Directory . . . 1843* (Chicago: Fergus Printing, 1896), 5; Andreas, *History*, I, 116, 142, 148–49, 178, 189, 420–21, 594, II, 555, III, 875; Moses and Kirkland, *History*, I, 86, 90–91, 95–96, 102–3, 113–15, 130–32, 137–39; Fremont O. Bennett, *Politics and Politicians of Chicago, Cook County and Illinois* (Chicago: Blakely Printing, 1886), 52–59, 73, 75, 97, 100–13, 118, 129, 134, 176–79, 589, 606–7;

Donald S. Bradley and Mayer N. Zald, "From Commercial Elite to Political Administrator: The Recruitment of the Mayors of Chicago," *American Journal of Sociology*, LXXI (1966), 154–60; biographical references in n. 4.

21. Andreas, *History*, I, 142; Moses and Kirkland, *History*, I, 102.

22. Bradley and Zald, "From Commercial," 154–60; biographical references in n. 4.

23. Andreas, *History*, I, 433–34.

24. *Industrial Chicago*, VI, *passim*; Moses and Kirkland, *History*, II, 153, 197–98; Andreas, *History*, I, 420–21; Arnold, *Reminiscences*, 133; Farwell, *Some*, 56.

25. James Nevins Hyde, *Early Medical Chicago* (Chicago: Fergus Printing, 1879), 12–33; Moses, *History*, II, 232–34, 263; Andreas, *History*, I, 465.

26. Hyde, *Early*, 43, 50; Moses, *History*, II, 259, 272–73; Andreas, *History*, I, 465, 471, 597–98, II, 535; Fergus, *Directory* . . . *1843*, 12.

27. Andreas, *History*, I, 518, 521, II, 511, 670–72; Moses and Kirkland, *History*, II, 128–29, 135, 390–91, 393; Wood, ed., *Chicago*, 322; J. W. Norris, *Norris' Business Directory of the City of Chicago for 1846* (Chicago: Fergus Printing, 1883), 28; Mrs. Lyman Baird, *Chicago Home for the Friendless* (Chicago: n.p., 1909), 1–5; Pierce, *History*, I, 256–57, 259; Cole, *Era*, 218–20.

28. Mary Drummond, "Long Ago," in *Chicago*, ed. Kirkland, 141.

29. Gladwys Spencer, *The Chicago Public Library* (Chicago: University of Chicago Press, 1943), 6.

30. Moses and Kirkland, *History*, I, 77, 82–84, 89–90; Andreas, *History*, I, 210, II, 102, 107–8; Pierce, *History*, I, 157, 212n, 271n, 283n–84n; Fergus, *Directory* . . . *1843*, 13.

31. Pierce, *History*, I, 239–42; Fergus, *Directory* . . . *1843*, 13; Estelle F. Ward, *The Story of Northwestern University* (New York: Dodd, Mead, 1924), 6–9; Thomas Wakefield Goodspeed, *A History of the University of Chicago, 1891–1916* (Chicago: University of Chicago Press, 1916), 10–18; Moses and Kirkland, *History*, II, 111; Andreas, *History*, III, 815–16.

32. Drummond, "Long," 141.

33. Bross, *History*, 40; Andreas, *History*, I, 357; Norris, *Business* . . . *1846*, 28–29; Fergus, *Directory* . . . *1843*, 8.

34. John V. Farwell, quoted in Mrs. Abby (Farwell) Ferry, *Reminiscences of John V. Farwell by His Elder Daughter*, 2 vols. (Chicago: Ralph Seymour Fletcher Publisher, 1928), I, 118, 150.

35. Jeremiah Porter, *The Earliest Religious History of Chicago* (Chicago: Fergus Printing, 1882), 58, 64–65, 67–70; Elizabeth Voluntine Rumsey, *Recollections of a Pioneer's Daughter* (Pasadena: Castle Press, 1936), 16; Philo Otis, *The First Presbyterian Church* (Chicago: Fleming H. Revell, 1913), 20, 30, 308; Bross, *History*, 39; Frederick A. Cook, *Bygone Days in Chicago* (Chicago: A. C. McClurg, 1910), 91–92; Arnold, *William B. Ogden*, 10–11; Moses and Kirkland, *History*, II, 334, 348–52, 354, 366–67, 369, 376–82; Andreas, *History*, II, 410.

36. John Wentworth, *Early Chicago* (Chicago: Fergus Printing, 1876), 44.

37. Spencer, *Chicago*, 45–62, 100–101; Andreas, *History*, I, 522, II, 512–15; Moses and Kirkland, *History*, II, 130–31, 133–34; Pierce, *History*, I, 288n–89n, II, 299–400, 413; Fergus, *Directory* . . . *1843*, 9; William Kern Higley, "Historical Sketch of the Chicago Academy of Sciences," *Special Publications of the Chi-*

cago Academy of Sciences, no. 1 (1902), 5–33; Angle, *Chicago Historical Society*, 16, 21; Scammon quoted on 45–46.

38. Moses and Kirkland, *History*, II, 6–8, 19; Andreas, *History*, I, 376–77, 384; Herbert Fleming, "The Literary Institutions of Chicago," *American Journal of Sociology*, XII (1905–6), 385, 502.

39. Eugenia Remelin Whitridge, "Art in Chicago: The Structure of the Art World in a Metropolitan Community" Ph.D. Dissertation, University of Chicago, 1946), 36–39.

40. George P. Upton, *Musical Memories* (Chicago: A. C. McClurg, 1908), 214–15, 271–73.

41. Samuel Eliot Morison, *Harrison Gray Otis, 1765–1858: The Urbane Federalist* (Boston: Houghton Mifflin, 1969), 59–61; Carl Seaburg and Stanley Paterson, *Merchant Prince of Boston: Colonel T. H. Perkins, 1764–1854* (Cambridge: Harvard University Press, 1971), 118–21; Moses and Kirkland, *History*, II, 566–67; Andreas, *History*, I, 476.

42. Wentworth, *Early*, 35; Moses and Kirkland, *History*, I, 145; Pierce, *History*, I, 140, 190; Cook, *Bygone*, 178–79.

43. John Dean Caton quoted in Charles Fenno Hoffman, *A Winter in the West* (Chicago: Fergus Printing, 1882), 14n; Charles Cleaver, *Early Chicago Reminiscences* (Chicago: Fergus Printing, 1882), 12–15.

44. Hoffman, *Winter*, 14; Caton quoted in *ibid.*, 14n; Wentworth, *Early*, 37; Joseph Turner Ryerson, "Gleanings from a Family Memoir," in *Chicago*, ed. Kirkland, 60, 71–72.

45. Cleaver, *Early*, 15, 28; Ryerson, "Gleanings," 60; Mrs. William Blair, "Out of the Past," in *Chicago*, ed. Kirkland, 75, 82; Drummond, "Long," 140.

46. Hoffman, *Winter*, 15n; Arnold, *William B. Ogden*, 24–26.

47. Harriett Martineau, "Society in America," in *Reminiscences*, ed. McIlwaine, 30; Mrs. Leander J. McCormick to Mrs. Martha A. Hamilton, Feb. 10, 1838, in *Chicago*, ed. Kirkland, 38; Wentworth, *Early*, 35.

48. Drummond, "Long," 130–31; Blair, "Out," 85–86; Caton quoted in Hoffman, *Winter*, 14n; Ryerson, "Gleanings," 71.

49. Ryerson, "Gleanings," 60; Drummond, "Long," 141.

50. Wentworth, *Early*, 38; Ryerson, "Gleanings," 59; Ferry, *Reminiscences*, II, 126–28; Andreas, *History*, I, 158, 522–23; Pierce, *History*, I, 210–11; Emmet Dedmon, *Fabulous Chicago* (New York: Random House, 1953), 37–38; Moses and Kirkland, *History*, II, 603; Martha Freeman Esmond to Julia Boyd, July 10, 1858, in, *Letters*, ed. Clark, 18.

51. Jonathan Y. Scammon, "William B. Ogden," in Arnold, *William B. Ogden*, 55.

52. Mrs. John H. Kinzie, *Wau-Bun*, 302; W. B. Ogden quoted in Goodspeed, *Biographical*, I, 39; W. B. Ogden to J. Allen, Jan. 15, 1840, in Hoyt, *One Hundred*, 40; Wentworth, *Early*, 37,

53. M. F. Esmond to J. Boyd, Nov. 3, 1854, in, *Dear*, ed. Clark, 13; John V. Farwell, "Diary," May 5, 1850, in Ferry, *Reminiscences*, I, 151.

54. Scammon quoted in Bushnell, *Biographical*, 29; Farwell, "Diary," Sept. 12, 1849, I, 128; Esmond to Boyd, Nov. 3, 1854, in *Dear*, ed. Clark, 13; Isaac N. Arnold, *Addresses Delivered at the Annual Meeting of the Chicago Historical Society* (Chicago: Fergus Printing, 1877), 7.

55. Farwell, "Diary," Aug. 15, 1859, I, 117–18.

56. Addie Hibbard Gregory, A Great-Grandmother Remembers (Chicago: A. Kroch and Son, 1941), 7; Ogden quoted in Arnold, William B. Ogden, 8; Ryerson, "Gleanings," 71–72.

57. Hoyt, One Hundred, 279–80, 483; Moses and Kirkland, History, I, 201, 229; Pierce, History, III, 20.

58. Hoyt, One Hundred, 440, 337.

59. Pierce, History, III, 154–56.

60. Moses and Kirkland, History, I, 294; Ernest L. Bogart and Charles H. Thompson, The Industrial State, 1870–1893 (Chicago: A. C. McClurg, 1922), 376–78.

61. Hoyt, One Hundred, 481; Bogart and Thomas, Industrial, 389; Ernest L. Bogart and John M. Mathews, The Modern Commonwealth, 1893–1918 (Springfield: Illinois Centennial Commission, 1920), 94–95, 97, 102, 104, 107, 392, 400; Riley, Development, 109, 128; Glenn E. McLaughlin, Growth of American Manufacturing Areas (Pittsburgh: University of Pittsburgh Press, 1938), 111, 166–70; Industrial Chicago, III, 596–630; Moses and Kirkland, History, I, 240–41, II, 447–48, 463.

62. James, Growth, I, 512; Wallace Rice, The Chicago Stock Exchange (Chicago: R. R. Donnelley & Sons, 1923), 35–36; Hoyt, One Hundred, 489; Melchior Palyi, The Chicago Credit Market (Chicago: University of Chicago Press, 1937), 8–9, 210–11, 215–31, 252–54; Charles G. Dawes, "Chicago as a Banking Center," The World Today, XIII (July 12, 1907), 914–15; Huston, Financing, I, 367; Industrial Chicago, IV, 176–84, 310; Moses and Kirkland, History, I, 532; Pierce, History, III, 201–3.

63. Samuel Kerfoot quoted in Andreas, History, II, 569.

64. Eighth Biennial Report of the Bureau of Labor Statistics of Illinois: Subject—Taxation (Springfield: E. F. Hartman, 1896), 342–51.

65. Lloyd Wendt and Herman Kogan, Give the Lady What She Wants! (New York: Rand McNally, 1952), 66, 81–83; Chicago Tribune, May 14, 1905, 1, May 20, 1884, 9, Jan. 17, 1906, 9; Chicago Record-Herald, Jan. 7, 1901, 1–2; Wayne Andrews, Battle for Chicago (New York: Harcourt, Brace, 1946), 187–88.

66. Hoyt, One Hundred, 117–85; Eighth, 66–68, 75, 78–80, 130, 132, 215, 256, 342–51; Robert M. Haig, A History of the General Property Tax in Illinois (Urbana: University of Illinois Press, 1914), 145–214.

67. Palyi, Chicago, 69–72; James, Growth, I, 455–56, 494–95, 501–5; Hoyt, One Hundred, 124.

68. Charles B. Farwell to Francis B. Cooley, May 15, 1863, Farwell, Recollections, facing p. 73; Potter Palmer quoted in Harold Irwin Cleveland, "Fifty-five Years in Business: The Life of Marshall Field," System, X (July-Dec., 1906), 22, 24; William McCormick quoted in William T. Hutchinson, Cyrus Hall McCormick, 2 vols. (New York: Century, 1930, 35), I, 122–23.

69. Hoyt, One Hundred, 84; James, Growth, I, 363.

70. John S. Wright, Chicago: Past, Present, Future (Chicago: Horton & Leonard, 1870), 148–49; Colbert, Chicago, 76–77.

71. Guy A. Lee, "The Historical Significance of the Chicago Grain Elevator System," Agricultural History, II (1937), 24.

72. The best account of the grain trade is Taylor, History, I–II, passim; cf.

Lee, "Historical," 16–32; Andreas, *History*, II, 359–82, III, 333–34; Moses and Kirkland, *History*, I, 308–62; Pierce, *History*, III, 65–91.

73. *The Third-Fourth Annual Report of the Trade and Commerce of Chicago, 1891* (Chicago: J. M. W. Jones, 1892), xxi.

74. Andreas, *History*, II, 354–55, 382; Pierce, *History*, II, 95–96; James, *Growth*, I, 356–61.

75. Ferry, *Reminiscences*, II, 19–21, 40, 60–78, 118–23; Wendt and Kogan, *Give*, 47, 51, 56; Robert Twyman, *History of Marshall Field & Co., 1852–1906* (Philadelphia: University of Pennsylvania Press, 1954), 11–12.

76. Twyman, "Potter Palmer: Merchandizing Innovator of the West," *Explorations in Entrepreneurial History*, IV (1951–52), 58–68; Twyman, *History*, 2–8; Wendt and Kogan, *Give*, 16–20, 36–37, 57–62; Bank of Commercial Ratings quoted on 39.

77. Farwell quoted in Wendt and Kogan, *Give*, 51; Farwell quoted in Cleveland, "Fifty," 462, 559, 561, 564, 567; McCormick quoted in Twyman, *History*, 16; Field quoted in Cleveland, "Fifty," 563, cf. 26.

78. Twyman, *History*, 19–30, 34–37, 51, 54–55, 99–101; S. H. Ditchett, *M. Field and Co.: The Life Story of a Great Concern* (New York: Dry Goods Economist, 1922), 70–75; Wendt and Kogan, *Give*, 203–4.

79. Harlow N. Higinbotham, *The Making of a Merchant* (Chicago: Forbes, 1906), 67–68, 96, 192.

80. Wendt and Kogan, *Give*, 65–171, 178–81, 184–238, 288–94; Twyman, *History*, 17ff., for sales and profits see 172; Cleveland, "Fifty-five," *System*, IX–XI (1906–7), 455–56, 556–67, 21–30, 129–38, 456–64, 574–82, 49–56, 123–32, 229–37, 361–68, 453–63; Ditchett, *M. Field and Co., passim; Eighth*, 66–67.

81. Palyi, *Chicago*, 62; "Investment Banking in Chicago," *University of Illinois Research Bulletin*, XXXIX (1931), 7–12, 40–41; Moses and Kirkland, *History*, I, 432–40, 453–62, 480–87; Pierce, *History*, II, 389–91.

82. Stennett, *Yesterday*, 4–5, 68–69, 75–76, 89–91, 93–94, 171–73, 180–81.

83. Chicago *Record-Herald*, Jan. 7, 1901, 1–2; Chicago *Tribune*, Jan. 17, 1906, 9; Julius Grodinsky, *Transcontinental Railway Strategy, 1869–1893: A Study of Businessmen* (Philadelphia: University of Pennsylvania Press, 1962), 183, 314–18, 328; Harper Leech and John C. Carroll, *Armour and His Times* (New York: D. Appleton-Century, 1938), 148–50; H. H. Porter, *A Short Autobiography* (Chicago: privately printed, 1915), 13, 22, 27–28, 31–33.

84. Cleveland, "Fifty," 55, 581–82; Hutchinson, *Cyrus Hall McCormick*, II, 593, 715–16; Charles Edward Russell, "The Greatest Trust in the World," *Everybody's Magazine*, XII (1905), 291–98, 503–61, 643–54, 779–92, XIII (1906), 56–66, 217–27; Pierce, *History*, III, 122.

85. John Roscoe Moore, "Taxation of Corporations in Illinois Other than Railroads since 1872," *University of Illinois Studies in the Social Sciences*, II (Jan., 1913), 94–95; John A. Fairlie, "Taxation in Illinois," *American Economic Review*, I (1911), 521, 526.

86. Pierce, *History*, II, 296, III, 318–19.

87. Palyi, *Chicago*, 46–48; Pierce, *History*, III, 216–18; Charles G. Dawes, *A Journal of the McKinley Years* (Chicago: R. R. Donnelly Sons, 1950), 418; *Forty Years of Investment Banking, 1882–1922* (n.p.: privately printed, n.d.), 8–14, 433; Twyman, *History*, 87; Willard E. Hotchkiss, "Chicago Traction: A Study in

Political Evolution," *Annals of the American Academy of Political and Social Science*, XXVIII (Nov., 1906), 27–46; Heilman, "Chicago," 2–22; Weber, *Outline*, 25–34; Forest McDonald, *Insull* (Chicago: University of Chicago Press, 1962), 55–132; Chicago *Tribune*, July 17, 1906, 4; Chicago *Record-Herald*, Jan. 7, 1901, 1–2; Andreas, *History*, III, 164–65; Samuel Wilbur Norton, *Chicago Traction* (Chicago: privately published, 1907), 26–107; Nicholas Komonos, "Chicago 1893–1907: The Politics of Reform," (Ph.D. dissertation, George Washington University, 1961), 157–71, 199–222; Sidney I. Roberts, "Businessmen in Revolt: Chicago 1874–1900," (Ph.D. dissertation, Northwestern University, 1960), 183–239; Moses and Kirkland, *History*, II, 533–35, 538–40.

88. *Eighth*, 237, 243.

89. Pierce, *History*, II, 320, III, 221–29; Rice, 75, 39–40; Goodspeed, *University of Chicago Biographical Sketches*, II, 206–12; McDonald, *Insull*, 52–132; Herbert N. Casson, *The History of the Telephone* (Chicago: A. C. McClurg, 1910), 185; Currey, *Manufacturing*, II, 171–73; Samuel Insull, *Public Utilities in Modern Life: Selected Speeches* (Chicago: privately printed, 1924), 342–43.

90. *Eighth*, 239–41, 244, 253.

91. *Industrial*, III, 595.

92. Andreas, *History*, II, 392; P. D. Armour to Kirk Armour, Oct. 26, 1900, in Leech and Carroll, *Armour*, 97–98.

93. Clemen, *American*, 136ff.; Louis F. Swift and Arthur Van Vlissingen, *The Yankee of the Yards* (Chicago: A. W. Shaw, 1927), *passim*; Goodspeed, *University of Chicago Biographical Sketches*, I, 84–95, 173–201; Edward J. Dies, *Street of Advent* (Boston: Stratford, 1935), 96–103; "Sketch of the Life of Philip D. Armour," Chicago *Record-Herald*, Jan. 17, 1901, 1–2; William T. Kane, *The Education of Edward Cudahay* (Chicago: Effingham Printing, 1941), *passim*; Dawes, *Journal*, 31; Russell, "Greatest," *passim*; "Armour Fortune," *Fortune*, III (Apr., 1931), 49; Leech and Carroll, *Armour*, 47–49, 52, 117–67, 235–320, 348; Pierce, *History*, II, 93–97, III, 108–39; J. Ogden Armour, *The Packers, the Private Car Lines, and the People* (Philadelphia: Altimus, 1906).

94. Swift and Van Vlissingen, *Yankee*, 137; "Armour Fortune," 49; Pierce, *History*, III, 108–9, 112–13; Leech and Carroll, *Armour*, 342, 348.

95. Moses and Kirkland, *History*, II, 421.

96. Hutchinson, *Cyrus Hall McCormick*, I, 6–22, 263–66, 274, 307–8, 321, 327–77, 452, 454, 466–68, II, 74, 100–101, 421–25, 435, 593, 715–16; Moses and Kirkland, *History*, II, 429–31; Herbert N. Casson, *Cyrus Hall McCormick: His Life and Work* (Chicago: A. C. McClurg, 1909), 78ff., McCormick quoted on 184; Casson, *The Romance of the Reaper* (New York: Doubleday, Page, 1908), *passim*.

97. Helen M. Kramer, "Harvesters and High Finance: Formation of the International Harvester Co.," *Business History Review*, XXXVIII (Autumn, 1964), 289–95; Cyrus Hall McCormick, Jr., "What 71 Years in Business Have Taught Us," *System*, XXX (1916), 224–29.

98. McCormick, Jr.: "What," 230, 360–61, 654; "Harvester Club Dinner, December 12, 1914," *Harvester World*, XXVII (July, 1936), 24–26: VI (Feb. 3, 1916), 41–42.

99. Moses and Kirkland, *History*, II, 409–11.

100. Wright, *Chicago*, 24–411; Schoff, *Industrial Interests*, 11–12; Riley, *De-*

velopment, 99–103; *Industrial*, III, 699–702; Andreas, *History*, II, 674–78, III, 676; Currey, *Manufacturing*, II, 14–15; Moses and Kirkland, *History*, II, 406–15; Porter, *Short*, 35; New York *Times*, Aug. 3, 1971, 28; Twyman, *History*, 86.

101. Moore, "Taxation," 70; *Eighth*, 239–40.

102. Joseph Husband, *The Story of the Pullman Car* (Chicago: A. C. McClurg, 1917), 24–28, 32–40, 47–48, 53, 103–4, 157; Twyman, *History*, 88; Cleveland, "Fifty," 575–78; Chicago *Tribune*, Jan. 17, 1906, 2; Moore, "Taxation," 96; *Eighth*, 239.

103. Richard Teller Crane, *The Autobiography of Richard Teller Crane* (Chicago: privately printed, 1927), 31–33, 38–43, 47–52, 55–56, 59, 66–69, 75–107, 110–13, 121–41, 213–14; "Crane Plumbing," *Fortune*, XIII (June, 1936), 124; Chicago *Tribune*, Jan. 9, 1912, 1–2.

104. *Industrial*, III, 678–84, V, *passim*.

105. Palyi, *Chicago*, 46–54, 58–60, 62–65, 216; Huston, *Financing*, I, 502, 519–20, 537, 542; James, *Growth*, I, 516, 558, 563, 565–66; "Investment Banking in Chicago," *University of Illinois Bureau of Business Research Bulletin*, no. 39 (1931), 7; *Forty*, 7, 39, A. G. Farr quoted on 39.

106. James, *Growth*, I, 488–89; Dawes, "Chicago," 914–15.

107. James B. Forgan, *Recollections of a Busy Life* (New York: Bankers' Publishing, 1924), 311–12. For the history of the First National Bank of Chicago see Henry C. Morris, *The History of the First National Bank of Chicago* (Chicago: R. R. Donnelley & Sons, 1902), *passim*; Guy Wickes Cooke, *The First National Bank of Chicago* (n.p.: privately printed, 1913), *passim*; Forgan, *Recollections*, 121–23, 126–27, 139–50, 230–31; James, *Growth*, I, 341–46, 430, 488–90, 510–12, II, 691–95, 698, 704–6.

108. Arthur D. Welton, *The Making of a Modern Bank—the Continental and Commercial Banks* (Chicago: privately printed, 1923), *passim*. For Field's and Armour's holdings see Chicago *Tribune*, Jan. 17, 1906, 9; Chicago *Record-Herald*, Jan. 7, 1901, 1–2. For data on Chicago banks and bankers see Morris, *History*; Cooke, *First*; Welton, *Making*; Forgan, *Recollections*, 116, 121–27, 131–33, 221–31; Dawes, *Journal*, 311–12; Gage, "Banks and Banking," 516–39; James, *Growth*, I, 284ff., II, 673–881; Huston, *Financing*, I, 250ff.; *Industrial Chicago*, IV, 188–93, 249, 286–87; Andreas, *History*, II, 626–41, III, 438–39, 449; Palyi, *Chicago*, 231, 238; Henry S. Henschen, *A History of the State Bank of Chicago from 1879 to 1904* (Chicago: Lakeside Press, 1905).

109. Gage quoted in Henschen, *History*, 47–48.

110. William H. Harper and Charles H. Ravell, *Fifty Years of Banking in Chicago: The Merchants Loan and Trust Co.* (Chicago: privately printed, 1907), 16–17, 25, 31–40, 63–72; James, *Growth*, I, 428–29; Andreas, *History*, III, 449.

111. Smith and Wentworth quoted in Andrews, *Battle*, 85–86; Gage, "Banks," 536; Forgan, *Recollections*, 125, 36; Dawes, "Chicago," 915.

112. Huston, *Financing*, I, 230–31, 237–38, 248–51, 308–15; James, *Growth*, I, 376–78, 445–56, 501–8, 580–87, II, 673–80, 704–6, 714–20, 828–29; Huston, *Financing*, I, 251, 264–76; Dawes, *Journal*, 397–400; Lyman J. Gage, *Memoirs of Lyman J. Gage* (New York: House of Field, 1937), 75–79.

113. James, *Growth*, I, 458, 595–98.

114. Bogart and Mathews, *Modern*, 443; *Eighth*, 24–31; Moore, "Taxation," 57–58.

115. Palyi, *Chicago*, 46–56; James, *Growth*, I, 564; Huston, *Financing*, I, 519–33, 537–42; Rice, *Chicago*, 9–25; *Forty*, 7–14, 39.

116. Goodspeed, *University of Chicago Biographical Sketches*, II, 135, 142; *Forty*, 41–42; Currey, *Chicago*, IV, 571–74; Insull, *Public*, 342–43.

117. Rice, *Chicago*, 75–80.

118. Andreas, *History*, II, 44–46, III, 461–70.

119. Ghent and Jaher, "Chicago Business Elite," 288–328.

120. G. F. Swift quoted in Andrews, *Battle*, 95.

121. Dawes, *Journal*, 426–27.

122. "Incomes of the First District of Illinois. List of Incomes Above and Including $3,000. Returned to the Assessor of Internal Revenue for the Year Ending December 31, 1863, upon Which a Tax of Five Percent Is Assessed," Chicago *Tribune*, Jan. 7, 1865, p. 9; Taylor, *History*, I, 334; Currey, *Chicago*, II, 193; Joseph T. Ryerson Estate, Chicago *Tribune*, Sept. 30, 1887, 2; Andrews, *Battle*, 155–56, 201; "Will of Joseph Medill," New York *Tribune*, Mar. 26, 1899, 2.

123. The list of high-income earners is taken from "Incomes." Biographical data on those on the list was derived from references in n. 4 and *Men of Illinois* (Chicago: Halliday Witherspoon, 1912); Glenn A. Bishop and Paul T. Gilbert, *Chicago's Accomplishments and Leaders* (Chicago: Bishop Publishing, 1932); *The Biographical Dictionary and Portrait Gallery of Representative Men of Chicago, Milwaukee and the World's Columbian Exposition* (Chicago and New York: American Biographical Publishing, 1892); *A Biographical History with Portraits of Prominent Men of the Great West* (Chicago: Manhattan Publishing, 1894); *Illinois and Its Builders* (Chicago: Illinois Biographical Association, 1925); E. R. Pritchard, *Illinois of To-day and Its Progressive Cities* (Chicago: Illinois of To-day, 1897); John Moses, ed., *Biographical Dictionary and Portrait Gallery of the Representative Men of the United States. Illinois Volume* (Chicago: Lewis Publishing, 1896); *Encyclopedia of Biography of Illinois*, 2 vols. (Chicago: Century Publishing, 1892); Edward F. Dunne, *Illinois, the Heart of the Nation*, 5 vols. (Chicago and New York: Lewis Publishing, 1933), vols. 3–5; George W. Smith, *History of Illinois and Her People*, 6 vols. (Chicago and New York: American Historical Society, 1927), vols. 4–6; *Centennial History of the City of Chicago: Its Men and Institutions* (Chicago: Chicago Inter Ocean, 1905); John J. Flinn, *The Hand-book of Chicago Biography: A Compendium of Useful Biographical Information for Reference and Study* (Chicago: Standard Guide, 1893); John M. Palmer, ed., *The Bench and Bar of Illinois*, 2 vols. (Chicago: Lewis Publishing, 1899); Henry Hall, ed., *America's Successful Men of Affairs*, 2 vols. (New York: New York Tribune, 1896), vol. 2. For a prosopagraphical analysis of an overlapping group see Ghent and Jaher, "Chicago Business Elite," 288–328.

124. Pierce, *History*, II, 481.

125. "American Millionaires," *Tribune Monthly*, IV (June, 1892), 12–15.

126. Ghent and Jaher, "Chicago Business Elite," 288–328.

127. The list is taken from "American Millionaires," 12–15. In addition to references in nn. 4 and 123 biographical data on the millionaires was derived from *Prominent Citizens and Industries of Chicago* (Chicago: German Press

Club of Chicago, 1901); John W. Leonard, ed., *The Book of Chicagoans: A Biographical Dictionary of Leading Living Men of the City of Chicago* (Chicago: A. N. Marquis, 1905); *Notable Men of Illinois and Their State* (Chicago: Chicago Daily Journal, 1912); *Notable Men of Chicago and Their City* (Chicago: Chicago Daily Journal, 1910); Mae F. Herringshaw, ed., *Clark J. Herringshaw's City Blue Book of Current Biography: Chicagoans of 1914* (Chicago: American Publishers' Association, 1914); *Who's Who in the Central States: A Business, Professional and Social Record of Men and Women of Achievement in the Central States, 1929* (Washington, D.C.: Mayflower Publishing, 1929). For a similar study see Ghent and Jaher, "Chicago Business Elite," 288–328.

128. Pierce, *History*, III, 515.

129. Field quoted on the elements of success in Currey, *Manufacturing*, I, 198; Field quoted in Cleveland, "Fifty-five," 457–58; Wendt and Kogan, *Give*, 178–81; Higinbotham, *Making*, 16, 27, 39–40. For McCormick's thoughts and the testimony of his family and associates see Casson, *Romance*, 31–32, 40–42, 391; Casson, *Cyrus Hall McCormick*, 53–54, 140–46, 186–87; Hutchinson, *Cyrus Hall McCormick*, I, 456, II, 746, 749, 754–55, 759–60, 761n, 769–70. For Swift see Helen Swift, *My Father and My Mother* (Chicago: privately printed, 1937), 33, 46, 58, 81, 116–17, 156; Swift and Van Vlissingen, *Yankee*, 3–23, 48–55, 82–110, 138–77, 194. For Armour see *Chicago Record Herald*, January 7, 1901, 1–2; H. I. Cleveland, "Philip Armour, Merchant," *World's Work*, VI (March, 1901), 547; Frank W. Gunsaulus, "Philip D. Armour: A Character Sketch," *American Monthly Review of Reviews*, XXIII (Jan., 1901), 169, 172–73, 176; Arthur Warren, "Philip D. Armour," *McClure's Magazine*, II (1893–94), 264, 266, 269–70, 278; Armour quoted in W. T. Stead, *If Christ Came to Chicago* (Chicago: Laird and Lee, 1894), 80–81; Leech and Carroll, *Armour*, 1, 23–24, 54, 66, 81, 84, 88, 121, 219–22; Poole, *Giants*, 139, 146, 152, 154, 156. For Crane see Crane, *Autobiography*, 15, 108, 213–14. For Gage see Gage, *Memoirs*, 97, 234. For Insull see Insull, *Public*, 20–21, 38–39, 185, 361.

130. Cyrus H. McCormick to William S. McCormick, May 15, 1845, in Hutchinson, *Cyrus Hall McCormick*, I, 462; Dies, *Street*, 215–16; Armour quoted in Leech and Carroll, *Armour*, 41; Mrs. Reginald De Koven, "The Influence of Great Riches upon the Rich Themselves," *The Independent*, LIV (May 1, 1902), 1063–64.

131. C. H. McCormick, Jr., to C. H. McCormick, Sept. 2, 1882, in Hutchinson, *Cyrus Hall McCormick*, 689.

132. Poole, *Giants*, 154; Leech and Carroll, *Armour*, 81, Armour quoted on 82; Philip D. Armour to Philip D. Armour Jr., and J. Ogden Armour, Dec. 19, 1899, in *ibid.*, 219–22.

133. Swift and Van Vlissingen, *Yankee*, 93; Swift, *My*, 116–17; Frazier Jelke quoted in Dedmon, *Fabulous*, 194.

134. C. H. McCormick, Jr., "Address before the North Central Academic Association, Mar. 15, 1918"; *Daily Princetonian*, Jan. 24, 1916; "Address before the Harvester Club, 1917," *Harvester World*, XXVII (July, 1936), 42, 44. For biographical data from which this table is derived see nn. 4, 20, 123, 127; Pierce, *History*, III, 539; Andreas, *History*, III, 182–84, 250, 846; Moses and Kirkland,

History, I, 139, 226, 233–34; Bennett, *Politics*, 140–51, 197, 363.

135. David Kinley, *The Spirit of the Union League Club, 1879–1926* (Chicago: Union League Club, 1926), 66–67, 71.

136. Joseph Medill and Robert R. McCormick quoted in Andrews, *Battle*, 65, 231.

137. Ernest R. May, *American Imperialism: A Speculative Essay* (New York: Atheneum, 1968), 45–76; Joseph Zimmerman, "Chicago and Imperialism" (Ph.D. dissertation, University of Illinois, 1971), 26–33, 136–45, 182–94.

138. Dawes, *Journal*, 369–70; Hutchinson, *Cyrus Hall McCormick*, II, 43–47, 59–60, 308–59; Leech and Carroll, *Armour*, 291–92.

139. F. W. Coyne, *In Reminiscence* (Chicago: privately printed, 1941), 200. John Coughlin and John Powers quoted in Ray Ginger, *Altgeld's America* (New York: Funk & Wagnalls, 1958), 112.

140. Michael Patrick McCarthy, "Businessmen and Professionals in Municipal Reform: The Chicago Experience, 1887–1920" (Ph.D. dissertation, University of Chicago, 1970), 7–22; Dawes, *Journal*, 416, 419–22; Leech and Carroll, *Armour*, 171; Ginger, *Altgeld's*, 133–34.

141. Lyman Gage quoted in Andrews, *Battle*, 134–37; cf. Ginger, *Altgeld's*, 58.

142. *Eighth*, xiii–iv, xviii, xxi–ii, and *passim*; Moore, "Taxation," 36–103; Fairlie, "Taxation," 519–34; Charles Edward Merriam, *Report of an Investigation of the Municipal Revenues of Chicago* (Chicago: City Club of Chicago, 1906), *passim*.

143. Merriam, *Report*, 4, 23, 30, 33–35; Bennett, *Politics*, 363.

144. Hutchinson, *Cyrus Hall McCormick*, II, 324; Roberts, "Businessmen," 49–51; Crane, *Autobiography*, 217; Pierce, *History*, III, 356–57; Henry Justin Smith, "Social Chicago Fifty Years Ago," *Illinois State Historical Society Transactions for the Year 1933*, no. 40, 39–41; Joel Arthur Tarr, *A Study in Boss Politics: William Lorimer of Chicago* (Urbana: University of Illinois Press, 1971), 34–35; Claudius D. Johnson, *Carter Henry Harrison I: Political Leader* (Chicago: University of Chicago Press, 1928), 118, 179, 184–99; Charles Edward Merriam, *Chicago: A More Intimate View of Urban Politics* (New York: Macmillan, 1929), 20–22; Bennett, *Politics*, 214, 264; Bruce Grant, *Fight for a City: The Story of the Union League Club of Chicago and Its Times, 1880–1955* (New York: Rand McNally, 1955) 69–80; Bradley and Zald, "Commercial," 163; Philip Kinsley, *The Chicago Tribune: Its First Hundred Years*, 3 vols. (New York: Alfred A. Knopf, 1943–46), II, 290–304, III, 9–10.

145. H. C. Taylor: "Romanism and Republicanism," *America*, I (July 7, 1888), 4–5; "Editorial," *ibid.* (Oct. 4, 1888), 2; "Naturalizing America," *ibid.* (July 21, 1888), 3–4; "The Indifference of the Intelligent Man to Politics," *ibid.* (Feb. 28, 1889), 2–3; *Chicago* (Houghton Mifflin, 1917), 97; Lyman J. Gage, "Chicago and Its Administration," *Open Court*, XI (1897), 198–99, 205–6; Franklin MacVeagh: "Presidential Address, 1874," *Addresses and Reports of the Citizens' Association of Chicago, 1874–1898* (Chicago: Hazlitt, 1898), 4; speech in the *Proceedings of the National Conference for Good City Government Held at Philadelphia, January 25–26, 1894* (Philadelphia: Municipal League, 1894), 84–86; "A Programme of Municipal Reform," *American Journal of Sociology*, I

(July-May, 1895–96), 551, 556–60; Andrews, *Battle*, 127–28; Kinsley, *Chicago*, II, 200–349.

146. *Addresses and Reports*; *Annual Report[s] of the Citizens' Association of Chicago, 1898–1935*; Sidney I. Roberts, "Chicago's Civic Profiles," *Union League Men and Events*, XXXIII (Sept., 1967), 5, 15–17, (Oct., 1967), 10–15; Roberts, "Businessmen," 18–23, 39, 71–79, 101–11; Hoyt King, *Citizen Cole of Chicago* (Chicago: Munroe & Southworth, 1931), 86–94, 120–22; Frank Mann Stewart, *A Half Century of Municipal Reform: The History of the Municipal League* (Berkeley and Los Angeles: University of California Press, 1950), 11; Kinley, *Spirit*, 82–83; Helen Horowitz, "Culture and the City: Philanthropy in Chicago from the 1880s to 1917" (Ph.D. dissertation, Harvard University, 1972), 71; Pierce, *History*, III, 252, 281.

147. Roberts, "Chicago," *Men and Events*, XXXIV (Feb. 2, 1958), 14.

148. Pierce, *History*, III, 375–76; Moses and Kirkland, *History*, I, 246; Merriam, *Chicago*, 105–6; Komons, "Chicago," 77–78, 155–56, 199–224, 262–63; Roberts. "Businessmen," 101–7, 119, 120–76, 200–239; King, *Citizen*, 42–43, 59–72; Graham Taylor, *Pioneering on Social Frontiers* (Chicago: University of Chicago Press, 1930), 51–81; Roberts, "Chicago," 15; Norton, *Chicago*, 68–77, 85–100, 113–17; Tarr, "Study," 80–81.

149. Gage, *Memoirs*, 69–70; Douglas Sutherland, *Fifty Years on the Civic Front* (Chicago: Civic Federation, 1943), 4–5, 8, 10–11, 15, 23–26, 30–31, 37–43, 87–98; Roberts, "Businessmen," 119–35; Komons, "Chicago," 54–57, 76–77, 248; Albion W. Small, "The Civic Federation of Chicago," *American Journal of Sociology*, I (July-May, 1895–96), 79–103; Roberts, "The Municipal Voters' League and Chicago's Boodlers," *Journal of the Illinois State Historical Society*, LIII (1960), 125; McCarthy, "Businessmen," 49–50.

150. Roberts: "Municipal," 129–32, 143; "Businessmen," 158–59, 170–76, 183, 200–230; Melville E. Stone, *Fifty Years a Journalist* (Garden City, N.Y.: Doubleday, Page, 1921), 157–63; Charles H. Dennis, *Victor Lawson: His Time and His Work* (Chicago: University of Chicago Press, 1935), 282–89, 317–29; King, *Citizen*, 36, 42–43, 59–72, 77, 81; Merriam, *Chicago*, 105–6; Komons, "Chicago," 262–63; Sutherland, *Fifty*, 16; Wendt and Kogan, *Lords*, 235.

151. Komons, "Chicago," 107, 197, 259, 274–75, 383–84, 398, 415; Tarr, *Study*, 184–85; Sutherland, *Fifty*, 23–26, 30–31, 37–43, 87–98; Merriam, *Chicago*, 107; McCarthy, "Businessmen," 66–81, 153–54, 159–60, 179.

152. For Field's views see interviews in the Chicago *Record Herald*, Oct. 18, 1905, 3; Chicago *Tribune*, Oct. 23, 1905, 1–2. For MacVeagh see Komons, "Chicago," 358. For anti-union sentiment see John Tebbel, *An American Dynasty* (Garden City, N.Y.: Doubleday, Page, 1947), 52–58; editorial in the Chicago *Tribune*, July 3, 1894, 6; Kinsley, *Chicago*, II, 200–349; Wendt, *Give*, 171; Twyman, *Marshall Field*, 164–66; Cleveland, "Fifty-Five," 575–78; "Mr. Pullman's Statement," New York *Tribune*, July 14, 1894, 1; Swift and Van Vlissingen, *Yankee*, 110, 180–81; Hutchinson, *Cyrus Hall McCormick*, II, 616–17; Leech and Carroll, *Armour*, 226, 230; Andrews, *Battle*, 106–9; Horowitz, "Culture," 76; Stone, *Fifty*, 77.

153. Franklin H. Head, "The President and the Facts," *America*, I (Dec. 20, 1888), 2; MacVeagh: "Programme," 558; "Presidential," 4.

154. Cole, *Citizen*, 81, 99–102; Kent, *William Kent*, 110.

155. Louise de Koven Bowen, *Growing up with a City* (New York: Macmillan, 1926), 166–67; L. Bowen to Francis B. Daniels, Apr. 13, 1911, Jan. 8, 1912, to Julius Rosenwald, Feb. 11, 1915, to C. H. McCormick, Jr., June 2, 1916, to Elbert H. Gary, Mar. 10, 1921, in Bowen, *Speeches, Addresses and Letters of Louise de Koven Bowen*, 2 vols. (Ann Arbor: Edwards Bros., 1937), I, 152–56, 168–71, 228–31, 320, 364, 401–3, 428–29, II, 624, 791.

156. Joseph Medill Patterson interview, Chicago *Record-Herald*, Mar. 30, 1906, 1, 4; Patterson, "Confessions of a Drone," *The Independent*, LXI (Aug. 30, 1906), 493–95; Patterson, "Marshall Fields' Will: A Socialist View of It," *Collier's Magazine*, XXXVII (June 2, 1906), 24, 26; Alfred Henry Lewis, "Joseph Medill Patterson: An Apostle of Hope," *Saturday Evening Post*, CLXXIX (Sept. 15, 1906), 3–5.

157. Ellen M. Henrotin, "The Attitude of Women's Clubs and Associations toward Social Economics," *Bulletin of the Department of Labor*, IV (July, 1899), 501–45; Jennie June Croly, *The History of the Woman's Club Movement in America* (New York: Henry G. Allen, 1898), 61–73; Henriette Greenebaum Frank and Amalie Hofer Jerome, *Annals of the Chicago Woman's Club* (Chicago: Chicago Woman's Club, 1916), 17–18, 125, 127, 130, 148, 168–69, 229, 243, 296, 328. For comparison among Chicago, New York, and Boston women see Croly, *History*, 60–73, 392–93, 588–675, 855–966.

158. Henrotin, "Attitude," 501–2; Agnes Geneva Gilman and Gertrude Marcelle Gilman, *Who's Who in Illinois: Women-Makers of History* (Chicago: Eclectic Press, 1927), 39, 48–49, 93, 152; Georgia L. Osborne, *Brief Biographies of the Figurines on Display in the Illinois State Historical Library* (Springfield: Illinois Government Printing Office, 1932), 127, 134; Ishbel Ross, *Silhouette in Diamonds* (New York: Harper & Bros., 1960), 60–64, 70–72, 105–8, 121–23, 178–81; Mrs. Potter Palmer: *Addresses and Reports of Mrs. Potter Palmer* (Chicago: Rand McNally, 1894), *passim*; "Speech to the Exposition, October 12, 1892," in *A History of the World's Columbian Exposition*, ed. Rossiter Johnson, 4 vols. (New York: D. Appleton, 1897), I, 277–80; Bowen: *Growing*, 102–41, 171–74, 182–83, 201, 208, 218; *Speeches*, I, 104, 107, 228–31, 305, 365–84, II, 536, 651.

159. Mrs. Palmer: "Address at the Opening of the Woman's Building, May 1, 1893," in Palmer, *Addresses*, 133, 136–39; cf., "Address to the Fortnightly Club of Chicago, April 10, 1891," *ibid.*, 44–45, 48–49; "Speech," Johnson, *History*, I, 278–80.

160. *Industrial*, VI, 53–56, 62, 122–26, 148–51, 170–72, 176–80, 286, 345–46, 447–49, 558–59, 649–50, 665–66, 826–28, 734; Andreas, *History*, II, 132–33, 454, 467, 469, 479, III, 103; Currey, *Chicago*, IV, 30–35, 132–38, V, 421–24; "American," 12–15.

161. *Industrial*, VI, 619–20, 872–74; Pierce, *History*, III, 395–96.

162. Arnold, *Reminiscences*, 153; Thomas Hoyne, *The Lawyer as Pioneer* (Chicago: Fergus Printing, 1882), 101–2; Elliott Anthony quoted in *Industrial*, VI, 737.

163. *Industrial*, VI, *passim*; Andreas, *History*, II, 479; Currey, *Chicago*, IV, 35, 132–38, V, 421–42.

164. Currey, *Chicago*, V, 733–34; Andreas, *History*, II, 395, 508, 522, 525–26,

III, 507–41, 547; Herma Clark, *The Elegant Eighties When Chicago Was Young* (Chicago: A. C. McClurg, 1941), 19–21; Goodspeed, *University of Chicago Biographies*, II, 205, 229.

165. Kinsley, *Chicago*, I, 43, II, 244, 278; Stone, *Fifty*, 50; Dennis, *Lawson*, 112, 390.

166. For Chicago newspaper history see Kinsley, *Chicago*, I–III; Tebbel, *American*; Stone, *Fifty*; Dennis, *Lawson*; Jack Alexander, "The Duke of Chicago," *Saturday Evening Post*, CCXIV (July 10, 1941), 10–11, 70–75; "Will of Joseph Medill," 2.

167. John Visher, *Hand-Book of Charities* (Chicago: Charles H. Kerr, 1894), 24–26, 35–38, 42–45; Wood, *Chicago*, 321–32; Baird, *Chicago*, 7–83; Clark, *Elegant*, 145–47; Moses and Kirkland, *History*, I, 211, II, 129, 135, 388–91, 393; Andreas, *History*, III, 604–12; Farwell, *Some Recollections*, 101, 131.

168. Visher, *Hand-book*, 51–55, 78–81, 85, 91, 95–96, 184–88, 199–200, 238–39; Clark, *Elegant*, 8–9; Wood, *Chicago*, 411; Moses and Kirkland, *History*, II, 259–60, 392, 394; Andreas, *History*, III, 519–22, 526, 609–12.

169. Visher, *Hand-book*, 42–45, 51–55, 95–96, 116–21; Moses and Kirkland, *History*, I, 211; Frank and Jerome, *Annals*, 369–78.

170. McCarthy, "Businessmen," 82–99, 104–5.

171. Sadie American, "The Movement for Small Playgrounds," *American Journal of Sociology*, III (1898), 159–60; Henry S. Curtis, "Vacation Schools and Playgrounds," *Harper's Monthly Magazine*, CV (June, 1902), 24; Walter Wood, "The Playground Movement in America and Its Relation to Public Education," Great Britain Board of Education, *Educational Pamphlets*, no. 27 (London: Eyre and Spottiswood, 1913), 8, 13; Joseph Lee, *Constructive and Preventive Philanthropy* (New York: Macmillan, 1902), 125; Clarence E. Rainwater, *The Play Movement in the United States* (Chicago: University of Chicago Press, 1920), 22–24, 56–57, 93–111.

172. Kenneth L. Kusmer, "The Functions of Organized Charity in the Progressive Era: Chicago as a Case Study," *Journal of American History*, LX (Dec., 1973), 672–74.

173. Jane Addams: *Twenty Years at Hull House* (New York: Signet Books, 1961), 251; *The Second Twenty Years at Hull House* (New York: Macmillan, 1930), 348; Bowen: *Growing*, 83–84; *Speeches*, I, 114; Louise C. Wade, "The Heritage of Chicago's Early Settlement Houses," *Journal of the Illinois State Historical Society*, X (1967), 411–41.

174. Baird, *Chicago*, 2, 12–13; Visher, *Hand-book*, 186–88, 238–39; Clark, *Elegant*, 95, 145–47; Bowen, *Growing*, 51–52, 54, 56–58, 60, 67–68, 83–84, 86; Andreas, *History*, II, 671, III, 519–20; Frank and Jerome, *Annals*, 42, 55–56, 72, 78, 82, 142, 243, 245, 270, 369–78; Croly, *History*, 61–73; Gilman and Gilman, *Who's*, 48–49, 93, 114; Hibbard, *Great-Grandmother*, 83, 93, 139.

175. *In Memoriam: Elbridge Gerry Keith* (Chicago: privately printed, 1906), 8–10, 13; Goodspeed, *University of Chicago Biographies*, I, 360–68, II, 30–49, 104–23, 234–51; *Industrial Chicago*, IV, 405–9.

176. Goodspeed, *University of Chicago Biographies*, I, 19–22, 111, 123, 142, 168–69, 283–87, 369–72, II, 52, 148–52; Chicago *Tribune*, Jan. 9, 1912, 2; Leech and Carroll, *Philip D. Armour*, 347; Chicago *Record-Herald*, Jan. 7, 1901, 2; Hutchinson, *Cyrus Hall McCormick*, II, 273n, 282n, 306n, 306–7; John Tebbel,

The Marshall Fields (New York: E. P. Dutton, 1947), 102; Ross, *Silhouette*, 251–52; Fehrenbacher, *Chicago*, 216; MacDonald, *Insull*, 134; Andrews, *Battle*, 156.

177. Dedmon, *Fabulous*, 45, 131, 182; Clark, *Elegant*, 224; Chicago *Record-Herald*, Jan. 17, 1909, IV, 2, Jan. 21, 1909, 11; Gregory, *Great-Grandmother*, 123; Carter H. Harrison, Jr., *Growing up with Chicago* (Chicago: Ralph F. Seymour, 1944), 53.

178. Bowen, *Growing*, 51–52; Frank and Jerome, *Annals*, 14.

179. C. H. McCormick to Joseph Anderson, Jan. 10, 1870, in Hutchinson, *Cyrus Hall McCormick*, II, 4–5; Armour quoted in the Chicago *Record-Herald*, Jan. 7, 1901, 2; Crane statement in the Chicago *Tribune*, Dec. 29, 1907, 1–2.

180. Mrs. Reginald De Koven, *A Musician and His Wife* (New York: Harper & Bros., 1926), 142.

181. Gage, *Memoirs*, 75–85; Johnson, *History*, I, 9–49, 90–105; Fuller, "The Upward Movement in Chicago," *Atlantic Monthly*, LXXX (1897), 534; Hamlin Garland, *A Daughter of the Middle Border* (New York: Macmillan, 1927), 2.

182. Otis, *First*, 69, 75, 81, 276; Cook, *Bygone*, 82–91; Andreas, *History*, III, 784, 790, 796, 806.

183. Gregory, *Great-Grandmother*, 42–43, 45, 95, 97–98; Clark, *Elegant*, 77–78, 100.

184. Andreas, *History*, III, 829; Hutchinson, *Cyrus Hall McCormick*, II, 6–36, 205–73, 302–3, 306–7.

185. Visher, *Hand-book*, 85–86; Pierce, *History*, III, 387, 394; Ginger, *Altgeld's*, 342.

186. Gilbert and Bryson, *Chicago*, 893; Clark, *Elegant*, 34; Bowen, *Growing*, 16; Ferry, *Reminiscences*, 133–38; Gregory, *Great-Grandmother*, 172; Arthur Meeker, *Chicago with Love* (New York: Alfred A. Knopf, 1955), 76.

187. Andreas, *History*, III, 508, 518–19, 532, 534–35; Ginger, *Altgeld's*, 353; Ward, *Story*, 11–12, 224, 327, 335–40.

188. Goodspeed: *History*, 82, 95, 174–76, 183, 224–25, 230, 273–75, 301–3, 328, 349, 468–69, 497–98, 500; *University of Chicago Biographies*, I–II, *passim*; Richard J. Storr, *Harper's University: The Beginnings* (Chicago: University of Chicago Press, 1966), 38–39, 41–43, 67, 351; Goodspeed quoted in Horowitz, "Culture," 4–8.

189. Meeker, *Chicago*, 76; Crane quoted in the Chicago *Tribune*, Jan. 9, 1912, 2; Insull, *Public*, 324; Field quoted in Andrews, *Battle*, 6.

190. Gregory, *Great-Grandmother*, 110; Robert Morss Lovett, *All Our Years: The Autobiography of Robert Morss Lovett* (New York: Viking Press, 1948), 62.

191. Angle, *Chicago*, 89, 92, 98, 106–7, 125, 138, 141–42, 166–69; Higley, *Historical*, 5–33, 38–39, 47–48; *Constitution and By-laws of the Chicago Academy of Sciences as Amended and Adopted December 12, 1882* (Chicago: Jameson & Morse, 1887), 13–14; Andreas, *History*, III, 412–13.

192. Andreas, *History*, II, 512–17, III, 428–29; Spencer, *Chicago*, 45–73, 100–101, 403.

193. Moses and Kirkland, *History*, II, 140–42; Katherine L. Sharp, *Illinois Libraries* (Urbana: University of Illinois Press, 1906–8), 588; Horowitz, "Culture," 80–82. For a list of trustees and Crerar quote see Goodspeed, *University of Chicago Biographies*, I, 377–78. For another upper-class injunction against

trashy novels and advice that boys should read uplifting, success literature see Farwell, *Some*, 210–11.

194. Moses and Kirkland, *History*, II, 584–85; Clark, *Elegant*, 233–34; Croly, *History*, 60–61, 392–93; Fuller, "Upward," 542–43; Gregory, *Great-Grandmother*, 124–25; Henrotin, "Attitude," 501.

195. Kirkland, ed., *Chicago*, 262, 266–67; Ralph Fletcher Seymour, *Some Went This Way* (Chicago: Ralph Fletcher Seymour, 1945), 158–59; Bernard Duffey, *The Chicago Renaissance in American Letters* (East Lansing: Michigan State University Press, 1954), 51–56; Anna Morgan, *My Chicago* (Chicago: Ralph Seymour Fletcher, 1918), 61–62, 138, 140, 160–63, 188–89; Fuller, "Upward," 544.

196. Horowitz, "Culture," 24–25.

197. Spencer, *Chicago*, 93, 160, 162–68, 276–81, 329, 347; Moses and Kirkland, *History*, II, 137.

198. Ross, *Silhouette*, 147–63; Whitridge, "Art," 41–43, 46, 51n, 62n–63n; Andrews, *Battle*, 155–56; Moses and Kirkland, *History*, II, 578–80; *Charter, Constitution and By-laws of the Chicago Academy of Design* (Chicago: n.p., 1874), 2–4, 13–14; Gregory, *Great-Grandmother*, 81.

199. Charles L. Hutchinson, "The Democracy of Art," *American Magazine of Art* VII (1916), 397–98; Hutchinson, "Chicago as an Art Center," *The World Today*, XIII (July-Dec., 1907), 913–14; Hutchinson, lecture before the art institute, Chicago *Saturday Evening Herald*, Mar. 31, 1888, quoted in Horowitz, "Culture," 83.

200. *Annual Report of the Trustees of the Art Institute of Chicago*, 33 (1911–12), 21–22; Hutchinson, "Chicago," 913.

201. *Annual Report[s]* (1–39), 1879–1918. For contributions see *ibid.*, 20 (1899), 55–57; 27 (1905–6), 13; Ross, *Silhouette*, 25; Andrews, *Battle*, 155–56; Whitridge, "Art," 62, 77n, 155–97.

202. Mrs. P. Palmer quoted in Ross, *Silhouette*, 158.

203. Thomas E. Tallmadge, *Architecture in Old Chicago* (Chicago: University of Chicago Press, 1941), 120; Henry Russell Hitchcock, *The Architecture of H. H. Richardson and His Times* (Camden, Conn.: Archon Books, 1961), 23, 129, 274, 279; John Drury, *Old Chicago Houses* (Chicago: University of Chicago Press, 1941), 35–39, 45; Wayne Andrews, *Architecture, Ambition and Americans* (New York: Free Press, 1964), 158–94; Louis H. Sullivan, *The Autobiography of an Idea* (New York: Press of the American Institute of Architecture, 1924), 319–20.

204. Harriet Monroe, *John Wellborn Root: A Study of His Life and Work* (Park Forest, Ill,: Prairie School Press, 1966), 24ff.; Charles Moore, *Daniel H. Burnham: Architect, Planner of Cities*, 2 vols. (Boston: Houghton Mifflin, 1921), *passim*; Willard Connely, *Louis Sullivan as He Lived* (New York: Horizon Press, 1960), 126; Dedmon, *Fabulous*, 173–75; Grant, *Fight*, 119–26; Leonard K. Eaton, *Two Chicago Architects and Their Clients: Frank Lloyd Wright and Howard Van Doren Shaw* (Cambridge: Massachusetts Institute of Technology Press, 1969), *passim*; Andrews, *Architecture*, 205–20, 250–87.

205. Charles H. Walker, "Chicago—Its Plan for a New City," in George E. Plumb, *Chicago: The Great Industrial and Commercial Center of the Mississippi Valley* (Chicago: Chicago Association of Commerce, 1912), 137–42; George C.

Sikes, "The New Chicago," *Outlook*, XCII (May-Aug., 1909), 997, 1000, 1003, 1007; Walter H. Moody: *Wacker's Manual of the Plan of Chicago* (Chicago: Calumet Publishing, 1916), xiii–iv, 55–137; *What of the City?* (Chicago: A. C. McClurg, 1919), 14, 91, 179, 320–21, 324, 326, 330, 332–34, 360–61, 381–82, 396, 402; Robert A. Walker, *The Planning Function in Urban Government* (Chicago: University of Chicago Press, 1950), 17, 137–40, 231–32; Moore, *Daniel H. Burnham*, II, 11–15, 97–98, 100–111; Burnham, "Address to the Merchants' Club (1907)," *Ibid.*, II, 100–102, 111.

206. E. E. Ayer quoted in Grant, *Fight*, 139; and in Frank C. Lockwood, *The Life of Edward E. Ayer* (Chicago: A. C. McClurg, 1929), 187.

207. Lockwood, *Life*, 185–98; Johnson, *History*, II, 500–501; Grant, *Fight*, 138–40; Stanley Field, "Fifty Years of Progress," *Field Museum News*, XIV (Sept.-Oct., 1943), 3–4, 10–12.

208. Andreas, *History*, III, 649–50; Upton, *Musical*, 286–89; Philo Adams Otis, *The Chicago Symphony Orchestra* (Chicago: Clayton F. Summey, 1924), 14, 17; Ferdinand W. Peck quoted in Dedmon, *Fabulous*, 175.

209. Andreas, *History*, III, 651; Grant, *Fight*, 118–26, 128; Upton, *Musical*, 305–6; Morgan, *My*, 63; Edward C. Moore, *Forty Years of Opera in Chicago* (New York: Horace Liveright, 1930), 51, 54–56, 116, 138–41, 143–44, 224–25, 237; Dawes, *Journal*, 438; Arthur Meeker, *Chicago*, 225–26, 234, Arthur Meeker Sr. quoted on 234.

210. Reginald De Koven: "Music as a Social Influence," *America*, I, (Nov. 29, 1888), 15–16; "Wanted an Orchestra," *ibid.*, II (May 9, 1889), 186, 188; "Music and Taxation," *ibid.* (July 4, 1889), 442.

211. C. Norman Fay, "The Theodore Thomas Orchestra," *Outlook*, XCIV (Jan.-Apr., 1910), 159–69, quote on 159; Rose Fay Thomas, *Memoirs of Theodore Thomas* (New York: Moffat, Yard, 1911), 367–68, 423–24, 511–19; George P. Upton, *Theodore Thomas: A Musical Biography*, 2 vols. (Chicago: A. C. McClurg, 1905), I, 387–94; Otis, *Chicago*, 25ff.; Grant, *Fight*, 128; George E. Adams, "Address at the Dedication of Orchestra Hall, December 14. 1904," in Upton, *Thomas*, 289.

212. Adams, "Address," 288–89, 294.

213. Hugh Dalziel Duncan, *The Rise of Chicago as a Literary Center from 1885 to 1920* (Totowa, N.J.: Buckminster Press, 1964), 137–38; Duffey, *Chicago*, 57–58, 70, 182–84; Slason Thompson, *Way Back When: Recollections of an Octogenarian* (Chicago: A. Kroch, Pulier, 1931), 283; Fleming, "Literary," 82–97, 114–18, 508, 514–16, 524–28; Harriett Monroe, *A Poet's Life: Seventy Years in a Changing World* (New York: AMS Press, 1969), 240–458; Garland, *Daughter*, 2, cf. 271.

214. Jack Alexander, "The World's Greatest Newspaper," *Saturday Evening Post*, CCXIV (July 26, 1941), 82–84.

215. Horowitz, "Culture," 61, 63, 67, 82–91, 229–37.

216. See nn. 199 and 210 for statements by De Koven and Hutchinson; Gage, *Memoirs*, 74; Arnold, *Addresses*, 16.

217. De Koven, "Influence," 1064; Chatfield-Taylor, *Chicago*, 123–26.

218. *The Bon-Ton Directory, Giving the Names in Alphabetical Order, Addresses and Hours of Reception of the Most Prominent and Fashionable Ladies Residing in Chicago and Its Suburbs* (Chicago: Blakely, Bronon & Marsh, 1879),

13–173; *The Elite Directory & Club List of Chicago* (Chicago: Elite Publishing, 1885), *passim*; Chatfield-Taylor, *Chicago*, 77–78, 97–98; Clark, *Elegant*, 1–3; Meeker, *Chicago*, 37; Gregory, *Great-Grandmother*, 103, 117; Drury, *Old*, 26ff.; Dedmon, *Fabulous*, 114; Cleveland Amory, *The Last Resorts* (New York: Harper & Bros., 1952), 191–92, 207; Rosewell Field, "Home Life in Chicago," *Harper's Weekly*, XLIX (Oct. 28, 1905), 1565–67.

219. Meeker, *Chicago*, 37.

220. Ferry, *Reminiscences*, II, 177; Bowen, *Growing*, 28–40; Gregory, *Great-Grandmother*, 39, 116; De Koven, *Musician*, 105; Meeker, *Chicago*, 56; Dedmon, *Fabulous*, 166; Elizabeth Voluntine Rumsey, *Recollections*, 42; H. C. Chatfield-Taylor, "Memories of Chicago," *Century Illustrated Magazine*, CX (May-Oct., 1925), 459.

221. Rumsey, *Recollections*, 42; M. F. Esmond to Julia Boyd, Apr. 20, 1873, in *Dear*, ed. Clark, 39; Ferry, *Reminiscences*, II, 151–52, 177–98; Mrs. B. F. Ayer, "Old Hyde Park," in *Chicago*, ed. Kirkland 184, 188–89; *ibid*., 271; Chatfield-Taylor: "The Yesterday of the House," *ibid*., 273–75; "Memories," 543–46; Gregory, *Great-Grandmother*, 39–40, 116, 122–23; De Koven, *Musician*, 83, 98–104, 106; Harrison, *Growing*, 51, 53; Meeker, *Chicago*, 54, 56, 77, 103–4, 108, 142–51, 160, 195, 197; Morgan, *My*, 145, 174–75, 195; Clark, *Elegant*, 139, 175, 205–6; Ross, *Silhouette*, 52–56, 111–17, 125–46, 166, 188; Fuller, "Upward," 542; Charles Dudley Warner, "Studies in the Great West. III—Chicago," *Harper's New Monthly Magazine*, LXXVI (May, 1888), 877; Dedmon, *Fabulous*, 116–33, 166, 182, 210–16, 302–4; Cleveland Amory, *Who Killed Society* (New York: Harper & Bros., 1960), 381–93; Drury, *Old, passim*; Poole, *Giants*, 149–50, 152–54; Swift and Van Vlissingen, *Yankee*, 93; Swift, *My*, 122–24, 127; Andrews, *Battle*, 92, 189, 211–12, 259–60, 296, 299; Warren, *P. D. Armour*, 279; Hutchinson, *Cyrus Hall McCormick*, II, 742–45; A. E. Hartzell, *Titled Americans* (n.p.: 1915), *passim*; Harvey O'Connor, *The Astors* (New York: Alfred A. Knopf, 1951), 241.

222. Harrison, *Growing*, 53, 187.

223. Gregory, *Great-Grandmother*, 116; Dedmon, *Fabulous*, 116.

224. Meeker, *Chicago*, 107; Ferry, *Reminiscences*, II, 196.

225. Dedmon, *Fabulous*, 121, 302–4; Kirkland, ed., *Chicago*, 262–64; Meeker, *Chicago*, 146–48, 156–57.

226. Gregory, *Great-Grandmother*, 7; Farwell, *Some*, 198, 209; Gunsaulus, "Philip D. Armour," 167–69; Dedmon, *Fabulous*, 182, 321; Ferry, *Reminiscences*, I, 177–79; Hutchinson, *Cyrus Hall McCormick*, II, 434–36, 747; Amory, *Who*, 400–403; Meeker, *Chicago*, 108.

227. Ross, *Silhouette*, 112–13, Palmer quoted on 222; Dedmon, *Fabulous*, 302–4; Clark, *Elegant*, 211; Meeker, *Chicago*, 128, 194–95, quote on 104.

228. For McAllister's comments and the responses of Chicagoans see *Chicago Tribune*, Apr. 10, 1893, 1, Apr. 16, 1893, 28, Apr. 23, 1893, 33–34; Dedmon, *Fabulous*, 224–25. For criticism from Philadelphia see Dedmon, *Fabulous*, 126–27. R. R. McCormick quoted in Waldrop, *McCormick*, 37; Julia Newberry, *Julia Newberry's Diary* (New York: W. W. Norton, 1933), 31, 42–43, 45, 81, 94–95, 142.

229. De Koven: *Musician*, 160, 234–35; "Influence," 1065; Waldrop, *McCormick*, 37–38.

230. Gregory, *Great-Grandmother*, 124; Clark, *Elegant*, 211; Higinbotham, *Making*, 16–17.

231. For an early list of memberships in these and other Chicago clubs see *Elite, passim; Charter: Articles of Association: By-laws: House Rules: Officers and Members of the Chicago Club* (Chicago: Chicago Club, 1932); Edward Blair, "The Chicago Club," *Chicago*, ed. Kirkland, 201–15; Andreas, *History*, III, 390–92; Meeker, *Chicago*, 206.

232. *Reception to the Settlers of Chicago prior to 1850 by the Calumet Club of Chicago* (Chicago: Fergus Printing, 1879), 1–8; Andreas, *History*, III, 392–93, 407–8, 581; Kirkland, ed., *Chicago*, 268.

233. Gregory, *Great-Grandmother*, 129; John J. Glessner, *The Commercial Club of Chicago* (Chicago: privately printed, 1910), 9–13, 102–25, quote on 21; *The Commercial Club of Chicago Year Book, 1938–39* (Chicago: Commercial Club, 1939), 41.

234. Robert S. Critchell, *Recollections of a Fire Insurance Man* (Chicago: privately printed, 1909), 126–27; Kinley, *Spirit*, 34–35, 48–51; Grant, *Fight*, 28, 35–38, 53, 128, 132, 175.

235. Washington Park Club Charter quoted in Andreas, *History*, III, 674–75.

236. *Elite*, 158–59; De Koven, *Musician*, 99–100; Andreas, *History*, III, 404–5; Dedmon, *Fabulous*, 117–18, Mrs. George Roswell Grant quoted on 117.

237. Andreas, *History*, III, 655–57.

238. For encomiums by upper-class Chicagoans see speeches of John D. Caton and Grant Goodrich, in *Reception*, 40, 64–65; Glessner, *Commercial*, 21; Chatfield-Taylor, *Chicago*, 117, 123–28. For an out-of-towner's praise of the city see Warner, "Studies," 869–79. For praise from a non–upper-class Chicagoan see Sullivan, *Autobiography*, 200.

239. Dedmon, *Fabulous*, 210–16; Pool, *Giants*, 197, 241; Gage, *Memoirs*, 160–67; Amory, *Who*, 400–403; Frank Waldrop, *McCormick of Chicago* (Englewood: Prentice-Hall, 1966), 30, 61–64; Meeker, *Chicago*, 56–60, 97, 268, quote on 60; De Koven, "Influence," 1065.

240. Ross, *Silhouette*, 209, 222; Clark, *Elegant*, 130; Meeker, *Chicago*, 59, U.S. Government Printing Office, 1952), 340, 346, 352, 358, 370; *ibid.* 1967, 1968, 1973, 470, 490, 510, 530, 550; *ibid.* 1972, 651, 687, 710, 747, 771.

241. Hoyt, *One Hundred*, 242, 265–76, 333, 470, 487.

242. *Ibid.*, 237, 481; *County and City Data Book, 1949* (Washington, D.C.: U.S. Government Printing Office, 1952), 340, 346, 352, 358, 370; *ibid.* 1967, 470, 490, 510, 530, 550; *ibid.* 1972, 651, 687, 710, 747, 771.

243. Hoyt, *One Hundred*, 381; "Chicago as a Money Market," *University of Illinois Bureau of Business Research*, Bulletin no. 17 (1928), 13; McLaughlin, *Growth*, 166–70, 326–30; *County and City*, 1949, 341, 347, 353, 359, 371; *ibid.* 1972, 650, 686, 710, 746, 770.

244. Palyi, *Chicago*, 1, 4, 8–9, 11, 16, 52–54, 62–64, 67–68, 84–95, 252–54;

245. Hoyt, *One Hundred*, 483; *County and City*, 1949, 384; *ibid.* 1972, 814–15.

245. Hoyt, *One Hundred*, 483; *County and City*, 1949, 384; *ibid.* 1972, 814–15.

246. Bishop and Gilbert, *Chicago's*, 177–79; Gilbert and Bryson, *Chicago*,

908, 1071; A. M. Sakolski, *The Great American Land Bubble* (New York: Harper & Bros., 1932), 266.

247. Herbert D. Simpson: *The Tax Situation in Illinois* (Evanston: Northwestern University Press, 1929), 20–21, 64; *Tax Racket and Tax Reform in Chicago* (Evanston: Northwestern University Press, 1930), 26, 74–79.

248. M. F. Werner, *Julius Rosenwald: The Life of a Practical Humanitarian* (New York: Harper & Bros., 1939), *passim*; Gilbert and Bryson, *Chicago*, 616, 643, 656, 712, 717–18, 893, 899, 917, 947, 1057, 1059; Bishop and Gilbert, *Chicago's*, 167, 427; Ferry, *Reminiscences*, II, 123; Tebbel, *Marshall Fields*, 134–35, 162; Ditchett, *M. Field and Co.*, 154–58; Wendt and Kogan, *Give*, 299–374; "Marshall Field & Co.," *Fortune*, XIV (Oct., 1936), 78–87, 134, 136, 138, 141.

249. "Crane Plumbing," 77–78, 124; New York *Times*, Aug. 3, 1971, 28; Bishop and Gilbert, *Chicago's*, 409–11, 445; Eaton, *Two*, 160–61, 207–9; Kane, *Education*, 153–54, 245; "Armour Fortune," 49–57, 158; Gilbert and Bryson, *Chicago*, 712, 915; "So Big, Armour & Co.," *Fortune*, IX (June, 1934), 58–68, 124–42; James, *Growth*, II, 936–38; Leech and Carroll, *Philip D. Armour*, 353–57; Andrews, *Battle*, 198–99; Meeker, *Chicago*, 80–81; Dies, *Street*, 163–64, J. O. Armour quote on 168–69.

250. *Harvester*, 4–5; Gilbert and Bryson, *Chicago*, 934; Edward C. Banfield, *Political Influence* (New York: Free Press of Glencoe, 1964), 286.

251. Insull, *Public*, 389; McDonald, *Insull*, 55–132, 188; Rice, *Chicago*, 52, 75; Gilbert and Bryson, *Chicago*, 654, 862, 892, 913; Eaton, *Two*, 185–88; Dennis, *Victor Lawson*, 390; Tebbel, *American*, 118–29, 146–47, 199–200; Alexander, "Duke," 71–72; Alexander, "World's," 82–89; "Battle of the Newspapers," *Time Magazine*, XXXVIII (Dec. 1, 1941), 60–65; Waldrop, *McCormick*, 14, 89ff.; Tebbel, *Marshall Fields*, 224–62; "PM's Little Brother," *Time Magazine*, XXXVII (June 2, 1941), 51, 62; New York *Times*, Nov. 2, 1944, 21; Stephen Becker, *Marshall Field, III* (New York: Simon and Schuster, 1964), 273–310; Jack Alexander, "Do-Gooder," *Saturday Evening Post*, CCXIV (Dec. 6, 1941), 15; Marshall Field, *Freedom Is More than a Word* (Chicago: University of Chicago Press, 1945), 93–125.

252. James, *Growth*, II, 930, 945–52, 1000–1004; Huston, *Financing*, I, 458–63, 465; Welton, *Making*, 26–30; Gilbert and Bryson, *Chicago*, 673, 678, 681.

253. Rice, *Chicago*, 75; Eaton, *Two*, 214–17; Gilbert and Bryson, *Chicago*, 923; "Marshall Field Interview," *Literary Digest*, XLIV (Mar. 27, 1920), 98; "Marshall Field, Tom, Dick & Harry," *Fortune*, I (May, 1930), 104–6, 140; nis, *Victor Lawson*, 390; Tebbel, *American*, 118–29, 146–47, 199–200; Alexander, "Duke," 71–72; Alexander, "World's," 82–89; "Battle of the Newspapers," *Time*

254. Chicago *Tribune*, Feb. 5, 1927, 8, June 3, 1936, 3; Meeker, *Chicago*, 154–55, 201, 273; New York *Times*, Aug. 26, 1932, 17; "Crane Plumbing," 124, 126; Waldrop, *McCormick*, 14.

255. Banfield, *Political*, 286, 291.

256. *Ibid.*, *passim*; Walker, *Planning*, 17, 137–43, 231–52, 272.

257. "Crane Plumbing," 124; Kane, *Education*, 259, 273; Harrison, *Growing*, 350; Bishop and Gilbert, *Chicago's*, 409; Bradley and Zald, "Commercial," 163; Harold F. Gosnell, *Machine Politics: Chicago Model* (Chicago: University of

Chicago Press, 1937), 12; Merriam, *Chicago*, 112–15, 179–90, 195–97, 200; Rosenwald quoted in Werner, *Julius Rosenwald*, 317.

258. Merriam, *Chicago*, 90–177, 197–200; Banfield, *Political*, *passim*.

259. Frank Mann Stewart, *The National Civil Service Reform League* (Austin: University of Texas Press, 1929), 273, 275; Sutherland, *Fifty*, 67; *Annual Report*[s] *of the Citizens' Association of Chicago, 1920–35*.

260. Merriam, *Chicago*, 102–6, 184; Grant, *Fight*, 224–26, 288–90, 329–35.

261. Grant, *Fight*, 267. For Medill McCormick see Chicago *Tribune*, Feb. 26, 1925, 4; New York *Times*, Mar. 6, 1919, 2, Nov. 23, 1920, 3, May 13, 1922, 14; *Congressional Record*, 66th Congress, 2nd Session, vol. 59, part 3 (Feb. 16, 1920), 2947–48; *ibid.*, 67th Congress, 2nd Session, vol. 62, part 6 (Apr. 14, 1922), 5512; Andrews, *Battle*, 248–52. For R. R. McCormick see Chicago *Tribune*, Apr. 13, 1939, 16, July 5, 1939, 4, Feb. 7, 1941, 6, Feb. 17, 1941, 7, Nov. 17, 1945, 12; Andrews, *Battle*, 283–90; Tebbel, *American*, 244–47. For Eleanor (Cissy) Patterson see "Cissy Fuss," *Time Magazine*, XL (July 24, 1944), 48; Andrews, *Battle*, 293–94; Tebbel, *American*, 310–11. For Joseph Patterson see Andrews, *Battle*, 291–93; Tebbel, *American*, 258–77. The best summary of his views is Marshall Field, *Freedom*.

262. Chicago *Tribune*, June 3, 1936, 3; Tebbel, *Marshall Fields*, 262, 271; "Marshall Field, III," *Life*, XV (Oct. 18, 1943), 103; Waldrop, *McCormick*, 281; Tebbel, *American*, 64–65; Chicago *Tribune*, Aug. 26, 1932, 2; Dennis, *Victor Lawson*, 454, 460–61; McDonald, *Insull*, 134, 239–49; Werner, *Julius Rosenwald*, 86, 104–5, 120, 171, 232, 282–86, 366.

263. New York *Times*, Aug. 3, 1971, 28; Gilbert and Bryson, *Chicago*, 901, 906, 923; Bishop and Gilbert, *Chicago's*, 101, 167, 409, 427; Eaton, *Two*, 207–9, 214–17; Becker, *Marshall Field III*, 342.

264. Joan W. Moore: "Patterns of Women's Participation in Voluntary Associations," *American Journal of Sociology*, LXVI (May, 1961), 592–98; "Exclusiveness and Ethnocentrism in a Metropolitan Upper-Class Agency," *Pacific Sociological Review*, V (Spring, 1962), 16–20, anonymous quote on 18.

265. Werner, *Julius Rosenwald*, 152, 273, 286.

266. For the Crerar Library see New York *Times*, Aug. 3, 1971, 28; Bishop and Gilbert, *Chicago's*, 427. For the historical society see Angle, *Chicago*, 221–29, 232–33; Gilbert and Bryson, *Chicago*, 628; Bishop and Gilbert, *Chicago's*, 411. For the academy of sciences see "The Chicago Academy of Sciences. Centennial Meeting, May 22, 1957," Chicago Academy of Sciences, *Special Publication*, no. 13 (1958), 3, 8; *Museum Activities*, no. 19 (1970), facing p. 1; for a list of officers and trustees in the 1930s see *Chicago Academy of Sciences: Progress of Activities*, 4 (July, 1933), 42. For the Union League see Grant, *Fight*, 323–25.

267. For donations see Chicago *Tribune*, June 3, 1936, 3; Dennis, *Victor Lawson*, 454, 461; Tebbel, *American*, 116–17; Waldrop, *McCormick*, 281; Becker, *Marshall Field III*, 367. For trustees see New York *Times*, Aug. 3, 1971, 28; Becker, *Marshall Field III*, 342, 476; Tebbel, *American*, 64–65; Bishop and Gilbert, *Chicago's*, 167, 427; "Marshall Field III," 103; Meeker, *Chicago*, 133.

268. *Annual Report*[s], *1918–1969*; Whitridge, "Art," 291–92, 308–9.

269. "Fifty," 10–12, 30; *Bulletin, Field Museum of Natural History*, 37 (June, 1966), 8, 23–24; "Ex-Field Museum," *Newsweek*, XXII (Sept. 27, 1943), 78.

270. Otis, *Chicago*, 355–56, 392–443; New York *Times*, Aug. 3, 1971, 28; Bishop and Gilbert, *Chicago's*, 427.

271. Meeker, *Chicago*, 252, 261–62; Moore, *Forty*, 239–41, 250–317, 378–92; McDonald, *Insull*, 240–49; Dedmon, *Fabulous*, 326–27; Chicago *Tribune*, Aug. 26, 1932, 2.

272. Moore, *Forty*, 378–92; *Annual Report*[s], 55 (1933), 6; 65 (1943), 2; Werner, *Julius Rosenwald*, 282–86; Gilbert and Bryson, *Chicago*, 737.

273. Meeker, *Chicago*, 177; De Koven, *Musician*, 194–95, 222; Tebbel, *American*, 286, 307; Gilbert and Bryson, *Chicago*, 923, 1057, 1071.

274. New York *Times*, Aug. 3, 1971, 28; Chicago *Tribune*, June 3, 1936, 3; Alexander, "Do-Gooder," 15, 107; Becker, *Marshall Field III*, 103, 151–52, 159, 187–93, 340, 342, 364; Tebbel, *Marshall Fields*, 271, 273; Werner, *Julius Rosenwald*, 366.

275. Eaton, *Two*, 214–17; Harvey W. Zorbaugh, *The Gold Coast and the Slum* (Chicago: University of Chicago Press, 1929), 35–36, 46, 48, 50–52, 58–62, 63–64, 66. For club memberships of elite Chicagoans see Eaton, *Two*, 188, 209, 217; Bishop and Gilbert, *Chicago's*, 167, 199, 327, 409, 427;Gilbert and Bryson, *Chicago*, 876, 886, 892, 901, 906, 915, 917; Chicago *Tribune*, June 3, 1936, 3; Gilman and Gilman, *Who's Who*, 29, 93, 131, 147, 150–151; Meeker, *Chicago*, 61, 107–8, 122–31, 141, 146–61, 177–85, 194–95, 258, 273, 275, 277, 280–81; Stanley Walker, "Cissy Is a Newspaper Lady," *Saturday Evening Post*, CCXI (May 6, 1939), 59; Andrews, *Battle*, 257; Tebbel, *American*, 289, 307; Amory, *Who*, 380–86, 389–91, 395, 397, 400–403; Waldrop, *McCormick*, 30, 54.

276. E. Digby Baltzell, *Philadelphia Gentlemen: The Making of a National Upper Class* (New York: Free Press, 1958), 29.

277. Chatfield-Taylor, "Memories," 459; Zorbaugh, *Gold*, 48; Amory, *Who*, 16; Meeker, *Chicago*, 103, 141, 200, 273–75, 277, 280–81, 284–87, quote on 291.

CHAPTER VI   *Los Angeles*

At various times in American history different cities—turn-of-the-century Chicago and present-day Los Angeles, for example—have dramatically symbolized the national spirit. At first Los Angeles appeared as remote from modern America as had Charleston. It was an exotic place in a country that steadfastly turned obstacles into achievements. A self-proclaimed Lotus Land, two-thirds of a continent away from the western outposts of industrial America, it lured settlers with promises of a life of ease amidst a climatic paradise. That tarnished jewel of southern California now epitomizes affluent, alienated, post-industrial society—informal, outdoor life; compulsive recreation; awesome commitment to consumption, lavishly displayed in amusement media and the fashion world; a birthplace of weird and ephemeral enthusiasms; and an absence of a city core (no Boston Common, Chicago Loop, or Times Square here). Its aerospace titans supplanted the lords of finance and steel as the glamor business elite, its "beautiful people" displaced the Four Hundred and Café society as the model for stylish swingers. Even more than in Chicago and New York each migrant wave imposed its ways on the community rather than defer to older elites. This intrusive imperialism made Los Angeles upper orders the least coherent of those examined in this study. Fluid leadership strata reflect the discontinuities in southern California society—tenuous roots, fragile group structures, and orientations to the present and future—that make the city and the region the mecca of modern America.

EL PUEBLO DE NUESTRA SEÑORA
LA REINA DE LOS ANGELES: 1781–1846

Three years after the village of Our Lady the Queen of the Angels was founded, the Spanish government in 1784 issued the first of twenty land grants that established the cattle baronies of Southern California, the social and economic basis of the original upper class. Rarely were these holdings less than 5,000 acres; the largest exceeded 150,000. They were deeded to retired noncommissioned officers and privates in payment for military service and to protect missions to the Indians. After independence in 1821, Mexico reaffirmed them and created hundreds of new estates by parceling out mission lands in California. Two hundred and fifty ranchos existed in 1830, a decade later, 600. Of ninety-one heads of families living in Los Angeles in 1816, seven were rancheros, and the *gente de razón* (rural gentry) comprised about one-tenth of Alta California (the Mexican territory of upper California) residents. At the time of the North American conquest several families had owned their estates for three generations.[1]

Ranchero fortunes derived primarily from hide and tallow exports. Cheap Indian labor, a self-sufficient food supply, and the absence of land or improvements taxes protected proprietary wealth from extensive production or upkeep expenditures. Low costs helped the gentry to survive a lack of education (many were illiterate), which precluded sophisticated business techniques and scientific agriculture or animal husbandry, and a prodigal life-style. The landed elite often went into debt to buy horses, cattle, clothing, and wine. Rancheros were noted for openhanded hospitality, costly households, resplendent dress, and love of dancing, fiestas, and horse racing. They bet thousands of dollars on their favorite steed, a single fiesta might cost the host $1,000, and a fancy dress suit the same sum. Thirty-room mansions with an additional score of rooms for servants' quarters in the outbuildings housed cavalier clans and their attendants.[2]

Alta California's gentry shared with South Carolina planters an affinity for gambling, horsemanship, hospitality, sartorial splendor, and courtliness. The Spanish-Mexicans displayed other squirearchical traits. Leading clans intermarried and the extended families of the patriarchal proprietors lived on the ranches.[3] "To be a kinsman of old man [Don Antonio Maria] Lugo was an assurance of an ample start in lands and cattle with which to commence the battle of life," reported American ranchero and early Los Angeles inhabitant Horace Bell. Juan Bandini gracefully but candidly assessed his class in recalling, "They were hospitable, and were capable of making great sacrifices to aid the afflicted. I do not believe there is one . . . who professes a trade; their occupation is tending stock, some small cultivation, and idling."[4] Despite the romantic and resplendent aura with which the rancheros and their contemporaries invested the group, they were a pale replica of the Spanish grandees. Lower-class beginnings, frequent illiteracy, and matrimony with American and European immigrants of equally obscure origins characterized the borderland gentry. These attributes and the recent advent of many native- and foreign-born proprietors as a result of grants under the Mexican Colonization Act of 1824 and the Secularization Act of 1833 more accurately categorize the California dons as a provincial elite.

Landed estates dominated Alta California and took up nearly all of what later became Los Angeles County. Colossal holdings stifled population and urban growth. In 1850 the Pueblo had 1,610 inhabitants and the county 3,530.[5] During the Spanish-Mexican era Los Angeles was a slow-paced, wide-open frontier cattle town. Sparsely populated and with few urban amenities or services (no primary schools until 1838, no newspaper, library, academy, college, or hospital), it was chiefly a market and exchange post for the ranchos. The original settlers had been illiterate and the passing decades did not appreciably raise the level of learning even in the upper class. In the 1830s no one could be found with the skills necessary to act as fiscal agent in the alcalde's (mayor's) court.[6]

Don José del Carmen Lugo "went into town only occasionally" and "returned without loss of time," but other rancheros resembled South Carolina planters with second homes in Charleston. They lived in townhouses located at the Plaza, the city center and exclusive neighborhood, and dominated the municipal government. In 1843–44 the provincial dons donated money for a government house and barrack and formed a short-lived elite social club.[7] Nine of the ten alcaldes then living in the Los Angeles district had high-status occupational listing in the 1836 census, the first census in the area: two were designated ranchero, four *propietario* (landowner), and three *comerciante* (merchant); the other was unlisted. Between 1811 and 1849 there were six other ranchero alcaldes, several of whom served more than once. Rancheros held the office thirty-one out of the thirty-eight years of its duration, and extensive kinship connections prevailed among the alcaldes. Members of the *gente de razón* also acted as *regidor* (town councillor), justice of the peace, and city treasurer.[8]

Los Angeles was the most populous town in Alta California and became the regional capital in 1835, largely through the efforts of the Bandini and Carrillo families. Their accomplishments indicated that the ranchero enclave was powerful on the provincial as well as the local level. In 1845–46 Don Juan Bandini was secretary of the province, Don

Ignacio del Valle treasurer, Don Manuel Requena a supreme court justice, and Don Pío Pico governor. Political power, wielded in the personal and familial manner characteristic of aristocratic rule, defended the interests of the landed patriciate. "You have always been a friend of mine, and are married to a daughter of one of my warmest friends," wrote Governor Pico to Benjamin D. Wilson, an American ranchero who married into the gentry. "What can I do for you?" Pico carved ranchos from mission territory for his friends and relatives and confirmed their land claims.[9]

In 1846 merchant Thomas Oliver Larkin, U.S. consul in California, rated the most important figures in Los Angeles on the basis of wealth, family, and political activity. In the order named, the top men consisted of Abel Stearns, Bandini, Pico, José A. Carrillo, Requena, Henry Dalton, and Luis Vignes. Bandini, Carrillo, and Pico were related by marriage. Six were rancheros and the seventh, Vignes, owned extensive tracts of land. Five held high government posts. Stearns, an American sailor turned merchant, wedded Bandini's daughter and became a ranchero and a prominent local officeholder. English-born Dalton was another rancher, and Frenchman Vignes was the initial vineyard owner and orange grower in southern California. Four were born into the upper class and another married into it; three were recent immigrants. Their prominence was disproportionate to the share of foreigners in the total population. Of the 1,846 inhabitants of the Los Angeles District in 1844, only fifty-two were not born in Mexico or California, twenty-five were North Americans, and seven came from England and Scotland.[10]

Before U.S. rule, several American and British settlers in the pueblo entered the patriciate, an expanding class due to land made available by Mexican secularization of the missions. The route to admission lay in acting as traders and financiers for the rancheros and in assimilating to the host culture. Newcomers learned Spanish, hispanicized their names, converted to Catholicism, married into the first families, and acquired ranches. Intermarriage, the strongest indicator of the ethnic assimilation, was so pervasive that in 1850 in only three Los Angeles families were both spouses North American born.[11] Larkin named Stearns and Dalton as the foremost Anglo-Americans and five years earlier the attaché to the French legation in Mexico called Stearns and John Temple "the leading citizens" of the American group. Massachusetts-born Stearns and Temple arrived in Los Angeles in the late 1820s, began as storekeepers, married into the rural gentry, and acquired ranchos. Stearns, a poor orphan, became the cattle barons' principal merchant and creditor, controlled commerce at San Pedro (the Los Angeles port), owned ships, and had lumber interests. Even before the gold rush he was California's richest resident. In the 1830s he served as *regidor* and *síndico* (legal and financial agent of the municipality) and in 1848 became alcalde. Temple opened the first store (1827) in the city. Like Stearns he was called "Don," and he used the Spanish version of his Christian name. Temple wedded the daughter of Manuel Nieto, master of the greatest cattle domain in Southern California, and in 1845 retired from trade to his own rancho. In 1849 Temple was appointed the last alcalde. Dalton also established residence in Los Angeles before 1830; he became known as Don Henrique Dalton and converted to Catholicism. During the 1830s he owned five ranches. The other non–Spanish-Mexican notables, Benjamin D. (Benito) Wilson, Isaac Williams, David W. Alexander, Alexander Bell, William Workman, Henry Mellus, Francis P. F. Temple, William Wolfskill, John J. Warner, John (Juan) Forster, Hugo Reid, and Vignes had similar careers. Except for Vignes, this group of fifteen stemmed from the United States or the British Isles. Seven of the nine Americans originated in the Northeast, four from Massachusetts. Early Los Angeles resembled early Chicago in the prominence of transplanted northeasterners. Like the originators of the Spanish-Mexican gentry, the newer segment of the patriciate was mostly first-generation. Six of the eight whose vintage of fortune could be definitely traced were self-made. Thirteen of the fifteen owned ranchos, eight married into leading indigenous clans, and five served in the pre–Mexican War municipal administration.[12]

Despite adaptation to native mores, these recent arrivals did not wholly pattern themselves after the Old Guard. Four of the Anglo-Americans or their children found spouses among the families of the fourteen leading Anglo-Saxons. Thirteen of the fifteen were merchants in addition to being ranchers. In the 1844 Los Angeles census most of the eminent immigrants were listed as *comerciante*, while only Bandini of the old elite was so designated. Conversely, none of the foreigners but the remainder of the Spanish-Mexican aristocracy were titled *propietario* or ranchero. A similar situation prevailed in contemporary San Francisco, where the Anglo-American contingent also became traders.[13] The agricultural practices of the newcomers were more diverse and innovative than those of the Latin cattle barons. Vignes and Wolfskill inaugurated citrus fruit planting, grape growing, and wine production in the area.[14] Cultural differences, impending conquest from the North, and the rapid advance of the Anglo-Americans to high status and affluence alarmed native squires. "We find ourselves suddenly threatened by hordes of Yankee emigrants . . . whose progress we cannot arrest," Pico allegedly said in 1846. These "perfidious people" are "cultivating farms, establishing vineyards, erecting mills, sawing up lumber, building workshops, and doing a thousand other things which seem natural to them, but which Californians neglect or despise."[15]

LOTUS LAND: 1847–85

From the northern conquest (1847) until the railroad boom of the mid-1880s Los Angeles remained an Arcadia aloof from the turbulence that produced an industrial superpower. Northern California surpassed southern California in regional development, and Los Angeles lagged behind San Francisco. Los Angeles had 11,183 people in 1880, an increase of under 10,000 in thirty years; San Francisco inhabitants numbered 34,776 in 1850 and 233,959 in 1880. Property assessments in Los Angeles County in 1855 amounted to slightly over $2.5 million, in San Francisco $53 million. Los Angeles County assessments in 1850 comprised one-thirtieth of the California total; two decades later they fell to one-fortieth. Property assessments in the municipality of Los Angeles in 1856 (five years after incorporation) were $1,858,196, and $7,259,598 in 1880–81. The county assessment in 1880 was $13.8 million in real and $2.6 million in personal property.[16] Los Angeles, whose first settlement antedated Chicago by twenty-two years, had yet to experience comparable growth. Its property assessments and population in 1880 were respectively less than one-fifth and one-tenth those of Chicago in 1860. Two hundred and sixteen Chicagoans earned a minimum of $10,000 in 1863; thirty Los Angeles County residents had incomes of at least $1,500 and one made above $10,000 in that year.[17] After a generation of U.S. rule Los Angeles remained an agricultural center with little trade, except for mining camps in the Southwest, and almost no industry. Total wealth in the city and county did not equal the individual fortunes of some New Yorkers.

Urban developments came late to the sparsely populated and poorly endowed farm market town. Banks, telegraph lines, gaslights, a volunteer fire company, and a professional police force first appeared in the 1860s. During the next decade were founded the initial fire department, transit line, dancing academy, public library, bookstore, four-story building, and chamber of commerce. The 1880s marked the arrival of cable cars, a theater, and paved streets.[18] Visitors, members of old families like Boyle Workman and Sarah Bixby Smith, and newer civic and business leaders like Harris Newmark and Jackson A. Graves, remembered Los Angeles from the 1850s to the 1880s as a violent, "sleepy, ambitionless adobe village," with a "meager population, streets unpaved, a town unsevered, a village condition of merchandizing, and an able bar constantly employed."[19] Their memories indicate that for several decades after the conquest, Los Angeles retained much of the character of the Mexican pueblo.

The Old Guard

In northern California, where economic change and the Yankee influx proceeded more rapidly, the Latin upper class lost its land by the end of the 1850s. Southward, the continued primacy of agriculture and the existence until the 1870s of a Mexican majority in Los Angeles and its environs prevented defeat from abruptly terminating the ranchero era. Unlike some conquests of one ethnic group by another, the native gentry was not immediately deposed. Nevertheless, U.S. rule precipitated circumstances culminating in the collapse of the old establishment. Validation of Mexican land grants inaugurated the decline of the *gente de razón*. Although the Land Commission of 1851 affirmed 604 of the 809 titles, legal fees involved in proving ownership consumed from one-quarter to one-third of the acreage of the successful claimants— one-tenth of the legitimate landholders failed as a result of the proceedings. Even more devastating were land taxes, high interest rates, inheritance disputes, extravagance, and inefficient agriculture and animal husbandry, which prevented effective competition with newcomers. Problems were compounded by falling cattle prices as North Americans moved in and more herds were raised. Natural disasters also destroyed the cattle industry. The drought of 1862–64, which killed 70 percent of the cattle in Los Angeles County, destroyed the basis of ranchero wealth. Before the drought the old Spanish-Mexican and Anglo-American elite owned nearly all the land tracts worth more than $10,000; by 1870 its holdings had shrunk to barely one-fourth of this prime proprietorship.[20]

At first the Mexican dons retained a large share of their riches. Of the fifty county residents who paid $100 or upwards in 1852 taxes, thirty-one were Spanish-Californians and at least half the rest had married into this group. Two of the top five and seven of the highest ten taxpayers came from the Mexican aristocracy.[21] Economic reverses in the 1850s diminished the presence of the dons among the richest county inhabitants, but the old elite continued to be well represented in the affluent enclave. Of forty-four partnerships or individuals assessed for at least $10,000 in 1858, twenty were Mexican-Californians. But only four native cavaliers were among the fourteen landowners aggregately assessed for half of the total county wealth.[22] Latin squires still constituted a sizeable portion of the wealthy stratum in 1860: fifteen of the twenty largest cattle owners in the county belonged to this group.[23] Three years later, however, rich natives had virtually vanished. The lone *paisano* who earned at least $1,500 in 1863 placed twenty-fourth among the leading thirty incomes in the county. The deterioration of the old families moved Benjamin Hayes, an important Los Angeles lawyer, county district attorney, and federal district court judge, to state in 1862 that "their fortunes have changed since 1852 . . . as the spirit of speculation begins to brood over and close around them."[24]

Some ranchos disappeared in spectacular financial debacles, but most proprietors gradually sold their acreage to meet mounting debts, the whole shrinking into nothing over several decades. By the 1880s the cavaliers had faded away. Pico and the Verdugos sank into poverty, José and Nicolás Sepúlveda turned to banditry, Juan J. Carrillo and Ygnacio Sepúlveda struggled to maintain a petit bourgeois respectability by respectively opening a grocery store and a boardinghouse. In the twentieth century one Verdugo peddled tamales and another repaired cars, one Alvarado taught high school and another became a court reporter.[25]

For many years after the conquest, southern California remained a rural society with land the most important form of property. Therefore, until the massive forfeiture of their estates was completed in the 1860s, Latin aristocrats still frequently served in the stage legislature, on the county board of supervisors and the city council, and sometimes even headed the municipal administration or acted as judges. They were well represented in the Los Angeles delegation to the state constitutional convention of 1849 and on the vigilante committees that policed the frontier village in the early 1850s.[26] Hayes's recollection of the first county elections in 1850 reveals the significance of the Mexican gentry, the informal and oligarchic politics of that era, and suggests the possibility that Latin ranchero officials fronted for the Americans. "A secret *junta* of all the leading Californians, at the residence of Don Augustín Olvera," selected Hayes for county attorney and slated other candidates. "Our ticket had a large majority. Native Californians were then in the ascendancy. Don Augustín Olvera became County Judge, Don Ignacio del Valle Recorder; Don Manuel Garfías, Treasurer; neither could speak or read English. Benjamin D. Wilson, Esq. was County Clerk." Officeholding enabled the cavaliers to obtain such benefits as low tax assessments but could not forestall the eclipse of their class.[27]

Mexican-Americans composed a majority of the city's population until the 1870s. Rancheros who could command the votes of their clans and clients, influence this ethnic group, and preserve a modicum of their former wealth and land were courted by Anglo-American politicians. But the erosion of their wealth and power and the relative decrease of their constituency ultimately reduced the Mexican enclave to a despised minority. Bigotry surfaced in the early 1850s: "American ladies form a society of their own," noticed Hayes. Don Manuel Domínguez was barred from acting as a witness in a law court. In 1872 the last Mexican served as mayor and by the 1880s the old Californians, now comprising only 10 percent of the urban inhabitants, were driven permanently from elective offices. A local resident, recalling his 1880 boyhood, could not remember hearing any Spanish or knowing any Mexican-Americans and asserted that history of the Mexican period was ignored in the schools.[28]

Antonio Coronel and Reginaldo del Valle were the last civic leaders from the Latin community. Mexican-born Coronel arrived in Los Angeles in 1834, began as a schoolteacher, enriched himself during the gold rush, bought a ranch, and kept his fortune and land. From the 1850s to the 1880s he held many posts, including state treasurer, mayor, and chairman of the Democratic county committee. He was a railroad promoter, newspaper publisher, a founder and original vice-president of the Historical Society of Southern California, a supporter of Los Angeles' first orphanage and college, a contributor to the Los Angeles County Museum, and president of the Spanish American Benevolent Society. Del Valle, son of a bankrupt ranchero and prominent politician, served in both state houses, as president of the state Democratic convention, on various municipal government commissions, and belonged to the fashionable California Club.[29]

Coronel and del Valle eventually became Mexican-American tokens in upper-class circles. In the 1850s, however, Olveras, Sepúlvedas, and Requenas patronized elite-sponsored cultural and charitable organizations, and recent northern immigrants who founded distinguished families continued to marry the daughters of the cavaliers.[30] The Mexican patricians, however, conscious of their imminent fate, began to express a hostility toward the gringos which intensified as their position worsened and their oppression increased. During the 1850s Ygnacio del Valle, father of Reginaldo, charged that Yankee thrift and literacy "eat us alive." Bandini grumbled that "our inheritance is turned to strangers. . . . Our necks are under persecution—we labor and have no rest."[31]

Alta California's immigrant contingent, more comfortable under the new order, fared considerably better than did the indigenous upper class. Of the fifteen leading members of the pre-conquest foreign-born elite, eleven ranked among the fifty greatest Los Angeles County taxpayers of 1852 and nine among the forty-four largest assessees of 1858. The highest 1858 county tax assessments were levied against Stearns, John Temple, and Wolfskill. Twenty-four of those assessed for at least $10,000 and eight of the thirteen with property valued at $25,000 and above in 1858 came from Europe or North America. Seven of the fourteen top county income earners of 1863 were among the fifteen preeminent immigrants to Mexican California.[32] Attrition among foreign-born members of the economic elite was much less than among native Californians in the *gente de razón*. Reid and Dalton failed in the 1850s but the other Anglo-Americans prospered. Until the drought Stearns had the greatest land and cattle empire in southern California. He owned the general store in Los Angeles and shipping interests in San Pedro, developed the Arcadia Block, encompassing the commercial district and containing the first modern brick buildings in town, and conducted extensive mining operations. The value of his property peaked in 1862, estimated for revenue purposes at $187,673. Temple, like Stearns, engaged in varied entrepreneurship. He, too, had great ranches, and the Temple Block rivaled Arcadia as a business center. At his death in 1866 Temple was worth $500,000. Wolfskill died in the same year, leaving an estate of $150,000. Unlike Stearns and Temple, his fortune exclusively derived from land—the cultivation of grapes, citrus fruits, and wine. Wolfskill, Stearns, and Wilson capitalized on the misfortunes of the native rancheros by purchasing their bankrupt properties. During the early 1850s Bandini's North American sons-in-law tried to discourage the don's extravagance, unwise investments, and inefficient cattle raising. They saved his home, but could not rescue his ranch. The effort on behalf of Bandini, however, was an exception to the usual practice, and family ties did not evoke unlimited generosity. Stearns paid his father-in-law's debts, but took Bandini's land in compensation. Wilson was unparalleled in gathering up the estates of the faltering cattle barons. Typical of eminent Anglo-Americans and of leading businessmen in new towns, he differed from the Latin elite by assuming the role of a general capitalist. Wilson was active in ranching, viticulture, citrus fruit growing, merchandising, steamship and railroad promoting, real estate, and oil. Workman, like Wolfskill, concentrated on ranching and fruit growing, but Alexander and Francis P. F. Temple (brother of John Temple) engaged in ranching, banking, trade, utilities, transportation, and real estate.[33]

Indigenous aristocrats raised mainly cattle, but Anglo-American survivors of the old establishment associated themselves with the economic growth of the region. Consequently, the passing of the rancho era was not a catastrophe for them. Stearns alone of these entrepreneurs was grievously hurt by the debacle of the 1860s, although most of them owned large cattle ranches. He lost his ranches but died rich. If versatile enterprise enlarged Old Guard fortunes, it sometimes contained hazards. Francis P. F. Temple and his father-in-law Workman came to grief in 1874 due to the failure of the Temple-Workman Bank (Workman's lone venture outside of ranching and fruit culture).[34]

Anglo-Americans prominent under Mexican rule became even more powerful after the conquest and used their influence to enhance their interests. During the 1850s and '60s they served as mayors and city councilmen, county administrators, and state legislators. In 1849 the city was first surveyed and the municipal administration promptly sold lots to speculators, including county clerk Wilson and city councillor John Temple. Temple and Wilson built business blocks on their property. In 1853 Stearns, who had extensive shipping interests in San Pedro, was appointed collector of customs at that port. State Senator Wilson in 1869 obtained the legislature's authorization for Los Angeles to vote a bond issue for the Southern Pacific Railroad to enter the city. The successful outcome of his initiative raised the value of his landed properties. In 1871 Wilson introduced a bill to make Wilmington a city, a measure which increased the worth of his holdings in Los Angeles' other maritime outlet.[35]

Old Guard Anglo-American predominance extended to civic, social, and cultural activities. Wilson and Wolfskill in 1855 funded the first local American public school and Wolfskill's subsequent support kept it alive. Wilson gave the site for the Mount Wilson Observatory and the land for Wilson College at Wilmington. Stearns, a member of the original school board, pledged land for a projected university. John Temple headed the city's earliest library, the Los Angeles Library Association (1858); Warner served as vice-president and also was a founder and first president of the Historical Society of Southern California (1883). These efforts were prompted by civic pride, the responsibilities of community leadership, material interests in developing Los Angeles, genuine intellectual curiosity, and a desire for genteel status. The last two motives impelled members of the elite to collect books, sit for portraits, give their daughters piano lessons, organize schools for their children and relatives, and in Wolfskill's case become a noted cultural figure.[36]

Philanthropic leadership came from the same group and for the same reasons. Stearns headed the committee that brought the Sisters of Charity to Los Angeles in 1851 to start an orphanage. Wilson and Workman belonged to the Los Angeles Lodge No. 42 of the Freemasons (1854), which raised money for charity. Many upper-class types were members of the lodge, which served social as well as charitable functions. The fact that none of the leading Latins belonged to it, despite the importance of Freemasonry in Mexico, reflected the widening distance between the Mexican and American elites and the deteriorating status of the former. The lodge gave formal balls, as did Wilson and Alexander. Many of these exclusive affairs occurred at Stearns's Arcadia Block. Society events integrated the elite in the same way as they did other urban patriciates and merged with leadership in civic rituals to provide yet another source of cohesion and ascendancy. Wilson and Alexander gave a dance on July 4, 1851, and the former presided over the 1872 Los Angeles independence day celebration.[37]

The New Elite

Between 1850 and 1885, by virtue of political power and office, wealth, leadership in business, professional, and civic organizations and affairs, and social prestige, 172 Angelenos belonged to the upper class.[38] Four were born in Los Angeles, and the arrival dates of 163 (97.0 percent) of the remainder were traced (see Table 1). As in Chicago, Denver, San Francisco, and other new cities, the upper order consisted largely of recent migrants.[39] Frequency of entry by decade coincided with the demographic growth of Los Angeles. During the prosperous 1850s the population rose from 1,610 to 4,385. In the next decade, however, agricultural disasters and the Civil War curtailed immigration and the 1870 population was 5,728. Between 1870 and 1880, a prosperous period, it increased to 11,183.[40]

Los Angeles later became a haven for elderly, retired people seeking a good climate and a relaxed atmosphere, but the affluent and powerful in these years came there in the prime of life (see Table 2). The age of entry for ninety-one (54.6 percent) of the migrants was ascertained. Unsurprisingly, in a new community with an elite composed mainly of self-made successes, nearly three-quarters of the upper class moved to the city in their twenties and thirties, an age of optimal contribution to the community and of minimal drain on its resources. Raised and educated elsewhere, they spent their most productive years in their new home and were amply repaid.

Of the elites examined in this book, the Angelenos had the most scattered birthplaces (see Table 3). Chicagoans, ranking next in this respect,

Table 1

Decade of Arrival of Upper-Class Los Angeles Residents: 1850–85

	Number	Percentage
Pre-1850	27	16.6
1850–59	66	40.5
1860–69	24	14.7
1870–79	37	22.7
1880–84	9	5.5
Total known	163	100

Table 2

Age at Migration of the Los Angeles Upper-Class: 1850–85

Age	Number	Percentage
0– 9	1	1.1
10–19	7	7.7
20–29	42	46.2
30–39	23	25.3
40–49	15	16.5
50–59	3	3.3
Total known	91	100

Table 3

BIRTHPLACES OF THE LOS ANGELES UPPER-CLASS: 1850–85

Birthplace	Number	Percentage
New England	20	13.6
Middle Atlantic	27	18.4
West (including the Old West and Old Southwest, but excluding California)	30	20.4
South	13	8.8
California	5	3.4
Mexico	1	0.7
Canada	5	3.4
Europe	46	31.3
Total known	147	100

hailed mostly from New England and the Middle Atlantic regions. Of the 85.5 percent with known geographical origins less than one-third came from these areas, virtually identical to the proportion born abroad. Nearly a quarter, including native Californians, came from the West, a slightly higher percentage than that component among the Chicago millionaires of 1892. Four were native to the city and one each came from Mexico and California, an indication of the passing of the cavaliers. The newness of the town and its distance from the older sections of the country accounts for the diverse roots of the eminent citizens. The large share of European immigrants is linked to the heavy representation of Jews in the upper stratum. The twenty-three Jews composed 13.4 percent of the group; twenty-two came from Europe. Historians of Los Angeles Jewry estimate about 150 Jews among the 15,000 county and city dwellers of 1870.[41] Relative to its share of the urban populace, the European-born segment was vastly overrepresented in the upper class. Los Angeles in 1890 had 50,000 inhabitants; a little less than one-sixth came from western Europe, the origin of all except one of the European-born in the elite. Immigrants from that continent comprised slightly over one-sixth of the residents. Conversely, Mexican-Americans were nearly one-tenth, but only three appeared in the upper order. Among upper-class North Americans by region of birth, New Englanders were two-and-a-half times their percentage of the population, the Middle Atlantic component slightly less than twice, and southerners approximately twice. The West (including the Old West, the Old Southwest, the Mountain and Pacific Coast regions) was underrepresented by nearly two-thirds and the native Californians by nine-tenths their respective portions in the city.[42]

Vintage of fortune of seventy-seven (44.8 percent) of the 172 was identified (see Table 4). While the relatively low share and small numbers of

Table 4

VINTAGE OF FORTUNE OF THE LOS ANGELES UPPER-CLASS: 1850–85

Wealth Generation	Number	Percentage
First	61	79.2
Second	7	9.1
At least two	5	6.5
Three or more	4	5.2
Total known	77	100

those traced in this category does not permit definitive conclusions, available evidence indicates an overwhelming presence of self-made types. The proportion of first-generation wealth is not surprisingly higher than among equivalent enclaves in older cities and falls almost equally between that of affluent Chicagoans of 1863 and 1892.

Business was the primary occupation of 114 (66.3 percent) members of this group. In this respect it differed little from other urban elites. It is impossible to establish frequencies of basic commercial activity because many were general entrepreneurs and their concerns often shifted, but the majority were merchants, real estate speculators, fruit growers, ranchers, and viticulturalists. Such heavy involvement in agriculture was at variance with San Francisco, Boston, New York, and Chicago upper classes. The fifty-eight professionals, which included forty-two lawyers and twelve physicians, also dealt extensively in real estate and often in commerce.

Despite diverse geographic origins and recent advent, family clustering in the upper class closely resembled that of more mature patriciates. Seventy-nine (45.9 percent) or their children had marital or consanguine relations with at least one other member of the group, a share double that of the high income earners of Chicago in 1863 and slightly more than that prevailing among the millionaire Chicagoans, Bostonians, and New Yorkers of 1892.

Contrasts between the early elite and peer groups in Charleston, Chicago, Boston, and New York must be qualified by the fact that the statistics used for the latter had a more concrete economic foundation in wealth, income, and tax assessment data. Unfortunately, the Los Angeles millionaires of 1892 were too scarce to be measured against their counterparts elsewhere. A more precise comparison can be made by analyzing the top income earners of 1863 in Los Angeles ($1,500 or more) and Chicago ($10,000 or more) and then relating these findings to the 1850–85 enclave, to those worth at least $100,000 on the assessment lists of New York in 1856–57 and Boston in 1860, and to the Charlestonians who owned 100 or more slaves on one South Carolina plantation in 1860. An objection may be raised that high income earners are more likely to be newcomers than those with high property valuations or those designated upper class by social and political position as well as by opulence. A huge income for a given year obviously takes less time to acquire than total property, or than prestige or power. Nonetheless, sixteen of the thirty Los Angeles high income earners of 1863 appeared among the thirty-eight largest assessees of 1858. Moreover, a prosopographical analysis of the 1863 rich derives from a quantifiable economic base, as do the profiles of the other elites, and confirms the conclusions obtained from the multivariate examination of the 1850–85 eminent Angelenos.

Newcomers composed a greater percentage of the economic elites of the relatively new towns of Chicago and Los Angeles than of the Eastern Seaboard enclaves, where many belonged to families that had resided in the same place since the eighteenth century. Slightly over half the high income earners of 1863 Chicago came to the city in the 1850s and '60s. The date of arrival was determined for twenty-one of the largest income earners in Los Angeles in that year: ten (47.6 percent of the knowns) came in the 1850s and none in the 1860s. The proportion of the 1850s entrants coincides with that of the wealthy Chicagoans and with the modal arrival decade of the more broadly selected 1850–85 patriciate.

Little difference existed between the percentages of the top income earners of Los Angeles (63.3) and Chicago (56.9) with traced birthplaces. No prosperous Chicagoan and only one Angeleno were natives of the city or state in which they lived in 1863 (see Table 5). The mid- and far western economic elites had a wider dispersion of birthplaces than did the easterners. Wealthy Angelenos had the most evenly distributed geographical origins and comprised the only rich group, other than insular Charleston, not dominated by transplanted New Yorkers and New Englanders. Moreover, the birthplace distribution of the 1863 top Los Angeles income earners closely resembled that of the 1850–85 upper class.

Table 5

BIRTHPLACES OF HIGHEST INCOME EARNERS
IN LOS ANGELES AND CHICAGO IN 1863

Birthplace	Los Angeles		Chicago	
	Number	Percentage	Number	Percentage
New England	4	21.1	45	36.6
Middle Atlantic	3	15.8	54	43.9
South	1	5.3	4	3.2
West	4	21.1	8	6.5
Abroad	7	36.8	12	9.8
Total known	19	100	123	100

The known vintage of wealth frequency was 43.3 percent for Los Angeles and 39.4 percent for Chicago (see Table 6). The two groups were also similar in generational distribution of fortune. They differed from the enclaves of Charleston and Boston in 1860 and New York in 1856–57, where inherited fortunes predominated. In the category of freshly minted wealth, the Los Angeles 1863 income elite exceeded the broader based upper class of 1850–85 by only 5.4 percent.

The highest 1863 income earners in Los Angeles and in Chicago also had similar rates of kinship linkage. One-fifth of the far westerners and 22.7 percent of the midwesterners or their children or grandchildren were or would be related by blood or marriage to those on subsequent elite compilations in their respective cities. Interrelatedness with those on the same list, however, was the single trait in which a significant gap existed between the Los Angeles income elite and the upper class. Kinship connections among the latter more than doubled those among the former.

Similarities between the income elites of Chicago and Los Angeles did not extend to political activity. Seventeen (56.7 percent) of the Angelenos and only 15.3 percent of the Chicagoans held public office. The two Los Angeles groups, however, resembled each other in this respect. Nearly two-thirds (111 of 172) of the 1850–85 establishment were in government service. Both California enclaves were well ahead of the great Charleston slaveholders, who had the next largest percentage among the elites of the five cities.

Economic Functions

The disappearance of the ranches and the growth of urban capitalism reshaped the economic base of upper-class Los Angeles. Agriculture continued to be the most important business activity, and leading grape and citrus fruit growers and wheat farmers were wealthy and influential citizens. Many great propertyholders, however, subdivided old estates to profit from the demand for small farms generated by newcomers

Table 6

VINTAGE OF FORTUNE OF HIGHEST INCOME EARNERS
IN LOS ANGELES AND CHICAGO IN 1863

| | Los Angeles | | Chicago | |
Wealth Generation	Number	Percentage	Number	Percentage
First	11	84.6	76	89.4
Second	—	—	1	1.2
At least two	—	—	5	5.9
Three or more	2	15.4	3	3.5
Total known	13	100	85	100

brought to Los Angeles by the completion of the Southern Pacific Railroad in 1876. Other eminent businessmen no longer, as had many of their predecessors, joined the country gentry. Even when large landowners, they remained devoted to urban enterprise.

Businessmen in more developed parts of the nation were increasingly specializing in one type of enterprise and were discarding partnerships and family firms in favor of the modern corporation, but the southern California commercial elite displayed the versatility and consanguinity typical of entrepreneurs in newly settled regions or previous eras. The city's first two banks, its largest wholesale grocery, many of its foremost mercantile establishments, and some of the county's greatest agricultural enterprises were family-controlled. Isaac N. Van Nuys owned wheat farms, operated wheat and flour mills, bought city lots, built a hotel and office building, and served as vice-president of the town's largest bank. Phineas Banning owned a general store, grew citrus fruits, developed San Pedro, promoted railroads, speculated in real estate, operated a stagecoach and freight wagon line, and headed the Pioneer Oil Co., southern California's first such venture. Harris Newmark, who arrived in 1853, noted "how little specialization there was in earlier days in Los Angeles." A dry-goods merchant and later a wholesale grocer, insurance underwriter, and realtor, he remembered, "it was not until about 1880 that this process, distinctive of economic progress, began to appear in Los Angeles."[43]

AGRICULTURE

The value of farm products in the county, $201,823 in 1870 and $1,865,056 in 1880, multiplied more rapidly and had a much higher dollar value than did trade or industry. Moreover, agricultural processing, citrus fruits, wine, and horticulture, until 1900, constituted the largest industry in Los Angeles. Commerce in the port of Los Angeles between 1870 and 1880 increased from 29,000 to 102,000 net tons and total value added by manufacturing in Los Angeles County between 1869 and 1879 rose from $430,000 to $657,000.[44]

The emergence of new types of elite landowners after the 1860s accompanied the replacement of the cattle range with sheep ranches, wheat fields, vineyards, and fruit groves. Unlike their Mexican forerunners, the newcomers were not always primarily interested in farming and husbandry. German-born horticulturalist and wine maker Leonard J. Rose, the preeminent orange grower in California, and his fellow countryman, Isaac B. Lankersheim, were mainly agriculturalists. Former New Yorker Van Nuys and New Englanders Llewellyn and Jotham Bixby, great sheep and wheat cultivators, and Irish immigrant Matthew Keller, vineyard owner, fruit grower, and wine merchant, divided their energies more equally between agriculture and urban and rural land speculation. Banning and Remi Nadeau, despite extensive agrarian interests, were chiefly urban businessmen. The leading husbandmen, viticulturalists, and farmers also manufactured and marketed their raw products. Grape growers Jean Louis and Pierre Sansevain were the original wine merchants in Los Angeles and the first to ship California wine to New York and Boston, and Lankersheim and Van Nuys milled their own wheat and flour and initiated the shipment of California wheat to Europe. Amidst much change persisted one similarity— agriculture remained to a large degree a kinship operation. Van Nuys managed and later inherited his father-in-law Lankersheim's estates, the Sansevain brothers bought the property of Vignes, their uncle and the original wine producer in California, and the Bixby brothers, in partnership with their cousins Benjamin and Thomas Flint, broke up several ranchos into small farms or converted them into sheep pastures and wheat fields.[45]

REAL ESTATE

The upper class, in common with elites of other eras and places, invested heavily in city lots and rural acreage. Ranchero indebtedness, new agricultural products and practices, development of port facilities, the arrival of the railroad, an influx of newcomers, the advent of nearby mining enterprises, and economic and population growth created opportunities for spectacular profits in real estate. Post–Civil War migration inflated Los Angeles land values 200 percent between 1865 and 1866 and another 500 percent in 1868. During a three-month span in 1868 business district properties tripled in value. As in early Chicago, busts invariably followed booms. The failure of the Temple-Workman Bank in 1875 triggered a financial panic that depressed the real estate market for five years. Isaias W. Hellman, the city's leading banker and an extensive land speculator, "added little if anything since 1875 to my capital." Before 1879 he annually netted $40–50,000 "but the shrinkage in real estate ate it all up. . . ."[46]

Virtually every leading businessman and politician bought and sold land, and their cumulative influence brought about alienation of the public domain. In 1850 the municipality owned 99 percent of the urban acreage but in the twentieth century retained only Pershing Square, Elysian Park, and the Old Plaza. Chicago and New York, on the contrary, succeeded in preserving large areas in the form of parks.[47]

Political and commercial activity influenced land values and offered incentives for officeholders and entrepreneurs to speculate in real estate. The municipality gave land to important businessmen and corporations in return for anticipated services. One grant went to Pioneer Oil for exploratory drilling, others to Banning for an artesian well and to Orzo W. Childs for a canal to supply water to the urban dwellers.[48]

Leading realtors typified versatility and kinship, the classic features of the early commercial elite: Childs was the initial commercial horticulturalist in Los Angeles, president of the Los Angeles Electric Co., trustee of the Farmers' & Merchants' Bank, a hardware dealer, and a streetcar line proprietor. Irish immigrant John G. Downey in 1865 inaugurated the subdividing of the old ranchos. During the 1870s he was the most successful acquisitor of foreclosed estates and built a business block that became the city's new commercial center. Downey arrived in Los Angeles in 1850 and opened a drugstore He quickly branched out into moneylending, which facilitated his seizure of debt-ridden estates. In the 1850s he served in the state legislature and as lieutenant governor and governor. He established the city's first bank in 1868, built the earliest artesian well in southern California, and financed the second streetcar line in Los Angeles. A railroad director and promoter, he helped the Southern Pacific Railroad gain entry into Los Angeles. J. DeBarth Shorb was associated with his father-in-law Benito Wilson in extensive speculations, including rancho subdivision, and in citrus fruit growing and marketing. Brothers Joseph P. and Robert Maclay Widney were effective local lobbyists for the Southern Pacific and for harbor improvements, and the latter helped organize the city's initial transit line. The Ohio-born Widneys, nephews of state senator Charles Maclay, another realtor, were respectively a Los Angeles district court judge and president of the Los Angeles County Medical Association, and both helped form the chamber of commerce. The Lankersheim-Van Nuys and Flint-Bixby connections also conducted vast real estate operations.[49]

TRADE

Trade, which launched the careers of most Anglo-Americans of the *gente de razón*, provided the same impetus for the elite of the next generation. Hellman began as a clerk in his cousins' stationery store in 1859 and later opened a dry-goods emporium. Banning, the real estate developer and transportation mogul, started out in a San Pedro general store. Charles Ducommun, Keller, Downey, and Childs were initially proprietors of small retail establishments. Canadian Prudent Beaudry, who came to Los Angeles in 1852, was the leading general store keeper of the1860s as well as a large real estate operator and president of the Los Angeles City Water Co. Merchandising structured itself along lines typical of business in new towns. Successful tradesmen often branched out into other endeavors and the family firm predominated.

The leisurely pace of trade enabled merchants to undertake other types of transactions, assume civic leadership, or just relax without any apparent loss of profit. "People were also not as particular about keeping places of business open all day," reminisced Newmark. "Proprietors would sometimes" spend "an hour or two for their meals, or to meet in a friendly game of billiards." Dry-goods merchant and realtor John Jones closed his store in the 1850s when he went north to buy goods.[50] Frontier conditions dictated a low level of specialization as well as a desultory rhythm. Although Downey, Ducommun, and Childs sold one line of products, many owned general stores and, like Banning, Solomon Lazard, the foremost dry-goods trader of the 1860s, Newmark, or Hellman, found that merchandising propelled them into other enterprises. Merchants bought urban and rural real estate, built roads and ships, ran wagons, or made harbor improvements to facilitate the movement of their goods, lent out surplus profits at high interest, and sold insurance.

Reliable partners were needed because goods had to be purchased in San Francisco or the East, thus necessitating long absences from Los Angeles. Jones regularly spent six weeks on buying trips. The family firm was a traditional means to secure trustworthy associates or assistants. French-born cousins Lazard and Maurice Kremer opened a dry-goods establishment in 1853; the Hellman brothers—Isaias M., Samuel, and Herman M.—began their stationery business, the dominant firm in this line, in 1854; Newmark first went into business with his brother Joseph in 1853 and twelve years later founded H. Newmark & Co., the greatest wholesale grocery in the city. At various times Newmark was in business with his cousin Maurice Kremer and his nephews Kaspare Kohn and Benjamin R. Meyer. Other renowned businesses that remained in the same family for several generations were Eugene Germain's wholesale commodity commission firm (1880), the largest in Los Angeles, Hellman, Haas & Co. (1871), a wholesale drug concern, Ducommun's wholesale hardware house (1850), Simon Norton's dry-goods firm (1878), and Simon Nordlinger's jewelery store (1868).[51]

German Jews, many mentioned above, comprised a large segment of the commercial elite, particularly in dry goods. In 1876 thirty-one of the thirty-seven dealers in that trade were Jewish. Although Jews were disproportionately prominent (relative to their share of the population) in the business life of antebellum Charleston and New York, they never matched the Hebrew community in early Los Angeles or San Francisco, or in another western town, Santa Fe, New Mexico.[52]

INDUSTRY

Long after industry overshadowed trade in the activities of New York, Chicago, and Boston tycoons, manufacturing was a sidelight in Los Angeles. In this respect the town lagged far behind San Francisco, its northern rival. Lacking financial resources and a market for finished goods, decades would pass before Los Angeles became a major industrial center (see Table 7).[53] Nevertheless, impelled by the benefits of

Table 7

PERCENTAGE AND RANK OF SELECTED INDUSTRIAL AREAS IN U.S.
TOTAL VALUE ADDED BY MANUFACTURING

	Percentage of U.S. Total Value Added by Manufacturing		Industrial Areas Ranked According to Value Added by Manufacturing	
	1869	1879	1869	1879
New York	13.2	15.8	1	1
Boston	7.8	7.4	3	3
Chicago	2.1	4.1	8	4
San Francisco	1.1	1.6	13	13
Los Angeles	0.02	0.03	32	32

vertical combination or seeking yet another source of profits sometimes related to, and sometimes remote from, their primary enterprises, local capitalists ventured into agricultural processing, mining, and oil ventures. A few businessmen even made manufacturing their main interest.

Van Nuys and Lankersheim's Los Angeles Farming and Milling Co. (1880), which milled the wheat grown on their farms, and the efforts of the Sansevains and other early wine producers exemplified industries linked to primary enterprises. The organizers of the Pioneer Oil Co. (1865), the Los Angeles Petroleum Refining Co. (1873), the Los Angeles Oil Co. (1877), and the Cerro Gordo silver mine ranged further afield from their other business concerns. Among the founders of the early oil companies were realtor John S. Griffin, Pico, Ducommun, Banning, Francis P. F. Temple, Childs, Keller, Wilson, and Downey. During the 1860s and '70s, however, southern California's oil deposits were usually developed by eastern or San Francisco capitalists, and the local organizations were not successful. Cerro Gordo, located 200 miles north of Los Angeles, was the other major extractive enterprise which attracted upper-class Angelenos. The mine was initially financed from San Francisco, but Beaudry's brother later became a part owner. Nadeau shipped the silver to Los Angeles, and Hellman, Haas & Co. and H. Newmark & Co. supplied the workers. During the 1860s and early 1870s the mine traffic constituted Los Angeles' chief interior trade; one-quarter to one-third of the exports from its harbor consisted of Cerro Gordo silver.[54]

Several upper-class Angelenos devoted themselves primarily to local manufacturing. German emigrant blacksmith John Goller, who arrived in 1849, was the town's first manufacturer. He made carriages and wagons and branched out into freight hauling. Another German, Louis Lichtenberger, who came in 1863, was also a carriage and wagon builder. Cabinetmaker William H. Perry moved from Ohio in 1854 and became the foremost furniture producer and president of a lumber company and served other industrial concerns.[55]

UTILITIES

Los Angeles, a city that emerged in an age dedicated to individualism, did not have the public service traditions of such older municipalities as Boston. Private ownership of utilities, like the selling of public land, was prompted by a strong commitment, uninhibited by past practices, to free enterprise. Water and power needs were met by businessmen in exchange for ownership and profit. Control over utilities was intimately connected with windfalls in such other fields as real estate. Since Los Angeles had a dry climate, those who controlled the water supply determined the pace and pattern of economic growth.

The first water franchise was granted in 1857 and six years later was transferred to Jean Louis Sansevain. In 1868 he conveyed the lease to Griffin, Beaudry, and Lazard, who used their political leverage in the city council to overcome rivals and obtain a thirty year monopoly to supply the city with water. Associated with other influential capitalists, they formed the Los Angeles Water Co. Within two years the company's municipal license fee was reduced almost 75 percent. Perry and Goller founded and headed the Los Angeles City Gas Co. (1867), which provided light and power, and Robert Maclay Widney, Childs, and George Chaffey were the main figures of the Los Angeles Electric Co (1882), which inaugurated the use of electricity and generated the power for the city's original electric railway. Electric power companies were innovative and efficient. Los Angeles was the first American city lighted exclusively by electricity and the rates, relative to other places, were cheap.[56]

TRANSPORTATION

Many of those who brought power and light initiated public transportation in Los Angeles. Here, too, civic needs were met by private enterprise. Robert Maclay Widney, Francis P. F. Temple, and their associates constructed the first streetcar line in 1874, Griffin, Perry, Downey, Childs, and Isaias W. Hellman soon organized other lines. These entrepreneurers were invariably large owners of urban real estate with surplus capital derived from land speculation and other businesses. They established transit systems to enhance the accessibility and, therefore, the value of their subdivisions.[57]

Profits depended upon population growth, the development of local markets, and the integration of southern California into the national economy. Consequently, the business elite promoted roads, railroads, and harbor improvements.

The beginning of a vast and complex transportation system between the town and its hinterland occurred in 1852, when Banning and Alexander organized southern California's first stagecoach line, which ran between San Diego and Los Angeles. Three years later a group of leading merchants and land speculators, desiring a connection with northern California, financed the construction of a road over the San Fernando Pass. During the 1850s and '60s Alexander and Banning were the most important freight handlers and ran wagons and stages from Los Angeles to San Pedro, Fort Yuma, Arizona, Salt Lake City, Utah, and Mojave, California. Banning, scion of a wealthy Delaware farming family that suffered reverses in his father's generation, became the premier transportation mogul. This strategic position brought many advantages. In return for free haulage of H. Newmark & Co. goods from San Pedro to Los Angeles, he received half the profits of that firm until Newmark bought him out. The only local freight agent to rival Banning was Nadeau, who controlled the silver shipments from Cerro Gordo to San Pedro. Nadeau and Banning notwithstanding, overland haulage was dominated by the eastern-owned Butterfield Overland Mail and Wells, Fargo companies.[58]

Banning was the prime developer of local maritime facilities. Like Stearns, his predecessor as Los Angeles' foremost capitalist, Banning began as a merchant and much of his influence and wealth accrued from his role as a trader and shipper. Banning, Stearns, Wilson, and Alexander were instrumental in making San Pedro a U.S. port of entry in 1853. Sixteen years later he put before Congress the original bill for federal support for improvements at San Pedro and in 1871 went to Washington to lobby successfully for the initial appropriation. The first Los Angeles Chamber of Commerce (1873) helped secure a congressional grant for harbor improvements. Banning had extensive interests in the port and founded and practically owned the town of Wilmington where it was located. He held the lighterage monopoly. ran vehicular lines to the city, and owned warehouses, wharves, and a fleet of freight schooners and steamers. Under Banning and his associates the port flourished. Between 1855 and 1875 the number of vessels arriving in the harbor increased from 59 to 326, import tonnage from 2,465 to 80,548, and export tonnage from 3,849 to 14,841.[59]

The most spectacular expansion occurred between 1870 and 1875, when ship arrivals rose by over 50 percent, import tonnage nearly quadrupled, and export tonnage more than doubled.[60] The main reason for this tremendous growth, especially in imports, was the coming of the railroad. Once again, Banning took the initiative. State Senator Banning in 1866 helped Los Angeles County get a railroad franchise between Wilmington and Los Angeles. As chief promoter of the line he successfully urged the city and county to issue public bonds to build the Los Angeles & San Pedro Railroad. When the municipality subscribed $75,000 and the county $150,000, Banning maneuvered the authorization for these bonds through the state legislature. He owned a majority of the stock, supervised construction, and with other upper-class capitalists was an incorporating director. The completion of the Los Angeles & San Pedro in 1869 almost tripled county property assessments and enriched its founder. Through control of the railroad he determined the prices of shipping goods from the port to the city and drove out competing carriers.[61]

The opening of the Los Angeles & San Pedro coincided with the beginning of a venture unprecedented locally in magnitude and significance. With business associate State Senator Wilson, Banning persuaded the legislature to authorize a bond issue vote to bring the Southern Pacific Railroad to Los Angeles. Banning became a Southern Pacific agent, merged his port and railroad interests with the larger line, contracted to build the Southern Pacific wharf at Wilmington, and that railroad advanced him credit to buy its lighterage business at San Pedro. He and other business leaders convinced the municipality to give the Southern Pacific $600,000 to come to the city. Since Los Angeles had 600 residents this amounted to $100 per capita, an extraordinary subsidy given the size and resources of the city. The commercial elite mobilized community support by organizing public meetings and writing pamphlets. It conducted the negotiations with Southern Pacific executives, drew up county right-of-way ordinances, lobbied in Congress and the legislature to compel the Southern Pacific to adhere to its original agreement to make Los Angeles a trunk line stop, and thus defeated the bid of San Diego as an alternate route.[62]

In 1872 Robert Maclay Widney urged the citizens to vote for the subsidy because the line would elevate land values, populate the town and hinterland, decrease costs, expand trade, increase shipments at San Pedro, attract capital, and encourage industry. These advantages would enable Los Angeles to overshadow San Francisco and San Diego and dominate the economy of the Southwest. Widney's pamphlet showed that the foremost capitalists had a bold and accurate vision of their city's destiny. Between 1869 and 1876 assessed value of urban property rose from $1,573,000 to $6 million and the city population tripled between 1870 and 1876. The citrus fruit industry benefited almost immediately when the first carload of fruit was shipped by rail in 1877 to St. Louis.[63] The arrival of the Southern Pacific in 1876 was the first great regional initiative undertaken by the business elite. It lobbied effectively at the local, state, and national levels to protect the interests of the city and its businessmen, convinced the community to raise money for the railroad, prevented Southern Pacific executives from choosing San Diego as a terminus, and took a crucial step in making Los Angeles the economic metropolis of the Southwest.

FINANCE

Banking, dependent upon the capital accumulation and the need for a medium of exchange associated with commerce, historically derived from trade. Financial institutions in frontier settlements recapitulated this process. The first bank in San Francisco, where the economy matured earlier and the businessmen were more sophisticated, appeared in 1849; nineteen years later one was established in Los Angeles. Before then local merchants and Wells, Fargo acted as bankers. Newmark backed Banning's undertakings, Downey lent money, the funds of large landowners and other wealthy Angelenos reposed in the safe in Isaias W. Hellman's store, and he, too, extended credit to friends, customers, and other entrepreneurs. In those days of risky ventures and scarce capital, exorbitant interest rates (customarily between 8 and 15 percent monthly) inhibited economic growth. Downey attributed the belated emergence of banking facilities to the "financial [in]-experience" of "the old American and foreign pioneers." To many rich ex-"mountaineers and trappers . . . establishing a bank" was "preposterous." Until 1868 "Los Angeles was without a bank, save the facilities offered by Wells, Fargo & Co. Every merchant who had a safe was a repository of money belonging to friends." Newmark noted that "twenty years after I arrived in Los Angeles, the credit system was so irregular as to be no system at all. Land and other values were extremely low, there was not much ready money . . . much longer time was then given on running accounts than would be allowed now."[64]

By the late 1860s economic resources and business enterprise were substantial enough to make financial institutions necessary and feasible. Eighty years after the first banks were organized by Eastern Seaboard commercial elites, Los Angeles' original bank, James A. Hayward & Co., was formed. Downey organized it, but San Francisco capitalist Hayward supplied the money. Hellman, Temple & Co. was incorporated later in 1868 by Workman, Francis P. F. Temple, and Isaias W. Hellman. After Workman and Temple left to start the Temple-Workman Bank (1870), Hellman and James A. Hayward & Co. merged as the Farmers' & Merchants' Bank of Los Angeles (1871). Hellman and Downey had previously cooperated in real estate deals and many of their allies in the commercial elite joined them as founding directors. When Downey soon resigned as president, Hellman became the foremost financier in Los Angeles. Until 1905 Farmers' & Merchants' remained the largest bank in the city. The other institutions incorporated in the 1870s were also organized by local entrepreneurs, frequently in combination with nonresident capitalists. In 1873 Leonard J. Rose and

Stephen H. Mott, lumber merchant and an organizer of the Los Angeles Water Co., assisted by San Diego businessmen, formed the Commercial Bank of Los Angeles. The Los Angeles County Bank (1874), the intital savings institution in the area, was founded by San Francisco and Los Angeles businessmen, and Jonathan S. Slauson, a lawyer, realtor, and viticulturalist, was the first president.[65]

Bank officers commanded the trust vital to attract depositors. Hellman associated with "large landowners and men of affairs who esteemed him for his practicality," wrote Newmark. Asked "often to operate for them in financial matters; he laid the foundation for his subsequent career. . . ." At the opening of Hellman, Temple & Co., the Los Angeles *Star* called Workman "a gentleman long known in this county, one of the early pioneers, possessed of extensive estates, and large accumulated capital besides"; Temple "a well known and opulent citizen of our county"; and Hellman "a young, enterprising, and intelligent merchant of this city, who will have charge of the business of the bank. Under such auspices, and with such responsibility, despositors may be assured of safety."[66] Such credentials attracted customers from the *gente de razón* as well as important businessmen.[67] Downey and Hellman told the public that the founders and trustees of Farmers' & Merchants' represented "the wealth and intelligence of the community." They "hope to give the New Bank, a permanence, stability, and reputation that will be alike credi[t]able to those interests" and "to the City" and will enable it "to perform its part in the brilliant future of Southern California." The *Star* supported their claims and announced in a tone of civic boosterism familiar in projects launched by the commercial elite: "The community generally will appreciate this accomodation, as the capital, instead of being transmitted to San Francisco, will be employed in forwarding and promoting local enterprises."[68]

Grandiose expectations of the press did not always materialize. The Panic of 1873 ruined San Francisco's Bank of California, thus causing a run on Los Angeles' financial institutions and the failure of Temple & Workman in 1875. The collapse of the latter stifled the economy because it held half the community banking resources and paid nothing on its liabilities. After the bank closed, real estate values fell and specie and credit disappeared.

Farmers' & Merchants', on the other hand, weathered the depression without missing a dividend. Hellman's prior career fitted him for banking much better than were cattle raisers Temple and Workman. The former bought out his onetime partners because he feared their rash extension of credit, an impulse that ultimately brought about their downfall. In Los Angeles, Hellman also innovated the policy of interest payments on time deposits, thus luring away those who banked in San Francisco. Downey, his associate, borrowed enough money from a San

Francisco banker in-law to tide Farmers' & Merchants' over the depression years. Moreover, it pursued a cautious lending policy and kept high reserves of cash on hand.[69]

Los Angeles emerged from economic infancy during the decade before the reversals of 1876. Utility companies were organized, railroads built, harbor facilities improved, banks founded, and a chamber of commerce established. These developments entailed an unprecedented scale of operations, which involved large amounts of capital, a thrust to dominate hinterland markets, and an expectation of interregional trade. They indicated the growing strength of the Los Angeles economy and the confidence of its leaders. Still in adolescence, the city and its entrepreneurial elite needed the resources of outside capitalists, especially for railroads and banking. But the town's preeminent businessmen organized and promoted ventures that laid the basis for a powerful metropolitan economy.

Politics

Governments sold land, granted franchises, gave subsidies, and levied tax assessments; Los Angeles was no exception to the historical nexus between power and profits. Its upper class resembled the preconquest dons and other patriciates in dominating the political as well as the economic life of the community. Assemblyman, county supervisor, lieutenant governor, and governor (1860–61) Downey had the most spectacular career among the leading businessmen. Rose and Banning were state senators, and many prominent capitalists served on the city council. Harris Newmark's brother was city attorney, Lichtenberger and Isaias M. Hellman city treasurers, Keller city assessor and county supervisor, Lazard and Kremer county treasurers, and Kremer headed the county board of supervisors.[70] Jews, overrepresented in the business elite, were frequently elected to public office. From 1850 until 1880 at least one Jew almost continuously sat on the city council or the county board of supervisors.[71]

Party bosses, especially Democrats, often were great entrepreneurs or their associates. Banker-realtor Stephen H. Mott's brother Thomas D. was the local Democratic potentate in the 1870s; during the next decade city attorney Meyer Newmark chaired the Democratic county committee and Shorb and Isaias W. Hellman were among the party leaders. The latter was also the party's chief financier, and during the 1860s and '70s two of his bank employees were both city and county treasurers and another was mayor.[72]

Through its government positions and voluntary associations the upper class preserved public order and safety. The Old Guard and the newer members of the elite in 1863 formed a company of rangers to halt crime and violence. Denver and San Francisco, other frontier towns, also resorted to vigilante organization.[73] During the 1860s and '70s leading businessmen, officials, and lawyers also belonged to the Los Angeles Volunteer Fire Company.[74] Several decades after fire fighting and crime control were professionalized and incorporated into older city administrations, many western communities, still in the early stages of urbanization, handled such matters through informal agencies. The scope and persistence of voluntary association also reflected the private enterprise outlook of the Los Angeles, San Francisco, and Denver citizenry.[75]

Political influence facilitated economic benefits. Until 1875 wagon roads were chartered by the state government and rates and road regulations set by the county supervisors. State land policies helped speculators and railroad agents accumulate large tracts which they then subdivided. The legislature passed fencing ordinances which favored wheat growers against the declining cattle barons and gave aid to viticulturalists. County supervisors underassessed, and thus undertaxed, personal and real property.[76] As previously mentioned, Banning used his influence in the legislature to promote his railroad and maritime interests. While in the upper house he was instrumental in the choice of Cornelius Cole as U.S. senator. We are "on the very best of terms," Banning wrote business partner Wilson in 1865, "and he fully understands what [I] have done for him. As far as my own business or the public improvements of our country are concerned, we are . . . well off" with Cole in the Senate. Banning was not disappointed. Cole introduced a Senate bill in 1870 for a $100,000 appropriation to improve San Pedro.[77] Local government was also manipulated to the advantage of local capitalists. The incorporators of the Los Angeles City Water Co., aided by the city council president, in 1868 won a thirty-year franchise from that body despite being underbid by competitors. City councillor William H. Workman convinced the municipality in the 1870s to bring water into land he acquired to new settlers.[78]

The Professions

LAWYERS

Early Los Angeles had neither the surplus wealth not the cultural traditions to support professors, artists, authors, ministers, and journalists, but in common with other urban elites a number of attorneys and doctors belonged to the upper class. Distinguished lawyers participated as professionals and as entrepreneurs with leading businessmen in commercial ventures, and because of their vocational expertise and community prominence frequently served in public office.

For over a generation after North American rule, real estate litigation constituted the major legal speciality. J. Lancaster Brent, who came to Los Angeles in 1850, defended ranchero title claims before the land commission. Volney E. Howard, who arrived in the city a few years later, also had many clients from old families and became an authority on land titles. The leaders of the bar represented the agrarian gentry.[79] [Andrew] "Glassell & [Alfred B.] Chapman had the best practice," asserted Henry W. O'Melveny, son of an eminent attorney and an influential counselor in his own right. It was "confined chiefly to real estate transactions, and they made their fortunes by being retained in the large petition suits." Even in the 1880s, according to O'Melveny's father, "The only staple of commerce or merchandise was real estate. The largest field of professional practice was in examination of abstracts of title. . . ."[80] Land litigation led attorneys into real estate operations. Chapman, Glassell, and Cameron E. Thom, acting for Julio Verdugo in the foreclosure of Rancho San Rafael, received large parcels of acreage from the estate. Benjamin S. Eaton became a great landowner in Pasadena, law partners Erskine M. Ross and Thom were also extensive realtors and Ross helped found Glendale. Henry W. O'Melveny reported that Chapman "would take his compensation in land, and nearly every final decree in partition would find that Glassell & Chapman had quite an acreage in severalty."[81]

Business interests were not restricted to land. Harvey K. S. O'Melveny and Henry T. Hazard helped arrange the Southern Pacific entry to Los Angeles and the contract between the railroad and the municipality was drawn up in their law office. Glassell, Chapman & [George H.] Smith represented the Los Angeles & San Pedro Railroad, and Jonathan S. Slauson became a bank president.[82]

Partnerships were the characteristic mode of practice. The first two lawyers in Los Angeles, Jonathan R. Scott and Benjamin D. Hayes, in the 1850s formed the original firm. During the 1870s the major firms were Thom & Ross, Glassell, Chapman, & Smith, and Hazard & O'Melveny. Subsequently, many attorneys associated with their kin, but the initial leaders of the bar did not practice with relatives. The one exception was Thom & Ross, the latter being the nephew and student of the former. During the 1860s the best lawyers made between $4,000 and $6,000 yearly, and in 1863 two ranked among the top thirty income earners in the country. Formal organization of the profession occurred when its leaders founded the Los Angeles Bar Association (1878), six years after a similar institution had been founded in San Francisco. But the bar could not yet sustain a professional organization and it lasted only a few years[83]

Typical of frontier settlements, litigation was conducted according to community values and habits instead of traditional judicial procedures or legal precedents. Violence in the young village penetrated the courtroom, where lawyers and judges became involved in arguments that ended in blows. Cases were often decided by common sense or sentiment rather than formal interpretation of the law. Nonetheless, attorneys, along with the doctors, were the best educated groups in Los Angeles; many noted lawyers had college and law school diplomas.[84]

Connections with the business and social elite, legal skills, wealth, and prominence resulted in a high rate of officeholding among luminaries of the bar. Stephen M. White and Cole became U.S. senators, Hazard and Thom mayors, and several were city councillors or state legislators. Ross and Harvey K. S. O'Melveny served as U.S. district court judges and the former sat on the federal court of appeals. Others were state, county, or municipal justices and frequently acted as city and county attorneys.[85]

PHYSICIANS

Physicians exhibited the same qualities and strategies as did lawyers to attain professional and communal eminence. Doctors, too, became entrepreneurs. John S. Griffin was a realtor and a director in several corporations, Joseph P. and Robert Maclay Widney were active in transportation enterprises and in the development of San Pedro, and Milton G. Lindley grew fruit and speculated in real estate. Profits from business deals and their practices placed two doctors among the thirty highest county income earners of 1863. Prestigious medical men such as Griffin, Joseph P. Widney, and Henry S. Orme served as municipal health officers and on the local, county, or state boards of health. The Los Angeles health officer and board of health were responsible for public health and sanitation, recording births and deaths, garbage collection, and inspection of milk and meat. Health Officer Walter Lindley in 1879 inaugurated a free vaccination system for public school children, improved garbage disposal, secured a sewer network for the main streets, and systematized birth and death registration. Physicians also held other government offices: two were mayors in the 1850s, Milton Lindley was a county treasurer and supervisor, several were on the board of education, one sat in the state senate, and James B. Winston and Griffin were city councillors.[86]

The medical and legal professions had many college-educated men but differed in that doctors were more likely than lawyers to come from the same families. Fathers and sons Joseph and Carl Kurtz and Milton and Walter Lindley, and brothers Joseph P. and Robert Maclay Widney belonged to the medical elite.

Formal organization, as well as kinship, developed earlier in medicine than in law. The Los Angeles County Medical Association began in 1871, seven years before the bar association. In professionalization, as in other aspects of urban sophistication and progress, northern California set the example. The San Francisco and Sacramento medical societies were founded in 1868. Doctors from the north were also more heavily represented in the California State Medical Society (1856) and on the state board of health. Not until 1879 did Orme break the San Francisco-Sacramento monopoly on the society presidency. Other aspects of professionalism, specialization, medical schools, and journals, also appeared first in northern California. Physicians prominent in economic and political life assumed leadership in professional organization. Griffin, Joseph Kurtz, Walter Lindley, Orme, and Joseph P. Widney headed the Los Angeles County Medical Association. The association, similar to those in other cities, recommended fees for medical services, established ethical standards and rules of practice, attempted to drive out unlicensed practitioners, and agitated for a municipal board of health and a health officer.[87]

Civic Activities

Los Angeles struggled to acquire the amenities long present in other cities. No school, library, Protestant church, or bookstore existed in 1850. Twenty years later the town had two Catholic and two Protestant shrines, two public and two private schools, a college, an orphanage, an infirmary, three newspapers, and a small park. During the 1850s appeared the Masonic Lodge and the Hebrew Benevolent Society, the first public school and printing press, and the Sisters of Charity Orphans' Asylum and Hospital. The next decade brought the first permanent newspaper, the French Benevolent Society, Central Park, the original book published in Los Angeles, and St. Vincent's College. In the following ten years were founded the public library, a free kindergarten association, and the Los Angeles Woman's Club. But before the 1880s the city had no theater, museum, opera company, orchestra, historical or scientific society, or central charity organization. Here, too, it lagged behind San Francisco, whose initial scientific society appeared in 1853, theater in 1851, art museum in 1874, symphony orchestra in 1865, and where the University of California started in 1869.[88]

CHARITY

During the 1850s the *Alta California* patriciate combined with upper-class newcomers to found the original humanitarian associations. Mayor Stephen C. Foster, Hayes, and Downey, for example, joined the Old Guard in aiding the Sisters of Charity in establishing Los Angeles' first orphanage. Within a few years, however, the *arrivistes* assumed control over philanthropy. The founders and early masters of the Freemasons' Lodge, which raised money for benevolent causes and whose members organized the public library and the first Protestant church, belonged to the new elite and included Jewish merchants. The latter also instituted the Hebrew Benevolent Society. The earliest welfare organization in the city, it gave alms to all faiths. In the 1870s their wives organized the Ladies' Hebrew Benevolent Society. Individually, as well as in concert, community leaders endowed charities. Hebrew Benevolent officer Isaias W. Hellman gave $5,000 to the orphanage and another $5,000 to the Protestant Los Angeles Orphan Home Society, and Beaudry donated the land for the Los Angeles Infirmary.[89] These efforts, even in the context of personal fortunes far smaller than those in Chicago, New York, or Boston, lagged behind the altruism of elites whose longer history encouraged greater civic responsibility. In Los Angeles, as in Denver and San Francisco, individualism, defined mainly as pursuit of personal gain, also undermined generous impulses.[90]

CULTURE

As was true in San Francisco and other cities, the upper class dominated cultural as well as philanthropic institutions.[91] The public school system was begun with the help of Downey and a master of the Freemasons' Lodge. Until 1869, when the post of school superintendent was taken over by professional educators, it was often filled by leading businessmen, physicians, and lawyers. Thereafter, members of the commercial and professional elite continued to sit on the board of education. The upper class was also active in the founding of Los Angeles High School (1873), and the wives of Robert Maclay Widney, Griffin, and Isaias W. Hellman were primarily responsible for the kindergarten movement, which in the 1870s organized the original public kindergarten in California.[92]

Emulating patriciates in older urban centers and in conjunction with survivors from the *gente de razón*, the new upper class inspired institutions of higher learning. A familiar pattern unfolded; *parvenus* displaced aristocrats as the chief supporters of colleges. Latin aristocrats and *nouveau riche* businessmen and their wives donated land and raised funds for St. Vincent's College. In 1875 Downey, Childs, and Isaias W. Hellman gave the site for the University of Southern California and the Widney brothers were the primary proponents of the school. With a typical mixture of civic commitment and personal gain, the land was contributed to enhance the intellectual life of Los Angeles and the donors' real estate developments in the vicinity.[93]

Newer members of the elite also cooperated with the Old Guard in attempting to refine the town by organizing libraries. They were active in the subscription library movement of the 1850s and '60s, and Downey, in 1872, presided over the original board of trustees of the Los Angeles Library Association. This body, which included many noted citizens, six years later founded the city's free public library, the initial municipal library on the West Coast.[94]

The elite strengthened its cultural hegemony when its members took charge of civic beautification projects and rituals, and acquired reputations for intellectual leadership. Wolfskill, Foster, Griffin, and Brent were the cultural leaders of the 1860s and '70s. Elijah Workman, while on the city council in the 1860s, gave time and money to landscape Central Park, and in 1870 a commission of urban luminaries improved the grounds. Renowned Angelenos also dominated celebrations that marked civic rites of passage and symbolized their own community salience. Banning headed the parade at the July 4, 1876, centennial celebration of the city's founding and its anticipated glorious future. Among his marshalls and aides were Meyer, Germain, and Lankersheim.[95]

At this time the town contained no professional authors, and newspapers were the chief source of literary activity. In the 1870s the *Express*, the *Herald*, and two other papers appeared. They reprinted essays, poems, and stories. Unlike early Chicago, however, the elite was not as yet heavily involved in journalism.[96]

Despite progress in other aspects of culture, the arts remained in a state of infancy. Museums, art galleries, and musical and opera ensembles existed in the East, Chicago, and even in San Francisco; but not until the mid 1870s did Los Angeles begin to support resident painters and hear amateur performances of classical music.[97] The absence of such institutions and of a local intellectual and artistic circle was partly due to the youth of the town. But San Francisco was not much older and, before the Mexican War, also had a *gente de razón*. In fact, the cultural void of the early years foreshadowed future trends. The elite continued to attract materialists—"go-getters" who devoted little time, had little interest, and saw little benefit in the contemplative or cultural life. Later upper classes would spend millions and make grandiose efforts to dispel, with mixed success, the philistine atmosphere. Even today many rich and powerful Angelenos resemble their predecessors. Aerospace, movie and TV executives are often ambivalent, if not hostile, to high culture, and Los Angeles retains much of its early reputation for vulgar materialism.

Society

Elites in Los Angeles, San Francisco, Boston, New York, Charleston, and Chicago developed modes of inner cohesion concomitantly with their achievement of urban leadership. Community dominion and group solidarity were mutually reinforcing. The Los Angeles enclave was integrated in the same way as other upper orders. Its members cooperated in business, political and civic matters, shared values, clubs, neighborhoods, social circles, and schools, and frequently intermarried.[98]

The *gente de razón* element in the upper class persisted through marriages between newcomers and descendants of Spanish-Mexican aristocrats. Winston, Foster, and county clerk and Democratic chieftain Thomas D. Mott wedded respectively the daughters of Juan Bandini, Antonio M. Lugo, and Jose Sepúlveda. Other *parvenu* leaders entered Anglo-American families established before the Mexican War, or made alliances with successful clans of their own vintage. Apart from previous examples, the children of Andrew A. Boyle and William H. Workman, Chapman and Scott, and George H. Smith and Banning intermarried, as did the sisters of Judge Hayes with Eaton and Griffin.[99] Cavalier traits supplemented connubial bonds in preserving continuity with the ranchero era. Several gentlemen fought duels. The Southern District Agricultural Society (1871), primarily founded by Rose, its first president, with the assistance of other distinguished citizens, held high-stakes horse races. The North Americans also perpetuated fancy dress and costume balls. They were organized chiefly by Winston and Harris Newmark and usually took place at the comparatively resplendent homes of society leaders Winston and Downey. Early society resembled glamorous *Alta California*, gallant Charleston, or gilded New York rather than dour old Boston or simple young Chicago. Its vitality even contained a risqué spirit. Boyle Workman, scion of two locally famous families, admitted that numerous sex scandals plagued the fashionables of the 1870s.[100]

As the village became urbanized, society adopted many customs found in older cities. Tendencies emerged toward formalization and segregation from the masses. By the 1870s the west side of Fourth Street and the Baker Block replaced the Plaza as the fanciest living quarter in town.[101] St. Vincent's College began as a preparatory academy as well as a college, and in the 1870s youths from the best families went there. Other upper-class children attended the Burton School (1865). Daughters of leading Jewish and Protestant as well as Catholic families studied at the Sisters of Charity School.[102] An increase in formality also marked convivial occasions. The first dancing academy opened in 1871 with Harris Newmark as one of its patrons. At this time evening dress became more customary at social events. The growth of exclusive social and educational institutions, a sign of more rigid stratification in the upper order, prompted the organization of selective clubs. The Social Club (1870), the original of its kind in Los Angeles, was founded, eighteen years after a similar one in San Francisco, by Thom, Harris Newmark, Isaias W. Hellman, and others in the elite. But the social and cultural atmosphere could not yet sustain the variety of associations that existed in other cities. The second club, the Woman's Club (1878), designed to pursue high culture, lasted only two years while identical organizations were permanently established in other places.[103]

Society gradually acquired the tone and structure of eastern and midwestern fashionable circles. Yet it was still simple, informal, and nonselective compared to older patriciates or San Francisco society. Although the latter was more egalitarian than its eastern counterparts, social arbiters began to appear in the 1850s.[104] Sarah Bixby Smith, daughter of Llewellyn Bixby, Harris Newmark, and Graves remembered the Los Angeles of their youth as an undifferentiated and unassuming town. Newmark, in a representative statement, recalled that "social life of those early days" lacked "foolish caste distinctions. . . . There were no such ceremonies as now; there were no 400, no 300, nor even 100." Only "two classes" existed, "the respectable and the evil element."[105] Newmark's nostalgia was at least partly evoked by the fact that Jews, as in San Francisco and Denver, were then assimilated into society.[106]

Not all the upper-class commentators, however, dwelled on the virtues of the early days. Boyle Workman felt that "the Pueblo [in the 1850s to the 1870s] itself offered little opportunity for gracious living." If Workman denigrated its style, Hayes criticized its snobbery. He "confess[ed]" in 1853, "society narrows itself within a very narrow circle, or rather several little circles. One must learn here to find consolation and 'company' at his own fireside."[107] Another type of complaint emanated from those who belonged to the preconquest patriciate. Declining elites habitually express bitterness over their displacement by condemning the groups that defeat them. Descendants of New York's Knickerbockers, Boston's Brahmins, Charleston's chivalry, Chicago's Gilded Age moguls, and Los Angeles' cattle barons vented their fury in this fashion. Such sentiments occurred more rarely and less intensely among the post-conquest upper class. When they did, as with Graves, Smith, or Newmark, they were often spurred by regrets over the passing of a pristine era rather than by the demise of a hierarchy that had tumbled the old establishment. Figures from leading families of the 1850s to the 1880s, even if they subsequently lost power or status, balanced their laments with praise for the accomplishments of Los Angeles and confidence in its future. Sarah Bixby Smith in 1925 might "wonder how soon the wheels of progress are going to stop rattling long enough for us to . . . develop some sort of cohesive social organism." In her childhood "there was less hurry. . . . We could stroll down the streets to do our errands, meeting friends at every turn." Now the "town is daily swamped with hordes of new and unrelated people. . . ." But this familiar litany of alienated upper classes was balanced by "pride in the vigor of her [Los Angeles'] life and . . . faith that when she really grows up and discovers a co-ordinated spirit to direct her overgrown body, she will earn a right to her queenly name." Boyle Workman, third-generation heir of an even more famous family, never subscribed to the golden age that Smith,

Newmark, and Graves glorified. This "city has been the birthplace of men of great vision," he proudly declared in 1936, and "strong men from all over the world have adopted it as their own."[108]

THE CITY EMERGES: 1885–1915

Between 1885 and 1915 the small town turned into a large city. Los Angeles had 11,183 inhabitants in 1880 and 319,000 in 1910. Its population quadrupled during the boom years of the 1880s, doubled in the next decade, and tripled between 1900 and 1910, far outpacing the growth rates of Boston, New York, San Francisco, Chicago, Detroit, Pittsburgh, Denver, Portland, and Seattle. The Midwest contributed the largest regional share of immigrants to Los Angeles. Residents originating in the east and west north-central states constituted one-third of the population in 1890 and two-fifths in 1910. Conversely, transplants from the New England and Middle Atlantic areas declined during this period.[109] The newcomers, who tended to be older, richer, more likely to emigrate in families, better educated, and with higher percentages of professionals and businessmen than the usual influx into urban centers, transformed Los Angeles from a boisterous frontier settlement into a decorous community. The insurgence of midwestern morality prompted in 1891 the Sunday closing of saloons; five years later gambling houses were shut down; and in 1906 the number of barrooms was sharply curtailed.[110]

As its economy and population expanded, Los Angeles acquired the attributes of a modern metropolis. In the 1880s there appeared cement-paved blocks, the telephone, the cable car, and electric light, and in 1890 the electric trolley. San Francisco, as usual, anticipated these innovations. Institutional development accompanied technological advances. The first great university in southern California appeared in Los Angeles in 1880, the historical society and the oldest permanent businessmen's organization in 1883, the original theater in 1884, the initial art club and a permanent chamber of commerce in 1888, the first public art exhibition in 1890, the symphony orchestra in 1887 and a permanent philharmonic in 1897, and the earliest museum in 1903.[111] Concomitant with these spearheads of urbanism were the proliferation of social clubs, churches, cultural societies, charities, hospitals, and colleges.

Demographic expansion, increased municipal services, and the multiplication and enlargement of civic institutions resulted from spectacular economic growth. Value added by manufacture to goods produced in Los Angeles was $657,000 in 1879 and $38.5 million in 1909, the largest increase in major American industrial centers during these decades. Ship tonnage entering Los Angeles harbor rose from 102,105 in 1880 to 1,660,975 in 1910. Banking interchanges at the Los Angeles

Clearing House expanded from $31,019,721 in 1890 to $1,145,167,110 in 1914. Heightened economic activity elevated total property assessments in Los Angeles from $49,320,670 in 1890–91 to $508,247,113 in 1914–15.[112]

An interlocking group of 381 business, professional, civic, and political figures, who were at least forty years old in 1885 and thus had reached or entered upon the apex of their influence, composed the multi-dimensional elite that provided the leadership for these achievements. A collective trait portrayal, similar to that of their predecessors, provides a structural analysis of the 1885–1915 group, and a basis of comparison with the earlier enclave and with Chicago, New York, and Boston elites.[113]

Like the upper class of 1850–85, a tiny segment of the elite (eleven members) were born in the city. The booming 1880s, the decade of the greatest proportional increase in the urban population, coincided with the largest single decade of entry for the elite (see Table 8). The newcomers were generally better established before moving than immigrants to other cities. Los Angeles was also a relatively new place undergoing growth and change; therefore recent inhabitants often entered the elite within a relatively short time. Indeed, a comparison between Tables 1 and 8 shows that the time lag between arriving and "making it" diminished in the later group.

Age of migration discloses another reason why it took less time for immigrants to enter the elite of 1885–1915 than for their forerunners (see Table 9). A comparison between Tables 2 and 9 indicates that over half of the earlier but only between one-third and two-fifths of the subsequent upper class came to the city before age thirty. During the later period Los Angeles was already widely touted as a haven for older people and the migrants among the elite, too, tended to be older than usual for newcomers to urban centers. Their relatively advanced age enabled

Table 8

ARRIVAL DECADE OF THE LOS ANGELES UPPER CLASS: 1885–1915

Decade	Number	Percentage
1850–59	1	0.3
1860–69	4	1.4
1870–79	38	13.2
1880–89	123	42.9
1890–99	79	27.5
1900–1909	42	14.6
Total known	287	100

Base percentage of group total: 77.6 (287 of 370)

Table 9

AGE AT MIGRATION OF THE LOS ANGELES UPPER CLASS: 1885–1915

Age	Number	Percentage
0– 9	9	3.8
10–19	13	5.6
20–29	63	26.9
30–39	90	38.5
40–49	42	17.9
50–59	15	6.4
60–69	2	0.9
Total known	234	100

Base percentage of group total: 63.2 (234 of 370)

many to accumulate money, complete their education, and establish themselves vocationally and thus come to Los Angeles with resources considerably above the average for urban immigrants.

Changes in the geographical origins of the earlier and later enclaves reflected modifications over time in the birthplaces for the entire city population. Comparing Tables 3 and 10, the midwestern component in the elite increased, New Englanders decreased, and the Middle Atlantic contingent stayed the same. The largest drop occurred among the foreign-born, a phenomenon connected to the disappearance of Jews. Identified Jews composed 13.4 percent of the earlier upper class and

Table 10

BIRTHPLACES OF THE LOS ANGELES UPPER CLASS: 1885–1915

Birthplace	Number	Percentage
New England	38	10.6
Middle Atlantic	68	18.9
South[a]	47	13.1
West[a]	129	35.8
Mountain and Pacific Coast states[b]	8	2.2
California	19	5.3
Los Angeles	11	3.1
Canada	14	3.9
Abroad[c]	26	7.2
Total	360	100

Base percentage of group total: 94.5 (360 of 381)

[a]See Table 3
[b]Excluding California
[c]Excluding Canada

only 2.3 percent (nine of 381) of the later. Relative to their 1890–1910 proportions of the municipality, immigrants from New England, the Middle Atlantic region, the Midwest, and from abroad were significantly overrepresented and southerners were slightly overrepresented in the elite. The development of the city and emergence of younger generations in old and influential families expanded the portions of California and Los Angeles natives compared to their representation in previous elites. Natives of the city and the state nevertheless remained grossly underrepresented; they constituted a share similar to that of indigenous Chicago millionaires of 1892 but smaller than those of native New Yorkers and Bostonians among the contemporary millionaires of those metropolises.

A comparison of Tables 4 and 11 reveals a decline in the percentage of self-made successes in the later group. Every category of inherited wealth increased in percentage and the rise was significant except in the variable of three or more generations. This resulted from the family founders of the 1850s and '60s bequeathing their riches to their progeny and from an influx of residents who came from affluent families in other places. Despite the lesser proportion of new wealth, the majority of those with discerned vintage of fortune were self-made. In this respect the elite was closer to the 1880s economic elite of San Francisco and the 1892 millionaires of Chicago than to New York and Boston millionaires of 1892.[114] Upper-class Angelenos, however, had a significantly lower level of Horatio Alger types in their ranks and higher shares in every inherited wealth vintage than did the Chicagoans. The midwestern metropolis was an older city with a slightly higher representation of indigenous residents in its elite; therefore the higher share of inherited wealth in the Los Angeles enclave was due to its attracting wealthier emigrants than did Chicago.

Despite the enlarged share of inhereited wealth, the 1885–1915 cohort lagged behind its predecessors of 1850–85 and contemporary counterparts in other cities in family clustering, an important index of group

Table 11

Vintage of Fortune of the Los Angeles Upper Class: 1885–1915

Wealth Generation	Number	Percentage
First	88	56.1
Second	35	22.3
At least second	23	14.6
Three or more	11	7.0
Total	157	100

Base percentage of group total: 41.2 (157 of 381)

cohesion. Only fifty-eight (15.2 percent) had connubial or blood ties with at least one other person in the group. This represented a two-thirds drop from the earlier upper class and a substantially lower level of interrelationships than prevailed among opulent New Yorkers, Bostonians, and Chicagoans of 1892. Kinship continuity with the 1850–85 echelon, another aspect of elite integration, was also low among the 1885–1915 leaders: forty-one (10.8 percent) were direct descendants or in-laws of those in the earlier elite. This portion was much smaller than those between earlier and later moneyed enclaves in Chicago, Boston, and New York. Conversely, thirty-one of the 172 (18.0 percent) of the members of the earlier enclave had direct descendants or in-laws among the subsequent aggregation. This measure of continuity, too, was much smaller in Los Angeles than between the mid- and late-nineteenth-century elites in the three other cities. Continuity and interrelationship were weaker in upper-class Los Angeles than elsewhere because the town's greater demographic and economic growth made the elite expand more rapidly and admit large numbers of newcomers.

Significant variations occurred over time in the occupational as well as in the social structure of the upper class (see Table 12). Increased specialization as the economy matured enabled an assignment of primary vocation to almost every member of the later elite, while such designations were impossible to make for most of the earlier group. Urban development also transformed Los Angeles from a cattle and farm market center into a city with a diversified economy, a transition reflected in the vast decrease of those primarily in agriculture. Advancing social sophistication of the city was reflected in the appearance of

Table 12
_____

Primary Occupations of the Los Angeles upper Class: 1885–1915

Occupation	Number	Percentage
Agriculture	5	1.3
Transportation	6	1.6
Utilities	8	2.0
Trade	17	4.5
Manufacturing	56	14.7
Finance	52	13.7
Real estate	22	5.8
General capitalist[a]	4	1.0
Professions	178	46.7
No occupation	33	8.7
Total	381	100

[a]No discernible primary occupation

those, chiefly women, with no occupation except club life and charity service.

The upper class shared a trend of avoiding government posts common among turn-of-the-century urban elites. Over two-thirds of the 1850–85 leaders held public office compared to seventy-four (19.9 percent) of their successors. Although its share of officeholders had shrunk, the later group was still slightly ahead of the affluent Bostonians and Chicagoans and appreciably ahead of the wealthy New Yorkers of 1892.

Economic Functions

New men, born and raised elsewhere, dominated the economic life of Los Angeles, but the nature of leadership remained constant. Business activity was still the basis of the multidimensional upper class, but commercial life changed in two important respects: the magnitude of operations was mammoth compared to the previous era, and the general entrepreneur (thirty years later than in San Francisco) gave way to the specialized capitalist.[115]

AGRICULTURE

Agriculture and associated enterprises remained an important element in the economy. Until 1900 horticulture was the area's chief industry and largest source of income. Citrus fruit growing and wine processing, however, constituted the main exception to the hegemony of the recently arrived magnates. During the 1880s and '90s Beaudry, Rose, Nadeau, and Shorb still owned the largest vineyards. The power of these Old Guard paladins enabled the growers to organize effectively to protect their interests. The chamber of commerce promoted and administered agricultural fairs, encouraged citrus fruit growers to unite for a favorable price schedule, and recommended higher tariffs on imported fruit. Shorb became president of the Southern California Protective Viticultural League (1889), which successfully lobbied for tax-free brandy. The Southern California Fruit Exchange, founded in 1893 to help the growers regulate market and shipping conditions, became the strongest pressure group in the region. As in so many other matters, however, northern Californians, outside of Shorb, instituted the most powerful protective associations.[116]

REAL ESTATE

Between 1885 and 1915 Los Angeles experienced an increase of population and wealth reminiscent of the 1830–60 growth of Chicago. Real estate operators in both cities were strategically positioned to take advantage of the boom years. The greatest inflation of land values that ever occurred in Los Angeles peaked when the Atchison, Topeka and Santa Fe Railroad entered the city in 1888. Competition between the

Santa Fe and the Southern Pacific drove down passenger fares and freight charges. New settlers, chiefly from the Midwest, flocked to southern California and boosted land prices. Aside from cheap transportation, the formula for attracting newcomers included widespread publicity of Los Angeles as an Edenic place of enormous economic promise and the expansion of the water supply and urban transit to stimulate and accommodate population growth. The chamber of commerce in 1888 started to propagandize the nation about local climatic, healthful, and commercial advantages. During its first three years the chamber distributed more than two million pieces of literature on Los Angeles, organized railroad excursions to the city and county, and exhibited local products at the world's fairs in eastern cities. Its efforts were supplemented by prominent land speculators Shorb and Harrison Gray Otis, publisher of the Los Angeles *Times*, and by the railroads, who indefatigably promoted the area.[117]

Unlike the viticulturalists, many of the foremost land speculators, even in the 1880s, were new men. Andrew M. Chaffey, an engineer, came in that decade, lawyers Jonathan S. Slauson, John D. Bicknell, and Moses L. Wicks, and banker John E. Hollenbeck arrived in the 1870s. During this decade, Old Guard remnants, Shorb and lawyers Chapman and Thom, who immigrated in the 1850s, and Don "Benito" Wilson were also prominent realtors. They purchased and subdivided ranchos and owned city blocks which were developed for residential or business purposes. At the height of the boom, between 1886 and 1887, county property assessments nearly doubled and city assessments more than doubled in value. Between June and August 1887 more than $10 million monthly in aggregate real estate deals took place. Spectacular personal fortunes were amassed. Between 1882 and 1886 the number of Angelenos worth more than $100,000 increased from seven to fourteen and those worth between $50,000 and $100,000 from nine to twenty-seven. During the boom, Isaias W. Hellman was alleged to have made $3 million and Bicknell at his death owned over $1 million in real estate.[118]

In 1888–89 land prices fell, banks curtailed credit, and over $14 million in real estate values disappeared in Los Angeles County. Total county property assessments diminished more than two-thirds between 1887 and 1890.[119] During the next quarter-century the leading land speculators, Otis and his son-in-law Harry Chandler, Henry E. Huntington, and brothers-in-law Eli P. Clark and Moses H. Sherman, were recent arrivals. Clark, Otis, and Chandler moved to the city in the 1880s, Sherman in the 1890s, and Huntington in the 1900s. Sherman and Clark were the predominant transit magnates of the 1890s and Huntington succeeded them in the next decade. They bought land along the routes of their prospective systems and when the lines were built the areas thus served were rapidly settled and property values rose dramatically. Through the efforts of the transit tycoons Los Angeles assumed its modern character; a shapeless and decentralized metropolis of strung-out neighborhoods and suburbs in search of a city center.

The greatest real estate deal of this period was transacted in 1905 when a syndicate composed of Huntington, Chandler, Sherman, Otis, banker Joseph F. Sartori, and viticulturalist Edwin T. Earl purchased most of the San Fernando Valley from Van Nuys for $2.5 million. The owners incorporated themselves as the San Fernando Mission Co. and subdivided the valley into tourist and suburban home sites. The combine prevailed upon the municipality to float a $25 million bond issue to build an aqueduct that brought water into the valley, thus encouraging its settlement. Another aid to the project was Huntington's Pacific Railway Company, which connected the valley with Los Angeles. The aqueduct was completed in 1913 and the syndicate resold its holding for an estimated $100 million profit. In 1915 most of the territory was annexed by Los Angeles.[120] The San Fernando venture illustrated the classic ingredients of land development in Los Angeles. Access to water and transportation raised land values by attracting settlers. The wealth and political power of the speculators made these resources available. The consequences of the project were the subdivision of large holdings which increased the population, expanded the economy, and contributed to the centrifugal disposition of the area.

Low assessments of real property constituted another example of political influence underwriting land speculation. In 1886 municipal assessments underrated actual property values by 40 percent and in 1910 by at least 60 percent.[121]

TRADE

Although realtors and viticulturalists diversified their enterprises, leading merchants tended to concentrate on trade. When Hellman decided to become a banker he left Hellman, Haas & Co. Specialization did not signify a total departure from tradition. Several historic family businesses, as previously noted, lasted until well into the twentieth century.

While older firms continued, recent arrivals, as in Chicago, dominated the department store, the largest and newest branch of trade. Asher Hamberger, proprietor of the People's Store (1882), the greatest emporium in turn-of-the-century Los Angeles, came to the city in 1881. Yankee trader J. W. Robinson arrived about the same time as Hamberger and established the Boston Store (1884), eventually the largest dry-goods house in southern California. A decade later ex-apprentice draper Arthur Letts emigrated from Seattle. He owned two department stores, an extensive ranch, and a large slice of downtown Los Angeles, belonged to several elite clubs, was a trustee of civic and welfare institutions, and headed the Los Angeles and National Retail Dry-Goods Associations. This multimillionaire owed his success to business methods virtually identical to those of his Chicago forerunner, Marshall Field. Both retailers worked hard, advertised widely, treated customers courteously, represented their wares honestly and allowed goods to be returned, operated on a one-price, no-bargaining system, believed in quick turnover of stock, promoted from within the organization, and were antiunion.[122]

INDUSTRY

Measured by increases in manufacturing employees and value added by manufacture, metropolitan Los Angeles between 1885 and 1915 was the fastest growing among the top thirty-three industrial areas in the United States. But it started from a tiny base and in 1899 still ranked thirty-third in total value added by manufacturing and in 1914 only twenty-fifth. In 1889 and 1909 its percentage of the national total of value added by manufacturing, respectively 0.12 and 0.45, was a fraction of New York's, Chicago's, or Boston's and less than half of San Francisco's. Until 1900 Los Angeles factories chiefly made products for local consumers and were agriculturally based, mainly in horticulture and citrus fruit processing. In the 1890s large-scale oil deposits were discovered in the region, and before World War I oil products comprised Los Angeles' sole significant contribution to the national industrial market.[123]

Los Angeles developed slowly as a manufacturing center because of sparse population, geographical distance from the East and Midwest and, until the discovery of oil, lack of a source of cheap power. Available capital in the 1890s usually went into traditional enterprises like real estate and trade, recalled John B. Miller, president of the Southern California Edison Company in the 1920s. Letts put his money in land while his Chicago counterpart, Field, invested heavily in U.S. Steel and in the Pullman Palace Car Co. Moreover, Los Angeles attracted an older population that sought an easy way of life incompatible with industrial endeavors. Business leaders, like banker H. S. McKee in 1915, noted that Los Angeles was "a residential . . . community," where "local . . . services . . . employ most of the working population." It lacked a "large industry . . . which produces a product far beyond local needs for sale and export to other localities. . . ."[124]

Although factories were a minor factor in the economy, several manufacturers belonged to the elite. Milo S. Baker, who moved to Los Angeles from Michigan in 1874, founded the Baker Iron Works. His successor and son Frederick L. was a city councillor, a water commissioner, president of the Merchants' and Manufacturers' Association, a director in land companies, and a member of exclusive clubs. London-born William Lacy entered Los Angeles in the same year as did the elder Baker. He founded the Lacy Manufacturing Company (1887), which made steel ties and other iron and steel products; had extensive oil, real estate, and mining interests; served on the board of education, as vice-president of the Farmers' & Merchants' Bank, and as president of the chamber of commerce; and belonged to fashionable social clubs. He, too, was succeeded by his son.[125]

In industry, as in trade, the major new development was largely the work of newcomers. Edward L. Doheny, a Wisconsin-born former jockey, came to Los Angeles in 1890 and two years later drilled the first oil well in the city and the largest in nineteenth-century California. Doheny became the premier oilman of the region, joined prestigious clubs, and, following a pattern not unusual among industrialists, took his son into his business. Aside from Doheny and Lacy, several prominent figures organized oil companies. Lyman Stewart, who migrated to Los Angeles in 1880, headed the Union Oil Co. (1890), the largest independent in the state. Its arch-rival, the Puente Oil Co. (1892), was formed by Lacy (its president) and William R. Rowland, realtor and scion of the *Alta California* gentry. Graves, the well-connected banker who arrived in the city in 1875, was business manager. Robert N. Bulla, a lawyer and state legislator who came to Los Angeles in 1883, helped organize and run the Central Oil Co. of Los Angeles (1900). Two years later the Associated Oil Co., the second largest independent in the area, was formed by producers in order to resist Standard Oil's bid for an oil monopoly in the region. Doheny's partner, Charles A. Canfield, was president and Graves later became a vice-president. Several business leaders formed the Pico Oil Co. (1909), a consolidation of several large local concerns including the Puente. William B. Scott, its president, was a son-in-law of a founder of Union Oil. Most of these tycoons, Scott, Canfield, Doheny, Graves, and Bulla, were self-made men and recent arrivals to Los Angeles.[126]

TRANSPORTATION

Adequate transportation and access to water were the necessary conditions for the growth of Los Angeles. The rate war between the Atchison, Topeka, and the Santa Fe and the Southern Pacific attracted settlers and enhanced the economy by lowering shipping costs between California and the rest of the nation. Mayor William H. Workman in 1887–88 played a key role in getting a right-of-way for the Santa Fe just as he had sixteen years earlier for the Southern Pacific. He owned large tracts of land in the city and county whose value was upgraded by the entry of an additional trunk line. Moses L. Wicks, who came to Los Angeles in the 1870s, was another Santa Fe promoter whose real estate holdings soared in value as a consequence of the railroad. James F. Crank also assisted the Santa Fe. An assemblyman, vineyard owner, citrus fruit producer, real estate speculator, traction magnate and bank executive, he arrived in the city in 1877 and organized the Los Angeles and San Gabriel Railroad Co. Crank sold the line to the Santa Fe in 1887, thus giving it ingress to Los Angeles. According to Charles D. Willard, chamber of commerce secretary and a prime Los Angeles booster, "The modern city of Los Angeles may be said to have entered its career in 1888" with the arrival of the Santa Fe.[127]

Twenty years later urban growth involved transformation of San Pedro into a harbor for ocean-going vessels. Los Angeles, unlike Chicago, Charleston, Boston, and New York, did not have a natural deep-water port. The crucial step was taken in 1897 when Congress funded San Pedro rather than the rival site of Santa Monica. The battle to develop San Pedro divided the upper class. Collis P. Huntington and his Southern Pacific, which had a monopoly of wharfage at Santa Monica, Cole, merchant-banker Kaspare Cohn, Slauson, and Lankersheim, all extensive real estate proprietors there, lobbied for that port. But the contingent favoring San Pedro—Otis, U.S. Senator White, William H. Workman, several prominent lawyers and bankers, the chamber of commerce, and the Santa Fe—prevailed upon Congress. They organized the Free Harbor League (1895), composed of leading businessmen, and outnumbered the Santa Monica proponents. Except for Lankersheim and Workman, the principals on both sides had come to the city in the 1870s or thereafter, but the San Pedro group generally had the more recent arrivals. Its triumph indicated that the upper class was powerful enough to vanquish a mighty force in California. Ultimately, however, this proved a partial victory because the Southern Pacific owned land and docks in the new harbor. By 1910 the San Pedro project, aided by a municipal bond issue, was completed and the port annexed to Los Angeles. A few years later the Panama Canal opened, setting off another boom and ensuring the maritime primacy of Los Angeles in the East-West trade.[128]

While shipping and transcontinental transport attracted settlers and promoted commerce, inter- and intraurban transit lines helped create the capacity to absorb the newcomers. Traction systems imposed on metropolitan Los Angeles a decentralized, suburban geographical structure. Trolleys preceded residents and opened up new towns. Company organizers were invariably large realtors who wished to make their subdivisions accessible to recent migrants. These entrepreneurs made Los Angeles the first city in California and the fourth in the country to have electric railways.[129]

During the 1880s William H. Workman, Victor and Prudent Beaudry, Wicks, and Cole constructed lines between the city and the suburbs, or within the city. Crank, the dominant traction magnate in the 1880s, and a syndicate of Chicago capitalists consolidated most of the lines in the city. In the next decade Sherman and Clark, backed by San Francisco capital, formed the Los Angeles Consolidated Electric Railway Co. (1890), which absorbed most of the urban lines. They organized the Pacific Electric Transit Co. (1895), eventually the largest American traction system, to link outlying towns with the city. Huntington succeeded Sherman and Clark. He inherited the Southern Pacific from uncle Collis P. Huntington, but was known mainly for a spectacular career in southern California transit. Funded by San Francisco investors, led by banker Isaias W. Hellman, now living there, in 1898 he bought the Sherman and Clark companies. Three years later Huntington founded the Pacific Electric Railway Co., the world's largest, and one of the best equipped and run, intercity transit company. At its height Pacific Electric operated over 1,000 miles of track and served the San Gabriel Valley, Pasadena, and had an exclusive track franchise in San Pedro. Huntington sold out to the Southern Pacific in 1910 and the following year organized the Los Angeles Railway Corporation, which consolidated the urban lines.[130]

Most of the tycoons were newcomers. Cole emigrated from San Francisco in 1880, Sherman and Clark from Arizona respectively in 1889 and 1891, and Huntington moved to Los Angeles in 1902. Traction entrepreneurs resembled other capitalists in recency of arrival, but differed from merchants and manufacturers in sources of financial support. Transportation projects, such as port improvements, the coming of the trunk lines, and the development of transit systems, required a scale of investment beyond the capacity of local resources. Therefore, unlike undertakings in agriculture, trade, or industry, financing came mainly from outside the commercial community. Hence, it was a milestone of local economic maturity when Huntington, within a few years of establishing Pacific Electric, acquired complete ownership of his enterprises.[131]

UTILITIES

Leading capitalists, especially real estate subdividers, were active in utilities enterprise. Six years after coming to Los Angeles George Chaffey, an extensive landowner, in 1884 became president of the Los Angeles Electric Company. Cohn helped organize the San Gabriel Light & Power Co. (1892), which tapped the waters of the San Gabriel Valley in order to generate hydroelectric power for the urban inhabitants, and several other gas and power corporations. Traction czar Huntington, the greatest landowner in southern California, in 1901 created the Pacific Light and Power Co., the largest independent electric company in the region. Pacific Light and Power exemplified the national trend toward vertical business combination; over three-fourths of its business was with electric railways and it supplied the power for virtually all the lines in southern California. Unlike the experience of other cities, proliferation of power utilities increased efficiency of service. By 1899 Los Angeles residents paid less for electric service per lamp than did the inhabitants of any other American municipality.[132]

Early efforts in meeting community needs for power, largely through private initiative, meant that upper-class entrepreneurs again controlled metropolitan growth. Los Angeles, unlike Philadelphia, New York, Chicago, or Boston, lacked access to coal, the conventional nineteenth-century source of power. Consequently, electricity was crucial to urban expansion. Electric companies, for example, were indispensable in the implementation of transit systems.

Electricity depended upon water power. Here again Los Angeles had to overcome a natural disadvantage absent in Charleston, Boston, New York, and Chicago. Upper-class Angelenos were intimately involved in the crucial Owens Valley Aqueduct. Frederick B. Eaton, former mayor, city engineer, and superintendent of the Los Angeles City Water Co., and son of state senator, lawyer, and landowner Benjamin S. Eaton, discovered the potential of the Owens River as a source of water for Los Angeles. Eaton bought land and water rights in the Owens Valley, anticipating a fortune if the municipality later purchased them. A 1907 municipal bond issue funded the construction of the aqueduct. City treasurer William H. Workman was instrumental in getting New York banks to underwrite the issue. Sherman, one of the members of the syndicate that bought up 47,500 acres of the San Fernando Valley, which would be served by the aqueduct, was president in 1909 of the Los Angeles Metropolitan Water District. The conveyance was opposed by the Southern California Edison Co., the most powerful utility in the region, but was supported by syndicate members Huntington, Chandler, and Otis.[133]

Aside from furnishing power and water and raising real estate values, the aqueduct contributed to the geographical and population growth and suburban character of Los Angeles. An annexation committee (1913), composed of civic and business leaders, recommended to the city council that outlying communities wishing to use the municipal water supply must become part of the city. The chamber of commerce, the Los Angeles Realty Board, and the *Times* backed the committee and the city council adopted its recommendation. Between 1915 and 1927 the San Fernando Valley and other areas joined Los Angeles. The additions totaled 257 miles, a 250 percent expansion of the city limits.[134]

Built and run by the municipal administration, the aqueduct represented the most dramatic departure from the traditional commitment to private enterprise in urban development. The movement for public ownership of utilities began in 1899 when, with Mayor Eaton's blessing, Hazard chaired a blue-ribbon committee for this purpose. In that year a bond issue enabled the municipality to take over the Los Angeles Water Co. City officials, prominent businessmen, the chamber of commerce, the Merchants' and Manufacturers' Association, and the *Times* advocated public ownership of water and power facilities. Not until 1914 did a significant rift occur over this issue among the elite.[135]

BANKING

Los Angeles, undergoing gigantic growth between 1885 and 1915, had a voracious need for capital. But its previously undeveloped economy prevented the amassing of financial resources. Los Angeles in 1890 had four savings banks and eleven commercial banks with only $2,764,350 in capital and $13,870,410 in total assets. Miller remembered the "little available capital in Southern California" in the 1890s.[136] San Francisco, by comparison, in 1885 had over half of the state's commercial bank capital and deposits and seven-eighths of the savings bank deposits. California's original savings institution was founded there in 1867, seventeen years before one appeared in Los Angeles. The state's first trust company was established in San Francisco in 1868, twenty-one years before one was incorporated in Los Angeles. The initial stock and bond house in Los Angeles was a branch of a San Francisco firm and no stock exchange existed until 1896. Further evidence of the ascendance of San Francisco was the fact that its capitalists funded some of the major electric and traction companies in Los Angeles, and the 1890 departure of Isaias W. Hellman for San Francisco.[137]

Although overshadowed by San Francisco, a sophisticated financial community gradually emerged in the thirty years before World War I. Hellman's Los Angeles Savings Bank (1884) was the first such institution in the city. Five years later the State Loan & Trust Co., the earliest local trust firm, was organized.[138] The appearance of trust companies showed that private fortunes were now large enough to sustain institutions devoted to investing and protecting personal wealth. The founding of bankers' organizations was another sign of progress. The Los Angeles Clearing House (1887) coordinated interchanges among the city's banks, forced unstable institutions to liquidate, and sustained healthy ones during financial crises. The California Bankers' Association (1891), organized chiefly by Los Angeles financiers, helped write state banking legislation. The National Currency Association of Los Angeles (1914) assisted banks to meet needs for liquid capital.[139]

Even in its early stages banking was a significant factor in the Los Angeles economy. Crank used his vice-presidency of the First National Bank of Los Angeles to obtain the credit necessary for his San Gabriel Railroad. Hellman's refusal to lend money to real estate speculators, a practice followed by other local bankers, pricked the land boom in 1888. Marco H. Hellman, nephew of Isaias W. Hellman and son of Herman W. Hellman, the founder and president of the Merchants' National Bank, in his capacity as vice-president of this institution helped sell aqueduct bonds when an eastern syndicate defaulted on its allotment of the issue.[140]

Now in San Francisco, Hellman still dominated Los Angeles finance. He headed Farmers' & Merchants', organized other banks, and made Farmers' & Merchants' executives their chief officers. Among these institutions was the Security Savings Bank & Trust Co. (1889), in 1915 the largest bank in the city. Hellman-controlled banks in 1915 held approximately one-fifth of the city's total banking assets of $225,742,000. He was the first president of the Los Angeles Clearing House Association and the original vice-president of the California Banker's Association, controlled credit during the great land boom, and through his political connections made Farmers' & Merchants' the repository of the Los Angeles county treasurer's funds.[141]

Farmers' & Merchants' was similar in its Old Guard directorship, interrelated management, conservatism, and eventual displacement from local preeminence to the Bank of New York and the Massachusetts First National Bank of Boston. Upper-class lawyers and businessmen and their sons served on the board of directors. The bank remained until 1920 in the hands of Hellman. His son and brother were vice-presidents. Graves, Hellman's successor, married the daughter of one of the bank's founders and his son-in-law also became a vice-president. Careful extension of credit, high cash reserves, and eschewal of high risk and high yield investments for safe U.S. government issues enabled Farmers' & Merchants' to escape embarrassment in times of national financial crises, sustain the high market value of its stock, and never miss a dividend after 1872. Caution also inhibited growth and ultimately caused the bank to lose ground to institutions headed by aggressive and imaginative financiers.[142]

Hellman-controlled institutions protected patrician Los Angeles by employing relatives of upper-class family founders. Apart from the Hellman and Graves clans, the Lankersheim-Van Nuys connection was thus nurtured. James B. Lankersheim, son of Isaac and brother-in-law of Farmers' & Merchants' vice-president Isaac N. Van Nuys, was president of the Main Street Savings Bank and Trust Co. and on the boards of other Hellman-controlled banks. Business ties reinforced kinship. Graves, before he turned to banking, was the Van Nuys family attorney.[143]

As indicated by the Hellman empire, leading bankers frequently held offices and directorships in several financial institutions. Graves at one time was an officer and director in fourteen banks in Los Angeles County. Ohio-born George H. Bonebrake, who came to Los Angeles in 1878, founded and headed four Los Angeles banks and several in southern California. At his death in 1898 Bonebrake was the largest owner of bank stock in the city.[144]

Particularly in the early years, versatile entrepreneurs Temple, Hellman, Downey, Graves, George Chaffey, Cohn, and Robert Maclay Widney organized and headed banks. Businessmen and lawyers were officers in major institutions. General capitalists who engaged in finance frequently founded family managed banks. In addition to Temple and his father-in-law and the Hellman clan, Cohn's sons-in-law inherited the Kaspare Cohn Commercial & Savings Bank (1914), and Andrew M. Chaffey succeeded his father as president of the American Savings Bank (1905). By the 1890s, as banking became a more complex and large-scale endeavor, executives were more often career financiers. First National president Stoddard Jess exemplified the professional banker. Son of a Wisconsin banker, he arrived in Los Angeles in 1898 and headed the Bankers' Association and the Clearing House.[145] Such bankers were less likely to preside over kinship-structured institutions. Under their leadership Los Angeles banking assumed the specialized professionalism long dominant in eastern financial institutions.

If bankers sometimes achieved their community standing through success in other enterprises, professional financiers often became civic leaders. Edward F. Spence, another First National president and a founder of the Banker's Association, moved to Los Angeles in 1875 and was mayor in 1884. Orra E. Monnette, son and grandson of Ohio bankers, immigrated to Los Angeles in 1906 and became president and the greatest shareholder in the Citizens' Trust & Savings Co. He headed the Los Angeles Library Board and served on the annexation and city planning commissions and the board of freeholders.[146]

BUSINESS ORGANIZATIONS

If the failure of the first chamber of commerce to survive the depression of the 1870s signified the fragile and rudimentary state of entrepreneurial Los Angeles, the founding of permanent business organizations in the 1880s heralded its coming of age.

The Los Angeles Board of Trade (1883) was the oldest permanent business organization. Most of the incorporators were early settlers of long-standing wealth and reputation. Since commerce established itself well before industry or banking, the city's first durable formal business association was unsurprisingly launched by merchants. The board aided mercantile interests by campaigning for appropriations for the Los Angeles Post Office Building, for the location of the Soldiers' Home in

Santa Monica, and for the placing of an army headquarters in Los Angeles. Presidents of the organization included Jacob Haas, Germain, banker William C. Patterson, and Bonebrake.[147]

The second Los Angeles Chamber of Commerce (1888) operated on a grander scale and became the city's foremost business association. Among its chief organizers were Otis and William H. Workman. Most of the founders and early members and officers were recent arrivals and leading capitalists in the city. Slauson, Meyer J. Newmark, Patterson, McKee, and Bulla served as presidents. Chamber membership in 1899 numbered about 1,000, including fifty-four lawyers, thirty-four physicians, both of California's U.S. senators, and three local congressmen. The organization advertised Los Angeles, lobbied government bodies for public improvements, and supplied information on business conditions and opportunities. Its efforts included the promotion of agriculture, trade, manufacturing, banking, transportation facilities, and water and power resources. The chamber contributed to the realization of such major projects as the improvement and annexation of San Pedro and the construction of the aqueduct.[148]

The Merchants' and Manufacturers' Association (1896) was founded to stimulate local economic activities but soon turned into the most potent antiunion force in Los Angeles. Before World War I, 750 firms and 80 to 85 percent of the larger establishments in the city belonged to the association. Industrialist Frederick L. Baker, its second president, and Otis, its chief creator, championed the open shop. The organization gave money to employers involved in labor struggles, brought in strikebreakers, and helped get court injunctions against picketing. Largely as a result of its efforts, Los Angeles became an antilabor citadel at a time when unions flourished in San Francisco.[149]

OUTLOOK AND IDEOLOGY

Successful entrepreneurs were the most avid civic boosters. Made sanguine by their triumphs, they expected urban growth to bring further gains. Isaias W. Hellman, Walter Lindley, Joseph P. Widney, Willard, Graves, Otis, Harris Newmark, Letts, Miller, and Huntington predicted that the city would become a great metropolis. Supreme optimists Letts, Huntington, and Newmark forecast that Los Angeles would become the nation's and possibly the world's premier metropolis.[150]

Hellman, Widney, and Lindley, while not ignoring the promise of economic growth and commercial profits, in the 1880s emphasized ideal living conditions resulting from a good climate and a fertile soil.[151] Subsequent enthusiasts also tended to attribute Los Angeles greatness to business advantages or entrepreneurial traits. "We possessed," claimed Newmark, "the spirit called . . . enterprise." If Newmark looked to character, Miller expected abundant natural resources, pleasant weather, and relative proximity to the Orient, the globe's future mammoth market, to make southern California "one of the great industrial and commercial as well as agricultural centers in the United States."[152]

Enthralled by its potential and encouraged by its accomplishments, Los Angeles enthusiasts, even before the twentieth century, compared it to America's preeminent metropolises. Amidst the depression of the 1890s Otis instructed "the merchants to cut loose and start a new era of prosperity upon a broader plane." Angelenos should cease "looking to San Francisco for inspiration," for "the rottenness of San Francisco must shoulder her own responsibilities. Los Angeles is a new world formed with higher motives, broader principles, and greater ambitions. The Chicago of the West—the ambitious, prosperous city of the Western Hemisphere." In 1889 Willard wrote, "Boston expressed culture, Philadelphia conservatism and regard for family, New York elegance and a certain aristocratic complacency, and Chicago is synonymous with enterprise. Los Angeles is destined to be one of the great cities of the Union." It is developing "those definite characteristics that will give it individuality among its sister cities."[153]

Prominent capitalists celebrated the place of their achievements and took pride in their lives. Hellman, Newmark, Graves, and Henry M. Robinson, who arrived in Los Angeles in 1907 and became a bank president, a corporate director, a member of national commissions and exclusive social clubs, and a trustee of cultural institutions, expressed gratification over their commercial success, community status, and personal happiness.[154]

Faith in themselves and their city helped win fame and fortune for great capitalists, and success, in turn, stimulated self-confidence and civic optimism. Innovative and imaginative in their careers, the character traits that the elite considered fundamental to success were a litany of clichés tirelessly invoked by businessmen throughout the country. Letts, Huntington, Graves, Doheny, and Norman Bridge, a Doheny partner who came to southern California in 1891, attributed their accomplishments to (and advised others to acquire) the self-regarding and achievement-oriented virtues of perseverance, aggressiveness, anticipation, and thrift.[155]

According to Doheny, Bridge, Newmark, Graves, and Widney the qualities that led to riches and commercial triumph also contributed to community well-being and national greatness. Widney, foreseeing a struggle for existence between the Anglo-Saxons and other peoples, claimed that "the Captains of Industry are the truest captains in the race war."[156] Impressed with their attainments and insulated by their ideology, eminent entrepreneurs were certain of their vocation, their values, their conduct, their rewards, and their contributions to the city, the nation, and the world.

Politics

The upper class wielded political power for the same reasons, in the same manner, and with the same effects as did other multidimensional elites. But members of old families appeared more rarely in public office than did Boston, New York, or Charleston patricians. Few scions of the *gente de razón* occupied government posts: Ygnacio Sepúlveda was a county superior court judge in the 1880s and Reginald F. Del Valle, an assemblyman and state senator in that decade, later became president of the municipal water and power commission. Descendants of the pre-Mexican War Anglo-American enclave fared little better. The Workmans were the outstanding Old Guard clan still active in politics. William H. Workman, the leading officeholder from this family, was a city councillor (1872–80), mayor (1887–88), park commissioner (1894–98), and city treasurer (1901–7). His brother Elijah was on the council and the board of education, and his son Boyle was a public service commissioner and city council president (1919–27). Post–Mexican War arrivals, or their children, bluebloods by Los Angeles standards, served with greater frequency in government positions. During the 1880s and '90s Rose sat in the state senate, Shorb and Mark G. Jones, son of a merchant-realtor and city councillor of the 1850s and '60s, were county treasurers, Thom and Frederick B. Eaton were mayors, Henry G. Weyse, scion of a pioneer vineyard owner and husband of a Wolfskill, was an assemblyman, and prominent merchant Jacob Kuhrts presided over the city council.[157]

A larger group of 1880s–90s officials entered the upper class more recently. Among them were mayors Spence and Henry T. Hazard; Bulla, who served in both houses of the legislature; county supervisor Milton G. Lindley; city councillors Frederick L. Baker and banker John T. Gaffey, who married a Bandini; and U.S. senator White. These figures, who came to Los Angeles after 1870, were or were close to major businessmen. Bulla, for example, counseled oil companies, and White, with partner Bicknell in the 1870s and 1880s, was involved in real estate, admiralty, corporate, and mining litigation, and represented the Southern Pacific, the Los Angeles Railway, and Otis.[158]

During these years party bosses also often came from the commercial and professional elite. Shorb and Hellman were still county Democratic leaders, and Gaffey became a power in the party. Among their Republican opposite numbers were noted attorneys Frank A. Gibson and G. Wiley Wells.[159]

Through such ties corporations and capitalists nurtured their ventures and fortunes. The Southern Pacific in the 1890s, notwithstanding its San Pedro defeat, still selected surgeons at Los Angeles hospitals to give medical testimony regarding injury suits rising from mishaps on its trains and also pushed through a franchise for additional city trackage.

The city council awarded to Otis's *Times* the municipal advertising contract in 1904 despite its bid being $10–20,000 above those of competing newspapers. In 1906 the council granted Huntington's Pacific Electric a free right-of-way franchise worth at least $1 million.[160] White's career illustrates the symbiotic relationship between political influence and the interests of the elite. Isaias W. Hellman suggested that White run for the California senate. There he voted for a new city charter despite his disapproval, giving priority to Hellman's wishes over his own. White also deferred to client Otis. He sought Otis's advice on reorganizing the county court system and in 1897 tried to obtain an appointment for the publisher as assistant secretary of war. Failing in this attempt he got Otis a brigadier-generalship during the Spanish-American War. White also secured for Ross, a former law partner, a U.S. district court judgeship. Probably the most powerful southern California politician of his day, White faithfully served the institutional as well as the individual interests of the ruling class. As a state senator he consulted the Los Angeles Bar Association on judicial candidates and on the reorganization of the county courts. When the chamber of commerce withdrew its instructions to vote against a bill dividing Orange County from Los Angeles County, he stopped opposing the legislation. In Washington he helped get appropriations for San Pedro, despite having once worked for the Southern Pacific.[161]

Political clout shaped public policy on even more vital matters such as labor relations and water and power development. Edwin T. Earl, Ross, Letts, Otis, Huntington, Baker, Graves, and the Merchants' and Manufacturers' Association defended the open shop. Their influence upon municipal and state governments, particularly that of Otis and the association, kept Los Angeles a nonunion town until the New Deal. Huntington and Otis defeated labor's attempts to organize the *Times* and the transit system. Earl, Otis, and the association prevailed upon old-line and Progressive city and state officials to pass antipicketing ordinances, arrest strikers, and defeat maximum-hour bills or attempts to ease union injunctions. Ross, a notorious antilabor jurist, guided the jury in handing down a conspiracy indictment against West Coast railroad walkouts during the Pullman Strike of 1894.[162]

From 1899 to 1914 the intertwined entrepreneurial and political elite also united on the issue of public ownership of water and power facilities. Eaton, Hazard, lawyer Joseph Scott, William H. Workman, del Valle, Huntington, Otis, Chandler, local Progressive party leaders, the chamber, the association, the Friday Morning Club, the Builders' Exchange, the Associated Jobbers, and the Municipal League supported bond issues to pay for city ownership of the Los Angeles Water Co., the aqueduct, and other milestones in the establishment of a municipally controlled water supply and hydroelectric power system. The business community first split on this issue in 1914 when Otis, Chandler, and the association defected on a public power bond issue. But the majority of the magnates and civic leaders, represented by the chamber, the City Club, the Municipal League, and the local newspapers except the *Times*, prevailed over the opposition. Public ownership encouraged civic reform and the expansion of the metropolitan economy while advancing the interests of eminent capitalists. An example of the latter consequence was the contribution of the aqueduct to the profits of the San Fernando Valley land syndicate.[163]

Apart from enhancing its projects and purses, the elite fostered urban development. Mayor Spence originated the municipal fire department, and Mayor Eaton encouraged municipal ownership of water and power resources. William H. Workman, in a series of public offices, supported the aqueduct, public ownership of the water supply, rights-of-way for the Southern Pacific and Santa Fe, public parks, inaugurated street paving, helped draw up a new city charter which modernized the municipal administration, donated land for school and park sites, and assisted in the organization of the city's high school.[164]

Public ownership became a major issue at the turn of the century. The Los Angeles Water Co. corrupted city politics and reformers felt that government control would eliminate the "water ring." In opposing the waterworks, however, as in their crusades for the initiative, referendum, and recall, the Progressives did not threaten the business elite. Their stand on these issues and their resistance to organized labor and socialism made them valuable allies of the tycoons. Although most of the Progressive chieftains did not belong to the upper class—Graves, and after 1902 Otis and Chandler, opposed the reformers—a few good government leaders had ties to rich and powerful citizens. Edward A. Dickson, an editorial writer for the Los Angeles *Express*, helped form the Non-Partisan Committee of 100 (1906) and the Lincoln-Roosevelt League (1907). The former supported local reform candidates and Progressives for state offices and the latter fought the influence of the Southern Pacific in local and state government. Dickson worked for Edwin T. Earl, the citrus fruit processor, antilabor agitator, land speculator, *Express* publisher, and a California Progressive party leader. John R. Haynes, another founder of the Lincoln-Roosevelt League, champion of public ownership, member of the board of freeholders, the Los Angeles Civil Service and Water and Power commissions, and the chief force behind the Direct Legislation League, was the physician and friend of Otis. The league was the main vehicle for the successful struggle for initiative, referendum, and recall. The Los Angeles Municipal League (1892), another public ownership–good government agency, was founded and run by chamber of commerce secretary Willard, and one of its presidents headed the Merchants' and Manufacturers' Association. The Civic Association (1899), the major women's good government organization, was formed by wives of leading lawyers and capitalists. Bar association president William J. Hunsaker, yet another organizer of the Lincoln-Roosevelt League, was counsel for the *Times* and the Santa Fe and chaired the Non-Partisan Committee. The latter's nominee for mayor was counsel for the leading real estate title abstract company in Los Angeles, a firm created and managed by conservative Republicans Graves, Gibson, and Bicknell.[165]

Los Angeles Progressives made municipal government more honest, efficient, and economical but did not challenge the establishment. Their interests, ideas, and associations linked them to the upper class. The inherent conservatism of the reformers surfaced on such crucial issues as labor relations and was highlighted in 1913 when they joined Otis and other foes of clean government to defeat a socialist mayoralty candidate.[166]

The Professions

Little alteration in role occurred from the earlier era, but in structure the professional elites underwent some change as the city matured. Medicine and law, like business, became more tightly organized vocations. The institutions which integrated these callings, again like commerce and banking, were dominated by members of the upper class. Contrary to some theories of modernization, as Los Angeles urbanized, kinship ties expanded at the apex of the legal and medical professions. Distinguished physicians and attorneys increasingly formed family dynasties as they bequeathed their status and practices to offspring or relatives. A final development in the professions during these years was the emergence of the newspaper publisher and the engineer as important civic figures.

LAW

Law remained the fundamental upper-class profession. Its primacy rested upon extensive interaction among legal, political, and business elites. The foremost law firms became advocates for the major financial and industrial corporations and tycoons. Graves and Henry W. O'Melveny were in a partnership from 1886 to 1903 that conducted the largest real estate conveyance business in the city, represented all but two Los Angeles banks, organized the Title Insurance and Trust Co., incorporated the Metropolitan Building and Loan Association, and handled the legal affairs of the board of trade. Houghton, Silent & Campbell, founded in the 1890s and an equal of Graves & O'Melveny, had clients in criminal, transportation, water, and mining litigation. Gibson, Dunn,

Bicknell, Trask, & Crutcher, another mammoth firm, represented Huntington's business interests, Southern California Edison, and the First National Bank. The business connections of several lawyers drew them from law to other undertakings. Monnette and Graves became bankers and George I. Cochran president of the Pacific Mutual Life Insurance Co. Typically, however, prominent attorneys remained in their firms while becoming corporate officers and directors. Graves, Bicknell, Stephen C. Hubbell, and Frank P. Flint probably had the most varied entrepreneurial involvements. Bicknell headed Title Insurance and Trust, an oil company, and was a First National vice-president. Graves organized the board of trade and engaged in numerous previously mentioned endeavors. Hubbell, a bank and oil company president and a traction company director, conducted a practice chiefly devoted to street railway litigation. An indication of the closeness between lawyers and capitalists was the selection of lawyers John D. Fredericks, Scott, and Bulla as chamber of commerce presidents.[167]

Luminaries of the bar participated as vigorously in politics as in business. White, Thom, Bulla, and Hazard were elected to government offices, and others spearheaded the movement for civic reform. Apart from their careers, discussed above, noted lawyers served in elective posts, as members of such municipal bodies as the board of freeholders (the city charter revision committee), the civil service and water and power commissions, the park, library, and education boards, state or national agencies, or became political party bosses. City attorney and superior court judge James W. McKinley chaired the state delegation to the 1904 Republican national convention. He was legal advisor to the Southern Pacific, chief counsel for Pacific Electric, and his firm was involved in important water suits. Ex-U.S. attorney for the southern district and U.S. senator (1905–11) Flint became a partner in the firm of Flint & McKay, vice-president and counsel for the Los Angeles *Evening Herald*, and president of several banking, lumber, shipbuilding, and investment concerns. Bradner Wells Lee, partner in the prestigious water rights litigation firm of Brunson, Wells, & Lee, chaired the Republican county executive committee from 1896 to 1910 and was on the Republican state central committee. U.S. senator John D. Works (1911–17) later joined the firm.[168]

With rare exceptions, the top-ranked lawyers moved to Los Angeles between 1870 and 1900. John G. Mott, however, was the child of a Sepúlveda and Thomas D. Mott, a merchant-realtor, county clerk, Democratic political boss, and assemblyman in the 1870s. The elder Mott was influential in bringing the Southern Pacific to the city; his son was an important figure in the aqueduct project and headed the bar association. For a time he was in partnership with Isidore B.

Dockweiler, another son of an early settler. Dockweiler served as president of the library board, on the executive committee of the Democratic national committee, on the U.S. board of Indian commissioners and, in 1902, was Democratic candidate for lieutenant governor.[169]

Although few renowned attorneys came from old families, kinship became increasingly visible in the profession. By the 1880s the Los Angeles bar, now thirty years old, resembled, in this respect, its counterparts in older cities. Elders wanted to establish family dynasties and relatives of the same generation often practiced together. Huntington's attorney George S. Patton practiced with his stepfather George H. Smith and his uncle Andrew Glassell in a firm specializing in real estate cases. James A. Anderson and his sons represented Edwin T. Earl, large southern California water companies, and played vital roles in harbor improvements and the aqueduct. Volney E. Howard and his son engaged in water litigation in the firm of Howard, Brousseau & Howard, and brothers Robert H. F. and William J. Variel were in a similar practice. James A. Gibson took his sons into Gibson, Dunn & Crutcher, and John D. Fredericks, Jr., joined his father in Fredericks, Hanna, & Morton, a firm which counseled leading manufacturers and conducted an extensive probate business. Many children of famous attorneys became noted in their own right without practicing with their parents. The O'Melvenys were an outstanding example of this type of continuity.[170]

Consanguinity solidified the legal elite. Its hegemony was reinforced by the emergence of a permanent local bar association and law school, both organized and controlled by distinguished attorneys. In 1888, a few years after the collapse of the original bar association, the foremost lawyers again attemped to organize the profession. This try foundered in the depression of the 1890s. A permanent institution was finally established in 1899. Presidents of the three Los Angeles bar associations included Glassell, Bicknell, Frank Howard, Robert H. F. Variel, Works, H. W. O'Melveny, Gibson, and James A. Anderson, Jr. Typical of such institutions, it sought to upgrade and limit entry into the profession by campaigning for higher standards of education, admission to practice and professional conduct, for a voice in the selection of local judges, and for such choices to be made on the basis of legal ability.[171]

Standards of legal education and admission to the bar were notoriously low in California. Hence in 1896 another step, the formation of the first permanent law school in the city, was taken by elite lawyers to improve the profession. A year after its founding the school became part of the University of Southern California. Its original trustees included Henry W. O'Melveny, R. H. F. Variel, and Ross. The law school was founded to raise educational requirements for lawyers and elevate standards of admission to the bar and thus maintain high income and

status.[172] The school and the association, with their interlocking directorates and common purposes, functioned in Los Angeles, as did similar
institutions elsewhere, as vehicles of vocational control for elite lawyers.

MEDICINE

Medicine accounted for the next largest professional group in the
upper class. Its importance exemplified the city's and state's fame as a
health center. By 1890 Los Angeles had more doctors in proportion to its
population than did any other city in the world and by 1900 California
had more doctors per capita than did any other state. Los Angeles became the center of tuberculosis treatment, the only medical speciality in
which it ranked ahead of San Francisco.[173] Doctors, by the nature of
their calling, participated less frequently and fundamentally in political
and economic activity than did lawyers or capitalists. On the other
hand, they were equally prominent in civic charity and culture. Physicians also shared with attorneys and businessmen a tendency to
specialize and to develop institutions of vocational cohesion, thus
reflecting, as did these other careers, the growing complexity and
sophistication of life in Los Angeles.

While lagging behind luminaries of the bar in their aggregate contribution to local and regional business and government leadership, elite
physicians played significant roles in these aspects of community
hegemony. Such endeavors, rather than medicine, gave Norman Bridge
and John R. Haynes, the most influential civic figures in the profession,
their power and prestige. Haynes arrived in Los Angeles in 1887, cared
for upper-class patients, made a sizeable donation to Good Hope Hospital, and held a professorship at the University of Southern California
Medical School. His patrician practice proved useful in launching a
career as a political and social reformer. Bridge had a more distinguished medical reputation as a professor at Rush Medical College and
the University of Chicago Medical School. He also was a member of the
Chicago boards of education and election commissioners. Moving to
southern California to recover from tuberculosis, he practiced in Los
Angeles and Pasadena and became a director of the Barlow and La Vina
Tuberculosis sanatoria. By 1906 he had given up medicine for bank and
oil company directorships, a partnership with Doheny, management of
educational and cultural institutions, and a membership on the board of
education.[174]

Surgeons and medical directors for railroads, traction lines, insurance
firms, and utilities forged the major link between the commercial and
medical elites. Occasionally these offices and other interests led to more
direct involvement in business matters. Wesley W. Beckett was vice-
president and director at the Pacific Mutual, whose medical program he
ran, and a director in several banks and land and water companies, and

Richard B. Chapman inherited and managed his father's real estate holdings.[175]

Doctors, unlike lawyers, held fewer government offices than in the previous era. Physicians now mostly appeared in public health posts or in upper-class sanctuaries associated with culture and philanthropy, such as the library and education boards. Walter Lindley, a member of the public library board, the board of freeholders, and the public utilities commission, was unusual in the breadth of his government involvement.[176]

Considerable overlap, illustrated by Joseph and Carl Kurtz, William R. Hitchcock, Milbank S. Johnson, H. Bert Ellis, and Beckett, existed between medical officers of major corporations and city health officers and members of the municipal health, library, and education boards. Doctors involved in entrepreneurship or government also achieved high professional status, as measured by affiliations, medical school faculty appointments, and medical society presidencies. Beckett, Joseph Kurtz, Lindley, health board member William L. Wills, and Ellis headed both the county and state medical associations. Practitioners without extensive political or business interests also rose to the top. Henry G. Brainerd became president of the California and Los Angeles County medical associations, and Francis M. Pottenger, W. Jarvis Barlow, and Frederick T. Bicknell headed the latter. Many of these figures held professorships at the University of Southern California Medical College or its successor institution, the medical department of the University of California. The elite also staffed the major hospitals. Brainerd was superintendent of Los Angeles County Hospital. Lindley, Hitchcock, and Bicknell founded and presided over the board of directors of California Hospital, Beckett was a director and treasurer of this institution, and Wills was a founder and chief surgeon of Children's Hospital. Barlow and Pottenger founded tuberculosis sanatoria in the region.[177]

Medical and legal elites achieved hegemony in similar fashion. An interlocking group of physicians controlled local professional societies, schools, and hospitals. The medical school and society, like their equivalents in law, aspired to raise standards of professional practice and admission and thus to restrict entry and maintain high income and status. These institutions were badly needed antidotes to the quackery that proliferated in California due to lax local health and state licensing legislation.[178] Joseph P. Widney, its first dean, assisted by Joseph Kurtz and Walter Lindley, founded the University of Southern California Medical College (1885). Earlier Kurtz and Widney had helped originate the county medical association and they and Lindley headed that body. This trio also initiated and edited the Southern California *Practitioner*, the first medical journal in the region.[179] By dispensing aid to the sickly poor, a key facet of public health and civic philanthropy, the medical elite assumed another dimension of professional and community leadership. Children's, Good Hope, and Los Angeles County hospitals catered to needy patients and Barlow's Sanatorium (1902) cared for indigent tubercular cases.[180] Thus did upper-class physicians, through their control over municipal health standards and services, local hospitals, medical charity, and professional schools, research, and societies, achieve comprehensive leadership.

Although none of the eminent physicians came from Old Guard clans, the previously observed trend toward medical dynasties continued during this era, giving the top echelon of the profession yet another source of cohesion. Carl Kurtz, like his father, taught at the University of Southern California Medical College, Haynes married Walter Lindley's daughter, husband and wife Frank and Rose D. Bullard became presidents of the county medical association, Melvin Moore and his son also headed this body, and Norman H. Morrison's son succeeded him as chief surgeon at Los Angeles Gas and Electric and the Santa Fe. Several members of the medical elite also had kinship ties with leaders of the bar. Bicknell was a brother of John D. Bicknell, Wills was the son of John Alexander Wills and married Patton's daughter, and Chapman was the son and grandson respectively of Alfred B. Chapman and Jonathan R. Scott.[181]

JOURNALISM

During the 1880s journalism became a prestigious occupation, and several newspaper owners entered the upper class. Los Angeles resembled Chicago and Charleston, whose upper strata did not denigrate the vocation. Boston journalists, unlike the city's highbrow magazine editors, were never admitted to genteel circles nor did they wield as much power as Los Angeles publishers. New Yorkers Horace Greeley and Joseph Pulitzer exerted enormous influence on the local and national scenes, but they, too, were never accepted into polite society. In a city striving to establish itself, civic boosterism was necessary and esteemed. Journalists thus became renowned citizens. Otis began life as an Ohio printer's apprentice and arrived in Los Angeles in 1882 and immediately purchased a quarter share of the *Times*. He also owned the Los Angeles Times-Mirror Co., the parent organization of the newspaper, other publishing enterprises, and large amounts of land in California and Mexico. For many years he was the town's leading citizen. Native Californian Edwin T. Earl, the next most powerful journalist, differed from Otis in almost every respect. Earl, like his father, made millions as a fruit processor and inherited California's greatest fruit-packing and shipping concern. Selling out in middle age, he bought the *Evening Express*. While the *Times* defended regular Republicanism, the *Express*, under Earl and Dickson, championed Progressivism. The *Ex-*

press also became a family enterprise and Earl's grandson eventually headed both the newspaper and its parent corporation. Chamber of commerce president Henry Z. Osborne, Earl's predecessor at the *Express*, was the third major editor in this era. Osborne came to Los Angeles two years after Otis and was also a self-made success. Otis and Earl did not seek public office, but Osborne was a congressman, a public works commissioner, and U.S. collector of customs at San Pedro.[182]

ENGINEERING

The need for water and power propelled engineers, rarely numbered among other urban upper classes, into the elite. Frederick Eaton, John H. Dockweiler, brother of lawyer Isidore Dockweiler, and George J. Kuhrts, son of Jacob Kuhrts the city councillor and merchant, belonged to old families. Dockweiler was city engineer in the 1870s. Kuhrts became chief engineer and president of Huntington's Los Angeles Railway Corporation and owned the Standard Boiler and Steel Works. Eaton was an important force in constructing the aqueduct and in the drive for municipal control of the water system. He served as mayor, city engineer, and chief engineer of the Consolidated Railway Co. Fred W. Wood, George Chaffey, and Seeley W. Mudd were self-made members of the upper class. Wood immigrated to Los Angeles in the 1870s and became general manager of the Huntington railway system and chaired the Republican county central committee. Chaffey, son of a wealthy Canadian shipowner, engineer, and lumberman, moved to the city in 1882. He became a bank president, a great land developer and irrigation project designer, and, as an organizer of Los Angeles Gas and Electric, constructed the town's first electric light system. Seeley W. Mudd, a millionaire mining engineer, moved to southern California in 1902 and became a benefactor of many cultural and educational institutions. The most noted engineers, William Mulholland and Ezra F. Scattergood, however, were civil servants with at best a peripheral association with the elite. Mullholland designed the aqueduct and other major water projects and was chief engineer and general manager of the municipal water system. Scattergood headed the municipal power agency and supervised the development of public hydroelectric energy.[183]

Civic Activities

The transition from town to city and the maturation of the upper class produced a growing magnitude and diversity of charitable and cultural institutions. Increasing in population, wealth, and size, Los Angeles encountered greater problems and pretensions and an enlargement of resources and incentives to cope with its needs and fulfill its aspirations. The same group that determined the economic and political strategies in metropolitan emergence also directed the major philanthropic and cultural activities. Los Angeles was long accustomed to private initiatives in benevolence as in business, hence the main ameliorative institutions were controlled by affluent lawyers, physicians, entrepreneurs, and men of inherited wealth and status. This elite, like its equivalent in older cities, had the leisure, fortune, connections, power, and community pride necessary for success in such endeavors. The organization of charities, parks, humanistic and scientific societies, museums, symphonies, libraries, schools, and colleges gave the establishment the visibility and leadership credentials that such accomplishments provided similar enclaves in older cities.

Civic activities, while corresponding to those in other communities, also captured the Los Angeles ethos. They resulted from voluntary association and reflected the midwestern evangelical roots of turn-of-the-century Los Angeles and the city's backwardness, relative to older and larger metropolises, in adopting the latest urban techniques and institutions. Los Angeles, once an unruly and casual frontier settlement, in 1907 reputedly had the largest Women's Christian Temperance Union branch in the nation and the greatest Young Men's Christian Association membership in the world. Although it forged rapidly ahead in morally crusading agencies, the community lagged behind other urban centers in creating the most advanced and professional social services. The first settlement house in Los Angeles appeared in 1894, twenty years later than in the East.[184]

CHARITY

A few examples of voluntary associations illustrate the temendous expansion of care for the dependent and the growing benevolence of the rich and powerful. Walter Lindley was president, consulting physician, and a founder of the Los Angeles Orphans' Home (1880), a bastion of upper-class humanitarianism with many organizers and directors who were spouses of renowned capitalists and professionals. Children's Hospital (1901), founded by Dr. William L. Wills and his sister for free treatment of poor patients under the age of fifteen, had a similar group of female sponsors and officers. In 1902 Kaspare Cohn gave the building for a tuberculosis hospital which eventually became the famous Cedars of Lebanon. Hollenbeck Home for the Aged, a gift of the wife of the deceased president of the First National Bank, had leading lawyers and bankers among its trustees.[185]

Upper-class organizations, as well as individuals, involved themselves in philanthropy. The Woman's Club, reinstituted in 1885, supported and managed the Flower Festival. The Flower Festival Society (1888) was founded and originally headed by Mrs. Joseph P. Widney. Proceeds from its sales, subsequently supplemented by money from the Woman's Club, established a home for poor working women. The latter was a favorite cause for upper-class ladies. The Friday Morning Club (1891), another elite female civic welfare association, funded a refuge for mentally retarded women and other charities. Religious bodies provided an additional impetus to philanthropy. The Episcopal Diocese of Los Angeles inaugurated several important charities. The wives of its well-born, well-placed, and well-heeled worshippers were directors of St. Paul's Hospital and Home for Invalids (1887), which gave free care to needy patients, and the Episcopal Mission to the Poor (1902), which consisted of social clubs, a kindergarten, and a dispensary. The rector of exclusive St. John's Church was a director of another Episcopal charity, the Seamen's Institute (patronized by the Bannings), and headed the Church Home for Children. The upper-class Hebrew community, responding to an influx of indigent eastern European Jews, also launched several welfare agencies. Cohn, his banker son-in-law Meyer, and Mr. and Mrs. Harris Newmark were active in the Cohn Hospital, the Jewish Alliance (1907), the Jewish Orphans' Home (1911), and the Federation of Jewish Philanthropies (1912).[186]

The benefactors and officers of welfare organizations often came from old families and dominated other phases of community life. The Willses, Bannings, Newmarks, Mrs. Joseph P. Widney, Mrs. Isaias W. Hellman, Mrs. Griffith, Cohn, and Slauson gave this group a somewhat larger representation of early settlers than the patrician element in the economic and political elites. The altruism of lawyer Joseph Scott, banker-realtor, church deacon, and chamber of commerce president Slauson, realtor Orson T. Johnson, and Dr. Lindley indicated that leaders in business and the professions were important philanthropists. Scott acted as attorney for the Los Angeles Orphans' Home, headed the community chest, and helped start the Knights of Columbus and Catholic Big Brothers. Slauson gave nearly $100,000 to churches and for playgrounds, helped organize the Boys' Home, the Los Angeles Orphans' Home, and the YMCA, and, with Otis, started the Salvation Army Rescue Home. Johnson donated $40,000 to Resthaven and the YMCA, built the Florence Crittenden Home (1914) for the aged, and financed a clinic for poor children and an apartment house for the indigent. Lindley headed the orphans' home, the Whittier Reform School for Boys (1890), the Los Angeles Humane Society, and the National Conference of Charities and Corrections.[187]

CULTURE

Until 1880 the cultural atmosphere of Los Angeles was even more arid than the climate. The boom of the 1880s, however, invigorated intellectual and esthetic life. Prosperity helped create the University of Southern California (1880), the Historical Society of Southern California (1883), Child's Opera House (1884), the city's first quality theater,

Occidental and Pomona colleges (1887), the original symphony orchestra (1887), and the Ruskin Art Club of Los Angeles (1888), the original art association. Economic collapse in 1888 suspended cultural efforts, but a brief recovery in the early 1890s generated the initial public art exhibit (1890), Throop University (later the California Institute of Technology) (1891), and Hollenbeck Park (1892). A depression-induced hiatus again intervened, but in 1895 the Society of Fine Arts of California appeared, Griffith Park was given to the city in 1896, and in 1898 a permanent symphony was established. The final spurt occurred in the early twentieth century and focused on such scientific societies and museums as the Marine Biological Laboratory at San Pedro (1901), the Southwest Society (1903) and its museum of local artifacts (1912), and the Los Angeles County Museum of History, Science and Art (1913). Almost invariably the earliest California appearance of such institutions took place in San Francisco. That city anticipated Los Angeles in scientific organizations by more than a generation, in museums by three decades, in a symphony orchestra by more than twenty years, and in theaters by about twenty years. San Francisco also became the literary center of the far West. Jack London, Ambrose Bierce, Joaquin Miller, and Gertrude Atherton lived there, and Los Angeles-bred Ina Donna Coolbirth, California's first poet laureate and the patroness of younger writers like London, moved to San Francisco in 1861.[188]

Public and private, associational and individual, initiatives sought to uplift Los Angeles. The municipality concentrated on primary and secondary schools and parks and playgrounds, conceiving of these enterprises as governmental responsibilities for the physical and spiritual edification of the city and its citizens. Higher learning and artistic, humanistic, and scientific activities were deemed the province of voluntary associations or individual patronage. Cultural leaders usually came from the interlocked business-political-professional-philanthropic elite. This was a familiar upper-class pattern, and the cultural managers of Los Angeles acted from impulses of class obligation, civic pride, and self-aggrandizement, and for purposes of community control and development, thus emulating their peers in Boston, New York, Charleston, Chicago and San Francisco.[189]

PUBLIC INSTITUTIONS

Although the administration of the public school system had been professionalized, distinguished figures like Patton, Scott, the Kurtzes, and banker John M. Elliott still frequently served on the board of education. The upper class also continued its activity in the kindergarten movement. The Public Kindergarten Association (1884), headed by Caroline M. Severance, campaigned to establish kindergartens for the poor. On its board of managers sat Mrs. Isaias W. Hellman, Mrs. Robert

Maclay Widney, and Mrs. John Alexander Wills.[190]

The public library was allied with public school as a means of educating local inhabitants. The board of directors of the Los Angeles Public Library was another elite bastion; its presidents between 1885 and 1915 included merchant Henry J. Newmark, banker Bonebrake, sugar tycoon J. Ross Clark (also president of the YMCA), realtor and board of education member William M. Garland, and Isidore B. Dockweiler.[191]

The public parks system was created in the 1890s. Hollenbeck Park was a joint gift of Mrs. John E. Hollenbeck and William H. Workman. Griffith Park (1878) was donated by Griffith J. Griffith, a British-born engineer who bequeathed Los Angeles $1 million for landscaping and a planetarium. Oil tycoon Canfield, chief benefactor of the McKinley Home for Boys, was a generous donor to the park. Park commissioners, like members of the school and library boards, were frequently upper-class figures.[192]

Speeches given by dignitaries at the Griffith Park opening captured the spirit of upper-class civic involvement. Griffith attributed his gift to "recognizing the duty which one who has acquired some little wealth owes to the community in which he has prospered and desiring to aid the advancement and happiness of the city that has been for so long, and will always be my home. . . ." Aside from *noblesse oblige*, the donor felt parks counteracted crowded, unhealthy, and hectic conditions of urban life. Lawyer Alexander Campbell emphasized civic pride and competition with San Francisco as motives for expending time, money, and energy on urban improvement. Acknowledging that "we are somewhat behind . . . San Francisco [in] generous contributions for public purposes," he hope[d] that Griffith's donation would set an "example." Los Angeles "aspires to rival the great city of the Golden Gate," therefore "our people must unite . . . in aiding by private benevolence the development of our large and growing city."[193]

Despite these gifts and proclamations, by 1902 Griffith and the *Times* were complaining that the government spent little on parks and allowed them to deteriorate. Griffith touched a sensitive chord, earlier sounded by Campbell, in pointing out that San Francisco, unlike his city, had generous patrons who kept up her parks and playgrounds and suggested that Los Angeles follow this example.[194] The creation of the board of parks commissioners redressed these grievances. The original board, the best in the history of Los Angeles, headed by Campbell's law partner and with Henry W. O'Melveny on it, reconstructed Pershing and Eastlake Parks.[195]

PRIVATE INSTITUTIONS

The major efforts of the upper class, typical of Los Angeles, focused on private rather than public endeavors. Private colleges, for example, attracted more of its attention and resources than did the public schools. Following the trend in older cities, early private organizations catered to elite and specialized participants and audiences, then came institutions aiming to reach the entire city. The historical society, the theater, several art associations, and universities were founded at a time when unsuccessful attempts were made to form institutions that reached a broader spectrum of the city. Not until 1898, after several tries, did a permanent orchestra emerge, and museums were established even later.

The University of Southern California, the first and major institution of higher learning founded in this era, was dominated by upper-class kinship units. Robert Maclay Widney drafted the articles of incorporation and was joined by his brother, Downey, and Spence on the original board of trustees. Joseph P. Widney was a founder and dean of the college of medicine and in 1902 president of the university. Like the law and medical schools, the college of theology was also dominated by the upper class. Great landowner Charles Maclay donated the site and his brother Robert became dean. A similar situation prevailed in the college of arts and sciences, where George I. Cochran was dean while his son served as treasurer of the university board and headed Pacific Mutual Life when that company in 1907 refinanced the USC debt. Among other benefactors and trustees were George and William Chaffey, who gave land for an agricultural college. George's son Andrew was a trustee and treasurer of the university. George F. Bovard and his brother served as USC presidents and a third brother was a vice-president.[196]

Dr. Widney, the outstanding early educator of Los Angeles, also headed the board of education. Shortly after retiring as USC president, he articulated a philosophy of education that emphasized democracy over elitism, pragmatism over scholarship, the present over the past, the California college over the eastern and European university, and the Pacific over the Atlantic Coast. Easterners schooled in that region and Europe "lose their originality," relevance, and force. They "go out from this atmosphere of a narrow overrefinement" looking "to the past." But those they "superciliously" regard "as crude and unlettered, men possibly without the university stamp are the men the world instinctively seeks out, and who do its work." According to Widney, the "distinctively American mental life is to be found rather west of the Appalachians, in the men of the log schoolhouse and the smaller colleges."[197]

Widney may have looked upon Occidental and Pomona as "the smaller colleges" of the West that captured the national spirit. Both institutions owed their existence to upper-class beneficence. Realtor James G. Bell was the primary founder of Occidental, and his sister-in-law, Mrs. John E. Hollenbeck, donated land. Bridge, Doheny, and Senator Flint and Patterson, respectively president and treasurer of the board, also provided financial assistance. Banker Elliott and transit magnate Clark were on the Pomona board and the Bixbys were trustees, donors, and students.[198]

Pomona imitated the New England liberal arts college, but Throop University, originally a secondary academy with few college students, more closely resembled Widney's vision and became a world-famous scientific school. Beginning in 1908, trustees Bridge, Robinson (the banker), and George Ellery Hale (head of the Mount Wilson Observatory) transformed the preparatory school into a scientific and engineering college.[199] Hale urged the changes in the pragmatic, but visionary, spirit that animated so many projects in the region. In 1908 he reported to the board that "in California the conditions and the need for technical education are unsurpassed." Consequently, "there is a place in Pasadena for a technical school of the highest class." Hale's hopes anticipated the scientific explosion that eventually made metropolitan Los Angeles a great national research and experimental center. Bridge shared Hale's instrumental view of education and Widney's democratic and utilitarian sentiments. The Throop board president praised changes in schools and colleges that emphasized work in "manual training and practical arts," which are "more interesting than any other [subjects and] start the student more directly into the work of life, even into actual vocations, and enable him to test his own powers, and find his own best life trail." He believed that "education should increase power to do things, to move the wheels of the world's progress."[200]

The four colleges had similar experiences. USC, Occidental, and Pomona were founded by religious denominations in the 1880s boom. Important donors and trustees came from the elite. During the lean years after 1887, particularly since their endowments consisted mainly of land, they struggled to survive. Occidental had six students in 1891 and, as at Throop, reverted to a preparatory school. USC barely retained its college status: in 1891 it had twenty-five undergraduates and concentrated on secondary education. Pomona, too, encountered setbacks in the recession.[201] The subsequent cultural and economic upsurge, however, rejuvenated these institutions.

An early sign of elite intellectual involvement, as in many cities, was the creation of a local historical society. Initiators of the Southern California Historical Society included former Mexican aristocrat Antonio F. Coronel, John J. Warner (the original president), who belonged to the pre-conquest Anglo-American elite, and early settlers Downey, Howard, and Joseph P. Widney. The society, typical of its counterparts in other places, affiliated with other cultural institutions. In 1908 it met at USC and after 1910 at the county museum, and George F. Bovard was president from 1910 to 1915. Despite the affluence and influence of its incorporators and its ties with other intellectual associations, the organization lacked community support, a deficiency that Campbell and

Griffith perceived in other civic projects. Its holdings were valued at $3,000 in 1898 and $4,000 in 1912. The society in 1913 owned approximately 6,000 books, 200 manuscripts, and 2,000 museum items, a collection miniscule in size and value compared to eastern historical societies and to the California Historical Society located in San Francisco. "The Southern California Historical Society has never had a permanent home," wrote its secretary in 1908, "its income is too small to rent a hall for its meetings, and none of Los Angeles' rich men have given free use of a room in their buildings."[202] These defects went unremedied for many years.

The historical society inaugurated a movement toward preserving and studying the regional past, a phenomenon common among local elites. The Society of the Pioneers of Los Angeles County (1897) was reminiscent of Chicago's Old Settlers' Society (1855) and of ancestral associations formed in the 1890s in Boston, New York, and Charleston. Most of its founders came from old families and Benjamin S. Eaton and William H. Workman were the first two presidents. The society consisted of pre-1871 settlers and published papers in local history.[203] The Southwest Society was also founded by the upper class to recover the regional past. The original officers included president Slauson, Otis, Bovard, Bridge, and Patterson. It collected relics and memorabilia of Los Angeles and conducted archaeological explorations.[204] Henry W. O'Melveny, a founder of the Pioneers and Southwest societies, and John G. Mott helped organize the Hispanic Society of California (1915), which sought to preserve Spanish-Mexican culture in the region.[205]

In 1894 Max Meyberg, who married a Hellman and helped start Los Angeles Gas and Electric, discerned a more profitable use of the past. With the assistance of the Merchants' Association and many civic and business leaders, he instituted La Fiesta de Los Angeles to divert people from the San Francisco Fair, revive the city from the depression, and promote tourism and permanent settlement. The Fiesta, repeated from 1894 to 1898, exploited local traditions for the purposes of civic boosterism, philanthropy, and private profit. One night of the festival was devoted to a grand ball for the Associated Charities under the patronage of virtually all the Old Guard society matrons.[206]

Shortly after the establishment of the historical society, Childs built a theater. Concerts, plays, and operas were given there by celebrated performers and companies. The elite now attended the same type of productions in the same setting as did upper-class Bostonians, Chicagoans, and New Yorkers. After 1902 high society patronized the Mason Opera House and the Belasco Theater.[207]

A few years after the construction of Child's Opera House the first organized art movement emerged. The Ruskin Art Club was an association of upper-class women dedicated to foster the study of art, at first among its members and later throughout the city. The public art movement accelerated during the 1890s when the Ruskin held a public exhibition of paintings and agitated for a public art gallery, and the chamber of commerce helped arrange a public show of works of native-born artists. In the early 1900s the Ruskin created a fine arts association to build an art museum, and the Society of Fine Arts of California was organized and headed by John D. Bicknell, Slauson, and Elliott. The society aimed to give exhibitions, lectures, and to assemble an art library "to advance the knowledge and love of art . . . and the promotion of general culture."[208] These various initiatives culminated in 1913 in the formation of the Los Angeles County Museum of History, Science and Art. A year earlier another art organization appeared which also resulted in the founding of a museum. The Pasadena Music and Art Association promoted music and art in this Los Angeles suburb. Its board consisted chiefly of the president and trustees of Throop University, and Huntington and Patton. The association's major achievement was to help convince Huntington to locate his library and art gallery in Pasadena.[209]

Art associations and museums signified a growing upper-class involvement in art and architecture. This impulse motivated Huntington's collection of Old Masters and a heightened interest in architecture. Beginning in the 1880s homes and public and commercial buildings replicated the eastern neoclassical, colonial, and Romanesque revivals, and their architects belonged to the upper class. Valentine J. Rowan was the son of a former mayor and Hellman employee. John C. Austin, builder for wealthy Angelenos, designer of the Erskine M. Ross house and one of the architects who worked on the City Hall, headed the chamber of commerce, the Los Angeles Humane Society for Children, and the Jonathan Club. Octavius Morgan, who built the Sisters' of Charity Hospital, the Hollenbeck Home, the Stock Exchange Building, the I. N. Van Nuys Building, and the Farmers' & Merchants' Bank, belonged to exclusive social clubs and served on the board of freeholders. John Parkinson, who designed the California Club, the Broadway Department Store, and the buildings of the Security National Bank, Los Angeles Gas and Electric, and the chamber of commerce, was also a member of prestigious clubs.[210]

The transition of musical performances, from entertainment for the elite to productions for the broader community, trailed the movement in art. The key to this development, the symphony orchestra, evolved in a manner characteristic of many upper-class endeavors. Early attempts to form a symphony, led by rich and influential figures, failed for lack of interest and money. After three tries, the Los Angeles Philharmonic Society, with contributions form Mrs. Edwin T. Earl and George A. Hancock, its treasurer, was permanently established. Its concerts were patronized mainly by the upper class, but after World War I the symphony reached a wider audience.[211]

Progress in science occurred later than in humanistic or esthetic fields because nineteenth-century academic and urban elites gave priority and derived more prestige from the latter activities. Metropolitan Los Angeles ultimately became a renowned scientific community. Before World War I, however, this achievement had barely begun. Noted lawyers and businessmen in 1901 financed the Marine Biological Laboratory at San Pedro.[212] During the mid-1880s Spence gave $50,000 worth of property to USC to locate an astronomical observatory at Mount Wilson. This project, like many started in the boom years, foundered in the subsequent collapse. Beginning in 1905 Hale revived the scheme, but it was not finally completed until 1917.[213] Another scientific activity got under way in 1901 when prehistoric animal and plant deposits were discovered on Rancho La Brea. Henry Hancock, original owner of the ranch, came to the city in 1850 and served in the assembly. His wife became one of the richest Californians when oil was discovered on her land. Their son, George A. Hancock, a force in civic culture and vice-president of several banks, gave the fossil pit to the Los Angeles County Museum.[214]

By 1915 several associations originally organized by and for a small elite now served the whole community. This transformation occurred even earlier in New York, Boston, and Chicago. It reflected the growing magnitude of business and governmental activities, the increased wealth of urban elites, their sense of duty, and their feeling that social problems and the defense of their own position required indoctrination of the lower orders in proper values and behavior. As in other cities, the vehicle for this broadened function was the museum movement. The Southwest Society organized the Southwest Museum to house its collections and exhibit them to the general public. The museum board, as usual in such enterprises, was dominated by eminent attorneys and entrepreneurs. Henry W. O'Melveny and board president Bridge were the chief fund-raisers. The latter, at the dedicatory ceremonies, stated the raison d'être of the society and museum and other agencies seeking to preserve the local past. Young communities, declared Bridge, obsessively "struggle for existence." The establishment of historical "institutions," like the museum, meant that Los Angeles was "old enough to have a perspective of history," and "prosperous enough to . . . take account of its more permanent treasures." Time had enriched and enlightened the upper class by enlarging the "considerable body of our citizens, . . .who conceive that possessions mean responsibility, and a duty to others which can be discharged only by giving some of their surplus—and with it giving themselves. . . ." They "glorify the city, enhance its ideals, ennoble its citizenship," and bring it to "the forefront of western enlightenment."[215]

Advancement in cultural outreach culminated in the Los Angeles County Museum of History, Science, and Art, which brought together the public art, park, and museum movements with specialized societies. Located in Exposition Park, it housed the collections of the Southern California Academy of Science, the Fine Arts League, the historical society, and the Cooper Ornithological Institute. Bovard and other representatives of these bodies sat on the museum board of governors.[216.] Thus were united the public and private elite proponents of civic health and beautification and intellectual improvement.

Upper-class culture differed from eastern patriciates in expressing stronger democratic and instrumental impulses. Here the establishment, as in the cases of Bridge and Widney, agreed with its Chicago counterpart. Except for this important variation, upper-class involvement in Boston, New York, Charleston, Chicago, and Los Angeles proceeded along similar lines. The foremost figures in this dimension of urban leadership were often active in several organizations and in other aspects of community hegemony. As the institutions that they directed enlarged from specialized clientele to community audiences their control expanded over high culture. Los Angeles also resembled the other cities in that the leaders of its intellectual and esthetic agencies often derived from distinguished families. The newly risen dominated economic, political, and professional life, but culture, like charity, remained an Old Guard stronghold. Mrs. John H. Jones, wife of the early realtor and city councillor, for example, was active in and distributed $190,000 among the YMCA, Barlow Sanitorium, the Protestant Orphans' Home, the Southwest Museum, and USC.[217] Joneses, Newmarks, Hubbells, Mesmers, Widneys, Bixbys, Downeys, Howards, Hancocks, and Coronels, like their peers in other places, compensated for commercial and political displacement by exerting considerable influence over culture.

Society

Accompanying economic expansion, rising affluence, and the multiplication of elite culture and charity societies was a more sophisticated upper-class life-style. High society corresponded to elite commercial, professional, and civic activities in becoming more formally organized through institutional development. In this respect and in clustering in selective neighborhoods, tribal marriages, rejecting Jews, and such rituals as cotillions and costume balls and evenings at the theater and opera, fashionable Los Angeles, with every passing decade, moved closer to the *haut monde* in San Francisco, Chicago, and the East.[218]

In common with other cities, formal dances culminated the social season. During the 1880s and '90s the Cotillion and Chesterfield Clubs gave these affairs, and the annual Cotillion Club Ball, attended by the city's first families, was the major social event. The ball, except for the characteristically puritanical Los Angeles touch of not allowing liquor, differed little from its analogues in older places. Similar to the activities of other urban elites, social and philanthropic occasions, as happened at the Masked Ball of the Fiesta de Los Angeles, sometimes merged.[219]

An elite custom, conspicuous in New York and noticeable in Boston, Philadelphia, and Chicago, had barely appeared in Los Angeles. There was but one Angeleno among the 454 American brides, by 1915, of titled or prominent foreigners. Lacking the assets accumulated by Atlantic Coast multimillionaires and remote in distance and orientation from Europe, southern California heiresses ranked far behind their sisters—even in Cincinnati, Baltimore, and Pittsburgh—in the search for coronets. San Francisco, a town more eastern in its ways and with a more affluent and mature upper class, recorded five alliances between society princesses and Old World aristocrats.[220]

If upper-class Los Angeles diverged from eastern equivalents in not wedding foreign nobles, its exclusion of Jews imitated the practice of these elites. Beginning in the late 1870s, New York Jews were black-balled from exclusive clubs to which they had once been admitted and even helped organize. A short time later they were barred from fashionable resort hotels. Before the German-Jewish migration, starting in 1848, Jews were accepted in genteel Philadelphia and married into this enclave. After the influx from Germany they were increasingly snubbed by the patriciate. In the late nineteenth century anti-Semitism surfaced in Brahmin Boston. Henry and Brooks Adams expressed the most consistent and comprehensive bigotry, but Henry Cabot Lodge, James Russell Lowell, and others also exhibited hostility. At president A. Lawrence Lowell's urging, Harvard instituted a quota system against Jews, and Boston bluebloods generally opposed the Supreme Court appointment of Louis Brandeis. According to the best historians of Charleston Jewry, that city's aristocracy did not exclude Jews, but Los Angeles followed the example of San Francisco, New York, Boston, and Philadelphia elites.[221] Jews historically achieved greater salience in Los Angeles than in these other cities. Until the 1890s they dominated trade and finance, regularly held elective offices, and were respected philanthropists. Jews helped start the selective social clubs initiated in the 1880s and '90s and were welcome at Los Angeles hotels. By the early twentieth century, however, the intensification of anti-Semitism throughout the country due to increased xenophobia and the mass influx of eastern Jews beginning in the 1880s led to Jews being excluded from the previously undifferentiated high society. After 1900 they ceased running for elective municipal posts. Hellman's Farmers' & Merchants' Bank had only four Jews among its twenty-eight directors in 1902, and entrepreneurs of this faith did not do business there. After 1900, the elite clubs blackballed candidates of Jewish background. According to Harris Newmark, capitalist, civic figure, and California Club member, "several Los Angeles clubs were organized in the early era of sympathy, tolerance and good feeling, . . . before the advent of men whose bigotry has sown intolerance and discord. . . ." The Hebrew community defensively formed its own organizations. Newmark made his indictment in 1916, but in 1891 elite Jews founded the exclusively Jewish Concordia Club. After 1900 they increasingly withdrew to endogamous charities, a striking departure from the ancient Hebrew Benevolent Society, which had given alms to the needy of all faiths and whose affairs were attended by upper-class Christians.[222]

Several clubs originated before 1880, but the proliferation of exclusive social and cultural associations in the 1880s and '90s reflected the increased cohesion and formality of the upper echelon and its tendency to imitate older urban establishments. The major clubs were the Los Angeles Athletic (1880), the California (1887), the Jonathan (1894), the Sunset (1895), the Los Angeles Country (1897), and the University (1898). They were created by the group that dominated the business, professional, political, and civic affairs of Los Angeles. In these organizations the Old Guard mingled with the newly risen.[223] Typical of Los Angeles and harbingers of the current California life style were the Athletic, the second oldest men's club in the city, and the country clubs. The latter resembled contemporary eastern institutions as the suburban movement of the 1890s began to draw upper strata out of the inner cities. Again typical of Los Angeles, the University, the lone club with intellectual pretensions, appeared years after its forerunners in other places.

Elite women's associations were more civic-minded than the men's clubs. In 1867 Caroline M. Severance, philanthropist, reformer and early suffragette, founded in Boston the initial Woman's Club in the United States. Eight years later she moved to Los Angeles and shortly thereafter formed another Woman's Club, which lasted until 1880. Severance revived the organization in 1885 and its members were the wives, sisters, and daughters of well-known business, professional, civic, and social figures. It campaigned to improve working and living conditions and obtain employment for females, placed a woman on the school board, contributed to the municipal art movement, and agitated for a juvenile court and detention home and better garbage disposal.[224] Severance also formed and headed the Friday Morning Club (1891). The two groups had the same type of membership, much of it overlapping, and similar interests. The Friday Morning supported the chamber of commerce drive for a nonpartisan school board, funded charities, gave scholarships, and pushed for women's suffrage.[225] The Ebell Club (1894) reached the same enclave and had aims identical with those of its sisters institutions. Mrs. Charles L. Strong, its originator and president, an inventor and water company president, belonged to the chamber of commerce, the state and county republican central committees, the Friday Morning and Ruskin clubs, and was vice-president of the Los Angeles Symphony.[226] These organizations, like their counterparts in other cities, began as cultural study groups and developed into civic reform and humanitarian societies. Several specialized upper-class institutions also appeared. The Ruskin Club, already discussed, and the Civic Association were the most notable. The association worked for a municipally owned water supply, public kindergartens, playgrounds, and parks, improved sanitation facilities, urban beautification, and a juvenile court. Its main initiators were Mrs. D. G. Stephens, president of the Los Angeles Orphans' Home board of trustees, and Mrs. Robert L. Craig, who succeeded her husband as head of a wholesale grocery company and was a member of the Friday Morning and the board of education.[227]

These organizations were the institutional equivalent of the society matron, a type common to many urban patriciates. Making her debut in Los Angeles in the 1880s, wife or daughter of a leading citizen, she participated in fashionable society and in culture and charity organizations and frequently in reform movements. In New York she concentrated on the former role, but in Los Angeles and Chicago she was more oriented toward community welfare and uplift. Charlotte Le Moyne Wills, for example, wife of a distinguished lawyer and mother of a prominent physician, helped found the Friday Morning and Woman's clubs and was a vice-president of the latter, of the Women's Industrial Exchange, and of Los Angeles' first kindergarten association, and a suffragette. Clara B. Burdette, the outstanding Los Angeles matron, helped organize and headed the Ebell and belonged to the Friday Morning and Ruskin clubs. She was an initiator and first president of the National Federation of Women's Clubs, vice-president of the Southwest Museum, trustee of the California Institute of Technology and Mills College, a state and national Republican committeewoman, a founder of the California branch of the League of Women Voters, an organizer of the Women's Legislative Council to further laws for the benefit of women and children, president of the Women's Athletic Club of Los Angeles, vice-president and chairman of the finance committee to build an auditorium for the philharmonic, and an author and hostess of a salon for artists and writers.[228]

Friendship and intermarriage fortified mutual business and political interests and joint associational affiliations in unifying the upper class. Graves numbered White, Downey, Isaias W. Hellman, and other community leaders among his best friends. Henry W. O'Melveny played cards with and entertained at his home leading lawyers and capitalists, and William H. Workman was intimate with the Hollenbecks and the Hellmans.[229] Matrimony between members of the Old Guard, between ancient families and *nouveaux riches*, and between children of the *parvenus* solidified the establishment. Aside from previously mentioned unions, the children of John Jones and James B. Lankersheim wedded each other, newly settled Patton married the child of pioneer Wilson, Harry Chandler was the son-in-law and successor of Otis, both self-made men came to town in the 1880s, Graves's son married a Banning, and Robert M. Widney was the father-in-law of Boyle Workman.[230]

Although upper-class Los Angeles assumed many attributes of older urban elites, its recent emergence from a frontier past, a constant influx of newcomers into the enclave, and rapid urban growth, as in Chicago, reinforced egalitarian beliefs. Unlike Philadelphia, Boston, New York, and Charleston, no residue of alienated aristocrats deprecated the American creed of democratic individualism. Since Los Angeles did not have a disgruntled leisured gentry, the comments of its leading citizens were generally optimistic. The establishment's most systematic thinkers, pioneer Joseph P. Widney and newcomer Bridge, elaborated the principles of pragmatic, present-minded egalitarianism. The "common people," said Widney, "often see [more] clearly the" essentials of American life "than do the statesmen or the universities." In contrast to disaffected gentlemen in the East, "the past" was "only a narrower and lived-out present. . . . New issues, new exigencies, require new departures." The former frontier army surgeon asserted that people should have equal rights and opportunities and that "labor is a blessing" while "idleness," whether due to "prison," a "strike," or "inherited wealth," diminishes the community. Only in dissenting against class welfare did Widney share the bleak sentiments increasingly voiced by patricians along the other coast. Affirming democratic individualism, he warned that "no class is permanently lifted up by pulling another down" and "the man who promotes class jealousy is an enemy to all, and to himself. . . ."[231]

Bridge expressed his instrumental egalitarianism in attacking the genteel manners, overrefined distinctions, and costly elegance that eastern aristocrats increasingly valued. While in Chicago he declared, "taste for taste's sake . . . is for the leisure of the race, for the time and state of lessened burdens and accumulated profits . . . expensive amusements and indulgences always cost and never save." Conversely, "utilitarian taste . . . means less expense in living, more resources for the future, more leisure for the workers." The "very rich are imbalanced . . . because exalted taste always leads to hyperesthesia." The Chicago physician, perhaps subliminally preparing for his future as an oil magnate, claimed that "the severest penalty of high taste . . . consists in its being an obstacle to career . . . ambitions" and "worldly and practical efficiency. . . ." Linking overrefinement to heredity, Bridge thought that "gifted families run out . . . until new blood from humbler, but for the weal of the race more promising, sources can enter them." For these reasons "the happiest people" are "the common middle class of folk, who are not censoriously particular about their tidiness or their grammar." Reflecting the crude entrepreneurial dynamism for which Chicago was then so famous, Bridge concluded, "the best taste is the power to take and do the thing that profits most; and the meaning of profit has references to both material needs and mental pleasure."[232]

MODERN METROPOLIS: 1915–70

Between the world wars the promise of the previous era was realized. Territorial annexations from 1915 to 1927 and a series of vast migrations to southern California resulted in Los Angeles between 1910 and 1920 surpassing in number of residents its arch-rival, San Francisco. Angelenos increased from 319,000 in 1910 to 1,238,000 in 1930; forty years later the population had doubled. Between 1870 and 1940, except for Detroit in 1910–20 and Seattle in 1870–1900, metropolitan Los Angeles grew faster than the other thirty-two largest industrial areas of the United States. It placed eighteenth in 1910, fifth in 1930, and is presently the second most populous of the top manufacturing centers. The city proper is now outranked only by New York and Chicago. Between 1900 and 1940 the national and greater Los Angeles population rose respectively by 73.3 and 1200 percent.[233] Los Angeles also became a major American commercial and manufacturing center and the premier Pacific Coast metropolis.

The emergence of three important institutions of higher learning, a great scientific community, a famous symphony orchestra, and a celebrated performing arts center and art museum made Los Angeles an intellectual match for San Francisco. Due to preeminence in the movie and television industries, a fashion industry second only to New York, and the spread of the rootless, sybaritic southern California life-style, Los Angeles now vies with New York as the country's cultural capital. But massive waves of in-migration and great social and economic changes have prevented southern California from developing coherent and cohesive traditions and institutions. During the interwar period the city forsook its midwestern evangelical past to become noted for extravagance, eccentricity, and self-destructive hedonism. Among the nation's cities of over 100,000 population in the 1920s, Los Angeles had the highest rates of suicides and drug addicts. In the next decade its divorce rate considerably exceeded that of the state, which, in turn, was higher than the national average and is presently the highest in the country. By the 1940s its divorce rate doubled the U.S. average, and its suicide rate exceeded the average for American cities of more than 100,000 people.[234] Many Americans now reject the creed of hard work and self-restraint and the rational calculus that created the globe's premier industrial power. Swept up in the post-industrial ethic of instant gratification and dedicated to "doing your own thing," the "now" generation found in southern California, and especially in Los Angeles, the model for its aspirations. In turn, this town of no past and no center, the home of celluloid dreams, became the manipulator of the current creed of narcissism.

Derived from the same biographical sources as the previous compilations of upper-class Angelenos, 313 inhabitants composed the multidimensional elite that presided over this phase of Los Angeles history.[235] A collective trait analysis of this group depicts its structure and provides a basis of comparison with its forerunners.

Like the earlier elites only a small number (thirty-six) were born in Los Angeles (see Table 13). Until the Depression and dust-bowl-driven migrants of the 1930s and the influx of war workers in the 1940s, newcomers tended to be richer, older, better educated, and more likely to have higher status occupations than did immigrants to other cities. The relatively deprived aggregate background of the 1930s and '40s arrivals accounted for their tiny representation in this enclave.

Table 13

ARRIVAL DECADE OF THE LOS ANGELES UPPER CLASS: 1915–70

Decade	Number	Percentage
1870–79	1	0.7
1880–89	26	17.7
1890–99	22	15.0
1900–1909	34	23.1
1910–19	38	25.8
1920–29	22	15.0
1930–39	2	1.4
1940–49	2	1.4
Total	147	100

Base percentage of group total: 53.1 (147 of 277)

The majority came to the city at a younger age than did the immigrants in the earlier upper strata (see Tables 2, 9, and 14). Nearly one-third moved to Los Angeles before the age of twenty and over two-thirds before the age of thirty. The more youthful age of entry than in the 1885–1915 group is explained by a large number of successful newcomers who bequeathed their status to their offspring, many of whom entered Los Angeles in childhood.

The trends observed in the comparison of geographical origins between the groups of 1850–85 and 1885–1915 (see Tables 3, 10, and 15) continued in the post-1915 upper class. The Midwest still contributed the largest, though a smaller, segment of the elite; the shares of former New Englanders, of those from the Middle Atlantic region, and of the foreign-born continued to diminish; representation from the Mountain and Pacific Coast areas and from California and the native-born Angelenos continued to rise. Given the westward settlement of the continent and the increased age and population of California and Los Angeles, these demographic developments are unexceptionable. Twenty-one Jews appeared among the leading post-1915 citizens, constituting 6.7 percent of the total elite. The Jewish contingent was smaller than in the earliest upper class but nearly three times its percentage in the 1885–1915 aggregation, a multiplication largely due to the advent of film industry moguls. Relative to their presence in 1920 and 1930 in the urban population, New Englanders and the foreign migrants among the elite were overrepresented, southern and Middle Atlantic emigrants were equally represented in the elite and the city, and those from the Pacific Coast and Mountain states, midwesterners, and natives of Los Angeles and California were underrepresented.[236]

Following a trend already marked in the previous elites (see Tables 4, 11, and 16) the proportions of self-made successes fell while those in the inherited categories rose. The decline of first-generation and the in-

Table 14

AGE OF MIGRATION OF THE LOS ANGELES UPPER CLASS: 1915–70

Age	Number	Percentage
0– 9	15	10.9
10–19	29	21.0
20–29	47	34.1
30–39	27	19.6
40–49	14	10.1
50–59	6	4.3
Total	138	100

Base percentage of group total: 49.8 (138 of 277)

Table 15

BIRTHPLACE OF THE LOS ANGELES UPPER CLASS: 1915–70

Birthplace	Number	Percentage
New England	15	5.4
Middle Atlantic	28	10.1
South[a]	45	16.2
West[a]	78	28.2
Mountain and Pacific Coast states[b]	9	3.2
California	37	13.4
Los Angeles	36	13.0
Canada	13	4.7
Elsewhere abroad[b]	16	5.8
Total	277	100

Group percentage of base total: 88.5 (277 of 313)

[a] See Table 3.
[b] See Table 10.

Table 16

VINTAGE OF FORTUNE OF THE LOS ANGELES UPPER CLASS: 1915–70

Wealth Generation	Number	Percentage
First	44	34.4
Second	33	25.8
At least second	25	19.5
Third or more	26	20.3
Total	128	100

Base percentage of group total: 40.1 (128 of 313)

crease of old wealth (at least second and third or more generations) was particularly large. Los Angeles, now a more mature city, at last joined Boston and New York in having a majority of its foremost figures stem from an affluent background.

Apart from inherited wealth, other dimensions of upper-class continuity—interrelatedness with those on the latest list or earlier compilations—showed contradictory movements from the 1885–1915 group. Only thirty-four (10.6 percent) of the most recent enclave had connubial or blood ties with at least one other member of the elite, a substantial decline from its immediate predecessors and from the earliest echelon. On the other hand, kinship continuity rose between the latest and earliest groups. Thirty-five members of the former (11.2 percent) belonged by blood or marriage to family founders of the 1850–85 era, a slight increase from those of 1885–1915 similarly connected with the oldest elite. Fifty-four (17.3 percent) of the leading citizens of 1915–70 had such bonds with their ancestors of 1885–1915. Conversely, thirty of the 172 (17.4 percent) in the 1850–85 enclave had descendants, by birth or marriage, on the latest list, only one fewer than the oldest upper-class descendants in the 1885–1915 group. Forty-five of the 381 (11.8 percent) members of the 1885–1915 upper stratum were so related to those on the subsequent list. The larger share of families persisting from the ancient elite helps explain the higher portions of at least second and third or more generations of wealth than second-generation fortunes among the 1915–70 upper class. Family clustering and continuity remained low because huge influxes of new settlers and enormous growth and change prevented the development of a large, kinship-structured elite component with extensive roots in the city's past.

As Los Angeles matured and industrialized, manufacturing and financers increased their representation compared to earlier upper classes (see Tables 12 and 17). Correspondingly, a contraction occurred in the older entrepreneurial vocations of trade, agriculture, utilities, and transport. Realtors also enlarged their presence, a reflection of the repeated land booms caused by twentieth-century population and economic growth.

Upper-class types in political office diminished, a trend already marked in the comparison between officeholders in the 1850–85 and 1885–1915 enclaves and a phenomenon that existed in many other American cities. Only thirty-eight (12.1 percent) of the most recent elite held public posts.

Table 17

PRIMARY OCCUPATIONS OF THE LOS ANGELES UPPER CLASS: 1915–70

Occupations	Number	Percentage
Agriculture	1	0.3
Transportation	1	0.3
Utilities	5	1.6
Trade	11	3.5
Manufacturing	66	21.1
Finance	71	22.7
Real estate	29	9.3
General capitalist[a]	4	1.3
Professions	121	38.7
No occupation	4	1.3
Total	313	100

[a]See Table 12.

Economy

By World War II metropolitan Los Angeles was the foremost commercial and manufacturing area on the West Coast and a national center of industry, trade, and finance. This transformation began in World War I when Los Angeles became a busy shipbuilding town. In the 1920s a land and oil boom and the tremendous growth of the film industry fueled the local economy. During the next decade airplane and rubber manufacturing propelled the area to a top place as a national industrial center. By 1910 Los Angeles had passed San Francisco as the richest California county in total property value. Although the city remained behind San Francisco in per capita income, by the 1930s it exceeded the California average. The state itself was rapidly becoming the richest in the union. By 1941 California ranked third behind New York and Pennsylvania in total personal income and in 1965 first in per capita income.[237] These accomplishments resulted from a gigantic population increase, a superb transcontinental highway and railroad network, development of hydroelectric and oil power sources, emergence of a scientific and engineering community, enlargement of local and regional markets, the integration of southern California into the national economy, and mammoth defense contracts in the world wars.

Growth in other fields, at least before World War II, did not cause Los Angeles County to lose its leadership in agriculture. In 1940 it ranked first in America in agrarian wealth and income. Without sacrificing the traditional base of its economy, the city and county became a great retail and wholesale market. By 1939 the municipality trailed only New York and Chicago in total volume of retail sales, a position it still held in 1967. But the gap between Los Angeles and Chicago closed significantly during these years. In 1967 it also stood third in wholesale transactions. Between 1948 and 1967 retail and wholesale business more than doubled. Maritime commerce also progressed at a dizzying pace. Between 1914–15 and 1939–40 ship tonnage entering Los Angeles harbor multiplied thirteenfold and total value of exports and imports twelvefold. In 1923 Los Angeles passed San Francisco as the premier Pacific Coast port.[238]

Los Angeles had long been an agricultural center, and its future greatness in commerce and trade was foreshadowed even before World War I. But its industrial potential really began to be fulfilled between the world wars. From 1919 to 1939 the dollar value of factory goods in Los Angeles County more than doubled and it climbed from twenty-seventh to seventh among the top U.S. industrial areas. During this time Los Angeles advanced from twentieth to sixth in value added by manufacturing, the highest rate of increase among the leading areas. In these two decades the value of its manufacturing products nearly tripled and the value added by manufacturing tripled. By 1939 manufacturing became the largest single source of income in the county. In 1935 Los Angeles led the nation in the movie, oil-refining, and airplane industries and ranked second in auto parts assembly and rubber products. During the 1920s Los Angeles surpassed San Francisco as the industrial center of California. Spectacular growth continued during and after World War II as the Los Angeles industrial area obtained the greatest proportions in the nation of government defense work. By 1949 it was the fourth or fifth largest manufacturing center. Between 1939 and 1965 value added by manufacturing in the municipality multiplied over eight times that of the entire county total in 1939.[239]

Business growth spurred capital accumulation. Los Angeles County bank deposits increased nearly four times between 1927 and 1949, and almost that between 1949 and 1970. By 1950 Los Angeles stood third among the nation's metropolitan areas in bank debits and deposits. Economic and demographic expansion also created, between 1920 and 1939, a threefold rise in assessed valuation of property in the city. In 1935 total municipal property assessment exceeded that of every California county save Los Angeles County. By 1970, as evinced by the national prominence of firms based there, the city and county had become a significant force in the American economy. Ranked by sales in that year, eight were among the top 100 U.S. industrial corporations and two held a similar position among the first fifty retail houses in the country. Ranked by assets, three placed in the top twenty-five banks, two were among the fifty largest insurance companies, and two occupied a similar position among the first fifty American utilities. Ranked by operating revenue, five made the upper fifty transport concerns in the nation.[240]

REAL ESTATE

In traditional enterprises, trade, banking, real estate, and publishing, several members or descendants of previous elites continued to embellish the family fortune and name. From 1920 to 1924 metropolitan Los Angeles underwent its greatest land boom since the 1880s. *Times* publisher Chandler organized the All Year Club in 1921 to promote tourism and elevate real estate values. That same year Chandler and other tycoons formed the Community Development Association, which under the presidencies of Andrew M. Chaffey and Garland, built the Los Angeles Coliseum. While the stadium was being planned Chandler and several business leaders founded the Central Investment Corporation, the company that constructed the Biltmore Hotel.[241] The hotel and coliseum, completed in 1923, enhanced property values in downtown Los Angeles. Letts, a principal in the association, headed several Mexican and southern California land and realty corporations. Chandler bought lots in Los Angeles, Hollywood, and the suburbs, and purchased and

subdivided the Wolfskill Ranch.[242] Between the world wars two men
who established themselves in the 1885–1915 era were probably the
foremost real estate dealers in metropolitan Los Angeles. Alphonzo E.
Bell, nephew of Hollenbeck and son of a great cattle rancher, made a
fortune in suburban developments. Garland, pre–World War I president of the Los Angeles Realty Board and head of the National Association of Real Estate Boards in 1917–18, developed Wilshire Boulevard
and other property in and around the city. He typified the classic Los
Angeles speculator-booster. After 1892 his advertising billboards predicted vast increases of population, and during World War II Garland
prognosticated, if "peace returns, people are going to make for southern
California." Bell and Garland were eminent civic figures. The former
presided over the Occidental College board, gave money to that school
and UCLA, was a delegate to the Presbyterian General Assembly, and
headed the Church Federation of Los Angeles. Garland sat in the 1890s
on the municipal library and education boards, served as a delegate to
the Republican national conventions of 1900 and 1924, headed the Athletic and California clubs and the California Chamber of Commerce,
and was instrumental in bringing the 1932 Olympic Games to the
city.[243]

Real estate, more than industry or finance, lent itself to kinship enterprise. Third-generation Workmans, Wolfskills, Bannings, and Bixbys
handled ancestral properties. Other prominent operators, e.g., Philo L.
Lindley, Robert A. Rowan, and, after 1948, the son of Garland, inherited firms founded by their fathers. Conversely, many of the great
operators, including several presidents of the realty board, were newcomers to the area. A few of the largest realtors, notably Joseph Top-
litzky and post–World War II suburban developer Louis H. Boyar, were
Jewish. Resident realtors, however, did not exclusively control the market. Even in the 1960s, when Los Angeles generated abundant local capital, the land and home building boom was partly funded by eastern,
chiefly New York- and Boston-based bankers, realtors, and industrial
corporations.[244]

TRADE

In trade, like real estate, old firms and families remained prominent.
Ducommun's hardware store evolved into the largest distributor of
tools, metals, and shop supplies west of Chicago and in the early 1940s
was still owned and operated by his descendants. H. Newmark & Co.,
the wholesale grocery, remained in the family until its liquidation in
1937. Drug jobbers Haas, Baruch & Co., originally Hellman, Haas &
Co., Eugene Germain's wholesale commission business in seeds and
plants, and Obadiah T. Barker's furniture store (1880) remained in family hands until the early 1940s. The Broadway Department Store, started

in 1896 by Arthur Letts and inherited by his son, in 1926 passed to his son-in-law. Old-timer Louis M. Cole, a Community Development Association organizer, treasurer of a great wholesale food distributor, married a Hellman, headed several land, insurance, and packing companies, was a bank director, World War I food administrator for Los Angeles, and president of the chamber of commerce. Many of the city's foremost merchants, including several department store proprietors, however, were recent arrivals and self-made successes.[245]

The bulk of the old firms were wholesalers. Retailers encountered more radical changes in business methods as the city decentralized and national chain store competition grew more formidable. Freeways and the advent of the automobile encouraged the horizontal expansion that made metropolitan Los Angeles the first of the flourishing suburban supermarket and shopping center regions and curtailed the business of downtown department stores and other retail outlets. In 1929 these department stores accounted for 75 percent of the total retail sales in the metropolitan area, a decade later 54 percent, and by 1959 only 18.2 percent.[246]

UTILITIES

During the 1920s Old Guard capitalists mobilized in two mammoth struggles that demonstrated both their immediate power and their inability to realize long-range goals and determine the course of urban development. After World War I, realtors, merchants, bankers, and others interested in preserving the downtown area worried about traffic congestion ruining business and lowering property values. Led by Sartori, the town's premier financier, Chandler and an assemblage of local heavyweights organized the Subway Terminal Corporation (1925) to put some of the transit line tracks underground. The fight to build the Union Terminal split the upper class. The chamber of commerce, the Pacific Electric Railway Co. and its influential president David W. Pontius, and other transit lines opposed the site of the terminal and balked at burying their tracks. But the *Times*, the Terminal Corporation, and William H. Workman supported the project, and city council president Boyle Workman cast the deciding vote for enabling legislation. The terminal was built but a subway system did not develop. Increased use of automobiles sent the intra- and interurban railways into a steep decline and traffic threatened property values and business volume in the business district.[247]

During this decade the Old Guard won another empty victory. The People's Economic League was formed by Garland, several Hellmans, Henry W. O'Melveny, and their peers to oppose the Boulder Canyon public power project. Assisted by the Chamber, the *Times*, and the gas and electric companies, they defeated public power advocates led by del

Valle, Haynes, the Hearst papers, and several highly regarded lawyers and civic figures. In the 1920s power bond issues failed at the polls, but one passed in 1930 and in 1935 Los Angeles Gas and Electric sold its electric system to the municipality.[248]

Upper-class leaders, more unified on the need for public development of water resources, here promoted community welfare and shaped urban development. The *Times* and the chamber supported municipal initiatives to expand the water supply, and in the 1920s a bond issue passed and the Metropolitan Water District of Southern California, controlled by Los Angeles, was created to tap the Colorado River via an aqueduct. Haynes and Pontius served as directors and the latter became comptroller of the water district.[249]

FINANCE

Bankers were members of the upper class, but financiers with blood or marital ties to distinguished families or who belonged to the traditional elite, even in the 1920s, did not match the Old Guard presence in trade or real estate. The patrician persistence in trade was explained above. Blueblood persistence in real estate may be accounted for by land inheritance. Banking, on the other hand, was more subject to corporate organization, liquid assets, and changing sources of capital, factors which made class and family continuity more difficult. During this decade the older leaders were Sartori, who headed California's second and Los Angeles' largest bank, the Security-First National; second-generation Chaffeys who controlled the California Bank, fifth largest in the city and twelfth in the state; Graves of Farmers' & Merchants', sixth largest in Los Angeles and thirteenth in California; and Benjamin R. Meyer, Cohn's successor at the Union. These men, however, were exceptions to the dwindling influence of the Old Guard. Other patricians headed smaller institutions and brokerage houses or functioned in secondary capacities, such as vice-presidents, of the larger banks. Since members of the older upper class died out and their descendants seldom participated in the areospace and movie industries or other new centers of capital accumulation and economic power, they gradually lost control of the largest financial institutions.[250]

Even Farmers' & Merchants', which had the most aristocratic leadership, replaced Graves in 1930 with Victor H. Rosetti, a Nevada-born self-made success, and its board became significantly less patrician in composition. During the 1950s and '60s the Union Bank stood second in Los Angeles and thirtieth in the nation in total assets and was the fastest-growing bank in the United States. It still concentrated on short-term loans to small businessmen, real estate financing, and extending credit to the city's clothing and fashion industry proprietors. Among its clients were many Jewish businessmen and its president was of the same faith. But the Union Bank was no longer in the hands of the Cohn clan.[251]

After World War II, Security-First National, still the greatest bank in the metropolitan area, was the last outpost, if not of patrician dominance, at least of Old Guard influence. In a paradox probably unappreciated by aristocrats involved in the transaction, the upper-class presence was strengthened by absorbing that citadel of respectability, Farmers' & Merchants'. In 1955, the last year of its independence, the management reverted to tradition by appointing Oscar Thom Lawler as president. Lawler was the son of a famous lawyer and counsel and director of the bank and other major corporations in southern California. According to Isaias W. Hellman, an extensive shareholder and grandson of the founder, a reason for the merger was the "proportion of stock [held] in absentee ownership. These absentee owners, particularly the Hellman family, are looked to for leadership which, under present day conditions, it is impossible to give." Lawler became senior vice-president and several Farmers' & Merchants' aristocratic directors went on the executive committee of Security-First National.[252] Thus ended the independent existence of the surviving stronghold of patrician finance. Its termination resulted, as Hellman had suggested, from absentee ownership, an attribute of inherited status and wealth that weakened many old families in Los Angeles and elsewhere.

In vivid contrast to the feeble admission of Hellman were the words of Harry Volk, who, in 1957, succeeded Meyer as Union president. "You can sense the vastness and opportunities of Los Angeles," he said in 1965. "Five years from now we should have fourteen to twenty-one regional headquarters." Volk's optimism impelled him to conduct a high-risk, high-interest rate, and rapid turnover business. Little wonder that this transplanted "go-getter" absorbed the Los Angeles booster spirit and impressed one bank analyst as "a great salesman, a great gatherer of business," and an eastern financier as someone to deal with "if you want something out of the ordinary. . . ."[253]

PUBLISHING

Newspaper publishing was another commercial endeavor marked by the persistence of kinship enterprise. Guy C. Earl, Jr., inherited his grandfather's headship of the *Express* and its parent publishing company and also a radio station.[254] Chandler controlled a greater publishing empire and became the foremost capitalist in Los Angeles during the interwar period. Upon the death of his father-in-law in 1917, this New Hampshire Yankee took over the *Times* and the Times-Mirror Company. During the 1920s he served as an officer and director in thirty-five California corporations, including banking, oil, irrigation, steamship, railroad, land, industrial, and areonautical enterprises. Chandler was the initial financier of aircraft manufacturer Donald Douglas and helped develop the San Fernando Valley, improve Los Angeles Harbor, and organize Western Airlines. Unlike the case of other upper-class clans, zeal and talent reappeared in subsequent generations. Control over the family business interests passed in 1941 to Harry's son. Assisted by his brothers, Norman considerably enlarged the empire. Between 1945 and 1956 he invested $29 million in various properties and projects, founded a local television station and afternoon newspaper, and the *Times* moved from twenty-first to top place among the nation's dailies in advertising lineage. As a result of these activities, in 1956, the family fortune exceeded $50 million. Although Norman inherited much of his holdings and affluence, his capacity for hard work matched the stamina of the legendary rags-to-riches magnate. In 1960 Norman's son Otis became head of the clan's enterprises. The three Chandlers improved the productive process and content of the *Times* and under the leadership of Otis it attained the third largest circulation among American newspapers and was widely considered the most profitable journal in the country. Capitalizing on southern California's suburban sprawl, young Chandler bought newspapers in Los Angeles, Orange, and San Bernadino Counties.[255]

Otis also ran the Times-Mirror Co., which controlled land, paper mill, TV, and various newspaper properties. After 1960, this conglomerate further diversified operations, acquiring the New American Library, then the country's second-ranked paperback house; leading publishers of road maps, aeronautical charts and flight manuals, law books, Bibles, and dictionaries; *Popular Science* and other magazines; an art-book house; a medical text firm; a bookbindery; a plywood corporation; and a scientific instrument maker. While expanding in new directions Chandler continued the tradition of using the *Times* to promote family interests. He supported the Feather River development, which would increase the Los Angeles water supply and enhance the value of real estate owned by Times-Mirror. The strategy of expansion, attuned to the growing professional, technically trained, better-traveled and -educated, and suburban segments of the population, proved highly successful. Between 1959 and 1963, its most profitable year, Times-Mirror sales increased by 80 percent, between 1960 and 1966 net profits tripled, by 1968 the company was the 273rd largest U.S. corporation, and over the previous ten years the twenty-seventh fastest growing. Within a decade it acquired twenty-two smaller firms and became the third largest American publishing empire. In consequence of these triumphs, the *Times*, before 1960 the financial base of the business, in 1964 contributed only 48 percent of the Times-Mirror profits.[256]

INDUSTRY

Old Guard magnates retained a residue of their former dominance in several businesses. But the essential weakness of their entrepreneurial position was revealed by their absence from the big growth industries that transformed Los Angeles from an agricultural market and processing center and a retirement and resort haven into the incarnation of modern America.

In 1917 Frederick L. Baker, head of the Baker Iron Works, assisted by Chandler, Flint, Sartori, Sherman, and several younger capitalists, founded the Los Angeles Shipbuilding & Dry Dock Company. Presided over by Baker, California's first major shipyard became the Old Guard's last significant manufacturing initiative. This group, in the same year, formed the Los Angeles Steamship Co., with Chandler's nephew as president, to operate and buy vessels and to handle harbor shipping. During World War I, Shipbuilding & Dry Dock received $70 million in defense contracts. When peace returned the industry lapsed until revived in 1941 under the leadership of newcomers like Henry J. Kaiser.[257]

During the 1920s Baker, and in that decade and the next George J. Kuhrts, Jr., of the Standard Boiler and Steel Works, and the second and third-generation Lacys of the Lacy Manufacturing Co., owned the outstanding older, family firms. Baker, whose career is depicted above, and Lacy were the most important upper-class manufacturers. William Lacy, Jr., served as a Farmers' & Merchants' vice-president and as a director in several banks and an oil company, and in 1924 headed the chamber of commerce. In 1932 his son took over Lacy Manufacturing. The overwhelming number of industrial concerns, however, were in the hands of recently arrived executives and magnates. Baker Iron Works passed from the family in 1929, absorbed by the Consolidated Steel Corporation, whose chief executive was born in Illinois.[258]

Oil refining and film making were the fastest-growing metropolitan Los Angeles industries in the 1920s. Throughout the subsequent decade and World War II, aircraft production took over as the flagship expansion industry. Rubber products, especially tires, automobile assembly parts, aerospace and electronics, the fashion and clothing industries, and the establishment of branch plants by national corporations also contributed to making Los Angeles a top national manufacturing center. In these fields it ranked first in California and, at various times, first or second in the country. These industries were begun or located in Los Angeles because of climate, favorable market conditions, defense contracts, a pool of technically trained and scientific personnel, a penchant for risk-taking in backing and implementing imaginative schemes that often characterizes entrepreneurs in newly developed areas of the country, and by southern California's increasing influence over American life-styles. In none of these activities, save Chandler's vital assistance in 1922 in launching the Douglas Aircraft Co. and his less crucial aid in 1919 to Warner Bros., did the Old Guard play an important part. In fact, the major financing and the direction of these ventures emanated usually from banks and corporations based mostly on the Atlantic Coast. Half the oil industry production was controlled by huge national corporations, and the leading independents were run largely by recent arrivals to Los Angeles. Motion picture enterprises were originated chiefly by humbly born Jews who hailed from Europe or New York and funded mainly from that city. The clothing industry, more locally financed, was also the creation of transplanted Jews. Aircraft, aerospace, and electronics firms were organized and managed by native Americans from similarly obscure backgrounds and also supported chiefly by eastern capital. Not until after World War II did the local leaders of these relatively youthful enterprises assume significance in the cultural and philanthropic aspects of community leadership.[259]

THOUGHT

Modern Los Angeles entrepreneurs acted from the same motives and values that inspired earlier capitalists. Indeed, their predecessors anticipated some of the notions heralded by mid-twentieth-century corporate chieftains. Bridge predicted in 1915 that "scientific management will sooner or later enter most lines of industry" because "it saves power and money. . . ." Eight years later President John B. Miller of Southern California Edison professed the managerial creed rapidly assuming biblical status for the modern executive. Miller consulted his aides and "specialists" before determining policy and assured the public that Southern California Edison's success was due to "adherence to the company's slogan 'Good service, square dealing and courteous treatment' " and "a fine spirit of teamwork."[260]

Conversely, the new breed of magnates sometimes modeled themselves on yesteryear's inner-directed captain of industry. North American Aviation president James H. Kindelberger, son of a West Virginia moulder, liked "nothing . . . better than being up to my tail in business." Donald Douglas, child of a minor official in a Washington, D.C., bank, avoided society, made all the important decisions in his aircraft company, and was succeeded by his son. But Douglas sought modern types of executives, "warm, balanced human being[s]," who "must be friendly, well-adjusted, with sympathetic understanding of human motives, limitations, and strength," and have "a sense of justice tempered with kindness, an instinct for teamwork, a sense of fair play, and a talent for helping and teaching their associates."[261]

Managerial solicitude still fell short of accepting the union shop or tolerating strikes. Strike-breakers crushed a 1919 walkout of the street railway employees. In 1937–38 the Merchants' and Manufacturers' Association, the chamber of commerce, and the Friday Morning Club opposed the teamsters' strike against local department stores. The city remained an open shop town, which made wages a lower cost-of-production item between 1929 and 1938 in Los Angeles industries than in San Francisco, Chicago, Cleveland, and Pittsburgh factories.[262] The New Deal policy of encouraging labor organization, however, undermined local resistance. The transit lines were unionized in 1934. Douglas, who located in Los Angeles partly to take advantage of lower wages in the area and who, in 1936, defeated an attempt to unionize Douglas Aircraft, capitulated the next year to the United Automobile Workers. The influx of branches of national concerns was another factor in this decade that breached the antilabor front. By World War II, unionization and the advent of service and technological enterprises had turned the metropolitan area into a relatively high-priced labor market. [263]

The new order also shared the confidence of its predecessors in the promise of southern California. Douglas, in 1955, had "great faith in aviation and in the future." Officers of manufacturing firms and branches of national corporations located in southern California from 1866 to 1940 gave as the primary reason for their move growing market opportunities in the region.[264]

Post–World War II businessmen sometimes succumbed to old time lures. A Carnation Milk vice-president named a pleasant climate as the incentive for the 1948 transfer of company headquarters to Los Angeles.[265] Other corporation officers, however, were attracted by the vigorous spirit of contemporary southern California. Asked to explain the company's relocation, another Carnation executive replied: "Nowhere else have I ever met so many people from other places. My point is, that such a fusion of ideas, cultures, and skills is productive of activity, growth and progress. It is what makes Los Angeles a dynamic city." Two years before the Carnation move, the board chairman of the Brand Names Foundation expressed a similar attitude: He sold "new products first in Los Angeles." The residents "would not think of all the reasons that old established communities can think of why it would not be successful," they would say: "Let's try it." After they "made a success of it then the old established cities accept it. If anything, that is the magic which has made Los Angeles great." Leaders of indigeneous businesses agreed with these pronouncements. The Security-National Bank president in 1949 remarked that the city's impulsive politics and exotic religious cults helped local industry: "It means that people coming out here are open to new ideas. They don't have commitments. They like to start something new." Spokesman from states threatened by the economic upsurge of California, especially its southern section, made the same evaluation. New York Senator Jacob K. Javits, in 1959, and Congressman John Tabor, in 1960, complained that their state lost out to California as the leading defense contractor because New Yorkers lagged behind the West Coast entrepreneurs in seeking government research funds and lacked the initiative of California's hungrier and younger capitalists.[266]

Los Angeles aerospace tycoons enthusiastically endorsed the volatility and venturesomeness that local magnates and their competitors from elsewhere attributed to the city, especially to its industrialists. "This part of the country has always been a little cracked," claimed president William Millar of Vultee Aircraft in a 1941 explanation for the airplane construction boom in Los Angeles. "It's the most wonderful place in the world to start an ism or a religion or a new business." In the 1950s and '60s Douglas, Lockheed Aircraft board chairman Daniel J. Haughton, son of an Alabama farmer and storekeeper, and other leaders in the industry proudly emphasized that they were "in the business of taking risks" and "processing . . . innovations." According to Douglas, "the most compelling characteristic of our industry is that it cannot . . . rest on its laurels."[267]

Entrepreneurial zeal, an apparently unbounded capacity for optimism and risk-taking, and economic growth accounted for the facts that approximately one-eighth of American businesses begun in 1946 started in southern California, mostly in Los Angeles County, and that in 1948 one-seventh of the nation's commercial failures occurred in this area.[268]

ORGANIZATIONS

During the 1920s the Merchants' and Manufacturers' Association and the chamber of commerce fulfilled their accustomed functions. By the 1930s, however, the association no longer stemmed the tide of unionism, and the chamber, representing traditional entrepreneurship, did not maintain leadership in the contemporary business community of aerospace firms, movie moguls, and branches and headquarters of national corporations. A dramatic sign of the chamber's weakness came in 1935, when, over its objections, the governor and state legislature implemented a personal income tax.[269]

From 1915 to 1930, chamber presidents, exemplified by attorneys Fredericks and Bulla, banker McKee, and manufacturer Lacy, usually derived from the older professional and business elite. At this time it was still powerful. Chamber-opposed water and power development bond issues invariably failed and it was consulted on all major initiatives by the Municipal Department of Water and Power. In 1916 the chamber instituted a World Trade Department, which aided in the development of local harbor facilities and maritime commerce, and in 1919 an Industrial Department, which stimulated manufacturing. The chamber

Transportation Department was instrumental in bringing several large auto assembly plants to Los Angeles, and in 1927 the organization helped start commercial air service to the city and fostered plans for an airport. Chamber influence extended to other civic matters. In 1918 it successfully campaigned to establish a local branch (UCLA) of the state university. Four years later it suggested the federation of the city's philanthropic institutions and shortly thereafter emerged the Los Angeles Community Welfare Organization. In the 1920s it had the largest membership of any local chamber of commerce in the world.[270]

After 1930 chamber presidents came from the younger capitalist group, but not from newer industries. In addition to occupation, they resembled most of their forerunners in not being natives of California.[271]

Politics

After World War I, the upper class, in common with other patriciates, rarely faced the voters. Boyle Workman, who left the city council in 1926, was the last descendant of the Anglo-American elite of Alta California in elective office. Newer business and professional leaders appeared more often in such posts. Wholesale grocer William D. Stephens and Fredericks, former chamber presidents, were Los Angeles congressmen respectively in 1916 and 1923, and Stephens in 1918 became governor of California. The rich, powerful, and a few of the well-born preserved much of their influence by manipulating officeholders and by dominating important public bodies not subject to voter approval. Joseph Mesmer, Haynes, and Louis D. Nordlinger, who succeeded his father as the town's leading jeweler, represented Los Angeles on the Metropolitan Water District Board. Mesmer, another former chamber president, served on the City Planning Commission along with financier Orra E. Monnette, the son of a Los Angeles bank president. Monnette was also a member of the board of freeholders, which framed the city charters, as was Dr. Milbank Johnson.[272]

The power of the commercial elite, wielded by these men and through such pressure groups as the chamber and the Downtown Businessmen's and the Property Owners' Tax associations, protected business interests and individual fortunes. Their efforts resulted in low corporate, personal income, and inheritance taxes and grossly underassessed property valuations.[273]

On issues where the upper class was less unified, as in public power development, even influential factions could lose out. During the 1920s Chandler and the *Times*, Southern California Edison, and Los Angeles Gas and Electric opposed Mayor George E. Cryer, a public power advocate, but could neither defeat him nor halt the Boulder Dam project which Cryer supported. The *Times* in 1938 unsuccessfully opposed another reform mayor.[274] This journal and its upper-class allies also failed, in this decade, to perpetuate the open shop.

At the time of the New Deal, Los Angeles was long noted as a conservative town dominated by the regular Republicanism of its transplanted midwesterners. Graves feared "the tyrannies and infamies of rabid labor unionism" even during the Harding and Coolidge administrations and while the open shop prevailed. He despised California Progressives and thought Woodrow Wilson "inclined toward socialism." Joseph P. Widney, like Graves a proponent of rugged individualism, argued that New Deal programs corrupted the American spirit.[275] The upper class recoiled in 1934 from the prospect of Upton Sinclair as governor. Campaigning on a strong public welfare platform, Sinclair was bitterly fought by patricians such as Isidore Dockweiler and Henry W. O'Melveny and his law firm, Robert A Millikan, president of the California Institute of Technology, and film studio chiefs.[276]

Beginning in the 1930s politics gradually liberalized. The old elite, rooted in local business activity and provincial in outlook, was overwhelmed by the forces that shaped contemporary Los Angeles: the trend toward decentralization as the city grew in size and number of residents and surrendered to the centrifugal thrust of the automobile and the freeway; an influx of poorer newcomers, many of them Blacks, seeking employment in defense plants and shipyards; the integration of Los Angeles into the national economy and its increasing dependence on international trade; the emergence of the aerospace industry, which needed federal government largesse; the advent of corporate managers who ran nationally based firms that were not diehard opponents of organized labor and whose primary priorities were not to maintain an open shop and low local property values and levies; and, finally, the development of Los Angeles as a counterculture haven.[277] Reflecting these changes, the *Times* by the late 1950s, under younger and more cosmopolitan Chandlers, was no longer a West Coast version of the Chicago *Tribune*.

The Professions

Elite professionals exhibited more cohesion with the past than did business leaders. Between the world wars a significant segment of the foremost attorneys and law firms derived from previous luminaries of the bar. Grandchildren and grandnephews of the founders of Brunson, Wells & Lee and of Anderson & Anderson now belonged to these firms. By 1950, four generations of Andersons and three each of O'Melvenys, Workses, Chapmans, Wellborns, and Meserves had been members of the bar association and most of them practiced in family firms. Additional examples of kinship were O'Melveny, Tuller & Myers, the largest firm on the Pacific Coast during the interwar period, Flint & McKay, and Dockweiler, Dockweiler & Finch. Henry W. O'Melveny headed O'Melveny, Tuller & Meyers and at his death in 1941 was succeeded by his son; Henry S. McKay, Jr., married the daughter of his partner, Frank P. Flint; and Isidore Dockweiler practiced with his children.[278]

During these decades members of noted legal dynasties, Henry W. O'Melveny (1919), Edwin A. Meserve (1920), and William H. Anderson (1934), presided over the bar association. Corporation counselors like Oscar Thom Lawler, whose firm represented Farmers' & Merchants', Standard Oil of California, Pacific Telegraph and Telephone, and Southern California Edison, also headed the association.[279]

Kinship ties also appeared among judges. Fathers and sons from the Shaw, York, Works, Wellborn, and Stephens families, all distinguished legal clans, served as justices. Nevertheless, prominent lawyers, like leading business men, were less likely than their predecessors to seek or hold political office.[280]

Elite medical families, not as cushioned by wealth and commercial connections, were less prevalent than elite legal dynasties. Wayland H. Morrison, who succeeded his parent as chief surgeon at Los Angeles Gas and Electric, Ernest C. Moore, president in 1925 and offspring of a former president of the county medical association, and William R. Maloney, Jr., head of this body in 1932 and son of an ex-president of the state medical association, were exceptions to the lack of intergenerational continuity. The infrequency of such relationships, however, did not preclude other ties to the past. Interlocking features of professional leadership, membership on civic health commissions, important posts in the local medical society, professorships at the USC Medical School, and service on the staffs of prestigious hospital and patrician charities still defined career eminence. Harlan Shoemaker, a faculty member at the medical school, became president of the Los Angeles Medical Society in 1936. Albert W. Moore also had credentials similar to those of illustrious doctors of previous periods. The nephew of a prominent Los Angeles merchant, Moore was on the municipal board of health, the orphans' home and Children's Hospital staffs, and a founder and vice-president of the Hamilton National Life Insurance Co. Prominent practitioners, however, like distinguished lawyers, rarely held public office, not even such appointive posts as the board of education.[281]

Law and medicine operated in traditional patterns, but professional life took on a new dimension with the advent of mathematicians, physicists, geologists, and engineers who, beginning in the 1920s, worked in the bourgeoning areospace, electronics, and oil industries. The scientific community emerged from the needs of these industries and from cooperation between the California Institute of Technology and airplane and electric companies. By the 1930s, Douglas Aircraft had a research and development brain trust drawn mostly from graduates of Cal Tech and helped finance and used the school's areonautical facilities to conduct experiments and implement technological advances. Southern California Edison had a similar arrangement and the oil industry was assisted by the school's development as a center of geological research and training. Since the late 1920s, Cal Tech professors have supplied ideas and students for the aircraft and missile companies and their students have founded postwar areospace and electronics firms. Beginning in World War II, Cal Tech received millions in government contracts to develop areospace inventions and hardware, which it subcontracted to local firms for production and marketing. By 1964, California had more scientists and Nobel laureates than any other state, including 17 percent of the nation's mathematicians and scientists trained in space research, 12 percent of the country's scientists, about half of America's Nobel Prize winners, and 22 percent of the National Academy of Science membership.[282]

Education

After World War I, upper-class cash and commitment to education focused almost exclusively upon higher learning. Cal Tech, located in the millionaire colony of Pasadena, offering services and with ties to the richest magnates in southern California, received the largest share of this type of *noblesse oblige*. Trustees Chandler, Bridge, Robinson, and Henry W. O'Melveny formed the California Institute of Technology Associates (1925) to raise money for the school. The group initially met at the home of Huntington, another associate, and in the first quarter-century of its existence raised over $2 million. Among the largest individual donors were Bridge, whose gifts totaled about $750,000, and trustee Arthur H. Fleming, a Pasadena multimillionaire lumberman, who donated about $5.2 million. By the 1930s Cal Tech, next to Stanford University, had the highest college endowment in California and ranked third behind Stanford and USC in the value of its physical plant. Its endowment, repute, and quality made the institute, along with the Massachusetts Institute of Technology, the nation's best scientific and technical school.[283]

In the 1920s USC had the next greatest claim on upper-class educational largesse. It had more difficulty in gathering funds than Cal Tech because its Methodist origins and ties inhibited contributions from affluent Angelenos. Despite problems of financing, it, too, forged bonds with the economic elite and during the interwar era grew into a major university. The relationship with Pacific Mutual Life continued after World War I under George Cochran's dual role as president of the company and USC treasurer. After one Pacific Mutual loan a faculty member remarked, "USC is merely an extension of Pacific Mutual." Like Cal Tech, USC assisted the gigantic growth industries recently located in the area. In 1928 a Department of Cinema was founded and funded by Cecil B. DeMille. USC drew on the old and new enclaves of the upper class for support, though not as successfully as Cal Tech. Allan Hancock and Seeley W. Mudd gave the university a marine biology center and the Mudds provided several trustees and large donations. The most generous contributor, however, was H. Leslie Hoffman, a Chicago-born electronics tycoon who came to California in 1929 and at his death in 1971 had given the university more than $2 million. Cal Tech and USC commanded support from the same enclave and several civic leaders were active in both institutions. The 1930 board of trustees consisted of Andrew M. Chaffey, Eli P. Clarke, Benjamin R. Meyer, and other older capitalists or their children. After World War II, however, newly risen entrepreneurs, such as Howard F. Ahmanson, banker, realtor, and insurance company organizer, Hoffman, and Franklin S. Wade, president of Southern California Gas, dominated the board.[284]

Occidental College trailed USC and Cal Tech in attracting upper-class funds and leadership and has never attained their academic reputation. Nonetheless, much of its support came from wealthy and influential residents of greater Los Angeles. A long-term board president, realtor Alphonzo E. Bell, donated more than $100,000, and Mrs. Norman H. Chandler served as a trustee. Newer members of the business elite, the treasurer of General Electric and the vice-president and general manager of the Southern California Telephone Co., also participated in college affairs. Similar in the source of its support, Occidental sometimes overlapped with USC and Cal Tech in contributors and trustees, e.g., Bridge, Doheny, and Huntington gave money to Occidental and USC and Fleming sat on both boards. Intimacy between Occidental and leading businessmen paved the way for its president in 1916 to leave the college for a vice-presidency and directorships in several important Los Angeles banks.[285]

The 1920s was a golden age for higher education in metropolitan Los Angeles. During this decade USC and Cal Tech became major institutions and the University of California branch at Los Angeles, established in 1919, began its development into the finest all-round university in southern California. UCLA in 1927 became co-equal, de jure if not de facto, of the main branch at Berkeley, largely through the initiative of the urban elite. *Express* editor Dickson and Dr. Ernest C. Moore conceived of the project, which was planned at the exclusive Jonathan Club. Civic leaders composed the Citizen's Committee to pick a campus site and in 1919 became the original University of California Regents from Los Angeles. Bell and the Arthur Letts estate donated respectively

$350,000 and $3.5 million to the new university by selling it land below the market price. During the 1920s Mrs. William G. Kerckhoff contributed $815,000, Doheny a building, the Mudd family more than $50,000, and William A. Clark, Jr., son of a Montana and Arizona copper-mining magnate, his library, house, and $1.5 million. Several of these benefactors were active in the affairs of other colleges in the area and all were community leaders. UCLA rapidly became, with Cal Tech, the chief object of upper-class patronage and emerged after World War II as a great university. The medical school was started in 1946 and, a year later, the law school and a theater arts school. Here, too, *parvenu* millionaires became a major source of support. In the 1960s Norton Simon, a University of California regent and a personification of the trend toward conglomerate capitalism as head of Hunt Foods & Industries, Wheeling Steel, the McCall Publishing Corporation, and Canada Dry, donated $75,000 worth of sculpture. David Bright, owner of America's largest closed-circuit television company, left the university half his art collection. Jules Stein, board chairman of the Radio Corporation of America, gave $2 million for an eye institute. Sharply breaking with the tradition that excluded Hollywood luminaries from upper-class civic affairs, movie celebrities contributed $4 million to the Jules Stein Eye Institute. In yet another example of the interaction between major universities and corporations, UCLA chancellor Franklin D. Murphy resigned to head the Times-Mirror Co.[286]

Culture

Advances in higher education, science, and technology spearheaded a trend that culminated in the 1960s with greater Los Angeles dominating American popular culture and becoming a powerful force in high culture. In 1913 a writer in the *Smart Set* described Los Angeles as a stronghold of transplanted midwestern provinciality, prudery, and spiritual aridity.[287] Fifty years later the city symbolized opulence, amusement, sensuality, and impulsiveness. It inspired a new American way of life through dominating the film and TV media, originating informal fashions in clothes, homes, and relationships, and epitomizing frenzied recreation and pecuniary accumulation. Less obvious was the advent of greater Los Angeles as a mecca of high culture. The area's colleges, scientific community, museums, theaters, art collections, and symphony—including a $14.5 million temple of art, a $4 million movie museum, a $6 million zoo, and a $33.5 million complex of music and performing arts auditoria—rivaled or surpassed those of San Francisco and made the metropolis a national intellectual center. The enormous increase of wealth in the region contributed to this achievement, for high culture has always flourished in affluent surroundings. Renowned universities, splendid art collections, fine musicians, and brilliant scientists required sizeable outlays of capital in the form of salaries, colleagues, equipment, acquisitions, and buildings. These needs were met in part from the purses of the princes of popular culture. Cinema stars and czars in the 1950s and '60s poured millions into the Los Angeles Music Center and the county museum. Bridges between popular and high culture, however, were paved with more than gold. Beginning in the 1920s the film industry hired major authors, lured by awesome salaries, as screenwriters, as well as musicians, painters, and dancers. Its celebrities became art collectors and patrons. Hollywood provided the themes for at least two major books by novelist-screenwriters, F. Scott Fitzgerald's *The Last Tycoon* and Nathaniel West's *The Day of the Locust*. And the motion picture ultimately became a serious art form in its own right. The intellectual and artistic community was also considerably enriched by the settlement of many expatriate European intellectuals, refugees from Hitlerian Germany, like Bertolt Brecht and Thomas Mann, or others who moved voluntarily, like Jascha Heifitz, Arthur Rubenstein, Arnold Schoenberg, Igor Stravinsky, and Aldous Huxley.

The heightened intellectual and esthetic life, however, was flawed by the materialism, superficiality, derivativeness, and vulgarity that had long plagued southern California. Hollywood and TV writers, for example, complained that their creativity was stifled and their sensibility violated by profit-inspired directives to cater to a national mass audience. Colossal contributions of money made possible the appearance of mammoth cultural monuments, museums, art collections, and orchestras, and inflated the egos and fame of their patrons. But these achievements were mostly imitative of eastern cities. Whether they exploited or encouraged talented artists, composers, and authors is an open question.

Nevertheless, the cultural level unmistakably improved. The transformation of the *Times* from a provincial and partisan sheet into a moderate and cosmopolitan newspaper resulted from community enlightenment. During the 1930s Washington reporters ranked the *Times* among the three most unfair and unreliable American journals. Polemical broadsides continued to mar its reputation in the 1940s and '50s. "We were kind of lopsided in those days," admitted Norman Chandler. "If we gave the Republicans a big story, we'd give the Democrats a small one. And we only gave management's side in labor disputes."[288] The Chandlers then differed little from the equally well-born McCormick-Patterson clan. But the forces that involved Los Angeles in national and global concerns, introduced more educated and sophisticated readers into the area, and upgraded its culture, ushered in a new order. Otis

Chandler, in the 1960s, increased the domestic and foreign news coverage and staff, hired eastern journalists from *Time, Newsweek,* and the New York *Times* and *Herald-Tribune* to head the overseas and domestic bureaus, and carried nationally known liberal columnists Robert Hutchins, Art Buchwald, and Walter Lippmann. Compared to that of his predecessors, Chandler's brand of journalism was professional and sophisticated. "I want the *Times* to be an Independent Republican newspaper," he said in 1964, "but we feel an obligation to present both sides of the political spectrum to our readers." The *Times* in 1964 and 1968 supported Nelson Rockefeller for the Republican presidential nomination, advocated the Civil Rights Act of 1964, grain sales to the Soviet Union, nuclear test-ban treaties, opposed the John Birch Society, and won a Pulitzer Prize in 1966 for its coverage of the Watts Riots. Democratic Governor Pat Brown even declared that he had been fairly treated by the paper.[289] An ex-*Times*man explained the difference between Otis and Norman Chandler as reflecting the shift of Los Angeles and its upper class from local to national involvement: "Part of the reason Otis wants to improve and expand is his desire to build a national reputation for the paper—and himself. His father, by contrast, took the attitude that anyone who really counted knew who he was already."[290]

The historical society was a unique exception to intellectual progress in metropolitan Los Angeles. Its president regretted in 1938 that lack of money and a permanent home virtually halted new acquisitions and that the organization failed to share in the massive funding of local museums, colleges, and scientific research. Twenty years later another president again complained about the absence of a permanent building and the niggardly public and private support compared to donations for similar institutions in eastern cities.[291] The society owed its relative poverty to the fact that it remained an Old Guard citadel while other institutions relied fundamentally upon more dynamic and opulent *parvenus*. Descendants of pioneer families proliferated among the officers and members and they lacked money and power to enlist the support of the municipal and county governments.[292] The affluent, influential, and largely self-made upper class conceived of Los Angeles as a city of the present and the future. Consequently, historical commitments and ancient roots were less cherished than in Boston, Philadelphia, or Charleston. This outlook prompted many businessmen to initially oppose celebration of the city's sesquicentennial anniversary because they felt its image would be tarnished if its true age were known.[293]

Believing that the fulfillment of Los Angeles' destiny lay in the future, prominent and wealthy citizens tended to be more interested in science than in history. Their assistance to Cal Tech included the bequest of Robinson's fortune for the purchase and maintenance of the world's largest telescope, they supported the USC and UCLA medical schools, and they financed the Mount Wilson Observatory. The latter was promoted by Hale, its first director, and funded by a Los Angeles industrialist. Like so many other scientific and technological projects, it aided local business. Mount Wilson became an ideal location for southern California's television stations.[294]

The Henry E. Huntington Library and Art Gallery (1917), like Mount Wilson Observatory and the historical society, was an upper-class project oriented toward a selective professional, social, or intellectual clientele. Huntington turned to books and art objects as he divested himself of business involvements. His great period of collecting began in 1910, when he retired from active entrepreneurship, and ended with his death in 1927. Although Huntington's interests changed, his methods remained the same. The ex-magnate bought books and paintings in the egotistic, aggressive, and imperial manner that he once acquired trolley lines. "I am an old man. I haven't much time," he said of the pecuniary efforts placed in the service of such possessiveness. Time for the newly converted bibliophile and art assembler would be used to win fame and bliss through ownership of old volumes and old masters: "I do not want [a] biography. . . . This library will tell the story. It represents the reward of all the work I have ever done and the realization of much happiness."[295]

The library and art gallery were housed in Huntington's Renaissance-style Palazzo and estate in San Marino. In 1919 the founder formed a trust for his holdings which consisted of himself, several relatives, a partner in Gibson, Dunn & Crutcher, which had handled his transit companies, attorney Patton, a friend and business associate, and Hale. From its inception the board has been dominated by Cal Tech trustees, administrators, and professors, and by principals from Gibson, Dunn & Crutcher and O'Melveny, Tuller & Myers. Other board members and presidents have been trustees of the Southwest Museum and of Claremont and Occidental colleges. Dohenys, Mudds, Bannings, O'Melvenys, and Shorbs were generous donors. In 1924 the library and gallery, along with securities, cash, and land valued at $13 million, the largest single sum ever donated by an individual benefactor in southern California, were given to the state. By 1967 the endowment fund and stockholdings of the institution exceeded $57 million. The gallery contained the best collection of eighteenth-century English paintings outside of Boston and New York, and the book collection included every important library on the market while Huntington was an active acquirer. The library, especially strong in English history and literature and western Americana, is a vital scholarly resource.[296]

The next greatest private library in southern California was the 18,000-book collection of William A. Clark, Jr. Clark, too, donated his library to public uses by giving it to UCLA. The upper class also continued to exert leadership in the municipal library. Orra E. Monnette (1916–35) and USC president Rufus B. Kleinsmid (1938–49) headed the Los Angeles Public Library Board.[297]

Previous cultural movements of Los Angeles were dwarfed by the building of a major music and theater center (1964) and an art museum (1965). These accomplishments came primarily from the new elite. An overlapping group of civic leaders and rich capitalists planned and funded both projects and secured county government assistance, and their efforts made Los Angeles a national music and art center.

The emergence of Los Angeles as an art capital resembled the growth of its public and private libraries. Wealthy individuals accumulated large collections and patronized artists (between 1956 and 1964 the number of local art galleries doubled) and then helped create public forums to exhibit their own and other acquistions.[298] The latter development in Los Angeles and elsewhere gave rise to the museum movement. Boston, Philadelphia, and New York housed the nation's great collections of traditional art, reflecting the tastes of their elites. Cities like Chicago, and its art institute, concentrated on the Impressionists because of the more modern preferences of their affluent enclaves and because the works of the Old Masters had been bought up by more ancient elites. Los Angeles patrons and collectors, guided by their passion for the modern and the futuristic, and because earlier modes were rarely up for sale, focused on post-Impressionistic painting.

Through the Los Angeles County Art Museum (1965) the upper class sought to refine community tastes, gain celebrity, and convince outsiders that Los Angeles was a great city. "It was our great collectors," asserted the original director of the museum, "who gave the funds to put up the new building." The largest museum constructed since Washington's National Gallery (1941), it replaced the art section of the Los Angeles County Museum of History, Science and Art. The new edifice and its holdings reflected the rapid arrival of Los Angeles as second only to New York, according to the associate curator of American painting at New York's Metropolitan Museum of Art, in volume of art sales and as a home of artists and collectors.[299] The money and energy of *noveau riche* local businessmen created the art museum. Chancellor Murphy was an organizer; Norton Simon, who had the finest art collection on the Pacific Coast, contributed over $2.8 million; Howard Ahmanson, another *parvenu* multimillionaire art collector, gave $2 million; electronics and aircraft firms and tycoons and several movie moguls and stars were also generous benefactors. Donations from the aristocratic Mudds and Chandlers were comparatively miniscule. The founders prevailed upon the county administration to donate five acres in Hancock Park as a building and grounds site and to transfer the holdings of the old county musuem to the new institution. Unlike early patrician trustees of Boston, New York, and Philadelphia museums, several self-made Jewish capitalists and an actor served on the first board. Its initiators reflected the fractious aggressiveness of the city's *parvenu* elite in their disputes over planning the museum. Simon and Ahmanson factions battled over whose name should appear on an art gallery, and when the former lost, their leader scaled down his original pledge from $1 million to $250,000. Bert Lytton of Lytton Industries reduced his promise of $750,000 to a reality of $250,000 after a defeat in his choice of pictures that should hang in the gallery named after him. This feuding also caused the resignation of the museum director and for several years prevented the purchase of new paintings.[300] One founder attributed strife among the "instant Medicis" to Los Angeles being "a frontier town" with "no real traditions. These are self-made people who really don't know where they stand, and that is why they are so self-assertive, so frightfully sensitive to criticism, so willing to blow up every minor disagreement into a passionate melodrama." Such defensiveness also may have motivated the museum patrons to hire their first director and chief curator respectively from New York's Frick and Guggenheim museums.[301]

A year before the opening of the museum another milestone was passed in Los Angeles' quest for cultural credentials. The prime mover behind the music center, a concert hall and several theaters completed at more than twice the cost of the museum, was Illinois-born Mrs. Norman (Dorothy Buffum) Chandler, president of the Southern California Symphony Association, head of a Citizen's Advisory Committee to locate and finance a music center, and chief fund-raiser for the project. The *Times* backed the center and the center's architect had designed Otis Chandler's home. Most of the money, however, came from the *arrivistes* responsible for the museum. More than half the contributors to each undertaking gave to both, and Ahmanson, the most generous original benefactor of the museum, donated $1.5 million. S. Mark Taper, a Polish Jew who came to southern California in 1939 and made a fortune in housing and in savings and loans, and oilman Edwin W. Pauley, who bestowed $1 million upon UCLA and was a University of California regent, each gave $1.5 million. The influence of the founders persuaded the county board of supervisors to give seven and a half acres of land for the center. Edward W. Carter, president of the Broadway-Hale department store chain, California's largest retail enterprise, Chandler's counterpart at the museum and her co-worker at the Music Center, and chairman of the University of California Board of Regents and of the Southern California Music Association, attributed the commitment to the music center to Los Angeles being "uniquely ready to spend money on culture. It is a center of artistic and musical activity, and spending money for their development is a prideful act. Besides, it tends to offset the image that the place is populated largely by kooks."[302] Recognition of the city's coming of age, civic loyalty, and self-aggrandizement inspired the creation of all the postwar cultural landmarks.

A decade before the realization of her pet project, Dorothy Chandler had been instrumental, as a member of the board of the Hollywood Bowl Association, in saving that stadium from bankruptcy. Built in 1919, it housed the Los Angeles Symphony and popular music concerts. Local patricians and several recently successful capitalists were the chief supporters of the bowl. After World War II, as occurred in other Old Guard–inspired institutions, Hollywood figures also became active in its management. When Chandler rescued the bowl, an actor headed its board.[303]

The appearance of the bowl coincided with the passing of the symphony presidency from George A. Hancock to William A. Clark, Jr. Under Clark's leadership and performing at the bowl, it reached a wider audience and became, as in other cities, an institution run by the elite to benefit the general public. During his presidency (1913–34) Clark gave $3 million to the orchestra. In the 1920s and '30s the directors were a Who's Who of the upper class. When the Maecenas of the symphony died in 1934 the Southern California Symphony Association, a group of businessmen, professionals, and society matrons, became the chief fund-raisers. Mrs. Chandler netted $400,000 for the symphony when, in 1955, she gave a party where actors and actresses performed gratis.[304] Typical of the contrast between culture in Los Angeles and in San Francisco in the 1960s, the Los Angeles conductor was Zubin Mehta, an innovative maestro sympathetic to contemporary music, while Joseph F. Krips led the more traditional San Francisco Symphony. When the *parvenu* elite assumed control, in music or art, the tendency was to go modern.

The benefactors of Los Angeles' premier academic, intellectual, and artistic institutions came from an intertwined cultural and economic elite. In the 1920s and '30s many of its members descended from patrician families, but after World War II newly risen entrepreneurs generally assumed leadership in cultural activities and narrowed the gap between proper Los Angeles and Hollywood figures. A similar situation prevailed in ritualistic and promotional civic celebrations. A Fiesta de Los Angeles in 1931 honored the sesquicentennial birthday of the first settlement. Isidore B. Dockweiler was president of the festival and a number of aristocrats were officers. Fifteen years later the city celebrated its centennial as a U.S. town. Old Guard Angelenos, many of them active in the earlier event, appeared on the centennial committee. But Hollywood newcomers joined in the ceremonies as committee members and as part of the motion picture and radio program of the entertainment. The two worlds merged when horse-opera hero Leo Carrillo, great-grandson of an Alta California governor, made an address.[305]

The upper class also engineered the most grandiose event in the city's history, the Olympic Games of 1932. Eleven years earlier editors Dickson and Harry Chandler moved to bring the contest to Los Angeles. They served on the Community Development Association, whose president, Garland, was an international Olympic committeeman and helped get the games for Los Angeles. The association sponsored the event and prevailed upon the city and county to finance the Coliseum, the stadium for the games.[306] The Olympics advertised Los Angeles abroad and at home, encouraged tourism and other forms of business, and the Coliseum upgraded urban real estate values.

Charity

Replicating the impulses and experiences of their forerunners and of civic leaders from other urban elites, rich and powerful Angelenos were usually simultaneously active in several cultural and charitable institutions. In the 1920s, Huntington endowed the Collis P. and Howard Huntington Memorial Hospital in Pasadena, Dorothy Chandler worked for Children's Hospital, and Judge Ross bequeathed over $245,000 to patrician-sponsored charities. Mrs. Albert Crutcher, wife of the eminent attorney, was long-time (1907–48) board president of Children's Hospital, and Jonathan S. Slauson's son headed the Barlow Sanitorium board. Marco H. Hellman served as a trustee of several Los Angeles orphanages and hospitals, and scions of the interrelated Newmark and Nordlinger clans were active in various Jewish welfare organizations.[307]

Despite these figures, Old Guard philanthropy gradually became overshadowed by attempts to professionalize and unify the disparate humanitarian agencies. This development culminated in the Los Angeles Community Welfare Organization, founded in 1924, and the Community Chest, which gained widespread acceptance in that year. As in other cities, new forms of coordination and dispensation ultimately displaced patrician benevolence with social workers and parvenu capitalists more comfortable with modern techniques. Several patricians, however, were able to make the transition. Jonathan S. Slauson's grandson was secretary of the Municipal Charities Commission, and William Lacy, Jr., headed the Community Chest. Those most active in the latter and other associations, however, tended to be parvenu entrepreneurs or corporate executives like David W. Pontius, also president of the symphony. The emerging group of distinguished lawyers and physicians also included some outstanding philanthropists. George H. Kress, dean of the University of California medical department, member of the city and state boards of health, and president of the state and county medical associations, headed the Charities Conference Committee of Los Angeles and the Associated Charities Board.[308] Although leaders and institutions changed, the new business and professional elites, like their predecessors, were active in charity organizations.

Society

Economic innovation and growth, cultural and social change, population expansion, recent settlement, and widespread commitment to now and tomorrow prevented the development of a stable establishment. The multigenerational networks that provided civic leadership in Boston, Charleston, Philadelphia, and San Francisco, and to a lesser extent in New York and Chicago, did not take hold in Los Angeles.[309] Its upper class had exclusive clubs, the Junior League, debutante balls, etc., that solidified high society in older places, but in Los Angeles money and publicity, not birth or tradition, dictated social rank. The Jonathan, Sunset, California, Ebell, and Friday Morning clubs admitted *arrivistes*, and daughters of newly-risen tycoons and Hollywood stars became debutantes.[310]

Café society devastated upper-class New York, Chicago, and Los Angeles. Originating in the eastern metropolis, it deposed the remnants of the Four Hundred. Next to New York, the new social order had its greatest impact in Los Angeles. Gossip columnists and press agents replaced society queens and their advisors as arbiters of fashion and included film celebrities as members of an international set that had dethroned the Astor and Palmer circles as sovereigns of stylish society. Commodore Vanderbilt's granddaughter commented on the changing of the guard at the 1935 wedding of her grandchild to the niece of Douglas Fairbanks, Sr.: "In my day we had the celebrities. Now, if it please, the celebrities have us." Social registrites and "debs" from other parts of the country married Hollywood figures or embarked on screen careers. Movie stars joined elite New York clubs, occasionally wedded royalty, or moved in court circles.[311]

The Hollywood elite, despite its new eminence, was, between the world wars, not yet accepted by polite society. The upper class denigrated Hollywood luminaries for dubious ethics, plebian antecedents, and Jewish origins. Undaunted by rejection, the film colony set up a parallel hierarchy, similarly based on wealth and power, and organized its own athletic, country, and woman's clubs, chamber of commerce, community chest, and welfare institutions. Fortified by conquests in café society, Hollywood figures responded to exclusion with contempt. Ethyl Barrymore, whose actress-niece "came out" in 1938 and who belonged to New York's prestigious Colony Club, felt that "Los Angeles Society is anybody who went to High School."[312] After World War II, the fortunes and fame of screen celebrities overcame the qualms of civic leaders and the stars gained admission to proper Los Angeles culture and philanthropy.

Amorphous Los Angeles society also encountered disintegrative forces from other quarters. New industrial magnates like Douglas shunned fashionable circles and, by the 1950s, *arriviste* tycoons, several of them Jewish, became prominent in charities and cultural projects.[313] An even more severe threat came when the Chandlers deserted high society. One of Dorothy Chandler's friends and co-workers at the music center attributed her success in this enterprise to having "all the weapons—the *Times*, the Chandler name, the real power."[314] By the 1960s, this family alone among the ancient clans was still influential. Chandler power derived from a sense of obligation. "I feel I should exercise a role of leadership in the community," asserted Otis Chandler, "especially in this community, where no one else is doing it." But the Chandlers now felt that their mission required withdrawl from the social set. The *Times* society page under Dorothy Chandler, the chief chronicler of the southern California *beau monde*, dutifully recorded elite bazaars, cotillions, balls, births, and betrothals. Otis, who disliked parties and disdained "the California Club crowd," dropped the section. "Inherited position [now] means less," said his mother of this decision. "People have to earn the right to appear on our pages by solid achievement."[315]

When General George Patton in 1945 returned to Los Angeles for a civic celebration of his victories, the municipality discovered that he was born there and belonged to the most distinguished Mexican and North American families in the city. Eighteen years later Remi Nadeau indicated the reason for the community's ignorance of the social origins of its famous sons. "Nowhere are the social elite more ignored," declared this descendant of a renowned civic and commercial figure of the early settlement. They "battle against eclipse by the film colony on the one hand and social ignorance of the public on the other." Californians are concerned with "gumption, and the foresight to study for a promising occupation" rather than "with the prestige of family names" or inherited wealth. California, "only two or three generations removed from the frontier," has "few of the artificial affectations and discriminations cherished by so-called mature societies" and has no "fixed leadership class." Its population and economy are "so dynamic that the energetic young enterpriser with a new idea can still revolutionize an industry. Personal success (including married to success) is still the first mark of respect in California."[316]

Nadeau's observation explains southern California society and is an epitaph for an aristocracy whose existence, beyond the wishes and intramural contacts of a few old dynasties, never had an impact on Los Angeles equal to the influence of patriciates in less volatile cities. Mexican and Anglo-American landlords, transplanted eastern and midwestern entrepreneurs, and cinema and areospace executives led different stages of urban development. Each enclave contributed to the growth of Los Angeles but was unable to perpetuate its ascendance. Successive stages of growth, creating dissimilarities in ethnicity and economic and social structure and perspective, brought the insurgence of new elites. Disruption at the top reflected and intensified the rootless, inchoate atmosphere of Los Angeles.

NOTES

1. Irving Berdine Richman, *California under Spain and Mexico, 1535–1847* (New York: Cooper Square, 1965), 207, 347–48; Charles Dwight Willard, *The Herald's History of Los Angeles City* (Los Angeles: Kingsley-Barnes & Neuner, 1901), 128; Carey McWilliams, *Southern California Country* (New York: Duell, Sloan, and Pearce, 1946), 52. For contemporary ranchero accounts of their class see Don José del Carmen Lúgo, "Life of a Rancher," *Historical Society of Southern California Quarterly* (hereafter cited HSSCQ), XXXII (1950), 187–236; Horace Bell, *Reminiscences of a Ranger or, Early Times in California* (Los Angeles: Yarnell, Caystille & Mathes, 1881), 26–28, 88–89, 174, 449–50. For another contemporary account see A. Robinson, *Life in California* (New York: Wiley & Putnam, 1846), *passim*. The best studies of the ranchos are Hubert Howe Bancroft: *History of California*, 7 vols. (San Francisco: A. L. Bancroft, 1884–86), I, 661–63, II, 349–50, III, 631–37, IV, 518–19, 532, 557–58, 629–35; *California Pastoral, 1769–1848: Works* (San Francisco: History, 1888) XXIV, 260–93, 396–435, 446–48; W. W. Robinson: *Ranchos Become Cities* (Pasadena: San Pasqual Press, 1939); *Land in California* (Berkeley and Los Angeles: University of California Press, 1948); Richman, *California*, 207, 340–50; Robert Glass Cleland: *The Cattle on a Thousand Hills* (San Marino: Huntington Library, 1964), 4–50; *The Irvine Ranch of Orange County* (San Marino: Huntington Library, 1952), 15–53; McWilliams, *Southern*, 50–54, 61–62; Charles C. Baker, "Mexican Land Grants in California," *Annual Publications, Historical Society of Southern California* (hereafter cited as *Annual*), IX, part 3 (1914), 238–43; Marion Parks, "In Pursuit of Vanished Days," *ibid.*, XIV, parts 1–2 (1928–29), 7–64, 135–208; Leonard Pitt, *The Decline of the Californios: A Social History of the Spanish-Speaking Californians* (Berkeley and Los Angeles: University of California Press, 1966), 11–13, 108, 128–29.

2. Cleland, *Cattle*, 19–33; J. M. Guinn, *History of the State of California and Biographical Record of the Coast Counties, California* (Chicago: Chapman Publishing, 1904), 117–18; Pitt, *Decline*, 12–13, 108, 128–29; Robinson, *Life, passim*; Thomas Workman Temple II, "Our Heritage from the Days of the Dons," *HSSCQ*, XL (1958), 70–76; Terry E. Stephenson, "Tomas Yorba, His Wife Vincente, His Account Book," *ibid.*, XXIII (1941), 142–46; George Shochat, "The

Case Adobe de San Rafael," *ibid.*, XXXII (1950), 279–80; Lúgo, "Life," 219–36; Cleland, *Irvine*, 15–35; Richman, *California*, 340–46, 350; Bancroft, *California*, 396–418; McWilliams, *Southern*, 61; Bell, *Reminiscences*, 26–28, 88–89, 291.

3. Robinson, *Land*, 86; Robinson, *Ranchos*, 52, 179; McWilliams, *Southern*, 52; Lúgo, "Life," 187; Bancroft, *History*, II, 783, III, 778–79, V, 783; Pitt, *Decline*, 11–12; Stephenson, "Tomas Yorba," 131; J. Gregg Layne, "The First Census of the Los Angeles District," *HSSCQ*, XVIII (1936), 87; Robinson, "The Story of Rancho Los Cerritos," *ibid.*, XXXIX (1952), 302–8; Shochat, "Casa," 279–80; Helen Tyler, "The Family of Pico," *ibid.*, XXXV (1953), 232; H. D. Barrows, "The Lugo Family of California," *Annual*, IX, part 1 (1912), 34; Barrows, "Pio Pico," *ibid.*, III, part 2 (1894), 55.

4. Bell, *Reminiscences*, 174; Juan Bandini quoted in Bancroft, *California*, 282.

5. Remi Nadeau, *Los Angeles from Mission to Modern City* (New York, London, Toronto: Longmans Green, 1960), 13; *U.S. Bureau of the Census, Fifteenth Census of the United States: Volume I. Population* (Washington: U.S. Government Printing Office, 1931), 18–19.

6. Richman, *California*, 152, 171, 286–87; Cleland, *Cattle*, 75–101; Bancroft, *California*, 251, 493–521; Barrows, "Don Antonio Maria Lugo," *Annals*, III, part 4 (1894), 32.

7. Lúgo, "Life," 236; Guinn, *A History of California and an Extended History of Los Angeles and Environs*, 3 vols. (Los Angeles: Historic Record, 1915), I, 365–66; Layne, "Annals of Los Angeles," *HSSCQ*, XIII (1934), 313; Bancroft, *History*, IV, 629n.

8. "Padron de la Ciudad de Los Angeles y Su Jurisdicción," reprinted in Layne, "First Census," no pp.; Layne, "Annals," 207, 211, 233; Bancroft, *History*, III, 633n, 635–37, 719–20, 766, IV, 633.

9. Bancroft, *History*, IV, 518–19, 557–58; Richman, *California*, 250, 255, 282. Pío Pico to Benjamin D. Wilson, ?, ?, 1846, in Benjamin D. Wilson, "The Narrative of Benjamin D. Wilson (1877);" Cleland, *Pathfinders* (Chicago, San Francisco, Los Angeles: Powell Publishing, 1929), 395; Susanna B. Dakin, *A Scotch Paisano: Hugo Reid's Life in California, 1832–1852, Derived from His Correspondence* (Berkeley and Los Angeles: University of California Press, 1939), 130–31; John D. Tanner, Jr., and Gloria R. Lothrop, "Don Juan Forster, Southern California *Ranchero*," *HSSCQ*, LII (1970), 208–9; Paul W. Gates, "Application of Spanish-Mexican Land Claims," *Huntington Library Quarterly*, XXI (1958), 217.

10. George P. Hammond, ed., *The Larkin Papers*, 10 vols. (Berkeley and Los Angeles: University of California Press, 1953, 1968), IV, 323–24; Marie E. Northrop, "The Los Angeles Padron of 1844," *HSSCQ*, XXXII (1960), 360–422.

11. Daikin, *Scotch*, 76; Robinson, *Life*, 34, 101; Willard, *Herald's*, 171; Layne, "Annals," 314.

12. Marguerite E. Wilbur, ed., *Duflot de Mofras' Travels on the Pacific Coast*, 2 vols. (Santa Ana, Calif.: Fine Arts Press, 1937), I, 184. For biographical data on the fifteen notables see H. D. Barrows, "Abel Stearns," *Annual*, IV, part 4 (1899), 197–99; Robinson, *Ranchos*, 52; Cleland, *Cattle*, 184–85; Marco R. Newmark, "Pioneer Merchants of Los Angeles," *HSSCQ*, XXIV (1942), 77–78,

81; John S. McGroarty, *California of the South: A History*, 5 vols. (Chicago, Indianapolis, Los Angeles: S. J. Clarke, 1933–35), V, 779–86; C. C. Baker, "Don Enrique Dalton of the Azusa," *Annual*, X, part 3 (1917), 16–35; John W. Caughey, "Don Benito Wilson: An Average Southern Californian," *Huntington Library Quarterly*, II (Oct.-July, 1938–39), 296–97; Wilson, "Narrative," 271–72, 383–84, 391; John C. Macfarland, "Don Benito Wilson," *HSSCQ*, XXXI (1929), 273–77; Roscoe P. and Margaret B. Conkling, *The Butterfield Overland Mail, 1857–1869*, 2 vols. (Glendale: Arthur H. Clark, 1947), II, 249; H. D. Barrows, "Don David W. Alexander," *Annual*, IV, part 1 (1897), 43–45; Lillian A. Williamson, "New Light on J. J. Warner," *ibid.*, XIII, part 1 (1924), 5–28; Barrows, "Captain Alexander Bell and the Bell Block," *ibid.*, III, part 3 (1895), 11–17; Barrows, "Memorial Sketch of J. J. Warner," *ibid.*, 23–29; Bancroft, *History*, II, 690, 715, IV, 634n–35n, V, 732–33, 775, 777, 779–81; Laurence L. Hill, *La Reina: Los Angeles in Three Centuries* (Los Angeles: Security-First National Bank, 1929), 20, 23, 25–26, 30, 43; M. R. Newmark, "The Workman Family in Los Angeles," *HSSCQ*, XXXII (1950), 316–18; Layne, "Annals," 210, 213–15, 223–24; Tanner and Lothrop, "Don Juan Forster," 197–98, 206, 208–9, 229–30; Daikin, *Scotch*, 7, 22–23, 61, 64–65, 81, 130–31; McGroarty, ed., *History of Los Angeles County*, 3 vols. (Chicago and New York: American Historical Society, 1923), I, 30–31; McGroarty, *Los Angeles from the Mountains to the Sea* (Chicago and New York: American Historical Society, 1921), 152, 154, 183, 186–87; Iris Higbie Wilson, *William Wolfskill, 1798–1866; Frontier Trapper to California Rancho* (Glendale: Arthur H. Clark, 1965), 19–34, 62, 72, 82, 87, 107, 113, 149, 162, 179, 196–97; McWilliams, *Southern*, 53; Willard, *Herald's*, 158–67; Northrop, "Los Angeles Padron of 1844," 360–422.

13. Northrop, "The Los Angeles Padron of 1844," 360–422; "Register of British and American Residents in California prior to 1840," Daikin, *Scotch*, 201–14; Gunther Barth, *Instant Cities: Urbanization and the Rise of San Francisco and Denver* (New York: Oxford University Press, 1975), 109–10.

14. Wilson, *William Wolfskill*, 87, 147, 149–51, 162; Vincent P. Carosso, *The California Wine Industry: A Study of the Formative Years, 1830–1895* (Berkeley and Los Angeles: University of California Press, 1951), 11–51; Herbert J. Webber and Leon D. Batchelor, eds., *The Citrus Industry*, 2 vols. (Berkeley and Los Angeles: University of California Press, 1943), I, 34–35; Iris Ann Wilson, "Early Southern California Viniculture, 1830–1865," *HSSCQ*, XXIX (1957), 242–50.

15. Speech attributed to Pío Pico, Robinson, *Land*, 59–60.

16. *Fifteenth Census*, I, 18–19; Cleland, *Cattle*, 118, 233; J. M. Guinn, "The Romance of Rancho Realty," *Annual*, VIII, part 3 (1911), 239; Guinn, *History*, I, 253–54.

17. *Alphabetical List of Persons in Division No. 7 of Collection District No. 2 of the State of California, liable to a tax under the Excise laws of the United States and the amount thereof assessed for 1863.* For the Chicago total see p. 492. For Chicago population and assessment figures see p. 453.

18. McGroarty, *History of Los Angeles County*, I, 194; William A. Spalding, *History and Reminiscences of Los Angeles City and County*, 3 vols. (Los Angeles: J. F. Frinnell, 1931), I, 151, 171, 175, 179, 247; Hill, *La Reina*, 47, 59, 68; Remi A. Nadeau, *City Makers* (Garden City, N.Y.: Doubleday, 1948), 98–99;

Boyle Workman, *The City That Grew* (Los Angeles: Southland Publishing, 1936), 115–17, 195; Harris Newmark, *Sixty Years in Southern California, 1853–1913* (New York: Knickerbocker Press, 1916), 427, 446, 519, 532; Cleland and Frank B. Putnam, *Isaias W. Hellman and the Farmers' and Merchants' Bank* (San Marino: Huntington Library, 1965), 15–16.

19. William H. Brewer, *Up and Down California in 1860–1864* (Berkeley and Los Angeles: University of California Press, 1964), 14; Sarah Bixby Smith, *Adobe Days: A Book of Memories* (Cedar Rapids, Iowa: Torch Press, 1925), 127–75; H. Newmark, *Sixty*, 650; Workman, *City*, 30, 50, 114; Jackson A. Graves, *California Memories* (Los Angeles: Times-Mirror Press, 1930), 100.

20. Cleland, *Los Angeles: The Transition Decades, 1850–1870* (San Marino: Huntington Library, 1937), 12; Robinson, *Land*, 1004–107; Cleland: *Cattle*, 87–89, 102–37; *Irvine*, 35–53; Gates "Application," 230–36; Pitt, *Decline*, 83–103, 108–16, 123–24, 127–29, 247–54, 257.

21. Los Angeles *Star*, July 17, 1852, 2; Cleland, *Cattle*, 314.

22. *Southern Vineyard*, Sept. 18, 1858, 2.

23. Layne, "Annals," 349.

24. *Alphabetical List . . . 1863*; Benjamin Hayes, *Pioneer Notes from the Diaries of Judge Benjamin Hayes, 1849–1875* (Los Angeles: privately printed, 1929), 217.

25. For the decline of the rancheros and the loss of their land see Robinson, *Ranchos, passim*; Pitt, *Decline*, 109–16, 146–213, 251–52, 264, 268, 275, 278; Robinson, *Land*, 87; Ella A. Ludwig, *History of the Harbor District of Los Angeles* (Los Angeles: Historic Record, n.d.), 111–12, 117; Harold D. Carew, *History of Pasadena and the San Gabriel Valley, California*, 3 vols. (n.p.: S. J. Clarke Publishing, 1930), I, 216; Ruth Waldo Newhall, *The Newhall Ranch* (San Marino: Huntington Library, 1958), 44–46, 102; McWilliams, *Southern*, 64–66; H. Newmark, *Sixty*, 178, 180, 237; Layne, "First Census," 87; Shochat, "Casa Adobe," 280–83; Gates, "Application," 231–32; Parks, "In Pursuit," 35–39, 41–42, 52–56, 159–69, 181–85, 190; Lúgo, "Life," 236; Robinson: "Story," 302–8; "Rancho Los Palos Verdes," *HSSCQ*, XXXVI (1954), 245–48; Hallock F. Raup, "The Rancho Palos Verdes," *ibid.*, XIX (1937), 13–14, 17. For accounts by contemporary upper-class citizens regarding the disintegration of the rancheros see Bell, *Reminiscences*, 449; Hayes, *Pioneer*, 217; Graves, *My Seventy Years in California* (Los Angeles: Times-Mirror Press, 1927), 138–66.

26. Winfield J. Davis, "Register of State Officers, 1849–1893," *History of Political Conventions of California, 1849–1892* (Sacramento: Publications of the California State Library, 1893), 605–64; Pitt, *Decline*, 132, 134, 136–37, 139–40, 156–57, 241, 269–73; Bancroft, *History*, IV, 288, 644n, 698n, 714n, VII, 253n, 271n, 305n, 319n, 363n, 410n, 422n, 644n, 657n, 698n, 714n; Layne, "Annals," 329–30.

27. Hayes, *Pioneer*, 186; Guinn, "Romance," 236–38.

28. Hayes to B. M. Hughes, Jan. 24, 1853, in Hayes, *Pioneer*, 91; Pitt, *Decline*, 123–24, 133, 202, 241–42, 273–74; Henry Carr, *Los Angeles: City of Dreams* (New York: Grosset and Dunlap, 1955), 137–38.

29. Pitt, *Decline*, 133–34, 136–37, 244, 251–52, 271–73; Margaret Romer, "Pioneer Builders of Los Angeles," *HSSCQ*, XLIII (1961), 102; Marco R. Newmark, "Antonio F. Coronel," *ibid.*, XXXVI (1954), 161–62; Barrows, "Antonio

F. Coronel," *Annual*, V, part 1 (1900), 78–82; M. R. Newmark: *Jottings in Southern California History* (Los Angeles: Ward Ritchie Press, 1955), 75–77, 273; "Pioneer Clubs of Los Angeles Founded during the Nineteenth Century," *HSSCQ*, XXXI (1949), 301–2.

30. Henry W. Splitter, "Education in Los Angeles: 1850–1900," *HSSCQ*, XXXIII (1951), 111–12; Laura C. Cooley, "The Los Angeles Public Library," *ibid.*, XXIII (1941), 6, 8; Barrows, "Juan Bandini," 243–46; Bell, *Reminiscences*, 140, 294; H. Newmark, *Sixty*, 181; "Tom D. Mott," *Annals*, VI, part 2 (1904), 184–86; McGroarty, *History of Los Angeles*, 700–701; Pitt, *Decline*, 124, 224, 267–68.

31. Ygnacio del Valle quoted in Pitt, *Decline*, 141–42; Juan Bandini quoted in Robert M. Fogelson, *The Fragmented Metropolis Los Angeles, 1850–1930* (Cambridge: Harvard University Press, 1967), 5.

32. Los Angeles *Star*, July 15, 1852, 2; *Southern Vineyard*, Sept. 18, 1858, 2. For the 1863 top income earners see *Alphabetical*, n.p.

33. Daikin, *Scotch*, 190; Baker, "Don Henrique Dalton," 16–35; Cleland, *Cattle*, 119–21, 184–98, 224–25; Spalding, *History*, I, 146–47, 167, 185, 198; Robinson, *Land*, 240; Layne, "Annals," 325–26, 344; Wilson, *William Wolfskill*, 149–51, 153, 157–58, 163, 175–76, 197–207, 210, 217; Newhall, *Newhall*, 44–46, 102; Robinson, *Ranchos*, 186–98; Cleland, *Irvine*, 43, 53; Carosso, *California*, 11–13; Pitt, *Decline*, 110–16; Macfarland, "Don Benito Wilson," 289; Caughey, "Don Benito Wilson," 286–92, 298; Maymie Krythe, *Port Admiral: Phineas Banning, 1830–1885* (San Francisco: California Historical Society, 1957), 35, 39, 133–34, 165–67, 173, 175, 185, 187–88, 198–201, 204–5; Barrows, "Don David Alexander," 43–45; Hill, *La Reina*, 25; M. R. Newmark, "Workman," 316–18; Nadeau, *City-Makers*, 48–50, 123–24, 132–33, 174–88; McGroarty, *Los Angeles*, 917–24.

34. H. Newmark, *Sixty*, 328–29; Barrows, "Abel Stearns," 197–99; Cleland: *Cattle*, 198–200; *Los Angeles*, 21–22; M. R. Newmark, "Workman," 317; Parks, "Pursuit," 144–57.

35. Davis, "Register," 605–64; Bancroft, *History*, VI, 644n, 657n, 698n, 714n, VII, 271n, 305n; M. R. Newmark, "Pioneer," 54–65; Wilson, *Wolfskill*, 192, 210–11.

36. Robinson, *Land*, 240; Krythe, *Port*, 48, 173, 185, 198–201, 204–5; Splitter, "Education," 104, 107; Workman, *City*, 234; William W. Ferrier, *Ninety Years of Education in California, 1846–1936* (Berkeley: Sather Gate Book Shop, 1937), 154, 258; Carr, *Los Angeles*, 120, 376; Cooley, "Los Angeles," 6; Guinn, *History*, I, 420; Manuel P. Servin and Iris Higbie Wilson, *Southern California and Its University: A History of the University of Southern California, 1880–1964* (Los Angeles: Ward Ritchie Press, 1969), 8; S. H. Hall, "The Historical Society of Southern California," *Annual*, IX, part I (1912), 13; Franklin Walker, *A Literary History of Southern California* (Berkeley and Los Angeles: University of California Press, 1950), 74–75; Caughey, "Don Benito Wilson," 298, 300.

37. Cleland, *Cattle*, 197–98; Splitter, "Education," 111–12; *Historical Review of the Freemasons of Los Angeles, Los Angeles Lodge, Number 42* (Los Angeles: Lodge No. 42, 1929), 51–77, 89–92; Maymie R. Krythe, "Daily Life in Early Los Angeles," *HSSCQ*, XXXVI (1954), 36–38, 229; Gwinn, *History*, I, 366.

38. The sources for upper-class Los Angeles are biographical articles in the *HSSCQ* and *Annual*; M. R. Newmark, "Historical Profiles," *HSSCQ*, XXXVII

(1955), 69–96, 177–87, 288–94, 357–74; Romer, "Pioneer," 97–103, 342–49; M. R. Newmark, *Jottings*; Hill, *La Reina*; McGroarty: *California*, III-V; *Los Angeles*, II-III; Bancroft, *History*, III-VII; Spalding, *History*, II-III; H. Newmark, *Sixty*; Nadeau, *City-Makers*; Willard, *History of the Chamber of Commerce*; W. W. Robinson, *Lawyers of Los Angeles: A History of the Los Angeles Bar Association and of the Bar of Los Angeles County* (Los Angeles: Ward-Ritchie Press, 1959); *Men of Achievement in the Great Southwest: A Story of Pioneer Struggles during Early Days in Los Angeles and Southern California* (Los Angeles: Los Angeles Times, 1904); Graves, *My*, 246–48; Alonzo Phelps, *Contemporary Biography of California's Representative Men* (San Francisco: A. L. Bancroft, 1882); Max Vorspan and Lloyd P. Gartner, *History of the Jews of Los Angeles* (San Marino: Huntington Library, 1970); Ira B. Cross, *Financing an Empire: History of Banking in California*, 4 vols. (Chicago, San Francisco, Los Angeles: S. J. Clarke, 1927), II-III; George L. Cole, *Medical Associates of My Early Days in Los Angeles* (Los Angeles: privately printed, 1930); Willoughby Rodman, *History of the Bench and Bar of Southern California* (Los Angeles: William J. Porter, 1909), 121ff.; Joseph C. Bates, *History of the Bench and Bar of California* (San Francisco: Bench and Bar Publishing, 1912).

39. Barth, *Instant*, 168–69, 173–74.

40. *Fifteenth Census*, 18–19.

41. Vorspan and Gartner, *History*, 32.

42. Fogelson, *Fragmented*, 80–81.

43. James R. Page, *I. N. Van Nuys: 1835–1912* (Los Angeles: Ward-Ritchie Press, 1944), 29–30; Graves, *California*, 89; Krythe, *Port*, 41ff., 133–34; McGroarty, *History*, III, 394–96; H. Newmark, *Sixty*, 280.

44. Fogelson, *Fragmented*, 56, 109; Glenn E. McLaughlin, *Growth of American Manufacturing Areas* (Pittsburgh: University of Pittsburgh Press, 1938), 160–61; Arthur G. Coons and Arjay R. Miller, *An Economic and Industrial Survey of the Los Angeles and San Diego Areas* (Sacramento: California State Planning Board, 1941), xiii.

45. L. J. Rose, Jr., *L. J. Rose of Sunny Slope* (San Marino: Huntington Library, 1959), 1–2, 67–68, 105; Smith, *Adobe*, 68–69; Graves, *My*, 406; Wilson, *William Wolfskill*, 110, 147–62, 197–205; Krythe, *Port*, 175; Cleveland E. Kindall, "Southern Vineyards," *HSSCQ*, XXXI (1959), 34–35; McGroarty, ed., *History*, I, 31–32, 197, II, 13–15, III, 394–96; Robinson: "Story," 306–8; "Rancho," 247–48; Cleland and Osgood Hardy, *March of Industry* (Los Angeles: Powell Publishing, 1929), 48, 82, 121–22; Rahno M. MacCurdy, *The History of the California Fruit Growers' Exchange* (Los Angeles: n.p., 1925), 4; Carosso, *California*, 7–8, 13–15, 22–23, 75, 85; H. Newmark, *Sixty*, 197–202, 381–82; Page, *I. N. Van Nuys*, 7–8, 14–15, 23; Barrows, "Andrew Boyle," *Annual*, V, part 3 (1902), 241–44; M. R. Newmark, "Historical," 91–93; John S. Hittell, *The Commerce and Industries of the Pacific Coast of North America* (San Francisco: A. L. Bancroft, 1882), 237; Webber and Batchelor, *Citrus*, 35.

46. Nadeau, *City*, 53, 60, 70, 221–22; Cleland, *Cattle*, 173; I. W. Hellman quoted in Vorspan and Gartner, *History*, 45.

47. Hill, *La Reina*, 43; Robinson, *Land*, 242.

48. Robinson, *Land*, 240.

49. Romer, "Pioneer," 101–2, 344; Robinson, *Lawyers*, 64–65; Earl Pomeroy,

The Pacific Slope (New York: Alfred A. Knopf, 1965), 140; M. R. Newmark, "Two Community Builders of Los Angeles," *HSSCQ*, XXXIII (1951), 135–46; Spalding, *History*, I, 208–9; Nadeau, *City*, 12–14, 44–47, 66–67, 123–33, 183–88; Nadeau, *Los Angeles*, 59; Carew, *History of Pasadena*, I, 270, 283, 292, 295, 316–20; Page, *I. N. Van Nuys*, 9–10, 13–15, 18, 23, 29–30; M. R. Newmark, "Historical," *HSSCQ*, XXXVIII (1956), 91–93; H. Newmark, *Sixty*, 302, 381–82; Smith, *Adobe*, 68–69; Robinson, *Land*, 240; Robinson, *Ranchos*, *passim*; Parks, "In Pursuit," *passim*; Krythe, "First Hotel of Los Angeles," *HSSCQ*, XXXIII (1951), 332.

50. H. Newmark, *Sixty*, 65; 81.

51. For memoirs of mercantile activity in early Los Angeles see H. Newmark, *Sixty*, *passim*; Barrows, "Reminiscences of Los Angeles in the 'Fifties and Early 'Sixties," *Annual*, III, part I (1893), 58, 60; Graves, *My*, 22, 89, 246. The best secondary accounts are Laura E. King, "Stores of Los Angeles," *Annual*, V, part 1 (1900), 5–8; Ana Begue Packman, "Landmarks and Pioneers of Los Angeles in 1853," *HSSCQ*, XXVI (1944), 88–91; Vorspan and Gartner, *History*, 8, 34–37, 75; M. R. Newmark, "Pioneer," *passim*.

52. Vorspan and Gartner, *History*, 34–36; Barth, *Instant*, 72–73; Peter R. Decker, *Fortunes and Failures: White-Collar Mobility in Nineteenth-Century San Francisco* (Cambridge: Harvard University Press, 1978), 81–83, 115–18, 238–39.

53. Table 7 is derived from McLaughlin, *Growth*, 160–61, 181.

54. Cross, *Financial*, III, 523–25; Page, *I. N. Van Nuys*, 30; Carosso, *California*, 7–8, 10, 11–15; H. Newmark, *Sixty*, 346; Krythe, *Port*, 133–34; Gerald T. White, *Formative Years in the Far West: A History of the Standard Oil Company of California and Predecessors through 1919* (New York: Appleton-Century-Crofts, 1962), 5–35, 45, 82; Nadeau, *City*, 31–35, 42, 88, 119–20; Spalding, *History*, I, 255–56.

55. McGroarty, *History*, II, 233–34; Spalding, *History*, III, 570–72; John E. Bauer, "John Goller, Pioneer Angeleno Manufacturer," *HSSCQ*, XXXVI (1954), 14–28.

56. H. Newmark, *Sixty*, 365–66; Vincent Ostrom, *Water & Politics: A Study of Water Policies and Administration in the Development of Los Angeles* (Los Angeles: Haynes Foundation, 1953), 40–45; Nadeau, *The Water Seekers* (Garden City, N.Y.: Country Life Press, 1950), 14–15; Workman, *City*, 84–89, 202–3; Graves, *My*, 249; Romer, "Pioneer," 101–2; Cross, *Financial*, III, 513–15.

57. Nadeau, *City*, 123–24; H. Newmark, *Sixty*, 460–62; Spalding, *History*, I, 208–9, II, 76–80; Glenn S. Dumke, "Early Interurban Transportation in the Los Angeles Area," *HSSCQ*, XXXII (1950), 319–20; Workman, *City*, 150–51, 182–83.

58. Cleland, "Transportation in California before the Railroads, with Special Reference to Los Angeles," *Annual*, XI, part 1 (1918), 61–67; Oscar Osburn Winther, *Via Western Express & Stagecoach* (Palo Alto: Stanford University Press, 1947), 10; Vernette S. Ripley, "The San Fernando Pass and the Pioneer Traffic That Went over It," *HSSCQ*, XXIX (1947), 9; Nadeau, *City*, 38–39; Spalding, *History*, I, 255–56; H. Newmark, *Sixty*, 343–44; M. R. Newmark: "Phineas Banning: Intrepid Pioneer," *HSSCQ*, XXXV (1953), 265–66; *Jottings*, 93–98; Krythe, *Port*, 3–10, 25–26, 47, 52–54, 61–68, 82, 157–58.

59. Krythe, *Port*, 25–26, 39, 47–48, 66, 81, 91–95, 109–10, 158–59, 180–81, 193–94, 198–201, 204–5; M. R. Newmark, "Phineas Banning," 270; H. Newmark, *Sixty*, 449–50; Clarence H. Matson, *Building a World Gateway: The Story of Los Angeles Harbor* (Los Angeles: Pacific Era Publishers, 1945), 24, 33, 42–43; Charles Dwight Willard, *The Free Harbor Contest at Los Angeles* (Los Angeles: Kingsley-Barnes & Neuner, 1899), 24, 38; A. T. Hawley, *Condition, Progress and Advantages of Los Angeles City and County, Southern California* (Los Angeles: Los Angeles Mirror Printing, 1876), 27.

60. Hawley, *Condition*, 27.

61. Nadeau: *Los Angeles*, 64–65; *City*, 26–29; M. R. Newmark, "Phineas Banning," 269; J. M. Guinn, "Pioneer Railroads of Southern California," *Annual*, VIII, part 3 (1911), 188; Stuart Daggett, *Chapters on the History of the Southern Pacific* (New York: Ronald Press, 1922), 128.

62. Krythe, *Port*, 174, 187–92, 195, 201, 214; Nadeau: *Los Angeles*, 66–67; *City*, 174–88; Vorspan and Gartner, *History*, 40; Workman, *City*, 159–60; Frank B. Putnam, "Serape to Levi," *HSSCQ*, XXXVIII (1956), 213–18; H. Newmark, *Sixty*, 440–42, 502–3; Daggett, *Chapters*, 128–29.

63. R. M. Widney, "Los Angeles Subsidy: Which Subsidy Shall I Vote For, or Shall I Vote against Both? Discussed from a Business Standpoint for the Business Community," originally published in 1872 and reprinted in *HSSCQ*, XXXVIII (1956), 347–62; Putnam, "Serape," 223; Guinn, *History*, I, 255; Nadeau, *City*, 123; Webber and Batchelor, *Citrus*, 39.

64. Downey, "The Banking System of Los Angeles," in Hawley, *Condition*, 97–98; Newmark, *Sixty*, 130–31, 346; Krythe, *Port*, 80, 116, 122; Cross, *Financing*, II, 530, 532–37; Cleland, *Cattle*, 115–16, 220–22; Cleland and Hardy, *March*, 231–32.

65. Downey, "Banking," 99–100; Nadeau, *City*, 46–47; Cleland and Hardy, *March*, 231–32; Graves, *My*, 316–20; H. Newmark, *Sixty*, 433; Workman, *City*, 153–57; Cleland and Putnam, *Isaias W. Hellman*, 15–30, 45; Cross, *Financial*, II, 537–46, 549–53; Vorspan and Gartner, *History*, 123; Willard, *History*, 255.

66. H. Newmark, *Sixty*, 346; Los Angeles *Star*, Aug. 8, 1868, 3; cf. Los Angeles *News*, June 2, 1868, quoted in Frank B. Putnam, "Pico's Building: Its Genealogy and Biography," *HSSCQ*, XXIX (1957), 77.

67. Cleland and Putnam, *Isaias W. Hellman*, 17.

68. Downey and Hellman notice in the Los Angeles *News*, Apr. 2, 1871, quoted in *ibid.*, 29; Los Angeles *Star*, Apr. 19, 1871, 3.

69. Downey, "Banking," 99; Workman, *City*, 153–55; Cross, *Financial*, II, 545, 553–54; Nadeau, *City*, 210–15; Cleland and Putnam, *Isaias W. Hellman*, 18, 35, 41–42, 45–46, 115, 119; Vorspan and Gartner, *History*, 123.

70. Davis, *History*, 605–74; McGroarty, *History*, I, 17–18; M. R. Newmark, "Pioneer," 64–65.

71. Vorspan and Gartner, *History*, 17–18.

72. Graves, *My*, 251, 256; H. Newmark, *Sixty*, 191, 323–24; Edith Dobie, *The Political Career of Stephen Mallory White* (Palo Alto: Stanford University Press, 1927), 75–77; Putnam, "Pico's," 78–79.

73. Bell, *Reminiscences, passim*; Layne, "Annals," 329–30; Krythe, "The First Hotel of Los Angeles," *HSSCQ*, XXXIII (1951), 54; Barth, *Instant*, 112, 118–20, 166–68, 203–4; Decker, *Fortunes*, 108–11, 120–43.

74. H. Newmark, *Sixty*, 446; Jacob Kuhrts, "Reminiscences of a Pioneer," reprinted in McGroarty, *California*, V, 100.

75. Barth, *Instant*, 156–68.

76. Gerald D. Nash, *State Government and Economic Development: A History of the Administrative Policies in California, 1849–1933* (Berkeley and Los Angeles: University of California Press, 1964), 45–46, 70–71, 120, 127–35, 210–12; William C. Fankhauser. *A Financial History of California* (Berkeley and Los Angeles: University of California Press, 1913), 186–87, 190–91.

77. Phineas Banning to Benjamin D. Wilson, Dec. 17, 1865, and Jan. 22, 1866, in Krythe, *Port*, 147–48, 177.

78. Ostrom, *Water*, 48; M. R. Newmark, "Pioneers," 5.

79. Robinson, *Lawyers*, 34–37, 47–48, 62–64; McGroarty, *California*, IV, 247–48; Marshall Stimson, "The Organized Bar in Los Angeles," *HSSCQ*, XXXIII (1951), 120.

80. Henry W. O'Melveny quoted in Robinson, *Lawyers*, 46–47; Harvey K. S. O'Melveny quoted on 69.

81. *Ibid.*, 46–47, 63–64; H. Newmark, *Sixty*, 51, 53; M. R. Newmark, "The Early Los Angeles Bench and Bar," *HSSCQ*, XXXIV (1952), 333; H. W. O'Melveny quoted in Robinson, *Lawyers*, 47.

82. Robinson, *Lawyers*, 51–53, 237; McGroarty, *California*, V, 355–58; Oscar T. Shuck, ed., *The History of the Bench and Bar of California* (Los Angeles: Commercial Printing House, 1901), 867–68.

83. H. Newmark, *Sixty*, 4–6, 34, 44–45, 50–51, 54–55; Graves, *My*, 113, 132, 406; Robinson, *Lawyers*, 33–34; Stimson, "Organized," 120; M. R. Newmark, "Early," 334; *Alphabetical*, n.p.

84. H. Newmark, *Sixty*, 55–57; Spalding, *History*, II, 65–70; McGroarty, *California*, V, 355–58; Shuck, ed., *History*, 657, 713–14, 841–42, 867–68.

85. M. R. Newmark, "Early," 328, 330–46; Robinson, *Lawyers*, 224, 318–25, 334–35.

86. H. D. Barrows, "Pioneer Physicians of Los Angeles," *Annual*, V, part 2 (1901), 106–8; *Alphabetical*, n.p.; M. R. Newmark, "Historical," 292–94, 361–62; McGroarty, *Los Angeles*, 603–4; Cole, *Medical*, 3–7, 13–16, 21–24, 50–53; George H. Kress, *History of the Medical Profession of Southern California* (Los Angeles: Times-Mirror Press, 1910), 19–21, 23–24, 153–54; M. R. Newmark, "The Medical Profession in the Early Days of Los Angeles," *HSSCQ*, XXXIV (1952), 75.

87. Henry Harris, *California's Medical Story* (San Francisco: J. W. Stacey, 1932), 146–47, 156, 218–21, 233, 264–319; M. R. Newmark, "Medical," 75–76; John W. Shuman, "California Medicine (A Review)," *New York Medical Journal and Records*, CXXXII (1930), 503; CXXXIII (1931), 38; Kress, *History*, 32–56.

88. Hill, *La Reina*, 47, 68; Cleland and Putnam, *Isaias W. Hellman*, 3, 7; Arthur Chapman, "Gifts Made to the City of Los Angeles by Individuals," *Annual*, X, parts 1–2 (1915–16), 71; J. M. Guinn, "The True History of Central Park," *Annual*, VIII, part 3 (1911), 214–15; Walker, *Literary*, 75–76, 93; Willard, *Los Angeles*, 292; M. R. Newmark, *Jottings*, 98–100; Ralph J. Roske, *Everyman's Eden, a History of California* (New York: Macmillan, 1968), 335–36, 339, 426, 433.

89. Newmark, *Sixty*, 189–90; Pitt, *Decline*, 224; *Historical*, 33–37, 41–47,

51–71, 101–29; Vorspan and Gartner, *History*, 20–22, 63–64, 80; M. R. Newmark, *Jottings*, 79; Workman, *City*, 59.

90. Barth, *Instant*, 180–81.

91. Decker, *Fortunes*, 139–43, for San Francisco.

92. Splitter, "Education," 104, 111–12, 232–38; Guinn: *History*, I, 380–83; "Pioneer School Superintendents of Los Angeles," *Annual*, IV, part 1 (1897), 76–81; "The Beginnings of the School System of Los Angeles," *ibid.*, VIII, part 3 (1911), 195–207; H. D. Barrow, "Pioneer Schools of Los Angeles," *ibid.*, parts 1–2 (1909–10), 62; Roy W. Cloud, *Education in California* (Palo Alto: Stanford University Press, 1952), 31–32; H. Newmark, *Sixty*, 105–6, 419; M. R. Newmark, *Jottings*, 98–101; Workman, *City*, 168; Ferrier, *Ninety*, 78, 168, 175.

93. Splitter, "Education," 113; Ferrier, *Ninety*. 259–60, 262; Vorspan and Gartner, *History*, 67–68; Workman, *City*, 79, 176, 186–87; Servin and Wilson, *Southern*, 5–6; G. S. Dumke, *The Boom of the Eighties in Southern California* (San Marino: Huntington Library, 1944), 246; Walker, *Literary*, 161.

94. H. Newmark, *Sixty*, 443–44; Cooley, "Los Angeles," 6, 8, 13; Faith H. Hyers, "A Brief History of the Los Angeles Public Library," *Forty-eighth Annual Report of the Board of Library Commissioners of the Los Angeles Public Library for the Year Ending June 30, 1936* (Los Angeles: n.p., 1936), 30–31, 35; Workman, *City*, 234; Guinn, *History*, I, 420–21.

95. Walker, *Literary*, 74–75; Chapman, "Gifts," 71; Guinn, "True," 214–15; Spalding, *History*, I, 222–26.

96. Walker, *Literary*, 75–76, 78.

97. Splitter, "Art in Los Angeles before 1900," *HSSCQ*, XXXXI (1959), 48; Carr, *Los Angeles*, 113.

98. Decker, *Fortunes*, 48–49, 61, 107, 203–6, 215–29, 231–32, for the behavior of elite San Francisco.

99. Spalding, *History*, III, 499–502, 592–95; McGroarty, *Los Angeles*, 3–8; H. Newmark, *Sixty*, 183; McGroarty, *California*, V, 247–48, 355–58; Robinson, *Lawyers*, 45; Bell, *Reminiscences*, 294.

100. Kuhrts, "Reminiscences," 99; Rose, *L. J. Rose*, 70; Nadeau, *City*, 46; Krythe, "Daily," 36–38; H. Newmark, *Sixty*, 39, 183, 400, 427; Workman, *City*, 170–71.

101. Workman, *City*, 118–19.

102. *Ibid.*, 176; H. Newmark, *Sixty*, 356; Samuel L. Kreider, "Volney Erskine Howard: California Pioneer," *HSSCQ*, XXXI (1949), 127; Vorspan and Gartner, *History*, 67–68.

103. H. Newmark, *Sixty*, 383, 400, 427; Vorspan and Gartner, *History*, 65–66; M. R. Newmark, "Pioneer Clubs of Los Angeles Founded during the Nineteenth Century," *HSSCQ*, XXXI (1949), 306–8; Jane E. Collier, "Early Club Life in Los Angeles," *Annual*, IV, part 4 (1899), 216–20. For San Francisco see Decker, *Fortunes*, 232.

104. Barth, *Instant*, 171–73.

105. Smith, *Adobe*, 127–75; H. Newmark, *Sixty*, 184–85; Graves: *My*, 437–38; cf. *California*, 6, 100.

106. Barth, *Instant*, 173.

107. Workman, *City*, 114; Hayes to Hughes, Jan. 24, 1853, in Hayes, *Pioneer*, 91.

108. Smith, *Adobe*, 154–55, 207–8; Workman, *City*, 5.

109. *Fifteenth Census*, 10–12; Fogelson, *Fragmented*, 81; McWilliams, *Southern California*, 127–30, 161.

110. McWilliams, *Southern California*, 127–28, 157; Willard, *Los Angeles*, 341.

111. H. Newmark, *Sixty*, 519, 531, 537, 589, 626, 647; Workman, *City*, 192, 367–68; Guinn, *History*, I, 430; Roske, *Everyman's*, 426, 437; McGroarty, ed., *History*, I, 203, 205, 212; H. Splitter: "Music in Los Angeles," *HSSCQ*, XXXVIII (1956), 315, 320–21, 332; "Art," 118, 135–36. For innovations in San Francisco see Barth, *Instant*, 222.

112. McLaughlin, *Growth*, 158–61; Coons and Miller, *Economic*, 23; Philip Neff, Lisette C. Baum, and Grace E. Heilman, *Production Cost Trends in Selected Industrial Areas* (Berkeley and Los Angeles: University of California Press, 1948), 16; Matson, *Building*, 12; Cross, *Financing*, II, 617, 704–5; Guinn, *History*, I, 253–55, 315, 375.

113. Note 38 for biographical sources. Fogelson, *Fragmented*, 80–81.

114. Decker, *Fortunes*, 167–69, 178–86, 231–33, 240–41, for San Francisco.

115. *Ibid.*, 52–53, for San Francisco.

116. Coons and Miller, *Economic*, xiii, 21–22; Walter Lindley and J. P. Widney, *California of the South* (New York: D. Appleton, 1888), 114–15; MacCurdy, *History*, 10–11, 14–15, 65; Willard, *History of the Chamber of Commerce*, 117–25; Carosso, *California*, 79–85, 150–51.

117. G. S. Dumke, "Advertising Southern California before the Boom of 1887," *HSSCQ*, XXIV (1942), 22–23; McWilliams, *Southern*, 125–29; Willard, *History*, 15–16, 76–77, 145–68.

118. Lindley and Widney, *California*, 113; Spalding, *History*, I, 286; Willard: *Los Angeles*, 331–33, *History*, 44; Dumke, *Boom*, 43, 55, 206–15, 259–68; Cross, *Financing*, II, 562–63; Vorspan and Gartner, *History*, 73; McWilliams, *Southern*, 121.

119. McWilliams, *Southern*, 129–30, 133; Spalding, *History*, I, 286–87, 319; Nadeau, *Los Angeles*, 108–17; Isaac F. Marcosson, *A Little Known Master of Millions* (Boston: E. H. Rollins & Sons, 1914), 8, 22–23.

120. McWilliams, *Southern*, 187–91; Robinson, "The Rancho Story of San Fernando Valley," *HSSCQ*, XXXVIII (1956), 232–33; J. Benton Van Nuys, "My Memories of San Fernando Valley," *ibid.*, 237–38; Nadeau, *Water*, 21–63; Page, *I. N. Van Nuys*, 30; Robinson, *Ranchos*, 94–95.

121. Lindley and Widney, *California*, 113; Marvel M. Stockwell, *Studies in California State Taxation, 1910–1935* (Berkeley and Los Angeles: University of California Press, 1939), 1–4. For the history of real estate operations between 1885–1915 see Workman, *City*, 198–99, 266–67; H. Newmark, *Sixty*, 474, 534–35, 555, 558–59, 561–62; Graves, *California*, 22–24; Carew, *History*, I, 320, 405–9; Robinson, *Ranchos*, *passim*; Edwin O. Palmer, *History of Hollywood* (Los Angeles: Edward O. Palmer, 1938), 83, 113–19; McWilliams, *Southern*, 127–30, 133–34, 154–61, 187–91; Dumke, *Boom*, *passim*; Nadeau, *Los Angeles*, 75–77, 108–17, 144–48.

122. M. R. Newmark, "Pioneer," 38–39; Vorspan and Gartner, *History*, 76; Workman, *City*, 184–85; Willard, *History*, 275; William H. B. Kilner, *Arthur Letts: A Biography* (Los Angeles: Young & McAllister, 1927), *passim*.

123. McLaughlin, *Growth*, 86, 100–103, 136–39, 152, 158–63, 181, 187, 212–14; Coons and Miller, *Economic*, xiii, 23–24; Frank L. Kidner and Philip Neff, *An Economic Survey of the Los Angeles Area* (Los Angeles: Haynes Foundation, 1945), 10–14; Neff, Baum and Heilman, *Production*, 16; Kidner, *California Business Cycles* (Berkeley and Los Angeles: University of California Press, 1946), 27–29.

124. John B. Miller quoted in B. C. Forbes, *Men Who Are Making the West* (New York: B. C. Forbes Publishing, 1923), 58; Kidner, *California*, 27–29; Fogelson, *Fragmented*, 120–21, H. S. McKee quoted on 123.

125. McGroarty: *Los Angeles*, 26–29; *California*, III, 49–52.

126. McGroarty, *California*, IV, 431–35; White, *Formative*, 126–27, 132–34, 152, 213, 230–33; Spalding, *History*, III, 42–45, 66; Joseph S. Bain, *The Economics of the Pacific Coast Petroleum Industry*, 3 vols. (Berkeley and Los Angeles, University of California Press, 1944–47), III, 5; Matson, *Building*, 147–49; *Men*, 134, 140–41; Cleland and Hardy, *March*, 179–80; McGroarty, *Los Angeles*, 34, 512, 872–73, 880–83, 925.

127. Workman, *City*, 230; M. R. Newmark, "Workman," 219; Spalding, *History*, III, 76–80; McGroarty, *Los Angeles*, 3–8; Dumke, "The Career of James F. Crank: A Chapter in the History of Western Transportation," *Huntington Library Quarterly*, VI (1943), 314–19; Willard, *History*, 21.

128. Willard: *Free*, 24, 38, 45–46, 57, 69, 95–96, 99, 104, 109, 111–19, 125, 127, 152–60, 165–66, 208–10, *History*, 126–42; *Los Angeles*, 351; H. Newmark, *Sixty*, 638, 642; Workman, *City*, 275, 283; Matson, *Building*, 56–57, 65; Marshall Stimson, "A Short History of Los Angeles Harbor," *HSSCQ*, XXVII (1945), 7–15.

129. Spencer Crump, *Ride the Big Red Cars* (Los Angeles: Crest Publications, 1962), 17–18, 95–96, 105–6; Spalding, *History*, I, 313.

130. Dumke, "Early," 131–35, 138–43; Palmer, *History*, 77; Dumke, "James F. Crank," 319–22; Workman, *City*, 266–67; H. Newmark, *Sixty*, 567, 612–13; Spalding, *History*, I, 281–87, 319; Willard, *History*, 318; Graves, *My*, 250; Crump, *Ride*, 40–41, 45, 51, 63, 66, 71–75, 88–91, 101–3; Marcosson, *Little*, 19–23; Dumke, "Early," 132–35, 138–43; Nadeau, *Los Angeles*, 108–17; George W. Hilton and John F. Due, *The Electric Interurban Railways in America* (Palo Alto: Stanford University Press, 1960), 406–13; Matson, *Building*, 50–51, 88–89, 133.

131. Crump, *Ride*, 71–75.

132. Spalding, *History*, I, 170, II, 138–42; Workman, *City*, 202–3; Stuart O'Melveny, *It's Best to Divide with Our Friends* (Los Angeles: Anderson, Ritchie & Simon, 1955), 8–9; Graves, *My*, 249; Marcosson, *Little*, 24–25; Crouch and Dinerman, *Southern*, 38–43; Crump, *Ride*, 66; Willard, *History*, 262.

133. Ostrom, *Water*, 11–14, 54–59, 80–83; Crump, *Ride*, 115–16; McGroarty: *History*, III, 482–85; *Los Angeles*, II, 308; Spalding, *History*, II, 76–80.

134. Ostrom, *Water*, 148–59.

135. *Ibid.*, 50–59, 80–84.

136. Cross, *Financing*, II, 570–71; Miller quoted in Forbes, *Men*, 58.

137. Leroy Armstrong and J. O. Denny, *Financial California* (Los Angeles: Coast Banker Publishing, 1916), 30; Cross, *Financing*, II, 559, 803–5, 810, 814;

Crouch and Dinerman, *Southern*, 92; Cleland and Putnam, *Isaias W. Hellman*, 56–57.

138. Cross, *Financing*, II, 49, 814.

139. *Ibid.*, 55, 605–6, 756–57, 935–52; Graves, *My*, 320–25.

140. Dumke, "Career," 314–19; Cleland and Putnam, *Isaias W. Hellman*, 55.

141. Graves, *My*, 318; Cleland and Putnam, *Isaias W. Hellman*, 49, 55, 75–76, 107; Cross, *Financing*, II, 514–16, 560–61, 566, 570, 605–6, 685; Vorspan and Gartner, *History*, 123; Armstrong and Denny, *Financial*, 99.

142. Cleland and Putnam, *Isaias W. Hellman*, 55, 59–63, 70, 73, 82–83, 93, 101, 108–15, 119; Vorspan and Gartner, *History*, 123.

143. Cleland and Putnam, *Isaias W. Hellman*, 55; Cross, *Financing*, II, 570, 689.

144. Cleland and Putnam, *Isaias W. Hellman*, 89; for Bonebrake and other examples see Cross, *Financing*, II, 560, II and III *passim*.

145. Workman, *City*, 353; Cross, *Financing*, II, 567, 655, 753, III, 354, 513–14. For Stoddard Jess see II, 551–52; for other professional bankers see II, III, *passim*.

146. Cross, *Financing*, II, 550–51, III, 330–33; for biographies of major Los Angeles bankers see II, III, *passim*.

147. H. Newmark, *Sixty*, 537; Guinn, *History*, I, 430.

148. Willard, *History*, II, 15–16, 59, 67, 69, 76–77, 117–69, 185–94, 207–27; H. Newmark, *Sixty*, 589; Guinn, *History*, I, 432–35; M. R. Newmark, "Short," 61–75; Hill, *La Reina*, 80–81, 92–95; "Chamber of Commerce Milestones," *HSSCQ*, XXX (1948), 205–7.

149. Louis B. and Richard S. Perry, *A History of the Los Angeles Labor Movement, 1911–1941* (Berkeley and Los Angeles: University of California Press, 1963), 21, 24–25, 135–36; Grace H. Stimson, *Rise of the Labor Movement in Los Angeles* (Berkeley and Los Angeles: University of California Press, 1955), 255; Guinn, *History*, I, 435–36; George L. Mowry, *The California Progressives* (Chicago: Quadrangle Books, 1963), 48–49; Ira B. Cross, *A History of the Labor Movement in California* (Berkeley and Los Angeles: University of California Press, 1935), 10–288.

150. H. Newmark, *Sixty*, 650–51; Miller quoted in Forbes, *Men*, 67–68; Huntington quoted in Crump, *Ride*, 15, 52; Hellman quoted in Vorspan and Gartner, *History*, 45, 71; Graves, *California*, 109; Arthur Letts to J. P. Logan & Sons, Apr. 25, 1906, in Kilner, *Arthur Letts*, 119; Willard, *Free*, 16–17; Lindley and Widney, *California*, *passim*; Los Angeles *Times*, Apr. 8, 1894, p. 3.

151. Lindley and Widney, *California*, *passim*; Hellman quoted in Vorspan and Gartner, *History*, 45, 71.

152. H. Newmark, *Sixty*, 650; Miller quoted in Forbes, *Men*, 67–68.

153. Los Angeles *Times*, Apr. 8, 1894, p. 3; Willard, *Free*, 16–17.

154. I. W. Hellman quoted in Vorspan and Gartner, *History*, 71; H. Newmark, *Sixty*, 650; Henry M. Robinson quoted in Forbes, *Men*, 280; Graves, *California*, 321.

155. A. Letts quoted in Kilner, *Arthur Letts*, 161; cf. 134, 160; Huntington quoted in Marcosson, *Little*, 29; Edward L. Doheny quoted in Forbes, *Men*, 100, 117–18; Norman Bridge, *The Rewards of Taste and Other Essays* (New York and Chicago: Herbert S. Stone, 1902), 3; Graves, *California*, 113; cf. 119, 144.

156. E. L. Dohney quoted in Forbes, *Men*, 99–100; Bridge, *Rewards*, 5; Graves, *California*, 117, 144; Joseph P. Widney, *Race Life of the Aryan Peoples*, 2 vols. (New York: Funk & Wagnalls, 1907), II, 309.

157. Davis, *History*, 605–74; M. R. Newmark: "Pioneer," 64–65; "Workman," 319, 322–23; McGroarty, *History*, I, 17.

158. M. R. Newmark, "Bench," 333–46; Davis, *History*, 605–74; McGroarty: *History*, I, 17; *Los Angeles*, 898–99; Spalding, *History*, II, 102–3, III, 69–71; Shuck, ed., *History*, 619–20, 642–46, 867–88; Robinson, *Lawyers*, 49–52.

159. Graves, *My*, 251.

160. Frederick L. Bird and Frances M. Ryan, *The Recall of Public Officers: A Study of the Operation of the Recall in California* (New York: Macmillan, 1930), 227–28, 233–34; Mowry, *California*, 38–39.

161. Dobie, *Political*, 75–76, 93–95, 167, 174–84, 223, 226–28; *Stephen M. White, Californian, Lawyer, Senator: His Life and His Work*, compiled by Leroy E. Mosher, 2 vols. (Los Angeles: Times-Mirror, 1903), I, 323–86.

162. Kilner, *Arthur Letts*, 129–30; Crump, *Ride*, 128–30; Nadeau, *Los Angeles*, 123–44; Graves: *My*, 249–50; *California*, 33–35; Perry and Perry, *History*, 24–25, 53, 70–93, 134–36; Stimson, *Rise*, 36–37, 72, 258, 264, 266–67, 342–43, 404, 420–30; Cross, *History*, 266–88; Harrison Gray Otis, "Testimony before the Commission on Industrial Relations," *Report*, 64th Congress, 1st Session, U.S. Sen. Doc. 415, 6: 5526, 5535; Mowry, *California*, 48–50, 144–47; Alexander Macdonald, "Erskine Mayo Ross: Courageous Jurist and Generous Benefactor," *American Bar Association Journal*, XXXIII (Dec., 1947), 1175.

163. Ostrom, *Water*, 53–59, 78–79, 244–46; Workman, *City*, 334–35; Spalding, *History*, I, 357.

164. McGroarty, *Los Angeles*, 3–8; Newmark, "Workman," 320–21; Spalding, *History*, II, 76–80; Workman, *City*, 209–10, 221–24, 230, 232, 237–38, 294–300.

165. Mowry, *California*, 38–56, 71, 86–88, 124–28; Graves, *My*, 266–67; V. O. Key, Jr., and Winston W. Crouch, *The Initiative and the Referendum in California* (Berkeley and Los Angeles: University of California Press, 1938), 427–41; Bird and Ryan, *Recall*, 29–33; Lorin Peterson, *The Day of the Mugwump* (New York: Random House, 1961), 234–37, 240–41; Peter C. MacFarlane, "What Is the Matter with Los Angeles," *Collier's* XXXXVIII (Dec. 2, 1911), 28, 30–31; H. Newmark, *Sixty*, 623, 646; Dana W. Bartlett, *The Better City: A Sociological Study of a Modern City* (Los Angeles: Neuner, 1907), 53–54, 172; M. Burton Williamson, "The Civic Association as a Factor of Greater Los Angeles," *Annual*, VIII, part 3 (1911), 180–87; J. Gregg Layne, "The Lincoln-Roosevelt League: Its Origin and Accomplishments," *HSSCQ*, XXV (1945), 79–101; Gustave O. Arlt, "Edward A. Dickson," *ibid.*, XXXVIII (1956), 3–8; John B. T. Campbell, "Marshall Stimson," *ibid.*, XXXIV (1952), 81–86; Spalding, *History*, I, 86–89, 319, III, 506–9; Robinson, *Lawyers*, 70–71, 110–14.

166. Mowry, *California*, 88–104, 201–5.

167. Graves, *My*, 290–93, 296; Robinson, *Lawyers*, 70–71, 97, 237; Shuck, ed., *History*, 514–18, 531, 873–74, 882, 933–34; H. Newmark: *Sixty*, 596–97; M. R. Newmark, "Early," 338, 343–44. Charles E. Haas, *Lawyers I Have Known and Their Cases* (Los Angeles: Los Angeles Daily Journal, 1954), 11–13; Bates, *History*, 324; McGroarty: *History*, III, 29–30; *California*, V, 307–8, 511–12.

168. Shuck, ed., *History*, 951–52; Bates, *History*, 258, 393–94; Spalding, *His-*

tory, II, 19–26; McGroarty, *California*, III, 99–101, 146–48; M. Anita Weyer, "Joseph Scott: A Life of Service," *HSSCQ*, XLVIII (1966), 254, 256–58. For other lawyers in public office see M. R. Newmark, "Early," 328–46; Robinson, *Lawyers*, 108, 110–11, 124–25, 224–25, 318–25, 332; McGroarty, *History*, I, 18.

169. Spalding, *History*, III, 550–53; McGroarty: *Los Angeles*, 29–30, 439; *California*, III, 357–58; M. R. Newmark, "Early," 341; Bates, *History*, 439; Shuck, ed., *History*, 1018.

170. Haas, *Lawyers*, 15–18, 21; Shuck, ed., *History*, 646–47, 791, 841–42, 946, 949, 964, 967, 1083–84; Bates, *History*, 324–25, 393–94; Spalding, *History*, II, 16–17, 45–49, 179–80, 394–95, III, 203–4; McGroarty, *California*, III, 418–25, V, 247–48, 291–93, 355–58.

171. Stimson, "Organized," 120–29; Robinson, *Lawyers*, 7, 83, 106–8, 314.

172. Robinson, *Lawyers*, 269–72; Servin and Wilson, *Southern*, 45.

173. John E. Baur, *The Health Seekers of Southern California, 1870–1900* (San Marino: Huntington Library, 1959), 48, 80–81; Harris, *California's*, 264–319.

174. Kress, *History*, 144; Cole, *Medical*, 55–58; Norman Bridge, *The Marching Years* (New York: Duffield, 1920), 90, 123, 153, 161–63, 211–12, 222.

175. Kress, *History*, 113, 137, 149, 153–54, 167, 518, 803–4; Cole, *Medical*, 67–70, 95; Spalding, *History*, II, 218–19, III, 623–24; McGroarty: *History*, II, 142, 443–44; *California*, V, 488–90; *Los Angeles*, 349, 854–55; Carew, *History*, II, 380–86.

176. M. R. Newmark, "Medical," 75, 154–55, 163–69; Kress, *History*, 23–24, 131.

177. M. R. Newmark, "Medical," 76; Kress, *History*, 32–56, 110–11, 126, 131–32, 144, 149, 153, 159, 172, 175–77; Cole, *Medical*, 21–27, 41–45, 47–53, 59–63, 105–6; Spalding, *History*, II, 395–96; McGroarty, *History*, II, 142, 433–34, 454–56.

178. Baur, *Health*, 86–87.

179. Kress, *History*, 70, 93, 153; Cole, *Medical*, 21–24, 50–53.

180. Baur, *Health*, 48; Kress, *History*, 488–90.

181. M. R. Newmark, "Medical," 167, 172; Kress, *History*, 114–15, 153–54, 166; McGroarty, *California*, V, 518–20; Spalding, *History*, III, 207–11, 623–24.

182. McGroarty, *Los Angeles*, 506–7, 840–44, 906–8; M. R. Newmark, *Jottings*, 103–6, 145; H. Newmark, *Sixty*, 623; *Men*, 78–79; Spalding, *History*, III, 171–73.

183. Spalding, *History*, II, 138–42, 311–12, 327–30; McGroarty: *History*, III, 482–85; *California*, III, 5–9; J. P. Alexander, *The Life of George Chaffey* (Melbourne, Australia: Macmillan, 1928), 10–22, 372; McGroarty, *Los Angeles*, 229–30; Ostrom, *Water*, 50–51, 168–93.

184. Bartlett, *Better*, 87–88, 107–8.

185. McGroarty, *History*, I, 700–702, II, 52–53; Palmer, *History*, I, 184; M. R. Newmark, "Medical," 172–73; Spalding, *History*, III, 426–27; Workman, *City*, 179.

186. Lindley and Widney, *California*, 105; Workman, *City*, 188–89; Collier, "Early," 220–21; Thelma L. Hubbell and Gloria R. Lothrop, "The Friday Morning Club: A Los Angeles Legacy," *HSSCQ*, L (1968), 87–88; Thomas C. Marshall, *Into the Streets and Lanes: The Beginnings and Growth of the Social Work*

of the Episcopal Church in the Diocese of Los Angeles, 1887–1947 (Claremont: Saunders Press, 1948), 24–25, 30–34, 45–46, 79; Spalding, *History*, III, 423–24; H. Newmark, *Sixty*, 643; Vorspan and Gartner, *History*, 146, 174–80.

187. M. R. Newmark, "Historical," 84–86, 292–94; *Men*, 44–45; Spalding, *History*, III, 32–35; Chapman, "Gifts," 70; McGroarty, *History*, II, 52–53, III, 287–88; Weyer, "Joseph Scott," 249–53, 259.

188. Roske, *Everyman's*, 336, 339, 425, 429–33.

189. For San Francisco see Barth, *Instant*, 170–71.

190. M. R. Newmark: "Pioneer," 64–65; "Bench," 332–46; Spalding, *History*, III, 45–46, 456–59; Splitter, "Education," 223.

191. Hyers, "Brief," 39, 44, 46, 52, 56.

192. Chapman, "Gifts," 69–70; Palmer, *History*, 99; M. R. Newmark, "Workman," 321; Workman, *City*, 224; Spalding, *History*, I, 364–65, III, 154; McGroarty, *Los Angeles*, 496–99; Lillian A. Van Aken, "History of Exposition Park," *Annual*, IX, part 3 (1914), 247–51; Griffith J. Griffith, *Parks, Boulevards and Playgrounds* (Los Angeles: Prison Reform Publishing, 1910), *passim*.

193. Griffith, *Parks*, 1, 5, 15–16, 21–22, 62–63; Alexander Campbell's speech, *ibid.*, 38.

194. Griffith, *Parks*, 47–53, 70.

195. Spalding, *History*, I, 364–65.

196. Servin and Wilson, *Southern*, 5–6, 13–14, 20, 22, 25–27, 30–31, 47, 49, 53, 61, 91, 126; Workman, *City*, 186–87; Rockwell D. Hunt, *The First Half-Century* (Los Angeles: University of Southern California Press, 1930), 5, 15.

197. J. P. Widney, *Race*, II, 99–101, 120, 154.

198. Robert Glass Cleland, *The History of Occidental College, 1887–1937* (Los Angeles: Ward Ritchie Press, 1937), 5, 7–8, 23, 25–26, 57; Andrew F. Rolle, *Occidental College: The First Seventy-five Years* (Los Angeles: Occidental College Press, 1962), 6, 48, 165–68; Smith, *Adobe*, 185; Charles B. Sumner, *The Story of Pomona College* (Boston: Pilgrim Press, 1914), *passim*.

199. Carew, *History*, I, 447–48; Helen Wright, *Explorer of the Universe: A Biography of George Ellery Hale* (New York: E. P. Dutton, 1966), 239–51.

200. Hale quoted in Carew, *History*, I, 448; Norman Bridge: *Fragments and Addresses* (Los Angeles: Bireley & Elson, 1915), 79–80; cf. *The Penalties of Taste and Other Essays* (Chicago: Herbert S. Stone, 1898), 145, 160.

201. Walker, *Literary*, 161–62; Cleland, *History*, 13; Smith, *Adobe*, 187.

202. N. Levering, "Origins of the Historical Society of Southern California," *Annual*, III, part 3 (1895), 9–10; J. M. Guinn, "Fifteen Years of Local History Work," *ibid.*, IV, part 2 (1898), 106–8; S. H. Hall, "The Historical Society of Southern California," *ibid.*, IX, part 1 (1912), 7–8, 73–74; Joseph B. Lockey, "The Historical Society of Southern California: What of its Future?" *HSSCQ*, XX (1938), 30; J. M. Guinn, "Twenty-five Years of Local History Work," *Annual*, VII, part 3 (1908), 156–57.

203. Guinn, "Pioneers of Los Angeles County," *Annual*, IV, part 1 (1897), 88–99, part 4 (1898), 176; Newmark, *Sixty*, 614.

204. Newmark, *Sixty*, 626; Guinn, *History*, I, 424; Spalding, *History*, I, 424.

205. M. R. Newmark, "Charles Fletcher Lummis," *HSSCQ*, XXXII (1950), 58; Robinson, *Lawyers*, 229.

206. M. R. Newmark, "La Fiesta de Los Angeles of 1894," *HSSCQ*, XXX

(1948), 101–11; H. Newmark, *Sixty*, 604–5; Christian W. Mead, "Las Fiestas de Los Angeles: A Survey of the Yearly Celebrations: 1894–1898," *HSSCQ*, XXXI (1949), 61–114.

207. Graves, *My*, 128; Workman, *City*, 192, 355.

208. Splitter, "Art," 118, 133–36; Jennie June Croly, *The History of the Women's Club Movement in America* (New York: Henry G. Allen, 1898), 246–47; Workman, *City*, 251–52; Bartlett, *Better*, 106–7; Charter of the Society of Fine Arts of California quoted in Splitter, "Art," 136.

209. Wright, *Explorer*, 373–86.

210. Harold Kirker, *California's Architectural Frontier, Style and Tradition in the Nineteenth Century* (San Marino: Huntington Library, 1960), 101; McGroarty: *California*, V, 531–32; *History*, II, 121–42; Spalding, *History*, II, 49–50, 266–67; M. R. Newmark, *Jottings*, 132–33.

211. Workman, *City*, 367–68; Splitter, "Music," 311–15, 321, 332; Donald Estes Smith, *The Philharmonic Orchestra of Los Angeles: The First Decade, 1919–1929* (Los Angeles: United Printing, 1930), 16–24, 27–29; Spalding, *History*, III, 26; Roske, *Everyman's*, 443.

212. M. Burton Williamson, "The Marine Biological Laboratory at San Pedro," *Annual*, V, part 1 (1901), 126.

213. Carew, *History*, I, 437–38, 441–45; Wright, *Explorer*, 181, 253; McWilliams, *Great*, 253.

214. Herbert Wynford Hill, ed., *Hancock Hall: The Allan Hancock Foundation for Scientific Research of the University of Southern California. Proceedings of the Dedicatory Exercises* (Los Angeles: University of Southern California Press, 1941), vii; Florence J. Seaman, "A Brief History of Rancho La Brea," *Annual*, IX, part 3 (1914), 253–56; Spalding, *History*, III, 26; McGroarty, *Los Angeles*, 82–83.

215. H. Newmark, *Sixty*, 647–48; M. R. Newmark, "Charles Fletcher Lummis," 55; Guinn, *History*, I, 424; Spalding, *History*, I, 337, III, 427–28; Robinson, *Lawyers*, 125, 258–59; Bridge, *Fragments*, 189–90, quote on 183–84, 194.

216. J. M. Guinn, "The Museum of History, Science, and Art," *Annual*, VIII, part 1 (1913), 5–7; Van Aken, "History," 250–51; Spalding, *History*, I, 370, 373.

217. McGroarty, *Los Angeles*, 930–31.

218. Decker, *Fortunes*, 203–6, 215–26, 228–29, 231–32, 239, 243, for San Francisco.

219. Workman, *City*, 212–18, 262–63.

220. A. E. Hartzell, *Titled Americans* (n.p.: n.p., 1951), 357.

221. Moses Rischin, *The Promised City: New York's Jews, 1870–1914* (New York: Harper Torchbooks, 1970), 261–62; Stephen Birmingham, *"Our Crowd:" The Great Jewish Families of New York* (New York: Harper & Row, 1967), 127, 239. For anti-Semitism in Philadelphia see Nathaniel Burt, *The Perennial Philadelphians: The Anatomy of a Ruling Class* (Boston: Little, Brown, 1963), 135, 231, 264, 565–73. For a discussion of the anti-Semitism of Henry and Brooks Adams see Frederic Cople Jaher, *Doubters and Dissenters: Cataclysmic Thought in America, 1885–1918* (New York: Free Press, 1964), 151–52, 155–56, 165–66, 171, 173, 185–86. For A. Lawrence Lowell's attitudes and the Harvard quota system see Henry A. Yeomans, *Abbott Lawrence Lowell, 1856–1913*

(Cambridge: Harvard University Press, 1948), 209–16; Samuel Eliot Morison, *Three Centuries of Harvard* (Cambridge: Harvard University Press, 1936), 416–17. For James Russell Lowell's feelings see Martin Duberman, *James Russell Lowell* (Boston: Houghton Mifflin, 1966), 307–10. For anti-Brandeis sentiment see A. L. Lowell to Henry Cabot Lodge, Jan. 31, 1916, John T. Morse to Lodge, Feb. 13, 1916, Barrett Wendell to Lodge, Jan. 28, 1916, and Lodge to Wendell, June 21, 1916, in Henry Cabot Lodge Papers, Massachusetts Historical Society; A. L. Lowell to Frederic Stimson, Feb. 1, 1916, in A. L. Lowell Letters, Houghton Library, Harvard University. For Lodge's attitudes toward Jews see Edward E. Hale to Lodge, Dec. 16, 1901, and Lodge to William Sturgis Bigelow, Feb. 22, 1913, in Lodge Papers. For Charleston see Charles Riznikoff and Uriah Z. Engelman, *The Jews of Charleston: A History of an American Jewish Community* (Philadelphia: Jewish Publication Society of America, 1950), 24–40, 69–70, 79–97, 104, 158–59, 179–82, 197–98, 239; Decker, *Fortunes*, 239, for San Francisco.

222. M. R. Newmark, "Pioneer Clubs," *passim*; Vorspan and Gartner, *History*, 63–64, 81, 84, 94, 123, 135–36, 139, 143–45, 205; H. Newmark, *Sixty*, 383, 545, 614, quote on 383.

223. M. R. Newmark, "Pioneer Clubs," 300–302, 310–16; H. Newmark, *Sixty*, 545; Workman, *City*, 251–52; Spalding, *History*, I, 312, 320, 333; Hill, *La Reina*, 62, 83; Lindley and Widney, *California*, 109.

224. Joan M. Jensen, "After Slavery: Caroline Severance in Los Angeles," *HSSCQ*, XLVIII (1966), 180–82; Collier, "Early," 216–21; M. R. Newmark, "Pioneer Clubs," 306–8; Hubbell and Lothrop, "Friday," 60; Bartlett, *Better*, 52–53.

225. M. R. Newmark: *Jottings*, 98–101; "Pioneer Clubs," 306–8; Hubbell and Lothrop, "Friday," 62–63, 66, 87–90; Bartlett, *Better*, 97, 100–101.

226. Bartlett, *Better*, 101; McGroarty, *History*, III, 279–82.

227. Williams, "Civic," 180–89; Spalding, *History*, III, 151–52.

228. Carew, *History*, III, 436–43; McGroarty, *California*, IV, 799; Hubbell and Lothrop, "Friday," 75–76, 78–79; Spalding, *History*, II, 111–12, 212, III, 36–40, 211–13, 426–27.

229. Graves, *California*, 98–99, 103–5; S. O'Melveny, *It's*, 19–20; Workman, *City*, 179–81.

230. Workman, *City*, 92–94, 158; M. R. Newmark, *Jottings*, 103–6; H. Newmark, *Sixty*, 363; McGroarty, *California*, IV, 685, V, 731–35.

231. Widney, *Race*, II, 63, 154, 328.

232. Bridge: *Penalties*, 5–6, 15–18, 21, 25; *Rewards*, 23, 150.

233. Richard Bigger and James D. Kitchen, *How the City Grew: A Century of Municipal Independence and Expansionism in Metropolitan Los Angeles* (Los Angeles: University of California at Los Angeles Press, 1952), 164–68; Neff, Baum, and Heilman, *Production*, 14; McLaughlin, *Growth*, 44–46, 54–55, 64–65, 71–72; Coons and Miller, *Economic*, xv–xvi; Fogelson, *Fragmented*, 78; *County and City Data Book 1972* (Washington, D.C.: U.S. Government Printing Office, 1973), 814.

234. Coons and Miller, *Economic*, 6; McWilliams, *Southern*, 238–39.

235. See note 38 and Wesley Price, "Merchant of Speed," *Saturday Evening Post*, 221 (Feb. 19, 1949), 48, 50; John Niven, Courtlandt Canby, and Vernon Welsh, eds., *Dynamic America: A History of the General Dynamics Corporation and Its Predecessor Companies* (New York: Doubleday, 1960), 245, 379–80; John B. Rae, *Climb to Greatness: The American Aircraft Industry, 1920–1960* (Cambridge: Massachusetts Institute of Technology Press, 1968), 8–11, 106, 126–28, 180; Harold B. Meyers, "For Lockheed Everything's Coming Up Unk-Unks," *Fortune*, 80 (Aug., 1969), 77, 81; Gertrude Jobes, *Motion Picture Empire* (Hamden, Conn.: Archon Books, 1966), 30, 59–60, 64–65, 70–71, 103–4, 134–35; Terry Ramsaye, *A Million and One Nights* (New York: Simon and Schuster, 1964), 585, 821, 829.

236. Fogelson, *Fragmented*, 81.

237. Cleland and Hardy, *March*, 274–75; Coons and Miller, *Economic*, 65–68; California State Chamber of Commerce, *Economic*, 336–37, 455; Roske, *Everyman's*, 581.

238. Coons and Miller, *Economic*, xiii, xix, 1, 4, 108; *County*, 1949, 340; 1972, 653, 814; Matson, *Building*, 12–13.

239. Coons and Miller, *Economic*, 12, 75–76, 123–26, 175–224; McLaughlin, *Growth*, 180–81; Neff, Baum, and Heilman, *Production*, 16; *Los Angeles: A Guide to the City and Its Environs* (New York: Hastings House, 1941), 60; James L. Clayton, "Defense Spending: Key to California's Growth," *Western Political Quarterly*, 15 (1962), 280–93; "The Undiscovered City," *Fortune*, 39 (June, 1949), 76; California State Chamber of Commerce, *Economic*, 60.

240. *Manufacturing and Foreign Trade Directory of Los Angeles County and District* (Los Angeles: Los Angeles Chamber of Commerce, 1928), vi; *County and City Date Book 1949* (Washington, D.C.: U.S. Government Printing Office, 1952), 39; *1972*, 61; Ostrom, *Water*, 167; *Los Angeles*, 55; Stockwell, *Studies*, 296n; "500 Largest Industrial Corporations, 1970," *Fortune* 79 (May, 1971), 172–87, 192–201.

241. W. W. Robinson, "The Southern California Real Estate Boom of the 1920s," *HSSCQ*, XXIV (1942), 25–30; Nadeau, *Los Angeles*, 155–57; Coons and Miller, *Economic*, 118; Spalding, *History*, I, 408, 411, 416–17; Hill, *La Reina*, 161–62, 170; McWilliams, *Southern*, 136; Grace A. Somberby, "When Los Angeles Was Host to the Olympic of 1932," *HSSCQ*, XXIV (1952), 125–27; M. R. Newmark, *Jottings*, 127–28.

242. "Who's Who—and Why: Serious and Frivolous Facts about the Great and Near Great," *Saturday Evening Post*, 198 (June 5, 1926), 52, 234; McGroarty, *Los Angeles*, 844–45; Kilner, *Arthur Letts*, 170–74.

243. John U. Pohlman, "Alphonzo E. Bell: A Biography," *HSSCQ*, XLVI (1964), 200–201, 207–8, 337–42; M. R. Newmark, *Jottings*, 127–28; McGroarty, *California*, V, 585–87; William M. Garland quoted in "City of Angels," 179.

244. McGroarty: *California*, IV, 599–600, V, 235–36, 245–49; *Los Angeles*, 152–53, 192, 306–7, 465–66, 624, 641–42; *History*, II, 15; Spalding, *History*, II, 81–82, 302–3, 391, III, 572–73, 612–13; Vorspan and Gartner, *History*, 233; Christopher Rand, "The Ultimate City," *New Yorker*, 42 (Oct. 1, 1966), 68, 73.

245. Graves, *California*, 108; M. R. Newmark, "Pioneer," 10–14, 18–25,

82–83; McGroarty, *Los Angeles*, 450–51, 647–50, 653–58, 682, 911–13; Spalding, *History*, III, 489–95; Kilner, *Arthur Letts*, 159; McGroarty, *California*, IV, 21–23, V, 739–41.

246. McWilliams, *California: The Great Exception* (New York: Current Books, 1949), 238; Crouch and Dinerman, *Southern*, 260.

247. Crump, *Ride*, 166–69; Hill, *La Reina*, 179–80; Workman, *City*, 372.

248. Ostrom, *Water*, 65–66, 78–79, 83–84, 99, 208–14, 244–46.

249. *Ibid.*, 83–84, 168–93; Workman, *City*, 387–91.

250. Cleland and Hardy, *March*, 284. For the careers of upper-class bankers see Cross, *Financial*, III, 358–61, 387–88, 393–94, 428, 432–34, 474, 513–15; McGroarty, *Los Angeles*, 82–83, 525, 534, 617–19; Spalding, *History*, II, 80–82, III, 274–75, 592–95. For the careers of the newer group of banking magnates and for officers and directors of the leading Los Angeles banks see Cross, *Financial*, II, 759, 764, 770–71, 777, 781, 784–87, III, 318, 348–51, 354, 364–65, 367, 369–71, 395–402, 405, 407, 431, 448–54, 461–65, 509–16, 525–26, and *passim*; Cleland and Putnam, *Isaias W. Hellman*, 108ff.

251. Cleland and Putnam, *Isaias W. Hellman*, 108ff.; Cross, *Financial*, III, 388–89; "Expanding to Unusual," *Business Week*, (Aug. 28, 1965), 69–70, 72; Vorspan and Gartner, *History*, 235.

252. Cross, *Financial*, III, 383–84; Cleland and Putnam, *Isaias W. Hellman*, 104, 107; I. W. Hellman quoted on 104.

253. Harry Volk quoted in "Expanding," 72; for the bank's policies, 70, 72; for the quotes from the bank analyst and eastern financier, 69–70.

254. Spalding, *History*, III, 171–73.

255. "Who's," 52, 234; "Those Tireless Chandlers," *Newsweek*, 47 (Apr. 30, 1956), 60, 62; "A Publishing Giant Takes a Long Step," *Business Week* (Mar. 14, 1964), 72; Peter Bart, "The New Look at the 'Times'," *Saturday Review*, 48 (June 12, 1965), 68, 79; "Newspapers," *Time*, 87 (May 13, 1966), 76–77; "How to Build an Empire," *Newsweek*, 69 (Jan. 2, 1967), 41–42.

256. "Los Angeles *Times* Revises Its Image to Reach Changing Market," *Business Week*, (Nov. 19, 1960), 120, 125; "A Publishing," 72–75, 77; Bart, "New," 71; "Happy Chandlers," *Newsweek*, 63 (June 8, 1964), 93; "How," 44–45; John M. Mecklin, "Times-Mirror's Ambitious Acquirers," *Fortune*, 78 (Sept., 1968), 99, 101.

257. Matson, *Building*, 127, 131–32; Spalding, *History*, I, 386, II, 19–26, 30–34; Coons and Miller, *Economic*, 197–99.

258. McGroarty: *Los Angeles*, 20–22, 26–29, 765–66; *California*, III, 5–9, 49–50; Spalding, *History*, I, 425, II, 26–29, 611, III, 72–75.

259. California State Chamber of Commerce, *Economic*, 460–62; Kidner, *California*, 108–10; Clayton, "Defense," 291; "Undiscovered," 76–77, 82–83, 148, 153–56; McLaughlin, *Growth*, 212–17, 224–25; Coons and Miller, *Economic*, xx, xxiii, 1–2, 4–5, 12–17, 109, 115–24, 127–28, 130–31, 134–35, 142–48, 151–58, 166–67, 175–224; Ostrom, *Water*, 165–67; McWilliams, *California*, 218–222, 225–26, 232–36, 339–47. For specific industries see Bain, *Economics*, I, 28–29, 42, III, 6–10, 40–45; Cleland and Hardy, *March*, 179–80, 274–75; Charles S. Goodman, *The Location of Fashion Industries* (Ann Arbor: University of Michigan Press, 1948), 25–29, 43–48, 51–53, 77–78; Jobes, *Mo-*

tion, 30, 59–60, 64–65, 103–5, 134–35; Ramsaye, *Million*, 585, 828–89; Palmer, *History*, 195, 223, 226, 231–40, 244; Benjamin B. Hampton, *The History of the American Film Industry from Its Beginnings to 1931* (New York: Dover Publications, 1970), 26–27, 113, 132, 227, 380, 410–14, 580–81; Leo C. Rosten, *Hollywood: The Movie Colony. The Movie Makers* (New York: Harcourt, Brace, 1941), 4, 8, 86–87, 164–65, 362–63, 372, 376, 378; Howard T. Lewis, *The Motion Picture Industry* (New York: D. Van Nostrand, 1933), 24, 29, 79, 398; Rand, "Ultimate," 86–115; Roske, *Everyman's*, 522–23, 525, 529–30, 555–56; G. R. Simonson: "The Demand for Aircraft and the Aircraft Industry, 1907–1958," *Journal of Economic History*, XX (Sept., 1960), 367, 375–77; "Missiles and Creative Destruction in the American Aircraft Industry, 1956–61," *Business History Review*, 38 (Autumn, 1964), 302–10, 312; Elsbeth E. Freudenthal, *The Aviation Business from Kitty Hawk to Wall St.* (New York: Vanguard Press, 1940), 88–107, 143, 252–53, 258–60, 295, and *passim*; Herman O. Stekler, *The Structure and Performance of the Areospace Industry* (Berkeley and Los Angeles: University of California Press, 1965), 6–7, 10–13, 17–18, 21, 23–24, 36, 78–102, 115–26, 137, 151, 159–60; Richard G. Hubler, *Big Eight: A Biography of an Airplane* (New York: Duell, Sloan and Pearce, 1960), 16–17, 20–22, 24–25, 28–30, 37, 78, 149; Kuhn, Loeb and Co., *Douglas Aircraft Co., Inc. and the Aircraft Manufacturing Industry* (New York: Kuhn, Loeb, 1954), 6, 8, 13, 59–60, 64, 70–71, 75, 77, 79, 83–84, 86–94, 101; Price, "Merchant," 48, 50; Niven, Canby and Walsh, eds., *Dynamic*, 245, 270, 337, 374, 379, 380, 410, 415, 418; Rae, *Climb*, 8–11, 16–18, 30–31, 46–47, 50, 61, 69–70, 91–92, 106, 126–28, 167–97, 206–7, 217–18; "City of Angels," 40, 91–93, 180; "The North American Way," *Fortune*, 23 (Mar., 1941), 99–100; "Success in Santa Monica," *ibid.*, 2 (May, 1935), 79–84, 170, 176, 178, 180, 185–86, 195–96; "Modern Flying," *ibid.*, 85, 192; "Six in the Money," *ibid.*, 31 (Aug., 1949), 136, 138, 141; "Lockheed Aircraft Corporation," *ibid.*, 22 (Aug., 1940), 50, 52, 90; Charles J. V. Murphy, "The Plane Makers under Stress," *ibid.*, 60–61 (June and July, 1960), 135–37, 228, 234, 240, 292, 294–300; Murphy, "Lockheed Scrambles for the Battle of the Primes," *ibid.*, 71 (Feb., 1965), 149–51; Meyers, "For Lockheed," 77–78, 81; Herbert Solow, "North American: A Corporation Deeply Committed," *ibid.*, 65 (June, 1962), 145–48, 164; John Mecklin, "Douglas Aircraft's Stormy Flight Path," *ibid.*, 74 (Dec., 1966), 167–68, 170–71; William Glenn Cunningham, *The Aircraft Industry: A Study in Industrial Location* (Los Angeles: Lorrin L. Morrison, 1951), 24, 29–30, 40, 43–44, 47–48, 56–57, 67–71, 97, 99–129, 154–56, 159–61, 164, 193; J. Keith Butters and John Lintner, *The Effect of Federal Taxes on Growing Enterprises* (Cambridge: Harvard University Press, 1944), 3, 8–11, 14; Crosby Maynard, *Flight Plan for Tomorrow: The Douglas Story, a Condensed History* (Santa Monica: Douglas Aircraft, 1962), *passim*; Frank J. Taylor and Lawton Wright, *Democracy's Arsenal* (New York: Duell, Sloan and Pearce, 1947), 23–27, 36, 38–39, 76, 79; Arlene Elliott, "The Rise of Areonautics in California, 1849–1940," *HSSCQ*, LII (1970), 15–16; Carl Rieser, "When the Crowd Goes One Way Litton Goes the Other," *Fortune*, 67 (May, 1963), 115–19, 220–28; Seymour Freedgood, " 'Dimjin': Architects for the Space Age," *ibid.*, 62 (July, 1960), 121–25, 177–84; Charles E. Silberman, "The Coming Shakeout in Electronics," *ibid.*, 126–30, 184–96.

260. Bridge, *Fragments*, 63; J. B. Miller quoted in Forbes, *Men*, 69.

261. James H. Kindelberger quoted in Price, "Merchant," 53; Hubler, *Big*, 16–17, Donald Douglas quote, 16–17.

262. Crump, *Ride*, 129–30; Perry and Perry, *History*, 473; Neff, Baum, and Heilman, *Production*, 38–39.

263. Crump, *Ride*, 129–30; Hubler, *Big*, 29; "City of Angels," 180; Perry and Perry, *History*, 534; "Undiscovered," 158.

264. Donald W. Douglas, *Wings for the World* (New York, San Francisco, Montreal: Newcomen Society of North America, 1955), 17; Frank Hugh Sparks, "The Location of Industry: An Analysis of Some of the Factors Which Have Affected the Location of Industry in the Ten Southern Counties of California," (Ph.D. dissertation, University of Southern California, 1941), 30–33, 57–67.

265. Alfred Ghormley quoted in "Undiscovered," 154.

266. Paul H. Willis and A. O. Buckingham quoted in McWilliams, *California*, 222; James H. Shelton quoted in "Undiscovered," 160; Jacob K. Javits quoted in the *Congressional Record*, 86th Congress, Second Session, June 23, 1959, 10522; John Tabor quoted in the New York *Times*, Apr. 18, 1960, 1.

267. William Millar quoted in "City of Angels," 40; Douglas, *Wings*, 17; Anonymous quote in Rand, "Ultimate," 135; Daniel J. Haughton quoted in Meyers, "For Lockheed," 77.

268. "Undiscovered," 160.

269. H. Dewey Anderson, *Our California State Taxes* (Palo Alto: Stanford University Press, 1937), 188–89.

270. M. R. Newmark, "Short," 62, 69–70, 73–75, 80; Ostrom, *Water*, 60–61, 65–67, 84; Matson, *Building*, 157–58, 179; *Manufacturing*, vi; "Chamber," 207.

271. M. R. Newmark, "Short," 80; McGroarty, *California*, II, 499–500, V, 341–42; Cross, *Financial*, II, 321.

272. M. R. Newmark, "Pioneer Merchants," 64–65; McGroarty, *Los Angeles*, 179–80, 203–4, 249–51, 710–11, 798–801; Cross, *Financial*, III, 330–33; Carew, *History*, II, 380–86; H. R. Newmark, *Sixty*, 544–45; Spalding, *History*, II, 132–36, 148–54; McGroarty, *California*, II, 191–93.

273. Anderson, *Our*, 86–91, 94, 217, 229, 241; Stockwell, *Studies*, 1–4, 125–44, 297; Crouch and Dinerman, *Southern*, 14–17, 126; Peterson, *Day*, 242–46; William Buchanan, *Legislative Partisanship: The Deviant Case of California* (Berkeley and Los Angeles: University of California Press, 1963), 35, 118, 124.

274. John T. Morgan, "Our American Mayors," *National Municipal Review*, XVII (Jan., 1928), 28–31; Francis M. Carney, "The Decentralized Politics of Los Angeles," *Annals of the American Academy of Political and Social Science*, 353 (May, 1964), 111.

275. Graves: *California*, 123–26; *My*, 447–50; Joseph P. Widney, *Civilizations and Their Disease and Rebuilding a Wrecked World Civilization*, 2 vols. (Los Angeles: Pacific Publishing, 1937), I, 42–43.

276. Upton Sinclair, *I, Candidate for Governor: And How I Got Licked* (New York: Farrar & Rinehart, 1935), 42.

277. Rand, "Ultimate," 99–100; Carney, "Decentralized," 118.

278. Haas, *Lawyers*, 15–18; Shuck, ed., *History*, 646–47, 841–42, 946, 949, 964, 967, 1083–84; Bates, *History*, 324–25, 393–94; Spalding, *History*, II, 16–17,

45–49, 179–80, 394–95, III, 203–4, 404, 550–53; McGroarty, *California*, III, 418–25, V, 248–49, 291–93, 355–48, 722; Stimson, "Organized," 139; Robinson, *Lawyers*, 230; M. R. Newmark, "Early," 334.

279. Robinson, *Lawyers*, 128–29, 165; Stimson, "Organized," 126–29; Spalding, *History*, III, 403.

280. M. R. Newmark, "Early," 328–46; Robinson, *Lawyers*, 224–25, 318–25, 332, 335.

281. M. R. Newmark, "Medical," 76–77; Kress, *History*, 166–67; Spalding, *History*, III, 518–20, 604–6; McGroarty, *California*, III, 41–42.

282. "Modern Flying," 85, 192; Robert A. Millikan, *The Autobiography of Robert A. Millikan* (New York: Prentice-Hall, 1950), 243, 247–59; Roske, *Everyman's*, 555–56; Rand, "Ultimate," 88–90, 93–97; Kuhn, *Douglas*, 79–80; Remi Nadeau, *California: The New Society* (New York: David McKay, 1963), 288; McWilliams, *California*, 263–64.

283. Millikan, *Autobiography*, 215, 220, 227, 238–40; Wright, *Explorer*, 337; Carew, *History*, I, 452; Roy W. Cloud, *Education in California* (Palo Alto: Stanford University Press, 1952), 165; Ferrier, *Ninety*, 364.

284. Servin and Wilson, *Southern*, 125–26, 194, 226, 241, 253, 260; Hunt, *First*, 20, 107; Hall, *Allan Hancock*, vii; New York *Times*, June 25, 1971, 34.

285. Rolle, *Occidental*, 48, 57–58, 107–8, 165–68; Cleland, *History*, 57, 73, 76–77, 88, 112–13; Pohlman, "Alphonso E. Bell," 337–41; M. R. Newmark, *Jottings*, 148; Carew, *History*, II, 5–7.

286. Andrew Hamilton and John B. Jackson, *UCLA on the Move during Fifty Golden Years, 1919–69* (Los Angeles: Ward Ritchie Press, 1969), 1, 8, 26, 41–42, 45, 69–70, 91–92, 116–18, 142, 145–47, 151; Spalding, *History*, I, 446, 481–90.

287. Willard Huntington Wright, "Los Angeles—The Chemically Pure," reprinted in Burton Rascoe and Groff Conklin, eds., *The Smart Set Anthology* (New York: Reynal & Hitchcock, 1934), 90–102.

288. William L. Rivers, "New Winds in the South, New Splash in the North," *Saturday Review of Literature*, 50 (Sept. 23, 1967), 75; Norman Chandler quoted in "How," 41.

289. "Los Angeles *Times*," 125–26; "How," 41–42; "Newspapers," 76–77; Bart, "New," 68, 71; Rivers, "New," 75; John Corry, "The Los Angeles *Times*," *Harper's Magazine*, 239 (Dec., 1969), 76, 81–2; "Happy Chandlers," 94, 114, Otis Chandler quote 114; cf. Chandler quoted in Bart, "New," 71.

290. Anonymous quote in "How," 41.

291. Lockey, "Historical," 31–32; Gustave O. Arlt, "Thoughts on the Event of Our Diamond Jubilee," *HSSCQ*, XL (1958), 207–8, 210.

292. Marion Parks, "The Golden Jubilee of the Historical Society of Southern California," *Annual*, XV, part 4 (1933), 116–17; Packman, "Landmarks," 90–91; *HSSCQ*, XXXIV (1952), 4; XL (1958), 215–19.

293. Laurence J. Hill, "A Great City Celebrates Its 150th Anniversary," *Annual*, XI, part 1 (1931), 8.

294. Millikan, *Autobiography*, 244–46; Wright, *Explorer*, 181, 253; McWilliams, *California*, 255–56, 263–64.

295. Henry E. Huntington quoted in Oscar Lewis, *The Big Four: The Story of Huntington, Stanford, Hopkins and Crocker and the Building of the Central*

Pacific (New York: Alfred A. Knopf, 1951), 269; Huntington quoted in Robert O. Schad, *Henry Edward Huntington: The Founder and the Library* (San Marino: Huntington Library, 1938), 32.

296. John E. Pomfret, *The Henry Edward Huntington Library and Art Gallery from Its Beginnings to 1969* (San Marino: Huntington Library, 1969), 32–34, 40–43, 46–55, 59, 70, 73–75, 104–7, 111, 116, 121, 128–29, 138–39, 147–49, 179–83, 206–7, 228; Lewis, *Big*, 268–69; Schad, *Henry Edward Huntington*, 11–29.

297. Hamilton, *U.C.L.A.*, 91–92; Hyers, "Brief," 60, 66.

298. "The City," *Time*, 84 (Dec. 18, 1964), 46.

299. Richard Brown quoted in Katharine Kuh, "Los Angeles: Salute to a New Museum," *Saturday Review of Literature*, 48 (Apr. 3, 1965), 30; Henry Geldzahler, "Los Angeles: The Second City of Art," *Vogue*, 144 (Sept. 15, 1964), 56. The art critic of *Saturday Review of Literature* was also impressed with the museum and the explosive growth of art in Los Angeles. See Kuh, "Los Angeles," 35.

300. Robert Wernick, "Wars of the Instant Medicis," *Life*, 61 (Oct. 28, 1966), 102, 105–6, 111–12; "Colossus in Los Angeles," *Newsweek*, 65 (Apr. 6, 1965), 84, 86; "Go West Go," *ibid.*, 70 (Apr. 24, 1967), 107; "Los Angeles Hoists the Flag of Culture," *Business Week*, (Nov. 21, 1964), 32; "Another String to Simon's Bow," *ibid.*, 178; Kuh, "Los Angeles," 29, 35.

301. Anonymous quote in Wernick, "Wars," 107; *ibid.*, 105; "Colossus," 86.

302. "Los Angeles Hoists," 32; "Colossus," 84, 86; "City," 46, 56–58; "Buff's Elegant Pavilion Opens in Los Angeles," *Life*, 57 (Dec. 18, 1964), 40; Mecklin, "Times Mirror's," 101; "How," 43; Henry A. Sutherland, "Requiem for the Los Angeles Philharmonic Auditorium," *HSSCQ*, XLVII (1965), 327–31; Edward Carter quoted in "City," 55.

303. Smith, *Philharmonic*, 99–100, 109–10, 112–13; Palmer, *History*, 210–11, 213; "City," 57; "Los Angeles Hoists," 32; McGroarty, *History*, III, 524.

304. Sutherland, "Requiem," 322–23; Smith, *Philharmonic*, 39–46, 77–78, 124, 143, 197–98; "City," 57.

305. Hill, "A Great City," 47; Roger J. Sterrett, "Los Angeles Celebrates Its Centennial," *HSSCQ*, XXVIII (1946), 130–33.

306. Somberby, "When," 125–27; M. R. Newmark, *Jottings*, 127–28.

307. Crump, *Ride*, 179; Schad, *Henry Edward Huntington*, 32; "The City," 57; MacDonald, "Erskine Mayo Ross," 1244; Marshall, *Into*, 91; McGroarty: *California*, IV, 21–23, 101; *Los Angeles*, 249–51; M. R. Newmark, "Medical," 172; Cross, *Financial*, III, 387–88, 432–33.

308. Newmark, "Short," 62; Melvin Scott, *Los Angeles: One Community* (Los Angeles: Haynes Foundation, 1949), 150–51; McGroarty: *Los Angeles*, 58; *California*, III, 50, IV, 801–2, V, 577–79; Spalding, *History*, II, 82–86, 347–50; Robinson, *Lawyers*, 235; Weyer, "Joseph Scott," 259; Haas, *Lawyers*, 61–62; M. R. Newmark, "Medical," 76; Kress, *History*, 152–53.

309. For comments on the absence of a coherent Los Angeles upper class see Carney, "Decentralized," 118; Nadeau, *California*, 48, 199–200; Lucy Kavaler, *The Private World of High Society* (New York: David McKay, 1960), 171, 199–201; McWilliams, *Southern*, 240.

310. M. R. Newmark, "Pioneer," 300–302, 306–8, 310–16; Hubbell and Loth-

rop, "Friday," 59–91; Cleveland Amory, *Who Killed Society* (New York: Harper & Bros., 1960), 167.

311. Amory, *Who*, 36, 110, 130, 142, 167, 221–26, 238–39, 498, 508–9, Mrs. Hamilton M. Twombly quote, 110.

312. Rosten, *Hollywood*, 60–64, 68–69, 72, 97–108, 164–65, 170–71, 177–211; Palmer, *History*, 223, 226, 231–37, 244; Carr, *Los Angeles*, 267–68; McWilliams, *Southern*, 335–39; Ethyl Barrymore quoted in Amory, *Who*, 36.

313. Hubler, *Big*, 28.

314. Anonymous quote in, "City," 56.

315. O. Chandler quoted in "How," 43, 45; "Los Angeles *Times*," 125–26. Dorothy Chandler quoted in *ibid.*, 126.

316. McWilliams, *Southern*, 240; Nadeau, *California*, 48, 199–200.

CHAPTER VII

Historical interpretation of leadership groups in Boston, New York, Charleston, Chicago, and Los Angeles becomes more significant by relating these case studies to other privileged ranks. Such comparisons indicate similarities in ruling groups in different eras and environments as well as those experiences exclusively American or unique to a region or a locality in this country. What follows is a brief review of the literature in this field, to illuminate, affirm, or generalize the findings on the upper orders of the five cities. This excursion proceeds from surveys of particular attributes of influential enclaves to more comprehensive studies of establishments in America and Europe.

Research on present-day elite and upper-class personality traits, cultural orientation, family structure, voluntary associations, and philanthropy provides evidence that verifies and broadens this investigation.

In 1941 two pioneering community stratification studies appeared. The surveys of Newburyport, Massachusetts, a maritime port that became an industrial town of 17,000 people, and "Old City," a deep South trading center of 10,000 inhabitants which served the surrounding plantations, employed similar research methods, and their findings agree with many characteristics of patriciates described in this book. W. Lloyd Warner and Paul S. Hunt discerned, through personal interviews, that the descendants of the old Yankee overseas traders—in contrast to more recently arrived elites—tended to respect parental authority. This group also cherished their ancestral homes, artifacts, and graveyards, belonged to genealogical societies and civic associations of ancient vintage and ascriptive membership, and loved family histories. Of all social classes in Newburyport, it was least likely to read self-improvement and social-climbing literature, a genre of particular appeal to those newly risen to riches and power. Allison Davis, Burleigh B. Gardner, and Mary R. Gardner, also on the basis of personal interviews, discovered that the equivalent echelon in "Old City," the progeny of the pre-Civil War planter gentry, similarly worshipped old ways, ancient organizations, kinship bonds, and ascriptive as opposed to the achievement values of *arriviste* elites. Psychologist Charles McArthur, studying Harvard undergraduates of the 1950s, found traits and priorities identical to those observed in the earlier investigations. The data showed that students of upper-class origins, compared to those of middle-class origins, tended to be underachievers oriented to the past and to tradition, to value leisure and deemphasize the work ethic, and to enroll in the liberal arts curricula rather than in more practical programs.[1]

William E. Henry's characterization of the modern business magnate, based on psychological testing and interviewing a sample of over 100 corporation executives, differs little from another finding in this work. He discovered that successful businessmen of the 1950s, like their eighteenth- and nineteenth-century predecessors, were high achievers, hard workers, driven by aspirations for upward mobility, decisive, aggressive, good organizers, and had a firmly integrated self-identity.[2]

The "Old City" survey replicated yet another finding of these five case studies. The offspring of the antebellum squirearchy, more than any other stratum in town, moved within a kinship network where, for example, married children stayed in the homes of their parents and where grandparents exerted great control over their grandchildren. The association of the extended family with upper-class status received further confirmation from Eugene Litwak's Buffalo, New York, family study conducted in the 1950s. Litwak defined the modern extended family as a more loosely organized unit than the classic three-generation household often containing collateral relatives, a usage also employed in this study. He found that the newer version, marked by deference to successful relatives and material and vocational assistance to kin in order to improve their status, tended to appear most frequently in upper-class Buffalo residents.[3] Their family structure and behavior recapitulates that of their forerunners in Boston, New York, Chicago, Charleston, and Los Angeles.

A host of other community examinations reveal similarity between contemporary and historical leadership groups in correlating with elite status a high frequency of participation and management in civic agencies and charitable, cultural, and professional societies. Recent research on local institutions scattered throughout the country and on national associations discloses that the most prestigious organizations had memberships drawn from people with the largest fortunes, the most esteemed occupations, the greatest power, the most exclusive residential addresses, the highest educational levels, and the best pedigrees in their community.[4] These data agreed with the information on voluntary association presented in the five case studies. Similarly, an investigation of philanthropic campaigns conducted in the 1940s and '50s in an eastern Canadian city revealed that civic altruism depended upon the direction and support of key business and social figures, just as did earlier efforts in American cities.[5]

Affluence ranked with power and ahead of distinguished lineage as a universal attribute, at least in their prime, of the enclaves described in this study. In nineteenth-century cities, young or old, wealth was distributed far less evenly than in rural counties or for the nation as a whole. According to the 1860 census, the richest 1 percent in Philadelphia and Worcester, Massachusetts, owned about 40 percent of the personally held wealth of their communities. In that year the same groups in Baltimore, New Orleans, and St. Louis owned respectively 38.5, 43.0, and 37.6 percent of the noncorporate wealth in their cities.[6] Given the commercial eminence of the richest stratum, there is little reason to assume that corporate-owned assets were any differently concentrated.

More comprehensive studies of American hegemonic groups, families, and figures in other places also resemble the elite and upper-class depictions in the previous chapters. Thomas J. Wertenbaker's and Clifford Dowdey's accounts of colonial Virginia note the mercantile origins of the Old Dominion aristocracy and its later shift to a baronial life-style, a transition also made by many family founders of the rural-urban gentry that comprised an extensive element of the Charleston planter patriciate. Nor was Charleston the only South Carolina low-country port. Georgetown and Beaufort merchants acted as rice and cotton factors for many planters, and the maritime elites in these towns resembled their Charleston equivalents in life-style and economic activity. By the 1820s, however, their share of the tidewater trade was annexed by Charleston, in much the same manner that, a generation earlier, Boston took over the commerce of Salem and Newburyport.[7]

Investigations of antebellum upper orders in other northern cities and other histories of such enclaves in New York and Boston affirm structural and functional patterns observed in the groups discussed here. Multifaceted leadership echelons composed of the wealthiest and foremost entrepreneurs (generally merchants) and professionals dominated local government, business, and civic activities and had the highest social status in Philadelphia; in Salem, Worcester, Northampton, Newburyport, and Springfield, Massachusetts; in Albany, Poughkeepsie, and Brooklyn, New York; in Providence, Rhode Island; and in New Haven, Connecticut. A number of urban centers exhibited similar variations in upper-class structure. By the 1850s and '60s old families had greater influence in Philadelphia, Salem, Northhampton, and Spring-field than in Albany, Poughkeepsie, Newburyport, Worcester, and New Haven, just as the aristocratic element dominated Boston and Charleston more than New York or Chicago.[8] The common experience of these upper strata is reflected in the parallel developments of their patrician families. The Browns of Providence, the Ganesvoorts of Albany, the Crowninshields, Derbys, and Grays of Salem, the Lowells and Tracys of Newburyport, the Cabots of Beverly, and the Shippens, Morrises, and Whartons of Philadelphia recapitulate, in their commercial origins and their subsequent predominance in the political, professional, civic, cultural, and social circles of their communities, the experience of the great maritime clans of New York, Boston, and Charleston. In effectively bequeathing to their offspring their multifunctional leadership they replicated the emergence of the Boston Brahmins, the Charleston gentry, and, to a lesser degree, the Knickerbocker and mercantile families of New York.

These patriciates also encountered similar difficulties in sustaining their position and eventually surrendered power and status to the same type of rising elites. The Old Guard weakened because of economic changes, usually the transformation from commerce to industry or the diversion of trade to a larger shipping center, or, in the South, the triumph of the plantation over the countinghouse, and demographic changes, usually an influx of European immigrants. Between 1830 and 1850 the Federalist-mercantile-professional upper class in Newburyport gave way to elites thrust up by the advent of Irish-Catholic settlement and industrialism. In the 1840s a similar establishment in New Haven was displaced by capitalists who headed new types of businesses and had humble antecedents. A decade later in Albany and during the 1870s in Springfield similar forces undermined ancient families.[9] The circulation of the higher ranks in these cities resembled the New York experience, where the traditional establishment was deposed by mid-century *nouveau riche* capitalists and ethnic political bosses.

Patrician Philadelphia, on the other hand, shared the experience of Brahmin Boston. These aristocracies absorbed newly risen capitalists and preserved community leadership until the end of the nineteenth century. Their cities developed from important colonial ports into major northeastern commercial centers. Similar historical background created parallel patterns of structure and behavior in their upper classes. Boston and Philadelphia family fortunes originated in trade and the professions, were supplemented by real estate speculation, and were sustained in the industrial era by investment in railroads and financial institutions and by marriage to *arriviste* industrial magnates. Both groups capitalized on regional natural resources. Philadelphia entrepreneurs formed Pennsylvania coal companies, and Boston magnates organized cotton manufacturing in Massachusetts. By the early 1800s these patriciates consolidated their ascendancy through intraclass kinship ties and the acquisition of prestigious social functions. Although not as politically active nor as intellectually distinguished as the Brahmins, Philadelphia gentlemen clearly constituted an urban aristocracy. Like proper Bostonians, Philadelphia bluebloods controlled the important commercial and older industrial family firms, investments banks, and law offices. They, too, were patrons of the city's art museum, symphony orchestra, and leading university, founded the state historical society, and were trustees of the oldest hospitals and most respectable charity agencies. Genteel Philadelphians and Bostonians also manifested the same pattern of gradual decline. New business interests represented by outside entrepreneurs overshadowed the upper-class family firm, politicians with ethnic minority backgrounds or constituencies preempted municipal government offices and party leadership, and exogamous marriage eroded patrician cohesion.[10]

The passing of the old upper class in Springfield, New Haven, Newburyport, and Albany created a situation closer to that of newer cities like Chicago and Los Angeles, or to post–Civil War Charleston and New York. Urban leadership now was exerted through alliances between business and political elites of diverse backgrounds and rapid turnover in membership. Political and economic activity was no longer directed by a coalition of old families and did not necessarily extend to public officeholding, high social status, and civic leadership.[11] This fragmentation of sovereignty occurred at different rates in communities of different ages, sizes, and geographical locations.

The "Old City" aristocracy underwent the same diminution as the Charleston chivalry. By the 1930s descendants of the antebellum rural gentry still maintained a self-contained social life but had forfeited economic and political control of the community to newly risen merchants, bankers, and lawyers. As a result they took little interest in the town and many had moved away. Upper-class New Orleans also shared the values and destiny of the Charleston establishment. Both cities served plantation-dominated districts and included many estate owners in their upper strata. Their aristocracies aspired to chivalry, honor, and elegance. Although the New Orleans enclave held trade in higher regard, the vocations of plantation ownership, law, medicine, banking, and politics were esteemed by both patriciates. Extensive intermarriage occurred within the upper ranks of both places. In New Orleans, as in Charleston, the old order never recovered from the Civil War. Since 1865, many descendants of distinguished families in these cities have lived in penury, and some reacted to their eclipse by becoming recluses and despairing the alleged postbellum degeneracy of their communities.[12]

The modern elites of Atlanta may have been even more fragmented. In an examination of the city's power structure published in 1953, Floyd Hunter found that the dominant group in the community consisted mostly of businessmen, especially financiers. These figures were not social registrites or holder of public office and achieved cohesive leadership through formal organizations like social clubs and informal associations such as luncheons. A portrayal of more divided leadership emerged from a 1961 study of the Atlanta elites. According to this investigation, the foremost capitalists competed with each other, alliances continuously shifted, and business and political leadership enclaves did not overlap.[13]

Birmingham, Alabama, differed from these other southern cities by lacking an antebellum past and, therefore, an aristocracy, and by belonging to the species of industrial centers that rose in mid- and late nineteenth-century America. A recent analysis of the Birmingham power structure from 1871 to 1921 shows that the business elite and the foremost lawyers corresponded to contemporary tycoons in New York, Chicago, Los Angeles, and Atlanta by determining issues, e.g. low property assessments and taxes, annexation of territory by the municipality, and antilabor policies, that they considered vital to their interests. As in other places, big businessmen divided on less important matters, e.g. street railways *vs*. railroads, the economic and social elites infrequently assumed public office, and leading citizens differed or did not assert control over style-of-life issues, e.g. prohibition, and allocation of municipal resources to services like schools, libraries, or public health. Neither a pluralistic distribution nor a monolithic concentration of power prevailed in Birmingham.[14]

The upper strata in New England, not as abruptly threatened or terminated by defeat and destruction in war, endured a more gradual contraction of power, affluence, and prestige. A survey of Salem elite, conducted in 1952–53 when the city had a little over 40,000 inhabitants, revealed a course of development reminiscent of its neighbor and former maritime rival. Like Boston, it originated as a trade center with a homogeneous population of native American stock and later became an industrial town with an ethnically mixed citizenry. The patriciate corresponded to the Brahmins in holding numerous positions in civic voluntary associations until well into the twentieth century, in serving, up to World War I, in the top offices in the municipal government, and in having a self-contained social life. After the war, however, the top economic leaders were industrialists and their attorneys; public officeholders generally represented ethnic minorities; and political power was shared by vestiges of mercantile clans, the industrial elite, and leaders from immigrant groups. Thus power and status hierarchies no longer coincided. Newburyport went through the same economic and demographic transition, and its waning aristocracy behaved like those in Salem and Boston. Warner and Lunt reported that the progeny of the mercantile patriciate formed a social circle based on intermarriage, residence in old family homes and exclusive neighborhoods, attendance at select private preparatory schools, and membership in ancient and exclusive voluntary associations dedicated to civic causes and genealogical matters. Although the blueblood life-style was a model for the newly risen and the aristocracy served in excess of its proportion of the total number of residents in local public office, the city government was dominated by elites of later origin. The *nouveau riche* had larger individual incomes but the patriciate had larger family incomes. Nevertheless, 17 percent of the old family descendants were clerks or salespeople. The old upper class felt that they had been displaced by newer elites and many had left town.[15]

Small cities in the interior, a more recently settled area of the United States, disclosed a pattern of elite circulation resembling that of Chicago, the region's major metropolis. A 1953 study of a Michigan city of 10,000 showed that the traditional upper class had lost its position to corporate executives recently arrived from larger urban centers. Old families still maintained their claims to high status but were unable to impose these claims on the larger community. A survey of a midwestern city with a population of 20,000, published four years later, disclosed sharp divergence between the commercial elite, composed of industrial corporation managers and directors and heads of banks, and civic association leadership, made up mostly of smaller businessmen. High municipal officeholders and members of the political elite were not usually leaders of these private community organizations. Yet another study of a similar-sized town in the Midwest came up with identical conclusions in 1958. Before 1900 the economic, political, and voluntary associational leadership had considerably overlapped. This interlocking establishment had since been supplanted by specialized elites. Economic control over the community now lies in the hands of absentee corporation executives, and political and civic leadership is exerted by middle-class businessmen and professionals.[16]

Although the Chicago upper class was less persistent and more permeable than were the Boston and Charleston aristocracies, it dominated the city for over fifty years. Leading Chicagoans also achieved a high level of group solidarity through clustering in exclusive neighborhoods and clubs and through extensive intermarriage. A similar situation existed in Pittsburgh, where iron and steel manufacturers and their banker associates controlled the economy. According to a 1959 study by Floyd Hunter, power in Detroit was also concentrated in a small group of industrial executives. But prominent citizens in Cleveland, Ohio, and Wheeling, West Virginia, again iron and steel magnates, had relatively low levels of integration. Compared to equivalent strata in Chicago, Pittsburgh, and Detroit, they lived in mixed neighborhoods and belonged to less selective local social clubs. In contrast to Chicago and Pittsburgh, Cleveland and Wheeling elites less frequently married within their enclave. The latter were more likely to leave their cities than were the relatively stable rich and powerful Pittsburghers or even the restless Chicagoans, to depart from the scene of their triumphs.[17]

Urban centers in the most recently developed parts of the country, the far West and the Southwest, appear to have a profile of leadership similar to that of other relatively new cities and epitomized by Los Angeles, the metropolitan giant in these regions. Between the 1850s and 1880s the business elite in Portland, Oregon, dominated their city in the same manner as did their counterparts in Los Angeles. It held high posts in the municipal government, controlled the economy, and assumed leadership in public and private civic, cultural, and charitable institutions. Old Guard magnates also met the same fate as did their opposite numbers in Los Angeles. After 1900, they were swept aside by a new enclave of Portland tycoons. A 1958 examination of hegemony in Seattle found that community leadership, as usual, was in the hands of a group consisting mainly of business executives and bankers who participated widely in civic agencies. None of these figures came from high-society circles and many were self-made men representing new interests and coalitions.[18] The power structure of Dallas, according to a 1963 study, had the same attributes: The "Dallas decision-maker is a businessman, often a banker," reported the author, "Most of them are 'self-made' men." Further evidence of the domination of businessmen, usually merchants and financiers, in the power structure of West Coast and southwestern communities appeared in a 1961 exploration of hegemonic groups in Denver, San Diego, El Paso, Tucson, and several other cities in New Mexico and Texas.[19]

A genteel and cultivated San Francisco establishment is often posited in invidious contrast to the aggressive *parvenus* of Los Angeles. But Peter R. Decker's work on early San Francisco shows considerable turnover in the upper class. A mercantile elite, whose style and rule largely recapitulated (and sometimes consciously imitated) the maritime enclaves of pre–Civil War Boston, New York, and Philadelphia, controlled the city between 1850 and 1870. This stratum, however, was mostly composed of self-made successes, and volatile business conditions created a vigorous circulation of personnel in the upper layer. Between the 1870s and 1890s the great merchants were replaced by manufacturers and their allies in finance. Unlike the Brahmins, the early elite was unable to make the transition to industrialism and thus shared the fate of New York's antebellum overseas traders. By the 1880s class lines tightened and the upper order in San Francisco became significantly less porous than in Los Angeles. Its grandiose life-style, however, resembled that of New York's Four Hundred. Conversely, the cultural and civic leadership of San Francisco's prominent families coincided with the role of Boston and Philadelphia patriciates rather than with the actions of the Astor set.[20]

Commercial elites in America have received esteem and deference from a society in which acquisition of wealth and success in business are reigning values. The attempts of these elites to buttress their status by assuming upper-class social and political functions and by adopting aristocratic attributes have been resisted by national beliefs and circumstances that promoted equality, democracy, and progress. Conversely, it has been claimed that in Europe rigid social stratification and residual feudal values made it more difficult to attain high status through personal, and especially through entrepreneurial, accomplishment, but that rank once acquired was protected by the institutions of an aristocratic society. Fortunes gained in business, after several generations of refinement, launched many a noble family. Acceptance from above, however, may have attenuated entrepreneurship because feudalism and medieval Catholicism left a legacy of anticapitalist values which permeated the outlook of the aristocracy. The creed of the old upper class glorified honor, largesse, courage, community, and continuity, and disdained capitalist virtues of thrift, rational calculation, increased productivity, systematic accumulation of wealth, triumph in open competition, and economic progress. Accordingly, a true gentleman would live on the land rather than in the city; he would derive his place in society from historical, familial, and communal ties, not from personal successes. Military prowess, genteel behavior, and a paternal concern for loyal and dependent peasants were traits deemed especially praiseworthy; the commercial achievements of the *parvenu* were considered vulgar and even dangerous. The aristocratic ideal held that society should be a closed system in which status and role are defined by birth, tradition, and standing in a static, hierarchical order.[21]

Historians have attributed significant differences in outlook between the American and European bourgeoisie to the continuing influence of the medieval past. European merchants who sought acceptance by a legally defined national aristocracy supported a hierarchical social system while their counterparts in the United States expressed pride at having risen in a democratic society. American businessmen derived greater gratification from their activities and won higher status for their accomplishments because they did not have to contend with the residual claims and values of feudalism. Consequently, Americans focused their resources and energies on business while European merchants and manufacturers frequently terminated their careers by retiring to landed estates, or diverted their efforts and capital to imitate the luxurious life-style of the aristocracy. The *haut bourgeoisie* hoped that emulation would ultimately lead to entry. If the first generation did not become aristocrats, at least by advantageously marrying off their daughters, by properly educating their offspring, by establishing a patrimony, and by acquiring landed estates they could eventually ennoble the family.[22] Extreme cases of such elevation and transformation occurred in Venice between 1381 and 1646 and in seventeenth-century Toulouse. The Venetian mercantile patriciate turned itself into a privileged caste based on inherited status and gradually divested itself of commercial functions while becoming a rural gentry. Its successors in the seventeenth and eighteenth centuries continued this tradition by using fortunes derived from trade and industry to acquire titles and land and thus to eliminate the stigma of commercial origins. In a related way, by the eighteenth century the Toulouse landed nobility completely absorbed the fifteenth- and sixteenth-century mercantile elite.[23]

Those who argue that the persistence of aristocratic values inhibited economic development assert that the more permeable and adaptable English nobility and gentry, with younger sons becoming commoners and wealthy capitalists sometimes rewarded with peerages, enabled Great Britain to surpass other European countries in commercial and industrial accomplishments. Conversely, Germany, where Junkerdom reigned in the nineteenth century, and France, held back by the spirit of the *ancien regime*, lagged behind.[24]

The influence of the feudal past offers a plausible, and even profound, rationale for differences between American and European elites and for variations among the latter. But the behavior of Old World aristocracies indicates that this theory, if not invalid, oversimplifies the situation. Available evidence shows wide-ranging diversification in the behavior of the nobility and gentry in different regions and at different times.[25] In Germany, for example, although Junkers acted atavistically in commercial matters, the sixteenth- and seventeenth-century Holstein nobility were the most innovative businessmen in the North Sea and Baltic region. Lawrence Stone, in *The Crisis of the Aristocracy, 1558–1641*, shows that the Tudor nobility evinced pronounced entrepreneurial interests and energies. It managed estates with an eye to maximizing profit, introduced new techniques in agriculture and husbandry, bought and developed city plots, organized and financed joint stock companies, fishing, trading, and colonizing expeditions, and ventures in mining, milling, and metallurgy. The eighteenth-century British rural nobility and gentry continued to participate vigorously in business either through exploitation of their estates (coal mining, agricultural processing, textile manufacturing, milling, ironworks, and stone quarries), through financing or organizing such undertakings as waterways and turnpikes which helped them move products from their estates to markets, or through capital investment in mercantile and banking endeavors. Victorian aristocrats also involved themselves in capitalistic activities. Many invested in railroads and several noted peers (though a small minority of the great lords) derived an extensive income from mining and urban real estate.[26]

Commercial achievement in aristocratic communities may vary with particular phases of the economy as well as with particular times and places. Nobles and lesser orders of landed gentlemen have fostered agricultural improvements and ventures in extractive industries (also closely associated with estate development and easily initiated because of control over the local labor force), while they condemned banking and retail trade, endeavors remote from local land ownership.[27]

Literary images and impressionistic characterizations of noblemen as obsolete types, romantic, indolent, spendthrift, traditional, contemptuous of trade, and impulsive are not always substantiated by historical evidence. Given the multitude of groups loosely called nobility, gentry, or aristocracy, it is difficult to generalize about traditions or traits that shaped class behavior. Furthermore, few noble families, due to failure to reproduce male heirs, or because of political disruptions, could trace their lineage more than several generations, much less back to the Middle Ages. Most families, in fact, were ennobled as a reward for military or civil services performed for the king, and thus owed their status to an antifeudal institution, the centralized state. Numerous others purchased titles with profits from commerce. The old and new nobility eventually intermarried and joined forces against the increasingly aggressive bourgeoisie, and the *arrivistes* were among the staunchest defenders of their order. Nonetheless, men whose talents and habits had brought them to the top in trade or in the government bureaucracy did not inevitably turn into romantic reactionaries when they received landed estates. Nor did so-called atavistic economic traits conventionally attributed to the aristocrat necessarily inhibit commercial endeavor. If landed gentlemen loved leisure and luxury, such tastes gave them time and incentive for profitable enterprise. Conspicuous consumption had to be financed, and debt spurred many a noble into more efficient estate management, or into milling or mining ventures that would enable him to live like a gentleman. Many aristocrats succumbed to idleness or sensuality. Others, however, dabbled in scientific agriculture, experimented with new metallurgical techniques, or built mills on their land to employ impoverished country people. Although ventures motivated by debt, curiosity, or humanity did not spring from the spirit of bourgeois capitalism, they were often entrepreneurial and sometimes profitable. The reckless romantic nature traditionally associated with aristocrats could also engender commercial activity. The plunger, the promoter, and the speculator share these traits. An impulsive outlook undoubtedly encouraged those Tudor, Spanish, and Portugese noblemen who financed and organized overseas trade and colonizing expeditions.[28] Nor is a rigid barrier between gentleman and businessman created by the old distinction between the flamboyant aristocrat, the public man of largesse, luxury, and courage, and the privatized Calvinistic burgher piling up gains through closeness, prudence, and thrift. Public men had power; they held government offices and exerted influence at court—no mean advantages in the mercantile economy of the early modern era. Even the traditional functions and privileges of the nobility could enhance as well as stifle enterprise. Remnants of feudal customs and laws in some areas precluded certain types of business activities for the nobility up to the nineteenth century, but legacies from the Middle Ages also conferred privileges, such as freedom from taxes or customs duties, which gave an edge to lords who competed with bourgeois businessmen. Ancient laws of servitude and tenancy also provided a cheap and stable labor supply which could be used for milling and mining. Rights vested in landownership gave access to natural resources, such as mineral deposits and water power, crucial to the commercial and industrial development of Europe. Land, the most secure collateral, gave estate owners access to credit unavailable to many middle-class businessmen in an age of scarce capital. Finally, the core functions, the raison d'être, of the aristocracy—landownership and war—served to stimulate entrepreneurship. Innovations in agricultural and military methods, organization, and instruments, and improvements in efficiency and productivity in these occupations over which the aristocracy presided, should give pause to those who conceive the class as a composite of Sir Galahad and Colonel Blimp.[29]

Comparisons between American and European social structures have emphasized entry into, as much as the quality of, the upper class. Tocqueville was not the first to assert that equality, upward mobility, and plentiful opportunity have made the United States an open society in contrast to the constrictions of tradition and exclusiveness imposed by the aristocracy upon Europe. The corporate society of church, guild, and lord, many observers have declared, stifled the emergence of elites based on achievement and merit, thus undermining democracy and, as discussed above, entreprenuerially inspired economic growth. Here again, however, caution must condition grandiose conclusions. The European upper class was rarely a closed caste. Accessibility varied from region to region and age to age depending upon the political situation, availability of land, birth and death rates, and the degree of expansion in the economy, the army, and the civil service.[30] An identical situation of variance between vigorous and sluggish turnover appeared in the circulation of personnel in urban elites. Sylvia Thrupp, in her study of London merchants from 1300 to 1600, argues that bankruptcy, biology, and acquisition of landed estates kept the class fluid. William G. Haskins observed the same phenomenon among the contemporary commercial elites of provincial British cities. And the Renaissance merchants who ruled Florence also absorbed *parvenu* talent and wealth. The Venetian commercial patriciate, on the other hand, evolved into a closed caste.[31] On the question of mobility-pattern comparisons between Europe and America, a study of such trends in the twentieth-century United States and northern and western European cities indicates that rates of status elevation are no higher in this country than in other industrial societies.[32]

It is difficult to gauge the effects of American democracy and European aristocracy upon liberty, equality, opportunity, and entrepreneurship if we do not know the extent to which their mobility patterns differ. Although calculations have been made for certain countries at specific times, much work remains before any general assessment of the permeability of the aristocracy can be reasonably accurate. And should such an approximation eventually materialize, we still face the problem of defining the qualities of the upper and middle classes and determining the substantive (as opposed to quantitative) differences between European and American social stratification. Evidence of a less exclusive and less reactionary aristocracy might force a revision of some conventional comparisons between the United States and Europe. As yet, even on specific issues in specific countries, controversy surrounds the relationship of aristocracy to society. Some experts, for example, claim that the enduring spirit of the *ancien régime* has prevented France from keeping pace with other advanced capitalist economies in developing standardized production, a mass market, and the large bureaucratic corporation. Failure to implement innovations in technology and business techniques has been attributed to the existence of anticapitalist, feudal beliefs which imposed upon bourgeois businessmen a traditional outlook, intense family loyalty, and contempt for the competitive *parvenu*. Other students, however, not only question whether the *ancien régime* has inhibited France, but assert the vigor and efficiency of French entrepreneurship.[33] But what if the aristocracy is atavistic? Does the imposition of feudal values upon those who enter that enclave necessarily cripple entrepreneurship? Given the state of knowledge about aristocracy and mobility, it is difficult to ascertain definitely the relationship of aristocracy to business enterprise. It is possible, however, to indicate some theoretical conditions which influence the effects of the aristocracy upon commerce. If movement from the middle class to the aristocracy is rare, the former may be so demoralized or so dependent on the latter that bourgeois values do not develop. Conversely, the aloofness of the gentility may enhance business enterprise by impeding entry into an alternative way of life. If the upper class is reasonably accessible, many talented businessmen may forsake commerce for land. Numerous transitions from the countinghouse to the castle may diminish the entrepreneurial talent available to the society. But if too many of the bourgeoisie gain entry, the aristocracy could be engulfed by an unassimilated influx of wealthy businessmen and prominent bureaucrats. Bourgeois values would then dominate society and enhance entrepreneurship. The relationship between aristocracy and entrepreneurship, however, is not governed solely by the interaction between the upper and middle classes. If the bourgeoisie is open to upward mobility, as well as itself being upwardly mobile, it can replenish skills that it loses to higher status by recruitment from below.

Important differences may exist between European and American urban establishments, but the literature on Old World cities abounds with evidence of coincidence. A major cause for this resemblance is that nations on both sides of the Atlantic developed from decentralized rural-agrarian into integrated urban-commercial-industrial societies. From their emergence in the eleventh century to the eighteenth century, rich and powerful enclaves in the northern European cities, in Florence, Venice, Milan, and Genoa, in London and Exeter, and in the English provincial towns anticipated many features of their analogues in the United States. On different continents and at different historical periods these upper strata originated as mercantile elites, frequently of humble rural stock. Eminent overseas traders became bankers and insurance underwriters, invested heavily in urban real estate, frequently acted together in commerce, and allied with leading lawyers and physicians or sent their sons into these callings. As they established commercial and professional predominance, entrepreneurs and lawyers gained control over local politics and proliferated in high municipal government offices. They also became the foremost philanthropists and patrons of culture in their communities, dwelled together in exclusive neighborhoods, joined the same clubs, attended the same churches, went to the same dinners, and were educated at the same schools. Now upper classes, intermarriage and inherited function, fortune, and status eventually made them patriciates. Even the variations among the urban establishments in Europe prefigured differences in elites in American cities. Renaissance Venice experienced a slower circulation in its great mercantile families than did London during the same period, just as Boston Brahmins and antebellum Charleston planters had lower rates of turnover than did the contemporary upper strata of New York and Chicago. Groups involved in similar activities usually share certain aspects of outlook and structure. It need scarcely be said that American and European capitalists avidly sought profit. Entrepreneurial skills, rational organization, and accessibility to investment capital were everywhere necessary. Fourteenth-century Italian overseas traders as well as merchants and manufacturers in New York, Boston, Charleston, Chicago, and Los Angeles were perforce concerned with establishing credit institutions, stable trade routes, effective transportation systems, and regular markets. Out of the necessity of protecting their enterprises and because of the very human desire to pass on their wealth, businessmen on both continents founded family firms. Desiring to secure their gains and grasp new opportunities, they agitated for political power in their communities. Commercial and political hegemony established the mercantile elite as the upper class in many towns. Wealth and social position gave this enclave a sense of community proprietorship which prompted its endowments to charitable and educational institutions. After having made their way to the top, entrepreneurs tried to perpetuate preeminence. The family firm, the exclusive guild, marriage with those of similar or superior station, and bequeathed status and role were the means by which they fought off newcomers. For the most part their resistance was unsuccessful because entrepreneurial skills were difficult to pass on, resources and talents were diverted to noncommercial activities, new opportunities were ignored or regarded as a threat, new techniques were considered vulgar, and new blood was rejected. In Exeter, London, Venice, Paris, Boston, New York, Charleston, and Chicago aggressive family founders gave way to rentier descendants interested in becoming a landed gentry, in military careers (more common in Europe than in the United States), in intellectual or cultural pursuits, in the professions (usually law or medicine), and in public service.[34]

Continuities between the urban upper strata here and abroad persist into the modern era. As in the United States, nineteenth-century bankers in Paris and Lyon were also merchants, and textile tycoons in Alsace and the Nord intermarried and dominated the politics and social welfare projects in their towns. By the 1870s British merchant princes, like their American counterparts, were losing commercial eminence to mass retailers and department store owners, and the great cotton-manufacturing families were socially established and assuming leadership in philanthropy. London bankers, like their American equivalents, often became financiers after success in trade or industry and had patrician ties. Plutocrats and their children in England and the United States went to prestigious boarding schools and colleges, where they were socialized by aristocratic students and genteel headmasters and professors. The urban business elites of both countries held the same values, served in similar political offices, and undertook leadership in great municipal improvement projects. The foremost banking and manufacturing families in Victorian Manchester and Birmingham and the iron-masters of Middlesbrough, in their respective communities, intermarried, headed the leading charitable and cultural organizations, served in high municipal posts, and represented the city boroughs (as did eminent businessmen in Boston, Charleston, and New York in their metropolitan congressional districts) in parliament. After 1870, like their American equivalents, they lost entrepreneurial zeal and hegemonic position. During the 1850s the preeminent businessmen of Hamilton, Ontario, also established an extensive kinship network through family firms and endogamous connubial connections, and achieved multi-dimensional sovereignty in this Canadian city by dominating local political and civic affairs.[35] A recent comparison between the power structures of Seattle, Washington, and Bristol, England, illustrates considerable coincidence in twentieth-century urban elites here and abroad. The largest group of influential figures in both metropolises consists of businessmen; labor leaders rank second, and professionals and government officials third. A virtually identical proportion of businessmen and professionals and government officials appears in the power elites of both cities. Variations between the leadership enclaves are relatively negligible. The labor component is larger in the Bristol elite, which also contains a contingent of affluent society leaders, an element absent in the American enclave. Traditional values also appear more strongly in the Bristol businessmen, perhaps due to the greater age of that city and to differences between American and English culture. They display more respect for scholarly pursuits and for a classical humanistic education than do the Seattle entrepreneurs. Additional evidence of correspondence between urban elites in the United States and foreign countries emerges from a study of southwestern communities. This survey, which includes two Mexican cities, reports no variation in the occupational structure of influential groups north or south of the national border. In all cases the local leaders are bankers or merchants.[36]

A more immediate interest than international comparison has captured the current attention of American elite studies. Social scientists, politicians, journalists, novelists, and other thoughtful citizens have long been concerned with the distribution of power, wealth, and status in this country. Pluralists claim that competing and countervailing interest groups have prevented a single class or enclave from monopolizing these resources. Revisionist critics assert that an interlocking directorate of corporation managers and high public officials rule the nation through control of vast wealth and circulation in key posts in great business organizations, influential government offices, and boards of important foundations and universities. They attempt to measure the concentration of contemporary power and wealth in the same way that I tried to ascertain these issues for historical times, through affiliational, reputational, and decisional criteria.[37]

The battle lines in this conflict have elsewhere been clearly drawn, but the proponents on both sides have done little to establish the historical dimension of their claims. Briefly put, they largely ignore the question of whether power or wealth is more concentrated than in the past. One of the most intriguing and significant paradoxes about America is that, from independence to the present, centrifugal impulses, territorial expansion, the widening area of settlement, and the proliferation of ethnic minorities have been accompanied by administrative and economic centralization and cultural homogenization. As the nation modernized, undergoing a gradual transition from a rural-agricultural society to an urban-industrial society, the forces of cohesion overcame the forces of dispersion. The growing power of the federal government, particularly the executive branch, the emergence of national productive, distributive, communication, and transporation systems, and the standardization of national tastes and values through mail-order houses, chain stores, and amusement media reduced local, regional, ethnic, and possibly even class differences. In these unifying developments lies the basis for the alleged domination of a national elite or ruling class.

The European nobility and gentry played an ambivalent role in political and commercial consolidation. Members of the upper orders sometimes assisted in the economic phase of this process while frequently resisting the development of modern capitalism. They displayed a similar dualism regarding the emergence of the nation state. Aristocrats led the national army and served as high judicial, fiduciary, and ministerial officials and royal advisors, but they also defended, on occasion to the point of rebellion, their local and traditional privileges and sources of authority. The dominant urban mercantile patriciates acted in a similarly ambiguous fashion, sometimes defending local independence and sometimes supporting centralized economic and administrative systems. The same contradiction occurred in hegemonic enclaves in the United States. Wealthy and influential Charleston planters, merchants, and capitalists contributed to the national economy by participating in interregional trade and furnishing rice and cotton for foreign export. Concomitantly, they organized banking, transportation, and industrial projects to strengthen local autonomy, tried to preserve the cultural uniqueness of the South, and ultimately seceded from the Union. In the North and West the contradictions between centralism and separatism did not as starkly emerge. Business elites and municipal bodies in Baltimore, Philadelphia, New York, Boston, Chicago, and Los Angeles, and the governments of the states in which they were located, built canals and railroads and founded banks not only in competition with each other, but in order to make their city the commercial center of the nation. Indeed, their vision of supremacy over other cities entailed their own establishment as the economic capital of the country. This quest for civic preeminence through national predominance, at least after the War of 1812, made the northern and western urban centers firm supporters of economic centralization and political unity. In other facets of community leadership, however, the urban upper orders were primarily insular. Their energy and money focused, especially before the Civil War, upon endeavors to improve the environment, uplift the spirit, and reflect the uniqueness of their own city. The champions of these efforts were aware that interurban competition existed in these aspects of civic life as well as in economic matters. But the contention in this sphere was for celebrity rather than mastery.

The attempt to overshadow in repute the charitable, intellectual, and cultural achievements in other places, by establishing the originality or greater magnitude of contributions in this aspect of metropolitan life and thus projecting beyond its borders the glory of the community, ironically led to widespread replication of forms and procedures. Emulation being an inextricable part of competition, interurban rivalry depended upon a comparison of similar activities.

In a more direct and fundamental way the upper orders in Boston, New York, Charleston, and Chicago participated in national unification. Defeat in Civil War destroyed the viability of the urban-rural gentry in Charleston, and their planter peers in other parts of the South, as a regional elite that might challenge the centralizing thrust of urban and industrial capitalism. During the first half of the nineteenth century, New York established superiority in commerce and finance over contending cities along the eastern seaboard. After the Civil War the Manhattan business elite, especially investment bankers and railroad magnates, increasingly dominated economic activity throughout the country and impinged on the autonomy of their counterparts in Philadelphia, Boston, Charleston, and Chicago.

The New Yorkers, however, did not command as much power in other areas of national life. Although drawn into the New York commercial orbit, Boston remained a bastion of high culture and exerted considerable leadership over the unification of elite life-styles that accompanied the development of a national economy. Beginning in the 1880s prominent citizens of Los Angeles, Philadelphia, New York, Cleveland, Pittsburgh, San Francisco, Chicago, and other places markedly preferred to send their children to exclusive New England preparatory schools, frequently run by Brahmin headmasters and trustees, and to Yale, Harvard, and Princeton rather than to local academies and colleges. Locally prestigious social clubs, charity organizations, civic associations, cultural institutions, and society affairs were modeled upon the high-minded customs and activities of genteel Boston and Philadelphia as well as on the antics of New York's Four Hundred.

Did these cultural and economic developments presage the appearance of a national power elite or upper class? Emulation is not absorption. Other upper strata could adopt the ways of the cultural or social elites of New York or Boston without surrendering local sovereignty in these sectors of community life. Nor did economic superiority entail supremacy in other, though admittedly less important, dimensions of leadership, a necessary condition for the emergence of a national upper class. But even at the zenith of its commercial predominance, New York never achieved monolithic economic rule. The robber barons of Manhattan incessantly squabbled among themselves. Daniel Drew, Jim Fisk, and Jay Gould warred against each other in the 1870s and '80s, and during the next decade mammoth struggles took place between the conglomerate empires of John D. Rockefeller and J. P. Morgan. In the Progressive Era, as Robert Wiebe noted in *Businessmen and Reform*, tycoons in New York and elsewhere often engaged in factional conflicts, dividing along regional lines or according to types of enterprise.[38] Finally, many local business decisions, real estate acquisition, zoning, resource exploitation, utilities enterprise, etc., were not dictated from Wall Street board rooms.

Since World War II, federal government defense spending, the decline of the steel and automobile industries, and the energy crisis have diminished the power of New York capital and the salience of northeastern and midwestern manufacturing. The newer and fastest-growing enterprises, aerospace and electronic firms, locate chiefly in southern California and Texas, and the corporate headquarters of older companies are moving from New York to Houston and Los Angeles. The demographic center of the country is also moving south and west, and the combined shift of population and commercial expansion enhances the political influence of the "rim" states. From 1960 to 1972 either the Democratic or Republican presidential nominee hailed from California, Texas, or Arizona, and from 1963 to 1974 natives of Texas and California served as chief executive, and an adopted son of California now sits in the White House.

A similar arrangement occurred in the cultural arena. Boston, Philadelphia, New York, and Chicago were famed centers of thought and culture as well as of trade, production, and finance. With the exception of high-society queens in New York and Chicago, the leading citizens of these places won repute for business acumen and acquisitiveness, or as educators, patrons, or practitioners in the arts, sciences, and philanthropy. They were praised for aggressiveness, seriousness, civic-mindedness, altruism, and other Victorian virtues. After World War I, Hollywood and café society broke the hold of older urban elites over fashion and style. Today, in an age dedicated to consumption, leisure, thrills, and youth, America admires film and rock stars, athletes, and newly minted oil and cattle millionaires, and worships the "sunbelt" life-style initiated and epitomized in Florida, southern California, Texas, Arizona, Nevada, and Colorado.

If a solitary ruling elite or class exists, it is territorially fluid and culturally adaptive. Nor is its personnel more constant. Outside of the descendants of a few persistent clans—the Roosevelts, Harrimans, and Rockefellers of New York; the Adamses, Saltonstalls, and Lodges of Boston; the McCormicks and Fields of Chicago, the Chandlers of Los Angeles, the Scrantons of Pennsylvania, and the duPonts of Delaware—the great post–World War II statesmen and capitalists do not come from the old urban aristocracy, or even from their successors, the late nineteenth-century captains of industry. Whether the contemporary power structure is pyramidic or polycentered, it is fixed neither geographically, culturally, nor hereditarily. Those who assert the existence of a national power elite do not claim that it depends upon recruitment from a narrow range of families or localities. If there is such a group, however, it has shifting geographical bases, high turnover in personnel, and great responsiveness to social and economic change. In these respects it differs little from historical leadership figures and echelons in this nation. Such conditions render this putative enclave either so amorphous that it cannot in a systematic and all-inclusive manner mobilize and therefore monopolize power, or so shrewd and comprehensive that its omnipotence is unchallengeable.

NOTES

1. W. Lloyd Warner and Paul S. Lunt, *The Social Life of a Modern Community* (New Haven: Yale University Press, 1941), 84–90, 93, 98–112, 120–25, 138–39, 142–44, 170–72, 198, 339–40, 380, 385, 428–29; Allison Davis, Burleigh B. Gardner, and Mary R. Gardner, *Deep South: A Social Anthropological Study of Caste and Class* (Chicago: University of Chicago Press, 1941), 63–64, 74–75, 84–99, 201–2; Charles McArthur, "Personality Differences between Middle and Upper Classes," *Journal of Abnormal and Social Psychology*, L (Mar., 1955), 247–54.

2. William E. Henry, "The Business Executive: The Psychodynamics of a Social Role," *American Journal of Sociology* (hereafter cited as *AJS*), LIV (Jan., 1949), 286–91.

3. Davis, Gardner, and Gardner, *Deep South*, 84–99; Eugene Litwak, "Extended Family Cohesion," *American Sociological Review* (hereafter cited as *ASR*), XXV (Feb., 1960), 9–21.

4. See the following articles in the *ASR*: Mirra Komarovsky, "The Voluntary Associations of Urban Dwellers," XI (Dec., 1946), 686–98; Mhyra S. Minnis, "Cleavage in Women's Organizations," XVIII (Jan., 1953), 47–53; John M. Foskett, "Social Structure and Social Participation," XX (Aug., 1955), 431–38; Mor-

ris Axelrod, "Urban Structure and Social Participation," XXI (Feb., 1956), 13–18; Wendell Bell and Maryanne T. Force, "Urban Neighborhood and Participation in Formal Organizations," XXI (Feb., 1956), 25–34; John C. Scott, Jr., "Membership and Participation in Voluntary Association," XXII (June, 1957), 312–25; Howard E. Freeman, Edwin Novak, and Lee G. Reeder, "Correlates of Membership in Voluntary Associations," XXII (Oct., 1957), 528–34; Charles R. Wright and Herbert H. Hyman, "Voluntary Association Membership of American Adults: Evidence from National Sample Surveys," XXIII (Mar., 1958), 284–94; Nicholas Babahuk, Ruth Marsey, and C. Wayne Gordon, "Men and Women in Community Agencies: A Note on Power and Prestige," XXV (June, 1960), 399–403.

5. Aileen D. Ross, "The Social Control of Philanthropy," *AJS*, LVIII (Mar., 1953), 451–60.

6. Lee Soltow, ed., *Six Papers on the Size Distribution of Wealth and Income* (National Bureau of Economic Research, New York: Columbia University Press, 1969), XXXIII, 1–24; Edward Pessen, *Riches, Class and Power before the Civil War* (Lexington, Mass., Toronto, London: D. C. Heath, 1973), 34, 36, 39; Robert Doherty, *New England Society, 1800–1860* (Amherst: University of Massachusetts Press, 1977), 46.

7. Thomas J. Wertenbaker, *The Shaping of Colonial Virginia* (New York: Russell and Russell, 1958), ii–iii, 2–3, 16–20, 31–32, 137–41; Clifford Dowdey, *The Virginia Dynasties* (Boston: Little, Brown, 1969), *passim*; George Rogers, Jr., *The History of Georgetown County, South Carolina* (Columbia: University of South Carolina Press, 1970), *passim*; "The Journal of Arthur Brailsford Wescoat, 1863," *South Carolina Historical and Genealogical Magazine*, LV (1954), 71–102; Frederick A. Porcher, "Historical and Social Sketch of Craven County," *Southern Quarterly Review*, new ser. IX (Jan.–Apr., 1854), 396–414.

8. Doherty, *New England, passim*; Bernard Farber, *Guardians of Virtue: Salem Families in 1800* (New York: Basic Books, 1972), *passim*; Robert E. Peabody, *Merchant Venturers of Old Salem* (Boston: Houghton Mifflin, 1912), *passim*; Ralph D. Paine, *The Ships and Sailors of Old Salem* (Boston: Charles E. Lauriat, 1924), *passim*; Joseph Duncan Phillips, *Salem in the Eighteenth Century* (Boston: Houghton Mifflin, 1937), *passim*; Floyd Hunter, Ruth C. Schaeffer, and Cecil G. Sheps, *Community Organization: Action and Interaction* (Chapel Hill: University of North Carolina Press, 1956), 3, 11–24, 100–102, 107–8; Benjamin W. Labaree, *Patriots and Partisans: The Merchants of Newburyport, 1764–1815* (Cambridge: Harvard University Press, 1962), *passim*; Warner and Lunt, *Social Life*, 78–79, 80–93, 98–102, 261–262, 371; Stephan Thernstrom, *Poverty and Progress: Social Mobility in a Nineteenth Century City* (Cambridge: Harvard University Press, 1964), 34–42; Michael H. Frisch, "The Community Elite and the Emergence of Urban Politics: Springfield, Massachusetts, 1840–1880," in *Nineteenth Century Cities*, Stephan Thernstrom and Richard Sennett, eds., (New Haven: Yale University Press, 1969), 277–296; Pessen, *Riches, passim*; Alice P. Kenney, *The Gansevoorts of Albany: Dutch Patricians in the Upper Hudson Valley* (Syracuse: Syracuse University Press, 1969), xiv, xxi–ii, 6–48, 108–87; E. Digby Baltzell, *Philadelphia Gentlemen: The Making of a National Upper Class* (Glencoe, Ill.: Free Press, 1958), 70–107 and *passim*; Nathaniel Burt, *The Perennial Philadelphians: The Anatomy of an*

American Aristocracy (Boston: Little, Brown, 1963), *passim*; James B. Hedges, *The Browns of Providence, Rhode Island* (Cambridge: Harvard University Press, 1952), *passim*; Robert A. Dahl, *Who Governs? Democracy and Power in an American City* (New Haven: Yale University Press, 1961), 11–32; Clyde and Sally Griffen, *Natives and Newcomers: The Ordering of Opportunity in Mid-Nineteenth-Century Poughkeepsie* (Cambridge: Harvard University Press, 1978), 40, 84–94.

9. Frisch, "Community," 284–96; Thernstrom, *Poverty*, 42–49, 53–56; Dahl, *Who*, 25–51; Kenney, *Gansevoorts*, 244–70.

10. Baltzell, *Philadelphia Gentlemen*, *passim*; Burt, *Perennial Philadelphians*, *passim*.

11. Thernstrom, *Poverty*, 42–49, 53–56; Frisch, "Community," 284–96; Dahl, *Who*, 63ff.; Kenney, *Gansevoorts*, 214, 244–270.

12. Davis, Gardner, and Gardner, *Deep South*, 63–64, 73–99, 201–2, 263–65, 490–98; Robert Tallant, *The Romantic New Orleanians* (New York, E.P. Dutton, 1948), *passim*.

13. Floyd Hunter, *Community Power Structure* (Chapel Hill: University of North Carolina Press, 1953), 1–25, 75–81, 105; M. Kent Jennings, *Community Influentials: The Elites of Atlanta* (New York: Free Press, 1961), *passim*.

14. Carl W. Harris, *Political Power in Birmingham, 1871–1921* (Knoxville: University of Tennessee Press, 1977), *passim*.

15. Hunter, Schaeffer, and Sheps, *Community Organization*, 3, 5–6, 11–35, 98–123; Warner and Lunt: *Social Life*, 38–39, 78–93, 98–102, 120–25, 135–36, 138–39, 142–49, 170–72, 198, 261–62, 290–21, 319, 329–38, 361, 371–74, 423–26, 428, 431, 433; *The Status System of a Modern Community* (New Haven: Yale University Press, 1942), 9–10, 27–31, 37–38, 41–50, 53.

16. George P. Stone and William H. Form, "Instabilities in Status," *ASR*, XVIII (Apr., 1953), 153–55; Robert O. Schulze and Leonard U. Blumberg, "The Determination of Local Power Elites," *AJS*, LXIII (Nov., 1957), 290–96; Schulze, "The Role of Economic Dominants in a Community Power Structure," *ASR*, XXIII (Feb., 1958), 4–9.

17. Floyd Hunter, *Top Leadership U.S.A.* (Chapel Hill: University of North Carolina Press, 1959), 43–55; John H. Ingham, *The Iron Barons: A Social Analysis of an American Urban Elite* (Westport, Conn.: Greenwood Press, 1978), 96–156, 177 ff.

18. Delbert C. Miller: "Industry and Community Power: A Comparative Study of an American and an English City," *ASR*, XXIII (Feb., 1958), 9–15; "Decision-Making Cliques in Community Power Structures: A Comparative Study of an American and an English City," *AJS*, LXIV (Nov., 1958), 299–310; E. Kimbark MacColl, *The Shaping of a City: Business and Politics in Portland, Oregon, 1885–1915* (Portland: Georgian Press, 1976), 18–37, 51–176, 180–82, 214–15, 360–63.

19. Carol Estes Thometz, *The Decision-Makers: The Power Structure of Dallas* (Dallas: Southern Methodist University Press, 1963), 85, 92, *passim*; William V. D'Antonio, William H. Form, Charles P. Loomis, and Eugene C. Erickson, "Institutional and Occupational Representatives in Eleven Community Systems," *ASR*, XXVI, (June, 1961), 440–46.

20. Peter R. Decker, *Fortunes and Failures: White-Collar Mobility in*

Nineteenth-Century San Francisco (Cambridge: Harvard University Press, 1978), *passim*; Julia Cooley Altrocchi, *The Spectacular San Franciscans* (New York: E. P. Dutton, 1946), 75, 101, 107–8, 112, 129–30, 157–273.

21. For studies of the European aristocracy and nobility which emphasize these traits see Franklin Ford, *Robe and Sword* (Cambridge: Harvard University Press, 1962); Ruth Kelso, *The Doctrine of the English Gentlemen in the Sixteenth Century* (Urbana: University of Illinois Press, 1929); Albert Goodwin, *The European Nobility in the Eighteenth Century* (London: Adam and Black, 1953); Arthur Ponsonby, *The Decline of Aristocracy* (London: T. Fisher Unwin, 1912); W. Lee Uslick, "Changing Ideals of Aristocracy, Character and Conduct in England," *Modern Philology*, XXX (Nov., 1932), 149–66; Sylvia Thrupp, *The Merchant Class of Medieval London* (Chicago: University of Chicago Press, 1948), 300–304; Lawrence Stone, *The Crisis of the Aristocracy, 1558–1641* (London: Oxford University Press, 1965); Ernest Kohn-Bramstead, *Aristocracy and the Middle Class in Germany* (Chicago: University of Chicago Press, 1964); Norbert Elias, *The Civilizing Process: The History of Manners* (New York: Urizen Books, 1978).

22. For aristocratic influences on mercantile and industrial urban elites see Ford, *Robe*, *passim*; H. Hauser, "The Characteristic Features of French Economic History from the Middle of the Sixteenth to the Middle of the Eighteenth Century," *Economic History Review*, IV (Oct., 1933), 257–72; Elinor G. Barber, *The Bourgeoisie in Eighteenth Century France* (Princeton: Princeton University Press, 1955), *passim*; John E. Sawyer, "Social Structure and Economic Progress: General Propositions and Some French Examples," *American Economic Review, Papers and Proceedings*, XLI (May, 1951), 321–29; David S. Landes, "French Entrepreneurship and Industrial Growth in the Nineteenth Century," *Journal of Economic History*, IX (May, 1949), 45–61; Sawyer, "Strains in the Social Structure of Modern France," in *Modern France*, ed. Edward Earle (Princeton: Princeton University Press, 1951), 293–312; Landes, "French Business and the Businessman," *Ibid.*, 334–53; Sawyer, "The Entrepreneur and the Social Order," in *Men in Business*, ed. William Miller (New York: Harper & Row, 1962), 7–23; Jesse R. Pitts, "Continuity and Change in Bourgeois France," in Stanley Hoffman *et al.*, *In Search of France* (Cambridge: Harvard University Press, 1963), 244–61; Stone, *Crisis*, 335–84; R. H. Gretton, *The English Middle Class* (London: G. Bell and Sons, 1917), 91–114, 124–26, 144–46; Roy Lewis and Angus Maude, *The English Middle Class* (London: Phoenix House, 1949), 44–50; Thrupp, *Merchant*, 144–61, 166–69, 224–32, 249–56; Wallace T. MacCaffrey, *Exeter, 1540–1640: The Growth of an English County Town* (Cambridge: Harvard University Press, 1958), 260–61, 266–67, 280, 289; W. B. Stephens, *Seventeenth Century Exeter* (Exeter: University of Exeter, 1951), 153; Maurice Dobb, *Studies in the Development of Capitalism* (London: George Routledge & Sons, 1946), 120–22; Alan Simpson, *The Wealth of the Gentry, 1540–1660* (Chicago: University of Chicago Press, 1961), 128–31, 137; George Mingay, *English Landed Society in the Eighteenth Century* (London: Routledge & Kegan Paul, 1936), 29–33, 93; F. M. L. Thompson, *English Landed Society in the Nineteenth Century* (London: Routledge & Kegan Paul, 1963), 20–21; Walter Arnstein, "The Survival of the Victorian Aristocracy," in *The Rich, the Well Born and the Powerful: Elites and Upper Classes in History*, ed. Frederic Cople

Jaher (Urbana: University of Illinois Press, 1974), 231–37; Frederic C. Lane, *Andrea Barbarigo: Merchant of Venice, 1418–1449* (Baltimore: Johns Hopkins University Press, 1944), 11–15; "A Symposium on the Aristocrat in Business," *Explorations in Entrepreneurial History*, VI (Dec., 1953), 77–130; Per Goran Ohlin, "Entrepreneurial Activities of the Swedish Aristocracy," *ibid.*, VI (Feb., 1954), 147–63; Miklos Szucs Nicholson, "Count Istvan Szecheyi (1792–1860): His Role in the Economic Development of the Danube Basin," *ibid.*, 163–80; Theodore Zeldin, *France, 1848–1945*, 2 vols. (London: Oxford University Press, 1973), I, 16–18; S. G. Checkland, *The Rise of Industrial Society in England, 1815–1885* (London: Longmans, Green, 1966), 292–95. See also the debate over the inhibiting tendency of aristocracy for entrepreneurship in *Explorations in Entrepreneurial History*, VI (1953–54). The relevant articles are Alexander Gerschenkron, "Social Attitudes, Entrepreneurship, and Economic Development," 1–20; D. S. Landes, "Social Attitudes, Entrepreneurship, and Economic Development: A Comment," 245–73; J. E. Sawyer, "In Defense of an Approach: A Comment on Professor Gerschenkron's 'Social Attitudes, Entrepreneurship, and Economic Development,'" 273–87. For the rejoinders and counter-rejoinders of Gerschenkron and Sawyer, 287–97. For a balanced view that incorporates the arguments of both sides see Charles Kindleberger, "The Postwar Resurgence of the French Economy," *In Search of France*, 129–36; Hans Rosenberg, *Bureaucracy, Aristocracy and Autocracy: The Prussian Experience, 1660–1815* (Cambridge: Harvard University Press, 1966), 151–52.

23. James Cashman Davis, *The Decline of the Venetian Nobility as a Ruling Class* (Baltimore: Johns Hopkins University Press, 1962), 15–20, 25–33, 106–15, 127; Oliver Logan, *Culture and Society in Venice, 1470–1790: The Renaissance and Its Heritage* (New York: Charles Scribner's Sons, 1972), 24–25; F. C. Lane, *Venice: A Maritime Republic* (Baltimore: Johns Hopkins University Press, 1973), 108–17, 151, 252–70, 427–31; Robert Forster, *The Nobility of Toulouse in the Eighteenth Century: A Social and Economic Study* (Baltimore: Johns Hopkins University Press, 1960), 24–27.

24. George U. Taylor, "Non Capitalist Wealth and the Origins of the French Revolution," *American Historical Review*, LXXII (Jan., 1967), 469–96; Rosenberg, *Bureaucracy*, 151–52.

25. A recent study of landed elites in nineteenth-century England, France, Germany, Spain, and Russia shows extensive national differences among these enclaves in industrial involvement, political power, wealth, size of estates, and degree of recruitment from other classes. See David Spring, ed., *European Landed Elites in the Nineteenth Century* (Baltimore: Johns Hopkins University Press, 1977), *passim*.

26. Hermann Kellenbenz, "German Aristocratic Entrepreneurship: Economic Activities of the Holstein Nobility in the Sixteenth and Seventeenth Centuries," *Explorations in Entrepreneurial History*, VI (Dec., 1953), 103–15; Stone, *Crisis*, 335–84; Mingay, *English Landed Society in the Eighteenth Century*, 100–101, 105–7, 189–201; Thompson, *English Landed Society in the Nineteenth Century*, 257–63; Spring, ed., *European Landed Elites*, 13, 30–47; Arnstein, "Survival," 229–31. For other regional aristocracies who displayed vigorous entrepreneurship see the following articles in *Explorations in Entrepreneurial History*: "Symposium," 77–130; Ohlin, "Swedish Aristocracy," 147–

63; Nicolson, "Count Istan Szechenyi," 163–80.

27. Fritz Redlich, "European Aristocracy and Economic Development," *Explorations in Entrepreneurial History*, VI (Dec., 1953), 89–90.

28. Richard Knoetzke, "Entrepreneurial Activities of the Spanish and Portuguese Noblemen in Medieval Times," *ibid.*, 115–21; Stone, *Crisis*, 363–77.

29. For a more detailed discussion of the points made in this paragraph see Kohn-Bramstead, *Aristocracy*, *passim*; Stone, *Crisis*, *passim*; Redlich, "European," 78–91.

30. Stone, *Crisis*, 51–161; Ford, *Robe*, 108–110, 128–46; Allan Everitt, "Social Mobility in Modern England," *Past and Present*, no. 33 (Apr., 1966), 56–73; Stone, "Social Mobility in England, 1500–1700," *ibid.*, 16–56; Simpson, *Wealth*, 28–29, 142–216; Thrupp, *London*, 256–87, 304–9; Dobb, *Studies*, 120–22, 153, 188–89, 191; Lewis and Maude, *English Middle Classes*, 29, 33–36, 42–43, 50, 62, 70–71; Mingay, *English Landed Society in the Eighteenth Century*, 6–16, 25–38, 68, 73–75, 91–100, 105–7; Thompson, *English Landed Society in the Nineteenth Century*, 1–3, 9–14, 17, 20–23, 109–31, 293–94, 297–303, 321–35, 342–44; Forster, *Nobility*, 24–27; Barber, *Bourgeoisie*, 10–11, 16–24, 101–5; Davis, *Decline*, 15–20, 25–35, 74, 100–101, 106–15, 123–37, 140–46, 158, 164–68, 171–78; Rupert Wilkinson, ed., *Governing Elites: Studies in Training and Selection* (New York: Oxford University Press, 1969), 82–83; Spring, ed., *European Landed Elites*, *passim*.

31. Thrupp, *London*, 194–232; William G. Hoskins, *Provincial England* (London: Macmillan, 1963), 74–78; Gene Brucker, *Renaissance Florence* (New York: John Wiley & Sons, 1969), 94–95.

32. Seymour Martin Lipset and Reinhard Bendix, *Social Mobility in Industrial Society* (Berkeley and Los Angeles: University of California Press, 1964), 11–76.

33. See the citations to Barber, Hauser, Sawyer, Taylor, Landes, Pitts, Gerschenkron, and Kindleberger in notes 22 and 24.

34. For accounts of behavior patterns in Eurpean mercantile communities from the late medieval period to the eighteenth century see M. M. Postan, E. E. Rich, and Edward Miller, eds., *The Cambridge Economic History of Europe*, III (Cambridge: Cambridge University Press, 1963), 31–33, 82–83, 221, 228–29; Thrupp, *London*, *passim*; MacCaffrey, *Exeter*, 21–45, 105–59, 166–73, 203–14, 222–25, 246–80; W. G. Hoskins, *Industry, Trade and People in Exeter, 1688–1800* (Manchester: University of Manchester Press, 1935), 11–20, 44–47, 118–19; N. S. B. Gras, *Business and Capitalism* (New York: F. S. Crofts, 1939), 72–223; Dobb, *Studies*, 98–154, 189–93, 277–81; Hoskins, "The Elizabethan Merchants of Exeter," in S. T. Bindoff, J. Hurstfield, and C. H. Williams, eds., *Elizabethan Government and Society: Essays Presented to Sir John Neale* (London: Athlone Press, 1961), 163–87; A. H. Dodd, "Mr. Myddleton the Merchant of Tower Street," in *ibid.*, 249–81; Hoskins, "Provincial," 74–78; Gino Luzzato, "Small and Great Merchants in the Italian Cities of the Renaissance," in F. C. Lane and Jelle C. Riemersma, eds., *The Entrepreneur and Secular Change* (Homewood, Ill.: Richard D. Irwin, 1953), 46–52; Armando Sapori, "The Culture of the Medieval Italian Merchant," in *ibid.*, 56–65; Lane: "Family Partnerships and Joint Ventures in the Venetian Republic," in *ibid.*, 87–99; *Andrea Barbarigo*, *passim*; Frank F. Foster, "Politics and Community in Elizabethan

England," in *Rich*, ed. Jaher, 110–38; Lewis and Maud, *English Middle Classes*, 29, 33–34, 44, 47–48, 51, 62, 70–71, 134–38; Davis, *Decline*, 15–20, 25–53, 75–80, 106–16, 127–29; Donald E. Queller, "The Civic Irresponsibility of the Venetian Nobility," *Explorations in Entrepreneurial History*, VII (1964), 234–45; Logan, *Culture*, 2–3, 6–7, 21–31, 35, 50–66, 148–61; Lane, *Venice*, 90–95, 100–101, 108–17, 138–40, 209–13, 219–20, 252–70, 331–32, 430–31; Brucker, *Renaissance*, 55–58, 68–78, 90–97, 102–5, 120–25, 135–51, 216–18, 222–30; Barber, *Bourgeoisie*, 19–20, 23–32, 38–43, 46–55, 85–89, 93–98, 101–37.

35. Zeldin, *France*, I, 65–66, 80–82; Checkland, *Rise*, 112–15, 129, 191, 292–95, 299–300, 312; Asa Briggs, *Victorian Cities* (London: Oldhams Press, 1963), 69–70, 106–7, 127, 206–7, 259–60, 263–64; Michael Katz, "The Entrepreneurial Class in a Canadian City," *Journal of Social History* (Winter, 1975), 1–29.

36. Miller, "Industry," 13–14, 20; D'Antonio *et al.*, "Institutional," 440–46.

37. The major recent works in support of the pluralistic position are Arnold M. Rose, *The Power Structure: Political Process in American Society* (New York: Oxford University Press, 1967); Ralf Dahrendorf, *Class and Class Conflict in Industrial Society* (Palo Alto: Stanford University Press, 1958); Nelson W. Polsby, *Community Power and Political Theory* (New Haven; Yale University Press, 1967); Richard A. Schermerhorn, *Society and Power* (New York: Random House, 1961); Dahl: *Who Governs?*; "Hierarchy, Democracy, and Bargaining in Politics and Economics," *Research Frontiers in Politics and Government* (Washington, D.C.: Brookings Institute, 1955), 45–69; "The Concept of Power," *Behavioral Science*, II (July, 1957), 201–15; "A Critique of the Ruling Elite Model," *American Political Science Review*, LII (June, 1958), 463–69; Raymond E. Wolfinger, "Reputation and Reality in the Study of Community Power," *ASR*, XXV (Oct., 1966), 636–44; Gideon Sjoberg, "Are Social Classes in America Becoming More Rigid," *ASR*, XVI (Dec., 1951), 775–83; Arthur Kornhauser, "Public Opinion and Social Class," *AJS*, LV (Jan., 1950), 333–45; Peter H. Rossi, "Community Decision Makers," *Administrative Society Quarterly*, I (Mar., 1957), 415–43; Daniel Bell, *The End of Ideology: On the Exhaustion of Political Ideas in the Fifties* (Glencoe, Ill.: Free Press of Glencoe, 1960), 43–67; Seymour Martin Lipset, *Political Man* (Garden City, N.Y.: Doubleday, 1960); Leonard Reissman, *Class in American Society* (Glencoe, Ill.: Free Press of Glencoe, 1959); Bernard Barber, *Social Stratification: A Comparative Analysis of Structure and Process* (New York: Harcourt, Brace & World, 1957); John Kenneth Galbraith, *American Capitalism: The Concept of Countervailing Power* (Boston: Houghton Mifflin, 1952). Galbraith has since moved to a more centralist belief on power distribution but sees influence moving from the entrepreneurial-managerial to the technocratic elite; see *The New Industrial State* (Boston: Houghton Mifflin, 1969).

The major proponents of a power elite or upper class are C. Wright Mills, *The Power Elite* (New York: Oxford University Press, 1956); Floyd Hunter, *Top Leadership*; Osborn Elliott, *Men at the Top* (New York: Harper & Bros., 1959); Richard H. Rovere, *The American Establishment and Other Reports, Opinions and Speculations* (New York: Harcourt, Brace & World, 1962), 5–21; E. Digby Baltzell, *The Protestant Establishment: Aristocracy and Caste in America* (New York: Random House, 1964); Paul M. Sweezey, *The Present as History, Essays and Reviews on Capitalism and Socialism* (New York: Monthly Review Press, 1953), 120–38, 158–88; G. William Domhoff: *Who Rules America?* (Englewood Cliffs, N.J.: Prentice-Hall, 1967); *The Higher Circles: The Governing Class in America* (New York: Random House, 1970).

38. Robert H. Wiebe, *Businessmen and Reform: A Study of the Progressive Movement* (Cambridge: Harvard University Press, 1962).

DeWitt, William C., 276
Dexter family, 531: Wirt, 510
Dial, The, 530
Dickey, Hugh T., 460, 482
Dickson, Edward A., 632, 638, 674, 682
Direct Legislation League, 632
Dix, Morgan, 229, 268, 311
Dixon family, 543: Arthur, 543; George W., 543, 548–49
Doane, John H., 480, 489
Dock Street Theater, 415
Dockweiler, Dockweiler & Finch, 672
Dockweiler family, 672: Isidore B., 634–35, 639, 643, 671–72, 681; John H., 639
Dodge family, 180–81, 249, 264, 266: Cleveland, 260; William E., 180, 198, 244
Doheny family, 678: Edward L., 621, 629, 636, 644, 674–75
Dole, George W., 459–60, 462, 465, 467–68
Domínguez, Manuel, 584
Donald, David, 55
Donnelley family, 543: Reuben H., 543
Douglas Aircraft Co., 667–68, 672
Douglas family, 667: Donald, 665, 667–68, 684
Dowdey, Clifford J., 713
Downey family, 645: John G., 595–98, 601–3, 607–8, 610, 627, 644, 653
Downtown Businessmen's Association of Los Angeles, 670
Drake family, 541: John B., 541
Drayton family, 328, 335, 374: John, 363, 368, 384, 388–90, 397; Thomas, 321; Thomas F., 360; William, 335; William (2), 368, 373–74, 383–84; William H., 390
Dreiser, Theodore, 530
Drew, Daniel, 250–51, 729
Drummond family: Mary, 465–66, 469–70, 472; Thomas, 465
Dry Dock Savings Institution of New York, 189, 239
Duane, James, 174, 211, 223
Ducommun family, 661: Charles, 595–97, 661
Dudley, Joseph, 18
Duer family, 172: John, 197; William, 172–73, 180, 191–92, 210; William A., 189, 217–18, 222, 226–28, 236, 247, 249–50
Duke, Doris, 280
Dun & Bradstreet, 478
Dunham, John, 462, 465
duPont family, 730
Dutch Reformed Church, 101, 168
Dutch West India Company, 161, 164
Duyckinck, Evert A., 233–34
Dwight family, 51

Dyer, Thomas, 462–63

Eagle Fire Insurance Co., 193
Earl family, 638–39: Edward T., 619, 631–32, 635, 638–39; Edward T. (Mrs.), 647; Guy C., Jr., 664
East Cooper River Community Chest Council, 413
East North Central States, 612. *See also* Midwest; Western states
Eastern Railroad, 51–52
Eastlake Park, Los Angeles, 643
Eaton family, 610, 624: Benjamin S., 605, 610, 624, 646; Frederick B., 624–25, 639
Ebell Club, 652, 683
Economic panics and depressions: in 1819, 343; in 1837, 182–84, 187–88, 454, 457; in 1857, 182, 187, 454, 462, 521; in 1873, 474, 489–90, 602; in 1893, 125, 274, 474, 489, 513, 539; in 1905, 489; in 1912, 489; in 1929, 93, 275, 414–15, 539–40, 544, 552, 655
Edict of Nantes, 325. *See also* Huguenots
Education and Schooling. *See* Private schools; Upper strata, cultural activities: education in Boston; Charleston; Chicago; Los Angeles; and New York City
Edward L. Brewster & Co., 490, 543
Eddy, Thomas, 172–73, 180, 192, 197, 239, 244
Eight-hour-day strike in Chicago, 505
El Morocco (restaurant), 280
El Paso, Tex., 718
Elgin National Watch Co., 486
Eliot family, 36, 262: Charles W., 36, 99–101, 103–8, 123–24, 263, 266; Samuel, 21, 33, 27–38, 54, 66; Samuel A., 36, 50, 54, 56, 58, 60–61, 75
Elliott family, 321, 331, 396, 402: Benjamin, 381, 385; Benjamin, Jr., 373–74, 381, 385; Stephen, 345, 348, 350–51, 371, 376, 381, 388–93; Stephen (2), 379; Stephen, Jr., 381, 385; William, 344, 352, 356, 361, 372, 390, 397, 399; William, Jr., 408
Elliott, John M., 642, 647
Elliott Society of Natural History, 384, 388–89
Ellis, H. Bert, 637
Elite Directory and Club List of Chicago, 531
Elmore, William, 346–47, 366
Empress of China, 176
Endicott family, 21, 257: William C., 99, 502
Engerman, Stanley, 432n
English Speaking Union of Charleston, 417